D1519082

THE MAKING
OF AN ENTERPRISE

―――――――――

The Society of Jesus in Portugal,
Its Empire, and Beyond
1540-1750

The martyrdom of Fr. Ignácio de Azevedo and his 39 companions en route from Portugal to Brazil in 1570. Augsburg, ca. 1730. Author's collection.

The Making of an Enterprise

The Society of Jesus in Portugal, Its Empire, and Beyond

1540-1750

DAURIL ALDEN

Stanford University Press
Stanford, California
1996

Stanford University Press
Stanford, California
© 1996 by the Board of Trustees of the
Leland Stanford Junior University
Printed in the United States of America

Published with the support of
the National Endowment for the Humanities,
an independent federal agency

CIP data are at the end of the book

Stanford University Press publications are
distributed exclusively by Stanford University Press
within the United States, Canada, Mexico, and Central America;
they are distributed exclusively by Cambridge University Press
throughout the rest of the world

To those who paved the way

Charles R. Boxer

Serafim Leite, S.J.

Josef Wicki, S.J.

Ludwig von Pastor

And, of course, to Leopold von Ranke

PREFACE

Among the most spectacular features of the expansion of Europe during the early modern period were the impressive evangelical campaigns undertaken by many religious Orders. These Orders included well-established, familiar ones such as the Dominicans, Franciscans, and Augustinians, as well as the newly formed Society or Company of Jesus. Like their Mendicant rivals, the Jesuits conceived of their spiritual enterprises as precious opportunities to emulate the apostles. The Jesuits believed that with sufficient resources they could revive and strengthen the beliefs of wayward Christians at home and convert the heathens beyond Europe to what Catholics were convinced was the true faith. As the Society's members distinguished themselves as educators of the young among Europe's elites, as confessors and advisors of its leaders, as orators, theologians, and scholars, and as missionaries on five continents, the Society gained the reputation of being one of the most dynamic Orders of the Church, one fervently admired by its supporters and friends, but passionately detested by its detractors and enemies.

A half century ago, a well-known Austrian admirer of the Society observed that "writings concerning the Society of Jesus may be numbered by the thousands; from the foundation of the order to the present day, every epoch, and almost every people and every tongue, has produced an extensive literature relating to the Jesuits. . . . Few . . . attempt to treat the subject objectively, while the remainder are all concerned either with reviling or accusing or with praising and defending."[1] Those comments are as valid today as they were when René Fülöp-Miller wrote them in 1930. Within the past decade or so, for example, besides Fülöp-Miller's own repeatedly reissued book, there have appeared four volumes that promise to reveal un-realized subtleties concerning Jesuit life and the Society's objectives. One by J. C. H. Aveling, a former Anglican priest and an ex–Benedictine monk, is a supposedly "definitive history" of the Society, although it uses not one archival source and is riddled with factual blunders. The same is true of a book by Manfred Barthel, a well-published German writer on religious topics, who revives the myths of Jesuit "riches" and their supposedly "sealed"

---

1. René Fülöp-Miller, *The Jesuits: A History of the Society of Jesus*, trans. F. S. Flint and D. F. Tait (1930; rpr., New York, 1963), iii.

archives. The best-known author of the lot, Malachi Martin, proprietor of "Malachi Martin Enterprises, Ltd.," an ex-Jesuit and an ex–curia official, offered a lurid account that made the *New York Times* best-seller list. He, too, is interested in myths; he unearthed the hoary one that portrayed the Jesuits as conspirators against legitimate authorities, but he dressed it up in modern garb. According to Martin, instead of allegedly fomenting regicide, today's leaders of the Society are intent upon attacking their special guardian, the pope himself, in order to destroy the very foundations of Catholicism. Of course, Martin offers no more proof of his assertions than did previous generations of anti-Jesuit mythmakers. Finally, there is the ambitious, archive-based study by a Yankee expatriate academician who teaches at a South Australia university. A. Lynn Martin's most recent book is an attempt to probe the "Jesuit mind" in late-sixteenth-century France, but his account falls short of fulfilling the promise of its title.[2]

This study is quite different in its conception, its objectives, and its evidentiary base from those cited above. Its focus is upon what the Society defined as the Portuguese Assistancy, a vast complex of administrative units that included the kingdom of Portugal and its empire, portions of the Indian subcontinent, Japan, China, Southeast Asia, and certain lesser territories. This is the first of two volumes. It begins with the founding of the Society and its entrance into Portugal in the early 1540s and extends to 1750, when the last Portuguese monarch sympathetic to the Society expired. A second volume, *The Destruction of an Enterprise*, currently in preparation, will show why the Jesuits were arrested and expelled from the empire and kingdom of Portugal, the first state to have welcomed them; what subsequently happened to members of the Assistancy; and what the state did with their far-flung assets.

Typically, writers concerned with the history of the Jesuits have been participants in an organized religion. Their adherence to a particular faith has inevitably shaped their judgments concerning one of the Church's most controversial Orders. I bear no religious affiliation and hold no brief for or against the Jesuits or any other religious body. Yet I confess that one of the reasons why I chose to study the Jesuits was to challenge my own sense of scholarly objectivity. I fully recognize that, like all ideals, complete objectivity is unattainable, but I remain convinced that it is the only legitimate road a historian ought to pursue.[3] Much has been written and will continue to be written concerning Jesuit contributions to theology, missiology, the arts, and the sciences.[4] Though I concede their importance, I have chosen to examine quite different themes.

One concerns the Society's perennial manpower problem within the Assistancy: despite enthusiastic promises of wholesale conversions of non-Europeans to what Catholics believed

2. In the order cited, the four books are J. C. H. Aveling, *The Jesuits* (1981; rpr., New York, 1987); Manfred Barthel, *The Jesuits: History and Legend of the Society of Jesus* (New York, 1984); Malachi Martin, *The Jesuits: The Society of Jesus and the Betrayal of the Roman Catholic Church* (New York, 1987); and A. Lynn Martin, *The Jesuit Mind: The Mentality of an Elite in Early Modern France* (Ithaca, N.Y., 1988).

3. I am naturally sobered by the findings of Peter Novick, *That Noble Dream: The "Objectivity Question" and the American Historical Profession* (New York, 1988). For an evaluation, see James T. Kloppenberg, "Objectivity and Historicism: A Century of American Historical Writing," *American Historical Review* 94, 4 (Oct. 1989): 1011–30.

4. László Polgár, S.J., *Bibliographie sur l'histoire de la compagnie de Jésus 1901–1980*, 6 vols. in 3 (Rome, 1981–90).

to be the true faith, there were never sufficient field-workers even to attempt to achieve such an objective. But where did Jesuits who served the Assistancy originate? Were most of those who labored in this Assistancy Portuguese or foreigners? Did they come from all parts of the kingdom or only certain sections? Who was excluded from membership? Why? What sorts of deviants were quietly eliminated, in part to safeguard the Society's carefully shaped public image? Who gained promotions to influential positions within the Society and who were condemned to be the hewers of wood, the haulers of water? Partial answers to these questions come from the Society's rich personnel records and from studies by its genealogists.

A major theme that shaped Jesuit activity from the outset was the Society's relations with the heads of government in Portugal and elsewhere. Is there evidence that in this Assistancy the Jesuits deliberately involved themselves in political affairs and, in fact, dictated their outcome? Or were they the creatures of capricious rulers and their self-serving lieutenants? Why did the Portuguese crown exploit the administrative and diplomatic talents of Jesuits to undertake tasks unrelated to their spiritual commitments? Could the Jesuits have declined to serve? What explains the shift in the crown's attitude toward the Society, from zealous devotion during the sixteenth century to near indifference by the mid-eighteenth century? The search for answers to these and related questions has required forays into the political, military, and diplomatic history of Portugal and its empire.

From the outset of this project I have sought answers to a series of fundamental questions. They include: Why, how, and to what extent did the Society become involved in the imperial economy? How lucrative were its financial enterprises? Did Jesuits really desert God for Mammon, as their opponents so persistently charged? Did they surrender their early spiritual commitment in order to pursue material goals? The quest for answers to such questions has led to inquiries into the magnitude of the crown's economic concessions to the Society and the regularity of the payment of its promised subventions. It has uncovered the identities of many of the Society's large and small benefactors— Portuguese and non-Lusitanian—and the extent of their contributions; and it has revealed the forms of infrastructure that the Jesuits built to support their ambitious enterprises. That infrastructure included the development of great estates producing wheat and other European grains, livestock, cane sugar, rice, coconuts, cacao, and other forest crops. As will be seen, the success of such activities provoked heated criticism from secular and religious rivals, and even from some members of the Order itself, and aroused the suspicions of the crown. But the crown's efforts to restrain the growth of the Society's latifundia were futile, and its efforts to compel the Jesuits to pay tithes upon their holdings were only partly successful. In Brazil, the development of vast rural estates presented the Jesuits with a serious dilemma: on the one hand, they were fervent opponents of the enslavement of the Amerindians, but on the other, they were the largest institutional owners of slaves of African origin or descent. How did Jesuits reconcile their seemingly contradictory position on the issue of human slavery? Were there viable alternatives to the activities of Jesuits as rentiers and landlords? Were their trading activities in cloth, gems, and other commodities conducted on a scale commensurate with the assumptions of their critics, then and now? How successful were the Jesuits as investors in maritime insurance and in personal and government annuities, and as lenders to their friends? Did the components of the Assistancy really need all of the capital they raised? How did they expend their income? And what accounts for the Jesuits' dismal record of achievement in Africa, their partial withdrawal from Asian portions of the Assistancy, their continued expansion in Brazil, and their cultural eclipse in Portugal during the first half of the eighteenth century? The chapters assembled in Parts III, IV, and V of this study offer answers to these and related questions.

The broad character of this inquiry has provided frequent opportunities for comparative insights. The geographic expanse and cultural diversity of the Assistancy make possible certain kinds of comparison, although it must be conceded that the paper trail of Jesuit enterprise is thickest for Portugal, Brazil, and India, where most Jesuits resided and performed, and consequently their activities in those lands receive greater emphasis than those in other parts of the Assistancy. The search for appropriate contexts in which to situate Jesuit problems and responses has required probing the general history of church–state relations during the Middle Ages, particularly the exceptionally rich literature pertaining to England before the ascendancy of the Tudors. Additional light has been shed by comparing Jesuit activities within the Portuguese Assistancy with Jesuit experiences in the French and Spanish Assistancies.

This project has occupied more than two decades and has necessitated extensive financial support. At critical junctures I have received aid from the American Council of Learned Societies, the American Philosophical Society, the American Institute of Indian Studies, the Calouste Gulbenkian Foundation (Lisbon), the Council for Research of the Economic History Association, the John Simon Guggenheim Memorial Foundation, the Andrew W. Mellon Foundation (via the Vatican Film Library, Saint Louis University), the Meyer Foundation (Melbourne, Australia), the National Endowment for the Humanities (via the Newberry Library, Chicago, and also a direct summer grant), and the Graduate School of the University of Washington. I remain exceedingly grateful not only to each of these institutions but also to my long-suffering referees and to the advisory committees that recommended acceptance of my proposals. Such aid has permitted me to conduct research on five continents in more than 35 archives and in general and specialized libraries, both public and private. I am deeply appreciative of the opportunities to work at liberty in such facilities, and I thank the directors and their staffs for their consistently excellent cooperation and service.

Though I have never enjoyed the services of a research assistant, I have been significantly aided, encouraged, and stimulated by a host of friends and colleagues. Several took valuable time away from their own studies to read and rigorously comment upon drafts of some of the chapters offered here in revised form. In particular, I wish to thank Roderick and Jean Barman; Rudy Bauss; Woodrow W. Borah; the late Ernest J. Burrus, S.J.; the late Manoel Cardozo; Tom Cohen; John Correia-Afonso, S.J.; Edith B. Couturier; James S. Cummins; Nicholas P. Cushner; Karubaki Datta; Anthony R. Disney; Francis A. Dutra; Neusa Rodrigues Esteves; George E. Ganns, S.J.; the late Maurício Gomes dos Santos, S.J.; Nigel Griffin; June E. Hahner; William F. Harrison; Mathias C. Kiemen, O.F.M.; John V. Lombardi (now president of the University of Florida); Thomas M. McCoog, S.J.; Joseph C. Miller; Charles O'Neill, S.J. (former director of the Society's Historical Institute in Rome); the late José Honório Rodrigues; Carla M. Philipps; Stuart B. Schwartz; Chandra

Richard de Silva; and Dorothy Winters Welker. I especially wish to express my gratitude to George D. Winius, well-known specialist on the eastern Portuguese empire, for his supportive reader's report.

Several members of my department have repeatedly responded to my queries with bibliographical and other sorts of information and have lent materials from their own libraries. I especially wish to thank Jere L. Bacharach, Frank F. Conlon, Mary O'Neill, and Joan C. Ullman, as well as my former colleague Caroline Bynum. I must also express my deep appreciation to Ruth M. Kirk, former head of the Interlibrary Borrowing Service of the library of the University of Washington, and her efficient staff and their successors for having obtained for me numerous materials cited in this study.

I acknowledge with profound gratitude publication subventions furnished by the Graduate School of the University of Washington and the National Endowment for the Humanities. I would also be remiss if I failed to express my deep appreciation to Mr. Hans Peters of London, who generously provided critical financial aid to defray additional publication expenses. The manuscript benefited enormously from the exceptional labors of my editors at Stanford University Press, Laura Bloch, Lynn Stewart, and Sherry Wert, and I am acutely sensitive of my debt to them. I must also express my sincere appreciation to Dr. Theodora MacKay for so skillfully preparing the camera-ready copy and to her husband, Pierre MacKay, for his technical skills. Felicia Hecker was indispensable in proofreading. The maps were drawn by Bill Nelson, to whom I am additionally grateful.

But my greatest debts are to those who have most decisively facilitated this study and its sequel. They include my ever-supportive, usually understanding wife, Beata, who generously equipped me with my first computer. My sons, Bryson and Grant, helped with solving some of its enigmas, but my principal gurus have been Drs. Asunción and David Lavrin, who have not only made me minimally computer-literate and enabled me to manipulate typed portions of the manuscript, but for more than two decades have also provided exceptional hospitality during my sojourns in Washington, D.C., and have assisted me in many other important ways. I also wish to record my thanks to the late Piedade Rato, longtime photographer for Portugal's Overseas Archives, who tirelessly filmed many manuscripts for me in various Lisbon archives. Nor can I forbear expressing my sincere appreciation to Grant Barnes, director emeritus of Stanford University Press, for his many years of warm friendship, and particularly for his faith in and support of this project.

Finally, my thanks to the pathfinders for whom this volume is dedicated. Without their ground-breaking work, the preparation of this study would have been impossible. I have been fortunate to know three of them: C. R. Boxer, Serafim Leite, and Josef Wicki; obviously, both Ludwig von Pastor and Leopold von Ranke belonged to an earlier generation, but they continue to serve as models of thorough, careful scholarship. For more than two decades, Charles R. Boxer, the doyen of Portuguese imperial studies, has been an exceptionally generous friend, first in Chicago at the now-famed Newberry Conference on Colonial Brazil, then at the Lilly Library at Indiana University, later in several Australian cities, but best of all in his remarkable library in his comfortable rural home in Hertfordshire. Even though we have disagreed on minor interpretations of Jesuit enterprise, Professor Boxer has been consistently supportive and ever generous by providing me with access to his unique manuscript and book collection and by inspiring me with exceptionally stimulating and informative conversations concerning Portuguese imperial history. At an early stage in this project, the late Serafim Leite, then nearing the end of his remarkably productive life, encouraged my undertaking while recognizing that my concerns were very different from what his had been. I am also grateful to him for placing me in contact with another venerable resident of the Lisbonense Jesuit center known as Brotéria, the late Maurício Gomes dos Santos, with whom I had many fruitful talks. In Rome, Fr. Josef Wicki, a superlative editor, kindly guided me to sources in the library of the Society's Historical Institute and to manuscript materials in its archives that I would otherwise have missed, whereas his former colleague, Fr. Charles O'Neill, frequently offered me genial, spirited, and always informative instruction in matters Jesuitica. To each of those mentioned and to others whose names I can no longer recall, I offer my deep-felt thanks. Naturally, for all the "faults escaped," as Thomas Hariot once wrote, I alone bear full responsibility.

Contents

Abbreviations		xxiii
Glossary		xxix
Editorial Conventions		xxxi

I. THE CREATION

1. The Founding of a Controversial New Society   3

   The Origins of the Society; The Organization of the Society; Unique and Controversial Features of the Society; Defining the Society's Mission; The Beginning of Hostility Toward the Society

2. Formation of the Province of Portugal, 1541–ca. 1615   24

   The Rise of Portugal; The Coming of the Jesuits; Beginnings of an Enterprise; Growth of an Enterprise; The Problem of Motivation

II. EXPANSION

3. Foundations of an Enterprise: The Distant Empire and Beyond, 1542–ca. 1615   41

   Beginnings of a Thalassocracy; The Achievements of Francis Xavier; The Goan Hub; The Northern and Southern Spokes; Jesuits Reach the Mughal Court; The Western Spokes; Alessandro Valignano Turns the Society Eastward; The First Eastern Spokes: Malacca and the Moluccas; Japan, "A World Apart"; The Chinese Spoke; The Beginnings of the Enterprise in Brazil; Jesuit Beginnings in Kongo and Angola

4. The Perils of Propinquity: The Jesuits and the Crown,
    1557–1640   79

    *The End of an Ideal King and of a Popular Dynasty; The Succes-
    sion Crisis, 1578–80; The Philippine Interlude, 1580–1640*

5. Years of Achievement and Disappointment: The Jesuits
    and the Crown, 1640–1706   101

    *The Jesuits as Collaborators of John IV, 1640–56; The Perilous Years,
    1656–68; The Petrine Interlude, 1668–1706*

6. Mandarins and Martyrs: Gains and Losses in the East
    During the Seventeenth Century   130

    *The End of the Japan Enterprise; The Restructured Japan Province;
    The Eastern Rival: The Enterprise in China; Expansion in the West;
    The Limits of the Possible*

7. An Empire and a Society in Peril: Consequences of
    the Anglo-Dutch Intrusions in the Eastern Seas,
    1600–1641   159

    *Beginnings of the North European Intrusions in the East; The
    First Major Territorial Losses; The Worsening Crisis in the East; Signs
    of Impending Collapse, 1636–41*

8. The Collapse of the Estado da India and Its Impact
    upon the Society, 1641–1700   181

    *The Troublesome Luso-Dutch Truce; The Lull Before the Storm, 1645–
    50; The Storm, 1650–63; The Transfer of Bombay: A Case of Un-
    fulfilled Promises; Arab and Indian Attacks on the Estado, 1661–98;
    The Rise of the Maratha Menace; The Waning of an Enterprise*

9. Vicissitudes of the Enterprise in the Atlantic World
    During the Seventeenth Century   206

    *The First Dutch Invasion of Brazil; The Second Dutch Intrusion; A
    Failed Enterprise: The Cape Verde Mission; A Troubled Enterprise: The
    Jesuits in Angola and Kongo; Recovery and Expansion in Brazil*

III. ORGANIZATION

10. The Governance of an Enterprise: The Hierarchy of
    the Portuguese Assistancy   229

    *Meetings, Periodic and Irregular; The Generals and Their Assistants;
    Intra-Assistancy Rivalries; Provincials, Rectors, and Other Superiors;
    The Visitors*

11. Recruitment for an Enterprise: The Pertinacity
     of Eurocentrism   255

     *The Exclusion of New Christians; Discrimination Against Colonial-
     Born Whites and Mixed Bloods; The Thorny Issue of the Admission
     of Nonwhite Clergy; The Problem of Other Europeans Serving in the
     Assistancy; A Prosopography of the Assistancy; Estimates of Jesuit
     Longevities; The Creation and Maintenance of a Public Image; Dis-
     posing of the Unfit: A Case of Double Standards*

12. The Fiscal Administration of an Enterprise   298

     *The Missions Procurators; The Provincial Procurators; The College
     Procurators; The Estate Managers*

              IV. FINANCING AN ENTERPRISE:
                 SOURCES OF CONTROVERSY

13. The Crown as Benefactor and Taskmaster   321

     *"By Robbing Peter He Paid Paul"; Other Royal Subventions; The Prob-
     lem of Delinquent Payments; "The Lord Giveth and the Lord Taketh
     Away"; Unwanted Burdens*

14. "Sharers in the Good Works": The Society's
     Other Patrons   345

     *Benefits to the Benefactors; Jesuit Benefactors; Other Ecclesiastical Bene-
     factors; Noble Patrons; Unranked Benefactors: Families and Couples;
     Unranked Benefactors: Bachelors and Widows; Less Conspicuous Bene-
     factors; Legacies as Mixed Blessings*

15. The Economic Foundations of an Enterprise:
     The Acquisition of Lands   376

     *Origins of the Church as Landowner; How the Jesuits Became a Ter-
     ritorial Power in the Assistancy; The Extent of the Jesuits' Patrimony;
     Some Further Considerations Concerning the Jesuits' Patrimony; The
     Emergence of Great Estates; Land Revenues from Villages; Sources of
     Urban Income*

16. The Economic Foundations of an Enterprise:
     The Utilization of Lands   402

     *The Jesuits as Landlords; The Jesuits as Stockmen; The Prevalence
     of Agriculture; The Jesuits as Reluctant Sugar Planters*

17. An Enterprise Under Attack: Attempts to Monitor,
     Curtail, and Eliminate the Jesuits' Patrimony   430

     *The Benevolent Years, 1541–80; Philippine Efforts to Check the Growth
     of Jesuit Latifundia; Criticism of Jesuit Landholding During the
     Restoration and the Petrine Years; The Second Threat by the State to
     Confiscate Jesuit Properties; The East India Company Versus the*

Jesuits; The Jesuits as Scapegoats: The Case of India; Increasing Complaints from Brazil; When Is Enough Enough?

18. God's Share or the King's? Jesuit Resistance to
     Payment of Tithes   461

     Background; Tithe Debates in the Kingdom; Disputes Concerning Tithes in the State of Brazil; Persistent Tithe Controversies in the State of Maranhão

19. Jesuit Efforts to Defend the "Freedom" of the
     Brazilian Indians   474

     Perceptions of the Amerindians; The Mission System and Its Consequences; Beginnings of the Conflict Between the Jesuits and the Settlers Concerning Indian Slavery; The Great "Tempest"; António Vieira and the Struggle for Indian Liberty; The Efforts of Pedro II to Protect the Brasis; The Conflict over "Indian Freedom" in Maranhão

20. Those Who Also Served: Bondsmen and Lay Servants   502

     The Labor Needs of the Society; Jesuit Attitudes Toward Slavery; Jesuit Reliance upon African Slavery in Portugal, Asia, and Africa; Jesuit Dependence upon Black Slaves in Brazil

21. For Piety or Profit? The Commercial Activities of
     the Jesuits in the Portuguese Empire   528

     Royal Ambivalence Toward Jesuit Commercial Activities; The Vehicles of Jesuit Commerce; The Jesuits' Role in the Japan Trades; The Macaonese Hub; The Alleged Jesuit Commercial Hegemony in India; Jesuit Involvement in the African Slave Trade; The Jesuits and the Brazil Trades; Myths and Realities Concerning the Jesuits' Trading Network

22. Alternative Forms of Risk-Taking: The Jesuits as
     Lenders and Borrowers   552

     The College of Santo Antão as Borrower and Lender; The Aveiro Loan Debacle; Investments by the Portuguese Province During the Eighteenth Century; The Anomaly of the Brazil Provinces; Investment Patterns Among the Eastern Provinces

                    V. AN ENTERPRISE QUESTIONED

23. Vicissitudes of a Beleaguered Enterprise: The Society on
     the Defensive, 1700–1750   571

     Of Rites and Wrongs: The Erosion of the Enterprise in Southeast Asia and China; The Beleaguered Provinces of Goa and Malabar; Brazil: An Expanding Enterprise; Tribulations of the Society in Joanine Portugal

24. Striking a Balance: For God or Mammon?   614

Poverty, "The Strong Wall"; Scrupulosity: Jesuit Record-Keeping; Patterns of Income; Patterns of Expenditure; Parameters of Shared Costs; The Persistent Preoccupation with Debts

25. An Enterprise with a Rich Past but an Uncertain Future   651

APPENDIXES

A. Concerning Coinage, Money of Account, and
    Conversions   665
B. The Society of Jesus as the Alleged First
    Multinational Firm   668
C. Relations Between the Society and the Portuguese
    Inquisition   670
D. Number of Jesuits Serving in the Portuguese
    Assistancy, 1549–1760   674
E. Inventory of Supplies, New St. Paul's College,
    Goa, 1707   677
F. The Fate of the Jesuits Serving in the College of
    Olinda and Its Dependencies at the Time of
    the Second Dutch Invasion, 1630   680

    Bibliographical Note   683
    Index   691

Maps follow p. xxxi.
Illustrations follow pp. 38 and 318.

TABLES

1.1	Growth of the Society of Jesus, 1556–1749	17
2.1	Polish Recruits' Views of the Society and the World, from 92 Autobiographical Statements, 1574–80	37
2.2	Why They Joined the Society of Jesus: Responses from 695 Jesuits in Spain and Portugal, 1561–62	37
3.1	Expansion of the Society in the Estado da India and Beyond: Administrative Units and Their Dependencies, 1549–1607	46
3.2	Growth of the Society of Jesus in the Province of Brazil, 1558–1600	74
8.1	Number of Jesuits Sailing from Lisbon to the Eastern Provinces During the Seventeenth Century	204
9.1	Jesuit Residents of the Insular and African Stations During the Seventeenth Century	212
9.2	Number of Jesuits Resident in the Provinces of Goa and Brazil and Number Sent There from Lisbon per Year, 1600–1759	219
10.1	Average Length of Provincials' Terms	244
10.2	Ages of Provincials When Appointed	245
10.3	Ages of Visitors When First Appointed	248
11.1	Non-Portuguese Jesuits Who Sailed to the Assistancy Overseas via Lisbon, 1541–1750	268
11.2	Native Origins of Jesuits Serving in the Vice-Province of Maranhão, 1690–1760	273
11.3	Native Origins of Jesuits Serving in the Japan Province, 1685–1753	276
11.4	Native Origins of Jesuits Serving in the Vice-Province of China, 1621–1755	276
11.5	Regional Origins of Jesuits Serving in the Province of Portugal, 1593, 1693, and 1749	277
11.6	Natal Bishoprics of Members of the Province of Portugal, 1593, 1693, 1749, and 1750	277
11.7	Average Ages at Death of Jesuits Serving in Selected Administrative Units of the Portuguese Assistancy, 1525–1777	279
11.8	Average Ages at Death of Fathers General, Provincials, and Vice-Provincials of the Portuguese Assistancy, 1541–1773	280
11.9	Comparative Life Spans or Expectancies of Jesuit Generals and Peer Groups	280
11.10	Admissions and Dismissals in the Brazil Province, 1566–1707	293
12.1	Schedule of Purchases by the Procurator of the College of Espírito Santo, Évora, 1606	311

13.1	Distribution of Contributions to the King by the Province of Portugal, 1641	330
14.1	Primary Beneficiaries of Jesuit Estate Renunciations, Province of Paraguay, 1609–1763	348
14.2	Prominent Non-Portuguese European Benefactors of the Portuguese Assistancy	355
14.3	Property Inventory of André Velho Freire and D. Felipa de Paredes, 1660	360
15.1	Steps in the Formation of the Vineyard of Valbom, 1582–97	388
15.2	Percentage of Annual Income Derived from Indian Villages by Colleges in the Provinces of Goa and Malabar, 1666 and 1730	395
15.3	Income Derived from Urban Properties as a Percentage of Total Income: Province of Portugal, 1736–37	397
15.4	Transactions Concerning Urban Properties Belonging to the College of Bahia, 1573–1621	399
15.5	Leading Sources of Income by Colleges in Brazil Province, 1683–1757	400
16.1	Estimated Production Levels of Key Jesuit Estates in Portugal, 1632–33	412
16.2	Account Between the Labruja Estate and the College of Santo Antão, January 1610 to 9 August 1612	413
16.3	Conspectus of Food Production, Province of Portugal, ca. 1733–37	414
16.4	Percentage of Collegial Income Derived from Sugar, 1683–1757	426
16.5	Sugar Output of Leading Jesuit Estates, 1745–60	426
17.1	"Manifesto of the Absolutism and Robberies of the English Committed Contrary to the Transfer Articles of Bombay," 1722	447
20.1	Indian and Kaffir Household Servants in Colleges Belonging to the Province of Goa, ca. 1730	515
20.2	Slaves Purchased in the Bahian Market for Engenho Sergipe do Conde, 1623–37, 1643–52	519
20.3	Average Number of Children per Household, Fazenda de Santa Cruz, 1768	522
20.4	The Slave Population of the Brazil Province, 1694–1757	524
20.5	Jesuit Slaveholding in South America, ca. 1760	524
21.1	Exports by Religious Orders from Belém to Lisbon, 1743–45	547
23.1	Growth and Decline of the Japan Province and the Vice-Province of China, 1700–1755	573
23.2	Average Age at Death of Missionaries Serving in the Vice-Province of China and the Province of Japan, 1500–1749	581
23.3	Jesuits Sent from Europe to the Eastern Provinces, 1700–1759	583
23.4	Estimated Income of the Provinces of Goa and Malabar, 1699–1746	583
23.5	Membership of the Provinces of Goa and Malabar, 1697–1756	596
23.6	Growth of the Brazil Province and the Vice-Province of Maranhão, 1690–1751	598
23.7	Distribution of Members of the Brazil Province and the Vice-Province of Maranhão, 1701–57	599
23.8	Jesuit Missions in the Province of Brazil, 1702–57	600
24.1	Estimates of Income by Major Units of the Portuguese Assistancy, ca. 1570–1757	622
24.2	Patterns of Expenditure in Six Jesuit Colleges	626

24.3 Expenditures of the College of Bragança, 1565–1756   626

24.4 Patterns of Expenditure of the Colleges of the Province of Goa, 1730   631

24.5 Patterns of Expenditure in the Provinces of Malabar, China,
      and Japan, 1730   632

24.6 Estimated Cost of Maintaining a Single Jesuit for One Year, 1550–1750   633

24.7 Wages of Hired Workers, Évora, ca. 1606   635

24.8 Comparative Expenditures by Four Contemporary Colleges, 1675–1700   637

24.9 Selected Salaries of Ecclesiastical and Imperial Officials, 1549–1750s   649

ABBREVIATIONS

ABAPP	*Anais da biblioteca e arquivo público do Pará*, 11 vols. (Belém, 1902–26; 1969)
ABNRJ	*Anais da biblioteca nacional* (Rio de Janeiro, 1876–)
ACE	*Assentos do conselho do estado*, ed. Panduronga S. S. Pissurlencar, 5 vols. (Bastorá, 1953–57)
ACL	Academia das Ciências de Lisboa
AERJ	Arquivo do Estado, Rio de Janeiro
AHR	*American Historical Review* (1895–)
AHSI	*Arquivum historicum societatis Iesu* (1931–)
AHU	Arquivo Histórico Ultramarino, Lisbon
AHU/LR	Arquivo Histórico Ultramarino, Lisbon, *livro[s] de registro* registry series
AHU/PA	Arquivo Histórico Ultramarino, Lisbon, miscellaneous papers by administrative unit
	BA = Bahia
	IN = India
	MA = Maranhão
	PA = Pará
	PB = Pernambuco
	RJ = Rio de Janeiro
	SP = São Paulo
AMB	Arquivo Municipal, Bahia
AMRJ	Arquivo Municipal, Rio de Janeiro
ANRJ	Arquivo Nacional, Rio de Janeiro
ANTT	Arquivo Nacional da Torre do Tombo, Lisbon
	/AJ = Armário Jesuítico collection
	/CJ = Cartório Jesuítico collection
	/LM = Livros das monções series
APB/	Arquivo Público do Estado, Bahia, Brazil
	CGVA = Cartas gerais a vários autoridades
	OR = Ordens régias
APO:1	J. H. da Cunha Rivara, ed., *Archivo Portuguez-Oriental*, 6 vols. in 9 (Nova Goa, 1857–76)
APO:2	A. B. de Bragança Pereira, ed., *Arquivo português oriental*, 11 vols. (Bastorá, 1936–40)
ARSI	Archivum Romanum Societatis Iesu

FG = Fondo Gesuitico
  Bras. = Brazil province
  Goa = Goa province
  JapSin = Japan province and vice-province of China
  Lus. = province of Portugal

ASCJ   António Franco, *Ano santo da companhia de Jesus em Portugal* (Porto, 1931)

ATC   Arquivo do Tribunal das Contas, Lisbon
  /CJ = Cartório Jesuítico collection
  /JI = Junta da Inconfidência collection

BA/JA   Biblioteca da Ajuda, Lisbon, Jesuítas na Asia collection

BAPP   Biblioteca pública do Pará, Belém, Brazil

BFUP   *Boletim da filmoteca ultramarina português*, 45 nos. (Lisbon, 1954–71)

BGJ   Franz Otto Busch, S.J., "Brasilienfahrer aus der Gesellschaft Jesu," in Ernste Reihe, *Aufsatze zur Portugiesischen Kulturgeschichte*, Band 11 (Munster, 1974), 215–96

BGUC   Biblioteca Geral, Universidade de Coimbra

BHCJ   László Polgár, S.I., *Bibliographie sur l'histoire de la compagnie de Jésus, 1901–1980*, 3 vols. in 6 (Rome, 1981–90)

BNL   Manuscript Section, Biblioteca Nacional, Lisbon
  CP = Coleção Pombalina, Pombaline collection
  FG = Fundo Geral, the general collection

BPE   Biblioteca Pública de Évora

CA   Afránio Peixoto, ed., *Cartas Jesuiticas*, vol. 2, *Cartas avulsas, 1550–1568* (Rio de Janeiro, 1931)

CB   Afránio Peixoto, ed., *Cartas Jesuiticas*, vol. 1, *Cartas do Brasil, 1549–1560* (Rio de Janeiro, 1931)

CCJ   Charles R. Boxer, *The Christian Century in Japan, 1549–1650* (Berkeley, 1951)

CCLP   José Justino de Andrade e Silva, comp., *Collecção chronológica da legislação portuguesa*, 10 vols. (Lisbon, 1854–59)

CeA   Eduardo de Castro e Almeida, comp., *Inventário dos documentos relativos ao Brasil existentes no Arquivo de Marinha e Ultramarina de Lisboa*, 8 vols. (Rio de Janeiro, 1913–36)

CJPM   Francisco Rodrigues, S.J., "A companhia de Jesús em Portugal e nas missões," *Revista de história* 10 (Lisbon, 1921): 161–201

CMP/*P*   Congresso do mundo português, *Publicações*, 18 vols. (Lisbon, 1940)

cod.   codex (a bound volume of documents)

CR   Carta régia, a royal provision intended to be a permanent directive

CSJ(C)   "The Constitutions of the Society of Jesus and Their Declarations," in George E. Ganss, S.J., trans. and ed., *The Constitutions of the Society of Jesus* (St. Louis, 1970)

CSJ(GE)	"The General Examen and Its Declarations," in George E. Ganss, S.J., trans. and ed., *The Constitutions of the Society of Jesus* (St. Louis, 1970), 75–118
CSPC/EI	Great Britain, Public Record Office, *Calendar of State Papers, Colonial* series, *East Indies* [title varies] 1–8 (1862–92)
CTEIP	Júlio Fermino Judice Biker, ed., *Collecção de tratados e concertos de pazes que o estado da India portuguesa fez com os reis e senhores com quem teve relações nas partes da Asia e Africa oriental desde o princípio da conquista até ao fim do século xviii*, 14 vols. (Lisbon, 1881–87)
cx.	*caixa* (box)
DH	Biblioteca Nacional, Rio de Janeiro, *Documentos históricos*, 110 vols. (1928–55)
DHA	Instituto do Açúcar e do Alcool, *Documentos para a história do açúcar*, 3 vols. (Rio de Janeiro, 1954–63)
DHJP	António José Teixeira, ed., *Documentos para a história dos Jesuítas em Portugal* (Coimbra, 1890)
DHMPPO	António da Silva Rego, ed., *Documentação para a história das missões do padroado português do oriente*, 12 vols. (Lisbon, 1947–58)
DHP	Joel Serrão, ed., *Dicionário de história de Portugal*, 4 vols. (Lisbon, 1971)
DI	Josef Wicki, S.J., ed., *Documenta indica*, 18 vols. (Rome, 1948–88)
DISP	Arquivo do Estado de São Paulo, *Publicação official de documentos interessantes para a história e costumes de São Paulo* (São Paulo, 1895–)
DM	Hubert Jacobs, S.J., ed., *Documenta malucensia*, 3 vols. (Rome, 1974–84)
DRI/LM	*Documentos remettidos da India ou livros das missões*, 5 vols. (Lisbon, 1880–1935)
DUP	Centro de estudos históricos ultramarinos, *Documentação ultramarina portuguesa*, 5 vols. (Lisbon, 1960–67)
DWIC	Dutch West India Company
EFI	William Foster, ed., *The English Factories in India, 1618–1669*, 13 vols. (Oxford, 1906–27)
EIC	East India Company
EJF	Pierre Delattre, S.J., ed., *Les Établissements des Jésuites en France depuis quatre siècles*, 5 vols. (Enghein, Belgium, 1949–57)
F/JM	D. Ferroli, S.J., *The Jesuits in Malabar*, 2 vols. (Bangalore, 1939–51)
HAG	Historical Archives of Goa
HAG/LM	Historical Archives of Goa, Livros das monções series
HAHR	*Hispanic American Historical Review* (1918–)
HCJAE	Antonio Astraín, *Historia de la compañía de Jesus en la asistencia de España*, 7 vols. (Madrid, 1902–25)
HCJAP	Francisco Rodrigues, S.J., *História da companhia de Jesus na assistência de Portugal*, 7 vols. (Porto, 1931–50)

HCJB	Serafim Leite, S.J., *História da companhia de Jesus no Brasil*, 10 vols. (Rio de Janeiro, 1938–50)
HIP	Fortunato de Almeida, *História da igreja em Portugal*, new ed., ed. Damião Peres, 4 vols. (Lisbon, 1968–71)
HJ	Henry Rule and A. C. Burnell, *Hobson-Jobson: A Glossary of Colloquial Anglo-Indian Words and Phrases*, 2d ed., ed. William Crooke (rpr., London, 1986)
HP	Ludwig von Pastor, *The History of the Popes*, trans. F. I. Antrobus et al., 40 vols. (London and St. Louis, 1898–1953)
HS:1	The Hakluyt Society, *Works*, 1st ser. (London, 1847–98)
HS:2	The Hakluyt Society, *Works*, 2d ser. (London, 1899–)
H/SAG	John Humbert, S.I., "Some Answers of the Generals of the Society of Jesus to the Province of Goa"
	H/SAG1 = *AHSI* 35 (1966): 322–46
	H/SAG2 = *AHSI* 36 (1967): 72–103
IAGHPB	Instituto archaeologico e histórico, Pernambuco
	OR = Ordens régias series
IHGB	Instituto Histórico e Geográfico Brasileiro
IHGB/MS	Instituto Histórico e Geográfico Brasileiro, Rio de Janeiro, J. C. Macedo Soares collection
IOL	India Office Library, London
JBBRAS	*Journal of the Bombay Branch of the Royal Asiatic Society* (1841–)
JMBRAS	*Journal of the Malay Branch of the Royal Asiatic Society* (1923–63)
JSM	Joseph N. Tylenda, S.J., comp., *Jesuit Saints & Martyrs* (Chicago, 1984)
*LAM*3	Alberto Lamego, *A terra Goytacá á luz de documentos inéditos*, vol. 3 (Paris, 1925)
LGM	"Livro grosso do Maranhão," *ABNRJ* 66 (1948) (= *LGM* 1) and 67 (1948) (= *LGM* 2)
LJI	Josef Wicki, S.J., comp., "Liste der Jesuiten-Indienfahrer, 1541–1758," in Hans Flasche, ed., *Aufsatz zur portugiesischen kulturgeschichte*, Band 7 (Munster, 1967), 252–450
LTC/RJ	D. Leite de Macedo, trans. and ed., *Livro de tombo do colégio de Jesus no Rio de Janeiro* (Rio de Janeiro, 1968)
m.	*maço[s]* (a bundle or bundles of archival documents)
MB	Serafim Leite, S.J., ed., *Monumenta brasiliae*, 5 vols. (Rome, 1956–68)
MHB	Ignácio Accioli de Cerqueira e Silva, *Memórias históricas e políticas da província da Bahia*, ed. Braz do Amaral, 6 vols. (Salvador, 1919–40)
MHE	*Memorial Historico Español*, 49 vols. (Madrid, 1851–1948)
MHJ	Josef Franz Schütte, S.J., ed., *Monumenta historica japoniae* (Rome, 1975)
NBBJC	Louis Pfister, S.J., comp., *Notices biographiques et bibliographiques sur les Jesuites de l'ancienne mission de China, 1552–1573*, 2 vols. in 1 (rpr., San Francisco, 1973)

NBL/GE	Newberry Library, Chicago, William B. Greenlee Collection
NCJ	Serafim Leite, S.J., ed. *Novas cartas jesuíticas (de Nóbrega a Vieira)* (São Paulo, 1940)
OLL	The Oliveira Lima Library, The Catholic University of America, Washington, D.C.
OM/*HP*	António Oliveira Marques, *History of Portugal*, 2 vols. (New York, 1972)
OSR	Victor Ribeiro, ed., *Obituários da igreja e casa professa de São Roque da Companhia de Jesus desde 1555 até 1704* (Lisbon, 1916)
PDH	*Portugal: Diccionario historico, biographico, bibliographico, heraldico, chorographico, numismatico, e artistico*, 8 vols. (Lisbon, 1903–13)
PRO/SP	Public Record Office, London [Chancery Lane], State Papers, Portugal
RACJ	Fernão Guerreiro, comp., *Relação anual das coisas que fizeram os padres da Companhia de Jesus nas suas missões*, ed. Artur Viegas, 3 vols. (Coimbra, 1930–42)
RADF	Arquivo Municipal, Rio de Janeiro, *Archivo do destricto federal; revista de documentos para a história da cidade do Rio de Janeiro*, 4 vols. (Rio de Janeiro, 1894–98)
RIHGB	*Revista do instituto historico e geografico brasileiro* (Rio de Janeiro, 1839–)
RJC	Joseph Dehergne, S.J., comp., *Repertoire des Jésuites de Chine de 1552 à 1800* (Rome, 1973)
RSI	Dionysius Fernández Zapico, S.J., comp., *Regulae Societatis Iesu (1540–1556)* (Rome, 1948)
S/*FX*	Georg Schurhammer, S.J., *Francis Xavier: His Life, His Times*, trans. M. Joseph Costelloe, S.J., 4 vols. (Rome, 1973–82)
VFL	Vatican Microfilm Collection, St. Louis University, St. Louis, Mo.
VMP	Josef Franz Schütte, S.J., *Valignano's Mission Principles for Japan*, 2 vols., trans. John J. Coyne, S.J. (St. Louis, Mo., 1980–85)
VOC	United Netherlands Chartered East India Company
VS/*HP*	Joaquim Veríssimo Serrão, *História de Portugal*, 10 vols. to date (Lisbon, 1977–)

GLOSSARY

aldeia: village; in Brazil, a mission settlement under religious supervision

alfândega: customs house

alvará: royal decree, nominally in force for one year, but often extended indefinitely

arroba: a unit of weight; in the Portuguese world, 32 lb. or 14.5 kg.

assistancy: administrative unit within the Society of Jesus based generally upon national considerations and consisting of provinces and vice-provinces. The Portuguese Assistancy included the provinces of Portugal, Brazil, Goa, Cochin, and Japan (Southeast Asia) and the vice-provinces of China and Maranhão.

auto-de-fé: act of faith; solemn public ceremony for the punishment of persons sentenced by the Holy Offices of the Inquisition

câmara: municipal council

carta régia: a royal provision intended to be permanently enforced

casa: house; in the Society of Jesus, a house of instruction, often an incipient college

coadjutor: literally, a helper; (1) *spiritual* (var. *espiritual*): curate; within the Society of Jesus, a priest who had taken simple vows; (2) *temporal*: lay brother

colégio máximo: senior Jesuit college; e.g., New St. Paul's, Goa; Bahia, Brazil

consultores: advisors to senior Jesuit administrators

conto: money of account, equal to 1 million *réis*

corregidor: royal magistrate

cortes: parliament

daimyo: Japanese baron

desembargador: senior royal magistrate; High Court justice

engenho: sugar mill; by extension, a sugar plantation

escrivão da [de] puridade: confidential royal secretary

Estado da India: the eastern Portuguese empire extending from Mozambique to Macao, its center being Goa, the viceregal capital

estáncia: stock ranch

fazenda: landed property devoted to the production of staples such as cereals, cacao, and sugar, as well as livestock

feitoria: fortress-factory

fidalgo: gentleman; member of lesser nobility

fidalguia: the nobility of Portugal

Institute: generally, the Society of Jesus; particularly, its *Constitutions* and later regulations

lavradores: farmers; *de cana*: share tenants on a sugar plantation

New Christians: In 1497, King Manuel I (the Fortunate) compelled all Portuguese Jews, an estimated 20 percent of the population, to convert to Christianity. The resulting so-called

New Christians were considered inferior, often suspect, by traditional Catholics, termed Old Christians.

ouvidor geral: district magistrate

Overseas Council: royal advisory council established in 1643; the primary link between the crown and its empire

padroado real: authority granted by late-fifteenth- and sixteenth-century popes to rulers of Portugal empowering them to nominate bishops, to license ecclesiastics and control their movements, to collect tithes, to approve the construction of religious edifices, etc., and charging them with the promotion and protection of the Catholic faith

procurator: within the Society of Jesus, a designation that applied to several types of official serving as business agents of a house, college, or group of colleges and representing the Society's interests at the courts of Portugal and Spain

provisão: royal edict

quinta: a landed property of a size varying from plot to plantation

real, pl. *réis*, rs.: Portuguese money of account, roughly the equivalent of the English farthing

Relação: High Court in Porto, Salvador, and Goa

Santa Casa da Misericórdia (Holy House of Mercy): a charitable fraternity with branches in leading Portuguese cities within the kingdom and abroad; its functions included the care of orphans, of women without husbands, and of prisoners; the lending of capital; and the transmission of funds entrusted to the House by persons residing abroad

sesmaria: a grant of land

third catalogues: periodic economic reports prepared in the name of a provincial and submitted to the fathers general and procurators-general in Rome

ultramar: generally, the lands beyond Europe; specifically, the Portuguese empire

Visitor: Jesuit administrative inspector and corrector, usually of a province or vice-province; the senior representative of the father general

EDITORIAL CONVENTIONS

Throughout this study several conventions have been employed. Although Luso-Brazilian orthography seems endlessly in flux, I have tried to follow modern Portuguese preferences with respect to accents and the spelling of names and terms wherever possible. Foreign terms are italicized only when first introduced. From 1580 to 1640 Portugal and its empire was ruled by three Spanish sovereigns—Philip II, III, and IV; I have used those designations, which are more common than the Portuguese alternatives—Philip I, II, and III. All units of weight, dry measures, and length are expressed in metric terms; for example, the standard Portuguese *arroba* (32 lb.) is 14.5 kilograms, and 1 mile is 1.6 kilometers. To present monetary data uniformly, I have converted the several forms of money or money of account employed in the lands east of the Cape of Good Hope into their equivalents in Portugal and its Atlantic empire. For details, consult Appendix A. The Gregorian Calendar was accepted by Portugal and other Catholic lands in 1582 but was resisted by England until 1752, when 3 September suddenly became 14 September. Until then, the Portuguese New Year began on 1 January, but for the English the year changed on 25 March. Before 1752, English consular and diplomatic officials sometimes adhered to what was termed Old Style (OS) dating and sometimes employed New Style (NS). In the notes I have generally followed the dispatch writer's preference but, where necessary, have adjusted the dates to be consistent with Portuguese practice. Unless specifically indicated, persons with identical surnames are not known to have been related.

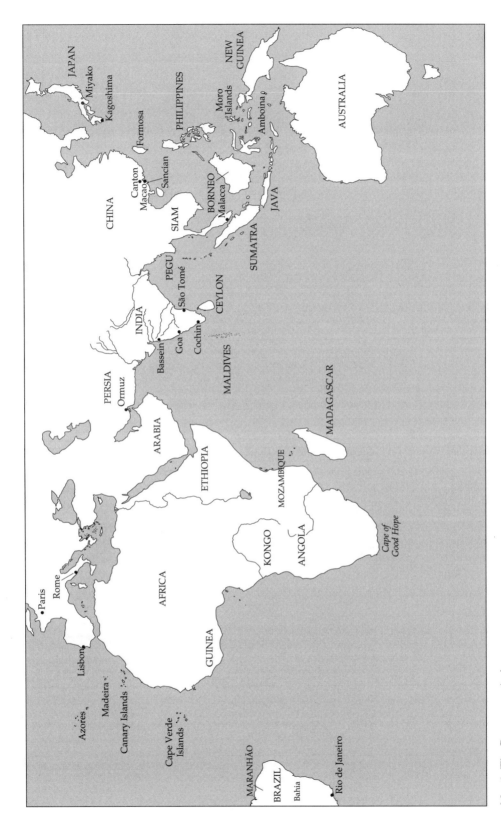

Map 1. The Portuguese Assistancy.

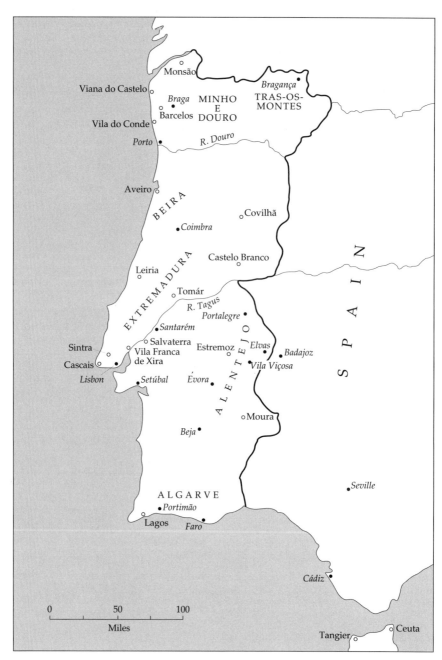

Map 2. Principal Jesuit installations in and near Portugal. *Italic type indicates Jesuit centers.*

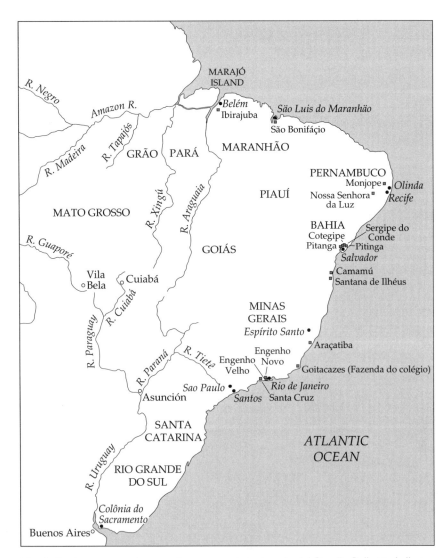

Map 3. Jesuit centers and supporting sugar estates in colonial Brazil. *Italic type indicates Jesuit centers.*

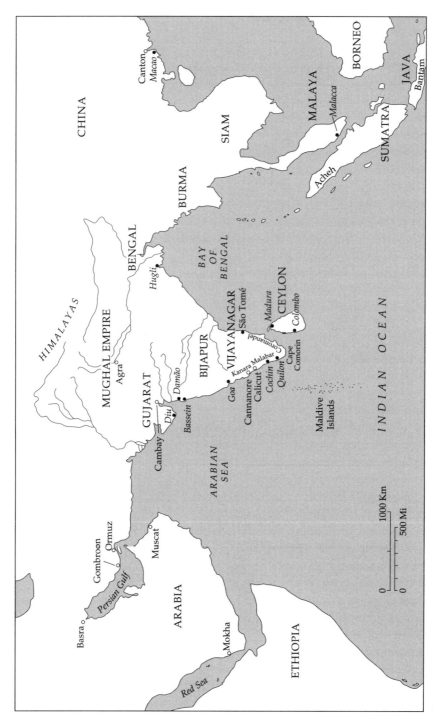

Map 4. The Estado da India. *Italic type indicates Jesuit centers.*

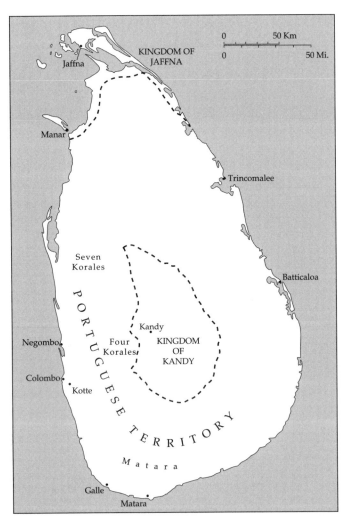

Map 5. Ceylon during the early seventeenth century.

KINGDOM OF
JAFFNA

0   50 Km
0   50 Mi.

Jaffna

Manar

Trincomalee

Seven
Korales

P
O
R
T
U
G
U
E
S
E

Batticaloa

Kandy

Negombo

Four
Korales

KINGDOM
OF
KANDY

Colombo

Kotte

T
E
R
R
I
T
O
R
Y

Matara

Galle

Matara

Map 6 (below). The city and
territory of Goa to the 1740s.

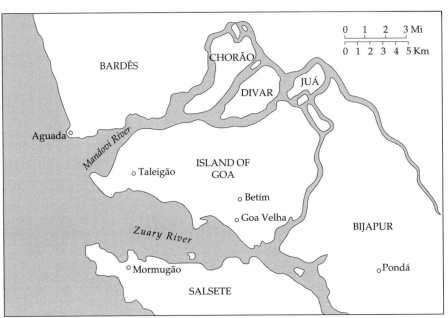

BARDÊS

CHORÃO

0   1   2   3 Mi
0 1 2 3 4 5 Km

DIVAR

JUÁ

Aguada

Mandovi River

ISLAND OF
GOA

Taleigão

Betím

Goa Velha

BIJAPUR

Zuary River

Mormugão

Pondá

SALSETE

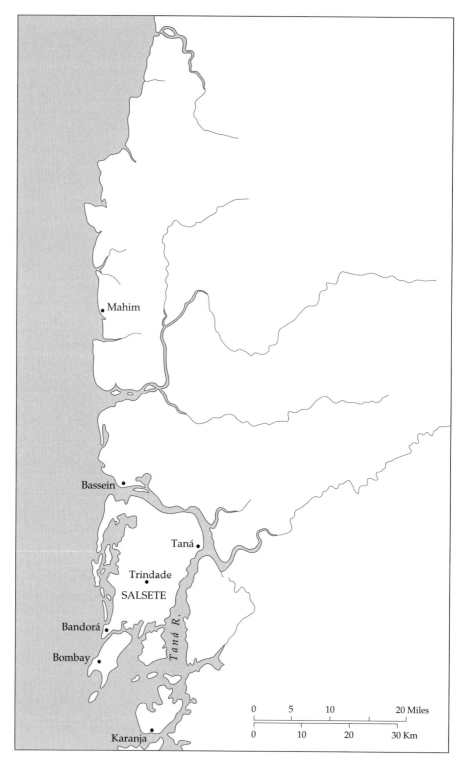

Map 7. Bombay and portions of the northern province.

PART I

The Creation

The Founding of a Controversial New Society

> The end of this Society is to devote itself with God's grace not only to the salvation and perfection of the members' own souls, but also with that same grace to labor strenuously in giving aid toward the salvation and perfection of the souls of their fellowmen.
>
> —Loyola, *General Examen*

> Whoever desires to serve as a soldier of God beneath the banner of the cross in our Society . . . should . . . keep . . . in mind [that he] is a member of a Society founded chiefly . . . to strive . . . for the defense and propagation of the faith and for the progress of souls in Christian life and doctrine.
>
> —Loyola, *Formula of the Institute of the Society of Jesus*

EUROPEANS IN THE first half of the sixteenth century witnessed a series of upheavals that would profoundly affect the course of global history. They discovered unsuspected new continents, unexpected civilizations, and undreamed-of wealth. They saw the Iberian Peninsula, home of the kingdoms of Spain and Portugal, emerge as the locus of political, military, and economic power within the European continent. They watched the rise of a menacing Muslim power in the East—the Turks, who threatened Christian control of the Mediterranean and Arabian seas and contiguous lands. They witnessed the shattering of Christian unity by militant Protestants, who gained control of England and portions of the Germanies and the Low Countries and threatened Catholic hegemony elsewhere. The Catholic Church responded to these challenges vigorously with the enactment of sweeping purifying and centralizing reforms by the Council of Trent (1545–63); improvements in the practices of some of the Church's venerable Orders, notably the Benedictines, Augustinians, and Franciscans; and the authorization of the formation of a new group of Orders that would include the Theatines (1524), the Barnabites (1533), the Somaschi (1568), and one that dared to call itself the Society of Jesus (1540).[1] This chapter examines the creation of the Society of

---

1. Competent recent surveys of these events include Steven Ozment, *The Age of Reform, 1250–1550: An Intellectual and Religious History of Late Medieval and Reformation Europe* (New Haven, 1980); and D. Lamar Jensen, *Reformation Europe* (Lexington, Mass., 1981). See also L. Cristiani, *L'Église à l'époque du concile de Trent*, in Augustin Fliche and Victor Martin, eds., *Histoire de l'Église depuis les origines jusqu'à nos jours*, no. 17 (Paris, 1948). Very much worth reading are H. Outram Evennett, *The Spirit of the Counter Reformation* (Cambridge, 1968), and idem, "The New Orders," *The New Cambridge Modern History*, vol. 2, ed. G. R. Elton, 2d ed. (Cambridge, 1990), 313–38, as well as T. M. Parker, "The Papacy, Catholic Reforms, and Christian Missions," *The New Cambridge Modern History*, vol. 3, ed. R. B. Wernham (Cambridge, 1968), 44–71. See also Jean Delumeau,

Jesus, its common and unique structural and policy features, its perceived objectives, and its early reception.

The Origins of the Society

The formation of the Society of Jesus, the most dynamic, successful, influential, and controversial of the new Orders created during the turbulent sixteenth century, was a remarkable but unplanned achievement by a remarkable man who, for much of his life, had no such aspiration. Iñigo López de Recaldo (b. 1491–d. 1556), who later adopted the name Ignatius de Loyola, was the son of a propertied Navarrese family who felt impelled to undertake a dramatic mid-life career change when a French cannonball ended his vocation as an adventurous, amorous knight during his participation in the defense of Pamplona (1521). While recovering from his grievous leg wounds, Iñigo read two tomes whose messages moved him profoundly and prompted his spiritual conversion. One was a volume of saints' lives, the other a Castilian translation of the *Life of Christ* by a Carthusian monk named Ludolf of Saxony. Iñigo was deeply impressed by what he learned about the experiences of the saints, particularly Saint Dominic and Saint Francis, founders of the two most popular Mendicant Orders of the late Middle Ages, and by Ludolf's vivid account of Christ's sufferings. Accordingly, he resolved to dedicate the remainder of his life to some form of holy service. Before he discovered his specific mission he undertook nearly two decades of intellectual and spiritual preparation as well as a good deal of travel.[2]

As soon as he had recovered from his injury, Iñigo went to a secluded Benedictine monastery near Barcelona. There he performed a dramatic gesture comparable to Saint Francis's act of stripping himself naked in front of his father and bishop: Iñigo gave away his knightly accoutrements and assumed the sackcloth of a humble pilgrim. He spent the next year in exhaustive spiritual exercises in a cave at nearby Manresa before he undertook the obligatory pilgrimage. Taking Saint Francis as his model, he indulged in severe mortifications that included holding long nocturnal vigils, fasting up to three days at a time, flogging himself with barbed chains, and engaging in the so-called Franciscan kiss with a diseased wretch—all acts that he would proscribe for his comrades later on. In addition to such external acts of piety, he absorbed the teachings of *The Imitation of Christ*, a famed handbook addressed to monks that is generally ascribed to Thomas à Kempis, the foremost writer of the "modern devotion," a religious movement particularly active in northern Europe at the time.[3] Inspired by such reading, Iñigo wrote his own spiritual guide, the famed *Spiritual Exercises*, a "shock-tactic spiritual gymnastic" (as Evennett so aptly described it) that the author continued to revise until the mid-1550s. Its purpose was the

Catholicism Between Luther and Voltaire (London, 1977); and John O'Malley, S.J., ed., *Catholicism in Early Modern History: A Guide to Research* (St. Louis, 1988).

    2. E. M. Rix, trans., *The Testament of Ignatius Loyola* (St. Louis, 1900). Far more has been (and continues to be) written on Loyola than on all other Jesuits. The most recent and complete bibliography is included in *BHCJ*, 1. See also S/*FX*, 1: 136 n. 232, 475–93.

    3. Harold C. Gardiner, S.J., ed., *The Imitation of Christ: Thomas à Kempis* (Garden City, N.Y., 1955); R. R. Post, *The Modern Devotion: Confrontation with Reformation and Humanism* (Leiden, 1968), esp. chap. 13.

transformation of the sinful man into an instrument of devotion, one absolutely attuned to the will of God.[4]

In 1523 Iñigo undertook a brief but unrewarding pilgrimage to the Holy Land. He returned certain that he was destined to aid troubled souls in achieving salvation and oneness with God, but convinced that he could not realize that destiny until he had obtained adequate instruction in Latin, letters, and theology. He enrolled in various Aragonese and Castilian universities but did not achieve the mastery that he sought, partly because he devoted so much of his time and energy to preaching and to the administration of his Spiritual Exercises to each person he persuaded to take them. His unorthodox activities inevitably aroused the suspicion of the Holy Office of Castile, and on three occasions he was incarcerated briefly.

Iñigo decided to follow the trail of other Peninsular students to the University of Paris, the leading international center of higher learning. As D. Lamar Jensen has observed, he entered its doors (1528) just as John Calvin was leaving.[5] The new Protestant dogmas were exciting many Parisians, but Iñigo was repelled by them. He began his studies at the Collège de Montaigue, but subsequently transferred to the Collège de Sainte-Barbe, a notable center of humanistic learning administered by Dr. Diogo de Gouveia, a Portuguese savant.[6] In both institutions Iñigo devoted himself to rigorous intellectual preparation for his still-undefined lifelong mission. Although not personally attracted to a scholarly life, he developed a profound reverence for learning, particularly for the philosophical teachings of Aristotle and the theological doctrines of Saint Thomas Aquinas.

The nearly seven years that Iñigo stayed in Paris were decisive for his career. As a symbolic gesture signifying his rejection of his previous life, in 1532 he dropped his family name, following the custom of many ecclesiastics—Francis of Assisi, for example—and replaced it with Loyola, the ancestral palace where he was born. Ignatius (Iñigo) de Loyola, or Loyola as he would henceforth generally be known, became a successful fund-raiser, obtaining money to sustain his fellow students. He also distinguished himself as the saintly spiritual leader of a coterie, six of whom became his original disciples. They included Diego Laínez, destined to become Loyola's immediate successor as head of the Order that Loyola would found, despite Laínez's part-Jewish lineage; Francis Xavier, who would become the most revered missionary in the history of the Society; and Simão Rodrigues, the stormy Portuguese-born founder of the Order in the kingdom of Portugal. Though each was younger and quicker to learn than Loyola, each also recognized his exceptional gifts of leadership and spiritual insight. All eventually agreed to submit to the rigors of his month-long Spiritual Exercises and to participate in frequent devotional activities with him at the Carthusian monastery of Montmartre, situated just outside of Paris. It was there,

4. Thomas Corbishley, S.J., trans., *The Spiritual Exercises of Saint Ignatius* (Wheathamstead, Hertfordshire, 1973). Evennett's understanding of the significance of the Exercises is superlative. See his *Spirit*, esp. 50–55, and S/*FX*, 1: 216 n. 186, both of which discuss the problem of the literary origins of the Exercises. Despite its age, Heinrich Boehmer, *The Jesuits: An Historical Study*, trans. Paul Zeller Stradach (Philadelphia, 1928), remains a stimulating analysis.

5. Jensen, *Reformation Europe*, 176.

6. For an excellent sketch of the origins and significance of the Collège de Sainte-Barbe, see S/*FX*, 1: 81–85. The Paris years of Iñigo and his companions are briefly discussed in George E. Ganss, S.J., *Saint Ignatius' Idea of a Jesuit University* (Milwaukee, 1954), chap. 2, and in S/*FX*, 1: 77–276.

on the Feast of the Assumption (15 August 1534), that Loyola led his six fellow theology students in taking their celebrated vow to surrender most of their possessions to the poor and to proceed to Rome to obtain the pope's consent to make a pilgrimage to Jerusalem, or, if that proved impossible, to "offer my services to the pope and perform whatever he commands me."[7]

Though that was not Iñigo's intention, the Montmartre oath became the first of a series of steps that led to the founding of the Society of Jesus.[8] In 1535 Iñigo and his companions separated. He returned to Navarre to recover his health and to attend to family matters. Meanwhile, his disciples fulfilled their promises and gave away all their possessions before proceeding on foot from Paris to Venice. Iñigo joined his companions in Venice in 1537. It was there that he and all but one of his disciples took the customary series of Holy Orders that led to their ordination on the feast of Saint John the Baptist (24 June 1537). However, because of an impending war in the eastern Mediterranean, Iñigo and his band soon discovered that it was impossible for them to fulfill their intention to sail to the Holy Land. While they waited for the conflict to be resolved, Iñigo successfully recruited additional followers and deployed them and his original disciples in a variety of activities. Some preached in public squares, begging for alms and shelter; others visited hospitals and prisons. Iñigo himself closely examined the practices of the new Theatine Order, then based in Venice, and also began to make important contacts in Rome. He also sent some of his men to several northern Italian universities to preach, to lecture on the scriptures, and to recruit. Other disciples performed spectacularly during a severe famine in the Eternal City (December 1538–February 1539), when they helped to feed thousands.[9]

Through these manifold activities, the sons of Loyola gained invaluable experience as well as increasing visibility, especially among people who counted. No one counted for more than Pope Paul III (1534–49), who regularly invited the Loyolans to his chambers during mealtimes. There they impressed him and his guests—groups of cardinals and scholars—by engaging in what the pope himself termed edifying theological debates. But access to the papal court was soon in jeopardy when a former recruit charged the Loyolans with being Lutheran heretics. Iñigo responded by asking for a prompt investigation by the papal inquisition and gained new prestige for his followers when that tribunal declared the allegations to be without foundation.[10]

By early 1539 the *prête parisiense* (one of the many sobriquets then applied to Iñigo's companions) had established themselves as zealous preachers, tireless workers, and well-informed debaters. Every month they received more invitations for service than their scant number permitted them to accept. It was time to decide whether their informal fraternal association was adequate for them to meet the increasing opportunities to discharge their religious commitment, or whether they ought to form an organization that would endure beyond their own time.

---

7. The oath is quoted in Boehmer, *The Jesuits*, 57; cf. S/*FX*, 1: 212–15.
8. The most recent account of the beginnings of the Society is John W. O'Malley, S.J., *The First Jesuits* (Cambridge, Mass., 1993). For the state of recent Ignatian scholarship, see Juan Plazaola, ed., *Ignacio de Loyola y su tempo: Congreso internacional de historia* (Bilbao, 1992).
9. S/*FX*, 1: 297–452.
10. Ibid., 1: 421–22.

During the Lenten and Easter seasons of 1539, Iñigo and his companions took the second step toward the creation of a new Order when they engaged in lengthy prayer and discussion concerning their future course of action. In June, Iñigo summarized their collective views in a document variously known as the *Summa instituti*, the *Formula instituti*, the Five Chapters, or the primitive constitution. Its preparation marked the third step toward the founding of the Society, for it was, in effect, a prospectus for what Iñigo and his companions decided to call a "Society in the name of Jesus." They pledged themselves "to engage in military service for God under the standard of the cross" and the leadership of a lifetime general. They announced their intention to remain activists rather than become a contemplative Order, to spread the faith "through the ministry of the word, spiritual exercises, and works of charity, and . . . the instruction of children," and to undertake whatever tasks the vicar of Christ (the pope) assigned them. To reinforce that pledge, they solemnly promised that in addition to taking the customary vows of chastity, poverty, and obedience, their most qualified members would also take a special vow of strict obedience to the commands of the supreme pontiff.[11]

Iñigo submitted this prospectus to Paul III at the end of June or the beginning of July 1539. Though the pope himself was very receptive, as were some members of his curia, others worried whether a new and unconventional Order would bring credit or embarrassment to the embattled Church. Some also questioned the need for another religious Order in view of the directives of the Fourth Lateran Council (1215) and the Council of Lyon (1274), both of which were opposed to the further proliferation of Orders.

Although the recent approval given the Theatines and the Barnabites had already muted these arguments, the determined, ever-resourceful Iñigo campaigned to win over key doubters. First, he ordered his companions to say 3,000 masses in honor of the Trinity. Second, knowing that he must win over Cardinal Bartolomeo Guidiccioni, a highly influential figure in the papal bureaucracy and former vicar general of Parma, Iñigo directed one of his companions to write the duke of Parma soliciting his intervention. The duke, in turn, contacted a brother who had recently been named cardinal and others whom he knew at the papal court, asking them to support the Loyolans' petition. The Loyolans also obtained a supportive statement from the city elders of Parma to their ambassador in Rome and prevailed upon D. Constanza Farnese, illegitimate daughter of Paul III and reputedly the most influential woman in Rome, who enlisted the assistance of the archbishop of Siena. And at the behest of John III of Portugal, whose enthusiasm for the Loyolans will be examined in the next chapter, the Portuguese ambassador to Rome, who had engaged Iñigo to be his personal confessor, used whatever influence he could to encourage the pope's approval.

Such wire-pulling was standard practice in governments then as today. Although the Jesuits would be accused of being particularly successful with such tactics, that charge is generally unprovable. In this instance, however, there can be no question that the well-orchestrated campaign was successful. After Iñigo agreed to make certain minor changes in the Five Chapters, Cardinal Guidiccioni recommended that Paul III accept the new Order. The pope did so in the bull *Regimini militantis ecclesiae* (25 September 1540), the fourth step in the Society's formation. Although that bull cautiously authorized an Order of limited size—a restriction soon removed—it provided the initial papal sanction for one of

11. Ibid., 1: 454–65.

the most dynamic but controversial Orders in the Church, one that would survive countless challenges in many parts of the world during the next 233 years. Nearly twenty years after those dark days at Pamplona, Ignatius de Loyola had finally found his mission in life.[12]

The Organization of the Society

As soon as Loyola's Order had been sanctioned, the founder became the Society's first general, or father general, and as such was the man primarily responsible for drafting of its constitution. He began that task in 1544 and was later assisted by key advisors, including Juan Polanco, a University of Padua–trained lawyer and priest who became the Society's first secretary (1547–73), and Jerónimo Nadal, Loyola's sometime vicar general.[13] In 1551 the first draft was experimentally implemented in places where the Society was then represented. After receiving suggestions for improvements, the founder continued to revise the text until his death in 1556. Two years later the Society's First General Congregation approved the *Constitutions*, which, with minor revisions, remained in force until the Order's suppression in 1773.

Just as the early Dominicans and Franciscans borrowed from each other and from earlier Orders, particularly the Cistercians,[14] so Loyola and his collaborators borrowed certain elements from existing Orders but rejected other features that they deemed incompatible with the founder's vision of a uniquely activist organization. Thus Loyola rejected the autonomist structure of the Benedictines, the early Cluniacs, the Premonstratensians, and the Augustinians, as well as the democratic model of the early Dominican Order.[15] He preferred the centralized structures of his own time as represented by the Dominican Order and increasingly by the papacy itself, as well as by secular governments.[16]

The result was an organization with a pyramidal system of government in which power flowed from the top, or "head," as Loyola termed it, to the members of the body of the Society. The early Dominicans and both the Spiritual and Conventual Franciscans of Loyola's time were governed by elective leaders who served for limited terms. In contrast, Loyola and his collaborators agreed that the Society would be best ruled by a

12. Ibid., 1: 466–74, 540–51; Boehmer, *The Jesuits*, 64–66; James Broderick, S.J., *The Origins of the Jesuits* (Garden City, N.Y., 1960). Each of the authors cited in the Preface considers the background to the Society's establishment.

13. *CSJ(C)*, 47–59; Richard H. Dowling, S.J., "Juan de Polanco, S.J.," *Woodstock Letters* 69, 1 (1940): 1–20; Manuel Ruiz Jurado, "Nadal y Polanco sobre la formula del Instituto de la Companía de Jesús," *AHSI* 47 (1978): 225–39.

14. Rosalind B. Brooke, *Early Franciscan Government: Elias to Bonaventure* (Cambridge, 1959), 225ff. and 293ff.; R. W. Southern, *Western Society and the Church in the Middle Ages* (Middlesex, 1970), 283–84.

15. Cf. William A. Hinnebusch, O.P., *The History of the Dominican Order: Origins and Growth to 1500*, 2 vols. (Staten Is., 1966), 1: 170ff.; E. K. Francis, "Toward a Typology of Religious Orders," *American Journal of Sociology* 4, 5 (Mar. 1950): 437–49. I am indebted to my colleague Joan Ullman for calling this dated but still stimulating article to my attention. It is sometimes said that the Cluniacs were among Loyola's models, but Giles Constable argues strongly against "the myth of the administrative centralization" of that Order during the late eleventh and twelfth centuries: "Cluniac Administration and Administrators in the Twelfth Century," in *Cluniac Studies* (London, 1980), 17–29.

16. Alexander Hamilton Thompson, "The Monastic Orders," in *The Cambridge Medieval History* (rpr., Cambridge, 1957), 5: 658–96, provides an excellent analysis of the structure of the major Orders. See also Jensen, *Reformation Europe*, 177.

general appointed for life. Such a director, called by the Jesuits a superior general or father general or simply a "general," in contrast to a master general (the head of the Dominicans and Spiritual Franciscans) or a minister general (the superior of the early Franciscans and the later Conventuals), possessed in theory and sometimes in practice exceptionally broad powers with respect to both the shaping of policy and administrative appointments. That authority could not be effectively checked by the general congregation, the collegiate body that was the Jesuit counterpart of the general chapter of the Mendicants. The general congregation convened only upon the call of the father general, his vicar, or some other designated agent. Participants in such assemblies included provincials (that is, territorial managers) and two representatives selected by each provincial congregation or named by the provincial. Although Loyola suggested that the general congregations might gather at regular three- to six-year intervals, their primary functions were to ratify measures decreed by the father general and, upon his death, to elect a successor. Unlike the Mendicant general chapters of the thirteenth century, Jesuit general congregations were not empowered to summon their general to account for his actions in behalf of the Society.[17]

The *Constitutions* authorized the general to govern the Society with the aid of a *socio* or companion, a secretary, a procurator-general, and several assistants. The procurator-general was the Society's chief legal officer and represented its interests in the papal curia; he also oversaw the accounting procedures of the Society's components. Originally there were four assistants, but their number later increased to five and then to six. Each served as liaison between the generalate and one of the major linguistic divisions within the Society— the Polish, German, French, Italian, Spanish, and Portuguese. The general congregation named or ratified the appointment of the general's assistants. None of them exercised any independent authority, for all decisions were undertaken only in the name of the father general himself.[18]

Since the curia was firmly situated in the Eternal City by Loyola's time, Rome also became site of the Society's permanent headquarters. The eighteen men who headed the Order between 1540 and 1773 rarely ventured outside of Italy, unlike the peripatetic early masters-general of the Dominicans.[19] As a consequence, they were dependent upon senior lieutenants, who administered large and small units of the Society beyond the limits of Rome. In theory, the father general appointed each of those administrators, although in practice he depended upon the recommendations of those who knew them best, their associates and peers. The duties and duration of service of such officials—territorial officers called provincials or vice-provincials, collegial superiors termed rectors, special investigators called Visitors, and other supervisors—will be explored in later chapters, especially Chapters 10 and 11.

Various writers have called attention to the supposed resemblance of the new Order to a military organization, suggesting that Loyola's soldiering background influenced his molding of the Society.[20] For example, C. R. Boxer has suggested that the Jesuits may be

17. *CSJ(C)*, pt. 8, chaps. 2–3; cf. pt. 9, chap. 1, par. 322.
18. *CSJ(C)*, pt. 9, chaps. 5 and 6.
19. Hinnebusch, *History*, 1: 202ff. and 124.
20. Cf. Evennett, *Spirit*, 82, and René Fülöp-Miller, *The Jesuits: A History of the Society of Jesus*, trans. F. S. Flint and D. F. Tait (1930; rpr. New York, 1963), 24–27.

likened to the United States Marines, implying that they were the spiritual shock troops of their time. However tempting such analogies may be, they are at best only partial fits. It is true that the Society possessed a strong chain-of-command structure extending from the most humble lay brothers through their intermediate superiors to the provincials and beyond to the assistants and the general, who for many early Jesuits became a father figure as well as Christ's lieutenant and an apparently nearly omnipotent commander of his forces. And it is true that there was provision in the *Constitutions* for harsh discipline. Though punishment did sometimes include penances such as the wearing of hair shirts, exile, and confinement in ecclesiastical jails, it never extended to corporal punishment comparable to the lashings administered to delinquent sailors, for example. Although the so-called Five Chapters twice refer to "military service for God" and pledge that members of the Society will labor "under the command of the Vicar of Christ," that is, the pope,[21] it should be remembered that the application of military symbolism to ecclesiastical bodies was commonplace long before the coming of the Jesuits. Indeed, it can be traced back to the clarion calls of the primitive church (2 Cor. 10:4–6) and was frequently employed during the Middle Ages. Thus, Federico Visconti, archbishop of Pisa, once described a stirring encounter between sin and virtue as a "battle of wits and words":

> O what a great battle takes place between the friar confessor and the penitent sinner. The sinner says . . . "I will do everything that you wish, but I can in no way whatever give up such a one as my lover, or usury, or hatred, or the grudge I have against so-and-so." Whence it is fitting that, as one knight fights another powerful, rebellious knight, the friar struggle and do battle with spears of reason and persuasion against the sinner, that he may conquer him spiritually.[22]

Somewhat earlier, King Edgar stated in the charter of New Minster, Winchester, that "the abbot is armed with spiritual weapons and supported by a troop of monks anointed with the dew of heavenly graces. They fight together in the strength of Christ with the sword of the spirit against the aery wiles of the devils. They defend the king and clergy . . . from the onslaughts of their invisible enemies." And Ordericus Vitalis wrote in his *Ecclesiastical History*: "Look carefully at the things which are provided for you by trained monks . . .; strenuous is the warfare which these castellans of Christ wage against the Devil; innumerable are the benefits of their struggle."[23] It is not surprising, therefore, that Loyola employed military terminology, especially at a time when much of Europe was torn by both theological and armed battles and when the Iberian powers were undertaking the conquest of the world beyond Europe.[24]

21. S/*FX*, 1: 462–63.
22. As quoted in Lester K. Little, *Religious Poverty and the Profit Economy in Medieval Europe* (Ithaca, N.Y., 1978), 199.
23. Southern, *Western Society*, 224–25.
24. Cf. *CSJ(C)*, 348–49.

Unique and Controversial Features
of the Society

The Society's organizational structure differed somewhat from that of many other religious Orders. But its unique features, rather than its organization, quickly became sources of suspicion, complaint, and controversy. One such feature was the specific standards that Loyola established for admission to the Society. Those standards were detailed in the *Constitutions* and in the General Examen, a manual that Loyola wrote (1546) and that was to be presented to each postulant.[25] Among those barred from admission were heretics, schismatics, homicides, substantial debtors, "legitimate" slaves, married persons, and immoral persons.[26] Nor could those who had already taken sacred vows to enter another Order gain entry into the Society, a stipulation that was intended to avoid the unseemly charge of raiding, which had characterized Franciscan–Dominican rivalries during earlier centuries.[27] Other impediments that precluded admission were physical or mental defects, the former since they would "not help toward the edification of the neighbors with whom . . . it is necessary to deal."[28]

The founder emphasized the importance of character and personality in the evaluation of a prospect's suitability for the Society. Thus, those given to uncontrolled passions, inconstancy, lethargy, excessive ambition, and indiscretions were not wanted. On the positive side, recruiters were urged to seek men who possessed good health and memories, "a pleasing manner of speech so necessary for communications with one's fellow men," and, in general, "a good appearance by which those with whom they deal are more usually edified."[29] Respectability was also vital, especially during the Society's formative period, when its leaders were sensitive to the shaping of its public image (see especially Chapter 11). Candidates were obliged to demonstrate their legitimacy and the orthodoxy of their forebears and to disclose the occupations and civil status of their siblings. Finally, in accordance with the requirements of other Orders, the recruit was to be asked whether he was "determined to abandon the world and to follow the counsels of Christ our Lord," and to obey all directives by His agents.[30]

As will be seen later in this chapter and elsewhere, when the generals and their agents considered particular circumstances compelling, certain of these restrictions could be—and were—set aside. Nevertheless, no other Order then functioning imposed such severe admission requirements. Nor did any other religious body provide such rigorous training for its members. That long process began with the novitiate, which lasted two years, twice as long as in other Orders. Whereas other religious bodies generally isolated novices from

25. For the text, see *CSJ(GE)*.
26. The Society's policy with respect to the admission of married persons was very different from that of the early Franciscans. See Paul Schwartz, O.F.M., and Paul Lachance, O.F.M., trans., "The First Rule of Saint Francis," in David Flood, O.F.M., and Thaddée Matura, O.F.M., *The Birth of a Movement: A Study of the First Rule of St. Francis* (Chicago, 1975), 63–65.
27. As Hinnebusch conceded, "All the Orders opened their arms to religious who had wearied of their first love," especially after the Black Death (1348–49). *History,* 1: 322–25.
28. *CSJ(C)*, pt. 1, chap. 3.
29. *CSJ(C)*, pt. 1, chap. 2.
30. *CSJ(GE)*, chap. 3.

professed members during the novitiate, Loyola prescribed a brief period of isolation and reflection for the novices, followed by a series of "experiences" or tests. In common with novices in many other Orders, particularly those that adhered to the Rule of St. Benedict, Jesuit novices learned the virtues of silence and of speaking only when specifically addressed. Their first "experience" was a month devoted to mental toughening, accomplished through close study of the Spiritual Exercises and meditation on their meanings, and accompanied by close monitoring. There followed a month of working in hospitals and another in which the novice made a pilgrimage "without money and even begging from door to door," after which came the performance of "various low and humble offices" in the novitiate, and then a period in which the subject was required to explain Christian doctrine "in public to boys and other simple persons, or . . . [teach] it to individuals." Then came the first "experience" of preaching or hearing confessions. During these initial two years, the candidate's will and general character were constantly subjected to various trials to determine his suitability for the Jesuits' way of life.[31] Candidates who demonstrated acceptable pliability, compliance, and talent were then permitted to take simple vows that bound them to the Society (but not vice versa) and to move on to the scholasticate, a much longer period of education in the humanities, philosophy, and theology, as well as in Latin, some Hebrew, and some Greek, a regimen that, as Evennett has written, was in Loyola's time a "radical innovation."[32]

When candidates entered the Society, or during their scholasticate, their superiors evaluated their talents, determined which of the several grades within the Society they seemed to fit best, and assigned them accordingly.[33] Because of the pledge that they took when they joined, the candidates recognized that they had no right of appeal, although some resentfully protested that they had been misled (see Chapter 20). Those who completed their training might be assigned to one of four grades. The first was that of the temporal coadjutors, who were lay brothers, the equivalent of the *conversi* of the Cistercians, though far less numerous in the Society.[34] Still, their number probably came to exceed Loyola's original expectation, and the variety of positions they occupied over time was far greater than he had contemplated.[35] The temporal coadjutors played a far more vital role in the activities of the Society than most Jesuit historians recognize (see Chapter 20).

If the temporal coadjutors were the *laboratori* of the trinity of medieval ranks, the remaining three grades were the equivalent of the *oratori*, for their members were all ordained priests. The lowest level was occupied by the spiritual coadjutors. They were considered sufficiently qualified to hear confessions, give exhortations, and teach Christian doctrine, but they were judged insufficiently learned in theology or in Latin to be admitted to the two

31. Ibid., esp. chap. 4.

32. Evennett, "New Orders," 333.

33. *CSJ(C)*, Index 1, 375.

34. The conversi were "second-class monks . . . illiterate and therefore unable to take a full part in the life of the [Cistercian] community. . . . Yet they were monks in the sense that they followed a simplified monastic regime." Southern, *Western Society*, 257–58. Though the number of conversi often exceeded that of the first class of monks by a ratio of 3:1 or 4:1, the number of Jesuit lay brothers never exceeded the number of priests. One must remember, however, that in Brazil and in other parts of the New World the Jesuits also became the owners of massive numbers of slaves of African origin. See Chapter 20.

35. Loyola defined their roles as cooks, stewards, doorkeepers, infirmarians, launderers, gardeners, alms-gatherers, and purchasers. *CSJ(C)*, pt. 1, chap. 2, pars. 148–49. Many were, but some attained far less humble positions within the Order.

higher classes, that is, the professed. Loyola expected that in time the percentage of such spiritual assistants would diminish. In fact, their number grew substantially throughout the balance of the sixteenth and the early seventeenth centuries, at least in part because of the persistent influence of the founder's confidant, Jerónimo Nadal, who impressed upon Ignatius's successors the need to maintain exceptionally high standards of learning for those allowed to join the ranks of the professed.[36]

The two classes of the professed included those who were judged to have sufficient learning to be qualified to take three solemn vows and those of "conspicuous" learning (meaning those who were especially proficient in Latin) who could take the famous fourth vow of special obedience to the pope.[37] Among the Jesuits, that pledge was first made in the Montmartre oath quoted above and was incorporated in each of the three key documents that Loyola submitted to the papacy to win approval for his organization in 1540.[38] The Five Chapters, for example, stipulated that the oath takers would obey any order from the pontiff and venture wherever he chose to send them "whether ... among the Turks or any other infidels, even those who live in the region called the Indies, or among any heretics whatever, or schismatics, or any of the faithful." One can, of course, find similar commitments in the vows of those who joined the chivalric orders, such as those of Spain. The inclusion of that vow became one of the obstacles that had to be surmounted when the Society's petition was being considered in 1540. Some, including the influential Cardinal Ghinucci, contended that since all Christians were obliged to follow the pontiff's directives the oath was superfluous.[39] That contention has been repeated many times since. Though it appears to have been a tactic intended to associate the Society with the papacy more closely than rival Orders,[40] it may ultimately have done the Society more harm than good. Except on a few occasions during the sixteenth century, popes rarely sent Jesuits on hazardous errands. Later on there would be occasions when leaders of the Society strongly opposed papal measures—such as the creation of the Propaganda Fide (1622), for example, a deliberate attempt by the papacy to play a more direct role in the activities of overseas missions—but could not openly express their differences. Besides the Society's appropriation of the sacred name of Jesus,[41] perhaps no feature of the Society became such a red flag for its opponents as the papal oath, particularly among those who feared or resented the perceived expansion of papal political authority.

The fact that Jesuits did not wear a distinctive garb but rather adopted the form of clothing that their leaders believed to be most appropriate in particular circumstances also aroused disapproval.[42] Another persistent point of criticism was Loyola's insistence that Jesuits not sing masses and offices in choir, as members of other religious bodies did.

---

36. Ladislao Lukács, "De graduum diversitate inter sacerdotes in Societate Iesu," *AHSI* 37 (1968): 237–316.

37. *CSJ(GE)*, chap. 1; *CSJ(C)*, 349–56.

38. "The Formula of the Institute of the Society of Jesus," in *CSJ(C)*, 63–74, at 68; *CSJ(GE)*, 79–80 and n. 18; *CSJ(C)*, 239, 268.

39. *S/FX*, 1: 470.

40. Cf. A. D. Wright, *The Counter-Reformation: Catholic Europe and the Non-Christian World* (London, 1982), 18.

41. *CSJ(C)*, 348–49.

42. The General Examen, for example, leaves to the superior of the novitiate whether novices may continue to wear their street clothes or should put on distinctive garments. *CSJ(GE)*, 84–85.

That stipulation appears explicitly in chapter 3 of part 6 of the *Constitutions*: "Because the occupations which are undertaken for the aid of souls are of great importance … and because our residence in one place or another is so highly uncertain, our members will not regularly hold choir for the canonical hours or sing Masses and offices." Loyola instituted that provision to free his members for endeavors more directly related to their apostolic goals, but it seemed heretical to conservative members of the Church. Near the end of his life, Loyola did agree to permit Vespers to be sung during Holy Week, but that was not enough to satisfy Pope Paul IV, who, in 1556, insisted that choir be mandatory. The pope died soon after, and Juan Polanco successfully prevailed upon his successor to rescind that order.[43]

Loyola also banned the keeping of musical instruments in Jesuit houses.[44] Yet, as T. Frank Kennedy and others have shown, the leaders of the Society soon discovered that music had an important place in its apostolic work. Liturgical and paraliturgical music was later performed within Jesuit churches and colleges and was also an important component of the vast corpus of Jesuit drama.[45]

Defining the Society's Mission

Further differences between the Society and its critics arose as the new Order's leaders sought to determine its specific mission. As Nicholas P. Cushner once remarked, at the time of its official sanction, the Society lacked a clear sense of purpose.[46] One of its objectives was to continue with the same lively preaching in which the Loyolans had engaged since their arrival in Venice in 1537. The Loyolans' aim was not only to reinforce the faith among wayward Catholics but also to win back disobedient Protestants and, in lands beyond the confines of Europe, to persuade devotees of non-Christian faiths to convert to what they, along with all Catholics, were convinced was the true faith. Through preaching, public disputations, counseling, and other techniques, the Jesuits tried to persuade Christians to purge themselves of their sins, to reform their lives in a manner acceptable to the Jesuits' understanding of God's will, and to demonstrate to pagans the superior wisdom and virtues of Christianity. But it was not the Jesuits' style to emulate Saint Francis, who appeared before crowds in filthy clothing, shouting fervent but disorganized threats at his listeners.[47] The Loyolans were as meticulous about their grooming as they were about their carefully prepared, eloquently delivered discourses. Their evangelical efforts will be considered in later chapters (see especially Chapters 3, 6, 9, 19, and 23).

43. Dowling, "Polanco," 13.

44. *CSJ(C)*, pt. 3, chap. 1, par. 268.

45. T. Frank Kennedy, "Jesuits and Music: Reconsidering the Early Years," Accademia nazionale di Santa Cecilia, Florence, *Studi musicali* 17, 1 (1988): 71–95. I am most grateful to the noted Oxford book and manuscript dealer Albi Rosenthal for sharing the text of this illuminating article with me. The most complete introduction to the vast literature concerning Jesuit drama is Nigel Griffin, comp., *Jesuit School Drama*, supplement 1 (London, 1986).

46. Nicholas P. Cushner, *Lords of the Land: Sugar, Wine and Jesuit Estates of Coastal Peru, 1600–1767* (Albany, 1980), 5.

47. Cf. Little, *Religious Poverty*, 162–63.

Participation in the confessional was a responsibility that the Jesuits had already begun to assume before September 1540, but the more notoriety the new fathers attained for their religious zeal and knowledge, the more pressure they faced to serve as confessors, especially to the high and mighty. According to Heinrich Boehmer, though it had long been customary for royal courts to include a chaplain and a preacher, the assignment of a father confessor for sovereigns and princelings was a practice that began with the Loyolans.[48] Initially the fathers general had misgivings about posting their members in royal palaces, where the confessors would inevitably be exposed to worldly temptations. But the sovereigns were insistent, and the Jesuits, as they often did when commanded by rulers, complied.

Although as father general, Claudio Aquaviva (1581–1615), the neglected Bonaventure of the Order,[49] issued general instructions (1602) cautioning confessors against mixing in court politics or becoming pawns of princes, he enjoined them to impress upon their noble penitents policies right in the eyes of God and beneficial to the Society. In practice, confessors were unable to avoid becoming drawn into the general concerns of their clients. Thus, for example, one duke who had benefited from the counsels of his Jesuit confessor for 26 years stated that he consulted him not only as his spiritual director but also as his financial advisor on the management of his estates, the payment of his workers, "and numerous other matters."[50]

By the early seventeenth century, Jesuits had become the principal confessors of the Catholic royalty of Europe and of many noble houses as well. Whether, as Boehmer has stated, the confessional "occupied the very center of the Order's pastoral activities" is debatable. Certainly it does not follow, as the German scholar contended, that the confessors' objective was to influence their charges "so that they would submit themselves to the priest's ministrations." It would be more judicious to say that they aimed to see that their spiritual dependents' conduct conformed as closely as possible to the requirements of God.[51]

If Jesuits became highly visible as court figures, both in Europe and abroad (particularly in Mughal India, Japan, and China), they also undertook, less conspicuously, other services not contemplated by Loyola nor explicitly authorized in the Society's *Constitutions*. One thinks, for example, of their performances in delicate diplomatic missions (see especially Chapters 4–8 and 23), as custodians and manufacturers of armaments (discussed in Chapter 6), and even as minters of coins (see Chapter 13). But they were particularly well known

48. Boehmer, *The Jesuits*, 120–21.
49. Although Aquaviva had more to do with the shaping of the Society than any father general after Loyola, no book-length study of the fifth general exists. See, however, Joseph de Guibert, "Le Généralat de Claude Aquaviva (1581–1615): Sa Place dans l'histoire de la spiritualité de la Compagnie de Jésus," *AHSI* 10 (Jan.–June 1941): 59–93; B. Schneider, "Der Konflikt zwischen Claudius Aquaviva und Paul Hoffaens," *AHSI* 26 (1957): 3–55; 27 (1958): 279–306; and Schneider's sketch in *The New Catholic Encyclopaedia* (1967), 1: 89–90. For a remarkably censorious but unconvincing assessment, see J. C. H. Aveling, *The Jesuits* (rpr., New York, 1987), 189–98. It should be noted that throughout this study the general's name will be written as indicated here, although it has become fashionable among Jesuit scholars in the House of Writers in Rome to revert to the antique spelling, Acquaviva.
50. Ernest J. Burrus, S.J., ed., *Kino Writes to the Duchess: Letters of Eusebio Francisco Kino, S.J., to the Duchess of Aveiro* (St. Louis, 1965), 60–61.
51. Cf. Boehmer, *The Jesuits*, 133. The activities of the confessors of the Portuguese royal family are considered in Chapters 4 and 5 below.

for educating laymen, also an activity that Loyola had not contemplated and, indeed, one he did not initially welcome.

As Fr. Pedro Leturia pointed out long ago, the founding fathers did not expect to have to provide humanistic and scientific training for their recruits.[52] Because they themselves possessed university educations before the Order came into being, they expected that their recruits would already be university-trained. Between 1540 and 1547, however, Loyola authorized the establishment of dormitory facilities, called colleges, exclusively for candidates for the Order, in major university centers like Paris, Louvain, Padua, Valencia, and Coimbra. Their residents merely lived there while attending university classes. But in 1545 the duke of Gandía, Francisco Borgia, later to become the Society's third general, established a college in Gandía that was at first intended exclusively for the training of Jesuit scholastics. After its rector invited members of the community to attend the students' philosophical disputations, some of the leading families begged that their children be permitted to attend classes at the new school. In 1546 Ignatius approved their request, and two years later Gandía became a model of a *collegium* that served both Jesuit scholastics and externs.

An even more radical move was made in 1548, when Ignatius answered the plea of an old friend, the viceroy of Sicily, who yearned to enhance the spiritual and cultural life of the island by establishing a college in the municipality of Messina. Ignatius sent ten men, five priests and five scholastics, to establish what became the first Jesuit school intended primarily for secular students. Three years later the general himself presided over the opening of the famed Roman College, which in 1584 became the Gregorian University (after its early patron, Pope Gregory XIII [1572–85]), and which remains an illustrious institution to this day.

By 1551, the year the Roman College was opened, Loyola's initial coolness toward a major Jesuit role in higher education had clearly been overcome. His shift in attitude may have been influenced by the actions of the Council of Trent, which urged Church leaders to promote education as a means of encouraging and solidifying knowledge of the faith. It may also have been affected by his recognition that the increasing urbanization of Europe necessitated more advanced-level schools, particularly for informed, zealous, capable Christian leaders.[53] Perhaps, too, he recognized that Jesuit colleges could become excellent recruiting centers, just as Dominican and Franciscan colleges had long been, and that proved to be the case. At any rate, in December 1551 Loyola issued a circular that announced the Society's commitment to what has been called "the apostolate of the classroom." The founder stressed that the establishment of new colleges, modeled on the Roman College, was consistent with the Society's goals and ought to be extended throughout Europe.

The response to that call was swift and impressive. By 1556, the year of Loyola's death, there were 46 Jesuit colleges established and authorized in Europe, Brazil, and

---

52. The following paragraphs rely primarily upon Fr. Leturia's "Why the Society of Jesus Became a Teaching Order," *Jesuit Educational Quarterly* 4, 1 (June 1941): 31–54; George E. Ganss, S.J., "The Origin of Jesuit Colleges for Externs and the Controversies About Their Poverty, 1539–1608," *Woodstock Letters* 91 (1962): 123–66; and William V. Bangert, S.J., *A History of the Society of Jesus* (St. Louis, 1972), 20–28.

53. *CSJ(C)*, pt. 4, 210–11.

TABLE 1.1

Growth of the Society of Jesus, 1556–1749

Year	Members (N)	Provinces and vice-provinces	Colleges	Seminaries	Novitiates	Professed houses	Missions and residences
1556	1,500	—	46	—	—	—	—
1579	5,164	21	144	—	—	10	—
1600	8,519	26[a]	245	—	—	16	—
1608	10,641	31[b]	293	—	33	21	96
1616	13,112	32	372	—	41	24	123
1626	15,544	38[b]	444	56	44	26	228
1679	17,655	35	578	88	48	28	266
1710	19,998	38[a]	712	157	59	24	540
1717	19,679	—	—	—	—	—	—
1749	22,589	39[b]	699	176	61	24	608

SOURCES: 1556: George E. Ganss, S.J., *St. Ignatius' Idea of a Jesuit University* (Milwaukee, 1954), 24. 1579, 1600, and 1608: idem, "The Origin of Jesuit Colleges for Externs and the Controversies About Their Poverty, 1539–1608," *Woodstock Letters* 91 (1962): 127. 1616–1749: Edmond Lamalle, S.J., "Les Catalogues des provinces et des domiciles de la compagnie de Jesus," *AHSI* 13 (Jan.–Dec. 1944): 77–101; and Alfred Hamy, *Documents pour servir à l'histoire des domiciles de la compagnie de Jesus dans le monde entier de 1540 à 1773* (Paris, 1892).

[a] Number includes one vice-province.

[b] Number includes two vice-provinces.

India. Their number had grown to 245 by 1600 and continued to increase thereafter (Table 1.1).[54]

The proliferation of such colleges had far-reaching implications and raised serious issues for the Society's leaders. One concerned how far its commitment ought to extend. Though Ignatius was sensitive to the need for improvements in primary education too, he insisted that the limited resources of the Order made it necessary for it to concentrate on secondary and higher education, a policy that his successors continued in Europe, although, as subsequent chapters will demonstrate, not always overseas.[55] A second concern pertained to the courses that Jesuit institutions should offer. Just as he had studied the rules and constitutions of other Orders as he was drafting ordinances for his organization, so Ignatius examined the constitutions of various universities, including those of Valencia, Salamanca, Alcalá, Coimbra, Paris, Louvain, Cologne, Bologna, and Padua, selecting the elements from each that best suited his views of what needed to be taught.[56] He rejected an elective system of courses in favor of a rigid sequence of what amounted to building blocks, so that students would acquire a solid foundation in Latin before attending lectures in the arts (logic, physics, metaphysics, mathematics, moral philosophy, rhetoric, poetry, and history). After studying the arts, students would move on to scholastic theology and learn some Hebrew and Greek, too. The result was a melding of scholastic and humanist learning with emphasis upon Quintilian rhetoric, Ciceronian grammar, Aristotelian science, and Thomistic theology.[57]

54. The standard work on the beginnings of Jesuit colleges remains Allan P. Farrell, S.J., *The Jesuit Code of Liberal Education: Development and Scope of the Ratio Studiorum* (Milwaukee, 1938).

55. Ganss, *Saint Ignatius' Idea*, 44.

56. Ibid., 38.

57. Ibid., 49.

Yet until Aquaviva's generalate, Jesuit education was far from standardized. In 1581 the Fourth General Congregation expressed concern about that issue and named a committee of twelve to prepare a standardized system. The father general played a major role in the preparation of the famous *Ratio studiorum*, the detailed regulations that would govern Jesuit schools from the late sixteenth century on. The first draft of the text was completed in 1586 and was subjected to a series of revisions until 1599.

The Aquaviva ordinances prescribed the texts to be used, how they were to be interpreted, acceptable student–professor relationships, the close surveillance of both teachers and students, and much else. They required all students, both scholastics and externs, to attend daily mass and monthly confession. Students were warned not to "come to class with arms, daggers, knives, or others of such nature as are forbidden according to the custom of the place or the time." They were enjoined to refrain from using abusive language or defacing "benches, the chairs, the stools, the walls, the doors, the windows, or any other part by drawing, writing with knives or in any other way," and cautioned to avoid "evil books and useless reading."[58]

While the *Ratio studiorum* was being prepared, the Society continued to debate the legitimacy of participation in the education of externs. Senior members of the Order were concerned that their very success in creating schools for seculars might be a violation of the *Constitutions* as well as a violation of the Society's commitment to poverty. The *Constitutions* had recognized two types of domicile for Jesuits: (1) the professed house, where Jesuits who had completed their training would apply themselves in preaching and administering the sacraments, and (2) the residence college of scholastics who were preparing themselves for life in the professed house. Loyola always insisted that the professed house must survive on voluntary contributions (alms) and must not have assigned sources of income; he ruled, however, that because of the students' involvement in their studies, neither they nor their superiors had sufficient time to beg for their sustenance. Consequently, the colleges were authorized to accept endowments and fixed incomes.[59]

Loyola and his colleagues assumed that because of the holy commitment of the occupants of the professed houses, there would be no difficulty finding sufficient donors to help establish those houses. They learned otherwise. Though many wealthy persons, both in Europe and overseas, came forward with offers of funds to build Jesuit churches and colleges, few wanted to contribute to professed houses. As a consequence, the number of colleges grew far more impressively than did the number of professed houses (see Table 1.1).[60]

Aquaviva, especially, became concerned about the steadily increasing number of colleges that were exclusively for externs and discouraged their establishment. In 1600 a congregation of procurators recommended that the Society establish residences for professed members not directly associated with colleges. It was hoped that such residences could evolve into professed houses. Eight years later the Sixth General Congregation decided that "not only the colleges which contain such seminaries, but also the others in which

58. Edward A. Fitzpatrick, trans., *St. Ignatius and the Ratio Studiorum* (New York, 1933), 119–254. The quotations are from 241–43.

59. Farrell, *Jesuit Code*, App. B.

60. T. M. McCoog, S.J., "The Finances of the English Province of the Society of Jesus in the Seventeenth Century: Introduction," *Recusant History* 18, 1 (May 1986): 18.

the pursuit of learning is carried on and classes have been opened for the benefit of our fellow men, are in accordance with our Constitutions and Institute."[61]

There the matter rested. By the mid-seventeenth century, the Society enjoyed exclusive control of higher education in Italy, Poland, and Portugal and administered more academies than any other entity in Spain, France, the Spanish Netherlands, or the Catholic-controlled regions of the Germanies and Hungary.[62]

But the Society's success in developing colleges that at one time existed on five continents was a mixed blessing. Sustaining those tuition-free institutions, which beyond Europe were also administrative and mission centers, involved a constant quest for sufficient income. As succeeding chapters will explain, meeting that demand led the Jesuits into unexpected roles as large-scale landlords, slaveowners, bullion brokers, investors, and traders, and brought about protracted controversies.

Later chapters will reveal many situations in which Jesuits reluctantly yielded to the importunities of secular officials and accepted tasks far beyond the intended scope of the Order's activities, as the fathers sometimes candidly conceded. But one opportunity Loyola firmly declined to take: to emulate the Mendicant Orders and create a second Order for women. It has sometimes been said that at one point Loyola did give consideration to the establishment of a female Order. If so, his experience with the likes of D. Isabel Roser and her nephew was so distasteful that he reached a contrary decision.

D. Isabel, a childless widow of a wealthy Catalan, had been a benefactress of Ignatius since the early 1520s. After her husband died in late 1541, she followed Ignatius to Rome, where she took up residence in the House of St. Martha and began a relentless campaign to persuade her old friend to admit her and some friends to the Society. For several years Ignatius evaded her pleas, but D. Isabel was unwilling to give up her ambition. Accordingly, at Christmastime 1545, she petitioned Paul III "to command Master Ignatius to accept my solemn vows" and handed over her remaining property to the Society. Evidently the pope gave in, for on Christmas Day that year D. Isabel and two friends knelt before Ignatius in a small church and pronounced their vows in the Society. As Fr. Hugo Rahner wrote in his delightful study of Ignatius's relations with women, "It was a far from welcome Christmas present for Ignatius." And, in fact, within the next several months D. Isabel made such a nuisance of herself that Ignatius successfully pleaded with the pope to release the three women from their vows.

In the meantime, two of D. Isabel's nephews arrived in the Eternal City. Distressed that they had been disinherited, one of them brought suit against the Jesuits in a papal tribunal. He insisted that "these Jesuits are rogues. Ignatius wished to steal all my aunt's fortune;

61. The foregoing is based upon the digest of Ganss, "The Origin." The quotation is from p. 165.
62. Boehmer, *The Jesuits*, 110. By no means were all Jesuit colleges established *de novo*. As George Huppert has demonstrated (*Public Schools in Renaissance France* [Chicago, 1984]), in France the Society responded to the crown's encouragement and took over a system of municipally founded, funded, and managed colleges. As will be seen in Chapter 2 and elsewhere, Jesuits were not always successful in maintaining control over schools they created. For one such setback, see John Patrick Donnelly, S.J., "The Jesuit College at Padua: Growth, Suppression, Attempts at Restoration: 1552–1606," *AHSI* 51 (Jan.–June 1982): 45–79.

he is a hypocrite and a thief." The court ruled otherwise and compelled the woman to sign a statement denying any wrongdoing by any member of the Society.

A few months later, in May 1547, Ignatius asked Paul III to exempt the Society permanently from the spiritual direction of women in organized communities.[63] By then he already had rejected a plan to establish a house of nuns in Gandía subject to the Society, partly on the ground that there were already enough such houses in that small community.[64] And about the same time, he warned his colleagues in Portugal that "I would not have any dealing with young women of the common people, except in church or in an open place. On the one hand, they are lightheaded, and whether there be foundation for it or not, it frequently happens that such dealings give rise to evil talk. Such females are in general more inclined to be giddy and inconstant in God's service." He then added a revealing qualification: "If I had to deal with women in matters spiritual, it would be with women of birth against whom no breath of evil rumor could arise."[65]

Consistent with this elitist bias—which, in fact, is central to an understanding of the mindset of the early Jesuits—is one of the few passages in the Society's *Constitutions* that concerns women. It stipulates that they are generally to be barred from physical entry into Jesuit facilities, "but if they are persons of great charity or of high rank as well as of great charity, the superior in his discretion will have the power to grant a dispensation for just reasons, that if they so desire they may enter to see it."[66]

One example of the exercise of such "discretion" concerns the admission of the only woman ever to become a Jesuit. Juana of Portugal was a fruit of the union of Charles V, Holy Roman Emperor (who was also Charles I of Spain), and his wife, Isabel of Portugal. Born in 1535, Juana married the heir apparent to the Portuguese throne in 1552. A sickly youth, her husband died in 1553, a few weeks before the birth of their son, the future King Sebastian, whose ill-fated adventures will be considered in Chapter 4. Soon after her spouse's demise, Juana made a vow to enter the Franciscan Order, but later changed her mind. During the summer of 1554 she entered into negotiations with Loyola to join the Society as a scholastic, employing the pseudonym of "Mateo Sánchez" in her correspondence. The following November the founder took a step that the *Constitutions* pledged that the Society would *not* take: he applied to the pope to commute Juana's earlier vow to join the Franciscans. After the pope acted favorably, the queen regent of Portugal was accepted into the Society. Unlike Isabel Roser, Juana never proved to be troublesome, and upon occasion she was helpful in defending the Society in Spain. She also contributed to the founding of a Jesuit college in Valladolid; but she applied most of her fortune to the establishment of a convent of discalced Poor Clares in her natal city, Madrid. A few years before her death in 1573, her longtime spiritual advisor, Francisco Borgia, became the Society's third superior general.[67]

63. The foregoing is based upon Hugo Rahner, S.J., ed., *Saint Ignatius Loyola: Letters to Women* (New York, 1960), 251–90. The quotations are from pp. 285, 287, and 290.

64. Loyola to Miguel de Torres, 10 Sept. 1546, in William J. Young, S.J., trans. and ed., *Letters of St. Ignatius of Loyola* (Chicago, 1959), 100–102. According to Rahner, there were several later attempts to dissuade Loyola from his opposition to second Orders, but none were successful. *Letters to Women*, 323–24.

65. To the members of the Society in Portugal, n.d., in Rahner, *Letters to Women*, 442.

66. *CSJ(C)*, pt. 3, chap. 1, par. 267.

67. Rahner, *Letters to Women*, 52–67. For consistency I shall refer to the third head of the Society as Borgia, though he is also known as Borja, the Spanish form of his name.

Juana's example was never repeated. There would be no Jesuit Order of nuns,[68] nor would there officially be third Orders of pious laymen. Such Orders were also common among the Mendicants. As Rosenwein and Little have written, they "provided alternatives to embracing fully the religious life; their members would continue in worldly pursuits but ... [also] engage in some of the friars' religious observances and enjoy some of their spiritual benefits, in a way analogous to that in which knights had associated ... with the monks by joining Cluniac confraternities."[69] Considering Loyola's exceptional understanding of the sources of political and economic power during his time, it is puzzling that confraternities did not play a conspicuous role in the Jesuit enterprise.[70] As will be seen in Volume 2 of this study, when the Jesuits did attempt to promote such organizations during the 1750s, the Portuguese crown directed that such plans be immediately abandoned. But by then the Society was embroiled in many controversies, the roots of which can be traced back to the sixteenth century.

The Beginning of Hostility Toward the Society

From beginning to end, the Society was embroiled in controversy. Between 1523 and 1540, Ignatius and his disciples were the subjects of ten inquisitorial processes in Spain, France, and Rome.[71] Soon after Ignatius reached Venice in 1537, he earned the enduring enmity of Giampietro Carafa, co-founder of the Theatines and the future Pope Paul IV (1555–59), when he criticized Carafa's lifestyle.[72] Although Paul III had been an ardent supporter of the Society, many of his sixteenth-century successors shared Paul IV's grave misgivings about the new Order, fearing that it was primarily a vehicle of imperialistic Philippine Spain.[73]

The sixteenth century was a particularly disputatious period in the religious history of Europe, not only because of the emergence of militant Protestantism, but also because of the appearance of profound divisions within the ranks of equally zealous Catholics. One has only to look at the bitter disputes between the Observant and Conventual Franciscans and their new rivals, the Capuchins.[74] Given the Jesuits' enormous zeal, their exceptional self-confidence, the unconventional aspects of their corporate structure, and their early successes in securing both ecclesiastical and secular support, it was doubtless inevitable that

---

68. Yet there would be a female Order modeled on the Institute of the Society: the Company of Mary, founded in 1607. See Pilar Foz y Foz, comp., *Fuentes primarias para la historia de la educación de la mujer en Europa y America: Archivos historicos Compañia de Maria Nuestra Señora* (Rome, 1989). I am indebted to Asunción Lavrin for having called this collection to my attention.

69. Barbara H. Rosenwein and Lester K. Little, "Social Meaning in the Monastic and Mendicant Spiritualities," *Past and Present* 63 (May 1974): 4–32, at 28.

70. As far as I am aware, Loyola never explicitly stated why he opposed confraternities. In the same directive in which he ruled against a Jesuit Order of nuns in Gandía, he also ruled against the establishment of confraternities there. See note 64.

71. Each is discussed at length in S/*FX*, 1.

72. According to Ludwig Marcuse, Ignatius came close to losing his self-control, perhaps for the first time since Manresa, when he learned of Carafa's election as pope. *Soldier of the Church: A Life of Ignatius Loyola*, trans. and ed. Christopher Lazare (London, 1939), 287.

73. Boehmer, *The Jesuits*, 105–6; Guenter Lewy, "The Struggle for Constitutional Government in the Early Years of the Society of Jesus," *Church History* 29 (1960): 141–60, and idem, *Constitutionalism and Statecraft During the Golden Age of Spain: A Study of the Political Philosophy of Juan de Mariana, S.J.* (Geneva, 1960), chap. 8.

74. J. R. H. Moorman, *History of the Franciscan Order* (Oxford, 1968), chap. 43; *HP*, II: 530–31.

they would find themselves the subjects of polemics from rival churchmen and academicians, especially those associated with the University of Paris, an institution notable for its earlier battles with the Mendicants.[75]

The Society was less than a decade old when it encountered its first serious challenges in Spain, where it opened five dormitory colleges between 1544 and 1546. Though many, particularly the duke of Gandía, applauded the Jesuits' achievements, others were hostile to their arrival. Indeed, Juan Martinez Siliceo, newly appointed archbishop of Toledo and primate of Spain, went so far as to label them heretics and pointedly prohibited any but parish priests from administering communion within his diocese. In 1547, when Loyola named Antonio Araoz to serve as the first Jesuit provincial in Spain, he unwittingly consigned his kinsman to a hornet's nest. In Saragossa, though supported by the prior of the Dominicans and many notables, the Jesuits were quickly condemned by the Carmelites, Franciscans, Augustinians, and certain members of the local clergy. The new fathers found their situation in Salamanca even more uncomfortable. Although Cardinal Francisco de Mendoza, bishop of Coria, had urged Loyola to open a college in Spain's oldest university, and to that end the Society was able to secure the support of a "learned and wealthy" benefactor, its arrival in Salamanca was strongly opposed by an erudite, highly respected Dominican, Melchior Cano, the ranking theologian at the university.

Fr. Cano became convinced that the Jesuits were "the forerunners of Antichrist," interestingly enough the same designation that William of St. Amour had applied to the Mendicants in thirteenth-century Paris.[76] During the Lenten season in 1548, Fr. Cano preached a university sermon in which he acidly declared that one of the curses of Christendom was "the shortsightedness of those prelates who, in order to please some pious souls, gave their sanction to new and laxly regulated orders. I mean orders whose members go to and fro about the streets like other people—an order of loungers . . .; given up to indolence, they take good care not to mortify the body, they procure for themselves permission to say their prayers out of the curtailed Roman breviary." He went on to accuse the Loyolans of being hypocrites and warned that "what is now deemed holy shall then be accursed and led down to hell" by the Jesuits.

Loyola recognized the Dominican's venom as a serious threat and once again resorted to pulling strings. He enlisted the support of Paul III, Queen Juana of Portugal, and the master general of the Dominican Order. Each issued statements strongly supportive of the Society. For a time, anti-Jesuit sentiment in Spain waned, but it would surge again later in the century when Jesuits and Dominicans locked horns over the doctrine of Grace, a dispute that would linger for two centuries.[77]

Elsewhere during the sixteenth century, other European critics resorted to hysterical diatribes against the sons of Loyola. The Jesuits were castigated as soul poisoners, igniters of public passions, usurpers of the name of Jesus, corrupters of youth (especially princelings),

75. Hastings Rashdall, *The Universities of Europe in the Middle Ages*, ed. F. M. Powicke and A. B. Emden, 3 vols. (Oxford, 1936), 1: 370–71; Moorman, *Franciscan Order*, 127–45.

76. Gordon Leff, *Paris and Oxford Universities in the Thirteenth and Fourteenth Centuries: An Institutional and Intellectual History* (New York, 1968), 260–70.

77. *HP*, 13: 92–95; *HCJAE*, 1: chap. 8.

subverters of episcopal authority, and models of immodesty.[78] If the archbishop of Dublin could warn that Jesuits were more dangerous than Martin Luther and "worse than the Jews," the author of a book published in the Germanies in 1593 could go even further when he accused them of being "assassins, ferocious wild boars, thieves, traitors, serpents, vipers . . . filthy billy goats [and] repugnant hogs."[79]

Notwithstanding such libels, the Society enjoyed a spectacular success during the sixteenth century, when it became a key instrument of the Counter-Reformation, a leading educator of European male elites, and one of the most celebrated, widely represented evangelical arms of the Church. Its numerical and institutional growth was especially impressive during the first five generalates, to the death of Aquaviva in 1615 (see Table 1.1). It is true that far fewer men were accepted into the Society than entered the two leading Mendicant Orders during their formative periods. Between 1212 and 1256, for example, 13,000 men joined the Dominican Order; by 1303 their number had increased to 20,650, the approximate size of the Order for the balance of the Middle Ages. Within its first century, the Order of the Friars Minor (the Franciscans) attained an enrollment of about 28,000 members.[80] It is likewise certain that the population of Europe was greater during the sixteenth than during earlier centuries. But the number of options for young men in commerce, warfare, and government administration, as well as in both branches of the Church, was also greater. Those options were clearly available in Portugal and its empire, where, as succeeding chapters will indicate, the sons of Loyola achieved some of their earliest and most striking successes.

78. A convenient summary of many such accusations by hostile churchmen and academicians is *Retrato dos Jesuitas feito ao natural pelos mais sabios, e mais illustres catholicos . . . desde . . . 1540 . . . até 1650* (Lisbon, 1761).

79. Alexandre Brou, *Les Jesuites de la legende*, 2 vols. (Paris, 1906–7), 1: 41–42, as quoted in A. Lynn Martin, "The Jesuit Mystique," *Sixteenth Century Journal* 4, 1 (Apr. 1973): 31–40, at 31.

80. Hinnebusch, *History*, 1: 330–31; Southern, *Western Society*, 285.

CHAPTER 2

Formation of the Province
of Portugal, 1541–ca. 1615

The Society of Jesus was instituted to serve or glorify the Lord and His Vicar
on earth, and especially to promote the spiritual progress of souls in Christian
doctrine and living, and the propagation of the faith, by means of a wide variety
of ministries.

—Loyola, *Constitutions*

As SOON AS papal authorization seemed assured, Ignatius began assigning his representatives
abroad to initiate evangelical, educational, and other activities. Within a generation the
Society became firmly planted in Italy, France, the Germanies, eastern Europe, and the
Iberian Peninsula. The Iberian Peninsula became the springboard for Jesuit enterprises on
four continents beyond Europe. Many of the Society's triumphs and not a few of its reverses
occurred in lands that Portugal sought to dominate. Before considering the foundations of
Jesuit endeavors in those lands, it is pertinent to examine how the Order became established
in Portugal, where so many Jesuits originated and were trained before venturing overseas.

The Rise of Portugal

Portugal, situated along the western reaches of the Iberian Peninsula, today is roughly the
size of the state of Indiana. But when it was created (1095) as a county of the interior kingdom
of León, it was a rectangular block of land between the Douro River in the south and Galicia
in the north. Its southward expansion occurred in a series of stages during the next century;
the liberation of Lisbon (1147) was one of the most important steps in the formation of an
independent kingdom, recognized as such by the papacy in 1179. By 1250 the last of the
longtime Muslim occupants of the country had been conquered and, with the exception
of one enclave lost to Spain at the beginning of the nineteenth century, Portugal assumed its
present dimensions. In 1415 Portugal led Europe's drive for global mastery when it captured
Ceuta, a North African caravan terminus and seaport that became the first step in the
establishment of the famed Portuguese thalassocracy. By the 1540s, Portuguese fortress-

factories (*feitorias*) were widely scattered along the coasts of Brazil, Africa, and Asia and, supplemented by warships, were symbols of Lusitanian efforts (never wholly successful) to dominate trade between the Sea of Japan and the Atlantic Ocean. If the kingdom itself produced only mundane exports such as salt, fish, olive oil, and wine, the empire yielded impressive quantities of gold, ivory, slaves, dyestuffs, textiles, spices, precious gems, and other exotic goods that made Portugal the envy of all Europe.[1]

Despite its increasing international importance, Portugal remained one of the most sparsely populated countries in Europe. By the second quarter of the sixteenth century its inhabitants numbered close to 1.3 million, compared with 7 million living in the neighboring Spanish kingdoms, 14 million in France, and 3 million in England.[2] According to Portugal's first national census, completed between 1527 and 1531, the kingdom contained 91 cities, towns, and villages, but only 12.5 percent of its population resided in such communities. Lisbon, the city by the Tagus, possessed between 50,000 and 70,000 inhabitants, almost four times as many as the second-ranking cities in the kingdom—Porto and Évora—each of which counted about 15,000 citizens. Santarém, Beja, and Elvas contained less than 10,000, whereas Aveiro, Estremoz, Viana, and Vila do Conde held about 4,000. Guimarães, Lagos, Portalegre, and Setúbal could claim no more than 1,600 inhabitants each.

Portugal was, therefore, mostly a rural country and would long remain so. Lisbon, the largest city in the Iberian Peninsula and third ranking metropolis in Europe after Paris and Constantinople, would surpass 100,000 inhabitants by mid-century and would contain 165,000 persons by 1619. The kingdom's leading seaport, the center of its burgeoning empire, and increasingly the official residence of the royal family, Lisbon welcomed the first Jesuits to enter Portugal.

The Coming of the Jesuits

In June 1540, the first two Jesuits reached the Portuguese capital. One, Francis Xavier, was destined to remain in the kingdom for only a year before beginning his spectacular decade of missionary endeavors in the East (see Chapter 3), but his companion, Simão Rodrigues, would reluctantly stay and become the controversial founder of his Order in the kingdom. Their arrival was gratifying to the Portuguese ruler, John III (1521–57), who had been anxious to recruit Jesuits to serve in his realm for many months. Even before the Society had gained papal approval, the monarch wrote to his ambassador in Rome that he had learned from Master Diogo de Gouveia in Paris

1. Concerning the evolution of Portugal, see OM/*HP*, vol. 1; and the early volumes of VS/*HP*. See also *DHP*, 3: 432–51. On the development of the empire, the best introduction remains C. R. Boxer, *The Portuguese Seaborne Empire, 1415–1825* (New York, 1969), but see also Bailey W. Diffie and George D. Winius, *Foundations of the Portuguese Empire, 1415–1580* (Minneapolis, 1977).

2. Vitorino Magalhães Godinho, *Estrutura da antiga sociedade portuguesa*, 3d ed. (Lisbon, 1977), 21–41. See also A[ntonio] de Sousa e Silva Costa Lobo, *Historia da sociedade em Portugal no século xv* (Lisbon, 1903), esp. chap. 1; Anselmo Braamcamp Freire, "Povoação da Estremadura no xvi século," *Archivo histórico portuguez* 6, 7 (July 1908): 241–84; Victor Ribeiro, "A vida lisboeta nos séculos xv e xvi," *Archivo histórico portuguez* 8 (1911): 308–37; and Maria de Lourdes Akola do Carmo Neto, "Demografia," *DHP*, 1: 796–97.

that certain learned clerics of exemplary life have left Paris ... [and] have taken a vow of poverty in the service of God and live only upon the alms of the faithful, and they preach and produce great fruit wherever they go ... [and that] it is their intention to convert the heathen; and they say that if it pleases our Holy Father ... they will go to India. Therefore it seems to me that since they are men of such character and intent, they would be of great service to our Lord there, and would produce great fruit for the faith.

Accordingly, the king directed his ambassador, D. Pedro Mascarenhas, to urge the pope to approve the establishment of the Society and to make every effort to recruit as many of its members as possible to come to his kingdom.[3] Not only because of his zeal to serve his ruler but also because he himself had engaged the services of Loyola as his personal confessor, Mascarenhas energetically complied with the king's directive.

Shortly after the arrival of "the Roman fathers," as these first Jesuits were initially called, they gained a private audience with John III and his wife, Catarina de Austria, who treated them "with a great display of benevolence."[4] The king, praised by some as John the Pious because of his support of ecclesiastical reforms and scorned by others as a fanatic because of his enthusiastic support of the Portuguese Inquisition (first authorized in 1536), his stifling of free thought in the national university (see below), and his ardent assistance to the Jesuits,[5] quickly became a great admirer of the Ignatians, as did members of his court, including his brothers, the infantes D. Luís (b. 1506–d. 1555) and D. Henrique, later Cardinal Henry (b. 1512–d. 1580).[6] After conversations with the new fathers, observation of their self-effacing, saintly characters, and the receipt of reports concerning their energetic spiritual work in Lisbon's hospitals and prisons, the king referred to them as "the apostles," the appellation Jesuits would employ in reference to themselves for centuries to come. Not surprisingly, John III told one of his nobles that he would like to have the entire Society come to his kingdom, even if that were to cost him part of his empire.[7]

The king's enthusiasm for these new "soul curers" may have stemmed in part from his need for religious consolation in the face of a long series of personal losses affecting most of his siblings and all nine of his children, none of whom survived to the age of twenty.[8] But it also derived from his conviction that the Jesuits could contribute significantly to the moral uplifting of both ecclesiastical and lay persons in his kingdom. During the late fifteenth and early sixteenth centuries, the need for such improvement was as well recognized in Portugal as it was in other parts of Europe. In that western kingdom, too, ecclesiastical simony, absenteeism, concubinage, inattention to spiritual duties, lack of discipline, excessive pomp, and preoccupation with worldly concerns were all too evident. Leading prelates set

3. King to Mascarenhas, Lisbon, 4 Aug. 1539, S/FX, 1: 543.
4. Baltasar Teles, Chronica da companhia de Jesu na provincia de Portugal, 2 vols. (Lisbon, 1645–47), 1: bk. 1, chap. 8.
5. Naturally, conservative historians in Portugal have always regarded John favorably, whereas their liberal opponents have denounced him as a reactionary. See the historiographical summary in S/FX, 1: 601; cf. J. D. M. Ford, ed., Letters of John III, King of Portugal, 1521–1557 (Cambridge, Mass., 1931), xvi–xviii, and OM/HP, 1: 215.
6. S/FX, 1: 608, nn. 102–3, provide biographical sketches of the two royal princes. See also note 33. Much more will be said about Cardinal Henry in Chapters 4 and 13.
7. Ibid., 1: 603–4.
8. OM/HP, 1: 215.

the tone by their opulent lifestyles, which tended to include legions of offspring, some of whom attained high positions in the Church; parish curates likewise lived openly with their concubines, and inmates of religious houses were accused of ignoring their vows of chastity. Both John and his predecessor, Manuel the Fortunate (1495–1521), supported efforts by leading Portuguese clergymen to purge the Church of such vices. In some Orders, such as the Recollects, the Capuchins, the Shod Carmelites, and the Dominicans, significant improvements were made before the arrival of the first Jesuits; but in others, particularly the houses of Benedictines, Augustinians, and Cistercians, there was resistance to their superiors' efforts to improve discipline and to instill greater religious fervor.[9] Consequently, the Jesuits arrived in Portugal at a propitious time, for they seemed well equipped by their training, moral fervor, experience, and dedication to assist prominent reformers like D. Frei Bartolomeu dos Mártires, O.P., archbishop of Braga and member of the Council of Trent, in their efforts to improve the quality of religious life in the kingdom.

The newly arrived Jesuits had intended to engage in the same activities they and their colleagues had been pursuing in Italy for the past several years. They preferred popular ministries, celebrating Mass in the major Lisbon hospital, attending to the spiritual and physical needs of its inmates and of doomed prisoners, and preaching in public squares. Instead, they found themselves spending most of their time at the royal court.[10] There they heard confessions of its members and of those who came to the palace on private business. They administered the Spiritual Exercises to prominent persons and enjoyed close relations with members of the nobility, leading government officials, and supportive ecclesiastics—contacts that would prove invaluable when the Jesuits began to erect their own facilities in the kingdom and elsewhere. As an obviously jubilant Xavier wrote, "This court has undergone a great reform, so much so . . . that it is more like a religious house than a court. So many go to confession and receive Communion every week that God must be given praise and thanks. . . . We are so busy hearing confessions that even if there were twice as many [of us] we would still have more penitents than we could handle. We are occupied the whole day and part of the night solely with the people at court."[11]

Though such an enthusiastic response may have been gratifying, it also proved to be an obstacle, for both Rodrigues and Xavier yearned to go on to India. The former worried: "Master Francis and I are somewhat concerned that we may be prevented from going. . . . It seems . . . that the king does not wish this, since he says that we are much needed [here]."[12] In the end the crown compromised: the king agreed that Xavier could sail to the East, as he did in April 1541, but insisted that Rodrigues must stay in the kingdom.

Although he was always frustrated by his inability to evangelize abroad, first in India and later in Brazil, Simão Rodrigues (b. 1510–d. 1579) rendered the Society invaluable service, first as superior (1540–46) and later as provincial (1546–52) of the Portuguese province—the

9. The most incisive analysis of the decadence of the Church in Portugal and of attempted reforms is José Sebastião da Silva Dias, *Correntes de sentimento religioso em Portugal (séculos xvi a xviii)*, 2 vols. (Coimbra, 1960), which, despite its title, really extends only to 1550. See also Henrique da Gama Barros, *História da administração publica em Portugal nos si'eculos xii a xv*, 2d ed., ed. Torquato de Sousa Soares, 11 vols. (Lisbon, 1945–54), 2: 13–289.

10. Teles, *Chronica*, 1:1, chap. 9.

11. S/*FX*, 1: 669–70.

12. Ibid., 1: 672.

first of a dozen formed during the generalate of Ignatius. The son of a member of the provincial nobility in northern Portugal, Rodrigues was "tall, [of] an olive complexion, with dark hair and beard, and a distinguished gate which [supposedly] betrayed his noble origin." Though his companions admired him for his achievements, they came to regard him as hot-tempered, as an indifferent but stubborn administrator, and ultimately as a source of embarrassment. Loyola was eventually compelled to use considerable tact to persuade his old friend to surrender his office and return to Rome.[13] Nevertheless, it was Rodrigues who took the first steps toward the permanent establishment of the Jesuit enterprise in the kingdom of Portugal, where it would flourish for more than two centuries and provide the kingdom and empire with many of its leaders.

Beginnings of an Enterprise

The first and always one of the most important of the Jesuit installations was the college of Santo Antão, situated in the district of Mouraria just north of Castle Hill, in the heart of today's downtown Lisbon. At one time the site was an exercise ground for horses. Later a Muslim mosque was built there, and around 1400 it was succeeded by a monastery of the fathers of Santo Antão, an Order that practiced the Augustinian Rule and was devoted to the care of the sick.[14] From about 1515 until 1539, Dominican nuns occupied the monastery, but in the latter year they were reassigned to another house. The monastery again briefly became the home of the fathers of Santo Antão, then a dying Order, but in 1541 its five houses were converted into an episcopal benefice, and the Order became virtually extinct. The same year, the king assigned the Jesuits title to the revenues of the vacant monastery of Cárquere, located 3 kilometers from the city of Lamego on the Douro River. Because Simão Rodrigues was anxious to have a Jesuit residence in Lisbon to accommodate an increasing number of recruits and to serve as a domicile for missionaries bound for the empire, he arranged to exchange the Cárquere property for that of Santo Antão.

The Jesuits took possession of the monastery, subsequently known as Santo Antão o velho (Old St. Anthony's), on 5 January 1542. For a decade it remained as a dormitory college, but in 1552 it became the Society's first Lisbon college for the education of both Jesuits and externs. Although the president of the Lisbon council (câmara) urged that admission of laymen be restricted to the sons of the nobility and others of genteel backgrounds, fearing that otherwise there would develop a shortage of artisans and others necessary to perform essential but humble tasks in the city, the Jesuits rejected this advice. They insisted that their classes would be gratis—the Society's customary policy—and that they would be open

13. Loyola to Rodrigues, 27 Dec. 1551; Loyola to Diego Mirón, 24 and 26 July and 3 Aug. 1553; in William J. Young, S.J., trans. and ed., *Letters of St. Ignatius of Loyola* (Chicago, 1959), 254, 302–4. Rodrigues has remained a controversial figure in the history of the Society. His earliest biographer, António Franco, S.J. (*Imagem da virtude em o noviciado da companhia de Jesus na corte de Lisboa* [Coimbra, 1717], bk. 1, chaps. 4–23), was very laudatory. Modern Jesuit assessments include *HCJAP*, 1:2, bk. 1, and S/*FX*, 1: 189–90. Ludwig Marcuse, *Soldier of the Church: A Life of Ignatius Loyola*, trans. and ed. Christopher Lazare (London, 1939), chap. 33, provides a popular account that is not wholly fair to Rodrigues. I have not seen José Carlos Monteiro Pacheco, *Simão Rodrigues: Iniciador da companhia de Jesus em Portugal* (Braga, 1987).

14. *HIP*, 1: 135 and 331.

to everyone, regardless of social station. As will be seen later, the latter policy was not always followed in their overseas colleges, which shaped admissions standards in accordance with the values held by local elites.[15]

Both the church of Santo Antão and that of the new novitiate and later professed house of São Roque (see below) became popular places of worship for members of the Lisbon aristocracy and the royal family. In 1555, for example, the first rector of the college reported that 1,200 persons confessed at both churches on Jubilee Sunday.[16] Santo Antão soon proved too cramped for the growing number of residents and externs. Accordingly, in 1579, construction of Santo Antão *o novo* (New St. Anthony's), a much larger facility, began. Fourteen years later the new college admitted its first students. By then the original college had been sold to Augustinians.[17] Both the original school and the successor college were more than educational facilities. They also served as the principal administrative headquarters of the Society in the kingdom and became the residence of the provincial and of several procurators who tended to the economic and personnel requirements of the overseas provinces (see Chapters 12 and 23). As will be seen later, Santo Antão was always in precarious financial shape, despite the fact that it was the only Jesuit college in the kingdom to own several sugar plantations in Brazil (see Chapter 16).[18]

In 1553, when Jerónimo Nadal visited the Portuguese province on behalf of Ignatius, he became convinced that the professed members of the Order ought to be housed separately from its novices and scholastics. At that point John III offered the Society five facilities, including the hermitage of São Roque, situated on a hill immediately to the west of the old city walls. The hermitage dated from the reign of Manuel I, when the kingdom was afflicted by plague and the ruler dispatched emissaries to Venice, where they procured relics of Saint Rock (ca. 1295–1327), a famous Montpellier-born plague-curer.[19] In 1506 a hermitage was constructed to preserve those relics. It was situated in an olive orchard on a hill beyond the São Roque gate and near a cemetery where plague victims were buried. Despite the objections of the custodial confraternity responsible for the hermitage, the king assigned it to the Jesuits and authorized them to transform it into a novitiate. He suggested that it include a grandiose temple in which he could be buried, but the fathers protested that this would be a violation of their devotion to poverty. In 1566 the Jesuits

15. *HCJAP*, 1:2, 290. One scholar has offered the startling suggestion that Jesuit colleges "had a student body that adequately represented the community. In general, there is evidence to show that normally the college was made up of youths predominately from the middle class, with a goodly fringe of nobles and of the poor." William H. McCabe, S.J., *An Introduction to Jesuit Theatre* (St. Louis, 1983), 9. Fr. McCabe's communities evidently consist solely of men! In any case, no such evidence survives concerning admissions to the colleges discussed in this study.

16. Inácio de Azevedo to Loyola, Lisbon, 31 Dec. 1555, *MB*, 5: 74–81, at 75.

17. Supposedly, the building was sold for 560,000 rs. [Anon.], *História dos mosteiros conventos e casas religiosas de Lisboa*, 2 vols. (Lisbon, 1950–72), 2: 36.

18. The founding of the two Santo Antão colleges is told in a late-sixteenth-century Jesuit account in ARSI, *Lus.*, 77, fols. 1–4, and in more detail in Teles, *Chronica*, 1: bk. 1, chaps. 16–17; *HIP*, 2: 170–71; [Anon.], *História dos mosteiros*, 2: 35–36; *HCJAP*, 1:1, 281–97, 617–19, and 1:2, 285–302. I. de Vilhena Barbosa, "Fragmentos de um roteiro de Lisboa (inedito): Antiguidades do governo intruso dos Felippes de Castella," *Archivo pittoresco* 5 (Lisbon, 1862): 369ff. António Lopes, S.J., *Roteiro histórico dos Jesuítas em Lisboa* (Lisbon, 1985), is a popular but also very useful account of the founding of all Jesuit institutions within the confines of the modern city; its maps and illustrations are particularly helpful.

19. A. Fliche, "Le Problème de St. Roch," *Analecta bollandiana* 68 (1950): 343–61.

began to replace their primitive chapel at São Roque with a much more ample church. It was designed by Felippe Terzo, an Italian architect who introduced in the kingdom a new single-nave style of architecture. In time that church became (and remains) one of the glories of Lisbon.

São Roque did not become a professed house until 1590. Before then it functioned as the province's first novitiate. When plague again visited the capital in 1569, the novices were shifted from there to other houses to escape the contagion. That action stimulated proposals to relocate the novitiate. In 1585 the Society acquired a farm in a locale called Campolide, situated on the northern outskirts of the capital. Construction of the new novitiate began soon after, and it functioned there from 1597 until 1603. In 1603 the provincial leaders decided to locate the facility on Monte Olivete da Cotovia in the Rato district. The Cotovia house, founded very close to the later site of the Academy of Sciences, was not finished until 1619.[20]

Like those of its rivals, the Society's houses became important recruitment centers. This was particularly true of two other Jesuit institutions in the kingdom. The first was the College of Arts at the University of Coimbra. Founded in 1290, Portugal's first national university was repeatedly shifted by its monarchs between Lisbon and Coimbra and was not definitively located in the north-central community until 1537.[21] When universities were first formed during the High Middle Ages, the religious Orders, especially the Mendicants, sought facilities in them to serve as recruitment and training grounds. During the 1540s and 1550s, Carmelites, Dominicans, Shod Augustinians, and other Orders followed this practice by establishing two kinds of boarding-house college at the Portuguese institutions, one for their own students who had taken simple vows, the other for the sons of wealthy aristocrats.

Shortly after their arrival in Portugal, the Jesuits, too, became interested in founding their own college at Coimbra. Indeed, Loyola responded to the king's plea that Simão Rodrigues remain in the kingdom when Xavier proceeded to India in part because he hoped that Rodrigues might establish a college in Coimbra that would train missionaries for service abroad.[22] In 1541 the Jesuit superior took the initial step toward that goal when he secured from the king the aforementioned income from the Cárquere monastic lands. The next year he visited Coimbra to select a site for what became the College of Jesus. Construction began in 1547.[23]

20. There is a brief coeval sketch of the founding of São Roque in ARSI, *Lus.*, 82, fols. 101a–101b[v]. More extensive early accounts of both that house and Cotovia are in Franco, *Lisboa*, 3, 5, 6, and 8; Teles, *Chronica*, 2:4, chaps. 20–28; *HIP*, 2: 171; *HCJAP*, 1:1, 619–29; 2:1, 181–85; [Anon.], "Santa Casa de Misericórdia: Antiga casa professa dos Jesuítas em S. Roque," *Archivo pittoresco* 5 (1862): 294–96, 311–12, and 408–9; [Anon.], "Noviciado dos Jesuítas em sitio da Cotovia," *Archivo pittoresco* 6 (1863): 244–46, 270–71. For an exterior view of São Roque, see Robert C. Smith, *The Art of Portugal, 1500–1800* (New York, 1968), pl. 35.

21. [José Maria] de Queiroz Velloso, "A universidade de Lisboa-Coimbra (1290–1537)," ACL, *Boletim*, n.s. 1 (1930): 771–94. The major histories of the university are the highly partisan account by Teófilo Braga, *História da universidade de Coimbra*, 4 vols. (Lisbon, 1892–1902), and the more dispassionate tomes of Mario Brandão and M. Lopes d'Almeida, *A universidade de Coimbra: Esboço da sua historia*, 2 vols. (Coimbra, 1937).

22. S/*FX*, 1: 672.

23. The establishment of the college and the later novitiate at Coimbra is described by Teles, *Chronica*, 1:1, chaps. 19–20, and 1:2, chap. 14, and by António Franco, *Imagem da virtude em o noviciado da companhia de Jesus*

Also in 1547, John III founded what was intended to become Portugal's premier humanistic college, the Royal College or College of Arts and Humanities, modeled after the Collège Royal, founded by Francis I in 1530.[24] By royal command, André de Gouveia, longtime principal of the Collège de Guyenne in Bordeaux, a leading French preparatory school, was summoned home to administer the new Portuguese college. Gouveia belonged to a remarkable pedagogical family whose members came from Beja and Coimbra and included his nephew, Diogo de Gouveia, then director of the Collège de Sainte-Barbe attended by Loyola and his disciples in Paris. André de Gouveia complied with the king's wishes and brought to Coimbra a distinguished faculty from his former school. They included French, Scottish, and Portuguese specialists in arts, mathematics, rhetoric, humanities, and classical languages.

The new college rapidly attracted more than a thousand students but very soon lost its initial director, for André de Gouveia died suddenly in 1548. His successor was Diogo de Gouveia, who came from Paris with another group of academicians. But almost immediately the Parisian and Bordeaux contingents began to quarrel over doctrinal matters. The newly founded Coimbra office of the Inquisition investigated allegations that one or the other faction was guilty of crimes ranging from heresy to homosexuality. Teófilo Braga, indefatigable historian of the university, contended that the Jesuits, anxious to gain control over the prestigious college, actually planted those accusations, but, as a leading Jesuit scholar, Francisco Rodrigues, pointed out, Braga submitted no convincing proof to support his charge.[25]

Whatever the merits of this dispute, the fact is that the Jesuits benefited from the doctrinal quarrel within the college. By 1550 the Holy Office had arrested several members of the Bordeaux faction, including the Scot George Buchanan and the Portuguese savant Diogo de Teive. But its staff failed to find evidence of their guilt and released them less than two years later. Buchanan promptly fled the country, but Teive briefly became head of the college.[26] In mid-1555, John III abruptly ordered Teive to transfer administrative control of his faculty to the Jesuits.[27]

The king provided no explanation for his startling directive. The contention by Braga and others that the Jesuits had conspired to gain control of this plum is as unproved as is Braga's assertion that the decadence of what had never been a first-class university stemmed

---

no real collegio de Jesus de Coimbra em Portugal, 2 vols. (Évora and Coimbra, 1719), 1: bk. 1, chaps. 1–4. See also *HIP*, 2: 172–74, and *HCJAP*, 1:1, 405ff. By the *alvará* (decree) of 5 June 1542, the king directed the Augustinian prior of Santa Cruz monastery (Coimbra) to arrange hospitality for the first Jesuits: *DHJP*, 120. By another directive of 26 Oct. 1542, the sovereign also instructed the aldermen of the city to issue a license permitting the Jesuits to acquire lands in Coimbra; ibid., 123.

24. On the creation of the College of Arts, see Mário Brandão, *O collegio das artes*, 2 vols. (Coimbra, 1924–33). The original statutes governing the college are printed in *DHJP*, 4–11; revisions issued during the reign of Sebastian (1557–78) are in ibid., 416–35. The anomalous relationship between the college and the university is somewhat clarified by the *provisão* of 12 Jan. 1550 (ibid., 51–53) placing the college under the supervision of the rector of the university.

25. Braga, *Historia da universidade de Coimbra*, 1: 529; cf. *HCJAP*, 1:2, 337 n. 1.

26. Mário Brandão, *A inquisição e os professores do colegio das artes* (Coimbra, 1948); Guilherme J. C. Henriques, "Buchanan na inquisição," *Archivo historico portuguez* 4, 7 (July 1906): 241–80. George Buchanan, a Latin tragedian, later became the tutor of Mary Stuart of Scotland and James VI of England.

27. Order of 10 Sept. 1555, *DHJP*, 180–81.

from the Jesuits' acquisition of its arts college.[28] Unquestionably the Jesuits used their new opportunity to purge the faculty of members unsympathetic to their views and to gain further concessions from the crown. In 1560, for example, students attending the college became exempt from payment of fees and from a requirement to take an oath of loyalty to university authorities. Another royal decree stipulated that Jesuits who had earned their degrees elsewhere would be regarded as having training equivalent to that offered at Coimbra. Most important of all, in 1561 a royal order prohibited any student from entering Canons or Laws without a degree from the College of Arts, a stipulation that enabled the Jesuits to screen out those whom they considered unfit to master those critical disciplines.[29]

For a time the Jesuits continued to operate both the College of Jesus and the College of Arts. In the late 1560s the two were housed together, and a few years later they were fully integrated. Within the next six decades the number of students enrolled in the College of Arts increased to about 1,800. Many of the college's graduates served with distinction as missionaries and royal officials throughout the kingdom and empire.[30]

Viewing the Jesuits' successful educational enterprises, a disgruntled Augustinian chronicler charged that leaders of the Society aspired to gain complete control over all levels of education within Portugal. There is no explicit evidence of such a plan, and it is easy to exaggerate the extent to which the Jesuits came to dominate the nation's cultural life. For example, the Society never possessed full authority over the University of Coimbra. Beginning in 1576 the institution came under the jurisdiction of the Mesa da Consciência e Ordens, a royal board charged with responsibility for religious affairs in the kingdom and its empire.[31]

Nevertheless, there was another university where the Society became clearly dominant. Since the fifteenth century, the crown had contemplated establishing a second national university. The site proposed was the old walled city of Évora. But the plans for its establishment were stillborn because of insufficient funds and a scarcity of teaching personnel.[32] The man who took the initiative in promoting the university was one of John III's brothers, Cardinal Henry.[33] In 1551, during the first of two occasions when he served as archbishop of Évora, Henry invited the Jesuits to open a university in his see to provide for the instruction

28. Braga, *Historia da universidade de Coimbra*, 1: esp. 529, 565, and 592; 2: 185 and 205; cf. Brandão and d'Almeida, *A universidade de Coimbra*, 1: 206, where the king's decision to assign the college to Jesuit administration is reported without editorial comment.

29. Brandão and d'Almeida, *A universidade de Coimbra*, 2: 205–6. That stipulation, however, merely reiterated the injunction in the alvará of 6 Apr. 1548, which directed that no student hear Laws, Canons, Theology, or Medicine "sem certidão do principal do collegio das artes"; *DHJP*, 25. See also the order of 9 Sept. 1556 concerning the granting of masters' degrees. Ibid., 217. No evidence has surfaced that would convincingly demonstrate that the Jesuits deliberately excluded qualified applicants from classes in the fields listed above.

30. Enrollment estimates for the late 1550s are given in Gonçalo Vaz de Melo to Diego Laínez, Lisbon, 26 June 1557, *MB*, 5: 131; *HCJAP*, 1:2, 366. For the college's subsequent growth, see Braga, *Historia da universidade de Coimbra*, 1: 568; *HIP*, 2: 175; and Eduardo de Freire de Oliveira, *Elementos para a historia do municipio de Lisboa* (Lisbon, 1901), 12: 140 n. 2.

31. OM/*HP*, 1: 298.

32. Ibid., 1: 196.

33. Henry became archbishop of Évora for the first time in 1540; five years later he was named a cardinal. In 1564 he served as archbishop of Lisbon, and in 1574 he again became archbishop of Évora.

of his clergy. Master Simão Rodrigues and nine of his followers accepted the challenge. Emulating Loyola's disciples (who, as seen in the last chapter, made their way on foot from Paris to Venice in 1537), they walked and begged their way from Coimbra to Évora. Late in 1551, the ten Jesuits formally opened the College of the Holy Spirit (Espírito Santo) in Évora; by 1554 its enrollment reached some 300 pupils, about half the number then attending Old St. Anthony's College in Lisbon.[34] Its first rector was Melchior Carneiro, who later became bishop of Ethiopia (see Chapter 3). In 1558 Cardinal Henry applied to Pope Paul IV to approve the new institution's status as a university and signified his intent to place it under Jesuit supervision. The pope consented, and on 1 November 1559 the Jesuits took formal possession of the incipient university. Subsequently the cardinal and other benefactors endowed several additional colleges, but Évora was never able to offer an array of classes as wide as Coimbra's.[35]

Soon after the Society began to administer the University of Évora, it also became responsible for three colleges in northern Portugal. In the late 1550s Francisco Borgia, formerly the duke of Gandia, but now special Jesuit commissioner in the kingdom, negotiated a series of agreements with local ecclesiastical dignitaries in the kingdom who were eager to facilitate the founding of Jesuit schools in their sees. The first to be founded was the college of São Lourenço, which opened its doors in Porto on the feast of St. Lawrence (10 August) in 1560. That act marked the fulfillment of three years of planning by the local bishop, the municipal council, and Jesuit representatives.[36] The second new college was that of São Paulo, founded in the ancient ecclesiastical center of Braga. Its archbishop had established an episcopal college in that community in the 1530s, but his distinguished successor, Fr. Bartolomeu dos Mártires, yearned to have the college grow and to entrust its administration to the Jesuits, whom he much admired. Borgia agreed to accept the school, and in 1561 it was formally proclaimed to be a Jesuit college.[37] The last of the trio was the remote college of Bragança, situated in the mountainous northeastern town of that name. Its creation owed much to the leadership of both Archbishop Mártires and the local ordinary, D. Julião Alva, who had hoped for such a facility for years by the time the school began to function in 1562. Within its first six years the new college reported that its enrollment had grown to 330 students.[38]

From 1562 until 1568 he also served as regent for his nephew, Sebastian, and, as will be seen in Chapter 4, was briefly king himself. S/*FX*, 1: 640 n. 103.

34. *HP*, 13: 190.

35. No adequate history of the College of the Holy Spirit seems to exist. Useful among contemporary sources are António Franco, *Imagem da virtude em o noviciado da companhia de Jesus no real collegio do espírito santo de Évora* (Lisbon, 1714), chaps. 1 and 4, and 881–82; Teles, *Chronica*, 1:3, chaps. 17, 19 and 21; 2:5, chaps. 14–26; António Franco, *Évora ilustrada: Extraída da obra do mesmo nome de Pe Manuel [F]ialho*, ed. Armando de Gusmão (Évora, 1945), bk. 3, 233–309. See also *HIP*, 2: 176–77; *HCJAP*, 1:1, 578–85, and 2:1, 85–110; José Maria de Queiroz Velloso, *A universidade de Évora: Elementos para a sua história* (Lisbon, 1949), is a series of sketchy chapters based upon half-century-old notes!

36. *HCJAP*, 1:2, 404–13.

37. Ibid., 1:2, 413–27. The beginnings of the college and the legal agreements assuring its financial support are detailed in *MB*, 5: 197, 242–55, 265–80, 328–29, and 387–88. Ernest Domingues, S.J., *Braga de 1560 a 1565 visto do colégio de S. Paulo* (Braga, 1973), is based upon these published sources and adds nothing new.

38. ARSI, FG, 1379/2; *HCJAP*, 1:2, 428–32.

During the remainder of the century, the province of Portugal expanded to the southwest and west and formed three insular colleges. The first, the college of Funchal, was created in the aftermath of a devastating raid on Madeira Island by French corsairs in 1568. Three Jesuit fathers accompanied the subsequent relief expedition to the island, and in the course of a year of spiritual ministrations inspired such enthusiasm among the locals that the islanders petitioned the crown to underwrite the establishment of a college in their capital city. Since both Francisco Borgia (by then the father general) and King Sebastian (1557–78) favored the project, the college was authorized. In 1570 a dozen Jesuits sailed from Lisbon and founded the college. Two years later the first of two colleges in the Azores was established at Angra on the island of Terceira, thereby fulfilling the ambition of a wealthy landowner who had sought such an institution for a dozen years. Another affluent islander came forward to endow a third archipelagic college, that of Ponta Delgada on the Azorean island of São Miguel, which began to function in 1591.[39]

These were the last educational and training facilities that the province of Portugal formed during the sixteenth century. The Irish seminary of St. Patrick, founded by a secular priest and located at the foot of Lisbon's famous Castle Hill, was already functioning in the 1590s, but Jesuits would not assume responsibility for it until 1605.[40] The openings of several additional institutions, including the province's second (and last) professed house at Vila Viçosa and colleges at Santarém, Elvas, Portalegre, and Faro, were already being planned as the Society's first six decades in the kingdom came to a close.[41]

Three features of the beginnings of Jesuit enterprise in Portugal and its Atlantic islands warrant further consideration. First, apart from their overseas missions and occasional preaching ventures into the countryside of the kingdom, the Jesuits, like their most prominent Mendicant predecessors, and unlike the earlier Carthusians, Premonstratensians, and Cistercians, preferred from the outset to erect their institutions in urban situations, rather than in rural areas. That urban emphasis was obviously consistent with the Society's activist, service-oriented character. Second, and contradictorily, the Order took a largely passive role in the creation of the educational institutions with which it would long be associated. But that situation was far from unique to the Portuguese province. As Marc Venard observed with respect to Jesuit institutional foundations in France, "It was rare when the Jesuits decided, by their own initiative, to establish in such or such a place. Most often, they were solicited by some authority, bishop, prince, or municipality."[42] That was, of course, also true of their educational beginnings in other parts of Europe as well. Third, the Jesuits' reception in Portugal was by no means uniformly supportive. The usually reliable Ludwig von Pastor was misinformed when he wrote that "the enmities and difficulties with

39. HCJAP, 2:1, 37–83.

40. The seminary, partly funded by Irish merchants in Lisbon, was intended to house a dozen Irish youths during their training for the priesthood. The facility was really a dormitory, and inmates attended classes at Santo Antão. The students resided in temporary quarters until 1611, when a Portuguese *fidalgo* purchased a former Carmelite convent to serve as their permanent residence. Teles, *Chronica*, 2:4, chap. 41; [Anon.], *História dos mosteiros*, 2: 95–102; HCJAP, 2:1, 134–38. By the 1630s the Dominicans also maintained a seminary for Irish refugee students in Lisbon, as they did in Andalucia as well. [Anon.], *História dos mosteiros*, 2: 123–30.

41. HCJAP, 2:1, 29–33, 112ff., 119–34. See also Chapter 4.

42. As quoted in A. Lynn Martin, *The Jesuit Mind: The Mentality of an Elite in Early Modern France* (Ithaca, N.Y., 1988), 16.

which the ... Society ... had to struggle in Spain, did not, happily, assail them in ... Portugal."[43] "Enmities" and "difficulties" surely existed there as well. Soon after the Jesuits took over Old St. Anthony's, the suspicious archbishop of Lisbon expressed misgivings about their spiritual aid to those who sought their help. He ordered them to abstain from hearing confessions and barred an Augustinian friar from preaching in St. Anthony's church. During the mid-1540s, rumors circulated in the kingdom that the pope had never really authorized the formation of the Society, that Simão Rodrigues had improperly claimed exemption from the jurisdiction of the heads of the secular clergy, and that Jesuit novices were being ordained within less than a month. Rival religious Orders, claiming to be "more perfect" (that is, more orthodox) than the Jesuits, engaged in what modern football coaches would recognize as "raiding" by attempting to persuade Jesuit recruits to switch their allegiance.[44]

If some warmly applauded the coming of the Jesuits to their communities, others remained markedly hostile. The forced sale of certain properties in Coimbra to the College of Jesus led to an incident in which a group of rowdies knocked down one of the walls of the college, provoking an indignant John III to demand that city authorities restore that structure promptly.[45] Although Archbishop Mártires wanted a Jesuit college in Braga, that community's aldermen did not, for they claimed that such a facility would violate the rights of other Orders already established there and that additional students in the community would lead to a shortage of foodstuffs.[46] In 1562 the Portuguese parliament (*cortes*) protested the Jesuits' growing number and affluence. A decade later the captain-donatary of Madeira opposed the founding of the college of Funchal because he was convinced that the Jesuits were really spies.[47]

Growth of an Enterprise

Despite the persistence of carping in certain quarters, the new Jesuit schools attracted increasing numbers of students, many of whom elected to join the Order. Among the recruits were some conspicuous members of the aristocracy. They included the brother of the duke of Bragança, a close relative of the king; the sons of the governor of the city of Lisbon; the secretary of the *casa da India*, the government agency charged with supervision of trade and navigation between the kingdom and its empire; and a son of the captain of Madeira.[48] Early chroniclers of the Society, such as the frequently cited António Franco, naturally gave prominent places in their accounts to the minority of aristocrats who entered their Order, but, as later chapters will demonstrate, many of its recruits were humble artisans, contrite businessmen, retired soldiers, government bureaucrats, and worn-out adventurers.

43. *HP*, 13: 190.
44. *HCJAP*, 1:1, 299–300, 335–44.
45. *DHJP*, 132–34.
46. *HIP*, 2: 173.
47. OM/*HP*, 1: 300; *HCJAP*, 2:1, 51–52 n. 4.
48. For these and other aristocratic recruits, some of whom played important roles in the establishment of overseas missions and colleges, see *HCJAP*, 1:1, 444–77.

At certain times during the Society's formative period, there were more recruits in the kingdom than the Jesuits were able to train. In 1546, for example, Simão Rodrigues took in thirteen applicants but rejected another 40. By 1552, scarcely eleven years after Rodrigues and Xavier first reached Lisbon, the province counted 318 members. But a crisis occurred that year when Jesuit leaders concluded that many of the recruits were unfit for their Order. Some appeared to display no disposition for learning but were inclined to leave school to engage in unauthorized pilgrimages or, in one notorious case, to streak bare-bottomed through the streets of Coimbra. Whether or not Rodrigues was responsible for the failure of discipline, that was the pretext that Loyola used to relieve his old disciple of his administrative post. Rodrigues's successors subsequently turned out between a third and a half of the province's novices.[49]

Nevertheless, within less than a decade after the great purge, the province was again burgeoning. By 1560, the Society's membership reached 350; within another fourteen years it had increased to 522. By 1579 there were 550 members, more than twice as many as in the two German provinces, and better than three times as many as in the Austrian province. By 1599 membership in the Portuguese province had grown to 591.[50] To be sure, that was far below the Society's representation in Spain, whose four provinces contained 1,747 members in 1587. Yet it must be remembered that the Spanish kingdoms' population was about six times that of Portugal.[51]

The 1599 personnel report concerning the Portuguese province discloses, not surprisingly, that most of its members came from the kingdom's capital and its two university towns. That year these cities provided 78 percent of the province's membership.[52]

The Problem of Motivation

Why did men, young and old, elect to join the Society during the sixteenth century? We shall be much better informed on that intriguing question when Thomas V. Cohen publishes his massive study of the social origins of the Order's European membership during its first six decades.[53] In the meantime, thanks to his already published research, we have some idea of the motives and objectives that impelled some of the Society's sixteenth-century adherents to enter its ranks. Two quite different sources throw light upon the recruits' aspirations. One is a collection of 92 spiritual autobiographies prepared by residents of the Polish province between 1574 and 1580. These residents were asked to explain their reasons for wanting to enter the Society. Cohen ingeniously organized their responses into a topology that matches the perceived advantages of the Society with the corresponding presumed shortcomings of the external world (Table 2.1).

49. *HCJAE*, 1: 608; cf. *HCJAP*, 1:2, 137ff.

50. Statistics for the growth of the Portuguese province in these decades are available in *HCJAP*, 2:1, 3–4. The comparisons are based upon William V. Bangert, S.J., *A History of the Society of Jesus* (St. Louis, 1972), 71.

51. *HCJAE*, 5: 241 n. 1.

52. "Catálogo 3.º que llaman de cosas de la prou.ª de Portugal hecho en Octobre de 1599," *HCJAP*, 2:1, 531–36.

53. In 1987 I was privileged to read a draft of his book-length manuscript, which bears the working title, "Where the Jesuits Came From: A Social History of the Order in the Sixteenth Century."

TABLE 2.1

Polish Recruits' Views of the Society and the World,
from 92 Autobiographical Statements, 1574–80

Perceptions of the Society of Jesus	Views of the world
Harmony	Chaos
Restraint	Unrestricted sensuality
Security	Peril
Eternal life	Fatality
Love unhindered by (personal) attachments	Marriage, office, entanglements
Preservation from avarice and pride	Egotism
Renunciation	Vain ambition

SOURCE: T. V. Cohen, "Why the Jesuits Joined, 1540–1600," in Canadian Historical Association, *Historical Papers 1974* (Toronto, 1974), 237–59, at 242. (I have slightly modified the categories the author employed.) See text for the circumstances that led to the preparation of the autobiographies.

TABLE 2.2

Why They Joined the Society of Jesus:
Responses from 695 Jesuits in Spain and Portugal, 1561–62

Motive	Percentage of responses
To serve God	38.4
To leave the world	23.9
The virtues of the Society	18.4
Self-mortification	12.7
A call from God	12.4
To serve mankind	5.3
To serve in missions abroad	1.4
To die a martyr	0.6
To combat heresy	0.3

SOURCE: See Table 2.1 and text.

It is clear that the Poles were attracted to the Society for the same reasons that have always drawn those who seek escape from the insecurities and imperfections of the world. They yearned to gain admittance to an organization that would provide an environment where they might live a spiritually pristine existence and avoid some of the troubling burdens of surviving in the external world.

Cohen's other source, a thirty-point questionnaire that Jerónimo Nadal distributed to the Iberian provinces in 1561 and 1562, is more directly applicable to the mindset of recruits in the Iberian Peninsula during the Society's formative period. Remarkably, 695 responses to that questionnaire survive. In view of the excitement generated by the coeval material and spiritual Iberian global conquests, these responses offer some surprises. Many of these recruits sought escape from the confusions and perils of their world, but about half of them were primarily concerned about their own souls rather than the welfare of others (Table 2.2). Shockingly few aspired to become soul curers in the distant reaches of the Portuguese empire and beyond. But as the next chapter will reveal, many were destined for such service.

*

From the outset the fate of the Society in Portugal was closely related to that of the crown itself. John III and his two immediate successors more ardently supported the activities of the new Order than did the leaders of any other European government. Both the king and his brothers, especially Cardinal Henry, actively helped the Society to become established in several of the leading urban centers in the kingdom and to assume an increasingly lively role in the educational and spiritual life of the Portuguese nation. In times to come, when the crown sustained major setbacks, so did the Society, as later chapters will show. But first we shall follow the Jesuits as they expanded, with the crown's favor, to the furthest reaches of the Portuguese thalassocracy and beyond.

1. Francis Xavier (?) assesses opportunities for evangelization in the Orient. P. Daniello Bartoli, *Dell'istoria della compagnia di Giesu l'Asia*, 3 vols. (Rome, 1657–63). Courtesy of the James Ford Bell Library, University of Minnesota.

2. A Jesuit priest and a Dominican friar preparing to enter China. C. R. Boxer, *Fidalgos in the Far East, 1550–1770: Fact and Fancy in the History of Macao* (1948; rpr., New York: Oxford University Press, 1968), pl. X. By permission of Oxford University Press and Kluwer Academic Publishers.

3. Jesuits at the Mughal Court (early seventeenth century). India Office Library, London. By permission of the British Library.

4. Arrival of Jesuit emissaries at Luanda on the eve of Angola's liberation (1648). Ernesto de Oliveira and Jorge Tavares, *Do cativeiro a restauração (1641–1647)* (Porto, 1971), 150.

5. The martyrdom of four Jesuits in Japan during the 1620s and 1630s. António Francisco Cardim, *Elogios e ramalhete de flores borrifado com o sangre dos religiosos da Companhia de Iesu, a quem os tyrannos do Imperio do Iappão tirarao as vidas por odio da Fé Catholica* (Lisbon, 1650). Courtesy of the Oliveira Lima Library, Catholic University of America, Washington, D.C.

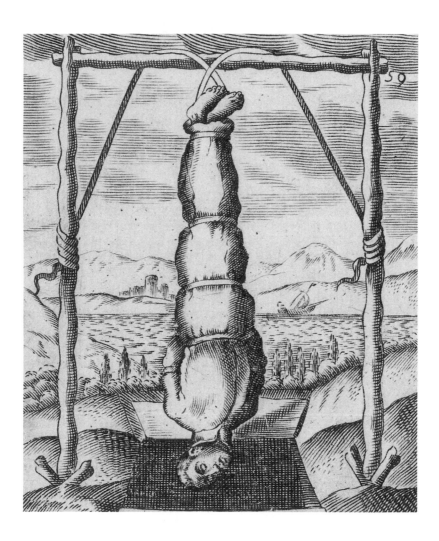

VNVS
NON
SVFFICIT
ORBIS

CHRONICA. DA. PROVINCIA. DO. BRASIL
PELLO P. SIMAM. DE. VASCONCELLOS

6. The *nau de província*, Brazil. Simão de Vasconcelos, *Chronica da companhia de Jesu do estado do Brasil* (Lisbon, 1663). Courtesy of the Oliveira Lima Library, Catholic University of America, Washington, D.C.

PART II

Expansion

CHAPTER 3

Foundations of an Enterprise: The Distant Empire and Beyond, 1542–ca. 1615

> May the Lord deign to send to His vineyard many such workmen that we may be ready to meet the wants . . . not . . . of Europe alone, but of Africa and Asia and India so that the whole world may be drawn to Christ Jesus, and that they may be "one fold and one shepherd."
>
> —Francisco Borgia, 1569

> This land is our enterprise. . . . We are working to lay the foundations of houses which will last as long as the world endures.
>
> —Manuel da Nóbrega to Simão Rodrigues, Bahia, 9 Aug. 1549

> Preparations are . . . being made here for an enterprise that will bring great glory to God and from which it [is] hoped to reap much fruit.
>
> —Br. Luis Frois to the Fathers and Brothers in Portugal, 1 Dec. 1560

ONE OF THE PRIMARY functions of the Jesuits' educational facilities in Portugal was to train missionaries to serve overseas. They set forth confidently on what they were convinced was a divinely inspired enterprise, one that would bring the unquestioned benefits of Christianity to non-Europeans and win back to the fold wayward Christians. The strategies they pursued to attain their objectives varied from land to land. Although the Jesuits operated simultaneously in many parts of the globe, it is best to consider their activities geographically, beginning with the subcontinent of India, for it was the spiritual opportunities there that initially prompted John III to solicit Jesuit assistance.

Beginnings of a Thalassocracy

Since the 1470s India had been the primary goal of the celebrated Portuguese argosies down the African littoral. By the time Vasco da Gama first arrived (1498), the subcontinent was divided, as it still is, between Muslims and Hindus, who together numbered an estimated 100 million.[1] In the Deccan, the powerful kingdom of Vijayanagar, "the focus of resurgent Hindu culture," in Sastri's words, was reaching its zenith, but five Muslim sultanates, which

---

1. Irfan Habib, "Population," in Tapan Raychaudhuri and Irfan Habib, eds., *The Cambridge Economic History of India*, 2 vols. (Cambridge, 1982), 1: 163–71.

relentlessly fought each other as well as the Hindus, contested its hegemony. One of them, Bijapur, controlled the protected insular port of Goa, 400 kilometers south of the future city of Bombay, centrally situated along the western littoral. Further south, a number of small Hindu rajas, including the sea raja of Cochin and his bitter rival, the Zamorin of Calicut, ruled the famous Malabar pepper coast.[2]

It was the international pepper emporium of Calicut that initially attracted da Gama and his early successors. Though they failed to capture it, they successfully negotiated a trading alliance with the rival raja of Cochin, who provided them with their first operational base along the littoral. Within a generation they successfully planted a series of feitorias between the Travancore coast in the south and the Gulf of Cambay. Those defenses, supported by powerful armadas that swept Muslim warships from the seas and supplemented by the seizure of vital international trading centers, notably Ormuz (Hormuz) and Malacca (Melaka), were designed, as D. K. Bassett reminds us, "to impair Mohammedan power in the Mediterranean by diverting the commerce that sustained it from the Red Sea and Persian Gulf routes to the new [Cape] route which they discovered and monopolized." The Lusitanians tried to control the flow of major commodities—pepper, spices, dyestuffs, and drugs—for which there was a strong European demand that they intended to satisfy exclusively, an ambition never fulfilled.[3]

By 1530 the capital of the so-called Portuguese State (Estado) of India, which extended from the Swahili coast of Mozambique to South China, was the city of Goa, successfully captured in 1510. Goa was situated on a large triangular island, Tissuary, between the Mandovi and Zuari rivers, some 24,000 kilometers by sea from the imperial capital of Lisbon. Long the prime port of entry for the horse trade between the Persian Gulf and South India, a notable shipbuilding center, and one of the two finest harbors along the west coast of the subcontinent, Goa became the principal port as well as the administrative and ecclesiastical center of the Portuguese eastern empire.[4] In 1541 it became the destination of the first Jesuit to reach the East.

The Achievements of Francis Xavier

The Jesuits were not, of course, the first Christian missionaries to reach India. According to tradition, Christianity was introduced there by St. Thomas, one of the original apostles. As early as the fifth century, there was an identifiable Christian caste living along the Malabar coast, and by the early sixteenth century, some 30,000 persons there were followers of the Syro-Chaldean rite under the spiritual aegis of priests ordained by the

2. S/FX, 2: 137–38; K. A. Nilakanta Sastri, *A History of South India from Prehistoric Times to the Fall of Vijayanagar*, 3d ed. (Oxford, 1966), 9, 277, and 285.

3. D. K. Bassett, "European Influence in the Malay Peninsula, 1511–1786," *JMBRAS* 33, 3 (1960): 10. The Portuguese also tried to control the internal or country trade, especially near India, by means of mandatory safe-conducts (*cartazes*) purchased by non-Portuguese ships. See also Michael N. Pearson, *Merchants and Rulers in Gujarat: The Response of the Portuguese in the Sixteenth Century* (Berkeley, 1976), 39–52.

4. For an excellent description of Goa and its environs, see S/FX, 2: 179–92. See also A. R. Disney, *Twilight of the Pepper Empire* (Cambridge, Mass., 1978), chap. 2.

patriarch of Armenia.[5] Between the 1290s and about 1350, a succession of Franciscan and Dominican friars visited India but left no lasting impression. Beginning in 1500, Franciscan friars accompanied the annual fleets that sailed from Lisbon to the subcontinent, but the first Observant Franciscan monastery was only established in 1518. By mid-century there were others at Cranganore, Cannanore, Cochin, Goa, and Bassein. Where the Observants led, others followed—the Jesuits (1542), the Dominicans (1548), the Recollect Franciscans (1566), the Augustinians (1572), the Discalced Carmelites (1607), and several minor Orders.[6]

It was the Observants who welcomed the newcomer, Francis Xavier, the dynamic, austere, restless founder of the Society in the East, at the end of a tiring thirteen-month voyage in May 1542. The son of a noble Navarrese family, he became one of Loyola's original and most devoted disciples. Accompanied by a single priest and a brother, he traveled to the subcontinent in a warship commanded by the new governor, the redoubtable Martim Afonso de Sousa, already well known for his exploits in Indian and Brazilian waters.[7]

Xavier came vested with responsibilities not only as missions superior (later, in 1549, first provincial), but also as papal nuncio. For him, passing the Cape of Good Hope had a special meaning; he was confident that beyond it he and his successors would be able to harvest an abundance of "fruit," meaning conversions. For the ensuing decade Xavier worked ceaselessly to convert pagans and to reform old Christians. He consoled the sick and the imprisoned, remonstrated with unscrupulous royal officials, and berated and dismissed fellow Jesuits who were unable to meet his severe ethical standards. His evangelical campaigns took him three times to the Fishery, Malabar, and Travancore coasts, twice to Bassein and Ceylon (Sri Lanka), five times to Malacca, and once to Amboina (Ambon), the Moluccas (Malukas), Japan, and the outskirts of the Chinese empire. Despite innumerable adversities, he retained his optimism until his final frustrating months in Malacca and on the Cantonese island of Sancian, where, physically (and perhaps mentally) exhausted, he expired in December 1552.

In his efforts to reach both the ruling classes and the humble elements in Asian societies, Francis Xavier used many techniques that his successors would emulate and improve upon. His mass-conversion campaigns, his remarkable courage, his incredible endurance, his almost limitless capacity to withstand personal austerities, his eternal optimism, his profound sense of spirituality and personal humility, his incisive understanding of the sources of political power, and his uncompromising leadership set standards that his successors would strive to match as they pursued their destinies in theaters where he had pioneered.[8]

5. A. Mathias Mundanan, C.M.I., *The Arrival of the Portuguese in India and the Thomas Christians . . . 1498–1552* (Bangalore, 1967), and idem, *Sixteenth-Century Traditions of St. Thomas Christians* (Bangalore, 1970).

6. "Mappa demonstrativo das ordens religiosas . . . neste estado . . . e que foram extinctas em 1835," in *Gabinete litterario das fontainhas* (Nova Goa, 1848), 119; Carlos Merces de Melo, S.J., *The Recruitment and Formation of the Native Clergy in India* (Lisbon, 1955), 45–46.

7. S/*FX*, 1: 701–3.

8. The massive four-volume life-and-times biography, S/*FX*, is a remarkable tour de force. Its author, Fr. Georg Schurhammer, devoted 60 years to the project. His matchless knowledge of his subject and his times, his commendable use of sources, and his exceptionally broad coverage make his study indispensable, despite his uniformly laudatory approach to his hero.

The Goan Hub

It was Xavier who took the first steps toward the institutional establishment of the Society in the East. Just as Lisbon became the center of Jesuit activities in Portugal, so Goa became the hub of their endeavors east of the Cape of Good Hope. Their initial and most important facility in the viceregal capital was the original college of São Paulo. Its origins trace back to a unique school created to train students from various parts of Africa and Asia to serve as secular priests among the indigenous populations. Its founders included Miguel Vaz Coutinho, the vicar general, and Diogo de Borba, possibly a Franciscan priest. In 1540 the zealous vicar general launched a drastic campaign to rid Goa of all vestiges of paganism by knocking down all pagan temples (*pagodas*) and idols around Tissuary, an undertaking completed there within a year but one destined to be resumed periodically elsewhere in India and in Ceylon by the Portuguese.[9] When the job was done in Goa, Vaz, Borba, and others organized the confraternity of the Holy Faith under the protection of Saint Paul, the apostle of the Gentiles, to promote the spiritual and temporal welfare of indigenous converts. With funds derived from the former temple lands, they built a church dedicated to the apostle and the seminary of the Holy Faith, which began admitting students in 1542. According to its 1546 statutes, the seminary was designed for non-Portuguese students between ages 13 and 15. Quotas were established for Indians, Kaffirs, Malays, and even Chinese. By 1548 the seminary, a prototype of today's well-known United World Colleges, housed students who spoke thirteen native languages.

Despite its promising beginning, the seminary posed a serious problem: who would be willing to administer it? The confraternity invited the Franciscans to do so, but though their commissary himself was willing, his chapter was not. The vicar general next approached the newly arrived Xavier, but he lacked sufficient personnel to assume responsibility for the school, though he promised that Jesuits would provide instruction there as soon as possible. In January 1547 both Vaz and Borba died, leaving the seminary's future in doubt. The governor, the royal secretary, and the bishop then insisted that the Jesuits fill the gap. By then Xavier possessed sufficient reinforcements to comply. Following approvals granted by Ignatius and John III, the Jesuits took formal possession of the seminary, the nucleus of the original St. Paul's college, in 1551.

Before long the college came to consist of several units. One unit was the residence, the administrative offices, and the major training facility of the Society in the East. Soon an orphanage, a catechumenate, and a novitiate were added, and a hospital was opened nearby. In time most of these facilities would be relocated in sites Jesuit leaders considered more

9. As the Romans did in Spain and the Spaniards were then doing in Mexico and Peru, the Portuguese replaced Hindu temples and Muslim mosques with their own churches. In medieval England the Venerable Bede pursued a wiser policy: he directed that pagan idols be smashed but that their temples be preserved, "for if the shrines are well built, it is essential that they should be changed from the worship of devils to the service of the true God." Bertram Colgrave and R. A. B. Mynors, eds., *Bede's Ecclesiastical History of the English People* (Oxford, 1969), 106–9. (I am indebted to Gordon Whatley for this reference.) Nationalist writers in India have long excoriated the Portuguese for the destruction of pagodas, forgetting that Muslims and Hindus have long defiled and razed their rivals' facilities too. K. A. Nilakanta Sastri, *The Culture and History of the Tamils* (Calcutta, 1946), 36; cf. S/FX, 2: 236, and Zahirudin Faruki, *Auranzeb and His Times* (Delhi, 1972), chap. 4, esp. 113–16, 128–29, and 132–33.

suitable. The seminary of the Holy Faith, soon separated physically from the college but situated on its grounds, became the source of a serious internal conflict. That conflict arose when the college's first director, Madeiran-born António Gomes, purged all indigenous students, replacing them with the sons of Portuguese residents. His intent was to make the college an Asian replica of the University of Coimbra, but Xavier repudiated his unauthorized action, recognizing that it was in violation of the conditions under which the Society took over the seminary. He soon dismissed Fr. Gomes from the Order. Between 1556 and 1607 the student body of St. Paul's grew from 110 to over 2,000 students, by far the largest number attending any Portuguese educational facility in the empire. Three years later, however, the leaders of the Society, seeking a healthier site, opened New St. Paul's (São Paulo *o novo*) on a hill a few kilometers away from the original college, now styled São Paulo *velho*, which remained the domicile for a handful of fathers who continued to instruct in the original seminary.[10]

The Jesuits also erected two other facilities in Goa and its vicinity. For some years they had been anxious to separate the original professed house from the first college. An opportunity to do so came in 1585 when some gardens and houses confiscated from Hindus on Cock's Square were put up for sale. Friends of the fathers purchased them at the request of the provincial, Alessandro Valignano, whose role in the expansion of the Society will be considered later. Additional parcels were needed to build a new professed house, and Valignano offered to exchange certain houses that the Society possessed with the owners of those parcels. While negotiations were under way, both the Franciscans and the directors of the Holy House of Mercy (Santa Casa da Misericórdia) began to object. The Franciscans insisted that the Jesuits already had more than enough facilities in the area, whereas the directors protested that the project would interfere with their ability to collect alms in the parish. By means of a nocturnal ruse, Valignano managed to occupy the disputed lands, an action that both the viceroy and the archbishop later supported. On 13 January 1586, the archbishop himself said Mass and laid a foundation stone for what became the professed house of the Good Jesus (Bom Jesús), today the only surviving Jesuit structure in Old Goa, where it continues to be a major religious shrine because it houses the remains of Saint Francis Xavier in a sumptuous, illuminated crypt.[11]

In 1548 a protracted war between the Portuguese and the sultans of Bijapur came to an end when Sultan Adil Khan renounced "forever" his rights to the districts of Bardês, the land of twelve villages north of Goa, and Salsete, a peninsula south of the capital consisting of 60 villages.[12] Subsequently the Franciscans were assigned exclusive evangelical responsibilities in the parishes of Bardês, whereas the Jesuits, who had become active in parish duties in Goa

10. No history of these first Jesuit educational institutions in the East exists, but see Merces de Melo, *Recruitment*, 65–109, and *S/FX*, 2: 235–43, 256–57, and 3: 456–70. There are many references to them in the *DI* series, e.g., the 1597 regulations of the Holy Faith seminary, *DI*, 18: 813–26. On the number of students attending the first St. Paul's, see *DI*, 3: 483–88, and 785–91.

11. On the establishment of the professed house, see Francisco de Sousa, *Oriente conquistado a Jesus Cristo pelos padres da companhia de Jesus da província de Goa* [1710], ed. M. Lopes de Almeida (Porto, 1978), pt. 2, 999–1001, and *DI*, 14: 24*–25*. In a signed statement dated 24 Dec. 1585, the archbishop wrote that he fully approved the establishment of the professed house, which "does not prejudice anyone." ARSI, FG, 1443/9/3 and /4.

12. *S/FX*, 3: 495–96. The peninsula of Salsete should not be confused with the island of the same name north of Bombay. The Portuguese designated the latter as Salsete do Norte.

TABLE 3.1

Expansion of the Society in the Estado da India and Beyond:
Administrative Units and Their Dependencies, 1549–1607

Location	Year						
	1549	1559	1571	1582	1587	1601	1607
Goa	20	68[a]	110	103	180	171	184
Bassein	2	10	18	36	13	23	24
Taná	—	5	3	6	10	16	14
Damão	—	—	—	5	5	8	8
Chaul	—	—	—	—	—	—	8
Diu	—	—	—	—	6	3	8
Ormuz	1	3	0	0	0	0	0
Ethiopia	—	6	5	3	2	—	5
Mozambique	—	—	—	4	—	—	3
Mughal Court	—	—	—	3	—	4	4
Cochin	0	7	15	—	22	35	60
Cranganore	0	0	0	0	0	0	10
Travancore coast	1	3	6	—	8	8	12
Fishery Coast[b]	7	6	13	—	20	—	37
Colombo	0	0	0	0	0	0	11
Malacca	3	5	5	—	6	8	8
The Moluccas	8	5	14	—	10	—	6
Japan	3	8	13	—	94	—	140
China	0	0	4	11	11	—	17[c]
Total	45	126	210	167	387	276	559

SOURCES: 1549: *DI*, 1: 517–23. 1559: *DI*, 4: 301–5. 1571: *DI*, 8: 414–18. 1582: *DI*, 12: 602–26, *MHJ*, 150–52. 1587: *DI*, 14: 788–800, *MHJ*, 216–23. 1601: *RACJ*, vol. 1, passim. 1607: *RACJ*, vol. 3, passim.

[a] Source lists 68 names but reports a total of 71 persons without explanation.

[b] Depending upon time, includes missions (later colleges) at São Tomé de Meliapor, Manar Island, Madura, and Bengal.

[c] Does not include college at Macao.

and in the nearby islands of Juá, Divar, and Chorão, were awarded exclusive spiritual duties in the peninsula.[13]　The first Jesuits entered Salsete in 1560; among their successors were Thomas Stephens, the first English-born Jesuit in India and the author or coauthor of the first published Konkani grammar, and Rudolfo Aquaviva, nephew of the fifth father general and leader of the first Jesuit mission to the Mughal court (see below), who was martyred in Salsete in 1583.[14]

The next Jesuit college, that of Salsete, was one of the fruits of another round of Lusitanian temple destruction in 1567, for the king assigned income from the confiscated properties to the fathers to erect another such facility.　First built in 1574 at Margão, the "village of the devils," the college was burned to the ground by Muslims in 1579.　The next year it was relocated in Rachol, 6 kilometers distant, under the protection of a fortress.　In

13. Anthony D'Costa, S.J., *The Christianisation of the Goa Islands* (Bombay, 1965).

14. Much has been written about Fr. Stephens (b. 1549–d. 1619), including J. Courtenay Locke, *The First Englishman in India* (London, 1930). See also *DI*, 11: 27*, 682–90 (a famous letter from Stephens to his father), as well as *DI*, 12: 903–4 and 918–32, and 17 and 18, passim. J. Stephen Narayan, *Aquaviva and the Great Mogul* (Patna, 1975), is an uncritical biography. See also *JSM*, 229–37.

1597 it was shifted back to Margão but was again destroyed in 1606, when it was definitively returned to Rachol, where it still exists as a center for the training of secular priests.[15] Highly respected for the quality of its instruction, which included language training in the local tongue, Konkani, the college also served as the administrative center for the Jesuit-supervised parishes in Salsete.[16]

For more than two centuries, Goa remained the major training center for Jesuits received and educated in the Far East and the principal reception center for partially prepared recruits arriving from Europe. The latter, for reasons discussed in a later chapter, far outnumbered the former. Xavier and his successors constantly pleaded for more hands, and Simão Rodrigues and those who succeeded him at home responded as promptly and as generously as their means permitted. The number of Jesuits sent from Europe to India increased decade by decade from the 1540s until the late 1620s: 26 arrived during the 1540s; more than 50 did so during the 1560s; 90 or more reached Goa during each of the remaining decades of the century; and even larger numbers were recorded for the first three decades of the next century. In 1575, 43 Jesuits arrived, a record for a single year not surpassed until 1602, when 62 recruits made the long voyage safely.[17] Many of those recruits remained in greater Goa for a significant time, but others were soon assigned to the Society's installations elsewhere in the subcontinent and beyond (see Table 3.1).

The Northern and Southern Spokes

Beginning during Xavier's regime, Jesuits began to radiate from Goa to establish other installations northward, between Chaul and Diu, and southward, from Cochin via Cape Comorin to São Tomé de Meliapor, today a suburb of Madras.[18] The first and most important center in the north was the city of Bassein, located on a projecting point of land partially surrounded by sea and swamps, north of the island of Bombay. The Portuguese mastered the city and its environs in 1534 and two years later erected their famous fortress there. In 1548 Xavier visited the city for the first time and discovered that a group of Recollects had founded a college there the previous year. The institution was struggling, not because of a lack of funding, for the king had already agreed to assign it revenues derived from former mosques, but because of a scarcity of personnel: one Franciscan had

15. At various times the college was called the college of Salsete, Espírito Santo, Todos os Santos, and Santo Ignácio, but in Jesuit documents it is usually termed the college of Rachol and will be so identified in this study.

16. For the origins and development of the college, see Sousa, *Oriente conquistado*, 819, 886–87; Merces de Melo, *Recruitment*, 181–84; and *DI*, 9: 335–43; 11: 276; and 17: 9*. The Konkani language center was one of several language schools that the Society maintained in India during the late sixteenth century. Another at Pulicat on the Fishery Coast provided instruction in Tamil and a third at Bassein offered Gujarati. *VMP*, 1: 156ff.

17. *LJI*, 269–93.

18. Alessandro Valignano, "Sumario de las cosas que pertencen a la província de la Yndia Oriental e al govierno della," in António da Silva Rego, comp., *Documentos para a historia da igreja em portuguesa oriente*, vol. 12 (Lisbon, 1958), 470–638, is especially helpful in determining the locations and chronologies of other early Jesuit facilities in India. This so-called "Indian Summary" went through several revisions between 1579 and 1583. *VMP*, 122–23. See also *DI*, 5: 164–88.

already died, and three others had decided to return to Portugal, leaving only two friars. One of the two urged Xavier to assume responsibility for the college, and the same year Xavier dispatched one of his lieutenants to supervise the school's activities. Subsequently, however, Franciscan reinforcements arrived in Goa, and their superior insisted that they would run the college. A compromise was reached: the Franciscans regained control of their college but agreed to split its income with the Jesuits. With additional funding provided by the crown, the Jesuits then purchased land for their own college in late 1559. They also obtained title to property within the town of Taná on Salsete Island (Salsete do Norte), nearly 20 kilometers south. There they constructed a large church and a grammar school for local boys. The latter became a *collegium inchoatum* (an incipient college) but was long one of Bassein's dependencies, as were another station at Bandorá (Bandra) and several nearby missions.[19]

The Society also gained three other facilities within or close to the Bay of Cambay, a densely populated, thriving textile, indigo, and commercial region of northwestern India. One facility was at Damão, 160 kilometers north of Bombay at the mouth of the Damagana River. The Portuguese annexed the port in 1559. A Jesuit mission soon followed, and in 1581 their college of the 11,000 Virgins, usually called the college of Damão, was opened there.[20] Between Bassein and Damão lay the harbor of Chaul, the chief port of the sultanate of Ahmadnagar, some 50 kilometers south of Bombay. In 1580 a Jesuit residence there was upgraded to a college.[21] The third of the Cambian outposts was situated at Diu, locus of the great Portuguese naval victory over the Turks (1509) and for a time during the sixteenth century a serious rival of Surat in the race to capture the trade of the declining port of Cambay.[22] Situated on an island off the Kathiawar Peninsula, Diu was strategically placed to monitor coast-hugging vessels traveling between the Gulf of Cambay, Ormuz, and Aden, and it survived two bitterly contested sieges (1538 and 1546). Xavier longed to send missionaries there, but none were permanently stationed at the fortress until 1600.[23]

The upper limit of the southern spoke was the insular city of Cochin, 160 kilometers south of Goa, situated in the midst of the labyrinthine littoral of the Malabar coast.[24] Cochin became the initial center of the Portuguese eastern empire, and it remained the second most important city long after the capital was shifted to Goa. Xavier stayed there on several occasions and initiated the dedicated, protracted, only partially successful Jesuit efforts to win over to orthodox Christianity both the raja and the Thomas Christians who lived along the coast. The college of Cochin (Madre de Deus), which also served as the regional administrative center for the Malabar, Travancore, and Coromandel coasts, was founded in

19. On the beginnings of these units, see S/*FX*, 3: 410; 4: 372–75; *DI*, 1: 417; 4: 714; 8: 119–20; and Sousa, *Oriente conquistado*, 81–82.

20. Sousa, *Oriente conquistado*, 142–44.

21. Ibid., 944–46.

22. Ashin Das Gupta, *Indian Merchants and the Decline of Surat, c. 1700–1750* (Wiesbaden, 1979), 2–3. For an excellent account of Portuguese efforts to wrest Diu from the Gujarati, see Pearson, *Merchants and Rulers*, map facing p. 58, and 68–82.

23. S/*FX*, 3: 587; *RACJ*, 1: 3.

24. See the map in S/*FX*, 2: 464.

1551 and thereafter flourished for some decades.[25] Several residences, which served as bases of operations for various priests who worked among the coastal and foothill communities, were also part of the college's responsibilities. One of the most important was the residence of Vaipicota (Vaipikotta) near Cranganore. During the 1570s and 1580s Jesuit authorities hoped to establish a seminary there in order to train young Thomas Christians to serve as priests, but the Franciscans opposed their plans, even though their own monastery at Cranganore did not attempt to minister to such people. Eventually the Jesuits secured the support of the presiding viceroy, and their seminary, offering instruction in Latin, Malayali, and Syrian, was opened in 1588.[26]

The peninsular town of Quilon, known to the Portuguese as Coulão, is situated 126 kilometers south of Cochin. It marks the northern boundary of the dry Travancore coast and was the site of a Portuguese feitoria. Xavier visited the coast more than once, and in 1552 the Jesuits established a grammar school there to accommodate 50 young men. By the beginning of the seventeenth century, the small Jesuit contingent posted there serviced 35 churches along the littoral and another seven inland.[27]

The Travancore coast ends at Cape Comorin, the southernmost point of India. Eastward lies the famous Fishery Coast. Extending for some 330 kilometers as far as the island of Manar, just off the Sinhalese littoral, the Fishery Coast was the home of Tamil-speaking Parava fishers who lived in villages scattered from the seacoast to a distance of more than 20 kilometers inland. The more affluent among them owned their own boats, fields of cotton, and a few fan palms, but the majority possessed little more than fishing nets and elementary catamarans. The Paravas were skilled divers, and the pearls they extracted were the most highly prized among those taken in eastern waters. But Hindu rulers who resided inland laid claim to the oyster beds and demanded tribute from the fishers, as did the more recently arrived Muslim intruders. Not to be outdone, the Portuguese themselves began to tax the fishers in 1524, igniting a furious conflict with the Muslims that dragged on for fourteen years. Caught in a three-way squeeze, the Paravas agreed to convert en masse to Christianity in the mid-1530s, provided that the Portuguese protected them from their rivals.[28]

Although thousands of Paravas reputedly accepted the new faith immediately, Xavier, who first worked along the coast in 1542–43 and returned on occasion to evangelize there, discovered that none of the secular priests knew Tamil and that the fishermen had no real understanding of the meaning of Christianity. Accordingly, he drafted a rough translation of the catechism, the creed, and the commandments and explained them to his hearers, summoned by his famous bell to his makeshift altar. When Xavier, whom the Paravas called "the great father," had successfully indoctrinated a village, he would persuade its occupants to level their temples and smash their images.[29]

Xavier is credited with thousands of conversions along the coast, but he never remained long enough to sustain the neophytes in their new faith. That became the responsibility

25. S/*FX*, 2: 289–90, 419, 493–94; *DI*, 17:12*–13*. K. M. Panikkar, *Malabar and the Portuguese* (Bombay, 1929), is hostile and superficial. Although deplorably organized, F/*JM* is indispensable.
26. *DI*, 14: 28*–31*, and documents cited there.
27. Ibid., 2: 1*–2* and 379; 5: 184–86. See also the inset map in S/*FX*, 2: 464, and *RACJ*, 1: 328–39.
28. S/*FX*, 2: 256–67, 306, and 311–21.
29. Ibid., 2: 308–10, 321–43, 406–8, 470–71, 534–35, and 641–42.

of a handful of secular priests and small groups of Jesuits who labored tirelessly along the coast at great risk to their own lives. Their adversaries included not only the resentful Hindu and Muslim leaders but also greedy Portuguese captains.[30] The first of many Jesuit martyrs on that coast, António Criminale, died as a consequence of the unscrupulous behavior of one such captain. Ordained at Coimbra in 1544, Fr. Criminale sailed for Goa the following year and was named missions superior on the coast in 1547, a responsibility that he met by working continuously, traveling barefooted, sleeping on the ground, and eating simple fare. While he was ministering to a group of fishermen, a Portuguese captain provoked an uprising by erecting a fortified toll station nearby to prey upon pilgrims. The Brahmans complained to their local lord, who responded by sending multitudes of Telugs to expel the Portuguese, causing many of the fishermen and their families to flee to their boats. Fr. António attended the panic-stricken neophytes as long as he could; then, in classic style, he faced his attackers, knelt down, raised his hands toward heaven, and was dispatched.[31]

Criminale's successor, Henrique Henriques (b. 1520–d. 1600), had a quite different impact upon the coast and, indeed, upon Jesuits throughout India. He was born in east-central Portugal in the town of Vila Viçosa, and his ancestors were conversos of either Jewish or Muslim origin, a stain that caused his dismissal from the Franciscan Order. While studying canon law at Coimbra, he came to the attention of Simão Rodrigues, who, surprisingly, admitted him to the Society and sent him as an ordained priest to Xavier. From 1547 until his death, Henriques served along the Fishery Coast, where he stoically survived years of physical disorders, occasional volleys of arrows, and a harrowing capture by hostile tribesmen. In 1551 he founded two hospitals at Pulicat, but one of his major achievements was the construction of the first European grammar in any Indian language—the famous Tamil grammar—completed by 1549 but revised by Henriques until 1566. He later roughed out a Konkani grammar as well, and it became one of the sources that Thomas Stephens consulted for his improved text, published in 1640. Henriques also published several works in Tamil, including a translation of the famous *Flos sanctorum*, the lives of the saints.[32]

Notwithstanding the fact that the Fishery Coast became one of their major successes in India, the Jesuits never managed to have more than a score of missionaries available to cover the coast, the island of Manar, and the adjacent Coromandel littoral during the remainder of the sixteenth century. More than once superiors complained that "the harvest

30. The beginnings of persisting conflict between the Jesuits and the captains may be seen in S/*FX*, 3: 447–48, 519–20, and 4: 353.

31. *DI*, 1: 486–89, 590–93; Sousa, *Oriente conquistado*, 248–56; S/*FX*, 3: 364–67, 4: 361–66.

32. António Franco, *Imagem da virtude em o noviciado da companhia de Jesus no real collegio de Jesus de Coimbra em Portugal*, 2 vols. (Évora and Coimbra, 1719), 1: 523–36; S/*FX*, 3: 711 and 4: 700–701 (s.v. "Henriques, Henrique"). There have been several illuminating modern studies of this remarkable missionary, notably Josef Wicki, S.J., "Father Henrique Henriques, S.J. (1520–1600)," *Indian Ecclesiastical Studies* 4 (1965): 142–56; 5 (1966): 36–72, and 175–89; idem, "The Confraternity of Charity of Henry Henriques," *Indian Church History Review* 1 (1967): 3–8; and Jeanne H. Hein's outstanding essay, "Father Henriques' Grammar of Spoken Tamil, 1548," *Indian Church History Review* 11, 2 (Aug. 1977): 127–57. Henriques' pioneering Konkani grammar is discussed in Hein, "Language Encounter in 16th Century Goa," Heras Institute of Indian History and Culture, International Seminar on Indo-Portuguese History, a working paper Mrs. Hein kindly sent me. She is preparing for publication a critical edition of his Tamil grammar.

is abundant, but the laborers are few," and lamented that serving there was no longer as appealing to zealous younger missionaries as it once had been because the coast had become a dumping ground for troublesome members of the Society threatened with dismissal.[33] Around 1600 there were about twenty Jesuits along the coast, some attached to small so-called colleges at Tuticorin in the southeast, others at São Tomé and Pulicat in the northeast. Still others resided on Manar or cared for one of the Society's 22 parishes, of which six were in the interior, most notably their residence in the important religious city of Madura (Madurai), where the controversial Roberto de Nobili would later flourish (see Chapter 6).[34]

Jesuits Reach the Mughal Court

With one exception, the Jesuits devoted most of their attention during the formative period of their enterprise to the dissemination of Christianity among the populations of the Indian littoral. The exception was the court of the Mughals, the dominant political force in northern India during the sixteenth and seventeenth centuries. By the reign of Jalal-ud-din Muhammad Akbar (1556–1605), Mughal rule extended from the Arabian Sea to the Bay of Bengal, from Kabul in the north to the Tapti River in the south. It was while the emperor was besieging the port of Surat in 1573 that the first Jesuits visited Akbar. The Portuguese wanted the port themselves but, impressed by Akbar's strength, they quickly withdrew and contented themselves with detailing a diplomatic mission to the Muslim ruler, who thereby gained his first real knowledge of the Portuguese. Six years later he responded by dispatching an embassy to Goa with letters to the viceroy, the archbishop, and the Jesuit provincial, whom he called upon to send him a delegation to explain the doctrines of Christianity. Although Portuguese authorities feared that the fathers might become hostages, they were eager to undertake the mission. Their first contingent left Goa for Fatehpur Sikri, Akbar's capital, in November 1579.

As one recent scholar has astutely observed, the participants in this mission were all non-Portuguese, seemingly selected to avoid giving Akbar offense. Their leader was 29-year-old Rudolfo Aquaviva, son of the duke of Atri and nephew of the Society's fifth father general. He was accompanied by Fr. António de Monserrate, a Catalan who became the main chronicler of the mission, and Francisco Henriques, a Persian convert from Ormuz, chosen because of his linguistic knowledge. There were obvious political and religious motives behind this mission and its successors. The Jesuits naturally hoped to achieve a major coup—the conversion of the most powerful ruler on the subcontinent. Akbar, eclectic in his religious interests and formally uncommitted to any faith, appears to have been genuinely curious about aspects of Christianity that he might adapt to his own empire. Both Portuguese and Mughal authorities were keen for intelligence that their emissaries could gather in their rivals' capitals.

The mission began with great expectations but ended in disappointment. The Jesuits brought the Great Mughal impressive gifts, including a copy of a large ninth-century

---

33. *DI*, 14: 272–74, 305, 361–63, and 419–20; and especially 15: 72–82, an excellent 1588 report concerning Jesuit activities and problems along the coast.

34. *RACJ*, 1: 31.

Madonna painting and a nearly complete set of the illustrated eight-volume Antwerp Polyglot Bible, commissioned by Philip II of Spain and published between 1568 and 1572. Akbar was exceedingly cordial to the fathers and permitted them the freedom of his court and an opportunity to instruct his son in the Portuguese language. He actively participated in their frequent disputations with his mullas and may (or may not) have favored the proposal that someone—the sources are unclear who—made that the validity of their respective religions be determined via an ordeal by fire. But he never gave any sign of being willing to adopt Christianity, and after a year the mission began to disband.[35]

The Jesuits undertook two additional missions to the Mughal court during the remainder of the century. The first (1590) was abruptly aborted, but the second began in 1595. It was led by Jerónimo Xavier (b. 1549–d. 1617), grandnephew of the founder of the Indian mission field, who spent twenty years at the Mughal court. If he did not succeed in winning over Akbar's son and heir, Jahangir (1605–27), who was no more than amused by any religion, at least he secured a permanent footing for the Society at Agra and Lahore, where a small number of Jesuits (usually two to six) maintained schools, ministered to small but devoted congregations for a century and a half, and kept Goan authorities informed concerning the Mughal's moods, intentions, and military operations that might concern the Portuguese.[36]

The Western Spokes

Just as Portugal served as the assembly point for Jesuits bound for the State of India, so India, especially Goa, became the springboard for Jesuit activities beyond the subcontinent in both the Far West and the Far East. In the long run, those in the Far West proved to be the least successful. This was true, for example, of the Jesuits who for a time served in the insular outpost of Ormuz in the narrow entrance to the Persian Gulf some 2,400 kilometers northwest of Goa. Captured by Afonso de Albuquerque in 1515, that rocky, desiccated island not only was a major emporium for the exchange of European silver and manufactures, Arabian horses, Persian carpets and silks, Indian cottons, Southeast Asian spices and drugs, and Chinese porcelain, but also was a center of clandestine arms traffic and a toll-collection point for Mecca-bound Muslims. Its population, estimated at about 40,000 at the beginning of the seventeenth century, consisted of Hindus from Sind and the

35. John Correia-Afonso, S.J., trans. and ed., *Letters from the Mughal Court: The First Jesuit Mission to Akbar (1580–1583)* (Bombay, 1980). See also C. H. Payne, trans. and ed., *Akbar and the Jesuits: An Account of the Jesuit Missions . . . by Pierre du Jarric, S.J.* (New York, 1926); Ashirbadilal Srivastava, *Akbar the Great*, 3 vols. (Agra, 1962), 1: 251–62; Saiyid Athar Abbas Rizvi, *Religious and Intellectual History of the Muslims in Akbar's Reign with Special Reference to Abu'l Fazl (1556–1605)* (New Delhi, 1975), 131–37; Edward R. Hambye, S.J., "The First Jesuit Mission to Emperor Akbar," in Christian W. Troll, ed., *Islam in India: Studies and Commentaries* (New Delhi, 1982), 3–13; and Ebba Koch, "The Influence of the Jesuit Mission on Symbolic Representations of the Mughal Emperors," in Troll, ed., *Islam in India* (1982), 14–29.

36. Edward Maclagan, *The Jesuits and the Great Mogul* (London, 1932), remains unsurpassed; see also C. H. Payne, *Jahangir and the Jesuits* (London, 1930), and H. Hosten, S.J., "List of Jesuit Missionaries in 'Mogor' 1580–1803," Asiatic Society of Bengal, Calcutta, *Journal and Proceedings*, n.s. 6 (1910): 527–42.

Cambay ports, Persians, Jews, and a few hundred Portuguese.[37] Famed for its immorality as well as its wealth, Ormuz ranked high on Xavier's list of places needing spiritual attention, but when Japan called, he sent in his stead a humble but determined Hollander, Gaspar Barzaeus.[38]

Barzaeus reached Ormuz in June 1549, after a difficult two-month sea voyage. Despite initial taunting by hostile Muslims, he quickly awakened the community through his fiery sermons, whose effect was strengthened by a series of earthquakes and aftershocks that terrified both Christians and Muslims. Within a short time, this pioneer Jesuit became a popular preacher and confessor, not only among civilians but also among soldiers, who vowed not to go into battle unless he was with them. By the time Barzaeus was recalled to Goa (in September 1551) to assume new duties, he had become so popular that he had to embark secretly to avoid causing a riot.[39]

The Society maintained a residence at Ormuz for the next three decades. Usually it was staffed by one or two fathers—in 1571 there were as many as five—but in some years there were none. In 1576 the Society's leaders in India recommended the mission's abandonment because of persisting Muslim hostility. Accordingly, in 1580 the Jesuit residence was turned over to Augustinians.[40]

Farther west, in the highlands beyond the Horn of Africa, lay a land where prospects for proselytism seemed far greater than at Ormuz. The ancient kingdom of Ethiopia appeared for a time to welcome the Portuguese and to be ready to abandon its schismatic traditions, dating from the fourth century A.D., and to recognize the authority of Rome instead of that of the See of Alexandria. At least that is what Portuguese sojourners there believed. In fact, Ethiopian rulers admired certain aspects of Western culture and wanted Western arms to defend their homeland against the Ottoman Turks. Following their capture of Mameluke Egypt (1517), the Turks advanced along the flanks of the Red Sea and encouraged local Muslim populations there to rebel against the Ethiopian emperor.[41]

The first Jesuits to visit the Abyssinian highlands went at the behest of both Lisbon and Rome in the mid-1550s. Their leader was João Nunes Barreto, who had previously served for six years in North Africa redeeming Christian captives.[42] Fr. Barreto bore the title of patriarch and was accompanied by two Jesuit bishops, André de Oviedo and Melchior Miguel Carneiro.[43] Their assignment was to persuade the king, Galawadewos or Claudius (1540–59), to forsake the spiritual aegis of Alexandria for that of Rome. But

37. The economic role of Ormuz forms the centerpiece of Niels Steensgaard's masterly study, *The Asian Trade Revolution of the Seventeenth Century: The East India Companies and the Decline of the Caravan Trade* (Chicago, 1973). See esp. 193–208 there.

38. For his background, see S/*FX*, 3: 496–98.

39. S/*FX*, 4: 375–403, 483–84.

40. *DI*, 10: 621.

41. Despite its age, A. H. M. Jones and Elizabeth Monroe, *A History of Abyssinia* (1935; rpr., New York, 1969), remains serviceable. See also Mordechai Abir, *Ethiopia and the Red Sea* (London, 1980); and Robert L. Hess, *Ethiopia: The Modernization of Autocracy* (Ithaca, N.Y., 1970). The approach of Charles F. Rey, *The Romance of the Portuguese in Abyssinia* (1929; rpr., New York, 1969), is indicated by its title.

42. Franco, *Coimbra*, 1: 243–61; *HIP*, 2: 694.

43. For a brief biography of Fr. Oviedo, see *JSM*, 209–11; on Fr. Carneiro, there is a brief essay by the prolific Fr. Manoel Teixeira, "Melchior Carneiro, S.J., bispo de Nicea e coadjutor do patriarca da Etiópia (1555–1566), delegado na China e no Japão (1566–1583)," *Boletim eclesiástico de Macao* (Jan.–June 1940): 227–33.

by the time the team reached Goa in 1557, it was apparent both to viceregal authorities and to Jesuit leaders that the ruler was faced with such serious internal problems that he could not have directed his clergy to abandon Alexandria even if he had wanted to do so. Consequently, Fr. Barreto remained in India while Bishop Oviedo led the first Jesuit mission to Ethiopia in 1557. Because of the Ethiopian king's death in battle two years later, the mission failed, although Fr. Oviedo, designated patriarch in 1560, remained there until his death in 1577 with a handful of colleagues who were scattered through the highlands attending primarily to the needs of about 1,000 Luso-Ethiopians. By the 1570s only two fathers remained but they were able neither to communicate regularly with the outside, nor to receive reinforcements, nor leave.[44] By the 1590s, the last members of this first Jesuit mission had died; but the Jesuits did not give up, and they later dispatched further missions to the highlands, where, for a brief time, the long-anticipated unification of the land of Prester John with the Eternal City seemed to be a real possibility (see Chapter 6).

The third and last western outpost of the Society, Mozambique, also proved disappointing to Jesuit leaders during the formative period of the enterprise. When Vasco da Gama first visited the Swahili coast in 1498, he found that a series of insular Arab city-states, including Sofala, Mozambique, Mombasa, Malindi, Kilwa, and Zanzibar, dominated its trade. By means of superior naval power, a series of alliances, and the erection of feitorias at Sofala and Mozambique Island, the Portuguese gradually subjugated or destroyed those communities during the next three decades.[45] The Lusitanians made no immediate effort to settle the vast interior of the adjacent mainland, although informal settlements consisting of shipwrecked sailors, deserting soldiers, and banished convicts began to appear along the Zambesi River by the 1530s.[46]

The first Jesuit mission to Mozambique arrived in 1560. That year three fathers, led by Gonçalo da Silveira, a former provincial and son of a count, sailed from Chaul to Mozambique, where they began to evangelize near Inhambane, south of Sofala. Encouraged by their early success, the fathers decided to ascend the great river. As they proceeded, Fr. Silveira set off alone for the land of the Mwene Mutapa, some two weeks by canoe beyond the upriver center of Tete. He succeeded in converting the ruler and several hundred of his tribesmen, but after someone—supposedly a Muslim—convinced the Mwene Mutapa that the Jesuit was actually a spy who intended to lead a Portuguese army to conquer their gold-yielding kingdom, Gonçalo da Silveira was strangled. A year later, his two former comrades returned to India.

Whether Fr. Silveira was, in fact, martyred at the instigation of a Muslim trader remains uncertain, but that was the story accepted in Lisbon, where vengeance was demanded. It was not forthcoming for nearly a decade, when it took the form of an expedition headed in 1569 by Francisco Barreto, former governor of India and later general of the galleys of the kingdom. Barreto sailed from Lisbon that year with a large force that included four

44. Valignano, "Sumario," 544–46, and *DI*, 14: 35*, and documents cited there.
45. Alexandre Lobato, *A expanção portuguesa em Moçambique de 1498 a 1530*, 3 vols. (Lisbon, 1954–60); Eric Axelson, *Portuguese in South-East Africa, 1488–1600* (Johannesburg, 1973).
46. M[alyn] D. D. Newitt, *Portuguese Settlement on the Zambesi: Exploration, Land Tenure and Colonial Rule in East Africa* (New York, 1973), 36.

Jesuits. His intent was to expel the Muslims from east-central Africa and to seize the gold mines of the Mwene Mutapa. Because of a grievous illness that afflicted everyone, including the fathers, as they ascended the Zambesi, Barreto did not fully achieve his objectives. Nevertheless, every Muslim the expedition captured was slaughtered. As Malyn Newitt has written, "For the greater glory of God some fifty . . . were impaled, blown from mortars, torn apart on tree-trunks, axed, or shot."[47] Two Jesuits perished during this bloody anabasis; the other two departed for Goa in 1574, the last members of their Order to visit Mozambique during the sixteenth century.[48]

Alessandro Valignano Turns the Society Eastward

It is clear that Jesuit efforts to establish flourishing enterprises west of India failed during the sixteenth century. That was no surprise to the man most responsible for shaping Jesuit enterprises in the East following Xavier's demise. Alessandro Valignano (b. 1539–d. 1606) was born in Chieti in the Abruzzi region of the kingdom of Naples. He came from a distinguished family that enjoyed close relations with the future Pope Paul IV, once a cardinal-bishop in Chieti. Valignano studied law at Padua, where he obtained his doctorate at age 19. Tonsured in the cathedral of Chieti in 1557, he traveled to Rome hoping to gain preferment from Paul IV. That ambition was dashed when the pope suddenly died. In 1561 Valignano returned to Padua for further legal studies, but the next year he was arrested after an altercation with a young woman, whose face he had slashed with a knife. For a time he was imprisoned in Venice. He was released through the intervention of Cardinal Carlo Borromeo, who may have been the same dignitary who then secured for him an administrative position in Rome. But Valignano did not retain the position for long. In mid-1566 he entered the Society. Four years later he was ordained and served briefly as master of novices in the Roman College before becoming rector of the college of Macarata. In August 1573 he was summoned back to Rome by Father General Mercurian, who appointed him chief administrative inspector (Visitor) to the province of India. Early the following month, Valignano made his profession of four solemn vows before Mercurian; 363 days later he was in Goa.[49]

Valignano spent the remainder of his energetic life in the East, not as a devoted missionary like Xavier, but as a forceful, talented, hard-working administrator. Like Xavier, he traveled frequently, especially between India and his beloved Japan. He wrote voluminously, not only perceptive, detailed administrative reports but also lengthy treatises on the condition of both the Church and the State in the East.[50]

47. Ibid., 41.

48. Axelson, *Portuguese*, 152–64; William Francis Rea, S.J., *The Economics of the Zambezi Missions, 1580–1759* (Rome, 1976), 44–45; Francisco Rodrigues, S.J., "Os Jesuítas portugueses na Africa Oriental (1560–1759)," *Brotéria* 3 (Sept. 1926): 118–22; but see esp. António da Silva, S.J., *Mentalidade missiológica dos Jesuítas em Moçambique antes de 1759*, 2 vols. (Lisbon, 1967).

49. Valignano's background is summarized by Paul A. Rule, "K'ung-Tzu or Confucius? The Jesuit Interpretation of Confucianism," Ph.D. diss., Australian National University, 1972, 56ff., and in *VMP*, 1: 30–39.

50. Many of his writings have disappeared, but the late and assiduous Fr. Schütte identified 428 items that survived. *VMP*, 1: 401–28.

One of the most impressive of Valignano's treatises is his famous "Indian Summary." In December 1575 he called to the island of Chorão near Goa a gathering of leading Jesuits, including the rectors of Bassein, Goa, and Salsete and old hands like Henrique Henriques, to advise him on what long-range policies the Society ought to pursue in the East.[51] After hearing their opinions, reading the reports of missionaries returning to Goa from all parts of the Estado, and reflecting upon his own travels between Mozambique and Malacca, Valignano drew up a lengthy report to the Roman headquarters on the status of the Society. In this report, composed and revised between 1577 and 1583, he reviewed the status of the Society in each area, emphasizing its problems and suggesting how they might best be resolved.[52] He candidly admitted that despite the efforts of more than four decades, the results of the mission did not match the expectations of the 1540s. Thousands had indeed been converted, but millions remained ignorant of the true faith, and although a few rulers, such as the king of the Maldives, had been won over, no major pagan ruler had yet been converted. Did the fault lie with the Jesuits themselves—their lack of sufficient talent or zeal or their pursuit of defective strategies? Or had the crown failed to respond adequately to the missionaries' needs? Valignano left no doubt that he considered the Society's limited achievements to be the results of misapplied resources. If he considered the African peoples to be

> a very untalented race … incapable of grasping our holy religion or practicing it [and] because of their naturally low intelligence unable to rise above the level of the senses [since] they lack any culture and are given to savage ways and vices, and as a consequence … live like brute beasts,

he found the Indians little better:

> A trait common to all these peoples (I am not speaking now of the so-called white races of China or Japan) is a lack of distinction and talent. As Aristotle would say, they are born to serve rather than to command. They are miserable and poor beyond measure and are given to low and mean tasks. Many … are very poor, but even the rich tradesmen have to hide their wealth from their tyrannical rulers. They go half-naked and live unpretentiously. More, they are all of a very low standard of intelligence.[53]

For Alessandro Valignano, the Italian-born aristocrat who reflected the conceits and prejudices of Europeans of his status and time, the obvious remedy was for his Society to concentrate upon the so-called "white" peoples of the East, and that meant finding effective means to reach the rulers and masses of Japan and China.

51. Ibid., 1: 122–23.
52. *DI*, 10: 228–315.
53. *VMP*, 1: 131–33.

The First Eastern Spokes:
Malacca and the Moluccas

As Xavier had before him, Valignano recognized Malacca, the crossroads of the monsoons, as an important stepping-stone to East Asia. Its capture in 1511 was one of Albuquerque's most celebrated achievements. At its peak during the sixteenth century, the city's inhabitants numbered some 40,000; another 150,000 resided within a radius of 60 kilometers. The emporium's diverse population included Malays, Persians, Arabs, Gujaratis, Tamils, Bengalis, Javanese, Chinese, and a small but powerful Portuguese minority.[54]

According to Fr. Schurhammer, in sixteenth-century Malacca, "The two reigning divinities ... were Mammon and lasciviousness."[55] When Xavier first visited there during the last quarter of 1545, he undertook the same remedies that he had employed in India, but he soon moved on to more fertile ground. Three years later he sent two of his lieutenants to open a house in that vital port, and the same year the bishop of Goa assigned the Society a small church there. The number of Jesuits residing in the entrepôt varied from none (in 1552, the year Xavier's body was temporarily interred there) to nine in 1576, but construction of the college that Xavier had planned was delayed for decades.[56]

Valignano was determined to establish that college. Even as he sailed from Italy to Portugal en route to the East in 1573, its founding was on his mind. He wrote Mercurian that a seminary in Malacca could serve as the headquarters for all of the Society's enterprises in East Asia. He discussed his plan with Portugal's King Sebastian and his uncle, Cardinal Henry, and the king offered to build a facility adequate for 60 to 70 residents.[57] But the Chorão conference (1575) recommended against such a grandiose structure because the Portuguese community in Malacca was small (it rarely exceeded 600 persons) and prospects for conversions among the predominately Muslim population were, as always, meager. In addition, Valignano's advisors pointed out that the city, dependent as it was upon external food supplies, was a notoriously expensive community, especially during its frequent sieges.[58]

54. Malacca lies at the meeting of the Northeast Monsoon from the China Sea and the Southwest Monsoon from the Indian Ocean. See the map in N. J. Ryan, *A History of Malaysia and Singapore* (New York, 1976), 19. For its evolution, see ibid., 15–38, and M. A. P. Meilink-Roelofsz, *Asian Trade and European Influence in the Indonesian Archipelago Between 1500 and About 1630* (The Hague, 1962), chaps. 2–4; Kernial Singh Sandhu, *Early Malaysia* (Singapore, 1973), 50–61; and C. W. Wake, "Melaka in the Fifteenth Century: Malay Historical Traditions and the Politics of Islamization," in Kernial Singh Sandhu and Paul Wheatley, eds., *Melaka: The Transformation of a Malay Capital, c. 1400–1980*, 2 vols. (Kuala Lumpur, 1983), 1: 128–61. Older but still useful is John Bastin and Robin W. Winks, eds., *Malaya: Selected Historical Readings* (New York, 1966).

55. S/*FX*, 3: 21–22. Easily the best analysis of Portuguese Malacca is I. A. Macgregor, "Notes on the Portuguese in Malaya," *JMBRAS* 38, 2 (May 1955): 4–47. See also Meilink-Roelofsz, *Asian Trade*, chap. 7, and Ryan, *A History*, chaps. 3–4.

56. S/*FX*, 3: 15–30, 420–24. See also R. Cardon, "The Portuguese Church of St. Paul," *JMBRAS* 12, 2 (1934): 38–43; Georg Schurhammer, S.J., "The Church of St. Paul, Malacca," *JMBRAS* 12, 2 (1934): 40–43; Lawrence A. Noonan, "The First Jesuit Mission in Malacca ... 1545 to 1552," *Studia*, no. 36 (1973): 391–457, and no. 37 (1974): 317–85; and Manuel Teixeira, *The Portuguese Missions in Malacca and Singapore (1511–1958)*, 3 vols. (Lisbon, 1961–63), vol. 1.

57. Valignano to Mercurian, Valencia, 16 Nov. 1573; Jerónimo Cotta to Mercurian, Santo Antão, 31 Dec. 1573, in *DI*, 9: 22, 48–49.

58. *DI*, 10: 292–93. Malacca underwent 25 sieges during the Portuguese regime, including five between 1551 and 1575. *DI*, 10: 394 n. 24. For a recent study of the consequences of one of those episodes, see

After the Visitor heard his confreres' reservations, he ordered the construction of a modest college, even though he recognized that the king's promised stipends would not cover a third of its running expenses. Construction of the Jesuits' second St. Paul's, their fifth college in the East, began in 1576. Though the college was completed within two years, its church was not finished until 1590.[59] Like many Jesuit facilities, the college was situated in a prime location: St. Paul's Hill, as it was later called, the highest point in the city and a navigational fix for vessels entering the harbor. In 1585 one occupant wrote enthusiastically that the college possessed "two verandas and has a fine view of the whole town, sea, islands, river, forests and gardens."[60] Decades later a Dutch conqueror described the college as "an excellent building, solid and pleasing, standing at the top of a hill right in the middle of the city ... [with] a strongly built tower, about 100 feet high, and a beautiful garden. The church has three altars ... all richly ornamented."[61]

Despite its location and amenities, the college never grew as rapidly as did its brothers in Goa and Cochin. Nor was it intended to do so, for, as I. A. Macgregor wrote, Malacca was a place where "people were always leaving ... to go somewhere else." That was as true of the Jesuits and other missionaries as it was of merchants, royal officials, soldiers, and sailors.[62] Portuguese Malacca, like sultanic Malacca, remained a transit station. And for the Jesuits, as for many others, beyond lay the Moluccas, Japan, and China.

Two thousand kilometers east of Malacca and a year's sailing time from Goa lay the fabled Spice Islands, the source of highly prized cloves, mace, and nutmeg. Included in those mostly volcanic islands were the Moluccas: from north to south, Ternate, its bitter rival Tidore, Mankian, Batchan, Moitir, and Galolo (or Halmahera), the Moros, Amboina, Seran (Ceram), and the Bandas. Through contacts with Javanese mercenaries who had served in Malacca and with Muslim traders, the islands had become Islamicized during the half century prior to the arrival of the Portuguese.[63]

As was the case in both India and Ceylon, the Jesuits reached the Spice Islands in the wake of the Franciscans, who first came to Ternate in 1522. Xavier spent a year and a half (January 1546 to June 1547) in the islands and assigned them to one of his lieutenants. After hearing reports of headhunters there, the missionary refused to serve, and Xavier

---

Pierre-Yves Manguin, "Of Fortresses and Galleys: The 1568 Acehnese Siege of Melaka," *Modern Asian Studies* 22, 3 (1988): 607–28.

59. *DI*, 11: 200.

60. Fulvio Gregorii to Ludovico Marselli, Malacca, 26 June 1585, in *DI*, 14: 39–42. For the college's location, see the reproduction of a Dutch map of 1656–63 in P. A. Leupe, "The Siege and Capture of Malacca from the Portuguese in 1640–1641," trans. Mac Hacobian, *JMBRAS* 14, 1 (1936): facing 176.

61. "Report of the Commissary Justus Schouten of His Visit to Malacca," 7 Sept. 1641, in *JMBRAS* 14, 1 (1936), 91.

62. Macgregor, "Notes on the Portuguese in Malaya," 6. See Didacus Pinto to Mercurian, Malacca, 25 Nov. 1580, in *DI*, 12: 144, for criticism of the constant movement of Jesuits, including rectors, in and out of the college. As will be seen elsewhere, Jesuit colleges at Macao, Mozambique, and even Lisbon also became transit facilities.

63. On the spread of Islam in Indonesia generally, see Ryan, *A History*, map 1; but cf. Uka Tjandrfasas-mita, "The Introduction of Islam and the Growth of Muslim Coastal Cities in the Indonesian Archipelago," in Haryati Soebadio and Carine A. du Marchie Sarvaas, eds., *Dynamics of Indonesian History* (New York, 1978), 141–60.

promptly dismissed him from the Society. A successor lasted less than a year, surviving repeated shipwrecks and attempted assassinations by Muslims before succumbing to what may have been poison.[64]

His experience was far from unique. Of 38 Jesuits who worked in the islands between 1546 and 1588, thirteen died there as a consequence of disease or Muslim militancy, and several of those who survived met early deaths elsewhere.[65] There were never more than ten Jesuits at a time to serve that insular expanse, and those who labored there met with hostility from the environment, Muslim leadership, and greedy Portuguese captains. Although the Society would be represented there until the mid-seventeenth century, the Spice Islands were always one of its least rewarding fields in the East. By contrast, Japan became its showcase.[66]

Japan, "A World Apart"

In December 1547, soon after returning to Malacca from the Moluccas and only four years after the first Portuguese reached Japan, Francis Xavier obtained direct information concerning spiritual opportunities in Marco Polo's Cipango, "The Land of the Rising Sun," from two informants. Accompanied by one of them—Anjiro, the interpreter, renamed Paul of the Holy Faith—and by two Jesuits and two servants, Xavier landed in southwestern Kyushu at Kagoshima, capital of Satsuma and the home of Anjiro, on 15 August 1549, the fifteenth anniversary of his Montmartre vows. He remained on Kyushu and neighboring Honshu for 26 months, during which he was cordially welcomed by several *daimyos* (barons) anxious for trade with the Portuguese and convinced that the holy men could facilitate it. The apostle also confronted and debated with Buddhist priests (*bonzes*), who became the Jesuits' principal intellectual adversaries in the archipelago.

It was during his six-week sojourn in Kagoshima that Xavier penned his famous assessment of the Japanese: "The people with whom we have thus far conversed are the best that we have yet discovered; and it seems ... that, among pagan nations, there will not be another to surpass the Japanese."[67] Despite a chilling Nipponese winter, he went to the imperial capital, Kyoto (Miyako), hoping to persuade the emperor to grant the Jesuits permission to spread their gospel throughout his land. He discovered, however, that the ruler was no more than a figurehead, unable, even if he had wished, to issue such authorization.

64. S/*FX*, 3: 52–207, 286–87; 4: 355–56.

65. António Marta, "Informações das Moluccas" (1588), in Artur Basílio de Sá, comp. and ed., *Documentação para a historia das missões do padroado português do oriente: Insulindia*, 5 vols. (Lisbon, 1954–58), 5: 89–129.

66. The best survey of Jesuit experience in the islands remains C[ornelius] Wessels, S.J., *Histoire de la mission d'Amboine, 1546–1605*, trans. J. Roebroeck, S.J. (Louvain, 1934); see also Paramita R. Abdurachman, "Moluccan Responses to the First Intrusions of the West," in Soebadio and Marchie Sarvaas, eds. *Dynamics* (1978), 161–88, which is based upon Portuguese archival materials. John Villiers, "Las Yslas de Esperar en Dios: The Jesuit Mission in Moro, 1546–1571," *Modern Asian Studies* 22, 3 (1988): 593–606, rests upon published sources.

67. Xavier to his colleagues in Goa, Aug. 1549, quoted in S/*FX*, 4: 82. In a similar vein, his Spanish-born companion and successor, Cosme de Torres, wrote, "These Japanese are more ready to be implanted with our holy faith than are all the other nations of the world. They are as prudent as can be imagined. They are governed by reason as much as, or more than, Spaniards." Ibid., 269.

Finally, leaving behind a thousand converts and his confreres to tend them, the future saint sailed away.[68]

The Jesuits reached Japan at a propitious time.[69] As Xavier learned, the centralized authority of the old Ashikaga shogunate had been destroyed by a long series of baronial wars dating from the 1460s, conflicts that deprived the emperor and the shoguns of effective control over the isles' 61 provinces. It was the daimyos, not the emperor, who were vital to the successful spread of Christianity, for if they were converted, most of their vassals and those merchants, artisans, and farmers who depended upon them would fall into line. That was why Jesuits there, unlike their colleagues who served on the Fishery Coast, pursued the strategy known as "from the top down." That strategy was, of course, fraught with peril, for a Christian daimyo could be toppled or succeeded by an adherent of Buddhism or, less likely, Shintoism, and one day's mass conversion could become the next day's mass apostasy.

Still, there were several reasons that Japan became an unusually tempting challenge for the Jesuits. First, they found that the many sects of Buddhism were badly splintered and that the sects' leaders were not always respected. Indeed, many bonzes bore a closer resemblance to crusading European Knights Templar than to contemplative monks, participating directly in the political struggles and engaging in immoral behavior that rivaled that of many secular priests in contemporary Europe. Though some Buddhists militantly and effectively opposed the emissaries of an alien faith, others became converts to it. Second, the missionaries learned that the Japanese were eager to engage in foreign trade. Because of long-standing depredations along the coast of China by the so-called Japanese dwarf-robber (*wako*) pirates, the great mainland empire had closed its doors to all legal trade with Japan the very year Xavier landed at Kagoshima.[70] The Japanese badly wanted superior Chinese silks, as well as the gold and European-made firearms that Portuguese traders, assisted by missionary interpreters and arbitrators, could supply. Third, unlike polyglotous India, Africa, or Brazil, the Nipponese archipelago was dominated by a single language, the mastery of which could facilitate the dissemination of Christian propaganda.

The Jesuit enterprise in Japan began slowly during the 1550s and escalated until the second decade of the next century.[71] It began on Kyushu and advanced to the main island,

68. S/FX, 4: bk. 1, which provides a close analysis of Xavier's experiences in and impressions of Japan and its people.

69. For concise introductions to the history of Japan at this time, see Mitsusada Inoue, *Introduction to Japanese History—Before the Meiji Restoration* (Tokyo, 1962), and the introduction to Adriana Boscaro, trans. and ed., *101 Letters of Hideyoshi* (Tokyo, 1975). Despite its age, the second volume of James Murdoch and Isoh Yamagata, *A History of Japan*, 3 vols. (London, 1925), is still serviceable, as is Sir George Sansom, *A History of Japan, 1334–1615* (London, 1961).

70. Kwan-wai So, *Japanese Piracy in Ming China During the 16th Century* (East Lansing, Mich., 1975). In a forthcoming study, Professor George Elison will revise our understanding of precisely who the wako were.

71. No satisfactory account of Jesuit enterprise in Japan exists. Charles R. Boxer, *The Christian Century in Japan, 1549–1650* (Berkeley, 1951), is remarkable for what it tells, but it leaves out much and does not provide a coherent narrative. Elegantly written and powerfully argued, George Elison, *Deus Destroyed: The Image of Christianity in Early Modern Japan* (Cambridge, Mass., 1973), is an intellectual study of high order but is concerned primarily with explaining the ultimate failure of the Jesuits, for whom the author has little sympathy. Often brilliant, Elison sometimes reaches beyond his evidence to perceive patterns of thought that I doubt existed. *VMP*, 1: chaps. 2–5, are indispensable. See also Donald F. Lach, *Asia in the Making of Europe*, 9 vols. to date (Chicago, 1965–), esp. 1:2, chap. 8, as well as Murdoch and Yamagata, *History of Japan*, 2: chaps. 7–9 and 13, and Sansom, *History of Japan*, chaps. 18 and 21.

Honshu, only in the late 1560s. Following the disaffection of the lord of Satsuma, the center of the enterprise first shifted to Bungo, whose rulers were in the process of conquering half the island, and then, beginning in 1571, moved to the rising port of Nagasaki. The enterprise became the responsibility of a succession of leaders whose strategies and procedures were not always congruent: objectives tolerated by one strongman might be repudiated by his successor.

From 1551 until 1570, the missions' superior was a Valencian, Cosme de Torres (b. 1510–d. 1570), whom Xavier had personally recruited.[72] Although Xavier's successors sent Torres as many men as they could spare, he never had more than thirteen, only seven of whom were priests, and often he had far fewer (see Table 3.1). Burdened by ill health and restricted by a limited vision of what might be accomplished, Torres nevertheless deserves credit for some notable conversions, including the lord of Bungo, who permitted the Jesuits to establish the archipelago's first hospital at Funai (Oita) in 1556. Torres also initiated negotiations that, after his death, led to establishment of the Society's headquarters at Nagasaki, and he persuaded Oda Nobunaga (b. 1534–d. 1582), the first of a trio of military strongmen who successfully centralized the quarreling provinces, to allow the Jesuits to preach in Kyoto and in the provinces that he controlled. When Torres died, he left a Christian population that approached 30,000.

The 1570s began inauspiciously for the Japan enterprise when the first Visitor and four companions perished off the Japanese coast in a typhoon.[73] But that decade and the early 1580s proved to be the "take-off" period for the enterprise. Initially under the leadership of the redoubtable patrician Francisco Cabral (b. 1528–d. 1609), kinsman of the discoverer of Brazil and commander of the second Portuguese expedition to India, and later under the decisive control of Alessandro Valignano, who undertook the first of three extended visitations of the archipelago between 1579 and 1582,[74] the numbers of Jesuits and neophytes rose dramatically. Besides the lord of Bungo, prominent converts included the daimyos of Omura and Arima in northwestern Kyushu, many Buddhist priests, and some renowned scholars. During the Jesuits' mass-conversion campaigns in northern Kyushu, zealous daimyos banished those who refused to adhere to the new faith and destroyed countless ancient temples and shrines.[75] No wonder Cabral observed that there were no better apostles in Japan than the daimyos themselves.[76]

72. Torres was a secular priest who for a time served as a Latin teacher on the island of Majorca. Persuaded by a Franciscan friend to go to Mexico, he became the chaplain of Don António de Mendoza, that colony's first viceroy, but after three and a half years there became restless and joined the ill-fated Villalobos expedition from Mexico to the Philippines. When he was shipwrecked on the island of Amboina, Xavier persuaded him to join the Society and later to accompany him to Japan. S/*FX*, 3: 115 and 4: 268.

73. *VMP*, 1: 315.

74. Valignano returned in 1590 and remained until 1592; he came back again in 1598 and stayed until 1603, three years before his death in Macao. *VMP*, 1: xvii–xviii. Fr. Cabral came to the East as an adventurer and joined the Order there in 1554. Before being posted to Japan, he held administrative positions in three colleges in India, to which he later returned to become provincial in the 1590s. Ibid., 188ff.

75. As in India, there remains the question of whether such conversions were wholly voluntary. In a lengthy directive in 1575, Mercurian equivocated, stating that although compulsory baptisms were to be avoided, missionaries ought "not to be too slow in encouraging prospective converts to enter the Christian fold—otherwise many souls might be lost whom we could have won for Christ." *VMP*, 1: 368.

76. Ibid., 1: 206.

Because Japan offered far greater opportunities than any other mission field in the East, it became the Jesuits' most favored assignment. There were 44 Jesuits in the islands by 1578, three times the number present at the beginning of the decade; by the end of the next year, that number had increased by eleven, and the fathers reckoned that there were 100,000 converts, three times as many as in 1571.[77] In that year Nagasaki became the terminus of the vital silk trade with Macao. Nine years later the baron of Omura took the unprecedented step of ceding the port's administration and part of its revenues to the Society.[78] The next year, the Japan missions became the Society's first vice-province within the Assistancy.

Though these steps pleased Valignano, he was far from satisfied with the condition of the Japan enterprise. He was not deceived by the growing number of converts, for he realized that few had had the opportunity to receive religious instruction. "Sometimes," he wrote, "eight or ten months pass without their seeing a single father, and when . . . they have him to themselves, it is only for a day or two."[79] He also knew that the pertinacity of the neophytes could evaporate because of the changing whims of their lords, the influence of unconverted members of their families, and the cunning of the bonzes. As Elison suggests, "The harvest had been great in quantity, but there was reason to doubt the quality of the fruit."[80]

The obvious solution was more frequent and better-quality instruction; but that meant additional manpower, and there were limits to how many Jesuits Europe or India could furnish. Some of those dispatched perished en route; others proved unsuitable. In the long run, Valignano concluded, the success of Christianity in Japan depended upon the development of an indigenous clergy. As he knew, the enterprise already relied heavily upon Japanese recruits, the *dojuku*, acolytes who, as Elison observed, "became the workhorses of the Society without actually belonging to it as members."[81] Although not permitted to take solemn vows, ostensibly because of their inadequate training, the dojuku served as preachers, translators, and advance men for the missionaries and were responsible for the conversion of key community leaders.[82] But the Visitor was shocked to observe that their morale was exceedingly low because his colleagues held them in utter contempt and complained about their unwillingness to adopt European ways. He insisted that since the Jesuits were strangers in an alien land, they must accommodate themselves to Japanese norms with respect to food, dress, hygiene, and manners. Valignano became convinced that the time was fast approaching when Japanese should be admitted to the Order.

His fellow patrician Francisco Cabral strongly disagreed. Although he himself had once favored taking in Japanese candidates, his years of experience in the archipelago caused him to turn increasingly cool toward such a prospect. Clearly burned out, Cabral was reassigned

77. *CCJ*, 242; *VMP*, 1: 269.

78. Diego Pacheco, S.J., "The Founding of the Port of Nagasaki and Its Cession to the Society of Jesus," *Monumenta Nipponica* 25, 3–4 (1970): 303–23; *VMP*, 1: 327–34.

79. *VMP*, 1: 298.

80. Elison, *Deus Destroyed*, 17.

81. Ibid., 16; *VMP*, 2: 39.

82. Arimichi Ebisawa, "Irmão Lourenço, the First Japanese Lay-Brother of the Society of Jesus and His Letter," *Monumenta Nipponica* 5 (1942): 225–33.

in 1579, leaving the Visitor a free hand to appoint as Japan's first vice-provincial, the experienced Gaspar Coelho (b. ca. 1531–d. 1590), who strongly supported Valignano's plans.[83]

The year after Cabral's departure, Valignano and Coelho established the first instructional facilities in Japan, the purpose of which was to train the sons of nobles to become Christian gentlemen, to qualify Japanese recruits for the priesthood, and to provide essential language instruction for European Jesuits. The new institutions included a novitiate and probationary house located within the Usuki fortress, 20 kilometers from the port of Funai, and a college at Funai, where instruction was offered in Japanese, Portuguese, Latin, and vocal and instrumental music, as well as religious doctrine. In addition, two boarding schools (seminaries) to train noble sons were opened, one at Arima, the other at Azuchi, where Nobunaga had just built a large castle.[84]

As soon as these institutions were operating, Valignano left Japan, confident that the entire archipelago could be converted if sufficient workers and adequate funds became available.[85] For a time his optimism seemed justified, despite the treacherous assassination of Nobunaga (1582) and the subsequent destruction of the Azuchi seminary. By 1586 there were 113 Jesuits, 20 residences, 200 churches, and an estimated 200,000 Christians in Japan.[86] In October 1587, however, there suddenly occurred the famous "thunderbolt of St. James' Day," when Toyotomi Hideyoshi (b. 1536–d. 1598), the peasant-born, misshapen soldier who had succeeded Nobunaga, peremptorily ordered the banishment of all Jesuits from the archipelago.

Authorities differ on whether Hideyoshi's action was the result of caprice or calculation. The fathers, who were caught completely off guard by the draconic decree requiring them to leave the country within twenty days (but exempting Portuguese traders from that stipulation), believed that the strongman acted because of a fit of pique or drunken fury. Later writers have suggested that Hideyoshi may have been moved by warnings from the bonzes that the Jesuits constituted a fifth column and were preparing the way for the European conquest of his homeland, or that he was simply implementing another phase of his centralizing campaign, which aimed at military rule.[87]

If the order was, indeed, a calculated move, it is puzzling that it was never implemented. It is true that Hideyoshi issued additional directives demanding the seizure of rosaries and relics, the removal of all flags and crosses, and the confiscation of Nagasaki and two other

83. *VMP*, 1: chaps. 4–5. Boxer's assertion that because Cabral did not share Valignano's views he "was sent packing to Macao" (*CCJ*, 73) ignores the fact that Cabral had been asking to be relieved for several years. His views on most issues do not seem to have differed fundamentally from those of Valignano, and I suspect that at bottom their disagreements were rooted in the fact that one was Italian, the other Portuguese, one an old soldier, the other an old lawyer. See *VMP*, 1: 188–247 and 376–78.

84. Alessandro Valignano, *Sumario de las cosas de Japon (1583) [y] Adiciones del sumario (1592)*, ed. José Luis Álvarez-Taladriz, Monumenta Nipponica Monographs, no. 9 (Tokyo, 1954), 143*–44*, 110–17; Naojiro Murakami, "The Jesuit Seminary of Azuchi," *Monumenta Nipponica* 6 (1943): 370–74.

85. Valignano, *Sumario*, chap. 6; Valignano to Aquaviva, Cochin, 12 Dec. 1584, in *DI*, 13: 598; Valignano to Fr. Manuel Rodrigues (Assistant in Rome), 27 Nov. 1587, in *DI*, 14: 654.

86. *DI*, 14: 38*, but cf. 673.

87. For differing views, see *CCJ*, 104, 145–47; Elison, *Deus Destroyed*, 116–17; Mary Elizabeth Berry, *Hideyoshi* (Cambridge, Mass., 1982), 92 and 225; Sansom, *History of Japan*, 346–48, and Murdoch and Yamagata, *History of Japan*, 2: 236–50. Hideyoshi's surviving correspondence fails to reveal his reasons for the expulsion, and Boscaro reasonably argues that his motivation "remains largely within the realm of conjecture." *101 Letters*, 32.

cities the Jesuits controlled. Some 60 out of nearly 250 Jesuit houses were destroyed, and for a time the fathers retired to the island of Hirado. Perhaps Hideyoshi merely intended to warn the Jesuits, though he might have acted far more severely had he known of Vice-Provincial Coelho's plans for armed resistance and his appeals to Macao, Goa, and even Spanish Manila for military aid. Less than three years later, the bellicose Coelho quietly expired, and the Jesuits began sifting back to their assignments under the protection of sympathetic daimyos.

Hideyoshi took no steps to punish such defiance, though he made it clear to Alessandro Valignano that henceforth he expected the fathers to abstain from all political activity and to maintain a low profile. He conveyed that warning in March 1591, when Valignano returned to Japan in his capacity as ambassador of the viceroy at Goa as well as Visitor. The inspector brought with him 28 Jesuits and four teenage noble youths from Kyushu who had completed a remarkable odyssey.

Valignano himself had organized their tour. In 1582 he assembled an expedition consisting of the sons of the retainers of prominent barons, several Jesuit escorts, and personal servants. The dual purposes of the trip were to acquaint Europe with the achievements of the Society in Japan and to impress upon the neophytes the attainments of European civilization. He himself accompanied the envoys as far as Goa, after which they sailed to Lisbon, traveled by land within the Iberian Peninsula, sailed from there to Rome, and journeyed throughout northern Italy. Everywhere, leading dignitaries, including the regent of Portugal, Philip II of Spain, and Popes Gregory XIII and Sixtus V, received them warmly.[88]

The mission was highly successful. If the awareness of Japan and of the Society's work there increased among leading Europeans, the Japanese too were impressed by the reports and gifts that the samurai youths brought back. The position of the Jesuits in the archipelago appeared to be more secure than ever. By 1592 there were 136 members in the islands, together with 180 dojuku and 380 servants, and the number of Christians they served rose to an estimated 300,000 out of a population of between 15 and 20 million.[89] But suddenly a new crisis developed.

There were two dimensions to that crisis, one internal, the other external; both involved competition. The internal threat (as it was perceived) was the fruit of Valignano's insistence that Japanese be qualified for admission to the Society. Until 1601 none had, in fact, been admitted to the priesthood, but by 1590 the number of novices had reached 70, more than twice as many as had existed a decade earlier, and even Valignano became concerned about the prospect of a Japanese majority within the enterprise in the islands and consequently restricted further admissions.[90] In distant Goa, where Francisco Cabral was now provincial,

88. Much has been written about the embassy. See J. M. Braga, "Os enviados Japoneses a Roma em 1582–1585," *Arquivos de Macao*, 2d ser. 1 (1945): 97–101; J. A. Abranches Pinto, Yoshitomo Okamoto, and Henri Bernard, S.J., *La Première ambassade du Japon en Europe, 1582–1592*, pt. 1 (Tokyo, 1942), covers the outbound voyage in detail with useful maps, but a planned second volume was apparently never published. Lach, *Asia*, 1:2, 688–706, is the fullest account in English. For additional bibliography, see Adriana Boscaro, *Sixteenth-Century European Printed Works on the First Japanese Mission to Europe: A Descriptive Bibliography* (Leiden, 1973), for which I am indebted to Donald Lach; as well as *BHCJ*, 2:2, 441–42.

89. Michael Cooper, S.J., *Rodrigues the Interpreter* (New York, 1974), 239; *RJC*, 326; Murdoch and Yamagata, *History of Japan*, 2: 70.

90. *CCJ*, 89.

the old foe of Valignano warned that "if one does not cease and desist admitting Japanese into the Society ... that will be the reason for [its] collapse ..., nay! of Christianity in Japan." In words that represented the very antithesis of those of Xavier and Torres a generation earlier, the provincial concluded, "I have seen no other nation as conceited, covetous, inconstant, and insincere as the Japanese," and he admonished European fathers serving in the islands not to trust their Japanese brothers.[91]

But could they trust other European missionaries? Wherever they served, members of each missionary group yearned for exclusive evangelical opportunities on the ground that a multiplicity of Orders would inhibit the success of their endeavors.[92] For close to 40 years the Society was the only Christian agency in Japan. Valignano very much wanted to maintain that situation. He devoted a chapter of his "Japan Summary" (1583) to an analysis of the reasons why it would be "inconvenient" for competitors to function within the country.[93] He urged Aquaviva to procure a papal bull confirming the Society's unique status in the islands, and in 1585 Gregory XIII responded with precisely the sort of brief that the Visitor wanted.[94]

Nevertheless, the Jesuits were not destined to remain the only spokesmen for Christ in Japan. Apart from a few strays, the first competitors, a Spanish Dominican monk and several Franciscans, arrived from the Philippines in 1592–93 at a time when Hideyoshi was actively exploring possible trade relations between Japan and the Spanish islands. Although formal relations were not established, the Franciscans remained on Honshu, much to the annoyance of the Jesuits. In October 1596 a typhoon compelled the *San Felipe*, one of the famed Manila galleons, to seek refuge in a Shikoku port, where it was fatally damaged on a bar. Although the passengers and a large quantity of silver bullion were saved, the local daimyo, acting upon Hideyoshi's instructions, confiscated the cargo. As Donald F. Lach observes, that was no mere act of caprice, for the *taiko*, or regent (Hideyoshi), had just met with a severe reversal in his effort to conquer Korea and badly needed silver to procure fresh war materiel. When a Spanish delegation, spurred by the Franciscans, protested too vigorously and the galleon's chief pilot was heard to boast that missionaries had already served as advance men in previous Spanish conquests, the regent responded decisively and shockingly. He ordered the immediate arrest of 26 Christians— six Franciscan friars, seventeen of their neophytes, and three Japanese Jesuit brothers—and accused them of being threats to the realm. On 5 February 1597, the 26 were crucified in Nagasaki.[95]

The Portuguese Jesuits were *not* directly involved in the Spaniards' troubles. It remains unclear why their Japanese brothers were among the Nagasaki victims. But the

91. Elison, *Deus Destroyed*, 16.

92. One thinks, for example, of the Dominicans' exclusive preserve in Timor and Solor, of the efforts of Dominicans and Jesuits to exclude Augustinians from Mozambique, and of the Jesuits' efforts to maintain exclusivity in the Amazon.

93. Valignano, *Sumario*, chap. 9; cf. *CCJ*, 156–59.

94. *CCJ*, 160.

95. For interpretations of the causes and significance of the *San Felipe* affair, see *CCJ*, 163–71; Elison, *Deus Destroyed*, 136–40; and Lach, *Asia*, 1:1, 308–9. See also C. R. Boxer, "Friar Juan Pobre of Zamora," *Indiana University Bookman*, no. 10 (Nov. 1969): 25–48. Pobre was a Franciscan witness to the martyrdom. The 26 martyrs were canonized in 1627.

Society paid in the aftermath, for more than 100 of its churches were destroyed by anti-Christian mobs. Their frenzy ceased with Hideyoshi's death (1598), but as the century closed, members of the Society were far less certain of their future in Japan than they had been a few years earlier. By contrast, Jesuit prospects in China were then better than ever.

The Chinese Spoke

China was a vastly different country from Japan. Its populatio outnumbered that of the archipelago by roughly five to one in the sixteenth century.[96] While Japan was being torn apart by civil wars, China remained static under the paternalistic rule of the Mings, who had overthrown the Mongols in 1368 and governed through a pyramidal hierarchy headed by remote but unchallenged emperors. In the empire, Buddhist and Taoist priests, unlike their Japanese counterparts, did not seriously challenge the political and military authorities and were, in fact, closely supervised by the ministry of rites (*li-pu*), which carefully restricted their numbers and activities.[97]

As in Japan, Portuguese traders preceded missionaries in imperial China. Beginning in the 1520s, Lusitanian smuggler-traders began to frequent Chinese waters to exchange pepper, sappanwood, ivory, and other products for foodstuffs, silks, and other goods.[98] The cessation of direct trade between Japan and China (1549) enabled them to serve as vital commercial intermediaries between the two hostile East Asian powers. In 1557 the Portuguese gained a precarious foothold on the south China coast when they were permitted to establish a permanent transit port, Macao, between the Pearl and West rivers, opposite Canton (Guangzhou).[99]

The Jesuits first reached Macao during the early 1560s, and by 1565 had established a house and a school there. But they did not found their famous college, Madre de Deus, until 1593. In time its church, of which only the four-tiered stone facade remains, became one of the city's most splendid ornaments.[100] Apart from its role as a training center for secular priests as well as members of the Society, the college would become a vital transit center for Jesuits bound for enterprises throughout East Asia.

96. For population estimates of Ming China close to 1600, see John D. Durand, "The Population Statistics of China, A.D. 2–1953," *Population Studies* 13, 3 (Mar. 1960): 209–56; Ping-ti Ho, *Studies on the Population of China, 1368–1953* (Cambridge, Mass., 1959), 22–23; idem, "An Estimate of the Total Population of Sung-Chin China," in Françoise Aubin, ed., *Études Song: In Memoriam Étienne Balazs*, ser. 1 (Paris [?], 1970), 33–53; and Lach, *Asia*, 1:2, 769 n. 208.

97. Charles O. Hucker, *The Traditional Chinese State in Ming Times (1368–1644)* (Tucson, 1961); and Ray Huang, *1587, A Year of No Significance: The Ming Dynasty in Decline* (New Haven, 1981).

98. C. R. Boxer, ed., *South China in the Sixteenth Century*, HS:2, 106 (1953), xxi–xxiv.

99. On early Macao, see C. R. Boxer, *Fidalgos in the Far East, 1550–1770: Fact and Fancy in the History of Macao* (1948; rpr., New York, 1968); idem, "Macao as a Religious and Commercial Entrepôt in the 16th and 17th Centuries," *Acta Asiatica: Bulletin of the Institute of Eastern Culture* 26 (Tokyo, 1974): esp. 64–65; and Austin Coates, *A Macao Narrative* (London, 1978), which is especially useful for its excellent photographs.

100. There is an excellent illustration of the church's facade in one of the endpapers of Coates's *A Macao Narrative*; the other endpaper locates the college on a hill within the heart of the city. For an appreciative description of the college's appearance in the seventeenth century, see Peter Mundy, *The Travels of Peter Mundy, in Europe and Asia, 1608–1667*, ed. R. C. Temple and L. Anstey, HS:2, no. 46 (1919): 162–63, 267–69.

One of the most appealing of those enterprises was the Ming empire, but, although poised on its very edge, Jesuits, like their missionary rivals as well as diplomats and traders, found it a difficult nut to crack. During Xavier's sojourn in Japan, his questioners provocatively asked him, "If yours is the true faith, why have not the Chinese ... heard of it?"[101] That question troubled the future saint, who yearned to go to the empire to meet and convert the emperor, but he got no closer than the island of Sancian (St. John's Island), 160 kilometers from Canton.[102] After the apostle's death there, several of his followers attempted to gain admission to the empire, without success. One of them, the Spaniard Juan Bautista Ribeira, who had been sent to China by his superiors in Rome, was disappointed in his endeavors to enter in disguise and ruefully returned to Europe convinced, like other frustrated missionaries, that the Chinese would have to be conquered before they could be saved.[103]

Between 1552 and 1583, 32 Jesuits, 24 Franciscans, 2 Augustinians, and 1 Dominican tried to obtain license to preach in China: all failed.[104] If Jesuits were to succeed where others had failed, a fresh approach was needed. Visitor Valignano, who was in Macao between October 1577 and July 1578, recognized the problem and discovered its solution. After reviewing the long record of missionary failures, he concluded that "the only possible method of penetration will be utterly different from that which has been adopted up to now."[105] That method was cultural accommodation, and for it to be successful its practitioners would need a sound knowledge of the Chinese language, something that none of the Jesuits then resident in Macao possessed. Fresh troops were necessary, notably the Italians recently arrived in India, among them two of Valignano's onetime novices.

The first of the new recruits to reach Macao was Michele Ruggieri (b. 1543–d. 1607). Born in Spinazzola in the kingdom of Naples, Ruggieri, like Valignano, was trained in law before he entered the Society (1572). Six years later he sailed to India with a number of other Italian-born Jesuits who would distinguish themselves in the East, including Matteo Ricci, Rudolfo Aquaviva, and Francesco Spínola. Just over a year after his arrival in Goa, Ruggieri responded to Valignano's summons, but by the time he reached Macao, the Visitor had already left for Japan. When he attempted to comply with Valignano's instructions to begin the intensive study of the Chinese language, he met with scorn from other Jesuits in the outpost, for they were convinced that "any attempt to win over [the Chinese] was a sheer waste of time, like trying to whiten an Ethiopian."[106] When Valignano came back to Macao, he remonstrated with Ruggieri's critics and demanded that

101. Lach, *Asia*, 1:2, 794.

102. S/*FX*, 4: 640–43.

103. Henry Bernard [Maitre], S.J., *Aux portes de la Chine: Les missionaires du seizième siècle, 1514–1588* (Tiensin, 1933), pt. 1; Lach, *Asia*, 1:2, 797–98. For bizarre Jesuit and other proposals to force open China's closed doors, see C. R. Boxer, "Portuguese and Spanish Projects for the Conquest of Southeast Asia, 1580–1600," *Journal of Asian History* 3, 2 (1969): 132–36. See also François Bontinck, *La Lutte autour de la liturgie chinoise aux xviie et xviiie siècles* (Louvain, 1962), 4 and nn. 11–12.

104. *RJC*, 325; Pascuale M. D'Elia, *Fonti Ricciane: Documenti originali concernenti Matteo Ricci e la storia delle prime relazione tra l'Europa e la Cina (1579–1615)*, 3 vols. (Rome, 1949), 1: 139–42 n. 5.

105. Quoted by George H. Dunne, S.J., *Generation of Giants: The Story of the Jesuits in China in the Last Decades of the Ming Dynasty* (Notre Dame, 1962), 17–18.

106. Louis J. Gallagher, S.J., trans., *China in the Sixteenth Century: The Journals of Matthew Ricci, 1583–1610* (1942; rpr., New York, 1953), 131.

they cease "portugalizing" their Chinese converts and commence "sinicizing" themselves in preparation for their mainland enterprise.[107]

That enterprise effectively began in 1583. In September Ruggieri and a companion traveled to Chao-ch'ing, capital of the viceregency of Kwantung and Kwansi provinces, where they established the first Jesuit mission in the empire. Within five years, however, Ruggieri was no longer associated with the China enterprise and was sent back to Europe. If he warrants credit as a pioneer and as the first to translate Christian doctrine into Chinese, it was his companion, Matteo Ricci (b. 1552–d. 1610), who would become the effective founder of the China enterprise, despite repeated reverses that discouraged even Valignano.

It was Fr. Ricci who devised the strategies that enabled Jesuits to survive and ultimately to attain considerable success in China. Ricci was born in the Adriatic town of Macerata in October 1552, less than three months before Xavier's death. Although sent by his pharmacist father to Rome to prepare himself for the legal profession, he emphasized philosophical and theological studies, as well as mathematics, cosmography, and astronomy. On Ascension Day (15 August) in 1571 he entered the Society, where his quick intelligence caught the eye of the master of novices, Alessandro Valignano. After volunteering for the eastern missions, he was sent to Coimbra and then to Goa for training, and he later taught rhetoric in St. Paul's in Goa and at the college of Madre de Deus in Cochin. In 1582 Valignano called Ricci to Macao to join Ruggieri and others in studying Chinese language and culture. His rapid progress made him the appropriate companion for Ruggieri. Except for brief visits to Macao, he stayed in China for the balance of his life. As gifted as his great contemporary, the resourceful administrator Valignano, or as his remarkable preaching predecessor, Xavier, Ricci proved far more serene and cerebral than St. Francis, less acerbic than his Italian superior, and far less severe and infinitely more patient in his relations with others than either. Neither could match his gift for languages or his scientific and technical abilities. Although he was just as fervent in his desire to spread Christianity, his methods were radically different from those of Xavier and more consonant with the views of Valignano.[108]

During the five years that Ricci remained at Chao-ch'ing, he perfected his knowledge of Chinese, aided by his photographic memory, and deepened his understanding of early Confucian classics in order to discover cultural bridges between ancient Chinese philosophy and Christian doctrines. The fruits of that study included a Chinese-Portuguese vocabulary (prepared with Ruggieri); a small treatise on friendship; the far more substantial and influential *True Account of God*, a work destined to be translated into major Asian languages; and his famous *mappamundi*, the first edition of which he completed before the end of 1584.[109] The multitalented Jesuit also painted and engraved sundials. They were among

107. Dunne, *Generation of Giants*, 18–19. By "portugalizing," he meant the customary Jesuit practice of requiring neophytes to assume Portuguese names, wear European clothes, and adopt other Lusitanian practices.

108. D'Elia, *Fonte Ricciane*, 1: ci–cxxxi; Dunne, *Generation of Giants*, 21–107; Gallagher, *China*, esp. xi–xiii; and especially Jonathan D. Spence, *The Memory Palace of Matteo Ricci* (New York, 1984).

109. Dunne, *Generation of Giants*, 29, 40, 44, and 96; Gallagher, *China*, 165–66. See especially Pascuale M. D'Elia, S.J., "Recent Discoveries and New Studies (1938–1960) on the World Map in Chinese of Father Matteo Ricci S.J.," *Monumenta Serica* 20 (1961): 82–164; idem, *Il mappamundo cinese del P. Matteo Ricci* (Rome, 1938). The third edition (of four) of Ricci's global map (the Vatican Library copy) is reproduced as plate 2 in the second volume of D'Elia's *Fonti Ricciane*.

the eye-catching gifts that he presented to friendly, bureaucrat-scholars, who were also impressed by other specimens of European technology, most notably glass prisms, watches, and chiming clocks.[110]

Although the technical innovations that Ricci and his successors made in or introduced to China may seem unrelated to their spiritual mission, they were, in fact, important elements in a program that was intended to replace the xenophobia and haughty cultural superiority of the Chinese intelligentsia with a yearning for Western ideas, including Christianity. "The Chinese are so self-opinionated," wrote Ricci, "that they can not be made to believe that the day will ever come when they will learn anything from foreigners which is not already set down in their own books."[111] But, as Ricci had hoped, scholar-magistrates in communities where he resided, as well as those from the provinces, became frequent visitors to the mission houses, where long scientific and philosophical discussions prepared the way for what Dunne has called the "apostolate by radiation."[112]

So, too, did the Jesuits' growing mastery of the Chinese language, their increasing understanding of Chinese culture, their adaptation of Chinese dress and customs. Initially the Jesuits entered China in the attire of Buddhist monks, but they discovered that the monks were held in lower esteem than were scholars, and in the mid-1590s they shifted to the dress of Confucian scholars. The first Jesuits also discovered that a respectable Chinese rarely employed his proper name but was commonly addressed by an honor name. "Up to this time," wrote Ricci, "the Fathers had always used their own names and were so called by their servants and domestics. To the Chinese this was ... quite unrefined. Therefore, in order to make themselves all things to all persons, and for the winning of souls to Christ [we] adopted the custom of taking an honor-name ... before entering [China]."[113] That, along with the wearing of the famous pigtails, became part of the process of sinicization that Ricci was convinced was essential if Jesuits were to achieve their goals in China. Under his leadership and that of his successors, the practice of cultural accommodation that Valignano so frequently urged went much further than in any other part of the Portuguese Assistancy.

There were other distinguishing features of the China mission. Ricci was keenly aware that the missionaries' stay in China was wholly dependent upon the sufferance of Ming authorities. There were no daimyos to protect them if they were at odds with powerful eunuchs or lesser officials; nor was there any realistic prospect of military support from outside. Therefore, he urged and practiced low visibility. He built no impressive churches or colleges situated in prominent places in Chinese communities. Indeed, there were no churches at all. In 1596 Ricci wrote, "I do not think that we shall establish a church, but instead a room for discussion and we will say Mass privately in another chapel, or perhaps use the reception hall for chapel; because one preaches more effectively and with greater fruit here through conversations than through formal sermons."[114] Not only were church spires, tolling bells, and fiery sermons absent, but so too were massive processions of converts

110. Gallagher, *China*, 169, 160–61, and 180.
111. Ibid., 142.
112. Dunne, *Generation of Giants*, 47.
113. Gallagher, *China*, 178.
114. Dunne, *Generation of Giants*, 46.

comparable to those that Jesuits and other missionaries organized in India and elsewhere. Nor were there any instances of mass conversions like those achieved by Xavier on the Fishery Coast or by his successors in Kyushu. Obviously forced conversions were out of the question in Ming China. Consequently, Christianity grew less spectacularly there than in Japan or India during the formative period. But that, too, was part of Ricci's strategy, for, unlike Xavier on the Fishery Coast, Ricci was far less concerned about the superficial conversion of today's multitudes who might become tomorrow's apostates than he was about intellectually achieved conversions of small cadres who might endure in bad times as well as good.[115]

The persistence of hostility toward those whom the Chinese consistently called the Southern Barbarians or (borrowing a Muslim term) the *Fo-lang-kis*, the Franks, meaning Europeans generally, all of whom Chinese leaders considered to be their cultural and moral inferiors, also retarded the enterprise in Ricci's time. Some Chinese considered the Jesuits to be alchemists, spies, and (as in Japan) advance agents of Portuguese merchants who wished to penetrate interior imperial markets.[116] On more than one occasion, mobs threw stones at Ricci and his colleagues, ravaged their gardens, and pillaged their residence.[117] Help was not forthcoming from timid imperial officials, who were anxious to receive the technological wonders the Jesuits brought but fearful for their jobs and their very lives because of their fraternization with foreigners.

The first of many predicaments that Jesuits faced in the empire occurred in 1588, the year after Hideyoshi's famous expulsion order, when a viceroy demanded that the Jesuits leave the country. Ricci eventually surmounted that threat by persuading the viceroy to accept a face-saving solution: the removal of the Jesuits from Chao-ch'ing to the interior city of Siuchow.[118] The establishment of a new residence there (1589) was followed by the founding of others at Nanchiang (1595), Nanking (Nanjing) (1599), and finally Peking (Beijing), where Ricci gained official acceptance in 1601 and where he spent the remaining nine years of his life.[119] But although he was able to send the emperor and others impressive gifts, including religious paintings, a clock, and a spinet, he was never able to fulfill the rest of Xavier's ambition: he was never permitted to meet, much less to have an opportunity to convert, the emperor; but then the Chinese emperor was far more remote from even his highest officials than were the Japanese strongmen from their advisors.

Until his last year Ricci had very few helpers. By 1610 his team had grown to sixteen—eight European priests and an equal number of Chinese brothers—who staffed four residences and attended 2,500 converts.[120] But Ricci had successfully cultivated many important friends, especially during his Peking years. A few years before Ricci's death, Valignano marveled that "the business of this mission ... has come to such a point that it seems more miraculous than human, for it would have been unbelievable that in a hundred

115. Ibid., 87. Cf. D. P. Walker, *The Ancient Theology: Studies in Christian Platonism from the Fifteenth to the Eighteenth Century* (Ithaca, N.Y., 1972), chap. 6, esp. 196–97.

116. Gallagher, *China*, 161, 186–89, and 231.

117. Ibid., 191–93.

118. Dunne, *Generation of Giants*, 31; Gallagher, *China*, 205–29.

119. Joseph Dehergne, S.J., "Les Crétientés de Chine de la période Ming (1581–1650)," *Monumenta Serica* 16 (Tokyo, 1957): 122; Dunne, *Generation of Giants*, chaps. 5–6.

120. Dunne, *Generation of Giants*, 67; Dehergne, "Les Crétientés," 122.

years Ours could have come to such credit in China as they have or could live [there] with such honor."[121] Nevertheless, there were those who wondered in 1610 whether the enterprise could survive without Ricci's impressive talents and tactful leadership. Time would show that it could (see Chapter 6).

The Beginnings of the Enterprise in Brazil

Although the activities of Xavier, Ricci, and others in the East were far more celebrated, it should not be forgotten that contemporaneously other Jesuits were establishing their enterprises along the flanks of the South Atlantic and that their Brazilian endeavors would eventually outperform those in the imperiled eastern theaters. On 29 March 1549, five and a half months before Xavier stepped ashore in Kagoshima, the first members of his Order reached the New World and sailed into the Brazilian harbor of All Saints Bay. Portugal claimed the territory of Brazil, which had been discovered by its second India-bound expedition in 1500, but did not attempt its formal occupation until the 1530s, when the crown entrusted the occupation, defense, and exploitation of segments of the littoral to a group of captains-donatary. Its aims were to facilitate the agricultural development of the colony and to deny it to Portugal's French rivals. Despite the successful introduction of cane sugar and the continued exploitation of timber, the dyewood known as brazilwood, and certain other commodities, the proprietary (captaincy) system was not a success. Accordingly, in 1549 John III acted decisively: having recently recovered title to the centrally located captaincy of Bahia from the heirs of its late captain-donatary, the king dispatched a royal governor and staff of officials to All Saints Bay with 1,000 men to erect what would become for the crown and the Society the Brazilian equivalent of Goa, the city of Salvador.[122]

When Simão Rodrigues learned of the king's plans for Brazil, he eagerly sought permission to lead the first groups there. In view of the glowing reports of Xavier's achievements in the East, the king authorized the dispatch of a group of Jesuits, but he again insisted that the provincial remain home. In his place, initially as missions superior and then, from 1553 until 1560, as provincial, went Manuel da Nóbrega (b. 1517–d. 1570), son of a High Court magistrate and nephew of a royal chancellor. Like Valignano and Ricci, he had studied law and theology, but he had done so at the universities of Coimbra and Salamanca. Having unsuccessfully competed for two academic posts, Nóbrega joined the Society in 1544. Over the next five years he earned a reputation as a humble, earnest, resolute priest, one who was able to withstand physical hardships and surmount his handicap as a stammerer to become an effective preacher.[123] Three priests and two brothers accompanied Nóbrega on his mission. The former included Leonardo Nunes and João de Azpilcueta Navarro, nephew of a noted Coimbra professor who was a cousin of Xavier.

121. D'Elia, "Recent Discoveries," 164 n. 263.

122. H[arold] B. Johnson, "The Portuguese Settlement of Brazil, 1500–1580," Leslie Bethell, ed., *The Cambridge History of Latin America*, 11 vols. (New York, 1984–94), 1: 249–86.

123. For Nóbrega's career, see *HCJB*, 9: 413–33, and Jerome V. Jacobsen, S.J., "Nóbrega of Brazil," *Mid-America*, n.s. 13 (July 1942): 151–87.

Brazil was certainly no India or Japan or China. Unlike those lands, Brazil was sparsely held by an estimated 1.5 to 2.4 million Indians (Brasis) who were culturally light-years removed from the sophisticated easterners. Of the more than 300 tribes with whom the missionaries and settlers would come into contact, the most numerous were the Tupi tribes, who had displaced more primitive hunter-gatherers—the Tapuias (peoples of the strange tongue)—along the seacoast a century before the coming of the Europeans. The most prominent among the Tupians, cultural relatives of the Guaraní of interior Paraguay, were the Tupinambá, who dwelt in or near the thick rain forest in isolated, semisedentary communities varying in size from a few hundred to several thousand members. Though mystically inclined, the Tupinambá lacked highly complex bodies of religious thought comparable to Islam, Buddhism, Hinduism, or Confucianism; nor did they possess any of the technological advantages long available in the East.[124]

Despite such differences, Nóbrega and his confreres expressed no regret about their assignment: they saw limitless opportunities for evangelization, not only among the tribesmen, but also among renegade Christians, whom they scolded for living immoral lives. Shortly after his arrival, the missions superior reported confidently, "This is our enterprise," and predicted that "much fruit" would be harvested for Christ. Initially the fathers found the Brasis warmly receptive, leading them to conclude that "conversion of these heathen is an easy matter." But the superior warned that "they can be kept in good behavior only with many workers, for they believe in nothing," lacking, as the early and oft-repeated proverb in Brazil put it, "religion, laws, or king."[125] Although the Indians appeared willing to become Christians, "they find it difficult to abandon their customs," especially sanguinary wars; reliance upon shamans (*pajes*), "the principal enemies we have here"; the practice of plural marriages; and the consumption of manioc beer.[126]

The fathers' early confidence in their ability to remold the character of the aborigines by example and persuasion evaporated in the face of the Brasis' resistance to continued intrusions by white settlers upon their fishing and hunting grounds and to the settlers' practice of enslaving Indians needed for their burgeoning sugar plantations. The missionaries warmly supported pacification campaigns undertaken by their close friend and benefactor, Mem de Sá, Brazil's third governor-general (1557–72), in the outlying districts of All Saints Bay and elsewhere along the coast.[127] In 1557 a chastened Nóbrega wrote, "By experience

124. For an able assessment of the Brasis and the results of European contact, see John Hemming, *Red Gold: The Conquest of the Brazilian Indians* (Cambridge, Mass., 1978).

125. That proverb, "não tem fé, nem lei, nem rei," was based not only upon direct observations but also upon the fact that the Tupi language lacked the letters f, l, and r. The origin of such a conviction goes back farther than even Robert Ricard recognized; see his *Études et documents pour l'histoire missionaire de l'Espagne et du Portugal* (Louvain, 1930), 204–5. Amerigo Vespucci first made the assertion ca. 1504, and both secular and ecclesiastical writers would repeat it endlessly over the next two centuries. Those who settled in New France came to the same mistaken conclusion. See [Ambrósio Fernandes Brandão], *Dialogues of the Great Things of Brazil*, trans. and ed., F. A. H. Hall, W. F. Harrison, and Dorothy W. Welker (Albuquerque, 1987), 308, 329–30 n. 19; and Cornelius J. Jaenen, *Friend and Foe: Aspects of French-Amerindian Cultural Contact in the Sixteenth and Seventeenth Centuries* (New York, 1976), 17 and 42.

126. For early Jesuit assessments of the Brasis, see *MB*, vols. 1 and 2, passim.

127. Herbert Ewaldo Wetzel, *Mem de Sá, terceiro governador geral (1557–1572)* (Rio de Janeiro, 1972), chaps. 4–6.

we see that [the Indians'] conversion by love is a very difficult business, whereas being a servile people, they do anything from fear."[128] The veteran Fr. Francisco Pires added, "I have always felt that success was impossible in these two parts without . . . the mercy of the Lord or his justice. . . . Recently justice has entered here, with the naked sword and . . . through the good industry of Lord Mem de Sá. . . . Because of it [the Brasis] are at peace, and since they have physical peace, we are working to give it to them spiritually."[129] A few years later José de Anchieta, a multitalented Canary Islander (b. 1534–d. 1597), who was a relative of both Loyola and Xavier and was later called the "Apostle of Brazil," even added his voice in favor of coercive measures: "We now think that the gates are open for the conversion of the heathen in this captaincy [São Vicente]. For these people there is no better preaching than the sword and iron rod. Here more than for any others it is necessary to adopt the policy of 'compelling them to come in' (Luke, xvi, 23)."[130]

Implementing that policy led to the creation of Jesuit-controlled Indian communities (*aldeias*) situated near white settlements, models of European civilization and Catholicism as well as markets for Indian-produced goods and Jesuit-supervised Indian labor (see Chapter 19). By the mid-1580s Anchieta reckoned that since 1549 the Jesuits had converted over 100,000 Brasis, but he ruefully admitted that only one out of five then remained under Jesuit influence, partly because of disease, especially smallpox, and flight, and also because of persisting enslavement by the settlers.[131] Despite such wastage, a Jesuit official reported in 1601 that the Society was ministering to 50,000 Brasis gathered in 150 aldeias situated along the coast and in the backlands stretching between northeasternmost Brazil and the plateau of São Paulo.[132]

Although the fathers expended much of their energy in rural situations, where they ministered to indigenous peoples and to newly introduced African slaves on the rapidly multiplying sugar plantations, they erected their most enduring institutions in the colony's incipient urban centers, thereby following the practice that also obtained in other parts of the Assistancy. During the formative period, the most conspicuous of those institutions were three colleges. The oldest was that of Bahia, also known as the *colégio máximo*, the same name by which New St. Paul's in Goa would be designated in the later seventeenth century. It remained not only the Order's largest college in Brazil but also its chief administrative center. When Fernão Cardim visited the two-story structure in 1583, he found its construction well advanced, though work continued there and at the other two colleges for the rest of the century. The colégio máximo had 30 large cubicles, many with splendid views of the harbor, organized around its single-nave church. Outside was a handsome garden of vines, fruit

128. Hemming, *Red Gold*, 105.

129. Pires to [Dr. Navarro], 2 Oct. 1559, in *CA*, 247–48.

130. Anchieta to [?], 1563, quoted in *HCJB*, 1: 291, and translated in C. R. Boxer, *Race Relations in the Portuguese Colonial Empire, 1415–1825* (Oxford, 1963), 92.

131. José de Anchieta, *Informação do Brasil e de suas capitanias (1584)*, intro. Leonardo Arroyo (São Paulo, 1964). On the beginnings of smallpox outbreaks in Brazil, see D. Alden and Joseph C. Miller, "Unwanted Cargoes: The Origins and Dissemination of Smallpox via the Slave Trade from Africa to Brazil, c. 1560–1830," in Kenneth F. Kiple, ed., *The African Exchange: Toward a Biological History of Black People* (Durham, N.C., 1987), 35–109.

132. Petition of the provincial, as cited by Stuart B. Schwartz, *Sovereignty and Society in Colonial Brazil: The High Court of Bahia and Its Judges, 1609–1751* (Berkeley, 1973), 129.

TABLE 3.2

Growth of the Society of Jesus in the Province of Brazil,
1558–1600

Year	Number of Jesuits	Year	Number of Jesuits
1558	25	1584	140
1568	61	1598	163
1574	110	1600	169

SOURCES: 1558: *MB*, 2: 459–61. 1568: *MB*, 4: 475–82. 1574, 1584, 1598, and 1600: ARSI, *Bras.*, 5. The 1600 catalogue is also published in *HCJB*, 1: 578–84.

trees, and even a spring.[133] The other two sixteenth-century colleges were situated in Rio de Janeiro and Olinda. Foundations of the former were laid in 1567, after Jesuits had played a significant role in helping Portuguese forces to expel the French from Guanabara Bay. In gratitude, Mem de Sá assigned them a site on Castle Hill in the northeastern quarter of the newly founded city of Rio de Janeiro. Like St. Paul's in Malacca, the college would long remain the most prominent architectural feature on the Carioca landscape, a symbol to be loved and loathed by the Society's friends and opponents. Classes began in 1573, the year the Bahian college awarded its first bachelor's degree.[134] In Pernambuco the college of Olinda was established in 1568, one year after its brother to the south.[135] Five instructional houses (*casas*) were also erected during the 1550s and 1560s in Ilhéus, Porto Seguro, Espírito Santo, São Vicente, and São Paulo de Piratininga. In time four of them would also be elevated to the status of college.[136]

As the number of missions, instructional houses, and colleges in Brazil grew, the need for helpers intensified. Although there were never enough sent from the kingdom or recruited in Brazil to satisfy local superiors, who must have understood that their province enjoyed a lower priority than did the eastern enterprises at this time, the Society's growth in the province during the second half of the century was impressive (see Table 3.2). The number of Jesuits serving in Brazil more than doubled between 1558 and 1568 and doubled again during the next sixteen years. By 1600 nearly three times as many Jesuits were serving there as had been the case in the late 1560s.[137]

There would have been even more Jesuits there had the province not sustained the greatest double catastrophe that would ever be experienced by any component of the Assistancy until the final expulsions of 1759–60. On 5 June 1570 the largest expedition of Jesuits ever sent to the Portuguese empire sailed from Lisbon under the leadership of Inácio

133. "Narrativa epistolar de uma viagem missão Jesuítica" [1590], in Rodolfo Garcia, ed., *Tratados da terra e gente do Brasil* (rpr., Belo Horizonte, 1980), 144. See also *HCJB*, 1: 47–70, esp. the plate facing p. 64.

134. "Historia dos collegios do Brasil," *ABNRJ* 19 (1897): 75–144, is a sixteenth-century Jesuit sketch of the development of the colleges of Salvador and Rio de Janeiro to 1574. See also *HCJB*, 1: 361–408.

135. Concerning its establishment, see *HCJB*, 1: 451–71, and *ABNRJ* 49 (1927): 5–54, a 1576 Jesuit account of the opening of the college.

136. *HCJB*, 1: 189–314.

137. The usually reliable John Hemming errs when he states that there were only 128 Jesuits in the province by the end of the century. *Red Gold*, 98.

de Azevedo. A onetime page in the court of John III, Azevedo possessed an exceptional record of service to the Society, which he had joined in 1548. After being named provincial of Brazil in 1569, he recruited 73 men to accompany him, mostly Portuguese but some Spaniards. They traveled aboard three ships, which first stopped at Madeira, where the governor warned the captains to be alert for French corsairs. On 15 July 1570, as the *Santiago*, bearing the provincial and 46 companions, neared the Canary island of Palma, Huguenots attacked the vessel, boarded it, and cast the provincial and 39 of his companions into the sea, where they drowned. Although a sister ship escaped, contrary winds compelled it to proceed to the Caribbean. After wintering there, the vessel tried for Brazil a second time. On 13 September 1571, it too was attacked near the Azores by another group of corsairs: twelve more Jesuits perished.[138] The loss of 52 recruits and their dynamic leader was a hard blow to the province, but it would not be the last (see Chapter 9).

Although badly shaken by these famous martyrdoms, the province did survive, and it would continue to expand for nearly two more centuries. The Society's situation was quite different in Brazil than in India or in Ceylon, for its agents arrived in what would become Portugal's most productive plantation colony before any other religious body had become successfully established there.[139] Nor would any ecclesiastical rival effectively challenge Jesuit preeminence in evangelical, educational, or cultural activities in the colony until the 1750s.

Jesuit Beginnings in Kongo and Angola

Jesuit achievements in Brazil were far more impressive than were the Order's beginnings on the opposite side of the South Atlantic, in the west central African kingdoms of Kongo (today Zaire) and Angola, whose seacoasts Portuguese navigators first traversed in the 1480s. In 1491 the king of Kongo became the first non-European ruler to accept Christianity, a faith that his son, the famous D. Afonso, and his grandson, D. Henrique, the first black African bishop, also maintained. Although Kongo attracted missionaries from several Orders—the Loios, Franciscans, and Dominicans—the faith did not prosper, in part because of the growing Portuguese involvement in the slave trade.[140] In 1547 Simão Rodrigues responded to a request by John III and dispatched four Jesuits to Kongo, but their mission soon became embroiled in political and economic conflicts, and they withdrew in 1552. A second foray (1553–55) fared no better.[141]

As Kongo declined in importance because of internecine strife, Portuguese interest shifted to the southern kingdom of Angola, where the dominant ruler, the Ngola, requested a Portuguese mission in 1560. Sensing an opportunity to evangelize in more fertile soil, two Jesuit priests and two lay brothers accompanied soldier-adventurer Paulo Dias de Novais,

---

138. Franco, *Coimbra*, 2: 63–139; idem, *Imagem da virtude em o noviciado da companhia de Jesus no real collegio do espírito santo de Évora* (Lisbon, 1714), 214–56; Serafim Leite, S.J., "A grande expedição missionária dos mártires do Brasil," reprinted in Leite, *Novas páginas de história do Brasil* (São Paulo, 1965), 207–46; see also *HCJB*, 2: 248–63, *HCJAP*, 2:2, 489–501, and *JSM*, 211–16 and 330–31.

139. The Benedictines began to build their first convent in Brazil in 1581 and were followed by Franciscans and Shod Carmelites (1584), Discalced Carmelites (1665), and various minor Orders. *MHB*, 5: 133–231, 468–69.

140. *HIP*, 2: 271–75; James Duffy, *Portuguese Africa* (Cambridge, Mass., 1959), 9–21.

141. *HCJAP*, 1:2, 546–56; Ralph Delgado, *Historia de Angola*, 4 vols. (Lobito, 1948–55), 1: 214–17, 224–29.

grandson of the discoverer Bartolomeu Dias, to Angola that year. But the old Ngola's successor turned against the Portuguese, imprisoning Dias de Novais for five years and Fr. Francisco de Gouveia, the missions superior, for the remaining thirteen years of his life. Nevertheless, Fr. Gouveia was able to send messages to Portugal in which he urged the king to conquer Angola to facilitate its Christianization and the exploitation of its mineral riches. Once released, Dias de Novais seconded that recommendation, but it was not until a major uprising occurred in neighboring Kongo that Lisbon named the adventurer governor-proprietor of Angola and sanctioned its military occupation.[142]

When Paulo Dias de Novais sailed from Lisbon in 1575, two Jesuit fathers and two brothers again accompanied him. The next year he founded as his base of operations the town of São Paulo de Luanda on the mainland opposite a long, low island. It was there that the Jesuits established their headquarters. Although they and their successors conducted occasional spiritual embassies to the interior, where they accompanied the endless, fruitless war parties of Dias de Novais, they achieved few conversions. Instead, they devoted most of their efforts to the care of Portuguese inhabitants in Luanda where in 1607 their little casa became a college, the only one that the Society possessed along the entire west coast of the continent. Angola, like the Moluccas, Mozambique, and Ethiopia, remained a hardship assignment for members of the Society. Between 1560 and 1593, eleven of the 26 Jesuits sent there perished from disease. In 1602 there were a dozen Jesuits serving in the colony; five years later all were dead.[143]

If, toward the end of his life, Claudio Aquaviva had commissioned his assistant for Portugal and its dependencies to prepare a progress report summarizing the Society's achievements within that assistancy, he might reasonably have marveled that so few had seemingly accomplished so much. Thanks to the zeal of Simão Rodrigues and his successors and to the ardent support of three successive monarchs, the Society had become the leader of reformed Catholicism and educational innovation in the kingdom. By the early seventeenth century, its agents had erected instructional centers, missions, and hospitals along the littoral of India. They had repeatedly penetrated the powerful Mughal court and were poised to enter Ceylon. Despite Muslim harassment, Jesuits enjoyed some success in the Moluccas, but their greatest triumphs were in Japan, where they survived two serious setbacks and by the end of the sixteenth century continued to enjoy the spiritual loyalty of tens of thousands of followers. Where others had failed, Jesuits succeeded in gaining permanent entry into imperial China, and were carefully building a small but devoted following there. As soon as the crown was ready to make a determined effort to preserve Brazil, Jesuits joined in

142. Joseph C. Miller, "Requiem for the 'Jaga,'" *Cahiers d'études africaines* 13, 1, no. 49 (1973): 121–49, supersedes earlier interpretations of the 1568 Kongo uprising and demonstrates persuasively that the intrusion of cannibalistic, barbarian hordes of so-called "Jaga" from the interior into the kingdom was an oft-repeated figment of many writers' imaginations.

143. For a brief account of early Portuguese interest in Angola, see David Birmingham, *The Portuguese Conquest of Angola* (New York, 1965), chaps. 2–3; see also Duffy, *Portuguese Africa*, chap. 3, and Delgado, *Historia de Angola*, 1: 269–349. For a glowing description of the Jesuit college, see António de Oliveira de Cadornega, *História geral das guerras angolanas* [1680], 3 vols., ed. José Matias Delgado (rpr., Lisbon, 1972), 3: 12 and n. 16. For Jesuit losses, see Baltasar Afonso, S.J., "Historia da residência dos padres da companhia de Jesus em Angola" [5 Jan. 1594], in António Brásio, ed., *Monumenta missionária Africana: Africa occidental*, ser. 1, 14 vols. (Lisbon, 1952–72, 1984–85), 4: 577–78; see also 3: 471ff.

the operation, embarking upon a continuing campaign to evangelize among the Brasis and to develop an educational system that no other religious Order ever matched there. Only in Africa were the Society's efforts patently disappointing, whether one looked in Ethiopia or Mozambique or Angola; but even there, the fathers remained optimistic about possible future successes.

In Europe, Jesuits were intimately identified with the forces of Catholic orthodoxy; abroad they became revolutionaries, not among the Europeans whom they hoped to reform, but among the indigenous multitudes whose basic systems of belief and customs they sought to alter through what today would be recognized as behavior modification. As ambassadors of what they, like most Europeans, were convinced was the true faith, they urged political leaders at home to undertake major conquests (e.g., China, Brazil, and Angola) to facilitate the spread of Christianity, and they encouraged local leaders and their subjects to destroy temples, smash images, and desert traditional spiritual leaders. They constantly urged those new in the faith to abandon such deeply rooted customs as polygamy, infanticide, concubinage, intertribal warfare, and even suttee. Although they preferred pacific approaches, the fathers were no more averse than their missionary rivals to the judicious use of force to expedite conversions when circumstances appeared to warrant such tactics. Compulsory conversions surely occurred in sixteenth-century Brazil (as in coeval Spanish America), in Japan, and very probably in India. But Jesuits did not resort to compulsion in China both because they realized that it would be folly to try and because they adhered to Ricci's more subtle and less offensive approach. In their religious as in their economic activities, the Jesuits became markedly skilled pragmatists.

With a few conspicuous exceptions, royal officials overseas applauded and wrote favorably concerning Jesuit achievements. Inevitably, however, the fathers had their critics. In Brazil, the best known during the late sixteenth century was Gabriel Soares de Sousa, a sugar planter, unsuccessful mining prospector, and author of a major chronicle and a secret report, both completed in the 1580s. As a chronicler, Soares de Sousa made favorable remarks concerning the fathers' work, but as a memorialist he expressed very different sentiments. In his report to the crown he presented a set of 44 "charges" against the Jesuits' conduct. He contended that they had become deeply involved in political intrigues in the colony; that they had forsaken their original spiritual mission and had become materialistically oriented; and that they were interested in the Indians primarily because they wished to exploit them for their own purposes. Despite Jesuit efforts to refute those allegations, they would be repeated in substance many times by generations of the Society's critics.[144]

About the same time that Soares de Sousa was attacking the Society in the West, Fr. Gaspar de Lisboa, the Franciscan commissary in Goa, also targeted the Society in the East. He wrote to Portugal's new Spanish monarch to protest the erection of the Society's new "sumptuous and large" professed house, Bom Jesús. Asserting that the Jesuits already possessed several other edifices in or near the capital, he urged the monarch to assign Bom Jesús to the Poor Clares on the ground that a new convent was more urgently needed in the capital than another Jesuit house. He accused the Jesuits of usurping Franciscan missionary

144. D. Alden, "Black Robes Versus White Settlers: The Struggle for 'Freedom of the Indians' in Colonial Brazil," in Howard Peckham and Charles Gibson, eds., *Attitudes of Colonial Powers Toward the American Indian* (Salt Lake City, 1969), 26–27 and sources cited there.

rights in nearby Salsete and claimed that wherever the Loyolans were present they became all-powerful, excessively rich, and troublesome. Though others might praise their activities in Japan, the Franciscan contended, their reckless behavior there had already endangered the future of Christianity in the archipelago.[145]

Significantly, both memorials were addressed to Portugal's new ruler, Philip II of Spain. Each was written during the 1580s, just after that monarch had gained control over Portugal and its empire. The ascendancy of the new regime posed increasingly difficult problems for the Jesuits as the triumphant sixteenth century gave way to the tumultuous seventeenth century.

145. Lisboa to king, Goa, 23 Dec. 1589, in *DI*, 15: 454–61.

CHAPTER 4

The Perils of Propinquity:
The Jesuits and the Crown, 1557–1640

> In the Society there should neither be nor be seen partiality to one side or
> another among Christian princes or rulers, but in its stead a universal love
> which embraces our Lord (even though they are adversaries to one another).
>
> —Loyola, *Constitutions*

> The order was given that you should at once give up political negotiations, which
> were inconsistent with our Institute and never had our consent.
>
> —Aquaviva to Henri Sammer, 1 Dec. 1585

LATE IN THE sixteenth century, the provincial of Goa wrote Aquaviva in response to
criticism that the Jesuits were seen at the viceregal court with unnecessary frequency. "Our
attendance," he insisted, "can not be avoided because of the many transactions (*negocios*)
we have concerning the affairs of the Company and of Christianity. It is impossible for a
single person to dispose of all of them because the Father of the Christians has his concerns
and the Provincial his." But the provincial promised to minimize Jesuit participation in
court affairs to the extent possible.[1] The extent to which the Jesuits ought to participate
(or refrain from participating) in the political affairs of the lands where they serve has been
the subject of debate among Church leaders from the sixteenth century to the present. In
our own time a pope has sharply admonished the Society to abstain altogether from political
involvements, thereby asking it to turn its back upon its own history, for the Jesuits, like rival
religious Orders and secular vested interest groups, have always found it convenient and
necessary to be close to the sources of power. For all his apparent unworldliness, Francis
Xavier himself had an acute understanding of the sources of political power and of accepted
techniques for bringing pressure upon the crown to grant the Society favors. Shortly before
his departure from Lisbon for India, he wrote Ignatius,

> It would be a great help if some of the cardinals who are friends of the king would write
> to him about this [the construction of a Jesuit house] and tell him how well the alms given for
> the construction . . . will be used. I believe that Cardinal [Rodolfo Pio de] Carpi is a friend of
> the king, since he is a great friend of Dom Pedro [Mascarenhas, the Portuguese ambassador

1. [Pedro Martins] to Aquaviva, Goa [Nov. 1571], in *DI*, 15: 626. The position of father of the
Christians was assigned to certain religious in Brazil and in India who bore special responsibilities for the
spiritual welfare of neophytes.

to Rome]. His letters would be useful, and those of [Cardinal] Santiquatro and those also of other cardinals who you discover are friends of His Highness. If they do not want to write to the king, then they should at least write to Dom Pedro so that he may speak to the king about it and take upon himself the burden of doing this good work.[2]

Envious outsiders always considered those Jesuits who occupied the sensitive position of royal confessor to enjoy exceptional opportunities to influence government policies in behalf of the Society. The perils of such appointments were appreciated by the early generals and the general congregations. In 1602 Claudio Aquaviva issued an instruction entitled "On the Confessors of Princes," a body of regulations confirmed six years later by the general congregation. That instruction stipulated that confessors remain fully under religious discipline and must reside in a local Jesuit house and be answerable to its superior. Mutio Vitelleschi, Aquaviva's successor, later enjoined the newly appointed confessor of Ferdinand II of Austria to take great care "lest he become involved in external and political matters. . . . Let [the confessor] . . . devote himself to those matters only that pertain to the conscience of the prince, or are related to it, and to certain other pious works." The rub came, of course, in defining precisely what were the "external and political matters" that could be separated from concerns of the royal conscience.[3]

As noted in Chapter 2, John III was the first European monarch to request that a Jesuit to serve as his confessor. His grandson, Sebastian, followed suit, as did two of the first three of Portugal's monarchs after 1640. Such requests, as Fr. Robert Bierley has recently observed, posed a serious dilemma for the Society:

> The Jesuits did not want to forego the influence they could exert for the advancement of the Church's interests through men close to the centers of power. Nor could requests for Jesuit confessors from generous benefactors and patrons of the order be turned down without causing ill-feeling and perhaps losing valuable support. But there were [also] disadvantages. Inevitably the popular mind associated the Society, through the confessor, with unpopular or questionable policies. . .; this burdened the Society's pastoral activity. Still greater liabilities were involved with factions in government and entanglement in the rivalries among princes.[4]

The years 1557–1640 represented a particularly trying period for Jesuit leaders in Portugal and in Rome. At the outset the fathers enjoyed exceptional, though unsolicited, influence at court. Later they shared the blame for the Moroccan debacle of 1578. When they failed to find a formula to save the old dynasty, the Portuguese Jesuits paid the price by witnessing the arrival of Spanish rulers, who denied them access to the highest levels of political authority. But during their years of obscurity, the fathers continued to champion the patriotic cause and saw their efforts bear fruit in a revolution they did not organize but whose success they certainly applauded.

2. Xavier to Ignatius, 18 Mar. 1541, in S/*FX*, 1: 719–20.
3. Robert Bierley, S.J., *Religion and Politics in the Age of the Counterreformation: Emperor Ferdinand II, William Lamormaini, S.J. and the Formation of Imperial Policy* (Chapel Hill, 1981), 11–12.
4. Ibid., 11.

The End of an Ideal King and
of a Popular Dynasty

On 4 August 1578, the forces led by a determined but inexperienced and reckless young monarch, Sebastian, suffered what one historian has termed "the most disastrous battle in Portuguese history," a battle that cost the nation its king and its independence.[5] Though there can be no question about the accuracy of that statement or about the king's responsibility for the disaster at Alcázarquibir, there remains widespread disagreement as to why the childless monarch undertook such a foolhardy, ill-conceived venture in the first place. From the sixteenth century to the present, many writers have insisted that the Jesuits bore ultimate responsibility for the king's action.

Sebastian had become king through one of those dynastic accidents that often bedeviled the Iberian kingdoms. John III (1521–57) and his wife, Catarina de Austria, brought forth nine children, but none survived to succeed to the throne (see Chapter 2). Prince John, their last living son, died eighteen days before his heir, Sebastian, was born in 1554. Soon after, Sebastian's Castilian-born mother, Juana, deserted him and returned to her homeland where, as seen in Chapter 1, she became the only female member of the Society. When John III died of apoplexy, his widow assumed a regency for her grandson but, fatigued by attending to the affairs of state and preoccupied by concerns for her own soul, she retired to a convent in 1562 after transferring the regency to her brother-in-law, Cardinal Henry, archbishop of Lisbon and grand inquisitor. Henry guided his nephew until 1568, when, at age 14, Sebastian was adjudged ready to assume the burdens of kingship. In reality, neither his grandmother nor his granduncle had done as much to prepare the young ruler for the duties of his office as had his educational and spiritual guides, the Jesuits.

The Jesuits assumed much, if not exclusive, responsibility for the young monarch's intellectual and spiritual formation. His instructor in reading and writing was Porto-born Amador Rebêlo (b. 1539–d. 1622), who later became one of the tragic king's early biographers. He also served as missions procurator (see Chapter 12), a compiler of mission accounts, rector of Santo Antão, and professor of humanities and theology at the same institution.[6] For a number of years, Rebêlo was also the "inseparable companion" of the alleged éminence grise of the boy king, Luís Gonçalves da Cámara.

Luís Gonçalves was a member of a distinguished Madeiran family. One of his brothers became the first count of Calheta; another, Martim, served as the ill-tempered *escrivão da puridade* (confidential secretary) in Sebastian's government, a post that gave that dour secular priest vast influence in the affairs of the realm.[7] Luís Gonçalves (b. 1518–d. 1575) entered the Society in Coimbra in 1545. After completing his novitiate in Valencia, he returned

5. OM/*HP*, 1: 312.

6. *PDH*, 6: 114.

7. The most extensive biography of Fr. Luís Gonçalves remains António Franco, *Imagem da virtude em o noviciado da companhia de Jesus no real collegio de Jesus de Coimbra em Portugal*, 2 vols. (Évora and Coimbra, 1719), 1: 21–54. See also [José Maria] de Queiroz Velloso, *D. Sebastião, 1554–1578*, 3d ed. (Lisbon, 1945), 119–20, 206–7; Luiz Augusto Rebello da Silva, *História de Portugal nos séculos xvii e xviii*, 4 vols. (Lisbon, 1860), 1: 44, 71. The office of escrivão da puridade was a powerful one that closely approximated that of royal chancellor. Henrique da Gama Barros, *História da administração publica em Portugal nos séculos xii a xv*, 2d ed., ed. Torquato de Sousa Soares, 11 vols. (Lisbon, 1945–54), 3: 230-37.

to Coimbra in 1547 as rector of the new Jesuit college. Less than a year later, however, he had a falling out with the provincial, the mercurial Simão Rodrigues, who dismissed him from his post and reduced him to the status of cook in order to teach him the meaning of discipline and humility. A short time after he accompanied Fr. João Nunes Barreto, the future patriarch of Ethiopia (see Chapter 3), to North Africa, where for five months the two Jesuits ministered to the needs of Christian captives of the Muslims. Although John III subsequently asked Luís Gonçalves to serve as his confessor, he declined and was transferred to Rome where he became assistant to the general for the Society's operations in Portuguese domains and also occupied the rectorship of the newly founded German college. In 1560 he was summoned back to Portugal at the behest of Cardinal Henry and with the apparent concurrence of the queen mother in order to serve as tutor and confessor to Sebastian.[8] In response to opposition within the court to his retention of both sensitive positions, he resigned his confessional office in 1566 and was briefly succeeded by an Augustinian friar; two years later, he resumed his spiritual duties at the insistence of Sebastian, who came to regard him as a surrogate parent and was so attached to him that he prevented Luís Gonçalves from going to Rome in 1572 as a delegate to the general congregation.[9]

Luís Gonçalves came from the same mold as Francis Xavier.[10] Like Xavier, he was given to great personal austerities: he fasted frequently and wore a hair shirt and a tattered cassock. Although a leading Jesuit historian contends that he was always scrupulous in his guidance to the young king, some scholars support the criticism expressed by court rivals—including, ultimately, the queen mother, who came to regard Luís Gonçalves's influence upon Sebastian as excessive and unhealthy. Especially alarming to such critics was the presence at court of two other Jesuits who occupied sensitive positions. One was Leão Henriques (b. 1524–d. 1589), a cousin of Luís Gonçalves, who served as rector of three Jesuit colleges in the kingdom before becoming a provincial and Cardinal Henry's confessor.[11] The other was Spanish-born Miguel de Torres, who, in the early 1550s, was charged by Ignatius with the delicate mission of investigating the conduct of Simão Rodrigues and later became first provincial of Andalucia before accepting the position of confessor for the queen mother.[12]

These three Jesuits pronounced themselves well pleased by the development of the young monarch. They asserted that he was quick to learn and capable of mastering difficult texts, though other contemporaries (and later historians) questioned the clarity of his mind. Sebastian was unquestionably extremely pious: he was a fervent witness at the *autos-de-fé* of the Holy Office and an ardent admirer of the exploits of the Society in its overseas missions. At the age of nine he wrote to the fathers of Santo Antão, "I pray God make me very chaste and very zealous in the spread of the Faith throughout the entire world."[13] Although Luís Gonçalves insisted on his deathbed that he had never asked the monarch for anything

8. Whether the queen mother initially favored or opposed Luís Gonçalves's appointment is the subject of a dispute between two prominent historians. Cf. *HCJAP*, 2:2, 253 n. 1, and Queiroz Velloso, *D. Sebastião*, 95 n. 9.

9. *HCJAP*, 2:2, 71.

10. *ASCJ*, 144–48.

11. Ibid., 188–91; *MB*, 4: 69*–70*.

12. *HCJAP*, 1:2, 664.

13. Ibid., 2:2, 259.

for his own family or for the Society, Sebastian generously supported the educational and evangelical efforts of the Jesuits both at home and abroad (see Chapter 13). For good reason, the fathers reported that Sebastian would become a great Christian leader, one who would do his utmost to assist the spread of the faith and the empire.[14]

Those denied the king's favor, on the other hand, insisted that Sebastian was badly educated by the Jesuits and molded by them into a fanatic, a throwback to the warrior-kings of the early Middle Ages rather than the statesman he should have been. Their criticisms find echoes in the writings of some modern historians; yet even they must admit that Sebastian was the product of a genetically explosive ancestry. As the fruit of six successive generations of cousin-german marriages, he possessed a very fragile constitution.[15] He had no interest in the usual forms of court recreation save hunting and fatiguing exercises related to the martial arts. Particularly suspicious in the minds of some was his lack of interest in marriage or, indeed, in women. His passions lay elsewhere: he enjoyed reading, especially accounts of wars between Christians and Muslims, Catholics and heretics.[16]

Because of their proximity to him, the Jesuits were blamed for the king's allegedly unhealthy interests. In 1570 there appeared in Lisbon certain anonymous letters thought to have been written by an exiled palace official. Whoever he was, the writer warned that the two Câmara brothers, Luís and Martim Gonçalves, were shaping Sebastian to become a captive king and predicted that within a short time he would become as powerless as the king of Ormuz.[17] On the basis of such "evidence," one prominent nineteenth-century liberal historian propounded the myth that the three Jesuits at court were deliberately following secret instructions from their general to make Sebastian the Society's puppet. Preposterous as that allegation is in the absence of convincing documentation, it finds acceptance with some modern historians.[18] Certainly it is true that the complaints of the Jesuits' critics reached the ears of the distressed queen mother (Juana), who prevailed upon Philip II of Spain to induce the Society's third general, Francisco Borgia, then traveling in the Iberian Peninsula, to remove Luís Gonçalves from his posts. Borgia tried but was unsuccessful, presumably because Sebastian was determined to keep Luís Gonçalves at his side.[19]

Whatever one may think of the notion that Sebastian had been no more than putty in Jesuit hands, by the mid-1570s he clearly began to act on his own impulses. Since the age of twelve he had been convinced that he was divinely chosen to direct some great Christian enterprise. He yearned, he said, to be "God's captain."[20] At first he considered sailing to India to lead his troops against the infidels. Once persuaded that such a venture was too risky, he set his sights on nearby Morocco, where Portugal had long-standing military and commercial interests dating from the capture of Ceuta (1415), opposite Gibraltar.

14. Ibid., 2:2, 256–62, and 342.

15. Queiroz Velloso, *D. Sebastião*, 101–14.

16. *HCJAP*, 2:2, 261.

17. Queiroz Velloso, *D. Sebastião*, 137; on the question of the authorship of the memorials, see *HCJAP*, 2:2, 275–76.

18. Rebello da Silva, *História de Portugal*, vol. 1, chap. 1; cf. Mary Elizabeth Brooks, *A King for Portugal: The Madrigal Conspiracy, 1594–95* (Madison, Wis., 1964), chap. 1.

19. *HCJAP*, 2:2, 278–79.

20. Ibid., 2:2, 262.

During the reign of Afonso V "the African" (b. 1432–d. 1481)—Sebastian's obvious model—the Portuguese "began to leapfrog south along the coast of Morocco, capturing Alcazar el-Saghir in 1458 and Tangier and Arzila in 1471." By the early decades of the sixteenth century they possessed a series of fortified outposts along the Atlantic littoral of Morocco that was intended to tap the interior trade of the western Maghrib, though in practice Portuguese military forays rarely extended inland more than twenty miles. Under Manuel I "the Fortunate" (1495–1521), the Lusitanians acquired several additional strong points, including Mazagão (El Jadida), Agadir, Safi, and Azemmour, so that they controlled the coast between Ceuta and Agadir.[21] In 1541, however, the Saadians mounted a holy war against the Portuguese and captured Agadir. Rather than take up the challenge, John III, mindful of the far greater promise of his eastern empire and the precariousness of his hold on Brazil, ordered the abandonment of Safi and Azemmour.[22] Prudent though that decision was, it was unpopular with hardliners in the kingdom, who viewed it as an act of cowardice and argued that the conquest of Africa was more important than that of India. Accordingly, Sebastian was taught to admire the spectacular exploits of Afonso V and Manuel I and to deplore the timidity of his grandfather.[23] As a young man he became aware of an exploit that epitomized Portuguese valor—the celebrated Portuguese resistance at Mazagão (1562), where a garrison of 2,600 successfully beat off repeated assaults by a vastly larger force under Mulai Mohammed and compelled it to break off its siege.[24] Twelve years later, Sebastian himself went to Africa, despite strong objections from the queen mother, Cardinal Henry, and his dying confessor, Luís Gonçalves. He spent two months near Tangier hunting "Moors" but accomplished little save for his insistent demonstrations of personal bravado.[25]

Those who hoped that Sebastian had gotten the notion of being a heroic conqueror out of his system were destined to be disappointed. In 1575 he lost his close friend, mentor, and confessor when a blind, crippled, and discouraged Luís Gonçalves died. The following year the other Cámara brother, Martim Gonçalves, fell from power as a result of palace intrigue. Distancing himself from Cardinal Henry and his remaining old advisors, the monarch surrounded himself with young hotheads who encouraged him in his obsessive plan to lead a large military force against the Moroccans.[26] To his delight, an internecine dynastic quarrel between two rival shereefs provided him with the opportunity to put his plan into effect. When Mulai Mohammed appealed for help after his uncle, Abd el-Malek, overthrew him, Sebastian was ready to answer the call—despite the misgivings expressed by his uncles, Cardinal Henry and Philip II of Spain, but with the support of Pope Gregory XIII and the reluctant compliance of most of the Portuguese nobility.[27]

What Braudel has termed "the last Mediterranean crusade" proved to be a miserable fiasco. The outfitting of Sebastian's expedition cost 40,000 *contos*, an amount equal to half the

21. Andrew C. Hess, *The Forgotten Frontier: A History of the Sixteenth-Century Ibero-African Frontier* (Chicago, 1978), 16 (from which the quotation is taken); Charles-André Julien, *History of North Africa*, trans. John Petrie, ed. C. C. Stewart (London, 1970), 213–15.

22. Julien, *History of North Africa*, 223.

23. Queiroz Velloso, *D. Sebastião*, 93; *HCJAP*, 2:2, 343.

24. E. W. Bovill, *The Battle of Alcazar* (London, 1952), 12.

25. *HCJAP*, 2:2, 352–58; Queiroz Velloso, *D. Sebastião*, chap. 6.

26. *HCJAP*, 2:2, 389–92; Queiroz Velloso, *D. Sebastião*, 204–15.

27. Queiroz Velloso, *D. Sebastião*, chap. 7.

crown's annual income, but the state did not foot the entire bill. The secular church provided a third of its yearly income for the venture, though whether the Jesuits subscribed, as they would during other critical military situations later on, is unknown. Taxes were increased and tax farmers were pressured to prepay their contracts. Loans from wealthy merchants were guaranteed by three years' income from the crown's Indian pepper monopoly. About a quarter of the funding came from the New Christian community (that is, descendants of persons of Jewish origin forcibly converted at the beginning of the sixteenth century) in return for a papal bull (soon after rescinded) promising that suspects arrested by the Inquisition would not automatically risk the loss of their property.[28]

The expedition sailed from Lisbon in late June 1578. Aboard the 800 or so ships were between 15,000 and 20,000 men, about two-thirds of them Portuguese. The rest consisted of mercenaries—Spaniards, Germans, Walloons, Dutchmen, and Italians. Most of the Portuguese troops were simple peasants, led by members of the high nobility. Prominent participants included the Spanish ambassador to Portugal, two papal representatives, two Portuguese and several Irish bishops, the inquisitor general of the Coimbra branch of the Holy Office, and a large number of other clergy. Among the latter were fifteen Jesuits headed by Fr. Maurício Serpe, who had succeeded Luís Gonçalves as the king's confessor.

The major landing was made at Arzila, and the king confidently led his forces overland toward the port of Larache. On 4 August he encountered a somewhat larger Muslim army directed by the terminally ill Abd el-Malek on the bank of the Wadi al-Makhazin, a tributary of the river Lukhus, about 80 kilometers south of Tangier. Although a fiery Jesuit father held aloft the cross to exhort the Lusitanians in the approved crusading style, they proved unequal to the task, for they were ill-trained, ill-disciplined, and ill-led. To be sure, the king fulfilled his ambition to die heroically: he had three horses shot out from under him and was last seen fighting frantically. Nevertheless, the battle, variously known as El-Ksar el-Kebir, Alcázarquibir, or the battle of the Three [Fallen] Kings, was an unmitigated disaster: half of the European forces were destroyed; all but 100 survivors were taken prisoner; and of the Portuguese nobles, 203 died in combat, another 11 later expired as a result of their wounds, and 228 were captured. Among the fallen was Fr. Maurício, who died a coveted martyr's death at the hands of a Muslim whom he deliberately insulted.[29]

The Succession Crisis, 1578–80

For many—but not all—the outcome of Alcázarquibir was a calamity. "There were none in Lisbon," wrote a contemporary, "but had some interest in this warr, who so had not his sonne there, had his father; the one her husbande, the other her brother; the traders and handi-crafts men who had not their kinsmen there ... did venture their wealth into it." Yet another observer, the Fugger agent in Lisbon, reported two and a half weeks after the

28. Ibid., 236–40; Rebello da Silva, *História de Portugal*, 1: 266–67.

29. Bovill, *Battle of Alcazar*, passim; Fernand Braudel, *The Mediterranean and the Mediterranean World in the Age of Philip II*, 2 vols., trans. Sian Reynolds (London, 1972), 2: 1178–79; Queiroz Velloso, *D. Sebastião*, chaps. 9–10; Brooks, *King*, 14–22; *HCJAP*, 2:2, 359–64. Six Jesuits became captives after the battle and one subsequently died in Ceuta; *HCJAP*, 2:2, 370. But one former prisoner, P. António de Azevedo, lived until 1632, when he died at 84. *OSR*, 16–17.

battle that "business here continues as though nothing untoward had taken place. The ships that arrived from India are being unloaded, the merchants ply their trade and go to sea; it is the nobility and the soldiers alone who have perished. No merchant has suffered thereby since they all stayed behind."[30]

Cardinal Henry did not share the merchants' equanimity. Aged and infirm, he was living in exile in Alcobaça when he received news of the disaster. He hastened to Lisbon, accompanied by Jorge Serrão, a veteran Jesuit administrator.[31] On 27 August the cardinal was acclaimed in the capital as Portugal's new king: "The heralds called out in loud tones throughout the city: 'Real! Real! Real!' These cries were heard almost all day." The Fugger agent concluded his remarks by praying, "May Almighty God give unto this King a long life and make his rule felicitous." But it was not to be.[32]

The 66-year-old monarch was suffering from gout and tuberculosis and understandably possessed diminished energies. Considering the precarious state of his health and the enormous pressures he experienced from rival factions within and without the country, Braudel's judgment that he was "an incompetent physician" to cure the nation's ills seems both excessively severe and unrealistic.[33] During his short reign, the new monarch confronted two major problems, one of which he could—and did—solve, the other of which he agonized about until his end (31 January 1580). The first concerned the redemption of thousands of Portuguese captives still in Muslim hands. Although it strained the kingdom's resources to assemble the necessary funds, the ransoming of the nobles was completed by October 1579 and was achieved through the intervention of several Jesuits and a score of Trinitarian friars.[34]

The other problem that the king faced was vastly more complicated and personally troubling to him, to his Jesuit collaborators, and to all other concerned Portuguese: who would succeed him? The earliest plan, one already bandied about when Henry was acclaimed monarch, was that he would obtain papal dispensation releasing him from his vows and enabling him to marry and father an heir. Whether or not his intended wife, the widow of France's Charles IX, was willing to save the dynasty by becoming its brood mare is uncertain; but the pope, under strong pressure from the adamantly opposed government of Spain, was unenthusiastic, and nothing ever came of the scheme.[35]

30. Girolamo Franchi di Conestaggio, *The History of the Uniting of the Kingdom of Portugall to ... Castille* [1585], Eng. trans. (London, 1600), often attributed to Juan de Silva, count of Portalegre, Spanish ambassador to Portugal during Sebastian's reign, and subsequently a member of Spain's Council of Portugal; but see Brooks, *King*, 144–45, and Diogo Barbosa Machado, *Bibliotheca Lusitana* [1741–59], 4 vols. (fasc. ed., Coimbra, 1965–67), 2: 750–52. For the Fugger agent's remarks, see Victor von Klarwill, ed., *The Fugger Newsletters* (New York, 1925), 27.

31. *ASCJ*, 437–38.

32. Klarwill, *Fugger Newsletters*, 28–29.

33. Braudel, *Mediterranean*, 2: 1179.

34. *HCJAP*, 2:2, 369–71; Queiroz Velloso, *D. Sebastião*, 412–20; idem, *O reinado do cardeal d. Henrique*, vol. 1, *A perda da independéncia* (no further volumes published) (Lisbon, 1946), chap. 1. In an article bearing the same subtitle, Queiroz Velloso states that the Trinitarians worked tirelessly to free the captives but that "alguns morreram cheios de trabalhos e desgostos; outros acabaram na prisão, por haverem fiado certos cativos, que depois indignamente se esqueceram dos seus fiadores." CMP/P, 6: 17. The Iberian crowns displayed far more interest in bringing back the nobles than their peasants. For a recent study of the Trinitarians, see Ellen G. Friedman, *Spanish Captives in North Africa* (Madison, Wis., 1983).

35. Queiroz Velloso, *D. Henrique*, chap. 3.

There was no lack of other would-be successors. The most active contenders were descendants of Manuel I, since John III had no remaining direct heirs. They included Catherine, duchess of Bragança, surviving daughter of Manuel's last son, D. Duarte; D. António, known as the prior of Crato, the illicit offspring of D. Luís, brother of John III; and Philip II of Spain, son of Manuel's eldest daughter, D. Izabel.[36]

Catherine was a member of the wealthiest, most prolific ducal family in the realm. The Braganças were direct descendants of an illegitimate son of the founder of the Aviz dynasty, John I, who created the dukedom in 1401 and assigned to it vast holdings of agricultural and mineral lands. Vila Viçosa, situated not far from the Spanish border town of Badajoz, was the center of the dukedom's far-flung financial and political interests, symbolized by a still-impressive ducal palace. The family fortunes suffered a serious setback in 1483, when the current duke had his throat slit because he was suspected of committing treason. The family fled to Castile, but it returned in 1496 during the regime of Manuel I and continued to augment its unrivaled real-estate holdings throughout the sixteenth century.[37] Catherine (b. 1540–d. 1614), whose eldest son, the count of Barcelos, was captured at Alcázarquibir, was eager to ascend the throne and to that end undertook a spirited diplomatic and legal campaign in support of her candidacy. But behind her back, her husband undermined her efforts by offending leading nobles and by negotiating with Philip II and the pope concerning the possible marriage of their daughter to Philip's son, or even to the recently widowed Spanish monarch himself. In the end, Catherine lacked both popular appeal and sufficient political clout to attain her goal.[38]

One who enjoyed both but suffered from other, more serious disabilities was the mercurial António, prior of Crato (b. 1531–d. 1595). Not only was he the bastard offspring of the king's brother, but his mother was a converted Jew. In accordance with his father's wishes, António entered the Portuguese religious Order of St. John and took minor orders, but he never advanced beyond the level of deacon. Lacking a commitment to the religious life, he became laicized about 1574. He was twice assigned to commands in North Africa before Sebastian induced him to participate in the ill-starred campaign of 1578, in which he became one of the many captives. Although an attractive figure in some circles, António was regarded in others as an opportunistic, spendthrift gadfly.[39]

Another opportunist, but one who possessed far more intelligence, cunning, pertinacity, and resources, was Philip II. Long the arbitrator of the family quarrels within the house of Aviz, Philip was anxious to realize the ambition of his ancestors by reuniting Portugal and Castile. He earned Portuguese gratitude by contributing generously to the ransom fund, but at the same time he menacingly arrayed his forces on the frontier. His agents aggressively blocked the diplomatic moves of his rivals, while D. Cristóvão de Moura (b. 1538–d. 1613), an ignoble Portuguese quisling in Philip's pay, constantly apprised his master of the changing moods of the Portuguese court and astutely corrupted threadbare Portuguese aristocrats,

36. A convenient genealogical table appears in Conde da Ericeira [Luís de Meneses], *História de Portugal restaurado* (1679), ed. António Alvaro Dória, 4 vols. (Oporto, 1945), 1: 465.

37. *DHP*, 1: 371–73.

38. Ibid., 1: 537; J. Gomes Branco, "A atitude dos duques de Bragança, D. João e D. Catarina na crise de 1580," CMP/*P*, 6: 77–102.

39. On the prior of Crato, see the cited works by Queiroz Velloso and *DHP*, 1: 157–59, where he is curiously declared to have been legitimate.

military captains, and prelates with lavish gifts of money, relics, and promises of forthcoming privileges and preferment.[40]

The convoluted maneuvering of the leading claimants placed the Jesuits in a difficult position. They fully recognized after Alcázarquibir that their own stock had tumbled seriously. Sebastiano Sabino, the Italian-born procurator of missions in Lisbon, wrote Gregory XIII that the Jesuits in Portugal were universally detested because of their close relationship with the late king. In 1579 a memorial couched in the name of the people of Lisbon informed the pope that the fathers were responsible for the nation's calamities because of their "unwise and sinister education" of the unfortunate monarch and contended that they had become so much the masters of the government that it was well known that "whoever seeks to expedite his petitions knows that he must frequent the *Limina Apostolorum*," that is, the Jesuit residences in the capital.[41] As would always be the case after Portuguese military reverses during the next two centuries, the Jesuits were the most convenient scapegoats available.

Sensitive to such criticism, Father General Mercurian wrote King Henry imploring him to dismiss Leão Henriques in order to spare the Society further harm. But the king refused to part with his confessor, who, along with Fr. Serrão, remained at his side throughout his brief reign.[42] The fact that the Jesuits stayed at court has allowed some writers to reach unwarranted conclusions concerning their role in the succession crisis. Many have followed Martin Philippson, who asserted that from the outset the Jesuits favored Philip II over other candidates because he offered them advantages that the others could not match.[43] That contention is defective in several respects. First, it implies that the Jesuits in Portugal were unpatriotic in failing to support a national candidate. (There is no evidence that they were.) Second, it ignores the fact that other religious, especially the Dominicans, played an even more active role in the crisis and ardently supported Philip's cause. Third, it fails to distinguish between the sympathies expressed by Jesuits in Spain and by those in Portugal. In 1580, as in 1640, the two national groups did not adopt a unified political stance; on the contrary, Jesuits in Portugal took their cue from their patron, King Henry, just as Spanish Jesuits lined up behind Philip II.

Initially the king's confessor supported Henry's plans to marry in order to produce an heir, but when that possibility became moot, the king and his Jesuit advisors considered other alternatives. António, prior of Crato, was dismissed as unacceptable. Both the king and the Jesuits strongly disapproved of his failure to become an ordained priest, his renunciation of his vows, and his persistent high living. Henry had serious quarrels with António and on several occasions compelled him to flee to Spain, the last time in 1579, when the king reversed the decision of an ecclesiastical tribunal that declared that the prior was, in fact,

40. One especially revealing biography of Philip's character is Geoffrey Parker, *Philip II* (Boston, 1978); on the crucial role of Moura, see *DHP*, 3: 114–15, and Queiroz Velloso, "A perda da independencia," *CMP/P*, 11–40, as well as his *D. Henrique*, passim. Moura first came to Spain in May 1554 as a member of the entourage of D. Juana, mother of Sebastian.

41. *HCJAP*, 2:2, 392.

42. Ibid., 404–5.

43. Martin Philippson, *Ein Ministerium unter Philip II: Kardinal Granvella am spanischen Hofe (1579–1586)* (Berlin, 1895), 92–95; cf. Roger Bigelow Merriman, *Philip the Prudent* (New York, 1934), 349 n. 3; Braudel, *Mediterranean*, 2: 1180; and Parker, *Philip II*, 143.

legitimate and therefore eligible to become Henry's successor. António then appealed over the king's head to Rome, a rash act that led to the confiscation of his properties and to his decision to go underground.

Relations between the Jesuits and António had begun cordially. In 1551 he became a student in their college in Évora and once vowed to found a Jesuit college with income derived from his priory, a promise never fulfilled. Precisely how the intense hostility between António and the fathers began is unclear, but it surfaced during a royal reception in 1576. As reported by a papal agent present, António encountered Fr. Maurício Serpe in the saloon and in front of many distinguished guests denounced the Jesuits as robbers and disturbers of the peace. The father indignantly declared that he was leaving the palace and would never return, prompting António to respond, "You do well to depart, and if you return I will personally throw you out the windows." That exchange created a breach that was never closed.[44]

For a time Henry and his Jesuit advisors favored the Bragança candidate, but by late 1579 the king appears to have reached the conclusion that his recognition of Catherine would simply provoke Philip II to impose his will on Portugal by conquest.[45] The kingdom had already witnessed enough calamities, for Alcázarquibir had been followed by a return of the plague for the second time in a decade and by a severe drought that compelled starving peasants to flee the wheat fields of the Alentejo and head for Castile.[46] As Henry began to waver in his opposition to Philip II, the Spanish sovereign increased the pressure on key Portuguese Jesuits. After receiving reports from Cristóvão de Moura in Portugal and from the Spanish ambassador in Rome that Leão Henriques and Jorge Serrão personally supported Catherine, the king instructed the Spanish ambassador to secure an order from General Mercurian directing the Portuguese Jesuits to maintain absolute neutrality in the succession crisis. With the aid of the Spanish assistant to the general, the ambassador was successful; Mercurian complied literally with Philip's demands.[47]

In fact, Philip did *not* want neutrality from the Portuguese Jesuits: he wanted their support. To that end he sent to Lisbon Luís de Guzmán, a Spanish Jesuit of aristocratic origins and an old friend of Leão Henriques. Ostensibly Guzmán was to serve as confessor to the Spanish ambassador, but his real mission was to persuade Henriques to advise the king to back Philip. Whether he conveyed such a message is uncertain, but it is clear that the Jesuit houses in Lisbon were embarrassed to provide Guzmán with hospitality at such a critical juncture and soon arranged for his return to Spain.[48] Hedging his bets, Philip II himself sent a personal letter to Fr. Henriques via Cristóvão de Moura, urging Henriques to use his influence to gain Henry's recognition of the Spanish king. Henriques respectfully but firmly declined the king's request.[49] But when Henry asked Fr. Serrão to undertake a delicate mission to Vila Viçosa late in 1579, the Jesuit official willingly complied. His mission (which failed) was to persuade the Braganças to accept Philip as Henry's successor

44. *HCJAP*, 2:2, 409–14.
45. Ibid., 400–401.
46. Conestaggio, *History*, 108; Rebello da Silva, *História de Portugal*, 1: 432–33.
47. Queiroz Velloso, *D. Henrique*, 120; *HCJAP*, 2:2, 408–9.
48. Queiroz Velloso, *D. Henrique*, 318–19; *HCJAP*, 2:2, 407.
49. *HCJAP*, 2:2, 406.

in return for their appointment as Portugal's perpetual viceroys.[50] In January 1580 the cortes convened in Almeirim to decide the succession question, but it proved unequal to the task. Although the clergy and half of the nobility favored the Spanish king, the remainder of the nobility and the popular representatives were opposed.[51] The failure of the cortes to relieve King Henry of his heavy burden may have contributed to his worsening condition. At any rate, on 31 January 1580, the king died while being assisted by Fathers Henriques and Serrão, who were joined by two Dominicans and a Franciscan.[52]

Henry's death left the succession problem unresolved. The five-man council of regency, headed by the archbishop of Lisbon, could think of no better plan than to try to persuade Philip to leave the ultimate decision to the pope; but the Spanish monarch would have none of that, and his concept of his rights to the Portuguese throne was sustained by the articulated views of certain Spanish Jesuits.[53] Exasperated by the refusal of the Portuguese to recognize his claim, Philip issued an ultimatum (16 April 1580) offering the Portuguese certain guarantes if they recognized him within twenty days, threatening vengeance if they did not. Nothing of consequence happened until 19 June, when António was proclaimed king in Santarém; four days later the triumphant pretender entered Lisbon.

Within a week Philip unleashed land and sea forces against Portugal. While the marquis of Santa Cruz maintained a partial blockade along the coast, the venerable duke of Alba emerged from disgrace to lead an army of around 40,000 men across the frontier at Badajoz. Alba met with only token resistance until he reached the fishing port of Cascais, west of Lisbon, which the Spaniards took and sacked (30 July). The decisive battle then occurred at the Alcántara ravine, along the approaches to the modern trans-Tagus bridge, on 24 August. Of the 10,000 Portuguese defenders, many of them irregulars led by António, one-fifth fell in the hand-to-hand fighting. The Fugger agent reported that "the dead lay heap on heap like swine.... All the streets are filled with dead men and horses, so that we had to walk across them as on a bridge.... Altogether it was a pitiable sight."[54] Alba's triumphant but undisciplined forces then plundered everything in sight, including the professed house of São Roque, where even the refectory forks were stolen.[55]

During these unsettling months and the subsequent pacification, the Portuguese Jesuits played a largely passive role, apart from patriotic sermons encouraging the defense of the

50. Ibid., 415.

51. Ibid., 401–2.

52. Queiroz Velloso, *D. Henrique*, 397.

53. *HCJAP*, 2:2, 422–23.

54. Klarwill, *Fugger Newsletters*, 49.

55. The most recent examination of Alba's final campaign is William S. Maltby, *Alba: A Biography of Fernando Alvarez de Toledo, Third Duke of Alba, 1507–1582* (Berkeley, 1983), chap. 14. See also Peter Pierson, *Commander of the Armada: The Seventh Duke of Medina Sidonia* (New Haven, 1989), 30–36. On António's retreat and the price Philip placed on his head, see Monsenhor J. Augusto Ferreira, "O Prior do Crato em o norte do pais ... e a sua fuga para França," CMP/*P*, 6: 103–16.

The Spanish occupation was facilitated by the plague that began in Évora in May 1580, spread throughout the kingdom, and by late July had claimed 1,000 lives. Jesuits and their students were among its victims, as they were during other outbreaks of plague in 1569 and 1599–1601. António Franco, *Imagem da virtude em o noviciado da companhia de Jesus no real collegio do Espírito Santo de Évora* (Lisbon, 1714), 327–47 and 375; idem, *Coimbra*, 1: 229, 234–42; 2: 570; OSR, 8, 26, 47–49, 82ff.

fatherland.[56] They comforted the survivors of Alcántara and provided temporary asylum for 500 persons in the college of Santo Antão. As Spanish forces chased the wounded and retreating António northward, the Jesuit rector at Coimbra sent two of his men to dissuade the Spaniards from ravaging the city. By the end of September, António made a final stand in Porto. After receiving reports that the Jesuits were keeping a Spanish spy in the college of São Lourenço, António drove the fathers from the city. Later, Spanish troops looted the college as they occupied the city. Although virtually the entire empire meekly accepted the new regime, the Azorean island of Terceira remained loyal to António, who arrived there with French assistance in 1582. Since the college of Angra did not share the islanders' enthusiasm for the pretender, António expelled its ten occupants, seized their properties, and walled up the college's doors and windows. When the Santa Cruz armada seized the island for Spain in 1583, it was accompanied by four Jesuits, who reclaimed their property.[57]

The Philippine Interlude, 1580–1640

For sixty years Portugal suffered the indignity of being ruled from Madrid. How much it suffered is a matter of dispute. Certainly some socioeconomic groups benefited immeasurably from the new regime by gaining lucrative positions, contracts, and privileges. They included members of the higher clergy, the landed aristocracy, the large wholesale merchants, tax farmers, importers of Castilian wheat, and exporters of slaves to the Spanish empire.[58] But the Portuguese Jesuits were not among the chief beneficiaries of Spanish rule. For the first time since the Society's founding they were excluded from the highest levels of political authority. Because the three Philips[59] were served by Dominican rather than Jesuit confessors, Portuguese Jesuits did not have access to the same quality of confidential information at court obtained by their predecessors, nor were they in positions to influence royal policies.[60] The Philippine sovereigns seldom visited the western kingdom; they administered it through

56. To be sure, a few Jesuits participated in the coeval military and naval campaigns of Philip II. Prior to the invasion of Portugal, the Spanish king requested that the province of Andalucia furnish seven of its members to accompany the royal armada that later entered the Tagus, but Aquaviva ruled that his men would only accompany armadas directed against infidels and heretics, not fellow Catholics. Nevertheless, when Santa Cruz sailed to the Azores in 1583, he was accompanied by one Spanish and three Portuguese Jesuits. Fifteen of the Jesuits who served in the armada of 1588 against England perished. Most of them were Spaniards or Portuguese. Francisco de Borja de Medina, "Jesuitas en la armada contra Inglaterra (1588)," *AHSI* 58 (1989): 3–42.

57. On the Jesuits' involvement in the Spanish occupation of Terceira, see *HCJAP*, 2:2, 421–35.

58. Vitorino Magalhães Godinho, "1580 e a restauração," reprinted in his *Ensaios*, 2 (Lisbon, 1968), 257–91; see also James C. Boyajian, *Portuguese Bankers at the Court of Spain, 1626–1650* (New Brunswick, N.J., 1983).

59. Philips II (1556–98), III (1598–1621), and IV (1621–56), respectively Philips I, II, and III of Portugal.

60. Spanish Jesuits continued to be privy to the highest levels of governmental information and rumor owing to their special relationship with Gaspar de Guzmán, count of Olivares and duke of San Lucar, who was the dominant minister of Spain from 1621 to 1643. See the invaluable series of Jesuit correspondence in *MHE*, vols. 13–19. From at least 1608, if not earlier, the province of Portugal maintained a special procurator in Madrid. The extent of the procurators' access to court gossip remains to be determined, but was evidently substantial, as is suggested by Fr. G. Simões to [?] (in India), Coimbra, 10 Mar. 1622, and Fr. Pedro d'Azevedo to Sebastião Gomes (superior, Cape Verde), Lisbon, 8 Mar. 1629, in ANTT/CJ/68, nos. 392 and 323. For references to four men who held the office, see Franco, *Coimbra*, 2: 618, 625, and 866, and idem, *Évora*, 853.

a series of single or multiple regencies and advisory councils, such as the Council of Portugal, which always remained with the king. More than half of the sixteen regencies were headed by Portuguese prelates, but no Jesuit was ever included; nor did any serve in the king's advisory bodies.[61]

When Philip II entered Lisbon in June 1581, the first religious house he visited was that of São Roque, presumably undergoing repairs after its violation by his soldiers. Upon his return to Castile in February 1583, he also inspected the Jesuit University of Évora.[62] Such perfunctory visits, however, did not symbolize a softening of Philip's attitude toward the Jesuits, which was consistently one of hostility toward their activities in Europe but supportive of their efforts overseas. If the king's suspicions of the Society were cultivated by Melchior Cano and other Dominican critics,[63] they were intensified by reports of Jesuit support of the Bragança candidacy both before and after Portugal's conquest. In 1581 the king ordered the exile of certain Portuguese Jesuits who questioned the validity of his claim to the throne. Two years later a concerned Father General Aquaviva directed Jesuits in Portugal to refrain from involving themselves in any political controversies. Evidence of ill feelings between Spanish and Portuguese Jesuits in the kingdom is suggested by the complaint of the former in 1584 that their colleagues were deliberately seeking to remove them from the province because of their national origins. Five years later Aquaviva directed a provincial inspector "for the good of Religion and the peace of the kingdom" to punish any Jesuits in Portugal who affected nationalistic sentiments, an order he found it necessary to repeat the following year. When rumors circulated in Portugal in 1595 that Philip II was terminally ill or possibly even dead, three Jesuits, one a former page of the duke of Bragança, were severely punished for contacting the duke and suggesting that he assume the crown.[64]

The Jesuits were certainly not alone in their desire to be rid of their Spanish overlords. The 1580s and 1590s saw the beginnings of a mystical movement in the kingdom known as Sebastianism. Although the mutilated body of the late king had been returned to Lisbon in 1582 and was interred in the venerable Jerónimite monastery in Belém, many persons refused to believe that the corpse was really that of the king and were convinced that he was either still in captivity or living in hiding and would return to liberate his kingdom at a propitious moment. Exploiting such sentiments, four impostors emerged to claim to be Sebastian, two in Portugal (1584–85), one in Spain (1594), and the last in Venice (1598). Each was exposed, and three were promptly executed.[65] Although there is no evidence that the Loyolans endorsed any of these crypto figures, some Jesuits, including Brazil's José de Anchieta, appear to have subscribed to the myth of Sebastian's survival and redemptive capacities.[66]

61. On the Council of Portugal, see Count-Duke of Olivares, "Grand Memorial," 25 Dec. 1624, in John H. Elliott and José F. de la Peña, eds., *Memoriales y cartas del conde duque de Olivares*, 2 vols. (Madrid, 1978), 1: 83. For the members of the regencies, see João Pedro Ribeiro, *Dissertações chronologicas e criticas sobre a historia e jurisprudencia ecclesiastica e civil de Portugal*, 5 vols. (Lisbon, 1860–96), 2: 195–99.

62. *HCJAP*, 2:2, 443–44.

63. Merriman, *Philip the Prudent*, 63–64, notes the unsuccessful effort of Philip to persuade Pope Sixtus V to revise the Order's *Constitutions*.

64. *HCJAP*, 2:2, 440–41; Francisco Rodrigues, S.J., "A Companhia de Jesus e a restauração de Portugal, 1640," Academia portuguesa da história, *Anais* 6 (1942): 329–31.

65. Brooks, *King*, 22ff.; J[oão] Lúcio de Azevedo, *A evolução do Sebastianismo*, 2d ed. (Lisbon, 1947).

66. Rodrigues, "Restauração," 332, where the indefatigable Jesuit historian admits that the evidence of the Jesuits' role in the dissemination of Sebastianism is murky. See also *HCJAP*, 3:1, 328–31, for other

Though most Jesuits may have remained skeptical of the likely survival of Sebastian the redeemer, others actively promoted the candidacy of a real alternative to the Philips, namely the Braganças. As Oliveira Marques has written, "By the 1620's and 1630's, most people started merging the hidden Sebastian with ... the Duke of Bragança, his lawful heir.... Sebastianism evolved into strict patriotism, and Sebastianists identified themselves with the opponents of the Iberian Union."[67] One such patriot was Fr. Bartolomeu Guerreiro (b. 1564–d. 1642), a well-known educator and chronicler. In November 1631 he responded to an invitation from the young duke to deliver a funeral oration in Vila Viçosa to honor the memory of his late father, D. Teodósio. In a text that was published and widely disseminated, despite the annoyance of Philip IV, Guerreiro emphasized D. Teodósio's saintly, Catholic, regal qualities, implying that his son possessed the same virtues.[68] Fr. Guerreiro followed another Jesuit supporter of the Braganças, Francisco de Mendóça (b. 1573–d. 1626), son of the chief armorer of Sebastian and an established poet, orator, and theologian. He dedicated the first part of his three-volume, oft-republished *Commentaries on the Books of the Kings* (1621–31) to Duke Teodósio in terms whose meaning was transparent: "To whom, may one ask, can a History of Kings be more appropriately dedicated than to you, scion of royal blood? For wherever one turns his eyes, kings present themselves to you, to whom they are so intimately related by ties of blood." Each of the succeeding volumes contained a similar message.[69] Four years after the publication of Fr. Guerreiro's sermon, the Jesuits provided a carefully staged regal reception for the duke at the University of Évora.[70]

Little wonder that relations between the Philippine sovereigns and the Portuguese Jesuits remained tepid and that royal support for Jesuit enterprises at home was wanting. But matters might have been worse. According to one informed contemporary, at the time of the Spanish takeover, "many were of the opinion that the King should suppresse the Universitie of Coimbra ... that the Portugals should go studie at the universities of Castill, where passing the heate of their youth, and growing familiar with the Castilians, they shoulde returne into Portugal more roially affected."[71]

The university was not suppressed, but the Philips did little to support education in Portugal. In France, the number of Jesuit facilities created during this period multiplied spectacularly; but only two institutions were established in Portugal during the first four decades of the seventeenth century, and neither was the result of direct royal initiative or support.[72] The first was the professed house in Vila Viçosa (1601), made possible by a restricted grant from the Braganças.[73] The second was the college of Santarém. Its

examples of Jesuit visions, and J[oão] Lúcio de Azevedo, *História de António Vieira*, 2d ed., 2 vols. (Lisbon, 1931), 1: 40–42.

67. OM/*HP*, 1: 319.

68. Rodrigues, "Restauração," 332–33, which includes the title page of Guerreiro's sermon, misdated 29 Nov. 1632. For his biography, see *PDH*, 3: 867.

69. Rodrigues, "Restauração," 333. Mendóça was the son of D. Alvaro da Costa, who opposed his son's entry into the Society at age 14, prompting the determined young man to change his name in order to join the Society. *PDH*, 4: 1026–27.

70. Rodrigues, "Restauração," 334–35.

71. Conestaggio, *History*, 250.

72. 26.5% of all Jesuit facilities in France were erected between 1550 and 1592, and another 58.3% between 1603 and 1649. *EJF*, passim.

73. For the terms of the Bragança seed grant, see *CCLP*, 1: 68–69.

creation was first proposed by a Jesuit father in 1575, when he donated certain houses to the Society for that purpose. Although his plan was supported by the archbishop of Lisbon, it was opposed by some townsmen, convinced by a hostile voice that the arrival of the Jesuits would be followed by the desiccation of their fields. Early the following century, another Jesuit contributed even larger resources to sustain a college, but by then the Jesuits were engaged in a quarrel with the archbishop of Lisbon over the payment of tithes (see Chapter 18). Accordingly, the archbishop strongly opposed the founding of the college on the ground that it was unnecessary. The Jesuits then appealed to the pope and to Philip III for protection and received it. The college opened in 1621 in the face of a warning from the archbishop's representative in Santarém, who threatened to excommunicate any who sent their sons to the new school.[74]

The existence of such hostility as well as royal indifference seemingly explains the Society's slow growth in the kingdom during the Philippine period. Though the membership increased by 22 percent between 1579 and 1599, it grew by only 8 percent during the next four decades.[75] In 1619 Vitelleschi ordered that the novitiates in Coimbra and Évora be closed, leaving only the Lisbon facility to admit recruits.[76] That directive may have been partly motivated by a disappointing number of recruits, but it may also have reflected two other factors: the virtual exclusion of Spaniards from the Portuguese province,[77] and the uncertain financial situation of that province because of two serious legal challenges concerning its right to hold landed property in the kingdom (see Chapter 17). The second round of disputes occurred in the early 1620s, when it was becoming increasingly evident that, notwithstanding the pledges that Philip II made at the cortes of Tomár (1581) to defend the Portuguese empire, his successors were incapable of doing so.

Apart from the foolish Moroccan campaign, Portugal was at peace when the empire was annexed by Spain. But Spain's adversaries immediately became Portugal's as well. The late 1580s and 1590s witnessed a series of English and French attacks upon Portugal and its Atlantic empire and the first Anglo-Dutch intrusions in the eastern empire. The French attempt to occupy northern Brazil (1612–15) failed for lack of crown support, but the 1620s saw a series of severe blows to the economy of the Portuguese empire, including the fall of Ormuz (1622) to Anglo-Persian forces, the beginning of the increasingly severe Dutch blockade of Goa (1623ff.), and the shocking Dutch capture of Salvador, capital of Brazil (1624). Even more serious losses occurred during the 1630s, when the Hollanders appropriated most of northeastern Brazil and some of Portugal's African slaving enclaves. The effects of these successes and of anti-Portuguese indigenous movements in Africa and South and East Asia upon the fortunes of the Jesuits will be considered in Chapters 7–9.

74. HCJAP, 2:1, 29–30; 3:1, 5–16. Several Jesuit petitions, including one by the Madrid procurator, in behalf of the Santarém college are in ANTT/CJ/68, nos. 456–60.

75. There were 484 members in the province in 1579, 591 in 1599, and 639 in 1639. ARSI, Lus., 44:I and 44:II, passim.

76. "Rezoens p.a nosso . . . geral ver sobre os noviciados da provincia de Portugal" [ca. 1647], ARSI, Lus., 82, fols. 187–90. The author, a former master of novices, argued that the closures had been economically unwise.

77. In 1639, for example, there was only one Spaniard among the province's 639 subjects. ARSI, Lus., 44:II, 570–93. The exclusion of Spaniards appears to have been a deliberate policy by the Roman headquarters, which may well have responded to Portuguese members' continued coolness toward their Iberian brethren.

Though it is true that Spain bestirred itself and, with Portuguese assistance, recovered Salvador (1625), other blows against Portugal's overseas interests were not similarly offset.

By the mid-1630s, the Portuguese were becoming more restive under the rule of an alien regime seemingly indifferent to Portuguese imperial commercial interests but increasingly determined to make Portugal more subservient and more lucrative to Spain. On 23 December 1634, the lady destined to be Portugal's last Spanish viceroy arrived in Lisbon. She was Princess Margaret of Savoy, widow of the late duke of Mantua and granddaughter of Philip II. She had not been the first choice of Spain's strongman, the count-duke of Olivares, for that assignment, but she was apparently the only noble distantly related to the former royal family of Portugal who was willing to serve.[78] Her appointment was part of Olivares's extensive reorganization of the government of Portugal. His aim was to strengthen the crown's control over the western kingdom and to increase royal income, as required by the onset of the very costly war with France (1635–59). Perhaps acting on Olivares's instructions, Margaret deliberately offended the sensibilities of the Portuguese aristocracy, many of whom silently withdrew from court, while surrounding herself with Spanish advisors.[79] But the dominant figure of her regime was Miguel de Vasconcelos, a zealous Portuguese quisling who was both brother-in-law and father-in-law of Diogo Soares, secretary of the Madrid-based Council of Portugal. Vasconcelos was Margaret's secretary of state and became responsible for creating new sources of royal income by measures comparable to those being undertaken in Spain.[80]

Early in 1635 Vasconcelos announced the raising of both excises and a consumptive impost known as the *real d'água* to be collected on every pound of meat and *canada* (2.26 liters) of wine. The real d'água originated in the late Middle Ages, when it was a source of revenue reserved to the municipalities, who were authorized to impose it during emergencies such as pestilence and famine.[81] Its imposition at this time was doubly troubling to the Portuguese, who had witnessed, since the late 1620s, rapid advances in the prices of meat, olive oil, rice, and wheat, and who resented the crown's takeover of a traditional municipal impost on the pretext that the revenues were needed for the defense of Brazil, though many suspected that the additional income would be used for purely Spanish projects.[82]

78. Ericeira, *Portugal restaurado*, 1: 79. Ericeira states that Olivares intended to name D. Francisco de Borja, prince of Esquilache, to the post since he was of Portuguese descent but was dissuaded by the prince's brother, the duke of Vila Formosa.

79. Sebastian Gonzales, S.J., to Rafael Pereyra, S.J., Madrid, 1 Apr. 1635, in *MHE*, 13: 155–56.

80. Vasconcelos was the son of Pedro Barbosa, a High Court magistrate and strong supporter of the Philippine regime until his assassination. The son became one of the most detested men in Portugal and was one of the first victims of the December 1640 revolution. One of his brothers was dean of the archbishopric of Braga, another was bishop of Leiria. *PDH*, 7: 330–32; CMP/*P*, 7: 132.

Parochial Portuguese historians who insist that Castile was attempting to suck Portugal dry ignore the fact that during precisely these years even heavier taxes were being assessed in Spain. Francisco Vilches, S.J., to P. Rafael Pereyra, S.J., 8 Aug. 1634; Bernardino de Alcocer to Pereyra, 3 May 1635; and Sebastian Gonzales to Pereyra, 8 May and 18 June 1635, in *MHE*, 13: 84–85, 183, 185, and 190–92, in the last of which the author notes that the king had raised 9 million ducats during the past three years.

81. *DHP*, 3: 540.

82. For increased prices, see Godinho, "1580 e a restauração," 275, and *DHP*, 4: 501–2, 505, and 507. Ericeira charges that Olivares wished to sweat the poor Portuguese to pay for the construction of the Buen Retiro palace, which Philip IV began constructing in 1631; *Portugal restaurado*, 1: 80. Although the Portuguese community in Madrid, especially the friends of secretary Diogo Soares, did contribute to its cost, Ericeira

Efforts to collect the taxes prompted a series of protest movements (autumn 1635–summer 1636) in various parts of the kingdom, especially in the far northern province of Tras-os-Montes. Those movements, which temporarily compelled royal magistrates (*corregidores*) to suspend collection of the imposts, revealed unexpectedly strong opposition to the Spanish regime. Although quashed, these movements were followed by a strike among Lisbon-based fishermen (July–August 1637) protesting a new license requirement. The strike caused a shortage of fish in the capital and led to violence when a fishing vessel from Setúbal attempted to land its catch in Lisbon. Anticipating the much later and more famous tea party in Boston, a mob hurled the fish into the Tagus and pelted the royal palace with stones.[83]

Although the Jesuits do not seem to have been involved in these preliminary challenges to Spanish authority, they did become entangled in the far more serious "disturbances" (*alterações*) that took place in Évora, the walled capital of the Alentejo, between August and October 1637. Riots began when the zealous corregidor attempted to collect the city's share of 200 contos that the crown said were necessary for the relief of Brazil. The municipal council (cámara) opposed his plan to increase taxes on salt, meat, wine, and other products. In order to exert pressure on two popular artisan representatives of that body, he invited them to his residence, where his threats caused the tribunes to appeal for assistance from a crowd assembled below. The crowd then swarmed through the residence, removing papers and furniture and subsequently burning them in the square below, while the terrified magistrate fled via the roof to the safety of a Franciscan church. Next the mob assaulted the royal tax offices and those of the public notaries and the courts, and then it proceeded to the public slaughterhouse to destroy the scales and to the jail to liberate prisoners. While the rioters controlled the city, the local nobility joined with ecclesiastical leaders, first in a church and later in the Jesuit university, and sought to defuse the dangerous situation. Such efforts were unavailing, as were those of a series of emissaries belatedly dispatched by Margaret and Olivares. Meanwhile the city was bombarded with daily proclamations issued in the name of a local buffoon called "Manuelinho" denouncing tyrannical government and those, like the bishop of Porto, who cooperated with it, decreeing the exile of the undesirable and the dismissal of unpopular officials, and calling the people to arms. The example of Évora inspired sympathetic revolts in many communities throughout the Alentejo and spread to the far south (the Algarve), to parts of Extremadura (as far north as Santarém and Abrantes), and even to the maritime north, notably Viana do Castelo and Porto.

These tumults infuriated the viceroy, who bitterly denounced the Church for permitting them to occur; otherwise she did little that was effective.[84] Only Madrid could supply the remedies, but the Spanish court, which at first downplayed the importance of the riots, was not disposed to provide ameliorative measures. In the end, responsible aristocrats, such as the duke of Bragança and the count de Bastos, and priests, including Jesuits, restored

---

seems in error. See Jonathan Brown and J[ohn] H. Elliott, *A Palace for a King: The Buen Retiro and the Court of Philip IV* (New Haven, 1980), 96–104.

83. VS/*HP*, 4: 124–30, a good summary of events from 1634 to 1636.

84. *Carta régia*, 2 Dec. 1637, in José de Seabra da Sylva, *Deducção chronologica e analytica*, 4 vols. (Lisbon, 1768), 1: 192, in which the duchess wrote, "As alterações que há havido em alguns lugares deste reino . . . tenho notícias que o principal fundamento de tudo são os religiosos e eclesiásticos, sendo, como são, interessados em que os povos não consintam no real da água." The text also appears in ANTT/AJ, cx. 29.

calm in some communities, while two Spanish armies, one led by the duke of Medina Sidonia, kinsman of Olivares and captain-general of Andalucia, pacified the Algarve and the Alentejo, punishing ringleaders by execution or by burning them in effigy.[85]

Precisely what role the Jesuits played in these disturbances has never been clear. The well-informed, multitalented Francisco Manuel de Melo (b. 1608–d. 1666) believed that the Évora faculty, particularly Sebastião de Couto (b. 1570–d. 1639), provided essential intellectual leadership for the uprising in that city. A modern historian concurs.[86] The ever-cautious Fr. Francisco Rodrigues, whose volumes are frequently cited in this study, found no firm evidence of Jesuit involvement, but he strongly suspected its presence.[87] So did the count-duke of Olivares, who demanded that the provincial of Portugal take action against any Jesuit who expressed support for the rioters. The provincial responded by threatening anyone who spoke favorably concerning the popular movements with excommunication and confinement. Two who defied his order paid the price. One was a professor of moral theology at Évora, who preached a sermon interpreted as favorable to the followers of Manuelinho and was promptly incarcerated. The other was Fr. Francisco de Macedo, who delivered sermons in Lisbon concerning unspecified but obvious public figures: a tyrannical king (Philip IV), a despotic minister (*valido*) (Miguel de Vasconcelos), and a simonical bishop (D. Gaspar do Rego da Fonseca, bishop of Porto). As a consequence, he remained in a dark cell in São Roque until he escaped to France and later to England.[88] In November 1637, the provincial received another directive from Madrid: he was to send four Jesuits to court for consultations concerning the recent riots. The fathers had little doubt that more than consultations lay in store for the four. Two of them, Frs. Couto and Alvaro Pires Pacheco, declined to go on grounds of ill health. A third, Fr. Diogo de Areda, implicated in the Castracani affair discussed below, went into hiding for the next two years. Only Fr. Gaspar Correia actually reached Madrid, where he was detained for a year before being returned with orders that he was to be confined in a remote northern monastery, an exile from which he would be released only after the December 1640 revolution.[89]

85. Two near-contemporary sources on the Évora rising are Ericeira, *Portugal restaurado*, 1: 81–96, and Francisco Manoel de Melo, "Alteraçoens de Évora" [1660], reprinted in Joel Serrão, ed., *Epanáforas de varia história portuguesa* (Lisbon, 1977), 34ff. See also *MHE*, 14 (1862): 189–92. Secondary accounts include Rebello da Silva, *História de Portugal*, 3: 433–53; VS/*HP*, 4: 130–36; *DHP*, 2: 146–48; A. Viñas Navarro, "El motim de Évora y su significación en la restauración portuguesa de 1640," *Boletin de la biblioteca Menéndez y Pelayo* 6 (Santander, 1924): 321–39, and 7 (1925): 29–49; and J. H. Elliott, *The Count-Duke of Olivares: The Statesman in an Age of Decline* (New Haven, 1986), 526–31 and 564, which demonstrates how Olivares misunderstood the depths of Lusitanian anti-Spanish sentiment. See also R. A. Stradling, *Philip IV and the Government of Spain, 1621–1665* (Cambridge, 1988), 162–63, 181–84.

86. José Felipe Mendeiros, "O oliventino Sebastiáo do Couto, mestre insigne da universidade de Évora e alma das alteraçóes de 1637," Academia portuguesa da história, *Anais*, 2d ser., 18 (1969): 17–32. Curiously, António Franco is silent on Couto's activities before or during the riots. *ASCJ*, 695–96.

87. Rodrigues, "Restauração," 337.

88. Francisco de Macedo had four brothers. The eldest became a Benedictine and the other three entered the Society, but only one remained a member for the balance of his life. Francisco later changed his name, joined the Franciscans, and became a philosopher in England. The most complete study of his career remains P. Iidio de Sousa Ribeiro, *Fr. Francisco de Santo Agostinho de Macedo: Um filósofo escotista portugués e um paladino da restauração* (Coimbra, 1951).

89. Ibid., 336–38; *HCJAP*, 3:1, 337–45.

If the crown's responses to these signs of popular unrest detracted from its efforts to promote loyalty and compliance among the Portuguese, its quarrel with an emissary of the pope (1637–39) diminished its appeal in the captive kingdom even more. That dispute, one of a series between papal agents and crown officers in Portugal since 1616, pitted a zealous career judicial official, Tomé Pinheiro da Veiga, a New Christian, against an equally intransigent apostolic collector, Alexandre de Castracani, who was charged with organizing remittances to Rome.[90] At issue was the crown's secularization of ecclesiastical chantries (*capelas*) left by decedents to assure masses for their souls. Although the crown attorney (*procurador da coroa*) and the collector played the leads in the drama that followed, each had an impressive supporting cast. That of Pinheiro da Veiga included the king, his viceroy in Portugal, and secretaries Diogo Soares and Miguel de Vasconcelos, while that of Castracani was led by two Jesuit jurists, the aforementioned Frs. Diogo de Areda and Nuno da Cunha.

The prelude to Act I of this not uncommon tragicomedy occurred in September 1635, when the rector of Santo Antão complained to the father general that the government was beginning to seize chantries belonging to the Society and to other Church entities. The fact that the crown was then making even heavier fiscal demands upon the Church in Spain did not lessen his indignation.[91] In Act I, the newly arrived Castracani learned of the seizures and responded by ordering edicts published in every church in the capital on Palm Sunday 1636, threatening all who participated in such usurpations with excommunication. While the king's representatives fulminated against the collector's defiance of the royal will, Castracani's legal defense was prepared by Frs. Areda and da Cunha. The act closed with Philip IV firmly supporting his crown attorney and ordering him to determine which ecclesiastics were behind the collector's outrageous threat.

Act II began with the case being considered by the supreme court of appeals (*casa da suplicação*) of Lisbon. That tribunal naturally found in favor of the crown and directed Castracani to remove his offensive edicts. He complied, but at the same time issued another insisting that he did not intend to challenge the crown's authority but merely to admonish the faithful of the consequences of wrongly taking the Church's property. That declaration hardly pleased the king's representatives, but they were even more indignant when Pope Urban VIII issued a bull (5 July 1638) fully supporting the position taken by his collector. The act closed with another Jesuit, Fr. Luís Brandão, being sent by the viceroy to persuade the collector to modify his position further. Brandão failed.

Act III commenced with a bombshell: on 25 June 1639 Castracani issued a solemn warning to all who menaced capela lands and imposed an interdict on all church services in the capital, the third time since 1616 that an apostolic collector had resorted to that dire threat. Princess Margaret immediately ordered the collector to leave the country, but he refused to budge from his residence. As a consequence, a magistrate accompanied by

90. For Pinheiro da Veiga's distinguished career, see *PDH*, 7: 362. I have not found a biographical sketch of Castracani. For a succinct account of the evolution of the office of papal collector, see G. Mollat, *The Popes at Avignon, 1305–1378*, trans. Janet Love (London, 1949), 326–29.

91. In 1634 Philip IV required the Church to contribute 600,000 ducats within a week's time. In subsequent years he demanded a tenth, and later a third, of its current income. *MHE*, 13: 59 and 186; 14: 284.

suitable reinforcements occupied the dwelling, confining Castracani to his room. After a week of cold dinners, the embattled collector left his quarters via a window and fled to a nearby Franciscan monastery. But he was soon hotly pursued by the king's men, who arrested him and dispatched him to a farm across the Tagus. A few days later, on 6 September 1639, Castracani was escorted by 50 guardsmen to the Castilian border town of Badajoz. As the final curtain fell, the papal agent parted company with his captors by excommunicating each of them.[92]

What effect, if any, the interdict had upon the persistence of unrest in various parts of Portugal in 1639 and 1640 is difficult to measure.[93] Still absent from participation in such public disorders were members of the aristocracy, whose leadership was vital if Portugal were to rid itself of alien rule. Olivares realized as much, and in mid-1638 he summoned to Madrid Portugal's three archbishops, the bishop of Porto, several senior magistrates, and a number of high nobles.[94] Ostensibly they were called for consultations concerning the situation in Portugal, but the cagy Spanish minister also knew that as long as they were out of the country the prospect of revolution was diminished. Missing from this group was the duke of Bragança, and it was rumored that he was to become the next viceroy of Portugal. Instead, he was designated as its supreme land and sea commander, an honor that justified his triumphal entry into Lisbon (June 1639), where the warmth of the reception arranged by ecclesiastics and others so impressed Princess Margaret that she sourly remarked that she did not welcome the prospect of Portugal having two kings.[95]

The series of catastrophes that Spain had sustained since 1638 not only further lessened Margaret's creditability but also persuaded the Portuguese aristocracy that the opportune moment for political action had arrived. The fall of the Alsatian city of Breisach, the essential Rhine bridge link between Spain's possessions in northern Italy and Flanders whose loss (December 1638) imperiled the famous Spanish road, had been the first of the disasters.[96] The alternative was to reopen a secure sea route between the northwestern port of La Coruña and the Low Countries, but the effort to do so (October 1639) cost Spain 43 out of 70 ships, including a large Portuguese galleon, sunk with 900 men.[97] The battle of the Downs, the worst naval disaster Spain had sustained in two generations, was followed by still another maritime calamity when the long-promised Luso-Spanish force intended for the relief of northeastern Brazil was defeated by the Dutch (January 1640), again with heavy losses.[98] Six months later, on Corpus Christi Day (7 June), the Catalans rebelled. To suppress revolution in that other peripheral kingdom, Olivares diverted 6,000 Portuguese

92. The fullest account of the Castracani affair is *HCJAP*, 3:1, 270–79, but see also *HIP*, 2: 320–21, and 585–86.

93. VS/*HP*, 4: 136. Other factors were probably also involved in motivating that unrest, including the continual financial exactions of Spain and the recruitment of troops to fight outside the realm.

94. Rebello da Silva, *História de Portugal*, 3: 468–70.

95. *HCJAP*, 3:1, 347–48.

96. John H. Elliott, *The Revolt of the Catalans: A Study in the Decline of Spain (1598–1640)* (Cambridge, 1963), 357; Geoffrey Parker, *The Army of Flanders and the Spanish Road, 1567–1659* (Cambridge, 1975), 55–56.

97. On the battle of the Downs, see *Diccionario de historia de España*, 2 vols. (Madrid, 1952), 1: 921–22. The loss of the Portuguese *Santa Teresa* is described in Rebello da Silva, *História de Portugal*, 3: 478.

98. The battle of Itamaracá is examined by Charles R. Boxer in *The Dutch in Brazil, 1624–1654* (Oxford, 1957), 89–94.

troops, raised at Portuguese expense and intended for campaigns in Italy, to Catalonia, and (to kill two birds with one stone) he ordered the *fidalguia* of Portugal, including the duke of Bragança, to campaign there too. They refused. Instead, some 40 of them staged a palace coup (1 December) that ended Spanish rule in Portugal and elevated the eighth duke of Bragança to the throne.[99]

Among the approving bystanders during the dramatic December days were Portuguese Jesuits, who realized better than most that it was one thing to proclaim independence, another to guarantee it. In truth, Portugal's times of trouble were far from over, and although the changing of the guard brought the Jesuits back to the royal palace, they would find themselves severely challenged for cultural hegemony in the kingdom in the years ahead by a powerful rival, the Inquisition.

99. John H. Elliott, *Richelieu and Olivares* (Cambridge, 1984), 143, and idem, *Count-Duke of Olivares*, 597–99, 603–4, 608, and 610, which discuss the Spanish court's failure to appreciate the widespread support for the coup, both at home and in the empire.

CHAPTER 5

Years of Achievement and Disappointment: The Jesuits and the Crown, 1640–1706

> The Fifth objection: Jesuites are dangerous men because they meddle in intrigues of State and thrust themselves into Court affairs. I answer that if ever any Jesuit doth do so, he transgresseth his rule and committeth a grievous sin against an express precept of obedience.
>
> —Martin Grene, *An Account of the Jesuites Life and Doctrine*

THE DECEMBER REVOLUTION ushered in one of the most critical periods in the history of Portugal and its empire and an anxious one for the Society of Jesus. The years 1640 to 1706 spanned the reigns of three kings and two regencies with whom Jesuit relationships were exceedingly uneven. For the initial 28 years, the nation was at grave risk, largely because of Spain's persistent refusal to accept the inevitability of Portuguese independence. Although that independence was definitively achieved by 1668, the cost had been heavy, and economic recovery was made difficult by the loss of the major sources of wealth in the Far East (see Chapter 6) and the onset of an extended depression (ca. 1670–95) that reduced earnings from the re-export of Brazilian staples. The Jesuits returned to the royal palace during the reign of John IV (1640–56) and enjoyed the king's confidence and gratitude, but their influence began to abate during the regency of his widow, Luísa de Gusmão (1656–62), and the Society found itself very much on the defensive during the troubled reign of Afonso VI (1662–68). Though the Jesuits were not responsible for toppling that unfortunate monarch, they rejoiced at the ascendancy of his brother Pedro, first as regent and in 1683 as king. Although the Jesuits enjoyed Pedro's favor in some respects, they found him less pliable than Sebastian had been. In the end they came to recognize the limits of the possible in one of Europe's most conservative kingdoms.

The Jesuits as Collaborators of John IV, 1640–56

John IV, founder of Portugal's third (and last) dynasty, has always been a controversial figure in his nation's historiography. Liberal historians have denounced him as cowardly and indecisive, and as a ruthless despot who was ungrateful to those who sacrificed so much for him; but conservative scholars have defended him as prudent, cultured, sagacious, statesmanlike, and heroic, and as the "soul" if not the leader of Portugal's struggle for independence.[1] Without assessing his leadership qualities, Richard Flecknoe, the English (or perhaps Irish) poetaster who visited the king's court in 1648, simply described him as "an honest plain man, . . . as homely as any farmer, and . . . as meanly clad as any citizen . . . [one whose] ordinary exercise is hunting and music."[2]

During the early years of his reign, John had little time for such recreations.[3] Slipping into Lisbon almost unnoticed on a rainy Thursday evening after the previous Saturday's successful coup, he and his wife, the daughter of the duke of Medina Sidonia, were subjected to three days of unrestrained festivities while the capital glowed with nocturnal illuminations. The new monarch found such euphoria inappropriate and remarked to one of the capital's aldermen, "Keep the rejoicing until later. We must now find the means to defend ourselves."[4]

John assumed the burdens of high office under conditions that would have deterred many other candidates. As the chanter of Évora observed in 1643, "This kingdom has reached the most miserable state in its history, without arms, without soldiers, without armadas, and without fortifications."[5] He might have added that it was also without funds until the recalled cortes voted extraordinary taxes in 1641, that it lacked papal support or any effective allies, that it was juxtaposed with a hostile neighbor that refused to recognize its right to a separate existence and provided asylum for the regime's enemies, that its empire was on the verge of total ruin, and that its ruler had only recently escaped a death plot in which some of the leading figures of the realm had participated.

The leaders of the conspiracy of 1641 intended to eliminate John IV and restore Margaret of Savoy, duchess of Mantua, and Philip IV as Portugal's rulers. Led by the primate, the archbishop of Braga, their number included two bishops, a duke, a marquis, three counts, the inquisitor general, the keeper of the national archives, two members of the supreme court of appeals, and various other bureaucrats, most notably Pedro de Baeta

1. Rodrigues Cavalheiro, "Os antecedentes da restauração e a posição do duke de Bragança," CMP/P, 7: 11–16; Luiz Augusto Rebello da Silva, História de Portugal nos séculos xvii e xviii, 4 vols. (Lisbon, 1860), 4: 183–84. For divergent views concerning John's character and achievements, see J[oão] Lúcio de Azevedo, História de António Vieira, 2d ed., 2 vols. (Lisbon, 1931), 1: 59–60; and VS/HP, 5: 8, 39–41.

2. Richard Flecknoe, A Relation of Ten Years Travels (n.p., ca. 1656), 56.

3. Despite its age, Martinho da Fonseca, comp., Elementos bibliograficos para a história das guerras chamadas da restauração (1640–1668) (Coimbra, 1927), remains a valuable survey of the Restoration period literature to 1920. For an excellent perception of the frantic activities of the regime during its first month, see João Pinto Ribeiro to Vasco de Andrade, 4 Jan. 1641, in CMP/P, 7: 127–35. The author (d. 1649) was a jurist who wrote a treatise demonstrating the reasons why the fidalguia could not be obliged to serve in alien lands. As the manager of the Bragança household at the time of the planning of the December coup, he served as go-between for the plotters in Almada, opposite Lisbon, and in Vila Viçosa. After the revolution he held a series of offices, including that of keeper of the national archives. PDH, 6: 265–66, which is more satisfactory than DHP, 3: 644–45.

4. Rebello da Silva, História de Portugal, 4: 184.

5. Manoel de Faria Severim, "Observação dos males que Deos permitio para bem de Portugal," 20 Sept. 1643, Archivo bibliographico, no. 18 (Coimbra, 1878): 341–43. The author was the nephew of the chronicler Manuel Severim de Farias (b. 1583–b. 1655) and died the same year as his uncle after a career devoted to the education of poor children. PDH, 3: 295. For another informed coeval assessment of Portugal's grim military and financial condition, see marquis of Montalvão to king, 1642, in Horácio Madureira dos Santos, ed., Cartas e outros documentos da época da guerra da aclamação (Lisbon, 1973), 151–59.

da Silveira, an immensely wealthy New Christian moneylender, and a number of other prominent New Christians. The plot was betrayed on 24 July, and two dozen conspirators were rounded up from Braga and Leiria in the north to Setúbal, Évora, and Lisbon in the center. What must have been especially galling to the king was the fact that many of the plotters had participated in his oath-taking ceremony only months before (15 December 1640). Appropriately, on the date commemorating the death of St. John the Baptist (29 August), twelve of the rebels were publicly executed in Lisbon's famous Roscío Square. They included a duke, a marquis, a count, and a gentleman, all of whom were beheaded, and seven others who were hanged, drawn, and quartered. Both the archbishop and the inquisitor general were confined to the tower of Belém. There the primate soon expired; the inquisitor general remained for a year and a half before he was released (for still-mysterious reasons) and restored to his offices and privileges.[6]

Although members of several religious Orders were implicated in the conspiracy, not a single Jesuit participated. Throughout John IV's reign, the Jesuits served the monarch as staunch and useful collaborators. Seemingly not privy to the plans of the plotters of the December revolution, the fathers rejoiced at the results since they had long promoted the Bragança candidacy. John recognized his indebtedness to the Jesuits when he remarked that the man most responsible for the "good fortune" that had come to his house and to the entire nation was his former confessor, Sebastião do Couto, who had died the previous year.[7] The Jesuits followed John into the royal palace, where they became advisors, confessors, and orators, but they also performed many other services. Immediately after the overthrow of the last Spanish regent, they persuaded the Lisbon artisan guild (the *casa dos vinte e quatro*) to support the new regime and prevailed upon the acting apostolic collector to lift Lisbon's fourteen-month interdict.[8] Just as Spanish Jesuits delivered sermons in favor of their nation's campaigns against the French, and French Jesuits exhorted the deity to bring victory to the forces of Louis XIII, so Portuguese Jesuits delivered patriotic sermons in support of their king and country.[9] Jesuit propagandists applied their quills with patriotic zeal, most notably perhaps in the treatise *The Prodigal Restoration of Portugal* (1643). Throughout the realm and

6. The fullest account of the conspiracy is Conde de Ericeira [Luís de Meneses], *História de Portugal restaurado* [1679], ed. António Alvaro Doria, 4 vols. (Oporto, 1945–46), 1: 297–22 and 499–511, the latter of which includes key documents, some of which were published in *Archivo bibliographico*, no. 18: 241–77. See also John Chandler, "consul of the English, Scotch, and Irish nations in Lisbon," to Charles I, Lisbon, 16 Aug. 1641, CMP/P, 7: 237, and James C. Boyajian, *Portuguese Bankers at the Court of Spain, 1626–1650* (New Brunswick, N.J., 1983), 31–32, 117, and 127. Much remains to be learned about the full ramifications of the conspiracy, the first of three attempts on the king's life (see Ericeira, *Portugal restaurado* 2: 237–39, for two botched attempts by a minor functionary in 1647), particularly its links with hostile emigré Portuguese aristocrats, most of whom were then living in Spain, where they risked the loss of their properties if they failed to heed the government's injunction to return to their homeland. For the emigrés' sentiments toward the "usurper" John IV, see *Archivo bibliographico*, no. 18: 277–86, 293–300, 317–24, and 333–41. For similar plots within Spain during these turbulent years, see R. A. Stradling, *Philip IV and the Government of Spain, 1621–1665* (Cambridge, 1988), 232–33.

7. *ASCJ*, 695; José Felipe Mendeiros, "O oliventino Sebastião do Couto, mestre insigne da universidade de Évora e alma das alterações de 1637," Academia portuguesa da história, *Anais*, 2d ser., 18 (1969): 19–32.

8. Francisco Rodrigues, S.J., "A Companhia de Jesus e a restauração de Portugal 1640," Academia portuguesa da história, *Anais* 6 (1942): 329–405.

9. Ibid., 341–42, 376–77, 380–83. Cf. Gregorio Marañon, *El conde-duque de Olivares (La pasión de mandar)*, 5th ed. (Madrid, 1965), 182 n. 2.

the empire, wherever there were Jesuit houses, there were organized popular demonstrations led by the fathers and their students to promote patriotism.[10]

After the exposure of the wide-ranging conspiracy of 1641, it is not surprising that John was hard pressed to find persons in whom he could place unlimited trust. He therefore repeatedly delegated Jesuits to undertake delicate missions. For example, although most of the empire readily accepted the return of the Portuguese monarch, the citizens of Angra, that onetime stronghold of António, prior of Crato, tempered their ardor when the Spanish commander of the 100-gun fortress that overlooked the city refused to surrender. To bring about his capitulation with as little damage as possible, the king called upon Fr. Francisco Cabral.[11] Ostensibly Cabral came to the island of Terceira as a Jesuit inspector, but he brought with him munitions (soon deposited in the church of the Jesuit college) and a royal warrant designating him as "superintendent of war" for the island. Fr. Cabral strengthened the islanders' resistance and, after a year-long siege, had the satisfaction of first seeing the fortress peacefully fall and then preaching a victory sermon in honor of the king.[12]

If the crown could reach a successful accommodation with the Dutch occupants, Brazil was potentially far more important to Portugal than the islands. Two Jesuits were therefore sent there on touchy missions. News of the December revolution reached Salvador on 15 February 1641, when a ship captain delivered secret dispatches to its viceroy, D. Jorge Mascarenhas, marquis of Montalvão. Although the viceroy had been appointed by the former regime and had close personal connections in Spain, he consulted with all important ecclesiastical and secular dignitaries, who unanimously recommended that he proclaim Portugal's independence. He did so, then named one of his own sons and two Jesuits—the longtime administrator and chronicler Simão de Vasconcelos, and the rising star António Vieira—as delegates to Lisbon to express the capital's support to the new monarch. At the same time Mascarenhas asked the Jesuit provincial, André Fernandes, future confessor of both John IV and his eldest son, to convey the news to Rio de Janeiro, where the powerful, opulent Salvador de Sá served as governor. There was some question about Sá's probable response since he was half Spanish and was married to the daughter of the viceroy of Peru, but that concern proved to be unfounded. When Fr. Fernandes informed the governor about the successful revolution on 10 March, Sá immediately called a meeting of notables, who gathered in the library of the Jesuit college. These dignitaries unanimously urged Sá to accept the new regime, and he immediately complied.[13]

Fr. Fernandes's mission contained fewer difficulties than that of Fr. Francisco de Vilhena, a veteran missionary in Brazil who had escaped the Hollanders (see Chapter 9) and was serving as a faculty member in Évora when John IV summoned him to embark on another

10. Rodrigues, "Restauração," 348–62, 374–76. For an impressive analysis of the sermons of Jesuit and other orators in behalf of the new government, see João Francisco Marques, *A parenética portuguesa e a restauração*, 2 vols. (Porto, 1989).

11. Francisco Cabral (b. 1588–d. 1652), one of several Portuguese-born Jesuits to bear that name, was born in Fornos de Algodres, Vizeu, and joined the Society in 1604. Known mainly as a preacher, he also served as rector of the colleges of Braga and Funchal, and the University of Coimbra. *ASCJ*, 572–73; Rodrigues, "Restauração," 365 n. 4.

12. Rodrigues, "Restauração," 363–65; VS/*HP*, 5: 91–94.

13. Charles R. Boxer, *Salvador de Sá and the Struggle for Brazil and Angola, 1602–1686* (London, 1952), 144–47; Rodrigues, "Restauração," 370–71.

mission to Brazil. Since two of Mascarenhas's sons had already fled to Spain and their mother remained under house arrest in Portugal because of her sympathies with the Spanish regime, the court questioned the viceroy's loyalty. Vilhena bore secret instructions to proceed to Salvador to determine whether the colony remained obedient to the king. If the viceroy seemed suspect, he was to be removed and replaced by an interim government. Vilhena appears to have exceeded his instructions when he arranged for Mascarenhas's removal and confinement (under guard) in the Jesuit college. However, an arriving Spanish ship brought evidence that seemingly confirmed the wisdom of the Jesuit's action: instructions from Philip IV ordering the viceroy to remain loyal to his government, and damaging family letters from Mascarenhas's wife and sons in which they expressed warm support for the old regime. Ironically, both the ex-viceroy and his Jesuit adversary ended their lives in confinement, Mascarenhas in a Lisbon fortress and Vilhena somewhere in North Africa, for his homeward-bound ship was apprehended by Algerian pirates.[14]

John IV also sent several Jesuits on diplomatic missions to various European courts. If those ventures proved less successful than he had hoped, their meager results were more a consequence of the precarious condition of the kingdom and its empire than of the fathers' lack of the requisite negotiating skills. The first mission was headed by Fr. Inácio Mascarenhas, son of an Alentejo aristocrat who had close connections with the Braganças. Fr. Mascarenhas and a companion, representing the second mission John had sent to Barcelona,[15] reached the Catalan capital on 24 January 1642, at a propitious time for the Catalans if not for the Portuguese. It is unclear whether Fr. Mascarenhas was supposed to negotiate a military alliance with the Catalans; if so, he arrived too late, for three days earlier they had agreed to become a French military protectorate, and two days after the Jesuits' arrival, the Catalans achieved their first major victory over the Spaniards. After some harrowing adventures escaping would-be Spanish assassins in Italy, Fr. Mascarenhas returned to Lisbon in late July with more than 50 Portuguese who had been serving in Catalonia. Their repatriation represented the only real fruit of his mission.[16] Even less was achieved by António Vieira, who undertook a series of embassies to Holland, France, and Rome between 1646 and 1650. The aim of his missions to Holland was to reach a satisfactory accommodation with the Dutch concerning the return of all (or part) of occupied Brazil (see Chapter 9). In France he tried to secure the marriage of the king's eldest son, D. Teodósio,

14. Rodrigues, "Restauração," 369–70. Mascarenhas's guilt may only have been by association, reason enough during the paranoia of the Restoration to justify imprisonment or worse, as Francisco de Lucena, former secretary, discovered in 1642, when he was executed on suspicion of being an agent of Philip IV; but there can be no doubt about the pro-Spanish sympathies of the marquis's wife or those of his two sons, some of whose letters are published in *Archivo bibliographico*, no. 18: 280–86 and 293–300.

15. The first efforts by the king to contact the Catalans ended disastrously when a party of 25, dispatched immediately after the December revolution, was taken to Cadiz by their treacherous Spanish captain and became prisoners of war. Eduardo Brazão, *A restauração: Relações diplomáticas de Portugal de 1640 a 1668* (Lisbon, n.d.), 45–46.

16. Rodrigues, "Restauração," 365–67. VS/*HP*, 5: 62–64; Brazão, *Relações diplomáticas*, 46–60. I have not seen Edgar Prestage, "Relação da embaixada do padre-mestre Inácio de Mascarenhas a Catalunha em 1641," *O Instituto* 73 (Coimbra, 1926), which includes the text of Mascarenhas's 1641 account. As Roger Bigelow Merriman wrote, the hoped-for Luso-Catalan alliance failed because neither side had anything in common with the other save its hostility toward Spain. Merriman, *Six Contemporary Revolutions* (Oxford, 1938), 135–38.

to the daughter of a French duke; in Rome he attempted to unite D. Teodósio with the only daughter of Philip IV of Spain! As a marriage broker and as a peace maker Vieira was a failure, though he could hardly be blamed, for Portugal did not enjoy much of a bargaining position.[17] The last of this series of Jesuit emissaries, Luanda-born António de Couto, was assigned the impossible task of renewing an old alliance with the ruler of Kongo, but his mission, too, failed.[18]

Nuno da Cunha, who became Portuguese assistant to the Society's head in 1646, was another Jesuit who performed diplomatic services for Portugal. Because of the papacy's refusal to recognize Portuguese independence, no formal diplomatic relations existed between Lisbon and Rome until 1669, when Pope Clement IX conceded recognition. Between the 1640s and the 1660s Cunha and his successors informally represented the crown's interests in the Eternal City.[19] But there was one intractable problem that they could not solve: until formal relations were restored, the Portuguese crown was unable to propose candidates for vacant episcopacies, whose numbers reached twenty in the kingdom and the Atlantic islands by the early 1660s. That, of course, meant that candidates for the priesthood in those lands found it increasingly difficulty to become ordained.[20]

Jesuits also defended Portugal's interests in a more direct way—through military service. When John IV first arrived in Lisbon as king, the fathers of Santo Antão paraded their students before him and offered them as defenders of the fatherland. That offer was not accepted, but Jesuits did serve as military chaplains and in other ways. The first to do so was a Gallway-born professor of mathematics known as Simão Falónio. Though assigned to instructional duties at Santo Antão, he also served as a designer of fortifications until his death in January 1642. Another who performed that function was a Flemish father called "Cosmander," also known as João Pasásio Ciermans. Born in s'Hertogenbosch (Bois-le-Duc), Brabant, in 1602, Ciermans entered the Society in 1619 and became a professor of humanities and mathematics in Antwerp and Louvain. In 1641 he came to Lisbon en route to the China missions. Learning of his engineering talent, the crown assigned him to supervise the construction or rebuilding of the kingdom's fortifications. He participated in several battles and was given the rank of colonel and the title of chief engineer. In 1647 Colonel Ciermans was wounded and captured by the Spaniards at Elvas. A year later he was a member of the forces Philip IV sent to attack Olivença (see below), and there the turncoat was mortally wounded.[21]

Other Jesuits participated in the first and second Portuguese attempts to recover Angola (1645 and 1648) from its Dutch occupiers (see Chapter 9) and in various Peninsular campaigns. When Fr. Francisco Manso, former procurator of the province of Portugal in

17. Vieira's frustrations as a diplomat have been discussed by many writers, perhaps best by Edgar Prestage, *The Diplomatic Relations of Portugal with France, England, and Holland from 1640 to 1668* (Watford, 1925), 30–31, 36–38, and 189–209. Vieira's first mission to Rome is detailed by Azevedo, *História de António Vieira*, 1: 172–83; see also Rodrigues, "Restauração," 385–88.
18. Rodrigues, "Restauração," 365–66.
19. Early in 1642, John IV sent a delegation headed by the bishop of Lamego to Rome to consult with the pope. Castilian factions at the curia prevented them from gaining a papal audience, and the Spanish ambassador publicly threatened to kill the bishop. Spanish troops attacked the delegates, causing the deaths of several Portuguese defenders. ARSI, *Lus.*, 74, fols. 276–281^v.
20. Rodrigues, "Restauração," 389–90; Brazão, *Relações diplomáticas*, chap. 7.
21. For a contemporary report of his end, see Madureira dos Santos, *Cartas*, 177–78.

Madrid and close friend of Diogo Soares, secretary of the Council of Portugal, came to Lisbon after the acclamation of John IV, he was immediately detained because of his past connections with the old regime, though there is no evidence that he bore any guilt. Nor was there evidence against Francisco Soares, a cousin of the Mascarenhas family headed by the imprisoned ex-viceroy of Brazil, but because of his familial connections, he was in trouble on two occasions. In 1642 he was confined to a windowless cell in São Roque for six months; seven years later he was back in the same cell because he had received a letter from a brother living in Spain. Upon his second release Fr. Soares became rector of the college of Elvas. When that city was attacked by Spanish troops in 1659, he insisted on leading his students against the enemy. During the defense of the famous "lines of Elvas," Francisco Soares and two fellow Jesuits were blown apart when a powder barrel exploded.[22]

Many of these activities became sources of embarrassment or annoyance to the six fathers general whose administrations spanned the Restoration years.[23] The most seriously concerned was Mutio Vitelleschi, who was nearing the end of his long administration when the uprisings began in the peripheral kingdoms of Spain. He recognized that these tumults could threaten Jesuit enterprises both in the Peninsula and overseas. Soon after the 1640 eruption in Catalonia on Corpus Christi Day (see Chapter 4), Vitelleschi issued a directive to the province of Catalonia ordering his subjects to remain absolutely neutral in the conflict: "In no way, neither by word nor by writing, nor in the pulpit or in private conversations," were they to express anything of an incendiary nature. He urged the provincial to remember "what the Company [of Jesus] owes to his Catholic Majesty and to his progenitors," particularly the colleges they had authorized, and he warned that it would be a "grave blow" if any member of the Society "committed the slightest inadvertence."[24] As Miguel Battlori notes, in insisting upon prudent behavior by members of the Society in Catalonia, the father general was adhering to precisely the same policy long pursued by the Holy See in the interminable quarrels between France and Spain, one of absolute neutrality. Nevertheless, Vitelleschi remained worried, and a year after sending his first directive he issued another in which he stressed that the Fifth and Seventh General Congregations (1593–94 and 1615) had expressly imposed "grave pains" upon members who allowed themselves to be drawn into affairs of state. He enjoined superiors to exercise "the greatest possible vigilance" to prevent "inconveniences" and to impose major penances upon those who failed to do their duty.[25]

The December 1640 revolution in Lisbon prompted quite a different response from Vitelleschi. Strangely, he seems not to have expressed any policy toward the Portuguese revolution until 1643, when he was compelled to act under pressure from Philip IV, the

22. Rodrigues, "Restauração," 390–94 and 397–401.

23. Five of these fathers general were Italians but only one (Carafa) came from Spanish-controlled territory. The sixth (Nickel) was German-born. They include Mutio Vitelleschi (1615–45), Vicente Carafa (1646–49), Francesco Piccolómini (1649–51), Aloysius Gottifredi (1652), Goswin Nickel (1652–64), and Giovanni Paolo Oliva (1664–81).

24. Vitelleschi to provincial, 11 Sept. 1640, as quoted by Miguel Battlori, S.J., "Los Jesuitas y la guerra de Cataluña: 1640–1659," *Boletin de la academia de la historia* 146 (1960): 141–98, at 143–44.

25. Vitelleschi to provincial, 8 Aug. 1641, quoted in ibid., 145. Battlori alludes (145 n. 10) to a further exhortation by the general the next year but does not supply the text.

Roman curia, and his own assistant for Spain and its empire.[26] That year he signed a dispatch drafted by the cardinal secretary of state and addressed to the nuncio in Madrid. Taking note of the fact that in Spain the Portuguese Jesuits were widely accused of responsibility for the ousting of Margaret of Savoy, the dispatch called upon the Portuguese provincial to undertake a diligent inquiry concerning Jesuits who might have violated the injunctions of the general congregations. When copies of this directive reached Portugal, they provoked a storm. Vitelleschi then wrote an explanatory letter to the provincial in which he admitted that he had been under grave pressure, that his directive was intended to calm the Society's critics in Spain, that he held the new king in high regard, and that he hoped the provincial would exercise prudence and charity in those difficult times.[27]

Among the critics of the revolution on the other side of the border were Spanish Jesuits, whose colleagues had enjoyed close and cordial relations with the count-duke of Olivares.[28] It is not surprising, therefore, to discover in the voluminous correspondence of Rafael Pereyra, the Seville-based missions procurator of Jesuit enterprises in the Spanish empire, unanimous condemnation of the December revolution and support for Philip IV. Pereyra's correspondents wrote him from Madrid, Salamanca, Badajoz, and other parts of Spain. They possessed excellent intelligence concerning conditions in Portugal and spoke of the "black treason" of the December revolutionists who proclaimed the "rebel duke" as their king. As the years went by, Pereyra's contacts expressed grave anxiety at the persistence of the rebellion of the Portuguese against their "legitimate king." They spoke of the existence of a "tyranny" across the frontier where the "intruder king" (precisely the term later applied to Napoleon's brother, Joseph) ruled.[29]

Just as Jesuits in Spain and in Portugal differed in their responses toward the Portuguese revolution, Jesuits in Catalonia and in Portugal also took different positions in their respective revolutions. In Catalonia, according to the research of Fr. Battlori, most Jesuits complied with Vitelleschi's insistence that they remain neutral. There was no place for neutrality in Portugal, however: one was either a patriot or a traitor, and most Jesuits became patriots.[30] But the two revolutions were very different. The Catalan rebellion was a social upheaval propelled from below; the December revolution was organized and directed from above. As Magalhães Godinho has written, "The people were absent on 1 December 1640."[31] It was much easier for the members of an elite Order to support an upper-class revolution than a lower-class one. Moreover, Spain's conquest of Portugal had occurred almost within living memory; whereas Catalonia was united with Aragon in 1137. Portugal had lost and regained its independence within two generations. John IV was its seventeenth Portuguese monarch; monarchy had no such record in Catalonia, where a suspect republic, generally

26. For the views of Alvaro de Arementa (assistant for Spain and its empire), see his dispatch of 21 Dec. 1641 to Fr. Rafael Pereyra, in *MHE*, 16: 196.

27. Rodrigues, "Restauração," 346–48.

28. Marañon, *El conde-duque de Olivares*, chap. 14.

29. E.g., [Sebastián Gonzalez] to Pereyra, Madrid, 31 Dec. 1640; Lic. D. Gabriel Ortiz Orve to Pereyra, Badajoz, 14 Oct. 1643; Gonzales to Pereyra, Madrid, 15 Dec. 1643; and Gonzales to Pereyra, 1 Mar. 1644, in *MHE*, 16: 104; 17: 310, 385, and 445. See also 19: 280.

30. Although Fr. Rodrigues would have us believe that all Portuguese Jesuits were ardent patriots, there were clearly dissenters. See Gonzalez to Pereyra, 22 Dec. 1640, in *MHE*, 16: 96–100.

31. Vitorino Magalhães Godinho, "1580 e a restauração," reprinted in his *Ensaios*, 2 (Lisbon, 1968), 281.

believed to be a front for French penetration of northeastern Spain, was proposed during the 1640s. Despite persisting peril, Portugal remained an independent entity; Catalonia became a satellite of France.

The evidence of the varied Jesuit reactions to radical change in Catalonia, Castile, and Portugal suggests an obvious truth that has eluded many critics of the Jesuits, namely, that the Society did not always speak with one voice. Despite the international composition of the Order and its professed nonsecular orientation, in times of crisis its members were as unable to resist nationalistic impulses as were ordinary civilians. For the Jesuits of Portugal and most of those in Spain, the ties of nationalism were obviously stronger than they were in Catalonia.[32]

The Perilous Years, 1656–68

The Jesuits' confidence in the Braganças was severely shaken by a series of political upheavals during the last dozen years of the Restoration, its most critical phase. At its beginning, one contemporary ruefully observed that "it was easy to make the duke of Bragança a king, but it was much more difficult to keep the crown on his head."[33] That was even more true between 1656 and 1668, when the fidalguia was bitterly divided over questions of leadership, power, perquisites, and national goals, and the kingdom was in despair because of the constant drain upon its human and material resources occasioned by the unending war with Spain and the continued crumbling of its empire. On 8 November 1656, the founder of the new dynasty died of complications from gout. John was to have been succeeded by his eldest son, D. Teodósio, whom Flecknoe described as "a prince of great expectation, learned, and of great wit and courage."[34] He was also profoundly devoted to the Jesuits, who seem to have expected as much of him as they once had of Sebastian.[35] Unfortunately for them—and perhaps the nation—Teodósio died of tuberculosis three years before his father.

Next in line was D. Afonso (b. 1643–d. 1683), a pathetic figure who suffered from a crippling childhood malady, perhaps meningitis, which damaged his central nervous system and left him with diminished capacities physically, mentally, and emotionally.[36] Because of his handicaps, some at court, including the Jesuits, favored passing him over in order to elevate his younger brother, D. Pedro (b. 1648–d. 1706).[37] After considerable soul-searching, the queen mother, Luísa de Gusmão, assumed the regency, which she retained for five years beyond the age when Afonso was supposed to be able to rule.

32. Cf. A. Lynn Martin, *Henry III and the Jesuit Politicians* (Geneva, 1973), 178–81. Martin found that the Jesuits in France during the 1580s were split between Gallican and "international" factions, a situation very different from the one that prevailed in the Iberian Peninsula in the mid-seventeenth century.

33. A free translation of the passage quoted by Caetano Beirão, "Vinte e oito anos de guerra," CMP/P, 7: 711.

34. Flecknoe, *A Relation of Ten Years Travels*, 56.

35. Azevedo, *História de António Vieira*, 1: 356.

36. Robert Southwell to [Secretary of State] Arlington, 5/15 Nov. 1667, in [Thomas Carte], *The History of Revolutions in Portugal: With Letters of Sir Robert Southwell* (London, 1740), 199–210, provides a devastating critique of the crudities and incapacities of D. Afonso. For the basic literature concerning the king, see *DHP*, 1: 44–46.

37. Godinho, "1580 e a restauração," 287; *HCJAP*, 3:1, 511.

From all accounts, Luísa discharged her trust responsibly and courageously.[38] When it was suggested that she should dismiss from court André Fernandes, the Jesuit father who bore the empty title of bishop of Japan and had served as confessor to the late king and his son, because the priest had been present at the deaths of both and was therefore an ill omen, she refused and named him as her own confessor. When Fr. Fernandes died in 1660, the queen mother declared that she had sustained the worst loss possible since the demise of her husband.[39] Perhaps so, but she had not used Fernandes as an advisor on public affairs, as had John IV. It may be suggestive of the waning influence of the Jesuits at court that instead of André Fernandes or any other Jesuit, the queen relied upon a Dominican priest, Domingos do Rosário (b. Daniel O'Daly), an experienced diplomat and founder of the Irish Dominican college in Lisbon, to serve as a member of her informal advisory council, the *junta nocturna*.[40]

It was during the queen mother's regency that the long-quiescent border war with Spain reached the flash point. Testing the new regime's resolve, Philip IV launched an invasion of the Alentejo in the spring of 1657. The Spaniards captured Olivença and Mourão, but successful Portuguese counterattacks drove them from both places and led to the abortive siege of Badajoz. The subsequent Spanish threat to Elvas (14 January 1659) was decisively repelled, leaving both nations exhausted and Portugal's future still in doubt. Its fate became even more grim after France, which had assured Portugal of its support, signed the seminal Treaty of the Pyrenees (8 November 1659) with Spain. That agreement, which brought to an end the 24-year war between France and Spain, freed Philip IV to concentrate his forces along the western frontier.[41]

As an uneasy nation viewed these developments with alarm, Portugal continued to seek a savior; but Afonso persistently demonstrated his inability to fill that role. His great passions were observing or participating in violence, whether in the court itself or in the capital's streets. On one occasion he and his low-life friends were passing the Jesuit novitiate when someone informed him that the fathers kept large mastiffs within. He demanded to see them. When the gatekeeper was slow in admitting the monarch, he threatened to break down the gates. Each morning the palace was filled with reports of the king's latest nocturnal escapades; as one critic wrote, "he was feared everywhere as a Wild Beast." During the late 1650s and early 1660s Afonso's principal confidant was António Conti, son of a peddler of Italian descent who sold trifles on the porches of the palace. So completely did Conti gain the king's confidence that the nobles became fully alarmed. Finally, in mid-June 1662, the duke of Cadaval took matters into his own hands, rounded up Conti and his brothers, the king's groom, and a discredited former Augustinian priest, and packed most of them off to Brazil.[42]

38. Hipólito Raposo, *Dona Luisa de Gusmão, duquesa e rainha (1613–1666)* (Lisbon, 1947), remains the standard, sympathetic biography.

39. *ASCJ*, 629–32, and more extensively in António Franco, S.J., *Imagem da virtude em o noviciado da companhia de Jesus na corte de Lisboa* (Coimbra, 1717), 592–65. Fr. Fernandes's predecessor was another Jesuit, João Nunes (d. 28 or 29 Dec. 1656), who was confessor of the commander of the Bahian recovery expedition of 1625 and later held various administrative posts. Ibid., 421–67. See also *HCJAP*, 3:1, 507–11.

40. VS/*HP*, 5: 43; Edgar Prestage, *Frei Domingos do Rosário—diplomata e político* (Coimbra, 1926), a work that I have not seen.

41. VS/*HP*, 5: 43–45.

42. Ericeira, *Portugal restaurado*, 4: 59–65; [Anon.], *The Portugal History: or, a Relation of the Troubles . . . in the court of Portugal in . . . 1667 and 1668* (London, 1677), esp. 41–56 and 77–82. The quotation is from p. 56.

If that power play was intended to teach the king a lesson and to strengthen the hand of Luísa de Gusmão, it proved to be a miscalculation. Instead, it made possible the ascendancy of Luís de Vasconcelos e Sousa, the young count of Castelo Melhor (or Castelomelhor). Son of a former governor-general of Brazil and himself a wounded war hero in his mid-twenties, the young count cannily contrived to fill the vacuum left by the departure of the king's friends. He persuaded Afonso to assume the reins of government himself, a demand with which Luísa de Gusmão reluctantly complied before escaping to an Augustinian convent, where she spent her four remaining years. For a slightly longer interval, Castelo Melhor dominated the king and the country. He occupied the palace apartment of the late D. Teodósio and persuaded Afonso to name him to the long-vacant office of escrivão da puridade, the same position once held by Martim Gonçalves da Câmara during the reign of Sebastian (see Chapter 4) and one that enabled the count to control fully Portugal's foreign and domestic affairs. After removing the members of the queen's party from court and replacing them with his own minions, the count, seen by some as the prototype of two of Portugal's more famous later strongmen, the marquis of Pombal and António de Oliveira Salazar, installed an uncle, a Benedictine, as the king's confessor, and a brother as a court factotum to keep watch on the ambitious infante.[43]

As Castelo Melhor was consolidating his power, a long-smoldering conflict between the Inquisition and the Society of Jesus was rekindled. At first sight such a struggle might seem implausible, for there were never any doctrinal differences between those two zealous defenders of orthodoxy. As seen earlier, the Jesuits were once offered supervision of the Holy Office in Portugal and rejected that opportunity. Nevertheless, both in the kingdom and in Goa, they retained close ties with the Inquisition (see Appendix C). Upon occasion a Holy Office even supported the Society. In 1634, for example, when someone in Spain distributed libels against the Ignatians, the Inquisition there sought to apprehend the authors and ordered their vilifying papers burned.[44] As recently as the early 1650s, D. Teodósio had proposed his confessor, Fr. André Fernandes, to become Portugal's next inquisitor general, but Fr. Fernandes said that he was unqualified to serve such an exalted position because of his humble birth. It is conceivable that had he been able to accept such an appointment, he might have been able to mitigate some of the serious conflicts that occurred between the Society and the Holy Office.[45]

The celebrated seventeenth-century conflicts between the Portuguese Inquisition and the Jesuits occurred at a time when the secular church was severely weakened by the suspension of relations between the crown and Rome and when other religious Orders were uncertain of their loyalties. As the two most visible ecclesiastical bodies of the realm, the Inquisition and the Society were fighting for primacy within the kingdom. The first

43. On the ascendancy of Castelo Melhor, see VS/*HP*, 5: 46–49; Ericeira, *Portugal restaurado*, 4: 68ff.; [Anon.], *The Portugal History*, 116ff.; and two studies by Gastão de Melo de Matos, "Um processo político do século xviii," CMP/*P*, 7: 631–68, and "O sentido da crise política de 1667," Academia portuguesa da história, *Anais*, 2d ser., 8 (1944): 337–440, the latter of which provides a valuable assessment of contemporary sources and reprints three obscure studies by an Azorean civil servant, José de Torres, without recognizing that Torres's accounts are no more than translations of *The Portugal History*. No modern biography exists, but see *PDH*, 2: 890–91, and *DHP*, 1: 525–26.

44. *MHE*, 13: 67–79.

45. *ASCJ*, 629–32.

of their quarrels occurred in the city of Évora in December 1642, significantly only a year and a half after the Holy Office's prestige had been tarnished by the complicity of the inquisitor general in the plot against the monarchy. The dispute turned on whether the Jesuit university was immune under its charter to assaults by the Holy Office and whether that tribunal was, as its officers affirmed, answerable only to God. The university operated a street fair and appointed a student to preside over transactions there as a market inspector (*almotacé*). When an argument ensued between a student and a buyer for the local Holy Office's prison concerning the ownership of a basket of apples, the almotacé intervened in behalf of the student. The Holy Office promptly summoned the almotacé to its quarters, but he ignored its call. He was subsequently seized by two of its agents, and paraded through the city as a common criminal, and locked up in a dungeon. Two months later the tribunal handed down a remarkably stiff sentence against the almotacé, prompting a vigorous protest by university authorities. One of them was himself detained and sent by the tribunal to the local Dominican monastery for incarceration. The Jesuits appealed to the king, but they were disappointed when he ultimately supported the actions of the Inquisition. Still dissatisfied, the Jesuits then imprudently appealed to Rome, thereby incurring the anger of John IV, who failed to alter his stand.[46]

During the next confrontation between the Inquisition and the Jesuits, however, the king demonstrated that when his own interests were directly involved, he could stand up to the Holy Office. By the 1640s it was evident to John IV, as it was to many others, that Portugal no longer possessed the resources to maintain its once-dominant position in the eastern seas and that the country's future was closely tied to the development of Brazil. But that development was severely handicapped as long as the Dutch occupied several key sugar-producing captaincies and exploited Portuguese naval weakness by capturing hundreds of sugar carracks en route to Peninsular ports.[47] As António Vieira astutely recognized, since the state lacked sufficient capital to build the warships necessary to protect such shipping, private enterprise must do it. He therefore proposed the formation of a trading company modeled on the successful Dutch and English commercial firms. In return for monopoly trading privileges in Brazilian ports, the Brazil Company was expected to furnish sufficient warships to safeguard the sugar fleets. Enough capital could be raised for the company, Vieira persuaded the king, if merchant-financiers, many of whom were New Christians, were assured that their assets would not be seized in the event that they were arrested on suspicion by the Inquisition.[48] In making that proposal, Vieira and his fellow Jesuits who endorsed it were swimming upstream, for many Portuguese were convinced that despite their enforced conversion, the New Christians remained true to their former faith and were responsible

46. King to provincial, 21 Aug. 1643, in ANTT/AJ/29. The Portuguese assistant was critical of the Évora faculty for allowing itself to become embroiled in the dispute. Nuno da Cunha to rector, Évora, 6 Apr. 1643, in ANTT/AJ/18, n. 13. The fullest account is *HCJAP*, 3:1, 479–91.
47. Charles R. Boxer, *The Dutch in Brazil 1624–1654* (Oxford, 1957).
48. Charles R. Boxer, "Padre António Vieira, S.J., and the Institution of the Brazil Company in 1649," *HAHR* 29, 4 (Nov. 1949): 474–97; David Grant Smith, "Old Christian Merchants and the Foundation of the Brazil Company, 1649," *HAHR* 54, 2 (May 1974): 233–59, who demonstrates that New Christian merchants predominated, but did not monopolize, the Lisbon capital market.

for Portugal's economic woes.[49] In the face of strong opposition from the Inquisition, the Brazil Company was established in 1649. It proved to be a successful venture for the country if not for its investors, but the Holy Office never forgave Vieira for subverting orthodoxy and yearned for an opportunity to strike back at him.[50]

Vieira himself provided such an opportunity. Between 1655 and 1661 he served as superior of Jesuit operations in the Amazon, where he oversaw the establishment of more than 50 missions. He also became engaged in a bitter conflict with Portuguese settlers, who expelled the Jesuits in 1661 (see Chapter 19). Upon his arrival in Lisbon, Vieira briefly returned to his former position as court preacher, but when his patron, Queen Luísa, was victimized by Castelo Melhor's coup, he was ousted as well and was banished to the college of São Lourenço in Porto. It was then that certain messianic writings Vieira had composed during his sojourn in the Amazon came to the attention of the Coimbra branch of the Holy Office, led by an old adversary. In those writings Vieira expressed support for the prophetic views of the presumed founder of Sebastianism and predicted that the late king (John IV) would rise from the dead and establish a universal Christian monarchy under Portuguese aegis. After reviewing such unorthodox remarks, the Holy Office ordered Vieira to be tried on a charge of heresy. Confined for a time to a cell, where he was even deprived of writing materials, the formidable Jesuit defended himself skillfully during 30 grueling hearings that were intended not only to humiliate him but also to embarrass the Society. When his sentence was delivered on Christmas Eve 1667, he was joined by the entire faculty of the College of Arts. They remained standing with him during the two-hour proceedings in silent protest against the practices of the Holy Office. Nevertheless, Vieira was silenced by the tribunal and confined for a time in a partially demolished structure attached to the college of São Lourenço. There he remained until the ascendancy of his old friend Prince Pedro made it possible for him to return to Lisbon and to obtain release from the strictures imposed by the Holy Office.[51]

While Jesuit attention was focused upon the fate of their superstar, the rest of the nation viewed with emotions ranging from enthusiasm to profound misgivings a series of events that occurred abroad, along the insecure frontiers, and within the faction-ridden waterfront palace, the *paço da ribeira*. As mentioned, the Treaty of the Pyrenees freed Spain to concentrate its forces along the frontier in order to reduce Portugal to submission. Portugal's only possible ally was England, with whom it had concluded a disastrous war in 1654; but that had been with the irascible Oliver Cromwell. During the summer of 1660, soon after Charles II ascended the restored Stuart throne, Francisco de Melo e Torres (d. 1667), the future marquis of Sande, perhaps Portugal's ablest diplomat during the Restoration, suggested to Charles, Europe's most eligible bachelor, a marriage treaty that revived an offer made to his late father and that in general terms approximated the recent

49. J[oão] Lúcio de Azevedo, *História dos cristãos novos portugueses*, 2d ed. (Lisbon, 1975), 238–39 and 460–62.

50. Ibid., 250–54 and 477–83, the latter of which includes the controversial alvará of 6 Feb. 1649, which protected investors against threats by the Holy Office to seize their assets.

51. The best account of Vieira's tribulations with the Holy Office remains Azevedo, *António Vieira*, 2: 5–85; see also his perceptive essay, "Os Jesuítas e a inquisição em conflito no século xvii," ACL, *Boletim da segunda classe* 10 (Lisbon, 1916): 319–45; and Robert Ricard, "Prophesy and Messianism in the Works of António Vieira," *The Americas* 17, 4 (Apr. 1961): 357–68.

Franco-Spanish agreement.[52] Portugal offered the 30-year-old monarch a wife, Catherine of Bragança (b. 1638–d. 1706), sister of Afonso VI and D. Pedro; a dowry of 800 contos, title to Tangier and the "port and island" of Bombay; and commercial concessions that exceeded those assured by the Anglo-Portuguese treaties of 1642 and 1654. After the king and his advisors had reflected upon his matrimonial options, his severe financial distress, and the depressed state of the English economy, Charles accepted the proposal in May 1661.[53] By an agreement signed the following month, he pledged himself and his heirs to settle upon Catherine a yearly sum, to provide two horse and two foot regiments and necessary naval support for the defense of Portugal, "to defend and protect all conquests or colonies belonging to the King of Portugal against all his enemies, as well future as present," and to mediate Portugal's unresolved wars with the Netherlands and Spain.[54]

As will be seen in Chapter 8, Portuguese interests in India and those allied with them, including the Jesuits, adamantly opposed the transfer of Bombay, which they correctly perceived as only the entering wedge of English penetration of the subcontinent. There can be no question that Charles II and his counselors fully appreciated Portugal's precarious condition and were determined, if possible, to extract further territorial and commercial concessions from their ally.[55] Except for the loss of Tangier, a Portuguese bastion since 1471 and still the home of several hundred Portuguese residents, no one in Portugal grumbled about the stiff conditions of the alliance.[56] Portuguese authorities warmly welcomed arriving

52. In accordance with the provisions of the treaty of 1659, Louis XIV married Maria Teresa, eldest daughter of Philip IV, and received a dowry of 500,000 crowns and former Spanish borderlands in the Pyrenees and in Flanders.

53. For Charles's marriage options, see Maurice Ashley, *Charles II: The Man and the Statesman* (London, 1971), 122–23. Concerning his financial problems, see G. N. Clark, *The Later Stuarts, 1660–1714* (rpr., Oxford, 1949), 6–8. The state of the English economy is explained by Charles Wilson, *Profit and Power: A Study of England and the Dutch Wars* (London, 1957), 149–51. See also David Ogg, *England in the Reign of Charles II* (Oxford, 1934), 183–88.

54. A convenient source of the text is George Chalmers, comp., *A Collection of Treaties Between Great Britain and Other Powers*, 2 vols. (London, 1790), 2: 286–96. The quotation is from the secret additional article. See also Clyde L. Grose, "The Anglo-Portuguese Marriage of 1662," *HAHR* 10, 3 (Aug. 1930): 313–52; and Edgar Prestage, "The Treaties of 1642, 1654, and 1661," in Prestage, ed., *Chapters in Anglo-Portuguese Relations* (Watford, Eng., 1935), 130–51, as well as idem, *Diplomatic Relations*, 142–49. The interpretation of Brazão, *Relações diplomáticas*, 249–62, closely follows Prestage.

55. See Charles II to Sir Richard Fanshaw, 23 Aug. 1661 (OS), in Great Britain, Historical Manuscripts Commission, *The Manuscripts of J. M. Heathcote, Esq.* (Norwich, 1899) [hereafter *Heathcote*], 18–19, in which the king admonished his envoy to remember that "one of the principal advantages . . . to ourself by this entire conjunction . . . is the advancement of the trade of this nation and the enlargement of our own territories and dominions." To that end, Fanshaw was to press Lisbon to concede to England Bassein, Goa, and the Brazilian sugar trade. Subsequently Fanshaw and his successors were directed to work for additional trading privileges with Portugal's Atlantic islands and Macao and to try to take over the salt port of Setúbal. Despite the costly loyalty of Portugal to Charles I, his son was patently no reliable friend. In 1656 Charles II signed a secret treaty with Spain and, in return for the promise of 6,000 troops to invade England, offered help in recovering Portugal. Ashley, *Charles II*, 78 and 93. Two years earlier Cromwell had toyed with a plan to divide the Lusitanian empire between England and Holland, a proposal that the earl of Clarendon suggested reviving during difficulties over the transfer of Bombay. See Chapter 8 below.

56. Thomas Maynard (consul) to [Sir Edward Nicholas (secretary of state)], 22 Jan. and 20–23 May 1661, in Charles R. Boxer, comp., *Descriptive List of the State Papers, Portugal, 1661–1780 in the Public Record Office, London*, 3 vols. (Lisbon, 1979–83), 1: 17–18. Maynard reported that everyone save the Inquisition favored the treaty and that the Portuguese were even willing to surrender their remaining possessions in India to save it. At the time, Tangier was considered more important than Bombay and was viewed as a future naval

English consular and diplomatic officials, and the morale of the people was strengthened by the presence of English naval units and by the coming of English and French mercenaries.[57] English warships patrolled off the Algarve and the bar of the Tagus, discouraging whatever sea-invasion plans Spain may have had, while the additional land forces, many of them veterans of Cromwellian or continental campaigns, distinguished themselves in the key battles that assured Portugal of its independence.

The long war with Spain rushed toward a climax between 1661 and 1665 in a series of short but furiously fought battles. In 1661–62, prior to the arrival of English and French mercenaries, Spain launched a general offensive in the north, center, and south.[58] The most successful was the center force, commanded by D. Juan of Austria, bastard son of Philip IV, who captured Évora in May 1663 and for a time threatened the Atlantic seaboard. The fall of Évora led to serious rioting in Lisbon, where noble houses and even the archiepiscopal residence were pillaged.[59] Less than two months later, however, Portuguese and mercenary troops led by Count Frederic Armand Schomberg, an Anglo-French soldier of fortune, scored a major victory in the field at Ameixial, 5 kilometers from Estremoz, and Évora was liberated soon after.[60] Almost exactly a year after Ameixial, the Portuguese gained a second victory at Castelo Rodrigo in the vicinity of Salamanca. Nevertheless, Spain was still capable of mounting a serious threat. It came eleven months later, on 17 June 1665; but Schomberg again defeated the Spaniards at Montes Claros near the Bragançan center of Vila Viçosa.[61] Whether or not because he saw the handwriting on the wall, Philip IV, that implacable foe of Portuguese independence, died three months later. But the regency that succeeded him still hesitated to betray his memory by making peace with Portugal. To compel it to do so and to lessen Portugal's dependence upon England, the Castelo Melhor regime fulfilled the ambitions of a quarter century of futile Portuguese diplomacy by signing two treaties with France (1666, 1667). The first provided the king with a wife and badly needed dowry funds, whereas the second promised that France would pressure Madrid to agree to peace.[62]

---

base comparable to that which Gibraltar later became. As R. C. Anderson pointed out, Tangier was, in effect, exchanged for Dunkirk, which Charles II sold to Louis XIV. Anderson, ed., *The Journal of Edward Montague First Earl of Sandwich . . . 1659–1665*, Naval Records Society (London, 1929), xxx–xxxi. But Tangier proved too costly and was abandoned in 1683, much to the annoyance of the Portuguese. When Louis XIV offered to lend King Pedro II funds to repossess it, the king wisely declined. Violet M. Shillington and A. B. Wallis Chapman, *The Commercial Relations of England and Portugal* (rpr., New York, 1970), 210–11. See also C. R. Boxer, "'Three Sights to be Seen': Bombay, Tangier, and a Barren Queen, 1661–1684," *Portuguese Studies* 3 (1987): 77–83.

57. *Heathcote*, 29, 80, 68, 111, 153; Boxer, *Descriptive List*, 1: 25–89.

58. Those offensives included the use of propaganda. One pamphlet of 1662 was addressed to the residents of the border town of Elvas. They were informed that the current siege was not intended to damage them or their countryside but to liberate them from their Portuguese oppressors, and royal clemency was promised to those who sided with Spain. ARSI, *Lus.*, 74, fols. 282–87.

59. The rioting, which began in the king's presence at the royal palace, did considerable property damage and cost at least 40 lives. Fanshaw to Sir Henry Bennet (Lord Arlington), 20–30 May 1663 (OS), in *Heathcote*, 92–96; "The Memoirs of Ann, Lady Fanshaw," in John Loftis, ed., *The Memoirs of Anne, Lady Halkett and Ann, Lady Fanshawe* (Oxford, 1979), 148.

60. Charles R. Boxer, "Marshal Schomberg in Portugal, 1660–68," *History Today* 26 (Oct. 1976): 653–63. Many of Schomberg's dispatches concerning his Portuguese campaigns are in *Heathcote*.

61. VS/*HP*, 5: 53–56.

62. Brazão, *Relações diplomáticas*, chap. 4; and Prestage, *Diplomatic Relations*, chap. 1.

Marie François Isabelle of Savoy, a cousin of Louis XIV best known as Mlle. Aumale, arrived safely in Lisbon on 2 August 1666 after her naval escort successfully eluded a Spanish fleet sent to intercept her.[63]   Although a huge crowd of dignitaries, including the king and the escrivão da puridade, welcomed her, both Afonso and Castelo Melhor were to rue the day.   So, too, was the queen.   Louis XIV expected her to influence Portuguese policies in favor of his own regime, but she found her way blocked by the king's chief minister. Within a short time she became as disgusted as others at court with the behavior of her husband, who continued his nocturnal debauches and his frequent rages but proved unable to consummate their marriage. In her frustration she turned to the king's younger brother.

As Gastão de Melo de Matos has written, we do not know when this discontented queen and her ambitious brother-in-law commenced their "understandings," but it is evident that each had important allies.   Those of the queen included members of the French embassy, especially her Jesuit confessor, Fr. François de Villes, whereas Pedro's supporters included disgruntled and displaced members of the senior aristocracy, military chieftains, the Lisbon cámara, the artisans' guild, and Manuel Fernandes, superior of the professed house of São Roque.   Their first test of strength occurred in August 1667, when the queen engaged in a shouting match with the secretary of state, António de Sousa Macedo, who proposed to reduce her household expenditures.   Professing herself deeply offended by his arrogant behavior, the queen prevailed upon the king to banish Sousa Macedo from the court and the city of Lisbon.[64]

Since Sousa Macedo, a well-known diplomat and writer, was a close collaborator of Castelo Melhor, the minister recognized his own vulnerability and took measures to strengthen his position.   He doubled the guards within and without the paço da ribeira and stationed units of cavalry and foot soldiers nearby.   But the infante immediately took umbrage at those measures and insisted to the king that they were intended as threats to his personal safety. Although Afonso VI (or his advisors) responded that the king himself had ordered the strengthening of the guards to prevent a recurrence of a recent incident in which an angry crowd pelted the palace with stones, the infante was far from assuaged.

As the factional intrigues within the palace intensified, each side appealed to the Jesuits to serve as intermediaries.   Castelo Melhor himself tried to enlist the help of Manuel Fernandes to calm the infante.   At a three-hour conference in Fr. de Villes's cell in São Roque, the queen's confessor was joined by the rector and two representatives of the escrivão da puridade.   The four men agreed to ask the queen to mediate between the quarreling brothers, and she pretended to do so. But the king refused to accept her intervention except on the condition that Castelo Melhor remain at his side.   Pedro responded that either he or the minister must permanently leave the palace.   As an increasing number of nobles deserted Castelo Melhor and joined the infante's camp, the count realized that he had been

63. António de Sousa Macedo recorded her reception in *Mercurio portuguez* [Aug. 1666], reprinted in J. E. Moreirinhas Pinheiro, ed., *Notícias históricos de Lisboa na época da restauração* (Lisbon, 1971), 50–69. António Alvaro Dória, *A rainha d. Maria Francesca de Sabóia* (Porto, 1944), the only biography, is based upon published materials.

64. Maynard to Arlington, 9/19 Sept. 1667, in PRO/SP89/8/211–13.

outmaneuvered, and on 15 September 1667 he withdrew from the palace, accompanied by 50 cavalrymen, who escorted him to a monastery in Torres Vedras.[65]

If the infante and the queen expected that Afonso would then offer them access to the government, they were soon disappointed. Two weeks after Castelo Melhor's departure, the king recalled Sousa Macedo and threatened to reappoint Castelo Melhor himself, an obvious ploy to demonstrate that he was still king. The queen and the infante responded by intensifying the pressure: on 14 November the tribune of the artisans' guild and members of the Lisbon cámara gained an audience with the king and insisted that he summon the cortes to debate the fate of the nation; Afonso complied reluctantly, realizing that the cortes was likely to depose him. One week later the queen suddenly left the palace and moved to a Franciscan convent. She explained her action in a letter to the king in which she observed that since their marriage had never been consummated, she was entitled to the return of her dowry and license to go back to France. The king responded with one of his predictable outbursts and rushed to the convent, where he was prevented from breaking down its doors by the timely arrival of the infante and friends. The next day (23 November), the king was roused from his sleep by a trusted noble, who informed him that he must either sign a statement voluntarily assigning his authority to Pedro or suffer the embarrassment of having the cortes declare him incompetent to rule. By now totally isolated, the king capitulated. Two days later Pedro issued a decree to the nation justifying his brother's removal.[66]

It is obvious that the Jesuits played only supporting, not principal, roles in this melo-drama. As such, their services continued to be in demand during the months ahead. When the cortes assembled (1 January 1668), it divided into three "congresses," representing the three estates. Each met in the house of one of the leading religious Orders. The nobles gathered in the church of the novitiate, where the Jesuits worked diligently to explain the reasons for the coup and to solicit support for D. Pedro.[67] One of the nation's most pressing concerns was finally addressed on 13 February, when Spain and Portugal signed a peace agreement that left all of the remaining portions of the Portuguese empire, save Ceuta, in Lusitanian hands.

But there remained the problem of dynastic continuity. The cortes urged Pedro to marry his sister-in-law, not only to assure the dynasty's succession, but also because the nation could ill afford to return the queen's dowry (400 contos). Jesuit theologians helped make that union possible by preparing learned statements in support of Marie François's suit of annulment. By a quite irregular procedure, a French cardinal who happened to be the queen's kinsman subscribed to a papal brief declaring her free to marry again. On 2 April, scarcely two weeks after the text of that brief reached Lisbon, the two were joined,

65. The struggle between D. Pedro and Castelo Melhor is reported in a series of dispatches by Southwell and Maynard to Arlington and Williamson in September and October 1667 in PRO/SP89/8/204–55; and in Robert Southwell, "A Narrative of the Proceedings in the Court of Portugal, Concerning the Discharge of the Conde de Castelmelhor . . . and Others," Lisbon, 5/15 Nov. 1667, in [Carte], *History of Revolutions*, 218–319, as well as in Southwell to Arlington, 15/25 and 18/28 Nov. 1667, ibid., 320–36. The count, compelled to reside abroad for many years, was accused of misappropriating large sums from the treasury.

66. In addition to the sources cited in notes 42 and 63, see Mário Sampayo Ribeiro, *1667–1668: A Deestronação de el-rei d. Afonso VI e a anulação de seu matrimónio* (Lisbon, 1938). Pedro's explanatory statement of 23 Nov. 1667 to the Lisbon council is published in Eduardo de Freire de Oliveira, *Elementos para a história do municipio de Lisboa* (Lisbon, 1893), 7: 16–17.

67. *HCJAP*, 3:1, 518–19; VS/*HP*, 5: 204–6.

causing shock throughout European courts and provoking a respectable modern historian to scold the royal couple for their "indecent haste."[68]

There was still the matter of obtaining Rome's blessing. To persuade the pope that these proceedings were legitimate, Fr. de Villes, that "most religious incendiary," as the English envoy labeled the queen's confessor, was dispatched to the pope.[69] But even before Clement IX sanctioned this curious fait accompli, the three estates met in the great hall of the paço da ribeira on 9 June to take their oath to Pedro as their new "governor, administrator, and curer of the kingdom."[70] Although the Jesuits' responsibility for this final act of the Restoration has sometimes been overstated, they had quietly contributed to its achievement. It remained to be seen whether the Society would regain the influence that it had enjoyed during the reign of John IV.

The Petrine Interlude, 1668–1706

The ascendancy of Pedro, first as prince regent and from 1683 until his death as King Pedro II, made possible a welcome interlude between the convulsive middle decades of the century and the superficial luster of the so-called age of gold during the reign of his son, John V (1706–50). Until his final years, Pedro successfully resisted temptations to become engaged in war, so that the nation enjoyed a rare, badly needed interval of peace. Institutionally the Petrine years became the seedbed of eighteenth-century absolutism: the cortes was convoked with decreasing regularity, and not at all after 1698. Royal policies were shaped by traditional councils, such as the councils of state, treasury, and overseas (that is, the empire), whose recommendations reflected the views of the two score or so great landed families that controlled the kingdom.[71]

One stark reality that confronted Pedro's policymakers was the heavy cost of independence and the state's reduced income base. Although no totals on the price of independence have come down to us, there is an abundance of evidence that it was nearly ruinous. In 1645 the cortes reported that annual defense costs ran to 860 contos but that receipts fell short of that amount by 268 contos. By the early 1650s, the annual deficit had been cut to 94 contos, but expenses rose dramatically during the 1660s, when the Spanish threat became most severe. In 1666 the English envoy, Robert Southwell, calculated the annual cost of the king's forces in the Alentejo at 1,440 contos and estimated that current revenues could cover only about 57 percent of that burden. But Southwell's estimate did not include the cost of the king's other armies and probably did not represent more than two-thirds of the cost of the kingdom's land defenses.[72]

68. Prestage, *Diplomatic Relations*, 88. See also VS/*HP*, 5: 204–6.

69. Southwell to Arlington, 10/20 Dec. 1667, in [Carte], *History of Revolutions*, 367; *HCJAP*, 3:1, 519–24.

70. The pageantry is described by Carl A. Hanson, *Economy and Society in Baroque Portugal, 1668–1703* (Minneapolis, 1981), 12–13.

71. Gaspar de Lemos Galvão, "A Description of the Government of Portugall," 15 Nov. 1665, in PRO/SP89/7/74–78, which is the basis of a similarly titled report by Thomas Maynard in the same codex, fols. 357–62. Cf. Hanson, *Economy and Society*, chap. 2.

72. Robert Southwell to Lord Arlington, 6 Nov. 1666 (NS), and an annex entitled "An Estimate of the Espence of the King of Portugalls Army for one yeare," in PRO/SP89/8/290–302. Cf. the breakdown of military and embassy expenses in [Alexandre da Paixão], *Monstruosidades do tempo e da fortuna (1662–1680)*, reprinted by Damião Peres, 4 vols. (Porto, 1938–39), 3: 118–24.

Throughout the Restoration and the Petrine years, the crown resorted to various expedients to raise revenue. Confiscated property, particularly that of "treasonous" families who sided with Spain, was put on the block. The Braganças themselves contributed heavily by selling rents on their vast holdings. The crown repeatedly persuaded the cortes to raise consumptive, customs, excise, and sales taxes: the hated real d'água was "temporarily" revived in 1641 and became permanent in 1668. Although its incidence fell upon commoners, all three estates were liable for the payment of the "military tenth" (*décima militar*), a 10 percent income tax. Despite complaints from the treasury council that price rises would invariably result, silver and gold coins were repeatedly devalued. When all such measures failed to bring in sufficient revenues, the crown resorted to forced loans from merchants and sold annuities (*juros*) to bridge the gap.[73]

One of the heaviest external burdens on the royal exchequer was the payment of Catherine's dowry. Article 5 of the treaty of 1661 specified that half the dowry, consisting of bullion, Brazilian sugars, and Indian jewels, would be placed aboard the fleet escorting the queen to England, whereas the remainder, to be paid in two installments, would be delivered within a year. When the earl of Sandwich called at Lisbon to collect Catherine and her dowry, he discovered that despite their frantic efforts to gather the pledged sums, Portuguese officials could not produce all that was assured and insisted on making up the difference with promissory notes, which, though unsanctioned by the agreement, the earl reluctantly accepted upon the plea of his new queen. Although Duarte da Silva, a prominent Lisbon tax farmer, accompanied the queen to England and declared that he had paid "more than 760,000 crowns" to various assignees, he was imprisoned for nearly a year for failing to provide more.[74] Sir Richard Fanshaw and his successors were continually urged by their superiors to press the Portuguese government for the balance due, but the dowry was not fully paid until about 1684.[75]

Indispensable though foreign mercenaries may have been to the achievement of Portugal's final victory over Spain, they, too, were expensive. Marshal Schomberg received the munificent sum of 7.2 contos per year, nearly as much as viceroys did in eighteenth-century India and 50 percent more than their counterparts did in Brazil. How much French troops in Portugal earned and how they were paid is uncertain; probably they were compensated out of the queen's dowry. The pay of English troops was constantly in arrears, and there were frequent threats to withdraw them because "they are almost starved to death" and "may soon molder away to nothing."[76] Even so, they were probably better off than Portuguese soldiers, among the most badly fed and paid in Europe. And while the soldiers fought not only the enemy but also the exchequer, the ex-king Afonso VI received as

73. Vitorino Guimarães, *As finanças na guerra da restauração (1640–1668) (separata)* (Lisbon, 1941); see also Hanson, *Economy and Society*, chap. 6.

74. Anderson, ed., *Edward Montague*, 125–30; *Heathcote*, 30–31.

75. The statement by Robert Latham and William Mathews, eds., *The Diary of Samuel Pepys*, 11 vols. (Berkeley, 1970), 3: 91 n. 1, that the dowry was never fully paid is mistaken. See Fanshaw to earl of Sutherland, 28 Aug. 1684, in Boxer, *Descriptive List*, 1: 223.

76. Bennet to Fanshaw, Whitehall, 20 Apr. 1663, annexed petition from English officers, in *Heathcote*, 86; Maynard to Arlington, 15 Mar. 1667, in Boxer, *Descriptive List*, 1: 70. Both volumes contain numerous complaints concerning the arrears owed the mercenaries.

part of the bargain by which he relinquished his throne the astounding sum of 16 contos per year.[77]

The economy of Portugal remained precarious throughout the 1670s and the 1680s, limiting the fiscal options the crown could exercise to restore either the domestic or the imperial economy.[78] There were several efforts to organize commercial companies to revive the eastern empire, but none proved successful. The future of the kingdom was, as John IV had said, dependent upon the economic development of Brazil and its satellite, Angola. But down to the early 1690s, both shared the general depression that afflicted the Atlantic world, reflected in falling values for Brazilian sugars and tobacco, the decline of the slave trade, and, in large measure, the cessation of the once-lucrative illicit silver trade between Brazil and the Spanish empire. Indeed, the scarcity of bullion was one of the factors in the contraction of Portugal's trade east of the Cape of Good Hope after 1640. By the 1690s the crown's short-lived efforts to create an industrial infrastructure at home were abandoned, a failing seemingly offset by the discovery of an abundance of gold in the Brazilian interior (see Chapter 23). Remittances from that bonanza were just beginning to reach spectacular levels as Pedro expired.[79]

The figure who presided over Portugal and its empire during these years of readjustment was, as Carl A. Hanson has written, "a complex and contradictory man whose moods ranged from deep and persistent depression to bawdy euphoria." Contemporary assessments of Pedro confirm Hanson's characterization.[80] Although much abler and more dedicated to the tasks of government than his enfeebled brother, Pedro was likewise more attracted to physical than to intellectual pursuits. He was an adept equestrian and loved to challenge the bulls. Like Afonso VI, he frequented the capital's bordellos but, unlike his brother, he made use of their services; as a consequence, by the 1670s he is reputed to have suffered from venereal disease. Although seemingly devoted to his two wives—Marie François, who

77. Southwell, "A Narrative of the Proceedings," 324. The sum was the equivalent of 100,000 English crowns.

78. During the 1670s and 1680s, English representatives to Portugal continually commented on the precarious state of its economy and on the crown's inability to provide forces to sustain the empire, especially in India. E.g., Consul Maynard to Arlington, 9 Dec. 1671 (NS), in PRO/SP89/11/244; Francis Parry to Joseph Williamson, 9/19 Jan. 1671/72, in PRO/SP89/12/3; Charles Fanshaw to [Sir Leoline Jenkins], 26 Oct. 1682, in Boxer, Descriptive List, 1: 195; Fanshaw to earl of Sunderland, 20 Nov. 1684 (NS), in PRO/SP89/16/131–32.

79. For an excellent survey, see Vitorino Magalhães Godinho, "Portugal and Her Empire, 1680–1720," The New Cambridge Modern History, vol. 6, ed. J. S. Bromley (Cambridge, 1970), 509–39; see also Hanson, Economy and Society, chaps. 5–11.

80. The most revealing contemporary accounts of Pedro are the "Mémoire touchant le Portugal" [ca. 1700], generally attributed to the French engineer Teofilo Daupineaut, translated and summarized by A. D. Francis in The Methuens and Portugal, 1691–1708 (Cambridge, 1966), 26–36; and [John Colbatch?], An Account of the Court of Portugal, under the Reign of the Present King Dom Pedro II (London, 1700). See also a series of assessments by Francis Parry to Williamson and Arlington, Sept. 1669 to July 1670, in PRO/SP89/10/135–280, and [da Paixão], Monstruosidades. Concerning the authorship of the Monstruosidades, see Gastão de Melo de Matos, "Panfletos do século xvii," Academia portuguesa da história, Anais, ser. 1, 10 (1946): 187–202. Francis Parry, who was miffed because Pedro for a time refused to accept his credentials, criticized the regent for being a poor Latinist and for being lazy, but other English representatives regarded him as superior to his brother and admired his physical fitness. Parry to Joseph Williamson, 19/29 May 1670, in PRO/SP89/10/224; Parry to Sir Leoline Jenkins, 28 July 1676, in Boxer, Descriptive List, 1: 171; Charles Scarburgh to [earl of Shrewsbury], 10/20 Sept. 1688, in PRO/SP89/16/367–68. I have not seen Tristão da Cunha de Ataide, Portugal, Lisboa e a corte nos reinados de D. Pedro II e D. João V: Memórias históricas de Tristão da Cunha de Ataide, ed. António Vasconcelos de Saldanha and Carmen M. Redulet (Lisbon, 1990).

died in 1684, and Marie Anna de Neubourg, whom he married four years later—Pedro, like Philip IV, fathered his share of royal bastards. Some were consigned to convents; others were shipped off to Brazil; one rose to become an archbishop.[81] But although he was a notorious womanizer, Pedro did nothing for Portugal's fledgling wine industry, for he was a teetotaler. He presided over a lackluster court that was devoid of the pageantry or cultural stimulus associated with those of two of his better-known contemporaries, Charles II of England and Louis XIV of France. Just as the court of his neighbor Charles II of Spain was divided into pro-French and pro-Austrian factions, his own was split between pro-English and pro-French cliques.[82] When confronted with major decisions, Pedro consulted with everyone of consequence, including his Jesuit confessors, before he reached a decision. Judging from the extensive marginalia that he added to the countless reports (*consultas*) the councils of the realm brought to his attention, he seems to have been better informed, tougher minded, and more fully cognizant of the limited options that he possessed than some contemporaries believed.[83] Though he could do little to reverse the long decline of Portugal's fortunes in the East, Pedro aggressively promoted Brazil's territorial expansion and economic development. He promised handsome rewards to prospectors who uncovered long-anticipated mineral deposits and to those who would help make the Amazon a spiceland to replace the sources of cloves, ginger, cinnamon, and nutmeg that Portugal had lost in the East. It was he who sanctioned the bold strike by which Portugal planted an outpost, Colônia do Sacramento, in the estuary of the Río de la Plata (1680) in defiance of Spain's claims of territorial exclusivity.[84]

Contemporaries extolled Pedro's piety and charity. John Colbatch, chaplain of the British Factory, observed, "He is a very Religious Prince, being constantly observant of the Set-Times and Seasons of Devotion; he is often heard . . . saying . . . his Ave-Marias and Pater Nosters. . . . He shews a great Zeal for the Conversion of Infidels . . . and is at great Charges in sending out Missionaries, and sometimes Ships on purpose for that end . . . above all, he is exceedingly charitable and, as I have it from good Hands, expends large Sums that way."[85]

Pedro's piety was reflected in the generally close relationship that he and his immediate family maintained with members of the Society of Jesus. Both of his wives had Jesuit confessors, as did Catherine of Bragança. Pedro himself was served successively by two devoted fathers. The first was Manuel Fernandes (b. 1614–d. 1693), superior of São Roque at the time of Afonso VI's dethronement. Previously he had served in the Azores and in the Algarve, and in the latter he had earned a glowing reputation for selfless service during another visitation by the plague. He had also been rector of the colleges of Fayal and

81. John V to "Dom Joze, arcebispo . . . de Braga, filho reconhecido do rey d. Pedro 2," 3 Oct. 1748, in a codex entitled "Obras de Alexandre de Gusmão," Manuel de Oliveira Lima Library, The Catholic University of America, fol. 1.

82. Parry to Arlington, 19/29 May 1670, in PRO/SP89/10/227–29^v.

83. This conclusion is based upon the reading of many such documents in both the AHU and the HAG.

84. D. Alden, "The Significance of Cacao Production in the Amazon," American Philosophical Society, *Proceedings* 120, 2 (Apr. 1976): 114–15; Mario Rodríguez, "Dom Pedro of Braganza and Colônia do Sacramento, 1680–1705," *HAHR* 38, 2 (May, 1958): 179–208.

85. [Colbatch?], *Account of the Court of Portugal*, 4.

Santarém, and he came to Pedro's attention during the negotiations leading to Afonso's resignation.[86]

From 1667 until his death, Manuel Fernandes was one of Pedro's closest advisors and always sat in on meetings of royal councils. Because he valued his administrative talent, Pedro named Fernandes to membership on the *junta dos três estados*, a board created in 1641 and charged with raising moneys for national defense. That appointment led to an amusing and revealing tempest in a teapot when the disgruntled António Vieira protested to the father general that Fr. Fernandes only accepted the post out of "blind ambition" and that holding it was contrary to the Institute of the Society.[87] This was quite evidently a case of sour grapes, since Vieira had once been an intimate advisor of John IV and was annoyed that he did not enjoy a similar relationship with Pedro. He seems to have mobilized Jesuit leadership in the kingdom against Fernandes, and the father general, Giovanni Paolo Oliva (1664–81), was persuaded to order Fernandes to resign from the board.[88] Fernandes did so only after Pedro's defense of his appointment was rejected by the holy pontiff upon Oliva's insistence. Oddly enough, when another Jesuit, the very able António Rodrigues da Costa, later served as a member of the Overseas Council under John V, no Jesuit complained that his appointment was contrary to the mysterious Institute.[89] In any case, Manuel Fernandes continued as the king's confessor and informal advisor for the balance of his life, although he became less effective after suffering a paralytic stroke in 1687.[90]

When Fr. Fernandes sensed that his end was near, he recommended as his successor Sebastião de Magalhães (b. 1635–d. 1709). Little is known about Fr. Sebastião's background save that he was born in Tangier, taught philosophy at Évora, and was successively rector of Santo Antão, provost of São Roque, and (at the time he became Pedro's confessor) provincial. He evidently came from a respectable family, for his brother served as Portuguese envoy to the court of St. James. Like his predecessor, Fr. Sebastião devoted long hours of each day to his duties at court, for which he received a small salary that he turned over to the procurate of his house. His critics contended that he often forgot to take time to eat and that

86. *ASCJ*, 311–12.

87. Whenever Jesuits found themselves in legal difficulties, they customarily fell back upon the argument that such and such was "contrary to the Institute," by which they meant not only their *Constitutions* but also the directives of the fathers general and the resolutions of the general congregations.

88. The campaign against Fr. Fernandes was carefully organized. Of the twelve Jesuit memorials written to the father general within a single week in November 1677, eleven were opposed to his membership on the board. ARSI, *Lus.*, 75, fols. 184–97. Curiously, neither the writers nor Vieira explained why it was acceptable for Jesuits to perform secular administrative tasks in the East but not in Europe. See Chapter 13.

89. For a sketch of the exceedingly competent and astute Fr. da Costa (b. 1656–d. 1732), see Charles R. Boxer, *The Golden Age of Brazil, 1695–1750* (Berkeley, 1962), 367–68.

90. António Franco, *Imagem da virtude em o noviciado da companhia de Jesus no real collegio de Jesus de Coimbra em Portugal*, 2 vols. (Évora and Coimbra, 1719), 1: 587–97. Both *HCJAP*, 3:1, 528–37, and Azevedo, *António Vieira*, 2: 194–96, explore Fr. Fernandes's role at court and his tribulations with Vieira. Edgar Prestage, ed., "Correspondencia do conde de Castelomelhor com o P. Manuel Fernandes e outros (1668 a 1678)," *O Instituto* 64 (1917): 387–404, 471–84, 558–74, 645–53; and 65 (1918): 82–98, 151–64, and 197–205, provide the text of 78 letters the count wrote to the confessor from exile in Spain, Italy, and France. They are replete with "proofs" of the count's diligence in office, lamentations about the "ruin" of his family and his estates since his fall, and pleas for the confessor's intervention in his behalf at court. One suspects that Prestage was correct in concluding that Fr. Fernandes, whose responses are missing, was not as friendly toward the onetime Jesuit foe as the count imagined and that he recognized the impossibility of Castelo Melhor's return as long as Marie François and the duke of Cadaval, a leading noble, were set against him.

he rarely left the palace before 10 or 11 P.M. because he was constantly reading dispatches submitted to him for his opinion. Because of his reputed sagacity, he was asked to continue working at the paço da ribeira after Pedro's death, but he declined in order to prepare his soul for the expected hereafter.[91]

As Colbatch reported, Pedro was always keenly interested in the development of the overseas missions, especially those of the Jesuits. When missionary representatives came to court, they found the king attentive to their accounts of the status of their enterprises and solicitous of their needs.[92] Pedro was often dissatisfied with the progress of other Orders in India and held up the Jesuits to them as models of zeal and dedication.[93] He rejected a petition by the Augustinians to found a seminary at Sena, Mozambique, stating that the site should be awarded to the Jesuits because "experience has shown that they are more disinterested and more zealous for the service of God and the conversion of souls" than any other religious body.[94] The king was especially concerned about the promising missions in China (see Chapter 6). Although he recognized that priests with scientific backgrounds, a short suit among the Portuguese, were in particular demand there, he insisted that as many Portuguese Jesuits as possible be sent to China, even if that meant stripping some of the other provinces.[95] When the settlers of Maranhão ousted the Jesuits in 1684, Pedro ordered stern measures against the rebels and strongly approved the drafting of the famous mission ordinances of 1686, the foundation of Jesuit preeminence in the Amazon during the following century (see Chapters 19 and 23).

In view of the king's apparent ardor for the Jesuits, it is curious that neither he nor his wives were especially liberal in their financial support of the Society. It is true that Pedro and Marie François built a chapel in the church of São Roque, where the French queen was later buried and to which she left a small bequest,[96] but Pedro, who required that 6,000 masses be said for his soul upon his demise and 500 a year thereafter, saw no need to contribute any of his substantial estate to the Jesuits or to any other religious body.[97] It is also true that Marie Anna de Neubourg made a contribution toward the construction costs of the new college of Beja, founded in 1695, and that the procurator-general of Portugal presented her with a *Life* of St. Francis Xavier prepared at her request by António Vieira, praised her aid to the Beja college, and pleaded with her for support for the Brazil province, but

91. Daupineaut, "Mémoire," 27. Although the English minister to Portugal did not fully trust Fr. Sebastião, he clearly respected him: John Methuen to earl of Nottingham, 28 Nov. 1693, in PRO/SP89/17:1/98. See also *ASCJ*, 403–5; Franco, *Coimbra*, 2: 603–9; and *HCJAP*, 3:1, 537–39.

92. Johan Philipe Betendorf, "Chrónica de missão dos padres da companhia de Jesús no estado do Maranhão" (ca. 1699), in *RIHGB* 72 (1909 [1910]): (369–97, 420–24).

93. King to Board of Missions, Estado da India, 22 Mar. 1687, and king to viceroy of India, 20 Mar. 1697, in HAG/*LM* 52, fol. 425ʳ and 61, fol. 263ʳ.

94. King to viceroy of India, 15 Mar. 1697, in George M. Theal, trans. and ed., *Records of South-East Africa*, vol. 4 (London, 1899), 489–90.

95. *CR*, 23 Mar. 1689 and 19 Mar. 1690, in HAG/*LM* 54, fol. 151ʳ and 55, fol. 189ʳ; king to viceroy of India, 12 and 18 Mar. 1693, in HAG/*LM* 58, fols. 45ʳ, 59, fol. 6ʳ; viceroy to king, 2 Jan. 1698, in HAG/*LM* 61, fol. 91ʳ.

96. "Testamento da rainha Dona Maria Francesca de Saboya," 20 Nov. 1683, CMP/*P*, 9: 92–95.

97. Pedro's testament, dated 19 Sept. 1704, is published in *As gavetas da Torre do Tombo*, vol. 6 (Lisbon, 1965?), 227–32. For his estate, see Virgínia Rau and Eduardo Borges Nunes, eds., *Inventário post mortem del-rei d. Pedro II* (Lisbon, 1969).

his appeal went unanswered.[98] In fact, all six Jesuit colleges founded in the kingdom and the Azores between 1645 and 1695 were privately endowed rather than state financed.[99]

Moreover, Pedro's personal affection for the Jesuits did not prevent him from opposing them whenever he saw fit. In the late 1680s and early 1690s, there was a serious clash between the king and the leading religious Orders over their refusal to divulge the extent of their land holdings. (The context of that dispute will be examined in Chapter 17.) A decade earlier an even more protracted controversy between the king and the Society occurred over the status of New Christians in the kingdom and proposed limitations on the powers of the Inquisition. The New Christian community, consisting of persons of Jewish origin, was imperiled in May 1671 when a young simpleton of New Christian background entered a village church northwest of Lisbon, stole some plate, and did some physical damage to the altar before making his escape. Even before the perpetrator was apprehended, tortured, and brutally executed, the New Christian community was held collectively responsible for his crime and became the object of widespread riots and protests. Pedro himself called for stern measures against presumed guilty parties, and the Holy Office was only too eager to comply. The Lisbon branch alone rounded up 90 merchants, including some of the crown's leading tax farmers, and cast them into dungeons; other New Christians were sent to Guarda and other places in the interior to be jailed on various pretexts. In May 1672, the inquisitor general invoked sumptuary laws against all persons previously convicted of charges of Judaism, depriving them of the right to travel by coach, by litter, or mounted on a horse, or to wear silks or display jewels or objects made of precious metals. In addition, all such persons and their descendants were forbidden to occupy governmental posts, receive honors, or bid on government revenue contracts. To defend the community against such threats, Manuel da Gama de Pádua, a wealthy New Christian merchant from Lisbon, went to Rome that same year to seek the papacy's protection.

The merchant's arrival in the Eternal City led to the Jesuits' involvement in the New Christian cause and to a renewal of their confrontations with the Holy Office. Manuel da Gama sought out António Vieira, who had been living in Rome since 1669 and was seeking the canonization of Inácio de Azevedo and the 39 martyrs killed en route to Brazil in 1570 (Chapter 3). Vieira and Manuel da Gama were old acquaintances as a result of the latter's services as a sugar broker for Vieira's brother in Bahia. After listening to the merchant's concerns, Vieira introduced him to Fr. Baltasar da Costa, the provincial of Malabar. Fr. Baltasar had come to Rome seeking assistance for his province, which had been devastated by the Dutch conquests of the 1660s (see Chapter 8). He was convinced that Portugal could recover lost ground in India because of the outbreak of war between France and Holland and because the Dutch had caused much resentment among the Hindu pepper potentates. Out of their discussions emerged a proposal that Fr. Baltasar presented to D. Pedro through the agency of his confessor, Manuel Fernandes. At first sight, the New Christian proposal seemed to promise a great deal to the state at little cost. The

98. [Colbatch?], *Account of the Court of Portugal*, 115–22, quotes at length from the procurator-general's address to the queen.

99. They included the colleges of Elvas (1645), Fayal (1652), Setúbal (1655), Portimão (1660), Alfama (Lisbon, 1679), and Beja (1695), though neither the church nor the college of the last-named was finished by the time of the Jesuits' expulsion. *HCJAP*, 3:1, 17ff., 25ff., 30ff., 34ff., 37ff., and 47ff.

community offered to form a commercial company modeled on the Brazil Company to revive Portugal's trade with India, to defray the cost of sending 5,000 troops to India immediately and additional reinforcements later on, to provide funds for the support of missionaries in the subcontinent, and to render other forms of financial assistance to the crown. All that the community required in return was a general pardon from Rome exempting its members from punishment, including the confiscation of their properties, by the Portuguese Holy Office for alleged religious transgressions.

Vieira and his colleagues warmly supported the New Christian plan. Vieira promised the king's confessor that he would do everything possible to advance it in the curia, but he added, "My endeavors will be very circumspect (*muito interiores*) because, as Your Reverence will comprehend, since it is opposed by the Inquisition, the father general does not wish any member of the Company [of Jesus] to work in its behalf openly, although everyone in the Company, including the father general, considers the measure is not only appropriate (*conveniente*) but necessary and urgent."[100] In the kingdom, the entire faculty of the University of Évora signed a petition urging the regent to permit the New Christian community to pursue its appeal to the pope. Another petition bearing the same message was signed by the confessors of D. Pedro and his queen, by senior Jesuit administrators from Lisbon to Coimbra, and by the archbishop of Lisbon, himself a former deputy of the Holy Office. Certain other prelates and several leading nobles also supported the appeal.

For a time, the Jesuits expected to defeat the Holy Office, and the papacy itself seemed to be in their corner. In an obvious gesture to curry favor with the regent, the pope approved a major ecclesiastical reform in Brazil, one that raised the prelate of Salvador to archbishop and created three new bishoprics. As the concerned English envoy Francis Parry noted, "All this is said to sweeten the Prince toward the Jews; whose businesse goes well in Rome."[101] As the years passed, death or a change of heart diminished the number of the Jesuits' supporters in the kingdom, but the Jesuits themselves remained nearly united in favor of the New Christian proposal until it became obvious that it stood no chance of success.

The bond that joined Jesuits and New Christians in seventeenth-century Portugal was not based upon doctrinal affinities, or even on personal friendships. Even António Vieira, the most visible champion of the community, though not (as one historian has contended) the campaign's directing genius, admitted that Manuel da Gama was his only close New Christian friend.[102] Despite the fact that the Society's third father general was himself a New Christian, the Society did not welcome New Christian applicants and, as will be seen in Chapter 11, gradually excluded New Christians already enrolled as it bowed to the socioreligious prejudices of the time. What drew Jesuits and New Christians together was partly their shared status as unconventional minorities who were convenient scapegoats for the failings of the state and its agents, partly their more rational views regarding the economic development of the empire, and partly their joint concern with the principles of elementary justice. It is worth emphasizing again that the Jesuits were *not* hostile toward the Inquisition per se. Even one of its most luminous victims, António Vieira, wrote, "It is a very

100. Vieira to Manuel Fernandes, 3 June 1672, in João Lúcio d'Azevedo, ed., *Cartas do Padre António Vieira*, 3 vols. (Coimbra, 1925–28), 2: 610.
101. Parry to Joseph Williamson, 30 Mar./9 Apr. 1675, in PRO/SP89/13/66.
102. Azevedo, *António Vieira*, 2: 123 n. 5.

holy tribunal, [one] absolutely necessary, but it can not be either holy or a tribunal if it is governed by procedures (*estilos*) that are unjust and unjustly practiced to the detriment of not only temporal affairs . . . but of innocence, of truth, and of the very faith itself. . . . Justice and more justice, innocence and more innocence, this is the foundation of everything."[103]

For a time Pedro appeared to be favorably impressed by the arguments advanced for the New Christian proposal. He recognized that neither the state nor Old Christian merchants were likely in those depressed times to achieve any real recovery in the East. Why not permit the New Christians to try? Louis XIV's war against the Dutch and the separate Anglo-Dutch conflict that also began in 1672 offered a rare opportunity for Portugal to regain some of the lost lands in the Orient. Accordingly, in July 1673, the regent again permitted the New Christians to submit their case to the pope and promised to support it.

By then, however, what Vieira termed the "fortress on the Roscío" was marshaling its own forces in opposition to the plan.[104] In March 1673, the council of the Inquisition circulated the proposal to each of its three branches. Each responded that it was absolutely opposed to any concessions to the New Christians. As Parry astutely observed, "The Inquisitors know very well that by *testimonias abertas e publicadas* it will be impossible to convict any Jew, therefore they make all the Interest they can to hinder it."[105] But the inquisitors claimed to see only duplicity, treachery, and heresy in the plan. They predicted that if the New Christians gained a general pardon, the kingdom would soon be swarming with crypto-Christians from foreign lands, a contention that must have carried special weight in a time of depression. The message from the Holy Office was clear: the recovery of India was not worth the corruption of Portugal's uniquely pristine form of Christianity.

The formidable allies of the Inquisition fully subscribed to its view. They included the Lisbon mob that went about the streets in hooded robes chanting, "Long live the faith. Death to Judaism." The crowd made menacing gestures to Jesuits hurriedly passing them, and its members posted threatening messages on the doors of Jesuit houses, especially São Roque. One Holy Office official was heard to suggest that a Jesuit church deserved to be incinerated because the fathers were protectors of heretics. It was even intimated that the royal confessor himself was worthy of burning. The tribune (*juiz do povo*) of the artisans' guild of Lisbon traveled to Caldas da Rainha and warned the prince regent that an insurrection in the capital was imminent. The archbishop of Évora also joined the lists as the self-proclaimed representative of the prelates of the realm. He beseeched D. Pedro not to protect heretics. One of the most prestigious of the prelates was Pedro Vieira da Silva, the septuagenarian bishop of Leiria who had served under both John IV and Afonso VI. Noting that every time the crown had made concessions to New Christians it had suffered reverses overseas, he implied that either the deity or the New Christians were responsible for all the setbacks Portugal had suffered. Members of other religious Orders duly signed memorials opposed to the grant of any concessions to the New Christians. Though the faculty of the University

103. Vieira to D. Rodrigo de Meneses, 31 Dec. 1672, and Vieira to Manuel Fernandes, 9 Sept. 1673, in Azevedo, *Cartas*, 2: 549 and 649.

104. This famous phrase appears in Vieira's letter of 5 May 1674 to Manuel Fernandes (Azevedo, *Cartas*, 3: 41) in which he observed, "Só faltava uma fortaleza por conquistar, que era a do Roscío, onde se encastelaram tantos traidores como naquele tempo [referring to the reign of Afonso VI] se experimentou e hoje se experimenta pôsto que com menos declarados pretextos."

105. Parry to Williamson, 30 Mar./9 Apr. 1675, in PRO/SP89/13/66–67.

of Évora supported the cause, that of the University of Coimbra (excepting its Jesuit College of Arts) opposed it.

For two years Pedro adhered to his promise to the New Christians. But his resolve was obviously shaken in September 1673 by the disclosure of a plot, encouraged by the Spanish ambassador and joined by a former secretary of state under Afonso VI and other supporters of the captive king, to kill the regent and his family, restore Afonso to his rightful throne, and marry him to the widow of the late Philip IV of Spain.[106] Although the conspiracy was quashed and its leaders executed, Pedro began to have second thoughts about the possibility of curbing the Inquisition's authority. In December he notified the Portuguese envoy to Rome that he was opposed to any changes in the regulations governing the activities of the Holy Office. Later, when the nuncio approached him, Pedro forbade him to speak about the New Christian affair.[107]

In January 1674, the cortes convened to approve the proposed succession of the infante as Pedro's heir and to vote the renewal of taxes. But the members were much more concerned about the New Christian question than about such matters. The ecclesiastical estate adamantly opposed any concessions to the community, even if the papacy mandated them. Some prelates even urged Pedro to expel the Jesuits from his dominions, or at least from Lisbon. A few members of the second estate spoke in favor of the New Christians, but in the end all three estates informed the regent in April that they were unanimous in their opposition to the concession of any liberties to the New Christians. The following month the queen herself wrote the pope to defend the "just and holy tribunal of the Inquisition." When he learned of her action, Vieira saw behind it the prompting of the turncoat Fr. de Villes, whom he suspected of having received orders from Versailles, which had ambitions itself in India and had no desire to see any improvement in Portugal's situation there.[108]

Despite the ominous news from Lisbon, Vieira remained optimistic that something could be salvaged from the New Christian plan. By May 1674, he knew that his adversaries in Rome had gained strength with the arrival of agents from the Portuguese prelacy and the Holy Office, sent in part because those interests distrusted the Portuguese resident.[109] Still, Vieira believed that the papacy might authorize a reform of the Holy Office's procedures if the cortes simply went home, the kingdom remained calm, and the Inquisition's methods could be demonstrated to be juridically defective.[110] Evidence soon arrived that its procedures were indeed faulty: acting in response to testimony furnished by its informers, the Évora tribunal had executed two 40-year-old nun siblings, despite the fact that they had lived religious lives for many years and protested to the end that they remained fervent Christians. Indignantly, the papal secretary of state, acting for the ailing pontiff, issued two briefs, one on 3 October, the other on 20 October 1674. By the first he suspended indefinitely all judicial proceedings by the Portuguese Inquisition until they could be reviewed in Rome. By the

---

106. For the several relocations of the deposed king, see VS/*HP*, 5: 209–10.
107. Parry to Williamson, 30 Mar./9 Apr. 1675, in PRO/SP89/13/66ᵛ.
108. Vieira to Ribeiro, 22 Feb. 1675, in Azevedo, *Cartas*, 3: 153–54.
109. Azevedo, *Cristãos novos*, 304–5.
110. Vieira to Manuel Fernandes, 5 May 1674, in Azevedo, *Cartas*, 3: 39–40.

second the papacy insisted that no matter what position the cortes adopted, all Catholics in Portugal retained the right to appeal their cases to Rome.[111]

Vieira saw in the papacy's action an opportunity to strengthen the regent's hand in support of the New Christians, but he was wrong.[112] The papal briefs merely stirred up new unrest in Portugal and inspired new anti-Jewish, anti-Jesuit placards. One declared, "Whoever wants to be a Jew, heretic, sodomite, and marry three times, go to speak with Padre Manuel Fernandes, confessor to His Majesty, and with Manuel da Gama de Pádua and Pedro Alvares Caldas, who have bulls from Padre Quintel [the papal nuncio] for everything."[113] Although the father general ordered all Jesuits to maintain absolute silence concerning the controversy, one father defended the rights of the Holy See so fervently that he was transferred from Lisbon to Santarém.[114] Vieira himself was under constant pressure from Pedro to return to the kingdom. Eventually he did so, but only after he obtained a rescript from the papacy permanently exempting him from the clutches of the Portuguese Holy Office and after submitting his final defense of the right of New Christians to solicit papal protection.[115] Vieira arrived in Lisbon in late August 1675, and soon discovered (as he had feared) that although the regent wanted him home, he was not prepared to find a place for him in the royal palace.

Vieira played no role in the last phase of the unsuccessful New Christian appeal; nor did any of his fellow Jesuits. Following Clement X's death in 1676, his successor, Innocent XI, asked that several of the Inquisition's files be sent to Rome for review. But its officers, acting on instructions from the crown, refused to comply, and for a time the government sealed the files. After a five-year stalemate, two files—one dating from 1611, the other from 1629—were finally forwarded. The papacy accepted such token compliance as adequate, and on 22 August 1681 it notified the inquisitor general that it found the evidence to be satisfactory. The fearsome autos-de-fé resumed the following January, but António Vieira was no longer in the kingdom to witness them. Resigned to the obscurity from which he had come, the old Jesuit had sailed to Bahia one year earlier, and there he remained for the final sixteen years of his turbulent life.[116]

Vieira and his colleagues learned important lessons from their disastrous—and ultimately fruitless—efforts to defend the legal rights of Portugal's New Christians. Influential though their Order was, it was no match for the fortress on the Roscío. Its doors could not be broken down without the strong resolve of the crown itself. It may be that Pedro lacked that resolve, but one must remember that he was in his mid-twenties when the controversy began, that he was only acting ruler as long as Afonso VI lived, and that after a half century of political turmoil and disasters overseas, no significant elements in the kingdom other

111. Azevedo, *António Vieira*, 2: 172.

112. Vieira to Manuel Fernandes, 15 Dec. 1674, in Azevedo, *Cartas*, 3: 132.

113. As quoted in Hanson, *Economy and Society*, 101.

114. *HCJAP*, 3:1, 500.

115. Azevedo, *António Vieira*, 2: 349–51.

116. Apart from the sources cited, the foregoing is based on Azevedo, *António Vieira*, 2: 118–47, 164–82, and 203–11. See also Azevedo, *Cristãos novos*, 290–322; *HCJAP*, 3:1, 491–502; Richard Graham, *António Vieira and the Economic Rehabilitation of Portugal* (São Paulo, 1978), 179–90; and Hanson, *Economy and Society*, 89–103.

than the New Christian community and the Jesuits wanted radical change. On the contrary, everyone else favored conformity and stability. The Jesuits always enjoyed a reputation for being realists. They doubtless recognized the conformist pressures under which Pedro labored. Certainly they did not condemn him for his reversal on the New Christian question. The year after Pedro's death, Miguel Dias, Portuguese assistant in Rome, delivered the customary laudatory sermon lamenting the sovereign's passing. He pronounced Pedro "one of the greatest sovereigns there has ever been in Portugal."[117]

The Jesuits should have learned another lesson from the experience of the 1670s: despite their reputation, they were not really cut out to be revolutionaries in any European society. Although proximity to the crown did not always ensure that they would have the royal ear, or that the measures they favored would sway the royal heart, the setbacks they suffered in the kingdom during this period were minor by comparison with the losses they and the state sustained during the seventeenth century in the empire and beyond, as will be seen in the next three chapters.

117. *Serman nas exequisas del rey N. S. d. Pedro II que pregou o r. p. Miguel Dias . . . assistente pelas provincias de Portugal em Roma: Na igreja de S. Antonio no anno 1707* (Rome, 1707), in ANTT/CJ/80, no. 140.

CHAPTER 6

Mandarins and Martyrs:
Gains and Losses in the East During
the Seventeenth Century

Enterprises in these parts are of great moment for God's service, lest the [other]
Religious should obstruct us in it later . . . as is their wont.

—Nicolas Pimenta to Aquaviva, 1 Dec. 1601

WHILE THE PORTUGUESE in the kingdom were preoccupied with problems related to national survival during the seventeenth century, most Jesuits serving in fields east of the Cape of Good Hope had very different concerns. Building upon its sixteenth-century foundations, the Society expanded its operations on a broad arc extending from the Japanese archipelago to the highlands of Ethiopia. Such activities led to unexpectedly severe reverses but also produced exceptional achievements. At times the Society's fundamental goal—the conversion of Asian and African leaders to the Christian faith—seemed within reach. If the Jesuits' activities aroused xenophobia and stimulated intense orthodoxy, both of which led to the Jesuits' permanent expulsion from two once-promising lands, Japan and Ethiopia, the Society found some compensation in new enterprises in Southeast Asia, Bengal, and Ceylon. But its most spectacular gains occurred, despite repeated persecutions and intense friction with competing religious Orders, in imperial China, where a group of multitalented, multinational fathers attained eminent positions of cultural influence and achieved coveted respectability for the Christian faith in Asia's largest nation-state.

The End of the Japan Enterprise

At the beginning of the seventeenth century, the vice-province of Japan was the most illustrious mission field the Society possessed beyond Europe. The death of Hideyoshi (1598) marked the end of the second phase of anti-Christian harassment by the shogunate. According to Fernão Guerreiro, the chronicler of the Society's achievements in the overseas parts of the Portuguese Assistancy at this time, "It appeared to the Christians that they had escaped from a great captivity and that after a dark and stormy night a new dawn had brought them a clear and serene day. Each looked at the other and they congratulated one another for the end of their travail because with the death of the tyrant they expected that the fathers would no longer be threatened and that the Christians would be spared further persecution."[1] In fact, the new dawn proved to be ephemeral. Increasingly threatening clouds led to an unexpectedly dark night during which the visible Society disappeared in Japan, a night after which there would be no tomorrow.

The opening years of the seventeenth century represented a period of apparent stability for the Society in the archipelago. Its facilities there included two colleges, one in Arima, the other in Nagasaki; a professed house; two seminaries (which were attended by more than 300 students); two rector's houses; and twenty residences. The number of priests, brothers, assistants (dojuku), and servants (*moços de serviço*) who constituted charges upon the Society's precarious resources exceeded 800.[2] During the years 1600–1614, twelve to twenty recruits a year arrived in Japan, a number barely sufficient to replace those who left for other assignments or died or were dismissed. In 1603 there were 122 fathers and brothers in the vice-province; eleven years later that number had grown by only four. To be sure, despite the misgivings of Fr. Cabral and others, the racial barrier was finally breached: the first two Japanese priests joined the Society in 1602, and the first Japanese secular priests were ordained two years later. Still, there were only ten indigenous clergymen in the islands by 1612, although by 1614 better than eight out of ten brothers were Japanese, as were upwards of 250 dojuku.[3] According to Guerreiro, in 1606 there were close to 750,000 Christians in Japan; modern scholars are convinced that the actual number lay somewhere between 250,000 and 300,000.[4] The Jesuits themselves claimed no more than 212,000 in 1609, and it is unlikely that this number was exceeded in later years.

Most of the new believers lived on the southern island of Kyushu, where they were especially concentrated in fiefdoms around Nagasaki. After 1599, the number of conversions began to fall precipitously. That year, 40,000 accepted the new faith, as did more than 30,000 the following year. By 1601–2, the number of neophytes fell to only 9,000. The annual letter for 1603–4 is conspicuously silent on the subject of conversions. That of 1605 states that the number of baptisms "for all Japan" exceeded 5,400, whereas the annual letter for 1606–7 claims that the number of new souls that year exceeded 7,500.[5] In his account for 1601–2, Fr. Guerreiro admits that the evangelical effort was somewhat disappointing, but assures his readers that the falloff in quantity was counterbalanced by the recruitment of many persons of high status. Though it is true that the Jesuits deliberately aimed at the conversion of the elite, they won few converts among the great lords. According to Murdoch, there were 200 daimyos in the empire. Only seven or eight became Christians. Considerably

---

1. *RACJ*, 1: 66.

2. "Catálogo das pessoas da vice província ... de Outubro de [1]603," *MHJ*, 441–55. The remarks that follow are based upon this catalogue and those of 1609 and 1614 (*MHJ*, 516–39 and 579–92), as well as the *RACJ* series.

3. Cf. *CCJ*, 226.

4. *RACJ*, 2: 220; *CCJ*, 230 and 187; and Charles R. Boxer, "The Clandestine Catholic Church in Feudal Japan, 1614–1640," *History Today* 16 (Jan. 1966): 54.

5. *RACJ*, 1: 78 and 169; 2: 7 and 220; and 3: 117.

more samurai and district bureaucrats did so, along with farmers, artisans, and traders.[6] But neither the Jesuits nor their rivals made successful inroads in the *bafuku*, the government of the shogunate.

The Jesuits were bedeviled in Japan by the admission of their spiritual rivals, the Franciscans, Dominicans, and Augustinians. As noted in Chapter 3, in 1585 a papal brief issued at the behest of Alessandro Valignano declared that the Society held a spiritual monopoly in Japan. But the Franciscans defied that brief in 1593 when they arrived from Manila. Despite Jesuit protests and the martyrdoms of 1597, the Friars Minor remained in the archipelago. In response to the Mendicants' pleas, Clement VIII modified the earlier brief in 1603: friars would be permitted to enter the archipelago provided that they came via Lisbon, Goa, or Macao. But the Franciscans were unwilling to accept such restrictions and joined with the Dominicans and the Augustinians to pry the door open even further. The result was the abandonment of all restrictions in 1608, when Paul V permitted the friars to enter Japan regardless of their base of operations.[7]

Despite all of the heat generated by the Mendicants' struggle to gain entry into Japan, few friars actually came. By 1614 there were only nine Franciscan priests and five lay brothers; nine Dominicans; and three Augustinian priests and one novice. Most of them resided in Kyushu.[8] But what they lacked in numbers, the Mendicants made up in fractious feuds with the Jesuits, echoes of the destructive internecine conflicts that discredited the Church in other missions, notably in Ceylon, Mozambique, and the Amazon. More critically, the feuds among the Orders and between Portuguese and Spaniards enhanced the misgivings of the chief regent, Ieyasu, concerning the presence of the Iberians within his domains.[9]

Tokugawa Ieyasu (b. 1542–d. 1616), founder of the house that was to supply Japan's shoguns for two and a half centuries, had been a rising star during the days of Nobunaga. He became Nobunaga's ally and, for a time, Hideyoshi's rival, until he married the latter's daughter. The lord of vast domains, Ieyasu made Yedo, the fortress-town that would later become Tokyo, his center in 1590. On the eve of Hideyoshi's death, he was named chief of the Board of Five Regents, but he was not content to be merely *primus inter pares* and subsequently took the field against his rivals, whom he defeated at Sekigahara in October 1600. In 1603 the emperor confirmed his dominance by naming him to the vacant office of shogun.[10]

Initially the Jesuits were enthusiastic about the ascendancy of Ieyasu, whom Fr. Guerreiro described as "a great king, a soldierly genius, a valiant captain," and "a friend of justice."[11] The Jesuits had some reason to subscribe to such an estimate, for Ieyasu had informed their leader that everyone in the islands was free to determine his own religious preference and that the Jesuits could be assured that neither they nor their neophytes would be molested in the Nagasaki district. In 1603, when the fathers were in financial difficulties

6. Ibid., 1: 169; James Murdoch and Isoh Yamagata, *A History of Japan*, vol. 2, *During the Century of Early Foreign Intercourse (1542–1651)* (London, 1925), 642.

7. *CCJ*, 239–41.

8. Pedro Morejón, "Acerca de la división de las províncias entre las religiones en Japón" (1614), in *MHJ*, 759–66; Lope de Vega, *Triunfo de la fee en los reynos del Japón*, ed. J. S. Cummins (London, 1965), fig. 2.

9. Lope de Vega, *Triunfo*, xxix–xxxv; Murdoch and Yamagata, *History of Japan*, 2: 490–91.

10. Murdoch and Yamagata, *History of Japan*, 2: 125, 271, 387–456.

11. *RAJC*, 2: 7.

because of the loss of a silk carrack in which they had invested, Ieyasu himself gave them a substantial donation. Over the span of two decades, João Rodrigues, the talented court interpreter and later the author of an invaluable analysis of Japanese culture, maintained a cordial relationship with Ieyasu. It was he who arranged for the official reception that Ieyasu granted Fr. Luís de Cerqueira, bishop of Japan, in 1606, as well as for the visit by Fr. Francesco Pasio, the vice-provincial, the following year.[12]

For quite different reasons, Ieyasu and Fr. Rodrigues, the vice-province's procurator, were both keenly interested in the silk trade. Whenever the silk ships came to Nagasaki, it was Rodrigues who mediated between the Portuguese merchants and their Japanese buyers, and it was Ieyasu who became accustomed to receiving tribute in the form of gifts from Portuguese captains. Ieyasu's desire to expand the silk trade led indirectly to the Jesuits' downfall. Since the early 1590s, several of the daimyos, taking their cue from the Portuguese, had outfitted vessels for ports in Indochina, Macao, Indonesia, and the Philippines to import silks and other luxuries. Ieyasu encouraged that trade but insisted on regulating it through the issuance of so-called red-seal passports.

The arrival of a red-seal vessel in Macao late in 1608 led to an unexpected series of crises. The Japanese sailors paraded belligerently through the port streets, alarming the Chinese community, which feared and hated the Japanese. The Chinese demanded action by the Portuguese authorities, who were caught in the middle. After a riot during which a Portuguese magistrate was wounded, the Japanese retreated to a pair of houses where they barricaded themselves and refused to surrender. The acting governor, André Pessoa, then attacked one of the houses and slaughtered its occupants. Through ecclesiastical intervention, the sailors confined to the second house agreed to leave in return for a promise of their liberty. But the governor seized their ringleaders, jailed them, and later ordered one of them strangled.

André Pessoa was also the commander of the next year's silk carrack. Before leaving for Nagasaki, he compelled the surviving Japanese sailors to sign a statement accepting full responsibility for the trouble they had caused. Although he expected that statement to protect him from reprisals, he soon discovered otherwise. Upon reaching the Japanese port on the *Madre de Deus* in late July 1609, he was greeted with unexpected hostility by the port governor. When his envoy went to call upon the shogun, he was kept waiting while Ieyasu dealt with representatives of the newly established Dutch factory on the island of Hirado, west of Nagasaki. Subsequently, when the shogun learned the Japanese version of the Macao affair from the survivors, who naturally asserted that the declaration they had signed had been exacted under duress, he contemplated teaching the Portuguese a lesson. He was further impelled to do so after conversations with a former acting governor of the Philippines, whose ships, bound for New Spain, had been driven to the Japanese east coast by a storm. The ex-governor encouraged Ieyasu to believe that the Spaniards could replace the Portuguese as silk suppliers and could also provide skilled miners from Mexico who would develop newly discovered silver mines in the archipelago. The shogun then ordered the daimyo of Arima, whose ship had been involved in the Macao incident, to confiscate the *Madre de Deus* and arrest Pessoa. When the Portuguese captain-major learned of the

12. *CCJ*, 180–83; Michael Cooper, S.J., *Rodrigues the Interpreter* (New York, 1974), 100–101, 194–95.

shogun's intentions, he tried to make a hasty departure from Nagasaki, but on Epiphany Day (6 January 1609) he found his ship becalmed and surrounded by 30 hostile vessels. After the attackers set the *Madre de Deus* afire, Pessoa deliberately lighted its magazine and blew up the ship rather than permit it and himself to fall into the hands of his adversaries.[13]

As Fr. Michael Cooper has written, "The sinking of the *Madre de Deus* was a heavy blow for the Jesuit mission in more ways than one."[14] Since most of the cargo of silks and silver went down with the ship and since the Jesuits owned a share of that cargo, they suffered severe losses, as did the Portuguese merchant community. Significantly, the Jesuits were rescued by a loan provided by a merchant who had recently been the beneficiary of a Jesuit decision in a commercial dispute between him and a Japanese Christian investor. Even though Ieyasu had insisted that the Jesuits determine the merits of the case, the fact that they had found against the Japanese plaintiff angered both the anti-Christian governor of Nagasaki, Hasegawa Sahyóe (Sahioye), and the city's magistrate, Murayama Tóan, then presumed to be a lapsed Christian. Those two convinced Ieyasu that João Rodrigues, the court interpreter, was a source of trouble between the shogunate and the Portuguese. Accordingly, in March 1609, Ieyasu ended Rodrigues's 33 years of service in the archipelago by banishing him. Rodrigues's successor was the famous "Kentish-man, born in a Towne called Gillingham" named Will Adams, but best known today as John Blackthorne.[15]

Between 1611 and 1614 the aging Ieyasu accumulated testimony adverse to the missionaries and their faith from various sources, including John Blackthorne, the representatives of the new Dutch factory, swaggering Spanish visitors, and militantly hostile Japanese foes. The most important of the last was Hasegawa Sahyóe, who addressed an influential memorial to the shogunate in which he labeled the Christians as "a fanatical and pernicious sect, dangerous to the Empire, and ripe for any mischief." What especially alarmed Ieyasu was the suggestion that unless he acted against the missionaries, then perceived by their critics as advance agents of Iberian imperialism, the daimyos would lose confidence in him and revolt.

The final decision came in two imperial edicts in January and February 1614 that charged the missionaries with disseminating "evil law," showing disrespect for traditional doctrines, and threatening national security. Therefore, the missionaries were ordered to leave Japan as soon as shipping could be arranged, and their neophytes were required to abjure their alien faith and become members of a Buddhist sect. Even though the Jesuits had had advance warning of the exclusionary decrees (gained from Hasegawa Sahyóe himself), they were unable to get them modified or rescinded. At a most inopportune time, their leader, Bishop Luís de Cerqueira, died. Hasegawa Sahyóe then blocked the provincial's efforts to

13. The Macao incident and the loss of the *Madre de Deus* have been recorded many times, most fully by C. R. Boxer, *The Affair of the Madre de Deus: A Chapter in the History of the Portuguese in Japan* (London, 1929), several times reprinted. See also Cooper, *Rodrigues*, 261–67. The most recent study of the ultimately unsuccessful efforts by Spaniards to negotiate a military, commercial, and cultural agreement with the shogunate is Josef Franz Schütte, S.J., "Don Rodrigo de Vivero de Velasco and Sebastián Vizcaíno in Japan," in Ernesto de la Torre Mesuco, comp., *International Congress of Human Sciences in Asia and North Africa* (Mexico City, 1981), 77–100.

14. Cooper, *Rodrigues*, 263 and 266 n. 1.

15. Blackthorne was, of course, the hero of James Clavell, *Shogun* (New York, 1975). On the beginnings of Dutch commercial activities at Hurado, see Grant K. Goodman, *Japan: The Dutch Experience* (London, 1986), 11–17.

send a representative to Ieyasu. When it became evident that the decision would not be reversed, there were extraordinary popular demonstrations of support for the missionaries in Nagasaki, some of them spontaneous, others orchestrated by the Jesuits. Nevertheless, on 7–8 November 1614, the visible Society came to an end in Japan with the deportation of 88 Jesuits and 50 dojuku as well as a number of friars. Two-thirds of the exiles boarded a silk carrack and a Chinese junk and sailed to Macao; the remainder made their way to Manila.[16]

But the invisible Society, together with members of the other Orders, persisted in Japan for another 30 years while their European and Japanese members tried to sustain the surviving believers against increasingly adverse odds. When the general expulsion occurred, 41 ecclesiastics remained more or less secretly behind. Among them were 27 Jesuits, 19 of whom were priests, and 5 secular Japanese priests. Small contingents of reinforcements slipped back to the archipelago almost yearly for several decades. By 1618 there were still 33 Jesuits in the islands, perhaps the apogee of the invisible Society, but their ranks were reduced to 17 nine years later. Although the daimyos who had supported the fathers in the past either had been liquidated or had apostatized, the underground priests were supported by networks of confraternities, and especially by loyal dojuku.[17] For a few years the fathers maintained a low profile and escaped the wrath of the shogun, who was preoccupied in 1615–16 with a titanic struggle against his rival, Toyotomi Hideyori, son of Hideyoshi. When the latter died after his castle in Kobe had fallen, five missionaries, two of them Jesuits, were among the survivors; but they were not menaced by the victors.[18] Ieyasu expired soon after, and the Jesuits briefly hoped that his successor would relax the expulsion order. That hope was dashed in September 1616, however, when the new shogun, Tokugawa Iemitsu, issued a decree reiterating the terms of the edicts of 1614, continuing the banishment of the missionaries, and forbidding Japanese, under threat of being deprived of their property and burned alive, to traffic with messengers of the alien faith or to offer them hospitality.[19]

By 1617 the new shogun began to crack down upon the foreigners. That year the first missionaries—one representative of each Order—were executed for their defiance of the edicts. Two of them, the Dominican vice-provincial and an Augustinian, deliberately sacrificed themselves in order to strengthen the resolve of Japanese believers to keep the faith. The first European layman to perish was Domingos Jorge, who was executed in 1619, in part for providing asylum for priests but also for serving as a conduit for messages from Macao to the faithful. A Dutch vessel that captured one of his ships gleefully turned over to Japanese authorities incriminating letters promising that as soon as the number of faithful reached sufficient strength, warships would be sent to assist them against the shogunate. Three years later, in September 1622, there occurred the famous "Great Martyrdom" in Nagasaki when 30 Christians were beheaded and 25 others were roasted to death. Among the victims were eight Dominicans, four Jesuits, three Franciscans, one Augustinian, and twenty brothers. That execution was witnessed by a crowd of thousands who, unlike the

16. *CCJ*, 308–27; Cooper, *Rodrigues*, 268; George Elison, *Deus Destroyed: The Image of Christianity in Early Modern Japan* (Cambridge, Mass., 1973), 161; *MHJ*, 629–30.

17. Boxer, "Clandestine Catholic Church," passim; *CCJ*, 328ff.; Cooper, *Rodrigues*, 330.

18. Murdoch and Yamagata, *History of Japan*, 2: chap. 17.

19. Ibid., 2: 612–17.

masses attending the autos-de-fé in Portugal or Spain, expressed their sympathy for the suffering martyrs by reciting prayers and chanting psalms.[20]

The executions were intended to convince the faithful of the futility of noncompliance, but the demonstrations indicated that far too many loyalists remained. Consequently, the government forbade future demonstrations and intensified the persecution. It also gained some notable apostates. One was Thomas Araki, a cashiered priest whom the Society expelled on morals charges and who repaid it by revealing its support networks.[21] The second was the famous ideologue Fabian Fucan, who in 1605 wrote a tract exalting the merits of Christianity compared with Buddhism, Confucianism, and Shinto, and in 1620, twelve years after abjuring his faith, wrote a second tract, *God Destroyed*, demonstrating the precise opposite.[22] From the perspective of the Society, however, the third apostate, Cristóvão Ferreira (b. 1580–d. 1650), was far more devastating to its image.

Ferreira, born in Torres Vedras, north of Lisbon, entered the Society at sixteen. After completing studies in philosophy and theology, he was assigned to the Japan station. By 1603 he was studying Japanese in Macao and became sufficiently proficient that he subsequently preached in that language. He went to the Japanese isles around 1610 and remained underground there after the general expulsion. In 1617 he took his final vows and traveled surreptitiously in the central archipelago, regularly sending out reports concerning the status of the Church and its notable martyrdoms. By 1633 Ferreira was vice-provincial, the most senior Jesuit remaining in the islands. That year he was captured and subjected to a newly devised form of torture by which the victim was bound, inverted, and suspended over a pit of excreta. Some lingered for days before expiring, though the torture's primary intent was to exact renunciations of the faith rather than to cause death. In Ferreira's case, that technique proved successful. He became a convert to Shinto, wrote tracts condemning Christianity, and served as a merciless interrogator of missionaries captured almost as soon as they landed on Japanese soil. The objective of some of those missions was to save the soul of this major delinquent, but Jesuit reports that Cristóvão Ferreira finally came to his senses and died in the pit seem to have no factual basis.[23] Ferreira's apostasy was far from unique. Two of five European Jesuits who arrived in Japan in 1642 also renounced their faith, as did nine of those who came the following year. Among them were another vice-provincial and the last Jesuits to set foot on Japanese soil for centuries to come.[24]

20. Ibid., 2: 616 n. 15 and 622; *CCJ*, 342–43. For biographies of Jesuit martyrs who perished in Japan, see *JSM*, 60–62, 159–62, 185–89, 274–76, 302–3, 319–24, 334–36, and 415–16. The Society celebrated the "glorious" martyrdoms of its members in Japan by printing detailed accounts of their sufferings. For one example concerning the deaths of ten members in 1627, see ANTT/CJ/68, no. 430.

21. *CCJ*, 334 and 389–90.

22. The second part of Elison's *Deus Destroyed* is a translation of Fucan's refutation of Christianity.

23. The most comprehensive account of Ferreira's activities during these years is Elison, *Deus Destroyed*, 185–91, 196–203, and 208–11.

24. *CCJ*, 391 and 445. António Franco, the leading biographer of Portuguese Jesuits, was among those writers who believed that Ferreira died a martyr to the faith: *Imagem da virtude em o noviciado da companhia de Jesus na corte de Lisboa* (Coimbra, 1717), 366–74. Shusaku Endo, *Silence* (1969), trans. William Johnson (New York, 1980), is a popular, controversial novel concerning Ferreira and other Jesuits who suffered during the persecution. The translator's allegation (p. ix) that by the end of the sixteenth century there was "a thriving Japanese [Christian] clergy" in the islands is nonsense.

Such missionaries traveled to Japan not with the aim of saving Christianity there but with the expectation of dying a martyr's death, the idée fixe of most of those who defied the edicts of 1614 and 1616. Even before Ferreira's recantation, it was obvious that the days of the invisible Society were numbered. In a desperate (but futile) attempt to save the silk trade, renewed in 1612, Macaonese officials refused to transport missionaries in the annual carrack after 1630. But that trade was doomed as Japan turned inward and became increasingly hostile toward nearly all foreigners. After an unprofitable decade, the English voluntarily gave up their factory in 1613; their later attempts to return were rebuffed. Only the Dutch would be permitted to trade via the island-prison of Deschima in Nagasaki harbor, and they did so under humiliating conditions.[25]

The end of Portuguese access to Japan, and with it the disappearance of the last hope of the Society to regain lost ground there, came in the aftermath of the Shimabara rebellion (1637–38), a long-expected uprising of Christians on a peninsula near Nagasaki and on the nearby island of Amusaka. The rebellion was preceded by famine and by merciless exactions from the peasants by greedy landlords. Most of the participants were peasants, but Murdoch and Yamagata insisted that the leadership was provided by ex-samurai Christians who lost their positions when the persecutions began in 1613–14. Although the uprising started as a form of economic protest, it became something of a religious crusade. An estimated 35,000 rebels occupied and fortified an abandoned castle, where for months they resisted a vastly larger force organized by daimyo clients of the shogun. Eventually the rebels ran out of food and powder and were overwhelmed.[26] Although neither the Jesuits nor Portuguese merchants had anything to do with provoking or directing the uprising, the bafuku believed that they had. Accordingly, in 1639, it closed the door from Macao to Nagasaki. The following year an embassy from Macao, one that contained not a single Jesuit, ended in the arrest and execution of all 61 of its members.[27]

The Restructured Japan Province

After the events of 1639, the Society had no realistic chance of returning to Japan, though it kept alive the vision of doing so by retaining the appellation "the Japan province." The college of Madre de Deus in Macao, where most of its members resided, became its headquarters.[28] The province's membership shrank disastrously: from a peak of 233 in 1609, it diminished to only 58 by 1648 and to about 45 for the balance of the century.[29] The province thus lost 75–80 percent of its staff during that dismal century. Nevertheless, about a third of its remaining members were redeployed from Macao to India (on educational or fiscal assignments), Tibet, Laos, Cambodia, Siam, and especially the two Sinitic states of Vietnam, Tonkin in the north and Cochin China in the center.[30]

25. Murdoch and Yamagata, *History of Japan*, vol. 2, chap. 23.

26. Ibid., chap. 22; *CCJ*, 375–83; Arimichi Ebisawa, "The Jesuits and Their Cultural Activities in the Far East," *Journal of World History* 5 (1959): 363ff.

27. *CCJ*, 383–85.

28. *RACJ*, 3: 115; *MHJ*, 1058–63 and 1068–81.

29. See Appendix B.

30. Besides the sources cited in the following notes, this section relies upon an undated but mid-seventeenth-century historical sketch of Jesuit activities in Southeast Asia written by Fr. João Alvares:

In 1615 the Society began hedging its bets by entering Vietnam. Late the preceding year, just as the refugees from Japan were arriving in Macao, a Portuguese silk merchant, Fernão da Costa, came back from a trip to the market center of Faio-fo, near Quang-nam, and informed the fathers that the inhabitants of Cochin China seemed ripe for conversion. As Alexander of Rhodes, one of the leading missionaries and publicists for seventeenth-century Vietnam, wrote, "Seeing the doors to Japan closed, our superiors believed God permitted this misfortune that those [sent] to Cochinchina might open it to the holy Gospel."[31] The man who led the way was Francesco Buzoni (b. 1576–d. 1635), a Neapolitan who, though apparently no great linguist, became mission superior in Cochin China in 1615 and remained there for the balance of his life. By 1620, Fr. Buzoni's staff consisted of three additional padres and one brother.[32] Four years later they were joined by five European priests, including Rhodes and one Japanese interpreter.[33] They arrived during the beginnings of what would become a half-century struggle between the rulers of Tonkin and Cochin China over certain sources of revenue.[34] That conflict proved to be both an advantage and a handicap to the Jesuits. Since the Nguyén rulers of the south controlled a smaller population than their rivals did, they were often willing to tolerate the Portuguese merchants and Jesuit missionaries as long as they received shipments of bronze cannon from a foundry in Macao, which then produced the finest artillery in the East. C. R. Boxer has contended that the Buddhist rulers of Cochin China remained "fundamentally hostile to the propagation of the Christian faith in their territory" but tolerated the doings of the missionaries as long as cannon and men to serve them came from Macao.[35] In any case, by 1625 the ten missionaries serving in Cochin China had succeeded in presenting their message in all of its major centers.[36]

The apparently successful beginning of Christianity in the south prompted Jesuit leaders to plan a campaign in the north. Because of the hostilities between the two kingdoms, the Jesuits were obliged to transfer missionaries from the south to the north via Macao. That is the route that Rhodes took in 1626–27, when he began a three-year campaign near modern Thanh-Hôa, south of Haiphong harbor. As Ricci and his successors did in China, Rhodes attempted to win over the king of Tonkin with presents of a clock and sandglass and with discussions of mathematics and astronomy. And, like Jesuit missionaries in Japan, northern

BA/JA/49-IV-66, fols. 77ᵛ–84ᵛ. George Bryan Souza, *The Survival of Empire: Portuguese Trade and Society in China and the South China Sea, 1630–1754* (Cambridge, 1986), 113–14, provides a brief account.

31. Alexandre de Rhodes, *Divers voiages . . . en la China e autres roiaumes de l'Orient*, 2d ed. (Paris, 1666); Solange Hertz, trans., *Rhodes of Viet Nam: The Travels and Missions of Father Alexander de Rhodes in China and Other Kingdoms of the Orient* (Westminster, Md., 1966), chap. 18.

32. "Catálogo . . . dos padres e irmãos que estam na missam de Cochinchina . . . anno de 1620," in *MHJ*, 884–85.

33. Rhodes, *Divers voiages*, chap. 18; Hertz, *Rhodes of Viet Nam*, 49. Rhodes wrote Nuno Mascarenhas (the Portuguese assistant) on the eve of his departure for the Orient reporting on his travels from Vila Viçosa to Lisbon via Évora and indicating with obvious enthusiasm how much he looked forward to his future service there. Rhodes to Mascarenhas, Lisbon, 2 Apr. 1619, in ARSI, *Lus.*, 74, fol. 148 (in Portuguese).

34. D[aniel] G[eorge] E. Hall, *A History of South-East Asia*, 4th ed. (London, 1981), chap. 24.

35. C. R. Boxer, "Asian Potentates and European Artillery in the 16th–18th Centuries: A Footnote to Gibson-Hill," *JMBRAS* 38, 2 (1965): 156–72, at 167.

36. Rhodes, *Divers voiages*, chap. 19; Hertz, *Rhodes of Viet Nam*, 51.

India, and Ethiopia, Rhodes and his successors pursued the strategy known as "from the top down"; that is, they sought to convert members of the royal palace, especially women, bureaucrats, and military officers, in the hope that the ruler would then become persuaded to impose Christianity upon his subjects. Although Rhodes enjoyed considerable success in Tonkin, he was banished by royal order in 1630 because of the Jesuits' insistence that converts become monogamous, a demand that infuriated the royal concubines and eunuchs. But others replaced him, and by mid-century the Jesuits claimed to have baptized more than 188,000 persons.[37]

One who remained skeptical of these achievements was Fr. Sebastien Manrique, an Augustinian monk who visited Cochin China in 1639. The Porto-born father observed that "those who talk about maintaining and increasing Missions, speaking merely on information more suited to the views of the speakers than to truth and reason, may see that it is by no means as easy as they imagine to maintain this Mission in Cochin-China ... [which] requires a new Moses with new wonders."[38] Though he may not have been exactly a new Moses, Alexander of Rhodes was a tireless evangelist. After his exile from the north, he worked in China, mainly around Canton, for a decade before returning to Cochin China, where he again labored from 1640 until 1645. There he found, as he put it, that "a single Jesuit counts as if he were a whole college."[39] Because of the constant threat of persecution, Rhodes remained concealed by day and traveled by sampan or hammock by night to minister to the Jesuits' increasing flock; but, as he himself admitted, their achievements were greatly facilitated by courageous catechists, both Vietnamese and Japanese, who took over much of the preparatory work before baptisms, risking and sometimes losing their own lives doing so.[40]

After being arrested on numerous occasions and threatened with death at least once, Rhodes was expelled from Cochin China in 1645. He made his way back to Europe, where he hoped to recruit hundreds of workers for the Vietnamese vineyard. He recognized that the Society could not provide such numbers itself and appealed to the pope for support. When that failed to produce more than the appointment of a few bishops—and those over the objections of the archbishop of Goa—Rhodes returned to France and interested the government of Louis XIV in his enterprise. The result was the founding of the first organization of secular missionaries, the Société des Missions Étrangères, in 1659. That group did send missionaries to Vietnam but lacked the resources to sustain that effort. By the end of the century, its members were replaced by Dominicans from the Philippines.[41] In protest against both papal and French intrusions in violation of the exclusive ecclesiastical rights earlier popes had conferred upon the rulers of Portugal, the prince regent, Pedro, ordered Jesuits under his control to leave

37. Rhodes, *Divers voiages*, chaps. 23–27; Hertz, *Rhodes of Viet Nam*, 76; António Francisco Cardim, *Batalhas da companhia de Jesus na sua gloriosa provincia de Japão* (1650), ed. Luciano Cordeiro (Lisbon, 1894), remains a major source on Jesuit operations in Vietnam.

38. *Travels of Fray Sebastien Manrique, 1629–1643*, trans. C. Eckford Luard and H. Hosten, S.J., *HS*:2, 61 (1927), 64.

39. Rhodes, *Divers voiages*, chap. 36; Hertz, *Rhodes of Viet Nam*, 101.

40. Rhodes, *Divers voiages*, pt. 3.

41. Hall, *History of South-East Asia*, 440.

Vietnam in 1682. Despite changes in spiritual representation, there were about 150,000 Christians in the two Vietnams in about 1700, an achievement of no small significance when compared with that of China, where far more missionaries were committed during the century.[42]

The Eastern Rival:

The Enterprise in China

The history of the Jesuits in China during this period bears striking similarities to their experience in the Japan province, but there are also significant differences. Here, too, were persecutions and occasions when the Society's members were driven underground. Here, too, were serious doctrinal differences between Jesuit pioneers and late-arriving religious rivals. As in Vietnam, the papacy intervened with disastrous consequences. But despite a relative lack of both personnel and financial resources, the Jesuits achieved about as many conversions in China by the end of the century as their colleagues in Japan had before 1614, and their leaders attained prestigious positions in the Ming and Ch'ing governments that were never matched by the Society in Japan.

Although Matteo Ricci's death was a serious blow to the China mission, then consisting of thirteen Jesuits serving in five residences, his self-selected successor, Niccolò Longobardo, elected to turn the founder's death to the mission's advantage.[43] He called upon the resourceful, talented, remarkably energetic Nicholas Trigault, a newly arrived Belgian priest, to proceed to Rome as his personal emissary to solicit urgently needed assistance for the mission.[44] He gave Ricci's manuscript, containing its impressive assessment of Chinese culture, to Trigault and asked him to translate it into Latin, the lingua franca of scholars of that time, and to arrange for its publication along with two annual letters, the second of which Trigault had prepared, concerning the status of the enterprise in China. The Belgian was also to persuade the papacy to authorize the use of the liturgy in Chinese for the Society's neophytes, to raise funds to relieve the mission of its critical shortage, to obtain as many as 50 recruits for the mission,

42. A[ntónio] da Silva Rego, *Curso de missionologia* (Lisbon, 1956), 580–81. In a series of annual letters between 1659 and 1696 (ARSI, *JapSin*, 48, fols. 26–82), the provincials presented a hopeful image of their province's potential, but those reports do not conceal the grim realities that they continually faced in the revamped province. Very little seems to survive concerning Jesuit activities in Siam in this period, but see J. Burnay, "Notes chronologiques sur les missions Jésuites du Siam au xvii⁰ siècle," *AHSI* 22 (1953): 170–202.

43. Longobardo (or Longobardi) (b. 1565–d. 1655), a Sicilian, was superior from 1610 until 1622 and served in China for 58 years. *RJC*, 153–54.

44. Trigault (b. 1577–d. 1628) was born in Douai in present-day Belgium and died after suffering a mental breakdown and hanging himself, a most unusual step for a Jesuit. *RJC*, 275–76. I have not seen C. Deshaisnes, *Vie du P. Nicolas Trigault* (Tournai, 1864). Edmond Lamalle, S.J., "La Propaganda du P. Nicholas Trigault en faveur des missions de China (1616)," *AHSI* 9 (1940): 49–120, is a masterly analysis of Trigault's mission to Europe and includes an annotated Latin text of his 2 Jan. 1617 report to his China confreres on his activities. See also George H. Dunne, S.J., *Generation of Giants: The Story of the Jesuits in the Last Decades of the Ming Dynasty* (Notre Dame, 1982). As Dunne correctly observes, Trigault's commission as procurator was technically improper, since the provincial had not approved his appointment.

and to persuade the father general to agree to a complete separation of the China and Japan enterprises.[45]

Trigault discharged his commission brilliantly.[46] It took him 22 months to reach Rome via a sea voyage to Goa and the caravan route from Basra. He arrived in the Eternal City seriously ill but with a nearly complete translation of Ricci, whose masterpiece became a best-seller and brought great prestige to the Society, as did publication of its annual letters.[47] Within a remarkably short time the papacy allowed the liturgical and other concessions the superior had requested. Paul V also provided the nucleus of the vitally important library of sacred and technical works that Trigault took back to China. As he traveled about Italy, the Germanies, Belgium, and the Iberian Peninsula, the procurator received many handsome gifts and promises of financial support for the mission. So many volunteered to return to China with him that he was obliged to restrict their number so as not to offend the xenophobic leaders of the dual Iberian empire. Nevertheless, when Trigault left Lisbon in the spring of 1618, he was accompanied by 22 recruits. Ten of them were Portuguese, but the most conspicuous were the Milanese Giacomo Rho (b. 1592–d. 1638), the German Johann Adam Schall von Bell (b. 1592–d. 1666), and the Swiss-born Johann Terrenz Schreck (b. 1576–d. 1630), best known as Terrentius. All three would become major disseminators of Western culture in China.[48] Five of the recruits died of fever off the coast of Africa, and two others, including Trigault's brother, expired soon after their arrival in Goa. Only 8 of the 22 recruits ever served in China, far fewer than Longobardo had sought. But the wastage of personnel during the long and difficult voyages from Europe would always be a serious handicap to the staffing of the China enterprise.[49]

By the time Trigault reached Macao, the China mission was under serious attack. Less than two years after the Society had been expelled from Japan, some of its members were arrested, detained, then deported from China while the rest remained underground.[50] In 1616 Shên Ch'üeh, vice-president of the Nanking Board of Rites and spokesman for certain Buddhist leaders and disapproving bureaucrats who opposed the presence of the Jesuits, wrote the first of three memorials to the throne in which he denounced the

45. Aquaviva agreed to the separation but died before essential paperwork was completed. His successor, Mutio Vitelleschi, left the final decision up to the Visitor, Francisco Vieira, who was reluctant to approve the division and did not authorize it until on his deathbed, so that the vice-province did not come into being until 1623. Dunne, *Generation of Giants*, 168–72.

46. Dunne was normally balanced in his assessments, but his conclusion that Trigault's trip was "a curious melange of scintillating success and over-all failure" (ibid., 179) seems excessively harsh. It is true that the concession to perform the liturgy in Chinese was never implemented, that the establishment of the vice-province was delayed, and that fewer recruits arrived in China than Longobardo wanted, but those failings were hardly Trigault's fault.

47. Ricci's commentaries appeared in three Latin editions (Augsburg, 1615; Lyon, 1616; and Cologne, 1617), an Italian edition (Naples, 1622), and a Spanish (1621) and a Portuguese (1623) edition. Samuel Purchas also excerpted Ricci in the first volume of his *Hakluytus Posthumus* (1625). Lamalle, "Propaganda," 100 n. 33.

48. For bibliographical data on each, see *RJC*, 215, 241–43.

49. According to the calculations of an eighteenth-century writer, 127 (33.7%) of the 376 Jesuits who set out from Europe for China between 1581 and 1712 died before reaching their destination. George Pray, *Historia controversarum de ritibus sinicis* (Budapest, 1787), 250, cited in *NBBJC*, 329. Since I have not seen Pray, I cannot vouch for the accuracy of his oft-cited statistics, which, for example, are uncontested by the compiler of *RJC* (see 324n).

50. Whether the Japanese expulsion decrees of 1614 sparked the anti-Jesuit persecution in China two years later remains a puzzle. I know of no authority who suggests a connection, but it seems likely.

fathers as agents provocateurs of a foreign power and accused them of having entered the empire illegally and of attempting to subvert traditional values. Their crimes were such, he maintained, that they deserved to be deported, if not executed. The Jesuits were staunchly defended by one of their most important converts, Shanghai-born Hsü Kuang-ch'i, a distinguished scholar-bureaucrat who would rise to become chancellor of the empire.[51] After the court ignored the memorials, the president of the Nanking Board of Rites simply ordered the arrest of the Jesuits and their supporters. Four Jesuits were seized in Nanking and temporarily imprisoned; their supporters were flogged, and some of their youthful converts were sent to Buddhist monasteries for reindoctrination. Elsewhere, however, the edict was indifferently enforced, and the Jesuits were able to find refuge among their sympathizers.[52]

Within a few years the heat was off, and additional Jesuits, including Trigault, Schall, and two of those expelled in 1616, were able to enter the empire. Then a new threat appeared: a Manchu invasion began in 1618 and put to flight Ming forces sent to repel it. Two years later Hsü Kuang-ch'i suggested that the court ask Portuguese authorities in Macao to send artillery and instructors to help ward off the Manchus. In September 1622 a demonstration of several Portuguese cannon occurred in Peking, but unfortunately one of the pieces burst, killing its Portuguese server and two Chinese assistants. That "unhappie accident," as one Jesuit called it, served as the pretext for another anti-Jesuit campaign by Shên, who contended that the fathers were associates of the antigovernment terrorist organization known as the White Lotus Society. Again the priests were compelled to go into hiding. But Shên soon fell from grace, and the persecution quickly abated, although the Jesuits remained for some years without official authorization to be in the empire and were prevented from opening Christian edifices and from preaching publicly.[53]

For several reasons, the Society's position began to improve during the remainder of the 1620s. First, the discovery (ca. 1623) of a Nestorian tablet dating from the eighth century and of evidence that several T'ang emperors had encouraged that form of Christianity gave the faith reintroduced by the Jesuits a respectability that it had hitherto lacked.[54] Second, by the mid-1620s Longobardo and Manoel Dias Júnior[55] were permitted to reopen a house Ricci had acquired in the capital twenty years earlier. They were authorized to do so after

51. See Lewis A. Maverick, "Hsü Kuang-Ch'i, A Chinese Authority on Agriculture," *Agricultural History* 14 (Oct. 1940): 143–60, which discusses the relationship that developed between this important Christian convert and the Jesuits.

52. John D[ragon] Young, *Confucianism and Christianity: The First Encounter* (Hong Kong, 1983), chap. 4, is the most recent of a substantial literature concerning anti-Christian movements in Ming and early Ch'ing China. For others, see the bibliographical note in John W. Witek, S.J., *Controversial Ideas in China and in Europe: A Biography of Jean-François Foucquet, S.J. (1665–1741)* (Rome, 1982), 2 n. 2. For the 1616 persecution, see Dunne, *Generation of Giants*, chap. 9.

53. Dunne, *Generation of Giants*, 157–60; Cooper, *Rodrigues*, 335–36; C. R. Boxer, "Portuguese Military Expeditions in Aid of the Mings Against the Manchus, 1621–1647," *Tien Hsia Monthly* 7 (Aug. 1938): 24–36, esp. 24–26, the source of the quotation.

54. Dunne, *Generation of Giants*, 193.

55. There were two Manoel Diases serving in the vice-province at this time. The elder (b. 1559–d. 1639) was called *o velho* or senior and the younger (b. 1574–d. 1659) *o novo* or júnior, a common practice employed within the Society to prevent confusion. *RJC*, 76–77.

they convinced members of the Board of War that Macaonese authorities would respond favorably to a new appeal from the Mings for cannon and instructors to ward off the Manchu threat. Third, such aid, in fact, was forthcoming: in November 1628, seven bronze and three iron cannon and a party that included the Jesuit Visitor and João Rodrigues, the quondam court interpreter in Japan, left Macao for Peking. Although most of the expedition proceeded only as far as Nanchiang, the two Jesuits got to the capital, where Rodrigues was able to present the first of a series of memorials in behalf of the Society.[56]

Then the Society began its long association with the preparation of the imperial calendar, the accuracy of which assumed exceptional importance in China because the emperor was considered to be the mediator between heaven and earth. The calendar was utilized to determine auspicious and ominous days to undertake or to avoid all sorts of public and private acts, including the launching of military campaigns, the appointment of officials, weddings, funerals, the planting and harvesting of crops, and many other activities of daily life. Inaccuracies in the calendar, therefore, reflected upon the stature of the emperor himself.[57] For years Chinese officials had been dissatisfied with the computations of the official astronomers, many of them Muslims. The approach of a solar eclipse in June 1629 provided an opportunity to test comparatively the predictive accuracy of the traditional Chinese method, the Muslim technique, and the Western method. After Hsü Kuang-ch'i appeared to demonstrate the superiority of Western computations, the emperor charged him with the establishment of a new calendar bureau and the preparation of a more reliable calendar. In September 1629, Hsü Kuang-ch'i named Longobardo, Terrentius, and two Chinese converts as members of that bureau. Although Terrentius, a onetime physician, mathematician, and academic associate of Galileo, died almost immediately, he was succeeded by Giacomo Rho and Adam Schall. By 1633 Hsü himself was gone, but by then Schall had effectively become head of the bureau.[58]

The new status attained by the so-called Peking Jesuits enabled members of the Society to intensify their proselytizing efforts both in the provinces and in the capital itself. By 1637 they claimed more than 40,000 Christians, a number said to have grown to between 60,000

56. Boxer, "Portuguese Military Expeditions," 24–31; Cooper, *Rodrigues*, 336ff.
57. Ho Peng-Yoke, "The Astronomical Bureau in Ming China," *Journal of Asian History* 3, 2 (1969): 137–57.
58. Dunne, *Generation of Giants*, 208–15 and 220. Whether the official calendar really required reform, as Ho Peng-Yoke and others contend, is disputed by Joseph Needham and Wang Ling, *Science and Civilization in China*, vol. 3 (Cambridge, 1959), 258–59, 422–47. That issue is part of a larger debate concerning the quality of the intellectual transmission of the Jesuits to China during the seventeenth and eighteenth centuries. Nathan Sivin persuasively argued that although at the outset the Jesuits' Chinese writings on scientific matters "reflected conservative but open-minded current thinking in Europe ... [they] gradually became hopelessly obsolete and out of touch with practice as well as theory" because of the Church's prohibitions on discussions of the implications of the Copernican heliocentric theory and of the Galilean system (1616, 1633). Whereas Pasquale M. D'Elia, S.J., contended that most Jesuits were "probably ... Copernicans at heart," Sivin argues precisely the contrary. Nathan Sivin, "Copernicus in China," *Colloquia Copernicana* 2 (Warsaw, 1973): 62–122, esp. 69, 85–86 n. 45, and 88–89. Cf. D'Elia, *Galileo in China: Relations Through the Roman College Between Galileo and the Jesuit Scientist-Missionaries (1610–1640)* (Cambridge, Mass., 1960), esp. vii, 51–52, and 57–59. Sivin's position is substantially that stated earlier by Needham and Ling (esp. 449–57), and both appear to accuse the Jesuits of responsibility for China's cultural backwardness in the later centuries, ignoring D'Elia's fundamental point: for the Jesuits, science was merely a means to a larger end, which was the conversion of China to Christianity, not the harmonization of Western and Eastern science.

and 70,000 within three years. By 1641 the Society possessed fifteen residences, "fifteen sturdy bulwarks," as its annual letter proudly reported. Twenty-three "soldiers for Christ" were distributed among eleven of the empire's fifteen provinces.[59] Among the converts were high mandarins, court ladies, eunuchs, relatives of the emperor, and a significant number of scholars.[60]

But such growth was accompanied by new perils. In the early 1630s the Jesuits' spiritual monopoly among Christians in China was ended by the arrival of the first Spanish Franciscans and Dominicans. Bypassing Macao, they landed on the coast of Fukien, where they behaved in a fashion more reminiscent of the Spanish spiritual conquest of Latin America than of the subtle approach favored by Ricci and his followers. The inevitable rivalries that developed between the Mendicants and the Jesuits immediately imperiled Jesuit operations in Nanking, where the Jesuit residence was reopened in 1634 after being closed for seventeen years, and in Fukien province. In the long run, the theological quarrels that ensued between Jesuit fathers and the friars led to a century-long fratricidal debate, the Chinese Rites controversy (see Chapter 23). That debate also created the specter, unsubstantiated by extant political realities, of an omnipotent Society of Jesus capable of doing whatever it pleased in the Chinese empire.[61]

It was during the early stages of this internecine strife that the Ming dynasty, oppressive, bitterly divided, and incompetently led, fell apart. In 1642, on the eve of its collapse, Adam Schall was called upon to assist with the defenses of the capital and to manufacture cannon, an assignment that gave him mandarin status. Schall's reluctant involvement in the foundry, which was expected to produce 500 small guns, ended his incipient school of astronomy but failed to save the dynasty, which was betrayed by its own officers.[62]

The collapse of Ming rule and the firm establishment of the Ch'ing dynasty throughout the empire required a decade and a half, beginning in 1644. Those were chaotic years for the citizens of the empire and for the Jesuits themselves. Seven of them perished in the fighting. The remainder were badly scattered. The Society's leadership in China became confused and indecisive. Some fathers attached themselves to the last Ming pretender, and one even served as his ambassador to the papacy. Others were apparently taken captive by a particularly bloodthirsty tyrant in the southwest.[63] But one who kept his head and his Japanese sword sharp was the redoubtable Adam Schall, who remained in the capital while it was being incinerated around him by a vengeful bandit and would-be emperor. Schall stood with sword in hand near the gate of his compound as looters prepared to enter. They quickly reconsidered.

Remarkably, before the end of 1645, less than eighteen months after the Manchus' arrival in Peking, Schall gained their confidence and appointment as director of the astronomy bureau, where he was soon joined by several companions. The significance

59. "Annua da vice província da China de 1641. Do estado temporal da China em comum," 7 Sept. 1642, in BNL/cod. 772, fol. 1ʳ.

60. *RJC*, 330.

61. Dunne, *Generation of Giants*, chaps. 14–15.

62. Ibid., 317–18. For an assessment of the causes of the Ming collapse, see Lawrence D. Kessler, *K'ang-hsi and the Consolidation of Ch'ing Rule, 1661–1684* (Chicago, 1976), 2–14.

63. Dunne, *Generation of Giants*, chaps. 11–12.

of that appointment has been perceptively summarized by Nathan Sivin: "Thanks partly to their technical skill, partly to the personal esteem which they commanded, and partly to their prompt support for the alien invaders, Schall and his colleagues ... had been given operational control of the Bureau ... [putting them] in the best possible position to make converts among highly placed Chinese, in fact the only really strategic position open to them."[64]

The years 1645–61 might well be called the "era of Adam Schall," for he was then the dominant Jesuit in China, and he attained an eminence there never before achieved by any missionary, any foreigner. A member of a wealthy Cologne family, he had entered the Society in 1611 and was a student in Rome when he met Trigault and became convinced that he was destined to become a missionary in China. His field experience was limited to a short stint (1627–30) in the northwestern province of Shensi. By then he had already composed his first book in Chinese on astronomy and had become an obvious choice to succeed Terrentius. Remarkably talented both linguistically and technically, Schall could be choleric, blunt, and morose, but he was also opportunistic, urbane, and unconventional.[65] He rose rapidly in the Manchu bureaucracy, ultimately becoming imperial chamberlain and court interpreter with the rank of mandarin first class, first division, a position that brought him into close contact with many members of the imperial household. With a sense of pride that would have incurred the rebukes of a Saint Ignatius or Saint Francis Xavier, he boasted, "Throughout the Empire my name was so spread that almost all knew of me. It was often useful to my companions situated elsewhere, to say they were my brothers or friends."[66] But he evidently spoke the truth, for Fr. Manoel Dias Júnior declared, "Would that we had a hundred Adams; ... he is so real a help to us that we need only to say that we are his companions and brothers and no one dares venture a word against us." Another father reported that "Schall has more influence upon the emperor than any viceroy or than the most respected prince, and the name of Father Adam is better known in China than the name of any famous man in Europe."[67]

Those words by Ferdinand Verbiest, Schall's distinguished successor, were written in 1661, just before the Society confronted its gravest crisis of the century in China. That year the emperor, Shun-chih, died unexpectedly, a serious blow to the Jesuits generally and particularly to Schall, who had enjoyed a remarkably close relationship with the ruler. Shun-chih had permitted Schall to sit in his presence in the palace and had become a frequent visitor in Schall's home, where they discussed matters of religion, state, and astronomy. But the emperor may have become bored by those discussions, for he turned increasingly toward Zen Buddhism during his last years. Nevertheless, Schall visited him during his final illness, and although he failed to convert Shun-chih, he did influence the emperor's decision to name as his successor his third son, K'ang-hsi, who was destined to become one of China's greatest emperors.

64. Sivin, "Copernicus in China," 89.

65. Jonathan Spence, *To Change China: Western Advisers in China, 1620–1960* (Boston, 1969), chap. 1, an incisive sketch. See also Irene Pih, *Le Père Gabriel de Magalhães: Une Jesuite portugais en Chine au xviie siècle* (Paris, 1979), chap. 3.

66. Spence, *Western Advisers*, 18.

67. Dunne, *Generation of Giants*, 325 and 348.

How much the Jesuits owed to the protection of Shun-chih soon became evident during the Oboi regency (1661–69).[68] As had been true elsewhere, the Jesuits' success invited hostile attack, especially from Buddhist and Confucian elements. By the 1660s the Jesuits were represented in all but two of the provinces, and the number of their followers approximately doubled during the first two decades of Ch'ing rule.[69] Soon after assuming power, the four regents-general sent out special commissioners to tour the provinces and to investigate charges brought against the Jesuits. Encouraged by Buddhist monks, provincial officials had accused the fathers of disseminating pernicious doctrines and of aiding enemies of the state. The Jesuits were therefore arrested and interrogated; their converts were harassed, and some were executed; Jesuit churches were destroyed.

Not until 1664 did this persecution affect the Peking Jesuits. Its chief spokesman was an eccentric, xenophobic archtraditionalist, Yang Kuang-hsien, who had made a career out of writing memorials to the throne critical of things he did not like.[70] He detested Christians generally and Adam Schall in particular. Beginning in 1659 he submitted a series of memorials critical of Schall's astronomical calculations, but he did not receive a serious hearing until 1664, when he formed an alliance with dissident Muslim members of the calendar bureau. In mid-September of that year, Yang Kuang-hsien delivered to the Board of Rites a series of charges against Schall and his co-workers, accusing them of serious miscalculations and of plotting against the state. Those charges led to the arrest, painful confinement, and repeated interrogation of Schall, his chief assistant, Ferdinand Verbiest, and two other Jesuits, along with their Chinese assistants. At one point the Jesuits were threatened with banishment, except for Schall, who was to be progressively mutilated. Then came what has been termed "a providential earthquake" (May 1665),[71] which was interpreted as a sign of the displeasure of the heavenly bodies. Although the sentences were modified with respect to the Peking Jesuits, who remained under house arrest until 1669, their five assistants lost their heads. Furthermore, all Jesuit properties were confiscated, and 25 Jesuits, 4 Dominicans, and a Franciscan were rounded up and either detained in Canton or compelled to withdraw to Macao.[72] Thus, from 1665 until 1671, Christianity was proscribed in China, just as it had been half a century earlier in Japan.

The pall was lifted by the actions of the new emperor and the ingenuity of Ferdinand Verbiest. In 1668 the 14-year-old K'ang-hsi assumed control of his government and dismissed the regents. The same year he responded to criticism of the official calendar, now prepared

68. The best account of the persecution of the 1660s relies upon Chinese as well as Western sources: Robert B. Oxnam, *Ruling from Horseback: Manchu Politics in the Oboi Regency, 1661–1669* (Chicago, 1970), 146–51. See also Pih, *Le Père Gabriel*, chap. 6.

69. *RJC*, 330.

70. Young, *Confucianism*, chap. 5.

71. The phrase is from Jacques Gernet, *A History of Chinese Civilization*, trans. J. R. Foster (Cambridge, 1982), 517.

72. Detention in China was less grim than some writers have made it appear. It was possible, for example, for missionaries to pass from there to Macao and to be secretly replaced by other missionaries. Obviously the missionaries did not wish to give up their foothold in the empire, even when they were kept under close surveillance. While in Canton, representatives of the several Orders engaged in lengthy, sometimes heated disputations concerning Chinese Rites (see Chapter 23). For a valuable summary of those disagreements, see James S. Cummins, ed., *The Travels and Controversies of Friar Domingo Navarrete, 1618–1686*, *HS*:2, 118–119 (1962), App. 1.

under the direction of the Jesuits' archenemy, Yang Kuang-hsien, who admitted that he lacked qualifications for the position. The emperor turned to Ferdinand Verbiest and asked him to review his rival's work. The Belgian had no trouble demonstrating its deficiencies and in 1669 replaced Yang as head of the bureau. That same year, the sentences against the Jesuits were reversed, their enemies were punished, and the persecution came to an end.[73]

Three years earlier the Society had lost a major luminary with the death of Schall, but Verbiest proved to be as talented a replacement and infinitely more tactful. The son of an estate bailiff in western Flanders, he entered the Society in 1641 and became an educator in his native land. Dissatisfied, he yearned to go to China, and in 1655 the father general, Goswin Nickel, granted his wish. Four years later he entered the eastern empire. In many respects, Verbiest's career paralleled that of Schall. Like the German, he began missionary work in Shensi; he, too, was called to Peking to assist with astronomical tasks. Like Schall, he became director of the astronomical bureau, a post he held until his death. Though lower in status, he, too, became a mandarin. As Schall had done, Verbiest formed a close relationship with the emperor and for years tutored him in higher mathematics, astronomy, and other subjects. Just as the Mings obliged Schall to produce cannon, so K'ang-hsi named Verbiest vice-president of the board of works and charged him with making heavy and light cannon, pulleys to move heavy stones, pumps to provide water for royal gardens, and other mechanical contrivances for various purposes. Somehow Verbiest found time to translate St. Thomas Aquinas into Chinese and Ricci's commentaries into Mongol. He also accompanied the emperor on his inspection trips as his scientific advisor.[74]

Although preoccupied with his technical duties, Verbiest never lost sight of his primary goal—the conversion of the emperor and the empire. Fulfillment of that ambition was still handicapped by the two problems that had always confronted Jesuit leaders in China, the shortage of manpower and the scarcity of funds. Although 82 men had been sent from Lisbon to the eastern missions between 1668 and 1678, only seven reached China.[75] In the latter year, Verbiest, then serving as vice-provincial (1676–80), addressed a general appeal to all Jesuit facilities in Europe urging them to send as many qualified persons as possible, especially those well trained in philosophy, theology, astronomy, and mathematics.[76] That appeal seems to have struck a responsive chord in the province of Upper Germany, where, according to Fr. Eusebio Kino,

> many men ... are most desirous of going to China, and they are undoubtedly more apt candidates because they are thoroughly versed, especially in mathematics and various branches of science; above all, they are richly endowed with religious virtues demanded by Father Berbiest [*sic*]. I am convinced that in no other Province ... are there so many Jesuits as in the Upper German Province who devote so much attention to mathematics and this particularly in order to go some day to the Chinese missions. ... I could easily

73. Kessler, *K'ang-hsi*, 61–64.
74. Spence, *Western Advisers*, 23–30; Arnold H. Rowbotham, *Missionary and Mandarin: The Jesuits at the Court of China* (Berkeley, 1942), 93–100; Young, *Confucianism*, chap. 7.
75. Witek, *Controversial Ideas*, 21 n. 21.
76. Verbiest to the Fathers of the Company in Europe, 15 Aug. 1678, in H. Jossen, S.J., and L. Willaert, S.J., eds., *Correspondance de Ferdinand Verbiest de la compagnie de Jésus (1623–1688)* (Brussels, 1938), 230–53. According to Witek, the original woodblock text was printed in Peking, and French and Latin copies were made in Europe within four years: *Controversial Ideas*, 21 n. 20.

name thirty or more.... As they see at every turn in the libraries and elsewhere in the Province the pictures representing Adam Schall and Martin Martini, they believe that they are unmistakably called to follow them by volunteering for China.[77]

Called they may have been, but the most important response to Verbiest's appeal came not from the Germanies but from France. There the director of the royal astronomical observatory in Paris proposed sending a team of Jesuit mathematicians to China to undertake certain astronomical measurements in order to produce improved navigational charts. Louis XIV, frustrated in his efforts to establish a commercial empire in the East that would rival those of Holland and England,[78] agreed to underwrite the cost of dispatching a group of Jesuits, called the royal mathematicians, to China to undertake such observations and to conduct research on ancient Chinese texts.[79] Among that team of six were two young theology students who possessed remarkable linguistic talent and Jean François Gerbillon, a mathematician whose diplomatic activities are noted below. Three of the six were members of the royal academy of sciences. Although the mission was strongly opposed by Pedro II, because it violated the Portuguese spiritual monopoly (the *padroado real*) in the East, the royal mathematicians nevertheless left Brest aboard the ill-fated Siam squadron in autumn of 1686.[80] They reached Peking on 7 February 1688, less than two weeks after Verbiest had died and, like Schall before him, had been given a state funeral.

One of Verbiest's last services was to persuade the dubious Manchu bureaucrats to admit the French mission. Another was to convince the emperor to name Fr. Tomás Pereira to the staff of a diplomatic-military expedition that went north to treat with representatives of the czar concerning the contested Amur border region. Verbiest hoped that Pereira might obtain Russian permission to use a trans-Siberian route as an alternative to the long sea voyage between Macao, Goa, Lisbon, and Rome.[81] But Pereira, a talented musician from

77. Kino to the duchess of Aveiro, Cadiz, 14 Dec. 1680, in Ernest J. Burrus, S.J., ed., *Kino Writes to the Duchess: Letters of Eusebio Francisco Kino, S.J., to the Duchess of Aveiro* (St. Louis, 1965), 93.

78. Holden Furber, *Rival Empires of Trade in the Orient, 1600–1800* (Minneapolis, 1976), 103–20.

79. The most recent study of the origins of the famous French mission is Witek, *Controversial Ideas*, 70–72. Witek insists, contrary to Pinot, that the mission was not intended to supersede the Portuguese-controlled vice-province but merely to achieve the stated scholarly objectives. Cf. Virgile Pinot, *La Chine et la formation de l'espirit philosophique en France (1640–1740)* (1932; rpr., Geneva, 1971). But even contemporaries appreciated that there were also commercial objectives behind the mathematicians' voyage: Furber, *Rival Empires*, 119–20. For additional bibliography on the French mission, see *BHCJ*, 2:2, 342–43. See also Theodore N. Foss, "A Western Interpretation of China: Jesuit Cartography," in Charles E. Ronan, S.J., and Bonnie B. C. Oh, eds., *East Meets West: The Jesuits in China, 1582–1773* (Chicago, 1988), 219–20.

80. Witek, *Controversial Ideas*, 39ff. E. W. Hutchinson, trans. and ed., *1688: Revolution in Siam: The Memoir of Father de Bezè, S.J.* (Hong Kong, 1968). As noted in Chapter 5, Pedro II took a keen interest in the China missions. He strongly opposed the dispatch of foreign missionaries to the empire and called for an increase in the number of Portuguese Jesuits assigned to the vice-province. King to count of Alves (viceroy), 23 Mar. 1685, in AHU/PA/IN, *cx.* 33, no. 72; *CR*, 23 Mar. 1689, in HAG/*LM* 54, fol. 151ʳ; viceroy to king, Goa, 24 Jan. 1690, in HAG/*LM* 54, fol. 153ʳ (pointing out the shortage of mathematicians in Portugal). The king demanded that the father general not assign foreign-born superiors to the State of India and warned that they would be forbidden entry. *CR*, 23 Mar. 1691, in HAG/*LM* 56, fol. 468ʳ. On the dispatch of the Portuguese so-called mathematician Fr. Luís Coelho to China, see Chapter 23. In 1693 Pedro sent ten Jesuits—nine Portuguese and one Savoyard—to China and directed the captain-general of Macao not to permit them to be diverted elsewhere. King to viceroy, 18 Mar. 1693, in HAG/*LM* 58, fol. 45ʳ.

81. Joseph Sebes, S.J., *The Jesuits and the Sino-Russian Treaty of Nerchinsk (1689)* (Rome, 1961), 94–102. One contemporary noted that dispatches sent from Peking via Macao, Goa, and Lisbon took up to two years to

the archdiocese of Braga who became K'ang-hsi's musical instructor, was a curious person to send on such an assignment since, as a loyal Portuguese, he was unalterably opposed to the opening of the land route.[82] Equally curious (and still unexplained) is his selection of Jean François Gerbillon as his companion, for Pereira also opposed the presence of the separate French Jesuit mission in China and only recently had bestowed an interdict upon its members.[83] Nevertheless, the two Jesuits played key roles in the negotiation of the Treaty of Nerchinsk (1689), the first international agreement entered into by a Chinese government.[84]

It was not uncommon for Jesuits to ask the state for a quid pro quo after doing it an important service. When, in 1691, the governor of the province of Chekiang undertook a local persecution of the Jesuits, Fr. Pereira protested to the emperor and reminded him of the many tasks the Society had performed for his government.[85] As a result, the Board of Rites framed the famous edict of 22 March 1692, which recounted the important contributions of the Jesuits to the conclusion of the Treaty of Nerchinsk and insisted that members of the Society "have ... rendered great service to the empire ... [and have] never been accused of any misdemeanor or of having caused any disorder. The doctrines that they teach are not evil nor are they capable of leading the people astray or of causing disturbances." Shên Ch'üeh and Yang Kuang-hsien must have rumbled to the contrary from their graves. No matter; the Board proceeded with its recommendation: "We must, then, leave all the churches of the empire in the condition in which they existed formerly and we must permit everyone to go there to worship God, without fear of molestation."[86]

When the emperor approved this famous edict of toleration, the members of the Society must have been jubilant, for after more than a century of effort, Christianity had finally become an acceptable faith in China. Little wonder that the number of conversions increased by the thousands. By 1700 there were approximately 300,000 Christians in the empire, about the same figure attained by the Jesuits in Japan long before. The vice-province had grown to more than 50 members by the end of the century, twice as many as had served there during the days of Schall and Verbiest.[87] If the royal palace still resisted the new faith,

---

reach their destinations and another two for responses to get back. Jossen and Willaert, eds., *Correspondance*, xvii–xviii.

82. Sebes, *Jesuits and Nerchinsk*, 139. See also *BHCJ*, 2:2, 343. Pereira, born in S. Martinho do Valle near Braga, entered China in 1672 and remained there until his death in 1708. He served as rector of the college in Peking (1688–91), as vice-provincial (1692–95), and as acting co-president of the board of mathematics (1688–94). He was the author of several volumes on musical theory and of the journal noted below. *NBBJC*, 381–85; *RJC*, 200–201; Sebes, *Jesuits and Nerchinsk*, 135–41.

83. Witek, *Controversial Ideas*, 49. Pereira took that action because the French fathers refused to take an oath to obey papal vicars in the Far East. The Portuguese fathers, pursuant to a directive from Pedro II, did take the oath. As Witek notes (44), this was the beginning of a fierce Luso-French rivalry among Jesuits in China, one destined to last until 1720.

84. The standard work on the treaty remains Sebes, *Jesuits and Nerchinsk*, which includes the previously unpublished journal of Fr. Pereira, the senior of the two Jesuit negotiators. For a different perspective, see "The Travels of Father Gerbillon, ... into Tartary," in Jean Baptiste du Halde, S.J., comp., *Description géographique, historique, chronologique, politique et physique de la Chine et de la Tartarie chinoise*, 4 vols. (Paris, 1735); Eng. ed. (London, 1736), 4: 214–380.

85. Sebes, *Jesuits and Nerchinsk*, 136.

86. For the full text, see Rowbotham, *Missionary and Mandarin*, 110. See also Joseph S. Sebes, S.J., "China's Jesuit Century," *Wilson Quarterly* (1978): 170–83.

87. *RJC*, 336.

at least it permitted the French Jesuits to reside within its confines in a house granted to them by the grateful K'ang-hsi, cured of a fever by quinine supplied by the French fathers.[88] But though it appeared that the Society was entering one of those celebrated golden ages, its painfully achieved respectability was about to be threatened by the papacy itself, as will be seen in Chapter 23.

Expansion in the West

Throughout the seventeenth century, the vice-province of China and the Japan province competed with the Indian provinces for the manpower that each required to support its ambitious undertakings. During the first three decades of the century, the arrival of an exceptionally large number of recruits from Europe permitted significant expansion in the West. Between 1600 and 1630, 413 Jesuits reached the redeployment center of Goa. The peak year of Jesuit sailings to the East (1541–1757) was 1602, when 62 fathers and brothers arrived safely in Goa without sustaining a single loss at sea. There were only six years during the first three decades of the century when no reinforcements came, and the yearly average for the remaining 25 years was 16.5 men, compared with 6.3 for the period 1541–99.[89]

Just as the growth of the Far Eastern missions led to the administrative separation of the vice-province (and later province) of Japan from Goa and later of the vice-province of China from Japan, so the enlarged concerns of the Society in the West led to the formation in 1601 of the vice province of Malabar, which was raised to a full province four years later.[90] Between 1605 and 1632, the manpower of the new province grew by nearly 100 percent, from 97 to 180. The headquarters of the vice-province was the college of Madre de Deus in Cochin, and its far-flung responsibilities included the Malabar, Travancore, and Coromandel coasts, Malacca, the Moluccas, the Bay of Bengal, the southern interior city of Madura and the island of Ceylon.

Jesuit interest in Bengal began before Malabar was separated from the province of Goa. As C. H. Payne once observed, Portuguese writers of the sixteenth and seventeenth centuries designated the Gangetic delta, the western district of Orissa, and the eastern kingdom of Arakan as parts of "Benguela."[91] Crown officers hoped to exploit the region's timber and mineral resources and also to establish a naval base there to intercept Muslim vessels bound from Bay of Bengal ports to Red Sea markets. The Jesuits were attracted to Bengal because it held a substantial Eurasian population, reckoned at about 2,500 in 1600, and because they feared that the Augustinians, who entered the region in 1598, a few months before the first Jesuits, were likely to preempt evangelical opportunities there. When a Jesuit scout returned to Goa after looking over possibilities in Bengal and urged the Visitor, Fr. Nicolas Pimenta, to send additional companions at once, the Visitor declined, stating that most of the available

88. Witek, *Controversial Ideas*, 61–63.

89. *LJI*, 269–94.

90. The man most responsible for the separation of Malabar from Goa was Fr. Alberto Laerzio, procurator for the Goa province in Rome. He returned to India in 1602 with 62 recruits and became provincial of Malabar on two occasions, 1602–1611 and 1626–1630. F/*JM*, 1: 276. See also *RACJ*, 1: 26 and 2: 302.

91. C. H. Payne, *Jahangir and the Jesuits* (London, 1930), 252 n. 2; see also Hall, *History of South-East Asia*, chaps. 15, 21, and 22.

men were being sent to Japan. Then the viceroy, Aires de Saldanha (1600–1605), intervened under circumstances that suggest the possibility of a prior understanding between himself and the Jesuit superior. In the presence of the archbishop and other ecclesiastical worthies, he threatened to put Pimenta in chains if he declined to provide men for Benguela. "I was surprised," reported Pimenta, "and said that the Company was his, that His Lordship could order, dispose, etc." He was curiously unruffled by Saldanha's threat because he was convinced, he said, that "enterprises in these parts are of great moment for God's service, lest the Religious [that is, the Augustinians] should obstruct us in it later, alleging possession, as is their wont."[92]

Acting under direct order from the viceroy, Pimenta sent three "quite picked subjects" to Bengal. One was Sicilian-born Fr. Natal Salerno. Fr. Salerno soon joined the resourceful Portuguese adventurer Felippe de Brito, a mercenary employed in the service of the king of Arakan, who seized the port of Syriam in Pegu and attempted to dominate the rest of Lower Burma between 1600 and 1613. Fr. Salerno and a companion ministered primarily to the needs of the Portuguese garrison at Syriam "because the people are still in a very unsettled state owing to the continual wars, and the fathers think it best to postpone this important work [evangelization] until the country is in a more tranquil state." Fr. Salerno undertook diplomatic missions for Brito and became a seagoing chaplain whose presence was considered indispensable to victory by Brito's fellow ruffians. In the end Fr. Salerno died in a sea fight, and Brito was strangled after the fall of his palisade fortress.[93]

Fr. Salerno's companions at Hugli, a few miles north of the nucleus of modern Calcutta, fared little better. Several died in prison; others perished from disease, shipwreck, and the consequences of military campaigns undertaken by the Mughals and the Arakanese. Although a college, the northeastern outpost of the Malabar vice-province, was established in Hugli about 1623, the number of Jesuits attached to it rarely exceeded five, and its finances remained precarious. The last Jesuit father at Hugli died in 1740.[94]

More spectacular and controversial was the mission established in the ancient Tamil-speaking religious center of Madura, northeast of Cape Comorin, by the remarkably talented and persevering Roberto de Nobili (b. 1577–d. 1657). Roman-born, the eldest son of a count, Roberto de Nobili joined the Society in Naples at age 20. After completing his religious studies and being ordained, he left Lisbon for Goa in 1604. Because of his linguistic talents, he was assigned to Malabar province. After a brief stint in Cochin, he was sent to the Fishery Coast and six months later went to Madura with a companion. His initial efforts at conversion proved unsuccessful. He concluded that the Tamils would not accept his teachings as long as he appeared to be an alien soothsayer. Accordingly, de Nobili assumed a disguise: as he wrote Paul V, he "professed to be an Italian Brahmin who had renounced the world, had studied wisdom at Rome ... and rejected all the pleasures and comforts of this world."[95] Thereafter he adopted the yellow garb of a Brahman *sanysasi* or penitent, restricted himself

92. Pimenta to Aquaviva, 1 Dec. 1601, in H. Hosten, S.J., ed., Asiatic Society of Bengal, Calcutta, *Journal and Proceedings*, n.s. 23 (1927): 103–4.

93. Payne, *Jahangir*, 201–2, 255 n. 10; Hall, *History of South-East Asia*, 270 and 300.

94. L. Besse, S.J., and H. Hosten, S.J., "List of Portuguese Jesuit Missionaries in Bengal and Burma, 1576–1742," Asiatic Society of Bengal, Calcutta, *Journal and Proceedings*, n.s. 7 (1911): 15–23.

95. De Nobili to Paul V, ca. 1622, in *Indian Church History Review* 2, 2 (Dec. 1968): 84–96; the quotation is on p. 85.

to a single vegetarian meal a day, and traveled on bare feet rather than accept a horse or the traditional litter. He mastered the essential languages (Tamil, Telug, and Sanskrit) and conducted lengthy discourses with prospective neophytes, 30,000 of whom he is credited with having gained for the faith. Despite his successes, de Nobili's adaptational approach aroused controversy even with members of his own Order. His critics accused him of mixing pagan rites and ceremonies with Christianity and of having accepted the caste system contrary to the teachings of Christ. De Nobili responded that the local customs he accepted were merely civic rather than superstitious in nature, and by 1623 even the pope approved his unconventional missionary style. Although de Nobili never had many companions or successors, his mission continued to prosper until the early eighteenth century (see Chapter 23).[96]

Jesuit activities in Ceylon did not endure nearly so long. Portuguese interest in that large pearl-shaped island dated from 1505–6, when D. Lourenço de Almeida, son of the famous viceroy, visited the island. By then the kingdom of Kotte, whose capital was situated a few miles east of Colombo, had lost its former dominance over the entire island, which was largely shared by three kingdoms. Kotte remained in control of the most populous districts, the fertile lowlands of the south and west, whereas the forested, mountainous interior was ruled by the sovereigns of Kandy, whose capital was located on the remarkably beautiful lake of that name. Both kingdoms were Sinhalese by race and Buddhist by faith, in contrast with the Hindu, Tamil-speaking kingdom of Jaffna, located on the far less prosperous or populous limestone peninsula of the north. Whereas Jaffna, whose capital remained Nallur until 1621 and thereafter became Jaffnapatão (Jaffnapatam), found natural trading partners with the Tamils of southeast India, Kotte traded with the Malabar through Muslim intermediaries.

Trading opportunities initially drew the Portuguese to the island, where they competed with Muslim rivals to purchase cinnamon (found exclusively in Kotte), elephants, areca nuts, coconuts, and precious gems. Although the first Portuguese fort at Colombo (1518–24) provoked such local enmity, probably fanned by Muslims, that it was soon demolished, the Portuguese established a factory on a spit of land south of the port. That factory became a beachhead for trade and intrigue. Shortly after its establishment, the three sons of the king of Kotte rebelled against their father, murdered him, and quarreled over control of the kingdom. The Lusitanians eagerly formed a commercial-military alliance with one of the unsavory trio, and in 1543 they recognized Dharmapāla, a grandson of their client, as the legitimate heir to the entire kingdom. In 1557 Dharmapāla became a Christian, 23 years later he designated the ruler of Portugal as his heir. After Dharmapāla's death (1597), the Portuguese took effective possession of the southern and western portions of the island.[97]

96. Much has been written about de Nobili. For two informative contributions, see Xavier Rajanikam, S.J., "The Newly Discovered 'Informativo' of Robert de Nobili," *AHSI* 39 (July–Dec. 1970): 221–65, and idem, "An Account of the Progress of the Madurai Mission During the Year 1627: A Letter of Roberto de Nobili," *Indian Church History Review* 11, 2 (Aug. 1977): 114–26.

97. K. M. de Silva, *A History of Sri Lanka* (Berkeley, 1981), is a recent, traditional survey; on the sixteenth and seventeenth centuries, see chaps. 8 and 9. There are several archive-based studies of Portuguese activities in Ceylon, notably Tikiri Abeyasinghe, *Portuguese Rule in Ceylon, 1594–1612* (Colombo, 1966); and Chandra Richard de Silva, *The Portuguese in Ceylon, 1617–1638* (Colombo, 1972). Although the book is primarily concerned with the Dutch, the early chapters of K. W. Goonewardena, *The Foundations of Dutch Power in Ceylon, 1633–1658* (Amsterdam, 1958), are helpful, as is Tikiri Abaysinghe, ed., *Portuguese Regiments on Sri Lanka* (Colombo, n.d.).

Goan authorities also became interested in the northern kingdom, for Jaffna controlled shipping between the Malabar and Coromandel coasts via the Palk Strait as well as the pearling beds off the island of Manar. Although the expedition led by Viceroy D. Constantino de Bragança (1560) failed to topple the ruler of Jaffna, it did seize Manar, where Christians from the Fishery Coast were subsequently introduced along with Jesuit missionaries, who gradually converted the island's inhabitants.

Until the administration of D. Jerónimo de Azevedo, captain-general of Ceylon (1594–1612) and viceroy of India (1612–18), Portuguese officials were content to control the peripheries of the island through client rulers. But the intrusion of the Dutch into the eastern seas (see Chapter 7) soon raised the prospect that the Hollanders might meddle in the internal affairs of the island to the disadvantage of the Portuguese. The Portuguese therefore elected to take preemptive action to conquer the entire island both physically and spiritually.[98] It was Azevedo, a brother of the Jesuit martyr Inácio de Azevedo, the leader of the ill-fated Brazil-bound expedition of 1570 (see Chapter 3), who invited the Jesuits to the island in 1602 with the concurrence of both the viceroy and the bishop of Cochin. The fathers responded to the call willingly, for they had been interested in establishing themselves there since Xavier's brief visit in 1545.[99]

The Jesuits' situation in Ceylon was a contrast to the positions they had long enjoyed in Brazil, Japan, and China, where they possessed spiritual monopolies among European missionaries for decades. In Ceylon they were latecomers, unwanted latecomers as far as the Franciscans were concerned. The latter had arrived in 1543 and had established a series of successful missions with thousands of converts in the Matara district at the southern end of the island. As recently as the 1590s, they had obtained a decree from Archduke Albert, regent of Portugal, confirming their exclusive spiritual rights to the island. Understandably, they protested the intrusion by the Jesuits and later by the Dominicans and Augustinians, who followed in 1606. Indeed, when the Jesuits delimited land assigned to them for a college in Colombo, the Franciscans pulled the fence down, and the Jesuits retaliated in kind.[100] By the early 1620s, each of the four Orders was allotted a separate zone on the island within which it was supposed to confine its activities: the Franciscans remained in the densely populated Matara district; the Augustinians were assigned the Four Korales, northeast of Colombo; the Dominicans gained the Sabaraguamuwa zone between the Four Korales and Matara; and the Jesuits were awarded the Seven Korales (north of Colombo and west of Kandy). The four Orders shared the Tamil north, annexed by the crown in 1619.[101]

The first Jesuits reached Colombo about 1602 and founded a collegial headquarters there three years later. In 1620 a separate house, sometimes also called a college, was

---

98. C. R. de Silva, *Portuguese in Ceylon*, 9ff.

99. Several Jesuits visited the island before the Society began formal work there. In 1552 Fr. Baltazar Gago sailed there with the viceroy and was struck, as were many Portuguese, by the island's rich economic and spiritual opportunities. Gago to Sociis Lusitanis, Cochin, 10 Jan. 1552, in *DI*, 2: 280. At the same time, Fr. Manuel de Morães served as chaplain of Portuguese forces stationed at Colombo and reported that he found that "the most wicked vices reigned supreme . . . and men were given to lewdness and lust. . . . I fulminated very strongly against these . . . in my sermons." In the mid-1590s Fr. António Schipari served as chaplain of a Portuguese expedition against Kandy and was briefly taken prisoner. S. G. Perera, "The Jesuits in Ceylon in the 16th and 17th Centuries," *Ceylon Antiquary and Literary Register* 1 (1915): 222 and 225.

100. Abeyasinghe, *Portuguese Rule*, 197–98.

101. C. R. de Silva, *Portuguese in Ceylon*, 243.

established at Jaffna. By 1627 the college of Colombo contained eighteen fathers, half of whom worked in the recently pacified Seven Korales, where they claimed 10,000 converts. Another sixteen Jesuits worked among the Tamils and by 1627 were responsible for the welfare of 40,000 neophytes. But the mountainous interior kingdom of Kandy continued to defy pacification probes by either soldiers or missionaries. The ascendancy of the resourceful Rājasinha II (1628–83) would ultimately spell disaster for the ambitions of both the crown and the Society (see Chapter 7).[102]

While the Malabar province was expanding in the southeast and northeast, the Goan province sent out new probes to the west. For a time, one proved fruitful. In 1607 two Jesuits explored the possibility of reestablishing the Society in Mozambique. Three or four years later, several Jesuits accompanied the newly appointed captain-general, D. Estévão de Ataide, who ascended the Zambesi in search of precious wealth in the interior, that is, the kingdom of the fabled Mwene Mutapa. Although Ataide was soon disgraced, the Jesuits remained. Their headquarters became the college of São Francisco Xavier on Mozambique Island (founded 1619), and they subsequently established a series of residences or missions on the Luabo, the fertile southernmost affluent of the Zambesi, and at several upriver stations or forts, notably at Sena, Chemba, Tete, Caia, and Marangue. As on Ceylon, the Jesuits were preceded in Mozambique by another Order, in this case the Dominicans (established by 1586), and the two remained serious rivals throughout the seventeenth century, although they joined together in the 1690s to block efforts by the Augustinians to gain entry to Mozambique.[103] Nevertheless, Mozambique remained a backwater of the empire: it never attracted a large number of settlers or priests. As with the Bengal enterprise, the Jesuits' residences on the Zambesi survived but never flourished.[104]

For a brief period, the Jesuits' position in Ethiopia seemed very much better. Shortly after Philip II assumed control of Portugal and its empire, he instructed the viceroy of India to "spare no labor or cost for the promotion and conversion of Ethiopia."[105] In 1589, two years after the king's directive was sent to Goa, the provincial assigned two priests to reinforce two aged fathers who still remained in the kingdom, where they ministered to the needs of 1,000 or so Christians, most of them of Portuguese descent.[106] The newcomers were Fr. António de Monserrate, a Persian-speaking veteran of the Mughal court, and the remarkable Pero Pais (Pedro Paes). Pais (b. 1563–d. 1622) was born in the town of Alcocer in the diocese of Toledo. He entered the Society at age 19 and arrived in Goa in 1588. There he was promptly ordained, even though he lacked formal training in theology.[107] In order to reach Ethiopia, Monserrate and Pais assumed the disguise of Armenian merchants and

102. Perera's previously cited article, which continues in the same journal (1: 217–26, 2: 1–28, 69–90, 224–35; 3: 19–35, 116–30; 4: 95–101, 150–56; 5: 31–41, 81–87, 125–37, 196–201; and 6: 33–38), was published between 1915 and 1921 and was also issued separately. Founded upon Jesuit sources, it remains basic to an understanding of the limitations of Jesuit enterprise on the island.

103. *APO*:1, 4:2, 211–13.

104. The most ambitious study of Jesuit activities in Mozambique is António da Silva, S.J., *Mentalidade missiológica dos Jesuítas em Moçambique antes de 1759*, 2 vols. (Lisbon, 1967). See also Eric Axelson, *Portuguese in South-East Africa, 1600–1700* (Johannesburg, 1960).

105. Quoted without source by Charles F. Rey, *The Romance of the Portuguese in Abyssinia* (1929; rpr., New York, 1969), 223.

106. *RACJ*, 1: 360.

107. *DI*, 15: 39* and 177.

planned to enter the kingdom from the north, traveling via Basra, Aleppo, and Cairo. But they were captured by Turks off the south coast of Arabia and found themselves prisoners amid a score of Christian captives in Yemen, where for a time they labored first as gardeners and later as galley slaves. Finally, in 1595, the two fathers were ransomed and returned to Diu. There Monserrate perished but Pais survived, determined to reach his goal.

He did so in 1603. That year he sailed from Diu, again posing as an Armenian merchant, and this time he successfully landed at Massawa. From there he made his way overland to Fremona, the Ethiopian capital. When he arrived, he found control of the kingdom being contested by three strongmen, one of whom, Za Dengel, emerged temporarily victorious. At first Pais maintained a low profile. A remarkable linguist who knew Latin and Greek and mastered Arabic during his captivity, Pais quickly gained a knowledge of Amharic and G'ez and began translating scriptural texts into the latter tongue for use as instructional materials in a school that he founded. Before long the impressive quality of his teaching brought him to the attention of Za Dengel, who summoned him to court. There, two of his star pupils amazed the emperor and his retainers with their knowledge and skill in debating dogma with the Monophysite clergy. In effect, the Jesuits employed the same techniques here that they had used at the court of Akbar and against shamans in Brazil during the sixteenth century. As in Brazil, these techniques produced the intended results. After extended conversations with Pais concerning the superiority of Roman Catholicism and the advantages of Western technology, Za Dengel expressed willingness to submit to Rome and wrote Philip II seeking a matrimonial alliance and military aid against his Gallas adversaries. But the emperor's precipitate action alarmed the Ethiopian clergy and nobles, who successfully rebelled and killed him.

After several years of turmoil, Susinyos, a soldier of fortune, became the new emperor in 1607. Like Za Dengel, he was impressed by the multitalented Pais, who by then had been joined by four additional fathers. Pais became a self-taught carpenter, tool designer, locksmith, and mason, and the architect of a unique two-story stone and clay palace for the new ruler.[108] Although Susinyos was initially tolerant of the Jesuits and permitted them freedom to travel about his kingdom, he did not formally proclaim adherence to Catholicism until he had consolidated his rule. Meantime, the Jesuits followed their customary strategy in the East by seeking to convert members of the elite—nobles and ecclesiastics—in order to reach the lower classes. The fathers won an important convert when the emperor's ambitious brother, Si'la Christos, became a Catholic in 1612 and assisted them in establishing a mission in his province, where he amassed vast properties taken from the traditional church. By the early 1620s, the number of Jesuit converts in Ethiopia approached 100,000 according to Society estimates, but, as always, one must be suspicious of such numbers. For a decade Susinyos continued to hope for signs of support from Rome and Madrid. Despite the absence of such signs, he formally accepted Catholicism in 1621 and issued a proclamation in which he abolished the traditional Saturday sabbath and other customary practices and required all his subjects to submit to the Roman rite. His submission and ban of traditional religious forms represented a triumph for Pais, but one that he did not long enjoy, for he expired the following year. He was thereby spared having to witness the actions of his

108. He also composed a three-volume history of Ethiopia during his spare time.

successor, Dr. Afonso Mendes, who soon set in motion forces that would lead to the rapid destruction of Christianity in Ethiopia.

If Pais had arrived in the highlands at an auspicious moment, his successor came at an unpropitious one, for the emperor's decision to adhere to Rome was already causing discontent. If the talented, patient Pais was the right man for the job, Mendes (b. ca. 1570– d. 1656) was distinctly not. Born in the district of Moura near Évora, Mendes entered the Society in 1593 and earned a doctorate in theology. For a number of years he served as professor of theology at the University of Évora, where he delivered a welcoming oration when Philip III visited there in 1619. Four years later he was named patriarch of Ethiopia.[109] Although he left Lisbon in March 1623, he did not reach Fremona for another 27 months. He entered the capital on a white horse leading a retinue that included four priests, two lay brothers, thirteen laymen, five musicians, and two personal servants.[110] Mendes was warmly greeted by the emperor and thousands of his subjects, but he found their enthusiasm to be transitory. For that he bore primary responsibility, since he was determined to implement a root-and-branch reform of the Ethiopian church. He insisted that Susinyos undergo the humiliation of kneeling before him and swearing fealty to him as a representative of the pope. Determined to expunge all forms of what he perceived to be Jewish-pagan corruption, he demanded that the entire population undergo rebaptism, that the clergy be freshly indoctrinated, and that their churches be remodeled in conformity with Roman custom and reconsecrated. Unlike Xavier, Mendes displayed neither affection, understanding, nor tact in dealing with those whom he regarded as cultural inferiors.

Yet for a time the Jesuit enterprise continued to grow. By the late 1620s, there were 21 fathers in the highlands distributed among thirteen residences (estáncias). Nevertheless, Mendes's reforms involved too many drastic changes in Ethiopian cultural and social values to gain passive acceptance. Instead, they provoked a series of revolts led by palace and country nobles, supported by leaders of the Monophysite church, who fought to defend not only their traditional institutions and customs but also their properties, their power, and the fatherland itself against a feared alien imperialism.[111] In 1632, after a four-year bloodbath in which thousands perished, Susinyos, disappointed that the promised military assistance from Spain had never arrived and sobered by the effects of the slaughter, moved to heal his polarized kingdom by restoring the traditional faith, while still permitting Catholicism to function. Then he resigned in favor of a son, Basilides (or Facilides).

Although the Jesuits soon labeled Basilides as a bloody, tyrannical apostate, Ethiopians have reason to consider him a nationalist and a savior. Within two years of his ascendancy, he put to death his powerful uncle, Si'la Christos, and 25 of his own siblings. Searching for ways to deal with the Jesuits, he first dismissed them from court, scattered them about the kingdom, and confiscated their properties and supplies of small arms. Then he recalled

109. For Mendes's biography, see *ASCJ*, 345–47.

110. The most remarkable of his companions was Fr. Jerónimo Lobo (b. 1595–d. 1678), who survived one failed attempt to sail from Lisbon to Goa, the loss of a second ship off Mozambique, nine years in Ethiopia, another shipwreck on the coast of Natal, and capture by the Dutch in the Caribbean: *The Itinerário of Jerónimo Lobo*, trans. Donald M. Lockhart, ed. C. F. Beckingham, *HS*:2, no. 162 (1984). Lobo awaits a James Clavell.

111. Ibid., xxii.

them to the capital. In the face of such treatment, the patriarch first fumed, then offered to compromise; but his gesture came too late. He also sent four priests, led by the chronicler-Visitor Manuel de Almeida, to India to secure troops to defend the Church. When Basilides learned that a large Portuguese force had landed on the coast near Mombasa, he concluded that it constituted a threat to his own kingdom.[112] Accordingly, he banished all Jesuits and other priests from his kingdom in 1634. After the patriarch slipped out of the capital and won protection from a dissenting governor, Basilides had several fathers killed and pressured the governor to surrender the patriarch to the Turks at Massawa. Confined for a time in irons and chains, Mendes was finally released after the payment of a large ransom. By mid-September 1635 he was back in Goa, where he remained for the balance of his life, a chastened man living in great austerity, grieving as the last Jesuits in Ethiopia were hanged (1641), and dreaming of a day never to come when the Society might return to the highlands.[113]

The Limits of the Possible

The destruction of Jesuit enterprises in Japan and Ethiopia constituted major setbacks within the Assistancy during the seventeenth century. But there were important lessons to be learned from each reverse. In both lands, Jesuit ambitions to effect complete conversions were entirely unrealistic. The fathers were tolerated in the archipelago and in the African highlands because they appeared to provide needed services. For some decades they served as vital interpreters and intermediaries in the silk trade, but the arrival of English and especially Dutch traders made the Ignatians expendable. In Ethiopia the Jesuits promised technical and military assistance from Spain that was never forthcoming and, considering that kingdom's international problems, never a real possibility. Both there and in Japan they provided useful educational programs; but those programs were patently designed to spread an alien faith that was intolerable to followers of much older, far more deeply rooted systems of belief. It seems significant that the Japan enterprise entered a critical phase after the passing of Alessandro Valignano, a hard-nosed but flexible realist.

At this time, Iberian Catholicism seems to have been less flexible, less imaginative than that practiced by other Europeans, especially Italians and Germans. Catholicism was introduced to imperial China by an Italian, and during the seventeenth century his greatest successors were another Italian, a German, and a Belgian. Their most conspicuous successors, in turn, were French savants. The Madura mission never prospered until the appearance of another Italian, Roberto de Nobili. It is inconceivable that if he had been

112. As will be seen in Chapter 7, Mombasa was lost in 1630 when its ruler, formerly a Christian, apostatized and massacred its garrison and priests. The Portuguese counterattack of 1632 was intended to recover the town and fort, not to menace Ethiopia.

113. The best contemporary account of the Mendes years in Ethiopia is Lobo's *Itinerário*, chaps. 8, 11–14, 20, 23–27. For Lobo's later efforts to persuade the count of Linhares, viceroy of India, and authorities in Madrid and Rome to send relief to his comrades in the highlands, see ibid., chaps. 28 and 36. Other helpful sources are Rey, *Romance*, chaps. 19–24; A. H. M. Jones and Elizabeth Monroe, *A History of Abyssinia* (1935; rpr., New York, 1969), 92–101; and Mordechai Abir, *Ethiopia and the Red Sea* (London, 1980), chaps. 9–10. Although the Jesuits did not return to Ethiopia, two parties of French Capuchins tried to do so in the late 1630s and again in the late 1640s, both times with fatal consequences: Jones and Monroe, *History of Abyssinia*, 99–100.

sent to Ethiopia he would have behaved as unwisely there as the Portuguese patriarch Afonso Mendes did.

Considering the paucity of Jesuits in Ethiopia, the lack of effective support from secular authorities in Goa or in Europe, and the complexity of the power structure in the highlands, one may well question whether the Jesuits ever stood any chance of permanent success there. The same, of course, applies to their enterprise in Japan. Jesuit approaches in Ethiopia might well have been different had they perceived the population as "white," as their comrades did the occupants of Japan and China, rather than black; for the Portuguese, like the Spaniards and the Italians, had far less admiration for dark-skinned cultures, such as those of India, Ceylon, or Africa, than they did for white-skinned groups. But whereas the reverses that the Society experienced in Ethiopia and in Japan were achieved by indigenous forces in locales where Portuguese military and naval power were nonexistent, other equally serious contemporaneous calamities beset the Society in places in the East, where Portuguese power was supposed to protect ecclesiastical enterprises. Those losses took place within the boundaries of the Estado da India, where the principal aggressors were North European heretics whose successes encouraged other indigenous foes of the Portuguese to join the assault on the Portuguese eastern empire.

CHAPTER 7

An Empire and a Society in Peril: Consequences of the Anglo-Dutch Intrusions in the Eastern Seas, 1600–1641

The King of Spain . . . would be the right King for these lands. He should take over the whole of India, all the kingdoms and provinces right into China . . . and unite under his rule his Spanish India with the Portuguese muncipalities: this he could accomplish with fifty thousand men.

—Report of the Fugger agent, Cochin, 10 Jan. 1580

By the beginning of the seventeenth century, the intrusion of two rival heretic nations, the Dutch and the English, had shattered Portugal's longtime hegemony in eastern seas. In the course of the next century, both interlopers appropriated much of the spice, cloth, gem, dye, and other trades that had served as the sources of Portuguese wealth in the East. Acting both independently and in concert, they exploited Portugal's weaknesses at home and overseas and gained mastery over most of its once-lucrative empire. But their gains were not only at the expense of the Portuguese crown and its subjects: they—and the indigenous forces they stimulated—deprived the Society of many of the spiritual outposts that Francis Xavier and his successors had planted so confidently during the previous century.

Beginnings of the North European Intrusions in the East

The Netherlands, one of the most economically and culturally dynamic parts of Europe, became dynastically attached to the Spanish crown in 1517. For religious, economic, and constitutional reasons, the Dutch rebelled against their Spanish overlords in 1568, thereby initiating an 80-year war.[1] In 1595 the Hollanders made their first direct voyage to the spice marts of the East. Its success inspired syndicates of Dutch merchants to sponsor ever larger argosies to trade with eastern ports during the next half-dozen years.

The Hollanders were not alone among Europeans who yearned to reap profits through eastern trades. In 1591 a group of London merchants underwrote the first English expedition to enter the East Indies since Drake loaded cloves in the Moluccas (1587), but, unlike

---

1. Geoffrey Parker, *Spain and the Netherlands, 1559–1659* (London, 1979).

159

his voyage, their venture was largely a failure. Nevertheless, a group of investors in the Levant Company petitioned the Privy Council to charter what became the East India Company (EIC) in order to protect England's future interests in eastern trade.[2] Its mission was commerce, not conquest,[3] unlike that of the rival Dutch firm, the United Netherlands Chartered East India Company (VOC), a fusion of formerly competing syndicates organized in 1602. The goals of the VOC were not only to pursue trade but also to wage war against the Luso-Spanish empire and to establish a rival territorial empire in the East. As the advocate Johan van Oldenbarneveldt declared pithily, the VOC was created to damage the enemy and to provide security for the fatherland.[4]

Initially the Dutch concentrated on the Indonesian archipelago. There they negotiated commercial agreements with spice potentates, collected intelligence concerning sources of supply, and began the disruption of Portuguese port-to-port trade, that is, the so-called country trade.[5] Although the Dutch sustained reverses, they were generally remarkably successful. After an initial attack on the Portuguese fortress at Tidore failed, the Hollanders appeared before Macao in September 1601, causing such panic that plans were made to move women and children to the Jesuit college for protection. But such asylum proved unnecessary. One of the Dutch craft fell prey to Portuguese defenders, twenty Hollanders were charged with piracy, and seventeen were executed, though not before the Jesuits convinced them to accept Catholicism and the authority of the pope.[6]

The pickings soon improved. In June 1603, the annual ship from Macao to Malacca, containing the proceeds of the previous year's trade with China and Japan and described by the distressed cámara of Goa as "the richest and most powerful ship that ever left China," was captured in the Singapore straits, as was a Macao-based junk carrying provisions to the same port. A month later the crew of the annual silk ship bound from Macao to Nagasaki abandoned ship rather than risk Dutch capture. The mere presence of a Dutch cruiser off Macao the next year discouraged merchants from outfitting another carrack for Japan. In March 1605, still another carrack sailing from Macao to Malacca was harried by Dutch pursuers and fled into the Malayan port of Patani, only to be turned over to the enemy by the port's queen.[7]

Portuguese responses to the intensifying Dutch offensive in the East proved ineffective. In April 1604, a fleet of five ships left Lisbon for India, but storms compelled three vessels to return to port, and a fourth was lost on the Natal coast of southeast Africa.[8] Noting the economic distress caused by the absence of shipping from the kingdom and the loss of vessels captured by the Dutch, the chief accountant of the Estado da India informed

2. K. N. Chaudhuri, *The English East India Company . . . 1600–1640* (London, 1965), 10–14.

3. Instructions of the Company to Henry Middleton, 3 Mar. 1603 (OS), in Sir George Birdwood and William Foster, comps., *The Register of Letters &c. of the . . . Company of Merchants of London Trading into the East Indies, 1600–1609* (London, 1893), 50–51. For the sake of uniformity with the Portuguese record, I have adjusted the dates mentioned in the text of this chapter to the Gregorian calendar.

4. C. R. Boxer, *Jan Compagnie in War and Peace, 1602–1799: A Short History of the Dutch East India Company* (Hong Kong, 1979), 1.

5. James C. Boyajian, *Portuguese Trade in Asia Under the Habsburgs, 1580–1640* (Baltimore, 1993).

6. *RACJ*, 1: 236–37; Francisco Paulo Mendes da Luz, *O Conselho da India* (Lisbon, 1952), 264.

7. *RACJ*, 2: 91. C. R. Boxer, "The Affair of the *Madre de Deus*: A Chapter in the History of the Portuguese in Japan," Japan Society, *Transactions and Proceedings* 26 (1928–29), 13.

8. Mendes da Luz, *O Conselho da India*, 273.

Philip III in 1605 that the State's situation was becoming increasingly desperate: provisions and munitions were in short supply, receipts from the subsidiary fortresses were diminishing while expenses were mounting, and Dutch craft were sailing with impunity in Indian waters because there were not sufficient warships to dispel them.[9]

But the Hollanders' interest in Indian waters was not merely the capture of Portuguese shipping. They were also following the trail of cloth and pepper to their Indian sources. Soon after the accountant wrote Philip III, the first Dutch commercial agencies (factories) were established near long-extant Jesuit outposts at Masulipatam and Pulicat, two important ports on the Coromandel coast. The next factory the Dutch established in the subcontinent, erected in the important Gujarati port of Surat in 1617, was also not far from several Jesuit facilities along the northwest coast.[10]

While the Dutch were opening these agencies and others in Indonesia and Malaya, they increased maritime pressure on the Portuguese. In 1606, one Dutch fleet blockaded Lisbon and prevented the dispatch of any shipping to the Estado, a tactic that the Hollanders would later pursue in the East with devastating effectiveness. Another fleet, consisting of a dozen ships and about 1,300 men, besieged Malacca, that vital link in the commercial chain extending from Goa to Macao and a major Jesuit way station between India, Japan, and China. After five months, during which plague accompanied famine, the Portuguese garrison was on the verge of surrender when the entrepôt was relieved by a powerful Portuguese armada commanded by a determined if not very astute viceroy, D. Martim Afonso de Castro (1605–7), a descendant of a former viceroy, Martim Afonso de Sousa, who had accompanied Francis Xavier to India. After an inconclusive sea fight, the Dutch withdrew to replenish their stores, but the viceroy unwisely split his forces, sending half of them to Bengal to protect a merchant fleet there. The Hollanders then attacked the remainder of his armada, capturing several vessels, causing the others to run aground, and killing two of the six Jesuits who were ministering to the sailors and soldiers.[11]

The loss of part of that armada was only one of several disasters that Goa reported to Lisbon and Madrid between 1604 and 1608. On three occasions Dutch forces ravaged Portuguese shipping near the Jesuit college on Mozambique Island, and once they came close to capturing the island's decrepit fortress.[12] But the Dutch achieved far greater success in Amboina and in the Moluccas, where they began their territorial empire. When fourteen Dutch sail appeared before Amboina on 22 February 1605, the commander of the Portuguese fortress surrendered without a fight. Within a week the conquerors had placed all Portuguese subjects, including two Jesuits, aboard an ill-provisioned vessel that somehow reached Manila without the aid of a pilot.[13] Subsequently the captain of the Portuguese bastion

9. [Jerónimo Pedroso de Brito], "Relação do estado em que estavam as coisas da India no ano de 1605," in ibid., 417–44.

10. Tapan Raychaudhuri, *Jan Company in Coromandel, 1605–1690* (The Hague, 1962), chap. 2; Kristof Glamann, *Dutch-Asiatic Trade, 1620–1740* (The Hague, 1958), 132–33. Ann Bos Radwan, *The Dutch in Western India, 1601–1632* (Calcutta, 1978), is a disappointing study.

11. Gabriel Towerson to his loving brother, Bantam, 30 Apr. 1607, in *CSPC/EI*, 1 (1862): 152; *DM*, 3: 48, 52, 57, and 85 n. 2.

12. Eric Axelson, *Portuguese in South-East Africa, 1600–1700* (Johannesburg, 1960), 16–29.

13. *RACJ*, 2: 127-28; C[ornelius] Wessels, S.J., *Histoire de la mission d'Amboine, 1546–1605*, trans. J. Roebroeck, S.J. (Louvain, 1934), 189–92.

on Tidore chose to fight the Hollanders, but after sustaining a six-day bombardment, he too surrendered. By 1607 the Dutch were in control of most of the Moluccas, the source of cloves, nutmeg, and mace, and the site of some of the most hazardous missions the Society maintained anywhere.[14]

These onslaughts were so effective that Fr. Luís Fernandes, the Jesuit superior on Ternate, warned the king that "these Hollanders travel in these parts as if they are masters and lords of the seas, so that if Your Majesty does not send a great armament to punish and expel them I am convinced that they will become masters of [all our] fortresses," including those in India. Nor was he exaggerating, for agents of the EIC reported that the Portuguese Estado had sustained "a wound almost incurable."[15] In fact, the only remedy that the Council of Portugal could propose was the dispatch of four 300- to 400-ton warships to Goa with 400 troops, as well as 32 contos extracted from the New Christian community.[16]

But Philip III's most intimate advisors had a better solution. Late in 1608, representatives of the United Netherlands and of Spain signed a truce in Antwerp. Although Spain was prepared to recognize Dutch independence, the negotiators could not reach a permanent agreement, because the Dutch refused to withdraw from the Indies as Spain insisted.[17]

Like most such agreements between European powers during the early modern period, the Twelve Years Truce (1609–21) failed to ensure a cessation of hostilities overseas, especially in the Far East. There, Portuguese forces from Negapatam and São Tomé erased the Dutch factory at Pulicat in 1612 but were unable to prevent the Hollanders from erecting a commanding fortress there the next year. Although a Dutch attack on Manila was repelled in 1615, an attempt in the same year by a Portuguese armada from Malacca to undertake a joint operation with Spanish naval forces to recover the Moluccas was aborted after the Dutch captured the Portuguese warships.[18] Still more ominously, in 1619 the VOC established its permanent headquarters close to the Sunda straits at Batavia, built on the ruins of Jakarta, Java, to which its agents soon lured Chinese, Indian, and Malayan merchants who formerly traded at Malacca.[19] The same year, Dutch and English representatives negotiated a twenty-year agreement, marked top secret to prevent the Portuguese from learning its contents, that

14. *DM*, vol. 3 (1606–82). The Moluccas mission survived precariously and never numbered more than a dozen Jesuits. Until 1654 they fell under the jurisdiction of the Malabar provincial, but thereafter they came under the aegis of Spanish Jesuits in Manila. Jesuit influence in the islands ended when the Dutch took over Ternate in 1663. Paramita R. Abdurachman, "Moluccan Responses to the First Intrusions of the West," in Haryati Soebadio and Carine A. du Marchie Sarvaas, eds., *Dynamics of Indonesian History* (New York, 1978), 161–88. For the remarkably costly efforts by Spain—not Portugal—to recover the Moluccas and Spain's ongoing war there with the Dutch for more than a generation, see Jonathan I. Israel, *The Dutch Republic and the Hispanic World, 1606–1661* (Oxford, 1982), 14–15, 68–69, 336, 368, and 370.

15. Luís Fernandes to Philip III, 27 Apr. 1608, in *DM*, 3: 96; M. A. P. Meilink-Roelofsz, *Asian Trade and European Influence in the Indonesian Archipelago Between 1500 and About 1630* (The Hague, 1962), 181.

16. Consulta of 11 May 1608, in Mendes da Luz, *O Conselho da India*, 493–97.

17. On the protracted negotiations, see Israel, *Dutch Republic*, 4–12; and Mendes da Luz, *O Conselho da India*, 291–302.

18. Raychaudhuri, *Jan Company*, 22–23; C. R. Boxer, "Portuguese and Spanish Rivalry in the Far East During the 17th Century," *Journal of the Royal Asiatic Society* 3–4 (Dec. 1946): 154; Israel, *Dutch Republic*, 26–27.

19. K. N. Chaudhuri, *The Trading World of Asia and the English East India Company, 1660–1760* (New York, 1978), 16–17; Meilink-Roelofsz, *Asian Trade*, 414, s.v. "Batavia."

ostensibly terminated their fierce commercial rivalry in Indonesia and promised future joint naval operations against the Lusitanians.[20]

Although the EIC would not be prepared for a number of years to concede the Indonesian trading area to the VOC, its agents were also drawn to India by opportunities to purchase pepper, cloth, and dyestuffs. As K. N. Chaudhuri has shown, the EIC's direct Asian trade during the first decades of the seventeenth century went through three stages: the Bantam to London phase (1602–7); the Red Sea phase (1608–12); and thereafter the most enduring phase, that of trade with Surat.[21]

Situated 22 kilometers up from the mouth of the Tapti River, which flows into the Bay of Cambay, Surat was the successor to Broach and Cambay as the dominant port of the Gujarat, a position it would maintain until the mid-eighteenth century, when it would be succeeded by Bombay. A dependency of the Mughal empire, the port was the eastern terminus of a major trade route that extended to the Red Sea ports of Mokha and Aden.[22] The first EIC ship arrived in Surat in August 1608, and for the next quarter century, Portuguese authorities in Goa, aided by a handful of Jesuits at the Mughal court, made every effort to exclude the English from trade with the Mughal empire. Ultimately, they failed.

William Hawkins, a Turkish-speaking merchant (no relation to the Hawkins of Plymouth), was the first EIC representative to seek an imperial rescript (*farman*) authorizing the English to establish a factory at Surat. He arrived in Agra in mid-April 1609, bearing broadcloth gifts for the emperor, Jahangir. If the gifts did not impress Jahangir, Hawkins's knowledge of Turkish did, and the emperor invited him to remain as a court official. Hawkins received a substantial allowance that enabled him to acquire an Armenian wife and a cache of jewels. He soon developed a strong antipathy toward the court Jesuits, who persuaded Jahangir that the English were merely sea robbers and that to trade with them would be to risk a merciless blockade of his coastline by the Portuguese.[23]

Although Hawkins failed in his mission, a series of events soon led Jahangir to change his mind, not only admitting the English to Surat but permitting them to open a series of factories there and throughout the Gujarat. The first of those events was a naval battle in 1611 in which English ships bested a much larger Portuguese armada. The next year Henry Middleton, "Chief Governor and Lieutenant General" of the Company's annual fleet, brought more attractive gifts to Jahangir and warned him against the "falce Jesuitts and their deceiptful promises ... [for] they are like serpents which thrust themselvs in princes affairs with their false reportes, thereby to induce them to warr one against annother." Middleton stated that his sovereign, James I, was surprised that Jahangir, "beeing soe greate

20. The agreement was reached on 16 July 1619 after the English had lost eleven sail to the Dutch, who also burned their factory at Jacatra. For a convenient summary of Anglo-Dutch spice-trade rivalry, see D[aniel] G[eorge] E. Hall, *A History of South-East Asia*, 4th ed. (London, 1981), 319–34; on the secret agreement establishing a defense council and promising joint fleet operations, see *CSPC/EI*, 2 (1870): ix.

21. Chaudhuri, *Trading World*.

22. Ashin Das Gupta, *Indian Merchants and the Decline of Surat, c. 1700–1750* (Wiesbaden, 1979), 1–19.

23. William Foster, ed., *Early Travels in India, 1583–1619* (rpr., Delhi, n.d.), 60–121. English representatives accused the Jesuits of poisoning them and of converting "as many as they can: which they doe, but alas, it is for moneys sake." "Extracts of a Tractate Written by Nicholas Withington" (1612–14), in Samuel Purchas, *Hakluytus Posthumus or Purchas His Pilgrimes*, vol. 4 (Glasgow, 1905), 165 and 174.

a monarke, to live as it weare in slavery to the Portugalls, in such sorte that your subjects shipps cannott make any voyage any where butt they must first paye tribute to the Portugalls; ... which is a great disgrace to the greatnes of your monarchie."[24]

What Jahangir thought of that approach we do not know, but he was deeply angered in 1613 when a Portuguese naval patrol seized a large vessel belonging to his mother. Even though the Mokha-bound ship bore a Portuguese pass, the cargo, valued at about £100,000, was seized, and 700 passengers were detained. Jahangir promptly expelled the Portuguese, including the Jesuits, from Agra and sealed the Christian churches there. He also threatened military operations against Portuguese positions along the Konkan coast.[25]

D. Jerónimo de Azevedo, the viceroy, acted promptly to make amends. A close friend of the Jesuits, he turned to one of the fathers, Jerónimo Xavier, grandnephew of Saint Francis Xavier, to help prepare a Luso-Mughal treaty (7 June 1615). That document called for a restoration of peace between the two courts, Portuguese payment for all damages caused by the confiscation of the Mughal ship, and the emperor's promise to expel the English and Dutch from Surat because they came "under the cloak of merchants ... to these parts to settle in them and to conquer lands therein, owing to their living in Europe in distress and poverty."[26]

It was an interesting ploy, but it did not work; Jahangir never signed the treaty. It is thought that he failed to do so in part because he was impressed by the outcome of a second Anglo-Portuguese naval engagement off Surat (1614), another English triumph achieved by smaller forces, and in part because of the arrival (1615) of England's first genuine ambassador, Sir Thomas Roe. Although Roe failed to persuade the emperor to oust the Portuguese from his empire, the ambassador did secure further confirmation of English trading rights within it. For a time Roe and the Jesuits sparred. Ultimately, however, the ambassador and an Italian father, Francesco Corsi, earned each other's respect, and each performed intelligence and other services for his rival. Yet their amiable personal relations did not prevent a further deterioration of Anglo-Portuguese relations after the expiration of the Twelve Years Truce.[27]

Although that agreement proved beneficial in certain respects to Spain and to the United Provinces, it also aroused strong opposition within each nation.[28] Given that Dutch overseas expansion had been especially costly to Portugal's interests in the East and that no Portuguese authority had been consulted before the agreement was signed, it is understandable that members of the Council of Portugal strongly opposed its renewal unless the Dutch agreed to

24. Middleton to the Great Mughal, Mocha, 18 May 1612, in William Foster, ed., *The Journal of John Jourdain, 1608–1617*, HS:2, 16 (1905): 223.

25. *CSPC/EI*, 1: liii.

26. H[enry] Heras, S.J., "Jahanger and the Portuguese," Indian Historical Research Commission, *Proceedings*, 9th meeting (Dec. 1926): 72–80, is mistitled. Rather than an analysis of Luso-Mughal relations, it provides Portuguese and English texts of the proposed treaty but fails to note that it was never ratified. For the reasons that it was not signed, see William Foster, ed., *The Embassy of Sir Thomas Roe to the Court of the Great Mogul, 1615–1619*, HS:2, 1 and 2, 1: 95–96 n. 2.

27. On the Anglo-Portuguese naval battles of 1611 and 1614, see H. G. Rawlinson, *British Beginnings in Western India, 1597–1657* (Oxford, 1920), chap. 4. See also *CSPC/EI*, 1: lvi; and Sir William Foster, *England's Quest of Eastern Trade* (London, 1933), chaps. 23, 28, and 32. Despite its age, Edward Maclagan, *The Jesuits and the Great Mogul* (London, 1932), remains fundamental. On the sparring at court between English agents and the Jesuits, see 75–90.

28. Israel, *Dutch Republic*, chaps. 1 and 2, analyzes in detail war and peace sentiments in both nations.

withdraw from the East Indies. It may be, as the English ambassador to Madrid reported in 1615, that Spanish authorities were already reconciled to the loss of the Estado da India, where they had never been either willing or able to make the sort of commitment contemplated by the Fugger agent at the onset of the dual empire.[29] Certainly the principal advisors of Philip III were more concerned about Dutch activities in the New World and in Europe. The Council of the Indies, the chief advisory body for the Spanish empire, was naturally preoccupied with the need to exclude the Dutch from the Americas, and, like the Council of Portugal, it favored a resumption of hostilities rather than an extension of the original agreement. Other councilors viewed with alarm Dutch support of Protestant forces during the evolving Thirty Years War and believed that another round of hostilities would prove more costly to the United Provinces than to Spain. The conflict resumed in Europe in late August 1621. Characteristically, it had started seven months earlier in the Far East.[30]

The First Major Territorial Losses

Although Spanish authorities were willing to gamble that their forces could outlast the Dutch and bring the Hollanders to the point of financial exhaustion, they were unprepared for the series of disasters that occurred in 1622–23. During those years the Anglo-Dutch allies were able to launch several spectacular attacks against their Iberian foes over a broad perimeter that extended from the Philippines to Mozambique. Against the allies' nearly 100 ships, the Iberians could muster but a few.[31] Of 34 ships that sailed from Lisbon or Goa between 1620 and 1623, eight were wrecked, two were captured, and nine were forced to return to port.[32] Five of the ships that failed to reach their destination belonged to the squadron of D. Afonso de Noronha, viceroy-designate of India. Their departure was delayed for a month by the absence of wind to carry them down the Tagus. When they finally got away, poor seamanship caused them to become becalmed off the Guinea coast of Africa, where spoiled provisions and spreading malignant fevers forced them to turn back. As Fr. Jerónimo Lobo, S.J., a disgusted passenger, later remarked, "If the Viceroy had been able to leave port [on] … time …, he would have arrived in India in October at the latest, whence he could have come to the aid of Ormuz … and [it] would not have been lost the following May."[33]

Perhaps so. Of all the disasters of 1622, none shocked the Lusitanians as much as the loss of Ormuz, the last of Albuquerque's great conquests, the so-called Portuguese Gibraltar. Strategically situated at the entrance to the Persian Gulf, Ormuz was the Malacca of the West, a once-thriving entrepôt where Near Eastern, Indian, and Indonesian goods were exchanged for fabled profits. Though that barren island may have seen its best days before the Jesuits withdrew from it in 1570 (see Chapter 2), as late as 1581 it supplied Goa with more

---

29. Sir John Digby to [Secretary Winwood?], Madrid, 16 June 1615, in *CSPC/EI*, 1: 412.

30. Israel, *Dutch Republic*, 96 and 118.

31. For estimates of the size of Anglo-Dutch forces and the limited number of Portuguese naval units, see Israel, *Dutch Republic*, 117; A. R. Disney, *Twilight of the Pepper Empire* (Cambridge, Mass., 1978), 65; and *CSPC/EI*, 4 (1630–33): lix.

32. John H. Parry, "Transport and Trade Routes," in E. E. Rich and C. H. Wilson, eds., *The Cambridge Economic History of Europe*, vol. 4 (1967), 195.

33. *The Itinerário of Jerónimo Lobo*, trans. Donald M. Lockhart, ed. C. F. Beckingham, *HS*:2, no. 162 (1984): chap. 1. The quotation is from p. 18.

than a fifth of the Estado's income. Thereafter its share of the State's revenue declined, partly because of troublesome privateering by local Arabs who menaced its small craft, and partly because of the recent Persian conquests of the Bahrain pearling beds (1602) and the vital water wells of nearby Gombroon (1615). In 1614–15, the Persians besieged the insular outpost, but the citadel's largely mercenary garrison and a powerful Portuguese galleon force stationed there prevented Ormuz's capture. Portuguese authorities in Lisbon and Goa were properly alarmed by the arrival of the English at nearby Jask, where an EIC factory existed between 1616 and 1619, not only because the English were anxious to divert the valuable Persian silk trade from Ormuz to their factory, but also because of the possibility that the English would join the Persians in an attack on their fortress. That, in fact, occurred: after a three-month siege, the garrison mutinied, and on 3 May 1622, Ormuz capitulated.[34]

Contemporaneously, Jan Pieterzoon Coen, the ambitious governor-general at Batavia, deployed four Anglo-Dutch fleets against the Iberians. One group of ten ships blockaded Manila Bay between January 1621 and May 1622, but the Dutch never had any luck with their Philippine assaults. A second fleet blockaded Malacca and induced Asian trading vessels venturing near there to take their cargoes to Batavia instead. One of Coen's major objectives was to wrest Macao from the Portuguese in order to initiate trade with China. To that end a Dutch force, consisting of thirteen ships and 1,300 men, appeared off the lightly guarded port on 21 June 1622. After an exchange of artillery, in which the Portuguese disabled one of the attackers, the Hollanders landed 800 troops on a northeast beach, from which 150 Portuguese and Eurasian defenders had just retreated. Under the cover of a smoke screen, the landing party confidently advanced toward the town, but the Jesuits were not prepared to give up their vital base without a fight. Led by their acting superior, they joined with other defenders to haul several bombards up a hill behind their college. Serviced by Giacomo Rho, Adam Schall, and others, the bombards began to fire upon the advancing Hollanders. Fr. Rho scored a fortunate bull's-eye when he succeeded in exploding a powder barrel in the midst of the invaders. During the ensuing panic, the attackers' leader was killed, and the survivors fled to their boats, hotly pursued by Portuguese soldiers, angry citizens, fearsome black slaves, zealous armed Jesuits, and other ecclesiastics. Many of the Hollanders drowned. Having suffered an estimated 300 casualties and the loss of one of his ships, the disgusted Dutch commander gave up the venture. Thus ended what Charles R. Boxer has termed "the most decisive [defeat] ever sustained by the Hollanders at the hands of the Portuguese in the East."[35]

But just over a month later, an Anglo-Dutch squadron achieved a major naval victory over the Portuguese near the island of Mozambique. Toward the end of March 1622, four

34. The best narrative of the final days of Ormuz remains C. R. Boxer, "Anglo-Portuguese Rivalry in the Persian Gulf, 1615–1635," in Edgar Prestage, ed., *Chapters in Anglo-Portuguese Relations* (Watford, Eng., 1935), 46–129; the most important fresh analysis is Niels Steensgaard, *Carracks, Caravans and Companies: The Structural Crisis in the European-Asian Trade in the Early 17th Century* (Copenhagen, 1972), pt. 2.

35. C. R. Boxer, *Fidalgos in the Far East, 1550–1770* (1948; rpr., New York, 1968), chap. 5. There are several accounts of the victory. They include: *Summa victoria lusitanorum in urbe Amachao contra hereticos Hollandas* (Lisbon, 24 June 1623), in ARSI, *Lus.*, 74, fol. 171; [Jerónimo Rodrigues, S.J.], *Relacion de la victoria que los Portugueses alcançaron en la cidade de Macao ... contra los Olandeses ... traduzida de la que embio el padre Visitador de la Compania de Iesus a los padres de seu colegio de Madrid* (Madrid, 1623, but printed by António Noguera Barrocos, identified as a Portuguese bookseller), James Ford Bell Library; and [Anon.], "Relação da victoria q' a cidade de Macao ... teve de Olandezes," n.d., in BA/JA/49-V-3, no. 18.

carracks, an advice boat, and two galleons prepared to leave Lisbon for the Estado. The galleons were bound for Ormuz, whose loss was not yet anticipated. The remaining vessels were bound for Goa with the Jesuit Jerónimo Lobo, still impatient after the disappointment of his aborted voyage the year before. But the most important personage aboard the flagship was D. Francisco da Gama, conde da Vidigueira.

The count, a grandson of Vasco da Gama, had served as viceroy of India at the end of the sixteenth century and was the son-in-law of a subsequent viceroy. He later became president of the Portuguese Council of India (1608–12) and served on the Council of State of Philip III. When D. Afonso de Noronha declined to tempt fate a second time after his unsuccessful voyage down the Guinea coast the year before, the count agreed to return to India to help organize the State's defenses. This time, according to Fr. Lobo, "the ships were prepared more energetically," and their departure went smoothly.

Apart from the loss of two of the squadron's units, which became separated from the others, the outbound voyage was uneventful until the remaining ships approached Mozambique Island. While about 50 kilometers south of that island, they were overtaken by what they initially presumed to be a pilot boat. Instead, it was one of several large warships forming part of the Anglo-Dutch "fleet of defence" that had left Batavia the previous December with instructions to patrol off Mozambique in order to apprehend any Portuguese vessels sailing up from the Cape of Good Hope. The result was a two-day running battle (23 and 24 July), at the end of which three of the four Portuguese ships ran aground within sight of their insular refuge. Lost were badly needed warships, part of their war chest, and, apparently, most of the private funds, which the Anglo-Dutch forces retrieved before setting the ships afire.[36]

Within the space of three months, therefore, the Iberians sustained two serious losses— Ormuz in May and the viceregal squadron in July—and survived one near miss when the Dutch assault on Macao in June miscarried. Less than two months after the Mozambique debacle, an even greater calamity occurred in the Caribbean, where 9 of 22 ships of the Spanish silver fleet were lost in a hurricane off the Cuban coast.[37]

Late in December of that black year, 1622, Vidigueira finally reached Goa via Cochin. He and his party were accorded the customary warm reception in the capital, but the count was not deceived: it was no longer the flourishing place he had known in his younger days. He reported to the crown that Cochin had hardly any trade left, that the loss of Ormuz had caused serious financial distress in Goa, that morale throughout his posts was low, and that India was bereft of adequate defenses.[38]

The count's grim report was not exaggerated. It is confirmed by the testimony of Pietro della Valle, an Italian patrician who visited Goa about this time and provided a far more

36. The foregoing is based upon *Itinerário of Jerónimo Lobo*, chaps. 3–4; and C. R. Boxer, "Dom Francisco da Gama, Conde da Vidigueira, e a sua viagem para a India no ano de 1622," *Anais do club militar naval*, nos. 5–6 (Lisbon, 1930) (separate).

37. On 21 July 1985, Treasure Salvors, Inc., of Key West, Florida, announced the discovery of the remains of one of the galleons of that fleet, the *Atocha*, still laden with millions of dollars in bullion and jewels. For an early analysis of the findings, see R. Duncan Mathewson III, *Treasure of the Atocha* (New York, 1986).

38. Viceroy to king, 1623, summarized in F. C. Danvers, ed., *Report of Portuguese Records Relating to the East Indies*, 2 vols. in 1 (London, 1892), 1: 27.

realistic assessment of conditions there than the rosy picture portrayed a few years earlier by Alexander of Rhodes. According to the Italian,

> Portugals there are not many; they us'd to be sufficiently rich, but of late, by reason of many losses by the incursions of the Dutch and English in these seas, they are ... rather poor. Nevertheless they live in outward ... splendor ...; however in secret they endure many hardships and some ... accounted ... Gentlemen ... lead very wretched lives, undergoing much distress, being put to beg every ... Evening.[39]

Vidigueira warned his superiors that they would be well advised to seek peace with the Dutch on any terms. The Council of Portugal, which had so recently urged the king to resume war against the Dutch, concurred and in September 1623 urged Philip IV to seek "some accord with Holland, for prospects for war become daily more impossible." But the Spanish Council of State disagreed. One of its members, a noble with long experience as a soldier in the Low Countries, optimistically wrote,

> The time for seeking the benefits of this war can not yet ... have arrived ... for the enemy must have mounted the utmost efforts of which he is capable, and if Your Majesty persists with the war ..., clearly they will not be able to keep it up ... the finances that they have for both undertakings [the European and the colonial wars] must decline so that ... they must weaken in such distant and costly conquests, and thus, even as regards Portugal's interests, Your Majesty can order nothing so useful as continuing the war.[40]

Six months later a powerful Dutch force occupied Bahia de Todos os Santos and the city of Salvador, capital of the State of Brazil and headquarters of Jesuit activities there, thus initiating three desperate decades of fighting for control of that colony's northeast sugar lands (see Chapter 9).

The Worsening Crisis in the East

Although the pace of Dutch conquests in the East slackened for some years while the VOC consolidated its positions, the Portuguese gained no respite during the late 1620s and the 1630s. The first crisis occurred in Ceylon, where, until the late 1620s, Portuguese rule seemed secure under the leadership of an energetic captain-general, Constantino de Sá de Noronha. As indicated in the preceding chapter, the Portuguese had become masters of two of the island's three kingdoms, Jaffna in the north and Kotte in the south and west. The remaining mountainous Sinhalese kingdom of Kandy had been weakened by a series of Portuguese campaigns during the first two decades of the century, and later by internal unrest. As late as the mid-1620s, Portuguese authorities remained confident of their ability to gain control of Kandy as well. Meanwhile, they relied upon a strategy of gradual encirclement to prevent the Kandyans from trading with the Dutch. By 1625 Sá had built

39. Edward Gray, ed., *The Travels of Pietro della Valle to India*, HS:1, 84 (1892), 157; cf. Solange Hertz, trans., *Rhodes of Viet Nam: The Travels and Missions of Father Alexander de Rhodes in China and Other Kingdoms of the Orient* (Westminster, Md., 1966), 11–18.

40. Both quotations are from Israel, *Dutch Republic*, 122. See also Council of Portugal to king, 23 Nov., 21 Dec., and n.d., 1622, in *DUP*, 2: 308–13, 321–22, and 386–87, as well as the "Relacion del estado en que quedavan las cosas dela India" [1622], in ibid., 316–19.

or strengthened half a dozen fortresses, including Colombo, Galle, and Negombo in the south and southwest, Jaffna in the north, and the capacious harbor of Trincomalee in the northeast. But his superiors in Goa and Lisbon remained concerned that Kandy might still establish contact with the Dutch via the eastern coastal lagoon of Batticaloa and therefore ordered it fortified.

In July 1628 Sá began the construction of a badly situated fort on an island about 5 kilometers inside the lagoon, thereby provoking the ruler of Kandy, Senerat, to undertake war. While Sá was at Batticaloa, Sinhalese forces advanced on Jaffna, provoking a general uprising in which two Jesuits perished. But the uprising was put down, and Sinhalese efforts to rouse Kotte failed. Sá responded by undertaking two raids into Kandy, burning the capital during his second foray; but he was badly punished as he descended from the mountains.

In late 1629, Senerat offered peace, but Portuguese authorities in Goa and on the island rejected that appeal. As a result, Sinhalese forces intensified the blockade of Batticaloa and lured Sá into a retaliatory strike. The decisive engagement occurred in the hill country of Uva on the field of Randeniwela (22 August 1630), where 12,000 Sinhalese surrounded Sá's army, consisting of 450 Europeans and 4,500 native auxiliaries or *lascarins*. When elements of the latter deserted, the Sinhalese carved up the Europeans, including the captain-general. The Kandyans briefly besieged Colombo, then moved back into the mountains. Thus began the final phase of the "fatal history" of Ceylon, one whose last chapter would be written in 1658.[41]

The Sinhalese annihilation of Portugal's largest military force on the island was one of three anti-Lusitanian indigenous movements in the early 1630s. In August 1631, Yusuf bin Hasan, the Christian apostate "king" or sultan of Mombasa, devastated Portugal's major fortress on the Swahili coast. Yusuf's father had been assassinated by order of the fort's commander in 1614, and he himself was sent to Goa for his education. There the Augustinians converted him and baptized him as D. Jerónimo Chingulia. By 1630 he seemed ready for the role of a puppet and was allowed to return to his Islamized homeland. The next year he was detected offering Muslim prayers before his father's grave and was marked for arrest and trial by the Holy Office in Goa. On 16 August 1631, Yusuf stole the march on his would-be captors by penetrating the fortress with a group of supporters. He conducted a bloodbath for two weeks, during which all but five of the fortress's 155 inhabitants were massacred. For two months (10 January to 19 March 1632) Yusuf held off a Portuguese relief expedition sent from Goa. Subsequently he withdrew from the settlement and turned to piracy; consequently the Portuguese were able to reoccupy the fortress the following August.[42]

---

41. On Sá's regime and his end, see Chandra Richard de Silva, *The Portuguese in Ceylon, 1617–1638* (Colombo, 1972), chap. 3; and George Davison Winius, *The Fatal History of Portuguese Ceylon* (Cambridge, Mass., 1971), chap. 2.

42. Justus Strandes, *The Portuguese Period in East Africa* (1899), trans. Jean F. Wallwork, ed. J. S. Kirkman (Nairobi, 1961), chap. 14; C. R. Boxer and Carlos de Azevedo, *Fort Jesus and the Portuguese in Mombasa* (London, 1960), 34–38; James S. Kirkman, *Fort Jesus: A Portuguese Fortress on the East African Coast* (Oxford, 1974), chap. 1. Unless one is interested in the abortive efforts to canonize three Augustinian martyrs killed by Yusuf, G. S. P. Freeman-Grenville, *The Mombasa Rising Against the Portuguese, 1631, from Sworn Evidence* (Oxford, 1980), is of scant value. As will be seen later, the Portuguese lost Mombasa at the end of the century (see Chapter 8). Jesuit financial assistance to bring about its recovery will be considered in Chapters 13 and 24.

But the reprieve on the east African coast was offset by another reverse in northeastern India. While Yusuf was engaging in piracy, troops of Shah Jahan, successor to Jahangir, overran the Portuguese outpost at Hugli, near the future city of Calcutta. The 200 Portuguese troops and 600 slaves of what had been Portugal's principal base in Bengal were subsequently removed to Agra, where they and the Jesuits who attended them languished in confinement for a decade.[43]

While the Portuguese were unable to liberate their comrades in the Mughal capital, all Europeans in India were equally powerless to cope with a series of natural calamities that afflicted the subcontinent from the late 1620s until the mid-1630s. In November 1630, the chief factor of the EIC agency at Masulipatam wrote his superiors, "On this coaste is a great and mortall death, which begann three yeares since and still increaseth." The next month his counterpart at Surat reported the existence of "an universall death over this continent, of whose like in these parts noe former age hath record." Failed rains followed by excessive flooding produced a mighty famine that extended eastward from the Gujarat to Golconda and southward as far as the Coromandel coast. In late 1631, the Portuguese viceroy reported that there had been an estimated 3,000,000 deaths in the Gujarat during the previous ten months. Two months later, a Dutch factor notified the VOC council in Batavia that 30,000 persons in Surat, including ten of the eleven English factors and three Dutch agents, had perished that year because of pestilence. Rice, the staff of life for millions of Indians, became extremely scarce, as did animal fodder, and the price of the former rose sevenfold in the course of a year. The effects of the great drought and associated maladies, both of which embraced the Portuguese enclaves as well, were still being felt as late as 1636.[44]

Portuguese authorities discovered no easy remedies to these problems. The Sinhalese revolt imperiled the vital cinnamon trade, whose growth for a time partially compensated for the loss of the rarer eastern spices. Throughout the 1620s, Portugal's share of pepper exports to Europe fell alarmingly and averaged less than half its sixteenth-century level. The crown's efforts to emulate the enemy by organizing a commercial pepper firm ended "in dismal failure" in 1634, five years after the venture began.[45] Scarcities of shipping and manpower made it impossible for the viceroys to assist Macaonese merchants, who were being squeezed out of Japan's silk trade by the Dutch and by Japanese intransigence, or to aid the Jesuits in Ethiopia during the persecution of the mid-1630s (see Chapter 6). It is not surprising, therefore, that D. Miguel de Noronha, conde de Linhares, viceroy of India (1629–34), vented his frustrations against Indian moneylenders, who failed to answer his pleas for loans to strengthen his defenses, and against the religious Orders, especially the Jesuits, who allegedly provided asylum for newly arrived recruits. Linhares accused the

43. Danvers, *Portuguese Records*, 1: 28; J. J. A. Campos, *History of the Portuguese in Bengal* (1919; rpr., New York, 1978), chaps. 12–13. See also Tapan Raychaudhuri, *Bengal Under Akbar and Jahangir: An Introductory Study in Social History* (1953; rpr., Delhi, 1969).

44. *EFI* (1630–33), xxi, 20, 79, 122, 166, 177–78, and 180–82; Anthony Disney, "Famine and Famine Relief in Portuguese India in the Sixteenth and Early Seventeenth Centuries," Fourth International Seminar on Indo-Portuguese History (separate, Lisbon, 1985). In late 1649, António Figueira, S.J., reported that the city and environs of Goa had suffered great hunger during the summer months, causing many deaths, but he failed to reveal its cause or the number of casualties. "Relação annual da província de Goa deste anno de 1649," in ANTT/CJ/56, no. 6.

45. Disney, *Twilight*, 61, 148, and passim.

Jesuits of insubordination and of taking advantage of Portugal's perilous state in India to enhance their own economic status there.[46]

Linhares's complaints about the economic activities of the Jesuits will be considered in later chapters (see Chapters 17 and 21). Suffice it to say here that the viceroy's quarrels with the Jesuits did not prevent him from attending mass in their churches or from relying upon them to help resolve one of Goa's most pressing problems—the persistence of maritime conflict with the EIC.[47] After the fall of Ormuz, that conflict had been carried on in a series of mutually costly engagements in two areas, the Persian Gulf and Swally Hole, the EIC's anchorage near Surat.[48]

Both sides had been anxious to end hostilities for some time. After the Amboina massacre (1623), the Anglo-Dutch alliance had turned sour. The same year, a member of the Council of Portugal proposed an alliance with England, reminding the king of the old duke of Alba's dictum, "Peace with England and war with the rest of the world."[49] Seven years later, England and Spain ended five years of hostilities by signing a peace treaty in which the status of English activities in overseas areas claimed by Spain and Portugal was deliberately left vague. In 1631, a year after two Portuguese efforts to prevent the EIC from trading at Surat ended in ignominious naval defeats, Thomas Rastell, president of the EIC factory there, contacted Jesuit fathers António Pereira and António de Andrade, residents of the college at Damão, and suggested that the 1630 peace be interpreted as extending to India. The response: only if England were willing to agree to an alliance against the Dutch. Also in 1631, Sir Francis Cottington, "lately returned out of Spain," advised officers of the EIC that the king and the Council of Portugal had been disposed to agree to extend the peace beyond the Cape of Good Hope until the arrival of reports of Portuguese victories in the East Indies caused them to resume their traditional stance,

46. The Jesuits and the other religious Orders repeatedly denied the Goan government's charge that they lured newly arrived soldiers to join them. E.g., Jesuit provincial to viceroy, 3 Jan. 1636, in ANTT/LM 35, fol. 183^r. Linhares considered the real traitors to be prominent Indians. He wrote in his diary, "Não são os olandezes do mar os que tanto perdem a Jndia quanto os olandezes da terra que estão nestes çidades do norte os quaes tem nomes de Sinais, Ganasinay, Ramasinay Vitulasinay, com os outros mais bramenes Canarinsa desta çidade que todos trazem conssigo sinais da perdição da Jndia, porque nem são gentios, nem mouros, nem christãos mas são todos huns alheos sem Deus, sem fee, sem ley, sem temer, sem vergonha." Entry of 23 July 1634, in Linhares, *Diário do 3.º* [*sic* for *4º*] *conde de Linhares, vice-rei da India*, 2 vols. (Lisbon, 1937–43), 2: 150.

47. English attacks on Portuguese shipping were harmful to all interests in the Estado, including the Jesuits. In 1618, for example, English raiders sank the flagship of a squadron of six vessels bound from Lisbon to Goa, resulting in the loss to the Society of 80,000 *patacas*. Hector F[e]r[nande]z to Br. António da Costa at São Roque, 1618, in ANTT/CJ/68/47.

According to the provincial of Malabar, bad blood between the Jesuits and the viceroy originated in a dispute over properties that Linhares had inherited in Portugal. "Do estado das couzas ao tempo q. se temou a conservatoria," Cochin, 4 Dec. 1632, in ARSI, *Goa*, 18, fols. 129–32.

48. For the continued maritime struggle in the Persian Gulf, see Boxer, "Anglo-Portuguese Rivalry," 93ff. Swally Hole or Swally Road was an anchorage 11 kilometers long and 1.6 kilometers wide, situated 19 kilometers west of Surat. It was protected from the reach of the sea by an extended sandbar, and English captains preferred it to the mouth of the Tapti River, which contained shifting shoals and allowed less maneuvering room. Rawlinson, *British Beginnings*, 49; Holden Furber, *Rival Empires of Trade in the Orient, 1600–1800* (Minneapolis, 1976), 344 n. 30.

49. Consulta of 29 Jan. 1623, in *DUP*, 2: 314–15.

which was that England had no right to be there.[50] The victories to which Cottington alluded were the successful defense of Malacca (October 1629) against massive forces assembled by the sultan of Acheh, Sumatra, and the destruction by Nuno Álvares Botelho, one of Portugal's most esteemed admirals, of a large Dutch ship off Jambi, in eastern Sumatra.[51]

Nevertheless, it seems clear that conversations and correspondence between the president of the agency and the Jesuits continued and that the fathers kept Viceroy Linhares fully informed.[52] Early in 1633 the viceroy reported one such conversation between the president and the mysterious Fr. Paulo Reimão, whom contemporaries described as either an Englishman or a Dutchman.[53] But Philip IV responded in March 1634 by forbidding any agreement with the English, contending that their presence beyond the Cape was a patent violation of the treaty of 1630. By then Thomas Rastell had been succeeded by William Methwold, who wrote Fr. Alvaro Tavares, the Jesuit provincial, then on an inspection tour in Damão, indicating that he would be willing to lay down arms if the viceroy would concur. Tavares responded promptly that he would do all in his power to facilitate such an agreement, that he was turning over the president's letter to local officials, and that he was dispatching two of his own men to Surat to help with the negotiations.[54]

Both Methwold and Linhares sensed that the time was ripe for the conclusion of an armistice, no matter what their superiors might think. As one EIC captain wrote his directors, because of Dutch naval patrols, "the pore Portingall cannot goe out of any thaire portes but the Dutch presantly taketh them." He predicted that the Portuguese could not long withstand continued Dutch maritime pressure. But he warned that if the Portuguese were crushed, the Company's trade would also suffer seriously, "for allreadye the Dutch hath as faire quartar in Surratt and Persia as the English have, and doth not faile to supplie those places with more goods than you doe of the same sort, and also such as you have none, viz, spises and Cheina ware of all sorts."[55] The captain's observations suggest the basic motives behind the accord signed in Goa in January 1635. The viceroy recognized that the Portuguese badly needed help if they were to continue to oppose the Dutch and to retain any hope of recovering lost ground. The English did not wish to see the Portuguese collapse completely and were anxious to trade in their ports, especially Goa, Malacca, and Macao. Furthermore, if Portugal had become a third-rate naval power in the East, the English were no more than second-rate. There was only one first-rate maritime force in the region—the Hollanders—whom both had reason to fear.[56]

50. *EFI* (1630–33), xxxvi; EIC, court minutes, 18 Mar. 1631 (OS), *CSPC/EI*, 4: 8 and 137.

51. C. R. Boxer, "The Achinese Attack on Malacca in 1629, as Described in Contemporary Portuguese Sources," in John Bastin and R. Roolvink, eds., *Malayan and Indonesian Studies: Essays Presented to Sir Richard Winstedt on His Eighty-Fifth Birthday* (Oxford, 1964), 105–21.

52. For one such exchange, see Fr. Paulo Reimão to Thomas Rastell, Damão, 22 June 1631, in *EFI* (1630–33), 220–21.

53. The English considered him to be of Dutch origins, while Linhares was uncertain, describing him as "de nação Ingres ou olandes." Linhares, *Diário*, 2: 264. Fr. Reimão is not listed by Fr. Wicki as among the Jesuits sent from Europe to the Estado da India.

54. Methwold to Tavares, 25 Dec. 1633, and Tavares to Methwold, 31 Dec. 1633, in *EFI* (1630–33), 331.

55. Captain Richard Allnutt, at Swally, to EIC directors, 31 Jan. 1634, first excerpted in *CSPC/EI*, 4: 517–19, and reprinted in *EFI* (1634–36), 6–9.

56. Cf. Foster's comments, *EFI* (1637–41), xlv.

Still, it required a year for Methwold and Linhares to get together. In January 1634, Linhares accepted the provincial's recommendation and issued a safe-conduct to Methwold. He stated that he did not believe that the treaty really applied to the East Indies but that he was willing to conclude a truce pending final confirmation by their European superiors. The safe-conduct, transmitted by two Jesuits in Surat, authorized up to ten English representatives to come to Goa. The Portuguese councilors at Damão wrote the president of their support for the meeting and praised the "holy zeal" of the Jesuits for opening the lines of communication. The fathers continued to maintain contact between the two sides throughout the year. In May, Tavares wrote Methwold that he rejoiced at the prospect of seeing him again and assured him that the Jesuits were preparing three of their houses in Goa to accommodate the English. In December, Linhares, who had repeatedly assured Methwold in letters conveyed to him by the Jesuit Fr. Reimão that he was anxious to get together, personally went to inspect the accommodations and found them acceptable.[57]

The English fleet, three ships and a pinnace, finally left Surat early in January 1635, a day after picking up Fr. Reimão at Damão to serve as interpreter. The fleet reached Goa on 17 January, anchored off the Aguada fortress, and saluted the port with 21 salvos, which were answered by all the fortresses and six Portuguese galleons and two carracks. Since Linhares was bedridden with fever, he sent his son in the viceregal barge to welcome his guests, who were housed in Pangim, the site of the present city of Goa but 8 kilometers away from its location at this time. Methwold and his colleagues were overwhelmed by their accommodations:

> The house is a stately one, and honorably furnished; our diett plentiful and accomodated by an abundance of goodly plate; the care of our enterteinment committed to persons of great quality both for office and estate; whilest the captaine of the guard and his whole company attended us; wherein we could all wish they would have been lesse officious, yet we conceive that to honor and serve us they received this imployment.[58]

With the assistance of three Jesuits, the terms of the truce were worked out during the next three days. The truce provided for an immediate cessation of arms, to last indefinitely unless denounced by the respective sovereigns and thereafter to remain in effect for an additional six months.[59] As soon as the document was properly signed, seven great ordnance announced the arrival of the English representatives at the viceregal palace, where the

---

57. *EFI* (1634–36), 2, 10, 21–22, 27, 31, and 34; Linhares, *Diário*, 1: 34–35 and 112–14; 2: 238–40 and 244.

58. Methwold et al. to the Company, Goa road, 19 Jan. 1635 (OS), in *EFI* (1634–36), 91. Despite existing scarcities, the viceroy ordered "se lhe desse tudo em super abundanssia assim aos da terra como aos do mar, E que a cada nao se mandassem duas pipas de vinho, seis vacas, doze carneiros, galinhas, e todo genero de fruitas, e quinentas padas de pão." Linhares, *Diário*, 2: 264.

59. The substance of the accord of 20 Jan. 1635 is given in *EFI* (1634–36), 88; the literal Portuguese text is in Linhares, *Diário*, 2: 267–68. The latter credits Methwold with having initiated the proposal "por meyo dos reuerendos Padres provinçiaes da companhia Antonio dAndrade e Alvaro Tavares, as grandes vtilidades e autoridades que se seguirião a dous Monarchas . . . não só çessão, mas vnião de armas contra os enemigos comús," whereas the English version simply begins, "The Fathers Provincial . . . having represented to the Viceroy, on behalf of the English, the profit and advantage likely to ensue to both nations in these eastern parts." Oddly, G. V. Scammell, "England, Portugal and the Estado da India, c. 1500–1635," *Modern Asian Studies* 16, 2 (1982): 177–92, ignores the agreement altogether.

bedridden Linhares gave his guests a two-hour reception: "Custome [and] the qualety of his dignity commanded us upon our knee," wrote Methwold, "where we endeavoured to have kist his hand: but he permitted it not, but embracing us raised us up one after another. And then, dismissing all but your President, he commanded a chaire to be brought, and him to sit down by him; and then, excluding all but Padre Paulo Reimaon, he spoke and heard out two full houres conference."[60] During those conversations the two rival officials exchanged information concerning recent Dutch activities[61] and discussed the possibility of future joint naval operations and trading opportunities. The viceroy offered the English all the facilities of the port, and the English agreed to supply him with "anie Europe commodities which are the natural grouth of our country," which Linhares promised to pay for in pepper. More than that, Linhares authorized an English ship to proceed to Macao to bring back urgently needed supplies, especially copper. Upon the conclusion of the meeting the president gave unspecified gifts to the viceroy for himself, his son, and the Jesuits amounting to 300 *pesos del ocho*, and the Portuguese reciprocated in kind.

Although the president and the viceroy parted with apparent cordiality, the long-standing distrust between their respective nations remained. As Methwold informed his superiors a few days later,

> As for their pretences of auncient amity and alliance betwixt the Crownes ..., with their acknowledgment that much English bloud continues still to runne in many of their most honorable veines, we must acknowledge the verity, but have cause to suspect the praetence: for whilest they are tainted with so much contradiction in religion as makes us unto them even an abhomination, we may feare the auncient position of the Jesuits: *cum haereticis fides non est observanda* [with heretics trust can never exist]. And so we will rather beleeve that not love towards us but hate to the Hollanders hath in pollicy humbled them.[62]

But, of course, the reverse was equally true.

Within two weeks Linhares wrote the crown a glowing report concerning the accord and its possibilities. He stated that William Methwold had assured him that Charles I would send a dozen galleons to protect Portuguese stations against the Dutch and that he had assured the president that Philip IV would dispatch a like number to India. With such forces, he predicted, it would be easy to recover Ormuz and Pulicat in less than six months. An alliance with the Mataram sultanate of Java would lead to the conquest of Batavia, thereby opening up opportunities for the recovery of the Spice Islands.[63] But the English ships proved to be visionary. No such armadas, no such joint operations, were ever to materialize. Although the English and the Portuguese both gained certain temporary advantages from

---

60. Methwold to EIC, 19 Jan. 1635, in *EFI* (1634–36), 92.

61. By the time Linhares met with the president, he knew from Fr. Reimão that the Dutch were encouraging the sultan of Bijapur to attack Goa and that two Portuguese ships loaded with cinnamon had been lost, presumably to the Hollanders. Linhares, *Diário*, 2: 254 and 260.

62. Methwold to EIC, 19 Jan. 1635, in *EFI* (1634–36), 96. The fullest coeval accounts of the final negotiations in Goa are in ibid., 89–99, and Linhares, *Diário*, 2: 261–69. See also Disney, *Twilight*, 148–54.

63. Linhares to king, 14 Feb. 1635, summarized in Alfredo Botelho de Sousa, *Subsídios para a história militar marítima da India, 1585–1669* [*sic* for *1650*], 4 vols. (Lisbon, 1930–56), 3: 593. The expansionist kingdom of Mataram controlled most of eastern Java and fought tenaciously against the Dutch intruders. Hall, *History of South-East Asia*, 304–8 and 336–49.

the accord, they were far fewer than either side had anticipated.[64] Preoccupied as it was with grave domestic and international problems, the Spanish court neither denounced nor ratified the agreement, whose terms were later incorporated in the Anglo-Portuguese treaty of 1642.[65] But in neither form did it prevent the continued erosion of Portugal's eastern empire.

Signs of Impending Collapse, 1636–41

The eastern empire's erosion owed much to the brilliant strategy devised by a Hollander, Antonie van Diemen, governor-general of Batavia (1636–45). As Charles R. Boxer has written, "No man had a better appreciation of seapower than this [onetime] clerk from Culemborg." By 1639 van Diemen had at his disposal 85 warships, and he knew how to deploy them: some were assigned to keep the Spaniards busy defending the Philippines and their positions in the Moluccas; most of the rest were ordered to patrol sea lanes utilized by Portuguese ships. Van Diemen's immediate aim was to reduce one Portuguese outpost after another. Once these outposts were in Dutch possession, the Hollanders could deal with their former English friends and then establish a commercial monopoly extending from Formosa and Nagasaki to Mozambique, one that would be far more powerful than the fragile Portuguese hegemony of the past.[66]

Van Diemen came remarkably close to achieving his ambition. One of the keys to his strategy was a seasonal blockade (late September until April or May) of Goa that lasted for eight years (1636–44) and consisted of six to twenty warships stationed off the port.[67] The warships' mission was to interdict shipping between Europe and Goa; to prevent reinforcements and supplies from being sent to the subsidiary centers of the State; and to disrupt the vital coastal convoys (*cafilas*) of small trading vessels that traveled under protective escort between Cochin and points further south and the capital, and between Goa, the Cambay markets, and the northern fortresses. In the past, as many as 300 vessels a year had participated in those semi-annual flotillas, but by the mid-1630s their number had fallen by nearly nine-tenths. Apart from the lost income from customs and passes, the decline of the cafilas made it difficult for Goan authorities to support the vital subsidiary centers and easier for the English and Dutch to appropriate former Portuguese trading

64. EIC ships brought Goa urgently needed naval stores, munitions, and copper, and occasionally provided safe transport for ecclesiastics and other passengers as well as cargo space for goods from Macao, Goa, and Mozambique bound for European markets. But the would-be allies were soon quarreling over English efforts to penetrate the Chinese market, to buy pepper in Kanara, and to expand their operations along the Coromandel coast. Portuguese ships pursued by Dutch patrols sometimes ran to the protection of English factories and forts, but even an English flag did not prevent their molestation. *EFI* (1634–36), xvii–xviii and 226–30; *EFI* (1637–41), xxiii, 19–20, 102, 105–6, 165, 177, and 217; *EFI* (1642–45), 14. See also *The Travels of Peter Mundy, in Europe and Asia, 1608–1667*, ed. Sir Richard Carnac Temple, *HS*:2, no. 45 (1919): 168, 173, 180, 182, 197, 202, 221, 226, and 292.

65. As Art. 12 of the "Articles of Peace and Commerce Between . . . Great Britain . . . and . . . Portugal," 29 Jan. 1642, in George Chalmers, comp., *A Collection of Treaties Between Great Britain and Other Powers*, 2 vols. (London, 1790), 2: 258–67.

66. Boxer, *Jan Compagnie*, 17; Israel, *Dutch Republic*, 277; Botelho de Sousa, *Subsídios*, 4: 18 and 20.

67. As Parry noted, the southwest and northeast monsoons governed entry and departure from Goa and maintained a natural blockade during the summer, when the entrance to the Aguada and Mormugão harbors was blocked by accumulated silt. Parry, "Transport," 193.

districts, especially the pepper ports of the Malabar. The blockade naturally disrupted Jesuit communications, too, and made it more difficult for men and supplies to be moved about the eastern provinces. Although never totally effective, the blockade seriously reduced sailings between Goa and Lisbon.[68]

Two major naval actions were consequences of the blockade. In January 1637, six Portuguese galleons sailed out of the Mandovi estuary and caught a dozen Hollanders by surprise. During the ensuing seven-hour fight, the Dutch lost three vessels but saved most of their crews, while the Portuguese lost a galleon and most of its men.[69] In September 1639, the Dutch squadron boldly entered the Goa roads and found what Boxer describes as "three of the finest galleons ever built in India." Two were careened and covered with straw beneath the Mormugão fortress. After the Dutch set the two ships afire, the third galleon approached to render assistance, but the Hollanders cut the cables of one of the burning galleons and sent it against the would-be rescuer, which was also torched. Not only were three fine vessels lost, but so were 400 soldiers and sailors, most of whom drowned. That also became the fate of Fr. Maurício Moureira, the Jesuit chaplain of the fleet, who was repelled by sword thrusts when he tried to climb aboard one of the attacker's vessels.[70]

The Portuguese were shocked by these losses and distressed by the effectiveness of the blockade, but van Diemen was naturally delighted. As he observed in December 1636, "Our blockade causes very slack trade at Malacca and consequently we find commerce here, at Batavia, growing daily."[71] The English also monitored the effects of the blockade. In December 1630, the president of the Surat agency wrote,

> This year they [the Portuguese at Goa] have no succor from Portugall; so that they are very much distrest and oppressed by the Hollanders at Goa, Zeiloan, and Mallacca; ... they are so much distracted for want of releife from Portugall, which makes some of them say (even men of cheife note among them) that if the King of Spaine cares no more for them, they will put themselves under some other Princes pertection who will affoard them readier and abler defence.... Of necessity they will bee inforct to desert some of theire forts to mainteyne those that are most usefull.... They are spread all alongst this coast and may well spare some of theire forts. Wee could heartily wish any one of them yours.

A month later he wrote further about the "miserable predicament" of the Portuguese: "Mallacca and Seiloan beseiged and (the Dutch say) as good as ceized; theire galleoons fired; theire souldiers decayed; themselves disheartned; and all precipitating them ... to utter ruine; whilst the insolent Dutch domineere in all places, stiling themselves allready Kings of the Indian Seas."[72]

68. On the cafilas, see Boyajian, *Portuguese Trade*, 340, s.v. "cafilas."

69. [Anon.], "Relação das grandes batalhas que os galeões do estado da India tiverão com o enemigo da Europa, que veo por cerco a barra da Goa o anno de 1637," in *DUP*, 1: 21–28; *EFI* (1637–41), x, 4, and 35; Botelho de Sousa, *Subsídios*, 4: 69–74.

70. *EFI* (1637–41), 217; Botelho de Sousa, *Subsídios*, 4: 149–51. On Fr. Moureira's death, see F/*JM*, 1: 447–48. The Boxer quotation appears in C. R. Boxer, "Portuguese and Dutch Colonial Rivalry, 1641–1661," *Studia* 2 (July 1958): 7–42, at 13. The Dutch celebrated their Mormugão victory with a painting by Hendrick van Anthonissen (1653), reproduced in Boxer, *Jan Compagnie*, 17. In addition to these three galleons, two were lost in March 1638 in Goa roads through negligence, both as a consequence of untended cooking fires. *EFI* (1637–41), 115–16.

71. As quoted in Israel, *Dutch Republic*, 277.

72. William Fremlen et al. to EIC, 9 [?] Dec. 1639 and 28 Jan. 1648, in *EFI* (1637–41), 216 and 230.

Malacca, the second of Albuquerque's conquests to fall and, as noted, a vital transit station for the Jesuits, had long been vulnerable to land and sea attacks. During the sixteenth century, it was assaulted on ten occasions by the sultans of Acheh or Johore. The Achinese returned in 1615 and 1629. On the latter occasion they sent 236 sail and over 19,000 warriors and coolies against the bastion, which was saved by the timely arrival of Nuno Álvares Botelho, whose armada blocked the invaders within the river where the entrepôt was situated. But by the time of the Dutch attack on Malacca, Botelho was gone, having been mortally wounded during his destruction of a Dutch carrack in May 1630.[73]

Three years later, the Dutch began an increasingly rigorous blockade of the port. The Portuguese viceroys turned to the English to run in urgently required foodstuffs, munitions, and other supplies. In 1636, one EIC captain found the port "wholey ruined by the Flemins continuall keeping those straights," and deserted by the Indian merchants who formerly brought to Malacca foodstuffs and cloth from Bengal and Coromandel.[74] Peter Mundy, who visited Malacca the following year, noted, "Provisons, as Bread, Flesh, butter, sugar etts. all extreame Deare; only [a]racke and Fruite Cheap."[75] As the Dutch tightened their blockade, the English resolved not to test it further. In August 1639, two EIC captains wrote the Company's agent in Golconda: "Your intended voyag ... for Mallacca and Goa is not further to be thought of ... ; nether will our President of Bantam ... aprove of any such projecte to send the Companyes shipps into the lyons claws ... our competitours the Dutch, who hath with the King of Acheem beeseiged Malacca by land and sea, soe that there canot a boate escape them."[76]

By April 1640, António Teles de Meneses, governor of India, recognized the precarious condition of the outpost but responded to pleas for relief from its cámara by explaining that there was little that he could do:

> When I arrived here ... I found the galleons in ashes, the treasury without a real and the State in debt.... But the war material had to be provided and to avert discouragement and dejection I did my utmost to raise the necessary funds ... for the equipment of eight galleons for the relief of Malacca. Meanwhile news was received of the war in Ceylon [see below].... We had to do what we could and therefore sent [the ships] to their relief. In view of Malacca's urgent need we have with great effort equipped these three galleons as best we could. I know very well that the provisions ... are not adequate but what shall I do?... The inhabitants of the city may rest assured that my heart is there and if I have not sent a bigger armada it is because it has not been possible to do so. But in any case a large part of it will go in September.[77]

That dispatch must have been comforting to the Dutch, who intercepted it. In fact, Teles de Meneses's successor was able to send only one ship with 60 soldiers, 200 barrels of powder, and some victuals, though whether that vessel was able to slip through the blockade

73. D. K. Bassett, "European Influence in the Malay Peninsula, 1511–1786," *JMBRAS* 33, 3 (1960): 11 n. 5 and 14 n. 14. See also note 51 above.
74. Henry Bornford to EIC directors, Surat, 29 Apr. 1636, in *EFI* (1634–36), 229.
75. *Travels of Peter Mundy, HS*:2, no. 45 (1919): 142.
76. Thomas Ivy and Thomas Morris to Andrew Cogan (at Golconda), Masulipatam, 1 Aug. 1639, in *EFI* (1637–41), 146. On conditions in Malacca during the 1630s, see Botelho de Sousa, *Subsídios*, 4: 40, 89–92, 130–33, and 169–70.
77. Teles de Meneses to cámara of Malacca, 24 Apr. 1640 in *JMBRAS* 14, 1 (1936): 163–64.

remains uncertain.[78] What *is* certain is that the Dutch, assisted by a large number of Achinese and 2,000 reserves from the sultan of Johore, erstwhile friend of the Portuguese, began their final siege in August 1640. But they found the citadel well fortified and more heavily gunned than they had expected. Pestilence—malaria and dysentery—decimated both sides; only its cumulative effects, together with famine and perhaps the irresolution of the inexperienced Portuguese commander, enabled the attackers to capture the entrepôt on 14 January 1641.[79]

When the dying Portuguese governor met his victorious but also terminally ill Dutch foe, he asked only that the city's miserable survivors be permitted to retain their liberty and possessions. The first request was granted but the second was denied. That refusal was later reversed, however. As the VOC's disgruntled fiscal officer reported after inspecting the remains of the ravaged city,

> The vanquished enemy was quite thoughtlessly allowed full liberty against all customs of war. Heeding the artful request of the Jesuits, the most qualified, the wealthiest and the most intelligent prisoners, both laymen and clergy together with the most prominent ladies, were permitted to sail to Negapatam in a yacht without any resolution of the Council [of Batavia] or inspection before their departure.... They carried off more than 100,000 rs. worth of gold and jewelry, besides the best slaves of both sexes, artists and musicians, in fact the best things in Malacca.... This foolish act robbed the [VOC] of at least 4 to 5 tons of gold. Further, the release of so many efficient persons strengthened our hereditary enemy.[80]

Among the clergy to whom the choleric commissary referred were a half-dozen Jesuits. Their Society lost heavily when Malacca, the Singapore or Dien Bien Phu of its day, surrendered. The Jesuits lost not only their sturdy college and its gardens, which even the Dutch admired, but also a prized library (1,300 books). In addition, they were deprived of important customs revenues to support missionary activities in East Asia, and they were barred by the victors' placards from further religious activity in Malacca.[81]

In reporting the capture of Malacca, a triumphant van Diemen assured his superiors,

> The fall of Malacca has caused great dejection among the Portuguese prisoners. They say openly "Now that Malacca is lost, there's no more India for us," and it is true. With [6,000 requested] reinforcements ... we shall be able to drive the Portuguese out of India within a short time. The ENGLISH and the DANES must then dry up and your honourable Company will have full control of the rich trade.[82]

It is curious that the governor-general failed to mention Ceylon, where the Dutch were already seriously committed. If Winius is correct, it was cinnamon rather than conquest that

78. Further reinforcements were ready to leave Goa in March 1641 when news of the capitulation arrived. C. R. Boxer, ed., *A Aclamação del rei d. João IV em Goa e em Macao* (Lisbon, 1934), 19–20.

79. The basic study of the fall of Malacca remains P. A. Leupe, "The Siege and Capture of Malacca from the Portuguese in 1640–1641," trans. Mac Hacobian, *JMBRAS* 14, 1 (1936): 1–178. See also Botelho de Sousa, *Subsídios*, 4: 193–203, and C. R. Boxer, "Karl Marx and the Last Days of Portuguese Malacca, 1640–41: A Reassessment," *Indica* 19, 2 (Sept. 1982): 123–28.

80. As quoted in Leupe, "Siege," 80. In fact, the 300 who sailed to Negapatam, including the Jesuits, had such a miserable voyage that 60 perished before the ship reached its destination. Ibid., 61.

81. "Cartel que os Olandeses fixão nas portas e lugares publicos da fortaleza de Malaca contra os P^es da Companhia de JESU e mais ecclesiasticas da religião catholica em Mayo de 1645," in ARSI, FG, 721/6.

82. Van Diemen to the Council of Seventeen, 8 Jan. 1642, as quoted in Leupe, "Siege," 49.

the Dutch first had in mind there.[83] By the mid-1630s, King Senarat had been succeeded by his third son, the victor over Constantino de Sá. The new king, who took the name of Rājasinha II after a celebrated Sinhalese foe of the Portuguese during the sixteenth century, styled himself as emperor and planned to unite the entire island under his rule, but he became convinced that to achieve that goal he required Dutch seapower. Accordingly, in September 1636, he sent an agent to the Dutch factory at Pulicat to offer the Dutch whatever they required to build a fort at Trincomalee or Batticaloa and to pay their expenses in return for their assistance against Portuguese outposts. After the fall of Batticaloa (April 1638), that promise was transformed into a treaty between the Dutch admiral and the emperor, an understanding (or misunderstanding) that a Dutch historian has termed the most advantageous agreement the Company ever made with an Oriental potentate. It designated the Dutch as Kandy's allies and protectors against the Portuguese, gave them exclusive access to the export of cinnamon and all other products of the island, and assured them that they would be fully compensated for all campaign expenses incurred in ridding Ceylon of the Portuguese.

Dutch naval forces, complemented by massed Sinhalese troops, moved efficiently against Portuguese outposts, which were designed to repel attacks from the land rather than the sea. In May 1639, thirteen months after a devastating bombardment had compelled Batticaloa's small garrison of 40 to surrender, the Dutch captured the commodious Bay of Trincomalee by the same means. Next they turned their attention to two citadels that guarded access to the principal cinnamon-producing lands: Negombo, 32 kilometers up the west coast from Colombo, and Galle, situated on a peninsula just over 100 kilometers south-southeast of Colombo. Both were captured during the early months of 1640, the former with ease, but the latter only after the loss of considerable blood on both sides. These setbacks were devastating not only for the Portuguese state but also for the Society. The next year, however, the Portuguese achieved one of their few successes in the East against the Dutch when they retook Negombo. Despite its recovery, a dispirited Fr. Manoel Sylveiro wrote in his annual report concerning the status of the Society on the island, "There is little or nothing to be said of the mission and the doings of the Christians, for it is now three years since everything is in tumult and the King of Candea and the Hollanders, whom he brought against the Portuguese, are up in arms for the destruction of the Portuguese. All this time the Fathers are retired within the walls of Colombo."[84] And there they remained until the end.

Except in the defense of Macao and the negotiation of the irregular Anglo-Portuguese agreement of 1635, Jesuits did not play primary roles in the reverses that Portugal sustained in the East during the first four decades of the seventeenth century. But those reverses affected the Society as well. In particular, its spiritual outposts in the Moluccas and in Ceylon were seriously imperiled, as were its missions in various parts of the Indian subcontinent. By 1641

83. The following two paragraphs are based mostly on Winius, *Fatal History*, 33–45; see also K. W. Goonewardena, *The Foundations of Dutch Power in Ceylon, 1638–1658* (Amsterdam, 1958), chaps. 2–3.

84. As quoted by S. G. Perera, "The Jesuits in Ceylon in the 16th and 17th Centuries," *Ceylon Antiquary and Literary Register* 5 (1920–21): 197. There were about sixteen Jesuits, all but two of them priests, left on the island. Ibid., 3 (1917–18): 35.

it had lost to the hated Dutch enemy only one of its colleges—Malacca—a harbinger of other calamities that would follow during the next two decades. As will be seen in later chapters, the heavy costs to the crown in defending the eastern empire lessened its ability to contribute to the expenses of Jesuit installations and therefore obliged the Society to devise new means to sustain its activities in the East. Although reports of the Portuguese recovery of Negombo were a source of some satisfaction after the recent loss of Malacca, they were overshadowed by the arrival of news of the December revolution. It remained to be seen whether the new regime in Portugal could prevent the further deterioration of its eastern empire.

CHAPTER 8

The Collapse of the Estado da India and Its Impact upon the Society, 1641–1700

The Indies are good and profitable only to the viceroys, governors, and some of the king's officers—not to the king, nor to the poor soldiers and mariners.
>   —François Pyrard de Laval, ca. 1610

I am afraid the missions of the East will be ruined completely.
>   —Fr. Francisco Barreto, annual letter, 28 Nov. 1658–Apr. 1659

The more Hell rises up in Opposition to us, the greater Conquests Heaven makes.
>   —Fr. Bouchet, S.J., to Fr. Le Gobien, S.J., Madura, 1 Dec. 1701

THE TERRITORIAL LOSSES that Portugal sustained in the East and the exclusion of the Society of Jesus from two of its once-promising evangelical fields—Japan and Ethiopia—during the first four decades of the seventeenth century proved to be the prelude to a series of far more devastating reverses that would affect both the crown and the Society during the century's remaining decades. As the new dynasty ascended the Portuguese throne in 1640, it was compelled to recognize that two important outliers of the eastern empire, Ormuz and Malacca, had already fallen or were about to be lost; that prospects for preserving its rule in Ceylon were bleak; and that vital communications between the kingdom and its Goan headquarters were endangered by the continuing seasonal Dutch maritime blockade. Portuguese authorities might have congratulated themselves that their enclaves in the Indian subcontinent, where the Society maintained extensive educational and military facilities, remained intact, but they realized that there was little that they could do if these facilities became imperiled. In the next six decades, many additional territories of the once-vaunted thalassocracy would be lost, some captured by aggressive Dutch and Afro-Asian warriors, others transferred to an imperial rival as a result of casual diplomatic negotiations. Despite repeated pleas by imperial authorities in the East for military and naval assistance, the hapless Portuguese monarchy proved incapable of preventing the continued decline of its eastern empire, a process that would have profound consequences for both the government and the Society.

The Troublesome Luso-Dutch Truce

Word of the December revolution reached Goa on 8 September 1641, and both there and throughout the State the reestablishment of Portuguese independence was enthusiastically welcomed.[1] But expectations that John IV would quickly form an alliance with the Dutch against Spain and send large reinforcements to Goa were quickly dashed. On 22 September, the second of two messenger ships dispatched from Lisbon arrived at Goa road bearing a safe-conduct from Dutch authorities in Europe. But Hendrik Quast, commander of the Dutch blockading squadron, refused to honor his government's pledge on the pretext that he lacked instructions from Batavia to do so.[2] Accordingly, he seized the ship, whose subsequent fate remains unknown. Quast's action proved to be a lugubrious omen for beleaguered Portuguese defenders. In despair, the viceroy, the conde de Aveiras (1640–45), sent an urgent message overland to his new sovereign in which he congratulated John IV upon his ascendancy but warned him that the preservation of the State of India was hanging in the balance. Its land and sea forces were so weak and the maritime power of the Dutch so overwhelming, said the count, that measures must be quickly undertaken to prevent the total loss of a state "of so much importance to the crown of that kingdom." First, the count declared, it was essential to conclude a peace, or at least an effective truce, with the Dutch in the East very promptly (*logo, logo*), and second, it was equally imperative to dispatch to India eight or ten strong galleons with troops, artillery, and as much money as possible.[3]

John IV needed no prompting to undertake negotiations with the Dutch, whose ships he permitted to return to Portuguese Peninsular ports barely a month after his assumption of power, despite the fact that the Hollanders still controlled much of Portugal's most important sugar colony and its principal sources of slaves, and menaced what remained of its eastern empire. When the king's emissary to Holland found it impossible to negotiate an immediate peace, John agreed to a ten-year truce that was to take effect in Brazil within six months of the exchange of ratifications, and in the East within one year of the conclusion of those essential formalities. Each side would retain what it possessed when the truce came into effect while the diplomats tried to work out a final agreement.[4]

The VOC naturally opposed the truce, and its agents in the East delayed its implementation as long as possible. The Dutch representative sent to Goa to work out terms insisted that two important cinnamon districts situated some distance from Galle be transferred to the VOC. When the viceroy refused to comply, the war resumed. In 1643–44, Dutch forces temporarily occupied the undefended Portuguese town of Negapatam on the Coromandel coast, recovered Negombo, repelled Portuguese efforts to take it back, and occupied the

1. C. R. Boxer republished a rare pamphlet concerning the reception of the new regime, *A Aclamaccão del rei d. João IV em Goa e em Macao* (Lisbon, 1934), originally printed by the Jesuit press at New St. Paul's, Goa, in 1643. Its author, Manuel Iacome de Mesquita, was an obvious lackey of the viceroy.

2. George Davison Winius, *The Fatal History of Portuguese Ceylon* (Cambridge, Mass., 1971), 52; Alfredo Botelho de Sousa, *Subsídios para a história militar marítima da India, 1585–1669* [*sic* for *1650*], 4 vols. (Lisbon, 1930–56), 4: 220–21.

3. Viceroy to king, 27 Sept. 1641, in *ACE*, 2 (1954): 573–78, esp. 574, a portion of which is quoted in Winius, *Fatal History*, 52–53.

4. Edgar Prestage, *The Diplomatic Relations of Portugal with France, England, and Holland from 1640 to 1668* (Watford, Eng., 1925), 171–82; see also Winius, *Fatal History*, 55–60; and C. R. Boxer, "Portuguese and Dutch Colonial Rivalry, 1641–1661," *Studia* 2 (July 1958): 14–15.

disputed cinnamon districts. Finally, in November 1644, Aveiras, sorely disappointed that the reinforcements for which he had hoped had never arrived and knowing that each year the VOC was sending thousands of troops and additional ships to strengthen its hand in the East, agreed to Dutch conditions for the proclamation of the truce. By then the VOC effectively controlled half of Ceylon's cinnamon traffic.[5]

The Lull Before the Storm, 1645–50

The next half-dozen years represented the last opportunity for the Portuguese to resolve their most persistent internal problems in the Estado and to make effective preparations to repel the next enemy onslaughts. The State's key internal problems had deep roots. Early in the century, a former viceroy advised the king that the Estado most urgently needed three things for its defense: money, ships, and men.[6] Virtually all of the administrations that served during the seventeenth century—26 viceroys and seven interim regimes—reiterated that warning, but with few positive results.[7]

If we take literally the complaints of those regimes, the coffers of the royal exchequer in Goa were perennially empty. That treasury was directly dependent upon Portuguese-controlled trade throughout the Estado. By the 1630s, Goa itself was responsible for about 40 percent of the State's income, and 71.5 percent of its receipts were derived from customs collections.[8] A few years earlier, one informant had stated that customs receipts were then half what they had been a decade before. It is, therefore, easy to understand why the fiscal condition of the State worsened in the 1630s and early 1640s after the loss of the silk and bullion trades between Macao and Japan, the fall of Malacca, the loss of much of the cinnamon traffic of Ceylon, and Anglo-Dutch inroads into the cloth and pepper trades in India.[9]

One of the heaviest burdens upon the royal exchequer both at home and in Goa was the cost of shipping necessary to defend and service the eastern empire. Carracks and galleons, those seagoing fortresses (as the old soldier Diogo do Couto called them), were the vital links that were supposed to hold together the chain of fortress-factories that extended from Macao to Mozambique. As Chapter 7 demonstrated, that chain was repeatedly broken by the Dutch and the English during the early decades of the century. Singly or in concert, they patrolled the key straits (Malacca, Sunda, Palk, and Ormuz),

5. The president of the Surat factory ruefully wrote, "The Dutch in these parts only prosper and flourish; . . . by their industry, patience, and indefatigable paines and unalterable resolutions [they] purchase [i.e., obtain] what they please; . . . they have now added to their other spices half the cinamon upon Ceiloan." Thomas Breton to EIC, Swally, 28 Nov. 1644, in *EFI* (1642–46), 217. See also Winius, *Fatal History*, chap. 5; K. W. Goonewardena, *The Foundations of Dutch Power in Ceylon, 1638–1658* (Amsterdam, 1958), chap. 4. For Dutch reinforcements in 1640–43, see Botelho de Sousa, *Subsídios*, 4: 293.

6. A. R. Disney, *Twilight of the Pepper Empire* (Cambridge, Mass., 1978), 63.

7. This statement rests upon the viceregal correspondence from the 1630s to the end of the century in HAG.

8. António Bocarro, "Livro das plantas de todas as fortalezas, cidades e povoações do estado da India oriental," *APO*:2, bk. 4, pts. 1 and 2, 1: 166–68. On Bocarro, see C. R. Boxer, *Three Historians of Portuguese Asia (Barros, Couto, and Boccaro)* (Macao, 1948), 23–28.

9. On the contraction of Portuguese commerce to ca. 1635, see Bocarro, "Livro das plantas," 1: 280–99. See also Disney, *Twilight*, 51.

lurked off favored Portuguese way stations (such as Mozambique Island), and, in the case of the Dutch, imposed increasingly severe blockades on major imperial ports, especially Macao, Malacca, and Goa. Though a few commanders, notably Ruy Freyre de Andrade and Nuno Álvares Botelho, were resourceful, courageous, and competent seamen, all too many conned their ships to disaster because of inexperience, ineptness, impetuousness, or pusillanimity. Those deficiencies, as much as superior English and Dutch gunnery and storm damage, accounted for one disaster after another. According to one seventeenth-century compiler, roughly one out of five ships that sailed from Lisbon to India between 1580 and 1640 was lost.[10] To the list of aborted or catastrophic voyages by large ships must be added the loss of hundreds of smaller service and supply vessels that made up the cafilas of small merchant vessels that the Hollanders relentlessly dispersed and destroyed. In 1622, a particularly disastrous year for the empire, one royal advisor candidly admitted that Portugal had lost control of the seas east of the Cape of Good Hope.[11] Nor was the empire ever to regain its former mastery there. The crown responded to the endless appeals by Goan authorities for naval reinforcements, but its ability to provide them diminished after the early 1640s because of its preoccupation with the defense of the kingdom and Brazil. But even if Portugal had been able to send much larger maritime contingents to India, most of them would have returned to Europe with empty holds, because most supplies of consumer goods in the East for which there existed a European demand were in the hands of Portugal's rivals.[12]

Apart from bullion, weapons, and munitions, the commodity that Goan authorities most frequently requested was manpower to defend the Estado. How many "volunteered" for service in the State during the century we do not know, but a fair guess would be close to 100,000, an impressive contribution for a small nation, but one that could not match the resources of the State's indigenous and European adversaries, who customarily outnumbered Portuguese forces wherever they fought. Both sides made use of indigenous troops, Kaffirs from Mozambique, Indians and Sinhalese (variously termed lascarins [or lascars] in early centuries and later sepoys), Southeast Asians, and Japanese. A large number of foreign mercenaries, especially Germans, Swedes, and Frenchmen, were attracted to serve the VOC by promises of pay and plunder. Prior to the Restoration, Spain required Portuguese troops to help fight its European wars, including the Catalan rebellion (see Chapter 5). After 1640, India's claim on available Portuguese manpower ranked far below those of the kingdom and Brazil. Most of the Portuguese so-called volunteers who went to the Estado were consequently raw recruits, swept from the fields or the streets of large and small communities, or released from jails to serve their country.[13] As Charles R. Boxer and several other commentators have observed, some were minors between the ages of six and fourteen, although what proportion of

10. Manuel de Faria e Sousa, *Asia portuguesa*, trans. Maria Vitória Garcia Santos Ferreira, 6 vols. (Porto, 1947), 6: 501–16.

11. Disney, *Twilight*, 65.

12. C. R. Boxer, *From Lisbon to Goa, 1500–1750: Studies in Portuguese Maritime Expansion*, Variorum Reprints Publications (London, 1984).

13. The most recent and extensive study of such "volunteers" is Timothy Joel Coates, "Exiles and Orphans: Forced and State-Sponsored Colonizers in the Portuguese Empire, 1550–1720," Ph.D. diss., University of Minnesota, 1993, chap. 4.

the total levies they represented is uncertain, as is whether they were intended to become immediate cannon fodder or were to be seasoned in the East before undertaking military duty.[14]

Certainly a disturbing proportion of the recruits Portugal sent east failed to arrive there in a condition that would have permitted them to fight anywhere. Either at sea or in the Jesuit-administered royal hospital in Goa, they succumbed to malignant fevers or to the consequences of putrid food and brackish water. An Augustinian chronicler may well have exaggerated when he asserted that 25,000 soldiers perished in the Goan hospital during the first three decades of the century, but Boxer assures us that death rates of more than 50 percent on the outward-bound voyages of East Indiamen were not uncommon.[15]

Many of the survivors chose not to tempt fate further or to trust their captains. Thousands deserted and served as mercenaries or in other capacities in the lands of Asian potentates from Indonesia to India. As reported in the last chapter, the count of Linhares complained that every year aggressive ecclesiastical recruiters snatched half of them, and his successors repeatedly complained about the religious Orders' unpatriotic penchant for offering refuge to such troops. Those complaints have led several commentators to conclude that all of the Orders were equally "guilty" of this offense, though there is no specific evidence to suggest that members of the Society of Jesus actually lured recruits into their houses. Considering the youth and perilous physical condition of many of the recruits, one might conclude that by offering them an alternative to almost certain death in the lines, the religious were simply discharging their humanitarian obligation.[16]

There was another aspect of the State's persisting manpower problem that its governors understandably rarely mentioned in their dispatches. Not only were there "never enough soldiers ... to meet the needs of the state," as Disney has said, but there were never enough qualified, ethically reliable persons to fill its administrative posts. From top to bottom there existed a web of corruption throughout the State that bound together viceroys, fortress captains, magistrates, customs collectors, and tax farmers, who sought to maximize their personal estates by defrauding the crown in every conceivable way: justice was sold; payrolls were padded; excessive charges were accepted for state purchases; and everyone in a position to do so traded on his own account or through cooperating intermediaries, who sometimes included the Jesuits (see Chapter 21). As Chapter 13 will show, the scarcity of competent administrators to run the royal hospital, operate royal mints, and supervise fortress warehouses was so great that the religious, especially the Jesuits, were pressed to occupy positions bearing no relationship to their vocation and embroiling them in countless

14. Boxer, "Portuguese and Dutch Colonial Rivalry," 27; Winius, *Fatal History*, 102; and Disney, *Twilight*, 67–68. Each of these authors expresses shock because of the apparently unique callousness of the Portuguese. But they ignore the statement of Hugh Lee, an English merchant in the Iberian Peninsula, who wrote that the youths were being sent east to become adjusted to endemic disorders there and that it was hoped that within a few years "they will be able to do good service" as their bodies adjusted to the climate. He added that "it were no evil course to follow in England for planting inhabitants in Virginia." Lee to Thomas Wilson, 26 Mar. 1609, in *CSPC/EI*, 1 (1862), 182.

15. C. R. Boxer, *Portuguese Society in the Tropics: The Municipal Councils of Goa, Macao, Bahia, and Luanda, 1510–1800* (Madison, 1965), 31–32.

16. See note 92 below.

conflicts with competing interests. The few top-level administrators who tried to introduce reforms found themselves stymied by lack of support from their superiors at home or their subordinates overseas.[17]

During the critical middle decades of the century—throughout the last years of the reign of John IV, the regency of Luísa de Gusmão, and the regime nominally headed by Afonso VI—leadership in the State was conspicuous by its absence. In 1643, a deranged governor of Macao murdered a bureaucratic rival and a slave boy who had intervened to try to save his master's life. Three years later, his successor was hacked to death by mutinous (and unpaid) soldiers. Six years afterward, elements of the Colombo garrison revolted and deposed the captain-general of Ceylon. The next year (1653), a cabal in Goa arrested the viceroy, a close kinsman of the king, and shut him up in a fortress. His successor lasted barely five months in office before he died mysteriously, perhaps a victim of poison. The death of the archbishop of Goa in 1652 led to a decade-long feud between the Jesuits and the other Orders in Goa concerning the election of his successor.[18]

The roots of these problems had been exposed for more than a century. In the 1580s, for example, both the astute Jesuit administrator Alessandro Valignano and the ironic Diogo do Couto, author of the *Soldado Pratico*, future chronicler of the State, and keeper of its records, testified to their extent and tenacity.[19] But one may go back even further to the 1550s, when a cantankerous dockmaster of Cochin, a veteran of 50 years of service in India, wrote John III that the viceroys and governors he was sending out

> are thieves of Your Highness's possessions . . . now there is no one in India who wants to bear arms and still less to fight; . . . they only want to lead a good life and to go around in badly cut silk clothes. . . . India is so full of great vanity and pomp that the people can not be maintained, since the salary which is paid to them is not at all sufficient for their dress, not to mention for a Negro who carries a parasol for them. . . . Everything is dissolving into vanities and thefts. . . . If India is in a state of turmoil, it is because the captains of Your Highness are great thieves and great tyrants, who plunder . . . the land.[20]

Nor did the quality of administration improve thereafter. As noted at the beginning of this chapter, a French sailor who became an involuntary sojourner in Goa observed that the East Indies were only profitable to the king's officers, not to the crown itself nor to its

17. Winius, *Fatal History*, 94–102; M[alyn] D. D. Newitt, *Portuguese Settlement on the Zambesi: Exploration, Land Tenure and Colonial Rule in East Africa* (New York, 1973), 117–20. For a more favorable view, see M[ichael] N. Pearson, "Corruption and Corsairs in Sixteenth-Century Western India: A Functional Analysis," in his *Coastal Western India: Studies from the Portuguese Records* (New Delhi, 1981), 18–40. Pearson argues that corruption was far more accepted in this period than it would be later on, but he ignores the fact that the paucity of king's officers who could be trusted compelled the crown to turn to the Jesuits to perform bureaucratic functions that had nothing to do with their spiritual mission. See Chapter 13.

18. C. R. Boxer, *Fidalgos in the Far East, 1550–1770: Fact and Fancy in the History of Macao* (1948; rpr., New York, 1968), 150–54; Winius, *Fatal History*, 122–29 and 134–39; H/SAG2, 88–90. Because of Rome's refusal to recognize Portugal's independence, the see of Goa remained vacant for 22 years. Carlos Merces de Melo, S.J., *The Recruitment and Formation of the Native Clergy in India* (Lisbon, 1955), 150 n. 3.

19. Valignano to Emmanuel Rodrigues, 31 Dec. 1575, in *DI*, 10: 390–411. The standard modern edition of Couto is that edited by M. Rodrigues Lapa, 2d ed. (Lisbon, 1954). See also C. R. Boxer, "Diogo do Couto (1543–1616), Controversial Chronicler of Portuguese Asia," in R. O. W. Goertz, ed., *Iberia: Literary and Historical Issues: Studies in Honor of Harold V. Livermore* (Calgary, 1985), 57–66, which updates his earlier essay in *Three Historians*, 13–22.

20. Joane Anes to king, 29 Jan. 1552, in S/*FX*, 4: 466–67.

impoverished soldiers and sailors.[21] By the 1640s, John IV and his advisors were reaching the same conclusion. Late in 1648, after the signing of the treaty of Münster-Westphalia, which brought to an end the long Hispano-Dutch war, the king asked his councilors, "Tell me by what means the kingdom can be defended against two so powerful enemies. It being exhausted of personnel and capital. . . . If this predicament necessitates withdrawing revenue from the customhouses, of which the greatest part must come from . . . India, how then will it be possible to reinforce India hereafter, just as it has not been reinforced to any considerable extent in past years?" Two members of his council of war responded that it was, indeed, fiscally impossible to defend the homeland and the empire against both Spain and Holland, that peace was preferable, but that if it proved to be impossible, "We should give up in Asia as much as we need to, in order to leave us free in Brazil, because whenever we are neighbors, the peace will never be too secure, nor our spices very valuable; besides which, Asia, by its distance and its size, is more difficult and costly and less useful to conserve."[22]

That conviction became the crux of Portuguese imperial policy thereafter. Employing a strategy similar to that agreed to by Roosevelt and Churchill during the early days of World War II, the famous Europe First plan, the Braganças became resigned to the loss of their eastern empire in order to save the kingdom and Brazil. It is true that the crown never explicitly conceded the loss of its remaining possessions in the Estado in its instructions to the State's administrators; but no one could have mistaken the intent of the advice that John IV gave the governing council of Goa in 1650: "In all things you must proceed with the necessary vigilance; do not spare the things you can do, sending help where you can, preventing what damage you can, or at least minimizing it through care."[23] Little wonder that the erosion of the Estado and of the Society's position in many parts of the East continued during the remainder of the century.

The Storm, 1650–63

By 1650, it became evident that there would be a resumption of conflict between Portugal and the United Provinces. The unexpectedly successful uprisings of the Brazilians against the Dutch intruders (see Chapter 9) made such a renewal inevitable. But the first blows against the Portuguese in the East came from Arab and Indian sources. In January 1650, the Imans of Oman, a maritime force that would repeatedly menace Portuguese fortresses in the Indian Ocean, successfully besieged Muscat, which together with the port of Kung (or Kongo) and a few others in the Persian Gulf had partially compensated for the loss of Ormuz. Muscat's garrison was forced to retire to Diu.[24] In 1653–54, the Dutch induced the Naik or princeling of Ikkeri to attack the Kanara fortresses of Onor, Cambolim, and Barcelor, compelling the Portuguese to withdraw from each and thereby to lose important sources of pepper, cardamom, and an inferior kind of cinnamon called cassia lignum. Finally, between

21. *The Voyage of François Pyrard of Laval to the East Indies*, trans. and ed. Albert Gray and H. C. P. Bell, *HS*:1, no. 77 (1888): 201.

22. Both quotations are from Winius, *Fatal History*, 116–17.

23. Quoted in ibid., 118.

24. Justus Strandes, *The Portuguese Period in East Africa*, trans. Jean F. Wallwork, ed. J. S. Kirkman (Nairobi, 1961), 225.

August and October 1654, the sultan of Bijapur, whose lands encircled the Goan territory, invaded the delta lands of Bardês and for a time imperiled the capital's food supply.[25]

But it was the Dutch who again delivered the most serious blows. News of the resumption of war reached Batavia in June 1652, and by September the Hollanders had reimposed their blockade of Goa.[26] Until late 1654, however, the VOC was preoccupied with devastating English shipping in the Indian Ocean as a consequence of the first Anglo-Dutch war.[27] Once that conflict was over, the Dutch were able to turn their attention to Ceylon and to the total exclusion of the Portuguese from the island. The Dutch siege of Colombo began in October 1655, but the defenders of its labyrinthine citadel, encouraged by Jesuits and other missionaries, fought tenaciously. Dutch artillery, famine, and plague finally wore down the defenders' resistance, and Colombo capitulated in May 1656.[28]

Next on the Dutch agenda were the remaining Portuguese positions along the Palk Strait. They included the island of Manar and the town of Tuticorin on the Travancore coast, both longtime centers of Jesuit enterprise and prominent pearling grounds; the Jaffna Peninsula, strategically important and a rich source of elephants; and the cloth-producing community of Negapatam on the Coromandel coast. The capture of all four was achieved by Rijcklof van Goens, a veteran VOC officer who rose from humble beginnings to the rank of admiral.[29] Largely unopposed, he seized Tuticorin in January 1658, then turned his attention to Manar, where ten Jesuits helped rally the defenders. Toward the end of February of that year, after 300 Portuguese had been killed and 400 had successfully escaped to Jaffna, the remainder surrendered. In Jaffna, the last Portuguese bastion on Ceylonese soil, the garrison held out for three difficult months but capitulated on 23 June 1658, when it became patent that no relief was in sight. A few weeks later, van Goens arrived at Negapatam with eleven ships and 700 soldiers, more than sufficient to convince the townsmen to surrender without a fight. Only São Tomé de Meliapor, 260 kilometers to the north, one of the last Jesuit centers on India's east coast, remained in Portuguese hands.[30]

Reviewing the Hollanders' recent successes, concerned English observers predicted that the Malabar coast would be the next to claim Dutch attention.[31] The Dutch had been interested in the area ever since their first squadron reconnoitered the littoral in 1604. Their ships visited it to purchase pepper when returning to Batavia after their seasonal blockades of Goa. By 1647, the VOC had an undermerchant posted there to facilitate such purchases.

25. Teotonio R. de Souza, S.J., *Medieval Goa: A Socio-Economic History* (New Delhi, 1979), 34–38; Winius, *Fatal History*, 145.

26. Viceroy to king, 12 Sept. 1652, in *ACE*, 3: 326–27. C. R. Boxer, *Portuguese India in the Mid-Seventeenth Century* (Delhi, 1980), 26.

27. *EFI* (1651–54), iii; H. G. Rawlinson, *British Beginnings in Western India, 1579–1657* (Oxford, 1920), 114–17.

28. Winius, *Fatal History*, 150–53 and 156–60.

29. For a biographical sketch, see C. R. Boxer, *Jan Compagnie in War and Peace, 1602–1799: A Short History of the Dutch East India Company* (Hong Kong, 1979), 40–41.

30. Goonewardena, *Foundations*, 178–80; S. G. Perera, "The Jesuits in Ceylon in the 16th and 17th Centuries," *Ceylon Antiquary and Literary Register* 5 (1920–21): 40 and 132; Tapan Raychaudhuri, *Jan Company in Coromandel, 1605–1690* (The Hague, 1962), 56–57.

31. For gloomy English assessments of Portuguese prospects in India after the fall of Colombo, see *EFI* (1655–60), 45, 55, 115–16, 153, 157, and 248–49. Francisco Rodrigues (archbishop, Cranganore) to the Portuguese assistant in Rome, Cochin, 8 Dec. 1653, in ARSI, *Goa*, 18, fol. 165, is a grim account of anti-Christian movements in Southwest India, famine in Manar Island, and administrative chaos in Goa.

Batavian officials therefore decided to campaign against the Portuguese there not only as the next logical step in their long war against the Lusitanians, but also in order to add Malabar pepper stocks to those they controlled in Sumatra, so that they could monopolize the pepper trade with Europe.

The Malabar campaigns soon reached their inevitable climax.[32] By the latter part of 1661, Batavian authorities felt an increasing sense of urgency about concluding the Malabar conquests. They knew that Portugal was close to signing a peace treaty with Holland and was also negotiating an alliance with England that might result in the transfer of the remaining Portuguese enclaves in India to England.[33] Accordingly, van Goens organized a powerful force of over 4,100 men, and on 7 December 1661, he landed near Quilon, which fell three days later. Next, he attacked Cranganore, some 34 kilometers north of Cochin. There the Dutch encountered unexpectedly stiff resistance organized by the fortress's Macaonese-born commander, Urbano Fialho Ferreira; but the Hollanders battered Cranganore into submission, and it fell on 15 January 1662.[34]

The major objective of the campaign was the capture of Cochin, the headquarters of the Jesuit province of Malabar, the second most important Portuguese city on the west coast, and an alternative port when the blockade of Goa was most effective. Despite limited resources and few soldiers, Cochin's commander, Inácio Sarmento de Carvalho, a kinsman of Fialho Ferreira, defended it well. After suffering heavy casualties, the Dutch were obliged to break off their initial attack. In October 1662, however, following the end of the monsoons, the Hollanders returned, this time augmented by native troops from Amboina and Ceylon and with local support. They subjected the town to a tight siege by land and by sea and to the relentless bombardment of 50 guns. Cochin surrendered on 7 January 1663. Five weeks later, Cannanore, the last Portuguese possession on the coast, also fell.[35]

Two weeks earlier, seven Dutch ships and two smacks had entered Goa road and delivered refugees from Cochin. They included 2,600 women, about 100 laymen, and an unspecified number of priests.[36] Whether Jesuits were aboard is unclear, for the Dutch initially jailed all those found at Cochin. Among the conditions they insisted upon before handing the port to their newly recognized raja was the stipulation, "No Catholic clergyman

32. Though T. I. Poonen, *Dutch Hegemony in Malabar and Its Collapse (1663–1795)* (Travendrum, 1978), which rests upon Dutch sources, represents an improvement over K. M. Panikkar, *Malabar and the Portuguese* (Bombay, 1929), and P. C. Alexander, *The Dutch in Malabar* (Annamalamagar, 1946), it is nevertheless sketchy and unsophisticated. See, too, Jonathan I. Israel, *Dutch Primacy in World Trade, 1585–1740* (Oxford, 1989), 248–50.

33. *EFI* (1661–64), 29.

34. C. R. Boxer, *Breve relação da vida e feitos de Lopo e Inácio Sarmento de Carvalho, grandes capitães que no século XVII honraram Portugal no Oriente* (Macao, 1940), which examines the career of the last Portuguese commander of Cranganore.

35. On the fall of Cochin, see John Harrington and Alexander Grigsby to East India Company president (at Surat), Malabar coast, 17 Apr. 1663, in *EFI* (1661–64), 246–48; and Jean-Baptiste Tavernier, *Travels in India*, trans. and ed. V. Ball, 2d ed., ed. William Crooke, 2 vols. (Oxford, 1925), 1: 187–94. For additional bibliography, see *ACE*, 4: 94 n. 1. Martinho Velho Barreto, former *veedor da fazenda* (senior treasury officer), attributed the fall of Cochin entirely to the "negligence" of the newly arrived viceroy, Martinho de Melo de Castro, who had ignored Barreto's advice and, in fact, confined Barreto to the Mormugão fortress, from which he wrote his laments of 12 May 1663 and 26 Jan. 1664 to the king, in AHU/PA/IN, *cx.* 25.

36. Viceroy to king, 1 Feb. 1663, in *ACE*, 4: 523.

should be tolerated in Cochin or dependent lands without special permission of the Company. The Jesuits and all other European priests should for all time be expelled."[37] Later, in discussing the terms of the Luso-Dutch peace treaty of July 1661, a Dutch general remarked to a Franciscan commissary that the Jesuits would never be permitted to return, for "they are the devil's blood. I would rather allow 1,000 Portuguese to stay near Cochin than a single Jesuit."[38]

The Transfer of Bombay: A Case of Unfulfilled Promises

It was one thing to be deprived of distant bases like Ormuz, Malacca, and Colombo, but it was quite another to lose Cochin, the site of the first Portuguese factory in India and the original capital of the Portuguese State. Its fall caused the council of state in Goa to declare that the Estado had reached its last straits (*ao ultimo aperto*).[39] But those officials were not only in despair; they were also angry because they felt betrayed by their English allies, whom they considered to be the unequal beneficiaries of the Anglo-Portuguese marriage treaty of 1661. And they were particularly indignant about the cavalier way that Bombay was ceded to the English.

Representatives of the EIC had long been yearning for such a port. For decades the Surat factors had wanted a secure anchor for their operations in western India and the Persian Gulf, one that would complement the presidency of Madras at Fort St. George, established in 1652. Swally Hole's shifting sand made it a less than ideal anchorage, and the factory at Surat depended upon the caprice of the city's governor, who took his orders from Agra. As early as 1636, President Methwold suggested the possibility of procuring the small island of Bombay, a neglected dependency of Bassein that measured 4.8 by 6.4 kilometers and whose 10,000 inhabitants cultivated rice, harvested palm trees, and fished. Although he would have been willing to take either Damão or Diu, Methwold preferred Bombay because "we are verily perswaded ... you might ... build a defencible house with fitting storehouses [on the island] ... so secure a place to winter in," and only two days' sail from Surat. During the first Anglo-Dutch war, one of Methwold's successors wrote the Company's directors, "We were never soe sencible of the want of a port in these parts (as that we might call our owne) as wee are at present." He suggested that either Bombay or Bassein "would bee very convenient for you." Later in the same decade, President Henry Rivington warned the Company that the Dutch appeared likely to take Goa and Diu, and that the Company would then lose all its trade with India.[40] In response, the

---

37. The terms of the treaty of 20 Mar. 1663 are given in Poonen, *Dutch Hegemony*, 34–37.

38. Quoted in F/JM, 2: 288.

39. Resolution of 3 Mar. 1663, in *ACE*, 4: 93–95. The same volume contains extended reflections (93–131) by Goan officials concerning the significance of the loss of Cochin. The state of the morale of Goan authorities is evident in their dispatches to Lisbon during the late 1650s and early 1660s. AHU/PA/IN, *cxs.* 25 and 26.

40. Methwold to EIC, Surat, 28 Apr. 1636, in *EFI* (1634–36), 222; [Jeremy] Blackman and Edward Pearce to EIC, Surat, 23 Mar. 1653, in *EFI* (1651–54), 169–70; John Spiller to [EIC], Isfahan, 10 Apr. 1654, in ibid., 272. For additional evidence concerning the perceived critical need to preempt the Dutch from fully dominating Indian Ocean and Persian Gulf trades, see Saffaat Ahmad Khan, "Anglo-Portuguese Negotiations Relating to Bombay, 1660–1677," *Journal of Indian History* 1, 3 (Sept. 1922) and separately printed (Bombay, 1922), 421–30; *EFI* (1655–60), 115, 153, 157, and 214; Benjamin Lannoy (English consul at Aleppo)

Company agreed in 1658 to authorize the purchase of "Denda Rajpore, Basseene, Bombay, or Caraptam, or such other healthfull place upon the coast of Malabarr ... for ... our shipping," provided that it did not cost more than £8,000.[41] The Surat factors evidently felt that it was improper for them to make the final choice without prior approval, but in January 1660 they warned the Company that it should "procure there a good port [which] may easily be obtained here, before the insulting Dutch gaine all." In midyear their president visited several possible sites, including Bassein and Bombay, "to experience how the Portugalls stood affected with parting from any of their ports unto us. Their civillity ... was great; and they ... declared a seeming willingness to enjoy such good neighbors. But they joyntly declared that it was not in their power to part with any port of their Kings without his commission."[42] Just as the factors tossed the ball back to London, so the unnamed Portuguese informants tossed it to Lisbon, and Lisbon changed its mind, or so it would seem.

When the Company offered to purchase the island in February 1660, the Portuguese ambassador to England seemed uninterested. Three months later, Charles II ascended the throne, and the Portuguese government promptly proposed a marriage alliance in order to secure the kingdom and what remained of its empire (see Chapter 5). One of the pieces of the bait that Portugal offered was the "port and island" of Bombay. Although Portuguese negotiators supposedly displayed a map showing its location, a map that later mysteriously disappeared, the lord chancellor, the earl of Clarendon, apparently never saw it, for he thought that Bombay lay close to Brazil! Sir William Foster, in his time the foremost authority on the actions of the Company during the seventeenth century, assures us that the Company itself never suggested the inclusion of Bombay in the proposed agreement.[43] Seemingly, therefore, Bombay became a throw-in, but one that excited neither the English crown nor, curiously, the directors of the Company.[44]

To prevent Goan authorities and Portuguese residents in Bombay from erecting any obstacles, the English and Portuguese agreed that the 44-gun English frigate *Leopard*, one of five vessels commanded by James Ley, third earl of Marlborough, would stop at Lisbon en route and take aboard António de Melo de Castro, whom the crown designated as high commissioner and governor of India, a title subsequently elevated to that of viceroy.[45] Melo de Castro was to accompany the squadron to Bombay and effect the transfer. Elements of Marlborough's squadron reached Bombay in mid-September 1662, but the *Mary Rose*, bearing the designated English governor, Sir Abraham Shipman,

---

to earl of Winchilsea, Aleppo, 7 Sept. 1661, in Historical Manuscripts Commission, *Report on the Manuscripts of Allen George Finch, Esq.*, 2 vols. (London, 1913), 1: 151; Lannoy to earl of Winchilsea, 12 Aug. and 13 Nov. 1662, in ibid., 209, 223–24.

41. Instruction to Nathaniel Wych, 7 Apr. 1658, in *EFI* (1655–60), 151.

42. Consultation of Matthew Andrews and other Surat factors, 22 June 1660, in ibid., 300.

43. *A Calendar of the Court Minutes, etc., of the East India Company, 1660–1663*, ed. Ethel Bruce Sainsbury, intro. William Foster (Oxford, 1922), xxi–xxii.

44. Ibid., xxii and 137. See also Khan, "Anglo-Portuguese Negotiations," 439–40.

45. King to Melo de Castro, 9 Apr. 1662, in J. Gerson da Cunha, *The Origin of Bombay*, *JBBRAS*, extra no. (1900): 244. The *Leopard* ascended the Tagus to fetch the viceroy just as the earl of Sandwich was embarking with the new queen and the first portion of her dowry. R. C. Anderson, ed., *The Journal of Edward Montague, First Earl of Sandwich ... 1659–1665*, Naval Records Society (London, 1929), 124 and 130.

commander of the 400-man English garrison, was not one of them. Accordingly, when Marlborough brusquely asked Melo de Castro to fulfill the transfer, the commissioner refused on the ground that he was empowered to do so only before Charles II's officially designated agent. Still smarting from affronts he claimed to have suffered aboard the *Leopard* during his five-month passage, the commissioner even refused to permit the famished and thirsty English soldiers to land. And when Shipman arrived the following month, Melo de Castro declined to honor his credentials, which he contended were defective.

Not until December did the troops and their commander finally land, but not at Bombay. Instead, Shipman, his aides (including a mysterious Jesuit, Fr. John Gregory, an interpreter), and the troops went ashore on Angediva Island, an unhealthy, uninhabited spot 19 kilometers southwest of Goa.[46] There they languished for nearly a year, during which half the men, including Sir Abraham, perished.[47]

Several reasons have been adduced to explain the viceroy's apparent obstinacy. The first is that he was simply being petulant, repaying the English for their ill treatment of him during the outbound voyage. The second is that after listening to the concerns of Portuguese landlords regarding the future of their estates on the island, he came to sympathize with their opposition to the transfer. The third is that he entered the pay of one of the island's principal landlords, the Jesuits, whom an English captain accused of bribing the viceroy with more than fourteen contos.[48] There is no evidence of such a bribe having been offered or accepted; nor is it necessary to assume that the viceroy did not honestly state his reasons for declining to deliver Bombay.

Those reasons were expressed in Melo de Castro's famous dispatch of 28 December 1662, in which he explained why he did not deem it "convenient" to hand over Bombay and some smaller islands that the English had also demanded. First, he pointed out that Shipman's warrant was not signed by the king, as was mandatory under Portuguese law. Second, he reminded his superiors that the Portuguese objective in negotiating the treaty was partly to secure English aid to protect its remaining outposts in India. He noted that no English squadron other than Marlborough's had been seen on the coast and that the earl had positively refused his appeal for assistance to relieve besieged Cochin. Third, he warned that Bombay was "the best port your Majesty possesses in India," and that its cession to the English would doom Portugal's remaining outposts in the north. Fourth, he proposed an alternative "remedy," namely that Afonso VI should offer to buy back the island. He assured his sovereign that "all in this State . . . would be pleased to be free from such a yoke,

46. Nothing is known concerning how or when Fr. Gregory entered English service. He may have boarded the *Leopard* in Lisbon and joined Shipman's staff because of his knowledge of Portuguese. For references to him, see Henry Gary to James, earl of Marlborough, 25 Jan. 1663 (two dispatches), in Khan, "Anglo-Portuguese Negotiations," 449–50.

47. Shipman to Marlborough, Angediva, 18 Nov. 1663, in ibid., 477. Shipman died the following April.

48. Dispatches of Henry Gary of 31 Dec. 1662 and 12 Jan. 1663 to EIC, in *EFI* (1661–64), 142–43; Sir George Oxenden to Lord Arlington, 6 Mar. 1665, in ibid., 144. Melo de Castro, who had a great talent for making enemies, later fell afoul of the Inquisition in Goa, in part for having stated that the Jesuits in India, unlike their companions in Europe, were only interested in furthering their own concerns and therefore resembled the Dutch! Pedro de Azevedo, "A Inquisição de Goa contra o vicerei Mello de Castro," *Revista de história* 1, 2 (Lisbon, 1912): 175–79. Melo de Castro was sent home in disgrace and was confined for a time in a fortress in Setúbal. Robert Southwell to Lord Arlington, 24 Oct./3 Nov. 1668, in PRO/SP89/9/127.

[and] would assist in carrying out that arrangement."[49] Where he gained such assurance, the viceroy did not say. Certainly there was nothing in the recent economic history of the Estado that could have led him to such a conclusion.

Such was the message that Melo de Castro entrusted to a Jesuit father, Fr. Manuel Godinho, to deliver to the king's closest advisors. He was to explain to them that the English were demanding not only Bombay but also all lands between that island and Bassein, that the earl said that his sovereign had nothing but contempt for Afonso VI, that if the English gained Bombay they would ruin the trade of the remaining Portuguese outposts, and that it would be far preferable to repurchase Bombay.[50]

Little is known about the background of the viceroy's messenger, but there is enough evidence concerning his conduct during his mission to suggest that Melo de Castro's confidence in him was misplaced. Manuel Godinho (b. 1630–d. 1712) was born in Portalegre or Lisbon and joined the Society sometime between 1645 and 1649. It is not known when he came to India or why the viceroy selected him as his emissary. The overland route that Fr. Godinho took, an alternative to the long, often hazardous sea voyage, had not been uncommon in the past but was rarely used by the Portuguese at that time.[51] Fr. Godinho left Goa in December 1662 disguised as a soldier and sailed to Bassein. From there he proceeded to Damão, where he adopted a Muslim trader's garb and sailed in an Arab ship to Basra. He then joined a caravan to Aleppo via Baghdad and continued on to Alexandretta, where he took a French vessel to Marseilles. Despite the urgency of his mission, Fr. Manuel celebrated the feast of St. Ignatius (31 July) with his confreres at the college in that port and remained with them for several weeks before journeying overland to Bordeaux. From there he proceeded to La Rochelle, where he took a ship for Portugal, landing in the port of Cascais on 25 October 1663.[52]

Because of the duration of the Jesuit's trip, both the English and the Portuguese governments were already aware of the unexpected hitch in the transfer before the viceroy's explanation reached the paço da ribeira. In mid-May 1663, Sir Henry Bennet, Charles II's secretary of state, indignantly blustered to Sir Richard Fanshaw, ambassador to Portugal, that Marlborough had reported that Bombay "is found to be far inferior to what it was represented"; nevertheless, Bennet declared that "less than the viceroy's head and satisfaction for all the damages and expenses of his Majesty ... will not suffice to pay ...

---

49. Melo de Castro's dispatch is printed in Gerson da Cunha, *Origin*, 245–48, and in several of the other cited sources.

50. The text of Melo de Castro's instructions to Fr. Manuel was discovered by Fr. John Correia-Afonso and is published in his "Some Portuguese Records on the Cession of Bombay," *Indian Archives* 27, 1 (Jan.–July 1978): 1–11.

51. Anthony R. Disney, "The Portuguese Overland Courier Service Between Europe and India in the Sixteenth and Seventeenth Centuries," *Don Peter Felicitation Volume* (Colombo, 1993), 51–63.

52. Fr. Godinho, who left the Society in 1667 and became a secular priest in Portugal, wrote a famous account of his journey, the *Relação do novo caminho da India para Portugal* (1665), ed. A. Machado Guerreiro (Lisbon, 1974), of which there is a competent English translation: Vitalio Lobo and John Correia-Afonso, trans. and eds., *Intrepid Itinerant: Manuel Godinho and His Journey from India to Portugal in 1663* (Bombay, 1990). A hitherto overlooked document, undoubtedly written by Godinho, concerning his reasons for refusing the father general's order to return to India is the undated and unsigned memo entitled "Rezoes que allego para me escuzar de tornar a India, como ordem a N. R. Padre Geral," BNL, cod. 177, fols. 219–20. See also John Correia-Afonso, S.J., "Postscript to an Odyssey: More Light on Manuel Godinho," *Modern Asian Studies* 22, 3 (1988): 491–502.

for this affront." Clarendon added that three days after Charles II had received an appeal from Afonso VI soliciting English mediation of Portugal's war with Spain, there arrived the first reports of the viceroy's duplicity, "an act . . . so foul that less than the head of the man cannot satisfy for the indignity, and for the damage his Majesty will expect and exact." He warned that if Afonso VI did not immediately make amends, "farewell the friendship with Portugal, and they are not to wonder if they hear that we and the Dutch are united in the East Indies, and that we do all else to their prejudice."[53] In Lisbon, Fanshaw demanded the viceroy's exemplary punishment and suggested that his master might be assuaged if Bassein were also "given into [his] hands," while in London the Portuguese ambassador was advised that Salsete do Norte and Taná must also be ceded to Charles II.[54] In short, while the Dutch were acquiring Portuguese possessions by force, the English tried to acquire them by bluster.

Lisbon responded with alarm and alacrity. Castelo Melhor, who had engineered the coup that ended the regency of Luísa de Gusmão (see Chapter 5), confessed to Fanshaw that his master could not understand why his explicit orders had not been fulfilled. Two months later he sent a reprimand in the king's name to the viceroy for having failed to comply with his instructions and directed him "to execute the said delivery with every punctuality and without the least consideration, as the matter does not admit of any, and the delay is very prejudicial."[55] Four months earlier, in February 1664, the king had dispatched a special agent to London to reassure Charles II of his sincerity, but also to see whether it might be possible, as Melo de Castro had suggested, to repurchase the contested island. It was, but not at a price that Afonso VI could afford.[56]

Although Fr. Godinho delivered the viceroy's fervent plea to the king in October 1663, Lisbon did not acknowledge it until the following February. Speaking for Afonso VI, Castelo Melhor again insisted upon explicit compliance with the crown's previous directive and advised the viceroy to assure worried estate owners in Bombay that their property rights would be protected by the new regime: "The only difference will be that they will live under the domination of the King of Great Britain, my brother, who will rule them with justice and in the freedom of the Roman Catholic religion. . . . The King of England also undertakes to protect the places I have in that State, and this was one of the reasons for my giving him that island. . . . This affair will admit no delay."[57]

53. Bennet (subsequently Lord Arlington) to Fanshaw, 24 May 1663, and Clarendon to Fanshaw, 26 May 1663, in Historical Manuscripts Commission, *The Manuscripts of J. M. Heathcote, Esq.* (Norwich, 1899), 87–90.

54. Fanshaw to Castelo Melhor, 26 June 1663, in ibid., 116–17; *Calendar of Court Minutes, 1660–1663,* xxviii.

55. Castelo Melhor to Fanshaw, 20 June 1663, in Historical Manuscripts Commission, *Heathcote*, 113; Afonso VI to Melo de Castro, 16 Aug. 1663, in Gerson da Cunha, *Origin*, 249; Khan, "Anglo-Portuguese Negotiations," 459. It was Melo de Castro's ill luck that Castelo Melhor was in power by the time his agent reached court. Although he enumerated eight nobles with whom Fr. Manuel ought to speak, Castelo Melhor was not one of them. The minister and the viceroy may well have been old adversaries. See note 48.

56. Clarendon set the price of £120,000 for the island and £109,862 14s. for the cost of the Marlborough fleet, sums that he knew Lisbon could not pay in addition to the already delinquent dowry payments. Prestage, *Diplomatic Relations*, 161.

57. King to viceroy, 8 Feb. 1664, in *ACE*, 4: 533–34; the English translation is in Historical Manuscripts Commission, *Heathcote*, 459–60.

Melo de Castro reluctantly submitted to the royal will, but he could not resist twisting the lion's tail a bit more. After a packet from Basra brought preemptory orders from Lisbon and amplifications of Shipman's instructions from London, Humphrey Cooke, a onetime shopkeeper in Lisbon and Shipman's successor, forwarded the documents to Goa. Since Marlborough had abandoned the survivors on Angediva, Cooke was obliged to hire Portuguese vessels to transport them to Goa, where their treatment proved very different from that accorded William Methwold and his associates 28 years earlier. A month passed, "the Soldjery and my selfe lying aboard in this hotte Sunn all the time," wrote the disgruntled Cooke, while the viceroy and the High Court deliberated whether Whitehall's orders addressed to Shipman could be executed by Cooke. In the end they concluded that they could be, but Melo de Castro had no intention of returning to Bombay himself. Instead, he sent the court's chancellor and his senior treasury officer (veedor da fazenda). He also compelled Cooke to accept fourteen interpretive articles that defined the cession as narrowly as possible.[58]

The transfer of Bombay was effected on Ash Wednesday (25 February) 1665. Five weeks earlier, the viceroy had written the king that he had reluctantly obeyed his orders: "I confess ... that only the obedience I owe your Majesty ... could have forced me to this deed, because I foresee the great troubles that ... will result to the Portuguese; and that India will be lost the same day in which the English nation is settled in Bombay."[59]

Unlike so many Portuguese prophecies concerning India, this one proved to be remarkably prescient. As the viceroy feared, Cooke immediately embarked upon a policy that his successors would also pursue: "My endeavours ... beeing to draw hither as many merchants (Banias as well as Moores and Persians) as possibly I cann from Suratt, Cambaya, Ahmadavid, Broach, Diu, Thana, etc. ... to exercise theyre religion publiquely in, no doubt but this will bee made a very famous and opulent port."[60] So it became, but not until a century had elapsed.[61] In 1668, the government of Charles II became so disenchanted with Bombay and its continued drain upon the treasury that it offered it to the EIC, whose directors, with feigned reluctance, accepted.[62]

The Portuguese came to rue the day they handed over Bombay, and the Society did too. The funds that Melo de Castro promised could be raised in India for its recovery never materialized, and all subsequent Portuguese plans to buy it back failed for lack of money.[63]

58. Protest by Cooke to Capt. Robert Bowen et al., Bombay, 13 Mar. 1665, in Khan, "Anglo-Portuguese Negotiations," 464–71; Melo de Castro to Relação of Goa, in ibid., 460; *EFI* (1665–67), 37ff. For the fourteen articles, see Khan, "Anglo-Portuguese Negotiations," 479–81. Cooke had no intention of respecting them, and Charles II did not denounce them until 25 Mar. 1677. Ibid., 482–83 and n. 66.

59. Melo de Castro to king, 5 Jan. 1665, in Gerson da Cunha, *Origin*, 258–59. When the first muster of the English garrison was taken, only 115 of the original 400 troops remained alive. *EFI* (1665–67), 43.

60. Cooke to Lord Arlington, 16 Feb. 1665, in *EFI* (1665–67), 51.

61. K. N. Chaudhuri, *The Trading World of Asia and the English East India Company, 1660–1760* (New York, 1978), 49, provides a cogent explanation of why the ascendancy of Bombay took so long.

62. *A Calendar of Court Minutes ... of the East India Company, 1664–1667*, ed. Ethel Bruce Sainsbury, intro. William Foster (Oxford, 1925), xxiv–xxv, 401, 408–9. The statement by the Company's governor that "had the Portuguese offered the island to them [the EIC] before the King had it, they would have refused it" is belied by the Company's instructions of 1658. See note 40 above.

63. Gerson da Cunha, *Origin*, 225, 259–60.

The crown might have been able to raise the capital from New Christian merchants, but, as demonstrated in Chapter 5, it rejected proposed aid from them. Notwithstanding the assurances Castelo Melhor gave, Portuguese landowners on the island, including the Jesuits, found that registering their titles with the new English masters of the island was a long, expensive process (see Chapter 17). But from the Portuguese perspective, the most serious shortcoming of the treaty of 1661 was that, contrary to the promises made by Charles II and the assurances given by Castelo Melhor, the transfer of Bombay did not prevent further threats to the integrity of the beleaguered Estado da India.[64]

Arab and Indian Attacks on the Estado, 1661–98

Taking advantage of Portuguese maritime weakness and Goa's preoccupation with the Dutch and the English, Arab and Indian adversaries repeatedly attacked outliers of the State during the last four decades of the seventeenth century. In 1662 the king of Golconda ordered the occupation of São Tomé de Meliapor, once an active market town on the Coromandel coast and the site of one of the two most distant surviving Jesuit colleges in the province of Malabar. Aided by a Dutch blockade of the port, the king successfully captured the town after a seven-month siege. The surviving Christians fled to the protection of Fort St. George (Madras), 16 kilometers to the north. A decade later, a French expedition, its commander supposedly encouraged by two Portuguese Jesuits who had remained in the outskirts of the town with their neophytes, occupied São Tomé but incurred such hostility from the English, the Dutch, and the Golcondans that it withdrew after less than two years. The Hollanders and Golcondans then destroyed what remained of the settlement.[65]

In the west, the Omani followed up their victory at Muscat (1650) by conducting a reign of terror over Portuguese outposts from East Africa to the Gulf of Cambay for nearly half a century.[66] In 1661 they assaulted the town of Mombasa but failed to take its fortress. Seven years later, they pillaged the island of Diu, which guarded access to the Gulf of Cambay, destroying the Jesuit college there along with many other buildings, kidnapping several thousand townsmen, and capturing large quantities of booty. Two years later, they took advantage of the absence of the captain-general of Mozambique, who was campaigning on the Zambesi with most of his forces, and attacked the island of Mozambique, mined

64. A secret article of the treaty stipulated that "in case . . . any towns, forts, castles, or any other place, shall be taken by the Dutch after the first of May . . . 1661, then His Majesty . . . doth oblige himself to send, the next monsoon . . . after the ratification of the treaty . . . a convenient succour to the East Indies, proportionable to the necessity of Portugal and strength of our enemies." George Chalmers, comp., *A Collection of Treaties Between Great Britain and Other Powers*, 2 vols. (London, 1790), 2: 196. No such "succour" was ever sent. It is, therefore, hard to agree with S. A. Khan that the treaty was "a one-sided bargain with all the advantages lying on the side of the Portuguese," and that "poor Charles II . . . found himself tricked at every turn . . . by the subtle Portuguese": "Anglo-Portuguese Negotiations," 440 and 570. There is no merit to Foster's contention that Cochin might have been saved had the Luso-Dutch peace treaty of 1662 been more promptly ratified: *EFI* (1665–67), 25–26. The Dutch had no intention of returning Cochin, and the English had no desire to compel them to do so.

65. *The Travels of the Abbé Carre in India and the Near East, 1672 to 1674*, trans. Lady Fawcett, ed. Sir Charles Fawcett and Sir Richard Burn, 3 vols., *HS:2*, 95–97 (1947–48), 96: xiii–xiv and chap. 4; *EFI* (1661–64), 146; S. P. Sen, *The French in India: First Establishment and Struggle* (Calcutta, 1947), a pedestrian account that ends with the founding of Pondichery (1683).

66. Strandes, *Portuguese Period*, chap. 16.

its fortress, and barely missed blowing it up. In 1674 they raided the agriculturally rich lands around Bassein and might have done even further damage on the island of Salsete do Norte had it not been for Jesuit cannon, which guarded the college of Bandorá on its southwest corner. But even the fathers could not prevent the return of the Arabs to Diu, which they sacked a second time in 1676. Twenty years later, Mombasa once again became a prime Omani target. Despite three Portuguese relief expeditions and the loss of nearly 1,000 men, its fortress of Fort Jesús fell on 13 December 1698, ending nearly two centuries of Portuguese efforts to rule the Swahili coast.[67]

The Rise of the Maratha Menace

Yet the most serious threat to the Estado in this period came from within the subcontinent of India. While the Europeans were fighting over its periphery, the heartland was beset by convulsive struggles between Hindus and Muslims. In the north and center of the Deccan, the three Muslim sultanates that had succeeded the Hindu empire of Vijayanagar—Ahmadnagar, Bijapur, and Golconda—were themselves successfully challenged by the imperialists of the north, the Mughals, who successively conquered Ahmadnagar (1633), Bijapur (1686), and Golconda (1687).[68] Mughal pressure on the Central Deccan triggered a revival of Hindu power there under the Marathas, who had lived dispersed throughout the interior since the thirteenth century, some as millet-raising peasants, others as mercenaries who fought in the armies of the sultans. From the 1640s to the end of the 1680s, two Maratha chieftains exploited the increasing weakness of Bijapur and persisting unrest in Ahmadnagar to create a roughly rectangular polity that extended southward from the proximity of the Tapti River to northern Kanara, and westward from the Western Ghats to the Konkan lowlands. The Marathas thus became a dangerous territorial power whose domains impinged upon all the remaining Portuguese enclaves in the subcontinent save Diu.[69]

With the rise of the Marathas, authorities in Goa faced a serious dilemma. Should they provide the Marathas with assistance in order to weaken their traditional Muslim adversaries? How strong could the Marathas be permitted to become before they represented a menace to the Portuguese? In the event they became too successful, could the Lusitanians expect help from their nominal English allies? If not, would they be compelled to turn to the Mughals for help, since precious little aid could be expected from Lisbon? If so, at what cost? The search for answers to those difficult questions occupied a succession of Goan

67. *ACE*, 4: 68–70, 123, 132, 135, 204–5, and 243. Eric Axelson, *Portuguese in South-East Africa, 1600–1700* (Johannesburg, 1960), 140, 155–75; Tavernier, *Travels*, 1: 28–30; *EFI* (1668–69), 257; Sir Charles Fawcett, ed., *The English Factories in India*, new ser., *1670–84*, 4 vols. (Oxford, 1936–55), 1: 115; John Fryer, *A New Account of East India and Persia, Being Nine Years' Travels, 1672–1681*, HS:2, 19–20 (1909–12), 19: 183, 191–95. For the location of Fort Jesús, see Frank Broeze, ed., *Bridges of the Sea: Port Cities of Asia from the 16th to 20th Centuries* (Honolulu, 1989), map 14, facing p. 200.

68. Holden Furber, *Rival Empires of Trade in the Orient, 1600–1800* (Minneapolis, 1976), 11; Sir Jadunath Sarkar, *History of Aurangzib* [1919], 2d ed., 5 vols. (Bombay, 1972–74), 4: passim.

69. Sarkar, *History of Aurangzib*, 4: 3–15; O. H. K. Spate and A. T. A. Learmouth, *India and Pakistan: A General and Regional Geography*, 3d ed. (London, 1967), 23–24, 654–56, 690–700; R. C. Majumdar, H. C. Raychaudhuri, and Kalikinkar Datta, *An Advanced History of India*, 3d ed. (London, 1973), 503–16. For a map of seventeenth-century Maratha territory, see Govind Sakharam Sardesi, *New History of the Maratas*, 2 vols. (Bombay, 1957), vol. 1, frontispiece.

regimes between the mid-1650s and the late 1680s and ultimately led to miscalculations that nearly resulted in the expulsion of the Portuguese from the Konkan lowlands.

The first Maratha warrior to challenge the Portuguese was Sivaji (b. 1627 or 1630–d. 1680), a son of a minor noble of Ahmadnagar and holder of a fief in Poona, who entered Bijapuri military service after the Mughals annexed his homeland. Sivaji exploited the disintegrating authority of Bijapur by undertaking his first campaigns in the mid-1640s, when he captured a series of hill forts, gained considerable booty, and recruited a band of armed followers. His subsequent raids upon Mughal-claimed districts in the north led to his defeat in 1657, but two years later he rebounded with a dramatic victory over an army of the sultan of Bijapur and captured its entire supply train.[70] In 1660 Sivaji occupied Poona and raided the South Konkan and the district of Kolhapur, northeast of Goa. Three years later he surprised and wounded the Mughal viceroy of the Deccan, a feat that led to his first attack on Surat in 1664. His forces burned two-thirds of that city of 200,000 and withdrew bearing vast quantities of loot, principally precious gems, cash, and bullion.[71] The next year, however, Sivaji was defeated by a Mughal force and was obliged to surrender much of his territory and travel to Agra as a penitent vassal. There he was placed under intimidating house arrest until he and his son, Sambhaji, made a spectacular escape.[72] Soon after, Portuguese officials in Goa found it necessary to reevaluate their estimate of Sivaji.

At first the Portuguese had considered him to be "a valiant and intelligent man" who might be useful to them.[73] They were disappointed when Damião Vieira, a Jesuit father who had survived the siege of Colombo and was sent to negotiate a treaty with the Maratha leader in 1665, found Sivaji indifferent to the making of such an agreement. In 1667, following Sivaji's escape from Agra, relations between the Portuguese and the Marathas began to deteriorate as Sivaji raided Bardês for cattle and for refugees who had escaped Bijapur because of his campaigns there. The viceroy, João Nunes da Cunha, count of São Vicente (1666–68), wrote his superiors, "I am worried with [Sivaji's] growing might in the sea, because he has built coastal forts which should have been prevented at the start, and he has a large number of [small] vessels."[74] São Vicente deputed another Jesuit, Fr. Gonçalo Martins, the "father of the Christians" of Salsete, to negotiate a treaty with Sivaji and to lecture him on the responsibilities of government. Evidently the warrior was unimpressed, because in December 1668, a year after making peace with the Portuguese, he violated the agreement by attempting to capture Goa by means of fifth columnists.[75] Their exposure

70. Sarkar, *History of Aurangzib*, 4: 35. The literature on Sivaji is vast. Useful starting places are Jadunath Sarkar, *Shivaji and His Times*, 6th ed. (Calcutta, 1961); and Surendra Nath Sen, *Foreign Biographies of Shivaji* (London, n.d. [ca. 1928]), which includes a translation of the earliest foreign biography, written by Cosme da Guarda (1695), an Indo-Portuguese resident of Goa.

71. *EFI* (1661–64), 296–316; Sarkar, *History of Aurangzib*, 4: 49–51.

72. Sarkar, *History of Aurangzib*, 4: 19–79.

73. Pandurang S. S. Pissurlencar [Pissurlenkar], *The Portuguese and the Marathas*, trans. P. R. Kakodkar (Bombay, 1975), 6. Except as noted, this paragraph is based upon chap. 1 of this indispensable but badly patched together volume. See also Alexandre Lobato, *Relações Luso-Maratas, 1658–1737* (Lisbon, 1965), which must be used with caution since its facts are not always reliable and it adopts an unwarranted rosy view of Portuguese motives.

74. Viceroy to prince regent, 1667, as quoted in Souza, *Medieval Goa*, 40.

75. *EFI* (1668–69), 113–15; Pissurlencar, *Portuguese and Marathas*, 28–29.

caused him to desist, and in 1670 he resumed his war against Aurangzeb, the Mughal emperor, by sacking Surat, again with devastating results.[76]

For the next decade, relations between the Portuguese and Sivaji remained strained. Each side seized shipping belonging to the other. The Portuguese attempted to buttress a local Muslim ruler near Chaul who was threatened by the Marathas, for, as the viceroy wrote, "we have come to the conclusion that the rule and neighborhood of such a mischievous enemy are not convenient to the State."[77] Sivaji responded by tightening his grip upon the Konkan lowlands, by threatening invasion of Bardês and Salsete, and by demanding from the Portuguese what racketeers call protection (*chauth*), a 25 percent assessment that he was already levying upon Surat and other cities that he had victimized.[78] In 1680, just as he appeared ready to undertake a full-scale campaign against Portuguese outposts, Sivaji, whom his Portuguese counterpart, António Pais de Sande, characterized as "a new Atila of India . . . brave, artful, and astute," a man who "robs and destroys everything wherever he goes," went to his reward.[79]

Sivaji's son, Sambhaji, was a very different sort of man. If Sivaji was abstemious, pious, relatively moral, administratively talented, and militarily gifted, as well as ruthless, treacherous, and greedy, the son shared his father's vices but lacked his virtues. Sambhaji was impetuous, prone to licentiousness, often lethargic, indifferent about the maintenance of military discipline, and disloyal to his own father, against whom he rebelled. His betrayal was the reason why he, the eldest son, was passed over in favor of his much younger brother, Rajaram, for whom a regency was established after Sivaji's death. But Sambhaji quickly exploited the factions engendered by that regency, gained a military following, and imposed himself upon the throne that his father had created six years earlier. On 16 January 1681, the usurper was crowned with customary pomp.[80]

Eight months later, Francisco de Távora, first count of Alvor, arrived in Goa to become its 33d viceroy. No one who held that office possessed better connections, and few exceeded the quality of his record of service. Born in the town of Moura in 1646, Távora was a grandson on his mother's side of the count of Linhares, the 23d viceroy of the Estado. At the age of nineteen he participated with distinction in the key battle of Montes Claros against the Spaniards (see Chapter 5). Four years later he arrived in Luanda to become mutinous Angola's new governor. His assignment was to restore order in the wake of a tumult that had resulted in the expulsion of his predecessor. Despite his youth, Távora fulfilled his responsibilities admirably. Angolans found him tactful, energetic, honest, pious, and caring. He not only regained their confidence but also supervised a successful campaign against black rebels

76. Fawcett, *English Factories*, new ser., 1: 195–98; Sarkar, *History of Aurangzib*, 4: 149–53. The emperor's name is also written Aurangzeb, the form used here.

77. António Pais de Sande (veedor da fazenda) to [crown], 28 May 1669, as quoted in Pissurlencar, *Portuguese and Marathas*, 30.

78. For Portuguese efforts to evade such payments, see A[nthony] D'Costa, S.J., "Correspondence Between Sivaji and the Government of Goa, 1678–1679," *Indica* 1 (1964): 187–97. Cf. Irfan Habib, *The Agrarian System of Mughal India (1556–1707)* (New York, 1967), 148. Habib contends that at Damão the Portuguese had been paying protection since the sixteenth century.

79. Sande to [crown?], 24 Jan. 1680, in Pissurlencar, *Portuguese and Marathas*, 53–54. For Sande's distinguished career, see *PDH*, 6: 551–52.

80. Sarkar, *History of Aurangzib*, 4: 192–97; Rajaram Vyankatesh Nadkarni, *The Rise and Fall of the Maratha Empire* (Bombay, 1966), 121–24.

in the interior and strengthened the colony's defenses. He maintained cordial relations with the pretentious cámara of the capital and with the Church, especially the Jesuits. Each Friday evening he attended mass dedicated to Saint Francis Xavier in the college's church. Very likely he considered the saint as his own patron. In the opinion of one important local dignitary who knew him well, Francisco de Távora was "the perfect governor," one whom the populace affectionately dubbed "the prudent lad." Exactly seven years after he assumed his post, he relinquished it and returned to the kingdom, where, in 1677, he married D. Ignes Catharina de Távora, daughter of his eldest brother, the first marquis of Távora, and a lady-in-waiting in the entourage of D. Marie François Isabelle of Savoy, wife of the prince regent. Four years later, D. Pedro named Távora to another challenging position with the expectation that he would instill a new sense of discipline and improve morale in the Estado. Sadly, his regime (1681–86) accomplished just the reverse, for if he was the right man for the job in Angola in the 1670s, he was the wrong man for the State of India in the 1680s, when the once-prudent governor became an imprudent viceroy, and an embarrassment even to the Jesuits.[81]

Initially Távora continued his predecessor's efforts to arrange a new peace agreement with Sambhaji, but those efforts foundered, in part because the viceroy insisted that the Maratha's envoy to Goa lacked proper credentials to sign a treaty (shades of Bombay!).[82] Then he decided to challenge Sambhaji. First, having learned that Sambhaji intended to occupy the island of Angediva, where poor Shipman and his comrades had perished, and fearing that the Maratha ruler would then admit the Omani to the island, thereby imperiling Goa's food supplies, the viceroy ordered the island fortified. Second, Távora warmly welcomed an envoy from Aurangzeb, the Mughal emperor, who had resumed his war against the Marathas in 1682, and granted the ambassador's request to permit Mughal forces free passage through Portuguese lands in the Northern Province, that is, the enclaves between Chaul and Damão, in order to attack the Marathas. A modern apologist declares that Távora maintained absolute neutrality between the Mughals and the Marathas at this time, but that contention is belied by the viceroy's effusive letter of 12 April 1683 to the Mughal emperor in which he asked for compensation for Portuguese assistance since "our state . . . has proved to be such a good friend of Your Majesty [and] . . . [Your] ambassador . . . always found me enthusiastic to help Your Majesty."[83] That proved to be Távora's first miscalculation, for by the time his letter reached Aurangzeb, the Mughal had abandoned his campaign.

Sir Jadunath Sarkar once observed that "in provoking war with Sambhaji by thus openly siding with Aurangzib, the Viceroy was backing the wrong horse," since he had no assurance of Mughal support and was far too weak to handle the Maratha leader alone.[84] Though it may be questioned whether the viceroy really had a choice, it cannot be denied that his

81. For a contemporary assessment of Távora's Angolan years, see António de Oliveira de Cadornega, *História geral das guerras angolanas* [1680], ed. José Matias Delgado, 3 vols. (rpr., Lisbon, 1972), 2: 298–371, esp. 334 and 366–67, and 3: 42. Cadornega, an old soldier, was senior alderman of Luanda in 1671 and clearly regarded Távora highly. So, too, did Angola's next major chronicler and another soldier, Elias Alexandre da Silva Correa, author of *História de Angola* [1782], ed. Manuel Múrias, 2 vols. (Lisbon, 1937), 1: 289–95. See also *PDH*, 1: 405–7. On the Overseas Council's high expectations concerning his viceregency, see Council to prince regent, 13 Jan. 1681, in *APO*:2, 1:3:1, LXXVIII–LXXX.

82. Lobato, *Relações*, 25–28.

83. Távora to Aurangzeb, 12 Apr. 1683, in Pissurlencar, *Portuguese and Marathas*, 81–87; the quotation is from p. 85. Cf. Lobato, *Relações*, 28.

84. Sarkar, *History of Aurangzib*, 4: 226.

actions provoked Sambhaji. The Maratha began by seizing Portuguese shipping and burning isolated villages throughout the Northern Province. In February or March 1683, Sambhaji attacked the undefended town of Tarapur, situated between Bassein and Damão. Early
in August he commenced the siege of Chaul, where years of neglected maintenance of the artillery nearly lost the fortress, and where the Marathas kidnapped a Jesuit and a Franciscan.[85]

Those actions provoked Távora's rash responses. First, he decided to emulate the
Marathas by encouraging the Canarins, the indigenous population of Goa, to burn and
plunder nearby villages under Sambhaji's control. Then he organized a so-called diversion-
ary operation whose conception only a Sebastian could have appreciated (see Chapter 4). In
late October he stripped his garrisons and even his warships to assemble a strike force of
1,200 Europeans, including 100 newly arrived troops, many of them underage, and 2,500
Canarins. The strike force marched toward the Maratha outpost of Pondá, situated at
the confluence of two creeks 18 kilometers southeast of Goa.[86] The viceroy's plan was not
only to destroy the fortress but also to persuade Sambhaji to lift the siege of Chaul. He
accomplished neither goal and left his capital exposed to enemy attack. After the strike
force slogged through incessant rain for five days, the Portuguese began to bombard the
fortress. Although they breached its walls, they were unable to penetrate them. Sambhaji
then arrived with a relief column consisting of several hundred mounted troopers. Távora
decided to retreat, but Maratha cavalry blocked his way, and the viceroy's withdrawal soon
became a disorderly rout, a miniature Alcázarquibir; and just as the Jesuits were blamed for
that debacle in the 1580s, so a century later they were alleged to be responsible for Távora's
foolishness. As soon as he reached the capital, the viceroy went into seclusion for four days.[87]

Sambhaji did not act for two weeks, perhaps waiting for the unseasonable rains to
abate. When he did, he terrorized the capital. Three kilometers northeast of the city lay
the small island of Juá (Santo Estévão). Its small fort was intended to protect the capital
from attacks launched from the nearby mainland. On the night of 24 November 1683, a
small contingent of Marathas waded across the channel separating the island from terra
firma, silently occupied the fort, and slew its garrison. The next morning, the viceroy,
properly alarmed, ordered all available boats to surround the island and assembled 400
men to recover it. The men were equipped mostly with spears, cutlasses, and swords,
hardly adequate weapons to oppose well-armed Maratha musketeers and cavalrymen, who

85. The basic Portuguese source for Luso-Maratha relations at this time is [Anon.], "Rellação
verdad[ei]ra do q. socedeo no estado da India desde dous de janeiro de 1683 athe vinte e sinco de janeiro de
1684," most of which is excerpted in *APO*:2, 1:3:1, CXIV–CXXX, and portions of which are translated
in Pissurlencar, *Portuguese and Marathas*, chap. 3. Its author contended that the Jesuits were largely responsible
for Portuguese reverses in India and accused the father charged with the custody of munitions at Chaul
of negligence because of defective equipment and powder, for which the fortress commander himself bore
obvious responsibility.

86. In 1665 Sivaji captured a Bijapur fortress at Pondá, which was not a Portuguese outpost, as some
authors have stated, but he evidently relinquished it when he made peace that year with the Mughals.
Between 1673 and 1675 he made several strong efforts to regain the fortress, and he succeeded in the latter
year. *APO*:2, 1:3:1, XLI, LXXIV–LXXVII.

87. [Anon.], "Rellação verdad[ei]ra," *APO*:2, 1:3:1, CXVII–CXVIII. The remainder of this report
and another participant account, Francisco de Sousa, S.J., *Oriente conquistado a Jesus Cristo pelos padres da
companhia de Jesus da província de Goa* [1710], ed. M. Lopes de Almeida (Porto, 1978), 583–86, are the basis
for the following two paragraphs. See also note 89.

outnumbered the Portuguese by about three to one. After a day of furious fighting, 150 of the Portuguese lay dead, and all of the remainder, including the viceroy, inadvertently(?) shot by his own servant, were wounded.

Early in December, the Maratha chieftain ordered a massive invasion of the Salsete and Bardês districts, which flank the capital on the south and north. A contemporary reckoned the Marathas numbered 20,000 foot soldiers, 4,000 to 5,000 horsemen, and ten war elephants. Whatever their actual number, the Marathas swarmed over the two districts from end to end. An anonymous Portuguese account, written the following year, condemned the Jesuits of Salsete for having abandoned their parish churches, stocked with provisions and munitions, and for having fled to the capital, but the writer admitted that three well-gunned forts in the two districts were also abandoned without a shot having been fired. For nearly a month, Sambhaji was master of all the Goan territory save the capital.

Recognizing that his forces were completely demoralized and convinced that no human relief was in sight,[88] Távora could think of nothing better to do than to attend mass in the church of the professed house of Bom Jesús, where the ornate, partially exposed crypt of Saint Francis Xavier, built at great expense early in the century with funds provided by an Italian noble, was situated (as it still is) to the right of the main altar. As a Jesuit chronicler, who was probably a participant, wrote a few years later, the viceroy,

> seeing himself attacked on so many fronts by a powerful foe, the people frightened and disconsolate, the paucity of the soldiers [at his disposal] . . . and everything threatened with total ruin . . . sought the protection of Saint Francis Xavier, and after the litanies, antiphonies, and the oration prayers, he walked down the sanctuary with the priests and joined them in a prolonged meditation (*huma large disciplina*). When this was over, torches were lit. The tomb of the saint was opened. The Viceroy gave the saint his baton, royal credentials, and a letter inscribed by himself . . . in which he committed to the Saint the defense and protection of the State. . . . With many sobs and tears, the Viceroy began to pray.[89]

88. Távora later wrote bitterly that "the Europeans who are in India are the greatest enemies we have. . ., particularly the English. They have supplied Sambhaji the artillery, the mortars, the gunpowder, the arms, and every sort of ammunition against us . . . [while] in no circumstances were they ready to sell us a grain of gunpowder." Távora to Pedro II, 25 Jan. 1684, in Pissurlencar, *Portuguese and Marathas*, 97 n. 14. He later complained about such favoritism to the governor of Bombay, who responded that his agents had done no more than the Portuguese had at the time of the first Maratha attack on Surat.

89. Sousa, *Oriente conquistado*, pt. 1, conq. 4, div. 1, 585. As A. B. Bragança Pereira indicates, there is also a less dramatic account of this famous scene provided by another Jesuit, Fr. Pierre Joseph d'Orleans, who published a study of Sivaji and Sambhaji in 1688. *APO*:2, 3:1:1, CXV. But Fr. d'Orleans was not present in Goa and depended upon a report, probably written by a Jesuit, sent to him. In contrast, Bahian-born Sousa (b. 1632–d. 1712), "the last great India historian of the Society of Jesus," as Schurhammer called him, was a Jesuit administrator in Goa at the time, took his fourth vow there that very year, and was then engaged in writing his chronicle, the first part of which was completed and approved by 1697. *S/FX*, 2: 650–52. I am, therefore, inclined to follow Sousa's version. The English translation in Pissurlencar, *Portuguese and Marathas*, 126, is infelicitous and woefully lacking in proper attribution.

Távora's exceptional devotion to Xavier echoed that of his immediate predecessor. See António Paes de Sande e Castro, *António Paes de Sande "O grande governador"* (Lisbon, 1951). The author claims more pro-Jesuit influence upon his forebear than the facts warrant. Curiously, half a world away, another imperiled viceroy presided over a similar ceremony in which Jesus Christ was acclaimed as captain-general of heaven and earth and Saint Francis as his admiral. *Chronicle of Colonial Lima: The Diary of Josephe and Francisco Mugaburu, 1640–1697*, trans. and ed. Robert Ryal Miller (Norman, Okla., 1975), 291. The actions of both viceroys are reminiscent of the behavior of Saint Leo the Great, the pope who compelled Attila the Hun to retreat from his attack on Rome in A.D. 452 by calling upon the ghosts of Saint Peter and Saint Paul, who reputedly stood

But it was not the saint who brought about the relief of Goa in January 1684; it was the approach of a Mughal army from Sambhaji's rear and the entry of a Mughal fleet into Goa road. And it was Mughal forces that kept Sambhaji on the run for the next five years, until they tracked him down and barbarously executed him in 1689. The Marathas would not seriously threaten Portuguese positions again until the 1730s, but when they did so they dealt crushing blows to the Society's enterprises throughout the East (see Chapter 23).[90]

The Waning of an Enterprise

At the beginning of the seventeenth century, a perceptive French sojourner in Goa, François Pyrard de Laval, concluded that "the revenues of the State can not at present be sufficient to pay and maintain the state . . . [for] the cost is greater than the value . . . indeed . . . but for the reputation and interest of the Catholic faith . . . they [the Portuguese] would long ere this have abandoned these lands."[91] Pyrard de Laval's conclusions seem even more compelling at the end of the century than they may have at its beginning. It would be hard to find sound economic reasons for preserving what was left of the Estado da India, the erosion of which seriously affected the Society of Jesus, too. During that dismal century, the Society suffered the loss not only of many of its valued positions, but also of the resources to sustain those that remained. It also possessed fewer personnel to staff the facilities that it had left.

As Chapters 11 and 23 will disclose, the Society's provinces east of the Cape of Good Hope were always far more dependent upon recruits sent from Europe than were those in Brazil. Table 8.1 indicates that more Jesuits sailed eastward during the first decade of the seventeenth century than in any later decennium: by the 1630s, when the Dutch initiated their blockade of Goa, only 56 percent of that number departed the kingdom; and during the 1660s, after Ceylon and the Coromandel and Malabar coasts had been lost, the total was only one-third that of the first decades of the century. Thereafter, recovery came slowly until the spurt in the 1690s, which reflected the increasing promise of imperial China.[92]

The membership of the province of Goa peaked at 304 in 1627. By 1649 its personnel had already diminished by a quarter, to 229. Perhaps because of refugee subjects from the stricken Malabar province, that number rose in the 1660s: in 1666 there were 258 Jesuits distributed among the province's 11 colleges, 9 missions and residences, 54 churches, and 50 parishes.[93] For the balance of the century, however, membership fluctuated at substantially lower levels, and in the first decade of the eighteenth century the number stood at 205, one-third fewer fathers and brothers than the province possessed during the 1620s (see Appendix D).

---

on either side of the pontiff as he intimidated the barbarian leader. C. Warren Holister, "The Phases of European History and the Nonexistence of the Middle Ages," *Pacific Coast Historical Review* 61, 1 (Feb. 1992): 8.

90. Sarkar, *History of Aurangzib*, 4: 235–36 and 334–44.

91. Pyrard de Laval, *Voyage*, *HS*:1, no. 77 (1888); *HS*:2, no. 210.

92. *LJI*, 282–312. In 1687 a Jesuit official expressed regret that it was impossible to prevent the continued decline of Goa province's membership because funds were not available to bring novices from the kingdom, and the Orders were expressly forbidden to recruit among the young soldiers arriving from there. Gaspar Afonso (provincial) to Távora(?), 27 Sept. 1687, in BNL, cod. 8538, fol. 49.

93. Manoel Barreto, S.J. (provincial secretary), "Lista das rendas e despezas da provincia de Goa da Companhia de JESV pera o s'nor conde v[ice]rey Joam Nunes da Cunha," 13 Dec. 1666, Cámara municipal, Elvas, ms. 6891.

TABLE 8.1
*Number of Jesuits Sailing from Lisbon to
the Eastern Provinces During
the Seventeenth Century*

Decade	Number	Decade	Number
1600–1609	171	1650–1659	102
1610–1619	103	1660–1669	57
1620–1629	109	1670–1679	74
1630–1639	96	1680–1689	98
1640–1649	88	1690–1699	149

SOURCE: *LJI*, 282–312.

Despite the loss of the Ethiopian salient and repeated Arab attacks on Diu, the province of Goa remained largely intact during the seventeenth century.[94] That was not true of the province of Malabar, which bore the brunt of the Dutch assaults from the Moluccas to Cochin. At its peak in 1632, the province boasted 180 subjects, but that number fell precipitously after 1640. By 1697, there were only 42 Jesuits left in the province, a quarter of the number that had served there 65 years earlier.[95] The few fathers who remained evidently had neither the motivation nor the opportunity to return to lands that the Dutch had successfully captured. Three years after the fall of Ceylon, for example, Malabar's provincial reported that there was little prospect of serving there as long as the Hollanders remained in control. That pessimism contrasts markedly with the determination of an earlier generation of Jesuits who willingly became martyrs in Japan after the Order had been expelled from the archipelago (see Chapter 6). There would be no underground church in Ceylon staffed by valiant young Loyolans. Indeed, in 1682, when two Orders contemplated entering that island legally, the Society was not one of them.[96]

After the fall of Cochin, the hill town of Ambalakad became the administrative center of the scattered remnants of the Malabar province, which was essentially an underground church. All its former facilities were gone, for the Dutch had destroyed some of them and converted others into storehouses and "preachers' halls." The only significant new undertaking of the province was the Mysore mission, situated in the south-central Deccan, southeast of Goa and west of Madras. Founded in 1648 by the Neapolitan Leonardo Cimmami, the mission, consisting of seven outstations and the headquarters at Canevacari, reached its zenith in the 1690s, when its 30,000 converts were tended by eighteen missionaries.[97]

In 1698 the provincial reported that Malabar still possessed five "colleges," though he admitted that they were no more than insecure mud huts. Indeed, even Ambalakad was not

94. Perhaps its most serious loss was the accidental destruction by fire of New St. Paul's College in 1663. According to Tavernier, *Travels*, 1: 197, the loss cost the province 12 contos. No information concerning that loss seems to survive in ARSI.

95. F/JM, 1: App. 1. The provincial became so desperate for personnel that he pleaded with the father general for permission to admit youths under age 15. Adriam Pedro to Gonzalez de Santalla, 23 Feb. 1694, in ARSI, *JapSin*, 166, fol. 9.

96. Robrecht Boudens, O.M.I., *The Catholic Church in Ceylon Under Dutch Rule* (Rome, 1957), 76–79, 82, and 87.

97. D. Ferroli, S.J., *The Jesuits in Mysore* (Kozhikode, India, 1955).

always safe: "A short time ago," the provincial reported, "we had to leave it and disguise ourselves as Franciscans." Those who continued to serve in the province and to attend to the spiritual welfare of the thousands of remaining Christians lived a peripatetic existence that permitted no amenities and was never free from grave risks. Indeed, the Jesuits' survival in the shattered province depended entirely upon the protection of sympathetic rajas, and the fathers risked death when they moved beyond their protectors' zones of influence.[98]

A few deliberately courted danger. The most conspicuous example was Fr. João de Brito. Born in Lisbon in 1647, Brito was the son of a member of John IV's household. His father served briefly as governor of Rio de Janeiro, where he died. Fr. João served in South India for twenty years, beginning in 1673. In 1686 he and several aides were arrested in the Marava district near Madura by the troops of a hostile prince. They were beaten, tortured, and left naked in the torrid sun. João de Brito rejoiced that he was about to die for his faith, but his time was not yet. Instead, he was rescued, and his superiors returned him to Lisbon. There Pedro II, impressed by his sterling character and intelligence, requested that Brito become his son's tutor. The father general, however, decided to return Brito to India and predicted that he was destined to become another St. Paul.

By 1691, Brito was back in Marava. Although the district was then involved in war with Madura, Brito claimed that he had made thousands of converts during the two years. But he made one too many, for one prince, after accepting the faith, renounced all his wives save the first. The discarded youngest wife then complained to the local raja, who accused the Jesuit of sorcery. Two days later, João de Brito was arrested, and on 31 January 1693, he was led to the place of execution, where, like António Criminale, he fell to his knees and embraced his executioners, who thereupon struck off his head and feet.[99]

Eight years later, the superior of the Madura mission reported with satisfaction, "Our mission . . . is more flourishing than ever. We have had four considerable Persecutions this Year. One of our Missioners has had his Teeth knockt out, and I am now . . . in the court of the Prince . . . to negotiate the deliverance of F. Borgese, who is of the Family of the Princes Borghese at Rome [and] has been now forty Days in Prison." He insisted that such persecutions were good for the faith, adding, "The more Hell rises up in Opposition to us, the greater Conquests Heaven makes."[100]

Perhaps so, but by this time many Jesuits seeking overseas assignment in the Portuguese Assistancy preferred Brazil, which, as will be seen in the following chapter, had weathered a protracted period of partial occupation by the Dutch and was becoming a far more promising enterprise for both the crown and the Society than the vestigial remnants of the Estado da India.

98. F/JM, 2: pt. 2, passim. When two Jesuits in occupied Malabar tried to foment rebellion against the Dutch, they were strongly admonished to desist because the crown feared that such action might provoke the Hollanders to resume war against Portugal. Viceroy to king, 29 Jan. 1667, and prince regent to Overseas Council, 21 Nov. 1668, in AHU/PA/IN, *cx.* 27.

99. Fr. Francisco Laínez (superior, mission of Madura) to the fathers of the Society, 10 Feb. 1693, in [Anon.], *Edifying and Curious Letters of Some Missioners of the Society of Jesus, from Foreign Missions* (n.p., 1707), 67–90; F/JM, 2: 80–87. The most extensive coeval biography of Fr. Brito is António Franco, *Imagem da virtude em o noviciado da companhia de Jesus na corte de Lisboa* (Coimbra, 1717), 755–847. See also JSM, 35–37.

100. Fr. Bouchet to Fr. Le Gobien, Madura, 1 Dec. 1701, in [Anon.], *Edifying and Curious Letters*, 25–26.

CHAPTER 9

Vicissitudes of the Enterprise in the Atlantic World During the Seventeenth Century

The islands [contribute] population ... wheat, excellent indigo, sugar, and other necessities of life. Brazil ... is an extremely fertile land for sugar and other things. . . . And from these lands we receive benefits that the conquest of India denies us. . . . It would have been better not to attempt the conquest of India [in the first place].

—Luís Mendes de Vasconcelos, 1608

This Conquest is a lion's den where many enter and few leave.

—College of Luanda to governor of Angola, 2 Nov. 1679

As the preceding five chapters have demonstrated, the seventeenth century was critical for the Portuguese nation and for the Society of Jesus both at home and abroad. At home, the alien monarchy of Spain was ousted and a Portuguese regime was restored and successfully defended, despite the opposition of Spain, the papacy, the Dutch, and sometimes even the English. Chapters 4 and 5 detailed the extent to which the Society contributed to these triumphs. That success was not matched, however, in the Estado da India, where the fragile thalassocracy was gravely weakened during the course of the century by the unrelenting pressure applied by rival European and Asian forces. The consequences were baneful and irreversible for both the crown and the Society (Chapters 6–8). During the same century, comparable challenges were faced in the Atlantic empire, but with markedly different results. For a time, the Dutch appropriated the lucrative sugar-producing littoral of northeastern Brazil and erased two of the Society's colleges and their dependent missions. A third college was lost in Angola when the Hollanders captured Portugal's principal source of slaves. In the end, however, the Dutch were driven out of both Brazil and Africa; the Society regained and rebuilt its installations and, with a greater number of recruits, staked out its spiritual claims to new territories. As a result, despite temporary setbacks, by the end of the century the Society was considerably stronger in the Atlantic empire than it had been a century earlier.

The First Dutch Invasion of Brazil

On 9 May 1624, a powerful Dutch force consisting of 26 ships and 3,300 men filed into All Saints Bay and trained its 450 guns on the sugar-laden ships anchored in the harbor and on the city of Salvador, capital of Brazil.[1] The arrival of this force occurred three years after the formation of the second great Dutch trading firm, the West India Company (DWIC), which, like its eastern model (the VOC), was intended to extend the war against the Luso-Spanish enemy throughout the broad Atlantic. The new firm's directors considered various targets, including the isthmus of Panama and the port of Havana, the rendezvous point for Spanish treasure fleets, but they ultimately decided upon an attack against Bahia. Its capture would satisfy several objectives: it would give the Dutch a vital harbor in the South Atlantic from which to strike other Luso-Spanish positions; it would enable the intruders to gain control over a substantial part of Brazil's sugar production; and it would severely disrupt Brazil's communications.[2]

Despite the fact that the Portuguese governor-general had advance warning of the armada's probable destination, he was ill prepared to resist the invaders. Nor could he prevent the pusillanimous flight of most of the city's inhabitants, including its garrison of nearly 4,000. Brazil's most important center fell to the Dutch one day after their arrival. The Hollanders' victory was sealed by the capture of the governor-general and the 40 men who had elected to stay with him.

Among those who escaped from the city were the occupants of the Jesuit college. Its staff and students successfully withdrew to the aldeia of São João, about 6 kilometers from the city, and to a recreational estate called Quinta do Tanque, about half that distance away (and close to Salvador's modern-day bus terminal). They avoided the Hollanders' clutches, but their provincial did not. He had been making an inspection in Rio de Janeiro and in Espírito Santo and was returning to Salvador two and a half weeks after its fall with nine companions when they were intercepted by an armed Hollander 75 kilometers south of All Saints Bay. The Dutch, who allowed members of the other religious Orders to return to the city, not only barred the Jesuits from doing so but spirited the ten captives to Holland, from which they were eventually ransomed.[3]

Although Dutchmen controlled Brazil's capital and its port, they were not masters of the hinterlands. The bush remained in the hands of the Portuguese and the mission Indians, who were led initially by Brazil's fighting bishop, D. Marcos Teixeira. Aided by several Jesuits who lent their Indian charges and their moral fervor to the cause, the defenders harried the Dutch whenever they sortied beyond the defense of their cannon, and captured or killed more than a hundred Hollanders.[4] Such harassment was annoying to the Dutch, but the defenders were not strong enough to dislodge the intruders. That became the task of the remarkable Luso-Spanish recovery expedition of 1625.

1. C. R. Boxer, *Salvador de Sá and the Struggle for Brazil and Angola, 1602–1686* (London, 1952), chap. 2.
2. C. R. Boxer, *The Dutch in Brazil, 1624–1654* (Oxford, 1957), chap. 1.
3. The standard source on Jesuit experiences during the Dutch occupation of Bahia is *HCJB*, 5: 25–54, which includes transcriptions of three coeval Jesuit accounts. The ransoming of the ten, and two others whom the Dutch also captured under circumstances that remain unknown, is mentioned in Manoel da Silveira Cardozo, "The Santa Casa da Misericórdia of Lisbon," *Revista de história* 100 (São Paulo, 1974): 217–55, at 224. Contrary to the author's surmise, the captives included lay brothers as well as priests. Cardozo reports that royal authorities rejected Jesuit efforts to recover the ransom levy—400,000 rs.—from funds reserved for the recovery of captives seized by North African pirates.
4. There is an excellent account of the resistance in Bartolomeu Guerreiro, S.J., *Jornada dos vassalos da coroa de Portugal* (1625; rpr., Rio de Janeiro, 1966), chap. 23.

The loss of Bahia, following as it did the fall of Ormuz two years earlier, was a calamity for the Society, the Portuguese, and the Spanish alike. With the fall of Bahia, the home of 80 of the colony's 191 Jesuits and of the oldest and largest of their three colleges in the colony, the Jesuits lost the nerve center of their operations in Brazil.[5] Portuguese leaders recognized that the loss of Bahia seriously weakened their hold upon the remainder of Brazil and rendered further Dutch encroachments likely. Spanish authorities feared that the Dutch lodgment would be a prelude to assaults upon the heart of Spanish South America, not only the Río de la Plata but even the silver-rich viceroyalty of Peru.[6] Accordingly, the normally quarreling Iberians put aside their differences and joined forces to recover Bahia. The hard-pressed crown turned to private contributors for much of the funding of the armada (which became known as the expedition of the vassals, less because of noble fighting men than because of noble financing). The great houses of the Portuguese kingdom contributed liberally to that funding, but so did merchants, foreign as well as domestic, and some prelates.[7] One might expect to find Jesuits among those contributors, but they seem to have been absent, though six fathers—four Portuguese and two Spaniards—accompanied the expedition.[8]

The combined Luso-Spanish fleets sailed into All Saints Bay on Easter Eve, 1625. Even though the Hollanders knew of the Iberians' intent, they were not ready to cope with the most massive force ever sent to the New World, some 52 ships loaded with 12,566 men, four times the strength of the Dutch force the year before. After a month's siege, the Dutch surrendered: their 51-week occupation of Brazil's first capital was over. First at Macao in 1622 and now at Bahia three years later, the Hollanders suffered rare and major defeats at the hands of the Iberians. On 1 May 1625, a victory service was celebrated in the church of the damaged Jesuit college. After the celebrating was over, the Jesuits calculated that the heretics' occupation had cost the Society 24 contos.[9] But the Society would soon suffer even greater losses as a result of the Hollanders' activities.

The Second Dutch Intrusion

The second time they invaded Brazil, in 1630, the Dutch established their beachhead at the northeastern captaincy of Pernambuco, which DWIC leaders had selected because of their conviction that it was less well defended than the refortified port of Bahia and equally

5. António Vieira to Mutio Vitelleschi, 30 Sept. 1626, in João Lúcio d'Azevedo, ed., *Cartas do Padre António Vieira*, 3 vols. (Coimbra, 1925–28), 1: 3–74, at 4.

6. Jonathan I. Israel, *The Dutch Republic and the Hispanic World, 1606–1661* (Oxford, 1982), 130–31.

7. Guerreiro, *Jornada dos vassalos*, chap. 9.

8. *HCJB*, 5: 57 and 58 n. 1.

9. That figure appears in a Jesuit memorial cited in Overseas Council to king, 1 Feb. 1642, in AHU/LR/44, 137ᵛ, per IHGB/MS, *lata* 29. But the figure given in 1642 by Simão de Vasconcelos, serving as procurator-general of the province, is even higher—28 contos—and evidently includes damages sustained in later Dutch attacks on Bahia, notably that of 1638 mentioned below. Those reported losses do not include half the sugar harvest of 1623–24 and all of that of 1624–25 of the Sergipe do Conde plantation since it belonged to, or was claimed by, the Lisbon college of Santo Antão. Those losses are detailed in Stuart B. Schwartz, *Sugar Plantations in the Formation of Brazilian Society: Bahia, 1550–1835* (Cambridge, 1985), 173.

valuable economically as the leading center of cane sugar production.[10] The attacking force—7,000 men on 67 ships—was twice the size of the 1624 armada, yet smaller than the retaliatory Luso-Spanish expedition of 1625. Still, the Dutch landed near the Pernambucan capital, Olinda, in mid-February 1630 and were soon in possession of the town despite bitter fighting around the Jesuit college, whose students joined in the battle and were among the casualties. The college, which the triumphant Hollanders renamed "the royal palace," became their initial headquarters. Within two and a half weeks, they also had gained possession of the port town of Recife, though not before Matias de Albuquerque, governor of the captaincy and brother of the private donatary to whom the captaincy belonged, had successfully destroyed by fire all of the shipping in the port as well as its warehouses.

As at Bahia six years before, the Hollanders found themselves restricted to the perimeters of the towns they had conquered, and their efforts to master the interior sugar-producing zone were frustrated by the resourceful Matias de Albuquerque. The governor blocked the trails inland by devising a series of labyrinthian defenses anchored at improvised fortified outposts, of which the encampment (*arraial*) of Bom Jesús was the most important. It was there that the governor (who also became interim governor-general of Brazil) made his headquarters and sought the advice of experienced Jesuit missionaries. One father died during the fighting in 1633 when he refused to leave a wounded man in the field. Albuquerque also organized effective search-and-destroy patrols, which, as in Bahia, harassed the invaders, and on one occasion nearly captured their commander.

The Jesuits, who administered five missions in Pernambuco and in adjacent Paraíba, contributed their charges to the resistance movement. One such patrol, consisting of several hundred Brasis from Paraíba, was led for a time by a Paulista-born father, Manuel de Morais (b. 1596–d. ca. 1651). Fr. Morais, a mixed blood (*mameluco*) who was proficient in the tongue of the Indians he served, was not lacking in resourcefulness or in self-confidence. The year after the Dutch invasion occurred, he took the unusual step of writing directly to the king suggesting more effective ways of utilizing Indians in the resistance. Albuquerque was so impressed by his abilities as a guerrilla leader that he bestowed upon Morais the grandiose title of captain-general of the Indians, but after two years of fighting, the Jesuit's superiors deemed such activities inappropriate for a priest, and Fr. Morais was obliged to turn over his command to one of his Indian protégés, António Felipe Camarão, who later became one of the heroes of the movement that resulted in the Dutch surrender.[11]

Such a turn of events seemed most improbable during the mid-1630s, when the Hollanders, having successfully beaten off the enfeebled and poorly led amphibious operations by Luso-Spanish forces, overcame Albuquerque's men. Under the leadership of the dynamic Johan Maurits, a great-nephew of William the Silent and governor-general of occupied Brazil (1637–44), the Dutch endeavored to revive the economy of Pernambuco and the six other northeastern captaincies that they subsequently conquered, and to reconcile Catholics

10. The most comprehensive analysis in English of the second Dutch occupation of Brazil remains Boxer, *Dutch in Brazil*. Equally informative and stimulating is Evaldo Cabral de Mello, *Olinda restaurada: Guerra e asucar no nordeste, 1630/1654* (São Paulo, 1975), which possesses a strong economic bent.

11. On the uncommon career of Fr. Morais, see *HCJB*, 5: 363–69 (which includes a lengthy bibliography); and Boxer, *Dutch in Brazil*, 267–69. His later adventures are mentioned below.

to live in peace with Calvinists and New Christians of Portuguese origins, whom the victors encouraged to settle in Netherlands Brazil.

As in the East and in Bahia, however, the Dutch considered the Jesuits to be personae non gratae. At the time of the invasion, there were 21 members of the Society attached to the college of Olinda, and another dozen assigned to its five dependent missions. Four of the 33 were foreigners (two Sicilians and two Spaniards), six were Brazilians, and the rest were Portuguese. There were twenty priests, nine brothers, and four students. Some of those who resided in the missions successfully led their flocks out of trouble by withdrawing to the safety of the small captaincy of Alagoas and later to northeastern Bahia. But the Hollanders captured seventeen and expelled them, mostly to the Netherlands. Ten perished in Dutch hands and another fell as a battle casualty (see Appendix F).

A few of the survivors attained distinction, meritorious and invidious. Fr. Francisco de Vilhena had been a close advisor to Governor Albuquerque and was among those priests captured after the fall of one of the resistance's last bastions, Fort Nazaré. Subsequently, he escaped from Holland and returned to Portugal. Soon after the ascendancy of John IV, the king dispatched him as a special agent to Bahia to determine the political predilections of the governor-general and his staff (see Chapter 5). Vilhena was bound for Lisbon to report to the king when his ship was seized by Algerian pirates, and he died in their hands. Francisco Ribeiro, a young Paulista, was still a student at the time of the Dutch invasion and became one of the invaders' captives. After incarceration in Holland, he returned to Brazil and completed his studies in Bahia. In 1650 he was elected provincial procurator to Rome, but his ship, too, was intercepted at sea, this time by Spaniards, and he was taken to Spain. Following his release, Ribeiro became vice-rector of the college of Bahia and died as rector of the college of his natal captaincy.

Fr. Ribeiro was a classic example of a student who made good, but the aforementioned Manuel de Morais became a rare example, at least within the Portuguese Assistancy, of a creditable Jesuit who became a serious embarrassment to the Society. After his capture in Paraíba in 1635, Morais, apparently convinced of the dictum "if you can't beat 'em, join 'em," renounced his faith, donned lay clothing, and, during his voyage to Holland, openly ate meat on Fridays. Such behavior and reports of his sexual lapses before his arrest convinced his superior to recommend his expulsion from the Society. Mutio Vitelleschi concurred, but that drastic action did not trouble the ex-Jesuit, who utilized his sojourn in Holland to marry a Protestant lady by whom he had a child and, following her demise, to marry another Calvinist by whom he had two more offspring. Morais then abandoned his second wife and progeny to return to Pernambuco, where he engaged in the brazilwood trade. After being apprehended by one of the chieftains of the renewed Luso-Brazilian resistance, he recanted, began preaching, and volunteered as a chaplain during one of the key battles against the Dutch in 1645. But Morais's dubious reliability led to his arrest and transportation to Lisbon, where he was tried by the Inquisition. After recanting again and professing repentance, he was sentenced first to a period of imprisonment. Because of ill health, Morais regained his freedom and was permitted to leave the kingdom for some Catholic land, possibly Brazil. In any case, Manuel de Morais is believed to have expired in 1651.

The Dutch always treated Jesuits with greater severity than other Catholic priests, partly because they were perceived to be the agents of the hated papacy, but also to symbolize their own apparent invincibility. And for a time the Hollanders did, in fact, appear unbeatable. They successfully captured one of Portugal's most celebrated outposts, the once-great commercial emporium of Malacca, early in 1641 (see Chapter 7). Despite the negotiation of a truce that year with the new Portuguese regime, Johan Maurits had aggressively seized additional Portuguese territory in Maranhão and in Angola (on the latter, see below). The only setback the Dutch leader had suffered occurred in 1638, when he personally led a large force of Europeans and Brasis into All Saints Bay but was frustrated in his efforts to recapture Salvador and withdrew with heavy losses. During the siege, the Jesuits supplied the city with grain and meat from their plantations and turned their college into an emergency hospital where they attended the wounded, thereby earning praise from Brazil's royal treasurer.[12]

Despite this rebuff, the Dutch were not in peril in Brazil until 1642, when uprisings began, followed three years later by the first of a series of land battles (1645–48) in Pernambuco that materially weakened them. A handful of Jesuits returned to Pernambuco to participate as chaplains in those campaigns. A private firm, the Brazil Company (1649), the fruition of a proposal made by Fr. António Vieira, was successful in protecting the sugar fleets with armed escorts, thereby weakening Dutch maritime power in the South Atlantic. Finally reduced to the enclave they had obtained during their initial 1630 landings, the Hollanders surrendered on honorable terms. When the Capitulation of Taborda was signed on 26 January 1654, the Jesuit superior of Pernambuco was among the witnesses. Several fathers participated in the ensuing Spiritual Exercises, which marked Portugal's greatest triumph over the Dutch. The victory had been costly to all concerned, including the Society, which had lost personnel as well as property during the hard-fought campaigns.[13]

A Failed Enterprise: The Cape Verde Mission

Despite the setbacks that the Society sustained during the Dutch war, it achieved remarkable growth and expansion in Brazil during the remainder of the century. Before we examine those achievements, however, it is necessary to consider other parts of the Atlantic world where Jesuit efforts ranged from modest successes to outright failures. The colleges in the Azores and in Madeira were examples of the former. They were, of course, western extensions of the province of Portugal (see Chapter 10). The membership of the college of Funchal remained virtually the same throughout the century (see Table 9.1). The same

12. Simão de Fonseca, S.J., to Nuno da Cunha (rector, Santo Antão), Bahia, 31 May 1638, in ANTT/CJ/68, no. 180. The abortive siege is discussed briefly by Boxer in *Dutch in Brazil*, 87; see also *HCJB*, 5: 60–64; and Pedro Cadena de Vilhasanti, *Relação diaria do cerco da Baia de 1638*, ed. Manuel Múrias (Lisbon, 1941), esp. 196–98.

13. Boxer, *Dutch in Brazil*, chaps. 5 and 6; idem, "Padre António Vieira, S.J., and the Institution of the Brazil Company in 1649," *HAHR* 29, 4 (Nov. 1949): 474–97; *HCJB*, 5: 397–403. The sources cited in note 9 state that through 1642 the damage to the college of Olinda and its supporting estates amounted to 8 contos. Presumably the subsequent War of Divine Liberty (1645–54) brought further losses, but there is no estimate of their magnitude. In his account to the general at the beginning of the war, the provincial indicates that the Jesuits contributed goods and slaves to the campaign. Francisco Carneiro to Vicente Carafa, Bahia, 24 Sept. 1646, in ARSI, *Bras.*, 3:I, 251–251ᵛ.

TABLE 9.1

Jesuit Residents of the Insular and African Stations
During the Seventeenth Century

Year	Funchal	Angra	Fayal	São Miguel	Cape Verde	Luanda	Kongo
1599	18	17	0	7	0	7	0
1619	17	16	0	10	3	10	0
1623	—	—	0	—	3	19	4
1628	24	17	0	15	3	11	4
1633	19	15	0	12	3	16	3
1639	16	18	0	13	5	16	—
1649	17	15	0	14	0	9	3
1655	—	14	6	11	0	—	—
1665	17	15	7	14	0	18	—
1672	18	15	8	16	0	10	0
1675	22	16	7	15	0	7	0
1678	18	17	9	16	0	14	0
1690	23	17	7	18	0	16	0
1693	22	13	9	13	0	18	0
1696	18	14	7	13	0	15	0
1700	19	18	9	15	0	16	0

SOURCES: 1599 and 1690: *HCJAP*, 2:1, 531–36, and 3:1, 545–52; the remainder: ARSI, *Lus.*, 44:II, 45, 46, and 47, passim.

was true of the college at Angra, which was joined by that of São Miguel (upgraded from a residence) and, beginning in the middle of the century, the residence at Fayal. Though the material resources of these institutions increased during the century, in other respects they appear to have changed very little. Stagnation rather than growth seems to have characterized the insular colleges during the century.

But at least they did not rank as failures, and the Society did have its share of those. For example, the Jesuits obtained their first footholds in Spanish America between Florida and the Chesapeake in 1568, but after four years they gave up and retreated, first to Cuba and later to New Spain.[14] Another instance of failure, the Society's abandonment of its Ormuz outpost, has already been discussed in an earlier chapter (see Chapter 3). The failed Cape Verde enterprise is a third example of voluntary withdrawal by the Jesuits from a spiritual outpost.

To give them their due, the Jesuits were not anxious to initiate a mission at Cape Verde: they were pressured to do so. In the 1590s, the new Philippine regime of Portugal suggested that it would be desirable for the Jesuits to establish a small college at Cape Verde to facilitate the spread of Christianity within the Guinea kingdoms. But the provincial responded that the Portuguese province lacked either the personnel or the financial means to do so. In 1600 the new monarch, Philip III of Spain (Philip II of Portugal), again urged the province to initiate such a mission. Three years later, the provincial congregation considered the matter but deferred to the judgment of Aquaviva. When the father general assented, the

14. There is an extensive literature on the ephemeral Jesuit missions in what is today the Atlantic seaboard of the United States. See *BHCJ*, 2:2, 189–93, especially items 8831, 8865, and 8867–69.

provincial recruited the initial mission, which consisted of three fathers and one brother. The leader of the mission was the master of novices at Évora, Fr. Baltasar Barreira, who had labored for fourteen years in Angola but was then 66 years of age, quite old for such a demanding assignment.

The Cape Verde enterprise began inauspiciously. One priest expired less than a month and a half after the arrival of the mission. A year later, another died while visiting one of the Cape Verde islands, thereby reducing the mission to its superior and the lay brother. Three other priests set out from Lisbon in 1607, and four more plus two brothers embarked in 1608, but the grim reaper claimed two of the first contingent the year of their arrival, and a third expired in 1609. In the course of nearly four decades, the Jesuits were never able to maintain more than five members to serve the mainland and the island of Santiago. Except for the founder, Fr. Barreira, who somehow lasted until 1622, few missionaries survived long on the mainland or in the islands. Replacements were hard to get: though an average of 14.6 missionaries annually sailed from Lisbon to India during the first four decades of the century, and six per year crossed the Atlantic to Brazil, fewer than one a year reached the Cape Verde mission.[15]

Another persistent problem for the mission was finances. From the outset, the crown had promised stipends of 80,000 rs. for each missionary who served in the mission; but since those funds were derived from locally collected taxes, most probably levied on slaves, unfriendly governors frequently withheld payments. This led to repeated pleas from the fathers, who insisted that the contentions of the governors and members of the cámara of Santiago that they possessed ample revenues were unfounded, a view with which the leading Jesuit historian of the mission agrees. During the 1630s, the fathers stationed at the mission repeatedly warned their superiors that these problems were insoluble, that they felt unwelcomed by the local inhabitants, and that the mission was literally fruitless.

Vitelleschi agreed. On 23 July 1642, the last three Jesuits sailed home from the ill-fated Cape Verde mission. But after their departure, the locals wanted them back. So did the Overseas Council, which, in 1647, urged the king to assure the Society of sufficient funds to maintain a mission of six to serve the islands and the adjacent mainland. The Jesuits steadfastly refused to return. In 1653 Fr. João Brisacier, the provincial Visitor, declared the Cape Verde enterprise "unprofitable for the glory of God and prejudicial to [the reputation of] the Company." Some years later, Portuguese Capuchins followed in the footsteps of the Jesuits, but without much success.[16]

A Troubled Enterprise: The Jesuits in Angola and Kongo

Of the five continents where the Society functioned during the years 1540–1773, Africa proved to be the least fruitful, as the abandonment of the Cape Verde mission, the Jesuits' modest achievements in Mozambique, their exclusion from Ethiopia, and their controversial

---

15. *LJI*, 282–96; BGJ, 241–45.

16. The foregoing is based primarily upon *HCJAP*, 2:2, 575–612, and 3:2, 193–236, and some of the archival sources that Fr. Rodrigues, whose account is exhaustive, first used. See also *HIP*, 2: 266–70; and Henrique Pinto Rema, "As primeiras missões da costa da Guiné (1533–1640)," *Boletim cultural da Guiné Portuguesa* 22 (July–Oct. 1967): 225–68.

activities in Central Africa demonstrate. The college of Luanda was established in 1607 (see Chapter 3), and it remained the nerve center of Jesuit activities in Angola (sometimes called Ethiopia Occidental) and in adjacent Kongo. Though its membership varied from decade to decade, the college and its dependencies averaged just under fifteen missionaries at a time, fewer than the complement of the colleges of Bragança or Funchal. Those who volunteered to serve in Central Africa could expect to remain there for decades unless death claimed them, as it did eleven fathers within one four-year period.[17]

The Dutch had long been interested in gaining possession of Angola and other West African slave entrepôts in order to assure an adequate supply of slaves for the restored Brazilian plantations as well as for newer ones that they and other Europeans were establishing in the Caribbean. Although the Hollanders' first attempt to capture São Jorge da Mina (1625) miscarried, they were successful on their second try (1637). Four years later, Johan Maurits dispatched an expedition from Recife to seize Luanda and the remaining West Coast Portuguese slave ports.[18] Since the bulk of Luanda's garrison was then inland preparing to launch an attack upon Kongo, 2,000 Hollanders under the well-known Admiral Cornelis ("Peg-Leg") Jol had no trouble seizing Luanda and the nearby agricultural lands of the Bengo River in August 1641. Although Benguela also fell, the Portuguese governor, who initially retired to a Jesuit plantation a few kilometers from his occupied capital, organized a defense at Massangano, 150 kilometers southeast of Luanda, and effectively interdicted the movement of slaves from interior Kongo and Angola to the seacoast. For the next seven years, a series of campaigns between the two European adversaries resulted in a stalemate, despite the fact that the Hollanders gained the support of most of the indigenous leaders, notably Nzinga, the female ruler of the interior kingdom of Matamba, some 400 kilometers east of Luanda, and Garcia II, ruler of Kongo. Just as the remaining Portuguese defenders were about to be overwhelmed, deliverance came from Brazil under the aegis of Salvador de Sá, governor of Rio de Janeiro and also of Angola.[19]

When Sá reached Luanda in mid-August 1648 with 1,200 to 1,500 men, including three Jesuits, he caught the Hollanders napping just as Jol had surprised the Portuguese seven years before. The port was defended by fewer than 50 soldiers, and exactly seven years to

17. *HCJAP*, 3:2, 277 n. 3. The Jesuits' Capuchin rivals suffered equally heavy losses. Between 1645 and 1665, 41% of the Capuchins who entered Kongo and Angola perished. António de Oliveira de Cadornega, *História geral das guerras Angolanas* [1680], 3 vols., ed. José Matias Delgado (rpr., Lisbon, 1972), 2: 488.

18. As Jan Vansina has pointed out, the Hollanders had, in fact, long shown interest in possessing slave colonies. In 1623, Dutch warships captured seven traders and temporarily occupied the Angolan port of Benguela. The next year they burned six ships in Luanda harbor and did further damage there later the same year. Vansina, *Kingdoms of the Savanna* (Madison, Wis., 1966), 135.

19. Boxer, *Dutch in Brazil*, 107, and *Salvador de Sá*, 240, restricts his attention to the successful Dutch attacks on the littoral. The best account of the stalemate is Anne Hilton, *The Kingdom of Kongo* (Oxford, 1985), 143–49. Cadornega, *História*, 1: 231ff., is a major contemporary source. See also Ralph Delgado, *História de Angola*, 4 vols. (Lobito, 1948–55), 2: pt. 3. The Dutch capture and subsequent loss of Angola provide the basic themes of one of the best of the late and prolific António da Silva Rego's books, *A dupla restauração de Angola, 1641–1648* (Lisbon, 1948), which utilizes all available published and manuscript sources, publishes the only contemporary narrative of the successful voyage by Salvador de Sá from Rio de Janeiro to Luanda, and describes the liberation of the latter: Fr. António do Couto to Fr. Jerónimo Vogado (provincial, Portugal), Luanda, 5 Sept. 1648, in ibid., 245–56. Ernesto de Oliveira, *Do cativeiro a restauração (1641–1647)* (Porto, 1971), supplies brief textual remarks to accompany the creative illustrations of Jorge Tavares depicting key events and figures of the Dutch occupation.

the day after the Dutch had seized it, they gave it up. The three Jesuits then repossessed their college, which had served as the Dutch governor's headquarters.[20]

In time the Jesuits restored their damaged college, but far more urgent problems dogged them for the next half-century. One was the appearance of unwanted rivals in Kongo and Angola. Although an occasional Dominican or Franciscan friar entered those kingdoms, the Jesuits had long possessed the only significant contingent of missionaries in Angola or Kongo. Though they considered Kongo to be part of their spiritual preserve, the Jesuits had done little evangelizing there. Not until the 1620s did they establish a so-called college in its capital, São Salvador, but that facility was never served by more than a couple of fathers assisted by a brother and offered only elementary instruction.[21]

The brief Dutch occupation of Angola permitted three ambitious political leaders to violate Portugal's spiritual monopoly in Central Africa and to introduce Italian and Spanish Capuchins. In 1615, D. Alvaro III, king of Kongo, appealed to the pope to send him a contingent of Capuchins, but although Paul V agreed in principle, the first Capuchins did not sail for Central Africa until 1640. When they arrived in Lisbon and learned that the Dutch had seized Luanda, they considered their mission impossible and returned to Italy. In 1645 a contingent of ten Capuchins—three Italians and seven Spaniards—sailed from Spain to Kongo with support provided by Philip IV of Spain, who was angry because of the Portuguese rebellion and anxious to develop Spanish interests in the African slave trade.[22] The mission was warmly received by Garcia II (1641–61), the last dominant ruler of Kongo for centuries. He was desperately seeking an alternative European ally to the Dutch, whose forces he considered insufficient to prevent the return of the Portuguese, who had menaced his sovereignty. Furthermore, Garcia II had rejected Dutch efforts to persuade him to embrace Calvinism and preferred papal support to assure the legitimacy of his patrilineal descendants.

The first Capuchins were quickly followed by several other substantial contingents—twelve friars in 1648, another sixteen in 1651, and additional levies thereafter, so that after twenty years, nearly 70 friars had been introduced, an impressive record when compared with that of the Society of Jesus. Garcia II saw to it that the Capuchins were enthusiastically received. They proved to be zealous, courageous missionaries, more willing to live in the bush and more adept at learning indigenous languages than were the Jesuits. The Capuchins' presence naturally did not inspire cheers from the Jesuits, who, as in the Far East and later in the Amazon, always wished to conduct spiritual operations without competition from other Christian bodies. In fact, one father darkly suggested that the Capuchins could be fifth columnists and ought to be expelled. Instead, they were permitted to wither away.

20. C. R. Boxer, "Salvador Correia de Sá e Benevides and the Reconquest of Angola in 1648," *HAHR* 28 (Nov. 1948): 483–513, relies upon Dutch as well as Portuguese sources and utilizes an eyewitness Jesuit account. See also Delgado, *História de Angola*, 2: 379–99.

21. *HCJAP*, 3:2, 323–60, is an unconvincing apology for the unimpressive Jesuit achievements in Kongo.

22. There is an extensive literature concerning the Capuchins. Apart from the sources cited in Hilton, *Kingdom of Kongo*, there are bibliographies in Boxer, *Salvador de Sá*, 276 n. 87; and in Cadornega, *História geral*, 2: 490–91. Apart from Hilton's fine study, the remarks here rest upon the notes of Delgado in Cadornega, ibid., 2: 485–89; António Lourenço Farinha, *A expansão da fé*, 3 vols. (Lisbon, 1942–46), 1: 193–201; and *HCJAP*, 3:2, 348ff.

The outbreak of fighting between the Portuguese and Kongo in the mid-1660s resulted in the destruction of the firm central government, and one by one the friars died or retired, so that by 1685 there were only seven left in Angola and Kongo. The death in 1666 of the redoubtable António de Couto, a longtime Jesuit missionary in Kongo, and the onset of political chaos in the region prompted the Jesuits to leave Kongo permanently three years later.[23]

The decision to withdraw must have been painful for the fathers, who were well aware that their very presence in Central Africa had become a source of controversy. At the center of that controversy were several governors who, during the second half of the century, taunted the Jesuits for preferring to live amid the relative comforts of Luanda rather than endure the hardships of the bush. The issue was an old one, reaching back at least to 1620, when Vitelleschi wrote the superior of Angola and inquired why the Jesuits were not venturing into the backcountry to evangelize effectively. The response was that the college lacked sufficient numbers to spare men for the bush and that the climate was excessively enervating.[24] When the crown itself asked why the Jesuits had not penetrated the interior, the provincial of Portugal weakly responded that the Society had never been specifically directed to do so.[25]

Nearly 40 years after Vitelleschi's inquiry, Luís Martins de Sousa Chichorro (1654–58) became the first of three Angolan governors to excoriate the Jesuits for their lack of missionary zeal and their preoccupation with their own welfare. Sousa Chichorro accused them of being primarily interested in their "temporal conveniences" instead of the spiritual welfare of the populace, and suggested that the crown ought to deny them its long-standing stipend, the elimination of which would alleviate the distress of the local exchequer. At issue was the so-called *ordinaria*, a stipend of 80,000 rs. per missionary per year for as many as ten religious. Philip III of Spain had initially conceded that amount in 1615, and the guarantee was renewed by his successors.[26]

As far as is known, Sousa Chichorro had no personal grievance against the fathers, but his successor, the redoubtable João Fernandes Vieira (1658–61), manifestly did. A Madeiran-born mulatto, Vieira became one of the leaders of the War of Divine Liberty and gained extensive rewards that included vast landholdings in the northeast and several administrative posts, among them the governorship of the captaincy of Paraíba and

23. Couto, whom Hilton insists was a mulatto, though no Jesuit source confirms that, was born either in Angola (as Rodrigues says) or in Kongo (as Hilton asserts) between 1610 and 1613 and entered the Society in 1631. He published an abbreviated indigenous catechism based on a manuscript prepared by an Italian Jesuit. Apparently educated in Portugal, he returned to Luanda with Salvador de Sá and spent most of his remaining years in Kongo, where he died. Hilton, *Kingdom of Kongo*, 181; cf. *ASCJ*, 366, and *HCJAP*, 3:1, 394–95 n. 5. On the Jesuits' retirement from Kongo, see ibid., 3:2, 356–59.

24. Mateos Cardozo to Vitelleschi, Luanda, 17 Aug. 1620, and Anon., "Enformação se convem aver em Angola missões e residencias" [1620], in ARSI, *Lus.*, 74, fols. 160–163ᵛ. The latter, retitled, is published in António Brásio, ed., *Monumenta missionária Africana: África occidental*, ser. 1, 14 vols. (Lisbon, 1952–72, 1984–85), 6: 551–53.

25. Pedro de Novais (provincial, Portugal) to king, 20 Apr. 1624, in ANTT/CJ/68, no. 32. Cf. consulta of 5 June 1624, incorrectly attributed to the Overseas Council (not active until 1643), in Brásio, *Monumenta missionária*, 6: 232–33.

26. Alvará of 14 Jan. 1615 and reconfirmation of 19 Jan. 1617, in Brásio, *Monumenta missionária*, 6: 187–89 and 271–72.

then that of Angola.[27] His contretemps with the Jesuits was the sort of fracas that occurred all too often during the colonial period in isolated posts where there were few diversions and meager rewards. It began immediately after his arrival in Luanda. The Luandan aldermen were determined to eliminate the annoying problem of stray animals wandering through the town's streets, and they passed an edict warning that such animals would be shot on sight. When troops attempted to enforce that edict at the expense of some porkers belonging to Jesuit slaves, the latter defended their animals and the shanties in which they lived, and were arrested. After learning that the slaves belonged to the Jesuit college, the governor ordered them released. Instead of allowing matters to end there, the fathers, who included a commissioner from the Holy Office, insisted on trying the governor and excommunicating him for violating ecclesiastical immunity. The governor, supported by a Dominican friar, defended himself in a petition to the Overseas Council, which exonerated him and, in the king's name, severely censured the Jesuits.[28]

While awaiting the Council's verdict, the governor exacted revenge against his adversaries by sending Afonso VI a report that reinforced his predecessor's assertions that the fathers had deserted God in favor of Mammon. Vieira observed that there were only five fathers saying mass at the college, and that most of the Jesuits in the colony devoted themselves to the administration of their vast patrimony, which included extensive urban holdings, thousands of slaves, 50 estates (*arimos*), and large herds of cattle. Therefore, the governor saw no justification for continuing the ordinaria and urged that its payment cease.[29]

It may seem surprising that the crown ignored Vieira's allegations altogether. Had they reached Lisbon during more tranquil times rather than in the midst of the regency, when the very survival of Portugal lay in doubt and authorities were preoccupied with weightier matters than Luandan backbiting (see Chapter 5), it is conceivable that the court might have acted decisively. Other chapters demonstrate that Pedro II, Afonso's successor, was on the whole favorably disposed toward the Jesuits and considered them to be Portugal's ablest missionaries. Despite continued questions by Angolan authorities regarding the legitimacy of the ordinaria, the prince regent ruled in 1672 that it would still be paid.[30] Eight years later, there appeared in Lisbon an anonymous pamphlet that offered a vigorous defense of Jesuit activities in Angola. Its apparent author was Fr. João Ribeiro (b. 1625–d. 1705), who had survived capture by a French corsair and served briefly in Funchal before being recalled to become one of the founders of the new college of Beja. He later spent some time in Angola, though seemingly not as rector, as Barbosa Machado believed.[31]

Shortly after its publication, that pamphlet came to the attention of Ayres de Saldanha de Menezes e Sousa, who had just returned to the kingdom in 1680 following four years of service as Angola's governor. Ayres de Saldanha, as he is usually called, was the son

27. Gonsalves de Mello's biography (see note 29) is standard, but Boxer, *Dutch in Brazil*, 273–76, provides an excellent brief sketch.

28. Even Fr. Rodrigues recognized the folly of the Jesuits' overreaction. *HCJAP*, 3:2, 293–97.

29. Vieira to king, 5 Nov. 1658, published in José António Gonsalves de Mello, *João Fernandes Vieira*, 2 vols. (1956; rpr., Recife, 1967), 2: 189–90.

30. *HCJAP*, 3:2, 301.

31. Diogo Barbosa Machado, *Bibliotheca Lusitana* [1741–59], 4 vols. (fasc. ed., Coimbra, 1965–67), 2: 734; cf. *ASCJ*, 48–49.

of a High Court official and had held a series of distinguished administrative and military posts.[32] Clearly infuriated by the pamphlet, he wrote a point-by-point refutation of its primary contentions. To the argument that it was necessary for most Jesuits to remain at the college in order to teach, he responded that the king had not granted the ordinaria to subsidize the education of the sons of the local elite but to fund missions in the bush.[33] To the statement that the college then had only fifteen members and needed another five to discharge their responsibilities, Ayres de Saldanha sarcastically replied that the king had sent Jesuits to Angola to become apostles, not porters. To the statement that the Jesuits *did* have missions in the interior, he responded that such missions were entirely chimerical and that one such station was occupied by a single father and was less than 5 kilometers from the capital. He then contrasted the Jesuits' disappointing record as missionaries with the far more impressive achievements of the Capuchins. Surprisingly, however, Ayres de Saldanha did not urge the crown to replace the Jesuits with members of that Order; instead, he recommended that Jesuits be assigned as chaplains to the interior presidios to attend to the spiritual needs of their garrisons and to carry the cross to the nearby indigenous folk.[34]

The Society's activities in Angola did not go undefended, however. One of its most conspicuous defenders was Salvador de Sá, an ardent patron of the Society, who not only was the liberator of Angola but also was well placed to protect the Society as a member of the Overseas Council and was the benefactor of the college of São Miguel in Santos (see Chapter 14). In 1656 Sá insisted that the Jesuits' endeavors in the colony were beyond reproach. Francisco de Távora, first count of Alvor, was another influential supporter. His tribulations as viceroy of India and his reliance upon the continued influence of Saint Francis Xavier have been noted in the preceding chapter. As remarked there, he had previously served as governor of Angola (1669–76), where he had come to admire the fathers and warned that if their stipend was cut off they would have to leave the colony. (That was an obvious bluff, for the ordinaria accounted for only a fraction of the college's income.) Despite his loss of nerve in India, Távora went on to serve in the Overseas Council, where he was clearly in a position to protect the Society against its accusers. He and the Jesuits must have drawn satisfaction from the report of another of Angola's governors in the 1690s, who found the Society more praiseworthy than any other religious agency in the colony.[35] But then, none could claim a record of much distinction.

Recovery and Expansion in Brazil

It is hard to escape the conviction that the Society failed to send its ablest members to the African stations during the period considered in this study. It may well be that the distressing conditions of life there robbed even those of ability and talent of the energy needed to be

32. The only sketch of his career that I have seen is Elias Alexandre da Silva Correa, *História de Angola* [1782], ed. Manuel Múrias, 2 vols. (Lisbon, 1937), 2: 238–39.

33. The text of the initial grant (see note 26) fails to support the ex-governor's contention.

34. The most convenient source of the pamphlet and the governor's refutation is Simão José Luz Soriano, *História do reinado de el-rei d. José e da administração do marques de Pombal*, 2 vols. (Lisbon, 1867), 2: 284–325.

35. Gonçalo da Costa Alcáçova Carneiro de Menezes (governor, 1691–94) to Pedro II, in BNL, cod. 1587, fols. 135ʳ–137ᵛ; published in *HIP*, 2: 285–86.

successful. Certainly Brazil offered more promising fields of endeavor once the Dutch had been removed.

The presence of the Dutch on Brazilian soil and their long hegemony in the South Atlantic inescapably inhibited the growth of the province of Brazil. Though the number of Jesuits attached to the province fluctuated somewhat during the first half of the century, there were about as many members there in the colony in the early 1650s as there had been five decades earlier (see Table 9.2). No new colleges were established during the first half of the century, and, as seen above, two of the oldest were temporarily lost and, though later recovered, were substantially damaged.

TABLE 9.2

Number of Jesuits Resident in the Provinces of Goa and Brazil
and Number Sent There from Lisbon per Year, 1600–1759

	India (Goa)		Brazil	
Years	*Residents (N)*	*Average number sent per year*	*Residents (N)*	*Average number sent per year*
1600–1609		17.2		5.1
1602	—		167	
1605	258		—	
1610–1619		12.4		2.4
1610	—		165	
1614	266		—	
1620–1629		11.0		2.3
1626	—		191	
1627	304		—	
1630–1639		9.7		0.4
1631	—		176	
1633	261		—	
1640–1649		8.6		3.2
1641	268		159	
1644	—		189	
1649	229		—	
1650–1659		10.4		5.6
1654	—		162	
1660–1669		5.7		7.7
1663	—		200	
1666	258		—	
1670–1679		7.6		2.4
1673	245		—	
1678	210		—	
1679	—		188	
1680–1689		9.9		6.2
1683	—		252	
1686	—		261	
1689	226		—	

Continued on next page

TABLE 9.2 *(continued)*

Years	India (Goa)		Brazil	
	Residents (N)	Average number sent per year	Residents (N)	Average number sent per year
1690–1699		15.0		7.8
1692	—		281	
1694	—		310	
1699	231		—	
1700–1709		13.3		4.5
1701	—		317	
1706	205		—	
1710–1719		9.8		6.4
1713	205		—	
1716	—		324	
1720–1729		9.9		8.5
1722	175		367	
1728	165		—	
1730–1739		15.1		8.2
1732	—		362	
1733	164		—	
1740–1749		9.8		5.2
1740	—		418	
1741	134		—	
1743	—		434	
1745	—		447	
1749	—		471	
1750–1759		14.2		5.3
1754	161		—	
1757	—		476	

SOURCES: *LJI*, 282–334; BGJ, 241–69; Appendix D.

The situation was very different during the second half of the century. The number of Jesuits in the province grew steadily: by 1701 there were almost twice as many as there had been a century earlier. As Table 9.2 demonstrates, during this century the province of Goa attracted considerably more recruits from Europe than did the Brazil province; yet, while the number of Jesuits assigned to the Indian province steadily declined beginning in the 1660s, the opposite occurred in the province of Brazil. Its membership began to exceed that of Goa in the 1680s, and it would continue to outdistance Goa for the balance of this period.[36] Despite the intrusions of the Hollanders in both India and Brazil, the latter clearly became the more attractive missionary theater.

One consequence of the increasing number of Jesuits available in Brazil during the latter half of the century was the founding of five new colleges and a celebrated so-called seminary. The first of these, the college of São Miguel in the port town of Santos, opened in 1653. The Society had maintained a residence (*domus*) there since the end of the sixteenth century but

36. See Appendix B. It needs to be borne in mind that Goa was the reception center for recruits assigned not only to that province but also to the other eastern provinces. It is not easy to determine what percentage of those who debarked in Goa during the century were permanently attached to that province. Among those who sailed from Lisbon to Goa between 1725 and 1754, 57.9% belonged to its province. *LJI*, 321–34.

was unable to upgrade it to a college until it found a patron to finance such expansion. Ultimately it was Salvador de Sá, a prominent benefactor of the Society (see Chapter 14) and a leading figure in the kingdom, who agreed to fill that need.[37] The following year, the province opened another college, that of Santiago in Espírito Santo, in a region where its members had labored since the early 1650s, thereby adding another link in the chain that extended from Olinda to São Paulo.[38] In 1678, benefactors financed the upgrading of the casa of Recife, which became a college that year.[39]

About 10 kilometers north of the tobacco-growing center of Cachoeira, across All Saints Bay from Salvador, lies the small hill town of Belém da Cachoeira. It was there in about 1686 that the fathers established their only interior educational facility in Bahia, the seminary of Belém, a preparatory school to train Christian boys in reading, writing, Latin, and music. Its founder and longtime rector was the remarkably long-lived Alexandre de Gusmão, a Lisbon-born pedagogue (b. 1629–d. 1724) whose remains lie in the floor of the seminary's bat-infested church, all that now remains of a once-large facility that served 70 or more boys a year.[40] The last two colleges erected during this period—N. S. da Luz in São Luís do Maranhão and Santo Alexandre in Belém do Pará—anchored what would become the vice-province of Maranhão, the most significant example of Jesuit expansion within the Assistancy during the turbulent seventeenth century. At that century's outset, such expansion was by no means a certainty.

In 1600, the settled seacoast of Brazil reached only to Rio Grande do Norte, the arid northeasternmost fragment of the Brazilian hump. Although the Portuguese claimed to own all of the territory between Rio Grande and the Amazon, a distance of some 2,400 kilometers, they had thus far failed to occupy it. The first Jesuit foray along the northern coast ended inauspiciously. In January 1607, two fathers, the Azorean Francisco Pinto and the Alentejano Luís Figueira, left Pernambuco in a salt-seeking vessel with 60 Christianized Indians to make contact with Tapuia tribesmen in what would become the captaincy of Ceará. When the ship reached its destination, the members of the expedition debarked and walked some 700 kilometers westward into the Ibiapaba Mountains, visited four years previously by a Portuguese slaver. The reception was not what they had expected, for the Tapuias indignantly set upon them, killing Fr. Pinto and many of the neophytes. Since he had no armed escort, Fr. Figueira precipitately retired to Pernambuco.[41]

Luís Figueira, along with the better-known António Vieira, was to become one of the founders of Jesuit enterprise in Maranhão. Until 1622, however, he was obliged to remain in Pernambuco, where he performed administrative duties. In the meantime, the Portuguese secured the Cearense coast by building a fort (Fortaleza) to assert their claim to it in 1610.

37. On the college's establishment, see *HCJB*, 6: 423–48, and Chapter 14 below.

38. Ibid., 6: 133–42. The casa or domus of São Paulo was upgraded to the rank of a college around 1631.

39. Ibid., 5: 460–64.

40. Ibid., 5: 167–98. On Gusmão's extensive publications, including what some consider Brazil's first fictional book, see ibid., 8: 289–98. As Serafim Leite cautioned (ibid., 6: 179n), there were three prominent figures named Alexandre de Gusmão. One became rector of the college of São Paulo; another was an eighteenth-century diplomat.

41. Serafim Leite, S.J., *Luiz Figueira: A sua vida heroica e a sua obra literaria* (Lisbon, 1940), 25–36; Luiz Figueira to Aquaviva, 26 Mar. 1608(?), in ibid., 107–52, is a full report on the disaster.

Five years later, two Jesuits accompanied Cristóvão de Moura on a military expedition to Maranhão, where an ephemeral French settlement had existed on a large island since 1612. When France chose not to contest Portugal's claim to Maranhão, the French evacuated, and Portuguese forces, accompanied by the two fathers, secured the settlement that became São Luís do Maranhão. The next year (1616) Portuguese forces laid claim to the Lower Amazon by founding the fortified outpost of Santa Maria de Belém do Grão Pará. But Jesuits were not involved in its establishment, and the two fathers who had accompanied Cristóvão de Moura to Maranhão returned to Pernambuco in 1618. Three years later, the three northern captaincies—Ceará, Maranhão, and Pará—were administratively separated from the rest of Brazil and became the State of Maranhão, a distinction maintained until the 1770s.[42]

Luís Figueira was able to return to the north coast in 1622, but for a number of years he and his colleagues played second fiddle to the Franciscans. By 1630 he had recognized that the Franciscans lacked the resources or the manpower to meet the evangelical needs of the State of Maranhão, and he urged Vitelleschi to authorize the Society to enlarge its commitment to the State. The general responded by directing Figueira to go to Lisbon and Madrid to inform the crown about the spiritual needs of the State and to offer the Society's services. Figueira agreed to do so but decided first to proceed to Belém to assess evangelical opportunities within the network of the Lower Amazon.

Fr. Figueira left São Luís in January 1636 and spent six months in Belém and traveling throughout the lower reaches of the Amazon as far as the Rio Xingú.[43] Upon the completion of his mission, he sailed to Lisbon, where his reflections on the Amazon's material and spiritual potential were published in 1637, four years before the appearance of the more celebrated *New Discovery of . . . the Amazons* (Madrid, 1641), written by the Spanish Jesuit Cristobal de Acuña. Like Acuña, Fr. Figueira was impressed by the Amazon's economic and evangelical opportunities. He observed that its immense forests could provide timber to build innumerable ships for the Portuguese merchant marine and that its verdant soils were suitable for the cultivation of Brazil's dominant crop, cane sugar. Fr. Figueira emphasized the loyalty of the Brasis during Dutch attacks but noted that there were too few clergy to attend to them or to the several hundred Portuguese residents. He urged that a senior ecclesiastical administrator be appointed to the region, since the bishop of Brazil was 3,000 kilometers away in Salvador and communications with him were regularly interdicted by Dutch cruisers.[44]

In Madrid, Figueira's memorial came to the attention of the Council of State in August 1637, the very month of the Évora disturbances and in the midst of the Lisbon strike (see Chapter 4). Nevertheless, the council devoted two days to the father's proposals. It

42. Ibid., 37–43.

43. Ibid., 57–62; [João Soares Avelar?], "Missão que fes o P. Luis Figueira . . . indo . . . à[s] capitanias do Rio das Almazonas no anno de 1636," in ibid., 181–203. Br. Avelar was Figueira's companion and subsequently left the Society to become a military commander in Pará.

44. "Memorial sobre as terras e gente do Maranhão & Grão Pará & Rio das Almazonas" (1637), in Leite, *Luiz Figueira*, 207–11. As is well known, the Spanish government quickly suppressed the first edition of Acuña's perceptive account for fear it would reveal to Spain's enemies the ease with which the mineral-rich viceroyalty of Peru could be approached via the undefended back door. Only two copies of Figueira's pamphlet are known to have survived. Did the government seize others for the same reason?

concluded that the Jesuits should be encouraged to found missions in the Amazon and that the Society should be assigned superior ecclesiastical authority in the State of Maranhão. That was more than Figueira had requested, and more than the Society's opponents were willing to concede. The bishop of Brazil protested when he learned that his nominal powers in the State would be imperiled, and the Portuguese board of religious affairs, the Mesa da Consciência e Ordens, was equally critical of the crown's decisions.

Fr. Figueira occupied himself by recruiting a band of missionaries who would join him in establishing the Amazonian enterprise, but six years passed before he was able to sail. During the interim, Fr. Acuña and a companion, the first Jesuits to descend the Amazon from Quito to Belém, returned to Spain to secure authority for the province of Quito to establish missions in Amazonia. That proposal might have led to an unseemly jurisdictional conflict between the two Iberian assistancies, but the December revolution in Portugal (see Chapter 5) intervened. Because of the new government's preoccupation with its survival and with the continued conflict with Holland, the Figueira expedition remained on hold until 1643.[45]

When Fr. Figueira, the missions superior, left Lisbon at the end of April 1643, his contingent of missionaries had been reduced from 22 to 17. Still, that was the largest number of Jesuits that would ever venture to the Amazon at one time. After a brief stop at the Cape Verdes, the ship continued on to São Luís do Maranhão but did not tarry, because the town was then occupied by the Dutch. As the vessel neared the island of Marajó, it was wrecked by a massive storm. Of the 173 aboard, only 45, including three Jesuits, survived. The remainder, including Fr. Figueira, either drowned or were killed by hostile Indians.[46]

The deaths of Fr. Figueira and thirteen of his companions—the second most severe loss of personnel that the Brazil province ever sustained, after the Azevedo martyrdoms of the 1570s (see Chapter 3)—was one of two blows that the Society suffered in Maranhão during the 1640s. The other was an Indian uprising not far from São Luís that claimed the lives of the only three Jesuits remaining in the State of Maranhão in 1649. By mid-century, therefore, there was not a single Jesuit in the State.[47]

The Society might well have elected to abandon northern Brazil at that point, and indeed, its leaders may later have wished that it had. Nevertheless, neither the king nor the heads of the Order were prepared to do that. The very year when the last Jesuits in Maranhão expired, John IV directed the provincial of Brazil to dispatch eight to ten fathers to the State, at least six of whom were proficient in the hybrid language called *língua geral*.[48] The Hollanders' continued maritime hegemony made it impossible to carry out the king's wishes, but a few years later, when Fr. Francisco Gonçalves was named procurator for the Brazil province to Rome, he urged his superiors to press for a renewed Jesuit presence in

45. Leite, *Luiz Figueira*, 63–68; Mathias C. Kiemen, O.F.M., *The Indian Policy of Portugal in the Amazon Region, 1614–1693* (Washington, D.C., 1954), chap. 3.

46. The major contemporary account is by an Azorean-born student, one of the three Jesuit survivors, who later became a priest: Nicolau Teixeira, "Successo da viage do Maranhão," Évora, 1 Aug. 1644, in Leite, *Luiz Figueira*, 229–34.

47. Kiemen, *Indian Policy*, 73–78.

48. Provisão of 11 Oct. 1649, quoted in José de Morães, S.J., "História da companhia de Jesus na extincta provincia do Maranhão e Para," in Candido Mendes de Almeida, comp., *Memorias para a historia do extincto estado do Maranhão*, 2 vols. (Rio de Janeiro, 1860), 1: 238–39.

the north.[49] In Lisbon, António Vieira, court preacher, disappointed diplomat, and royal confidant, also supported the Society's return to Maranhão and was gratified when John IV promised financial aid for as many as ten fathers in the State.[50]

Such assistance, when actually provided, contributed only part of the support necessary to finance the Society's activities in the State during the ensuing decade. In 1652, two contingents—eleven fathers and four brothers altogether—sailed from Lisbon to São Luís and to Belém. Those Jesuits proved to be the harbingers of 48 who entered the State during that decade, nearly twice as many as went from the kingdom to the Brazil province and roughly half as many as proceeded from Portugal to the eastern provinces during those years. There can be no question, therefore, that the Society was beginning to make a serious personnel commitment to Maranhão. So, too, did the crown, at least as long as John IV reigned. When António Vieira, the king's trusted advisor, became superior in the State, he was equipped with full powers to establish missions wherever he deemed them to be appropriate. The same sovereign also awarded the Jesuits exclusive responsibility for converting the Amerindians of the State and, in effect, designated them as the Amerindians' protectors and as mediators between the settlers and indigenous laborers.

The Jesuits took full advantage of their privileged position, not only with the Amerindians but also with the State's governors, whom the king charged with assisting them. Vieira dispatched his men throughout the Lower Amazon and its principal affluents, and within less than a decade they founded 54 missions that were supposedly occupied by 200,000 souls. But their very success led to their undoing, for the fathers became targets of criticism from less-advantaged ecclesiastics and from settlers who had never favored the return of the Jesuits in the first place. Serious anti-Jesuit riots ensued, first in São Luís and then in Belém, in May and July 1662. In both instances the fathers were arrested, removed from their fledgling colleges, placed aboard the first available vessels, and dispatched to the kingdom.[51]

One might have expected that such shoddy treatment of the fathers—the second such instance in Brazil in little more than two decades (see Chapter 19)—would have prompted the crown to assert its authority vigorously and severely punish the rioters. That did not happen. Fortunately for the rebels, the regency of Luísa de Gusmão fell six months later in the Castelo Melhor coup. As a result, when António Vieira returned to the royal court, instead of the strong support that he had expected, he found himself to be persona non grata because he was associated with the unsuccessful forces backing the young prince and future monarch, Pedro II. Vieira was therefore banished from Lisbon and soon had his hands full defending his convictions against the accusations of the Holy Office (see Chapter 5). Though the new regime permitted the Jesuits to return to

49. *HCJB*, 4: 33–34.

50. The crown promised up to 350,000 rs. for the ten, one-half derived from revenues collected in Bahia, the rest from tobacco duties assessed in Lisbon. When the crown found it impossible to furnish the latter, it assigned the Rio de Janeiro exchequer the responsibility of providing the remainder of the stipends. Provisões of 24 July and 12 Sept. 1652, in *CCLP*, 9: 203–5. António Vieira to Francisco Gonçalves (provincial, Brazil), 14 Nov. 1652, in Azevedo, *Cartas*, 1: 274–90, is fundamental for an understanding of the careful preparations that Vieira made for the Jesuits' return to northern Brazil.

51. The foregoing is based primarily upon *HCJB*, 4: 32–60; Kiemen, *Indian Policy*, chap. 4; and John Hemming, *Red Gold: The Conquest of the Brazilian Indians, 1500–1760* (Cambridge, Mass., 1978), chap. 15.

Maranhão, it utterly failed to punish their opponents; instead, it weakly pardoned them.[52] Furthermore, the regime not only declined to restore the Jesuits' former authority in mediating Indian–white relations but also eliminated their special evangelical privileges. Nevertheless, between 1663 and 1680, 42 Jesuits entered the State of Maranhão, nearly as many as came during the years of Vieira's leadership. Theirs was a frustrating assignment, for every day they witnessed the severe mistreatment of the indigenous population but were powerless to arrest it.[53]

That changed when the prince regent (soon to be Pedro II), always a strong supporter of overseas missions, restored the Jesuits to their former positions of preeminence in the State. Following proposals made by Vieira, who, though he never returned to Maranhão after 1662, retained a keen interest in the welfare of the Amerindians there, the Overseas Council in 1680 again assigned the Jesuits exclusive missionary responsibility and gave them a major voice in all aspects of Indian–white relations. But the settlers soon challenged that action. In 1684 the citizens of São Luís attacked both the Jesuits and the officers of a newly formed company intended to provide African slaves as an alternative source of labor. The company failed, and the Jesuits in the captaincy of Maranhão (but not that of adjacent Pará) were again ousted.[54]

This time prominent Jesuits debated the wisdom of attempting to continue their work in Maranhão. One who recommended that they follow the example of the Cape Verde mission and give up altogether was the Swiss-born academician and administrator Jodoco Perret (or Peres) (b. 1633–d. 1707). A onetime professor of philosophy in two German universities and in the college of Bahia, Perret came to the State of Maranhão in 1678. Because of his inability to master indigenous tongues, he served as an administrator until the São Luís rioters arrested him in 1684. Perret was dispatched back to Lisbon with his comrades, but his ship was seized by pirates, and he and his companions were left on an island near Belém, from which they were eventually rescued. Perret then took another vessel to the kingdom to argue that the settlers' hostility toward the fathers was so great and the lack of support from the king's officers so blatant that the father general ought to terminate the enterprise. After all, he argued, the apostles once withdrew from Judea because of their persecution.[55]

But another foreign-born veteran of the Maranhense missions did not share Perret's pessimism. He was the famous Luxembourger and future mission chronicler Johan Philipe Betendorf (or Bettendorff) (b. 1625–d. 1698), who had come to northern Brazil in 1660 at the behest of António Vieira and served there many years as a missionary, linguist, and administrator.[56] Although he, too, had been exiled by the rioters, Betendorf remained optimistic that the fathers could succeed in their enterprise provided that the crown gave them adequate backing. As Vieira had during the reign of John IV, Betendorf enjoyed entrée

52. Provisão of 12 Sept. 1663, in *LGM*, 1: 31–32.

53. Kiemen, *Indian Policy*, chap. 5; J[oão] Lúcio de Azevedo, *Os Jesuítas no Grão-Par'a: Suas missões e a colonização* [1901], 2d ed. (Coimbra, 1930), chap. 5.

54. A recent study of the second revolt, Maria Liberman, *O levante do Maranhão "Judeu cabeça do motim": Manoel Beckman* (São Paulo, 1983), was a master's thesis prepared under the direction of Anita Novinsky. Though a useful survey of the sources, it is repetitive, diffuse, and contextually incomplete.

55. *HCJB*, 4: 87–89. For Perret's biography and extensive writings, see ibid., 9: 44–47.

56. Ibid., 8: 98–106.

to the royal palace.[57] Certainly his views were known to Pedro II, who responded precisely in the ways that Fr. Betendorf had urged.

The king insisted that the Jesuits would be given the crown's full support in Maranhão. This time the rebels did not escape with pardons but were severely punished. Moreover, in 1686, the Overseas Council, after reviewing the conflicting testimony of the missionaries supporters and opponents, drew up the seminal missions ordinances that would continue to define the parameters of Indian–white relations in Maranhão until the middle of the eighteenth century. Those regulations ostensibly gave the Jesuits a dominant voice in the determination of Indian–white relations in Maranhão (see Chapter 19).[58]

Assured of the crown's direct interest and protection, Jesuits elected to make the Maranhense missions one of their major enterprises in the Assistancy. Between 1687 and 1700, recruiters in the kingdom dispatched 62 members to Maranhão, compared with only 50 who sailed for the province of Brazil, and around 20 who ventured to the eastern provinces during those years. As will be evident in a later chapter, after the turn of the century, the older Asian provinces would lose their luster, whereas the vice-province of Maranhão would shine increasingly brightly. One suspects that António Vieira would have been gratified but not surprised.

The seventeenth century proved to be a time of repeated trials for both the crown and the Society of Jesus. The leaders of the Society viewed sorrowfully the elimination in the East of some of their most promising fields of endeavor, most notably Japan, Ethiopia, and Ceylon. They also witnessed the successes of their hated rivals, the heretical Hollanders, in the West. But unlike those in Malacca, Ceylon, and South India, the losses in Brazil and Angola proved temporary, albeit costly to the crown and its subjects, including the Jesuits. If the recovery of Angola failed to lead to the flowering of Jesuit enterprise there and in adjacent Kongo, there were still compensations across the Atlantic, where new colleges and missions were founded. At the beginning of the century, there were only three Jesuit colleges in Brazil—Pernambuco, Bahia, and Rio de Janeiro. By the century's end, Ignatian citadels of learning and missionary enterprise extended from Belém do Pará in the far north to Santos and São Paulo in the south. By 1700, Brazil had already entered its first golden age, one that Jesuits and other ecclesiastics would contend ought to have spiritual as well as material dimensions. Before considering the development of the Assistancy during the first half of the eighteenth century, it is best to examine how it was organized, how it was financed, and how Jesuit efforts to sustain their enterprises created the image of a Society that had allegedly deserted God for Mammon.

57. Ibid., 4: 89–90. Fr. Betendorf was not alone. Another Jesuit reported that on the eve of his departure with four junior members of the Society for São Luís, the missionaries were invited to the royal palace to kiss the king's hand and that the queen escorted them to a chamber where the infante was playing, attired in the garb of a Jesuit! "Relação da viagem que fez o P. Fructuoso Correa," São Luís do Maranhão, eve of the feast of the Holy Spirit, 1696, in ARSI, *Bras.*, 9, fols. 416–19[v].

58. See, however, *HCJB*, 4: 91ff.; Kiemen, *Indian Policy*, chap. 6; and Hemming, *Red Gold*, 416ff.

PART III

Organization

CHAPTER 10

The Governance of an Enterprise: The Hierarchy of the Portuguese Assistancy

> Even in the angels there is the subordination of one hierarchy to another; and in the heavens, all the bodies that are moved, the lowest by the highest, and the highest, in their turn unto the Supreme mover of all.
>
> —Loyola, "On Obedience"

> The Jesuit "General" . . . was a commander in chief in fact as well as in name . . . and he exercised virtually unchecked and undisputed control over all the manifold activities and ramifications of the Company from his headquarters. . . . He alone nominated to every office in the Society, and he could appoint or remove at his pleasure the provincials, vice-provincials, superiors, and rectors, in the same way as a military commander in chief could appoint or dismiss his subordinates in time of war. . . . Mobility and missionary activity were of the essence of the Society . . . , whose founder extolled his institution as the cavalry of the Church, ready to go anywhere or to do anything at a moment's notice.
>
> —Charles R. Boxer, *The Christian Century in Japan, 1549–1650*

THE IMAGE OF the Society of Jesus as a finely tuned machine whose parts always worked together smoothly and efficiently in response to the dictates of the chief engineer is a pervasive one. That is how the founders intended their organization to perform, that is the tone that imbued directives from the Roman headquarters, and that still seems to be the popular impression of how the Society functioned. In reality the Society never hummed as harmoniously or as efficiently as is often thought. Two obvious factors—time and distance—made it impossible for the generals to exercise personally the omnipotent authority granted to them by the *Constitutions*. As the enterprise expanded around the globe, the heads of the Order found it necessary to delegate portions of their powers to distant lieutenants, who performed their duties in the name of the generals and were, of course, answerable to them for their actions. Power *did* flow from the general to the provincial, from the provincial to the local superior, and from the local superior to the "subject," that is, the individual member, just as the *Constitutions* prescribed,[1] but the chain of command that linked the subject and the general through the sacred principle of absolute obedience frequently proved to be flawed. The Society *did* become one of the best-organized bureaucracies of its time, but the flow of paper did not move as expeditiously as intended. The Order was created by Europeans within a European context, where distances were relatively short

1. *CSJ(C)*, pt. 8, chap. 1, 666.

and communication reasonably swift; but those conditions did not obtain beyond Europe, so that the continuous exchanges envisaged in the *Constitutions* between Jesuit houses and provincials and between provincials and the central headquarters often proved unfeasible.[2]

As already observed, the founders drew upon their own experience and those of the older Orders when designing the Society. Considering their objectives, they selected well, but they could not anticipate all of the challenges posed by the unstable times in which they and their successors lived. It is ironic, for example, that the Society was conceived as a supranational organization at a time when nationalistic sentiments and assertions of regal power were growing ever more insistently. The founders did not expect that the national origins of their members would become a significant consideration in the allocation of personnel, but the leaders of the Society soon discovered that they had to pay close attention to the demands of secular authorities concerning acceptable appointments, territorial organization, and other state concerns. Though the fathers general and the general congregations repeatedly directed their subjects to abstain from secular affairs, especially in the political and economic sectors, the Jesuits found it impossible to avoid them.

As the membership grew from a handful to hundreds and later to thousands, the generals could no longer know personally the qualifications of each subject for positions of responsibility, nor were they able to shunt subjects about with the martial precision that some writers imagine. Accordingly, they became dependent upon those closest to the scene, who were most familiar both with the available pool of talent and with the urgent problems that that talent might effectively address.[3] If a sound knowledge of theology and Latin was essential for those who were professed and were thus supposedly the most capable of the three levels of the Society's priests, seniority, social origin, and age seem to have counted at least as heavily as previous administrative experience in the selection of those who led the Society between its founding and the mid-eighteenth century.[4]

In the chapters that follow I have divided the history of the old Society into three somewhat arbitrary periods: (1) the formative period (1540–1615), when most of the major policies that would guide the Society until its suppression were formulated; (2) the period of stability (1615–1704), when relatively few changes in the Society's operations occurred; and (3) the period of stress (1704–73), when the Society was beset by increasingly severe challenges, both European and extra-European in origin. The present chapter will first consider the functions of the general congregation, the Society's major legislative body, and its relationship to the generals. Next, it will examine the Society's leaders—the

2. Ibid., pt. 8, chap. 1, 674.

3. The files of the ARSI are replete with letters from superiors and consultores to the fathers general with recommendations of persons they considered fit for administrative duties. E.g., Pero Rodrigues to Aquaviva, Bahia, 18 Feb. [1]606, in *Bras.*, 5:I, 59; Gregorius Rois, "Patris qui videri apte ad functionis sequentes videntur," 25 Dec. 1681, in *Goa*, 35, fol. 227; Emanuel Carvalho (provincial) to Tamburini, 20 Jan. 1707, in *Goa*, 9:II, fol. 395; and "Informatio ad gubernatio prov.ª Malabar . . . 1720," in *Goa*, 60. The last evaluates 26 persons according to criteria that include knowledge of philosophy and theology, administrative experience, piety, religious discipline, relations with peers, general character, and aptitude for administration.

4. Nuno Rodrigues to Aquaviva, Goa, 13 Dec. 1595, in *DI*, 18: 447–65, esp. 448–49. The now-classic study of the grades of membership within the Society is Ladislao Lukács, "De graduum diversitate inter sacerdotes in Societate Iesu," *AHSI* 37 (1968): 237–316. See also Léo Moulin, "L'Organisation du gouvernement local et provincial dans les constitutions des Jésuites," *Revue internationale des sciences administratives* 21 (1955): 485–523.

fathers general, provincials, rectors, and Visitors—with special reference to the Portuguese Assistancy, analyzing their responsibilities and identifying some of the rocks that made their paths anything but smooth. Turning from leaders to subjects, Chapter 11 will consider the sorts of people within the Portuguese Assistancy that the Society accepted, dismissed, or excluded as it strove to fulfill its mission and to protect its reputation. Next, Chapter 12 will focus upon the kinds of people charged with the several levels of fiscal management of the Enterprise.

Meetings, Periodic and Irregular

The *Constitutions* provided for two types of gatherings of Jesuit representatives in Rome. One was a periodic assembly of provincial procurators, who met at regular intervals to discuss problems common to the Society and those of special concern to particular provinces. Membership was restricted to the father general, his assistants, and the procurators elected by each province. Forty such meetings took place between 1568 and 1749, one about every 4.5 years. If minutes and conclusions survive, they await analysis and publication.[5]

Far better known is the Society's general congregation. As the Society's chief governing body, it met on sixteen occasions between 1558 and the mid-eighteenth century. The longest session was the eighth, which lasted for 145 days between 1645 and 1646; the shortest was the sixth, which met in 1608 and dissolved after only 36 days. Each province was entitled to send three delegates—the provincial and two professed members—but political restrictions, wars, and local problems reduced the actual number of participants. The first meeting (1558) saw only 20 members in attendance, whereas 96 delegates gathered at the eighth meeting, the largest.[6]

The general congregation's most vital and urgent task has always been to elect (by secret ballot) the father general's successor and his assistants, but it also has other responsibilities. One is to serve as an ecclesiastical court to consider charges of serious misconduct against a serving general. Another is to examine proposals (*postulatus*) submitted on behalf of the provinces suggesting possible changes in the Institute.[7] The general congregations also define major policies of the Society.

Although spokesmen both for and against the Society always made much of its special relationship with the popes, the general congregations no more welcomed papal intervention in their affairs than did any other body in Christendom. Thus, when Pope Gregory XIII (1572–85) indicated to representatives of the Third Congregation his opposition to the election of a fourth successive Spaniard as general, they momentarily balked before electing the pope's preferred candidate, Everard Mercurian, a Belgian born in the Spanish Netherlands.

5. One of the few sources that discusses the procurators' meetings is Moulin, "L'Organisation," 488–89. A listing posted in the reading room of ARSI, "Congregationes et praeposti generalis SJ," gives the dates of such meetings but not the sources upon which it is based.

6. The fundamental source concerning the decrees enacted by the general congregations is *Institutum Societatis Iesu*, 3 vols. (Florence, 1892–93). John W. Padberg, S.J., "The General Congregations of the Society of Jesus: A Brief Survey of Their History," *Studies in the Spirituality of Jesuits* 6, 1 and 2 (Jan.–Mar. 1974), is a convenient summary and is the source primarily followed here.

7. The "Institute" is a term that encompasses the *Constitutions*, the directives of the fathers general, and the decrees of the general congregations.

The Fifth General Congregation (1593–94) was an extraordinary meeting in more than one respect. It was the first to be called during the lifetime of a serving general, and it assembled to consider fundamental constitutional changes proposed by Spanish dissidents who were strongly supported by Philip II of Spain and who enjoyed the sympathy of two popes. Despite the Spanish origins of the Society and the fact that its first generals were Spaniards, the king was always suspicious of its centralized authority in Rome and its special relationship with his political rival, the pope. Six years before the convocation of the delegates, the king badgered Pope Sixtus V (1585–90) until he ordered a papal agent to inspect all religious Orders in Spain. The intent of that inquiry was to expose the unorthodoxy of the Jesuits with respect to the making of their vows, their appointment procedures, and their special dependency upon the papacy. Before that investigation had proceeded very far, Claudio Aquaviva, then the Society's general, managed to persuade the pope to suspend it. Soon after, Sixtus V died.

But Aquaviva's Spanish opponents were not finished. They insisted that the generals' authority was too broad and should be curtailed by the vesting of additional powers in the provincial congregations.[8] Pope Clement VIII (1592–1605) was impressed by the Spaniards' concerns and directed Aquaviva to convoke a general congregation. The father general did so, no doubt reluctantly, but he successfully maneuvered to exclude his most vociferous critics. After extended debate, the congregation exonerated the general of charges that he had abused his authority and affirmed that, on balance, he had governed the Society well. Urged by the Spanish ambassador to Rome, however, the congregation also considered various *postulatus* designed to weaken the general's authority, but it rejected each of them. In what amounted to a slap against the Spanish dissidents, it voted in favor of a decree that stipulated "in virtue of holy obedience" that no member of the Society "is to involve himself in public or secular affairs of princes ... and [members are] never to take the liberty of occupying themselves with political interests or affairs."[9]

Aquaviva had won the battle, but the campaign was not yet over. A few years later, Philip III of Spain prevailed upon Clement VIII to order the general to undertake a visit of Spain. But Aquaviva's sudden illness, confirmed by the papal physician, prevented him from accepting the king's unwanted and inconvenient invitation.[10]

There were no further attempts to intervene in the government of the Society by either a pope or a secular ruler for half a century. But when the Eighth Congregation met to select Carafa's successor, Pope Innocent X (1644–55) directed it to examine a series of proposed

---

8. Provincial congregations met under the aegis of the provincial and included the superiors of each house and other senior members. Visitors, however, were barred from participation. Though they did not possess legislative authority, the delegates discussed common problems, drafted postulatus, elected procurators to represent the interests of the province in Rome and elsewhere in Europe, and named delegates to the general congregations. Though there were plans to hold such meetings at regular three- or six-year intervals, those in sixteenth-century India and Brazil gathered irregularly, and, because of distance and other considerations, some were abbreviated so-called chapter meetings, not to be confused with the house chapter meetings regularly held by other Orders. After 1600, provincial leaders seem to have met less regularly. *DI*, 14: 833, par. 6, and 15: 31*; *HCJB*, 2: 500–504; 7: 105–7, 261–62; and 8: 258 and 263. See also *VMP*, 2: 33–34.

9. Padberg, "General Congregations," 18.

10. The constitutional crisis is nicely summarized by Padberg, "General Congregations," 17–18, and is examined in extenso in *HCJAP*, 3: 400–597.

reforms. They included automatic meetings by the general congregation every nine years, restriction of all superiors to triennial terms, and permission for provincial congregations to elect their provincials. Although the delegates favored regular meetings for themselves, they were opposed to the other suggested changes. But the pope wanted them, and in January 1646, while the delegates were still deliberating, he ordered that henceforth the congregation would assemble every nine years and that the terms of all officials save the generals would be limited to three years.[11]

Seventeenth-century secular rulers also interfered in the Society's internal affairs on several occasions. One instance pertaining to the Portuguese province is discussed below. The next major intervention by a pope or head of state occurred during the third quarter of the eighteenth century, with consequences that will be noted in this volume's sequel.

The Generals and Their Assistants

Though a few popes attempted to modify the Society's machinery, no general congregation ever restricted the authority of the generals or attempted to compel them to conform to the delegates' views. Between 1541 and 1773, eighteen men headed the Society.[12] Four were Spaniards, ten were Italians, two were Belgians, one was a German, another was a Bohemian, and none were Portuguese. Several came from illustrious families. Saint Ignatius was a member of the minor Basque nobility and Aquaviva (1581–1615) the son of the duke of Atri. Carafa (1646–49) was related to Pope Paul IV and to the counts of Montorio; Piccolómini (1649–51) came from a prominent Siena family that had contributed a fifteenth-century pope; Visconti (1751–55) was a descendant of a once-dominant Milanese family. Unrivaled in terms of his lineage, Saint Francisco Borgia [Francisco de Borja y Aragón] (1565–72) was the fourth duke of Gandía and a great-grandson of both Pope Alexander VI and Ferdinand, king of Aragón. Though previous experience and administrative talent were doubtless important factors, considerations of birth and social standing appear to have strongly influenced the congregations' ballotings.

There was considerable variance in the ages of the fathers general at the time of their elections. At 37, Aquaviva was the youngest; Nickel (1652–64) and Centurioni (1755–57), both 70 when elected, were the oldest to assume office. The first five generals averaged 49.6 years of age at the time of their election; the next eight, 65.3 years; and the remaining five, 61.6 years. As will be seen in Chapter 11, despite the burdens of their office, the generals lived to quite respectable ages. Laínez was the youngest at his death, at 53, whereas Vitelleschi (1615–45) lived longest, expiring in his 85th year.

The preparation of the generals for their exalted post varied considerably. Half were, in effect, generals-designate, having served as vicars general during the last year or years of their immediate predecessor's terms, a strategy evidently intended to provide administrative continuity. Borgia clearly held the widest variety of major administrative posts before becoming the third general. Five of the generals were former provincials, college rectors, or

11. Padberg, "General Congregations," 23.
12. The analysis that follows is based upon a review of the relevant bibliographical articles in *The Catholic Encyclopedia*, 15 vols. (New York, 1913), the *Encyclopedia universal ilustrada europea-americana*, 50 vols. (Barcelona, 1923), *The New Catholic Encyclopedia*, 18 vols. (New York, 1967), and fugitive references.

house superiors. Three were ex-assistants, two were former provincial Visitors (see below), and two had been secretaries of the Society. Laínez was one of three papal theologians who attended the Council of Trent (1545–63), but several generals, including Lorenzo Ricci, the last general, had no background in international or administrative affairs. Of particular significance to this study, none had any overseas experience, though Gonzalez de Santalla (1687–1705) was bound for an African mission at the time of his election.

Much less is known about those who served as assistants (sometimes termed assistants general) in terms of their backgrounds, reasons for selection, duties, or influence upon the generals' decisions. The *Constitutions* merely state that the assistants should be "persons of discretion and zeal for the good of the Society," and that a new team ought to be selected by the general congregation when it elects a new general. Whenever replacements are necessary, the general is empowered to name them with the concurrence of a majority of the provincials, presumably those of the affected assistancy.[13] The assistants, of whom there were initially four and later six,[14] are intended to be the general's helpers or senior advisors and to assist him in "settling the problems of doctrine and action which require greater thought." All final decisions remain with the general, with one exception: in the event that serious charges arise concerning a general's conduct, it would become the assistants' responsibility to convoke an extraordinary general congregation and to serve upon a secret committee to determine the merit of such charges.[15] It has never been necessary to implement that provision.

No complete list of Portuguese assistants has come to light. The writings of António Franco, the Assistancy's indefatigable genealogist, and the manuscript personnel catalogues for the Portuguese province provide data concerning 30 of those who served between 1556 and 1751.[16] Several of the assistants were among those considered for the position of father general, suggesting that they commanded exceptional respect among their peers. Most of them possessed substantial academic and/or administrative experience, though none had served overseas. Some, like António do Rêgo, were elected to their positions after assisting their immediate predecessors. Those named during the formative period were somewhat older than the generals they advised: their average age at the time of their appointment was 49.6 years. The assistants who served during the period of stability were 3.7 years younger than their superiors. Those who served during the initial period held office for an average of 5.2 years, whereas their successors seem to have served nearly twice as long. Fathers Rêgo (1687–1709) and Nuno Mascarenhas (1615–37) held office longest within the Assistancy, Nuno Mascarenhas having succeeded his brother, António (1607–15). Although there was no constitutional requirement that assistants be natives of the Assistancy they served, all but

---

13. *CSJ(C)*, pt. 9, chap. 5, 779–81; Moulin, "L'Organisation," 489–90.

14. As noted in Chapter 1, the assistancies were organized along linguistic lines. By 1558 there were four: Italiae, Lusitaniae, Hispaniae, and Germaniae. Galliae (the French assistancy) was added in 1608, and Polaniae (the Polish assistancy) in 1755. Edmond Lamale, S.J., "Arquivum Romanum Societatis Iesu," reprint in ARSI, 145.

15. *CSJ(C)*, pt. 8, chap. 2, 681; pt. 9, chap. 5, 782–85.

16. I have relied primarily upon biographical data in António Franco's *ASCJ*, supplemented by his *Imagem da virtude em o noviciado da companhia de Jesus no real collegio de Jesus de Coimbra em Portugal*, 2 vols. (Évora and Coimbra, 1719), 2: 619–21 and 626; and idem, *Synopsis annalium Societatis Iesu in Lusitania ab anno 1540 usque ad annum 1725* (Augsburg, 1726); as well as ARSI, *Lus.*, 46–49.

two of the Portuguese assistants identified were of Lusitanian origin, reflecting the Society's deference to the Portuguese crown's nationalistic sensibilities.

We await a careful study of the relationship between the assistants and their generals in order to assess the extent of their influence upon the Society's policies. We know, for instance, that Valignano's assistant, Pedro da Fonseca (1573–81), claimed full credit for Valignano's appointment. As he wrote to the Visitor, "I alone, against much opposition, took in hand and put through your appointment.... When not a few of the fathers objected to your youth and short time in the Society I did not abandon the struggle."[17] Because many of the reports that field officers throughout the assistancies prepared were routed by the Society's secretary to the assistants, it is reasonable to conclude that their influence upon the selection of personnel and the formation of policies must have been considerable.

Intra-Assistancy Rivalries

The Portuguese was the oldest and geographically most extensive of the Society's assistancies. Ultimately it consisted of five provinces and two vice-provinces. When the Order was formed, it was anticipated that additional provinces would be created wherever there existed great spiritual promise, adequate financial resources, and a sufficient pool of recruits.[18] Within a decade of the establishment of the province of Portugal, it became obvious that its head could not effectively administer the extensive enterprises being undertaken in India and Brazil. Accordingly, in 1549, three years after the Portuguese province itself was created, the province of Goa was formed, followed in 1553 by that of Brazil. Thereafter the province of Portugal consisted of the kingdom itself, the Atlantic islands, and Portugal's West African enclaves. In time the province of Goa also proved too vast for oversight by a single administrator; indeed, its dimensions exceeded those of all the European provinces combined. Therefore, it spawned Japan (a vice-province in 1583 and a full province by 1611), Malabar (a vice-province in 1601 and a full province in 1605), and China (effectively a vice-province in 1623).[19] The vice-province of Maranhão (1727) was organized because of the difficulty of communications between the northern parts of Brazil and the provincial headquarters (Salvador) and because of the Society's increasing missionary commitment in the Amazon region. Partly for political and partly for economic reasons, long-standing plans to divide the Brazil province into separate northern and southern provinces and also to raise Maranhão to the status of a full province remained inactive throughout the first half of the eighteenth century; thereafter, implementation of such schemes became impossible.[20]

The founders expected new administrative units to flourish; they did not anticipate that some might wither or that their members would develop intense loyalties and engage in fierce intra-assistancy rivalries. One example of such hostility is that between the province

17. *VMP*, 1: 46.

18. *HCJB*, 1: 12.

19. The dependency of a vice-province upon the mother province is clearly spelled out in the detailed regulations establishing the vice-province of Malabar and suggests why members moved rapidly to gain independent status: "Orden q. se ha de guardar entre el prou[incia]l dita prov^a de Goa y el v. prov[incia]l dela v. prov^a del Malavar y partes del sul," ca. 1600–1601, in ARSI, FG, 1443/9/44.

20. *HCJB*, 7: 261–63.

of Goa and the exciting Japan missions, which spokesmen for the mother province insisted ought not to be detached from Goa.[21] Another is the rivalry between the colleges of Malacca and Macao to become administrative centers in the Far East after the collapse of the Japan enterprise.[22]

Persisting friction also developed, especially in the seventeenth century, between those fathers who identified with the Japan province and those who served in China. Late in 1614, on the eve of the Jesuits' expulsion from Japan, a provincial congregation met in Nagasaki and vowed to oppose the creation of a separate administration for China, which Fr. Nicholas Trigault, representative of the superior of China, was expected to negotiate while in Rome. Accordingly, the Japan province sent two procurators to the Eternal City, one via Goa, the other via Acapulco. They were instructed to do whatever they could to impede the creation of the unwanted vice-province.[23] When the pope nevertheless sanctioned the establishment of a vice-province, the disappointed leaders of the Japan province delayed its effective formation until 1623. Thereafter, officials of the reformed Japan province and those of the new vice-province competed for recruits and for financial resources, neither of which was ever adequate (see Chapters 23 and 24). In 1686 Ferdinand Verbiest, the vice-provincial, complained to the general about the long-standing practice of the province of Japan of deliberately retaining in Macao missionaries sent from Europe specifically for the China enterprise and pleaded (unsuccessfully) that the vice-province be raised to a full province.[24] Until the 1720s, the two rivals shared training and dormitory facilities in Macao in the college of São Paulo, but during that decade the casa (domus, sometimes termed college) of São José was erected exclusively for missionaries destined for imperial China.

Another persistent rivalry was that between the provinces of Goa and Malabar. According to the historian of the Malabar province, "From the very beginning . . . [the Malabar province] found herself unwelcome by her elder sister, the Province of the North, as Goa was then called, and since the elder sister had to be foster mother to the younger child, the child was stinted. The best men were kept in Goa, the fattest alms never found their way to the South."[25] This statement reflects the bias of the administrators of the southern province, especially its founder, the Italian Alberto Laerzio, who had been sent from Goa to Rome as procurator in 1598 and who returned three years later with 35 recruits. Fr. Laerzio subsequently complained that Goan authorities permitted him to take less than a dozen of those he enlisted to Cochin. In 1604 he protested, "What grieves me most is the little help which the Province of Goa gives us . . . to judge from what has taken place last year . . . they do their best to prevent us from organizing ourselves and from being independent, they

21. See the strongly negative reactions of Frs. Francisco de Monclaro, Cristóvão de Castro, and Gomes Vaz to Aquaviva, 26 Oct. to 21 Nov. 1593, in *DI*, 16: 182–201, 402–9, 415–21. Cf., however, Francisco Cabral (provincial) to Aquaviva, 15 Dec. 1593, in ibid., 521–22. Cabral, an old hand in Japan, favored its separation to end its ability to divert the best men coming from Europe from Goa to the islands.

22. Valentim Carvalho (rector, Macao) to João Alvares (assistant), Macao, 4 Nov. 1606, and Manuel Coelho to Mutius Vitelleschi, 12 Feb. 1621, in *DM*, 3: 46–47 and 436–39.

23. Edmond Lamalle, S.J. "La Propaganda du P. Nicholas Trigault en faveur des missions de Chine (1616)," *AHSI* 9 (1940): 54 n. 13, and 92 n. 6. See also Chapter 6 above.

24. John W. Witek, S.J., *Controversial Ideas in China and in Europe: A Biography of Jean-François Foucquet, S.J. (1665–1741)* (Rome, 1982), 54.

25. F/*JM*, 1: 267.

do not want to give us any one. This Province finds in Goa neither help nor remedy for its troubles. It is useless to write there. They do nothing for us."[26]

Despite the devastating effects of the Dutch conquests, the members of the southern province persistently opposed reunion with Goa. Proposals for reunion were made in 1630 and again in 1650, but in both cases the Malabar zealots successfully resisted them. The issue arose once more in 1698, when Fr. João da Costa was sent as Malabar's procurator to Rome. There he seems to have exceeded his instructions: recognizing that the province had lost all of its sources of economic support, that its membership had shrunk by nearly 75 percent since the 1640s, and that its so-called colleges were then mere mud huts, the procurator strongly recommended reunification with Goa. Both the general and his assistants favored such an arrangement, but the Portuguese assistant urged that before proceeding they ought to consult members of the Malabar province.[27]

The province's reaction was militantly negative. In 1699 its provincial directed Fr. Virgilio Mansi to inform the secretary of the Society that his subjects viewed with grave alarm the prospect of reunification. Mansi responded with a passionate dispatch in which he denied that the province had become "chimeric and nominal," as the procurator had contended, and reminded his superiors that Malabar had the honor to be "the eldest daughter of the great Xavier, and the only support of Christianity in the whole East," a palpable exaggeration. He argued that reunion would bring "disastrous consequences" because the "interests" of the two provinces were diametrically opposed:

> If the Goan laxity were joined to the Malabar fervor it is evident that vice would have the better of virtue. That spells spiritual ruin. The Dutch ... will—once they come to know of this reunion—renew the past persecutions. That means temporal ruin. And how can the Fathers, when they are in trouble, have recourse to a Superior, when they have to wait one year for his answer? Instead of diminishing the expenses, they will be doubled by the long voyages, and especially with Religious who are dissatisfied, and the lovers of comfort.

It is clear that the embattled Jesuits in Malabar considered themselves spiritually superior to their colleagues in Goa, and that they believed that they alone retained the apostolic zeal of the heroic Xavier, whereas those who resided in Goa had become "lovers of comfort." In view of Malabar's heated opposition, the general, Gonzalez de Santalla, yielded to the pleas of the provincial spokesmen. The proposal was therefore tabled and there it remained.[28]

It is tempting to suggest that such provincial loyalties were unique to the eastern provinces of the Society, for there is no evidence of such conflicts occurring in Brazil between the original province and the vice-province that it spawned. But an even more serious fissure occurred in the province of Portugal during the seventeenth century. An ambitious minority in the southern reaches of that province gained a powerful ally in the person of John IV, who presented a series of short-lived fathers general—Vicente Carafa, Francesco Piccolómini, Aloysius Gottifredi, and Goswin Nickel—with the gravest problem

---

26. Ibid., 280 and 271, the quotation being from the latter.

27. The crown also asked the viceroy whether he saw any impediments to the plan. *CR*, 23 Mar. 1699, in HAG 63, fol. 115ʳ.

28. *F/JM*, 2: 265–67. (The quotation appears on p. 267.) In addition to rivalry between the two Indian houses, there existed serious conflicts in the sixteenth century between members of Old St. Paul's, the Chorão novitiate, and the professed house in Goa. See *DI*, 16: 5*, and sources cited there.

the Society had ever experienced in its relations with the Portuguese crown. Less than two years after the revolution of December 1640 (see Chapter 4), a determined minority in Portugal revived an old plan to create a separate province for the south, that is, the kingdom of the Algarve and the province of the Alentejo. The plan dated back at least to 1604, when Francisco Guerreiro, the well-known chronicler, advised the Portuguese assistant that many Jesuits believed that such a separation was warranted. The provincial congregation that met at São Roque two years later strongly disagreed and brushed aside the proposal. Nevertheless, in 1642 the provincial himself, António de Sousa, who came from the town of Cadafais, Extremadura, lent his support to the proposal and instructed Matias de Sousa, rector of the college of Santarém and recently elected as procurator to Rome, to explore the subject with Mutio Vitelleschi; but the ailing and aging general turned a cold shoulder to the idea. The separatists, who represented less than 10 percent of the province's members, then responded to the provincial's directive by memorializing the Society's secretariat in favor of such a division. Shortly afterward, the provincial died. The separatists then turned to the king, himself an Alentejano. Initially John IV was understandably preoccupied with graver national problems (Chapter 4) and gave the matter little thought. But when Fr. Sebastião de Abreu, an Alentejano from the town of Crato, came to see the king en route to Rome to assume his duties as censor (*revisor geral*), he found the monarch supportive. Yet Abreu, too, was unable to discuss the matter with Vitelleschi because of the general's increasing infirmities. In 1645, following the general's death, three Jesuit delegates from Portugal attended the general congregation to elect his successor. Among them were Nuno da Cunha, a Lisbonense who strongly opposed separation, and Bento de Sequeira, an Alentejano who ardently favored it. Sequeira hoped to take up the matter with the new general, Carafa, but was unable to approach him and instead devoted his energies to an unsuccessful effort to block Nuno da Cunha from being elected Portuguese assistant. But Carafa did receive communications concerning the proposal from two influential Jesuits who were staunchly opposed to separation. One came from the venerable António Mascarenhas, a veteran administrator who had just completed an unprecedented third stint as provincial of Portugal; another emanated from the current vice-provincial, Francisco de Távora. Mascarenhas stressed the economic difficulties that separation would pose, whereas Távora expressed his opposition in terms of the "certain ruin" that division would bring to the Society's enterprises in the kingdom and the empire.

Frustrated in Rome, the separatists, now joined by the exceedingly influential royal confidant António Vieira, tried a different tactic. They appealed to Fr. João de Matos, the new Visitor of the province. When he displayed no enthusiasm for their plan, they turned again to the king and appealed to his pride as an Alentejano and as Portugal's popular new monarch, who, they said, must defend his prerogatives. The separatists induced the monarch to write the Visitor to inform him that the crown itself favored separation and that he therefore ought to order it. But Matos responded (quite correctly) that he lacked authority to approve such a division. That response infuriated the separatists, who urged the king to sign a second, stronger letter, one allegedly drafted by Vieira himself. In it the king insisted on compliance with his wishes and defined the proposed second province as embracing not only the Algarve and the Alentejo but also the colleges of Santarém and Funchal, and the four Jesuit installations in Lisbon.

By 1647 the Visitor reluctantly agreed to forward the plan to Rome, but the king, doubtless prodded by ardent factionalists, himself wrote to three prominent Jesuits in the Eternal City and insisted upon compliance with his wishes. Those Jesuits were Nuno da Cunha, by then the Portuguese assistant; Sebastião de Abreu, the censor; and Carafa himself. When the general responded equivocally, the separatists, led by the fiery Abreu, denounced him as a Spaniard (he was from Naples) and asserted that his assistants, including Nuno da Cunha, were hispanophiles. The dissidents insisted that they had the support of many of the most eminent Jesuits in the realm and that the "peace and tranquility" of the Society in the kingdom required separation.[29]

Following the arrival in Lisbon of news of Carafa's death, a provincial congregation met to select delegates to the meeting that would choose his successor. There the antiseparatists committed a tactical error: the king indicated that one of the three delegates ought to be Fr. Inácio Mascarenhas, his nephew and an ardent supporter of separation. Mascarenhas lost by a narrow margin, much to the fury of the monarch.

Next, the crown applied pressure upon the provincial, Pedro da Rocha, and ordered him to accomplish the separation and to name new heads of houses within the proposed second province. Like João de Matos, the provincial properly stated that he did not have authority to yield to the royal will, causing John to threaten to expel all Jesuits opposed to the division and to name only Alentejanos to govern Jesuit houses in the kingdom. Alarmed, the provincial convoked a meeting of a half dozen senior Jesuits, who decided to appeal to the queen through her confessor; but that strategy failed to reduce the growing tensions between the rival factions.

The newly elected general, Francesco Piccolómini (1649–51), was determined to defuse the increasingly tense relationship between the Society and the crown. He offered to separate the Alentejo and the Algarve from the rest of the province and to appoint a special Visitor to govern the South. But that left in doubt the future administration of the Lisbon houses. A meeting of eleven Jesuits in the capital voted 8 to 3 against permitting the Alentejanos to govern the most eminent of those houses, Santo Antão. Upon learning of their decision, John angrily ordered the rector of Santo Antão, the humanist Baltasar Teles, exiled to the North; António Barradas, superior of São Roque and a leading opponent of separation, and the oft-maligned Nuno da Cunha, now returned to the kingdom, were exiled even farther away from the capital.

In June 1651 Francesco Piccolómini died. The general's death led to a further crisis, for the king peevishly refused to allow the customary provincial congregation to assemble to elect delegates to the next general congregation, so that Portugal was unrepresented when Aloysius Gottifredi began his ephemeral term (21 January to 12 March 1652). As the feuding between the rival factions continued, the unitarians indicated that they would agree to the formation of the Alentejo province provided that a third province—Lisbon and the remainder of Extremadura—was also sanctioned.

That suggestion was too much for the king, who concluded that he had heard more than enough about the internal problems of the Society. Consequently he ordered the rector of Santo Antão to retire immediately and named an Alentejano in his place. He decreed

29. Memorial of Abreu to Carafa, 1647, in *HCJAP*, 3:2, 14.

that no Jesuit would henceforth be permitted to communicate with the father general and severely reproved the Visitor of the Alentejo for continuing to do so.[30] John IV also ordered all Portuguese Jesuits living in Rome, including the Portuguese assistant, to return to the kingdom immediately.

Gottifredi's response was to dispatch, successively, three prominent French Jesuits to try to resolve the crisis. The first two expired before they were able to assume their posts. The third succeeded only because he yielded completely to the implacable will of John IV. In June 1653 the old province of Portugal was formally split into two units: the southern province, after much discussion simply called Alentejo, included the key Lisbon houses, the college of Évora, the professed house of Vila Viçosa, the colleges of Portalegre, Elvas, and Faro, the island of Madeira, and Angola. The rest was left to the shrunken province of Portugal, centered in Coimbra.

But the discord that this innovation was intended to eliminate persisted. In exasperation, the next general, Goswin Nickel (1652–64), stated that the two Portuguese provinces caused him more headaches than all the other provinces combined. His successor, Giovanni Paolo Oliva (1664–81), also lamented the continued factionalism in the formerly prospering province of Portugal. What particularly irked him was the emergence of a new feud between the sons of Coimbra and Minho on the one hand and those of Beira on the other over which natives ought to be superiors of the houses in the North.

John IV's death in November 1656 gave Nickel hope that the two provinces could be reunified, especially when he was assured by a senior secular ecclesiastic that he could now govern the Society in Portugal in conformity with the Order's Institutes and without further crown interference. That assurance seemed confirmed when the queen mother, Luísa de Gusmão, regent for her son, Afonso VI, assured her confessor that she had no wish to intrude in the Society's internal affairs. But Oliva, then vicar general, proceeded cautiously, testing the queen's resolve. He soon discovered that she was, in fact, opposed to reunification in deference to the wishes of her late husband. Indeed, Luísa notified him that she expected that he would name as heads of Jesuit houses in the kingdom only persons acceptable to her. Oliva assured the queen mother that he would respect her wishes and that he would make no move to reunite the provinces as long as she remained opposed.

The queen mother's opposition continued until June 1664, two years after she was forced from power and into a convent (see Chapter 4). It was from that domicile that she finally wrote Oliva that he should do whatever he thought best "for the greater service of God . . . and his . . . glory." When he read those lines Oliva must have uttered a great sigh of relief. In March 1665 his decree abolishing the joint provinces and restoring the ancient province was read in Lisbon and elsewhere in the kingdom. There were no protests, but there were no celebrations either, for every Jesuit in Portugal realized that the stature of the Society in the kingdom had been seriously compromised by the protracted divisional dispute. Possibly the same was true in the Lowlands and in Sicily, where self-determination also became a divisive issue at this time.[31] Despite the pleas of some of the injured parties,

30. In 1688, Louis XIV did the same after the general refused to name a special vicar general for France, but he yielded after an appeal by the five provincials of that kingdom. *HCJB*, 7: 103 n. 2.

31. Padberg, "General Congregations," 24.

especially Nuno da Cunha, for retribution, none was ever exacted, though bitter memories of the division lingered for the remainder of the century.[32]

In his masterly narration of this acrimonious affair, the Assistancy's leading historian, Francisco Rodrigues, depicts the conflict as one between Lisbonians and Alentejanos. Such a distinction is misleading, however. Although many of the dissidents were associated with the University of Évora and were natives of the bishoprics south of the Tagus River, many of those who resided in the principal Lisbon houses—São Roque and Santo Antão—were not natives of Lisbon or its suburbs. According to the personnel catalogue of 1639, the one closest in time to the beginning of the crisis, only 22.4 percent of the occupants of the professed house were from Lisbon or its vicinity, whereas 16.3 percent were from Évora, 14.3 percent from Coimbra, 30 percent from the North (the sees of Porto and Braga), and the balance from other parts of the kingdom. But it may be argued that São Roque, many of whose residents were of advanced years, was not a typical Jesuit house. The same could not be said of Santo Antão; the 1639 catalogue reveals that only 13.3 percent of its members were from Lisbon, while 24.4 percent came from the archdiocese of Braga and another 20 percent from Coimbra and its environs. The mixing of residents from many parts of the kingdom was not accidental: it was the result of a little-known but deliberate policy intended, in part, to remove members from contact with their families and friends.[33] The composition of the Évora staff, which included 42 priests, 71 brothers, and 10 novices, was an exception: 60.5 percent were from Évora and four other Alentejano dioceses, whereas 16.8 percent came from Lisbon, 9.2 percent from Coimbra, and the rest from elsewhere within the Assistancy.[34] It may be argued that the separatists felt a strong sense of regional identity, whereas the unitarists seem to have been bound by collegiality and institutional loyalty, that is, loyalty toward their own residences. What unfortunately divided the two groups was the quest for pride, place, and power. Ignatius, Xavier, Valignano, and their generations would have been horrified!

Provincials, Rectors, and Other Superiors

Within the assistancies, each province or vice-province was headed by a provincial or a vice-provincial who supervised a corps of rectors and superiors. That corps administered the Society's colleges, novitiates, professed houses, seminaries, missions, and properties. The *Constitutions* state that the supervisors are "to do what they ought to do for the universal

32. The foregoing is based upon *HCJAP*, 3:2, 3–91, an outstanding example of Fr. Rodrigues's scholarship. Curiously, in his standard biography (*História de António Vieira*, 2d ed. 2 vols [Lisbon, 1931]), João Lúcio de Azevedo ignores António Vieira's purported role in the conflict. Nor is there any reference to it in Vieira's published correspondence, even though he was in contact with some of the leading principals, especially Nuno da Cunha, André Fernandes, and John IV, during the years 1653–61, when he was superior of the Maranhão missions.

33. To my knowledge, the only other scholar who has recognized the existence of such a policy is Nigel Griffin, "'Virtue versus Letters': The Society of Jesus, 1550–1580, and the Export of an Idea," European University Institute, Working Paper no. 95 (Badia Fiesolana, 1984), 23 and n. 57. The implementation of that policy is evident in the many surviving personnel catalogues, particularly of the Portuguese province, in ARSI, *Lus.*, 44–49.

34. "Catalogi primi Lus," ARSI, *Lus.*, 44:II, fols. 570–97. I also consulted for this analysis the less detailed 1642 and 1645 personnel catalogues, fols. 604–22 and 630–49.

good of the Society."[35] They are charged with instilling moral fervor in their subjects, with enforcement of the Institute, and with defense of the Society's interests in its relations with the crown and with other religious bodies.

As the Society increased in number, geographical extent, and responsibility, its generals delegated certain powers to the provincials and vice-provincials, but reserved for themselves final approval of their lieutenants' acts. The *Constitutions* authorized a provincial or vice-provincial to grant enumerated dispensations, to approve publication of books or pamphlets issued by the provincial press, to confirm admissions and dismissals, to reassign personnel, to assemble and preside over provincial congregations or chapters, and to serve as one of three provincial delegates to general congregations. Both administrators exercised such responsibilities in consultation with four *consultores* appointed by the general or by the Visitor, his deputy. Consultores were defined as "grave and authoritative" subjects who were expected to render advice and also to keep watch on their superior's conduct and to report on his performance to the general. They lacked any collective decision-making authority, however.[36]

Broad as their powers were, the provincials and vice-provincials were specifically enjoined not to exceed their authority. They could not, for example, confer either the third or fourth vow upon any subject without license from the general. With rare exceptions, they were forbidden to intercept and read dispatches from Rome intended for other members of their province.[37] They could not alienate the Society's property beyond a stipulated amount, nor divert funds or goods intended for one unit of the Society to another. They were forbidden to dismiss their consultores or to grant exemptions to those classed as temporal brothers, so that, for example, they might undertake courses of study, unless such study pertained to the acquisition of literacy that would better equip them to perform tasks assigned to them.[38]

The *Constitutions* admonish the provincials to keep the general "informed of every-thing ... important."[39] In practice, provincials devoted a great deal of time to reading and preparing reports. If those who served overseas found it impossible to comply with the constitutional provision to write monthly to the general, they sent him lengthy annual reports and responded as often as possible to specific directives from headquarters. They also supervised the preparation of periodic personnel reports, known as first and second catalogues, which provided their superiors with basic biographical information on each member and assessments of his spiritual, intellectual, and physical

35. *CSJ(C)*, pt. 9, chap. 5, 778.

36. E.g., *CSJ(C)*, pt. 4, chap. 10, par. 431, and chap. 17, par. 490; see also pt. 9, chap. 6, par. 810.

37. One exception: dispatches intended for the Jesuit contingent in Ethiopia were read and copied in Goa before being forwarded to the highlands, a measure taken because of the possibility that such correspondence might be lost in transit.

38. The duties of the provincials are outlined in *CSJ(C)*, pt. 1, chap. 2, 141; pt. 2, chap. 1, 206; pt. 4, chap. 17, 490 and 491; pt. 8, chap. 4, 682 and 684; pt. 9, chap. 3, 747 and 759. See also Claudio Aquaviva, "Instrución para el nuevo provincial de la India Oriental," 22 Dec. 1582, in *DI*, 12: 686–700; idem, "Facultates concessae provinciali Indiae," Jan. and Mar. 1585, in *DI*, 13: 830–31 and 838–40; and especially Alessandro Valignano, "Summary of the Rules for the Provincial of India," Apr. 1588, in *DI*, 14: 828–98, which summarized in a highly organized fashion the decrees of the fathers general pertaining to the office as well as the responsibilities of Visitors and other superiors.

39. *CSJ(C)*, pt. 8, chap. 1, 662.

capabilities.[40] Provincials were also charged with sending Rome periodic economic reports, often called third catalogues, identifying the sources and amounts of income and expenditure of each facility within their jurisdictions.[41] When they considered it appropriate, they wrote directly to their king and his ministers, to actual or prospective benefactors, and to other provincials. They also responded to regular reports submitted to them by subordinate administrators and by field workers. Whenever Visitors were present, they also corresponded with them.

The provincial normally resided in a professed house, but he was often out of town on inspection tours. The *Constitutions* state that such visits ought to be conducted "when [the provincial] thinks by [them] greater service will be given to God," but they caution that he should always remain in places from which he can communicate effectively with the general and his subjects.[42] In practice, the provincials tried to visit each of their facilities once during their term, interviewing their heads and staffs, assessing their qualities, resolving disputes, scrutinizing their records, altering whatever needed to be corrected, and participating in the spiritual life of the community. When the province of Goa reached from Mozambique to the Moluccas and to Japan, visits to distant parts of the province became impossible, and the provincial assigned a nearby superior to undertake a visitation in his stead. Even so, a newly appointed provincial could look forward to many days of difficult travel by canoe, frigate, litter, or other form of conveyance. Considering the manifold duties they bore and the advanced ages of many at the time of their appointments, it is not surprising that some provincials literally worked themselves into the grave.[43]

The *Constitutions* empowered the general to appoint provincials "commonly for three years, although he may shorten or lengthen this period when he thinks that this will be conducive to [the] greater glory of God."[44] A review of 312 men who served as provincials within this Assistancy indicates that the triennium was generally the norm in the kingdom, but longer stints were more common for those who served overseas during the formative period (see Table 10.1). One of the most broadly experienced was the Madeira-born Sebastião de Morais (b. 1535–d. 1588), longtime confessor of the duke of Parma, whom he accompanied to Flanders and Italy, and biographer of his wife, the duchess. In Italy he became rector of the college of Parma, Visitor of the Italian provinces of Romana and Milan, and, from 1580 to 1588, provincial of Portugal. He surrendered the latter post when he was consecrated bishop of Japan, but met his death off Mozambique before he

40. Many of the first (*primus*) catalogues are cited in Chapter 11. A good example of the second (*secundus*) reports is the "Catalogus per dotes et qualitate sociorum tantum modo pertinentum ad provinciam goanam," ca. 1709, in ARSI, *Goa*, 26, fols. 34ʳ–45ʳ. See also *DI*, 16: 927–89. Until 1761, all such reports were laboriously copied by hand, but in that year the Society began for the first time to use printed forms for the first, second, and possibly third catalogues. ARSI, *Lus.*, 49, fols. 223–329ᵛ.

41. John Correia-Afonso, S.J., *Jesuit Letters and Indian History: A Study of the Nature and Development of the Jesuit Letters from India (1542–1773) and of Their Value for Indian Historiography* (Bombay, 1955), esp. chap. 1.

42. *CSJ(C)*, pt. 8, chap. 1, 670.

43. Four of those who served in Portugal died in office. Only two of those who held office in Brazil and China did so, but seven who occupied the post in Goa and eight of those who did so in Malabar and Japan expired while holding office. I have assembled basic biographical data concerning the provincials from *CJPM*; *ASCJ*; *HCJB*, 2: 243–46, 459–98, 7: 3–60, 115–40, 8 and 9, passim; HAG, 2089; and *RJC*.

44. *CSJ(C)*, pt. 9, chap. 3, 757.

TABLE 10.1

Average Length of Provincials' Terms

(Years)

Province or Vice-Province	Period 1	Period 2	Period 3
Portugal	3.8	2.8	3.1
Brazil	6.6	3.8	3.3
Maranhão	—	—	2.9
Goa	5.5	2.6	2.8
Malabar	5.0	3.3	3.1
Japan	9.7[a]	3.3	2.6
China	9.0[b]	3.8[c]	3.5
Average for period	6.6	3.3	3.0

SOURCES: See note 43.

NOTE: Period 1 = 1546–1615 (Portugal); 1553–1615 (Brazil); 1549–1615 (Goa); 1605–15 (Malabar); 1549–1617 (Japan); 1583–1610 (China). Period 2 = 1615–1703 (Portugal); 1615–1705 (Brazil); 1615–1704 (Goa); 1615–1705 (Malabar); 1617–1704 (Japan); 1610–1704 (China). Period 3 = 1703–60 (Portugal); 1705–60 (Brazil); 1727–60 (Maranhão); 1704–60 (Goa); 1705–61 (Malabar); 1705–62 (Japan); 1704–65 (China).

[a] Includes three superiors plus one superior who later became a vice-provincial.

[b] Includes three superiors.

[c] Includes two superiors.

could take up his new position.[45] António Quadros was vice-provincial of Goa for three years prior to his thirteen-year regime as provincial. In Brazil, José de Anchieta remained as provincial for a decade, and one of his predecessors, Luís de Grã, held that position for a dozen years. A handful of those who served as provincials, vice-provincials, and superiors served more than one term.[46] Fr. José de Seixas bore the unique distinction of being provincial of Brazil (1675–78) before assuming the same position in Portugal (1681–85). As the burdens of the office intensified and as the pool of administrative talent deepened, the terms of the provincials were gradually shortened until they approximated the ideal triennium.[47]

While the length of the provincials' term shrank, their age at the time of their appointment significantly increased between the sixteenth and the eighteenth centuries (see Table 10.2). During the formative period, when administrative talent was scarce, most provincials were first appointed in their early to mid-forties. When the number of candidates became greater and the Order's leadership became increasingly conservative, there was a marked rise in the ages of those named provincials, especially those in Portugal and Brazil. The upward trend in the ages of such appointees appears to have continued in the last period, except in the vice-province of China.[48]

45. Franco, *Coimbra*, 1: 105–14.

46. One repeated in Maranhão; two in Goa; four each in Portugal, Brazil, and Malabar; and six in China; but none in Japan.

47. In 1646, Innocent X mandated three-year terms for all superiors save the generals and their assistants. Today the normal term is six years.

48. Insufficient biographical data for those serving in eighteenth-century Portugal make it impossible to determine the ages of those who assumed such appointments there during the last period. Similar lacunae

TABLE 10.2

Ages of Provincials When Appointed

Province or vice-province	Period 1	Period 2	Period 3
Portugal	45.0	65.6	n.a.
Brazil	42.9	62.1	65.0
Maranhão	—	—	50.6
Goa	44.8	—	—
Japan	46.0	52.7	55.5
China	46.0	56.1	49.6

SOURCES: See note 43.

NOTE: Period 1 = 1546–1615 (Portugal); 1553–1615 (Brazil); 1549–1605 (Goa); 1549–1617 (Japan); 1583–1610 (China). Period 2 = 1615–1703 (Portugal); 1615–1705 (Brazil); 1617–1704 (Japan); 1610–1704 (China). Period 3 = 1704–58 (Portugal); 1705–58 (Brazil); 1727–60 (Maranhão); 1705–62 (Japan); 1707–62 (China).

Most provincials in the Assistancy were born in the Iberian Peninsula, as were most royal executive officers, magistrates, and prelates who served there or overseas. The only two non-native provincials of Portugal were Sebastião de Morais and Sebastião de Magalhães, born in Madeira and Tangier respectively. Forty-two out of 54 provincials of Japan were also Portuguese; one was a *mestiço*, the son of a Japanese mother and a Portuguese father, and eleven were foreigners. Twelve of 38 who served as provincials of China were also foreign-born. Except for Cristóvão Semedo, a Malabar provincial who was the offspring of Portuguese parents residing in Quilon, no creoles appear to have become provincials east of the Cape of Good Hope. By contrast, eight of the provincials of Brazil and two of the vice-provincials of Maranhão were born in Brazil.

The *Constitutions* are conspicuously vague about the qualifications needed to become a provincial, except to say that provincials must be "men worthy of great confidence."[49] Several, including three provincials of Portugal—António Mascarenhas, António de Abreu, and Luís Lobo—came from noble backgrounds, as did Saint Francis Xavier and Gonçalo da Silveira, both provincials of Goa. Some, like Portugal's Mascarenhas and Goa's Quadros, were brothers of prelates in the kingdom. Probably no other provincial in Portugal could approach the record of missionary service abroad achieved by Jerónimo Vogado (b. 1579–d. 1652), who served in Angola for 24 years before becoming provincial (1645–48), but such a record was not exceptional among those who administered the provinces of Brazil, Goa, and Malabar or the vice-provinces of Maranhão and China. Many of these provincials had spent portions of their careers as masters of novices and as academicians, particularly as professors of philosophy and theology. And most had served one or more stints as superiors or rectors of houses, thereby gaining the experience and contacts that enabled them to persuade senior colleagues to recommend them to the generals as men who possessed the requisite piety, probity, tact, and administrative ability to become provincial heads.[50]

account for the omission of those who served in Goa during the second and third periods and all those who held the post in Malabar province.

49. *CSJ(C)*, pt. 9, chap. 5, 778.

50. E.g., see the assessments by the provincial of Portugal and his consultores in G. Serrão to Mercurian, Lisbon, 28 Feb. 1574, in *DI*, 9: 196.

Although few provincials served more than one term, many rectors held the post of superior several times. The *Constitutions* are more explicit in defining the criteria to be satisfied in the selection of a rector than those that must be met in the naming of a provincial. The rector should be

> a man of great example, edification, and mortification of all his evil inclinations, and one especially approved in regard to his obedience and humility. He ought ... to be discreet, fit for governing, experienced both in matters of business and of the spiritual life. He should know how to mingle severity with kindness at the proper times. He should be solicitous, stalwart under work, a man of learning and ... one in whom the higher superiors can confide and to whom they can with security delegate their authority.[51]

Rectors were normally appointed to three-year terms, but during the formative period, especially in the East, their tenures often lasted as long as a decade. The rector bore significant burdens. He set the rules of his house and was responsible for its spiritual welfare. He appointed and supervised members of its staff and those of the smaller houses (casas and *residencias*) annexed to his college or university. He controlled access to the library and saw to it that both teachers and students fulfilled their duties; he dismissed students who made inadequate progress in their studies. In consultation with the provincial, he admitted recruits and dismissed members who proved unfit. He presided over his house's formal activities, including festivals and graduations, and over faculty meetings. Like most departmental chairmen or deans of academic institutions today, he was obliged to listen to any complaints from the faculty but not to heed their recommendations, provided that he notified the provincial of his reasons for dissenting from such advice. Rectors worked closely with the provincials, furnishing them with recommendations on policy and personnel matters when requested. They attended provincial congregation meetings and prepared personnel and economic reports for the summaries that provincials submitted to Rome. In addition, they maintained close contact with civil authorities and with field missionaries and estate managers. Unlike the provincials, they were directly responsible for the management of the temporal goods belonging to their college and were therefore charged with supervising the record-keeping and, where possible, with augmenting college income and reducing expenditures.[52]

Evidence derived from eleven personnel catalogues suggests that the average age of those who became rectors or house superiors was about the same as that of the provincials, and that as the Society aged, so did its rectors. Between 1587 and 1611, the average age of rectors in the Portuguese province rose from 45.7 to 51 years (1603), but then fell back to 45.2 years. By the late 1630s, however, it had risen to 53.3 years. In the eighteenth century, it varied between a low of 57.9 (1754) and a high of 59.4 (1705) years.[53]

Similar patterns existed overseas. The average age of the three rectors in Brazil in the 1560s was 47; 25 years later, it had risen to 56.3. In 1601 it declined to 52, and it remained at

---

51. *CSJ(C)*, pt. 4, chap. 10, 423. The duties of the rector are further laid out in Francisco Rodrigues, "Regimento da ordem e oficios de casa: Regras do rector" [1545–46], and in Jerónimo Nadal, "Officium rectoris" [1553–54], in *RSI*, 22–23 and 346–61.

52. *CSJ(C)*, pt. 4, chap. 10, 424, 435, and 437; pt. 8, chap. 1, 662; and pt. 4, chap. 2, 326.

53. Primi catalogi (1587–1611): ARSI, *Lus.*, 44:I, 1–17, 25–25ᵛ, 65–84, 129–50, 168–96ᵛ, 214–36; (1639): 44:II, 570–93; (1705): 47: 63–96; (1740): 48: 207ʳ–40; (1754): 49: 130–81ᵛ.

that level for the balance of the century. By 1755, however, the average age of rectors in the province was greater than in the kingdom: 61.7 years.[54] In 1588, the ages of the ten rectors or house superiors in Goa province averaged only 39.7 years at the time of their appointments. Nine years later, however, that average had climbed to 47.1 years. By 1760 it was nearly the same: exactly 48.[55] Similarly, in East Asia, the average age of ten rectors appointed between 1582 and 1685, most of them heads of the college of Macao, was 50.[56]

The Visitors

The provincial Visitor (*visitator*), sometimes called the visitor general, was an exceptional rather than a regular appointee and outranked both the provincial and the rectors.[57] His authority derived directly from the general who named and instructed him. As Aquaviva wrote when he confirmed Valignano's authority, "We devolve on you a portion of our responsibilities in government and hereby appoint and declare you Visitor of the East Indian and Japan province, its colleges and residences, with that full authority which we would have were we present ourselves."[58] The Visitor was required to examine as many facilities within the province as possible to determine their spiritual and material states, to suppress abuses, resolve conflicts, and provide remedies; to identify talent for future assignments, remove any official, including the provincial, found defective, and assign subjects to new positions; to convene special meetings of senior priests to discuss major concerns; and to acquaint the general with everything he considered important for him to know. As Mercurian wrote in his "Instruction for the Office of Visitor," a Visitor must "have eyes and ears open to the needs of all concerned. Remembering that he belongs more to others than to himself, he should devote mind and heart to their welfare as one who will have to account to God for the manner in which he has discharged his office."[59]

The Visitors tended to be mature members of the Society of about the same age as the other members of the hierarchy already discussed (Table 10.3). At age 35, Alessandro Valignano was the youngest ever appointed in the Assistancy; the octogenarian António Vieira was the eldest. As with the posts already considered, the ages of the Visitors increased substantially between the formative period and the period of stability, though somewhat younger men gained the appointment in the period of increased stress.

54. 1560–1601: José de Anchieta, *Informação do Brasil e de suas capitanias (1584)*, intro. Leonardo Arroyo (São Paulo, 1964); *HCJB*, 1: 578–84, 8 and 9: passim; 1679: ARSI, *Bras.*, 5:II, 39–48, and *HCJB*, 8 and 9; 1755: *HCJB*, 7: 435–53, and 8 and 9.

55. 1588: *DI*, 15: 170–201; 1597: *DI*, 18: 843–56; 12: 14*; 16: 931–80; 1760: John Humbert, S.J., "Catalogus patrum et fratrum Societatis Iesu ex India anno 1760 expulsorum," *AHSI* 31 (July–Dec. 1962): 324–59.

56. The evidence comes from a variety of sources, including *MHJ*; *RJC*; ARSI, *JapSin*, 26/D; and BA/JA/49-IV-56.

57. For the general responsibilities of the inspectors of religious Orders, see Georges Baccrabere, "Visite canonique du supérieur religieux," in R. Naz, ed., *Dictionnaire de droit canonique*, 7 vols. (Paris, 1935–65), 7: cols. 1595–1605.

58. *VMP*, 1: 52.

59. Ibid., 1: 47. The powers and duties of the Visitor are discussed further in the same source, esp. 47–52 and 165–66. See also Guy Philippart, S.J., "Visiteurs commissionaires et inspecteurs dans la Compagnie de Jésus de 1540 a 1615," *AHSI* 37 (Jan.–June 1968): 3–128, and 38 (Jan.–June 1969): 170–291.

TABLE 10.3

Ages of Visitors When First Appointed

Province or vice-province	Period 1	Period 2	Period 3
Portugal	42.8	62.5	—
Brazil	44.3	63.0	54.0
Maranhão	—	47.3	55.5
India[a]	42.0	51.6	53.5
Japan-China[b]	46.0	58.3	53.0

SOURCES: See note 62.

NOTE: Period 1 = 1566–1610 (Portugal); 1566–1607 (Brazil); 1568–96 (India); 1574–1611 (Japan-China). Period 2 = 1624–53 (Portugal); 1622–1702 (Brazil); 1667–83 (Maranhão); 1618–82 (India); 1616–1703 (Japan-China). Period 3 = 1716–25 (Brazil); 1717–55 (Maranhão); 1704–37 (India); 1703–71 (Japan-China).

[a] Visitors were responsible for both Goa and Malabar.

[b] See text.

Other qualifications of the men selected for those delicate assignments varied greatly. Valignano had served only a year as rector of Macerata when Mercurian summoned him to begin what turned out to be a 32-year career either as Visitor or as provincial in the Far East, a record that no other Visitor in the Assistancy ever matched. But Valignano was a doctor of civil law with a degree from the venerable University of Padua, and the general had in mind his legal training as well as his character when he made the assignment. Another who had undertaken legal studies was Cristóvão de Gouveia, Valignano's counterpart in Brazil and certainly one of that province's most notable Visitors. But Gouveia had already been rector of three colleges and vice-rector of another, as well as Visitor to Madeira and secretary to the provincial of Portugal, before being sent to Brazil to undertake what became a six-year visitation (1583–89). José de Seixas, who served as Visitor of Brazil about a century later than Gouveia, was 25 years older than his predecessor when he began that assignment. He was a professor of Latin, philosophy, and theology at the University of Évora and was then successively twice rector of Portuguese Peninsular colleges and provincial of Brazil before being designated to undertake that province's inspection. Another academician-turned-bureaucrat was Dr. Nicolas Pimenta (1546–1614), who taught at Évora for a number of years, then became rector of the College of Arts at the University of Coimbra, and later was procurator in Rome before being sent to India, where he undertook two visitations (*visitas*).

Pimenta's career suggests what may have been the single most important criterion applied in the selection of Visitors, namely, the trust they inspired. Trust may have counted for more than previous experience in the minds of the generals and the assistants as they strove to find the men best qualified to undertake the burdensome and sensitive assignments as Visitors. Abuse of the broad authority entrusted to them could cause serious embarrassment to the Society and deflect its subjects from their spiritual, educational, and other goals. Though many Visitors had been rectors on one or several occasions and some, particularly those who served in China and Japan, were also former provincials, a surprising number, including Ricci's translator Nicholas Trigault (see Chapter 6), had been delegates (that is, procurators) from their provinces to the Roman headquarters. The position of procurator, one of the few elective posts within the Society, was an especially demanding one, for a procurator was part ambassador, part fund-raiser, and part recruiter for his province.[60] Consequently, only persons who commanded the respect and confidence of their senior colleagues were likely to be selected for such duties. Pimenta possessed credentials that inspired Aquaviva's confidence: he was the son of a respected magistrate (*desembargador*) and alderman of Lisbon, he held a Ph.D. in theology from Évora, and he had served as chief administrator of the College of Arts at Coimbra for nine years and as procurator for his province in Rome.[61]

It is clear that place of birth was an important consideration in the selection of those assigned to serve as Visitors within this Assistancy. Out of 81 men who served as Visitors general, vice-Visitors, commissioners, or regional Visitors, only two were born overseas.[62] Both were Brazilians: one was the Bahian Bernabé Soares, who served briefly in Maranhão before it became a vice-province; the other was the Paulista Francisco de Toledo, whose tribulations in the same vice-province during the 1750s will be examined in the second volume of this study. The striking preference for appointees of European origin for this position reflects the marked Eurocentrism of the Society's leadership and its willingness to defer to the prejudices of the Portuguese crown, which, like that of Spain, was well known for its bias against colonial candidates for high office.[63]

Europeans who were not natives of Portugal or its empire were largely barred from such posts as well. The Portuguese crown and the interests that it represented also viewed with grave suspicion the naming of foreigners to positions of authority within its domain. Of course, the crown was not unique in harboring such hostility; the same was true of the governments of Spain and France. Except in the Far East, few foreigners served as Visitors in the Assistancy. True, Dr. Miguel de Torres served twice in the mid-sixteenth century as Visitor to the Portuguese province, and another Spaniard, Diego Mirón, held that office on one occasion, but these two were noted for executing Loyola's order to purge the Portuguese province of unfit members (see Chapter 11), and they were the last Spanish Visitors to function within the Portuguese domain. Not even during the period of Spanish rule (1580–1640) did the Society dare to name Spaniards to undertake inspections of Portugal. During the crisis between the Society and the crown in the 1650s when, as already seen, a Visitor seemed urgently needed, no Portuguese candidate was acceptable because of the likelihood that he would possess ties with either the unitarists or the separatists. Given the continuing war with Spain, appointing a Spaniard was patently impossible. Accordingly, Jean Brisacier became the third of the three Frenchmen to draw that unenviable assignment, and, as already observed, Brisacier's principal task was not to conduct an inspection but to make peace with the obdurate king. The only other foreigner to serve as Visitor to Portugal, the

---

60. There was another type of official, also called a procurator, a financial and legal officer whose duties will be considered in Chapter 12.

61. Franco, *Coimbra*, 1: 491–98; *DI*, 17: 51*–52*.

62. The remarks that follow are based upon *ASCJ*; *CJPM*; *HCJB*, 2: 244, 489–93; 4: 225–32; 7: 8–131; 8 and 9: passim; *HCJAP*, 4:1, 170 n. 4; and *RJC*.

63. Henry III of France once rejected the appointment of a Frenchman as Visitor in his kingdom and insisted that Aquaviva name an Italian in his place. A. Lynn Martin reaches the unwarranted conclusion that the king objected because "it seemed improper for a French provincial to be named to France." *Henry III and the Jesuit Politicians* (Geneva, 1973), 199. There was absolutely nothing improper about such an appointment. The literature concerning Portuguese prejudice against colonial-born subjects attaining high office is extensive. E.g., C. R. Boxer, *The Portuguese Seaborne Empire, 1415–1825* (New York, 1969). See also Chapter 11 below.

Milanese Carlos António Casnedi (1721–24), seemingly gained his position because he had served for twenty years as the confessor of an immensely wealthy emigré, the admiral of Castile, a major benefactor of the China missions (see Chapter 14). When Casnedi allowed himself to be drawn into another quarrel with the crown, the results were his expulsion and the abandonment of the practice of periodic Jesuit visitations of Portugal.[64]

As already suggested, the ethnic pattern of Visitors was very different in the Far East, where 23 of the 41 Visitors and vice-Visitors were non-Portuguese. Significantly, only three of them, all Italians, were named before the mid-seventeenth century; but from the 1680s onward, only two Portuguese held either position, reflecting Portugal's declining control over the Japan and China missions (see Chapters 6 and 23).

Only one foreigner ever became Visitor to the province of Brazil, but his regime was both brief and tumultuous. Jacinto de Magistris was born in the Po Valley in the diocese of Cremona, best known for its fine-quality violins. He entered the Society at age 21 and was assigned to the province of Malabar, where he remained as a missionary for two decades and witnessed the collapse of that once-promising province. At the beginning of the 1660s he was sent as procurator to Rome, where he reported on the grim consequences of the collapse of Portuguese power in Ceylon and South India. The Genoa-born vicar general, Giovanni Paolo Oliva, who was soon to become father general, was so impressed by Magistris's zeal and seriousness of purpose that he decided that he was precisely the man needed to undertake the touchy assignment of Visitor of the Brazilian province, where a number of thorny problems that had been simmering for a long time urgently required solution. They included the final settlement of an embarrassing dispute between the colleges of Santo Antão and Salvador concerning the inheritance of Brazil's third governor-general, Mem de Sá, of which more will be said in a later chapter; the imposition of restrictions on the number of novices that could be admitted in Brazil; and the procurement of additional recruits in Europe.

Magistris's troubles began as soon as he reached Lisbon. To his chagrin, he discovered that the conde de Obidos, the viceroy-designate of Brazil, refused to see him because of a recently enacted law forbidding foreigners to serve as superiors of Brazil. That law did not prevent the queen mother from cordially receiving the Visitor, and eventually the conde and his wife agreed to do so as well, though the viceroy took care to see that he and the Visitor sailed in separate ships. Even before departing Lisbon, the Visitor, pursuant to his instructions from Oliva, began to assert his authority in ways that offended resident representatives of the Brazilian province. He directed that certain debts that the province owed to the provinces of Portugal and Japan be promptly settled. He supervised the signing of the final agreement by the two competing colleges concerning the Sá properties. He ordered certain reforms undertaken in the economic bureau of the Brazil province in Lisbon (see Chapter 12) and reprimanded its head for his unwillingness to purchase copies of certain Jesuit chronicles for the province.

Magistris left Lisbon for Salvador on 19 April 1663 with a Portuguese companion and nine Italian fathers. Simão de Vasconcelos, an old Brazil hand and former provincial, sailed in a second vessel with another ten missionaries. Both contingents arrived in Brazil's capital

64. *HCJAP*, 4:1, 438.

less than three months later, and the Visitor immediately stirred up discontent by expressing disapproval of the program of studies designed for novices in the local college and criticizing both Vasconcelos and the current provincial, José da Costa, for having admitted an excessive number of Brazilian novices. Magistris directed certain fathers holding positions of authority in the city to withdraw to the missions and replaced them with men satisfactory to him. And when members of the college community, contrary to the admonitions of several generals, informed persons outside of the Society about their troubles with the Visitor, he rebuked them severely.

Word of the distress of Brazilian-born sons of the Society filtered down to the south, where the provincial, the Sicilian-born José da Costa, was on an inspection trip. He immediately returned to Salvador, where he convoked a meeting of six elder Jesuits, read them a decree enacted by the Ninth General Congregation (1649) that stated that a provincial or Visitor could be deposed when there was evidence that he was physically or mentally incapable of exercising his authority, and persuaded his colleagues that Magistris was an apt candidate for deposition. After five votes, they concurred, and on 22 September 1663 the provincial informed not only his fellow Jesuits but others in the capital that the Visitor had been removed from his office because of mental incapacity.

The "Jacintada," as this episode is known in Brazilian history, understandably infuriated Oliva, elected general on 31 July 1664. Nine weeks after his election, Oliva addressed a stinging rebuke to the cabal and denounced their action as, according to the paraphrase of Fr. Serafim Leite, "seditious, precipitate, temerarious, unjust, invalid, scandalous, and incongruous." He removed from office those who had supported the coup and insisted that Magistris, who had returned briefly to Lisbon and then sailed on to Genoa, retained his full authority. Oliva gave the Visitor the option of returning to Brazil or going back to India. Magistris preferred the latter and died on the subcontinent in 1668. Meanwhile, in 1665, Oliva named Gaspar Alvares, rector of Coimbra, as the new provincial and appointed Antão Gonçalves, a respected professor at the University of Évora and a future provincial and later an assistant, as commissioner and Visitor, charged with carrying out the assignment formerly entrusted to Magistris.[65]

Whether the "Jacintada" was simply a symptom of the crisis in leadership in the Portuguese empire in the mid-seventeenth century, as Leite suggests, whether it arose because Magistris lacked requisite tact, or whether it stemmed from the personal dislike of a Sicilian for a man from Cremona remains unclear to this day. It would seem that Oliva was ill advised to send a man who had no experience either as an administrator or as a missionary in Brazil on such a difficult venture.

Certainly the reception accorded Magistris was frigid compared with that enjoyed by many Visitors, whose arrival was traditionally an occasion for celebration. When Nicolas Pimenta visited the province of Malabar in 1610, an "academy" was held in the college of Cochin in his honor. The actors, garbed in costumes estimated to have cost thousands of *cruzados*, performed a "dialogue" on Christian doctrine that was apparently edifying to their audience. Fernão Cardim accompanied Cristóvão de Gouveia

65. Fr. Leite's account of the "Jacintada" (*HCJB*, vol. 7, bk. 1, chap. 2, based upon a large file in ARSI, FG, 721:II) is a magisterial summary. See also *HCJAP*, 3:2, 165 and 181–82.

to Brazil and provides excellent testimony of the Visitor's enthusiastic reception during his travels and his close spiritual relationship with the communities of the houses that he visited.[66]

Behind such external marks of respect, however, there often lurked suspicion, misgivings, and concealed hostility, for the Visitors were, by design, fault-finders who were enjoined by the generals to insist upon the elimination of signs of laxity and upon strict compliance with every detail of the Institute regardless of local conditions. Their appearance was also resented because, in the cases of Brazil, India, and even the province of Portugal until the later sixteenth century, they were newcomers. Indeed, Mercurian named Valignano, an Italian, partly because he had no previous connection with the Jesuits in Portugal or in the Far East. Valignano was almost gleefully aware of the animosity that his appointment generated: "I see clearly that this independent status ... carrying such wide powers with it, is highly displeasing to them ... it is a bitter pill, which they find it hard to swallow, that control of India is taken out of their hands."[67]

Even though Nicolas Pimenta had spent a decade and a half in India before undertaking his visita of Malabar in 1610, he was still considered an outsider. The Italian founder of the province, Alberto Laerzio, protested to Aquaviva that

> Fr. Visitor has changed at will, without seeking anybody's advice ... [all of my appointments]. The personnel of the college of Cochin has been partially changed, beginning with the Rector. All the consultores of the Province have been changed. Your Reverence will understand that there are objections to a manner of government so absolute. ... The Visitor has ordered the courses of Philosophy to begin in November, instead of June. Fr. Levanto was rector of São Tomé [de Meliapor]. He was *persona grata* to the king of [Vijayanagar] and to the bishop of Meliapor, and was endeavoring to maintain the Christian Community in Chandragiri and Vellore. Fr. Visitor has replaced him with Fr. de Sá. Foolishness.

Laerzio's strong admirer, the Catalan archbishop of Cochin, was in full agreement with the provincial's criticism of Pimenta: "Fr. Visitor has taken the wrong road; and if he continues along it, he will not come to a good end." A year later the provincial again lamented: "Fr. Visitor does not love us much. In two years he has taken ten padres and six brothers for Goa and has given us only five fathers and five brothers [in return]."[68]

The effectiveness of a Visitor depended upon many factors, including the extent of support he received from headquarters, his tact, the respect he earned, his energy, his sense of dedication, and his administrative talent, as well as the cooperation he obtained and the duration of his assignment, which automatically ended with the death of the general who had appointed him. The most successful Visitor east of the Cape of Good Hope no doubt was the oft-mentioned Alessandro Valignano, who did much to encourage the Japan enterprise, to rationalize the Society's administration in the East, and to seek effective ways to provide for the economic security of the Society's enterprises there.[69] Cristóvão de Gouveia rendered

66. F/*JM*, 1: 282; Fernão Cardim, *Tratados da terra e gente do Brasil*, ed. Rudolfo Garcia (Belo Horizonte, 1980), 143, 151, 165, and 167.

67. *VMP*, 1: 82.

68. F/*JM*, 1: 283.

69. Valignano's career warrants further study. The late Fr. Schütte's two volumes (*VMP* 1 and 2) are indispensable, but they reach only to 1582.

comparable service to the Brazil province. Together with his secretary, Fernão Cardim, he tirelessly visited each Jesuit house, renewed vows, heard confessions, went to missions and sugar estates, and sought to reconcile conflicts between planters and missionaries concerning the use of Amerindian labor (see Chapter 19). Like Valignano, Gouveia was profoundly concerned about the need for stable financial support for the province; like other early Visitors, he left behind meticulous rules for the governance of the houses of the province.[70] In Portugal, the aged but still energetic Visitor João Alvares (1610–13) not only visited most of his province but prepared more than 200 pages of detailed instructions for its spiritual and material welfare.[71] But many other Visitors seemingly left no impact upon the provinces or vice-provinces they inspected.[72] Whether, on balance, many of the inspections were worth the commotion they sometimes caused remains to be determined.

The hierarchy described in this chapter included the most visible members of the Society—those with whom important outsiders, especially royal officials and other ecclesiastics, were likely to be in contact. Most of the officers of the Society were mature men in their forties, fifties, and sixties, chosen for their posts because of their previous experience, their perceived piety, and their personal connections. They were predominately European by birth and by training. In the Portuguese Assistancy, a large proportion of the leaders were natives of Portugal. Their selection reflected not only the preponderance of Portuguese members in the Assistancy but also the deference of the Roman headquarters to the xenophobia of the rulers of Portugal. Only in the Far Eastern missions, the farthest removed from the centers of Portuguese authority, did other Europeans gain a large share of the senior administrative positions.

Toward the end of the sixteenth century, one longtime provincial lamented that he had been a Jesuit for 29 years but a subject for only three. It is improbable that many joined the Society with the expectation of becoming career administrators, but in this Assistancy, and probably in the others as well, a striking number of men became professional managers, moving almost continuously from one administrative assignment to another, often after having spent little time as educators or missionaries. Though a few eventually returned to apostolic labors, many careerists died in harness, exhausted after long administrative service.[73]

The hierarchy to which this select group belonged did not always function as smoothly as the designers of the Society had intended. When the Jesuit managers were required to define the meaning of the Society's famous motto—"For the greater glory of God"—they were inclined to do so narrowly, in terms of the interests of the immediate jurisdiction

70. Gouveia's inspection is discussed extensively in *HCJB*, 1: s.v. index, and 8: 279–83. See also J. Manuel Espinosa, "Gouveia: Jesuit Lawgiver in Brazil," *Mid-America* 24 (Jan. 1942): 27–60. The ordinances that he left, "O que pareceo ao p.ᵉ visit.ᵒʳ Christóvão Gouveia ordenar na visita deste coll.º [Salvador] da Baya 1 de janeiro de [15]89," are in ARSI, FG, XVIII, *Collegia*, 1369/7.

71. "Visita da provincia de Portugal pelo P. Joao' Aluarez," in ANTT/AJ, *antiga cx.* 1, *m.* 5.

72. E.g., see the comment of Johan Philipe Betendorf concerning the inspection of Pedro de Pedrosa (1679–81) in Maranhão. *HCJB*, 4: 226.

73. Cf. J. C. H. Aveling, *The Jesuits* (rpr., New York, 1987), 236. For some further examples, see *RJC*, 285–86 for the career of Tomé Vaz in China, and Humbert, "Catalogus patrum," 355, for the administrative profiles of Manuel da Silva and Eusebio de Matos. The manuscript personnel catalogues in ARSI provide many other cases.

to which they were tied, rather than broadly, in terms of the larger goals of the Society. One of the tasks of the fathers general, sometimes shared by the general congregations, was to remind every member what those goals were. But although there was more dissent within the Society than is sometimes recognized, there was widespread agreement on many issues, particularly those pertaining to whom the Society ought to admit and whom it should exclude.

CHAPTER 11

Recruitment for an Enterprise:
The Pertinacity of Eurocentrism

Send many to India, for they will greatly enlarge the boundaries of Holy Mother Church.

> —Xavier to Simão Rodrigues, Cochin, 27 Jan. 1545

This land is so vast that a hundred thousand fathers would not be sufficient to catechize everyone.

> —Joannes da Beira to [Loyola], Malacca, ca. Aug. 1547

The harvest is great but much is lost because of the scarcity of reapers.

> —António Pires to the brothers of the Society in Portugal,
> Pernambuco, 2 Aug. 1551

The number of religious that the Company possesses in these three provinces [Goa, Malabar, and Japan] is almost 600; although that appears to be a lot, they are very few in comparison with those necessary for the doors of that immense heathenism that are open and continue to open daily to receive the gospel. Even if all the colleges and houses of the Company in Europe were to be emptied and their members sent here, they would be insufficient for the great harvest represented by the innumerable multitude of people in [this so-called] ant hill of the world; for which reason those already there continually ask those here for more companions.

> —Fernão Guerreiro, 1601

WITHIN THE IMMEDIATE decades after its founding, the Society of Jesus became a victim of its own success, for its leaders were beset by far more requests for service than they could fulfill, given the limits of existing manpower, their Eurocentric attitudes toward suitable recruits, and their restricted financial resources. For centuries, the Society's leadership grappled with the problem of how to expand its personnel discretely in order to meet perceived evangelical challenges without diluting the quality of that personnel and thereby risking the loss of support by the European elites upon whom the Order so heavily depended. The spectacular growth of the overseas salients of the Portuguese Assistancy provided one challenge that the Society never fully met. Appeals for additional helpers there had to be balanced with requests for orators, teachers, apostles, and confessors within Europe itself and elsewhere abroad.

Initially the province of Portugal bore the full burden of furnishing manpower for the expanding assistancy, and it continued to supply a large share of the personnel who served overseas throughout the period embraced by this study. Almost as soon as the provinces of Goa and Brazil were formed, their superiors and subordinates began to bombard the home province with requests for additional hands to meet the seemingly limitless challenge posed by multitudes of red, black, brown, and yellow peoples who appeared to be "ripe" for harvest by emissaries of the True Faith.[1] The provincials responded as best they could by dispatching recruits as quickly as they became available. But they were restricted in their ability to comply with all the appeals they received. The province of Portugal itself was never large: its membership stood at 350 in 1560, 665 in 1615, 701 in 1690, and 818 in 1754 (see Appendix D). Some members were attached to colleges in Coimbra and Évora that were intended to provide missionaries for overseas service. But others belonged to colleges founded to educate members of the local elite to serve immediate, not remote, needs. Nor was every young Jesuit in Portugal anxious to leave familiar places for distant lands with the attendant risks of travel and of life in a hostile environment. That is evident from the Nadal questionnaire discussed in Chapter 2. The responses suggest that during the formative period of the enterprise, only a small minority of the recruits came into the Society because of a desire to serve mankind either at home or abroad.

To be sure, enthusiasm for overseas service vastly increased after the 1560s, as reflected by the 15,000 applications to the generals for such assignments in Jesuit archives.[2] Such interest was stimulated by the publication of missionary accounts of exotic peoples and places, of triumphs and tragedies, and of opportunities to serve God more actively than seemed possible in Europe. The carefully sanitized annual letters prepared by deputies of the provincials and published by the Society were partly intended to help with recruiting. So were the energetic campaigns undertaken throughout Europe by zealous provincial procurators such as Brazil's Inácio de Azevedo, India's Alberto Laerzio, and China's Nicholas Trigault.

For some, permission to serve in a distant mission came only after years of waiting and prayer and must have seemed to be the fulfillment of a dream. It was so for Alexander of Rhodes. He states that he felt destined for Japan while he was still a novice: "I began laying plans for Japan at the very time the persecution began there. I presented a memorandum to that effect to . . . Aquaviva. . . . I continued to importune his successor . . . Mutio Vitelleschi throughout my four years of theology . . . [and] made a pilgrimage to Loreto seeking the intervention of the Virgin." On Easter Sunday in 1618, Vitelleschi summoned Rhodes to his quarters. The general informed him that he had prayed at length on the matter and had decided to accede to his wishes.[3] Three years later, Jerónimo Lobo, a student at Coimbra,

---

1. *HCJB*, 2: 424–29.

2. Ernest J. Burrus, S.J., "Research Opportunities in Italian Archives and Manuscript Collections for Students of Hispanic American History," *HAHR* 31, 3 (Aug. 1959): 441. Unfortunately, few petitions by volunteers from this assistancy seem to have survived. A group of 65, dated 1611–1717, indicates 25 requests for posting in East Asia, 24 for India, and 11 for Brazil. Some members applied for such authorizations repeatedly, sometimes writing in the vernacular, sometimes in Latin. ARSI, FG, 757/II.

3. Solange Hertz, trans., *Rhodes of Viet Nam: The Travels and Missions of Father Alexander de Rhodes in China and Other Kingdoms of the Orient* (Westminster, Md., 1966), 3.

had a very different experience, one that suggests that assignment to a remote land could come about swiftly and without apparent warning:

> I was informed in Coimbra of my assignment to the India mission on the Friday before Low Sunday, April 16, 1621. . . . I was notified at a quarter to ten, and at three in the afternoon of the same day I left the College and began my journey. On the following Monday at midnight I arrived at the main door of Santo Antão. On Tuesday morning I was ordained a subdeacon. . . . On Wednesday and Thursday, [I was] ordained a deacon and priest. On the following Sunday I said my first Mass.[4]

In time, certainly by the generalate of Aquaviva, each province or vice-province assumed primary responsibility for augmenting its membership. But the parameters of who could be taken in, who must be weeded out, and who should be turned away were set by the leadership, a leadership that was exceedingly cautious and seemingly less concerned about the conversion of all of mankind than about the defense of the Society's public image. This chapter will examine those parameters and their impact upon the overseas branches of the Portuguese Assistancy.

The Exclusion of New Christians

Although both the General Examen and the *Constitutions* enumerate various impediments sufficient to deny admission to the Society, nowhere do they specifically mention Jews or New Christians.[5] During the early decades of the Society some New Christians attained important positions within the Order, the most notable being Diego Laínez, the second general who, as already noted, was one of the papal theologians present at the Council of Trent.[6] Paulo Ferreira, chancellor of the University of Évora, Vasco Baptista and Gaspar Vaz, both of whom held chairs in the same institution, Gonçalo Simões, who occupied the important post of master of novices at the University of Coimbra, and Inácio Tolosa, fourth provincial of Brazil, were New Christians, or at least were widely believed to possess that stain.[7] In the State of India, nearly a score of Jesuit priests and brothers of Jewish descent served, though most of them, like Henrique Henriques, were assigned to places of peril, such as the Fishery Coast or the Moluccas, rather than to places of relative comfort and security, such as Goa or Cochin.[8]

As observed in Chapter 5, during the seventeenth century the Jesuits in Portugal repeatedly championed the efforts of the New Christian community to gain exemption from the Holy Office and were popularly and derisively labeled "Jew lovers." In fact, they were anything but. Both Simão Rodrigues and Francis Xavier were strongly opposed to the admission of New Christians, as was Alessandro Valignano.[9] When the Third

4. *The Itinerário of Jerónimo Lobo*, trans. Donald M. Lockhart, ed. C. F. Beckingham, *HS*:2, no. 162 (1984): 1.

5. *CSJ(GE)*, chap. 2, pars. 22–31, and chap. 3, par. 41; *CSJ(C)*, pt. 1, chap. 3, 165–76.

6. Charles W. Reinhart, S.J., "An Apostle of Europe: Father James Laynez, S.J. (1512–1565)," *Woodstock Letters* 71 (1942): 153.

7. *HCJAP*, 2:1, 340; *HCJB*, 2: 443 and n. 2, 9: 162–63.

8. *S/FX*, 4: 368, 495 n. 104, and 540; Josef Wicki, S.J., "Die 'Cristãos-novos' in der Indischen Provinz der Gesellschaft Jesu von Ignatius bis Acquaviva," *AHSI* 46 (1977): 342–61.

9. *HCJAP*, 2:1, 336; *S/FX*, 4: 540; *VMP*, 1: 137.

General Congregation assembled in April 1573 to select a successor to Francisco Borgia, the odds-on favorite to become the next general was the Society's longtime secretary, Juan Polanco. As observed in Chapter 10, Gregory XIII, who opposed the election of still another Spaniard, was joined in his efforts by the Portuguese delegation, which opposed Polanco partly because its members believed him to be a New Christian. Both King Sebastian and Cardinal Henry implored the pope not to accept a New Christian for the position, contending that such an appointment would grievously harm the reputation and work of the Society.[10] In 1579, Everard Mercurian, the pope's choice, notified the provincial of Brazil that New Christians must not be admitted because of possible scandal to the Order.[11]

The Fifth General Congregation enacted a decree that reinforced Mercurian's order. After rejecting efforts by dissident Spaniards to curtail the general's authority and to augment that of the provinces, the victorious supporters of Claudio Aquaviva declared that most of the absent Spaniards were "false sons" of Jewish or Moorish ancestry, and not only banished them from the Society, but also stipulated that henceforth no one of such origins could become a member without special dispensation.[12] The following year, Frs. Baptista and Vaz were both sacked from their chairs at Évora, and Fr. Simões was removed from his position as master of novices. Although the next general congregation (1608) modified the exclusionary decree slightly, permitting persons with unblemished records who were five generations removed from New Christian ancestors to enter the Society, and although a few New Christians, such as Alexander of Rhodes and his brother, were granted exemptions, the Society continued to keep out most New Christians until 1946, when it abrogated the 1593 decree.[13]

Discrimination Against Colonial-Born Whites and Mixed Bloods

The Society's decision to bar New Christians reflected its willingness to yield to Iberian prejudices,[14] and the same was true of its skepticism concerning the qualifications of whites who had served many years abroad, those who had been born abroad, and those of mixed ancestry. Xavier himself doubted that creoles could be of much service to the Society. In his last letter to Simão Rodrigues, he wrote that those who had been received in India, including not only creoles but also European sojourners, were really only fit for domestic offices and as companions of priests trained in Europe, since they lacked adequate knowledge themselves to be ordained for the priesthood. Xavier, therefore, thought in terms of an expanding

10. *HCJAP*, 2:1, 345–61.

11. Ibid., 443 n. 2.

12. John W. Padberg, S.J., "The General Congregations of the Society of Jesus: A Brief Survey of Their History," *Studies in the Spirituality of Jesuits* 6, 1 and 2 (Jan.–Mar. 1974): 18; *HCJAP*, 2:1, 340. Remarkably, Fr. Rodrigues, writing during the 1930s, still approved of the 1593 decree. See esp. 2:1, 336 and 340–41.

13. Padberg, "General Congregations," 18. See also John Patrick Donnelly, S.J., "Antonio Possevino and Jesuits of Jewish Ancestry," *AHSI* 55 (Jan.–June 1986): 3–31. For the admission of the Rhodes brothers, see Hertz, *Rhodes of Viet Nam*, xii; and *RJC*, 215–16.

14. That decision was also in keeping with the position adopted by the Orders of friars since the late Middle Ages. For the development of anti-Semitism in their ranks, see the illuminating study by Jeremy Cohen, *The Friars and the Jews: The Evolution of Medieval Anti-Judaism* (Ithaca, N.Y., 1982), especially chap. 10.

enterprise staffed entirely by priests trained in Europe.[15] Alessandro Valignano also took a dim view of those born in India to Portuguese parents and urged that great caution be exercised in their admission because of the alleged defects of the subcontinent's climate and the shortcomings of their education.[16] Nevertheless, the personnel catalogue of 1584 reveals that 14.6 percent of the 350 members of the Society serving in the Estado da India and in Japan had been born in the empire. They included 2 subjects from Madeira, 3 from the Azores, 15 from Cochin, 32 from Goa, and 5 from Malacca; the remainder were from Ormuz, Bassein, and Chale.[17]

Valignano's opposition to the admission of colonials was shared by Mercurian and Aquaviva, as well as by Francisco Cabral, the sometime provincial of Goa, and other administrators in India. Their opposition applied not only to colonial-born whites but especially to most Eurasians.[18] These prejudices persisted well into the next century. In 1648, for example, D. Afonso Mendes, erstwhile patriarch of Ethiopia, urged the general to dispatch a Visitor to India to undertake urgently needed reforms, and recommended that "very few individuals should be admitted to the Society here, because all our ills originate with this rabble, since they have very little learning and a great deal of envy and hatred against those of us who came from Europe." As Charles R. Boxer reminds us, Mendes was reflecting a sentiment that peninsulars (Reinões) had long held regarding creoles (Indiáticos), whether lay or ecclesiastic. But it appears that both groups dipped their quills in the same venomous ink. A few years after Mendes wrote, Fr. Jerónimo Lobo, that much-traveled father whose odyssey has been mentioned before, averred that the Indiáticos sent false reports to Rome about their European colleagues and mocked them in broadsides and satires. Having served as the superior of several houses between Goa and Bassein, he came to the conclusion that the creoles lacked adequate theological qualifications and that their only advantage over their European brethren was their knowledge of Indian tongues. Like Mendes, Lobo believed that the Society's enterprises in the East ought to be staffed primarily by European recruits.[19]

European Jesuits serving in Brazil adopted a similar position. The founding of the early colleges there—Salvador, Piratininga, and Olinda—led a number of students to seek admission to the Society. Although the first provincial congregation recommended against accepting Brazilian-born candidates in 1568, by the mid-1570s a few had gained admission.[20] In 1584, Visitor Cristóvão de Gouveia wrote Aquaviva that the Brazilians provided a useful service because of their knowledge of Indian languages and their acceptance by the Amerindians. His observations reflect his disagreement with Mercurian's decision in 1579 to bar further creole admissions. In 1596, Aquaviva not only reaffirmed his predecessor's policy, but also ruled that Portuguese who had merely resided in Brazil for many years were unsuitable candidates. Two years later the provincial delegation pleaded for the Society

15. S/*FX*, 4: 548. As noted in Chapter 3, Xavier recommended sending Flemings and Germans to Japan since they were accustomed to low temperatures and to other climatic adversities. Ibid., 447–48.

16. *VMP*, 1: 137.

17. *DI*, 13: 601–58.

18. *DI*, 11: 750; 16: 25*, 26*, 70, 230, and 370–72. In one instance, Valignano agreed to admit a Eurasian, Francisco Taveira, whose father was Portuguese and mother Chinese. Ibid., 16: 667–68.

19. C. R. Boxer, *Portuguese India in the Mid-Seventeenth Century* (Delhi, 1980), 16–17.

20. "Postulados na primeira congregação provincial do Brasil," Bahia, June 1568, in *MB*, 4: 465–68.

to admit Brazilian- and Portuguese-born sons and to consider admitting even mamelucos (half-breeds) and persons of Indian ancestry to the fourth degree. Aquaviva replied curtly that experience had shown that such groups were, in fact, unsuitable. Seemingly, both Mercurian and Aquaviva were convinced that those who had lived in Brazil were unable to adhere strictly to the vow of chastity and lacked sufficient dedication to remain in the Society. The latter point was underscored by Jacome Monteiro, secretary to Visitor Manuel de Lima, who calculated in 1610 that only six or seven of the Brazilians admitted to the Society had stayed until their deaths. Though Fr. Serafim Leite questioned the accuracy of that assertion, the real point is that Monteiro's conclusion went unchallenged by higher authorities in either Brazil or Rome.[21]

Persuaded that Brazilians were unsatisfactory material for the Society, Aquaviva's successors continued to prohibit or limit severely their entry. By the mid-seventeenth century, each provincial was permitted to accept no more than a dozen colonials during his triennium. It may be recalled that one of the issues that provoked the crisis with Visitor Magistris in 1663 was his condemnation of the liberalism of two provincials in the admission of Brazilians. Simão de Vasconcelos received 26 Brazilian novices; his successor, José da Costa, admitted another 18.[22]

It was José da Costa who responded forcefully to a complaint by the cámara of Bahia that Brazilian sons were not allowed to assume important posts in the Society to the same degree that Europeans were. He contemptuously dismissed the charge as the work of the devil and contended that regardless of their origins, all Jesuits were considered "sons of the Company" and were treated alike. He demonstrated which Brazilians then held leadership positions in the province:

> Who governs the college of São Paulo? Is it not Francisco Ribeiro, a son of this State? And who administers the college of Santos? Is it not Manuel Nunes, a son of Bahia? And who governs the college of Rio [de Janeiro]? Has not Francisco Madeira, a native of Pernambuco, just completed his term and been succeeded by Francisco de Avelar, a son of this State? And who is superior of Espírito Santo? Is it not Mathias Gonçalves, a son of this State? Who formerly was rector of the college of Pernambuco? Was it not Francisco Dias, a son of Porto Seguro? And who is his successor? Joam Pereira, a son of this Bahia. And who governs Recife? Is it not Diogo Machado, another son of this Bahia? Open your eyes and consider the basis for your complaint.[23]

The provincial went on to identify several Brazilians who held chairs in the colleges of Salvador and Rio de Janeiro. Whether all of those he mentioned were truly Brazilian-born cannot be fully verified.

Despite the Sicilian's efforts to dispel the notion that the Society was prejudiced against its Brazilian members, there is additional evidence for such a prejudice. An anonymous Jesuit document of the second half of the seventeenth century reveals its depths. As in the Far East, Brazilians were alleged to suffer from the shortcomings of a tropical climate, one that the writer noted had produced the savage Amerindian. Brazilians were, therefore, considered to be both physically and mentally inferior to Europeans. Furthermore, instead

21. *HCJB*, 2: 432–36.
22. Ibid., 36–37.
23. Provincial to cámara, n.d. [ca. 1665], in ARSI, *Bras.*, 9.

of being suckled at their mothers' breasts, as was customary in Europe, Brazilians were nursed by blacks and mulattas, whose milk was claimed to be inferior. European sons were brought up by strict fathers who maintained discipline over their offspring, whereas Brazilian fathers were notoriously lax in the formation of their children's characters. In a land where lasciviousness was considered the norm, there seemed to be a strong likelihood that Brazilians suffered from blood corrupted by probable African or Amerindian antecedents and by possible exposure to syphilis. Finally, whereas in Europe the Society was able to attract recruits from members of the titled nobility, most Brazilians were, after all, plebeians.[24]

Many Jesuits subscribed to such convictions, which reflected the views held by most Europeans at the time, and did not attempt to modify them. But others, especially Brazilian-born members of the Society, actively sought to combat that prejudice. For example, the provincial congregation that met in Salvador in 1660 memorialized their general, Goswin Nickel (1652–64), to relax the triennial quota. Nickel responded that he found no compelling reason to overturn a policy firmly set by his predecessors. By 1679, however, Nickel's successor, Giovanni Paolo Oliva, did agree that for a five-year trial period the number of Brazilians who might be admitted could be increased until they equaled the number dismissed during those years. One of his successors, Tirso Gonzalez de Santalla (1687–1705), the last Spanish-born general of the old Society, relaxed admission standards even further, at least in theory, when he ruled that candidates who were mamelucos or mestiços beyond the fourth degree could be taken in, provided that they demonstrated appropriate deportment and came from "definite and ancient" noble stock.[25] But few superiors were willing to risk a repetition of the bizarre career of Manuel de Morais (see Chapter 9), so the number of those of mixed Indian and white ancestry admitted for the balance of the period was probably negligible.[26]

Despite their alleged handicaps, the percentage of Brazilian-born members of the Society in the province of Brazil gradually increased from 14.5 (1574) to 37.2 (1698) and to 45.3 (1732), but it is unlikely that Brazilian-born members ever became a majority, as colonial-born (creole) members did in both Peru and Mexico at the time of the expulsion (1767).[27] Comparable gains were not registered in the vice-province of Maranhão. There, the percentage of Brazilian-born members actually declined from 11.4 (1697) to only 4.7 (1740), in part because the Society's leadership repeatedly refused to sanction the establishment of a novitiate, even though local administrators contended that it would be far cheaper to train candidates in the vice-province than to import recruits trained in Europe.[28] Oddly enough, by 1760, only 20.5 percent of the Jesuits serving in the two Indian provinces had been born in the colonies, whereas half of them had originated in Brazil.[29]

24. *HCJB*, 7: 233–35, which is based upon ARSI, *Bras.*, 3:II, 294–294^v.

25. *HCJB*, 7: 238–39.

26. Ibid., 5: 363–69.

27. According to the calculations of David Block, creoles represented 63% of the members of the province of Peru and 62% of those serving in New Spain in 1767: *Mission Culture on the Upper Amazon: Native Tradition, Jesuit Enterprise, and Secular Policy in Moxos, 1660–1880* (Lincoln, Neb., 1994), 106, table 9.

28. *HCJB*, 7: 240. For the generals' refusal to authorize the novitiate, see ibid., 4: 235–36.

29. Ioanne [John] Humbert, S.J., "Catalogus patrum et fratrum Societatis Iesu ex India anno 1760 expulsorum," *AHSI* 31 (July–Dec. 1962): 324–59.

The Thorny Issue of the Admission of Nonwhite Clergy

Theoretically, missionaries ought to work themselves out of a job. If their endeavors are wholly successful, the seed of the faith is firmly planted and thereafter can be nourished by a carefully trained indigenous clergy rather than by outsiders. But in the centuries surveyed here, there existed a wide gap between theory and practice.[30] Although the Jesuits devoted great efforts to the protection and conversion of the Amerindians, no priest, not even António Vieira, ever advocated their admission to the Society, nor, for that matter, did any spokesman of any other Order in Brazil or elsewhere in the Americas.[31] Partly because of their own involvement in black slavery and (to some degree) in the slave trade itself, and partly because of Iberian biases against persons of African origins, the Jesuits likewise excluded Africans from membership in their Order.[32]

In Portuguese India, the seminary of the Holy Faith, founded in 1541, was a pioneer effort to train an indigenous clergy. As noted in Chapter 3, the Jesuits soon acquired control of that facility, which was housed on the grounds of the original St. Paul's. Some of its African and Asian graduates were ordained as secular priests; others became catechists and auxiliaries in the religious Orders. But Xavier gloomily reported to Ignatius at the beginning of 1549 that "experience" had demonstrated that Indians were unfit to join the Society, a view that the seminary's first Jesuit rector fully shared.[33] Ignatius, however, remained more sanguine, and the year before his death suggested that "of the boys who are being educated in the college . . . those who are more talented and stronger in the faith, better behaved and more presentable, could be admitted . . . although, because they come from infidelity, they should be more tried than the others; nevertheless they should not . . . be welcomed less heartily."[34] That suggestion seems to have fallen upon deaf ears. Still, Francisco Borgia directed Gonçalo Alvares, the first Visitor in the East, to determine whether "some of those nations are worthy to be admitted to the Company."[35] The Visitor responded cautiously: "Experience has taught us that it is not now convenient to admit the natives of the land into the Society . . . even if they are mestiços. The Superiors of

30. Hubert Cieslik, S.J., "The Training of a Japanese Clergy in the Seventeenth Century," in J. Roggendorf, S.J., ed., *Studies in Japanese Culture* (Tokyo, 1963), 41–78.

31. Ignácio de Azevedo to Borgia, Bahia, 19 Nov. 1556, in *MB*, 4: 368; see also *HCJB*, 2: 429–30.

32. In Bahia, in deference to the prejudices of white families, the local Jesuit college also barred mulattoes from attending certain classes. After the mulattoes protested that they were not excluded from taking courses at Coimbra or Évora, the Overseas Council urged that they be admitted in Bahia, and Pedro II so ordered. Consulta of 30 Jan. and alvará of 28 Feb. 1689, in AHU/PA/BA, 1st cat., cx. 16; see also *CCLP*, 10: 187. For Jesuit advocacy of seminaries for black clergymen in Angola, see C. R. Boxer, *The Church Militant and Iberian Expansion, 1440–1770* (Baltimore, 1978), 8–9. The intent, never realized, was to train an inferior indigenous clergy to serve as parish priests, but the Jesuits did not offer to assume responsibility for such training or to accept such ecclesiastics within their own ranks. Although Dominicans in East Africa admitted a few blacks, the Jesuits never did.

33. Xavier to Ignatius, 12 Jan. 1549, in S/*FX*, 4: 338 n. 18; António Gomes to Ignatius, Cochin, 16 Jan. 1551, in *DI*, 2: 176.

34. Carlos Merces de Melo, S.J., *The Recruitment and Formation of the Native Clergy in India* (Lisbon, 1955), 165.

35. Ibid., 166 n. 1, where the instruction is undated. I have not found the original. Borgia's instructions to Alvarez, dated 10 Oct. 1567 and 7 Jan. 1569, in *DI*, 7: 304–13 and 627–29, do not mention such possible admissions.

the other Orders are strongly of the same opinion. Still, I am convinced that if they are well trained and indoctrinated, some could assist the Ordinary, and eventually we may even be able to admit a few since Christ our Lord died for us all."[36] Six years later Pero Luís, a Christian Brahman, was ordained as a member of the Society. Ironically, in the same year Alessandro Valignano reported that neither Africans nor Indians appeared to have any chance of qualifying for ordination (see Chapter 3). It was apparently on the basis of Valignano's pessimism that Mercurian decided in 1579 to bar both Asians and Eurasians from entry, a policy that Aquaviva reaffirmed six years later.[37] Although Fr. Luís served meritoriously until his death in 1596 and begged the general to admit additional Indians, even if the trial period were to be doubled, he was the only one ever to become a priest in the old Society.[38] Where the Jesuits led, others followed: by the early seventeenth century, the Franciscans and other Orders had also erected color bars, which remained in place until at least the late eighteenth century.[39]

Even though entry into the Orders in India was denied, it was possible for a determined, resourceful, high-caste Indian to be ordained in Rome. One who succeeded not only in doing so but also in being designated a bishop in India was the famous Christian Brahman Matias de Castro (b. ca. 1594–d. 1677). Born on the island of Divar near Goa, Castro studied Latin and grammar for five years at the Franciscan seminary of Reis Magos above Aguada Bay. Although strongly recommended for ordination by the vicar general of the Carmelites and the archdeacon, he was denied priestly orders by the archbishop of Goa, who had vowed never to ordain a Brahman. Castro then traveled to Rome, where he was befriended by Monsignor Ingoli, the powerful secretary of the Sacred Congregation of the Propaganda of the Faith, created by Gregory XV in 1622 to oversee the missions beyond Europe. Castro not only was ordained but also obtained a doctorate in theology at the Collegio Urbano in the Eternal City. In 1637 D. Matias, by then bishop of Chrysopolis, returned to India as vicar-apostolic of Bijapur, the first representative of the Propaganda Fide in India; but Portuguese authorities refused to honor his credentials, contending that they had been fraudulently obtained. Among Castro's adversaries in Goa was the venerable ex-patriarch, D. Afonso Mendes, who dismissed him as "a bare-bottomed Nigger," to quote Charles R. Boxer. D. Matias responded in various memorials to Rome that the Jesuits were the most detestable of God's creatures and were responsible for the ruin of Christianity in the subcontinent. He also criticized them for erecting colleges that were nominally for Indians but restricting their graduates to domestic service and denying them opportunities for advanced studies because of their alleged intellectual deficiencies, a charge he denied by pointing out his own intellectual attainments, including the mastery

36. Alvarez to Borgia, Goa [Dec. 1568], in *DI*, 7: 573, also translated by C. R. Boxer, "The Problem of the Native Clergy in Portuguese India, 1518–1787," *History Today* 17, no. 11 (Nov. 1967): 774–75.

37. The order is quoted by Merces de Melo, *Recruitment and Formation*, 166 n. 2. See also Aquaviva to Valignano, [18 Jan.] 1585, in *DI*, 14: 920.

38. C. R. Boxer, "The Problem of the Native Clergy in the Portuguese and Spanish Empires from the Sixteenth to the Eighteenth Centuries," in Geoffrey J. Cuming, ed., *Studies in Church History*, vol. 6, *The Mission of the Church and Propaganda of the Faith* (London, 1970), 89–90. For Fr. Luís's plea, see Luís to Aquaviva, Quilon, 2 Jan. 1589, in *DI*, 15: 219–20; but for continued Jesuit opposition to the admission of Indians from the subcontinent, see ibid., 13*, 118, par. 10, and 625.

39. Boxer, "Problem . . . in Portuguese India," 775.

of nine languages. But such arguments failed to sway Jesuit leadership or that of any of the other Orders.[40]

The malady that Fr. George Dunne appropriately labeled "the virus of Europeanism" was only slightly less virulent in the Japan and China enterprises.[41] It may be recalled that both Xavier and Valignano were convinced that the Japanese were particularly apt subjects for evangelization and that Valignano, knowing fully how much the Japan enterprise depended upon the labors of the dojuku, became a strong advocate of the admission of some Japanese to priestly orders in the Society. His views provoked strong opposition, however. As observed in Chapter 3, Francisco Cabral, onetime superior of the Japan mission, reversed his early positive views and doubted that the Japanese possessed adequate steadfastness to serve as priests. Celso Confalonieri, experienced master of novices, wrote in the mid-1590s that the Japanese were so young in the faith that none should be considered for admission for another half century. Likewise, two other veterans of Japan, Francesco Pasio, a future vice-provincial, and the interpreter João Rodrigues, urged great caution in accepting Japanese candidates. Partly because of such opposition and partly because of hostile political conditions within the archipelago after 1581, the elaborate educational structure envisaged by Valignano to train a native clergy did not begin to become operative until about 1600. The next year, two Japanese priests were welcomed by the Society; by 1614 there were fourteen Japanese priests in the islands, half of them Jesuits.[42] But their presence still caused grave doubts, and the Nagasaki congregation, which gathered in October of that year, recommended against ordaining more Japanese or admitting them to the Society as lay brothers. Five members of that group signed a memorandum that condemned the Japanese as secretive and insufficiently motivated for a religious vocation.[43]

A number of Japanese candidates accompanied Jesuit exiles to Macao that year. Whatever hopes they may have entertained for full admission into the Society were soon dashed. In 1618 the Visitor, Francisco Vieira, indicated that there were no plans to ordain them in the East and warned that if some "vagabonds" showed up in Rome they should be turned away: "To be a priest in Japan is considered a matter of honor and of profit ... self-conceit is their inborn nature; they are faddists addicted to novelties ... therefore, should they return to Japan as priests and, separated from [the European] priests of the Society, draw close again to their pagan relatives and friends ... [they might cause] great damage to the faithful in Japan."[44]

One of the "vagabonds" whom the Visitor had in mind was Pedro Casui Kibi, who, denied an opportunity to become a priest in the East, made his way to Rome in 1620. There he impressed Jesuit authorities with his qualifications and was ordained and received into the Society. A decade later he returned to his homeland via the Philippines and successfully served as a member of the Christian underground for nearly nine years, until

40. Memorial of 14 Dec. 1646, in ARSI, FG, 1443/9/23; Merces de Melo, *Recruitment and Formation*, 36–37, 154–55, and 215–20. For the quotation, see Boxer, *Church Militant*, 13.
41. Dunne, *Generation of Giants: The Story of the Jesuits in China in the Last Decades of the Ming Dynasty* (Notre Dame, 1962), 174. See also the index entry "Europeanism."
42. Cieslik, "Training," passim.
43. Dunne, *Generation of Giants*, 166.
44. George Elison, *Deus Destroyed: The Image of Christianity in Early Modern Japan* (Cambridge, Mass., 1973), 196–97.

he was unmasked by the apostate Cristóvão Pereira. Unlike that erstwhile Old Christian provincial, Pedro Casui Kibi died a martyr to his new faith. Even so, his example did not encourage Jesuit superiors to believe in the steadfastness of Japanese candidates for the Society. The catalogue of 1650 shows that out of 41 priests in the Japan province, only one was of Japanese birth.[45]

The record of the vice-province of China with respect to the admission of native-born Chinese to the Society was no better. Despite the paucity of European missionaries able to enter the empire during the late sixteenth and seventeenth centuries, Aquaviva ruled in 1606 that Chinese must not be ordained as members of the Society because they were too new to the faith. In vain did Niccolò Longobardo, Matteo Ricci's enthusiastic successor, protest that Chinese brothers had repeatedly demonstrated their loyal service to the Order and were as fit to enter it as were the Japanese or the Europeans themselves.[46] The first Chinese to become a priest was Fr. Gregorio Lopez (Lo Wen-tsao), ordained as a Dominican in 1654. Not for another ten years was a Chinese Jesuit, Emmanuel de Siqueira (or Cheng Ma-no Wei-hsin) (b. 1633–d. 1673), admitted.[47]

As Fr. Emmanuel, trained in Italy and in Portugal, was making his way by stages from Lisbon to Macao in the mid-1660s, the persecution in China was approaching its zenith (see Chapter 6), prompting the religious Orders there to debate the future of Christianity in the empire. One of the issues upon which the Orders seriously differed was the wisdom or necessity of further ordinations of Chinese. The Jesuits themselves were badly divided upon that question. On the one hand, the three fathers confined to the court of Peking in 1664 (see Chapter 6)—the Belgian Verbiest, the Portuguese Magalhães, and the Italian Ludovicio Buglio—were in agreement that the faith could not possibly prosper without the aid of Chinese catechists and priests. They conceded that the Chinese had great difficulty mastering Latin (just as Europeans did Chinese) but urged that Rome sanction a simplified Latin form of the most important Masses and honor its long-standing promise to approve the saying of Mass in Chinese.[48] These so-called court Jesuits recommended that candidates for the priesthood be restricted primarily to scholar-gentry or literati and, given the perilous state of Christianity in the empire at that time, requested permission to ordain several as soon as possible. The Macao Jesuits and those detained with members of the other Orders in Canton, on the other hand, strongly disagreed. Their spokesman was the aged António de Gouveia (b. 1592–d. 1677), who had served in the empire since 1636 and would soon become vice-provincial.[49] All his experience led him to the conclusion that the Chinese were unsuitable for the priesthood or for admission to the Society because they were so "full of vices, irresolute, and inconstant." The hard-liners were convinced that, as priests, the immoral Chinese would bring ruin to the faith.

45. *MHJ*, 1068–81. A seventeenth-century instruction to the economic procurators of the Japan province warned them against engaging a Japanese companion or loaning money to persons of Japanese ancestry because of the possible loss of respect for the Society. BA/JA/49-V-8, no. 94, fols. 635–49.

46. Dunne, *Generation of Giants*, 164.

47. Francis A. Rouleau, S.J., "The First Chinese Priest of the Society of Jesus, Emmanuel de Siqueira, 1633–1673," *AHSI* 28 (Jan.–June 1959): 3–50, a model of historical detection.

48. The basic study of the problem of the Chinese liturgy is François Botinck, C.I.E.M., *La Lutte autour de la liturgie chinoise aux 17e et 18e siècles* (Louvain, 1962). See also Dunne, *Generation of Giants*, chap. 10.

49. For his career, see *RJC*, 115–16.

Their views were effectively rebutted by the Belgian François de Rougement (b. 1624–d. 1676), who had been in China only a dozen years before he submitted a forceful statement in behalf of Chinese candidates.[50] He contended that even if the government relaxed the persecution and the faith were permitted to thrive, maintaining the enterprise would require the services of far more priests than Europe could provide or than the empire would permit to enter. De Rougement condemned negative stereotypes of the Chinese, observing that throughout its history Christianity had always coped with some who were corrupt, weak, and unreliable. He argued that for eight decades Chinese catechists and converts had repeatedly demonstrated their steadfastness in the faith despite the suffering to which they had been subjected. Then he came to the crux of the issue, which so many nay-sayers in India, Japan, China, and elsewhere conveniently chose to ignore: "Are we, then, more engaged with maintaining our authority than with maintaining and spreading the Faith?" But De Rougement was no radical: he simply urged only that elderly catechists and lay brothers who had demonstrated loyal service for many years be considered for the priesthood.

That was the position that the Sicilian Prospero Intorcetta took when he arrived in Rome in 1672 as procurator of the vice-province. He urged Giovanni Paolo Oliva to permit the induction into the Society of well-screened men of proper lineage (that is, the scholar-gentry or literati class) who possessed unblemished records of service and were over the age of 40. Oliva directed that a small number of such candidates be admitted, provided that they met with the approval of the Visitor and two-thirds of the European missionaries.

Despite the relaxation of restrictions upon the exercise of Christianity by Emperor K'ang-hsi (see Chapter 6) and the persisting shortage of missionaries in the empire, the Jesuits applied Oliva's dictum with extreme caution. It was not until 1688 that three aged Jesuit catechists were ordained. They were followed by another pair four years later. But the Dominicans were even more reluctant to admit Chinese candidates to the priesthood. Despite the services performed by Fr. Gregório Lopez, no other Chinese priest was accepted by their Order until 1730. As late as 1739, there were still only eighteen Chinese priests in the empire, compared with 76 Europeans. Eleven of those eighteen were Jesuits. But even in the eighteenth century, prominent Jesuits in the empire continued to debate the desirability of admitting younger Jesuits to the Society. Whereas Ehrenbert Xavier Frideli, the Austrian-born rector of the Portuguese college of Peking, informed the general, Michelangelo Tamburini, that it was "absolutely necessary either to found seminaries in which young Chinese can be trained, or to allow the Chinese [priests] to administer the sacraments in their own language, or ... the mission will not be able to maintain itself, let alone expand, without a miracle," another veteran missionary, the Alsatian Romain Hinderer, Visitor in 1722, strongly opposed the training of young Chinese for the priesthood. Nor was a consensus achieved among Jesuits concerning the admissibility of Chinese to the Society during the remaining years of the old Order.[51]

50. Ibid., 232–33.

51. The foregoing relies primarily upon C. R. Boxer, "European Missionaries and Chinese Clergy, 1654–1810," in Blair B. Kling and M. N. Pearson, eds., *The Age of Partnership: Europeans in Asia Before Dominion* (Honolulu, 1979), 97–121.

The Problem of
Other Europeans Serving in the Assistancy

The fact that the Jesuits, like the other Orders, discriminated against the peoples of the host nations in which they served never aroused significant criticism from Portuguese authorities. What disturbed those officials far more, particularly after 1580, was the presence of non-Portuguese Europeans in Jesuit enterprises overseas. The founders of the Society, of course, did not consider their members as nationals after they entered the Order. As the provincial of France assured Henry III, his men were "all dead to the world," and the king could be assured of their love and respect regardless of their national origins.[52] Portuguese sovereigns, like France's Henry III, however, became convinced that the primary loyalty of foreign-born fathers remained with the rulers of the lands of their birth. Consequently, they became increasingly suspicious of other European religious in their overseas domains. Faced with urgent requests for additional hands in both the eastern and the western enterprises, the Portuguese delegates to the First General Congregation reminded their colleagues that Portugal was a small country and appealed to them for recruits from other provinces. The members of the congregation assured their brethren that they would help to the extent that they could. Three years later, in 1561, Fr. Nadal responded to a plea from Fr. Gonçalves da Câmara and wrote Laínez suggesting that robust but not terribly bright recruits who served no useful purpose in Germany would be very helpful in converting the heathen overseas.[53]

Initially the kings of Portugal raised no obstacles when the Society sought to send its subjects, regardless of nationality, to lands where the rulers insisted they possessed exclusive patronage (*padroado*) rights. As Table 11.1 indicates, nearly half of the missionaries who sailed east of the Cape of Good Hope during the reigns of John III, Sebastian, and Cardinal Henry came from other parts of Europe, and the same was true of more than a fifth of those who went to Brazil. The table also indicates that the Spanish provinces then furnished nearly two-thirds of the foreigners assigned to Brazil and to the Estado da India. In 1575, however, Lisbon received a report from an unnamed fortress captain in the East that Spanish missionaries there were urging Philip II to undertake the conquest of China, which Lisbon considered within its sphere of influence. The court immediately became alarmed. Fr. Alessandro Vallareggio, the missions procurator, wrote Mercurian that Lisbon considered prejudicial to its interests the presence of Spanish fathers in India, China, the Moluccas, and Brazil, and that in the future the court would license only Italians, Portuguese, and Germans to travel to the East and would not approve the dispatch of Spaniards, Frenchmen, or Englishmen to Brazil.[54] Although some Spaniards continued to sail from Lisbon to the eastern missions during Portugal's Philippine period, their number fell precipitously, and none went to Brazil after 1583. Their place was taken primarily by Italians, whose disunited land lacked overseas colonies, and secondarily by Germans, whose homeland also posed no threat to Portugal.[55] The Italians went primarily to the Malabar province and to China,

52. A. Lynn Martin, *Henry III and the Jesuit Politicians* (Geneva, 1973), 96–99.
53. *HCJB*, 2: 437.
54. Ibid., 439.
55. When Aquaviva learned in 1601 that the Spanish government was attempting to ban Italians from service in the dual empire, he wrote a vigorous defense of their service and loyalty to the king and protested

TABLE 11.1

Non-Portuguese Jesuits Who Sailed to the Assistancy Overseas via Lisbon, 1541–1750

Period	Destination India^a (N)	Destination Brazil^b (N)	Percentage non-Portuguese India	Percentage non-Portuguese Brazil	Percentage of total Spanish India	Percentage of total Spanish Brazil	Percentage of total Italian India	Percentage of total Italian Brazil	Percentage of total German^c India	Percentage of total German^c Brazil	Percentage of total Other^d India	Percentage of total Other^d Brazil
1541–1580	226	164	45.1	21.3	28.3	14.6	12.4	3.7	—	—	4.4	3.0
1581–1640	701	138	36.2	10.1	4.4	0	26.8	9.4	0.9	0.7	4.1	0
1641–1706	627	332	24.0	9.3	0	0	15.2	4.5	3.8	0.6	4.5	4.5
1707–1750	506	264	22.7	6.0	0.4	0	12.2	3.0	8.5	2.3	0.7	0.7

SOURCES: *LJI*, 269–331; *HCJB*, 1: 560–72; 4: 333–59; and 6: 589–605.

NOTE: Totals for India do not include French Jesuits sent to Southeast Asia or to China beginning in the 1680s because they did not pass through Lisbon. Percentages do not always add up because of rounding.

^a That is, the State of India (Mozambique to Macao) as defined in the text.

^b Includes the province of Brazil (1549–1739) and the vice-province of Maranhão (1727–1750).

^c Also includes Austrians.

^d Includes French, Flemings, English, Irish, Swiss, and a few Asians.

and the latter also became the destination of most of the German fathers who sailed from Lisbon. In addition, there were small numbers of Austrians, Poles, Belgians, Swiss, and Flemings, a few Englishmen, and an occasional Irishman. The Restoration governments of John IV and Afonso VI severely reduced the number of foreigners permitted to travel overseas, and both Pedro II and John V continued to restrict the number of foreign Jesuits permitted to function beyond the kingdom, especially in Brazil.

The presence of foreigners in the Assistancy became a source of frequent complaint by Portuguese Jesuits and by royal officials. During the generalate of Everard Mercurian, there were several signs of hostility between Portuguese and Spanish fathers. Fr. Villareggio's concern has already been mentioned. In addition, sometime during the 1570s, the general's secretary, the Italian-born António Possevino, submitted to Mercurian a memorandum in which he urged the general to circularize the Society, exhorting its members to work together in union and charity without distinction between races and nations. The secretary clearly had in mind the Portuguese province, where there was considerable resentment over the prominence achieved by certain Spanish fathers, especially Miguel de Torres, who had held one post after another there from 1552 until 1578. Another who was concerned about Iberian disharmony was Jorge Serrão, provincial of Portugal from 1570 to 1574. Toward the end of his term, he acknowledged the existence of such factionalism, and he wrote Mercurian that he considered it to be of the utmost importance for the general to stress "the union among nations" and that for Jesuits "there must not be Italians nor Spaniards nor Portuguese but only perfection and the Company of Jesus." Since it was Mercurian himself who issued the 1579 order barring from membership in the Society both Brazilians and Asiatics, it seems unlikely that he effectively acted to reduce hostility between the Portuguese and their rivals.[56]

---

that their exclusion would seriously hurt the labors of the Society because neither Spain nor Portugal could provide the Assistancy with all the men that it urgently needed. Aquaviva to Philip III, 1601, in ARSI, FG, 1452/2.

56. *HCJAP*, 2:1, 332–33.

The union of the crowns in 1581 did not reduce the antipathy between Portuguese and Spaniards serving in the Assistancy. Despite Aquaviva's efforts to promote harmony between the two Iberian contingents, their hostility toward one another in the East became notorious.[57] The same was true in Brazil. In 1594, for example, the provincial of Brazil defended himself against criticism from Aquaviva, who censored him for naming only Portuguese as his appointees. The provincial observed that Portuguese subjects in the province resented the fact that a Spaniard, Inácio Tolosa, was rector of the college of Bahia and that several other Spaniards and an Italian held other positions of authority in the province. Three-quarters of a century later, Fr. José Soares, secretary to António Vieira, observed in a letter to a colleague in Portugal that though there were many potential recruits in Italy, caution should be exercised so that "at least half" of the missionaries in Brazil were always Portuguese, for if they were outnumbered by foreigners the situation would become reprehensible (*coisa muito repáravel*). In 1691, when a copy of that letter fell into the hands of Giovanni António Andreoni, secretary of the Brazil province and future author of a major economic treatise on Brazil, it added further fuel to his long-standing quarrel with Vieira himself. The next year, the provincial suggested that his province be reserved exclusively for Portuguese recruits and that Italians and Germans be restricted to the Asian missions, where most of the Jesuits serving were Portuguese.[58] For that reason the papal nuncio in Lisbon doubted that it would be convenient to mix the Portuguese with the Italians "because the genius of the two nations does not mesh well together, nor do the Portuguese view favorably Italian missionaries."[59]

The vice-province of China became another arena where Portuguese Jesuits quarreled with those of other nationalities. Their disapproval of the manner by which French Jesuits reached China during the 1680s has already been discussed (see Chapter 6).[60] Later the Germans also became targets. In 1750 Fr. António Gomes, the vice-provincial, observed, "It is incredible that the Germans govern here. Were it not for the religious patience I am obliged to maintain, I would be capable of uttering imprecations against those who sent so many here; however, for those already here there is no other remedy than patience. But in the future they should be kept in Europe."[61]

Colonial officers, notably the viceroys of India, shared the Portuguese Jesuits' hostility toward foreign-born missionaries. That aversion was particularly strong in the Malabar province, whose founder, the Italian-born Alberto Laerzio, brought back 31 Italians out of a contingent of 60 missionaries, and, to the chagrin of his Portuguese subjects, immediately assigned several Italians to administrative posts in the new province. Antonino Schipani became rector of Cochin; Nicholas Spinola, a member of a noble house that would contribute

57. *DI*, 16: 258–64, 402–8, 581–89; 17: 30, 191–200, and 243–44.
58. *HCJB*, 7: 97, 101–2.
59. *HCJAP*, 3:1, 136.
60. According to a listing of 1688, the nationalities of the 114 Jesuits who had "entered" China between Xavier (1552) and that date were: Portuguese (38), Italians (33), Germans (11), French (11), Belgians (9), Spaniards (6), Poles (3), and Other (3). In addition, the Dominicans had sent 31 Spaniards, Mexicans, and Italians between 1635 and 1681; the Franciscans, 20 Spaniards and Mexicans (1633–81); and the Augustinians, four Spaniards (1681–83), in addition to four secular priests who arrived in 1684. BA/JA/49-IV-66, fols. 62ᵛ–66.
61. *HCJAP*, 3:2, 136.

a martyr to Japan, was superior of Quilon; Fr. Levanto held the same post at São Tomé de Meliapor; and several other Italians also occupied conspicuous positions.[62] In 1619 the Visitor, André Palmeiro, wrote the assistant,

> They will tell you that some Portuguese do not get on well with the Italians ... one thing which I often hear and which I see with my own eyes, is a source of discord. It is generally believed that the Italians write to Rome to complain about the Portuguese for every little trifle.... When Fr. General sends his advice, they are even more convinced that this is so, and they say, "If you wish to live in peace, venerate the Italians." The matter is deplorable; but they are not cured; rather they get angry with all these advices from Rome.... It is being said that Fr. Laerzio will bring orders from Rome ... that the higher Superiors will be Italians. Have they not this year made an Italian rector of Colombo?[63]

The quarreling between the Italians and the Portuguese in the province persisted. In 1630 the conde de Linhares reported that the Jesuits there were divided into two camps (*bandos*); the dominant one was the foreign-born, but the other camp, the Portuguese, was supported by the bishop of Cochin. The count declared that the Jesuits of Goa behaved themselves better than those of Malabar because they were Portuguese. The obstreperous ones, he said, were those in the south, especially the Italians and the Flemings, "who are more sovereign on the [Fishery] Coast than the king," a charge that the missions procurator for India stoutly denied.[64] Toward the end of the century, another viceroy reported the arrival of a French squadron bearing half a dozen Jesuits, mostly foreigners. He expressed misgivings about them because "wherever the Portuguese fathers of the Company serve they are well accepted with friendship and harmony; however, when they are mixed with Flemings everything degenerates into affronts, distrust, and commotion."[65]

The crown was not unmindful of these concerns and repeatedly acted to exclude foreigners from the Assistancy, particularly those designated for supervisory positions. In 1601 the provincial of Portugal and the general found it necessary to make a special appeal to Philip III to permit Italians to sail to India, but in 1609 a special tribunal in Madrid ordered that all foreign missionaries in India be sent back to Europe and that no more be permitted to go there. After the papacy intervened, that order was set aside, but the same tribunal later issued another directive stating that only Italians who were subjects of His Catholic Majesty or of the Supreme Pontiff himself might sail to the East.[66] A few years later, when Nicholas Trigault, the energetic procurator of China, arrived in Lisbon with a large number of recruits, he encountered serious opposition from Madrid, where a royal council stipulated that he could take no more than ten non-Portuguese with him.[67] In 1620 the Philippine regime issued a royal order directing that no foreign missionaries might proceed to India

62. F/*JM*, 1: 281. Ferroli defends Laerzio's selections, contending that he was simply appointing the best men for the positions, regardless of nationality.

63. Ibid., 378–80.

64. Linhares to king, 2 Dec. 1630 and 6 Feb. 1635, in *BFUP*, 2: 514–16 and 509; procurator to king, ca. 1635, in BGUC, cod. 4359, fols. 215ʳ–216ʳ.

65. Dom Pedro A. de N. Albuquerque to king, 16 Dec. 1696, in ASL, col. *Vermelho*, cod. 513, fol. 83ʳ.

66. *HCJAP*, 3:2, 132–34.

67. Edmond Lamalle, S.J., "La Propaganda du P. Nicholas Trigault en faveur des missions de Chine (1616)," *AHSI* 9 (1940): 78ff.

without its consent and that no royal license would be issued unless superiors presented a list of the names and nationalities of those they planned to lead overseas.[68]

The Society encountered further difficulties in arranging authorization for missionaries to travel overseas in the Assistancy during the Restoration. At a time when the papacy refused to recognize Portuguese independence, John IV barred all Italians from embarking for India. His son, Afonso VI, went even further and prohibited any foreign missionaries from proceeding to the East. The court's ire was aroused partly because of rumors that some foreign Jesuits in India were still proclaiming the Spanish sovereign to be their legitimate king. It was also stimulated by reports of the conclusion of a Jesuit expedition from China to Europe via Central Asia, undertaken by two Austrians, a Belgian, and a German between 1656 and 1664. Although that expedition's purpose was to determine the feasibility of a land route that would be safer for the movement of missionaries to China than the existing sea route, still menaced by the Dutch, the count of Castelo Melhor became convinced that its real intent was to circumvent the Portuguese padroado. Thus, when Martino Martini, the missions procurator for the vice-province of China, arrived in Lisbon with a dozen Italian and four Belgian recruits, he ran into a stone wall: the court would not permit any Spaniard or anyone from Spanish territories, including Belgium and the Two Sicilies, to venture to the East. Eventually the procurator defused the court's irritation over the land expedition by pointing out that it had been sanctioned by the Portuguese Visitor of Japan and China, but he managed to conceal the fact that it was actually Goswin Nickel who had originally approved of the expedition, chosen two of its participants, and prepared their instructions. Nevertheless, Martini did not gain the court's approval for his expedition to sail until the king's sister, Catherine of Bragança, personally intervened on the Jesuits' behalf. In the end he was able to take only seven missionaries—five Italians, one Belgian, and the previously mentioned Chinese priest, Fr. Emmanuel Siqueira.[69]

Although in this instance the crown ultimately relented and permitted Martini to depart, Pedro II, despite being keenly supportive of the Society's evangelical enterprises, remained opposed to their being staffed by foreigners. As noted in an earlier chapter, Pedro II protested in vain against the dispatch of the French mathematicians to China because the French government had ignored Portuguese demands that they must clear through Lisbon. In 1692 the king issued an order stating that no foreign missionaries were to exercise supervisory positions in any part of Brazil, not even the administration of a single Amerindian village, and demanded assurances from both Jesuit leaders and his own lieutenants that his orders were being observed.[70] The Petrine policy remained in force in the province of Brazil and in the vice-province of Maranhão for the balance of our period. It also applied in Portugal, where the ill-fated visitation of António Casnedi (1721–24) was the only exception. Other than the term of António Broglia Brandolini, Visitor from 1737 to 1742, it applied in India as well. But the policy was often ignored in the province of Japan and the vice-province of China, where Portugal possessed no effective control. The next

68. *CR*, 22 Sept. 1620, in *CCLP*, 3: 29; also published in Paiva Manso, *Historia do Congo* (Lisbon, 1877), 169.

69. Rouleau, "First Chinese Priest," 21–23; *HCJAP*, 3:2, 134–35.

70. *CR*, 21 Feb. 1692, in *MHB*, 2: 284; António Luís Gonçalves da Cámara Coutinho (governor-general) to king, Bahia, 9 July 1692, in *DH*, 34: 65–66. See also *HCJB*, 7: 97–98.

volume of this study will demonstrate how serious an issue the presence of foreigners in one critical area, the Amazon, would become during the final years of the old Society in the Portuguese Assistancy.

A Prosopography of the Assistancy

For better or for worse, therefore, the provinces and vice-provinces of the Assistancy depended primarily upon Portuguese nationals for service at home and overseas. Their identities, birthplaces, and ages, both at the time of admission and current, are indicated in the periodic catalogues, initially called the *catálogo primeiro* and later termed the *catalogus personarum*, that administrative heads periodically sent to Rome. Such registers are essential to determine the national origins of members of the Assistancy and the parts of the kingdom where they originated. In the analysis that follows, that kingdom has been somewhat arbitrarily divided into the North, the Center, and the South. The North was the original county of Portugal, that is, north of the Douro River, and therefore included the archbishopric of Braga and the bishopric of Porto in the west as well as the bishoprics of Miranda and Bragança in the northeast. The Center, the largest, most populous of the three divisions, embraced the bishoprics of Lamego, Viseu, and Coimbra in the north-center, those of Guarda, Portalegre, Évora, and Elvas in the east, and the archbishopric of Lisbon in the west. The South included the bishopric of Beja and the old kingdom of Algarve, especially the city of Faro.[71]

Four catalogues provide data on Jesuits serving in the province of Brazil. One was compiled in 1600, another in 1654, the third in 1701, and the last in 1757.[72] The earliest of this series reveals that two-thirds (66.6 percent) of the province consisted of Portuguese-born subjects, 13 percent were Brazilians, 10 percent came from other parts of the empire, another 10 percent came from elsewhere in Europe. The 1654 catalogue, completed the same year as the Dutch surrender of all Brazilian territories (see Chapter 9), shows that the percentage of Brazilian members had climbed to 37.6, compared with 51.2 percent who were from Portugal, and another 11.2 percent who came from the Atlantic islands and parts of Italy. Those percentages held in 1701: Portuguese Jesuits stood at 50.2 percent and Brazilians at 38.2 percent, leaving 5.4 percent who came from other parts of Europe, and over 6 percent who were natives elsewhere within the empire. By the 1750s the proportions of Portuguese and Brazilians were nearly equal (46.5 percent compared with 45.5 percent), the remaining members being divided between the empire and other European lands.

71. No reliable demographic statistics exist for the kingdom during this period. In addition to those cited in Chapter 2, see Joaquim Veríssimo Serrão, *Uma estimativa da população portuguesa em 1640* (Lisbon, 1975). His estimates are more conservative than those of OM/*HP*, 1: 164–67, 271, 379–80, which demonstrate the inadequacy of our knowledge of the changes in Portugal's population during the centuries that pertain to this study.

72. The 1600 catalogue is published in *HCJB*, 1: 578–84; that of 1701 in ibid., 5: 581–87; and that of 1757 in ibid., 7: 421–34. The "Catalogus primus sociorum qui in Brasilia ... apr.... 1654" is in ARSI, *Bras.*, 5:I, 183^r–190^v. Biographical data come mainly from *HCJB*, vols. 8 and 9, supplemented by *ASCJ*. *PDH*, vols. 1–7, are indispensable for determining diocesan origins. I have used these auxiliaries throughout this section.

TABLE 11.2

Native Origins of Jesuits Serving in the Vice-Province of Maranhão, 1690–1760

Year	Total (N)	Portugal and Atlantic Islands (%)	Brazil (%)	Foreign (%)
1690	54	63.7	16.6	16.6
1708	55	76.4	14.5	7.2
1720	64	84.4	10.9	4.7
1740	128	87.5	4.7	7.0
1751	148	91.0	4.0	5.0
1760	155	85.0	9.2	5.6

SOURCES: ARSI, *Bras.*, 27 and 28. The 1760 catalogue is also published in *HCJB*, 4: 363–67.

These same catalogues reveal changing patterns of recruitment for Brazil within the kingdom. In 1601 a biographical sample of 40.1 percent (69 out of 172) discloses that 65.2 percent of the recruits came from the central bishoprics, compared with 21.7 percent from the southern bishoprics and 13 percent from the northern sees. By mid-century, northerners represented 48.7 percent of the Peninsulars, whereas 45 percent were natives of the central sees and only 6.5 percent came from those in the south. The 1701 sample (50.2 percent of the total) shows that the North's share had increased to 57.2 percent, whereas the Center's had fallen to 37.1 percent, and the South remained about the same (5.6 percent). A sample (46.7 percent) taken from the last of the series, the catalogue of 1757, again demonstrates that more than half (53.6 percent) of those who served in the Brazil province came from the kingdom's northern sees; the remainder came from the Center.

Seven catalogues depict the Society's native origins in the vice-province of Maranhão between 1690 and 1760.[73] The earliest indicates that 63.7 percent of the members were from Portugal, compared with 16.6 percent who were from other parts of Europe, and an equal percentage who were natives of Brazil. As Table 11.2 demonstrates, the more the Society increased its commitment to Maranhão during the next seven decades, the more heavily the kingdom contributed personnel to the vice-province. Biographical data are available on the 48 Peninsulars listed in the 1697 catalogue. The Center provided 47.9 percent, the North 37.5 percent, and the South only 14.6 percent of the vice-province's personnel. The Center's contribution was even greater in 1760. Of the 78.1 percent whose native origins are known, 74.1 percent were from the Center, 19.8 percent from the North, and only 5.6 percent from the South.

The most useful among the several detailed sixteenth-century personnel catalogues concerning the Goan province is that of 1584.[74] It reports that the kingdom supplied

73. They include the 1690 catalogus personarum, in ARSI, *Bras.*, 27, fols. 7–10; that of 1697, in Bento da Fonseca, S.J., "Catálogo da missão do Maranhão .... 1697," which is interspersed in his "Catálogo dos primeiros religiosos da companhia da vice-província do Maranhão com notícias históricas," *RIHGB* 55, 1 (1892): 407–31, at 417–22; the 1720, 1730, 1740, and 1751 catalogues are in ARSI, *Bras.*, 27, fols. 19–33ᵛ, 51–52ᵛ, 95–104, and 162–63; for that of 1760, see *HCJB*, 4: 463–68.

74. The Goan catalogues discussed in this section are: (1584) *DI*, 13: 601–58; (1647) ARSI, *Goa*, 25, fols. 84ʳ–121ʳ; (1706 and 1726) ibid., FG 627; for the 1760 catalogue, see note 29 above.

57.1 percent of the province's 350 subjects; that 20.8 percent came from other parts of Europe; and that about the same percentage originated elsewhere within the empire. Three catalogues compiled during the next century and a quarter show convincingly the province's heavy dependence upon Peninsular personnel: that of 1647 reveals that 91.4 percent of Goa's subjects were from the kingdom; only 7.6 percent came from other parts of Europe; the remaining 2 percent were born in Africa or Asia.[75] Six decades later, the proportions were largely unchanged: by then five subjects (2.4 percent of the province's 205 Jesuits) were from Brazil, two from the Atlantic islands, nine from non-Iberian parts of Europe, and the remaining 189 (91.4 percent) from the kingdom.[76] The 1726 catalogue, prepared a few years before the devastating Maratha invasion of Goa's northern province (see Chapter 23), showed that out of 176 members, there were three Brazilians (1.7 percent), another trio from the Atlantic islands, ten from East Asia (5.7 percent), one Cuban, one Spaniard, and five Italians (together 3.9 percent); the remaining 153 members (87 percent) were from Portugal.[77] The last of this series of catalogues concerns the 127 fathers and brothers who were forcibly sent to the kingdom in 1760. That catalogue indicates that despite the existence of a long-hoped-for novitiate in Lisbon to train young men for the Indian field, the kingdom had provided only 71 members (55.9 percent); two subjects came from the Atlantic islands and a dozen (9.4 percent) from Brazil. But six other European countries furnished 23 members, more than half of whom were from Italy. What is surprising is that Asia provided nearly as many members as did the Italian peninsula.

Most of the Portuguese recruits who sailed to India came from the kingdom's central dioceses. Of the 198 Peninsulars listed in the 1584 catalogue whose origins are ascertainable, 55.7 percent were from those sees; 22.2 percent came from the North and 14.1 percent from the South, leaving 8 percent undetermined. The first catalogue of 1647 reveals that 96 Portuguese communities furnished the province with 217 members. By then the Center's share had increased to 73.5 percent; the North's remained about the same (22.4 percent), but the South's had fallen to only 4 percent. The 1706 catalogue demonstrates about the same percentage for each of the three regions and shows that 97 communities in the kingdom were represented in the Goan province. Twenty years later, however, the Center's share had fallen to 66 percent, whereas the North's had grown to 23.5 percent and the South's had doubled to 10.4 percent. More than 90 Peninsular communities still contributed sons to the province. In 1760, when members of both Indian provinces were expelled, 55.9 percent came from the kingdom, 18.1 percent were from other European lands, and the balance were from the empire. This final register demonstrates that long-established patterns still held: the northern sees provided 25.4 percent of the members, the Center 68.6 percent, and the South only 5.9 percent. This time only 45 communities supplied the 71 members who were from the kingdom.

The Japan province demonstrates a strikingly different racial pattern among its personnel. Five catalogues (1588, 1593, 1604, 1620, and 1648) are particularly informative.[78] According to the 1588 catalogue, the kingdom provided only 26.5 percent of the future

75. The origins of 9.7% of those listed in the catalogue are unknown.
76. It is not possible to determine the place of origin of 19.1% of those who came from the kingdom.
77. The birthplaces of 21.8% of those born in the kingdom are undetermined.
78. They are published in *MHJ*, 234–60, 306–39, 579–92, 952–65, and 1058–81.

province's membership, compared with 23.9 percent who were from other parts of Europe, leaving 9.7 percent who were Luso-Asians. The percentage of Japanese brothers increased during the next quiennium to 43.5, compared with 25.4 percent who were Peninsulars, 23.9 percent who were from other European lands, and 6 percent who were non-Japanese Asians; the rest were unspecified. According to the 1604 catalogue, the Japanese, now including the first priests, represented 44.3 percent of the province, the Portuguese 29.6 percent, and other Europeans 20.9 percent; the remainder came from other parts of Portugal's Asian holdings. By 1620, six years after the expulsion, the province's membership had fallen slightly from 115 to 106; Portuguese represented 50 percent of that total, compared with 19.8 percent other Europeans, 27.4 percent Japanese, and the remainder Luso-Asians. The last of the series, the 1648 catalogue, reveals that the province's membership had fallen to only 58, of whom 43.1 percent were Portuguese, 37.9 percent came from elsewhere in Europe, and the remaining 19 percent were from various Asian lands, though only one was Japanese, whereas two were Chinese and six Macaonese.

This series of catalogues demonstrates once again that most Portuguese Jesuits in the Japan province came from the kingdom's central dioceses. In 1588, for example, 62 percent were from the Center, 31 percent from the North, and 6.9 percent from the South; the origins of the remainder were hidden. In 1593 the Center's share of the future Japan province's membership fell to 43.7 percent, whereas that of the South rose to 17 percent. The North's share increased slightly to 34.3 percent, leaving a small percentage undetermined. In 1604 the Center provided Japan with 58.8 percent of the Peninsular Jesuits, compared with 20.6 percent for the North and South. The Center's share was 64.2 percent in 1620; the South remained steady at 20.7 percent, but the North fell to 15.1 percent. By 1648, 80 percent of the shrunken membership originated in the central bishoprics, compared with 12 percent from the South and only 8 percent from the North.

A second series of catalogues, extending from 1685 to 1753, contributes additional data concerning the ethnic origins of those who served in the reconstituted Japan province, that is, primarily mainland Southeast Asia.[79] Between one-third and three-quarters of them came from Portugal (see Table 11.3). Although other parts of Europe, especially Italy and the Germanies, provided significantly fewer Jesuits during the eighteenth century, Asia's share remained relatively steady. Unfortunately this series is unhelpful with respect of the origins of Portuguese members of the province.

Europeans normally constituted between two-thirds and three-quarters of the membership of the rival vice-province of China (see Table 11.4), excluding subjects of the separately administered French mission (see Chapter 6). The catalogues from which these data were taken do not clearly indicate the Peninsular origins of Portuguese members, but two standard biobibliographical aids suggest that during the last years of the Society's formal presence in China, the central dioceses of Portugal provided more than three-quarters (76.1 percent) of those who came from the kingdom, compared with 19.6 percent who came from the North and only 4.3 percent who were from the South.[80]

79. The catalogues are in ARSI, *JapSin*, 25 and 26/D.
80. The analysis is based upon *NBBJC*, 622–909, and *RJC*, passim.

TABLE 11.3

Native Origins of Jesuits Serving in the Japan Province, 1685–1753

Year	Portuguese (N)	Portuguese (%)	Other European (N)	Other European (%)	Asian (N)	Asian (%)	Total (N)
1685	13	32.5	16	40.0	11	27.5	40
1691	16	35.5	11	24.4	18	40.0	45
1698	21	42.0	12	24.0	14	28.0	50[a]
1714	37	68.5	8	14.8	9	16.6	54
1734	43	76.8	2	3.6	8	14.3	56[a]
1753	33	55.9	10	16.9	16	27.1	59

SOURCES: ARSI, *JapSin*, 26/D, fols. 39–40^v, 45–48^v; 25, fols. 235–38, 269–271^v.

[a] Three members not identified.

TABLE 11.4

Native Origins of Jesuits Serving in the Vice-Province of China, 1621–1755

Year	Portuguese (N)	Portuguese (%)	Other European (N)	Other European (%)	Asian (N)	Asian (%)	Total (N)
1621–							
1624	10	35.7	11	39.3	7	25.0	28
1645	10	35.7	14	50.0	4	14.3	28
1683	4	19.0	11	52.4	6	28.6	21
1688	6	20.0	17	56.6	7	23.3	30
1702	18	43.9	15	36.6	8	19.5	41
1741	16	35.5	14	31.1	15	33.3	45
1751	20	42.5	12	25.5	15	31.9	47
1755	25	54.3	9	19.6	12	26.1	46

SOURCE: ARSI, *JapSin*, 134, fols. 301^r–447^r.

NOTE: Figures are exclusive of the French mission.

It is pertinent to see whether the regional patterns observed among Jesuits who served overseas mirrored similar patterns among those who were members of the Portuguese province. It will be recalled that the province included not only the kingdom but also Portugal's Atlantic islands and Angola. Three representative catalogues, those of 1593, 1693, and 1749, reveal that, as might be expected, most of those attached to the province's houses were native sons.[81] The first of that series demonstrates that only 5.7 percent of the 571 members, including thirteen Spaniards, came from the empire or other parts of Europe. The latter two catalogues show even higher percentages of native sons: 97.5 percent in both 1693 and 1749.

Though it is clear that the kingdom itself provided nearly all of those members who served in the province, it is equally evident that most of them came from the central dioceses and from the archdiocese of Lisbon. As Table 11.5 shows, the Center furnished from two-thirds to three-quarters of the province's membership during these years, whereas the North's share varied from over a fifth to nearly a third. The sparsely populated South,

81. The sources of the three catalogues are: (1593) ARSI, *Lus.*, 44:I, fols. 65–84; (1693) ibid., 46, fols. 245–298^v; and (1749) ibid., 49, fols. 2–59^v.

TABLE 11.5

Regional Origins of Jesuits Serving in the Province of Portugal, 1593, 1693, and 1749

Region	Total (N)	North (%)	Center (%)	South (%)
1593	530	30.9	67.2	1.9
1693	650	25.2	71.7	3.1
1749	823	23.4	75.6	0.9

SOURCES: ARSI, *Lus.*, 44:I, fols. 65–84; 46, fols. 245–298ᵛ; and 49, fols. 2–59ᵛ.

TABLE 11.6

Natal Bishoprics of Members of the Province of Portugal, 1593, 1693, 1749, and 1750

(Percentages)

Region	1593	1693	1749	1750
North				
Braga	65.2%	69.5%	58.5%	61.1%
Bragança	3.0	4.8	0	0
Miranda	0	0	12.9	8.6
Porto	31.7	25.6	28.5	30.3
Center				
Lamego	6.2	4.9	6.6	5.9
Viseu	8.7	6.6	7.7	7.9
Guarda	6.7	3.6	2.2	2.4
Coimbra	17.7	34.1	35.2	33.2
Portalegre	5.3	3.9	3.9	3.7
Elvas	5.6	2.4	1.9	2.7
Évora	21.1	18.9	15.1	15.0
Lisbon	28.6	25.5	27.3	28.7

SOURCES: See Table 11.5 for 1593, 1693, and 1749. The analysis for 1750 is based upon BNL, *cx.* 59, doc. 23, which also indicates that the North contributed 23.3 percent of the members of the province, the Center 75.3 percent, and the South a mere 1.3 percent.

which sent few sons to the overseas provinces, did not provide many candidates for the Peninsular colleges either. Braga furnished at least twice as many members as did the rest of the northern diocese, but its prominence is less evident among those who went to the overseas stations (see Table 11.6). On the other hand, the archdiocese of Lisbon, which sometimes produced fewer recruits than did the diocese of Coimbra, sent a much larger proportion of its youths abroad than did either Évora or Coimbra. Presumably, Lisbon's dominant role as the kingdom's chief port and its clustering of several Jesuit houses explain why it regularly provided a large percentage of the recruits who went to distant lands.

Estimates of Jesuit Longevities

In December 1574, Visitor Valignano sadly reported to Rome that during the previous four years 58 members of the Indian province had perished.[82] Considering the perilous and lengthy sea voyages between Lisbon and the outliers of the Assistancy, the primitive conditions of overland travel beyond Europe, radical changes in diet, exposure to epidemic and parasitical diseases, and the hostility of both indigenous and foreign rivals, high death rates among the Jesuits come as no surprise. Indeed, every personnel catalogue included a lament for those who had expired since the previous report. More surprising is the fact that so many Jesuits lived as long as they did.

Table 11.7 presents a series of estimates concerning the longevity of Jesuits who served in various parts of the Assistancy between the sixteenth and mid-eighteenth centuries. Those estimates are based upon the Society's periodic personnel catalogues, listings of Jesuits who had died in particular localities, and published biographical sources. Owing to the exceptionally comprehensive work by Fr. Serafim Leite, we possess very detailed biographical information for Jesuits who served in Brazil and Maranhão. But Fr. Leite's data are skewed in favor of the more prominent fathers and reflect the limitations of the Society's files with respect to lower-ranking members of the Order. The same limitation applies to the two very useful biographical dictionaries of Jesuits who served in the vice-province of China. The absence of such dictionaries for Portugal and the two provinces of India remains a serious handicap.

For Portugal the catalogues are most detailed from 1690 to about 1740 and show that Jesuits who labored within the kingdom generally lived into their mid-fifties. Rather surprisingly, those who worked in the Brazil province survived as much as a decade longer. Although Jesuits who served in the vice-province of Maranhão during the first half of the eighteenth century died younger than their peers in Brazil or Portugal, those who were arrested in the vice-province at the time of the general expulsion fared better and lived well into their sixties. Jesuits who functioned in the province of Goa lived about as long as those who resided in Portugal, but it seems clear that Jesuits who suffered the privations of the general arrest of 1759–62, the long sea voyage back to the kingdom, and further detention there lived significantly shorter lives. Until the general expulsion, Jesuits who served in imperial China appear to have outlived their colleagues in the kingdom of Portugal by five to nearly ten years; however, their life spans were significantly reduced during the second quarter of the eighteenth century, when the Society experienced serious persecution in China (see Chapter 23).

One might think that the burdens of administration would shorten life spans, but that does not appear to have been the case within the Portuguese Assistancy. As Table 11.8 indicates, the mean duration of life for senior administrators within the Assistancy actually increased between the first and second periods considered here, though in several cases it declined during the stressful eighteenth century.

It is interesting to compare the completed lives of the fathers general with other Europeans who came from about the same social class. Table 11.9 compares the ages

82. *VMP*, 1: 136.

TABLE 11.7

Average Ages at Death of Jesuits Serving in Selected
Administrative Units of the Portuguese Assistancy, 1525–1777

Province or vice-province	Period of death	(N)	Percentage of total	Average age at death
Portugal	1690–1693	43	79	54.8
	1700–1705	86	76	53.1
	1737–1739	56	17	55.3
Brazil	1600–1604	20	60	62.3
	1661–1665	17	74	65.1
	1702–1709	9	100	60.2
	1710–1714	20	51	56.9
	1730–1734	20	82	65.4
	1750–1754	20	69	62.5
Maranhão[a]	1699–1749	22	69	51.8
	1760–1777	15	36	63.9
Goa	1625–1716	47	77	59.6
	1679	9	100	54.6
Goa and Malabar	1760–1777	49	100	52.8
China[b]	1500–1524	7	100	61.0
	1525–1549	25	100	55.3
	1550–1574	39	100	62.8
	1575–1599	48	100	56.9
	1600–1624	80	100	55.0
	1625–1649	54	100	58.7
	1650–1674	126	100	60.5
	1675–1699	58	100	64.6
	1700–1724	66	100	57.4
	1725–1749	28	100	50.6

SOURCES: Portugal: (1690–1693) ARSI, *Lus.*, 46, fol. 303; (1700–1705) ibid., 47, fols. 61r–62v; (1737–1738) ibid., 48, no fols. Brazil: (1600–1604) *HCJB*, 1: 578–84, and vols. 8 and 9, passim; (1661–1665) ARSI, *Bras.*, 7, fols. 14–15, and 5:I, 183–92; (1702–1709) *HCJB*, 5: 581–82, and vols. 8 and 9, passim; (1710–1714) ARSI, *Bras.*, 7, fols. 21–22, and 6:I, fols. 2–8v; (1730–1734) ibid., 7, fols. 26–28, and 6:I, fols. 132–40; (1750–1754) ibid., 6:II, fols. 314–320v, 342–348, 388–394v, and 7, fols. 31–34. Maranhão: (1699–1749) BNL, cod. 4518, fols. 2–15; (1760–1777) *HCJB*, 4: 363–68, and vols. 8 and 9, passim. Goa: (1625–1716) "Noticia . . . dos religiozos que falecerão nesta provincia" [1724], *AHSI* 39 (Jan.–June 1970): 106–51; (1679) ARSI, *Goa*, 25, fol. 312. Goa and Malabar: (1760–1777) *AHSI* 31 (July–Dec. 1962): 335–58; China: *NBBJC*, 622–909, and *RJC*, passim.

[a] Data derive from a list of Jesuits buried in the college church in São Luís do Maranhão.

[b] The calculations for the vice-province of China are organized by quarterly intervals of birth rather than by dates of death.

at death of the leaders of the Society with four peer groups in three periods. The first period extends from the birth of Ignatius until the death of Aquaviva, from the birth of the eighth to the death of the thirty-sixth governor of India,[83] from the time of Pope Julius II until the death of Pope Leo XI. The data from this period also include estimates of the average future life spans of male members of the high aristocracy in Europe during the sixteenth century and of male members of British ducal families from the late fifteenth to

83. Although many of the senior Portuguese administrators of the State of India were styled viceroys, all were also called governors, the best encompassing designation that fits here.

TABLE 11.8

*Average Ages at Death of Fathers General, Provincials,
and Vice-Provincials of the Portuguese Assistancy, 1541–1773*

	Period 1	Period 2	Period 3
Generals	49.9	65.3	61.6
Provincials and vice-provincials			
Portugal	71.9	77.6	n.a.
Brazil	42.9	76.6	74.8
Maranhåo	—	—	69.1
Japan	62.0	64.3	67.7
China	59.3	70.1	67.9

SOURCES: See Chapter 10, notes 12 and 43.

NOTE: Period 1 (generals) = 1541–1615; (provincials) = 1546–1615 (Portugal), 1553–1615 (Brazil), 1549–1617 (Japan); (vice-provincials) = 1583–1610 (China). Period 2 (generals) = 1615–1705; (provincials) = 1615–1703 (Portugal), 1615–1705 (Brazil), 1617–1704 (Japan); (vice-provincials) = 1610–1704 (China). Period 3: (generals) = 1706–73; (provincials) = 1705–54 (Brazil), 1705–62 (Japan); (vice-provincials) = 1723–60 (Maranhão), 1707–62 (China). The fits are approximate and minor overlaps exist.

TABLE 11.9

*Comparative Life Spans or Expectancies of
Jesuit Generals and Peer Groups*

	Years	Average age at death
Period 1		
S.J. generals	1491–1615	49.9
Popes	1487–1605	68.6
Viceroys, India	1496–1617	50.8
Ruling families	1500–1599	[45.9][a]
Ducal families	1480–1679	[42.7][a]
Period 2		
S.J. generals	1563–1705	65.3
Popes	1582–1700	76.2
Viceroys, India	1565–1702	63.4
Ruling families	1600–1699	[45.2][a]
Period 3		
S.J. generals	1648–1757	61.6
Popes	1649–1774	76.8
Viceroys, India	1646–1756	68.2
Ruling families	1700–1799	[54.5][a]
Ducal families	1680–1779	[52.8][a]

SOURCES: Chapter 10, note 12; [A. Gonçalves Pereira], *Tratado de todos os vicereis e governadores da India* (Lisbon, 1962), 87–183; J. N. D. Kelly, *The Oxford Dictionary of Popes* (New York, 1988); Sigismund Peller, "Births and Deaths Among Europe's Ruling Families Since 1500," reprinted in D. V. Glass and D. E. C. Eversley, eds., *Population in History: Essays in Historical Demography* (Chicago, 1965), Table 10; and T. H. Hollingswoth, "A Demographic Study of the British Ducal Families," in ibid., Table 12.

[a] Extrapolated from the expectation of life for this group at age 15.

the late seventeenth centuries. Both estimates are based upon an average future life span at age 15, the approximate age at entry of most Jesuits who later achieved prominence. The second period begins with the birth of Mutio Vitelleschi and ends with the death of Tirso Gonzalez de Santalla. It also covers the terms of the thirty-third to the sixtieth governors of India and those of Popes Paul V through Innocent XII. In addition, the data for this period include Peller's estimate of the life expectancy of European aristocrats during the seventeenth century. The third period commences with Michelangelo Tamburini's birth and closes with the death of Aloysius Centuroni. It also includes the pontificates between Clement XI and Clement XIV, and the series of Portuguese governors of India from the birth of the fifty-sixth until the death of the seventieth. Finally, the data for this period include projected average life spans for the two aristocratic family groups.

Admittedly, these calculations are somewhat crude. Assuredly there is a significant difference between a completed life span and expectations of future life. Nevertheless, the data assembled in Tables 11.8 and 11.9 are suggestive. During the initial period, the generals' lives were about as long as those of the governors and several years beyond the life expectancies of the aristocrats, but were markedly shorter than the popes'. The provincials of Portugal and Japan had strikingly longer lives than any of these groups save the popes, although provincials of Brazil were substantially younger when they died. However, the age at death of senior Jesuits serving in Brazil in 1600 was 38.5 percent greater than the age at death projected for the aristocrats. In the second period, the generals outlived the governors of India by nearly two years, and their lives were about 31 percent longer than those projected for the aristocrats. Again, the popes enjoyed by far the longest lives. The longevity of the provincials and the professed members in Brazil is even more impressive, although the average age at death of members of the Goan province, which included those who performed apostolates in Ethiopia and Mozambique, was significantly lower. In the last period, the governors outlived the generals by an average of 6.6 years; the popes exceeded them by more than 15 years. The significant improvement in the life expectancies of the aristocrats then was unmatched by the completed lives of the Jesuits surveyed, probably because of the physical hardships of the general expulsion, although the provincials still seem to have lived impressively long lives.

Though these tables demonstrate that popes consistently outlived other peer groups, they also suggest that senior Jesuits survived longer in most instances than the average aristocrat, and longer than the governors of India. Why they were able to do so takes us into the realm of conjecture, although some factors may seem more obvious than others. First, the Jesuits' dedication to chastity must have spared them the consequences of venereal disease, which ravaged many of their peers. Second, though they frequently engaged in verbal combat, the Jesuits normally refrained from the kinds of physical encounters to which dueling aristocrats and fighting soldiers were prone, though, of course, Jesuits perished violently in shipwrecks, sea battles, and martyrdoms. Still, such deaths were the exceptions rather than the rule: many Jesuit leaders spent only a brief time in missions or other hazardous situations and remained for most of their lives in the relatively secure urban houses of the Society.[84] Third, the Jesuits enjoyed the reputation of being unrivaled in their pharmacological knowledge. Some of their remedies (such as bezoar stones) possessed no therapeutic value, but others (such as quinine) obviously did.[85] It may be, therefore, that the Jesuits, and those to whom they extended medical remedies, enjoyed better health than did their peers, although the catalogues are full of references to nagging maladies with which both Europeans and non-Europeans were seemingly constantly afflicted. Perhaps the best explanation of why Jesuits enjoyed exceptional longevity may simply have been their uncommon concern about maintaining a balanced diet, a subject considered in Chapter 24.

The Creation and Maintenance of a Public Image

During the formative period of the Society, its leaders were profoundly concerned about the maintenance of the Order's internal discipline and the creation of an external image of the Society as a spartan, uncorrupted agency of the Church. Accordingly, the Society's directors sought not only to instill and preserve in each subject the fullest possible religious understanding and commitment but also to circumscribe minutely his deportment.

Students who entered the Order received a handbook, generally entitled "Rules of the Company," which they were expected to master. Such manuals provided a short summary of the *Constitutions* and added detailed instructions for the personal conduct of the novice. The Évora edition of 1603 placed great emphasis upon the deportment expected of the novice both within and outside a Jesuit house. Inmates were to remember that poverty was "the strong bulwark of religion" and to emulate the poor in their food, dress, and even sleeping accommodations. No one should possess any money or entrust any to the care of an outsider. All should refrain from intervening in purely secular matters, such as serving as executors of estates. Members were forbidden to sleep in cubicles with open windows or doors or to retire unclothed. They should never leave the premises without first obtaining permission from their superior and must never appeal an adverse decision from one superior to another. When addressing superiors, inmates were to speak with great reverence and gravity. Gravity should also be the hallmark of their relations with persons of authority outside the Society. They must never look such persons directly in the face but always cast their eyes lower down. They should refrain from shifting their heads from side to side or wrinkling their foreheads, much less their noses, and should moderate pressure on their lips so that they appeared to be neither pursed nor excessively open, "because exterior serenity is a sign of what resides within." The message of the rules of conduct was clear: so far as relations with others were concerned, the aim of a Jesuit was to present a grave, deferential, and contented exterior.[86]

84. This generalization applies to the Portuguese Assistancy, but it does not fit the experience of Jesuits elsewhere. According to David Block, among Jesuits who served during the eighteenth century in the Moxos missions of the province of Peru, situated east of Santa Cruz de la Sierra, "long service was buttressed by a pronounced tendency to stay in the same station for many years." *Mission Culture*, 112–13.

85. Serafim Leite, S.J., *Artes e ofícios dos Jesuítas no Brasil (1549–1760)* (Rio de Janeiro, 1953), 85–96. On bezoar stones, see Chapter 21.

86. Ignatius Loyola, "Regulae Modestiae" edition of Jan. 1555, in *RSI*, 518–25. There is a copy of the Portuguese edition of 1603, *Regras da companhia de Iesu* (Évora, 1603), in the Newberry Library, Chicago, and another in the private collection of Charles R. Boxer. I have consulted both. For a more available

A manual given to a young Jesuit who had just taken his first vows in Coimbra in 1559 includes the text of the famous "Letter on Obedience" written by Ignatius six years earlier and addressed specifically to the Portuguese province. The text also includes a list of qualities that a new Jesuit was expected to cultivate. Among them are honesty, sobriety, charity, humility, piety, modesty, submissiveness, chastity, and the suppression of concupiscence.[87]

The early rectors, provincials, and Visitors also issued detailed instructions to their subordinates regarding individual conduct. In 1552, for example, Gaspar Barzaeus, first vice-rector of Old St. Paul's, laid down 33 rules governing the conduct of students in that institution and residents in its dependencies. They were admonished to proceed quietly whether in church, in the house, or on the street. They were forbidden to borrow, to lend, or to consider anything their personal property, for "everything will be [held] in common." They were not to remove any object from the common rooms without permission, make marks in books they read, or skip breakfast. Whenever the tocsin rang to summon them, they were to drop whatever they were doing and hasten to the required destination. They were to refrain from taking any medications without prescription or undertaking unauthorized penances. Anyone who knew of the existence of such activity was obliged to report it to the rector. Students were not permitted to send out letters without first giving them to the rector to read, nor were they to receive communications from the outside unless the rector had already read them. They were to make their beds each morning and to sweep out their cubicles every second day. No one was to proceed from his cubicle to another's after lights out. Barzaeus mandated that such instructions were to be read weekly, presumably during mealtimes, to the entire house, and drafted similar instructions to house masters and other functionaries concerning their duties and deportment. Those rules, too, were to be reviewed weekly.[88]

Xavier was also very much concerned about the personal behavior of his subjects and repeatedly counseled them to be humble, self-effacing, and agreeable. They were to refrain from carping at or quarreling with other religious or secular priests.[89] He shared with Ignatius uneasiness about proper relations with women:

> Converse with [them] ... in an open place, for example, in the church, and never go to their homes except in case of extreme necessity.... Since women are generally inconstant and of little perseverance, and take up much time, you should take great care and work with their husbands so that they come to God; and spend more time in producing fruit among husbands than among their wives since ... men are more constant.... Do not believe the pious impulses of women when they say that they would serve God more if they were separated from their husbands rather than being with them, for these are only pious impulses which are of short duration and which are seldom executed without scandal. Avoid giving blame to the husband in public even though it lies with him.... Even if the wives are not to blame, do not excuse them as they excuse themselves, but rather show them the

---

example of such instructions, see "Common Rules Pertaining to Studies," in Allan P. Farrell, S.J., *The Jesuit Code of Liberal Education: Development and Scope of the Ratio Studiorum* (Milwaukee, 1938), facing 431.

87. *Regras pera os estudantes*, in BNL, cod. 4214.

88. "Regulae collegii Goani," Sept. or Oct. 1552, in *DI*, 2: 337–68.

89. S/*FX*, 4: 87, 526–27, and 542.

obligation which they have to put up with their husbands. . . . When you cannot reconcile them, send them to the Lord Bishop or to the vicar general.[90]

From time to time the generals also issued directives concerning personal behavior. Aquaviva, for example, became alarmed that Jesuits in the East might be observed swimming publicly and ordered the practice prohibited. Valignano assured him that although others, including the Franciscans, followed that practice, his men refrained from it. He admitted that his men might take an occasional discreet dip in a stream where they secretly washed themselves, but he observed that India was a very hot country where one sweated profusely.[91] The same general also worried about reports that the fathers often went alone through their parishes and insisted that they always be accompanied by companions. Again, the Visitor pointed out that the eastern lands were vast and teeming with people, that parishes were large, and that there were few fathers available to cover them.[92] Some years later, Aquaviva returned to the problem and instructed the vice-provincial of Portugal to prohibit "severely" the custom of Jesuits traveling unaccompanied in public because of the risk of scandal. He made an exception in the case of houses with fewer than twenty residents and authorized the procurators or buyers of such houses to go out alone, but only on the most urgent business.[93] In India, no Jesuit was to travel singly or make use of a *palanquin*, a litter supported on the shoulders of bearers.[94]

One acutely sensitive topic that concerned the generals was the extent of their subjects' compliance with the vow of poverty (see especially Chapter 24). Toward the end of his long career, Aquaviva circularized the Society, reminding every subject that acceptance of gifts from a relative or friend without his superior's permission was strictly forbidden.[95] Even the offer of a small portable writing desk by a craftsman in India to one father aroused Vitelleschi's indignation, and he sternly ordered that such gifts belonged to the house, not to the individual.[96] Soon after assuming the generalate, Michelangelo Tamburini addressed a lengthy circular to the members of the Brazil province on the topic of poverty. He reminded them that Ignatius had admonished that poverty was "the strong bulwark of religion" and that the Twelfth General Congregation (1682) had issued a series of decrees that condemned violations of that sacred vow. Then Tamburini turned to particular violations

90. Ibid., 544.

91. Valignano to Aquaviva, [Cochin], 22 Dec. 1586, in *DI*, 14: 459.

92. "Instrución para el nuevo provincial de la India Oriental," 22 Dec. 1582, in *DI*, 12: 690, par. 10.

93. Aquaviva to vice-provincial of Portugal, 13 Nov. 1607, in ANTT/CJ/68, no. 260. Toward the end of the century, the papal nuncio to Portugal complained about "the greave inconveniences" of the religious traveling about Lisbon without their companions and called upon the crown to prohibit the practice. The result was the decree of 1 Sept. 1692, in *CCLP*, 10: 299–300.

94. Order of Goswin Nickel, 16 Dec. 1655, in H/SAG2, 78. For reasons that are unclear, the crown itself opposed the use of litters by the Portuguese, except for those aged 60 and above, and even they were required to obtain license from the viceroy for one or two days' use. *Carta de lei*, Jan. 1602, renewed in 1631 and 1634. José Ignácio de Abranches Garcia, comp., *Archivo da relação de Goa*, 2 vols. (Goa, 1872–74), 1: 33 and 451. Palanquins, called *andoras* when covered, were evidently a status symbol in India. For contemporary descriptions of their appearance and use, see Surendra Nath Sen, ed., *Indian Travels of Thevenot and Careri* (New Delhi, 1949), 76 and 160; and J. Ovington, *A Voyage to Surat in the Year 1689*, ed. H. G. Rawlinson (London, 1929), 152. Upon occasion during the sixteenth and early seventeenth centuries, Jesuits also traveled by litter in Brazil and in parts of Africa.

95. Aquaviva to the Society, 16 July 1613, in BA/JA/49-IV-56, n. 17, fol. 197[r].

96. Vitelleschi to João Baptista (Visitor), 20 Dec. 1637, as quoted in H/SAG1, 336.

that had been brought to his attention—one suspects by envious Portuguese-born members in the province. No one, he declared, should be permitted to retain expensive clocks (*relógios de rodas*), relics, or images, or to furnish his quarters with clothing, jewelry, or anything not necessary for the common life. Tamburini reminded his subjects that they were forbidden to administer estates or to keep money, either in their own hands or in those of others. He closed by exhorting all to remember the vow that they had taken, warning them that it was fundamental and sacred, and that the reputation of the Society depended upon their literal adherence to it.[97]

Another matter that disturbed the generals was the propensity of their subjects to gossip. They repeatedly remonstrated with their subjects against discussing Society affairs with outsiders and urged them to maintain a low profile in the public arena.[98] Two years after succeeding Aquaviva, Vitelleschi circularized the Society in the East, urging each to emulate Xavier by being humble and reverent. He pointed out that in recent years unnamed enemies had accused the Jesuits of greed, arrogance, boastfulness, and preoccupation with amassing riches, and of being politically rather than spiritually oriented. Vitelleschi contended that such charges were based upon unwise utterances.[99]

The propensity of superiors to regulate the lives of their subordinates even extended to household servants. The ordinances prepared by Visitor João Alvares stipulated that each servant was to go to confession once a month and was to receive regular religious instruction. No one might leave the residence without permission from the brother in charge (the *ministro da casa*) and from the superior. Servants were required to sleep every night in their rooms with their doors firmly shut. They were permitted to play ball games or billiards "but not other games" on feast days, and to play musical instruments provided that their noise did not disturb the fathers. Each new employee was required to have the rules of the house read to him and to signify by sign that he understood them. By that declaration the employee pledged himself to remain on the job until the period for which he had contracted service was completed and to accept whatever punishment was appropriate for his errors and negligence.[100]

Compliance with the endless admonitions concerning personal behavior must have varied from place to place, and from time to time, and was probably dependent upon the amount of zeal a superior was willing to devote to enforcement. One suspects that many petty regulations were read, digested, and forgotten. If the vaunted discipline of the Society had truly been as formidable as some writers imagine, reiterated scolding would have been unnecessary.[101]

97. Tamburini to provincial, Brazil, 30 Sept. 1709, in *LAM* 3, 368–77.
98. For two of many such admonitions, see H/SAG2, 100–101, and Charles W. Polzer, S.J., trans. and ed., *Rules and Precepts of the Jesuit Missions of Northwestern New Spain* (Tucson, 1976), 89.
99. Vitelleschi to the Fathers and Brothers [of the State of India], 2 Jan. 1617 (Rome, [printed]), in Maggs Brothers, *Bibliotheca Asiatica*, pt. 1 (London, 1924), 62. I have consulted the copy in the library of Charles R. Boxer.
100. "Visita da provincia de Portugal pelo P. João Alvarez feito no ano de 1610 até 1613," ANTT/AJ, no. 5, tit. 9, chap. 14, fols. 98–99.
101. Not untypical is Boxer's view that "rigid discipline and blind obedience were inculcated as the cardinal virtues in members of the Society." *CCJ*, 45–46. I do not question that these values were "inculcated," but I do dispute the extent to which they were practiced. See also Polzer, *Rules and Precepts*, 95 and 122, concerning efforts by superiors to root out card playing in Jesuit houses.

It is not difficult to discover examples of nonconformist behavior. Although several generals condemned the use of litters, Jerónimo Lobo, the venerable missionary who served in Ethiopia, India, and Portugal, candidly recorded in his memoirs that he had traveled from Damão to Bassein "as is the custom, in hammocks on the backs of men called bois. . . . The chair is restful and very comfortable, for a person travels in a reclining or sitting position with bed made and writing desk at his feet. . . . It has very convenient protection against the sun. . . . In this manner I traveled twenty leagues or so."[102] In Cochin China, Alexander of Rhodes, one of the most admired Jesuits of the seventeenth century, wrote, "[I] often had myself carried according to the native custom in a hammock borne about the neck by two men. . . . I used this convenience not only to remain concealed, but also to catch a little sleep while traveling, because once [I] arrived at my destination, I had to expect to work night and day."[103] One can be certain that the two fathers considered their actions not as defiance of headquarters, but simply as the most expedient way to travel in order to accomplish their apostolates.

The use of litters by Jesuits in India appears to have lessened in the eighteenth century, although that may not have been due only to injunctions from Rome. There is ample evidence, however, to demonstrate that another of the generals' campaigns failed. From Vitelleschi to Nickel, from 1637 to 1653 and perhaps beyond, a succession of generals issued bans on the use of tobacco. Vitelleschi described smoking as "pernicious to body and soul" and lamented that in India there were fathers who wasted money purchasing tobacco by the pound and shared it with their friends. Carafa stipulated that no one might indulge in the habit without authorization of the house health officer and the approval of the provincial. Violators were threatened with public flagellation for the length of a *De profundis*. Nickel reaffirmed his predecessors' orders and noted that other religious bodies were undertaking a similar campaign, one thus far ineffective in the Goan province.[104] The generals' orders were duly recorded in the "book of obediences" of each house, and during their visitations, provincials and Visitors were enjoined to verify that the ban remained in effect.

Periodically they did succeed,[105] but as is so often the case in modern times as well, this behavior modification campaign failed. The detailed inventory of New St. Paul's in 1707 lists 23 kilograms of tobacco on hand, whereas the procurator of the college in Macao reported in 1719 that it possessed 18 kilograms.[106] From the 1720s through the 1750s, the household accounts of three other Jesuit houses reveal nearly monthly entries for purchases of as much as 14.5 kilograms of tobacco, consumed in pipes and as snuff, and show that one superior of the professed house in Goa had a very considerable habit—as much as 1.8 kilograms a month![107]

102. Lobo, *Itinerário*, 75.
103. Hertz, *Rhodes of Viet Nam*, 102–3.
104. H/SAG1, 336, 341–42; H/SAG2, 75–77.
105. In 1682, for example, the provincial of Goa reiterated Oliva's dictum that the unauthorized consumption of tobacco was a grave sin, a reminder that Visitor Alessandro Cicero repeated two years later. ARSI, *Goa*, 35, fols. 235ʳ, 272–74ʳ.
106. ARSI, *Goa*, 9:II, fols. 400–404ᵛ; *JapSin*, 23, fols. 376–79ᵛ.
107. "Contas do colégio do Bom Jesús," 1724–36, "Receita e despeza do colégio de Rachol" 1725–30, 1748–56, in HAG, cods. 2098, 2048, and 2049; "Livro da receita e despeza q.al o coll.º de Brag.ᶜᵃ [fez]," 1754–59, ATC/JI, cod. 35.

Like the efforts of one early general congregation to prohibit beards—never effective in China—the Society's antismoking campaign was quietly forgotten.

Though the efforts of Jesuit leaders to shape and circumscribe the conduct of their subjects may seem excessive, frivolous, and sometimes fruitless, one must remember that each religious Order attempted to control the behavior of its members and that the Jesuits were, after all, the new kids on the block. From the perspective of the leadership, it was essential for the Society to project a public image that convinced outsiders of the members' rectitude, piety, reliability, and gravity, for those were the qualities expected of religious by the larger societies in which they functioned and upon which the Society was dependent for recruits, financial assistance, and other forms of aid. But it must be remembered that some novices, some brothers, and even some priests failed to measure up to the standards set by their superiors and left the Society, voluntarily or otherwise.

Disposing of the Unfit: A Case of Double Standards

The Society strove for perfection, but its founders recognized the imperfection of man and the need to separate those whose conduct was deemed harmful to God and to the Society. In some instances, separation might be temporary and involve an indefinite period of rigorous confinement in the cell of a house other than the customary residence of the offender.[108] More often, however, separation meant permanent removal from the Society. Sometimes this removal was voluntary, but during this period it usually was not. Authority to banish a member was vested in the general and delegated by him to provincials, rectors, and Visitors.[109] Causes for dismissal included inability to restrain passions or to eliminate vices; defects termed "incorrigibility"; impediments concealed at the time of admission, including prior marriage, burdensome debts, and (after 1593) New Christian origins; lack of vocation or capacity to perform useful service; and propensity to promote disharmony within the Order.[110] The *Constitutions* stipulated that whenever a superior considered a subject to be in jeopardy because of misbehavior, he should confer with his *consultores* and order prayers in the house to determine the will of God, though concealing the name of the target. They also provided that when it became necessary "to send away" a separated member, he was to be informed, publicly or privately.[111] That was not always done. In one instance, the superior of a misbehaving subject in Brazil arranged for him to be sent back to the kingdom. As soon as the offender's ship was safely at sea, "a trustworthy man" handed him a letter informing him of his immediate termination.[112] Those dismissed were given opportunities to redeem themselves, and superiors were authorized to readmit them if satisfied that they had purged themselves of the defects that had led to their severance.[113]

---

108. Examples of such imprisonment, a penalty common during the Middle Ages and one seemingly more frequently practiced in this period by other Orders, will be found in ARSI, *Lus.*, 37:I, fol. 196; 44:II, fol. 357; and 78, fol. 25.

    109. *CSJ(GE)*, chap. 6, pars. 119–20; *CSJ(C)*, pt. 2, chap. 1, par. 206.

    110. *CSJ(C)*, pt. 2, chap. 2; pt. 8, chap. 1, pars. 664–65.

    111. Ibid., pt. 2, chap. 3.

    112. *HCJB*, 2: 449.

    113. *CSJ(C)*, pt. 2, chap. 4.

Although the *Constitutions* declared that those dismissed were to leave their house "without shame or dishonor" and "with as much love and charity . . . and as much consoled in our Lord as possible," that did not mean that their former colleagues wanted them to remain in the community.[114] In 1573 the provincial of Brazil obtained a royal order advising officials in Brazil that certain former Jesuits were injuring the reputation of the Society by attacking it and its members. The king directed that such troublemakers be rounded up and removed to captaincies where no Jesuit facilities existed.[115]

Ostracism of former members also occurred in India. Fr. Julião Vieira, a former member born in Cochin, complained to the Spanish regent of Portugal that although Valignano had dismissed him and relieved him of his vows, the provincial stipulated that for a period of six years he must not reside within 90 kilometers of a Jesuit facility. He insisted, rightly it would seem, that since he no longer had any ties with the Society, he ought to be free to reside wherever he wished, and that since his father resided in Goa, he wanted to go there. Aquaviva urged Valignano to exercise greater leniency in such cases, but the Visitor responded that it was necessary to prevent easy egress from the Society.[116]

The greatest purge ever to occur in the Assistancy took place in Portugal at the end of 1552, following the disgrace of the founding provincial, Simão Rodrigues (see Chapter 2). He was replaced by two Spaniards, Diego Mirón, former rector of the college of Valencia, who became provincial, and Dr. Miguel de Torres, ex-rector of the college of Salamanca, named as Visitor by Ignatius with instructions to cleanse the province of its impurities. Precisely what ailed the province is still unclear, but it is known that the general received reports that some Jesuits were indulging in luxury, that discipline had become lax, and that subjects were daring to question decisions made by their superiors.[117]

Dr. Torres took his assignment seriously: after interrogating various members of the province, he concluded that many were incapable of adhering to the discipline required by the Society and promptly expelled them. How many he let go became the subject of a vigorous debate between two leading Iberian Jesuits. In 1912 António Astráin, then beginning to publish his still-standard multivolume history of the Spanish Assistancy, concluded that Torres had dismissed 130 subjects, or about half the entire province. Nearly two decades later, Francisco Rodrigues, the Portuguese-born author of the counterpart history of the Lusitanian assistancy, reviewed the evidence, accused his colleague of misinterpreting a key document, and in 1931 announced that Astráin's figures were highly inflated. He pointed

114. Ibid., par. 225. Members of the Society even seem to have taken unchristian pleasure in keeping track of the unhappy fates of former members. According to one authority, there is a file in ARSI entitled "Deserters from the order and their unhappy ends." Thomas H. Clancy, S.J., "Priestly Perseverance in the Old Society of Jesus: The Case of England," *Recusant History* 19, 3 (May 1989): 286–312, at 287.

115. The text of the provisão of 24 Feb. 1573 is given in *LTC/RJ*, 20; Leite dates it 1563, not 1573. *HCJB*, 2: 453.

116. Vieira to [Cardinal Albert, Jan. 1586?], Aquaviva to Valignano, [18 Jan.] 1585, and Valignano to Aquaviva, 26 Dec. 1585, in *DI*, 14: 7*–8*, 311–13, 919–21, and 250–57. Did former members of the Society retain a stigma? That seems suggested by a complaint from an official in Maranhão stating that a onetime Jesuit brother, expelled more than a quarter century earlier, had married, become a carpenter, and "despite his evident incompetence" had been favored by several governors, one of whom made him a fortification contractor. Matias da Costa e Sousa to king, 10 Sept. 1733, in AHU/PA/MA, *cx.* 24 (orig.).

117. *HCJAE*, 1, pt. 2, chap. 19; and *HCJAP*, 1:2, liv. 1, chaps. 4–5.

out that between the province's founding and the arrival of Dr. Torres, 318 persons had been admitted to the province, of whom 90 had already left, voluntarily or involuntarily, and that two contemporary sources indicated that the maximum number Torres actually ousted was 33 out of a total of 135 subjects. Therefore, Rodrigues reduced Astráin's total by 97 and his percentage of dismissals from 50 to only 24. In triumph, Rodrigues concluded that the Portuguese province was not as "worm eaten" as his Spanish colleague had thought.[118]

The only available figures on the number of dismissals in the Portuguese province after the great purge date from 1599 and 1690. In his report for 1599, the provincial declared that 130 persons had been received into the Society that year, but that 40, including sixteen novices, had been dismissed, a ratio of 30.8 percent, higher than during the purge of 1552. In 1690, admissions were up to 159 and dismissals fell to 30, or 18.9 percent.[119]

As founder of the province of India, Xavier himself zealously weeded out those whom he considered inadequate to meet the Society's needs. He once counseled a subordinate, "Avoid being singular, and put aside the favor of the world, and abhor all vain opinion of yourself. This presumption . . . does harm to many of our Society. I have dismissed many . . . because I found them subject to this vice and to others. Take great care that you do not do something for which you would be dismissed . . . live in humility in our Society."[120] One of those whom Xavier separated was his companion in Malacca. After João d'Eiró accepted a small sum of alms given to him for Xavier himself, the saint exiled him to an island off the port and directed him to fast and repent. When the unfortunate d'Eiró later denied seeing a vision that Xavier was certain he had observed, the provincial gave up and ordered him to become a Franciscan. He dismissed another of his original companions, Francisco Mansilhas, as well. Mansilhas refused an assignment to the Moluccas because of reports of the presence of headhunters. Xavier sent him to the bishop of Cochin and ordered him to serve God as a secular priest. A third, and more conspicuous, colleague who tried Xavier's patience excessively was Fr. António Gomes, a scholarly Madeirense patrician who was considered to be a fine theologian and a fiery orator but who proved to be a tactless, excessively rigid administrator. At one point Xavier assigned him to Ormuz, but Gomes resorted to his political connections in the capital to remain in Goa. Later the provincial exiled him to the new Jesuit house at Diu, but Fr. António continued to displease Xavier, who dismissed him and returned him to Portugal.[121]

Just as he strove for perfection in his own life, so Xavier sought perfection in the lives of his subordinates. During his final months, the saint was clearly preoccupied by the problem of unfit subjects. He complained to Simão Rodrigues that he had found it necessary to dismiss "those whom you sent here three years ago (in 1549), since they are not well trained there; for, when they left . . . Coimbra with much zeal, but without experience . . . they were like novices here; and things happened which came to the attention of the people and made it necessary that they be dismissed." In his last letter to the trusted Gaspar Barzaeus, Xavier warned against the admission of too many into the Society and stipulated that "those who

118. Cf. *HCJAE*, 1: 607–8; and *HCJAP*, 2:1, 137–41.
119. *HCJAP*, 2:1, 531; 3:1, 545.
120. Xavier to Gonçalo Rodrigues (superior, Ormuz), 1551, in S/*FX*, 4: 523.
121. Fr. António failed to reach his destination: his ship was wrecked at the mouth of the Great Fish River near the Cape of Good Hope. S/*FX*, 3: 267, 286–87, 554, and 595; 4: 337, 404, 420, and 478–79.

have already been received should pass through many tests, since I fear that some have been received whom it would be better to dismiss, as I have with Alvaro Ferreira," who had refused to attempt to enter China because he feared for his life. Again, Xavier sent him to another Order.[122]

Xavier's ruthless weeding out of undesirables was in accordance with the views of the early generals, particularly Ignatius, Mercurian, and Aquaviva, who were deeply concerned about preventing a few rotten apples from spoiling the barrel. The saint's successors, especially Valignano, maintained a vigilant attitude, particularly toward non-European-born members of the Society, lest they fall by the wayside. Echoing Aquaviva, Valignano admonished his lieutenants that "it is necessary to purge with great resolution useless and damnable people from the Company."[123]

Though many of those discharged in the East during the later sixteenth century were obscure novices and brothers, mostly let go for sexual lapses, lack of promise, and sometimes chronic illness, a few were persons who achieved prominence before or after their association with the Society. One was Fernão Mendes Pinto (b. ca. 1510–d. 1583), a wealthy merchant, soldier of fortune, and "ubiquitous traveler," to use the words of Charles R. Boxer. Recruited by Xavier, he briefly became a brother (1554–56) and loaned the Society a substantial sum of money (evidently later repaid), but he found its discipline intolerable and left by mutual agreement. He later returned to Portugal, where he wrote his famous Peregrinations, whose authenticity continues to fuel scholarly debate.[124]

Another notable onetime Jesuit, António Erédia (b. 1518), was born in Bragança, entered the Society in 1545, and sailed to India in 1551. Initially appointed to the new college in Cochin as its superior (1551–53), he was later assigned to Ormuz but left after a brief stint because of ill health. He served for a time in Bassein and Chorão. By 1560 he resided at the original college of São Paulo and seems to have become disillusioned with his vocation and with the Society's prospects. In 1561 he returned to Portugal (perhaps without authorization), where he wrote a long account of adverse reflections upon the Society's missionary program, a critique that led to his immediate expulsion.[125]

Manuel Godinho de Erédia (b. 1563–d. 1623), the famous Luso-Malayan cosmographer, cartographer, ethnographer, engineer, pirate pursuer, and so-called Portuguese discoverer of Australia, was briefly a student at St. Paul's before he, too, was terminated, either because of physical infirmities (as he later claimed) or because of his unconventional speculative fancies (as others averred). Certainly he bore the Society no malice, for he once wrote Aquaviva

122. S/FX, 4: 457 and 639. Xavier, gifted with remarkable stamina, was convinced that only younger men ought to serve in the eastern missions. Therefore, despite the fact that he had been confessor to Simão Botelho de Andrade (1509–post-1560), an exceptionally able, incorruptible official, a courageous soldier, a fiscal expert, and the compiler of a major cadastral survey (1546–54), Xavier refused to admit him because he was already 45. Botelho then joined the Dominicans and became a very successful fund-raiser. S/FX, 3: 16–17.

123. Aquaviva, "Instrución para el nuevo provincial de la India Oriental," 22 Dec. 1582, in DI, 12: 686; cf. Valignano, "Summary of the Rules for the Provincial of India," Goa, Apr. 1588, in DI, 14: 834–38.

124. For an excellent review of Pinto's career and of scholarly judgments concerning the reliability of his account, see CCJ, 18–24 and 453–54, and S/FX, 4: 260–91, esp. 291 n. 86. Cf. Rebecca D. Catz, trans. and ed., The Travels of Mendes Pinto: Fernão Mendes Pinto (Chicago, 1989), esp. xxxix–xliv.

125. Anthony D'Costa, S.J., The Christianisation of the Goa Islands (Bombay, 1965), 70; S/FX, 4: 423 and n. 22.

pleading for permission to wear a Jesuit insignia on his breast, connoting his respect for the Order.[126]

Manuel Godinho de Erédia had been a mestiço, whereas Francisco Dionisio was one of the few mulattoes ordained by the Society. Although he was the son of a Spaniard and an African woman, he impressed Valignano as a sound scholar, and the Visitor named him as rector of the college of Cochin. There Dionisio was accused of consorting excessively with lay persons. In 1578 he was relieved of his post, an action not displeasing to him, since for several years he had been secretly negotiating to enter the austere Carthusian Order. After being removed, he fled to the Dominicans, who, despite Jesuit protests, offered him refuge. Eventually he yielded to pressure from his superiors, repented, and agreed to live in the novice house in Goa, but by 1580 his superiors had concluded that his attitude remained unacceptable and sent him to Portugal, where he was promptly dismissed.[127]

The *Constitutions* did offer opportunities for readmission, but that seems to have been the exception rather than the rule. One who gained a second chance was Fr. António Vaz (b. ca. 1526). In 1554 he was assigned to Ternate in the Moluccas, where he improperly assumed the title of missions superior and was dismissed on the charge of usurpation. Vaz returned to Goa and successfully appealed for reentry. Subsequently he served in Goa, Cochin, Diu, Damão, Ormuz, and Bassein. In 1573 he wrote Francisco Borgia that he still hoped to be permitted to take his fourth vow, but that ambition apparently remained unfulfilled, for by December 1574 he was no longer listed as a member of the Society.[128] His experience raises a question, unanswerable at this point: once separated from the Order, could one ever expect to be fully accepted again?

By the 1580s and early 1590s three or four persons a year were sent away in the Goan province. Between 1588 and 1594, for example, 26 were dismissed. Among those discharged in 1591 were Fr. Francisco Luís, for being turbulent, inconstant in his vocation, and disobedient; Br. Inofre Rodrigues, for having demonstrated little talent, for being disobedient, and for writing a love letter to a woman; and Br. Gaspar Gonçales, for exercising poor judgment and exhibiting an unpleasant disposition.[129]

126. Josef Franz Schütte, S.J., "Manoel Godinho de Erédia, 'Entdecker' der Terra Australis," *AHSI* 39 (1969): 292–312; *DHP*, 2: 68–69; Armando Cortesão and A. Teixeira da Mota, *Monumenta portuguesa cartographica* (1960), 4: 40. I have not seen Jorge Faro, *Manoel Godinho de Erédia Cosmografo* (Lisbon, 1955).

127. *VMP*, 1: 359–60. Fr. Dionisio was not the only Jesuit to seek admission to the Carthusians, who, however, did not maintain a monastery in the East. For the troubled career of another Jesuit who tried to enter the same Order, see *DI*, 11: 164–98, 202–9, and 853; see also *HCJB*, 2: 447. No Order liked to have its members shift to one of its rivals, and the Church normally took the view that the practice ought to be permitted only when an ecclesiastic sought to "go higher up," meaning to pursue a more austere form of life. Even then permission was required from the Order he was leaving to preclude the suspicion of the sin of "levity." Douglass Roby, "Philip of Harvengt's Contribution to the Question of Passage from one Religious Order to Another," *Analecta Premonstratensia* 49 (1973): 69–100.

128. Vaz to Borgia, Bassein, 8 Dec. 1573, and "Catalogus patrum et fratrum Provinciae Indicae," [Goa, Dec. 1574], in *DI*, 9: 283–85, 474–80. Cornelius Wessels, S.J., *Histoire de la mission d'Amboine, 1546–1605*, trans. J. Roebroeck, S.J. (Louvain, 1934), 209–10, states that Vaz lived until 1589, but I suspect that he confused him with another António Vaz who came from Leiria, entered the Society in 1565, and was eleven years older than the Vaz mentioned in the text. See *DI*, 13: 646.

129. *DI*, 12: 7*–8*; 13: 7*–8*; 14: 7*–9*; 15: 12*; and 16: 20*–21*; for those dismissed in 1591, see *DI*, 15: 730–31.

How many members were dismissed from the India and Japan provinces in later years remains unknown. There are two contradictory lists concerning dismissals by the Japan province. One, of about 1595, gives the names of 25 persons separated since 1554; another, of 1590–92, enumerates ten brothers who were sent away, but only one of them appears on the first list. Among the ten, seven were Japanese, two were Europeans (or Eurasians) born in India, and one was Portuguese. Many of those reported by the 1595 list were also Japanese. The customary reasons given for separation in both sources included unfitness, instability, corruption, desertion, and apostasy.[130] Whether similar reasons prevailed among those separated in the vice-province of China requires further study.

We possess better statistical data concerning the rate of dismissals from the Brazil province during the sixteenth, seventeenth, and early eighteenth centuries than we do for any other part of the Assistancy. According to Fr. Serafim Leite, the two principal reasons for discharge during the sixteenth century were disciplinary breakdowns and violations of the vow of chastity. He observed that many of the 83 who were separated between 1578 and 1603 were interpreters who had close relations with the indigenous population. One was John Vincent Yate (b. ca. 1551), the first English-born Jesuit in Brazil, who was sent away in 1601 for fornication.[131]

In 1688 Giovanni Antonio Andreoni, an official in the college of Bahia and later the author of a famous analysis of the sources of Brazil's wealth, became curious about the patterns of admission and expulsion in the province. Accordingly, he extracted the relevant data from registers kept in the archives of the novitiate of Salvador. Those records have unfortunately disappeared, so that it is not possible to verify the completeness of Andreoni's survey. Still, it is evident that between 1556 and 1675, between a quarter and a third of those admitted were subsequently discharged, and that there was a greater likelihood of the Brazilian minority to fail than there was for the Portuguese Peninsular contingent to do so (see Table 11.10). Two later lists reporting dismissals between 1681 and 1759 reveal that most of those dismissed were students or brothers. Less than 20 percent were priests, none of them members of the elite who had taken the fourth vow, and possibly only one was born outside of Luso-Brazilian territories.[132]

The calculations of Andreoni and those derived from a list disclosing dismissals between 1681 and 1707 indicate that 29.6 percent of those admitted to the province suffered discharge from it. The three sources also indicate that the province usually experienced one to three dismissals per year. Some years, no one was separated; during exceptional years, as many as ten to twelve were turned out.

130. "Dos [padres e irmãos] em Japão se forão ou despedirão da Companhia," n.d., BA/JA/49-IV-56, fols. 9ʳ–9ᵛ; "Catálogo delos despedidos, muertos, y recebidos en este trienio en la dicta provincia de Japón, [15]90, 91–92," in *MHJ*, 335–37. According to Fr. Rouleau, four seminarians at Nanking were dismissed in the 1680s, one for immoral conduct, one for lack of talent, a third for lack of motivation, and the last for being overbearing. Rouleau, "First Chinese Priest," 39 n. 93.

131. *HCJB*, 2: 447–54.

132. "Noticia de provᵃ Brasiliensi," Apr. 1688, in ARSI, *Bras.*, 3:II, fols. 248–251ᵛ (includes both Portuguese and Latin texts); "Catalogus dimissorum e Societate in Provinciae Brasilica ab anno 1681 usque ad annum 1707," in ibid., 6; "Cat.al de personis prov. Brasiliae, confectus Romae, c. 1760," in ibid., 7, fols. 39–40.

TABLE 11.10

Admissions and Dismissals in the Brazil Province, 1566–1707

	Total	Portugal		Brazil		Atlantic islands		Angola		Other		Percentage of
	(N)	(N)	(%)	(N)	(%)	(N)	(%)	(N)	(%)	(N)	(%)	those admitted
Admissions												
1566–1608[a]	[247][b]	131	53.0	63	25.5	42	17.0	0	0	11	4.5	—
1608–1675	475	226	47.6	170	35.8	34	7.2	7	1.5	38	8.0	—
1676–1688	173	76	43.9	77	44.5	9	5.2	4	2.3	7[c]	4.0	—
Dismissals												
1566–1608[a]	61	28	45.9	19	31.1	9	14.8	0	0	5	8.2	24.7
1608–1675[d]	[165]	79[e]	47.9	65[f]	39.4	10	6.0	0	0	[11]	6.6	34.3
1676–1688	29	9	31.0	13	44.8	4	13.8	0	0	3	10.3	16.8
1689–1707[g]	107	60	56.1	38	35.5	4	3.7	0	0	5	4.7	n.a.

SOURCES: *HCJB*, 2: 436–37 n. 3; ARSI, *Bras.*, 3:II, 248–251ᵛ and 6.

[a] Because of a scribal error, there are slight overlaps for the year 1608.

[b] I have corrected Andreoni's total.

[c] Not included: 7 Italians.

[d] Because of a scribal error, the inclusive years in the text (1606–88) overlap the last period.

[e] Includes 31 from Lisbon.

[f] Includes 37 from Bahia.

[g] Omits those from 1681 to 1688 given in the second source in order to prevent duplication.

How the failure rate in Brazil compares with that in other parts of the Assistancy or in other assistancies remains to be determined. Likewise, until further studies have been undertaken, it is impossible to state how the termination rate in this assistancy compares with that of other coeval religious bodies. Although the turnover rate was undoubtedly substantial, and even costly, it does not seem to have been out of line with the experience of modern firms, which report annual termination rates of 24–31 percent.[133]

Probably no human organization ever fully satisfies its manpower problems. Certainly the Society of Jesus did not. Confronted with seemingly limitless opportunities to convert millions of non-Western peoples to what most Europeans then still considered to be the only true faith, it never found sufficient personnel even to attempt to realize that ambition. In the Portuguese Assistancy, the scarcity of Peninsulars presented the leaders of the Society with various alternatives, of which some were politically unacceptable to the host regime, others socially unacceptable either to the members of the Society or to the larger European societies upon which they depended. The reluctance of the Roman headquarters to admit a significant number of colonial-born whites in Brazil and elsewhere and the determination to exclude most colonials from the highest levels within the Order reflect the widespread prejudice of Europeans, including the Portuguese, toward whites born overseas. With respect to the admission of nonwhites, and especially their ordination in the Assistancy, the record of

133. Anon., "Personnel Turnover: AMS' Latest Findings," *Administrative Management* 29, 7 (July, 1968): 43–46; Victor R. Linquist, "Trends in the Employment of College and University Graduates in Business and Industry 1986," *Northwestern Endicott Report* (Evanston, Ill., 1985). I am indebted to my graduate student, Gordon Aamot, head of the Business School Library, University of Washington, for both references.

the Society is not one of conspicuous achievement. Since one of the declared objects of the Order was "to labor strenuously in giving aid toward the salvation and perfection of the souls of their fellow men,"[134] and since it was manifestly impossible to fill its staffing needs entirely from European sources, the Society's reluctance to admit nonwhites to the priesthood may seem surprising. But the Society's record was, in fact, no worse than that attained by other religious Orders beyond Europe during this period. In a short article devoted to Franciscan policy toward the admission of indigenous candidates in Portuguese India, Fr. Achilles Meersman, a distinguished Franciscan scholar, has observed that

> the Portuguese were in a sense ill-equipped to expand Christianity into a country with an ancient culture such as India. They inhabited the extremities of western Christendom and had little or no contact with other cultures. The Catholicism they inherited from their forefathers ... they tenaciously clung to. Every rule or custom was sacrosanct. No formulation of a doctrine could be improved upon. This tendency was later strengthened by the enactments of the Council of Trent.[135]

It would be hard to accept that argument in its entirety. First, the contention that the Portuguese had had only minimal contact with other cultures is fundamentally mistaken: long before Vasco da Gama reached India, the Portuguese had had extensive contact with the peoples of north, west, and west-central Africa as well as with those who inhabited the Canary Islands. Second, whether Spaniards, Italians, Germans, or Belgians were any better equipped to establish Christianity in India or elsewhere abroad is unprovable. Third, the parameters of Jesuit activities in India and elsewhere were set primarily by non-Portuguese superiors, among them Xavier, a Spaniard; Mercurian, a Belgian; and Aquaviva and Valignano, both Italians. On the other hand, it is true that the Iberians were rigidly legalistic and intolerant of deviations from perceived norms, especially norms sanctified by law or by the agents of the law. And there can be little question that centuries of embittered relations between the followers of Christ and those of Mohammed led Iberians to develop contemptuous attitudes toward dark-skinned peoples whom they encountered overseas and whom they derisively and generically labeled as *mouros* or Moors.

To be fair, however, one must remember that other Europeans also took a jaundiced view of non-Westerners, and that not all of them were Catholics. In 1703, for example, the directors of the English East India Company warned its field agents that "the Chinieses are a Subtill Cunning People and are very dexterous in putting Cheats upon all that Deal with them and must be managed accordingly."[136] Later in the same century, the British Board of Trade wrote, "The general or rather total want of integrity among the natives [of India] is too well known." Reports from EIC agents in India led the Board to conclude that

> the depravity, ignorance and misconduct of native Hindoostanny agents ... has often been [described] as being notorious, lamentable, and irremediable ... the generality of the natives of this province, particularly the Hindus, are absolutely lost to every sentiment of religion

134. *CSJ (GE)*, 1: 3.

135. Meersman, "The Question of Admitting Indians to the Franciscan Order," *Neue Zeitschrift für Missionwissenschaft* 13 (1957): 29–34.

136. "Orders and Instructions Given by the Court of Managers for the United Trade to the East Indies," London, 29 Jan. 1703, in IOL, Letter Book ser. 12 [E/3/95], fol. 20.

and morality, when their temporal interests, their prejudices, or their possessions interfere ... [and the Indians are] a race of people who from their infancy are utter strangers to the very idea of common faith and honesty.[137]

When it came to racial prejudice, the Iberians enjoyed no monopoly. Wherever the Society operated within the Portuguese Assistancy, its leaders were bound to consider seriously the social biases of the dominant Lusitanian (or nominally Lusified) population. But those leaders also included Italians, Germans, and other Europeans who were as accustomed to resort to derogatory racial stereotypes when referring to the talents, virtues, and intellectual potentials of non-Europeans as were the Iberians. It may be argued that the Jesuits ought to have used their exceptional influence and prestige, especially during the formative period, to correct or improve prevailing social attitudes expressed by European laymen abroad, but the Society did not consider that to be a part of its mission. Besides, its members were as convinced as other contemporary ecclesiastics that the imperfections of terrestrial existence were insignificant compared with the blessings that those properly prepared would enjoy in paradise.[138]

Some apologists have denied that the Jesuits were ever racists and have attributed the Society's meager record regarding the ordination of nonwhites to the "unfortunate failures" of a few non-Western candidates who failed to adhere to the high moral and theological standards that the Jesuits and others sought to maintain.[139] Undeniably some Indians, Japanese, Chinese, and other Asians wavered in their vocations, but so did some Europeans. Cristóvão Pereira, after all, was an Old Christian, a professed priest, a provincial, and an apostate. It is hard to resist the conclusion that the Jesuits applied higher standards of conformity to nonwhites than they did to Europeans. They were even willing to bend their rules for some Europeans but were disinclined to do so for other ethnic groups. Simon Rangel was a triple homicide who had once been a member of a Franciscan house in Coimbra. The *Constitutions* explicitly state that murderers and persons who have previously been attached to other Orders are to be barred from membership, yet Simon Rangel was taken in, first as a brother and later as an ordained priest. He enjoyed the backing of two Visitors and two generals. One of those Visitors, Alessandro Valignano, wrote that Rangel appeared to possess the requisite "virtue" to become an accomplished humanist and to have a sound knowledge of theology. Rangel was sent to the Moluccas, where his ardor for the Society soon evaporated and he sought permission to leave it.[140] Would a Chinese, a Japanese, or an Indian applicant with the same background have been given as much consideration as Simon Rangel?

137. P[eter] J. Marshall, "Indian Officials under the East India Company in Eighteenth-Century Bengal," *Bengal Past and Present* (1965): 95–120, at 105. See also Kenneth Ballhatchet, *Race, Sex and Class under the Raj: Imperial Attitudes and Policies and Their Critics, 1793–1905* (London, 1980).

138. E.g., Valignano to Aquaviva, Macao, 25 Sept. 1589, in *DI*, 15: 341–44. The Visitor thanked the general for admitting his nephew and declared that he wished that his other nephews would also join, so that they would be free from the deceits of the world and able to serve God.

139. E.g., Cieslik, "Training," 72; and Lawrence A. Noonan, "The First Jesuit Mission in Malacca ... 1545 to 1552," *Studia*, no. 36 (1973): 435.

140. Valignano to Mercurian, Goa, 15 Nov. 1576; Rangel to Mercurian, Goa, 2 Nov. 1580; and Aquaviva to Rangel, Rome, 19 Feb. 1582, in *DI*, 10: 776–77; and 12: 140–41, and 574–76. Interestingly enough, knowledge of Rangel's previous shortcomings was declared "secret."

One wonders how right the China missionary François de Rougement was when he asked, "Arc wc . . . more engaged with maintaining our authority than with maintaining and spreading the Faith?"[141] Could Jesuits, Franciscans, Dominicans, diocesan clergymen, or European laymen have accepted a situation in which nonwhites exercised a preponderance of power within European-conceived organizations? Did not the Jesuits and others mistake power for virtue, conformity for talent, and image-making for piety?

The growth of the Society in the Assistancy was influenced by its success in recruitment and in the retention of those admitted. Except for the relatively few who resigned from the Society voluntarily and with the concurrence of their superiors, most of those discharged represent failures in the processes of selection and the inculcation of discipline. It may be, for example, that during the regime of Simão Rodrigues, some unsuitable young men were taken in because of pressure applied by important families, anxious for the social status conferred by having a relative who belonged to an Order that enjoyed so much royal favor. It needs to be remembered that most of those marked for the priesthood entered as teenagers, few of whom could fully comprehend what they wished to do with their lives, and that many joined because of familial pressure.[142] Though such families may have felt shame when their sons were passed over as candidates for the priesthood, some of those not selected to undertake academic programs became frustrated because of their inability to realize their religious goals. It is easy enough to say that when they joined they understood that such decisions would be made for them, but it is equally possible to empathize with their disappointment and to understand why they lost confidence in their futures within the Society and wanted out.[143] Many of those destined to become brothers or coadjutores were recruited for their urgently required nonacademic skills. Some were artisans, others were linguists, and still others possessed business experience. Many of them entered when already in their mid-twenties or later, after having lived vigorous, sometimes unrestrained lives. It is not surprising that some, like Mendes Pinto, found the Society's discipline intolerable and asked to be released.

According to the personnel catalogues and other coeval sources, a high proportion of those discharged were novices and students; very few were professed. That was in keeping with the constitutional provision stipulating that those newest in the Society could be released most easily and that those more senior could be separated only with greater difficulty.[144] Discipline in the Society, that internal policing system so often lauded by its admirers, was, in fact, relative, not absolute. Young men who wrote love letters to old flames back home could expect to be dismissed, as could those who, like several of Xavier's companions, refused assignments.[145] But when Fernão Rebelo (b. 1547–d. 1608), a theology instructor at Évora, was assigned to teach his specialty in Brazil, he informed the provincial that it would be impossible for him to go because the sea air caused him to become addlepated. Presumably it was only long voyages that provoked this disorder, for

141. As quoted in Boxer, *Church Militant*, 25.

142. E.g., Scholastic Jorge Barradas to Aquaviva, Goa, 25 Nov. 1593, in *DI*, 16: 437, par. 2.

143. E.g., Br. Juan Martín to Aquaviva, Cochin, 26 Dec. 1588; Br. Michael Rodrigues to Aquaviva, Cochin, 9 Jan. 1594, in *DI*, 15: 160–61, and 16: 613–16.

144. *CSJ(C)*, pt. 2, chap. 1, par. 205.

145. E.g., António Pires to Luís Rodrigues, Ilhéus, 17 July 1565, in *MB*, 4: 261.

the next year he traveled to Madeira on administrative assignment, and he later made a voyage to Italy.[146] The militant separatists who disrupted the Portuguese province during the middle decades of the seventeenth century were never punished for their conduct, nor was the provincial of Brazil who engineered the overthrow of Visitor Magistris. Those who wrote love letters or who declined to do a job were expelled as object lessons, but those who caused the Society far more damage escaped without significant punishment. Why? In part because of their senior status, but also because they enjoyed the protection of their rulers, and the Jesuits, who understood the meaning of power very well, respected that protection and knew when to yield to it. They were prepared to do so because they were dependent upon the political arm to assist the Society with its enterprises, including its financial support, the subject of the next chapters.

146. Virgínia Rau, "Aspectos do pensamento económico portugues durante o século xvi," *Revista "Comércio português"*, nos. 171–73 (Jan.–Mar. 1961): 5.

CHAPTER 12

The Fiscal Administration
of an Enterprise

> If such business affairs occur in connection with the colleges, they should have
> a procurator to take care of them and defend their rights. If such affairs arise
> in connection with the houses of the Society or its whole body, to enable the
> Society itself to preserve its peace, the same procurator, or another coadjutor,
> or some person from outside the Society . . . could defend the Society's rights for
> the greater glory to God.
>
> —Loyola, *Constitutions*

THE FATHERS GENERAL, assisted by the general congregations, set the Society's general
policies. As Chapter 10 indicates, the implementation of those policies depended upon the
energy, tact, and initiative of the senior field officers, the provincials, the Visitors, and the
college rectors. These officials governed by means of personal contact, written correspondence, and standing instructions issued to subordinate officials of the Society. Prominent
among the latter were those charged with the management of the Society's economic affairs.
They included several types of managers—the missions procurators, the provincial (or vice-
provincial) procurators, the house procurators, the estate supervisors, and others. Though
the procurators frequently became the targets of criticism, if not derision, from their spiritual superiors and have rarely inspired appreciative remarks by Jesuit historians, the Order
could hardly have functioned without their acuity, initiative, experience, resourcefulness, and
probity. Their tireless labors made economically possible many of the Society's celebrated
spiritual achievements. For that reason, and because their work frequently brought them into
close contact—and conflict—with the Society's leading critics including royal officials, rival
religious, and indigenous leaders, it is necessary to understand the range and scope of their
duties and the ways in which they reported their stewardship of the assets entrusted to them.

The Missions Procurators

One of the most demanding responsibilities in the Society was the office of the missions
procurator.[1] Initially the provisioning of the incipient Jesuit missions overseas fell to crown

---

1. Fundamental for an understanding of the origins of the office are Josef Wicki, S.J., "Die Anfange
der Missionsprokur der Jesuiten in Lissabon bis 1580," *AHSI* 40 (Jan.–June 1971): 246–322, and *HCJB*,

officers. They were assisted by an Italian brother, Bernardino Excalceato, who took the name dos Reis when he joined the Society in 1542.[2] A dozen years later, Fr. Manuel Godinho became the first of at least two procurators of the province of Portugal who were also aides to the overseas missions.[3] As the Society's evangelical enterprises in India, Japan, and Brazil expanded and their needs intensified, it became apparent that they placed a heavy burden upon Godinho's successors. Accordingly, in 1573 and 1574, Mercurian authorized the appointment of missions procurators in Lisbon for the Portuguese Assistancy and in Seville for the Spanish Assistancy.

The first to occupy the post in Lisbon was Alessandro Vallareggio (b. 1529–d. 1580), who served in India, Macao, and Japan briefly before being sent to Rome as procurator for the Japan enterprise. There he evidently came in contact with Alessandro Valignano, who recommended his fellow Italian for the new position and drafted his instructions. Vallareggio did not prove to be a happy choice. Afflicted with stomach problems and a choleric temperament made worse by the slothful Portuguese bureaucracy and by rigid spiritual superiors,[4] he offended both Jesuits and non-Jesuits in the kingdom and incurred the ire of Valignano for being an alleged spendthrift, a complaint often leveled at his successors as well.[5] In 1576 Vallareggio was succeeded by another Italian, Sebastiano Sabino, whose service proved to be equally unsatisfactory to his masters in the East. In 1580 Sabino surrendered his office, and the following year he became one of the fourteen apostles who embarked for India.[6]

Partly because of complaints about the administration of the early missions procurators from abroad and partly because certain Portuguese Jesuits, notably the provincial of the kingdom, resented the fact that the occupant was not under their full control and expressed

---

1: chap. 2. See also Felix Zubillaga, S.J., "El procurador de las Indias Occidentales de la Compañía de Jesús (1574)," *AHSI* 22 (Jan.–June 1953): 367–417. Both the Wicki and the Zubillaga articles contain valuable appendixes. The latter includes the text dated "hacia 1577" of an instruction detailing the responsibilities of the office. For a later, updated version, for which the suggested date is "a principios de outubre 1578," see Antonio de Egana, S.J., comp., *Monumenta peruana*, vol. 2, *1576–1580* (Rome, 1958), 469–74.

2. *S/FX*, 1: 716 n. 16; *ASCJ*, 164.

3. The second appears to have been Francisco Henriques (b. ca. 1530–d. 1590), a onetime gentleman of the royal bedchamber who was successively procurator of the arts college of Coimbra and rector of Santo Antão before becoming secretary of the province and procurator of Portugal and the missions, 1558–64. *ASCJ*, 148–49; *MB*, 3: 82*–83* and 383–85.

4. The missions procurator and his assistant were given cramped accommodations at the college of Santo Antão. Vallareggio complained that the college rector and monitor forbade them to write dispatches or to work on their accounts on Sundays and holy days and accused them of risking mortal sins for attempting to do so. Vallareggio to Mercurian, 4 May 1575, in Wicki, "Die Anfange," 310. The status of such "guests" in the college is discussed further in Chapter 24.

5. *VMP*, 1: 88; Valignano to Aquaviva, 20 Nov. 1587, in *DI*, 14: 697ff.; "Respuestas dadas en enero . . . de 1594 al memorial del provincial del Brasil . . . Marcal Belliarte," in ARSI, *Bras.*, 2; Emanuel de Almeida (provincial) to Vitelleschi, Goa, 12 Sept. 1638, in ARSI, *Goa*, 22, fol. 136. These and similar complaints relate to the unperceived wave of inflation that washed over Iberia beginning in the 1580s and continued until at least the mid-seventeenth century. Earl J. Hamilton, *American Treasure and the Price Revolution in Spain, 1501–1650* (1934; rpr., New York, 1965), 272, 278, 290, and tables 28 and 29. For some indications of comparable advances in Lisbon, see *DHP*, 4: 500–504.

6. *HCJAP*, 2:2, 461. His predecessor, Vallareggio, participated in the ill-fated Alcázarquibir battle, where he became a captive of the Muslims. After his release, Vallareggio worked for the ransoming of other captives until he succumbed to the plague in Ceuta in 1580. *RJC*, 281.

concern lest the eastern missions be wholly dominated by foreigners, Mercurian appointed a committee of three senior fathers to make recommendations concerning the future of the office. The committee urged that the office be suppressed and that its duties be reassigned to the Peninsular procurator.[7] That was done, but with unsatisfactory results. Superiors in the missions criticized the shortcomings of the Peninsular procurator, Fr. Jerónimo Cardoso, an experienced administrator, whereas both he and his superior, the provincial, insisted that he lacked sufficient space or personnel to discharge his duties.[8] The provincial defended Cardoso and advised Aquaviva that he was trying to find persons to assist him but that the task was not easy, for "some lack the stamina for the job which is burdensome (*grande*)," while others lacked the talent. By 1585 Aquaviva had decided to reestablish the post of missions secretary, but it was another two years before he found someone to fill it.[9]

The new occupant, who, like his successors, lived at Santo Antão, was Fr. Amador Rebêlo, who had an unusual background. He was first admitted to the Society in 1553 at about age 14, "but did not persevere." A decade later he gained readmission. The next year Rebêlo became an aide to Fr. Luís Gonçalves da Cámara, preceptor of Sebastian (see Chapter 4), a post he held for a dozen years. While serving as rector of Santo Antão (1577–81), he was involved in negotiations for the redemption of captives from Morocco after the 1578 catastrophe. In 1586 he went to Madrid, apparently to become court procurator (see below), but he was recalled to Lisbon to assume the missions procurate.[10]

Fr. Rebêlo fared no better than his predecessors, for he soon became the target of criticism from Goa. He was accused of mismanaging the province's accounts, of failing to trade its commodities in Lisbon profitably, of sending bills of exchange to the East that could not be honored, of being untalented for his assignment, and of being too old for his job—though he lived on until 1622! Such criticisms came from Francisco de Monclaro, superior of the mission contingent sent out in 1592,[11] as well as the provost of New St. Paul's and two provincials, the second of whom, the splenetic Francisco Cabral, advised the general that it would be "a great charity and profit to the province" to remove Rebêlo, a sentiment echoed a year later by the fourth provincial congregation in Goa.[12] By the date of the congregation's deliberations, Aquaviva had already decided to replace Rebêlo.[13]

A decade later, Aquaviva finally recognized that the demands of the office of missions procurator exceeded the abilities of a single manager. In 1604 he created a second procurate

7. Francisco Martins, S.J., et al. to Mercurian, 12 Dec. 1580, in *DI*, 12: 160–66.

8. For a brief biography of Cardoso (b. 1548–d. 1605) see António Franco, *Imagem da virtude em o noviciado da companhia de Jesus no real collegio de Jesus de Coimbra em Portugal*, 2 vols. (Évora and Coimbra, 1719), 2: 571–72.

9. Sebastião de Morais (provincial) to Aquaviva, 26 Apr., 2 June, 7 and 30 Nov. 1585, and Jerónimo Cardoso to Aquaviva, 25 Jan. and 6 Sept. 1586, in *DI*, 14: 25–27, 32, 52, 61–62, 310, and 331–36.

10. *ASCJ*, 245; *DI*, 14: 61 n. 1.

11. Of the five ships dispatched from Lisbon to Goa in 1592, only Monclaro's reached its destination; two were sunk, one was captured by the English, and the Portuguese destroyed the other off the coast of Mozambique to prevent its seizure by the English. *DI*, 16: 182 n. 1.

12. [Pedro Martins (provincial)] to Aquaviva, ca. Nov. 1591; Francisco de Monclaro to Aquaviva, 26 Oct. 1593; Cristóvão de Castro to Aquaviva, 29 Oct. 1593; Jerónimo Xavier (provost) to Aquaviva, 12 Nov. 1593; Francisco Cabral to Aquaviva, 15 Dec. 1593; Acts of the Fourth Provincial Congregation, par. 15, in *DI*, 15: 624–25; 16: 201, 208, 248, 528–29, and 658.

13. It is not clear who Rebêlo's successor was. Wicki (*DI*, 16: 658 n. 63) says that it was Fr. João Soeiro. There was such a father serving in China at this time, but he does not appear to have returned to Europe. *RJC*, 257, no. 801.

for Brazil, a reform that had been repeatedly urged since 1558.[14] Within the next decade or so, the same father general further subdivided the eastern procurate into two positions, one for the two Indian provinces and the other for the province of Japan and the vice-province of China. Other reorganizations reflected the changing fortunes of Jesuit overseas enterprises. In 1711 there was one missions procurator for Japan and Malabar, a second for Goa, and a third for Brazil, including the Maranhão missions. In the 1720s a fourth position followed the formation of the vice-province of Maranhão. By the late 1750s, five missions procurators served Goa, Japan and Malabar, China, Brazil, and Maranhão.[15]

Those who held the post of missions procurator were, of course, appointed by the fathers general upon the recommendation of senior Jesuits in the affected provinces. It seems obvious that politics as well as merit influenced such recommendations. In 1706, for example, Francisco Sarmento, the ailing provincial procurator of Goa, wrote to Tamburini stating that he had heard that the missions procurator for his province had submitted his resignation. He urged that it be rejected, insisting that the missions procurator was a person of exceptional ability and zeal and had become the target of certain unnamed jealous persons who aspired to his position. Evidently Fr. Sarmento wrote without consulting his chief, Provincial Emanuel Carvalho, for a few months later the latter recommended to the general three other candidates for the position, one the deceased Sarmento's successor, the second his own companion and a former estate manager, and the third the rector of the novitiate of Chorão.[16]

If little is known concerning those who served as missions procurators for the eastern provinces, we are better informed about those who represented the interests of Brazil and Maranhão in Lisbon, mainly because of the researches of Fr. Serafim Leite. Of the fourteen for whom we possess biographical data, three were born in Brazil, two in Angola, and the remainder in the kingdom. The first, Fr. António Colaço (b. 1568–d. 1647), held office only a short time before he became procurator at the court of Madrid, a position he held until his death.[17] One of his early successors, Pero (Pedro) da Cunha, was accompanying his provincial on an inspection trip between Bahia and Rio de Janeiro when they were apprehended by the Dutch in 1624. He and his companions were sent to Holland, where they were shut up in a former monastery for two years. Upon his repatriation to Lisbon in 1626, Cunha became missions procurator for Brazil, an office that he held until about 1640. During the 1630s he petitioned to be reassigned, but though the assistant general reported that he was worthy of such favor, no one had come from Brazil who was suitable to replace him. Cunha did manage to return to Brazil in 1641 and probably died there.[18] During the 1660s and apparently the 1670s, the office was held by João Pimenta, who, though born near

14. It was urged initially by Visitor Inácio de Azevedo (Azevedo to Laínez, 2 Nov. 1558, in *MB*, 5: 191–93), subsequently by Visitor Cristóvão de Gouveia (1582–89; *HCJB*, 1: 135 and 142), and also by the embattled Jerónimo Cardoso (Cardoso to Aquaviva, 6 Sept. 1586, in *DI* 16: 333–34).

15. ARSI, *Lus.*, 77: 69; "Conta que derao os pp. procurators das prov.ªs da Companhia de Jesus em o ultramar, . . . 1758–1759," ATC/CJ, no. 266.

16. Sarmento to Tamburini, 26 Aug. 1706, and Carvalho to Tamburini, 20 Jan. 1707, in ARSI, *Goa*, 9:II, fols. 384 and 395.

17. Diogo Barbosa Machado, *Bibliotheca Lusitana* [1741–59, 4 vols.] (fasc. ed., Coimbra, 1965–67), 1: 242–43; and António Franco, *Imagem da virtude em o noviciado da companhia de Jesus no real collegio do Espírito Santo de Évora* (Lisbon, 1714), 853.

18. ARSI, *Bras.*, 8:II, 432a; *HCJB*, 1: 580; 5: 33, 35, 47, and 50; and 6: 593.

Lisbon, entered the Society in Rio de Janeiro in 1646. Though a master of Tupi, Pimenta was so sickly that his superiors decided to return him to the kingdom, where he became missions procurator, a position he seems to have held until his death in 1677.[19]

One of the most visible men to hold the office was Baltasar Duarte. Born around 1646 in Lisbon, Fr. Duarte sailed to Brazil in 1665 and for a decade served as professor of humanities at the college of Bahia (1673–83). While in Salvador, he became the confessor of the archbishop and a confidant not only of three governors-general but also the formidable António Vieira. During his six years as procurator in Lisbon (1689–95), Duarte was responsible for sending 65 men to serve in his province. He enjoyed close relations with Pedro II, who kept him at court for three years after he surrendered his post. Fr. Duarte returned to Brazil in 1698 and became rector of the college of Rio de Janeiro for a triennium, but in 1701 he sailed back to Lisbon, where he died four years later. Little seems to be known about his immediate successor, Paulo Carneiro, except that he was born and died in Pernambuco, where he had served as rector of both Jesuit colleges before becoming missions procurator.

The case of Miguel Cardozo, who was born in Luanda in 1659, is especially illuminating. Cardozo joined the Society in Bahia in 1674 and, because of his knowledge of Bantu, was assigned to care for slave gangs on the Bahian plantations and to provide spiritual care for newly arrived chattels. After a stint as rector of the college of Recife (1702–5) he was elected procurator to Rome. The next year (1707), he went to Lisbon to become missions procurator, a post he occupied until 1715, when he returned to Brazil. There he served as rector of the college of Rio de Janeiro (1716–19) before becoming provincial, dying in harness at Santos in 1721.

Another Luanda-born Cardozo, António (b. 1669), possibly Miguel's brother, followed a similar career. He, too, entered the Society in Bahia in 1684 and worked among the Bantu-speaking slaves. He excelled as a preacher and was renowned for his ability to work with nonecclesiastics. Perhaps for that reason he became one of the negotiators during the celebrated invasion of Rio de Janeiro by the Breton corsair René Duguay-Trouin in 1711. Cardozo later served twice as rector of the new seminary at Belém da Cachoeira and as vice-rector of the college of Rio de Janeiro before being posted to Lisbon as missions procurator from about 1722 until 1727. He died in Rio de Janeiro in 1750. His successor was Martinho Borges (b. ca. 1677–d. 1755), a Lisbonense who entered the Society in 1693 and sailed for Brazil the next year. He was briefly rector of the small college of Santos (1724–26) before being assigned to Lisbon as missions procurator, a job he performed from 1727 until about 1740.

The last of the missions procurators in Brazil for whom we have data is José Giraldes (b. 1697–d. 1760), who was already a secular priest in his early thirties when he joined the Order. It is unclear when or in what capacity he served in Brazil. He was missions procurator in the 1740s, but at the end of that decade he returned to Bahia as rector of the novitiate of Jiquitaia, and later as consultor of the rector of the college of Bahia.[20]

19. In 1669 Pimenta advised the father general that when he had assumed his duties seven years earlier he had found the procurate to be in debt more than 12,000,000 rs., but that its obligations had been settled. Pimenta to Oliva, 11 Aug. 1669, in ARSI, *Bras.*, 3:II, 84.

20. The foregoing is based largely upon *HCJB*, 8 and 9.

Only three men occupied the position of missions procurator for the vice-province of Maranhão between its establishment in 1727 and its suppression at the end of the 1750s. Two of them became highly controversial. The first was Jacinto de Carvalho, who was born near Coimbra in 1677 and died there in 1744. After entering the Order in 1699, he spent thirteen years as a missionary in the Amazon. Because of ill health, he was sent back to the kingdom. When the vice-province was formed, Carvalho was an obvious choice to become its missions procurator because of his field experience; two years after assuming that position, however, he agreed to return to Pará with the State of Maranhão's new governor, João da Maia da Gama (1722–28). In Pará, Carvalho served as Maia's confessor and as mission Visitor. For a time he was also confessor to Maia's successor, the choleric Alexandre de Sousa Freire, but the two broke over Indian policy (see Chapter 19). In 1730, Carvalho returned to Lisbon and resumed his former position, one that João Teixeira (born in Lisbon in 1676; died in Pará in 1758) had occupied during the interim (1724–31), having previously been a missionary in Maranhão and rector of both of its colleges. When Fr. Carvalho relinquished his office a second time in 1739, he was succeeded by another ex-missionary, Bento da Fonseca (b. 1702–d. 1781). In 1720 Fonseca sailed from Lisbon to Maranhão, where he completed his studies and became a professor of philosophy and theology and the head of a mission. When Fr. Carvalho's years caught up with him, Fonseca was summoned back to Lisbon and remained as the vice-province's often embattled missions procurator until his Order's suppression.[21]

Each of these fourteen men had had considerable field experience in Brazil before being named to the demanding position of missions procurator. Most had important standing with members of the elite, who would be inclined to treat them and their requests with respect. But none had known business experience before assuming tasks that required extensive knowledge of accounting procedures, exchange rates, market values, and the like. For such expertise, the missions procurators were dependent upon their assistants, who were often brothers rather than priests. Missions procurators came and went, but the assistants provided the knowledge and experience so necessary to the discharge of their office.[22]

Those duties were undeniably complex, time-consuming, and often frustrating.[23] The procurators were expected to forward all dispatches between the overseas provinces and the

21. The preceding is based principally upon *HCJB*, 9: 154, 149–50, and 8: 243–52, as well as much of the correspondence of Frs. Carvalho and Fonseca cited elsewhere in this study.

22. Two examples: Br. Bastian Gonzales (b. 1541–d. 1604) entered the Society in 1559 and made his vows as a temporal coadjutor about 1577. From at least the mid-1580s until his death, he was the assistant to the missions procurators. *DI*, 14: 333 n. 12. Br. António Homem, another *coadjutor temporal*, served as a companion of nine missions procurators during a 23-year period. "Catalogo [da] provincia de Portugal . . . 1639," ARSI, *Lus.*, 44:II, 570–93. Homem received unusually extensive mention in *ASCJ*, 29–30, apparently because of his saintly demeanor; the suggested date for his demise (1693) is probably a typo for 1673, however, since he entered the Society in 1599.

23. Some of the duties of the missions procurators are summarized in *VMP*, 1: 86. Specific instructions include Alessandro Valignano, "Memorial de lo que ha de hazer el P.e Alexandro Regio despues de mi partida," Feb. 1574; Mercurian, "Instrución para el procurador de la India y Brasil," 6 Mar. 1575; and Valignano, "Regimento para el procurador de la India que reside en Portugal," 7 Dec. 1587; in *DI*, 9: 188–89, 618–21, and 14: 747–60. Cf. Aquaviva, "Ultima instruccion para el procurador de las Indias occidentales," ca. 1577, in Zubillaga, "El procurador," 400–402. The same author published an extract from a memoir of a Spanish missions procurator dated 1651 (pp. 395–97). I have not seen any comparable document for the Portuguese missions procurators. See also note 1 above.

Roman headquarters. They worked closely with the *procurador da corte*, who resided with the king and reported on all matters of concern to the Society.[24] They assisted with the recruitment of candidates for the overseas missions and arranged for their education and temporary accommodation until they were ready to sail.

A substantial part of the instructions drafted by Visitor Francisco Vieira in consultation with the provincials of Goa and Malabar pertains to the duties of the missions procurator with respect to such departures. As soon as he learned of the date set for the sailing of the East Indiamen, the missions procurator was to inform the general so that he could arrange passage to Lisbon for recruits from other provinces. They were to arrive at least a month before the intended sailing to facilitate their spiritual and physical preparation for the voyage. At least two weeks prior to their sailing, the procurator was to assemble the contingent so that they could be sent to a retreat to rest for the ensuing voyage, normally six months. The procurator was directed to distribute members of the Society so that there were at least two per ship and was cautioned to see that supplies were carefully stowed so that perishables were easily accessible and not liable to spoil when the ships reached the tropics. He was also to consider as criteria for his designation of the superior of the voyage age, prudence, charity, and a pleasant disposition.[25]

Another major part of the procurators' responsibilities pertained to marketing. Procurators were expected to sell at the most favorable prices goods sent to Europe by the provinces as well as those brought by the procurator-delegates to Rome to defray their expenses. Missions procurators also distributed gifts sent from overseas to prominent benefactors and to the fathers general.[26] In addition, they tried to fill the want lists submitted to them by the provincial procurators (see below). They collected income due the provinces as a result of crown subventions, earnings on annuities, and loans, as well as that derived from urban properties and estates belonging to the overseas provinces.

The missions procurators must have been mired in paperwork. They kept books in which the instructions of their office were set down, as well as records of all legal rights the provinces enjoyed and the texts of all royal licenses they obtained demonstrating the crown's confirmation of the vital titles to lands owned by the overseas colleges (see Chapter 15). They were required to report monthly to the fathers general concerning the status of all negotiations affecting the overseas stations assigned to them. They maintained accounts

24. Fr. Gabriel Afonso (b. 1527–d. 1585) appears to have been the first Jesuit to hold the office of procurador da corte. He did so in 1565–66 and again in 1577. When Madrid became the locus of the Portuguese empire, Afonso moved to the Spanish capital. One of his longtime successors was the aforementioned António Colaço. Another was Francisco Manso (b. ca. 1598–d. 1674), who was serving in Madrid at the time of the Restoration and secretly returned to the kingdom, where he was briefly incarcerated because of suspicions that he held pro-Spanish sympathies. He subsequently held a series of administrative posts in the province of Portugal and was briefly provincial of the separate Alentejo province. *ASCJ*, 136. On the functions of the procurador da corte, see Aquaviva, "Instrucion para el procurador de las provincias de Portugal, Brasil y India Oriental que reside en corte de Valladolid catolica, hecha en enero de 1584," in *DI*, 13: 475–86.

25. "Regimento pera os P^{es} e Ir[mão]^s da Comp.^a que se embarcao' de Portugal pera a India feito em janeiro de [1]616," ARSI, FG, 721:II/3/2.

26. E.g., Alessandro Vallareggio to Mercurian, Lisbon, 4 Nov. 1574, in *AHSI* 40 (Jan.–June 1971): 306–7, reporting the forwarding to the general of 30 boxes of quince jam, 6 boxes of fine Madeiran sugar, a barrel of rose sugar, 16.8 kg of ginger, and unspecified quantities of cinnamon, cloves, and pepper.

with each province and each college assigned to them. Once a year they sent each unit a statement showing whether it was a creditor or debtor of the office of missions procurator. They retained one copy for their own files and prepared another for review by the office of the procurator-general in Rome.[27] Through their contacts with the procurador da corte and others at court, the missions procurators kept tabs on pending legal matters that were of concern to the provinces and shared whatever intelligence they gained.[28] In their free time, they conducted a wide-ranging correspondence with college procurators, businessmen, and prominent Jesuits throughout the Assistancy.[29]

In short, the post of missions procurator was a demanding one, the more so because its occupants were obliged to try to please several different masters, including the overseas provincials and procurators and sometimes, as in the case of Valignano, the Visitors. In addition, missions procurators acted upon instructions from both the fathers general and the procurators-general. In spiritual matters a missions procurator and his assistants were answerable to the rector of Santo Antão, where they resided. Little wonder that missions procurators repeatedly confessed their inability to discharge their many obligations and sought relief from them.

The Provincial Procurators

In the *ultramar* (the lands beyond Europe) the provincial procurators were among the chief correspondents of the missions procurators. Their duties varied with their stations,[30] but

27. Several specimens of the missions procurators' accounts survive: "Co[n]ta do p.dor da provincia de Portugal co. a provincia do Brasil," 20 July 1586, in ARSI, *Bras.*, 5, fols. 51–52; an undated memo concerning the same province, probably for 1589, in ibid., 11, fols. 333ᵛ–34; "Livro da receita e despeza da provincia de Goa ... 24 de mayo de 1613 ... [até 24 de mayo] de 1626," ARSI, FG, 1443/9/16; "Orsamento de contas das 3 prov.ᵃˢ da India ... Japan, China," 7 Aug. [1]629, in ibid., *Lus.*, 77, fols. 94–95; "Contas do Pᵉ Luís Pinheiro com as prov.ᵃˢ de Japão e China desde o primeiro de 1618 até o 19 de março do dito anno," in ibid., FG, 721/V/E; "Exemplum de Ratiocenus etatis ... proveratoris brasiliae" (1695), in ibid., *Bras.*, 3:II, 347–48ᵛ; and "Conta da procuratura da prov.ᵃ de Goa com a deste coll.° [Santo Antão] dos segundos seis mezes ... de 1750," in ANTT/CJ/68, n. 83.
There is remarkably little in the *Constitutions* defining the functions of the procurator-general. His responsibilities included representing the assistancies in their relations with the Vatican (e.g., concerning proposals for beatification or sainthood) and reviewing the accounting procedures of the divisions of the Society. Diego Mirón to António Araoz, Almeirim, 13 Dec. 1564, in *MB*, 4: 116. For a critique of the account submitted by António Cardozo in 1724, see ARSI, *Bras.*, 11, fols. 465ff. The procurator-general did *not* orchestrate the economic activities of the Society's component parts.
28. [Jacinto de Carvalho?], "Cartas q. não tem baixado resultas," n.d., a series of dispatches concerning the Jesuits and Indian policy in the Amazon, 1723–31, for which action was still pending, BNL/FG, 4517, fol. 105ʳ.
29. Some fascinating examples of that correspondence, dating from the 1740s and 1750s, are contained in a bundle of about 450 documents in ANTT/CJ/68. Missions procurators, deservedly or otherwise, had the reputation of being wire-pullers. Thus, for example, when the well-known Eusebio Kino wanted to be reassigned from northwest Mexico to the Marianas Islands, he wrote the duchess of Aveiro, the islands' patroness, that "I ... will take up the matter with the Procurator at Lisbon, for he is very devoted to me." Kino, of course, failed to obtain his wish. See Ernest J. Burrus, S.J., ed., *Kino Writes to the Duchess: Letters of Eusebio Francisco Kino, S.J., to the Duchess of Aveiro* (St. Louis, 1965), 90, where the date (6 Dec. 1688) should be 1680.
30. Apart from Mercurian's previously cited general regulations, the duties of the provincial procurators are detailed in the "Visita da provincia de Portugal pelo P. João Alvares" [1610/1613], ANTT/AJ, *antiga cx.* 1, *m.* 5, tit. 10, chaps. 4 and 5 (the latter pertaining to the obligations of companions); Anon.,

all were responsible for the receipt, disbursement, and accountability of the assessments (*fintas*) that each college and some missions contributed to the province's general expenses. They also assisted their chief, the provincial, in the collection of data necessary for the preparation of the periodic economic reports, the third catalogues, sent to the Roman headquarters (see Chapter 23). Provincial procurators also forwarded correspondence between the colleges and missions and destinations in Rome and other European cities. In the province of Portugal and possibly elsewhere as well, provincial procurators, with the approval of their superiors, arranged for the investment of funds entrusted to them by collegial units of the province.

One of the duties of the overseas provincial procurators was the preparation of yearly want lists that reflected requests sent to the provincials from colleges and missions for goods from Europe. The resulting shipments, which the provincial procurators and their staffs verified, cleared through customs, and distributed to the colleges and missions with which they maintained accounts,[31] included various qualities of Italian-manufactured paper, quills, and sand clocks; occasional dried vegetables such as chickpeas as well as seeds for the growing of European vegetables; wine for mass and other purposes; dried fruit, olives, olive oil, and cane sugar; provisions such as dried cherries, reserved for invalids; Brazilian tobacco; religious medals (*verónicas*), tiny bells, crosses, and other items intended as gifts to neophytes; Latin grammars, lives of the saints, the Exercises of Loyola, and other devotional works; and both bills of exchange and specie.[32]

Specie remittances were always more important to the Far Eastern enterprises than to any other in the ultramar. As seen in later chapters, during its heyday the Japan province relied substantially upon both crown and papal subventions, that is, silver sent from Lisbon to Goa and forwarded via Malacca to Macao for investment in the silk trade and for other purposes. After the end of Jesuit activities in the Japanese archipelago and the termination of papal support for the eastern missions, the Japan province and the vice-province of China depended heavily upon remittances representing earnings on their properties in the kingdom and in India (see Chapter 24). In addition, Jesuit installations in Brazil and India sent silver to Macao to purchase altar cloths and other objects to adorn their churches. Bullion was one of the commodities that procurator-delegates to Rome took with them to defray their expenses during their sojourns in Europe. From time to time provincial

---

"Regimento para o procurador da vice provincia da China" [1622], BA/JA/49-V-7, fols. 309ʳ–310ᵛ. The requirements of the office of the Japan procurator were originally drafted by Alessandro Valignano and augmented by Visitors Francisco Pasio and Francisco Vieira: "Regimento para o procurador de Japão que reside na China" [ca. 1611–17], BA/JA/49-IV-66, no. 1 (fols. 10–15ᵛ), but they were further elaborated in the well-known "Couzas que podem servir para os procuradores," [1629], BA/JA/49-V-8, no. 94 (fols. 635–49), of which C. R. Boxer provided a partial summary in "Macao as a Religious and Commercial Entrepôt in the 16th and 17th Centuries," *Acta Asiatica* 26 (Tokyo, 1974): 71–72. I have not seen specific instructions for the provincial procurators of Goa, Malabar, or Brazil, or for the vice-provincial procurator of Maranhão.

31. For the eighteenth-century provincial procurate of Goa, two codices of such accounts survive: HAG 2094 and 2557.

32. Two invaluable codices in HAG (nos. 2570 and 1945) make it possible to trace both want lists and shipments from Lisbon to the Goan province between 1676 and 1740. Contrary to the assumptions of the Society's critics, neither reveals any incriminating European merchandise that conceivably could have been sold by the Jesuits to outsiders.

procurators in Goa also sent specie to Lisbon to balance their accounts with the missions procurator there.[33]

Though most of the tasks of the provincial procurators were uncontroversial, the same cannot be said for those performed by the provincial procurators of Japan during the boom years of that enterprise. The Jesuits possessed important shares in the bullion and silk trades between South China and the Japanese archipelago (see Chapters 14 and 21). The 1629 observations on the office of provincial procurator emphasize that he should conduct his duties with great secrecy and that he should always remember that "the procurator of Japan, unlike that of any of the other provinces, is a simple merchant (*um puro negoceador*) and for that reason his duties ought to be discharged by a civilian rather than a member of the Society."[34]

Whether secular persons ever served as provincial procurators is uncertain. We possess only fragmentary data about those who held that post. Available information suggests that it was normally filled by mature members of the Society who had considerable field experience. If not the first, one of the earliest provincial procurators in Brazil was Rodrigo de Freitas (b. ca. 1519–d. 1604), a member of the lesser nobility who had come to Brazil as a treasury officer in 1549. Widowed, Freitas joined the Society in 1560 and became successively superior of the incipient college of Olinda, Visitor of the southern captaincies, and an advisor to several college rectors before being named provincial procurator.[35] The data are unclear, but it appears that Fr. Rodrigo was a spiritual helper (coadjutor spiritual) rather than a professed priest. Estevão Lopes (b. 1533), who had served as a missionary in Mozambique, bore the title of coadjutor spiritual when he became procurator of Goa in 1579, a post he seems to have held until 1584.[36] His successor, Gomes Vaz (b. 1542), a New Christian, had served as a missionary in Bassein before being recalled to Goa, where he took his fourth vow in 1584 and became provincial procurator. Aquaviva directed that he be relieved of his duties, however, contending (erroneously) that the *Constitutions* stipulated that those who had taken the fourth vow were reserved for more important responsibilities than those of procurators.[37]

Br. Manoel de Figueiredo (b. 1589–d. 1663) served as pharmacist and procurator of the vice-province of China for 24 years.[38] That was an unusually long stint, for the rate of turnover was usually much higher among provincial procurators than among missions procurators, college procurators, or estate managers. A register of those who occupied the position of procurator of Goa from 1706 to 1755, the only such listing that we have,

33. The foregoing is based primarily upon the sources cited in note 32. HAG 1945 indicates, for example, that during the monsoon of January 1722, the Goan provincial procurator sent 1,221,000 rs. to the Portuguese capital to balance his accounts. The same codices illuminate specie flows from Goa to Macao, as do the "Contas do Padre Manoel Borges da receita e despezas desta procurat.rª de Macao" [1616–17], BA/JA/49-V-712 which indicate that just over 1,105,000 rs. were sent from India that year to Macao.

34. See "Couzas que podem servir para os procuratores" [1629], cited in note 30.

35. *HCJB*, 8: 261.

36. *DI*, 13: 635, and 16: 937.

37. Ibid., 13: 444, 602–3; Aquaviva to Valignano, 24 Dec. 1585, and Valignano to Aquaviva, 20 Dec. 1586, in *DI*, 14: 158 and 443. As Fr. Wicki points out, the passage in the *Constitutions* (pt. 9, chap. 6, par. 12) concerns the qualifications of procurators-general, not provincial procurators.

38. The 1659 catalogue indicates that he held office for 28 years (*RJC*, 93), but Figueiredo himself stated that he assumed his responsibility in 1621 and did not surrender it until 1645. "Lembrança do irmão Manuel de Figueiredo," 21 Feb. 1661, in BA/JA/49-V-5, no. 127.

shows that two men held office on three occasions and that the average length of service was just over two years.[39] It is possible that provincial procurators served relatively short terms because their assignments coincided with those of their direct superiors. Whatever the explanation, their duties were less onerous than those of the college procurators, who, along with the estate managers, were the most visible officals among Jesuits concerned with economic affairs.

The College Procurators

Each Jesuit house had one or more officials who were concerned with its internal management, with the purchase of commodities that it required, with the keeping of its fiscal and legal records, and with the representation of its interests before civil authorities.[40] At the beginning, all these tasks were often carried out by one person, and that continued to be the practice in the smaller colleges; but in larger institutions there were separate house managers (ministros or *oeconomi*), buyers (*compradores*), and procurators. All three offices were derived from the old Benedictine office of cellarer or steward. According to the Benedictine Rule, that official was to be elected by the congregation. He was expected to be "wise, mature in character, sober, not given to much eating, not proud, not turbulent, not an upbraider, not tardy, not prodigal, but fearing God: a father, as it were, to the whole congregation." His duty was to "take care of everything" but to undertake nothing without the consent of the abbot.[41]

The same was true in the Society, where such administrators relieved rectors and other superiors of all tasks related to the economic affairs of the house. House managers, also called house ministers, supervised the activities of their staffs, including cooks; cleaning personnel; the *ostiarius* or porter (*porteiro*), who was a guard, doorkeeper, and sometime janitor; the infirmarian; and the buyer. They also kept inventories of supplies on hand and personnel records.[42] Like the post of master of novices, that of minister was sometimes the first step in a long administrative career. Yet some ministers were so highly regarded for their stewardship that they were retained for decades in their positions.[43]

Where a separation of functions existed, the college procurators bore primary responsibility for the receipt and expenditure of funds belonging to the house, as well as for

39. HAG, 2089.
40. *EJF*, 1: xix.
41. David Knowles, ed., *The Monastic Constitutions of Lanfranc* (London, 1951), 85–86; idem, *The Monastic Order in England . . . 940–1216* (Cambridge, 1963), 430. See also Abbot Gasquet, *English Monastic Life* (London, 1904), 72–77; and Maarten Ultee, *The Abbey of St. Germain des Près in the Seventeenth Century* (New Haven, 1981), 64–65. Some Orders, such as the Augustinians, also employed the term "procurator" for the office, but others, such as the Mercedarians, preferred the designation "commander." Cf. Donna U. Vogt, "Economic and Social Structures in Eighteenth-Century Manila: Padre Pedro Núñez and his 'Manual for the Use of Friars Serving as Procurators in the Convent,' " *Indiana University Bookman* no. 11 (Nov. 1973): 43–68; and James William Brodman, *Ransoming Captives in Crusader Spain: The Order of Merced on the Christian-Islamic Frontier* (Philadelphia, 1986), 52–53.
42. The duties of the minister are detailed in several instructions prepared between 1549 and 1554. See *RSI*, 170–71, 226–29, and 362–79. For the obligations of the porter, comprador, and infirmarian, see *RSI*, 30–37 and 456–58.
43. For some examples of long service by ministers, see *OSR*, nos. 5 and 159; Franco, *Coimbra*, 1: 550–75; and idem, *Imagem da virtude em o noviciado da companhia de Jesus na corte de Lisboa* (Coimbra, 1717), 587.

the keeping of financial and legal records, including the texts of all bequests; royal licenses; decrees and instructions from the fathers general, the general congregations, and other Jesuit authorities; and copies of pertinent royal legislation. Whenever necessary, they utilized such materials in the preparation of documents they submitted to crown authorities in defense of their colleges' property rights.[44] The Society's first procurator was a rotund ex-canon, Pietro Codacio (b. 1507–d. 1549), a Lombardian who became the first Italian to join the new Order. As Schurhammer has written, he was "a godsend ... [for he] took over the care of the temporal needs of the house ... looking after the food, clothing, and everything else that was needed by his confreres so that they might carry on their apostolic labors without hindrance."[45] During the formative years of the Society, however, it was hoped that outsiders rather than the Order's own members could perform sordid economic tasks. Thus in 1552 Xavier instructed that "when the rents are collected, ... [they] should be not made by your person nor by anyone of the Society ... since it would be a source of scandal. Some friend or laymen who are spiritual friends should do this ... [especially] pious individuals who frequently go to confession. ... And if it should be possible ... these persons who collect the rents ... [should be] rich and prosperous and above all good."[46]

But there was the rub. In sixteenth-century Mexico, the Jesuits were able to find outsiders to manage the financial affairs of their colleges.[47] In India and elsewhere within the Portuguese Assistancy, however, it was difficult to find reliable, affluent laymen willing to put aside their own affairs to manage those of a Jesuit house. It is true that licentiate Manuel Alvares Barradas, a former judge in Malacca and Cochin, was recruited to administer the revenues of Old St. Paul's, but he was succeeded by that college's former rector, Baltasar Dias, chosen "because of the experience that he already possesses in this land."[48] Another former rector who became college procurator was Francisco Lemos (b. ca. 1563–d. 1628), nephew of a fellow Jesuit, Fr. Gregório Serrão. Lemos was a member of the expedition that conquered Rio Grande do Norte in 1597 and then traveled by land to Bahia, where, in 1601, he bore the title of procurator-general of the colleges of Bahia and Rio de Janeiro.[49]

But the employment of senior Jesuits in such positions was unusual, at least in the sixteenth century. More typical were Francisco Henriques, António Viegas, and António de Fonseca. Henriques, born in Ormuz around 1553, was a Persian who entered the Society in 1557 and served for many years as a lay brother. In 1588, he took vows as a coadjutor spiritual, a rare instance of such a procedure, at least within this assistancy. For a decade or more during the 1580s and 1590s, Henriques served as procurator of Old St. Paul's and of several other Goan houses. Eventually he returned to Bassein, where he had joined the Order, to serve as minister of the house there.[50] Viegas (b. 1558), a Goan described as an

44. The duties of the college procurator are spelled out in several early instructions. See *RSI*, 24–25 and 410–21.

45. S/*FX*, 1: 505–6.

46. Ibid., 4: 482.

47. Cf. Félix Zubillaga, "La província jesuítica de Nueva España: Su fundamento economico: siglo XVI," *AHSI* 38 (Jan.–June 1969): 3–169, at 168.

48. Xavier to Barzaeus, 6/14 Apr. 1552, in S/*FX*, 4: 534; *DI*, 3: 527.

49. *HCJB*, 8: 315.

50. Henriques is mentioned frequently in the *DI* series, notably at 3: 715 and 788; 12: 51; 13: 609; 15: 172, and 424; and 16: 964, 998.

indiano but possibly of Luso-Indian parentage, was also a coadjutor spiritual who served as house manager of Old St. Paul's in the late 1580s before becoming vicar of Assalona.[51] António de Fonseca (or Afonseca) was born in Lisbon about 1533 and joined the Society in 1584 as a lay brother (coadjutor temporal). Soon after completing his probation, he was assigned as house manager of the novitiate and the probationary house, positions that, by 1594, he had occupied for eight and a half years.[52]

These men appear to have shared several qualities. First, they probably came from humble backgrounds that did not provide them with the education or social polish necessary for selection for the higher ranks within the Society.[53] Second, each had already reached adulthood when he joined the Society and therefore possessed useful experience in the secular world, specifically a knowledge of buying, selling, and record-keeping, as well as an ability to work with laborers, suppliers, and tenants, skills that many more exalted members of the Society lacked.

It is evident from a study of a small octavo notebook kept by two early-seventeenth-century procurators of one of the colleges of the University of Évora that the job of house procurator was a demanding one.[54] This notebook discloses that the manager kept track of prevailing wage rates for all types of both skilled and nonskilled workers that the college and its supporting estates required, as well as the costs of all sorts of commodities (such as provisions, earthenware, pewter, paper, cloth, and tanned leather) used by the college. The Évora procurator also needed to know the dates of the fourteen annual fairs in his region—the Alentejo—between 30 January and 30 November so that he could arrange for necessary purchases at each. He kept a list of the hours when the sun rose and set throughout the year because they governed the hours of meals and religious services. In winter, inmates of the college of Espírito Santo rose at 5 A.M., had their principal meal (*jantar*) at 11 A.M., supped (had *cea*) at 7 P.M. and retired at 10 P.M., whereas in summer they began the day at 4 A.M., dined at 10 A.M., ate again at 6 P.M., and went to bed at 9 P.M. The notebook also specifies the portions of meat, vegetables, bread, and other foodstuffs to which each member was entitled. Table 12.1 shows the annual schedule of purchases that the house procurator, assisted by his inevitable companion and his indispensable errand boy (*moço de sombreiro*), annually made in behalf of his house.

The college procurators also periodically prepared want lists for submission to their superiors and for the use of the provincial procurators. Either the minister or the procurators maintained and regularly inventoried the contents of storage rooms with confirmation by their superiors. As Appendix E indicates, the supplies kept by some colleges were diverse and

51. Ibid., 13: 615; 15: 176, 367; and 16: 960, 281, 998, 1020.

52. Ibid., 13: 623; 14: 628, 782, 793; and 16: 955, 997.

53. Very informative concerning the socioeconomic origins of temporal coadjutors in sixteenth-century Europe is an unpublished study by Thomas V. Cohen, "Where the Jesuits Came From: A Social History of the Order in the Sixteenth Century," chaps. 5 and 7. I am indebted to Professor Cohen for an opportunity to read his impressively researched manuscript.

54. "Varias lembranças pera hum procurador ... feito no anno de [1]606," BNL/FG, 4254. I am indebted to an Indian scholar, Karubaki Datta, for obtaining a film of this unique codex for me. It was begun in 1606 by Br. Affonso da Rocha, procurator of the college of Espírito Santo in Évora, and was later continued by Br. António Homem (see note 22 above). I know of no comparable surviving notebook for any part of the Portuguese Assistancy. The discussion that follows is based upon this invaluable codex.

TABLE 12.1

*Schedule of Purchases by the Procurator of the College of
Espírito Santo, Évora, 1606*

Month(s)	Special purchases
January and March	Linens for towels, tablecloths, and caps
April and May	Tunny fish from the Algarve; black cloth for cassocks; coarse woolen cloth for grape sacking
June and July	Raisins, figs, almonds, mustard, Setúbal salt, hides, saffron from Spain
August	Sheep skins; fruit from the Algarve
September	Nuts from Estremoz; lentils from Évora; apples from Montemor o Novo; linen from Campo d'Ourique
October and November	Dried fish from Lisbon; cod from Porto; sardines; sugar from Madeira
December	Wine; olive oil; ground chestnuts; pork to make hams; lentils, capers, and chickpeas

SOURCE: See note 54.

ample.[55] It is not surprising, therefore, that Jesuit superiors repeatedly cautioned that such stocks should be concealed from the eyes of inquisitive outsiders, for they seemed to provide evidence that the Jesuits maintained, as their critics claimed, "magazines" or factories where goods were allegedly sold to secular friends of the Society. But it should be remembered that certain colleges, such as Santo Antão in the kingdom and the colleges of Salvador, New St. Paul's, and Macao abroad, supplied other colleges, missions, and other facilities as well as themselves.[56] House procurators often corresponded with their counterparts elsewhere, but they maintained even closer relationships with the administrators of their colleges' estates.

The Estate Managers

As observed in Chapter 1, in 1546 Loyola created, with papal approval, two inferior grades of members to assist senior-level priests who had taken third or fourth vows. One group consisted of "spiritual aides," or coadjutores spirituales, and the other of lay brothers, or coadjutores temporales. Both types of coadjutor were customarily entrusted with the management of the Society's estates. Generally the coadjutors were recruited from lower socioeconomic strata than were the senior priests and had had only limited education before entering the Society. In particular, they lacked solid training in Latin or theology. They appear to have joined the Society at more advanced ages than did those who became

55. Very few inventories of institutions within the Portuguese Assistancy have survived. Besides the 1707 inventory, somewhat compressed in Appendix E, I know of two others: a rather primitive inventory of the new college of Luanda, Angola, in 1596 (ARSI, FG, 1361/6), and the very detailed "Memorial das couzas da procuratura desta prov.ª" of supplies for the Japan province kept at Macao in 1616 (BA/JA/49-V-5, no. 79).

56. Cf. Nicholas P. Cushner, *Lords of the Land: Sugar, Wine and Jesuit Estates of Coastal Peru, 1600–1767* (Albany, 1980), 170, for the comparable role played by the college of Buenos Aires.

senior priests. Many of the lay brothers had been craftsmen, such as carpenters, smiths, tailors, or weavers; some had been peasants, others personal servants.[57] The skills they brought to the Society were essential to its success. That was especially true of those who assumed the burden of managing the Society's properties in the kingdom and in the ultramar.

The assignment of estate managers began during the early 1550s, and by the early eighteenth century there may have been as many as a hundred men throughout the Assistancy who held such posts. The names of only a few are recorded in the Society's annals, but more show up in its correspondence files. One was Br. António Mendes, a coadjutor temporal who died in one of the Évora colleges in 1609. According to António Franco, the foremost necrologist of the Portuguese province, Mendes managed the college's farms and estates for almost 30 years unstintingly and without complaint. "Many times he went the entire day with only bread and water and slept at night in the open air with the farm hands (*homens do campo*)." He regularly fasted twice a week and, after his sight failed, occupied himself during his last three years with spiritual exercises.[58]

By no means were all Jesuits who administered properties as contented with their assignment as Br. Mendes. Some protested to their superiors, including the fathers general, that they were unsuited for such duties and begged for reassignment. In seventeenth-century Goa, coadjutores spirituales were most reluctant to supervise estates, claiming that such duties were fit for lay brothers, but not for priests, who had a higher calling.[59] Nearly a century later Fr. Pedro Teixeira, the gouty administrator of the sugar estate of Santana de Ilhéus in southern Bahia, complained about his three years' "penance" in his assignment: the slaves were notoriously unruly, his assistants were prone to immoral conduct, and the red wine sent from Salvador turned to vinegar within two weeks of its arrival.[60]

Both Ignatius and Xavier would have been shocked and indignant at such complaints, for both were adamant that a good Jesuit did whatever his superiors required of him without any semblance of selfish lamentation. As early as 1552, for example, Loyola wrote to Fr. Manuel Godinho, one of the earliest Portuguese recruits, who had complained to him concerning his transfer to a property at São Fins, near Galicia. St. Ignatius replied,

> Although the charge of temporal affairs seems to be and is distracting, I have no doubt that by your good and upright intention you turn everything you do to something spiritual for God's glory. . . . We rightly hold any operation whatever in which charity is exercised to God's glory to be very holy and suitable for us and those activities even more so in which the infallible rule of obedience to our superiors has placed us.

57. The generalizations offered here rely upon chaps. 5 and 7 of Cohen's "Where the Jesuits Came From" and upon evidence cited in Chapter 20 below.

58. *ASCJ*, 151.

59. Francisco Ferreira Senior to General, "Informação 2ª pera nosso m.ᵗᵒ r.ᵈᵒ P. Geral sobre as freg.ᵃˢ de Salsete," 26 Oct. 1642, in ARSI/FG, 1443/9/21.

60. Teixeira to P. Simão Estevens, 20 June and 19 Aug. 1731, in ANTT/CJ/68, nos. 343 and 347. Teixeira was slated for promotion to the more important fazenda of Sergipe do Conde, which, like Santana, belonged to the Lisbon college of Santo Antão. But after observing his behavior for two weeks, Fr. Mathias de Sousa called for his removal, declaring that he was incapable of managing slaves, and that he regarded his posting as the equivalent of purgatory. Sousa to Estevens, Santana de Ilhéus, 16 Oct. 1731, in ibid., no. 354.

He then added that if Fr. Godinho still felt that "in God's service this office is unsuitable for you, confer with your superiors . . . and they will do what is proper."[61]

Yet many superiors found no alternative but to retain coadjutors on their farms, plantations, and ranches for many seasons because suitable replacements were unavailable. In the case of the large polycultural Mexican estate of Santa Lucia, which belonged to the Colégio Maximo in Mexico City, Herman Konrad found that the average manager served for thirteen years. That was roughly twice as long as administrators remained at the large Jesuit sugar hacienda of Villa in Peru between 1675 and 1751. But in Oaxaca, in southern Mexico, a Jesuit report composed during the first half of the eighteenth century lamented that "one can hardly find overseers or administrators for the Nexapa trapiche [sugar mill], since they quickly die or become ill after going there."[62]

The handful of biographies of estate managers in the Portuguese Assistancy that we possess suggest that managers served lengthy terms—some would call them purgatories—on the properties entrusted to them. The personnel catalogue of the Portuguese province of 1639 refers to a certain Fr. Pedro Correia who had been in the Society for twenty years, most of that time as procurator on the Azorean island of São Miguel.[63] In Brazil, Fr. Manuel de Oliveira appears to have managed the giant sugar plantation of Sergipe do Conde for the last third of the seventeenth century. Manoel de Figueiredo, the irascible Pedro Teixeira's predecessor, served at Santana de Ilhéus for about 23 years. Luís Veloso was also one of that estate's managers. He began his managerial career at Santana about 1698. By 1717 he had been promoted to Sergipe do Conde, where he remained in charge of the plantation until sometime in the 1730s. Other estate administrators were relieved after much shorter stints. The well-known Estevão Pereira, for example, lasted only four years at Sergipe do Conde.[64] In the East, Br. António Dias served for more than fifteen years in India as resident manager of estates, including Taleigão, belonging to the Japan province and the vice-province of China. His colleague, Luís Silva, administrator of the Bettim estate, situated in Bardês, owned by the province of Malabar, appears to have served nearly as long.[65] But another coadjutor, Miguel Vieira (b. 1681–d. 1760), may have set something of a record for service as an estate manager in India. Born in the kingdom, he volunteered for the China missions and was a pharmacist in Macao for six years until he was overcome by "melancholia" and was transferred to India, first to the royal hospital in Goa, but from at least 1725 until 1752 as the manager of the vice-province's estates in the subcontinent. Arrested by crown officers during the general roundup of members of the Society in 1760, he died at sea three days before his ship reached Lisbon.[66]

61. Loyola to Godinho, 31 Jan. 1552, in William J. Young, S.J., trans. and ed., *Letters of St. Ignatius of Loyola* (Chicago, 1959), 254–55.

62. Herman W. Konrad, *A Jesuit Hacienda in Colonial Mexico: Santa Lucia, 1576–1767* (Stanford, 1980), 131–33; Cushner, *Lords,* 78; William B. Taylor, *Landlord and Peasant in Colonial Oaxaca* (Stanford, 1972), 183.

63. "Catalogo [da] provincia de Portugal . . . de 1639," ARSI, *Lus.,* 44:II, 570–93.

64. On the Madeiran Oliveira, see *HCJB,* 9: 26. For the others, see Stuart B. Schwartz, *Sugar Plantations in the Formation of Brazilian Society: Bahia, 1550–1835* (Cambridge, 1985), 399–402; on Frs. Pereira and Veloso, see *HCJB,* 9: 39 and 185.

65. Statements of Luís Silva and António Dias to Miguel de Amaral (Visitor, Goa), 9 and 11 Oct. 1708, in ARSI, *Goa,* 9:II, 434–38.

66. ARSI, *Goa,* 9:II, 481; *RJC,* 292.

From the Society's perspective, a long period of service on a single estate offered both advantages and disadvantages. Obviously managers had the opportunity to master their jobs and, presumably, to operate their properties at maximum efficiency. Some served so long without respite that they became cranky and indifferent to the improvements that their estates required. And some administrators, like the already mentioned Brs. Luís Silva and António Dias, identified with their estates so intimately that they were reluctant to participate in the religious life of the community to which they were attached.[67]

Whether administrators born in the colonies were any more likely than those born in Europe to prefer the far greater independence that they enjoyed on the estates to the more structured life in the colleges they served can only be surmised. The strong preference in the overseas enterprises for Jesuits from Europe, and especially from the Peninsula (as observed in Chapter 11), also seems to have applied to the selection of estate managers. According to Konrad, 66 percent of the coadjutores who served in New Spain between 1572 and the 1650s came from Spain; but by the 1760s, the Peninsular proportion had fallen to only 30 percent, whereas 42.2 percent of the managers then were born in Mexico. Cushner found that most Jesuit managers who worked in the Andean basins of Chillos, southeast of Quito, were colonial whites, that is, creoles. The only available listing of coadjutores for the Portuguese Assistancy is one that Fr. Serafim Leite published concerning the Brazil province. It reveals that 91.9 percent of the 120 persons who served in that colony as administrators, shepherds, and farmers during the two centuries beginning in 1549 were from the kingdom; the remainder came from Madeira, the Azores, and Brazil itself.[68] It would not be surprising to discover that about the same proportion occupied managerial positions on estates east of the Cape of Good Hope.

The responsibilities of these property managers depended upon what their estates produced.[69] In the kingdom and the Atlantic islands, those duties included the threshing of oats and wheat, the crushing of grapes and olives, the clipping of wool, the preparation of such products for shipment to market, and the remittance of the proceeds to owner

---

67. The residents of the professed house of Bom Jesús, Goa, repeatedly complained to the generals that the guest procurators preferred to live on their estates rather than reside in their house. As Br. Luís Silva noted, the issue was raised by the fathers general on four occasions between 1685 and 1706. See note 65. On the other hand, as will be noted below, some superiors were reluctant to have their managers leave their estates, fearing that their work forces might get out of hand during the administrators' absence.

68. Konrad, *Jesuit Hacienda*, 133–35; Nicholas P. Cushner, *Farm and Factory: The Jesuits and the Development of Agrarian Capitalism in Colonial Quito, 1600–1767* (Albany, 1982), 87; Serafim Leite, S.J., *Artes e oficios dos Jesuítas no Brasil (1549–1760)* (Rio de Janeiro, 1953), 77–79.

69. The responsibilities of estate managers form the subject of a number of instructions handed down by their spiritual superiors. In the Portuguese Assistancy, surviving examples include the "Ordens do P.e Visitor da prov.ia de Japam p.a ao provedor q. reside em Bandar[a]," Jan. 1644, in BA/JA/49-V-13, no. 12; "Ordens que o P.e Visitador Fran.co Barreto deixou visitando a igreja e fazenda de Assalona no anno 1661," in ARSI, FG, 1443/9/30; Barnabé Soares, "Instructio ab iis qui officinam sacchaream administrant, servanda," 27 Dec. 1692, in ARSI, *Bras.*, 11, fols. 132–35.v (said by Serafim Leite to have been a major source of Antonil); and Jerónimo da Gama, "Ordens q' com visita dou ao ir[mão] comp[anheir]o do P. Sup[intendent]e deste eng.o [Santana de Ilhéus] e aos q' lhe succederem," 20 Oct. 1752, in ANTT/CJ/54, no. 5. For comparable instructions in the New World reaches of the Spanish Assistancy, see François Chevalier, ed., *Instrucciones a los hermanos Jesuitas administradores de haciendas* (Mexico City, 1950); Pablo Macera, ed., *Instrucciones para el manejo de las haciendas Jesuitas del Peru (ss. xvii–xviii)* (Lima, 1966); see also Konrad, *Jesuit Hacienda*, 116ff.; Cushner, *Farm and Factory*, 85–86; and idem, *Jesuit Ranches and the Agrarian Development of Colonial Argentina, 1650–1767* (Albany, 1983), 42–45.

colleges. Both at home and overseas, estate administrators also collected dues, symbolic and monetary, from their often reluctant tenants. With respect to the direction of the Society's sugar properties in Brazil, the superintendent, according to Fr. Veloso, "keeps the slaves . . . well controlled and instructed, so that they do not bother anyone. . . . He sees to the confessions and the last rites. . . . He makes a good division with the *lavradores* [tenants] . . . and helps them cut and transport the cane and gives accounting of the sugar . . . ; he pays and treats the employees of the mill with punctuality as with all those others who supply the engenho."[70] But, of course, the manager had many other responsibilities as well. He determined which fields would be planted during a particular season and which would lie fallow, and he supervised the critical phases of the manufacture of the several qualities of sugar, as well as their curing, crating, and distribution, whether through local sales or by dispatch to Lisbon for disposal by the missions procurator there.[71] Those administrators who directed the operations of large multifunctional estates, such as São Bonifácio (in Maranhão) and Santa Cruz (west of the city of Rio de Janeiro), had additional burdens, since such properties produced not only sugar, fruit, legumes, and livestock, but also bricks, ceramics, and other fabricated items made and usually sold at the estate.

The tasks of such managers in the western parts of the Assistancy are familiar enough; those handled in India by the administrators of the Society's indispensable coconut plantations are less well known. Apart from an oft-reprinted anonymous account attributed to a Jesuit, the fullest description that we possess of the yearly operations of such a plantation comes from a statement by Br. António Dias, procurator of Japan and China and manager of the Taleigão estate at the beginning of the eighteenth century.[72] According to Dias, unless a carrack was readying to leave Goa for the kingdom, January was otherwise a quiet month when the manager caught up on his paperwork. Beginning at the end of January, however, and continuing into March, the manager supervised the digging of ditches around the trees and their fertilization with ash. Dias reports that there were so many trees—upwards of 8,000, suggesting a planting of about 68 hectares—that six to seven years were required to complete that process for the entire estate. During April and May, Dias averred that

70. As quoted in Schwartz, *Sugar Plantations*, 285.

71. The classic description of the duties of the manager of a sugar estate is that of Fr. Giovanni Antonio Andreoni, who first published his *Cultura e opulencia do Brasil por suas drogas e minas* in 1711 employing the pseudonym André João Antonil. The standard modern edition is that ably translated and edited by Andrée Mansuy (Paris, 1965). Andreoni served as a major source of inspiration and information for the outstanding recent analysis of the cane sugar industry by Schwartz (*Sugar Plantations*), which also relies upon surviving documentation for two Santo Antão–owned mills in Bahia, Santana de Ilhéus and Sergipe do Conde, which are heavily represented in the ANTT/CJ series.

72. There is also an anonymous account attributed to a Jesuit coconut estate manager and originally published in 1841 and 1852 by Felipe Neri Xavier in his *Bosquejo historico das comunidades*, printed in Goa. It was republished in Lisbon in 1872 by Bernardo Francisco da Costa in *Agricultor indiano*, 141–68, again in 1896 by J. I. de Lisboa in *Cultura indiana*, and in 1918 by the Geographic Society of Lisbon, *Arte palmarica*, a 36-page pamphlet printed in Nova Goa. I have consulted this last edition and gratefully acknowledge the assistance of Karubaki Datta in locating two copies of it in the library of the Sociedade Geografica de Lisboa, as well as that of Fr. John Correia-Afonso of St. Xavier's College, Bombay, who first called the text to my attention during our sojourn in Rome. The procedures outlined in this account and that of Dias cited in note 74 may be compared with the recommendations made in several modern studies, notably Jaspar Guy Woodroof, ed., *Coconuts: Production Processing Products* (Westport, Conn., 1970); C. M. John, *Coconut Cultivation* (New Delhi, 1970); and P[alakesseril] K[umaran] Thampan, *Coconut Culture in India* (Cochin, 1972), the most helpful modern treatment.

he was "incredibly busy" because of the arrival of the annual ship from Macao, for he had to attend to the provinces' share of the cargo as well as the cleaning of drainage ditches on the plantation and the bleeding of the trees in preparation for winter. In June and July, 500 new trees were set out, and protective screens were erected to shelter them from the coming monsoon. In August, trenches were excavated, salt and ash were dug in at the feet of recently planted and mature trees, and additional protective bamboo screens were installed. Those activities continued into September and October, when the manager and his assistants gathered the quitrents from the rice farmers who leased paddies on the estate. Dias stressed that it was essential to collect them before the growers harvested their crops to prevent the inevitable frauds.[73] December could be the "laziest" month of all, according to Dias, unless a carrack was readying to depart for the homeland, in which case the procurator was continually busy preparing shipments and paperwork.[74]

As it was for the other types of procurator discussed in this chapter, paperwork was one of the fundamental chores of the estate managers. The managers kept inventories of the properties entrusted to them to display to their superiors and to be countersigned by their successors. They maintained accounts of goods supplied to and received from owner colleges. Managers of Indian properties belonging to the Japan province and the vice-province of China were required to submit status reports on their estates to the provincial procurators several times a year. The managers also kept well-guarded strongboxes for cash received and paid out, as well as files of all legal documents pertaining to the estate. Though juridical challenges to the ownership of such properties were the responsibility of spiritual superiors, the managers kept a watchful eye out for those tempted to encroach upon their estates and, when urgently necessary, armed themselves and organized resistance to bandits and other types of intruders.[75]

Upon occasion, such managers were accused of excessive zeal and other shortcomings.[76] In the early 1680s, some anonymous memorialists in Goa complained vigorously to the father general about the activities of his subjects in India. They alleged that the estate administrators persistently enlarged their plantations by buying land during the winter season and then charged as much as the traffic would bear for the commodities they produced during the summer. In response, the provincial assured Father General Noyelle that the complaint was unfounded. He admitted that the Society possessed the best

73. Modern Indian landlords evidently face the same problem. Cf. Irfan Habib, *The Agrarian System of Mughal India (1556–1707)* (New York, 1967), 241.

74. António Dias to Miguel de Amaral (Visitor, Goa), 11 Oct. 1708, in ARSI, *Goa*, 9:II, 435^v–38.

75. E.g., declaration of Francisco Travacos (ouvidor, Salsete de Goa), 30 Oct. 1621, in ANTT/CJ/90, no. 106. The magistrate testified that on two occasions Br. Fernão de Almeida rendered important services to Philip III by defending the villages of Velly, Ambely, and Assalona against Muslim intrusions and that on the second occasion he risked his life by capturing nine "robbers" and delivering them to a royal justice. Other managers were authorized to arm themselves against pests. Thus, an alvará of 14 Sept. 1736 confirmed the right of the padre shepherd of the *quinta* of Val de Rosal to carry a musket and lead between October and January of each year to protect livestock and fruit from unspecified types of pests. ANTT/CJ/39, no. 94.

76. For instance, when a drunken mulatto slave-catcher physically attacked a slave belonging to Engenho Sergipe do Conde in Bahia, the militant supervisor of the mill, the aforementioned Fr. Luís Veloso, sent a group of armed slaves to seize the offender. During the ensuing melee, the slave-catcher was killed, and Fr. Veloso was temporarily placed under house arrest. Schwartz, *Sugar Plantations*, 279–80. For reasons unclear, Veloso was subsequently recalled to Lisbon; however, he later returned to Bahia and resumed direction of the estate. *HCJB*, 9: 185.

estates in the vicinity of Goa but insisted that that was because their managers constantly sought to improve them, whereas their competitors, both religious and secular, were merely interested in collecting rents from their properties.[77] When attacked by outsiders, the Jesuits, like any other group within the Portuguese empire, rallied in defense of their brethren. That did not necessarily mean that spiritual superiors always trusted those charged with temporal affairs.

For the convenience of analysis, the temporal administrators whose functions have been examined in this chapter have been separated from their spiritual supervisors, but it should be remembered that they did not constitute a separate hierarchy within the Society. Rather, they were links in a chain that extended from the most recently entered novice to the father general. Each was merely a subordinate, a helper to his spiritual superior. Both his standing instructions and his superior's special orders continually reminded him that he possessed only delegated authority and that final responsibility for decisions affecting the temporalities that he tended lay with his superior. Each procurator was given specific spending limits, beyond which he was obliged to consult his superior before undertaking any action affecting the assets he managed. No procurator could alienate property entrusted to his custody or obligate the unit he represented without the approbation of his superiors. Estate managers who labored close to their owner colleges were kept under close surveillance by their superiors, but even those on detached duty, notably the procurators who served the college of Santo Antão on the Bahian sugar estates and those who managed the interests of the Japan province and the vice-province of China in Goa's northern province (the Bassein district), were explicitly placed under the spiritual control of the nearest college rector. Provincials visited some of the more conspicuous estates, and rectors were expected to do the same as often as possible. One purpose of such visits was to inspect the estates' facilities and to determine the completeness and accuracy of their accounts; another aim, as Cushner astutely observes, "was to remind [Jesuit administrators] symbolically and actually of the ties that bound them to Jesuit activity in colleges and residences, activity that was considered by some more directly apostolic."[78] Estate managers and their companions were enjoined that when it was necessary for them and their companions to travel to their colleges on business, they ought not to tarry in town or to visit other Jesuit estates. Superiors sometimes praised their procurators for exceptional service, but they were more prone to scold them for real or presumed shortcomings: for extravagance, carelessness, and negligence; for excessive chastisement of slaves or others working under their direction; for the sale of estate goods to outsiders; for lending equipment or money

---

77. Simão Martins to the general, Goa, 28 July 1683, in ARSI, *Goa*, 35, fols. 252–57, in response to a memorial that begins, "Cousas que se notaram nos religiosos da Companhia que vivem na India e principalmente na província de Goa, ... anno 1682," ibid., fols. 247ʳ–48ᵛ. Jesuit superiors were clearly sensitive to the problem of parish priests also serving as custodians of estates. Francisco Barreto recognized that such activity "hardly comports with the diligence and perfection expected of Ours in the cultivation of souls," but he perceived no realistic alternative to assigning men who had been trained as missionaries to manage estates whose revenues were essential to sustain the Society's endeavors in the East. "Ordens que deixou o P. Francisco Barreto, visitador, pera se goardarem em toda a provincia de Goa ... anno de 1660," in ARSI, FG, 1443/9/27.

78. Cushner, *Lords*, 76 and 78.

to unauthorized laymen; for misappropriating goods entrusted to them; and for keeping sloppy books.[79]

The fact that the performances of these officials sometimes fell short of what was expected of them is less astonishing than is the record of their achievements. After all, most managers began their assignments without any special training for the direction of an economic enterprise. Few possessed prior accounting experience. Many, especially those in Brazil, labored in remote situations in the midst of work forces that were indifferent, if not hostile. Considering the human, environmental, technological, and other obstacles that confronted them, most managers appear to have performed competently and zealously, if not efficiently. Although managers rarely advanced to positions of major authority within the Society, they provided much of the financial means that permitted the Society's heads to strive to fulfill its major educational and evangelical goals.

The chapters that follow will examine in greater detail the economic basis of those educational and evangelical programs in the Portuguese Assistancy and the economic sources of the Society's conflicts with its critics. They will also provide evidence necessary to consider the validity of the hypothesis, suggested some years ago by C. R. Boxer, that the Society of Jesus constituted "the world's first multinational corporation."

79. The preceding is based largely upon the sources cited in notes 69 and 77. For a different view, see Konrad, *Jesuit Hacienda*, 115 and n. 14.

7. Interior of the church of the professed house of São Roque, Lisbon. Robert C. Smith, *The Art of Portugal, 1500–1800* (London: George Weidenfeld and Nicolson, Ltd., 1968), pl. 55. By permission of the publishers.

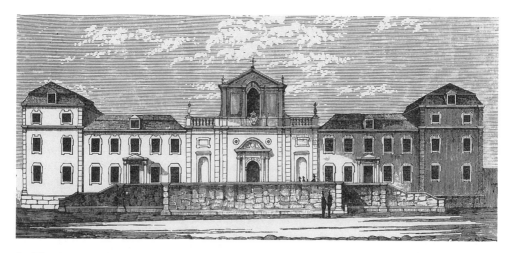

8. The Cotovia Novitiate, Lisbon, which was destroyed by fire in 1813. *Archivo pittoresco: Seminario ilustrado*, 11 vols. (Lisbon, 1858–68), 6: 245. Courtesy of The Newberry Library, Chicago.

9. Ruins of the College of Santo Antão, Lisbon. *Archivo pittoresco: Seminario ilustrado*, 11 vols. (Lisbon, 1858–68), 5: 365. Courtesy of The Newberry Library, Chicago.

10. Courtyard of the University of Évora. Robert C. Smith, *The Art of Portugal, 1500–1800* (London: George Weidenfeld and Nicolson, Ltd., 1968), pl. 40. By permission of the publishers.

11. Facade of the church of the College of São Lourenço, Porto, built 1614–22. Robert C. Smith, *The Art of Portugal, 1500–1800* (London: George Weidenfeld and Nicolson, Ltd., 1968), pl. 42. By permission of the publishers.

12. The Jesuit Church and College of São Paulo, Brazil. Acervo do Museu Paulista/USP.

13. The Jesuit College of Jesus, Rio de Janeiro, atop Castle Hill. LTC/RJ, after xxxi. Biblioteca Nacional, Rio de Janeiro.

14. Ruins of Engenho Novo, Rio de Janeiro. Instituto do Açúcar e do Alcool, *Brasil açucareiro* 65, 3 (Mar. 1965): facing 40.

15. A mid-nine-teenth-century lithograph of the Jesuit college, now cathedral, in Salvador, Bahia. Collection of Weston J. Naef, curator of photographs, The J. Paul Getty Museum.

16. A mid-nineteenth-century lithograph of the Jesuit college, garden, and wharf in Recife. *HCJB* 5: facing 466.

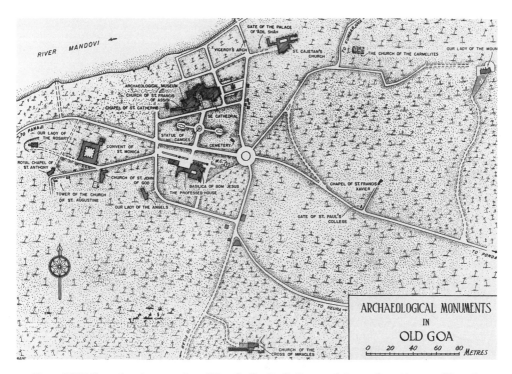

17. Plan of Old Goa, showing remains of New St. Paul's College and the professed house of Bom Jesús. S. Rajagopalan, *Old Goa* (n.d.). © Archaeological Survey of India.

18. Facade of the church of the College of Salsete (Rachol), Goa, Mário T. Chicó, "Algumas observações acerca da arquitectura da Companhia de Jesus no distrito de Goa," *Garcia de Orta: Revista da Junta das missões geográficas e de investigações do ultramar*, special no. (1956). Ministério do Planeamento e da administração do território. Instituto de investigação científica tropical. Centro de documentação e informação, Lisbon.

19. Portal of the church of the Jesuit college in Bassein. Mário T. Chicó, "Algumas observações acerca da arquitectura da Companhia de Jesus no distrito de Goa," *Garcia de Orta: Revista da Junta das missões geográficas e de investigações do ultramar*, special no. (1956). Ministério do Planeamento e da administração do território. Instituto de investigação científica tropical. Centro de documentação e informação, Lisbon.

PART IV

Financing an Enterprise:
Sources of Controversy

CHAPTER 13

The Crown as Benefactor
and Taskmaster

It would be a great help if some of the cardinals who are friends of the king would
write him about this and tell him how well the alms given for the construction of
this house will be used. . . . If they do not wish to write to the king, then they
should at least write to Dom Pedro so that he may speak to the king about it
and take upon himself the burden of doing this good work.

—Xavier to Loyola, Lisbon, 1541

FOR CENTURIES THE Jesuits have enjoyed a well-deserved reputation for their ability to
cultivate the high and the mighty. Their leaders, fully aware of the process of decision
making in their time, quite deliberately sought the support of influential persons who could
advance their undertakings, as did spokesmen for other privileged interest groups. Loyola,
Xavier, and Valignano, for example, recognized that the king's backing was necessary to
assure the success of Jesuit enterprises at home and abroad. Without question, John III, his
grandson, Sebastian, and his brother, Cardinal Henry, were exceedingly generous—some
would say reckless—in their support for the Society, which they endowed with lands, rents,
and both direct and indirect subventions. Though less bountiful in their bequests, the
Philippine rulers and their Bragançan successors generally reconfirmed the privileges and
immunities conferred by the initial trio of royal patrons and nominally continued their
support of certain units of the Society within the Assistancy. But, as this chapter will
demonstrate, the Jesuits soon discovered that the lavish promises made by Portugal's rulers
were often not honored by their agents overseas. And later chapters will show that the
uncertainty and insufficiency of the royal bounty led the Society to assume a far more
active role in the imperial economy than its leaders had initially contemplated or than some
of its members ever considered wise. The Jesuits soon discovered what earlier religious
Orders had painfully learned:[1] there was always a price tag attached to royal favors, and,
particularly in the eastern empire, the services to the crown that they were obliged to
render often represented significant departures from their Institute. But the performance

1. Cf. C. H. Lawrence, *Medieval Monasticism: Forms of Religious Life in Western Europe in the Middle Ages*
(New York, 1984), 114.

of extraordinary duties did not assure the Society of exemption from the assessment by crown agents of what amounted to forced loans during military crises, borrowings for which repayment was probably never expected and was certainly never forthcoming.

"By Robbing Peter He Paid Paul"

Like some other European rulers, the last three members of the House of Aviz provided seed grants for certain, but not all, new Jesuit colleges in the kingdom. In part, that was accomplished by reassigning properties and revenues formerly enjoyed by others, including religious institutions, to the Society of Jesus.[2] For example, John III assiduously endowed the College of Arts of the University of Coimbra after he entrusted it to the Jesuits. The former Augustinian monastery of N. S. de Cárquere, situated 15 kilometers from the town of Lamego, was the first of many properties he conveyed to the college. The Augustinian monastery of S. João de Longosvalles, on the left margin of the Minho River close to the northwestern border with Spain, was also given by the king to the college.[3] When John III shifted 1,400,000 rs. from the university's general budget to the Jesuit college, university authorities vigorously protested, and the crown agreed to provide 200,000 rs. of that sum from its Aveiro customs collections. Shortly after its founding, the Coimbra branch of the Inquisition confiscated a vineyard and the estate of Vila Franca, situated on the Mondego River outside of town, and they became part of the arts college portfolio.[4] In addition, Sebastian assigned to the college the income of fourteen churches formerly attached to the ex-Benedictine monastery of São Fins in the archdiocese of Braga.[5]

John's brother, Cardinal Henry, became the founder of the new University of Évora. With the blessing of the pope, he assigned to the university various ecclesiastical properties, including the income of the monastery of S. Jorge, a former Augustinian facility near Coimbra; that of the famous Paço de Sousa, a Benedictine monastery 24 kilometers from Porto; and that of the town of Monte Agraço, situated near Lisbon and formerly part of the fabric-lands of the archepiscopacy of Évora.[6] The same patron directed the reluctant chapter of that archdiocese to contribute two pensions, each valued at 200,000 rs. annually. He also ordered the archepiscopal cellar to provide the university with 23,000 liters of wheat

2. E.g., Elizabeth M. Hallam, "Henry II as a Founder of Monasteries," *Journal of Ecclesiastical History* 28, 2 (Apr. 1977): 113–32. Cf., however, A. Lynn Martin, *Henry III and the Jesuit Politicians* (Geneva, 1973), 27, who observes that "contrary to many other royal families, the French monarchy did not finance the foundation of any Jesuit colleges, possibly because of the suspicions regarding the Society's [alleged] Spanish character."

3. The canons of Santo Antão were formed in Portugal shortly after its establishment as a county of Leon-Castile in 1095. They possessed monasteries in Guarda, Pinhel, Santarém, Lisbon, and the bishopric of Viseu, but each was largely empty at the time the Society was created. In 1550 Pope Julius III sanctioned the transfer of their properties to the Jesuits. João Bautista de Castro, *Mappa de Portugal*, 3d ed., 4 vols. (Lisbon, 1870), 2: 77.

4. *HCJAP*, 1:2, 379–87; 2: 199ff.; *DHJP*, 245–52, 276–80, 285, 290–92, 293–307, 323–24, 327–33, 358–66, 690–92, and 703–14.

5. "Informacio para las tres pacacis q la comp.ª quiere hazer en elRey de Portugal de los padroados de las iglesias anexas al collegio JESU de Coimbra," n.d. (ca. 1570), in ARSI, *Lus.*, 84:II, 523–24. The conveyance included all income from a dozen churches (estimated at 778,000 rs.) and half the income of two others (amount unspecified).

6. Fabric-lands were intended to provide secure income for a church to underwrite the cost of routine maintenance and repairs.

and 7,800 liters of barley annually. By his command, the archdiocese also assigned to the university a portion of its tithes from the town of Estremoz, as well as thirteen or fourteen prebendaries within the confines of Évora. In addition, the cardinal allocated 25,000 rs. yearly to the university pharmacy from the royal customs house in the city.[7]

Contemporaneously, the same rulers provided undeveloped lands or established rural estates for Jesuit colleges overseas. Those in Brazil included four land grants (*sesmarias*) issued to the college of Bahia between 1550 and 1566, and another in Rio de Janeiro in 1567.[8] In Angola, the famous captain Paulo Dias de Novais awarded the Jesuits tribute paid by the native potentates to compensate them for the inadequacy of the royal alms.[9] In Goa, after the Portuguese destruction of Hindu temples (1541, 1562, and 1574), the crown authorized the transfer of their income properties—the so-called pagoda lands—to the Jesuit colleges of São Paulo (*o velho*) and Salsete (Margão). Such properties were often small, but they were abundant. As one Jesuit brother wrote, the Konkani "were much given to pagodas, so . . . that there were 360 in this island [Salsete], each with its separate revenues, which were spent on the day of its feast, on the ministers serving the pagodas, and on the public women and danceresses who lived in the pagoda for all their impurities."[10] In 1605, D. Jerónimo de Azevedo, captain-general of Ceylon and brother of Inácio de Azevedo, the martyred leader of the 1570 expedition to Brazil (see Chapter 3), bestowed upon the Jesuit college of Colombo and the Society's missions on that island revenues from 64 villages, and awarded income from other properties on the island to the college of Cochin.[11]

Other Royal Subventions

Besides such land endowments, the crown assisted certain Jesuit entities with subventions in goods and cash. John III, for example, provided the college of Santo Antão with nine *moios* (8,900 kilograms) of wheat and a quantity of wood each year.[12] His successors, Sebastian and Philip II, supplied the college of Angra in the Azores with 680,000 rs. per year, of which 600,000 came from customs revenues and the balance from sales of wheat belonging to

7. António Franco, *Évora ilustrada: Extraída da obra do mesmo nome do P^e Manuel [F]ialho*, ed. Armando de Gusmão (Évora, 1945), chap. 26; *HCJAP* 2:1, 220–25.

8. *MB*, 1: 195 and 299–301; 3: 521–32; 4: 343–45 and 349–53. Serafim Leite, "Terras que deu Estácio de Sá ao colégio do Rio de Janeiro: A famosa sesmaria dos Jesuítas," *Brotéria* 20 (1935): 90–108. See also *MB*, 4: 219–39.

9. "Declaração de Paulo Dias de Novais," 7 Jan. 1588, in António Brásio, ed., *Monumenta africana*, vol. 3 (Lisbon, 1953), 357. See also *HCJAP*, 2:2, 531 n. 2.

10. H. Hosten, S.J., ed., "Father A. Monserrate, S.J., on Salsete, Chorão, Divar, and the Molucas [*sic*] 1579," Asian Society of Bengal, *Journal and Proceedings*, n.s. 28 (1922): 349–69, at 363. For additional references to the temple lands, see also P. S. S. Pissurlencar, ed., *Regimentos das fortalezas da India* (Bastorá-Goa, 1951), 58–59; *DI*, 1: 760–63; 2: 44–47; 7: 387, 396; 9: 274–82, 329–30; *DHMPPO*, 7: 221–23; 12: 239–45; *S/FX*, 4: 532; Ricardo Michael Teles, "Ordens religiosas e seus conventos," *Boletim do Instituto Vasco da Gama*, no. 59 (1944): 132–38; and Anthony D'Costa, S.J., *The Christianisation of the Goa Islands* (Bombay, 1965), 29–30, 32–33. Although it applies most directly to Tamil South India, Burton Stein, "The Economic Foundation of a Medieval South India Temple," *Journal of Asian Studies* 19 (Feb. 1960): 163–76, is helpful for understanding the role of temple lands in western India as well.

11. Tikiri Abeyasinghe, *Portuguese Rule in Ceylon, 1594–1612* (Colombo, 1966), 222.

12. Cristóvão Rodrigues de Oliveira, *Sumario em que brevemente se contem algumas cousas (assim eclesiasticas como seculares) que ha na cidade de Lisboa (1551–1554)* (Lisbon, 1938), 56.

the king. About 1574, Sebastian authorized the college of Funchal, Madeira, to collect half of its income from locally gathered tithes.[13] That year Sebastian also promised to support each missionary serving in Angola with a fixed annual pension of 42,500 rs., an amount raised to 80,000 rs. by 1617. By the 1650s total royal stipends reached 800,000 rs. One hostile governor questioned whether such support was still necessary in view of the Society's sources of revenues in the colony, but in 1672 Pedro II directed that the Jesuits' pensions be continued.[14]

The crown also provided assistance to Jesuits serving in Brazil. Initially it instructed the colony's first governors-general to assist the fathers with whatever manioc, rice, and clothing they required for their maintenance. Between the mid-1560s and the 1570s, the crown assigned to three colleges—Bahia, Rio de Janeiro, and Olinda—a portion of the income that it received from tithes paid in sugars in accordance with the padroado real agreements. Later it provided annual subsidies for the living expenses of Jesuit missionaries serving in Maranhão.[15] One of the most important of the indirect subsidies the government awarded Jesuits serving in Brazil was their total exemption from customs duties, a subject discussed in Chapter 21.

Jesuit facilities in India were also beneficiaries of crown subventions. During the sixteenth century, virtually every college and mission within the province of Goa gained all or a substantial part of its income from the crown, which assigned portions of its revenues and allotments of foodstuffs. In the mid-1590s, for example, the king's annual pledges to the professed house in Goa included 9,072 kilograms of wheat, three kinds of Indian rice amounting to about 6,000 kilograms, 226.8 kilograms of butter, quantities of coconut and olive oil, 53.2 kilograms of almonds and raisins, half that amount of prunes and wax, six boxes of marmalade, and six pipes of wine.[16]

Until the early seventeenth century, the crown also furnished subventions to the Jesuit college in Malacca and to Jesuit missions in the Moluccas. But the spectacular Japan enterprise claimed the crown's greatest assistance. In 1574 Sebastian awarded the enterprise 400,000 rs. annually, less certain quitrents owed by the Japan enterprise on two communities (aldeias) it possessed in Goa's Salsete do Norte province. Six years later, Cardinal Henry increased that amount fivefold for a lustrum, and his successor, Philip II, extended that grant for another equal term. In 1596, however, Philip reduced his support to 800,000 rs., one-half derived from his Malacca customs and the remainder from his income in Salsete do Norte. That level of royal support persisted until at least the mid-seventeenth century and probably beyond.[17] The crown also provided monetary subsidies, derived from its Malacca customs,

13. "Rol da renda que o collegio ... de Angra ... tem [h]oje 27 de julho de 1592," ARSI, *Lus.*, 79, fols. 129ʳ–130ʳ. For Funchal's tithe income, see Chapter 18, note 26.

14. *HCJAP*, 2:2, 553ff.; 3:2, 292–93 and 300. For the sterling equivalent, see Pere Michael Angelo of Gattina, "A Voyage to Congo, in the Years 1666 and 1667," in A. Churchill, ed., *A Collection of Voyages and Travels*, 6 vols. (1704; London, 1732), 1: 561.

15. *CR*, 1 Jan. 1551; provisão of 2 Dec. 1559, in *DH*, 35: 96, and 36: 3–5. For the subtraction of tithe yields to the colleges and to the Maranhense missionaries, see Chapter 18, note 27.

16. Francisco Paes (*provedor mor*), "Tombo dos contos de Goa e mais ilhas anexas e Bardês, Salçete ... até 1595," University of London, Kings College Library, Marsden Collection.

17. Alessandro Valignano, *Sumario de las cosas de Japon (1583) [y] Adiciones del sumario (1592)*, ed. José Luis Alvarez-Taladriz, Monumenta Nipponica Monographs, no. 9 (Tokyo, 1954), 8–9; *DI*, 11: 537; *APO*:1, 3: 640–41; alvará of 6 Feb. 1616, BA/JA/49-V-76; ANTT/CJ/80, no. 57; *CR*, 19 June 1649, in *CCLP*, 9: 191.

for the China enterprise. The magnitude of such subventions increased from 120,000 rs. per year in 1586 to 600,000 rs. in 1612 and to double that amount by the end of the 1660s; by 1731, however, the crown's contribution to the vice-province had fallen to just under 900,000 rs. per annum.[18]

In addition to such financial assistance, the crown contributed monetary assistance for Jesuits who were obliged to travel. Each missionary sent from Lisbon to Brazil received 20,000 rs. in 1581, an amount increased to 35,000 rs. in the early 1690s.[19] The travel allowance was much higher for India-bound missionaries, whose arduous voyage was two to three times longer than passage to Brazil. In 1594 the procurator of Goa complained that although the king furnished 400,000 rs. per man, the actual cost of the trip was 640,000 rs.[20] Travel within the East was much less expensive: in 1586 the king furnished 12,000 rs. for Jesuits voyaging from Goa to Malacca, and an equal amount for those sailing from Malacca to Macao.[21] The crown also assisted provincials and their companions who conducted the Society's triennial inspections. In 1575 the king provided for that purpose 80,000 rs., an amount raised to 100,000 rs. by 1589 and to 150,000 rs. by 1628.[22]

The Problem of Delinquent Payments

Several points need to be made concerning the promised royal assistance described above. First, it was available only to some Jesuit facilities, not to all. Second, levels of support increased over time in some instances, but not in all. Third, and most critically, what the king promised, his overseas agents did not always provide. As Nicholas P. Cushner has written with respect to the Spanish crown and missionaries in its empire, "There always seemed to be enough . . . in the coffers to send priests to America and the Philippines, but once . . . [they] arrived at their destinations, royal beneficence became less evident. The great number of missionaries' letters in the Archive[s] of the Indies asking the Crown for wine, oil, salaries, and *limosnas* [alms], bears eloquent testimony to the truth of this."[23] Cushner's observations are equally applicable to the Portuguese Assistancy.

There are several reasons why governors, treasurers, customs officers, and others charged with making payments to Jesuits and to other ecclesiastics often failed to provide

---

The level of royal subventions actually sent from India to Japan between 1610 and 1613 is indicated in HAG 1890, fols. 11^v ff.

18. Report of the veedor da fazenda, Malacca, 1612, in BA/JA/49-V-5, no. 47.

19. *HCJB*, 2: 439–40 n. 3; ARSI, *Bras.* 3:II, 347–348^v.

20. Fr. Francisco Lameira to Aquaviva, [Goa], 7 Nov. 1594, in *DI*, 16: 760. In the mid-1630s, a Jesuit official complained to the viceroy that although the king insisted that foreign-born Jesuits serving in India be sent back to Europe, he provided nothing to defray the cost of Jesuit return voyages. Manuel d'Almeida to [Linhares?], ca. 1636, in ARSI, *Goa*, 25, fol. 63.

21. *DI*, 14: 499.

22. The alvará of 13 Feb. 1575 states that such expeditions were to be defrayed "tudo a custa de minha Fazenda." *LTC/RJ*, 13. The same year, Visitor Gouveia found the actual cost to be 80,000 rs. J. Manuel Espinosa, S.J., "Gouveia: Jesuit Lawgiver in Brazil," *Mid-America* 24 (Jan. 1942): 39. For the 1628 order by the provedor mor of Bahia to provide such assistance, see *DH*, 15: 185–86. Chapter 24 offers more detailed consideration of the transportation costs of Jesuits serving within the Assistancy.

23. Cushner, "Merchants and Missionaries: A Theologian's View of Clerical Involvement in the Galleon Trade," *HAHR* 47 (Aug. 1967): 360.

such funds. One was the chaotic character of royal finances: there never was any concept of budgeting and, especially in the East, every administrator able to do so endeavored to enrich himself at the expense of both the king and his subjects. Despite many royal directives requiring full accounting of moneys received and expended, the resulting reports were capriciously compiled, often were out of date by the time they were received in Lisbon, and sometimes failed to reach the kingdom because they were lost at sea.[24] If the king's finances were in a precarious state by the 1540s, the very decade when Jesuits first went to the extremities of the Lusitanian empire,[25] they only became more so during subsequent decades because of increased military expenditures, crippled commercial activity, consequent falloffs in customs receipts, and, as indicated in Chapters 5–9, devastating wars resulting in territorial losses, permanently in the East and temporarily in the West.

Jesuit complaints regarding tardy and insufficient payments from the king began as early as 1549 and did not abate until the end of the Restoration (see Chapter 5). As in the Spanish Assistancy, many missionaries, both Jesuit and non-Jesuit, continually lamented to their superiors that promised stipends were delayed, paid only partially, offered in depreciated currency, or entirely delinquent. They constantly reported that "the king's officers pay badly and tardily," and that whenever they applied for their stipends they were treated with rudeness that bordered on contempt.[26]

Such complaints began during the reign of John III. In 1549, for example, António Gomes, the choleric rector of the first St. Paul's, Goa, complained to the king that only two-thirds of the funds promised for the new Bassein mission were forthcoming. Xavier himself expressed concern that the crown was falling behind in its payments to the Society, and Barzaeus observed in 1552 that the crown already owed St. Paul's 210,000 rs. The following year, Manuel da Nóbrega, who four years earlier had led the Jesuits to Brazil, reported from São Vicente that the promised clothing and provisions allowances were both lacking.[27]

Treasury officers were always quick to defend their custodianship and to accuse the missionaries of being spendthrifts. Thus in 1552 Simão Botelho, a famous controller of the treasury of the State of India, observed,

> The friars of this land want to spend so freely and give so many alms at the expense of Your Highness's Treasury that a goodly part of the money is spent on that and, moreover, some of them want to be so lavish with Christianity that many of the rents are lost and the lands deserted, especially those in Bassein [because of the fathers' intolerance of pagans]. I well believe that it is all done in good and honest faith and that Our Lord and Your Highness are well served thereby, but it seems that they could strike a fair mean.[28]

24. Although the statements made here are based upon documents that I have studied in various archives pertaining to both Brazil and the eastern empire, they are supported by the writings of many other scholars cited in this study, most notably C. R. Boxer, Anthony R. Disney, Michael Pearson, and George Davison Winius. For one recent assessment, see Winius, *The Black Legend of Portuguese India: Diogo do Couto, His Contemporaries and the Soldado Pratico* (New Delhi, 1985).

25. See S/*FX*, 4: 481–82 n. 19.

26. E.g., *HCJB*, 1: 118.

27. Gomes to John III, 25 Oct. 1549, in *DI*, 1: 529–30; Xavier to Barzaeus, 24 Apr. 1552, in S/*FX*, 4: 576 and n. 29; Nóbrega to Simão Rodrigues, 12 Feb. 1553, in *MB*, 1: 423.

28. Botelho to king, Cochin, 30 Jan. 1552, in António da Silva Rego, comp., *Documentos sobre os portugueses em Moçambique e na Africa Central, 1497–1840*, vol. 7 (Lisbon, 1971), 282–83.

There were occasions even during the reign of the boy king Sebastian, that ardently pro-Jesuit monarch, when the crown's stipends were delinquent. In 1572, for example, the provincial of Portugal wrote Jerónimo Nadal, the vicar general, that 500 ducats that the king had pledged for an annex of the College of Arts of the University of Coimbra had failed to arrive. Inácio Tolosa, Nadal's counterpart in Brazil, reported three years later that the tithe yield promised the three Brazilian colleges was not being paid and that the king owed them 4,400,000 rs. As it often did, the crown responded to such complaints by directing its subordinates to fulfill its guarantees to the missionaries.[29]

Understandably, the Jesuits found it increasingly difficult to collect their stipends during the Philippine period (1580–1640), when Portuguese commerce and domains were continually victimized by Spain's enemies (see Chapters 7–9). In 1583 Valignano advised Aquaviva that the Malacca customs had yielded the Japan enterprise nothing for the past nine years; the same year, the Visitor to Brazil reported that the arrears due the colleges of Salvador and Rio de Janeiro continued to grow. Their concerns were echoed by Jesuit leaders in Goa and Cochin, who complained that the lack of royal support was harmful to the spread of Christianity.[30]

The problem escalated during the 1590s. By 1596 missionaries in Angola had gone unpaid for a decade, and those serving in China had been without subventions for a lustrum. The next year, the provincial of Goa protested that his subordinates serving in Damão were being paid in depreciated currency that reduced the king's contribution by 50 percent. A few years later, the provincial of Portugal charged that the archbishop of Braga and the bishop of Coimbra, taking their cues from the crown, had become delinquent in their assignment of tithe revenues to the Coimbra college of arts and to the college of Porto.[31]

Collections became even more difficult after the turn of the seventeenth century, when the Dutch began to swarm into eastern seas, capturing Portuguese vessels and besieging key entrepôts. In 1607 the novitiate of Lisbon reported that the crown had embargoed interest payments on an annuity that it held in the India House.[32] The same year, the fiery Italian provincial of the Malabar province protested that royal officials refused to provide any stipends to his men serving in the Moluccas. He declared that they had not been paid for five years, and warned that if conditions did not improve he would withdraw them. Philip III acknowledged the problem, ordered the arrears paid, and directed the missionaries to

29. Serrão to Nadal, São Fins, 11 Aug. 1572, in *DI*, 8: 556; Tolosa to Aquaviva (?), 17 June 1575, in ARSI, *Bras.*, 11, fol. 329; memorandum of directives by Cardinal Henry to Goan authorities, 9 Mar. 1579, in *DI*, 11: 541.

30. Valignano, *Sumario* [1583], 69–70 n. 8 and 117; "Lo que parescio al Pe... Gouvea," in ARSI, *Bras.*, 11, fol. 162; José de Anchieta, "Informação da província do Brasil para nosso padre" [1585], in A. de Alcântara Machado, ed., *Cartas, informações, fragmentos históricos e sermões de Joseph de Anchieta* (Rio de Janeiro, 1933), 413 and 421; *DI*, 15: 152, 204, and 217; 16: 490.

31. William Francis Rea, S.J., *The Economics of the Zambezi Missions, 1580–1759* (Rome, 1976), 56; José Luis Alvarez-Taladriz, "Inversion de plata del Peru en la India oriental para la mission de Japon (1590–1598)," *Tenri Daigaku Gakuho* [Bulletin of Tenri University], no. 107 (Mar. 1977): 50; provincial, Portugal, "Noticia e informação que deram os PP. da Companhia das pensões que recebiam, feitas por D. Henrique" [ca. 1599], in *RIHGB*, 43: 156–63, at 159–60.

32. "Rol da renda q. tem a casa de N. Sra. da Asumção do noviciado de Lisboa em Dezembro de 1607," in ARSI, *Lus.*, 82, fols. 128–29.

remain at their posts. Though some funds were briefly forthcoming, Jesuits who survived in the islands remained precariously financed.[33]

The absence of royal stipends was acutely felt in the peripheries of the Assistancy, which lacked alternative sources of income. As indicated in Chapter 6, Jesuit activity in Ethiopia seemed to show real promise during the first decades of the seventeenth century. The king ruled that missionaries serving there would be paid out of his Diu customs, but the fathers found it exceedingly difficult to obtain funds from that source.[34] The Japan province, which was supposed to receive most of its support from customs revenues in Malacca and other royal sources in Goa's northern province, Salsete do Norte, was especially hard hit. In 1620 the provincial reported that the province had not received funds from oft-besieged Malacca in fifteen years, nor any from India in five years. Even funds promised by the pope (see Chapter 14) had not been paid during the previous four years. Although the provincial detailed one of his men to Malacca to see what could be done about collecting the arrears, the young father soon reported that there was little prospect of collection because whatever funds the *alfândega* produced went to the captains and their soldiers.[35] The vice-province of China was in an equally precarious condition, for the royal subventions (also to be paid out of the Diu customs) never arrived. The vice-province accumulated alarming debts and was sustained only by borrowing from the Japan province, which also became a substantial debtor. The Dutch invasion of northeastern Brazil (see Chapter 9) compelled the crown to reduce its contributions to the remaining Jesuit colleges there. By 1638 the college of Rio de Janeiro had not received a contribution in nine years, and when payments were resumed, they were reduced by a third.[36]

The crown was not insensitive to Jesuit complaints and repeatedly admonished its subordinates to pay "promptly" what it owed to the Society's various installations.[37] What the crown failed to do, however, was to suggest to hard-pressed viceroys, treasurers, and customs collectors where they could obtain the promised funds.[38]

As indicated in Chapter 5, the Restoration was a desperate time for Portugal. It is not surprising, therefore, that the crown was often unable to honor its monetary promises to

33. Alberto Laerzio to Fr. Niccolo Spinola (procurator-elect), Cochin, 8 Dec. 1607; Philip III to viceroy, India, 11 Dec. 1607, in *DM*, 3: 87 and 90; see also ibid., 165–66, 173, 250–51, and 278–79.

34. Raymundo António de Bulhão Pato, ed., *Documentos remettidos da India, ou livros das monções*, vol. 1 (Lisbon, 1880), 246–47; *APO*:1, 6:2, 851–52.

35. *MHJ*, 869; Manoel Coelho to general, Malacca, 12 Dec. 1621, in ARSI, *Goa*, 18, fols. 54ʳ–55ᵛ. Jesuit bishops in Japan suffered as well. In 1603 Bishop Luís de Cerqueira reported to the pope his frustrating efforts to gain his stipends from India. Hubert Cieslik, S.J., "The Training of a Japanese Clergy in the Seventeenth Century," in J. Roggendorf, S.J., ed., *Studies in Japanese Culture* (Tokyo, 1963), 65.

36. *MHJ*, 969. For the diminished stipends to the Rio de Janeiro college, see *DH*, 17: 120–22. Jesuit installations in Mozambique likewise failed to receive subventions during much of the seventeenth century. Rea, *Economics*, 57.

37. E.g., *BFUP*, 1: 528, 541–42, 573, and 577; C. Beccari, ed., *Rerum aethiopicarum scriptores occidentales*, vol. 12 (Rome, 1912), 125, 144–45, 168, 240, and 325. Both sources provide a sampling of royal admissions from 1601 to 1638. In addition, king to viceroy, India, 23 Mar. 1627, and provisão of 16 Mar. 1630, in *Arquivos de Macao*, 2d ser., 1 (1945): 220 and 388, demonstrate Philip IV's concern that Jesuits serving in Japan, China, South Asia, and Ethiopia receive their stipends.

38. Conde de Linhares to king, 3 Jan. and 12 Feb. 1630, in *BFUP*, 2: 78 and 137. But in his marginal note of 14 Oct. 1633, Linhares denied that his treasury had missed a single quarterly payment to the ecclesiastics. Ibid., 3: 297–98.

the Jesuits and to other missionaries. In 1644 the vice-provincial of China reported that his enterprise had not received any pensions for more than 30 years and that the arrears then stood at 18,000,000 rs., or roughly fifteen times its annual income.[39] Two years later, the procurator for the Japan province disclosed that funds owed it from Naples, Spain, and India amounted to 6,700,000 rs.[40] Because of the Dutch war in the East, the royal stipends promised to the Malabar province virtually ceased long before that province was devastated by the Hollanders.[41] At the end of the 1650s, the co-governors of Goa reported to the king that there were no funds to pay ecclesiastics because the treasury's coffers were empty.[42] Likewise in Brazil, the royal stipends promised to Jesuits serving in the Maranhão mission had been long suspended when the viceroy ordered them to be resumed if their payment did not interfere with moneys owed the garrisons.[43] Two years later, in 1668, the rector of Bahia again complained about the difficulty of obtaining his college's share of the royal tithes.[44]

The close of the Restoration period seems to have marked the end of Jesuit protests about their royal stipends. But the cessation of such complaints was less a consequence of the government's improved finances than an indication of the Jesuits' resignation that they must fend for themselves by expanding their landholdings, increasing investments, and engaging in other income-producing ventures. Ironically, their financial successes made them inviting targets, along with branches of Portugal's famed charitable institution, the Santa Casa da Misericórdia, for forced loans exacted by the crown itself and by agents overseas.

"The Lord Giveth and the Lord Taketh Away"

On the one hand, the Portuguese crown posed as a generous supporter of the faith generally and of the Society of Jesus in particular; on the other, it frequently extracted large loans from the Jesuits as well as other interest groups within its realm in order to meet extraordinary state expenses that were primarily related to military considerations. One such occasion was Sebastian's reckless campaign that ended so tragically at Alcázarquibir in 1578. To raise funds for that exceedingly costly affair, the king borrowed from foreign traders, extorted a large contribution from his New Christian community, "borrowed" funds from the accounts of orphans, deceased persons, and absentees, sold promissory notes, offered discounts to farmers who paid their taxes in advance, and appealed to the Church for a contribution that amounted to 60,000,000 rs., about two-thirds the sum obtained from the New Christians.[45] Whether the Society of Jesus contributed financially to that ill-fated venture is unknown. It would not be surprising if it did, in view of the Order's exceedingly close relationship

39. AHU/PA/IN, *cx.* 13, docs. 1, 16, 99, per Teotonio de Souza, S.J., *Medieval Goa: A Socio-Economic History* (New Delhi, 1979), 170. A quarter century later, another vice-provincial reported that it was still very difficult to collect the 900,000 rs. that the crown had promised to pay out of its Damão customs. António de Gouveia, "Cathalogus rerum v. provincia Sinensis," 6 Oct. 1669, ARSI, *JapSin*, 134, fols. 160–61ʳ.
40. Antonius Franciscus Cardim, "Informatio pro provincia Japponiae" [1646], in *MHJ*, 1026–27.
41. F/*JM*, 2: 14.
42. Francisco de Melo de Castro and António de Sousa Coutinho to king, 20 Jan. 1659, in *BFUP*, 9: 190.
43. Petition by the Jesuits, ca. 20 Nov. 1666, and response by conde de Obidos, in *DH*, 22: 359–60.
44. Mᶜˡ. de Oliveira to Nuno da Cunha, Bahia, 12 Sept. 1668, in BNL/CP, cod. 575 (orig.).
45. [José Maria] de Queiroz Velloso, *D. Sebastião, 1554–1578*, 3d ed. (Lisbon, 1945), 236–40.

TABLE 13.1

Distribution of Contributions to the King by the Province of Portugal, 1641

Facility	Amount (000 rs.)	Facility	Amount (000 rs.)
Coimbra	500	Funchal	200
Évora	400	Angra	150
Santo Antão	66	São Miguel	20
Campolide (novitiate)	80	Luanda	100
Santarém	120	Faro	20
Porto	133	São Roque (professed house)	20
Braga	100		
Bragança	100	Total	2,009

SOURCE: ANTT/CJ/68, no. 433.

with the youthful monarch. With but one exception—a loan to the crown by the college of Cochin and the Santa Casa da Misericórdia of the same city in 1610 to facilitate the purchase of pepper—an obligation still unpaid by the late 1620s—there seems no evidence that entities of the Society lent to the crown during the Philippine interlude.[46]

During the critical years of the Restoration, the crown repeatedly demanded that the facilities of the Society contribute monetarily to the defense of the realm. In 1641 the colleges and houses of the province of Portugal contributed over 2,000,000 rs. to John IV, allocated in proportion to their income (Table 13.1). Throughout the 1650s, the same houses were assessed a levy that appears to have amounted to 10 percent of their income. In 1661, when the treasury reported that the arts college of Coimbra was behind in its contributions, the crown threatened to confiscate all of its current income. The procurator-general responded that the recent Spanish invasion of the Minho had deprived the college of revenues from one of its major estates and pointed out that since 1657 it had turned over 2,520,960 rs. to the royal coffers.[47]

The crown also turned to the Society's overseas provinces for financial aid. In 1656 the provincial of Goa reported sadly that the fortress captain of Diu had confiscated for alleged defense needs a long-anticipated bequest from a rich merchant in Diu amounting to 6 contos. That money had been intended to support the missions and college in Mozambique. The same year, all colleges of the province were burdened with an annual assessment of 1,500,000 rs. to defray state obligations. How long that assessment continued is unclear. Three years later the governors of tightly besieged Goa reported that the exchequer was exhausted and that because there were no funds to pay the troops and it was crucial to offset Dutch bribes to a native potentate with their own gifts, the city had to borrow 7,500,000 rs. from the Jesuits and others, an amount the governors deemed sufficient to pay urgent bills only for six

46. Petitions of the procurator-general, Indian provinces, ca. 1627, in ANTT/CJ/90, nos. 76 and 117. The unpaid balance amounted to about 10,400,000 rs., a substantial sum, by the late 1620s.

47. *CR* to Jesuit Visitor, 9 Apr. 1652; *CR* to provincial, Alentejo, 9 Dec. 1656 and 17 Aug. 1658; in BNL/CP/476, fols. 271, 269ʳ, and 273ʳ. Petition, procurator-general (Portugal) to king, 1661, in ANTT/CJ/68, no. 435. In 1672 the provincial reported that during the war the Spanish occupation of part of Tras-os-Montes province cost the college of Bragança 600,000 rs. per year, and that the college of Braga was deprived of another 800,000 rs. in yearly income. BNL/CP/475, fol. 413.

weeks. Six years later, following the devastating fire at New St. Paul's, the Jesuits requested repayment of that loan. It is unlikely that the exchequer was able to oblige.[48]

Several years earlier, the signing of the Anglo-Portuguese marriage treaty of 1661 (see Chapters 5 and 8) had prompted Afonso VI to double the size of excises for two years and to establish a new tax on exports of Brazilian sugars and tobacco to help defray Catherine of Bragança's dowry. When officials attempted to assess the new duties upon Jesuit exports, the rector of the college of Bahia protested that such an assessment was contrary to canon law. Strangely, he did not cite the long-standing exemption of the Jesuits from the payment of all customs duties with respect to their shipments to and from Brazil. The crown's response in this instance was to direct the tithe contractor to reserve 200,000 rs. of the king's contribution to the college for the payment of the college's share of the dowry.[49]

In India the viceroy, the combative António de Melo de Castro, reported in 1665 on his efforts to comply with a royal directive to impose a new tax on the king's subjects amounting to 12.5 percent of current income in order to raise funds to assure peace with the Dutch. Everyone, it seemed, was willing to fall in line save the Jesuits, who "obstinately" refused. But there was another side to that story, as Fr. Francisco Barreto, former provincial and current Visitor, reported to the king. He enclosed a detailed list (unfortunately now missing) demonstrating that the exchequer owed the province of Goa 6,900,000 rs. loaned for the defense of Ceylon and Macao, the payment of troops during the last Mughal attack on Goa, and the cost of improved defenses in Diu. He also observed that the college of New St. Paul's at its own expense had built a bulwark on Chorão island, that the college of Rachol had contributed 1,000,000 rs. to repel the same Muslim invasion, and that when the exchequer of Cochin was exhausted during the desperate defense against the Hollanders (see Chapter 8), the Jesuit college had contributed its silver. He added that during the previous two years, the province had contributed 2,700,000 rs. to the hard-pressed royal treasury and would have been willing to furnish even more had it not been for the incineration of New St. Paul's.[50] Nevertheless, the viceroy continued to apply pressure upon the Society's estates, insisting that everyone, both ecclesiastics and lay estate owners, in the Portuguese enclaves in India contribute 12.5 percent of the yield of their properties for the indemnity. The Jesuits eventually complied.[51]

In 1672 the Portuguese envoy to Rome applied to the pope to authorize an ecclesiastical subsidy comparable to that exacted from the Church during the Restoration. The crown needed an additional 20 contos per annum for six years, it said, to revive its navy so that it

48. Third catalogue, Goa, 1656, in ARSI, *Goa*, 25, 160ʳ–160ᵛ; deliberations of Council of State, Goa, 17 June 1659, and report to East India Company, 10 Dec. 1659, in *ACE*, 4:2–4; Afonso VI to viceroy, India, 4 Apr. 1665, cited in *BFUP*, vol. 10 (page no. missing). Around 1680, António Pais de Sande, acting governor of India, assigned the Jesuits income from the tolls of a river, which the Portuguese called the Brancavara, to compensate them for the loss of the bequest of Bartholomew Lopes, the Diu merchant.

49. *CR*, 13 Oct. 1662, in *DH*, 65: 242; petition by Jacinto de Carvalho, S.J., 9 June 1664, and conde de Obidos to provedor mor, 29 June 1664, in *DH*, 7: 159–60 and 180–81.

50. Overseas Council to king, 26 Sept. 1665, summarizing Melo de Castro to king, 6 Jan. 1665, in AHU/PA/IN, *cx*. 26, no. 204; Francisco Barreto to king, 24 Jan. 1664, in ibid., no. 35.

51. *BFUP*, 10: 414; 11: 499, 502, and 504–5. Viceregal decree, 27 Feb. 1665, and Melo de Castro to João de Sousa (Jesuit provincial), 14 June 1665, in HAG/*LM*, 35, fols. [158ʳ] and 165. In reporting his triumph the viceroy boasted that it required "a viceroy made of bronze" to deal with the Jesuits. Viceroy to prince regent, 29 Jan. 1666, in ibid., fol. 96ʳ.

could recover lost possessions in the East seized by Dutch heretics. In 1675, Clement X acceded to the prince regent's request. Two years later, the squadron paid for by the ecclesiastical subvention, consisting of eleven ships, most of them newly built, 3,000 soldiers, and 1,000 sailors, sailed from Lisbon, but not to the Far East; rather, it went to Algiers to hunt down pirates. Weeks later it sailed up the Tagus, having accomplished precisely nothing. Nor was it ever used for offensive operations against the Dutch or any other alien power.[52]

The funds generated for the creation of this useless squadron might better have been used in Goa to defend Portuguese positions in India against the very serious incursion of the Maratha chieftain Sambhaji in 1683–84 (see Chapter 8). The viceroy, Francisco de Távora, who it may be recalled entrusted the defense of the capital to St. Francis Xavier, first appealed to the king's subjects, especially the religious, for a massive donation of 90,000,000 rs. and then asked all of the religious to strip their churches of silver and loan the exchequer an additional 30 contos,[53] pledging to repay the loan out of the customs derived from the Persian Gulf port of Kung.[54] When it proved impossible to honor that promise, the crown ordered repayments to be made from its tobacco monopoly, but in 1691 the governors of Goa reported to Pedro II that because of the exhaustion of the exchequer, it was no longer possible to make payments from that source either.[55]

The treasury was bereft of funds and the religious went unpaid primarily because of the expense of the planned relocation of the capital from the island of Tissuary to the high bluff overlooking Mormugão harbor. The project was conceived about 1670, when the governors of India suggested that the bluff was more defensible than Goa. Sambhaji's invasion and the outbreak of an epidemic convinced Viceroy Távora that it was time to go ahead with the plan. Although the cámara of Goa strongly favored relocation, the archbishop and the heads of all of the religious Orders, including the Jesuits, opposed it because they were reluctant to abandon their existing facilities and rightly questioned where the money for the new city would come from. In practice it came from moneys owed them. Although the religious heads, fiscal officers, and other royal officials in Goa repeatedly urged that the plan

52. Francis Parry to Joseph Williamson, Lisbon, 26 Nov. 1672, in PRO/SP89/12, fol. 186; memorial of Gaspar de Abreu to Clement X, 1672, in ibid., /16, fol. 242 (copy in Portuguese); the papal brief, dated 23 Feb. 1675 but improperly attributed to Pius X, stating that the funds were to be used expressly to assist the "conquests of the states of India and Brazil invaded by enemies of the faith," is in AHU/PA/IN, cx. 30, no. 58, where the text is in Latin. Details concerning the composition of the squadron and its inconclusive Algerian campaign are given in Parry to Williamson, 20/30 July 1675, and Parry to Mr. Secretary Coventry, 12/22 Oct. 1675, in PRO/SP89/13, fols. 94^r–94^v, 43^r–43^v, and 114^r–116^v.

53. Assentos of 24 Nov. 1683 and 13 Mar. 1684, ACE, 4: 410–12 and 428–32.

54. Following the loss of Ormuz (1622), the Portuguese shifted their commercial and evangelical interests in the gulf to Muscat, but the Omani drove them from the Arabian Peninsula by 1650. Thereafter their only base in the gulf was at Kung, confusingly called Kongo. It was situated 6.4 to 12.8 kilometers east of the town of Linga. The Portuguese built a factory there in 1625 and were supposed to receive 50 percent of the customs from the shah of Iran, but when Abbé Carré visited there, the shah was no longer making such payments. Kung was lost in 1711. The Travels of the Abbé Carré in India and the Near East, 1672 to 1674, trans. Lady Fawcett, ed. Sir Charles Fawcett and Sir Richard Burn, HS:2, 95, 106–13; Arnold T. Wilson, The Persian Gulf: An Historical Sketch from the Earliest Times to the Beginning of the Twentieth Century (London, 1928), 153–56; C. E. Bosworth, "Linga," in Encyclopaedia of Islam, 2d ed., vol. 5 (1983), 765.

55. CR to governor of India, 8 Jan. 1689; governors to king, 22 Dec. 1691; in HAG/LM, 54, fol. 5^r; 56, fol. 30^r.

be shelved until remedies could be found for the shortfall in royal income, Pedro II became captivated by the idea and repeatedly insisted that every effort be exerted to build the new city and to undertake its fortification. For the balance of the seventeenth century, as much as 6,000,000 rs. a year were spent on the Mormugão project. Then, suddenly, inexplicably, it was abandoned altogether.[56]

During the War of the Spanish Succession (1702–13), the provinces of Portugal and Brazil came to the assistance of the crown. The former, in what amounted to a patriotic gesture that its leaders probably hoped would not be accepted, offered all of its landed properties to assist the crown in financing the defense of the realm.[57] In 1711, after the French corsair Duguay-Trouin had captured Rio de Janeiro, the Jesuit college there contributed not only to the fund for the redemption of the capital, but also to the expenses of the garrison and the panic-stricken settlers.[58]

But there were limits to the Jesuits' spirit of giving. In 1726 the cámara of Macao was confronted by a serious problem: Alexandre Metello de Sousa Menezes arrived in port on an embassy to China. The crown expected the city fathers to contribute the lion's share of the 7,400,000 rs. budgeted for his expenses. After the cámara had raised 1,200,000 rs., it turned to the college of São Paulo for a major contribution. The vice-rector, noting that the last time his institution had been approached for such a purpose it had been obliged to borrow 1,200,000 rs., for which it apparently had never been repaid, declined to contribute a second time. The ambassador himself intervened, and in the end the province of Japan furnished 400,000 rs.; the always impoverished vice-province of China supplied half that amount.[59]

56. This was not the first proposal to relocate the capital of the State of India. Early in the century there was a possibility that it might be shifted to Colombo, Ceylon. The documentation on the capital's transfer is substantial. See assento, 12 Jan. 1684, in *ACE*, 4: 421–26; HAG/*LM*, 52, fols. 177ʳ–78ʳ; 54, fol. 117ʳ; 55A, fol. 122ʳ; 58, fol. 36ʳ–37ʳ; 59, fol. 129; and 63, fol. 169ʳ. Additional documentation will be found in AHU/PA/IN, *cx.* 34, no. 72, and *cx.* 38, nos. 19 and 65. The arguments against the move, largely financial, are best indicated by the opinions filed in BNL, cod. 8538, fols. 18ᵛ–25ᵛ, whereas the king's determination to press ahead as late as 1697 is indicated in *CR*s, 6 and 8 Mar. 1697, in BNL/CP/439, fols. 171 and 184. Jesuit concerns are indicated in Alexandre Cicero (Visitor) to P. Joseph Tisanier (provincial, Japan), 4 May 1684, in ARSI, *Goa*, 35, fol. 276. As late as 1702, New St. Paul's was spending 15,000,000 rs. on a new professed house being built on the promontory. Anon., "Pro providendo de opportuno remedio collegio Goano D. Pauli tria pra habenda sunt, tamquam fundamenta," ca. 1702, in ARSI, *Goa*, 36:1, fol. 27ʳ. Despite its age, the two-part article by J. F. Ferreira Martins, "Mudança da cidade de Goa para Mormugão," *O oriente portugués*, 2d ser., 7 (1910): 34–42 and 89–100, is still worth reading.

57. BGUC, cod. 617, fols. 40ʳ–41ʳ.

58. There is a discrepancy as to the extent of the Jesuit contributions. The "Relação das pessoas e das quantias com que contribuirão para o resgate desta cidade, rendida pelos francezes em 11 de setembro de 1711," *RIHGB* 21 (1858): 30–31, shows that the college provided 4,866,000 rs. (out of 246,500,464 rs.) for the ransoming of the city. The Jesuits later said, however, that they furnished a much larger sum—16,000,000 out of 240,000,000 rs., in addition to 100 chests of sugar and 200 oxen—for the city's recovery, the payment of the garrison, and assistance to its citizens. It seems clear that the Jesuits expected to be repaid for all or part of their expenses. Provisão of 9 Feb. 1714, in AHU/LR 225, fols. 42ʳ–42ᵛ.

59. See the relevant correspondence in *Arquivos de Macao*, ser. 1, 2 (1930), where the pagination is defective. Although a Jesuit father, Francisco Pimentel, had accompanied an earlier Portuguese diplomatic embassy to China, the Jesuits do not appear to have been among the financial supporters of that expensive, ultimately fruitless mission. C. R. Boxer and J. M. Braga, comps. and eds., *Breve relação da jornada que fez a corte de Peken o Senhor Manoel de Saldanha (1667–1670), escrita pelo Padre Francisco Pimentel e documentos contemporaneos* (Macao, 1942), reprinted in *Arquivos de Macao*, 2d ser., 1 (1945): 25–36, 87–96, 229–36, 289ff., and 339–53.

The Jesuits were much more responsive when their friend João de Saldanha da Gama approached the provincial for a large loan to underwrite the cost of the ill-fated expedition sent from Goa to Mombasa in 1728. Outfitting that expedition cost 74,198,100 rs., of which the fathers of the Goan province provided a loan of 50.5 percent.[60] Such assistance did not assure the Jesuits of the good will of the crown's agents in subsequent years. During the late 1730s, not only did the Society lose its northern colleges in India when they were overrun by the Marathas, but for a time its revenue sources for the college of Damão and some of its facilities in Goa were confiscated (see Chapter 23).[61]

According to a memorandum of computations in the accounting bureau in Goa, the Jesuits remained a heavy creditor of the crown in India. That statement does not agree with Governor Saldanha's 1728 report, which states that the treasury only owed the Jesuits 37,500,000 rs. as a result of the 8 percent loan negotiated in October 1727, plus an additional 4,200,000 rs. borrowed at the end of the following year. It is clear that because of the Maratha war, liquidation of those loans proceeded slowly; nevertheless, they were substantially reduced by the late 1740s. By 1751 the balance owed stood at 4,573,800 rs., but two years later the exchequer again borrowed a substantial sum from the Jesuits—24,000,000 rs.—but this time at 5 percent interest, since the new regime in the kingdom had recently arbitrarily reduced to that level the licit maximum rate of interest.[62]

It should be clear, therefore, that in various parts of the Portuguese Assistancy, Jesuit facilities repeatedly came to the aid of the crown in times of need. The scale of Jesuit giving and lending was greater than that of any other entity within Portuguese dominions, save for some of the branches of the Santa Casa da Misericórdia, custodians of funds belonging to orphans and to European heirs, funds repeatedly and shamelessly raided by agents of the crown and seldom repaid.[63] The roles of both the Jesuits and the Holy Houses of Mercy as lenders to the crown have never been recognized, nor have the administrative services that Jesuits often, albeit reluctantly, provided.

Unwanted Burdens

The *Constitutions* state explicitly: "That the Society may be able to devote itself more entirely to the spiritual pursuits pertaining to its profession, it should abstain *as far as possible* from all

60. Saldanha to king, 20 Jan. 1728, in AHU/PA/IN, *m.* 14. The 8% loan was to be defrayed by assigning to the fathers revenues from the islands of Panele and Curique, also known as Panelem and Corjuvem. A complication arose when Joseph Barbosa Leal, fiscal of the Strait of Ormuz and the Red Sea, petitioned for the right to collect the income from the same islands to compensate him for his services. The conde de Sandomil, Saldanha's successor, pointed out that 89.6% of their annual yield (3,724,650 rs.) was assigned to the Jesuits. Sandomil to king, 9 Jan. 1733, in ibid., *m.* 74. The extent to which the Jesuits contributed to the expenses of the earlier (1698) relief expedition to Mombasa is unclear. Since the vice-province of China supplied a token amount (215,400 rs.), it seems likely that the two Indian provinces furnished even more, but I have seen no evidence that they did. HAG 1497, fols. 34^v and 36^v.

61. The Jesuits petitioned for the restoration of their properties, and in 1743 the crown ordered that done. Interim government to king, Goa, 25 Jan. 1744, in AHU/PA/IN, *m.* 78.

62. "Copia da liquidacao' feita no tribunal dos contos en 11 de janeiro de 1751," HAG 2096, tucked into one of the account books of Bom Jesús at fol. 181^r.

63. The files in HAG contain many flagrant examples of the crown borrowing such funds without any indication of repayment.

secular employments."[64] In the Portuguese Assistancy, particularly in the State of India, it often proved impossible for the Jesuits to resist demands by the crown and its agents that members of the Society discharge commissions that many fathers were convinced were contrary to the provisions of their Institute. Just as Chinese emperors required that Jesuits perform secular duties such as the preparation of official calendars, the casting of cannon, and the execution of various engineering tasks as the price of tolerating the presence of missionaries in their midst, so the rulers of Portugal insisted, despite repeated objections from leaders of the Society, that Jesuits undertake responsibilities that were more appropriate for persons in secular garb, or for secular churchmen, than for representatives of the Society.

In the Spanish Indies, the scarcity of secular clergy during the first half of the sixteenth century led to a special papal authorization enabling members of the religious Orders to perform the duties of parish priests. A comparable situation occurred in western India, where Jesuits around Bassein and in Goan Salsete exercised the same functions. Though the Bassein parishes do not seem to have become subjects of conflict with the archbishops of Goa, the Salsete parishes were constantly the focus of contention between Jesuit leaders and senior prelates. The fathers first established their presence in the Salsete parishes during the 1560s, but withdrew in 1573–74 in response to a complaint from the archbishop. They returned in 1583, the year Rudolfo Aquaviva and his four companions were martyred in the district (see Chapter 3). By 1586 Jesuits were serving 14,000 Christians and 1,500 catechumens in the region.[65] In 1591 D. Matias de Albuquerque, archbishop of Goa (1591–97), petitioned Philip II to transfer the parishes to his jurisdiction, and Claudio Aquaviva called for a report on whether the Jesuits ought to yield the parishes. Three years later, Fr. Thomas Stephens, the English-born rector of Margão (the first home of the college of Salsete, to which those who served the parishes belonged), pointed out that all but one of those priests knew Konkani and therefore were competent to confess their flocks in their own language, something that secular priests then and later were unable to do. At the same time, his colleague, Fr. Jerónimo Cota, rector of St. Paul's, strongly opposed transfer of the Salsete missions; nevertheless, that year Aquaviva ruled that they should be turned over to the archbishop.[66]

Typically, the Jesuits' withdrawals from the Salsete parishes were of short duration because the archbishops invariably found that they could not staff the district with Konkani-speaking clergymen. Although their critiques questioned whether the Jesuits themselves were linguistically competent to work in the parishes, there is positive testimony in their behalf. In 1618, seven indigenous aldermen (*gancares mores*) signed a statement attesting to the fact that the Jesuits who served their communities and participated in their feasts spoke and confessed in Konkani without reliance upon interpreters.[67] Still, some Jesuits continued to oppose service in the parishes. For example, in the early 1640s, one senior father recommended to Vitelleschi that most of the parishes be surrendered because parish

64. Chap. 3, par. 591. Emphasis added.

65. *DI*, 14: 33*.

66. Alessandro Valignano to Mercurian, 7 Aug. 1574, in *DI*, 9: 408–9; Fr. Nuno Rodrigues to Aquaviva, Goa, 3 Dec. 1591, in *DI*, 15: 718–19; Stephens to Aquaviva, 18 Nov. 1594; and Cota to Aquaviva, 21 Dec. 1594, in *DI*, 16: 831 and 1026–27; extracts of letters from Aquaviva to Francisco Cabral (provincial), Rome [late 1594], in *DI*, 16: 1044–45.

67. Declaration signed at Rachol, 15 Nov. 1618, in ANTT/CJ/90, no. 109.

duty was inappropriate to members of his Order. Nevertheless, he admitted that there were no secular priests competent to replace his colleagues.[68]

Senior Jesuits continued to share their misgivings about the retention of the parishes. Though one of the consultores of Fr. Fernão de Queiróz strongly endorsed the presence of the Jesuits in the parishes in 1670, a decade later he himself expressed reservations. In 1677 the Jesuits again gave up the missions, and Queiróz stated that it was best that they stay out of them. He noted that there had been 25 Jesuits serving the parishes, that it required six months to a year for each to become competent in Konkani, and that he was convinced that such personnel could be better utilized elsewhere. But the royal board of missions, the Mesa da Consciência e Ordens, disagreed and urged that the Jesuits be directed to return. They did return, but in 1693 they again petitioned Pedro II for permission to withdraw. This time it was the Overseas Council that insisted that the fathers, then serving 100,000 persons in the district, remain, since it was in the king's interest that they do so. Pedro II agreed.[69] The Jesuits stayed in the parishes, but in 1703 the provincial inspector recommended to the general that it was in God's interest that the Order withdraw from them. It was not, however, in the king's interest, as the new monarch, John V, declared in 1708.[70] Nevertheless, a bitter quarrel between the Jesuits and the archbishop led to their abandonment of the Salsete parishes in 1723, an action that bewildered the aldermen of Rachol, who petitioned the general in 1726. The aldermen insisted that they had never criticized the fathers, nor had they wanted them to give up the parishes. They implored the general to ignore any criticism of the Jesuits' conduct there.[71] In spite of all the pulling and tugging, the Jesuits were still working in those parishes as late as December 1758.[72]

The Jesuits also performed a variety of services as trustees. For example, when Sebastian assigned to the College of Arts at Coimbra income from the old monasteries of São Fins and Longosvalles, that college assumed the responsibility of paying the stipends of a number of curates whose income derived from those institutions. In effect, the crown transferred the burden of payment from itself to the Society.[73] From time to time Jesuit colleges, like those of other religious Orders and especially the Holy Houses of Mercy, served as custodians of funds belonging to persons who died overseas and bequeathed their estates to heirs in Europe. Fulfilling the conditions stipulated by the decedents' wills was time-consuming and sometimes fraught with unexpected difficulties; often the work involved was hardly worth the alms that the house received for its services. In 1661, for example, Br. Manoel de Figueiredo, longtime procurator of the pharmacy of the college of Macao, reported that in 1649 Mathias da Sylva, a benefactor of the Society, had expired after being admitted as a brother. He left a substantial inheritance amounting to 10 contos and requested that it

68. Francisco Ferreira Senior to general, 26 Oct. 1642, in ARSI, FG, 1443/9/21 (/22 is a second copy).

69. "Parecer q. o P.ᵉ P.ᵃl Fernao de Queiros pedir ao P.ᵉ Fr.co Nog.ra sobre aceitarmos ou nao as igr.as de Salsete," 8 Sept. 1670; memo of Queiroz, 7 Oct. 1680; Mesa da Consciência to king, 16 Mar. 1680; in ARSI, FG, 1443/9/37, /40, and /42; Overseas Council to king, 26 Feb. 1693, in AHU/PA/IN, cx. 37, no. 7.

70. King to provincial of Goa, 7 Apr. 1708, ARSI, Goa, 9:II, fol. 419.

71. Declaration of Francisco Joseph de Payo(?) (vice-rector, New St. Paul's), 5 Jan. 1723, in AHU/PA/IN, m. 14, bk. 2; two memorials from procurator, India, to king [no month, no day], 1724, in ARSI, Goa, 9:II, fols. 580ʳ–83; cámara to general, 11 Jan. 1726, in ibid., fol. 604.

72. HAG, cod. 2557, fol. 72.

73. "Informacio para las tres pacacis q. la comp.ᵃ quiere hazer ... de las iglesias anexas al collegio JESU de Coimbra," n.d., in ARSI, Lus., 84:II, 523–24.

be sent to his heirs, who lived in the town of Arroyos in the kingdom. Except for a small sum that he retained as alms, Figueiredo sent the funds in silver to Goa and asked the procurator representing the Japan province there to forward them to Europe. Because of the Dutch war, shipping was scarce, and the distressed procurator concluded that only just half of the funds that he had forwarded had been remitted to the kingdom.[74]

The transmission of the estate of the late Vicente de Aristendo posed vexing problems for the rector of the college of Rio de Janeiro. Aristendo was a Biscayan who spent many years in Rio de Janeiro, one suspects as a commission merchant, where he died around 1690. He left a sizable estate to be sent to his childless wife and his nephews. One nephew had also expired; the other had left his natal city, Deba, supposedly because of his corrupted mulatto blood. Though the rector reported difficulty collecting from Aristendo's creditors in Brazil, a labor of charity, he claimed, rather than obligation, despite the *grossa esmola* (the large, but unspecified, alms the deceased had left the college), he had sent some 4,000,000 rs. to Lisbon, where the procurator of Brazil had attempted to locate the heirs. Several impostors had presented themselves bearing false papers to claim the inheritance. They were exposed and jailed for their trouble. The rector suggested that the Spanish assistant arrange with the father general to have the funds remitted to the college closest to the Biscayan heirs, and that when the negotiation had been completed, the appropriate affidavit be remitted to the Rio de Janeiro college via the Portuguese assistant in Rome and the procurator for Brazil in Lisbon.[75]

Sometimes the well-intended role of a college as the custodian of an outsider's possessions caused embarrassing problems. One such instance occurred in 1605, when the college of Santo Antão was sued by a couple and their daughters-in-law, who alleged that a quantity of money, rings, necklaces, pearls, and other valuables entrusted to the college by the wife's father had disappeared. A royal court found the claims without foundation and condemned the complainants to pay charges.[76] Three decades later, the president and council of the English East India Company complained that Abraham Aldington, accountant for the first English voyage to China, had overcharged the Company for his expenses in Macao and failed to account for 700 teacups brought to Goa. He was fined 300 pieces of eight out of funds that he had entrusted to the rector of the college of Damão.[77] For good reason, one procurator strongly recommended against any college accepting deposits belonging to laymen, "because we lose much credit with them and also much silver because the procurators expend it" in fulfilling the demands placed upon them. Vicente Carafa prohibited the practice in 1647, and in 1682 the Twelfth General Congregation did likewise, but, as the Aristendo case suggests, the prohibition was not always respected.[78]

The best-known facilities that the Jesuits maintained in the field of health care were their pharmacies. In Portugal, both the College of Arts at Coimbra and the University

74. Statement of Manoel de Figueiredo, Macao, 21 Feb. 1661, in BA/JA/49-V-5, no. 127.

75. Francisco de Matos (rector, College of Rio de Janeiro), "Directorio para a ultima entrega dos bens de Vicente de Aristendo a seus herdeyros e legatarios," 1693 (no day or month), in ARSI, *Bras.*, 11:II, 427–28.

76. "Sentença aplica contra dom fr.ᶜo de [N]oronha e sua mulher e cunhadas," 22 Dec. 1605, in ARSI, FG, 1453/5/24.

77. William Methwold and council, consultation of 1 Aug. 1636, in *EFI* (1634–36), 275.

78. Anon., "Couzas que podem servir para os procuradores" [1629], in BA/JA/49-V-8, no. 94 (fols. 635–49), par. 16; H/SAG2, 72–73.

of Évora operated pharmacies that were available to the public. The cámara of Évora extolled the local Jesuit facility, stating that the city itself was ill provided with pharmacies, that it had "great faith" in the remedies the Jesuits dispensed, and that though the pharmacy did not exist to earn profits, its surplus income assisted the local poor.[79] In Brazil, every college maintained a pharmacy, often the only one in the community and a significant source of income.[80] The situation was different in the Goan province, where pharmaceutical services were centralized in New St. Paul's, which supplied drugs to each of the outlying colleges. The colégio máximo also maintained an infirmary that served the entire province and was doubtless open to Jesuits in transit to other provinces in the East as well.

Though the Society of Jesus is not known as a hospital order, it did operate a number of hospitals in the State of India as well as the usual clinics attached to its colleges in the kingdom and in Brazil. The most conspicuous one entrusted to the Jesuits in the East was the royal soldiers' hospital in Goa. It was first commended to the Society in 1579, when the viceroy, dissatisfied with the high death rate among inmates and reports of gross mismanagement, asked the provincial to assume responsibility for it. Although the provincial raised objections, he yielded on an interim basis. The report of the rector makes it clear why most of those who entered emerged to be taken to burial grounds; the Jesuits found the hospital in deplorable condition. Because of an insufficiency of beds and bedding, most victims, suffering from an assortment of fevers, dysentery, and venereal diseases, were strewn about the floor amid their own filth, to which purges of wild amaranth and fish continually contributed. The Jesuit father and brother who took charge cleaned up the hospital, obtained suitable bedding and covers, introduced better food and superior sanitary conditions, and reduced costs by 50 percent. In 1584 the Jesuits drew up basic rules governing the hospital's management. One may still pity the patients, for whom the day began with a 5 A.M. mass![81]

Was it appropriate for the Society to supervise such an institution? Neither Mercurian nor Aquaviva believed that it was, and both directed the provincial to terminate Jesuit management. He complied in 1583 or 1584, but Philip II soon appealed to the Order to resume the hospital's direction. After an exchange of views between Jesuit leaders in Goa and in Rome, Aquaviva instructed Valignano to prepare to take over the hospital from the local Holy House of Mercy when the king issued the order. The Jesuits

79. "Rasoes' que offerecem os vereadores, cidadões, e povo da cidade de Évora pera o nosso collegio lhes haver de dar as mezinhas da nossa botica por seu dinheiro," n.d. (but clearly the first half of the seventeenth century). ARSI, *Lus.*, 80, fols. 334–35.

80. According to the periodic economic reports submitted by the provincials of Brazil to the Roman headquarters, the pharmacies generally provided between 3% and 10% of a college's income, but sometimes far more. ARSI, *Bras.*, 5:I, 5:II, 6:I, and 6:II. In 1732 the procurator for the vice-province of Maranhão reported that the *botica* of Pará earned up to 600,000 rs. per year. ARSI, *Bras.* 25, fol. 56[v]. See also Serafim Leite, S.J., *Artes e ofícios dos Jesuitas no Brasil (1549–1760)* (Rio de Janeiro, 1953), 83–100.

81. On the initial takeover of the hospital by the Jesuits, see Gomes Vaz to [Mercurian], 20 Oct. 1578; and António de Monserrate to Mercurian, 26 Oct. 1579; in *DI*, 11: 272–73 and 664–65. Christophorus de Castro (rector, Cochin) to Aquaviva, 5 Jan. 1582, in *DI*, 12: 581–82, provides vivid before-and-after descriptions of the quality of health care in the hospital. See also Anthony Coke Burnell and V. A. Tiel, eds., *The Travels of John Huyghen van Linschoten to the East Indies*, HS:1, 70: 237; and the "Regimento do hospital real da cidade de Goa," 28 May 1584, in *DI*, 13: 867–73.

returned in 1591, after the king assured them of sufficient funds derived from taxes on food, soap, and opium.[82]

Because the old hospital, built in the 1540s, was falling down, the Jesuits supervised construction of a new and presumably larger facility between 1594 and 1598.[83] One of the early and certainly one of the most enthusiastic patients of the new facility was a French sailor, François Pyrard, who was a patient there in 1608. In an oft-cited passage, Pyrard described the hospital as

> the finest in the world, whether for the beauty of the building and its appurtenances, the accommodation being in all respects excellent, or for the perfect order, regulation, and cleanliness observed, the great care taken of the sick, and the supply of all comforts that can be wished for. . . . Some Jesuit novices are employed in searching for and collecting old linen throughout the town for the use of the hospital, for new would not be proper. The Jesuit Fathers . . . most worthily acquit themselves there in; were it in the hands of others it could hardly be maintained upon twice the present revenue. In this hospital are apartments for each ailment.[84]

Not everyone was prepared to write such glowing reports concerning the Jesuits' administration of the royal hospital. About 1670, for example, the jewel merchant Jean Baptiste Tavernier averred that though the hospital had once been "renowned throughout all India," it had declined, its patients being "badly treated, and many Europeans who enter it do not leave it except to go to the tomb." But Tavernier's account was based upon hearsay, as was that of a malicious Italian, Nicolao Manucci, who contended that the Jesuits badly exploited the inmates and shamelessly pocketed their estates.[85] A fellow countryman, globetrotter Giovanni Francesco Gemelli Careri, charged that "thousands, particularly wretched Portuguese Souldiers," died in the hospital. The only surviving mortality figures for the late seventeenth century show that 78 persons—hardly a shocking number—expired in the hospital between January 1690 and January 1691. It is likely that many of them arrived after becoming mortally ill aboard East Indiamen during their long and difficult voyages from Lisbon.[86]

There is no evidence to support Manucci's assertion of wrongdoing by the Jesuits with respect to deceased persons' property, but there *is* evidence by the late seventeenth century that the quality of care at the hospital was declining, owing to the shortage of doctors and

82. See the excellent summary in *DI*, 15: 6*–7*. See also ibid., 606–8 and 738–39. The latter indicates clearly that the Jesuits were reluctant to resume the hospital's administration and constitutes an adequate refutation of the charge by the historian of the Santa Casa da Misericórdia of Goa that the Jesuits took the administration away from the Santa Casa "because of their natural tendency to monopolize everything." José F. Ferreira Martins, *Historia da misericórdia de Goa (1520–1910)*, 3 vols. (Nova Goa, 1910–14), 2: 317.

83. S/*FX*, 2: 201 n. 2.

84. *The Voyage of François Pyrard of Laval to the East Indies*, trans. and ed., Albert Gray and H. C. P. Bell, *HS*:1, 77 (1888): 5–8.

85. Jean Baptiste Tavernier, *Travels in India*, trans. and ed. V. Ball, 2d ed., ed. William Crooke, 2 vols. (Oxford, 1925), 1: 197–98; Nicolao Manucci, *Storia do Mogor or Mogul India, 1653–1708*, trans. and ed. William Irvine, 4 vols. (London, 1906–8), 3: 283–84.

86. Surendra Nath Sen, ed., *Indian Travels of Thevenot and Careri* (New Delhi, 1949), 194; "Lista dos defuntos q. fallecerão nesta hosp.^l desde janr.º de 1690 thé oje 20 de janr.º de 1691," HAG/*LM*, 55B, 385^r–390^r.

the scarcity of funds.[87] In 1691 Pedro II directed the rector of the College of Arts at Coimbra to dispatch two doctors to Lisbon so that they could be sent to India to teach medicine. It is unlikely that they ever arrived, for two years later the viceroy reported that there was only a single doctor in the entire capital.[88] In 1698 another viceroy, António Luís Gonzales da Cámara Coutinho, proposed that the Jesuits be superseded as hospital managers by an Order that specialized in health care, namely that of St. John of God, but Pedro II opposed such a change. He doubted that the latter Order possessed sufficient manpower for the task, and he was convinced that it would be difficult to amalgamate its members with the Jesuits in the administration of the hospital; further, he was reluctant to alter an arrangement that had been in place for so many years.[89] Once again, it was the crown rather than the Jesuits who insisted that they continue to perform a service entirely unrelated to their spiritual calling.

A century earlier, in 1597–98, the provincial had withdrawn his personnel from the hospital because the promised royal funding was lacking. A dying Philip II capitulated and authorized a voyage from Goa to Macao to raise funds to support the institution. If Pyrard's information is accurate, the funding level was twice as large in 1608 as it had been twenty years earlier.[90] Nevertheless, financing the hospital became a continual headache for its administrators. In 1670 the father administrator stated that it lacked an ambulatory ward for convalescents and asked for the assignment of the land revenues from a particular village. *Eighteen* years passed before his petition was approved. In 1673 the administrator reported that neither the ships' officers nor the officials of India House would honor a concession from the crown permitting the hospital to ship certain goods to the kingdom without payment of duties.[91] Despite the persistence of Jesuit dissatisfaction, the fathers continued responsible for the soldiers' hospital for the balance of our period.[92]

If the crown had had its way, the Jesuits would have remained in charge of all such facilities in the East. In 1601, Nicolas Pimenta, the Visitor of the Goa province, ruefully advised Aquaviva that the provincial had complained to Philip III about "the annoyance and trouble which the burden of the hospital at Goa gives us." The king responded that "so great is the service rendered in this to God by the Company that we should take charge not only of . . . [that] hospital . . ., but also of those in all other cities and fortresses . . . and the Lords viceroys and archbishop insisted." To which he added, "I wish that he had not waked up those who were asleep."[93]

87. Governors of India to king, 23 Jan. 1691 and 23 Jan. 1693, in HAG/*LM*, 55B, fols. 366[r] and 396[r].

88. Overseas Council to king, 22 Mar. 1691, in AHU/PA/IN, *cx.* 35, no. 80; viceroy to king, 11 Dec. 1693, in HAG/*LM*, 57, fol. 240.

89. Cámara Coutinho to king, 15 Dec. 1698, in AHU/PA/IN, *cx.* 40, no. 66; copy in HAG/*LM*, 62, fol. 211[r]; Overseas Council to king, 6 Feb. 1700, in AHU/PA/IN, *cx.* 41, no. 85; king to viceroy, 1 Mar. 1700, ibid., *cx.* 43, no. 58.

90. *APO*:1, 3: 526, 689, 692–93, and 805.

91. Overseas Council to king, 8 Jan. 1688, in AHU/PA/IN, *cx.* 34, no. 69; Luís de Mendonça Furtado (viceroy) to prince regent, 11 Oct. 1673, enclosing "Informação das queixas que mandou o procurador deste hosp.[al] real de S.A.," in HAG/*LM*, 38A, fols. 217[r]–219[r].

92. Fr. Mathias Alvares (administrator) to king, 6 Jan. 1730; Overseas Council to king, ca. Mar. 1736, in AHU/PA/IN, *m.* 54 and *m.* 34. HAG 2481 is the daybook of the hospital procurator for the years 1747–55.

93. Nicolas Pimenta to Aquaviva, Margão, 1 Dec. 1601, ed. H. Hosten, S.J., Asiatic Society of Bengal, *Journal and Proceedings* 23 (1927): 106–7.

The Jesuits, in fact, already operated several other hospitals in the East. They had founded that of Funai, the first such institution in the history of Japan, around 1557. One of its wings was a leprosarium; the other was for abandoned, sick children and victims of curable diseases. In 1587 the troops of a hostile daimyo destroyed it.[94] Another was a hospital for the poor, originally founded in Goa but shifted to Margão about 1570. The Society maintained it throughout our period.[95] For some time, the Jesuits also managed a hospital in Mozambique. If Carvalho is correct, it passed to the brothers of St. John of God in 1681.[96]

The fathers also briefly managed a hospital in Malacca.[97] In 1605 Philip III announced that as a result of an agreement with Aquaviva, the Jesuits were taking over the management of hospitals "under my protection in the places where the Society has residences." One of those facilities was situated in Malacca, where the fathers were charged with building a new hospital to replace one established by the bastion's conqueror, Afonso de Albuquerque, a century before. In 1611 the Jesuits left the hospital to protest the insufficiency of royal funds promised to support it. In this instance, in contrast with their behavior in Goa, they persistently resisted the king's subsequent pleas to return to the hospital.[98]

But the Jesuits were less successful in avoiding other administrative chores imposed by the crown. One that involved frequent disputes between Jesuit managers, fortress governors, and other personnel was the fathers' role as superintendents of four key Indian northwestern fortresses—Bassein, Chaul, Damão, and Diu—and those of Onor in the south and Mozambique in the west. P. S. S. Pissurlencar, the able former archivist of the Historical Archives of Goa, suggested that Jesuit responsibility for the munitions, weapons, and other stores, and royal revenues kept for those fortresses, began in 1635, but he was clearly mistaken. In the 1601 statement by Fr. Pimenta quoted above, the Visitor observed that the king "ordains urgently that we should take care of the fortification of Damão."[99] The next year, the "nonperpetual" instructions left by the Visitor at the Damão college contain the following admonition: "Responsibility for the fortification ... urged by the viceroy should not be accepted because it is a matter alien to our Institute and is fraught with grave inconveniences as

94. Fr. Manuel Teixeira, *Luis de Almeida, S.J., Surgeon, Merchant, and Missionary in Japan* (n.d., n.p.). See also Dorotheus Schilling, O.F.M., *Os portugueses e a introdução da medicina no Japão* (Coimbra, 1937), and P. J. Peregrina da Costa, *Medicina portuguesa no extremo-oriente* (Bastorá, 1948).

95. The hospital is mentioned in *DI*, 5: 170; 7: 573–74; 8: 189; 10: 279 and 419–20; 12: 199; *BFUP*, 1: 572; and Linhares to king, 12 Nov. 1630, in HAG/*LM*, 14, fol. 31, no. 177. The last reference misled Ferreira Martins, *Historia*, 2: 343, who mistakenly believed that the hospital was founded that year. A century later it was responsible for 4.8% of the expenditures of the college of Salsete. Enc. in Saldanha to king, 23 Jan. 1731, in AHU/PA/IN, *cx.* 35.

96. Sebastião José de Carvalho, "Alguns subsidios para a historia da organização dos serviços medicos e hospitalares nas conquistas do oriente portugues nos seculos xvi, xvii, e xviii," Sociedade de Geografia de Lisboa, *Boletim* 54 (1936): 263–302.

97. They also cared for the sick at Cochin, especially those arriving in disease-infected ships from the kingdom, but it is not clear whether the hospital there was under their jurisdiction. *DI*, 12: 222.

98. *CR*, 17 Feb. 1612, in Bulhão Pato, ed., *Documentos*, 2: 180–81; Manuel Teixeira, *The Portuguese Missions in Malacca and Singapore (1511–1958)*, 3 vols. (Lisbon, 1961–63) 1: 413–14. The hospital was destroyed in 1641 during the final Dutch bombardment. P. A. Leupe, "The Siege and Capture of Malacca from the Portuguese in 1640–1641," trans. Mac Hacobian, *JMBRAS* 14, 1 (1936): 94.

99. See note 93. Cf. P. S. S. Pissurlencar [Pissurlenkar], *The Portuguese and the Marathas*, trans. P. R. Kakodkar (Bombay, 1975), 93 n. 8. See also *ACE*, 5: 397 n. 1, where Pissurlencar again cites a carta régia of 30 Mar. 1635 as marking the beginning of Jesuit administration of the fortresses. In fact, it simply renewed their authority to do so.

past experience has demonstrated." With a tone of resignation, someone added "Aceitosse," meaning that the assignment had been accepted.[100] A series of documents dated 1620 demonstrates that the Jesuits already bore such responsibilities for Onor and Chaul.[101]

The Jesuits came to rue the day they accepted those assignments, for they became sources of continual complaints by fortress governors, magistrates, customs collectors, cámaras, and certain viceroys, particularly the prickly count of Linhares and the truculent António de Melo de Castro. Such officials protested that the fathers exceeded their authority, were uncooperative, and refused to account for the funds entrusted to them.[102] Vitelleschi, who was clearly uncomfortable with the Society's assumption of such duties, cautioned that all records concerning the custody of public funds should be kept in separate books.[103]

As with the administration of the hospitals of Goa and Margão, the Jesuits discovered that once they had accepted a job they could not escape it. Beginning in 1633, the procurator-general for India petitioned the king to relieve his Order of administrative responsibilities for Damão and Chaul.[104] A dispute between leaders of the Society and Viceroy Melo de Castro led to another attempt to resign from the posts, but the Jesuits found the viceroy unwilling to name a successor.[105]

Despite their willingness to surrender their administrative chores, the Jesuits not only retained them but acquired further responsibilities when the crown decided to shift the capital to Mormugão. The person charged with overseeing its fortification was Fr. Theotonio Rebello, S.J.[106] As late as 1724, the provincial of Goa was still pleading for his seriously reduced corps to be relieved of their fortress duties, citing persisting disputes with the captains. Characteristically, the Overseas Council opposed the Jesuits' removal but recommended that a magistrate investigate their complaint and proceed with the punishment merited.[107] Ironically, it was the Maratha campaign during the next decade that finally ended Jesuit responsibility for the northern fortresses (see Chapter 23).

The crown also burdened Jesuit rectors with supervision of the minting of small coins called *bazarucos* or *bousurque*. These coins were usually made of copper but sometimes of tutenay (copper, zinc, and nickel) and were the equivalents of farthings. In Linchoten's time

100. "As cousas perpetuas q' ordenou o P^e Viz^{or} no coll^o das 11 mil virgens de Damão visitando em fev^{ro} de [1]600," in ARSI, FG, 1407A/44/8 (second and third copies).

101. *BFUP*, 4: 97, 150–51, and 154. See also the opinion of the High Court of Goa attached to a finding (assento of the Council of State dated 14 Feb. 1629), in *ACE*, 1: 29–30.

102. E.g., marginal note of conde de Linhares, 6 Oct. 1633, and conde de Linhares to king, 5 Dec. 1634, in *BFUP*, 3: 302–3 and 411; Linhares to king, ca. Mar. 1636, in ANTT/LM35, fol. 156. Cf. *Diario do 3° [sic for 4°] conde de Linhares, vice-rei da India*, 2 vols. (Lisbon, 1937–43), 2: 186; and Overseas Council to king, 24 Oct. 1668, in AHU/PA/IN, *cx.* 27, no. 141, concerning a complaint by the cámara of Chaul against Jesuit "interference."

103. Vitelleschi to provincial, Goa, 20 Dec. 1637, quoted in H/SAG1: 335.

104. King to Linhares, 22 Jan. 1633, in *BFUP*, 3: 302–3.

105. Assento of 22 Mar. 1666, in *ACE*, 4: 153. The fullest Jesuit statement concerning the origins of their involvement in the management of the fortresses and a defense of their conduct is P^e Manoel Barreto (provincial secretary), "Informacam sobre as administracois de Chaul, Bacaim, Damam, Dio p^a o P P[rocurado]^r da India informar a S. Mag^{de}," 5 Jan. 1666, in ANTT/CJ/80, n. 1. It is nicely summarized by Fr. John Correia-Afonso, "The Jesuits and the Fall of Bassein," *Indica* 15, 2 (1978): 107–20, at 110–11.

106. Overseas Council to king, 7 Feb. 1699, in AHU/PA/IN, *cx.* 41, no. 20, indicating a viceregal recommendation of a stipend for Fr. Rebello and his companion.

107. Overseas Council to king, 18 Jan. 1724, in AHU/PA/IN, *m.* 14, bk. 2.

(the 1580s), they were worth 0.8 rs. or 75 per *tanga* (60 rs.). Bazarucos were important for petty market transactions in Portuguese-controlled communities and were apparently also collected for the payment of a 1 percent tax used to support the maintenance of the northern fortifications. They were subject to counterfeiting, and in 1606 the crown insisted that they could be minted only in the kingdom.[108] The ensuing maritime war with the Dutch made such a scheme impractical, and the Dutch blockade of Goa may have been the reason why the viceroy, Rui Lourenço de Távora, authorized the city of Damão to produce bazarucos in 1611, a concession that his successor nullified two years later.[109] At some later time during the century, both Damão and Diu were minting bazarucos, but because of allegations of embezzlement, the viceroys turned to the Jesuit rectors of both fortresses and charged them with supervising preparation of the coins. Inevitably there were complaints against the fathers' management, and in 1748 the rector of Damão sought relief from the responsibility. None was forthcoming until the general expulsion a dozen years later.[110]

The Jesuits were also assigned the care of public granaries. In the villages of western India, grain storehouses have existed since the fifth or fourth century B.C.[111] Considering the periodicity of seventeenth-century famines[112] and the scarcity of rice—the indispensable staple of the Portuguese enclaves—during the long maritime wars, it is not surprising that Portuguese authorities created rice reserves in Goa, Bassein, Damão, Chaul, and Diu during the 1680s and 1690s. In Goa the administrators of the *celeiros*, as the storage facilities were called, were the superior of the professed house, the Franciscan guardian, and "one of the most zealous and intelligent citizens" of the community, but in the other fortresses the management of those facilities was exclusively the rectors' responsibility. According to an anonymous report of 1731, the Jesuits discharged that responsibility well, selling rice for less than going prices and gradually building up significant cash reserves to increase stocks on hand.[113]

It may seem puzzling that the Jesuits resolutely discharged tasks that had absolutely nothing to do with their educational or spiritual mission. They did so in part because they always found it difficult to refuse service appeals by the high and the mighty, but they also recognized, as did perceptive royal officials, that the king had precious few persons overseas

108. Alvará of 23 Feb. 1606, in *BFUP*, 1: 497. The problem of counterfeiting is discussed in viceroy to king, 24 Jan. 1688, in AHU/PA/IN, *cx*. 34, no. 80.

109. *APO*:2, 4:2:3, 264–67.

110. Ibid., 267ff.; 4:2:2, 534–35; António Francisco Moniz, "O cofre dos Jesuitas em Damão," *O oriente portuguez* 5 (1908): 365–67.

111. A. S. Altekar, *A History of Village Communities in Western India* (Bombay, 1927), 63.

112. The devastating famine of the early 1630s is mentioned in Chapter 7. For a list of others, see Radhakamal Mukerjee, *The Economic History of India, 1600–1800* (Allahabad, 1967), 19–20.

113. Conde de Alvor (viceroy) to king, 20 Jan. 1685, and Anon., "Representao' se a S.M. os inconvenientes q. se podem seguir da execução do [real] decreto" (1731), in AHU/PA/IN, *cxs*. 33, no. 30, and 46, no. 62. Noting that the absence of a rice reserve in Macao was the cause of "great suffering" for the people, who were dangerously dependent upon the will of the Chinese, the cámara asked the provincial in Japan to arrange with the fathers of the house of São José, which in fact belonged to the vice-province of China, to erect a celeiro. Cámara to provincial, 28 June 1733, in *Arquivos de Macao*, 3d ser., 6, 6 (Dec., 1966): 341. The well-known granary in Bahia, the first of its kind in Brazil, was not established until 1785, long after the Jesuits' removal from the colony. "O celeiro da Bahia (1785)," *Revista do instituto geographico e historico da Bahia* 3, 10 (1896): 565–80.

whom he could trust to do a job competently and honorably. As one crown attorney stated during the seventeenth century, "This republic is not administered by Angels but by sinful men. It is possible, indeed probable, that some injustices are committed; however this harm stems from weakness and human wickedness which can not be wholly helped."[114] Corruption doubtless existed throughout the empire, and in other kingdoms as well, during this period, but it was especially prevalent in the State of India, as Diogo do Couto, Francisco Rodrigues de Silveira, and Fr. Fernão de Queiroz made abundantly clear in their critiques of Portuguese rule.[115] It is not surprising that viceroys and their masters turned to ecclesiastics—especially the Jesuits, who were the most numerous—to help the state accomplish essential tasks, both administrative and diplomatic.[116] Whether in Europe or abroad, the Jesuits' relationship with the crown and its agents was never an easy one. Certainly the crown was a far more demanding patron than were private benefactors, whose assistance to the Society forms the subject of the next chapter.

114. Opinion of Manuel Lopes de Olmeiro (procurador da coroa), n.d., quoted in Luisa da Fonseca, comp., "O Maranhão (roteiro dos papeis avulsos do sec. xvii do Arquivo Historico Colonial)," CMP/P, 11: 197.

115. Winius, *Black Legend*, passim. The ever fault-finding António de Melo de Castro grumbled about the "great thefts in the royal treasury of Goa because persons who receive and dispense public moneys treat more of their own profit than of the service of His Majesty." Viceroy to king, 29 Jan. 1664, quoted in Overseas Council to Afonso VI, 3 Feb. 1665, in AHU/PA/IN, *cx.* 26, no. 167.

116. The role of the Jesuits as diplomats during the Restoration is considered in Chapter 5. For examples of their diplomatic assignments in India, see *ACE*, 2: 556–58, and 3: 523–35, 546–49, 565–71, 582–87, and 599; and 4: 510–11. See also cámara of Macao to Fr. António Soares, S.J., 18 Jan. 1721, in *Arquivos de Macao*, ser. 1, 1 (1929): 157ff.

CHAPTER 14

"Sharers in the Good Works": The Society's Other Patrons

> True nobility does not consist in knowing who our parents were; but in the works that we have fathered.
>
> —João de Medeiros Correia, *Perfeito soldado e política militar*

> The founders and benefactors of such colleges become in a special way shares in all the good works of those colleges and of the whole Society.
>
> —Loyola, *Constitutions*

> Far more attention has been paid to the religious houses than to their founders.
>
> —Jennifer C. Ward, "Fashions in Monastic Endowment"

THOUGH JESUITS IN the Portuguese Assistancy counted heavily upon the financial support of the rulers of Portugal, especially during the sixteenth century, the rapid growth of their enterprises coincided with the crown's increasing financial difficulties, compelling the Society to turn to private benefactors for financial aid for its far-flung undertakings. Donors—nobles and plebeians, sinning bachelors, virtuous widows, childless couples, persons of modest means as well as those of formidable wealth, Europeans and Asiatics—responded generously to Jesuit appeals. They furnished capital, annuities, and landed properties that enabled the Jesuits to complete and maintain churches, colleges, and other institutions, to undertake hazardous missions, and to realize other important objectives. But it often proved as difficult to collect sums promised by private donors as it was to obtain the stipends that the crown had assured.

Benefits to the Benefactors

The practice of soliciting funds from donors for ostensibly meritorious purposes is an ancient one and continues to this day. Churches sell glass panes in so-called cathedrals for thousands of dollars; universities name professorial chairs after obscure persons in return for munificent endowments; a prominent research library even has a schedule of "naming opportunities" for those willing to endow its rooms, scholars, and senior administrators.[1] The terms that

---

1. "Naming Opportunities at the John Carter Brown Library," a promotional leaflet issued by the library administration at Brown University in 1989. During the late 1970s Robert Schuller, a well-known television preacher, wooed 10,000 persons who contributed $500 each to have their names engraved on

the Jesuits offered their donors were far less generous than those conceded earlier by, for example, the Benedictines.[2] Those who became "sharers" in the Society's "good works" were not accorded any role in the spiritual, moral, or intellectual life of the community they supported; nor were they promised that their sons, nephews, or other family members would be admitted to the Society. And since all appointments were made by the Roman headquarters, founders and other benefactors had no voice in the selection of local Jesuit leadership. Nor did they assume some of the responsibilities common to the founders of other houses, who often served as protectors and guarantors of the monasteries' privileges. Whereas founders of medieval monasteries often reserved sumptuous accommodations for themselves and other members of their families and expected to be lavishly entertained in their houses, those who established Jesuit installations were never accorded such treatment.

The *Constitutions* thus make it clear that those who contributed financially to the Society could expect none of the traditional rights, privileges, claims, or responsibilities of earlier founders. Nevertheless, founders and other prominent patrons were promised the customary masses in perpetuity, both weekly and monthly. On Founder's Day, a special wax candle, embossed with the founder's coat of arms or the "emblems of his devotions," was presented to the founder or to one of his close relatives. And whenever a college was opened, the father general was required to notify the entire Society so that three masses could be said for its founder and benefactors if living, and for their souls if departed. Founders and certain other patrons were customarily buried within the Order's sanctified church premises, but although the Society promised them spiritual support, it did not offer them material aid. Its policy was set against accepting legacies to which strings were attached, although, as will be seen, the Jesuits sometimes acquired bequests that included elaborate debt settlement requirements.[3]

Jesuit Benefactors

Given the vow of poverty that each Jesuit took upon joining the Order, it was axiomatic that he should not retain any property that he possessed at the time of his entry or subsequently

---

mirrored glass panes above the altar of his Crystal Cathedral. It is reported that the donors could read their names with the aid of binoculars. Steve Bruce, *Pray TV: Televangelism in America* (New York, 1990), 146.

2. The statements that follow concerning ecclesiastical patronage *before* the founding of the Society of Jesus are based especially upon Geoffrey Baskerville, *English Monks and the Suppression of the Monasteries* (New Haven, 1937), 48–55; H. M. Colvin, *The White Canons in England* (Oxford, 1951), 292–95 and 304–14; Susan Wood, *English Monasteries and Their Patrons in the Thirteenth Century* (Oxford, 1955), introduction and chap. 6; Joel T. Rosenthal, *The Purchase of Paradise: Gift Giving and the Aristocracy, 1307–1485* (London, 1972), 55–59, 67–69, 73–77, 102–3, 108–9, 118–22, 130–33, and app. 1; Kathryn L. Reyerson, "Changes in Testamentary Practice at Montpellier on the Eve of the Black Death," *Church History* 47, 3 (Sept. 1978): 253–69; Penelope D. Johnson, *Prayer, Patronage, and Power: The Abbey of La Trinité, Vendome, 1032–1187* (New York, 1981), 86–95; J[ennifer] C. Ward, "Fashions in Monastic Endowment: The Foundations of the Clare Family, 1066–1314," *Journal of Ecclesiastical History* 32, 4 (Oct. 1981): 427–51; Kathryn Norberg, *Rich and Poor in Grenoble, 1600–1814* (Berkeley, 1985), 115–22, 124, 130, 244–57; and Ann K. Warren, *Anchorites and Their Patrons in Medieval England* (Berkeley, 1985), chap. 6. See also Barbara H. Rosenwein, *To Be the Neighbor of Saint Peter: The Social Meaning of Cluny's Property, 909–1049* (Ithaca, N.Y., 1989); and Sara T. Nalle, *God in La Mancha: Religious Reform and the People of Cuenca, 1500–1650* (Baltimore, 1992), esp. 182–85.

3. *CSJ(C)*, pt. 4, chap. 1, pars. 309–10, 312–15, 317–19; chap. 7, par. 398; and chap. 11, par. 442; Aquaviva to Valignano, 27 Jan. [?] 1587, in *DI*, 14: 596–97; *Institutum Societatis Iesu*, 3 vols. (Florence, 1892–93), 2: 214.

inherited. The *Constitutions* make it clear that before a candidate was admitted "Each one [might] do what he [pleased] with his property, but after his entrance he ought to dispose of it . . . in a manner which is proper for a man who is leading a spiritual life." Novices were not permitted to retain any money and understood that within their first year as members they should seek the advice of seniors, "persons of learning and goodness," to distribute their estates in a manner that "is pleasing to God."[4]

Cynics might suspect that such a provision would enable seniors to pressure young, possibly emotionally stressed novices to make over their assets to the Society. Though one cannot be certain that such pressure was never exerted, there is evidence suggesting that if was applied, it was not effective. The evidence comes not from the Portuguese Assistancy, for which such data do not seem to be available, but from Fr. Pedro Grenón, S.J., a historian of the province of Paraguay in the Spanish Assistancy. Fr. Grenón examined a thousand bundles and notarial registers in the archives of Córdova, Argentina, and extracted all property renunciations made by Jesuits within that province between 1609 and 1763. The results, summarized in Table 14.1, show that the Society became the beneficiary of fewer than one-third of the bequests made by novices in Paraguay between 1609 and 1701, and that its share declined to a mere 1.5 percent between 1702 and 1763. But even that percentage is misleading, since two of the bequests were to be shared by the Society, in one instance with the donor's brother and sister, in the other with his brother. Also, the assignment by a native of Ouro Preto, Brazil, in favor of the college of Rio de Janeiro is included, but that gift was made three years *after* the crown sequestered the institution!

It is uncertain why the Society's share of such renunciations in Paraguay fell so dramatically during the eighteenth century. Possibly the diminution reflected a determination by the Society's leadership to protect the Order against the increasingly common accusations that it had become primarily interested in Mammon. Although no such directive is known to exist, there is suggestive evidence, found in a 1741 decision by Joseph Moreira, S.J., superior of the professed house of São Roque, who granted license to Fr. Diogo da Cámara to dispose of his *legítima* (inheritance) bequeathed by his parents "by any means that appears proper to him and he may give it to any person of his choice." That determination was, in fact, consistent with the constitutional provision that members who inherited properties *after* they joined the Order ought *not* to give them to a Jesuit facility, a stipulation evidently intended to protect the Society against unseemly accusations or litigation, but one that was not always consistently enforced.[5]

4. *CSJ(C)*, pt. 3, chap. 1, par. 256. A legal problem arose in Portugal, where the law prohibited minors under age 25 from disposing of their property. The Society argued that such a stipulation was a source of embarrassment, and in Sebastian's name the queen regent signed a decree authorizing Jesuits who reached the age of 20 to renounce their estates. Provisão of 23 June 1562, in *DHJP*, 229–32; reissued on 5 June 1572, in *LTC/RJ*, 17–19.

5. License signed by Fr. Moreira, 30 July 1741, in ANTT/CJ/68, no. 466. For the foregoing, see *CSJ(C)*, pt. 3, chap. 1, pars. 256 and 258; see also *CSJ(GE)*, chap. 4, pars. 56-A and 57-4. For some puzzling deathbed bequests by Jesuits, see Francisco da Fonseca, S.J., "Livro da fazenda ou noticia das rendas e obrigações das provincias da assistencia de Portugal . . . anno 1730," ARSI, FG, 627/B, where this longtime financial specialist of the Assistancy indicates that P. António do Rego, a Jesuit member of the papal college of confessors (the Penitencieri), left upon his death in 1709 4,697,900 rs., to be distributed to the province of Malabar, to that of Japan (or, if extinguished, to the vice-province of Maranhão), to the Lisbon novitiate, to the University of Coimbra, and to the vice-province of China (or, if extinguished, to that of Maranhão).

TABLE 14.1

Primary Beneficiaries of Jesuit Estate Renunciations,
Province of Paraguay, 1609–1763

Beneficiary	1609–1701		1702–1763	
	(N)	*(%)*	*(N)*	*(%)*
Father	6	5.8	21	10.9
Mother	8	7.8	22	11.5
Both parents	6	5.8	27	14.1
Brother(s)	8	7.8	49	25.6
Sister(s)	13	12.6	38	19.9
Family	5	4.8	4	2.1
Society of Jesus	31	30.1	3	1.5
Other pious works	1	0.9	5	2.6
Other persons	3	2.9	3	1.5
Unknown	22	21.3	19	9.9
Total	103	99.8	191	99.6

SOURCE: Pedro Grenón, S.J., "Las renuncias de bienes en la provincia del Paraguay: Siglo xvii," *AHSI* 24 (July–Dec. 1955): 402–17; idem, "Las renuncias de bienes en la provincia del Paraguay: Siglo xviii," *AHSI* 27 (Jan.–June 1958): 121–31.

C. R. Boxer once observed that "contrary to popular belief, wealthy novices were rare in the Society."[6] Though that statement is correct, it needs to be recognized that Jesuit benefactors did provide crucial support for many of the Society's facilities. One of the earliest nonregal benefactors of the College of Arts of the University of Coimbra was Gonçalo da Silveira, son of the count of Sortelha, and a Jesuit novice who assigned the college an annual pension of 50,000 rs.[7] Between the late sixteenth and early eighteenth centuries, 23 fathers and brothers made contributions to the University of Évora.[8] The college of Santo Antão became the recipient of several Jesuit renunciations. Inácio de Azevedo, leader of the 40 martyrs of 1570, had endowed it with 600,000 rs. a decade earlier. In 1562, the son of a desembargador, Fr. Francisco Cabral, who was stationed in Bassein, assigned the college of Santo Antão some houses, silver, slaves, and wheat farms on the island of Terceira in the Azores, other properties in the Cape Verdes, and between 600,000 and 800,000 rs. in cash. Another father who expired in India, Fr. Balthazar Gago, left the college wheat land in the district of Sintra. Since the land was burdened with a quitrent of 20 *alqueires* of grain due the Santa Casa da Misericórdia of Lisbon, the college purchased the *foro* in the 1580s in order to gain clear title. At the beginning of that decade, Fr. Nuno Rodrigues and his sister agreed to endow the college with one of its most famous properties in the Portuguese realm,

---

Similarly, P. Pedro Bello, who also served in the headquarters of the Assistancy and died at 86 in 1707, left the Society 4,374,000 rs., whereas P. Donato Castrellani, S.J., a member of the province of Naples, left 5,458,000 rs. to the incipient college of S. Jose de China in Macao. One must assume that such funds were alms given to the fathers, but for some reason previously undistributed by them.

6. *CCJ*, 116.

7. *DHJP*, 287–89.

8. António Franco, *Évora ilustrada: Extraía da obra do mesmo nome de P.ᵉ Manuel [F]ialho*, ed. Armando de Gusmão (Évora, 1945), 270–71.

the *quinta* of Caniços in Torres Novas.[9] In 1609, two years after he became a novice, Duarte da Costa, grandson of Brazil's second governor-general, became the founder of the college of Santarém. His endowment included the farm of Labruja, another agricultural property in Loures, houses in Lisbon, and income from a private captaincy in Brazil.[10] Four years later, Lourenço Lombardo, a rich Flemish merchant, gave the Coimbra novitiate the large sum of 12 contos when he joined the Order.[11] And in 1631, Fr. Simão de Almeida became another college founder in the kingdom when he assigned his extensive inheritance from his wealthy parents to establish the college of Portalegre.[12]

The relative importance of Jesuit contributions to the Society's enterprises varied from province to province. In the case of the Brazil province, for example, Serafim Leite found that fewer than a half dozen members became benefactors during the formative period.[13] One was the father of a mestiço member of the Society who joined the Order in 1561 as a brother and later became a priest. The member's father contributed "a good fazenda" in Bahia to the new college there. Nearly a century and a half later, the Bahian Fr. Inácio Pereira provided 2.4 contos to found the seminary of Belém da Cachoeira, situated in the hills above the town of Cachoeira, west of the capital. A much more prominent Bahian, Col. António Alvares da Silva (d. 21 Jan. 1755), who expired as a brother in the Order, gave the Bahian college its last sugar estate, the engenho Cotegipe.[14]

Those gifts may not have been vital to Jesuit operations in Brazil, but a trio of Jesuit benefactors *did* make fundamental contributions to the activities of the Japan province. The first was the famous Fr. Luís de Almeida (b. ca. 1525–d. 1583). Born in Lisbon, Almeida studied humanities and later acquired a diploma in surgery. About 1550 he went to the Orient on business and became a successful merchant. Six years later he joined the Society and contributed his assets, estimated at between 1,600,000 and 2,000,000 rs., the seed money that Valignano used to get the Society started in the famous silk trade. Later, Fr. Almeida founded the first hospital, Funai, in the Japanese archipelago for abandoned children and victims of diseases, including leprosy.[15] The second benefactor was an anonymous father who joined the Society in Japan and provided the funds used to purchase one of the villages in the Bassein district that helped to support the Japan enterprise.[16] The last donor was Fr. Diogo Brandão, an ex-lawyer who entered the Order about 1609 and three years later contributed the vastly important wine-producing farm of Carcavelos, situated about

9. Azevedo was descended from the royal treasurer of Afonso V. For his award, see P. Miguel de Torres to Diego Laínez, Lisbon, 11 June 1560, in *MB*, 5: 237–38. Fr. Cabral's donation of his legítima, 19 Nov. 1562, is in ARSI, FG, 1453/5/ n. 1. The testament of Fr. Gago, 18 Oct. 1568, is in ANTT/CJ/2, no. 1. For Fr. Rodrigues' gift, see *HCJAP*, 2:1, 218.

10. ANTT/CJ/57, no. 26, fol. 19; *HCJAP*, 3:1, 5–7.

11. Teófilo Braga, *História da universidade de Coimbra*, 4 vols. (Lisbon, 1892–1902), 3: 352.

12. "Verbas do testamento do P. Simam de Almeida pertencente ao collegio de Portalegre do qual he fundador," 27 Aug. 1655, in ARSI, *Lus.*, 84:II, fol. 321; *HCJAP*, 2:1, 122.

13. *HCJB*, 1: 162.

14. Manuel da Nóbrega to Francisco Henriques, São Vicente, 12 June 1561, in *MB*, 3: 353; *HCJB*, 5: 170–71 and 259.

15. Leon Bourdon, "Luis de Almeida chirurgien et marchand avant son entrée dans la Compagnie de Jesus au Japan, 1525(?)–1556," in *Mélange d'études portugais offert à M. Georges Le Gentil* ([Lisbon], 1949), 69–85; Fr. Manuel Teixeira, *Luis de Almeida, S.J., Surgeon, Merchant, and Missionary in Japan* (n.d., n.p.).

16. *DI*, 14: 495.

19 kilometers from Lisbon across the Tagus, as well as houses and other properties. This gift assured the Japan province of a source of income in Europe to defray the expenses of its procurators and recruits and to pay for supplies sent to the East.[17] Just before the midpoint of the seventeenth century, another Jesuit, Br. Ignácio Coelho, contributed 720,000 rs., which were used to purchase land for a goat farm to provide milk for inmates of the college in Macao.[18]

Other Jesuits helped to fund the Society's activities in India. One of the better known is Br. Gaspar Viegas, who had made a fortune trading via Macao. When Frs. Ruggieri and Ricci were desperately seeking funds to enter China, it was Viegas who assisted them. Later he moved to Goa, where he decided to endow the novitiate of Chorão by purchasing several properties, including the village of Carmona in Goan Salsete, an estate at Taleigão on the island of Tissuary, and the small island of Zuari. Shortly before his death (1593), Viegas asked to be admitted into the Society, and his request was granted.[19] A dozen years earlier, another brother, Thomé Gonçalves, had left a substantial sum (5,040,000 rs.) to endow the future professed house of Bom Jesús. During the 1660s, Gonçalo Pinheiro de Freitas left the Society a house valued at nearly 3,000,000 rs. The same decade brought a significant contribution from João Martes Cabral (d. Chaul, 1666), who was twice married and had a daughter by his first union. His daughter's son fell into Dutch hands and died a captive. Either the daughter expired or Cabral found no need to provide for her. In any case, he left the professed house 3,235,459 rs.[20]

Still others furnished or raised funds for Jesuit activities in the south of the Indian subcontinent. When the Neapolitan(?) Jerome Scaraggi de Bitonto entered the Society in 1622 at age 42, he gave 6,000,000 rs. to found a college at Madura. The previous year, Antonio Vico, who served in Roberto de Nobili's famous enterprise, had written to the father general and explained that several years before he had written to his father seeking "substantial alms" for the mission to found a school. His mother had replied that his father had died, leaving him 1,000 florins in the central Italian town of Montalto near Ascoli. Vico asked Vitelleschi to arrange its collection for his school. A few years later, in 1638, Luíz Fernandez also wrote to Vitelleschi for assistance. He reported that the Cochin college was in miserable financial shape but that he had learned that an anonymous brother in a European novitiate wished to contribute 20,000,000 rs. to "the missions of India," and that there was no better place in which to invest than the poor province of Malabar, which, he warned, would otherwise die on the vine.[21] Despite that dire warning and the reverses

17. Dominicus de Brito, Praty Japona, "Informação do estado temporal da provincia de Japam," Macao, 14 June 1727, in BA/JA/49-V-28, no. 107. Brandão died (29 Oct. 1619) in his fifties and was buried at São Roque. OSR, no. 173.

18. "Despeza da prata da receita dos dous mil pardaos q. o Ir' Ignácio Coelho deixou ao Coll.º de Macao," 1646, in BA/JA/49-IV-66, no. 38, which includes a breakdown of the costs of the dairy.

19. Louis J. Gallagher, S.J., trans., China in the Sixteenth Century: The Journals of Matthew Ricci, 1583–1610 (1942; rpr., New York, 1953), 145–46; DI, 16: 10*, 129–34, 317–18, 444–51, and 530–31.

20. DI, 12: 411; "Bemfeitores da casa professa do Bom Jesu de Goa," n.d. [late seventeenth century], in ARSI, FG, 1443/9/48.

21. Scaraggi's gift is mentioned in Edmond Lamalle, S.J., "La Propaganda du P. Nicholas Trigault en faveur des missions de Chine (1616)," in AHSI 9 (1940): 94 n. 14. See also Antonio Vico to Vitelleschi, Madura, 9 Feb. 1621, in ARSI, Goa, 18, fols. 44–45; and Luíz F[ernand]ez to Vitelleschi, 8 Feb. 1638, in ibid., fol. 153.

that it sustained as a consequence of Dutch intrusions (Chapter 7), the province did survive, though the funds supposedly offered by the brother were never forthcoming.

On another continent, another Jesuit brother, the famous Gaspar Alvares, became one of the Society's most controversial contributors, for it was he who provided a massive infusion of capital to the fledgling college of Luanda, Angola, on the eve of his death. Lisbon-born Alvares was a leading slave dealer in Angola who supplied both Brazilian and Platine markets with black captives. After a bizarre sexual experience with one of his slaves, he became guilt-ridden and begged the Jesuits to admit him as a neophyte. Ten days after his admission, he was dead (1623), leaving an estate rumored to total 160,000,000 rs. The value of the estate proved to be considerably less than that staggering amount, and only a portion of it went to the Jesuits. Nevertheless, their share was substantial: it included 4,000,000 rs. assigned to one of the Society's Lisbon houses, apparently to defray the cost of masses for Alvares's soul; two ranches, one of sheep, the other of cattle; slaves valued at 12 contos; a grain-storage facility in Kongo appraised at 4 contos; lands in the city of Luanda, where Alvares urged the fathers to build two rental units (*moradas de casas*); and an additional 4 contos for investments. These bequests were intended to underwrite a college in Kongo and to support a seminary in Luanda for the sons of poor families in the kingdom. Neither facility was ever opened. Although the crown expressed concern that the Jesuits had obtained the merchant's estate through improper means, no fault was found with the preparation of his will, and the Alvares bequest long sustained the college of Luanda.[22]

Other Ecclesiastical Benefactors

Ecclesiastics who were not members of the Society also made important contributions to it. As is well known, the popes of the late sixteenth and early seventeenth centuries became enthusiastic supporters of the Japan enterprise. In 1583 Gregory XIII (1572–85), keenly hopeful about the Society's prospects for converting the Japanese but concerned about its participation in the silk trade, took the most unusual step (not duplicated elsewhere in the Portuguese Assistancy by any pontiff) of promising the Japan missions an annual subvention of 1,600,000 rs. for twenty years. Two years later, Sixtus V (1585–90) enthusiastically increased the papal subvention by 50 percent and declared it to be a permanent award. His successors found it impossible to honor that commitment, however, and Clement VIII (1592–1605) directed that only the original stipend would be paid.[23]

22. António de Oliveira de Cadornega, *História geral das guerras angolanas* [1680], 3 vols., ed. José Matias Delgado (rpr., Lisbon, 1972), 3: 312–13; "Testamento de Gaspar Alvares" [23 Feb. 1623], in António Brásio, ed., *Monumenta missionária africana: África occidental*, ser. 1, 14 vols. (Lisbon, 1952–72; 1984–85), 7: 89–95; see also 7: 228–31, 279–84, 394–95, and 405–6. A decade after Alvares's death, another slave dealer emulated him and also became a significant patron of the Luanda college. Santarém-born Francisco de Chaves, having no recognized heirs, left the college food farms and 80 slaves valued at 4 contos in return for a document signed by the general recognizing him as a brother in the Society. Rector (Luanda) to Vitelleschi, 30 Jan. 1633, in Brásio, *Monumenta missionária*, 8: 218–22.

23. The best brief histories of the papal subvention are Fonseca, "Livro da fazenda" cited in note 5 above, and Anon., "Titulo dos bens de raiz de Jappao," n.d. [ca. 1620], in BA/JA/49-IV-66, no. 50. For a lucid discussion of the duties of the papal collector and his staff, see William E. Lunt, *Papal Revenues in the Middle Ages*, 2 vols. (New York, 1934), 1: 34–51; see also G. Mollat, *The Popes at Avignon, 1305–1378*, trans. Janet Love (London, 1949), 326–29.

The popes' lead was followed by a handful of other secular priests. In the 1570s, for example, the bishop of Miranda, D. Juliam Dalva, generously supported the fledgling college of Bragança by the assignment of several benefices and an annuity of 100,000 rs.[24] Another generous ecclesiastical benefactor was Fr. Luís Alvares de Távora, who bore the title of chief commander of the Order of Malta and in 1614 left an imposing sum, 12,000,000 rs., to found the college of São Lourenço in Porto.[25] In the late 1630s, Fr. Paulo dos Santos, a controversial Japanese secular cleric known as "the commercial priest" because of his trafficking, endowed a seminary for a dozen Japanese youths in Macao with 4,800,000 rs. Later, when it became impossible to recruit the youths, the invested funds were used to support a Jesuit mission in South Vietnam.[26] Fr. Emanuel Fernandes Lica, a Porto-born secular priest who was educated by the Jesuits at their college in Rio de Janeiro, retained his affection for the Society, and in 1700 left the college 6,400,000 rs. in the form of a dozen black slaves, a field of sugar cane, two substantial houses, silver, and cash.[27] Perhaps the last example of a secular priest providing financial aid to the Society was Tomé Carvalho da Silva, vicar of the capital of the Brazilian captaincy of Piauí, who, "moved by zeal in the service of God and the salvation of souls," offered a cattle ranch valued at 4,800,000 rs. so that the Jesuits could establish a grammar school in his community.[28]

Noble Patrons

As indicated in the previous chapter, the Jesuits successfully cultivated their connections with members of the European nobility, both within the Portuguese kingdom and elsewhere on the continent. Jesuits traveling overseas commonly sailed aboard warships with viceroys, governors, and other important dignitaries, and the Society provided such luminaries with hospitality in its colleges. It may be recalled, for example, that Xavier went to India in the company of Governor Martim Afonso de Sousa. In 1574, when Spanish-born Quirício Caxa (b. ca. 1538–d. 1599) made his profession in Salvador, his witnesses included two of Brazil's governors-general.[29] Sixteen years later, the ship bearing Francisco de Sousa, Brazil's new governor-general (1591–1602), Visitor Cristóvão de Gouveia and his companion, Fernão Cardim, to Brazil was obliged to put in to Madeira for needed repairs. During the ensuing

24. "Lista dos benefícios unidos in perpetuu ao collegio ... de Bragança," Nov. 1572, in ARSI, FG, 1379/2.

25. António Franco, *Synopsis annalium Societatis Iesu in Lusitania, ab anno 1540 usque ad annum 1725* (Augsburg, 1726), 211, par. 10.

26. For references to this controversial figure, see C. R. Boxer, "Macao as a Religious and Commercial Entrepôt in the 16th and 17th Centuries," *Acta Asiatica* 26 (1974): 68–69; and idem, *The Great Ship from Amacon, 1555–1640* (Lisbon, 1963), 325–29. "Treslado do testam.ᵗᵒ do P. Paulo dos S[antos]," in BA/JA/49-V-11, no. 81. HAG 825 is an account book of the endowment and tells how it was used.

27. Lica to father general, Rio de Janeiro, 12 June 1700, in ARSI, *Bras.*, 4. Another who retained his admiration for the Society was D. Miguel de Argão, formerly Miguel Bonafre. Though expelled from the Society (for undisclosed reasons), he left the professed house in Goa 1,944,300 rs. "Bemfeitores da casa professa" (see note 20).

28. Overseas Council to ouvidor of Mocha (capital, Piauí), 31 Mar. 1731, in AHU/LR/270, fol. 187ʳ; provisão of 1 Apr. 1733, in *DH*, 64: 79.

29. *HCJB*, 1: 65.

ten days the governor resided in the college of Funchal.[30] In 1681, the procurator of Goa, Francisco Sarmento, was in Lisbon attending to the affairs of his province. He was supposed to travel on to Rome to consult with the father general, but after receiving an invitation from Francisco de Távora, viceroy-designate of India, to sail back with him and the new archbishop, Sarmento hastily changed his plans. He informed Giovanni Paolo Oliva that it seemed to him vital to take advantage of his good fortune, that he really had no pressing business in Rome, and that he was sending him a gift via the procurator of Malabar![31] Six years later the carrack bearing Távora, the much-stressed ex-viceroy (see Chapter 7), arrived in All Saints Bay and was discovered to be unseaworthy. Until he was able to resume his voyage, Távora was housed in a cell of the Jesuit college and, according to António Vieira, participated fully in its spiritual activities.[32] Half a century later, when the acting governor of Rio de Janeiro reached the dock to welcome D. Luís de Mascarenhas, incoming governor of São Paulo, to invite him to stay at the governor's palace, he was disgusted to find that the new governor was already in the Jesuit college; he complained, "I could not separate him from the cassock wearers."[33] Provincials like Valignano regularly wrote to kings, their secretaries, prominent nobles, and other important figures at home, as did António Vieira, Roberto de Nobili, and numerous other well-placed fathers.[34] Jesuits not only performed economic favors for important friends (see the previous chapter) but also were viewed as wire-pullers for colonial officials who believed themselves targeted by their enemies.[35]

Such contacts were invaluable to the Jesuits when they faced legal and other difficulties, but they were also helpful in establishing close relations with well-heeled potential donors. Local officials kept the generals informed of events in the lives of important persons, who often received letters from the generals themselves or from their assistants.[36] Similarly, those

30. Fernão Cardim, "Narrativa epistolar de uma viagem e missão jesuítica," Bahia, 1 May 1590, in *Tratados da terra e gente do Brasil*, ed. Rudolfo Garcia (Belo Horizonte, 1980), 141–42.

31. Francisco Sarmento to Oliva, 9 Sept. 1680, in ARSI, *Lus.*, 75, fol. 227.

32. Vieira to Diogo Marchão Temudo, 1 June 1687, in João Lúcio d'Azevedo, ed., *Cartas do Padre António Vieira*, 3 vols. (Coimbra, 1925–28), 3: 542.

33. José da S[ilv]a Paes to Gomes Freire de Andrada, 27 Dec. 1738, in ANRJ, col. 84/9/190^r.

34. For a sample of Valignano's correspondence with such worthies, see *DI* 14: passim. The Vieira letters cited in note 32 also contain numerous examples. See, too, Joseph Wicki, ed., "Sei lettere inedite del P. Roberto Nobili, S.J., 1606, 1607, 1615," *AHSI* 37 (Jan.–June 1968): 129–44. Jesuit leaders tried to restrict communications between field workers and important crown officials by requiring that such correspondence be left open to be read by superiors, but such stipulations were not always obeyed: Valignano, "Summary of the Rules of the Provincial of India," Apr. 1588, in *DI*, 14: 873, par. 34; "As cousas perpetuas q' ordenou o P^e Viz.^{or}," [1]600, in ARSI, FG, 1407A/44/8, par. 14; and "Ordens gerais q. deixou p.^{a} toda a provincia o P^e Cicero, visitador das provincias da Goa e Malabar," 15 Jan. 1685, in ibid., *Goa*, 35, fols. 291–96, par. 1. Cf. Charles W. Polzer, S.J., trans. and ed., *Rules and Precepts of the Jesuit Missions of Northwestern New Spain* (Tucson, 1976), 63–64, 100, and 122. See also Ernest J. Burrus, S.J., ed., *Kino Writes to the Duchess: Letters of Eusebio Francisco Kino, S.J., to the Duchess of Aveiro* (St. Louis, 1965), esp. the introduction.

35. An interesting example concerns a dispute between the Carioca-born landowner and royal treasurer, Francisco Cordovil de Siqueira Melo, and the treasury fiscal and his scribe. Melo to Raphael Mendes, S.J., Rio de Janeiro, 18 Apr. 1739, in ANTT/CJ/68, no. 277, a copy of a letter sent via the Bahian fleet.

36. For example, the superior of the Moluccas mission advised the general that Don Pedro de Acuña, the Spaniard who recovered Ternate in 1606, "merece ser honrrado de VP asi diante de su Rey como de Su Santidade, y particularmente por el amor que tiene a la Compañía," so much so that he was expected to become an important benefactor of that mission. Unfortunately, three weeks after his return to the

who became founders, or at least were prominent contributors to the Society, received letters of thanks from the fathers general.[37]

Several members of the Bragança family became Jesuit benefactors, though less bounteous than one might guess. In 1604 D. Teodósio II established Portugal's second professed house in his residential town, Vila Viçosa, though never with sufficient funds so that it could truly flourish.[38] It may be recalled that the Jesuits were instrumental in facilitating the shocking marriage between Afonso VI's ex-wife and his brother, Pedro II (see Chapter 5). Prior to the queen's death in 1683, she asked to be interred in the Jesuit novitiate in the capital and left it a relatively modest contribution—2,000,000 rs.[39] But when the royal couple's daughter, D. Isabel, expired seven years later, she left only 400,000 rs. in memory of her Jesuit confessor.[40] The provisions of the will of the dowager queen, Catherine of Bragança, must have been disappointing to the fathers. She was supposedly much attached to the Society, particularly its Maranhense missions, and was decidedly well-off when she returned to Lisbon to spend her last years. Catherine died in 1705, leaving bequests amounting to over 55,000,000 rs.; less than 3 percent of her estate went to the Society.[41] D. Mariana of Austria, wife of John V, gave the Order 12,000,000 rs., but that was nothing compared with the fortune in jewels she left to others.[42]

Philippines, he died of poison. Luis Fernandes (superior) to Aquaviva, Ternate, 2 May 1606, in *DM*, 3: 28 and 41 n. 3.

The leadership was especially solicitous of the Braganças. When the duke was blessed by the birth of his first son, the duke of Barcelos, in 1604, he received a letter of congratulations from the assistant general. Exactly 30 years later, his son received a similar letter when his first son was born. For acknowledgment of the two letters, see Duke Teodósio II to João Alvares, 10 Sept. 1604, and Duke Duarte to Vitelleschi [?], 16 Dec. 1634, in ARSI, *Lus.*, 74, fols. 32 and 248. Catherine of Bragança, ex-queen of England, was also the recipient of warm correspondence from the generals. Manoel Pires to Tirso Gonzales de Santalla (general), 17 Sept. 1697 and 26 June 1702, in ibid., 75, fol. 27; and 76, fol. 38. See also William J. Young, S.J., trans. and ed., *Letters of St. Ignatius of Loyola* (Chicago, 1959), 64–67, 225–26, 310–11, 314–15, and 437–39.

37. E.g., Aquaviva to D. Pedro de Castro, 25 Nov. 1588, in *DI*, 15: 128 (expressing gratitude for the gift of three important villages in India—Assalona, Velim, and Ambelim). Diogo Gonçalves, another old India hand and the founder of the college of V. N. de Portimão, received a similar letter. *HCJAP*, 3:1, 34.

38. "Condições da fundação da casa professa . . . em Vila Viçosa," 20 Mar. 1604, in *CCLP*, 1: 68–69; *HCJAP*, 2:1, 116 and n. 1; António de Morães (superior, São Roque) to Vitelleschi, 4 Aug. 1635, in ARSI, *Lus.*, 74, fol. 258.

39. The testament of D. Marie François Isabelle of Savoy, 20 Nov. 1683, is published in Centro de Estudos Históricos Ultramarinos, *As gavetas da torre do tombo* (Lisbon, 1967), 6: 235–36.

40. The testament of D. Isabel Luísa Josefa, 11 Oct. 1690, is published in ibid., 218–23.

41. When Catherine returned to Lisbon in 1689, she brought with her a "large and precious library," which she gave to the college of Espírito Santo, Évora. António Franco, *Imagem da virtude em o noviciado da companhia de Jesús no real collegio do Espírito Santo de Évora* (Lisbon, 1714), 740, where further details are omitted. Her testament, dated 14 Feb. 1699, is published in Centro de Estudos Históricos Ultramarinos, *As gavetas da torre do tombo*, 6: 208–17. Examples of Jesuit reports concerning her supposed inclination toward the Society include Manoel de Andrade to Gonzales de Santalla, 6 Jan. 1697; Manoel Pires to Gonzales de Santalla, 17 Sept. 1697; and Manuel Pires to Gonzales de Santalla, 26 June 1702; in ARSI, *Lus.*, 75, fols. 270 and 277; and 76, fol. 38. Readable but not searching biographies include Janet MacKay, *Catherine of Braganza* (London, [1937]), and Virginia Rau, *D. Catarina de Bragança, rainha de Inglaterra* (Coimbra, 1941). See also Rau, ed., *Inventário dos bens da rainha da Grã-Bretanha D. Catarina de Bragança* (Coimbra, 1947).

42. For Mariana of Austria's testament and the codicil dated 23 Oct. 1753, see Centro de Estudos Históricos Ultramarinos, *As gavetas da Torre do Tombo*, 6: 245–53; cf. the 1760 inventory of her jewelry, 257–325.

TABLE 14.2
Prominent Non-Portuguese European Benefactors of the Portuguese Assistancy

Patron	Year	Amount per year	Beneficiary
Duke of Bavaria	1616	500 florins	Vice-province of China
"Madonna of Rhodes"[a]	?	180,000 rs.	Vietnam and Iran missions
Ferdinand III of Austria	1654	1,000 florins	Vice-province of China (?)
Max Henry, Elector of Cologne	1654	100 imperials	Stipend to support 1 missionary in China
Prince of Simiana[b]	1670	800,000 rs.	Vietnam missions
Duchess of Gravina[c]	ca. 1670	6,000,000 rs.	Jesuit installations in India, Southeast Asia, and China
Lady Inez Catarina Finx of Bamberg	1697	4,500 florins	Support for 2 missionaries and 8 catechists in Malabar
Juan Tomás Enrique de Cabrera, Admiral of Castile	1708	63,428,000 rs.	Novitiate in Lisbon to train missionaries for India and China
Duke of Arcos[d]	1709	800,000 rs.	Vice-province of China

SOURCE: Except for Admiral of Castile, see Francisco da Fonseca, S.J., "Livro da fazenda ou noticia das rendas e obrigações das provincias da assistencia de Portugal . . . anno 1730," ARSI, FG, 627/B. For the admiral, see the text and the accompanying notes.

[a] Sister of Alexander of Rhodes.

[b] Possibly Syme or Simi, an island in the Dodecanese, northwest of Rhodes.

[c] I.e., Naples.

[d] Income from an annuity. The duke was the son of the duchess of Aveiro, well-known benefactress of Jesuit missions in the Marianas. Her branch of the family moved to Spain during the Restoration.

If members of the Bragança family (excepting Pedro II, whose benefactions are noted in an earlier chapter) were parsimonious in their financial support of the Society, so too were members of the nobility of the realm. Not a single member is known to have been a substantial giver to the Order. On the other hand, some well-known bluebloods from other parts of Europe did make contributions to the Society's overseas enterprises. Those known to the accountant of the procurate of the Assistancy are indicated in Table 14.2.

The most conspicuous member of this group is the famous admiral of Castile, a man of fabulous wealth. D. Juan Tomás Enrique de Cabrera, eleventh admiral of Castile, duke of Medina de Rio Seco, count of Modica, Ossona, Melgar, and Rueda, viscount of Cabrera and Bas, lord of Castroverde, Aguilar, Rueda, and Mansilla, was one of the ranking grandees of Spain and the head of one of its wealthiest houses. Related to the Portuguese Braganças, he was born in Genoa in 1646. He held numerous military and administrative appointments during the reign of the enfeebled Charles II of Spain, including that of field master of a battalion of Lombardians in Italy (1670), ambassador extraordinary to Rome (1676), governor of Milan, and viceroy of Catalonia. In 1691 D. Juan was named councilor of state, lieutenant general, and grand master of horse, positions that he held for the balance of the Hapsburg regime. A decade later he had fallen from favor, and he suffered personal humiliation when the new Bourbon administration deprived him of all his offices and exiled him to France with the title of ambassador. But he never took up that post, for as his impressive entourage—300 persons and 150 carriages—was ostensibly proceeding toward the Pyrenees, the admiral suddenly gave orders to turn west, and he sought asylum in Portugal, arriving in Lisbon on 24 October 1702.[43] There, accompanied by Carlos António Casnedi, his longtime Jesuit confessor, he took up residence in a palace of the duke of Cadaval in the Sete Rios district of the capital. Piqued by his deprivation of office, the admiral offered his services to the Austrian ambassador and thereby became a champion of Archduke Charles, the pretender to the Spanish throne. Inevitably he became one of the leaders of the Austrian party in Portugal, a frequent intermediary between Vienna, London, and the Lisbon court. But as he was preparing to reenter Spain at Badajoz, the admiral suddenly fell ill, and in late June 1705 he died of suspicious causes near Estremoz.

The admiral, who was childless and unmarried, left an enormous fortune. His incredible art collection was acquired for a paltry sum by the Austrian archduke and sent to Vienna.[44] Pedro II obtained some of his vast jewelry collection, but most also went to the archduke, whose campaign in Spain was substantially funded by the admiral's estate, which contributed 176,000,000 rs. to that inglorious cause. The Jesuits' share, while impressive by the standards of their principal patrons, was nevertheless relatively small. It was, moreover, conditional: apart from provisions to pay for 10,000 masses for his soul, and a modest allowance for his confessor (288,000 rs. per year), most of the amount earmarked for the Society would go to the archduke should he successfully ascend the Spanish throne. The admiral named as trustees of his ecclesiastical assignments the Jesuit provincial, the procurators of the Indies and China, his confessor, and a fourth cleric whom I have not been able to identify.[45] His intention was found two colleges, one in Madrid to train clergy for the New World, the other, less amply funded, in Lisbon. The latter facility was really a novitiate, intended to alleviate the alarming shortage of Jesuits in India and in the Portuguese vice-province of China by attracting recruits in the kingdom.[46] The admiral had extensive funds invested in Vienna, Naples, Milan, and elsewhere. It is uncertain how much of the proceeds were remitted to Portugal. According to one memorandum, between 1716 and 1726 the remittances to Lisbon reached the impressive sum of 63,428,000 rs., by far the largest donation furnished by any patron of the Assistancy.[47]

It should not be forgotten that Asian potentates also contributed both land and revenues to Jesuit enterprises. In India a wealthy (but unnamed) Brahman gave 1,818,000 rs. to the fledgling Goan enterprise seven years after Xavier's arrival in the East. In the late 1580s the clansmen (ganvkari) of villages in Goan Salsete contributed land to aid the incipient college of Salsete. Near the end of the century, a ruler in the kingdom of Vijayanagar authorized the Jesuits to build a church, assigned a village's taxes for its support, and made an outright gift of 900,000 rs., whereas two unknown rajas in Bengal furnished 240,000 rs. to build

43. For biographical data, I have relied primarily upon Gastão de Melo de Matos, "O ultimo almirante de Castela em Portugal (1702–1705)," *separata* of *Trabalhos da associação dos arqueologos portugueses*, vol. 2 (Lisbon, 1937) (separately paginated). The admiral is frequently mentioned in A. D. Francis, *The Methuens and Portugal, 1691–1708* (Cambridge, 1966), s.v. index, "Almirante of Castile."

44. It included 30 Titians, 9 Correggios, 3 Raphaels, 1 Perugino, 2 Michelangelos, 1 Breughel, 26 Van Dykes, 34 Tintorettos, and 22 Rubenses!

45. A Spanish copy of the admiral's testament, dated 11 Apr. 1705, is in ANTT/CJ/85, no. 17.

46. Authenticated copy, dated 21 May 1713, of an earlier letter from Fr. Carlos Casnedi to the father general, in ARSI, *Lus.*, 76, fols. 119^r–119^v. Carlos Casnedi to Tamburini, Lisbon, 17 Mar. 1706, in ARSI, *Informationum, Procurator Generalis*, bk. 142, 673–74.

47. "Fundatione del Grande Almirante de Castila" (1727), in ARSI, *Lus.*, 79, fol. 7.

Jesuit churches there. In 1609 the raja of Travancore furnished the house at Quilon with an annual income of 30,000 rs., and in the north, the Mughals assigned the Jesuits lands in Agra for a cemetery and for gardens.[48]

Other local or imperial rulers aided Jesuit activities in Japan and China. During Xavier's celebrated visit to the islands, the lord of Yamaguchi furnished the Jesuits with "a very large piece of property so that we might build a college upon it." Later, Christian daimyos and wealthy samurai offered the fathers land and money to further their efforts. Only three years before the expulsion (1614), the governor of Nagasaki built "a very beautiful and large church" and established a perpetual source of income to support it.[49] When Matteo Ricci first entered China bound for Peking, the viceroy of Kainsi province gave him funds to facilitate his journey. Half a century later, the emperor, moved by the death of Fr. Giacomo Rho, gave his colleagues 800,000 rs. to invest in income-producing properties and ordered that Adam Schall should receive a regular stipend.[50] These are but examples of the financial assistance that Asian leaders provided to the Society during its formative years in the East.

Unranked Benefactors: Families and Couples

If certain members of the European nobility were moved by considerations of noblesse oblige and piety to support the religious Orders, including the Jesuits, during the early modern era, commoners, who were likewise convinced of the necessity to attain salvation and escape perdition through pious deeds, also offered the Society such support.[51] About 1556, 45-year-old Henrique Nunes de Gouveia, a descendent of Cornelio Dutra, discoverer and captain-major of the island of Fayal in the Azores, made major decisions that would lead to the alienation of his family's substantial possessions and to its breakup. He gave away his properties, some of them to the Society, and determined that he and his 14-year-old son, Cristóvão, would join the Order, and his wife and their daughters would enter a convent of the Poor Clares. Although the patriarch-novice soon died, Cristóvão became successively Visitor to Brazil, Provincial of Portugal, and bishop-elect of Japan (see Chapter 10). While the Gouveia family's experience was unusual, it was not uncommon for families in Portugal, as elsewhere in Europe, to become passionately devoted to the

48. Gaspar Barzaeus to the Coimbra colleagues, Goa, 13 Dec. 1548, in *DI*, 1: 401; Francisco de Sousa, S.J., *Oriente conquistado a Jesus Cristo pelos padres da Companhia de Jesus da província de Goa* [1710], ed. M. Lopes de Almeida (Porto, 1978), 887–88; F/*JM*, 1: 283 and 285; H. Hosten, S.J., "Mughal Farmans, Parwauaks, and Sauads Issued in Favour of the Jesuit Missionaries," *Catholic Herald of India* (Calcutta), 30 Aug., 6 and 13 Sept. 1916; rpr. in *The Examiner* (Bombay), 10 and 17 Mar. 1917. Copy available in ARSI, *Collectinea maioria 2/2*.

49. S/*FX*, 4: 270; C. R. Boxer, "The Affair of the *Madre de Deus*: A Chapter in the History of the Portuguese in Japan," Japan Society, *Transactions and Proceedings* 26 (1928–29): 35; Hubert Cieslik, S.J., "The Training of a Japanese Clergy in the Seventeenth Century," in J. Roggendorf, S.J., ed., *Studies in Japanese Culture* (Tokyo, 1963), 71; "Catalogo dos fundadores dos collegios e residencias da provincia de Jappao e dos bemfeitores da mesma provincia," in ARSI, *JapSin*, 23, fols. 1–4, is a list that includes ten Japanese donors and the amounts they contributed.

50. George H. Dunne, S.J., *Generation of Giants: The Story of the Jesuits in China in the Last Decades of the Ming Dynasty* (Notre Dame, 1962), 54 and 310.

51. Philippe Aries, *Western Attitudes Toward Death from the Middle Ages to the Present*, trans. Patricia M. Ranum (Baltimore, 1974), 63–65; idem, *The Hour of Our Death* (New York, 1981), esp. 181–83, 188–96.

support of a particular religious Order such as the Society of Jesus. With respect to Brazil, for example, one thinks of the famous Sá family, whose members, from Mem de Sá, Brazil's third governor-general (d. 1572), to Salvador de Sá (b. 1602–d. 1686) enjoyed an intimate relationship with the Society and alienated both their own property and some of the crown's to aid the Jesuits in their endeavors. The controversial bequest of Mem de Sá's daughter, the countess of Linhares, to the Society will be considered later in this chapter. His Jesuit-educated grandson, Salvador, was always an ardent defender and admirer of the Society. In 1643 Salvador informed Vitelleschi that he considered himself to be "a slave and brother of the Company" and expressed the desire to establish a small college at Santos and to be recognized as its founder. Nearly a decade later, he and his wife transferred to the Society some of their rental properties in the city of Rio de Janeiro for that purpose.[52]

A less well-known example is that of the Araujo family in Rio de Janeiro. As Simão de Vasconcelos explained in 1655, the college of Rio de Janeiro needed a new and sumptuous church but lacked the funds to build it. Vasconcelos approached António de Sylva Pimentel, one of the leading fidalgos in the city, who promised assistance and introduced him to members of the sugar-producing Araujo family. Captain Francisco Gil de Araujo offered to build the principal chapel of the church in return for the title of founder and promised to contribute 12,000,000 rs. over the next decade and double that amount if the harvests of his "copious estates" prospered. Sylva Pimentel himself pledged eight crates of sugar at once and promised 100 *arrobas* per year for an unstipulated period. Pedro Garcia, another member, offered 800,000 rs. toward the cost of a chapel, while two brothers each gave half that amount. Sylva Pimentel's brother-in-law, a nephew of the governor-general, also contributed 400,000 rs. toward the church's completion.[53] Fifteen years later, thirteen citizens in the town of Beja in the Alentejo region of the kingdom conjoined and pledged 40,000 rs. in cash and properties worth ten times that amount to establish a Latin school in a new Jesuit college. Despite opposition from an unnamed local noble and delays that lasted for 23 years, their petition was finally approved by Pedro II.[54]

Couples, especially those who had no children or whose children had already perished, were also important Jesuit benefactors. The *Monita Secreta*, that spurious document attributed to the Society's leadership, called attention to such couples' susceptibility to Jesuit entreaties: "What has been said, in relation to widows [see below], must be made use of towards merchants, rich citizens, and married people who are childless; whole entire estates the Society may often acquire [providing that they were prudently approached]."[55] One such couple was Fernão Teles de Menezes and his wife, D. Maria de Noronha, who, in 1578,

52. Sá to Vitelleschi, 2 June 1643, in ARSI, *Bras.*, 3:I, fol. 223; cf. Manoel Fernandes (provincial) to Vitelleschi, 28 June 1643, in ibid., 229. C. R. Boxer, *Salvador de Sá and the Struggle for Brazil and Angola, 1602–1686* (London, 1952), 154, 287, and 401; *HCJB*, 6: 423–28, which includes the full text of the letter quoted above.

53. Vasconcelos (vice-rector) to Francisco Gonçalves (provincial), 9 Oct. 1655, in ARSI, *Bras.*, 3:I, 162^r–162^v.

54. Citizens of Beja to Oliva, 26 Nov. 1670, in ARSI, *Lus.*, 75, fol. 128; "Dificuldades e inconvenientes q. occorrem acerca das condições com q. se dis que S. Mag.^{de} . . . se ha de servir de dar licença para a fundação do collegio . . . de Beja" [1693] in ibid., 79, fols. 290–90a.

55. *Monita Secreta: The Secret Instructions of the Jesuits* (London, 1723), chap. 9.

pledged their estate, valued at 8,000,000 rs., to found the probationary house in Lisbon in return for their recognition as founders and their exclusive interment in its chapel. They contributed the quinta of Monte Olivete, situated near Lisbon, which D. Maria had inherited from her mother and which was valued at 2,400,000 rs.; several annuities, two of which represented claims upon the capital's customs house and its abattoir; and capital loaned at 6.25 percent interest.[56] Another childless couple, Francisco de Utra de Quadros, captain-major of the island of Fayal in the Azores, and his wife, D. Isabel da Silveira, who claimed descent from the Flemish nobility, gave their entire estate (extent undisclosed) to found the college of Horta, opened in 1652.[57]

André Velho Freire (d. 1657) and his widow, D. Felipa de Paredes (d. 1663), likewise childless, became the patrons of not one but two Jesuit colleges in the kingdom. During their lifetimes, the couple contributed pearls, diamonds, worked gold, and silver valued at 1,200,000 rs. to the new college of Faro. As soon as Freire, a member of the Order of Christ and a prominent merchant, perhaps in Setúbal, expired, his Spanish-born widow arranged to convey their entire estate to found the college of Saint Francis Xavier in Setúbal. Their assets, summarized in Table 14.3, provide a rare glimpse of substantial wealth in Portugal in the midst of the most desperate years of the Restoration. The inventory is, in fact, incomplete, for other appraisals estimated the estate to be worth between 13,000,000 and 16,000,000 rs.[58]

It would be possible to extend the list of couples who financially assisted the Society with their estates,[59] but one last example may suffice. It concerns Mirza Zu'lqarnain (variously spelled) (b. 1592–d. 1656), son of a Christianized merchant from Aleppo, possibly an Armenian, who served at the Mughal court. The son also became a court functionary. Yet both he, his wife, and their several children all became Christians as a result of Jesuit efforts and generously supported Jesuit endeavors in Bombay, Agra, and, for a time, Tibet. Zu'lqarnain advanced the funds that resulted in the purchase of the villages of Parel (Parela) and Vadala in Bombay, major sources of income of the "incipient college" of Agra, of which he became the worthy founder. By 1628 the fathers estimated that his

56. "Treslado ad verbvu da doaçam q. Fernão Teles de Menezes e Dona M.ª de Noronha ... f[azem] p[a]ra a casa de p[ro]vação de Lxª," 26 Dec. 1578, in ARSI, *Lus.*, 77, fols. 21ʳ–21ᵛ. The donation was accepted by the previously mentioned Cristóvão de Gouveia. Since the probationary house was situated in a Lisbon district known as Cotovia, it is usually known by that name. Its location is fixed in António Lopes, S.J., *Roteiro histórico dos Jesuítas em Lisboa* (Lisbon, 1985), 31–33. For the difficulties in identifying founders for the facility, see *HCJAP*, 2:1, chap. vi.

57. *HCJAP*, 3:1, 25–28.

58. D. Felipa also left 20,000 rs. to a nun in Madrid (or to her convent if she was deceased), liberated a female slave, directing the fathers-administrators to give her 60,000 rs. and a bed, and left two other servants 35,000 rs. apiece. In addition to the source cited in Table 14.3, the foregoing is based upon Franco, *Synopsis annalium*, 1657, no. 7, and 1663, no. 13; in ARSI, *Lus.*, 75, fols. 29ʳ and 31ʳ, and 84:I, 3–4ᵛ. See also *HCJAP*, 3:1, 31–32.

59. E.g., Luís Fernandes de Almada (d. 1620) and his wife Isabel Gomes (d. 1610), founders of the Jesuit-administered Irish seminary (ARSI, *Lus.*, 75, fol. 20), and Manuel Martins Vieira and his wife, Ines Neta, who, in 1684, offered to endow a college in Paraíba, Brazil, with ten parcels of properties worth 6,400,000 rs. (ARSI, *Bras.*, 11, fol. 491; cf. *HCJB*, 5: 492–93). There are many further examples, especially for the seventeenth century, in ANTT/CJ/85, and others for the Japan province in "Catalogo dos fundadores dos collegios e residencias da provincia de Jappao e dos bemfeitores da mesma provincia," n.d. [ca. 1630s], in ARSI, *JapSin*, 23, fols. 1–4ᵛ, and a second copy, 5ʳ–8.

TABLE 14.3

Property Inventory of André Velho Freire and D. Felipa de Paredes, 1660

(000 rs.)

Description	Value	Annual yield
Two salt pans, which produce 2,730,000 liters/year	1,300	290
Four other salt pans	5,600[a]	[1,276]
Landed estate "Molinhola"	500	—[b]
Family residence	650	25
Six groups of rented houses	1,400	114
Warehouse	100	8
Worked gold, silver, and jewels	1,200	—
Cash on hand	1,200	—
Money at interest (6.25%)	1,211	750
Other loans	—	85
Quitrents	—	150
Houses already purchased for college	—	1,200
Money already spent on church	800	—
Personal effects (clothing, furniture, bedding, china, pots, pans, images)	739	—
1 box white sugar, to be sold in Pernambuco, and 5 quintals of ivory, to be sold in Angola	—	ca. 100
Total	14,700	3,998+

SOURCE: "Lista da faz.ᵈᵃ dos Sʳᵉˢ Andre Velho Freire e de sua molher D. Philipa de Paredes e lhe o dote do Coll.º de S. Fran.ᶜº Xavier de Setubal," ca. 1660, in ARSI, *Lus.*, 75, fols. 33ʳ–33ᵛ; other copies in ibid., 84:I, 5ʳ and 11–12.

[a] Because of scribal error, the estimated value of the four salt pans is situated in the wrong column in the manuscript texts. Since their value is 4.3 times that of the first two salt pans, I have estimated their value with minor rounding.

[b] The yield—1,560 liters rye, 31,200 liters wheat, 1 pig, and 2 chickens—cannot be indicated in monetary terms.

gifts of funds and goods exceeded 40,000 rupees, and further support followed during later decades.[60]

Unranked Benefactors: Bachelors and Widows

Single persons of both sexes, both Europeans and Asians, were often moved to make bequests to religious Orders, including the Jesuits. Single males seem to have been more inclined to become patrons overseas than within the kingdom itself. The only obvious examples for Portugal date from the 1670s, when Manoel Azeitão, brother of a Jesuit and son of a general, offered to assist in founding the college of Beja, but precisely what property he could furnish he did not reveal. During the same decade, Jorge Fernandes Vilanova (d. 1677), described as

60. In his 1666 report on the state of Jesuit finances in the Goan province, the provincial observed that the income of the Agra mission—1,200,000 rs. per year—derived from the Parel village and from two coconut orchards in Goan Salsete, was owing entirely to the worthy late benefactor. "Lista das rendas e despezas da provincia de Goa," 13 Dec. 1666, câmara municipal, Elvas, ms. 6891. The most convenient summary of what is known about Zu'lqarnain and his family is Edward Maclagan, *The Jesuits and the Great Mogul* (London, 1932), chap. 11.

"rich, noble, and virtuous," left his entire estate to establish a college in the Alfama district of Lisbon dedicated to his patron, St. Francis Xavier. Although his proposal met with stiff opposition, it was supported by the powerful duke of Cadaval and by Pedro II: the new college offered its first class in 1686.[61]

The propensity of affluent, ailing adventurers or merchants to seek admission to the Society on the eve of their demise has already been noted in this chapter. That tendency, whose roots go back to the Middle Ages, appears to have been more common overseas, especially in India, than at home. In the ultramar, unmarried or widowed adventurers and merchants frequently became the Society's benefactors. Less than a decade after the Jesuits' arrival, the captain of Cochin was so moved by a fiery sermon preached by the mercurial António Gomes that he donated to the fathers a large coconut orchard and provided in excess of 440,000 rs. and other funds to begin a college there.[62] Another early benefactor of the college of Cochin was Cristóvão Carvalo, who died about 1564 leaving a fortune of close to 16,000,000 rs. and a Eurasian son who, as the Jesuit reporter said with obvious relief, was illegitimate and was therefore not a legal heir, so that the college of Madre de Deus gained the bulk of Carvalo's fortune.[63]

Among the donors to the Society in India during the later sixteenth century was Nuno Alvarez de Faria, a Portuguese settler who resided for 30 years in the vicinity of Meliapor on the Coromandel coast. In 1579 he donated property situated 60 kilometers south of present-day Madras, with several buildings and an oratory, to the Goan province. He stipulated that this was a free-will gift, made without any pressure whatsoever.[64] Another benefactor was Diogo Mendes, a merchant or sailor, who died at sea and left his small estate for a chantry in the Malacca college, to be distributed among the poor, and to redeem a Jesuit martyr in Ireland.[65] Far more important was the controversial donation of D. Pedro de Castro to the novitiate of Chorão of the leaseholds of three South Goan towns, Assalona, Velim, and Ambelim. After Castro participated in a punitive campaign against those accused of murdering Fr. Rudolfo Aquaviva and his companions in the early 1580s (see Chapter 3), a grateful viceroy assigned the towns to the captain, an action that Philip II approved. But when Castro subsequently conveyed the towns to the new novitiate of Chorão, his right to do so was challenged by Peninsular tribunals, and it became necessary for the provincial to dispatch a special agent to Europe to persuade the king to reverse his initial negative decision. As will be seen later, those villages, especially Assalona, provided vital income to several Jesuit enterprises.[66]

The number of such donors seems to have declined in seventeenth-century India, but there were still several important bequests. One came from Bartholomew Lopes, a rich merchant who appears to have engaged in the ivory and slave trades of Mozambique and other parts of East Africa. In 1641 he promised to endow the colleges of Diu and

61. Azeitão to Oliva, Beja, 12 Dec. 1670, in ARSI, *Bras.*, 3:II, fol. 109; *HCJAP*, 3:1, 47.

62. Fr. Baltasar Gago to the fathers at Coimbra, Goa, 14–20 Oct. 1549, in *DI*, 1: 599.

63. Fr. António Quadros to Laínez, Goa, 8 Dec. 1563, and Fr. Amator Correia to the members in Portugal and other parts of Europe, Cochin, 20 Jan. 1564, in *DI*, 6: 73 and 170.

64. *DI*, 12: 81–84.

65. Fr. Gabriel Afonso to Mercurian, 12 July 1579, in *DI*, 11: 599–600; see Manuel da Costa, "The Last Years of a Confessor of the Faith, Father David Wolf," *AHSI* 15 (1946): 127–43.

66. *DI*, 14: s.v. index, 934; 16: 10* and sources cited there.

Mozambique with 6,000,000 rs. in cash. The money became available by 1656, but the viceroy confiscated it for military expenses, and although the Society was eventually assigned the right to collect tolls on a river in India, the bequest was essentially lost.[67] It was rare for high public officials to grant large bequests to the Society. One who did so was Dr. Sebastião da Costa, a member of the High Court (Relação) of Goa. As if he had something to conceal, he insisted that his donation of 15,000,000 rs. to the professed house of Bom Jesús be kept entirely confidential, but nevertheless he asked that he be inhumed next to the house's founder, D. Jerónimo Mascarenhas, and that his picture be exhibited and be of the same size as that of the founder![68] One of the last major donors in India was João Dias Ribeiro, proprietor of an island off Cape Dalgado, Mozambique, who died in 1690 and was buried with "great pomp" in the church of the College of Eleven Thousand Virgins, Damão, of which he became the official founder by reason of his legacy of 6,000,000 rs.[69]

The Far Eastern enterprises of the Society attracted a few bachelor patrons but undoubtedly hoped to gain more. One contributor was Duarte António de Algarve, a Castilian who came to Japan via the Philippines, probably in the 1590s, and at an undisclosed date died leaving the province a relatively large legacy—7,200,000 rs.[70] Another was Andrés Coutinho, a wealthy man, presumably a merchant, who returned from the East about 1585 and offered to found in Lisbon a probationary house for missionaries to be assigned to Japan or India. Although he promised the Society 9,600,000 rs., 8,000,000 in cash, and the remainder in debts owed him in India and in the kingdom, his proposal was deemed insufficient for the intended purpose and was rejected.[71] Whether that decision was shortsighted may be questioned. At any rate, as already seen, such a facility was not established until the massive bequest by the admiral of Castile in the eighteenth century. Other than the offer of one Bras da Sylva, about whom nothing is known, to purchase the village of Morosy in Salsete do Norte for the support of the mission in North Vietnam, no significant additional donations by bachelors in the East appear to have been made.[72]

In Brazil, bachelors did not emerge as prominent supporters of the Society until the late seventeenth century. As already noted, the only Jesuit college in Pernambuco was that of Olinda, founded in the 1570s, lost during the Dutch occupation, and rebuilt after the liberation. But the citizens of the rival port city of Recife yearned for their own college. The

67. The Lopes "foundation" is mentioned as received in the third catalogue of 1653, as "borrowed" in that of 1656, and as not returned in the reports for the remainder of the century. ARSI, *Goa*, 15, fols. 80–81ʳ, 135ᵛ–136ʳ, 160ʳ, 200ʳ–201ʳ, et seq.

68. "Proposta que fas Doutor Sebastião da Costa debaixo de todo o segredo ao . . . Pᵉ Simão Ferreira. . . provincial . . . de Goa," 6 Nov. 1678, in ARSI, FG, 1443/9/38.

69. Sousa, *Oriente conquistado*, 144. It is probable that the merchant João Machado, who left the procuratorial office of the professed house in Goa 300,000 rs. for the redemption of Portuguese captives, made his bequest in the late seventeenth century. It is mentioned in an order of the provincial of 9 Aug. 1717, in HAG, 2660, fol. 1.

70. Nothing seems to be known about him, other than his legacy, which is mentioned in the donor list cited in note 59.

71. Sebastião de Morais (provincial) to Aquaviva, Lisbon, 30 Mar. 1585, in *DI*, 13: 847–48; cf. *HCJAP*, 2:1, 195ff.

72. The offer by Braz da Sylva is mentioned in Overseas Council to king, 13 Mar. 1693, in AHU/PA/IN, *cx.* 37, no. 14. The council recommended approval to liberate the royal treasury of the need to continue to support missionaries in Tonkin, but it stipulated that the quitrents that the village owed the crown must still be paid.

problem was that the crown was not prepared to underwrite its cost. In 1675 a wealthy landowner, Captain António de Gouveia, offered to do so himself. He stated that he was about 40 years old, that he had a 90-year-old father in Viseu who could not be his heir, and that his surviving brother was a clergyman who had his own church and was therefore financially secure. Claiming that he already had some knowledge of Latin and that he was then studying it with the aid of Jesuits, he asked to be admitted to the Society to prepare himself for the priesthood. "Moved by God and for the benefit of his soul," he offered to provide 6,400,000 rs., half invested in cattle, the remainder in rental property in the port, and stipulated that his bequest was irrevocable even if he failed to pass muster in the Society.[73] In 1693 the college attracted a second major benefactor when António Fernandes de Matos offered it 12,000,000 rs. to construct an impressive church that survived until the present century.[74] The same year, a wealthy Bahian, Bento Maciel, became the first of several major benefactors of the new seminary of Belém da Cachoeira, which he offered to endow with his entire estate, estimated to be worth 10,000,000 rs.[75]

Easily the greatest patron of the Society in the empire was the celebrated Domingo Afonso, who, because of the years he spent opening up cattle lands northwest of Bahia, proudly added to his name "Sertão" and was nicknamed "O Mafrense" because he was born near the site of the future monastery of that name 80 kilometers northwest of Lisbon. Domingo appeared in Bahia about 1671, and by 1674 he had participated in the pacification of the future cattle barony of Piauí, where in the course of two decades he established 30 ranches. By the early 1690s he had become one of the wealthiest men in northeastern Brazil. His fortune was based not only upon cattle sales but also upon loans he made to other landowners, merchants, and royal officials in the colony, as well as income from rented rural and urban properties. He also became a prominent official in the royal government, most conspicuously as royal treasurer. Domingo Afonso Sertão was on good terms with several religious Orders but was personally attracted to the Society of Jesus. In 1704 he negotiated a lengthy, surprisingly tough agreement with local leaders of the Society. They had long wanted to establish a novitiate separate from the probationary house in Salvador. Domingo agreed to finance its construction, pledging the princely sum of 25,600,000 rs. for that purpose and leaving the bulk of his estate for the support of the novitiate of Jiquitaia, erected on the outskirts of Salvador, and to assist the college of Bahia. Among the conditions he attached were that he be buried as a lay brother in the church of the novitiate, that thousands of masses be said for his soul until eternity, and that stipulated grants be made to his natural daughter, to a large number of children of his servants, to his relatives in the colony and the kingdom, and to his slaves, many of whom he freed. Apart from various

73. "Informação da proposta que o Capitam António de Gouvea fes ao P^e Manoel da Costa, visitador do collegio de Pernambuco ... sobre a fundacao' da caza de Recife em Collegio," Bahia, 10 Feb. 1675, in ARSI, *Bras.*, 3:II, 130^r–130^v; notarized statement by Gouveia, Recife, 10 May 1677, in ibid., FG, 1477/25.

74. Emanuel Correa to Gonzalez de Santalla, 2 June 1693, in ARSI, FG, 1569/2; ibid., *Bras.*, 11, fols. 485–86; cf. *HCJB*, 5: 463–64, 467, 477–78. There is a brief sketch of the benefactor, who also endowed the third Order of St. Francis in Recife and built a fortress at his own expense, in António José Victoriano Borges da Fonseca, "Nobiliarchia Pernambucana," *ABNRJ* 47 (1935): 76.

75. ARSI, FG, 1373/4; *HCJB*, 5: 170. In a most unusual arrangement, Maciel was permitted to live in the seminary and died there in 1709 as a brother in the Society. For other benefactors, see *HCJB*, 5: 170–77.

charitable gifts to the poor and to several other religious Orders in Salvador, he left his 30 ranches in Piauí to the Society in the form of a chantry (capela), the proceeds of which were intended to defray the costs of certain pious causes, including the care of indigent prisoners, dowries for white Old Christian girls, and, of course, the financial requirements of the novitiate and the college of Bahia.[76]

Single women also became important sources of support within the Assistancy. Females, especially widows, were supposedly particularly susceptible to entreaties by representatives of religious Orders.[77] The author of the *Monita Secreta* was especially scornful of Jesuit efforts to woo feminine supporters:

> Let the greatest sums be always extorted from widows, by frequent remonstrances of our extreme necessities. . . . For the managing . . . [of approaches to female prospects] let only those of advanced age, of a lovely complexion and agreeable conversation be chosen . . . and the minute they begin to show any affection towards our order, then 'tis time to lay before them the good works and merits of the Society. . . . They . . . may be well admonish'd, especially to a constant perseverance in their state of widowhood . . . by . . . praising the advantages and felicity of a single life . . . [and] the inconveniences of wedlock, especially when 'tis repeated. . . . When we have thus far gain'd our point, the widow must be, by little and little, excited to the performance of good-works . . . [and] dispose of what she has in favour of the Society. . . . If any widow does not in her life-time make over her whole estate to the Society; whenever opportunity offers, but especially when she is seiz'd with sickness, or in danger of life, let some take care to represent to her the poverty of the greatest number of our colleges.[78]

It is impossible to ascertain whether Jesuits were actually any more persistent or skillful than members of other religious Orders in their appeals to unattached women. Certainly Loyola conducted a lengthy and not always easy correspondence with influential women. And Jesuits did enjoy remarkable successes in their appeals to some wealthy women, a few of whom resembled the stereotype depicted by the author of the *Monita Secreta*.[79]

The most important financial supporter of the Lisbon college of Santo Antão was unquestionably D. Felipa de Sá, countess of Linhares, the last surviving offspring of Mem de Sá, Brazil's third governor-general. When her father died (1572), D. Felipa was living

76. The foregoing is based mainly upon the author's unpublished study of cattle-ranching in colonial Piauí, but see especially *HCJB*, 5: 141–50 and 574–76; C. R. Boxer, *The Golden Age of Brazil, 1695–1750* (Berkeley, 1962), 230, 234–36, and 243; and A. J. R. Russell-Wood, *Fidalgos and Philanthropists: The Santa Casa da Misericórdia of Bahia, 1550–1755* (Berkeley, 1968), esp. 118, 125, 150, and 255. See also "Testamento de Domingo Afonso Certao," Bahia, 12 May 1711, in *RIHGB* 20 (1857): 140–50. The most important ARSI references are *Bras.*, 4, 173–74, and 11:I, 160–61, 166–79.

77. For examples of important benefactresses, see Rosenthal, *Purchase of Paradise*, 67–68; and Constance H. Berman, "Women as Donors and Patrons to Southern French Monasteries in the Twelfth and Thirteenth Centuries," in Constance H. Berman, C. W. Connell, and J. R. Rothschield, eds., *The Worlds of Medieval Women* (Morgantown, W.Va., 1985), 53–68. I am indebted to Dr. Berman for a copy of her essay.

78. *Monita Secreta*, pp. 11, 39, 43, 51, and 55.

79. See Hugo Rahner, S.J., ed., *Saint Ignatius Loyola: Letters to Women* (New York, 1960). One fascinating example of a specific solicitation for funds to establish a chantry for the support of the precariously financed Malabar province is João da Costa (procurator, Malabar) to "Ex.ma Sra," Lisbon, 23 Feb. 1700, in Newberry Library, Chicago, Greenlee Collection, no. 336. See also Burrus, ed., *Kino*, esp. the introduction. It may be objected that Kino and his colleagues, who wrote to the famous patroness from China, India, and elsewhere, were simply keeping her informed of developments in Jesuit enterprises, but it would be naive to adhere to such a view.

in a Dominican convent in Évora, where she had resided since the age of 12. Her surviving brother, Francisco, a secular priest, was supposed to succeed their father, but he expired within a few months. Someone decided, therefore, that D. Felipa should leave the convent and make a suitable marriage. In 1573 she and D. Fernando de Noronha, future count of Linhares, were wed in what proved to be a barren union. For several decades the two enjoyed not only the fruits of the count's properties in the kingdom but those of his wife's properties in Brazil. They included two sugar estates founded by her father, Santana de Ilhéus and the famous Sergipe do Conde, also known as Sergipe da Condessa. In 1617 the count expired, and his widow prepared to meet her end. Five years earlier she had contracted to build a suitable church for the college of Santo Antão, founded in 1593 but still lacking an appropriate spiritual edifice. To finance its construction and to defray the expenses of members of the Order who served in it, the countess pledged 1,000,000 rs., consisting of income properties in the capital, certain annuities, and her residential estate at Talhares.[80] As her health deteriorated, the condessa decided to bequeath the rest of her estate, namely, the sugar properties in Brazil, to the same college. She died on 1 September 1618, very likely oblivious to the fact that her bequests conflicted with the terms of her father's will. That contradiction would lead to decades of litigation among the designated heirs of the father and the daughter.[81] As will be seen later, the Bahian sugar properties presented the leaders of the college with endless problems.

Less than a dozen years later, another widow, D. Joana Perestrella, expired, probably not far from Coimbra. Although the *Constitutions* warned that Jesuits ought not to accept the burdens of "executors or mandates," she nevertheless had designated as the executor of her will a nephew who was a Jesuit resident in the College of Arts at Coimbra and named her confessor, another Jesuit, as his alternate.[82] She directed that her body be interred in the church of that college, that 300 masses be said the day following her death, and that her landed property be sold to build a new chapel within the church to house her body and that of her late husband. She declared herself debt-free and directed that the obligations of her married daughter be settled, but that she be otherwise disinherited. Beyond making minor provisions for her servants, she had no other instructions save to ask her nephew to sign her will, since she was incapable of doing so.[83] Such terms not only demonstrate the traditional piety that still characterized rural landowners in the kingdom but also suggest that the counsel of Silvian de Marseille, the fifth-century theologian who contended that it was more fitting for parents to leave their wealth to the Church than to their offspring, was still taken seriously in Portugal.[84]

80. Schwartz's contention (see note 81) that the agreement was reached in 1617 is incorrect, as is evident from the contract summary in ARSI, *Lus.*, 76, 19–20[v], and Francisco Sarm.[to] et al. to procurator general, Santo Antão, Lisbon, 1 June 1702, in ibid., *Informationum, Procurator Generalis*, bk. 142, fols. 679–80.

81. On the condessa and her famous bequests, see Stuart B. Schwartz, *Sugar Plantations in the Formation of Brazilian Society: Bahia, 1550–1835* (Cambridge, 1985), app. A; but see also *HCJAP*, 2:1, 187–90; *HCJB*, 5: 243ff.; and Herbert Ewaldo Wetzel, *Mem de Sá, terceiro governador geral (1557–1572)* (Rio de Janeiro, 1972), chap. 12.

82. *CSJ(C)*, pt. 6, chap. 3, par. 591.

83. "Treslado do testamento de D. Joana Perestrella," 20 Feb. 1629, in ARSI, *Lus.*, 84:I, 212.

84. Jack Goody, *The Development of Family and Marriage in Europe* (Cambridge, 1983), 100–101.

Two other significant benefactresses in the kingdom made no demands for special masses in return for contributing their estates to the Society. One was Philippa Mendes, who died in 1650 in the district of Villar do Monte, close to 30 kilometers from the city of Bragança. She was the mistress of extensive wheat lands as well as of a farm and a complex of urban houses, all of which she left to the college of Bragança unconditionally, asking for "not even a single mass."[85] About the same time, D. Ana da Silva, who lived in the fertile community of Vila de Pernes, 15 kilometers south of Torres Novas, left her farm, São Silvestre, and untold funds to establish a Jesuit college of twelve in her community. But either her proposed foundation appeared too meager or someone in the government was opposed. In any event, following her death in 1661, a Latin school was opened there, but never the college she had hoped for.[86]

Widows also proved to be vital donors to the province of Goa. In his invaluable financial survey of the province in 1586, Valignano mentioned four who had made major gifts to the Society that year in the Bassein district. The most important was D. Isabel de Aguiar, a Portuguese woman who lived for a time in Ormuz, where she met Fr. Gaspar Barzaeus. When he returned to India, she accompanied him. She followed Fr. Barzaeus's advice and married a Portuguese stationed in Bassein. After his death, she decided against remarrying (thereby obviously pleasing the Jesuits, though whether in response to their advice is unclear). After making provision for her mother-in-law, she assigned to the Society three villages in Salsete do Norte to which she had title, reserving for herself their income for the balance of her life. Since these villages became the foundation of the college of Bassein, the Jesuits acclaimed her as its founder, its "worthy benefactress." According to the chronicler Francisco de Sousa, her example was followed by many other matrons in the district.[87] Another "rich widow" who made an important contribution was Mercia Roiz of Ceylon. In 1613 she endowed the new college at Colombo with funds totaling 3,119,040 rs., and upon her death around 1620 she left the same institution an additional 162,000 rs.[88]

The most celebrated patroness of Jesuit missions in India was D. Juliana Dias da Costa (d. 1734), a prominent lady-in-waiting at the Mughal court. Her father was a Portuguese adventurer, born in Cochin, who was captured at Hugli in 1633 when it was overrun by Mughal forces and brought to Agra, where her Indian mother was a slave. Christianized, D. Juliana was married, but no one is certain to whom. In any case, she became an early widow with several sons. Resourcefully, she supported Bahadur Shah against his rival brother following the death of their father, Aurangzeb, in 1707 and was handsomely rewarded with hoards of jewels and the revenue of four villages. She became a valued friend of the Jesuits and, curiously, of the Dutch as well. Her services to the Jesuits

85. Rector and consultores of Bragança to Aloysius Gottifredi, 1650, in ARSI, *Lus.*, 79, fols. 496–99.

86. *HCJAP*, 3:I, 50–51.

87. Alessandro Valignano, "Sumario de todos os colegios e casas. . . no anno de 1586," in *DI*, 14: 480–84; Sousa, *Oriente conquistado*, 172–73; [Francisco Cabral] to Laínez, [11 Dec. 1564], in *DI*, 6: 347–48. D. Isabel's benefactions are frequently mentioned in *DI*, 4: 341–42, 347–48, 404, 575, 594, and 662. One enthusiastic father described the three villages as "as milhores que ahi nestas terras," noting that the founder conveyed them with no conditions whatsoever. Fr. Ferdinand da Cunha to the colleagues in Portugal, Bassein, 11 Dec. 1564, in *DI* 6: 341–42.

88. S. G. Perera, "The Jesuits in Ceylon in the 16th and 17th Centuries," *Ceylon Antiquary and Literary Register* 2 (1916–17): 7, and 3 (1917–18): 22.

drew praise not only from them but also from the viceroys, who considered her very influential at the Mughal court. Her most important assistance was to the Agra station after the English had cut off its principal sources of revenue by seizing the villages in Bombay that had supported it (see Chapter 17). About 1707 she gave the province of Goa a fortune variously estimated at between 40 and 150 contos, sufficient so that in 1712, Father General Tamburini officially proclaimed her "mistress and mother" of the Society in a document that was personally delivered to her by a Jesuit messenger in 1714. When she died twenty years later, the Goan personnel report of 1735 included a most unusual statement sorrowfully advising the general of the death of the "worthy benefactress of the college and mission of Agra."[89]

From time to time, benefactresses provided significant assistance to other provinces as well. In 1640, for example, a certain D. Angela de Lemos of Macao left a substantial quantity of silver to the perennially fiscally strapped Japan province as seed money for a future (but never realized) college in Vietnam. At an undetermined point during the seventeenth century, another Macaonese, Isabel Reigota, furnished the Visitor with 760,000 rs. so that he could undertake an inspection of the Vietnam missions, and several Chinese ladies of mandarin status provided between 800,000 and 4,800,000 rs. to the equally precariously financed vice-province.[90]

No biographical details are available concerning these patronesses, but rather more survives concerning Brazil's D. Catarina da Costa. She was first married by Fr. António Vieira to the captain-major of Gurupi, a private captaincy in the Lower Amazon, in the 1660s. When her husband died, about 1674, he left a new sugar estate, the fazenda de Ibirajuba, to his widow provided that she did not remarry. In the event that she did so, the college of Pará was to become its new owner. After she married another prominent settler, her new husband agreed to pay the college 1,600,000 rs. in lieu of the estate. Following her second husband's death (1691), D. Catarina left the mill and additional lands to the college, for which she received grateful thanks from the father general. As will be seen elsewhere, Ibirajuba became a major Jesuit property in the eighteenth century.[91]

Less Conspicuous Benefactors

Although the Jesuits, like members of other religious Orders, lavished praise on their most conspicuous patrons, the Society also received important contributions from faithful

89. Such a remarkable lady has naturally attracted a good deal of attention. The most extensive summary of the literature, including a helpful bibliography, is Maclagan, *Jesuits*, chap. 12. She is mentioned in several viceregal dispatches of 1715 and in a response by the Overseas Council. See *CTEIP*, 5: 310–17; *ACE*, 5: 218 and 295–98; and *APO*:2, 1:3:2 (1939), passim. Several writers state that she contributed a *lakh* (100,000 rupees) to the province. If a rupee then equaled 400 rs., that would amount to 40,000,000 rs. See Anthony D'Costa, S.J., ed., "Tombo de Baçaim, 1610–1730," *Indica* 6 (1969): 106–18, at 107 n. 9, where the equivalency is unfortunately undocumented. The Jesuits' economic report of 1713 refers to the "new and magnificent foundation" by D. Juliana amounting to 500,000 xerafins, or the higher figure given in the text. ARSI, *Goa*, 16, fol. 52^r. Her death is reported in the "Catalogus sociorum" of Jan. 1735, in ibid., 27, fol. 165^v.

90. Praty Japona, "Informação do estado temporal da provincia de Japam," 1727 (cited note 17); "Catalogo dos fundadores ... da provincia de Jappão," in ARSI, *JapSin*, 23, fol. 4^v; "Rol dos fundadores da vice provincia de China" (1727), in ARSI, FG, 722/17.

91. *HCJB*, 3: 303–4.

adherents of modest means.[92] Such benefactors, ignored in the Society's annals, gave small amounts of silver, small plots, orchards, grain supplies, or other property to adorn churches, to provide masses for their special saints, to underwrite the costs of festivals, to endow small chantries, and for other purposes. Within nine years of its establishment, the novitiate of Chorão received alms from various persons amounting to 10,800,000 rs.[93] One report prepared around 1700 lists nineteen contributors of chantries to the professed house in Goa with a total value in excess of 17,000,000 rs.; another account, dated 1710, records the legacies of 23 persons totaling 20,510,700 rs.[94]

Small contributions were especially important in the Far East, where financing was always precarious. Though less wealthy donors often conveyed the bulk, if not the whole, of their estates to particular religious bodies or houses, some, like Maria Gaya, preferred to spread around their modest savings. In her testament (1607), Maria Gaya left the Jesuit college of Macao about a third of her estate, valued at 334,800 rs., but allotted the remainder to twenty religious bodies and individuals, whose legacies ranged from 2,000 rs. to 60,000 rs. each.[95] An undated seventeenth-century record of founders of residences in the Japan province includes the names of seventeen Asians who contributed under 300,000 rs. each.[96] In 1636 a dozen persons in Macao, some of them representing deceased relatives, joined together and pledged 9,600,000 rs. to found a Jesuit college in Hanchow, one that they optimistically expected to house 40 members. An undated seventeenth-century report from the same city shows more than a score of persons who gave the Jesuit college between 16,000 rs. and 240,000 rs. for pious works; another report, dated 1677, states that during the half century between 1622 and 1672, about two score persons contributed over 25,000,000 rs. to the vice-province.[97]

Surviving records suggest that such contributions were relatively more important in the East than in the West. They may have been particularly significant during the formative period. A report of the Brazil province of 1577 states that the new college of Olinda was already the recipient of "many large alms" ranging from 4,000 rs. to 40,000 rs., and that without such moneys, its twenty subjects would be unable to feed themselves.[98] A 1761 analysis of chantries established for the college of Bahia and three other nearby facilities states that 27 donors left properties consisting of cattle ranches, sugar fields, and urban income

92. Cf. Gustave Dupont-Ferrier, *Du collège de Clermont au lycée Louis-le-Grand (1563–1920)*, 3 vols. (Paris, 1921–25), 1: 91.

93. Alberto Laerzio (master of novices) to Aquaviva, 28 Nov. 1593, in *DI*, 16: 451, par. 19.

94. "Titulo das capelas legados mandas e deixas que deixaram varios devotos a esta igr.ª e casa professa [Bom Jesús]," n.d. [ca. 1700]; report of Manoel Carvalho (provincial), 5 Sept. 1710, in ARSI, *Goa*, 9:II, 467–473ᵛ. The previously cited "Bemfeitores da casa professa do Bom Jesu" (note 20 above) dates from the late 1660s but is not restricted to small donors. Total annual income from contributions, including the uncertain share from the king, is calculated at 15,151,630 rs.

95. Testament dated 2 Aug. 1607, in BA/JA/49-V-5, no. 29.

96. "Catalogo dos fundadores ... da provincia de Jappão," cited in note 90.

97. "Titulos dos benefeitores menos principaes' deste coll.º de Macao," n.d., in BA/JA/49-IV-66, no. 59; "Treslado do contracto que fez a Companhia de Jesus com os doze fundadores do collegio ... de Hancheo," Macao, 27 Dec. 1636 (signed copy), and "Rol dos fundadores da vice provincia de China" [1677], both in ARSI, FG, 722/17.

98. Serafim Leite, ed., "Emformação dalgumas cousas do Brasil [por Belchior Cordeiro, 1577]," Academia portuguesa de historia, *Anais*, 2d ser., 15 (1965): 186.

property that provided an annual income in excess of 2,000,000 rs.[99] Although these minor donors did not receive the publicity accorded the principal benefactors, their contributions nevertheless helped keep the Society's churches and other facilities functioning.

Legacies as Mixed Blessings

Invaluable though these benefactions were, they nevertheless posed knotty, frequently protracted, and sometimes insoluble problems for their recipients. First, since the Jesuits were more successful than their religious rivals in obtaining the favor of opulent patrons, they were victimized by rumors that vastly exaggerated the size and number of the legacies they received. In 1596 an envious Franciscan claimed that the previous year the Japan missions had received 24,000,000 rs. from a single donor in India, compelling Valignano to deny the existence of both the benefactor and his legacy.[100] Nearly three decades later, Diogo Ximenes Vargas, a slave dealer in the Cape Verdes, expired, leaving his entire estate to the Society. The local cámara protested against the fulfillment of the bequest, asserting that it was worth 20,000,000 rs., when in fact only 7 percent of that amount was netted.[101]

Sometimes a well-intentioned benefactor wittingly or otherwise exaggerated the amount his estate could contribute to a pious objective. W. K. Jordan found that the same difficulty existed among philanthropists in early modern England: "In a few cases the enthusiasm of donors outran their estates or an estate melted away in adversity, fire, or mismanagement between the date when the will was drafted and the time of probate."[102] When Margarida de Paz expired in the Portuguese kingdom in 1560, she left a Jesuit institution (apparently the arts college of Coimbra) a legacy of about 1,600,000 rs., but the disappointed fathers soon learned that because of encumbrances, her estate would yield far less than that.[103] The just-mentioned Vargas bequest is another case in point. Though Jesuit administrators found the estate to be worth over 10,000,000 rs., after settling the decedent's bills and discounting uncollectible credits, it netted only 1,437,156 rs.[104] Forty years after Salvador de Sá enthusiastically endowed the college of Santos with various urban properties, that college remained one of the smallest and most poorly funded in Brazil because the houses constantly deteriorated and repairs ate up their income.[105] In 1711 António de Argão Menezes, a Bahian cattle baron, and his wife pledged 8,000,000 rs. to the new seminary of Belém da Cachoeira, but Argão died without fulfilling that promise, and the Jesuits

---

99. "Relação dos bens sequestrados aos regulares proscriptas e expulsos da Companhia . . . de JESVS onerados com encargos pios," Bahia, 19 Apr. 1761, in AHU/PA/BA, 1st cat., no. 5586.

100. J. L. Alvarez-Taladriz, "Inversion de plata del Peru en la India oriental para la mission de Japon (1590–1598)," *Tenri Daigaku Gakuho* [Bulletin of Tenri University], no. 107 (Mar. 1977): 34–57, at 33.

101. *HCJAP*, 3:2, 213.

102. W. K. Jordan, *Philanthropy in England, 1480–1660* (London, 1959), 33.

103. P. Miguel de Torres to Laínez, Lisbon, 11 July 1560, in *MB*, 5: 237. Since Torres mentioned both the arts college and the new facility at Braga, I cannot be certain which became the recipient in this instance.

104. "Memoria do q. importou a faz.^da do Capitao Diogo Ximenez Vargas, e como se despendeo," Lisbon, 8 June 1647, in ANTT/CJ/37, nos. 26–29. There is further documentation in /57.

105. *HCJB*, 6: 426–27.

took his widow to court to compel her to honor her late husband's commitment. As a result, she was obliged to sell five ranches.[106] Even the massive endowment of Domingo Afonso Sertão proved insufficient to maintain the Jiquitaia novitiate: in 1757 the endowment provided 42 percent of its running expenses, while the colleges within the province supplied another 31.5 percent.[107]

On receiving a legacy, the Jesuits often had to deal with claims submitted by disappointed heirs. Toward the end of the sixteenth century, João Lopes Anriques left the incipient college of São Miguel in the Azores 20 contos and was acclaimed its "worthy benefactor," but his bequest was bitterly contested by a disappointed brother, and his suit dragged on for years with unknown results.[108] At an uncertain date during the seventeenth century, Afonso Rodrigues de Guevara, former secretary of state for the State of India, went to his reward, leaving the Society as his sole heir. Somehow he had forgotten that he had a wife back in the kingdom, but when she learned of her erstwhile spouse's demise, she applied for her share of his relatively small estate, just under 3,000,000 rs. In the end, the fathers were obliged to sell some houses in Lisbon in order to meet her claim. They were, however, less sympathetic to the challenge that another claimant lodged with Aquaviva concerning the estate of his late brother, António Guedes Morais, who left the new province of Malabar a welcome 9,000,000 rs. The provincial responded to queries from Rome by stating, "Your Paternity has not been well informed. We owe nothing to this man. He was only half-brother to our Benefactor.... Fr. Ottavio Lombardo [the procurator] ... will explain everything."[109] Whether or not Lombardo alleviated the concern of headquarters, there can be no doubt that litigation over bequests embarrassed the Society and provided evidence to support critics who accused the Jesuits of chicanery, greed, uncharitableness, and unscrupulous behavior.

The influence that the Jesuits possessed (or were believed to possess) in the making of wills by persons *in articulo mortis*, that is, at death's door, sometimes caused the Society embarrassing problems. McManners found in France that during the first half of the seventeenth century, more than two-thirds of all wills were drafted when the testator was nearing death, and that the practice became significantly less common by the second half of the eighteenth century.[110] Certainly many of the Jesuits' patrons *were* close to death when they dictated the terms of their wills, but whether Portuguese practice followed the French example remains to be studied. As previously noted, the *Constitutions* urged members of the Society to refrain from becoming executors of wills. No doubt, however, Jesuits, like other churchmen, gave solicited advice to their spiritual charges when the latter neared death. Rightly or wrongly, such advice led to tongue-wagging about deathbed assignments. The

106. "Relação dos bens sequestrados aos . . . expulsos da Companhia . . . de JESVS." For the family's supposed devotion to the Society, see *HCJB*, 5: 171–74, where, however, no reference will be found to the litigation mentioned here.

107. *HCJB*, 5: 148.

108. "Informaçam dos bens de raiz que os collegios da Companhia . . . tem neste reyno" [ca. 1611], ANTT/CJ/57, no. 26, fol. 23.

109. F/JM, 1: 275. Another example of a contested will appears in Gaspar Fernandes (procurator [?], Malabar) to Vitelleschi, Cochin, 25 Nov. 1632, in ARSI, *Goa*, 18, 127–28.

110. John McManners, *Death and the Enlightenment: Changing Attitudes to Death Among Christians and Unbelievers in Eighteenth-Century France* (Oxford, 1981), 239.

problem was not new, and Norberg probably understates its severity when she writes, "The testator's state of health at the time he dictated his will may well have had some effect upon his decision to make religious bequests."[111] Certainly leaders like Valignano recognized the danger. In 1585, Valignano wrote Aquaviva that an unnamed Portuguese had recently died and left the house (and future college) of Damão a large and valuable garden that was never to be alienated from that facility, a condition that Valignano said was very likely suggested by the Jesuit father who had been the donor's spiritual advisor. He strongly recommended that members of the Order be barred from influencing the terms of wills because of the "inconveniences and risks" that could follow. Nearly a century later, António de Melo de Castro indignantly wrote Afonso VI that although he had prohibited the religious from assisting in the preparation of wills in which they were beneficiaries, the Jesuits ignored his admonition. He pointed out that a dying vicar in Bassein had a Jesuit confessor and left a village leasehold to a nephew in Goa who had a Jesuit connection, "and this is the way they do with all testaments."[112] Whether or not the viceroy's charge was true, it was, as Valignano had warned, another source of uneasiness to Jesuits concerned about their public image.

Although critics may have been unaware of it, legacies sometimes placed heavy burdens upon Jesuits charged with executing the terms of complex wills. In the case of the Vargas bequest discussed above, more than two decades elapsed before the estate was settled. Though the *Constitutions* stipulated that legacies should be accepted unconditionally, the fathers sometimes were obliged to accept legacies that required a great deal of negotiation before the files could be closed. An example is the living trust (*inter vivos*) made to the college of Bahia by Rev. Joseph de Andrada e Sá, a secular priest who lived at the south end of Itaparica Island in All Saints Bay. In 1689 he made an "irrevocable" bequest to the college that included extensive lands, 28 slaves, 74 cattle, 15 oxen, 30 goats, and credits of 751,000 rs. for chests of sugar and other considerations owed by five members of the Bahian community, including a prominent member of the High Court. The priest charged the rector of the college with settling his debts in excess of 138,000 rs. owed to several Lisbon merchants, to the count of Castanheira (a quitrent), and to a tithe collector who resided in Pernambuco. He also admonished the rector to pay "for the good of his conscience" any other debts that he might have forgotten, and to reserve funds for masses to be said on his birthday, as well as for alms for a *pardo* (mulatto) blacksmith's apprentice in the college's employ and for the education of two black boys.[113]

Despite their best efforts, the fathers sometimes were unable to execute the wishes of testators in a timely manner because of formidable opposition. As noted earlier, the citizens of Beja yearned for a college in the late seventeenth century and petitioned the crown for its establishment. Although a wealthy couple agreed to become its founders and the father general favored the request, Pedro II preferred another professed house to a college. The Jesuits tried to sway the king through his second wife, but the queen expired in 1699 without

---

111. Norberg, *Rich and Poor*, 124.

112. Valignano to Aquaviva, 25 Dec. 1585, in *DI*, 14: 212 and 217; Overseas Council to king, 1 Mar. 1669, commenting on Melo de Castro's report of 28 Jan. 1668, in AHU/PA/IN, *cx*. 28, no. 36.

113. "Escrita de doação entre vivos ... q. fas o R.^{do} Joseph de Andrada e Saa aos m.^{tos} R.^{dos} p.^{es} da Companhia de Jesu deste coll.° da B.ª," 22 July 1689, in ARSI, FG, 1469/7/11.

the issue having been decided. Sixty years later, neither the college nor its church had been finished.[114]

One further example. In 1723 António de Figureido Ferreira was close to death. He and his wife, longtime admirers of the Society, wishing to do something for their souls and for their community, decided to found a college in Gouveia, one that would train home missionaries. To that end, they promised 16,000,000 rs. Soon after the negotiations were completed, António expired. Three years later, his ailing wife appealed to Michelangelo Tamburini for action. She expressed bewilderment that the matter remained unresolved and pleaded because of her poor health for the peace of mind that a quick solution would assure. The problem was not that the Society was dragging its feet, but that a local parish priest had raised a furor against the establishment of the college. Eventually his opposition was overcome: the first stones were laid in 1739, and Portugal's last Jesuit college opened in 1754.[115]

The Jesuits also found that, as with royal subventions, their most exasperating problem with legacies was collection. In addition to the factors already mentioned, sea disasters, wars, and political considerations contributed to the difficulty in obtaining what they had been promised. Consider, for example, the problem collecting the papal subventions intended for the support of the Japan missions. As seen earlier in this chapter, Gregory XIII assigned that enterprise 1,600,000 rs., an amount that his successor increased by 50 percent, though later popes reduced it to the original figure. The funds came from Christmas dues paid to the papal collector in Spain, who forwarded the money to Lisbon; from there it was sent to Goa, and then on to Macao. The money was used for general expenses of the province, including clothing, wine, and other necessities, but sometimes it never reached its ultimate destination. In 1585 the loss of an East Indiaman cost the Japan missions about 70 percent of the year's stipend. Shipments in the 1590s were irregular, probably because of intensified maritime warfare among Spain, England, and Holland. Payments appear to have been rather regular during the first decade of the seventeenth century, but by 1620 they were four years in arrears. Even so, some funds were remitted annually between 1617 and 1625. No known surviving records testify whether the subsidies were dispatched during the next fifteen years. As could be expected, one of Spain's responses to the December revolution of 1640 was to interdict payments of the subvention for most of the 1640s, but a catch-up effort was made by papal authorities between 1648 and 1654. Thereafter, however, the record is silent on any further papal payments to the Japan province.[116]

114. *HCJAP*, 3:1, 37–41.

115. António de Figureido Ferreira to Father Visitor, Gouveia, 7 Mar. 1723; Brigida de Távora (his wife) to Tamburini, 22 Feb. 1726, in ARSI, *Lus.*, 76, fols. 170^r–173^r. The "Lembrança das fazendas que tem a caza de António de Figureydo Ferreyra e sua molher" indicates that the couple's estate consisted of their residence, 40 rented large and small farms, and various quitrents paid in wheat, beans, olive oil, wine, and livestock. In *HCJAP*, 4:1, 258–60, Rodrigues incorrectly refers to the male donor as António Ferreira de Figureido.

116. The loss of the *nau Santiago* is reported in a document of 1586 (*MHJ*, 190); the absence of a payment in 1591 was disclosed by Fr. Francisco Lameira (procurator) to Aquaviva, Goa, 1 Dec. 1591, in *DI*, 15: 712–13; transmittals from Goa to Macao during the first decade of the seventeenth century are indicated in HAG 1890; payments for the years 1617–24 are recorded in ARSI, *JapSin*, 23, fols. 51–52^v, 55, 59–60; and for 1624–25 in *MHJ*, 1: 966–69. The last known payments (1648–54) are mentioned in ARSI, *Lus.*, 79, fols. 98

The Jesuits discovered that many private benefactions in the Assistancy, as in early modern England, melted away before they were able to claim them. D. Jerónimo Mascarenhas was a member of a distinguished family that contributed four sons to the Society. Two, as noted in a previous chapter, were successive assistants general; a third became rector of the University of Coimbra and bishop of the Algarve. D. Jerónimo, the remaining brother, amassed a fortune, estimated at 16,000,000 rs., as captain of Cochin and later Ormuz, where he died in 1593, leaving his entire estate for the construction fund of the new professed house in Goa. A priest and a brother were sent by the provincial to Ormuz bearing letters from both the viceroy and a magistrate in Goa urging local authorities to cooperate with them in their efforts to collect the legacy. They discovered upon their arrival that most of the captain's possessions had already been stolen. By the end of 1594, the Society had managed to recover only about 20 percent of the Mascarenhas inheritance.[117] Also in 1594, it was discovered that most of the inheritance (8,000,000 rs.) of the ex-merchant Gaspar Viegas, a Jesuit brother mentioned previously, had been lost when the Cochin fleet of 1592 bound for the kingdom failed to reach its destination.[118]

A few years later, Pedro de Heredia, Spanish governor of the Moluccas, offered the equivalent of 4,800,000 rs. to found a college to train missionaries for the islands, which fell administratively under the Malabar province centered at Cochin. One of the consultores of that college expressed serious misgivings concerning the offer, not because Heredia was a Spaniard, but because the consultor feared that if the crown got wind of the proposal, it would cut off its subvention to the college. He also pointed out that since Heredia's assets were in Philippine lands, it would be necessary to dispatch a brother to that archipelago to collect the annual income, an inconvenient solution. Since Heredia insisted that a college be established in the Moluccas and the Cochin fathers believed that the funds should be sent to their college to educate missionaries for the islands, an impasse was reached and negotiations broke down. In the end, the Jesuits got nothing.[119]

Other bequests were lost in part or entirely as well. It may be remembered that in Bahia, Bento Maciel was the first to offer to underwrite the cost of the Belém da Cachoeira seminary. In 1693 he promised 10,000,000 rs., but by 1709 only 72 percent of that amount had been gathered.[120] Still, that was better than the record of collections from certain other legacies. A grant by the duke of Bavaria to the vice-province of China was faithfully paid by his agents and heirs from 1616 until 1689, when the Turks overran his estates and they were lost. Similarly, part of the vast estate of the admiral of Castile was invested in half annates in the city of Milan, but because of the outbreak of war in

---

and 105–11. Since there is no reference to the receipt of any papal contributions after 1654 in surviving fiscal documents for the Japan province, I suspect that they terminated about this time.

117. "Dom Jerónimo Mascarenhas, fundador da igreja da casa professa do Bom Fim [*sic*] Jesu de Goa," n.d., in ARSI, FG, 1443/9/47; *DI*, 16: 5*, and sources cited there, as well as 170–71. Jerónimo's three Jesuit brothers earlier had assigned their own inheritances to the Lisbon novitiate. António Franco, *Imagem da virtude em o noviciado da companhia de Jesus na corte de Lisboa* (Coimbra, 1717), 18.

118. Alberto Laerzio to Aquaviva, 16 Nov. 1594, in *DI*, 16: 822.

119. Fernandes to Vitelleschi, 25 Nov. 1632 (see note 109); *DM*, 3: 469, 484–85, 488, 501, and esp. 508–9.

120. *HCJB*, 5: 170.

1732 they proved uncollectible.[121] The same was true of the bequest of William Godolphin, an English Catholic lord who left 4,000,000 rs. to the vice-province of China upon his death around 1713, but whose English relatives ignored Jesuit appeals to execute his pledge. A few years earlier, the duke of Arcos, a member of the Aveiro family, offered a small annuity of 720,000 rs. in support of the same vice-province, but until at least 1730 there was no record of payment. And when the prince of Simiana, earlier noted as a benefactor of the Vietnam missions, died in 1670, his heirs declined to honor his commitment, and between that date and 1724, all efforts to persuade them to do so failed.[122] In short, as with the king's assistance, it proved easier for private donors to make promises than to fulfill them.

Despite the difficulties that they sometimes presented, the bequests of a great variety of donors were as essential as royal grants to the operations of the Society in the Assistancy, especially during the Order's formative period. They provided the Society with a vast array of rural estates (developed and otherwise), urban income property, annuities, and other assets that it would not otherwise have possessed. It would appear from the available evidence that the high point of such patronage occurred during the seventeenth century. Did it really decline in the Portuguese Assistancy during the eighteenth century, as may have been the case in France?[123] Our evidence is too fragmentary to be certain. On the other hand, the kinds of donor who supported the Society may well have shifted by the eighteenth century. Contributions by entering Jesuits appear to have tailed off. Merchants, too, along with royal officials, seem to have been less inclined to remember the Society in their testaments than was the case during the sixteenth century.[124] Perhaps, like Sir John Banks, prominent trader and director of the East India Company, they spurned the Church in their wills.[125] They may have preferred to leave their estates to their families, to other

121. Annates, so-called first fruits, consisted of papal assessments on the revenues that accrued to vacant benefices.

122. These examples are drawn from the invaluable "Livro da fazenda . . . das provincias da assistencia de Portugal . . . anno 1730," by Francisco da Fonseca (see note 5).

123. The revealed evidence is not, in fact, conclusive. The number of bequests to the college of Louis-le-Grand reached 71 between 1626 and 1650, but fell during the eighteenth century to 35 (1700–24), 19 (1728–48), and 23 (1750–64). Dupont-Ferrier, *Collège de Clermont*, 1: 93 and 3: app. D. See also McManners, *Death and the Enlightenment*, 240–41; but cf. Philip D. Hoffman, *Church and Community in the Diocese of Lyon, 1500–1789* (New Haven, 1984), 119–27 and 171–73.

124. Revealing, for example, is the pattern of bequests of D. Felipa de Noronha, an exceedingly wealthy daughter of the marquis of Cascais who managed extensive properties and investments before entering the Poor Clares convent in Lisbon. Upon her death (1738), she left an estate worth over 141 contos and specified that 34.2% of it go to public-assistance institutions, 3.1% to individual ecclesiastics, and 39.5% to other religious facilities. The Jesuits were not among her beneficiaries. Manuel Felipe Cruz de Morais Canaveira, "A fortuna de uma nobre portuguesa no século xviii: D. Felipa de Noronha e a sua testamentaria," *Revista de historia economica e social* 13 (Jan.–June 1984): 93–140. Only further research can determine whether D. Felipa was exceptional or typical of her time and socioeconomic station.

125. Banks (d. 1699) possessed a fortune of about £170,000 but left nothing to the Anglican church. D. C. Coleman, *Sir John Banks, Baronet and Businessman: A Study of Business, Politics, and Society in Later Stuart England* (Oxford, 1963), 190. Jordan found an abundance of evidence in England that by about 1480, donors "distrusted the church as feoffee [recipient of a fief] for social change and amelioration because they knew that the ancient church had been . . . an inefficient, they . . . said faithless, custodian of social wealth and because in certain areas of need . . . it had stubbornly resisted progress." Jordan, *Philanthropy*, p. 20. Such a view seems to have been extremely rare in Portugal, at least until after 1750.

religious bodies, or to charities such as the Holy Houses of Mercy.[126] We simply do not know. As the sources summarized here suggest, the traditional conservative landowners, especially childless couples and bachelors, continued to make bequests to the Society to the 1750s. It is possible that in some parts of the Assistancy, most notably the provinces of Goa and Brazil and the vice-province of Maranhão, private support was less vital in the eighteenth century than it had been earlier because the Jesuits, realizing that they could not depend exclusively upon donors, whether royal or private, had by then successfully developed an infrastructure that enabled them to cover most of their expenses with their own earnings. Succeeding chapters will examine how Jesuits in the Assistancy utilized the assets given them to sustain their bold enterprises.

126. According to Russell-Wood, *Fidalgos and Philanthropists*, 151–52 and 165, an important shift occurred in the aims of legacies given to the Bahian Santa Casa da Misericórdia about 1700. Prior to that date they seem to have been made primarily because of religious fervor and the quest for personal salvation; after that date donors intended their estates to alleviate social distress. Was that true elsewhere in the Portuguese empire?

CHAPTER 15

The Economic Foundations
of an Enterprise:
The Acquisition of Lands

Until the last century, world capital consisted primarily of cultivated land and
houses. The instruments of production, plows, ships, or looms, occupied only
a minor place in this inventory.

—Paul Veyne, as quoted by Philippe Aries, *The Hour of Our Death*

INITIALLY THROUGH THE beneficence of its donors, royal and private, and subsequently
through an aggressive program of acquisitions by purchases and other means, the Society of
Jesus became a major property holder in lands where Portugal ruled or pretended to govern.
Its properties included grain farms, olive orchards, and vineyards in the kingdom and the Atlantic islands; vast livestock ranches, sugar plantations, and multipurpose fazendas (estates)
in Brazil; coconut and rice estates in India; and expansive subsistence plantations called arimos in Angola and *prazos* in Mozambique. The Society also derived land-based income from
villages and temple lands in India, and from rentals of both rural and urban parcels. This
chapter will examine some of the ways by which the Society became an impressive patrimonial Order and will provide estimates of the extent of its holdings at various times in several
parts of the Assistancy. It will also demonstrate that although some colleges owned properties
concentrated in their vicinity, other colleges held properties that were remarkably widely dispersed. And it will show that though the Order's rural properties were its most visible assets,
its less easily identified urban holdings often produced higher rates of return. Chapter 16
will focus upon how the Jesuits utilized their vast landed portfolio, and Chapter 17, the last of
this series, will focus upon the growth and extent of criticism of the Jesuits as prominent lati-
fundists and upon the responses of the Portuguese and other governments to that criticism.

Origins of the Church as Landowner

In a classic study, David Herlihy demonstrated that the growth of the Church's landed
properties in medieval Europe was uneven and underwent several stages. The first occurred

during the pre-Carolingian period, from about the fall of Rome until the mid-eighth century, when the Church first became a significant landowner. The second stage, from 751 until 825, featured a threefold increase in its holdings to more than 30 percent of the developed lands in the European continent. During the third stage, centered in the tenth century, the first serious attacks upon Church property occurred. Some property was secularized, but such losses were often offset by additional "generous donations of land." In the fourth stage, from the mid-tenth to the mid-eleventh century, "the attrition of Church property [was] temporarily halted and even reversed," especially in Spain, southern France, and, somewhat later, Italy. Still, Herlihy concluded that by 1200, the Church claimed about 15 percent of the land in those parts of Europe for which measurable data survive.[1]

No comparable estimate of ecclesiastical properties exists for the kingdom of Portugal during the Middle Ages, but it is clear that there, too, the Church became a major recipient of pious bequests of developed and undeveloped lands. During the initial formation of the nation (1095–1250), its rulers, like their counterparts in the two eastern Iberian kingdoms, were lavish in their awards to the Church in return for its support of the *reconquista*, the liberation of the Christian homeland from its Muslim invaders. Though the pace of such territorial transfers doubtless declined once the entire kingdom was under Christian hegemony (that is, by the mid-thirteenth century), the ravages of the Black Death (1348) prompted many pious persons in the kingdom to bequeath their estates to churches and monasteries.[2] Two centuries later, the arrival of the Jesuits triggered another round of gift-giving to an ecclesiastical entity, and also spurred opposition to such territorial alienation.

How the Jesuits Became a Territorial Power in the Assistancy

During the second half of the sixteenth century, when the Assistancy was undergoing a period of rapid growth in both personnel and installations, its leaders and Portugal's supportive sovereigns, especially Sebastian and Henry, recognized that the financial security of the Society's operations required stable, guaranteed sources of income. In the context of the times, that meant the acquisition of landed properties, both developed and undeveloped, at home and overseas. Such properties were obtained by various means: royal largesse, private benefaction, direct purchase, exchanges, and (occasionally) land transfers caused by defaulted obligations.

As seen in Chapter 13, the crown contributed impressively to the landed endowments of many of the early Jesuit colleges in the Assistancy. In the kingdom, that support included the transfer of monastic lands from decadent Orders to the arts college of the University of Coimbra and to the new University of Évora, and the assignment of revenues from customs and from the archepiscopacy of Évora to enable the arts college of Coimbra and the colleges of Santo Antão, Braga, and Porto to purchase income-producing properties to sustain their operations. Both Sebastian and Cardinal Henry authorized such awards, but it was their

1. David Herlihy, "Church Property on the European Continent, 701–1200," *Speculum* 36, 1 (Jan. 1961): 81–[105], also in Bobbs-Merrill Reprint Series in European History, E-102.
2. Henrique da Gama Barros, *História da administração publica em Portugal nos seculos xii a xv*, 2d ed., ed. Torquato de Sousa Soares, 11 vols. (Lisbon, 1945–54), 6: 161–78; *HIP*, 1: 109–13, and 309; J[oão] Lúcio de Azevedo, *Épocas de Portugal económico*, 2d ed. (Lisbon, 1947), 46.

predecessor, John III, who sanctioned the issuance of the first land patents (sesmarias) to the colleges of Bahia and Rio de Janeiro and the initial assignment of temple (pagoda) lands to the colleges of Old St. Paul's and Rachol, a practice that Sebastian continued.[3] The crown's assent was, of course, necessary to sanction the Society's acquisition of privately owned property, and, as will be seen later, procuring such licenses involved procedures that were often lengthy, tedious, and fraught with pitfalls; nevertheless, the Jesuits were usually successful in having legal obstacles to ecclesiastical ownership of lands waived (see Chapter 16).

As indicated in Chapter 14, the Jesuits also obtained property from private parties in various ways. Some persons elected to convey their estates to the Society by means of inter vivos trusts that allowed them to enjoy the fruits of their estates for the rest of their lives. That was true, for example, of the widow Isabel de Aguiar, who donated several Indian villages to the Society. Similarly, about 1595, Fernão Carvalho and his wife, residents of the island of Madeira, made an agreement with the new college of São João Evangelista in Funchal promising to assign to it their farm, known as Pico do Cardo, in return for an initial payment of 100,000 rs. and installments of 30,000 rs. per year for the rest of their lives. Since they lived for another seventeen years, the college's expenditures in behalf of Pico do Cardo ultimately reached 610,000 rs. Some living trusts, however, cost recipient institutions very little. At the beginning of the seventeenth century, Gaspar Alvares, the famous slave merchant in Luanda, made an inter vivos agreement with the local college by which he promised to pay 20 contos upon his death; months later he expired as a Jesuit brother.[4]

Colleges also obtained lands through exchanges with other ecclesiastical proprietors, a long-established custom. As Charles Parain wrote with respect to that practice during the Middle Ages, "There were constant exchanges of land between ecclesiastical lords. Very often the object was merely the rounding off of their estates," or, as he goes on to say, the evasion of canonical barriers against the alienation of ecclesiastical property.[5] Sometimes Jesuit colleges found it convenient to swap lands to achieve greater administrative efficiencies. One such instance occurred in the mid-1580s, when the arts college of Coimbra applied to Rome to sanction a land exchange with its sister college in Évora.[6] About the same time, the college of Bahia exchanged some houses with a local widow, and a piece of undeveloped land with another party.[7]

Though mere administrative convenience may explain these transfers, another motive —evasion of canon or secular law—may have been involved when, in 1590, José Adorno and his wife Catarina exchanged several leagues of land west of Rio de Janeiro for a mere

3. For the assignment of temple lands in the Konkan to the Jesuits, see *APO*:1, 5:1, 182–85, 231–34, 246–54, 286–90, 330, 335–37; 5:2, 694–97, 835–39, 992–93; *DI*, 2: 539–41; and *BFUP*, 1: 599 and 2: 454.

4. António Simão Lobo de Matos, "Relação da fundação do colégio de São João Evangelista," Funchal, n.d., in AHU/PA/Madeira, *cx.* 1, no. 229; *HCJAP*, 2:2, 570.

5. Parain, "The Evolution of Agricultural Technique," in *The Cambridge Economic History of Europe*, ed. M. M. Postan (Cambridge, 1966), 1: 201.

6. Sebastião de Morais (procurator) to Aquaviva, Lisbon, 24 Apr. 1586, in *DI*, 14: 28. Between 1579 and 1611, the same college expanded its quinta of Vila Franca through the addition of 26 parcels, four of which were obtained by exchanges. "Informaçam dos bens de raiz que os collegios da Companhia de JESV tem neste reyno de Portugal," ca. 1611, in ANTT/CJ/57, no. 26, fols. 5ᵛ–7ᵛ.

7. *DH*, 64: 11–15; *HCJB*, 1: 150–51.

88 meters of land along the São Vicente–Santos road in neighboring São Paulo. The beneficiary of that transaction was the new college in Rio de Janeiro, and the Adorno exchange became a key addition to its famous Santa Cruz estate (see below).[8]

Long before the coming of the Jesuits, ecclesiastical bodies were accustomed to rely upon third parties to facilitate property transfers that may have been illegal, or at least would have inflamed "public opinion" had the real owner's identity been revealed. The Jesuits used this technique to advantage in both the Spanish and the Portuguese assistancies.[9] In 1585 the fathers in Lisbon had an opportunity to purchase the quinta of Campolide on the northern outskirts of the capital, a desirable recreational facility for the members of the professed house (São Roque). To prevent gossip, the fathers procured the services of André Lopes, prior of the parish of Santo André and brother of a Jesuit father, who bought the property, ostensibly for himself. He then made over the title to São Roque, which assigned the property to the new Lisbon novitiate in 1624.[10] As the *cartório jesuítico* in Portugal's National Archives demonstrates, third parties assisted several Jesuit institutions in the kingdom in acquiring houses and fragments of rural estates from the late sixteenth to the mid-eighteenth century.[11]

Third parties also facilitated the enlargement of some of the Jesuits' famous estates in Brazil. In 1649, for example, a couple purchased some cane lands in the parish of Passé, Bahia, and immediately sold them to the local college for 220,000 rs., precisely what they had paid for them.[12] During the late seventeenth and early eighteenth centuries, at least four parcels that were attached to the engenho Santana de Ilhéus were acquired through the intervention of third parties.[13]

The most famous example of such intervention is the role of Salvador de Sá, onetime governor of Rio de Janeiro, royal councilor, wealthy landowner, ambitious entrepreneur, and founder of the college of Santos, in facilitating Jesuit acquisition of much of northern Rio de Janeiro—the celebrated campos de Goitacazes. In 1617 the fathers gained their first foothold in the area when they founded the mission (aldeia) of São Pedro. The same year, the college received one-third of a sesmaria, the balance being assigned to the aldeia. In 1630 the Jesuits petitioned the governor of Rio de Janeiro in behalf of the Goitacá Indians for additional lands between the Macaé and Paraíba rivers, claiming that their charges had been crucial in defending the district against Dutch intruders. But since some of the lands they wanted had already been awarded to a group of landed magnates known as the "seven captains," the fathers received only part of what they sought. Then, in 1648, Salvador de Sá arranged for a new division of lands in the Goitacazes that was notoriously beneficial to the Jesuits, the Benedictines, and Sá himself. As a result, the fathers gained a quarter of

8. *HCJB*, 1: 421.

9. Cf. François Chevalier, *Land and Society in Colonial Mexico: The Great Hacienda*, trans. Alvin Eustis, ed. Lesley Byrd Simpson (Berkeley, 1966), 243–44; and Herman W. Konrad, *A Jesuit Hacienda in Colonial Mexico: Santa Lucia, 1576–1767* (Stanford, 1980), 23.

10. *HCJAP*, 2:1, 199. Strangely, Fr. Rodrigues failed to point out that, in accordance with the *Constitutions*, professed houses were forbidden to own real property. See also António Franco, *Imagem da virtude em o noviciado da Companhia de Jesus na corte de Lisboa* (Coimbra, 1717), 8.

11. ANTT/CJ/84, passim.

12. "Trespasse que fez Manuel de Souza Dalpoim e sua mulher, Maria Rabela Correia, aos . . . padres da companhia," 26 June 1649, in *DH*, 63: 281–86.

13. Inventory of Santana, 27 July 1759, in AHU/PA/BA, 1st cat., no. 4947.

the disputed lands, which were organized into three large cattle and sugar properties: the fazenda dos campos de Goitacazes (also known as the *fazenda do colégio*), Campos Novos, and Macaé.[14]

Though the use of proxies and intermediaries contributed significantly to the buildup of Jesuit patrimony, most lands were acquired by donations (see Chapter 14) and purchases. During the sixteenth century, as Nicholas P. Cushner and several other scholars have pointed out, Jesuit land acquisitions in Hispanic America were primarily the products of donations or endowments; thereafter, however, the colleges purchased far more property than they were given. Herman W. Konrad also suggests that "by the late 1580s, the Jesuits [of New Spain] adopted a policy of active land acquisition," one they continued to pursue until the general expulsion.[15]

I suspect that similar patterns existed in the Portuguese Assistancy, although the balance between gifts and purchases seems to have varied from place to place and from period to period. Of the nearly 170 parcels obtained by the college of São Lourenço, Porto, between 1562 and 1619, 36 (or about 21 percent) were gifts; the remainder were purchases.[16] Between 1550 and 1590, the college of Salvador, Bahia, benefited from thirteen property acquisitions, of which four, including a leasehold, were purchases, all made in the mid-1580s. All nine parcels that the college added between 1636 and 1650, during the Dutch war, were direct purchases.[17] Between its establishment in 1567 and 1616, the college of Rio de Janeiro acquired thirteen parcels of land, of which six represented direct purchases.[18] As disclosed in Chapters 13 and 14, gift-giving by the crown and private donors continued to be a major source of acquisitions in India into the eighteenth century.

The Extent of the Jesuits' Patrimony

No complete survey of Jesuit territorial holdings in the Portuguese Assistancy exists, but there is a variety of evidence that attests to the success of the Jesuits in acquiring an impressive patrimony to help defray the expenses of their institutions. Konrad has suggested that in colonial Hispanic America, "the timing of the [Jesuits' land] acquisitions varies but not the patterns."[19] In Portugal, the major accumulation of properties appears to have occurred between the late 1570s, when the previously mentioned crown seed grants were issued to enable certain colleges to purchase real estate, and the second decade of the seventeenth century, when the Jesuits' legal right to their properties was first seriously

14. A good deal has been written about the Jesuits' controversial Goitacazes acquisitions. For some of the sources, see *LTC/RJ*, 300–303, 306–9, and the documents following. See also Alberto Lamego, "Macaé a luz de documentos ineditos," *Anuario geográfico do estado do Rio de Janeiro* 11 (1958): 1–152; *LAM*3: 228–30; C. R. Boxer, *Salvador de Sá and the Struggle for Brazil and Angola, 1602–1686* (London, 1952), 286–87; *HCJB*, 6: 78–84; and William Harrison, "A Struggle for Land in Colonial Brazil: the Private Captaincy of Paraiba do Sul, 1533–1753" (Ph.D. diss., University of New Mexico, 1970), 33–34 and 57–71.

15. Nicholas P. Cushner, *Lords of the Land: Sugar, Wine and Jesuit Estates of Coastal Peru, 1600–1767* (Albany, 1980), 28 and sources cited there; Konrad, *Jesuit Hacienda*, 49.

16. "Enformação das fazendas q. tem o coll.º do p.to feita em 12 de jan.ro de 1619," in ANTT/CJ/57, no. 31.

17. *HCJB*, 1: 149–54; *DH*, 63: 249–350, passim.

18. *LTC/RJ*, 33–259, passim.

19. Konrad, *Jesuit Hacienda*, 410–11 n. 8.

contested (see Chapter 17). In a special report, the province disclosed that between 1579 and 1611, the college of Santo Antão had acquired 46 properties, led by the quintas of Caniços, Enxobregas, and Val do Rosal. By the latter date, the arts college of Coimbra also possessed three large estates—the quintas of Canal, Vila Franca, and Cheira—as well as 85 other properties ranging from houses and small plots to sizable hectarages. By 1611 the college of Braga owned 42 parcels; that number had increased to 47 by 1618. Even the small colleges, both those already established and those still being formed, had significant holdings by that date: that of Bragança possessed ten properties, Faro in the Algarve owned seven, and Luanda, Angola, held thirteen. In the same year, the incipient college of São Miguel in the Azores reported that its holdings, mostly wheat lands, consisted of four parcels on the island of São Miguel and another thirteen on Fayal. Its lands were valued at 2,375,000 rs. and annually produced nearly 110,000 kilograms of grain. Most surprising of all, the college of São Lourenço, Porto, owned nearly 170 properties by 1619. Among them were eighteen houses, four or five farms, six vineyards, three stores, and a balance consisting of various segments of cereal-producing plots or farms.[20]

Some colleges continued to add to their holdings for decades. In 1655, for example, the minor college of Faro boasted 21 parcels of income-yielding property, including a farm, an orchard, several vineyards, wheat lands, and groups of houses—three times the number of properties that the college of Funchal, Madeira, then reported.[21] But such holdings were modest compared with those enjoyed by some of the Brazilian colleges. For example, by the 1750s, the possessions of the college of Santo Alexandre, Pará, included three agricultural estates, eight cattle ranches, 25 small plots, assorted houses, and a staggering total of more than 2,000,000 kilometers of land.[22] An eighteenth-century report by the college in Maranhão lists 21 properties but curiously omits its massive sugar estate, São Bonifácio.[23] The other major colleges in the colony, Salvador and Rio de Janeiro especially, possessed comparable holdings.[24]

Brazil, of course, was a vast colony that occupied much of a continent, so the existence of Jesuit latifundia there is not surprising. What *is* startling is the success of the fathers in gaining extensive holdings in the subcontinent of India, where, as seen in other chapters, the Portuguese never held more than shallow enclaves and, by the eighteenth century, were hard pressed to retain even those. A report of 1635–36 limited to the Bassein-to-Damão stretch of the west coast reveals that several houses, including the colleges of Bassein, Damão, New St. Paul's, and Taná and the province of Japan, possessed 82 properties in

20. This paragraph rests primarily upon ANTT/CJ/57, nos. 26, 31, 57, 83, and 86.

21. "Catalogo das fazendas E rendas do coll.º de Faro no anno de 1655," and "Catalogo 4 das fazendas do coll.º de Funchal," ca. 1655, in ARSI, *Lus.*, fols. 137 and 133.

22. The sources utilized for this analysis include several summaries dating from ca. 1761 in AHU/PA/PA *cx.* 14, an estate inventory of 1761 in ibid., *cx.* 21, and the indispensable codex ARSI, *Bras.*, 28, esp. fols. 9–22.

23. "Rol das fazendas e terras que possuem os pp. da Companhia de Jesus no Maranhão," n.d. [perhaps ca. 1734], in *LAM3*: 361–62.

24. A report entitled "Titulos de todos os bens de raiz e propriedades que possui o colegio da Bahia," 5 July 1693, in ATC/CJ, no. 235, 118 fols., is less comprehensive than the title suggests, for it presents the licenses and confirmations for the college's land acquisitions that, with the exception of a single entry for 1650, were restricted to the 1550s through the 1590s. A more detailed analysis of the property holdings in each Brazilian college will be presented in the second volume of this study.

that district. They included coconut orchards, rice paddies, vegetable gardens, and salt pans.[25] A cadastral survey completed in 1716 reveals that the colégio máximo of São Paulo then possessed 147 parcels of land, mostly coconut groves, in the vicinity of Goa. Between 1725 and 1750, the number of coconut orchards that the college of Salsete (or Rachol) possessed increased from 20 to 27.[26] By 1730 most of the other colleges attached to the provinces of Goa and Malabar derived between 18 and 100 percent of their income from estates.[27] Though further accumulation of property in India thereafter was undoubtedly retarded by the highly destructive Maratha campaign (see Chapter 23), it is nevertheless easy to agree with Konrad that "the transfer of land from indigenous control . . . eventually into Jesuit control was an unabating process," one that continued until the uprooting of the Society.[28]

Some Further Considerations Concerning the Jesuits' Patrimony

According to the *Constitutions*, only probationary houses and colleges were authorized to possess landed property, a restriction not removed until the Twenty-fourth General Congregation (1892). Although leading Jesuit scholars have assumed that the restriction was always honored,[29] they failed to consult the Society's abundant surviving accounts, which disclose that incipient colleges, missions, or so-called residences, and even provinces and professed houses, acquired lands and depended upon their incomes.[30] The 1611 provincial report mentioned above reveals that the future colleges of Santarém, Portalegre, and São Miguel already possessed several estates, and that the Cape Verde residence owned three blocks of houses in Lisbon. In the East, the Mysore, Qatar, Sunda, Pedania, and Agra missions attached to Goa province relied upon assured sources of income derived from lands in India, as did the missions in North Vietnam.[31] Even the Japan province owned estates, both in India and in the kingdom, and the vice-province of China also possessed lands in the Indian subcontinent. Sometimes, for administrative purposes, properties were temporarily assigned to established colleges until arrangements could be worked out to

25. "Lista das pacarias e aldeas que possuem os padres da Companhia de Jesus na cidade de Baçaim e em Tanna e Bandora," ANTT/LM, 35, fols. 357–60. The list was authenticated in Bassein on 28 Feb. 1635 by the desembargador, Luís Mergulhão Borges, and was countersigned in Goa on 8 Mar. 1636 by Sebastiam Soares Paes, another royal functionary. I am indebted to Anthony R. Disney for calling the document to my attention and to Karubaki Datta for very kindly transcribing it for me.

26. HAG 7593, an elephant folio of 100 leaves, is a priceless register of New St. Paul's lands as confirmed by the college procurator, several village chieftains (*gancares*), and the desembargador juiz do tombo. Their deliberations began on 25 Feb. 1715 and concluded on 22 Feb. 1716. The identities of Rachol's palm orchards are recorded in "Receita e despeza do colegio de Rachol, 1725–1730 e 1748," in HAG 2048–49.

27. Reports of income and expenditures, 15 Nov. 1730 and 10 Jan. 1731, encl. in João de Saldanha da Gama to king, Goa, 23 Jan. 1731, in AHU/PA/IN, *m.* 35.

28. Konrad, *Jesuit Hacienda*, 137.

29. E.g., *HCJB*, 4: 167; *DI*, 14: 212 n. 12.

30. The constitutional restriction that supposedly prevented professed houses from owning properties or enjoying certain revenues did not prevent them from having recreational properties.

31. See notes 6 and 26. The "L[ivr]o da receita e despeza das fazendas vindas das missoes e collegio de Macao 1693 [*sic* for 1692]–[1736]," HAG 1497, is an invaluable record of remittances derived from rice, coconuts, fish dues, quitrents, and loans in the northern province that were sent to Macao. The accounts are divided into funds due the Japan province, those belonging to the college of Macao, and those for the North Vietnam mission.

place them under the control of the intended beneficiary. For example, until about 1620, the trans-Tagus quinta of Carcavelos, a key estate of the Japan province, was administered by Santo Antão, which also was in charge of another estate, the quinta of Labruja, likewise left by a Jesuit for another facility, in this case the new college of Santarém.[32] Similarly, in India, the villages surrounding Assalona, discussed below, were allotted to the province of Japan before being reassigned to that of Malabar.

The acquisition of a landed portfolio was primarily the responsibility of each college. The properties that a college obtained were subject to the restrictions imposed by the *Constitutions* and the Institute, and required the approval of either the provincial or the Visitor. Cushner observes that "until 1699 ... [there was] no clear directive ... by the Jesuit central office in Rome about the process of acquiring land. It was more or less left up to each college to determine the quantity and quality of its acquisitions," another unrecognized illustration of the decentralized structure of the Society. Cushner reports that in 1699, Father-General Tirso Gonzalez de Santalla tried to reduce the likelihood of unwise accretions of land by insisting that anticipated income and expenditures be estimated before further parcels were accepted or purchased; if the rector and his advisors urged their acquisition, that recommendation was to be reviewed, and approved or rejected by the provincial and his consultores.[33] Presumably it was also intended that such scrutiny occur within the Portuguese Assistancy, but I have never seen evidence of it, nor any reference to the 1699 decree.

The 1699 directive was apparently intended to prevent colleges from being burdened with excessive or unproductive properties. Though some writers subscribe to the myth of the "dead hand of the Church," that is, the belief that once an ecclesiastical body gains control over land it is forever lost to the tax rolls and to the market,[34] in fact Jesuit institutions often disposed of unwanted properties with the consent of the fathers general. In 1594 the original premises of Santo Antão were sold to another religious Order, since the Society no longer needed them.[35] The next year the college of Rio de Janeiro vended a recently donated parcel measuring 1,023 meters by 3,300 meters to the Carmelites, who owned an adjacent property.[36] In 1612 both the provincial of Goa and the Visitor agreed that certain houses in Salsete do Norte (the northern province) should be sold because they were wasting resources.[37] Five years later the provincial of Portugal recommended the disposal of two properties belonging to the University of Évora, one because it did not pay for itself, the other because the extrusion of salt had destroyed the fertility of its soil.[38] In the mid-seventeenth century, the arts college of Coimbra also reported the sale of a substantial

32. "Informação por parte do p. p[rocurad]or geral ... da prov.ª de Portugal sobre a materia de dizimos," n.d. [ca. 1611], in ANTT/CJ/80, no. 6; "Contas feitas entre o collegio de S. Antão e a quinta de Labruja desde jan.ʳᵒ de 1610 ate 9 de agosto de 1612," in ANTT/CJ/58, no. 4.

33. Cushner, *Lords*, 38.

34. For a recent expression of this myth, see Joel T. Rosenthal, *The Purchase of Paradise: Gift Giving and the Aristocracy, 1307–1485* (London, 1972), 141. William B. Taylor long ago discredited the substance of the myth with respect to most church lands, excepting, of course, chantries, other pious gifts, and dowries. See *Landlord and Peasant in Colonial Oaxaca* (Stanford, 1972), 194.

35. *HCJAP*, 2:1, 208.

36. *RADF*, 3 (1896): 251.

37. HAG 1890, fol. 30ʳ.

38. Francisco Pereira to Vitelleschi, 14 May 1617, in ARSI, *Lus.*, 74, fol. 138ʳ.

estate for 90,000 rs., but it did not reveal the reason for its disposal.[39] Between 1646 and 1670, the college of Santo Antão, which owned the massive engenho Sergipe do Conde in Bahia (see Chapter 16), sold half a dozen parcels of that plantation, also for reasons undisclosed.[40] Yet such sales were the exception, not the rule, for wherever possible the colleges retained the properties they acquired and developed.

Sometimes donors themselves mandated the sale of certain lands to raise funds for devotional or other purposes, especially perpetual masses or the support of special schools.[41] In 1653 a Jesuit official reported the sale of lands worth more than 2 contos in the Cape Verde Islands, from which the Society had withdrawn in 1642 (see Chapter 9).[42] Nearly four decades later, the college of Olinda sought permission from Jesuit headquarters to sell two parcels of land in Pernambuco because of protracted litigation, sterility of the soil, and remoteness from the owner institution.[43]

A quite different situation prompted the liquidation of the Japan province's real-estate holdings in Bombay, where the agents of the East India Company were making life increasingly unpleasant for the Jesuits after the island's transfer in 1665 (see Chapters 8 and 17). Seeing the handwriting on the wall, Fr. Manoel Henriques, the province's resident procurator, began selling 48 pieces of land on the island, mostly coconut orchards, in 1675. Within a quinquennium he had disposed of nearly all of them, as well as ten groups of houses situated in the new English town. In 1687–88 he invested the proceeds—14,578,800 rs.—in the large, relatively safe estate of Taleigão, situated in the village of that name on the island of Tissuary, where Goa was located.[44]

The practice of disposing of unneeded property continued in the eighteenth century. In 1730, for example, the father general approved a petition by the college of Maranhão to sell various small parcels in the captaincy that yielded modest amounts in order to purchase others adjacent to the college. A few years earlier, sometime before the triennial report of 1722, the college of Rio de Janeiro sold a sugar estate near its famous *engenho velho* property for 5,200,000 rs. in order to build a sumptuous mansion in the city. The intent of that transaction was to employ the mansion's rental income to embellish a new church that the college planned to erect.[45]

39. "Terceiro catálogo das cousas da província de Portugal [1649]," in ARSI, *Lus.*, 44:II, 559–61.

40. *DH*, 62: 199–210, 237–54, 351–80. It also sold another parcel in 1710. Ibid., 341–45.

41. E.g., "Titulo das capelanas legados mand.[as] e deixas que deixaram varios devotos a este igr.[a] e casa professa [Bom Jesús]," ca. 1700–1709, HAG 2092; AHU/PA/BA, 1st cat., no. 5586. Sometimes donors of chantries (capelas) left money to be invested in lands to generate income for perpetual masses. About 1710, Baltazar da Veiga left 1,350,000 rs. in estates that were to be sold so that their proceeds could be invested in the existing Bamboly property to underwrite the cost of such a mass. ARSI, *Goa*, 9:II, 467–73[v].

42. António Dias, "Sobre se aver de vender as faz.[das] de Cabo Verde," Lisbon, 20 Feb. 1653, in ANTT/CJ/80, no. 11.

43. Two Latin petitions, one dated 5 Aug. 1692, the other 9 Feb. 1693, both in ARSI, FG, 1477/25.

44. Memorandum that begins "Tem esta prov.[a] de Japão as fazendas q. se comprarao em Taleigão, ilha de Goa, [*sic*] q. custarao' 52,623 xerafins e 14 rs.," BA/JA/49-IV-66, fol. 97. The Bombay sales provided 92.3 percent of the purchase price of the Taleigão property. In 1595 the island of Tissuary was divided into 31 villages, including that of Taleigão. Francisco Pais *(provedor mor dos contos de Goa)*, "Tombo da ilha de Goa e das terras de Salcete e Bardes," *Boletim do instituto de Vasco da Gama*, no. 62 (1945): [73–192], at 81, 92, 95, and 100.

45. General (either Michelangelo Tamburini [d. 1730] or Francisco Retz, his successor) to commissioner general and provincial of Portugal, 1730 (no month or day), in ARSI, *Bras.*, 25, fol. 49; *HCJB*, 6: 73.

The Society's properties were sometimes situated near the owner colleges, but that was not always the case. Though many of Braga's properties were near the college, others were located as far as 50 kilometers distant.[46] Braga's northern brother, the college of São Lourenço, possessed lands not only within the confines of the kingdom's second city, Porto, but also as far away as Barcelos and Torres Vedras. The latter community, 42 kilometers north of Lisbon, included São Lourenço's major estate, the quinta of Arneiro, a major olive producer. The possessions of Santo Antão were even more scattered. They included the quinta of Caniços, in the district of Torres Novas, about 110 kilometers north-northeast of Lisbon; some liens (*censos*) on properties in Santarém, 75 kilometers northeast of the capital; the celebrated Val do Rosal estate near Almada, opposite Lisbon; some pasture lands on the island of Terceira, in the Azores; and two famous sugar engenhos in Brazil, Santana de Ilhéus and Sergipe do Conde, of which more will be said in the following chapter.[47] Similarly, the University of Évora collected revenues from the village of Monte Agraço (see below) and drew income from S. Salvador de Paço de Sousa, a tenth-century monastery erected on the left bank of the Rio Sousa, 7 kilometers from Penafiel and 28 kilometers from Porto. The supporting lands of the Lisbon probationary house were also widely dispersed: many were situated in the Alentejo, some as far east as Estremoz, others as far north as Vieiros (apparently S. Miguel de Vieiros, in the district of Braga).[48]

In Brazil, properties tended to be clustered near owner colleges, but a very different pattern existed in the East, where the Indian subcontinent provided estates that supported Jesuit enterprises from South Asia to Mozambique. As seen in an earlier chapter, beginning in the 1570s the leaders of the Japan enterprise, acting upon the suggestion of Father General Borgia, began acquiring estates in the vicinity of Bassein.[49] The heads of the vice-province of China, which was always precariously financed, also hoped to acquire revenue-producing lands. To that end, a Bohemian father, Wenzel Pantaleon Kirwitzer, who had arrived in Macao in mid-1619 with Adam Schall, was dispatched to Goa with "some pieces," presumably Chinese slaves, to sell to the Mughals in order to raise funds to buy property in Goa or in the northern province. After Kirwitzer signaled that both Mughal and Portuguese authorities were hostile to such a plan, Manoel Coelho was sent from Macao to Malacca to see whether property could be obtained there. Coelho found the local Jesuit superior supportive and reported that "lands are very fertile and abundant and cheap," that he had been assured that he could buy some on good terms, but that because the Malays were naturally lazy, it would be necessary to import Chinese coolies to serve as an estate work force.[50]

Since Malacca was soon a major Dutch target and was also subjected to raids by the Sumatrans (see Chapter 7), nothing came of Coelho's recommendations. In the end, the

46. "Rol das terras do colegio de Braga," Nov. 1618, in ANTT/CJ/57, no. 57.

47. By virtue of the mixed endowment that Fr. Duarte da Costa provided—the quinta of Labruja, a leasehold in Loures, some houses in Lisbon, and the revenues of the private captaincy of Peruacú in Bahia—the college of Santarém also drew income from Brazil for a time. *HCJAP*, 3:1, 5ff.

48. This paragraph rests especially upon the 1611 report on Jesuit properties in the kingdom: "Informaçam dos bens de raiz que os collegios da Companhia de JESV tem neste reyno de Portugal," in ANTT/CJ/57, no. 26.

49. Francisco Borgia to Gundislavus Alvares, 10 Jan. 1570, in *DI*, 8: 189. See also Chapter 3.

50. Coelho to Vitelleschi, Malacca, 12 Dec. 1621, in ARSI, *Goa*, 18, fols. 54^r–55^v.

vice-province, like the Japan province and several colleges of the Goa province, obtained some properties in the vicinity of Bassein, but whereas the Japan province withdrew from Bombay in the 1670s and bought property close to Goa, the others did not follow suit, with disastrous results after the successful Maratha invasion of the 1730s (see Chapter 23). Combarjuá, one of the islands near Goa, provided a large part of the revenue of the three clusters of missions in Mozambique, where the much-discussed prazos appear to have served merely as subsistence farms.[51]

The dispersed patterns of Jesuit landholdings were, of course, hardly unique. Tavistock Abbey, situated in Devon, possessed 27 parcels in three counties, whereas Westminster Abbey enjoyed income from 110 "principal estates" distributed throughout nineteen counties.[52] In Portugal the properties of venerable monasteries such as Alcobaça and Tibães were also dispersed over hundreds of kilometers.[53] The prevalence of Jesuit properties at home and abroad made the Society an obvious target for those critics who responded to centuries-old concerns about the extent of ecclesiastical holdings in the realm. As will be seen in a later chapter, such critics did not distinguish between parcels in a given community that belonged to the local college and those owned by more distant houses. In their eyes, the Jesuits were simply land rich while most of the king's other subjects were desperately poor. But what most attracted the critics' attention was the startling success of the Jesuits in assembling great estates that became the envy of their rivals, both ecclesiastics and laymen.

The Emergence of Great Estates

During the Middle Ages, many landlords, whether ecclesiastical or secular, utilized every opportunity to consolidate their estates by acquiring, through fair means or foul, nearby or contiguous properties in order to form great estates that became a source of admiration and indignation among their neighbors.[54] So, too, the Jesuits. Nearly a generation ago,

51. At least, that is the impression given by the meager coeval documentation, such as the periodic economic status reports (i.e., the third catalogues) sent to Rome from Goa. On the prazos see William Francis Rea, S.J., *The Economics of the Zambezi Missions, 1580–1759* (Rome, 1976), 84ff., and M[alyn] D. D. Newitt, *Portuguese Settlement on the Zambesi: Exploration, Land Tenure, and Colonial Rule in East Africa* (New York, 1973). Combarjuá Island is first mentioned as a source of income for Mozambique in the 1666 report (see note 87 below); by 1730 the western missions received two-thirds of its yield, the remainder being assigned to Old St. Paul's. See also note 27.

52. H. P. R. Finberg, *Tavistock Abbey: A Study in the Social and Economic History of Devon* (Cambridge, 1951), 5–6; Barbara Harvey, *Westminster Abbey and Its Estates in the Middle Ages* (Oxford, 1977), map II, following p. 470.

53. Cf. Aurélio de Araujo Oliveira, *A abadia de Tibães, 1630/80–1813*, 2 vols. (Porto, 1979), 1: chap. 2, which discusses the distribution of the Braga-based Benedictine abbey's landholdings. The topic is not mentioned in the otherwise illuminating study by Fernando de Sousa, "O rendimento das ordens religiosas nos finais do antigo regime," *Revista de historia economica e social* 7 (Jan.–June 1981): 1–27; but cf. Iria Gonçalves, *O património do mosteiro de Alcobaça nos séculos xiv e xv* (Lisbon, 1989), map facing p. 22.

54. The process is described by many writers, e.g., R. W. Southern, *Western Society and the Church in the Middle Ages* (Middlesex, 1970), 264; François Louis Ganshof and Adriaan Verhulst, "Medieval Agrarian Society in Its Prime: France, the Low Countries, and Western Germany," in Postan, ed., *Cambridge Economic History of Europe*, 1: 299–300; see also Georg Ostrogorsky, "Agrarian Conditions in the Byzantine Empire in the Middle Ages," in ibid., 214–15; J[ohn] Gilchrist, *The Church and Economic Activity in the Middle Ages* (New York, 1969), 99–100; and Penelope D. Johnson, *Prayer, Patronage, and Power: The Abbey of La Trinité, Vendome, 1032–1187* (New York, 1981), 53 and 59.

François Chevalier reminded his readers that in northern Mexico during the colonial era the fathers "systematically built up their rich estates in an amazingly short time and without difficulty. Relying on their powerful backers and lawyer friends (many of whom had attended their schools), they did not allow obsolescent clauses in title deeds to deter them from attaining ends that they felt justified the means: maintaining their colleges … and aiding their missions."[55] As Colmenares, Cushner, and Macera have demonstrated, the Jesuits also rapidly augmented their properties in various parts of Spanish South America.[56]

It is no surprise, therefore, to discover that the same process occurred in the Portuguese Assistancy. In 1565 the College of the Holy Spirit, Évora, purchased the quinta of Loredo about two kilometers from the city. In quest of a closer estate that could serve as a recreational facility for the students and their instructors, the college acquired the vineyard of Valbom in 1582.[57] As Table 15.1 demonstrates, between the date of its purchase and the end of the century, the Jesuits enlarged the nuclear estate through fifteen transactions, most of which involved purchases. Although we cannot determine the size of the original quinta, of the one added in 1593, or of the three pieces acquired four years later, we may assume that the *courela* (var. *coirela*) was the standard narrow agricultural strip measuring 220 by 22 meters, so that the 11 courelas contributed a further 53.24 kilometers to the property. In 1571 the Coimbra branch of the Holy Office awarded the Jesuit-administered arts college the quinta of Vila Franca, a large olive-producing property situated along the Mondego River seized that year from its New Christian owners. By 1611 the Jesuits had successfully enlarged the estate by means of 26 transactions, mostly purchases, that involved primarily the acquisition of additional olive orchards, although part of the estate was devoted to the production of wine, vegetables, and citrus fruit and the raising of ducks. In short, Vila Franca became a classic demesne, or what in medieval England was termed the home farm.[58]

55. Chevalier, *Land and Society*, 242.

56. German Colmenares, *Las haciendas de los jesuitas en el nuevo reino de granada* (Bogotá, 1969), 61–67 (I wish to thank Herbert Klein for kindly making available to me a copy of this scarce book); Nicholas P. Cushner, *Farm and Factory: The Jesuits and the Development of Agrarian Capitalism in Colonial Quito, 1600–1767* (Albany, 1982), 42 and 56; idem, *Jesuit Ranches and the Agrarian Development of Colonial Argentina, 1650–1767* (Albany, 1983), 17 and 19; Pablo Macera, ed., *Instrucciones para el manejo de las haciendas Jesuitas del Peru (ss. xvii–xviii)* (Lima, 1966), 14–16.

57. *HCJAP*, 2:1, 219–20, where the statement that Valbom was less expensive than Loredo is incorrect: Valbom cost twice as much.

58. "Os bens de raiz da Comp.ª neste reino" [ca. 1611], in ANTT/CJ/57, no. 26. The citrus trees were clearly planted by the Jesuits themselves. In 1579 the college reported the estate's income at 114,000 rs. and set its expenditures at 146,000 rs., but the rector confidently stated that because of the new trees and vines, it would yield a profit in the near future. "Renda q. tem o collegio de Coimbra em abril de 1579," in ARSI, *Lus.*, 84:I, fols. 69–71. His prediction proved correct: by 1619 Vila Franca possessed an income of 400,000 rs. "Rol das rendas do coll.º [de Jesus, Coimbra] desde … 1583 … ate … [1]619," in ibid., fols. 209ª–209ᵇ. A few years later, however, a severe flood led to expenditures of 800,000 rs. "Catalogo 3.º da provincia de Portugal … 1628," in ARSI, *Lus.*, 44:II, 474ᵛ–479ʳ. By about 1640, the estate's income had fallen by more than half. "Lista das rendas q. tem o coll.º de JESU da cidade de Coimbra," ca. 1640, in ARSI, *Lus.*, 84:I, 170–71.

On the traditional ecclesiastical home farm, see R. A. L. Smith, "The Benedictine Contribution to Medieval English Agriculture," in *Collected Papers* (New York, 1947), 105–6; Michael M. Postan, "Medieval Agrarian Society in Its Prime: England," in idem, ed., *Cambridge Economic History of Europe*, 2: 577–79; and Joyce Youings, "The Church," in H. P. R. Finberg, gen. ed., *The Agrarian History of England and Wales*, vol. 4, *1500–1640*, ed. Joan Thirsk (Cambridge, 1967): 314–15.

TABLE 15.1

Steps in the Formation of the Vineyard of Valbom, 1582–97

Year purchased	Transaction	Price (000 rs.)
1582	Quinta purchased from António Lopes Dalbergo	1,200
1582	Courela purchased from Francisco Inguarte	95
1582	Another courela purchased from Countess Bras	40
1582	Another courela purchased from Bras Godinho	38
1584	Another courela purchased from Luis Nunes	45
1584	Another courela purchased from Rodrigo Fernandes	50
1585	Another courela purchased from António Moreno	35
1585	Courela exchanged for a *farragem* owed by Brites de Cunha	50
1586	Another courela purchased from Mateus P.iz Pires	48
1586	Another courela purchased from D[oming]os Lopes	30
1590	Another courela purchased from F[rancis]co de Estremoz	80
1590	Another courela purchased from D.os Per.a	80
1593	Another quinta purchased from D.os Per.a	400
1597	Vineyard purchased (fee simple) from D.os Per.a	80
1597	Small vineyard purchased from Elena Gaga	14
1597	Leasehold (*util dominio*) of same purchased from Marcal P.iz	14
	Total cost to 1 December [1597]	2,300

SOURCE: "Rol das vinhas, q. comprou o Coll.º de Évora em Valbom," ca. 1597, in ANTT/CJ/57, no. 52.

The same college enjoyed similar success in expanding two grain-producing monastic properties assigned to it by John III (see Chapter 2). One was the ancient Benedictine house of São Fins, situated above the Tuy River in the municipality of Valença on the northwest frontier. With papal approval, the college took over that monastery and its lands in 1548; by 1611 it had added 33 properties by purchase, 3 by gift, and several others that had been seized for debts. Between 1600 and 1618, it made 23 additions to the estate: seven in 1600; five in 1602; two each in 1604 and 1605; one each in 1610, 1613, and 1614; and four in 1618.[59] The heads of the arts college also augmented its other former monastic property, S. João de Longosvales, a former Augustinian house located on the left margin of the Minho River near the town of Monsão. It was assigned to Coimbra in 1551; by 1611 the nuclear estate had grown through the acquisition of twenty parcels—fifteen by purchase, three by gift, and two as a result of litigation.[60]

Sometimes Jesuits moved with exceptional alacrity to augment new acquisitions. That appears to have been the case with the quinta of Labruja, an olive orchard situated near the town of Golega, about halfway between Santarém and Torres Novas and 5 kilometers west of the Tagus. The quinta was part of the inheritance of Duarte da Costa, a novice who joined the Society in 1609 and expired four years later. The son of Portugal's chief armorer, who perished with Sebastian in 1578, Costa bore the name of his grandfather, Brazil's second governor-general (1553–57). Labruja became the

59. ANTT/CJ/57, nos. 26 and 63. Perhaps the most conspicuous Jesuit resident at São Fins was Simão Rodrigues, who sulked there for a time after being removed as Portugal's first provincial. Franco, *Lisboa*, 95.

60. ANTT/CJ/57, no. 26.

demesne of the college of Santarém, which did not open its doors until 1621. Prior to that date, as indicated above, it was administered by Santo Antão. According to its records, between 1613 and 1619, the property was enlarged through eleven purchases and three exchanges.[61]

It is possible to trace the same step-by-step process in the growth of two famous Jesuit plantations in Brazil: Santana on the south coast of Bahia in the district of Ilhéus, and Santa Cruz, situated 56 kilometers west of the city of Rio de Janeiro. The origins of Santana trace back to the regime of Brazil's third governor-general, the celebrated Mem de Sá (1557–72), who induced the private donatary of Ilhéus to assign to him a grant measuring 1.5 leagues by 1 league (about 9,450 by 6,300 meters) along the south bank of the Rio Santa Ana. Subsequently, with the evident concurrence of royal authorities, the limits of the grant were construed to extend along both banks of the river, an obvious advantage when water was the most expeditious way of moving cane from field to mill. Before his death, Sá obtained two further parcels, each half a league in extent. Santana became part of the governor-general's controversial inheritance and ultimately came into the possession of the Lisbon college of Santo Antão. Between the mid-1640s and 1716, eight of the college's resident managers successfully purchased nineteen additional, mostly contiguous, parcels of cane and woodlands for the engenho.[62]

We have no very clear idea of the extent of the enlarged Santana plantation, but we know that the fazenda of Santa Cruz became the grandest property that the Society possessed in Brazil. On 6 January 1576, Cristóvão Monteiro, described as an old resident of the town of São Vicente, received a sesmaria to certain lands that measured "four good leagues" along the seacoast. Eleven years later his widow, the marquesa Ferreira, divided the property between her surviving daughter and the Jesuit college in Rio de Janeiro. Then, on 12 February 1590, her married daughter and son-in-law elected to donate their share to the college in return for some modest plots in the vicinity of Santos. Accordingly, the college formally recognized the couple as its benefactors.

The remaining three acquisitions came as a result of purchases rather than gifts. In 1616 the college paid cash for a section measuring 1.1 kilometers by 3.3 kilometers. Nearly a half century later, in 1654, Tomé Correia de Alvarenga sold the college another three leagues of contiguous land, and two years later his brother-in-law sold it the final parcel, another three leagues. Thus by 1656, what Fr. Serafim Leite called "the most important property of the Fathers in the South of Brazil," and indeed its largest estate in the colony—some 63 square kilometers—was complete. In the eighteenth century, as many as 11,000 head of cattle grazed on the estate's extensive pastures. Its fields produced rice, beans, manioc, cotton, and sugar. Although it lacked a sugar mill, one was under construction at the time it was sequestered (1760). It boasted a carpentry, a manioc flour mill, a rice-husking plant, a limekiln, a tannery, a pharmacy, a fishery, and a boat-building yard capable of constructing canoes and large, ocean-going smacks. Like some other Jesuit estates in Brazil, its factories produced serviceable bricks, pots, and cotton

61. "Apontamentos da fazenda q. se comprou de rais neste coll.º do ano de [1]611 [até ca. 1619]," ANTT/CJ/57, no. 58. Internal evidence suggests that the property discussed in the memo was Labruja. For the donor, see *ASCJ*, 72, and *HCJAP*, 3:1, 5–6 n. 3.

62. Inventory of 27 July 1759, in AHU/PA/BA, 1st cat., no. 4947.

cloth. In short, Santa Cruz became a prime example of what Fr. Leite was fond of calling Jesuit polyculture.[63]

These are only a few of the many latifundia that the Jesuits successfully constructed in various parts of the Assistancy. Their primary function was to provide support—foodstuffs, other commodities, and cash from sales—for the owner colleges, but some had other advantages as well. In the midst of an outbreak of plague in 1590, the rector of the college of Espírito Santo sent all unnecessary personnel to the Loredo farm outside of Évora to escape the contagion.[64] Some estates served partially or entirely as convalescent and recreational facilities. A prime example is the famous quinta of Val do Rosal purchased by Santo Antão in 1559 in the district of Almada across the river from Lisbon. It was there amid vegetable gardens, vines, and citrus groves that the members of the ill-fated expedition led by Inácio de Azevedo prepared themselves physically and spiritually for their intended voyage to Brazil in 1570 (see Chapter 3). Val do Rosal also served as an assembly point for those embarking on the long voyages to India and other points east. In the end, following the Jesuits' arrest (1759–60), it also functioned as a concentration camp.[65]

The degree to which an owner college was economically dependent upon its demesne naturally varied with the magnitude of its income sources. Of the estates mentioned, Vila Franca contributed 2.1 percent of Coimbra's income in 1579, and only 2.8 percent in the mid-seventeenth century.[66] Loredo and Valbom together yielded 4.3 percent of Évora's revenues in 1582, but only 1.4 percent in 1606. In 1725, "the most abundant in these times," Loredo produced 2.8 percent of the funds entering the University of Évora.[67] On the other hand, Carcavelos, a major wine producer situated across the Tagus, left by Fr. Diogo Brandão to the Japan province (Chapter 14), was long a vital source of European funds for that province. In 1646 it provided 43.5 percent of the province's total income; in 1758–59 it still contributed 49 percent of the province's European revenues.[68] Near Goa, the same province's Taleigão estate contributed 14.3 percent of its non-European income in 1699; by 1730 that percentage may have doubled.[69]

The leaders of another precariously funded province, Malabar, desperately sought to recuperate from the devastating Dutch conquests of the mid-seventeenth century (Chapters 7–8) by finding a wealthy donor who would give them sufficient funds to buy a revenue-producing estate in India. About 1667, they succeeded in obtaining between 4,000,000 and

63. *HCJB*, 1: 420–22; 6: 54–66. See also Richard Graham, "Slave Families on a Rural Estate in Colonial Brazil," *Journal of Social History* 9 (Spring 1976): 382–402.

64. António Franco, *Imagem da virtude em o noviciado da companhia de Jesus no real collegio do Espírito Santo de Évora* (Lisbon, 1714), 361–62.

65. Baltasar Teles, in a most unusual passage, waxed eloquent about Val do Rosal: *Chronica da companhia de Jesu na provincia de Portugal*, 2 vols. (Lisbon, 1645–47), 2: bk. 4, chap. 8. See also António Franco, *Imagem da virtude em o noviciado da companhia de Jesus no real collegio de Jesus de Coimbra em Portugal*, 2 vols. (Évora and Coimbra, 1719), 2: 79–80. See also *HCJAP*, I:2, 478; and *MB*, 4: 74*.

66. ARSI, *Lus.*, 84:I, fols. 69–71, 170–71.

67. Ibid., 80, fol. 18; "Varias lembranças pera hum procurador . . . feito no anno de [1]606," BNL/FG, fols. 49–50; ARSI, *Lus.*, 81:II, fols. 570–72^v.

68. António Cardim, S.J., "Informatio pro provinciae japponiae" [1646], in *MHJ*, 1026–27; "Conta que derao os pp procuradores das prov.ªˢ da Companhia de Jesus em o ultramar," ca. Dec. 1758–Feb. 1759, ATC/CJ/266, fol. 4^r.

69. ARSI, *Goa*, 36:I, fol. 71; BA/JA/49-V-28, n. [130]. The 1730 estimates cited earlier (note 27 above) put Taleigão's share at only 15.8 percent.

4,800,000 rs. from the duchess of Naples and purchased a large coconut orchard in the Bardês peninsula, northwest of Goa, called Betím (Bety). By 1673 the viceroy had advised Lisbon that the Jesuits had been diligent in making improvements so that Betím was already *hua grande fazenda*, a large estate. In 1734 that estate, whose revenues were earmarked for the support of the Madura mission, supplied the province with 11.4 percent of its income.[70]

Considering the tangled political conditions that so often prevailed, one might not expect to find a Jesuit agricultural property in the Far East. The college of Macao possessed a fruit basket near the town, however. Its name was Ilha Verde, a small island that forms part of the port's inner harbor. The "green island" became a much-appreciated source of fruit—pineapples, figs, and peaches particularly—for the inmates of the local college. In Peter Mundy's day (1637), its surpluses even produced a small profit for the college.[71] Still, surprising as it may seem, considering the attention they attracted, estates in some parts of the Assistancy produced less income than the Jesuits garnered from other sources.

Land Revenues from Villages

Villages provided one additional source of income for the Jesuits. The taxable incomes of villages were sometimes assigned to the Society by the crown, sometimes bequeathed by pious donors, and sometimes purchased by administrative units of the Society. Charles Parain once remarked that during the Middle Ages, "the ownership of whole villages by ecclesiastical lords was by no means a general thing." Possibly not, but in England the practice was certainly not unknown. Raftis, for example, found that by 1086, Ramsey, one of the Fenland Abbeys near The Wash, a Benedictine house founded during the previous century, possessed income from 24 villages.[72] Whether that custom was widespread in Portugal needs to be determined. Only in one instance did a Jesuit institution in the kingdom receive income from such a source. In 1553, two years after the establishment of the College of the Holy Spirit, Évora, its founder, Cardinal Henry, with the pope's blessing, severed the revenues of the village of Sobral de Monte Agraço from the archdiocese of Évora and assigned them to the new college. That community, chartered by D. Manuel on 20 October 1519, is situated 40 kilometers north of the capital. Its claim to fame is that it formed the center of the famous defensive perimeter known as the Torres Vedras lines during the Peninsular campaigns against Napoleon's forces. Monte Agraço, as it was usually called, furnished the college, and subsequently the university, with between 2.8 and 8.5 percent of its revenues for the next two centuries.[73]

70. Undated memo, in ANTT/CJ/90, no. 66; *CR*, 11 Apr. 1668, in HAG/*LM*/34, fol. 259ʳ; Luís de Mendonça Furtado (viceroy) to prince regent, 11 Nov. 1673, in HAG/*LM*/38B, fol. 9ʳ; F/*JM*, 2: 346.

71. "Titolos dos bens de raiz deste collegio de Macao," [1] Jan. 1617, in ARSI, *JapSin*, 23, fol. 312; Peter Mundy, *The Travels of Peter Mundy, in Europe and Asia, 1608–1667*, ed. Sir Richard Carnac Temple and L. Anstey, *HS*:2, no. 45 (1919): 269. For Ilha Verde's location, see George Bryan Souza, *Survival of Empire: Portuguese Trade and Society in China and the South China Sea, 1630–1754* (Cambridge, 1986), map 4.

72. Parain, "Evolution of Agricultural Technique," 201; J. Ambrose Raftis, *The Estates of Ramsey Abbey: A Study in Economic Growth and Organization*, Pontifical Institute of Medieval Studies, *Studies and Texts* 3 (Toronto, 1957), 20.

73. For a brief history of the community, see *PDH*, 6: 1004; estimates of the revenues that the Jesuits collected from it appear in ARSI, *Lus.*, 80, fols. 18 and 226–27; "Varias lembranças pera hum procurador . . . [1]606," fols. 49–50; ANTT/CJ/80, no. 6; and ARSI, *Lus.*, 82:II, 570–72ᵛ.

In the East, certain Indian villages in the district of Salsete near Goa and in the northern corridor between Damão and Bassein—that is, Salsete do Norte, the northern province—provided vital revenues for the three eastern provinces and the vice-province of China. Land revenues, foros or quitrents, were an ancient source of taxes in India. In western India, according to Altekar, "ever since the foundation of our village communities during the fifth and fourth centuries B.C. the tax has been in existence."[74] In 1579 a Jesuit father, António de Monserrate, provided a unique description of how the levy was determined in Goan Salsete: two men from each of the dozen principal villages (aldeias) assembled in an agreed place with a scrivener to determine the tax rate. "When they have settled what has to be done, the scrivener gives a shout, like a crier at an auction ... which is their common agreement. . . . [The king's] revenue is limited in such a way that that amount is always given him, whether the lands yield much or little. And if an aldeia was lost and had no harvest, the others pay for it."[75]

Procuring income from villages was attractive to the Jesuits because it appeared to be less troublesome than operating plantations and less risky than making investments (see Chapter 22). The Jesuits' acquisition of village revenues seems to have begun in 1568, when the crown assigned four unnamed villages to Old St. Paul's in lieu of the wine and olive oil that it had pledged in 1552.[76] In 1571, Sebastian sanctioned the transfer of the revenues of two other villages to the same college.[77] That year the king also commuted a customs lien earmarked for the support of the college of Cochin to the revenues of the island of Divar in the vicinity of Goa.[78] During the next decade, Valignano, seeking to lessen the Japan missions' dependency upon the controversial silk trade, secured royal consent to obtain four villages near Bassein for the support of those stations.[79] By 1635 the Japan province and the colleges of Old St. Paul's, Bassein, Taná, and Damão could claim the land revenues of 29 villages, district centers (cassabes), or village wards (pacarias) in the northern province.[80]

The college of Cochin also claimed revenues from one of those 29 villages, that of Quirol (Kirol). With the consent of the dying King Henry, Quirol's revenues were purchased in 1580 with proceeds derived from the sale of certain houses left to the college by various donors. By 1586 Quirol was providing 16.5 percent of the college's income.[81] The village continued to furnish the Malabar Jesuits with important revenues until the English confiscated it in the late seventeenth century (see Chapter 17).

Situated in the southwestern part of Goa territory near the Salt River were three other villages whose income became vital to more than one Jesuit facility: the town of

74. A. S. Altekar, *A History of Village Communities in Western India* (Bombay, 1927), 63–64.

75. The passage was originally published in translation by H. Hosten, S.J. in "Father A. Monserrate, S.J., on Salsete, Chorão, Divar, and the Molucas [*sic*] 1579," Asian Society of Bengal, *Journal and Proceedings*, n.s. 28 (1922): 349–69, at 363, and was republished by Irfan Habib, *The Agrarian System of Mughal India (1556–1707)* (New York, 1967), 124. See also ibid., 240ff.; H. Fukazawa, "Maharastra and the Deccan: A Note," in Tapan Raychaudhuri and Irfan Habib, eds., *The Cambridge Economic History of India*, 2 vols. (Cambridge, 1982–84), 1: 196; and Habib, "Agrarian Relations and Land Revenue," in ibid., 239–44.

76. *DI*, 8: 405; cf. 2: 606–7.

77. *DI*, 8: 404–5.

78. Ibid., 16: 11* and sources cited there.

79. *MHJ*, 188.

80. See note 25.

81. *DI*, 14: 487–88.

Assalona (modern Assolna) and its two neighbors, Velim and Ambelim.[82] The three had been confiscated as a result of a campaign that Portuguese forces undertook in the mid-1580s to punish those accused of responsibility for the deaths of Rudolfo Aquaviva and his three fellow martyrs (see Chapter 3).[83] The crown granted title to those villages to the commander of the punitive force, D. Pedro de Castro, who, in 1587, assigned their income to the college of Cochin.[84] For a brief time their revenues assisted the Japan enterprise, but by 1616 the viceroy, D. Jerónimo de Azevedo, determined (why, we do not know) that they belonged exclusively to Cochin.[85] Subsequently the novitiate of Chorão claimed a share of their yield, but in 1644 an arbitrator in Rome, assigned by Father General Vitelleschi, ruled against the novitiate and in favor of Cochin.[86] Nevertheless, in 1653 the triennial economic report from the province of Goa listed one-half of the revenues from the three villages as contributing to the income of Old St. Paul's; thirteen years later Chorão appears in the records with the half share formerly enjoyed by Old St. Paul's.[87]

In the 1660s, when the Dutch virtually destroyed Jesuit operations in the Malabar province (see Chapter 8), Cochin's share of the revenues from Assalona and its two sisters became vital to the stricken province's survival. Between 1664 and 1670 the villages contributed 7,419,900 rs. to the province's income. Those funds were used to ransom Jesuit prisoners, to furnish living allowances for the handful of missionaries still active in Travancore and along the Fishery Coast, to provide travel expenses for small contingents of missionaries who slipped back into the occupied Malabar littoral from Goa, and to sustain an unspecified number of Franciscans, likewise expelled by the Dutch from Malabar, who had no funds of their own for their maintenance.[88] As late as the 1730s, Assalona and its sisters supplied the vestigial Malabar province with a substantial part of its income.[89]

Farther north, the village of Parel, situated at the northern end of Bombay Island about 4 kilometers from Bandorá, performed a comparable service during much of the seventeenth century for the Agra mission, the Jesuit outpost in the Mughal empire. In 1619 a mysterious benefactor, Mirza Zu'lqarnain (see Chapter 14), provided the funds that enabled the mission superior to purchase the village.[90] A decade and a half later, the Jesuits reckoned Parel as the

---

82. José Julião do Sacramento Almeida, *A aldeia de Assolna: Esboço historico-arqueologico e geografico* (Goa, 1958), a collection of previously published essays that Fr. Josef Wicki kindly called to my attention. There is a copy in the library of the Historical Institute of the Society in Rome.

83. Essential documents include *DI*, 12: 921 n. 19, 977, and 993. See also 7: 51*.

84. *DI*, 14: 628–37, 639–43; 15: 109, 128, 248 n. 16, 483, 539, and 653.

85. BA/JA/49-IV-66, n. 50. In 1610 Assalona supplied the Japan province with about 400,000 rs. in income, an amount reduced to a mere 159,900 rs. the next year. HAG, cod. 1890, fol. 29^r.

86. "Parecer do grande Padre Antonio Peres, lente de theologia, Colegio Romano, a favor do collegio de Cochim na controversia q. ouve entre o d.^{to} collegio e o noviciado de Goa sobre as aldeas," 7 Sept. 1644, in ANTT/CJ/90, n. 113.

87. Third catalogue, province of Goa, Dec. 1653, in ARSI, *Goa*, 25, fols. 135^r–136^r; "Lista das rendas e despezas da provincia de Goa . . . pera o Snor' Conde V. Rey Joam Nunes da Cunha," Goa, 13 Dec. 1666, in Cámara Municipal, Elvas, ms. 6891.

88. Francisco de Lucas, "Lista . . . tirado do livro das receitas E desp.^{as} dos rendimentos de Assolona depois da perda do coll.^{o} de Cochim," Goa, 20 Nov. 1670, in ARSI, *Goa*, 84^r–85^r, a detailed accounting for the years ending 30 May 1664 to 1670.

89. The 1730 report (see note 27) indicates that Assalona contributed 43.8 percent of the province's income, whereas the triennial report of 1734 estimated its share at 34.2 percent. F/JM, 2: 346.

90. Edward Maclagan, *The Jesuits and the Great Mogul* (London, 1932), 175–76. Maclagan states that the revenues of the village of Vadala were purchased at the same time, but I have seen no reference to this.

second most lucrative property they held in the northern province. By 1666 it furnished 75 percent of Agra's income, but late in the century it, too, was confiscated by the English.[91]

The crown continued to sanction the assignment of land revenues from villages to needy Jesuit institutions. In the early 1630s, for example, the count of Linhares, no real friend of the Society, authorized the small college of Damão to obtain the revenues from the nearby village of Nargol for its support. By the mid-1660s, Nargol contributed 45 percent of Damão's income.[92] Three decades later, another viceroy recommended that the Japan province, whose income had been severely curtailed during the century, be permitted to buy the revenues of the village of Morosi in the northern province near Bombay.[93] Three years later, the Japan province purchased rights to the income of another village, Malara, also situated in the northern province, to finance the pharmacy in the Macao college.[94] In 1700, Pedro II approved the purchase of the village of Gantacomprem on Tissuary Island to support two of Malabar's most imperiled outposts, São Tomé de Meliapor and Bengal. Finally, during the 1720s, the vice-province of China purchased the income from two villages in the northern province.[95] This appears to have been the last acquisition of that type made by Jesuits in the Assistancy.

It is difficult to be certain how lucrative such land revenues were for the Jesuits in the East.[96] According to Teotonio de Souza, the foro in Goa represented about 20 percent of the gross income of a village.[97] But a 1635 report of Jesuit holdings in the northern province indicates that the average yearly return from 28 of the 29 communities was only 2.68 percent of gross income.[98] Yet, as suggested by Table 15.2, many of the Jesuits' facilities in the Indian Ocean area drew a substantial share—in several instances an expanding share—of their income from village revenues.

The same may be said for those in the province of Japan and the vice-province of China. In 1719, 81.2 percent of the income from India came from villages; eleven years later villages still furnished 77.1 percent of the revenues from the subcontinent.[99] The income from the two villages in the northern province that the vice-province of China purchased in

91. See notes 25 and 87 for sources.

92. See note 87.

93. Souza, *Survival of Empire*, 190.

94. Malara was purchased in 1693. HAG 1497 is a register of its yield.

95. See note 27. The vice-province purchased Paspuly in 1722 and Olnem in 1729. Revenues from both were, of course, lost as a result of the Maratha invasions of the 1730s.

96. Habib reminds us that "the fiscal burden borne by each village did not ... consist entirely of land revenue." He adds that there were also assessments on particular trades as well as market and transit levies. *Agrarian System*, 243. Nevertheless, the documents that I have consulted indicate that the sums the communities paid the Jesuits came entirely from lands.

97. Souza, *Medieval Goa: A Socio-Economic History* (New Delhi, 1979), 78.

98. "Lista das pacarias e aldeas que possuem os padres da Companhia de Jesus na cidade de Bacaim e em Tanna e Bandora e do procurador de Jappao e na cidade e fortaleza de Damão," in ANTT/LM, cod. 35, fols. 357–58. (I am grateful to Karubaki Datta for transcribing the text for me.)

99. Joseph Anselmo, "Informe das rendas q. tem na India as provincias de Jappam e China," 6 Jan. 1719, in BA/JA/49-V-27, no. 197; Francisco Maria del Rosso (provincial secretary), ["Income and Expenses of Japan Province in India to 15 Nov. 1730"], Goa, 9 Jan. 1731, in BA/JA/49-V-28, no. [130], which incorporates data submitted, presumably by the procurator for the eastern provinces, to the crown concerning the income and expenses of the province of Japan, the vice-province of China, and the province of Malabar, 15 Nov. 1730 to 10 Jan. 1731, in AHU/PA/IN, *m.* 46. HAG 1497 provides an annual summary of remittances from the northern province to Macao in behalf of the Japan province from 1691 to 1735. The document is published

TABLE 15.2

*Percentage of Annual Income Derived from Indian Villages by Colleges in the Provinces of
Goa and Malabar, 1666 and 1730*

Institution	1666	1730	Institution	1666	1730
New St. Paul's	49.9	63.3	Damão	45.4	68.6
Novitiate (Chorão)	45.5	—	Mozambique	80.0	94.4
Bassein	69.8	80.0	Mughal mission (Agra)	75.0	—
Taná	100.0	79.5	Malabar province	—	62.5

SOURCES: "Lista das rendas e despezas da provincia de Goa," 13 Dec. 1666, Câmara Municipal, Elvas, ms. 6891; enc. of 15 Nov. 1730 and 10 Jan. 1731, in Manoel João de Saldanha da Gama to king, Goa, 23 Jan. 1731, in AHU/PA/IN, *m.* 35.

the 1720s accounted for 28 percent of the funds its agents collected in India in 1730, but that enterprise then also drew moneys from Europe and from China itself, so that the Indian villages accounted for only 9.6 percent of the vice-province's total revenues.[100] Nonetheless, when the Marathas overran the northern province later that decade, they severely crippled the finances of the vice-province of China and of many other Jesuit administrative units in the East.

Sources of Urban Income

Despite the Jesuits' commitment to rural evangelism, the Society was very much an urban Order. It was in the cities that it maintained its permanent facilities—preparatory schools, seminaries, colleges, probationary and professed houses. Each, especially the distinctive Jesuit churches with their massive, boxlike structures, their soaring vaulted ceilings, and their impressive but often spartan facades, reminded passersby of the Society's prominent, often dominant position in the community.[101] Less evident to such viewers were the income-producing properties that the Jesuits owned in the towns where they were represented. The Society was not, of course, the only religious Order to hold extensive urban real estate. In England, for example, before the dissolution of the monasteries, two-thirds of London and substantial parts of Lincoln, Exeter, Chester, and many other communities belonged to religious entities, especially Benedictine and Cistercian houses.[102] Judging from

---

in Souza, *Survival of Empire*, 193, table 7.2. Remittances peaked in 1703 and fell by about two-thirds by the mid-1730s.

100. "Estado de todas as rendas da v. provincia da China em 1731," in ARSI, FG, 627.

101. On Jesuit architecture, see particularly Lúcio Costa, "A arquitetura dos Jesuitas no Brasil," *Revista do serviço do patrimônio histórico e artístico nacional* 5 (1941): 9–100; Robert C. Smith, "Jesuit Buildings in Brazil," *Art Bulletin* 30 (Aug. 1948): 187–213; J. B. Bury, "Jesuit Architecture in Brazil," *The Month*, n.s. 4, 6 (Dec. 1950): 385–408; and Mário T. Chicó, "Algumas observações acerca da arquitetura da Companhia de Jesus no distrito de Goa," *Garcia de Orta: Revista da junta das missões geográficas e de investigações do ultramar*, special no. (1956): [257]–72.

102. R. A. Donkin, "The Urban Property of the Cistercians in Medieval England," *Analecta sacri ordinis cisterciensis* 15 (Rome, 1959): 104–31; Dom S. F. Hockey, *Quarr Abbey and Its Lands, 1132–1631* (New York, 1970), 92; C. H. Lawrence, *Medieval Monasticism: Forms of Religious Life in Western Europe in the Middle Ages* (New York, 1984), 111–12.

More than three decades ago, Dom David Knowles observed that "monasteries in . . . London or on its outskirts . . . owned much house property and urban land, but only in a few cases . . . did such revenues amount to more than half of the temporal total." *The Religious Orders in England*, vol. 3 (Cambridge, 1959), 249.

the distribution of urban holdings of Alcobaça, the same seems to have been true in medieval Portugal.[103] Although the Society's rural holdings contributed heavily to the financing of its urban institutions as well as to its missions and were among its most controversial assets, Jesuit institutions also possessed impressive urban portfolios whose yield sometimes equaled and occasionally exceeded the institutions' income from all other sources of support. That portfolio included shops, warehouses, single- and multi-story houses, blocks of apartments, and even a few mansions. Some came as gifts; others represented purchases or structures that Jesuit entities themselves built.

The crown itself encouraged Jesuit colleges to obtain urban properties. Sebastian's endowment of 40 contos to the college of Santo Antão was specifically intended to enable the college to acquire income-producing urban properties. Between 1569, when the grant was made, and about 1580, the college commissioned the construction of a number of houses and shops in the capital and purchased others.[104] There survives a single codex showing the properties that the college let in Lisbon during the year 1698.[105] Most of the 22 units were modest dwellings, rented to carpenters, shopkeepers, and soldiers. Despite the devastating effects of the Lisbon earthquake (1755), many of the college's rental units survived. Ten lots, nine of them dating from Sebastian's grant, containing 48 rental units, were still providing the college with a handsome income at the time of the Order's expulsion (1759). According to a report of 1770, these lots yielded a remarkably high return—9.9 percent of their appraised value, compared with only 4.4 percent for the college's rural estates.[106] The small college of São Lourenço, Porto, also utilized part of its royal seed grant to purchase urban real estate. As elsewhere, some buildings were demolished to permit the erection of the centrally located college and its grounds. By 1619, São Lourenço reported that it possessed eighteen blocks of houses.[107]

The Jesuits' acquisition and retention of property, whether urban or rural, depended upon both opportunities and policies that were set by the college with the approval of the provincials and possibly authorities in Rome itself. For example, though Santo Antão, São Lourenço, and certain other colleges mentioned in this section were committed to the ownership of substantial urban holdings, the University of Évora was not. In 1582 it reported that less than 1 percent of its income came from urban properties.[108] It is doubtful that that percentage was ever greater. The possession of townhouses represented a minuscule percentage of the income of the colleges in the Atlantic islands, too.[109]

The percentage of income that urban properties in the kingdom contributed to their owner colleges in the 1730s is summarized in Table 15.3. Their average is remarkably close to the 8 percent figure reported a century later for the surviving religious Orders, whose

103. Gonçalves, *O patrimonio*, map facing p. 108.
104. "Titulos que pertencem a acerca do colegio de S. Antão," in ANTT/CJ/2, nos. 12–24.
105. "L[ivr]º 6 dos alugeis de cazas do coll.º de S.ᵗᵒ Antam" [1698], in ANTT/CJ/102, no. 9.
106. "Autos que se processaro' para a avaliacao' e confrontacao' dos bens de raiz da caza que foy collegio de Santo Antao' desta cidade" [1770], in ATC/CJ/100.
107. "Enformação da fazenda q. tem o coll.º do Pᵗᵒ em 12 de jan[ei]rº de 1619," in ANTT/CJ/57, no. 31.
108. "Pauta de renda q. o collegio d'Evora te' nos annos por outrosa feita ao prim.ʳᵒ de dezembro de 1582," in ARSI, *Lus.*, 80, fol. 18.
109. Less than 1% in the cases of the incipient college of São Miguel, the Azores, and Funchal, Madeira. ANTT/CJ/57, no. 83; ARSI, *Lus.*, 45, fol. 133.

TABLE 15.3
Income Derived from Urban Properties as a Percentage of Total Income:
Province of Portugal, 1736–37

Facility	Total income (000 rs.)	Urban income (%)	Facility	Total income (000 rs.)	Urban income (%)
Braga	5,704	0.3	Santo Antão	5,470	11.9
Porto	3,609	2.3	Professed House, Lisbon	1,702	36.8
Coimbra	28,071	0.3	St. Patrick's Seminary	1,082	6.9
Portalegre	1,451	1.1	Setúbal	4,970	0.5
Elvas	1,046	12.2	Faro	688	9.0
Santarém	4,589	2.9			
			Average	5,307	7.7

SOURCE: "Ratio status temporalis domus et collegiani provincia Lusitania" [1736–37], in ARSI, FG, 627A/2. Income for Bragança and Évora was not reported.

properties were nationalized in 1834.[110] In some parts of the ultramar, that percentage was exceeded, but that was not the case everywhere.

In the Far East, first the Japan province and later the vice-province of China relied upon income from rentals of shops and houses to augment their always precarious finances. In 1609, for example, 6.9 percent of the Japan province's income came from property rentals in Macao, but by 1616–17 that had shrunk to 4.1 percent. During the dark year 1620, however, when the situation in the Japanese archipelago was becoming increasingly desperate and Dutch raiders were interdicting sea traffic, the province invested heavily in houses in Macao in the hope of providing assured income at the seat of its operations for its dangerous ventures elsewhere.[111] In the late 1630s, Fr. Paulo dos Santos, a former missionary in Japan, bequeathed the province a substantial fortune (4,800,000 rs.) to finance a seminary in Macao to train a dozen Japanese youths; two-thirds of his bequest was subsequently invested in urban properties.[112] By the mid-1640s, income from Macaonese properties accounted for 21.8 percent of the province's funds.[113] Just over a century later, the province also possessed eight housing units that it rented in Lisbon for 1,176,000 rs. a year.[114]

The vice-province of China also relied upon urban properties for part of its support. During the seventeenth century, these properties were situated exclusively in Macao, where their yield furnished the vice-province with between 10.1 and 33.7 percent of its annual income.[115] Forty years later it possessed houses and shops in Peking, the fruits of some

110. Sousa, "O rendimento," 18.

111. João Coelho, "Narração breve do número das casas, da gente, da renta, e gastos da companhia de Jappão," 12 Nov. 1609, in ARSI, *JapSin*, 23, fols. 33–40ᵛ (published in *MHJ*, 516–39); "Contas do Padre Manoel Borges . . . desta procuratura de Macao" [1616–17], in BA/JA/49-V-712; "3.º catalogo da provincia de Japam, feito em setembro de 1620," in *MHJ*, 868–69.

112. HAG 825 is a unique codex that shows how the earnings of the fund were employed from its founding until 1762. Because of a lack of suitable students, the proceeds were devoted to support a mission in Vietnam beginning in 1700.

113. António Cardim, "Informatio pro provincia japponiae" [1646], in *MHJ*, 1026–27.

114. "Conta que derao os PP procuradores das prov.ᵃˢ da Companhia de Jesus em o ultramar," ca. Dec. 1758–Feb. 1759, in ATC/CJ, no. 266, fols. 5ʳ–5ᵛ.

115. *MHJ*, 969 (for 1624); BA/JA/49-V-11, no. 76 (1661/67); ARSI, FG, 721/II/6 (1669); and ARSI, *JapSin*, 134, fols. 360–61 (1690/91).

19 contos contributed by Chinese and other supporters. Their net yield in 1731 represented 21 percent of the vice-province's income.[116]

The Goan and Malabar provinces preferred not to rely heavily upon income derived from urban properties. As early as 1575, when Valignano convened the famous Chorão meeting of Jesuit leaders, the delegates agreed that it was better to sell the town properties that the Society then possessed in India because rent collection was difficult and had become a source of "scandal and many complaints."[117] As a consequence, when urban properties were donated to Jesuit houses in India, they were sold and the proceeds invested in either village revenues or rural estates. Consistent with that policy, about 1612 both the Visitor and the provincial of Goa recommended that the Japan province liquidate some houses that it possessed in the subcontinent.[118] But that province continued to retain certain urban holdings until the 1670s, when its leaders directed the sale of ten lots of houses in Bombay. In 1730 only three Jesuit houses in the eastern provinces—Mozambique, Taná, and Diu— reported any urban income, and only in the case of Mozambique did it amount to as much as 5.6 percent.

Jesuit administrators in Brazil took a different view of urban properties. They were eager to acquire them, feeling that it was easier to collect rents in towns than it was to administer any other form of real estate, and that such income was at least stable, whereas earnings from plantations depended upon the vagaries of weather and international market conditions.[119] The board of guardians of Bahia's major charitable institution, the Santa Casa da Misericórdia, did not agree: they considered lending money at the legal rate of interest (6.25 percent until 1757) to be a wiser form of investment, and in the 1650s petitioned the crown for permission to dispose of unrestricted lands and houses given to the Santa Casa. Permission was granted in 1657; thereafter, the Santa Casa discouraged property legacies.[120]

But the Jesuits in Brazil never did. Beginning in the 1570s, the colleges of Bahia and Rio de Janeiro started to acquire parcels of urban property by donation, exchange, and purchase. Table 15.4 summarizes the known transactions of the college of Bahia over a half century. A surviving register suggests that the college of Rio de Janeiro was equally involved in obtaining urban holdings, for it records a dozen negotiations for such property between 1577 and 1639.[121] Later, the colleges of both Olinda and Recife secured urban holdings in Pernambuco and in adjacent Paraíba.[122] The other colleges in the two Brazilian provinces also utilized opportunities to acquire urban properties. In the 1730s, the college of Bahia

116. "Estado de todas as rendas da v. provincia de China em 1731," in ARSI, FG, 627.

117. "Deliberationes . . . in Insula Chorão inter 6 et 18 Decembris 1575," *DI*, 10: 271.

118. HAG 1890, fol. 29ʳ. Both Goan officials viewed such assets as "wasteful" investments.

119. *HCJB*, 5: 163–65.

120. A. J. R. Russell-Wood, *Fidalgos and Philanthropists: The Santa Casa da Misericórdia of Bahia, 1550–1755* (Berkeley, 1968), 93, 163–64, and 198.

121. *LTC/RJ*, 53–55, 109–12, 116–18, 123–24, 139–42, 150–51, 173–75, 185–87, 221–22, 226–36, and 285–88. There is, of course, no certainty that the register is complete.

122. In 1658 one Jesuit critic observed that the college of Olinda possessed thirteen houses in the Pernambucan capital and that they were the best that renters could obtain. João Fernandes Vieira to king, 5 Nov. 1658, as quoted in José António Gonsalves de Mello, *João Fernandes Vieira*, 2 vols. (1956; rpr., Recife, 1967), 2: 189–90.

TABLE 15.4

Transactions Concerning Urban Properties Belonging to the College of Bahia, 1573–1621

Year	Transaction	Value (rs.)
1573	Purchase of houses and gardens	6,000
1573	Purchase of houses	90,000
1581	Proceeds from the sale of houses to the widow Helena Borges to pay debts	90,000
1582	Exchange of houses owned by the college with a private party	—
1586	Lots given to the college	4,000
1596	Purchase of houses	50,000
1597	Purchase of houses	100,000
1599	Purchase of houses	450,000
1600	Gift of houses sold to Helena Borges (see 1581) made by son Francisco de Lemos after he joined the Society	not given
1607	Exchange of houses	—
1608	Purchase of houses	922,000
1612	Exchange of houses	—
1619	Purchase of house	320,000
1621	Gift of houses	370,000

SOURCE: *DH*, 63: 241, 244–49, 357–63, 366–69, 370–74, 378–83, 386–91; 64: 11–19, 21–23.

regularly dedicated funds to new urban construction.[123] By 1759, that college possessed 186 urban properties—more than any other unit of the Assistancy—valued at 152,165,000 rs. The rate of return was 6 percent, very likely several times the net income from plantations. Bahia's urban holdings were nearly three times the size of those of Rio de Janeiro, which had 65 houses worth 66,275,000 rs. By contrast, Olinda possessed 21 and Recife 42 urban rentals about the time of the Jesuits' expulsion.[124]

From at least the seventeenth century onward, urban properties represented a major share of the income of several Brazilian colleges. As indicated in Table 15.5, the college of Bahia's earnings from urban real estate exceeded its income from its major agricultural staple—cane sugar. In the case of the college in Rio de Janeiro, houses and shops constituted the leading or second most important source of its income; for the college of Recife, urban properties provided the second- or third-ranking source of receipts. These three institutions in the province, and possibly others as well, were far more dependent upon earnings from urban sources than were Jesuit colleges in Spanish South America.[125]

123. "Catalogus tertius temporalis . . . Brasiliae," 1736 and 1739, in ARSI, *Bras.*, 6:I, fol. 230; 6:II, fol. 276.

124. [Inventory of urban properties belonging to the college of Bahia], ca. 27 Aug. 1759, in AHU/PA/BA, 1st cat. no. 4952, which is a more complete list than that published by Leite, in *HCJB*, 5: 578–79; interim governors of Rio de Janeiro to Francisco Xavier de Mendonça Furtado (colonial minister), 21 Mar. 1763, in AHU/PA/RJ, 1st ser. não cat., *cx.* [1] of 1763 (orig.), and published in *RIHGB* 254 (Jan.–Mar. 1962): 242; the urban holdings of Olinda and Recife may have been larger than suggested here. The only account of them represents properties still unsold: enc. in *junta da inconfidencia*, Pernambuco, to marquis of Pombal, 31 Jan. 1772, in AHU/PA/PB, *cx.* 58.

125. E.g., Macera, *Instrucciones*, 8; Colmenares, *Las haciendas*, 26; Luis Martin, *The Intellectual Conquest of Peru: The Jesuit College of San Pablo, 1568–1767* (New York, 1968), 175.

TABLE 15.5

Leading Sources of Income by Colleges in Brazil Province, 1683–1757

College	Year	Total income (000 rs.)	Sugar (%)	Urban (%)
Bahia	1694	10,812	27.7	33.8
	1701	10,032	29.9	36.5
	1722	13,000	32.3[a]	49.2
	1736	11,400	35.1[a]	43.9
	1739	12,300	32.5[a]	44.7
	1743	12,300	24.5[a]	21.5
	1757	22,600	34.5	32.7
	Average	13,206	30.7[b]	37.5
Rio de Janeiro	1683	13,100	44.6	9.6
	1694	10,600	37.7	11.3
	1701	11,400	35.1	10.5
	1722	15,231	44.8	34.9
	1736	13,800	40.6	36.2
	1739	19,800	18.2	24.2
	1743	16,200	6.2	29.6
	1757	23,603	33.9	20.4
	Average	15,467	32.6	22.1
Recife	1701	1,665	48.1	21.0[c]
	1722	1,850	43.2	21.6[c]
	1743	1,574	35.7	21.1[c]
	1757	3,094	32.3	33.6
	Average	2,046	39.8	24.3

SOURCES: Rio de Janeiro, 1683: ARSI, *Bras.*, 11, fol. 70; the remainder is derived from the third catalogues in ibid., 5:II, 6:I, and 6:II, passim.

[a] Includes both sugar produced and income from lands rented.

[b] Average only of 1694, 1701, and 1757.

[c] For the years indicated, livestock was the second-ranking source of income, and urban rentals were the third. In 1722 their yields were identical.

*

Contrary to the conviction of the Society's critics, the vast majority of the Order's capital was invested in traditional kinds of property—buildings and lands. The latter included developed and undeveloped properties—farms, gardens, orchards, plantations, ranches, both vast and minuscule hectarages. Apart from the structures utilized for administrative, educational, and evangelical activities, some of the Society's entities owned impressive quantities of urban real estate, rented out for businesses and domiciles. Surviving evidence suggests that in the kingdom and to some extent overseas as well, the period of most rapid patrimonial growth occurred between about 1570 and 1620. With certain exceptions, to be noted in the next chapter, the nuclei of many of the Society's most celebrated properties in the Assistancy were acquired during those decades.

In his study of Jesuit activities in colonial Quito, Nicholas P. Cushner found that by 1767, when the Society was expelled from the Spanish Assistancy, it no longer held title to many of the properties that it had possessed there at the beginning of the eighteenth century, for they had been sold, exchanged, or otherwise liquidated. Cushner concluded that "very few Jesuit landholdings spanned the entire period of the Jesuit presence in Quito."[126] That is indeed surprising, for such a massive turnover may have been the exception rather than the rule in the history of ecclesiastical tenure generally and in that of the Society in particular.[127] Though the fathers in the Portuguese Assistancy regularly disposed of unwanted properties, they retained control of the bulk of them from the date of their acquisition until their sequestration by the crown. That was true of many of their urban holdings as well as their rural estates and the villages from which they drew land revenues. Even the Jesuits' enemies marveled at their skill in amassing vast holdings. How vast those holdings actually were became a source of persistent dispute, as will be shown in Chapter 17. What made the Jesuits' real estate especially inviting targets for the Society's critics was the fathers' tireless and successful development of their holdings, the subject of the following chapter.

126. Cushner, *Farm and Factory*, 64.
127. Cf., e.g., Youings, "The Church," 308–9. Maarten Ultee found that most of the agricultural property that the abbey St. Germain des Prés possessed in the seventeenth century had been on its rolls for 900 years. *The Abbey of St. Germain des Prés in the Seventeenth Century* (New Haven, 1981), 67.

CHAPTER 16

The Economic Foundations
of an Enterprise:
The Utilization of Lands

> Once land was acquired . . . the landowner could exercise several options. The
> land could be worked for a predetermined use; it could be rented or leased,
> allowed to lie fallow, partially cultivated, or sold to a third party. Jesuit colleges
> exercised all of these options at one time or another.
>
> —Nicholas P. Cushner, *Jesuit Ranches and the Agrarian Development of*
> *Colonial Argentina, 1650–1767*

THE CONSTITUTIONS OF the Society are remarkable not only for what they say, but also for what they leave out. For example, they exclude words such as agriculture, crops, farm, plantation, and ranch. Indeed, they contain few direct references to food at all. To be sure, they do remind candidates that their "food, drink, clothing, shoes, and lodging will be what is characteristic of the poor" and that members ought to have sufficient nourishment to be able to perform "God's service and praise," and they do suggest that during mealtimes "food should also be given to the soul" through meditation on edifying readings.[1] The Jesuits did not set out to become coconut or sugar planters, grain farmers, herdsmen, grape growers, or owners of giant latifundia. During the middle decades of the sixteenth century, they anticipated that their food requirements would be met through alms contributed by the crown and the faithful. As already suggested in preceding chapters, by the last quarter of that century, the Jesuits had discovered that they could not rely exclusively upon such sources to sustain themselves or their enterprises but needed to find ways of maximizing the returns from the lands that the crown and private benefactors had contributed, directly or indirectly, to the Society's houses. The solutions that the fathers adopted made the Society an active and significant participant in the imperial economy. Though the implementation of these plans seemingly reduced the Jesuits' financial peril, it also exposed the Society to unwanted criticism, carping, and condemnation, and thereby engendered problems that neither Loyola nor any of his cofounders could have anticipated.

---

1. *CSJ(GE)*, par. 81; *CSJ(C)*, pars. 294, 296, and 251; see also ibid., pars. 304 and 435.

The Jesuits
as Landlords

According to Postan, "the chief source of money" of the Benedictines in England during the late twelfth and thirteenth centuries "was rents and other rent-like payments of tenants."[2] The Jesuits in the Portuguese Assistancy also drew substantial income from rentals and leases. In the kingdom and in the Atlantic islands, colleges customarily rented or leased most of their holdings, including portions of their demesnes that they regarded as marginal or beyond their ability to exploit.[3] In 1725, for example, seven of the University of Évora's thirteen estates were leased for sums that represented 47.4 percent of the income that it garnered from agriculture.[4] Twenty-five years later, the Lisbon college of São Francisco Xavier reported that all thirteen of its rural holdings were occupied by tenants.[5] In 1770 the custodian reported that six rural estates of the former college of Santo Antão awaited purchasers. According to the appraisals, five of their tenants paid an average of 4.4 percent of the properties' estimated value.[6]

Whereas in other parts of eighteenth-century Europe, landlords often received cash payments for lands let out, the Jesuits were still accepting payments in kind as well as in money. The rental of only one small plot belonging to the college of São Francisco Xavier was paid entirely in money; the rest was remitted either in commodities or in goods plus cash. Altogether the thirteen properties paid the owners 111,750 rs. in cash and 13,883 kilograms in wheat and barley, as well as token obligations that included ropes of onions, baskets of grapes, and chickens. The college at Ponta Delgada in the Azores possessed 51 tenants who paid 230,740 rs. in cash and an additional 193,493 kilograms of grain for their use of the land.[7] The same pattern of mixed payments can be seen in the accounts of the college of Santo Antão. One of its renters, for example, annually paid the owners 356 kilograms of wheat; another paid 266.9 kilograms of barley, plus two chickens, two goats, and six fryers; and a third tenant annually furnished the University of Évora with 115,000 rs. and 27 cheeses for a property that he leased.[8]

By the eighteenth century, the standard rental agreement made by the Society's representatives in the Portuguese Assistancy extended for three years.[9] In the early days, however, when the Society became the recipient of far more land than its units could effectively exploit,

2. Michael M. Postan, "Medieval Agrarian Society in Its Prime: England," in *The Cambridge Economic History of Europe*, ed. Postan (Cambridge, 1966), 1: 577.

3. The Carcavelos property of the Japan province was partially rented to a half dozen tenants in 1758–59. "Conta que derao os pp. procuradores das prov.ᵃˢ da Companhia de Jesus em o ultramar," Dec. 1758–Feb. 1759, in ATC/JI/266, fol. 4.

4. "Folha da receita e despeza do coll.º de Évora no anno de 1725," in ARSI, *Lus.*, 81:II, 570–572ᵛ.

5. "Livro dos juros, foros, e faz.dᵃˢ do coll.º de S. Fr.cº Xᵉʳ 1750," BNL, 4464.

6. "Autos que se processarao' para a avaliacao' e confrontacao' dos bens de raiz da caza que foy collegio de Santo Antao' desta cidade" (1770), in ATC/JI/100.

7. "Autos de inventario e entrega . . . dos bens e fazendas que forao dos . . . [Jesuitas]," 11 May 1765, in ATC/JI/246, "A." The rental conditions had not changed since the expulsion six years earlier.

8. ATC/JI/100, fols. 18ᵛ and 20ʳ.

9. E.g., contract dated 13 Sept. 1718 made by the rector of Santo Antão with Manoel Francisco Galvão, in ANTT/CJ/2, no. 8. Herman Konrad found that the longest rental contract negotiated by the managers of the hacienda of Santa Lucia was nine years, but that "two-year contracts appear to have been more common." *A Jesuit Hacienda in Colonial Mexico: Santa Lucia, 1576–1767* (Stanford, 1980), 390 n. 90.

it was not uncommon for its overseas colleges to arrange leases for up to three lives, that is, three generations. Believing that the owner institutions would lose revenues through such generosity, Aquaviva condemned the practice.[10] In some instances, college administrators may have believed that it was better to have lands their institutions did not immediately require occupied by tenants who paid token rents than to risk having them taken over by squatters or sequestered by agents of the crown. For example, in 1587 the college of Rio de Janeiro authorized two tenants to utilize lands along a tributary of the Rio Macacu in the Goitacazes district for twenty years in return for the payment of a single chicken.[11]

Lease agreements could also extend for indefinite periods. Thus in 1602 the rector of the college of Rio de Janeiro signed a contract with a couple who leased 3.5 square kilometers in the Inhauma district of the city "from this day forward" (*aforava em fatiosim deste dia pera todo sempre*). The tenants promised to plant canes on the land and within two years to erect a sugar mill (engenho) and annually to deliver to the college 65 kilograms of sugar (two parts white, one part brown) or, until their mill became operational, 16,000 rs. A few years earlier the same college had leased a property close to its own garden to a carpenter and his wife for the period of two lives. The couple agreed to pay a modest annual rent (320 rs.) but promised never to open a door or window or build a terrace that faced the college upon threat of voiding their lease.[12]

Most tenants appear to have paid their Jesuit landlords in cash or commodities; some contributed personal service instead. That was true, for example, of the 101 Indians living on the Arasiguama cattle ranch in São Paulo, who gave three days of labor per week in return for the huts in which they lived and the plots where they grew subsistence crops.[13]

As time passed, the Jesuits negotiated stiffer terms with their tenants than they had initially. That is evident in the agreements that the college of Rio de Janeiro made during the 1750s. For example, José Ribeiro da Silva agreed to pay 76,800 rs. for pastures belonging to the engenho velho estate in Rio de Janeiro. He was permitted to graze 32 oxen but was required to have them guarded at night by a black cowboy to prevent the stock from damaging nearby cane fields. For a yearly payment of 16,000 rs., Captain Severino Pães rented a plot of uncertain dimensions that was also in the northern part of the city. He was specifically authorized to plant manioc and vegetables but was forbidden to sublet or sell any of his leasehold, to have a relative live there, to graze stock, to cut wood and make charcoal, or to undertake any unauthorized improvement exceeding 50,000 rs. without the college's express consent. He recognized by his signature that failure to heed these strictures could lead to his expulsion from the college's property.[14]

This register suggests that as long as the conditions of tenancy were honored, leases were automatically renewable, but that was not always the case. In 1662, for example, one Nazianzeno da Fonte wrote the father general that for the past nine years he had leased certain cane fields from the college of Rio de Janeiro. He insisted that he had always been

10. *HCJB*, 1: 159; *DI*, 16: 776–77.

11. Agreement between the college and Gaspar de Magalhães and Francisco da Fonseca, 3 Feb. 1587, in *LTC/RJ*, 138–39.

12. *LTC/RJ*, 177–83, 289–90.

13. "Relações dos bens apprehendidos e confiscados aos Jesuitas da capitania de S. Paulo," 14 Dec. 1762, in *DISP* 44 (1915): 337-78.

14. *RADF*, 1: 426–31.

punctual with his payments, that he had respected the owners' insistence that he refrain from cutting any timber, and that he and his family had always been devoted to the Society. He pointed out that two of his uncles were members of the Society, that for half a century his father had provided legal aid to the college, that one of his brothers was its current doctor and another its chapel master. Despite such credentials, the college had unaccountably refused to renew his lease. He protested that he was an honorable but poor man and assured Goswin Nickel that Simão de Vasconcelos, former rector of the college and former provincial, was prepared to testify in his behalf.[15] Unfortunately we do not know whether his plea was successful.

The tenants mentioned thus far produced crops or stock on lands that the Jesuits owned but did not care to exploit directly, but there were other kinds of tenants, known as *lavradores de cana*, who grew sugar cane and sometimes subsistence crops on sugar plantations, including those managed by the Jesuits themselves. The activities of these cane farmers have been closely studied by Stuart B. Schwartz.[16] The Jesuits, like other sugar magnates, made agreements with such tenants, who were assigned parcels of land varying in size from under 3 to more than 8 hectares. The duration of their leases (*arrendamentos*) was usually between six and eighteen years, though some were conceded for even longer terms. The tenants obligated themselves to mill all of their sugar in the owner's engenho or sugar-grinding apparatus and to give their landlord one-half plus an additional quarter or third of all the cane that they grew. Such terms were apparently standard in colonial Brazil's sugar industry, though by the late seventeenth century, when that industry was in the doldrums, lavradores de cana were able to insist upon more generous conditions. The number of these tenants varied with the plantation and the time. Schwartz's evidence suggests that during the seventeenth century, the number of tenants on Santo Antão's famous Sergipe do Conde property in Bahia ranged from approximately 25 to as few as five.

It is not known how many lavradores de cana were associated with other Jesuit sugar plantations in Brazil. The Rio de Janeiro register contains agreements made with 270 tenants during the 1750s, but they clearly were mostly subsistence farmers, truck gardeners, and small-scale grazers.[17] That register is unique; none comparable is known to survive for any other part of the Assistancy. We cannot be certain, therefore, that its stipulations were typical of the lease agreements that the Jesuits were making at that time with such tenants.

Clearly the conditions spelled out in the contracts contained in the Rio de Janeiro register reflect the Jesuits' long experience with tenants who, there and elsewhere, were likely to challenge the fathers' control over their actions whenever opportunities permitted. Though the relations between landlord and tenant may sometimes have been mutually supportive and even affectionate, each, like landlords and tenants the world over, probably viewed the other with a certain suspicion. Valignano once remarked to Aquaviva that even if the Jesuits could purchase agricultural lands in Japan, their exploitation would be difficult

15. Letter of 28 Nov. 1662, in ARSI, *Bras.*, 3:2, 18ʳ.

16. Especially in "Free Labor in a Slave Economy: The *Lavradores de Cana* of Colonial Bahia," in D. Alden, ed., *Colonial Roots of Modern Brazil* (Berkeley, 1973), 147–97; see also Schwartz, *Sugar Plantations in the Formation of Brazilian Society: Bahia, 1550–1835* (Cambridge, 1985), chap. 11 and elsewhere.

17. "Livro do arrendamento e assentantes de foros e fazendas que foram dos Jesuitas 1751–1758," AERJ 40-2-21, a nineteenth-century copy of a lost original; partially published in *RADF*, 1: 426–31, 455–60; 2: 9–17, 62–68, and 69–74.

because the peasants "steal or hide everything they can lay [their] hands on, with the result that the owner gets practically nothing in return."[18] In India the Jesuits had the reputation of relentlessly squeezing their tenants for as much rent as they could bear, but, as Fr. Dominico Ferroli wrote, "the religious landlords had great difficulty in getting their dues from their tenants. They had often recourse to litigation. And so they were hated." But, without displaying any evidence, he assures his readers that "when compared with other landlords, they were kind and considerate," though he admits that "they were often called the pest of India."[19] The manager of the Taleigão estate observed that during the autumn months, one of his major tasks was to collect the rents due from the rice tenants before they had harvested their crop; otherwise they would steal the fathers blind. But tax collectors in Mughal India were equally eager to collect the government's share of the *rabi* crop before the peasants had cleared the fields.[20] As Joyce Youings has written with respect to early Tudor England,

> Monastic tenants would no doubt have regaled the stranger with talk of crippling rents, low prices, neglected repairs, and inescapable tithes. At the abbot's table the tale would have been a different one, of miserably low rents, quite unrelated to the profit being enjoyed by his tenant farmers, of the high cost of foodstuffs and of the other bare necessities of the convent, and of the profitless task of improving such parts of the estate as could . . . be taken in hand.[21]

One may surmise that the relationship that existed between Jesuit landlords and their tenants was about the same.

The Jesuits as Stockmen

One of the familiar images of the Jesuits in the popular literature is that of the padre on horseback. Indeed, one longtime admirer of the Order, Herbert E. Bolton, wrote a biography of a famous Jesuit with precisely that title. Meat—beef, lamb, pork, and veal—constituted an important part of the Jesuit diet, so it is not surprising to find that Jesuits became conspicuous stockmen both in the kingdom and in Brazil. In 1708 the University of Évora reported that four of its properties contained 2,535 sheep, 530 pigs, 544 goats, 200 cows, and 152 oxen. By 1725 the cattle herd had increased to 250 head, and 30 head were slaughtered per year, the same number of yearlings that the herd produced. The university's wool clip was then valued at 900,000 rs., and its estates manufactured some 900 cheeses.[22] Coimbra, Bragança, and other Jesuit facilities also possessed livestock, but the extent of their herds remains unknown.[23]

18. *VMP*, 2: 37.

19. F/*JM*, 2: 350; cf. Teotonio de Souza, S.J., *Medieval Goa: A Socio-Economic History* (New Delhi, 1979), 71–72, 227–28.

20. Statement by António Dias, procurator of Japan and China, Goa, 11 Oct. 1708, in ARSI, *Goa*, 9:II, 434–38, par. 6. Cf. Irfan Habib, *The Agrarian System of Mughal India (1556–1707)* (New York, 1967), 241.

21. Youings, "The Church," in H. P. R. Finberg, gen. ed., *The Agrarian History of England and Wales*, vol. 4, *1500–1640*, ed. Joan Thirsk (Cambridge, 1967), 307. Comparable complaints regarding the negligence and unreliability of tenants in Portugal are included in rector and consultores of the college of Bragança to general, 1650, in ARSI, *Lus.*, 79, fols. 496–99.

22. ARSI, *Lus.*, 76, fols. 69–71; 81:II, fols. 570–72^v.

23. A document of ca. 1611 that gives the annual yield of Jesuit estates throughout the province of Portugal includes five mentions of income from the sale of cattle, but in each instance the income

In Brazil the Jesuits turned to stock-raising on a modest scale soon after their arrival. Their first superior, Manuel da Nóbrega, confronted by the appearance of the first batch of so-called orphans from Lisbon in 1550, appealed to the authorities for some cows to provide milk for his charges. As a result, when John III sent a shipment of cattle from the Cape Verdes to Brazil in 1552, the Jesuits received a dozen head. The next year Nóbrega arranged for another ten to be supplied his lieutenants in São Vicente, the future captaincy of São Paulo.[24] By 1561 he reported that the Vincentian nucleus had grown to a hundred head and predicted that if authorization could be obtained from the crown and the general, the Jesuits could soon take care of their financial needs with very little effort by selling excess meat, milk, cheese, and hides.[25] But although the crown approved of the Jesuits' desire to raise some cattle, Father General Borgia ruled that such activity did not comport with the Institute.[26]

Borgia's opposition and the caution with which the Jesuits generally pursued what could be regarded as "mercantile" activities during the sixteenth century appear to have effectively blunted Nóbrega's optimistic plan.[27] Until well into the seventeenth century, the Jesuits' use of livestock seems to have been limited to slaughtering for their own needs and employing draft animals upon their sugar plantations, which, as will be seen below, only began at the start of that century.[28] As early as 1641, however, cattle, especially the sale of hides, became a significant source of income of one college, that of Rio de Janeiro. From that date until 1701, livestock and their byproducts accounted for between 23.9 and 41.5 percent of that college's income.

Not until the 1694 triennial economic report of the province do we have data on livestock-raising by other Jesuit colleges. Both that document and the next surviving one in the series, that of 1701, demonstrate that by the turn of the eighteenth century, several Jesuit colleges were becoming significant stock producers. The Bahian college possessed five ranches along the São Francisco River, whereas the college of Rio de Janeiro counted 17,050

---

is undifferentiated from other sources, so that it is impossible to know how many animals were being marketed. "Informação por parte do p. p[rocurad]ᵒʳ geral da comp.ᵃ de IESU da prov.ᵃ de Portugal sobre a materia de dizimos," in ANTT/CJ/80, no. 6. Évora's herds were vastly larger than those possessed by the Benedictine abbey of Tibães, which possessed 20 head in 1680 and in 1760. Aurélio de Araujo Oliveira, *A abadia de Tibães, 1630/80–1813*, 2 vols. (Porto, 1979), 1: 237.

24. *HCJB*, 1: 34 and 174.

25. Nóbrega to Francisco Henriques, São Vicente, 12 June 1561, in *MB*, 3: 348–49.

26. Ibid., 353; Francisco Borgia to Fr. Inácio de Azevedo, 30 Jan. 1567, in *MB*, 4: 376–77. However, he asked Azevedo, then serving as Visitor, to look into the matter further. Borgia to Azevedo, 22 Sept. 1567, in *MB*, 4: 417.

27. In 1577, for example, a disgruntled Jesuit reported that meat was in short supply in Brazil except in Bahia. "Geralmente fallando, se padece muito no comer, assi polla falta que ha, como polla qualidade dos comeres, que todos os do Brasil sao insipidos e sem sostancia." Serafim Leite, ed., "Enformação dalgumas cousas do Brasil," attributed to Belchior Cordeiro, S.J., 1577, in Academia portuguesa de historia, *Anais*, 2d ser., 15 (1965): 194.

28. E.g., in an inventory of 1676, the temporary custodian of the sugar estate of Santana de Ilhéus, discussed below, reported that the fazenda possessed eighteen oxen, eight goats, and eleven pigs, but curiously no horses. Br. Manuel da Costa, "Treslado do inventario do engenho de Sancta Anna de que entregou . . . ao P.ᵉ Procurador Joseph Teixeira," 13 Aug. 1676, in ANTT/CJ/54, no. 7. A half century or so later, the manager reported that the estate possessed 49 head: 18 oxen, 2 horses, and 29 cows. Pedro Ferreira, "Estado em que achey e fez integra do eng.ᵒ Sta Anna dos Ilheos ao P. Manoel de Fig.ᵈᵒ aos 7 de agosto de 1730" [but dated 30 June 1730], in ANTT/CJ/15, no. 23 (no. 24 is a clearer but incomplete copy).

cattle distributed on 47 ranges (called *bovilibus* or *currais*), plus another 1,800 horses and sheep. Each of the two northern colleges, Olinda and Recife, reported over 1,200 head of cattle, and the incipient college of Espírito Santo had over 1,600 head on its Muribeca ranch, which straddled the boundaries of the captaincies of Rio de Janeiro and Espírito Santo. However, the two Paulista colleges were still far less committed to livestock production: Santos had only 58 cattle, whereas São Paulo claimed 475 head plus another 58 horses and oxen.[29]

Spurred by persisting economic imperatives, by the increasing demand for hides in the kingdom, by urban growth related to Brazil's gold boom, and very possibly by a deliberate search for a cash earner that would become a viable alternative to the troubled sugar industry, the Jesuits expanded livestock production in the eighteenth century until nearly every house from the Amazon to the incipient college in Paraná possessed one or more ranches with several hundred head of stock. In the far north, cattle and horses were first introduced during the 1650s, when António Vieira served as missions superior. The Jesuits gained a foothold on the eastern grasslands of the Belgium-sized island of Marajó (or Joannes, as it was then called) shortly before 1689, when a secular priest gave them his livestock. By 1718 the college of São Alexandre already possessed the fazenda of Marajó, which boasted about 30 kilometers of river frontage. That fazenda was soon joined by another half dozen ranches inherited from pious persons. Situated along the Arari River, they measured 18.9 kilometers by 31.5 kilometers. According to a rough count made in 1759, the Marajó ranches possessed 134,465 head of cattle and another 1,500 or so horses.[30]

The college of Maranhão also possessed a half dozen ranches. In 1760 they were estimated to hold 15,600 head of cattle and other large animals and some 500 horses, far fewer, therefore, than the Marajó herds, and fewer than the herds that the Jesuits developed on 39 ranches in the interior captaincy of Piauí.[31] Thirty of those ranches belonged to the complex and controversial bequest of the famous Domingo Afonso Sertão, one of the original developers of Piauí and, as a result of his agreement with the college of Salvador in 1706, the founder of the Bahian novitiate of Jiquitaia (see Chapter 14). As many as 1,200

---

29. The preceding is based upon the periodic provincial economic reports (the so-called third catalogues) for 1641, 1658, 1694, and 1701. They are gathered in ARSI, *Bras.*, 5:I and 5:II, and the 1701 text is published in *HCJB*, 5: 588–96. I have also utilized António de Oliveira (provincial), "Resumo do que recebeo este collegio do Rio de Jan.ʳᵒ desde o pr.º de mayo de 1683 ... athe o ultimo de mayo de 1684," in ARSI, *Bras.*, 11, fol. 70.

30. *HCJB*, 5: 247ff. The inventory, taken after crown agents seized the ranches, was first reported by António Pinto da Silva to Pascoa de Abranches Madeira (*ouvidor da comarca*) on 22 Mar. 1759, in AHU/PA/PA, 1st ser., *cx.* 19 (signed copy), and on that day the magistrate forwarded those figures to the captain-general, Manuel Bernardo de Melo e Castro. Abranches Madeira to Melo e Castro, 22 Mar. 1759, in BAPP, cod. 2, nos. 5 and 6. The captain-general transmitted the details to Lisbon in his report of 30 July 1759 to Tomé Joaquim da Costa Corte Real, which was first published in *ABAPP* 2 (1902): 152–53 n. 2 and again in 8 (1913): 56–59. Fr. Leite, preferring to rely upon the memory of a Jesuit exile in Italy (ARSI, *Bras.*, 28, fol. 12), contended that the actual number must have been closer to 50,000, but he offered no convincing evidence to support his conviction.

The only contemporary description of livestock-rearing in the Amazon region of which I am aware is João Daniel, S.J., "Tesouro descoberto no Rio Amazonas," pt. 4, chap. 10, *ABNRJ* 95, 2 (1976): 71–80, which, though it provides a useful analysis of the problems of stock-raising in the eighteenth century, does not specifically refer to Jesuit ranches.

31. ARSI, *Bras.*, 28, fols. 24ᵛ and 29ᵛ. Cf. *HCJB*, 3: 158–90.

beeves from the Piauense ranches were annually trailed to Capuame, the major livestock fair in the northeast situated just north of Salvador, where they were sold. Only two estimates were ever given of the size of the Piauense herds: 30,000 cattle and 1,500 horses in 1739, and 32,000 head, by 1757, a modest increase for nearly two decades.[32]

Because they belonged to two chantries, these cattle did not contribute income to the college of Bahia. However, the college's five São Francisco River ranches supplied it with 600 head per year for slaughter. The size of the herds varied from 7,000 to 10,000 cattle and from 200 to 400 horses between 1725 and 1757. In addition, by the mid-1750s, the Belém seminary had 400 cattle, the professed house another 300, and the college's two sugar plantations, Pitanga and Cotegipe, another 300 cattle and 120 horses.

Such herds were several times larger than those of the colleges of Olinda and Recife. The latter also owned a dozen ranches along the São Francisco with herds that doubled in size between 1736 and 1757 (to 3,000 head of cattle), but the herds of the college of Olinda remained about half that size. These figures do not include several hundred livestock that the fathers possessed in Paraíba and Rio Grande do Norte, or another 2,000 that helped to support the Jesuit house in Ceará. Nor do they include the several hundred cattle, horses, sheep, and goats that belonged to the Indian villages the Jesuits administered in the captaincies of Pernambuco and Bahia. Two Indian villages in Espírito Santo also had some livestock, but the principal producer for the Jesuits there remained the giant Muribeca ranch, where the number of cattle increased from 1,741 in the mid-1730s to 2,346 by the late 1750s; by the latter date, the same ranch possessed more than 500 horses, an increase of better than 75 percent in two decades.

In São Paulo, the only significant Jesuit livestock producer at this time was the fazenda of Santana, whose herds never contained more than 300 cattle in this century. By the 1750s far more stock—2,030 cattle and 1,020 horses—contributed to the support of the incipient Jesuit college in Paraná.

With a few exceptions, the most important of which were in the captaincy of Rio de Janeiro, ranches in colonial Brazil were deliberately confined to marginal areas not suited to the cultivation of sugar. This restriction stemmed from royal legislation designed to protect the sugar lords from the trampling of their unfenced fields by stock animals,[33] but it inevitably meant that meat in the colony was always tough (because the animals were trailed long distances and were not fattened before slaughter) and expensive. Even the Jesuits' ranches in the captaincy of Rio de Janeiro were situated far from their natural urban market. The Santa Cruz estate was nearly 70 kilometers west of the city; the other two major ranches, the Campos Novos de São João and the Goitacazes estate, were 150 and 390 kilometers, respectively, from the metropolis. Of course the captaincy of Rio de Janeiro was not one of colonial Brazil's major centers for livestock-rearing. If the usually well-informed Jesuit administrator Giovanni Antonio Andreoni is to be believed, at the beginning of the eighteenth century the captaincy contained only about 60,000 head of

---

32. I have studied these ranches before and after the crown sequestered them in a lengthy but still unpublished essay, but the substance of this paragraph will be found in *HCJB*, 5: 550–65.

33. Caio Prado Júnior, *The Colonial Background of Modern Brazil*, trans. Suzette Macedo (Berkeley, 1967), 216–17. His chapter on stock-raising (pp. 213–46) remains a very helpful introduction to the subject.

cattle.[34] That would suggest that the fathers possessed about a third of the captaincy's herd. We cannot be certain that the college of Rio de Janeiro enjoyed such a dominant position at the time, but it is clear that the number of livestock it possessed increased substantially during the first six decades of the eighteenth century. By 1757, eight Jesuit estates, led by Goitacazes, Santa Cruz, and Campos Novos, reported herds totaling 28,277 cattle and 5,782 horses. Over a quarter century, the number of cattle had increased nearly 50 percent, far more than the growth in the number of horses. In addition, five Jesuit-administered missions owned 364 cattle and 149 sheep.[35]

The estimates that we possess suggest that from the Amazon to Paraná, the Society possessed over 200,000 head of livestock, mostly cattle, by the mid-eighteenth century. That number may not seem impressive, for one could find as many head upon a single large ranch in eighteenth-century New Spain, and probably nearly that many on an estancia in the Río de la Plata.[36] But livestock ranching, often marginalized by the favored sugar producers, was not nearly as developed in Brazil as it was in Hispanic America. Early in the seventeenth century, a ranch with 1,000 head in Brazil was reckoned to be a large property, though by Andreoni's day some held 6,000 to 10,000 or even 20,000 head.[37] Though such ranches were modest compared to those elsewhere in the Americas, the livestock properties of the Jesuits in Brazil were obviously relatively large. Indeed, the scale of these properties was greater than that of Jesuit stock holdings elsewhere in Latin America.[38] According to the province's periodic economic reports, ranching provided an important share of the incomes of several of the colleges. In Bahia, the ranching sector's share increased from less than 4 percent (1694–1701) to 24.5 percent (1743); in Rio de Janeiro, the college garnered just over one-third of its income from stock-rearing between 1683 and 1757, whereas livestock provided the two Pernambucan colleges, Olinda and Recife, with 21.8 to 22.6 percent of their revenues during the eighteenth century. Ranching then represented the third-ranking source of their income.

34. André João Antonil [pseud. for Giovanni Antonio Andreoni], *Cultura e opulencia do Brasil por suas drogas e minas* (1711), trans. and ed. Andrée Mansuy (Paris, 1965), 474 and 476.

35. The statistics summarized in these paragraphs and in the next one are derived from the provincial third catalogues for 1707, 1722, 1725, 1732, 1736, 1739, 1743, and 1757, in ARSI, *Bras.*, 6:I and 6:II, passim.

36. E.g., Lesley Byrd Simpson, *Exploitation of Land in Central Mexico in the Sixteenth Century*, Ibero-Americana series no. 36 (Berkeley, 1952); François Chevalier, *Land and Society in Colonial Mexico: The Great Hacienda*, trans. Alvin Eustis, ed. Lesley Byrd Simpson (Berkeley, 1966), chap. 3, 105–14; Ricardo Levene, *Investigaciones acerca de la historia economica del virreinato del Plata*, 2d ed., 2 vols. (Buenos Aires, 1952), 2: chap. 4; and Héctor H. Bruit, "Notas e documentos sobre a pecuária do Rio de Prata no século XVIII," *Estudos históricos* (Marília, São Paulo), no. 8 (1969): 177–95.

37. Ambrósio Fernandes Brandão, *Dialogues of the Great Things of Brazil*, trans. and ed. F. A. H. Hall, W. F. Harrison, and Dorothy W. Welker (Albuquerque, 1987), 264; Antonil, *Cultura e opulencia*, 478.

38. Cf. German Colmenares, *Las haciendas de los jesuitas en el nuevo reino de granada* (Bogotá, 1969), 109–11; Nicholas P. Cushner, *Lords of the Land: Sugar, Wine and Jesuit Estates of Coastal Peru, 1600–1767* (Albany, 1980), 146; and idem, *Jesuit Ranches and the Agrarian Development of Colonial Argentina, 1650–1767* (Albany, 1983), 76–77. In the kingdom of New Granada, for example, the Jesuits possessed 32 livestock ranches, but the largest of them had only 14,229 head in 1767. In Chihuahua, New Spain, the 28 missions that the Jesuits administered possessed in 1767 a total of 20,491 livestock, including cattle, horses, mules, and lesser animals. Harold Bradley Benedict, "The Distribution of the Expropriated Jesuit Properties in Mexico, with Special Reference to Chihuahua (1767–1790)," Ph.D. diss., University of Washington, 1970, 377, table 14.

The Prevalence
of Agriculture

Though stock-rearing was of special importance in the kingdom and in Brazil, the production of foodstuffs was the most widespread form of economic activity throughout the Assistancy. In some cases the Jesuits themselves raised or processed the commodities that they consumed and marketed; in others they received them as tribute from tenants. In the kingdom, those commodities included cereals, dairy products, fruit, and vegetables, most of which were supplied to the owner institutions for their own needs.[39] Surpluses were marketed, but we do not know how that was done. They consisted of familiar staples that Portugal grew and processed: cereals, particularly wheat, but also barley, millet, and sometimes rye; wines; and olive oil.

From the outset, the Peninsular colleges became significant grain producers. Within a few years of its founding, Bragança reported that its income for 1565–68 included 163,800 liters of wheat and a remarkable 270,000 liters of rye. That income was much larger than that of the new University of Évora, whose lands produced 77,400 liters of wheat and 27,450 of barley in 1582.[40] In 1611, three Lisbon houses—the novitiate, the probationary house, and Santo Antão—reported that altogether their properties supplied a total of 316,350 liters of wheat.[41]

By the early seventeenth century, the demesne of the Peninsular colleges were also producing considerable amounts of olive oil and wine. Table 16.1 summarizes the estimated levels of production of some of the best known of those estates. They were clearly substantial properties, but it is hard to speculate about their relative size in the kingdom, because the extant literature is bereft of meaningful comparisons.[42] Each estate was oriented primarily toward its owner, whose requirements it attempted to satisfy, but, as Table 16.2 demonstrates, each estate also borrowed and lent to other Jesuit estates, thereby creating a sort of agricultural co-op, a network that would later arouse deep suspicions among the Society's critics. The Order's Peninsular facilities continued to receive impressive quantities

39. Those needs were considerable. In November 1705, the cellar of the University of Évora had 120 moios (108,000 liters) of wheat, but two months later its steward found it necessary to purchase an additional 37 moios (33,300 liters) in the open market. Three years later, the university reported that it had only 92 moios (82,800 liters) of wheat, rye, and barley on hand. "Assento do estado temporal em q. fica este collegio de Évora," 14 April 1708, in ARSI, *Lus.*, 76, fols. 69–71.

40. "Renta, gasto y deudas del collegio de Bragança de los anos 1565, 1566, '67 [y] 1568," in ARSI, FG, 1379/2; "Pauta da renda q. o collegio d'Evora te' . . . annos por outros feita ao prim.ᵒ de Dezembro de 1582," in ARSI, *Lus.*, 80, fol. 18.

41. "Informação por parte do P. P[rocurad]ᵒʳ," cited in note 23 above.

42. The closest may be R. C. Hoffmann and H. B. Johnson, "Un Village portugais en mutation: Povoa d'El Rey a la fin du quatorzième siècle," *Annales, economies, sociétés, civilisations* (Sept.–Oct. 1971): 917–40, and H. B. Johnson, "Les Comptes d'un hopital portugais, 1379–1383," *Études rurales: Revue trimestrielle d'histoire, geographie, sociologie et economie des campagnes*, no. 51 (Paris, 1973): 67–84, both cited from reprints.

More than a quarter century ago, B. H. Slicher van Bath observed that "it is still difficult to obtain enough quantitative data from the Late Middle Ages on the areas cultivated and the harvest yields. There is no material covering a whole country or any considerable area of land. One or two accounts from a few large landed estates contain the required information." *The Agrarian History of Western Europe, A.D. 500–1850*, trans. Olive Ordish (London, 1963), 170. Those observations are still applicable to Portugal during the early modern period.

TABLE 16.1

Estimated Production Levels of Key Jesuit Estates in Portugal, 1632–33

Owner	Number of residents	Estate	Commodities produced	Annual yield (liters)
Santo Antão	41	Caniços	Wheat	20,700
			Barley, rye, millet	27,000
			Vegetables	4,500
			Olive oil	4,000
			Wine	11,924–14,309
			Cheese, honey, wool	?
		Enxobregas	Wheat, vegetables	900
			Olive oil	847.5
			Wine	14,308–19,078
		Val do Rosal	Wine	14,308–19,078
Probationary House	54	Campolide	Olive oil	240–320
			Wine	23,848
Santarém	10	Labruja	Wheat, rye	450
			Olive oil	480–640
		Alagoa	Millet, rye	900
			Vegetables	225
Porto	26	Arneiro	Wheat	650
			Wine	9,539
		Vacaria	Olive oil	360
			Wine	23,848
Braga	30	Ricase	Wheat	26
			Wine	7,200
Faro	11	S. Cristóvão	Wheat	18,000
			Wine	9,539–11,924

SOURCES: "Catalogo 3° das cousas da provincia de Portugal," May 1633, in ARSI, *Lus.*, 44:II, fols. 512–518ᵛ; Sebastião de Morais (procurator, Portuguese province, in Madrid) to king, "Informação do estado da causa dos dízimos neste anno de 1631" (printed), in BNL/CP/475, fols. 263–268ᵛ.

of cereals, olive oil, and wines from their home farms and their tenants well into the eighteenth century, as is evident from Table 16.3.

Grain and wine also figured prominently among the commodities that the Jesuits' estates on the Atlantic islands produced. The college of Angra enjoyed a 75 percent increase in its supply of wheat between 1592 and 1625; by the latter date, it received as much as 108,000 liters a year from its properties. The incipient college of São Miguel obtained about a third of that amount in 1612 from nineteen properties. One of them, the quinta of Fayãa, also contributed 315 quintals (18,289 kilograms) of woad that year.[43] The principal estate that supported the college of Funchal, Madeira, was also a supplier of wheat, rye, barley, beans, and chickpeas, as well as wine.[44]

43. "Rol da renda que o collegio ... de Angra ... tem ... [h]oje 27 de julho de 1592," in ARSI, *Lus.*, 79, fol. 129ʳ; "Recopilação do temporal do coll.° de Angra," 1625, in ibid., fols. 133–34; "Catalogo das avaliações das terras e propriedades q. tem esta residencia de S. Miguel," ca. 1612, in ANTT/CJ/58, no. 83.

44. The only data on yields that I have found are for 1761 (wine) and 1765–69 with respect to the other commodities. ATC/JI/257, *caderno* V.

TABLE 16.2

Account Between the Labruja Estate and the College of Santo Antão, January 1610 to 9 August 1612

Charge, item	Total (rs.)
Cash on hand at the estate, January 1610	114,340
67 chickens sold to college @ 120 rs.	8,040
4 fryers (*frangos*) sold to college @ 25 rs.	100
6.5 dozen eggs sold by Fr. Manoel Roiz	260
2 rams sold to college	800
2 rams that Fr. Roiz gave to Val do Rosal	2,000
Balance of 34 rams sold to college	920
Freight paid to son of Luis Pereira who went with Fr. Roiz in the bark	300
17 chickens sold to college	1,920
Quitrent paid in money	240
Cash loan to a brother of quinta of Caniços	3,000
Paid Joam F[e]r[nande]z for pigs from Caniços	1,200
Miscellaneous bills paid for college	370
70 bundles of wood @ 30 rs.	2,100
Wages of two men who cleared land	400
1,300 *lanias* (bovine teeth?) @ 4 rs. per hundred	52
Carriage for lanias	80
12 *alqueires* of rye sold to college	1,200
7 alqueires of barley sold to college	490
120 bundles of wood @ 30 rs. and cleaning of same	141,610
Credit Santo Antão for six heifers sold to quinta of Caniços	29,000
Lodgings provided sometimes to tenants of Loures	240
Lodgings provided workers (*moços*) at various times between January 1610 and 15 April 1611	500
Money spent to fetch Fr. Duarte da Costa [donor of the estate] when he fell ill	910
Additional expenses to go after Fr. Duarte da Costa	1,262
Three ropes for well and six "de lear"(?)	400
Cost of a long cloak (*manteo*) that father provincial ordered for Fr. Manoel Roiz when he went to Portalegre	4,000
A new hat authorized by father provincial for Fr. Roiz	550
4 *almudes* of wine @ 440 rs. each plus carriage sold to Br. Daniel de Miranda	1,860
Portion (subsistence allowance) of Fr. Manoel Roiz from January 1610 to January 1611 as authorized by father provincial	30,000
Portion of Br. Joam F[ernandez], January 1611 to January 1612	30,000
Six alqueires of wheat sold for farm	800
80,000 rs. for two years ending 4 March 1612, consisting of alms that Fr. Duarte da Costa donated for each year that he lived in the college @ 40,000 rs. less the 181 days that he stayed at the farm, leaving a net of	6,520
	155,042 [*sic*]
Credit the farm	141,610[a]
Credit the college	13,432[b]

SOURCE: ANTT/CJ/58, no. 4.

[a] Meaning unclear. Repeats the amount paid for 120 bundles of wood.

[b] That is, sales of commodities *to* the owner college.

TABLE 16.3

Conspectus of Food Production, Province of Portugal, ca. 1733–37

(liters)

Unit	Period	Wheat	Barley	Millet	Wine [a]	Olive oil
Braga	1 July 33–30 Sept. 35	3,450	—	24,750	22,914	—
Coimbra	Apr. 34–30 Mar. 36	8,700	22,350	126,900	22,896	17,381
Probationary house, Lisbon	1 Mar. 33–31 July 36	18,600	2,115	13,140	—	—
Elvas	1 Jan. 35–31 Dec. 36	4,500	3,000	—	1,260	9,275
Évora	1 Jan. 35–31 Dec. 36	49,800	43,800	—	20,880	13,000
Faro	1 Nov. 34–1 Oct. 36	40,140	—	—	3,888	—
Portalegre	1 Jan. 35–31 Dec. 36	10,125	—	—	2,340	1,209
Pernes [b]	1 Oct. 33–10 June 36	1,980	—	1,400	4,875	3,380
Portimão	1 Sept. 34–Oct. 36	11,700	—	—	1,950	—
Santarém	1 Oct. 33–30 June 36	—	—	1,050	4,050	300
Setúbal	1 Feb. 35–28 Feb. 37	10,200	255	9,750	2,160	9,360
St. Patrick's Seminary, Lisbon	1 Jan. 37–3 June 37	750	600	3,250	—	—

SOURCE: "Ratio status temporalis dormus et collegiani provincia Lusitania" (1733–37), in ARSI, FG, 627/A/2.

NOTE: The college of Bragança was omitted; the college of Porto was included, but there were no data on the production of foodstuffs. Atlantic island colleges were also omitted.

[a] Wines were expressed in terms of *almudes* and *alqueires*, converted at one almude = 18 liters and one alqueire = 15 liters.

[b] A residence belonging to the college of Santarém.

In the subcontinent of India, the counterparts to cereals, olive oil, and wines were rice and coconuts. Though the Jesuit fathers themselves harvested the latter, they obtained the former from their renters and lessees.[45] According to Raychaudhuri and Habib, paddy rice or baty was "the most important foodgrain of southern India" and of the west coast, too.[46] The best contemporary description of the rice-planting cycle comes from the quill of John Burnell, who wrote at the beginning of the eighteenth century:

> The baty grounds are prepared in April . . . at which time they burn the stubble that remains of last season's baty, and add . . . straw or dung, to extract the vegetal salt. . . . They [then] let it lie fallow till the monsoons are well set in and hath well soaked the earth; they plow it knee deep in mud, forcing it up with a wooden colter [blade]. . . . When the plow hath made the earth fit for seed they sow the baty, which is rice well soak'd in water and laid in straw till such time as it shooteth forth. . . . When it is about six or eight inches high, they transplant it, taking it up in handfuls and placing them in regular furrows, where it grows six or eight

45. Teotonio R. de Souza stated confidently that "the religious proprietors [of Goa] . . . cultivated their paddy fields" with local labor, but he supplied no evidence that they actually did so. *Medieval Goa*, 73. I have not seen any evidence suggesting that the Jesuits themselves ever farmed rice: every reference to the grain that I have found is to supplies contributed by tenants. Apart from the sources cited in the following notes, there is the testimony of António Dias, S.J., procurator for Japan and China and manager of the Taleigão plantation, who stated that it was necessary to collect the rice from its tenants before the harvest. Statement of 11 Oct. 1708, in ARSI, *Goa*, 9:II, 434–38. The only place where it is certain that the Jesuits themselves were rice planters is the captaincy of Rio de Janeiro. *RADF*, 2 (1895): 64, par. 1.

46. Tapan Raychaudhuri and Irfan Habib, eds., *The Cambridge Economic History of India*, 2 vols. (Cambridge, 1982), 1: 227–28, and 233. The quotation is from p. 227. See also Sanjay Subrahmanyam, "The Portuguese, the Port of Basrur, and the Rice Trade, 1600–1650," *Indian Economic and Social History Review* 21, 4 (1984): 432–62, an illuminating study of the west coast rice trade from South India to Goa and points north.

inches deep in water, shooting forth an ear like to oats. As the monsoons go off, it ripens, turning a pale yellow, and when thoroughly ripe it is reaped and carried into the [granary], where the rice is trod … by buff[a]los.[47]

The Jesuits obtained rice from lands around Bassein and Goa. In 1635 the yearly payments in rice submitted to the colleges of Bassein, Taná, and Damão, the residence of Bandorá, and the procurate of Japan by tenants and villages in the north totaled nearly 500 metric tons.[48] Toward the end of the seventeenth century, the same sources supplied the Japan province with 378 metric tons and provided about half the income that the province received from the northern province in the subcontinent.[49] At the beginning of the eighteenth century, the seminary of Bassein shared with the seminary of Santa Fé, Goa, an income from a single village that included over 15 metric tons of rice.[50] Except for the villages and estates in the vicinity of the capital, all of the rice income was lost when the northern province fell into the hands of the Marathas (see Chapter 23).

If the fathers obtained revenues from rice indirectly, they gained income from coconuts as a result of their own careful management of plantations, of which, as suggested in the preceding chapter, they possessed a large number both in the north and around Goa. When the agent for the Japan province liquidated its holdings in the north in the late 1670s, he sold off palm groves with 7,259 trees, which he claimed annually produced 297,000 fruit, a remarkably high yield if true.[51] The funds from the sale of those properties, as observed in the last chapter, were invested in the Taleigão estate, which by 1708 possessed some 8,000 trees.[52] If they were planted at 150 or so trees per hectare, that would suggest that 53.3 hectares were devoted to coconuts.[53] Three fragments of accounts from Jesuit coconut plantations reveal how profitable they could be. Between 1717 and 1722, the gross profit of the estate of Betalbaty belonging to the college of Rachol averaged 26.4 percent; that of an unidentified estate belonging to the long-suspended Tibet mission was almost as high, averaging 25.7 percent for most years between 1716 and 1732; and the yield from a palm orchard owned by New St. Paul's produced a remarkable 48.7 percent between 1749 and 1759.[54] Though net profits from the Society's coconut plantations were undoubtedly considerably lower, they appear to have been far higher and, except for the occasional typhoon, less risky than those

47. Burnell, *Bombay in the Days of Queen Anne*, ed. Samuel T. Sheppard, *HS*:2, no. 72 (1933): 60–61.
48. "Lista das pacarias e aldeas que possuem os padres da Companhia de Jesus na cidade de Baçaim e em Taná e Bandora e do procurador de Jappão e na cidade de … Damão," Goa, 8 Mar. 1636, in ANTT/LM, 35, fol. 357.
49. "L.º da receita e despeza das fazendas vindas das missões e collegio de Macao, 1693 [*sic* for 1692]–[1736]," HAG 1497; summarized in George Bryan Souza, *The Survival of Empire* (Cambridge, 1986), 193, table 7.2. Souza, *Medieval Goa*, 172, states that the price of rice in the Goan market rose nearly 10% during the seventeenth century but ignores the continued depreciation of Portuguese currency at the time. See Appendix A.
50. "Lista de todas as fazendas que tem este seminario [Bassein]," 1709, in ARSI, *Goa*, 9:II, 441ʳ.
51. Statement of P. Manoel Henriques, ca. 1688, in BA/JA/49-IV-66, fol. 97ʳ. Cf. P[alakesseril] K[umaran] Thampan, *Coconut Culture in India* (Cochin, 1970), 33, table 4.1, which indicates yields of 53.5 to 95.1 per tree.
52. See note 45.
53. C. M. John states that it is usually appropriate to plant 150 to 200 trees per hectare. *Coconut Cultivation* (New Delhi, 1970), 20.
54. HAG 2092, 2661, and 2085, passim.

derived from the Jesuits' most heavily capitalized agricultural enterprise, the production of cane sugar.[55]

The Jesuits as Reluctant Sugar Planters

Cane sugar, introduced to Brazil perhaps as early as 1526, became that colony's leading staple after 1549, but the Jesuits did not become directly involved in the industry until the start of the seventeenth century.[56] From the beginning, the fathers received small quantities of sugar as gifts from supporters, and the royal stipends to the colleges of Bahia, Olinda, and Rio de Janeiro were paid—often belatedly—in sugar (see Chapter 12). Manuel da Nóbrega, that prescient founder of the Jesuits' enterprise in the West, clearly longed for an opportunity to send sugar to the kingdom in order to produce income to meet the requirements of new missions and houses. Although Diego Laínez sanctioned its dispatch in limited quantities, Borgia ruled against the planting of canes by members of the Society, fearing that such activity might violate canon-law prohibitions against mercantile activity and become a source of scandal.[57] By 1590, however, Aquaviva—moved by disturbing reports of the Brazilian colleges' mounting debts, by Jesuit pleas that their Benedictine and Carmelite rivals in Brazil were already growing sugar, and by Valignano's persuasive arguments in support of another kind of trade, the silk traffic in the Orient—had relented and authorized the college of Bahia to plant canes. As in the province of New Spain, where Jesuits debated the wisdom of becoming grain farmers,[58] there remained lingering opposition among Jesuits in Brazil to the Society's direct participation in the colony's dominant industry. Interestingly enough, that opposition was still based upon legalistic considerations, not upon concerns about the capital investment that might be required or about the inevitable reliance upon servile labor. By 1594, Aquaviva had been persuaded that neither the *Constitutions* nor the Institute would be violated if the Brazilian colleges were to grow sugar. Accordingly, the Jesuits' long and intimate association with colonial Brazil's best-known export began in August 1601, about a decade after Jesuits in New Spain turned to the production of sugar, and four decades before their colleagues in Peru did so.[59]

During the seventeenth century, the fathers acquired five sugar plantations in the captaincy of Bahia. Three belonged to the local college, the other two to Santo Antão in

55. According to an anonymous memorandum of 1700, a good estate in India was expected to return a net of 7% per annum. ARSI, *Goa*, 36:I, fol. 27^r. The earliest published Jesuit account of the production of coconuts is the general essay of Fr. Jerónimo Lobo, whose *Itinerário* is cited frequently in these pages. It appears as an appendix in his *A Short Relation of the River Nile*, trans. Peter Wyche (London, 1673), 57–104. He makes no specific reference to Jesuit coconut plantations.

56. This section is a revision of D. Alden, "Sugar Planters by Necessity, Not Choice: The Role of the Jesuits in the Cane Sugar Industry of Colonial Brazil, 1601–1759," in Jeffrey A. Cole, ed., *The Church and Society in Latin America* (New Orleans: Tulane University, Center for Latin American Studies, 1984), 139–70. I am indebted to the Center for permission to utilize this material in another context. The most recent and comprehensive study of the sugar industry is Schwartz, *Sugar Plantations*.

57. Nóbrega to Francisco Henriques, 12 June 1561, in *MB*, 3: 348; Diego Laínez (general) to Nóbrega, Trent, 16 Dec. 1562, in *MB*, 3: 516; Francisco Borgia to Luís de Grã, 10 Jan. 1566, and Borgia to Inácio de Azevedo, [24 Feb. 1566], in *MB*, 4: 292 and 329.

58. Cf. Konrad, *Jesuit Hacienda*, 35–44.

59. *HCJB*, 1: 181–82; James Denson Riley, *Hacendados jesuitas en Mexico: El colegio maximo de San Pedro y San Pablo* (Mexico City, 1976), 32ff.; Cushner, *Lords*, 29.

Lisbon. Shortly after 1601, the Bahian college began construction of the engenho Mamõ in the Passé district at the head of All Saints Bay, where the college had first acquired land as early as 1562.[60] However, when after a few years, members of the college expressed misgivings concerning the legitimacy of its participation in cane production, the mill was closed. An Indian uprising in the Ilhéus district, south of the capital, soon focused the fathers' attention upon neglected lands that the college had owned there since 1563. As soon as the Indians were quieted, Fernão Cardim, the rector, led a team to inspect those lands, which were situated along the Rio Trindade. He and his advisors concluded that the best way to secure their interests in the property was to develop it. Accordingly, the construction of the engenho Camamú began in 1604. That mill, too, became a source of internal controversy. In 1607 a Jesuit inspector urged that it be shut down, even though 8,000,000 rs. had already been expended on the plantation. But Camamú remained active until 1640, when Dutch intruders torched it. Fearing future enemy attacks, the college decided against rebuilding the mill, and thereafter its lands produced lumber, cacao, and cinnamon.[61]

The loss of Camamú caused Jesuit leaders to revive the engenho Mamõ in 1642. But it was again shut down and possibly sold when the college found an opportunity to acquire a more promising neighboring property, the engenho Pitanga. Both its owners and the college claimed title to the same cane fields. Rather than engage in litigation, the parties agreed to an amicable solution: in 1643 the college simply purchased Pitanga and its 21 slaves for 2,800,000 rs. Over the next seven years, the new administrators expanded the property, partly through successful litigation but especially through purchases that nearly equaled the engenho's original purchase price.[62] By mid-century, Pitanga reportedly yielded a gross annual profit of 2,000,000 rs. and was reputed to produce some of the colony's best-quality sugars. Still, there were those within the college who were displeased by its role in the industry and therefore urged that the mill be sold. It is unclear whether their recommendation was based upon moral concerns or upon a recognition of sugar's increasing lack of profitability due to a prolonged depression afflicting both Portugal and Brazil. In 1685 the college offered to sell Pitanga, but the market proved to be so poor that the Jesuits discovered that they would reap only a quarter of the 24,000,000 rs. they considered the property to be worth; consequently, they withheld it from the market. Pitanga remained one of the mainstays of the college for another 75 years.[63]

The remaining two seventeenth-century Jesuit properties in Bahia—Santana de Ilhéus and Sergipe do Conde—became the sources of the most serious internal economic dispute within the Assistancy and were ultimately awarded to Santo Antão, the only Peninsular college to own sugar estates in Brazil. The origins of those properties and the protracted controversies in which they figured have been described many times and may be briefly summarized here.[64]

60. "Carta de sesmaria da terra dos indios da aldeia do Espirito Santo," 7 Sept. 1562, in *DH*, 63: 337–42.

61. What little is known about the history of Camamú is summarized in *HCJB*, 5: 199–203.

62. For the original purchase agreement and the subsequent acquisitions, see *DH*, 63: 268–332.

63. *HCJB*, 5: 256–59.

64. Because of the disputes over ownership and because the accounts of the two properties were kept in Lisbon, where far more Jesuit documentation has survived than has been the case in Brazil, much has been

Sergipe do Conde, the larger and more productive of the two estates, began with a tainted transaction negotiated by Brazil's third governor-general, Mem de Sá (1557–72). About 1559, Sá arranged for an oversized sesmaria (12.6 by 25.2 kilometers), situated at the north end of All Saints Bay about 75 kilometers from the capital, close to the present town of São Francisco do Conde, to be awarded to a court official who was a personal friend. The next year, in what seems to have been a clear instance of collusion, the court provisioner renounced his claim in favor of the governor-general's son, Francisco de Sá. Further additions to the property were made during the 1560s, and in 1571 Francisco de Sá was reconfirmed as the legitimate owner of the estate. But although the son was the nominal owner, the estate's real and active manager was his father. It was he who built the first mill and also developed a second sugar plantation, Santana de Ilhéus, described in the preceding chapter.

Mem de Sá died in March 1572, leaving only two survivors among his once-numerous progeny. One was the aforementioned Francisco, a priest, and the other was a daughter, Felipa. Upon learning of his father's death, Francisco decided to give up his profession in order to manage his vast inheritance. Why he took that step is uncertain, for there was no prohibition against secular priests being property owners, and many were, in Brazil and elsewhere. In any case, within months Francisco expired. Before doing so, he bequeathed his estate, which included properties in the kingdom as well as those in Bahia, to his sister.

In order to secure her inheritance, Felipa emerged from a Dominican convent in Évora, where she had been sent by her father in 1560 at age 12. In 1573, a year after her father's death and months after the loss of her brother, D. Felipa was married to D. Fernando de Noronha, later to become count of Linhares. Although they never visited their Brazilian properties, the two invested heavily in their development over the next four decades, and Sergipe became renowned, first as Sergipe do Conde and later as Engenho da Condessa, after its two absentee owners. In 1617 D. Felipa's husband died, and she herself became seriously ill. Perhaps because of her condition or perhaps because she was ignorant of the terms of her father's will, D. Felipa, a childless widow, signed a testamentary document whose terms violated the stipulations of her father. Mem de Sá had specified that in the event that neither of his surviving children had direct heirs, the Brazil properties were to be sold and the proceeds divided into three parts. One portion was to go to the college of Bahia; another to the local charitable institution, the Santa Casa da Misericórdia; and the remainder to impoverished orphans in Salvador. However, under the influence of a spiritual advisor who was *not* a Jesuit, D. Felipa left all of her estate to Santo Antão.[65]

In September 1618, D. Felipa followed her husband into the hereafter. Three years later, the first of many lawsuits between the Jesuit colleges in Lisbon and Bahia and the

---

written concerning the two properties, whose history has been most fully told by Schwartz, *Sugar Plantations*, 489–97 and throughout his volume. For other sources, see Alden, "Sugar Planters," n. 32.

   65. Schwartz errs when he refers to it as "the newly created . . . College." *Sugar Plantations*, 492. As indicated in an earlier chapter, the original Santo Antão was founded in 1553. It proved to be too small. In 1579, with the sanction of that persistent Jesuit benefactor, Cardinal King Henry, the foundations for a replacement college, Santo Antão *o novo*, were laid, but its doors were not opened until 1593. Thereafter, however, the most serious problem that confronted its leaders was the inadequacy of its endowment. Why D. Felipe's confessor, the prior of Lumiar, steered her to name Santo Antão as her sole beneficiary is an interesting puzzle.

other concerned parties began. By 1663 a basic settlement had been worked out, partly through the intervention of the ill-fated Jacinto de Magistris, Visitor to the Brazil province (see Chapter 10), but representatives of Santo Antão did not gain complete possession of the engenho until 1676.

Sergipe do Conde became the largest plantation in seventeenth-century Bahia, probably in all of Brazil. In 1625 Dutch invaders heavily damaged the mill, but it was soon rebuilt. By 1635 the plantation extended for 80 square kilometers. Apart from its imposing crushing mill and curing houses, the engenho possessed extensive woodlands, abundant pastures (indispensable for the primary motive power—oxen), and a dozen cane fields, some of which were cultivated by share tenants, the lavradores de cana. That year, the estate's gross income was estimated at 3,874,000 rs. and its expenses at 3,308,635 rs., leaving an apparent gross profit of 8.5 percent.[66] Such a profit was uncharacteristic of the great mill. There survive sufficient details to compute the mill's income and expenses for 43 of the years between 1611 and 1680; only eighteen of those years ended profitably.[67] By the late seventeenth century, Santo Antão also contemplated selling the mill, but its administrators failed to find buyers with sufficient capital.[68] Why the Jesuits, who could profitably operate large sugar estates in Peru, were unable to render Sergipe do Conde consistently profitable remains a conundrum.[69]

The other Bahian sugar estate that the condessa bequeathed to Santo Antão was Santana, situated nearly 190 kilometers south of Salvador, inland from the seacoast along the Santana River.[70] Acquired by Mem de Sá in 1560, the mill prospered for a few years until an Indian uprising destroyed it. The first known inventory, that of 1572, states that the estate was worth a modest 1,252,100 rs., of which 58.3 percent was invested in its 112 slaves, many of them Indians.[71] Thereafter the property languished for decades. An inventory in 1618 lists only 34 slaves; eleven years later, a Jesuit inspector reported that the estate lacked a functioning mill or usable curing facilities.[72] Fr. Estevão Pereira, who visited Santana in 1629 and again in 1633, undertook to revitalize its operations, and the next surviving inventory, that of 1639, reveals some of the fruits of his labors and those of the estate manager. The plantation's value had grown to 7.2 contos, a sum that compares favorably with the coeval

66. Estevão Pereira, S.J., "Dase rezao da fazenda que o coll.º de Sᵗo Antao tem no Brazil e de seus rendimentos," 25 Aug. 1635, in ANTT/CJ/13, no. 20; published most reliably in the Mansuy edition of Antonil, *Cultura e opulencia*, 513–27. Pereira was the administrator of the estate between 1629 and 1633. His invaluable report is the oldest account that we possess concerning the operating expenses of a Brazilian sugar estate. Cf. Schwartz, *Sugar Plantations*, 220, 224, 229–30, for an unreasonably severe critique of Pereira's accounting procedures. It is hardly fair to expect a nonprofessional to observe twentieth-century accounting principles, and Schwartz's suggestion that Pereira must have been "skimming" (p. 230) is without foundation. Had Pereira done so, he would have been guilty of violating one of his fundamental vows, for which the penalty would have been immediate dismissal. There is no evidence that he was ever charged with malfeasance or expelled. If he was guilty of sloppy bookkeeping, he had a lot of company in the Society.

67. Schwartz, *Sugar Plantations*, 233, table 8.6.

68. "Perguntasse se he conuente vendese o eng.º de Sergipe do Conde," n.d. [late seventeenth century], in ANTT/CJ/56, no. 59.

69. Cf. Schwartz, *Sugar Plantations*, 229ff.

70. Pereira's "Dase rezao" (note 66) contains useful data on the beginnings of Santana.

71. "Inventario do engenho de Sant' Ana," 13 Mar. 1572, in *DHA*, 3: 84–155.

72. "Auto de envent.º da fazenda ... de Santa Ana," 23 Aug. 1618, in ANTT/CJ/15, no. 12.

evaluation of Sergipe do Conde, some 8 contos.[73] Fr. Serafim Leite's contention that the mill's recovery dated only from the 1660s thus appears suspect.[74] Another inventory, completed in the mid-1670s, states that the slave population had increased to 119 and that the mill was able to process 10,160 kilograms of sugar per year, a far cry from the capacity of Sergipe do Conde—some 61,000 kilograms or more—but about the level that Santana appears to have produced a century earlier.[75]

Bahia was one of three Brazilian captaincies where the Jesuits had sugar mills during the seventeenth century. Shortly before 1666, the college of Olinda, Pernambuco, constructed the fazenda of Monjope, situated a few leagues distant from that regional capital. But that was not the Jesuits' first sugar estate in the captaincy. About 1614 the college sold an earlier estate (name unknown) for the substantial sum of 5,600,000 rs. How that property was acquired and how long the college utilized it are also unknown. We are simply told that it was sold when the college became embroiled in a dispute with a local contractor over tithe payments.[76] Very little is known about Monjope save that in 1692 its labor force included 100 slaves whose toil provided a third of the college's income. For reasons undisclosed, the fathers became dissatisfied with Monjope, and in 1693 they purchased a second mill, Engenho de Cotunguba. Thereafter Monjope became one of the Society's many recreational facilities.[77] During the same decade, Olinda's brother college, Recife, also constructed a mill, Nossa Senhora da Luz, but it did not commence operations until 1701.[78]

Two of the southern colleges also became involved in the production of sugar during the seventeenth century, one briefly, the other more permanently. In 1644 a benefactor gave the college of Espírito Santo a nearby engenho named Carapina, but the heads of the college did not consider the property worth keeping and soon sold it.[79] In the northern sectors of the city of Rio de Janeiro is a ward called Engenho Velho. Its name is derived from a fazenda originally called São Francisco Xavier but best known as Engenho Velho. It originated in the erection of a hermitage in that district in the late sixteenth century. Initially its lands were rented to tenants, but sometime during the seventeenth century the college of Rio de Janeiro decided to plant them with canes, and at an uncertain date it erected the oldest of the college's several mills to process them. By the 1680s, sugar, much of it presumably from this estate, constituted 44.6 percent of the college's income.[80]

73. "Papeis do coll.º [Santo Antão] . . . de 1639," in ANTT/CJ/20, no. 1.

74. *HCJB*, 5: 221.

75. "Treslado do inventario do eng.º de Sancta Anna," 22 Aug. 1676, in ANTT/CJ/15, no. 23 and no. 24, the latter being a clearer copy; also /54, no. 7.

76. [Report concerning the extent of the properties of religious Orders in Brazil] (1614), AHU/LR, 284, fols. 162ʳ–163ᵛ. I am indebted to Stuart B. Schwartz for calling my attention to this anonymous report, which was intended to demonstrate why the Orders ought to pay tithes. I suspect that it was written by a magistrate recently returned to the kingdom from Brazil.

77. "Catalogus rerum temporalium Brasiliae," Bahia, 24 June 1694, in ARSI, *Bras.*, 5:II, fols. 136–45; *HCJB*, 5: 423–25.

78. *HCJB*, 5: 477–78.

79. Virtually nothing is known about the engenho. Ibid., 6: 151.

80. "Resumo do que recebeo este collegio do Rio de Jan.ʳº desde o prº de mayo de 1683 . . . athe o ultimo de mayo de 1684," in ARSI, *Bras.*, 11, fol. 120. The beginnings of this famous property remain murky. See *HCJB*, 6: 67–69.

The eighteenth century witnessed a further expansion of the Jesuits' role in Brazil's sugar industry. At first sight this seems surprising since the industry, beset by problems of overproduction and persisting low prices since the 1670s, continued to be in the doldrums.[81] But the Jesuits were excluded from the burgeoning mining districts of Minas Gerais and Mato Grosso and, confronted by steeply rising costs (particularly for African slaves) and expanding mission opportunities (especially in the Amazon region), they continued their commitment to the sugar industry even while, as suggested in the preceding chapter, they were enlarging their investments in urban real estate.

During Brazil's so-called golden age, several additional colleges became mill owners. In the north, the college of Nossa Senhora da Luz, Maranhão, operational since about 1670, developed the already-mentioned polycultural complex of São Bonifácio during the eighteenth century. Situated on the island of Maranhão close to the town of Viana and a nearby Jesuit mission, São Bonifácio became what Serafim Leite termed "the nerve center" of the college and was one of only five engenhos in the entire captaincy, another being owned by the Carmelites. Besides several cane fields, that complex included a saw mill and a brandy distillery. In addition to sugar, the plantation produced manioc, cacao, bananas, citrus, and indigenous fruit, as well as brandy. After the Jesuits' removal, São Bonifácio, already in decline, was appraised at nearly four times the value of Sergipe do Conde.[82]

In the neighboring captaincy of Pará, the college of Santo Alexandre, founded in 1668, lacked a sugar mill until it inherited one in about 1722. Sometimes called São Francisco de Borja but more commonly known as Ibirajuba, it was located on the right bank of the Moju River, four hours by canoe south of Belém. The estate, one of 25 sugar plantations in the captaincy, consisted of about 6.3 square kilometers of land containing a mill and several cane fields; an island measuring about 9.6 kilometers in circumference and containing five additional cane fields; and a third parcel with an additional 3.1 kilometers of land. Like São Bonifácio, Ibirajuba was also a multifunctional plantation, for it grew not only sugar but also cacao, coffee, and manioc, and likewise produced brandy. By 1760 its cane fields, its cacao and coffee groves, its manioc fields and melon beds, and its carpentry, blacksmithy,

81. For the sugar depression, see Frederic Mauro, *Le Portugal et l'Atlantique au xviie siècle, 1570–1670* (Paris, 1960), esp. 233–34; Vitorino Magalhães Godinho, "Portugal, as frotas do acucar e as frotas do ouro (1670–1770)," reprinted in idem, *Ensaios* 2 (Lisbon, 1968): 295–315, esp. 300ff.; and J. H. Galloway, "Northeast Brazil, 1700–50: The Agricultural Crisis Re-examined," *Journal of Historical Geography* 2 (1975): 21–38. The statements in this paragraph also rest upon my "Price Movements in Brazil Before, During, and After the Gold Boom, with Special Reference to the Salvador Market, 1670–1769," in *Essays on the Price History of Eighteenth-Century Latin America*, ed. Lyman L. Johnson and Enrique Tandeter (Albuquerque, 1990), 335–71.

82. *HCJB* 3: 120–21, 190–91; Joaquim de Melo e Póvoas (governor) to Francisco Xavier de Mendonça Furtado (colonial secretary), 28 Aug. 1765, in AHU/PA/MA, *cx.* 40, reporting the value of São Bonifácio at 80 contos. In 1740, following a complaint by the cámara of Belém concerning the extent of ecclesiastical properties, the Overseas Council instructed the governor of the State of Maranhão to discover how much property each Order possessed. Each mission superior was directed to disclose his Order's complete assets, but the rector of the college of Maranhão somehow overlooked São Bonifácio in his report! João de Abreu Castelbranco to Overseas Council, 20 Feb. 1741, in AHU/PA/PA, *cx.* 10.

locksmith shop, pottery, and canoe works were served by 102 slaves. At that time it was valued in excess of 19 contos, about a quarter the appraisal for São Bonifáçio, but nearly as much as the older Bahian properties belonging to Santo Antão.[83]

In Pernambuco the two colleges continued to rely upon sugar for a substantial share of their income. In 1701 the college of Olinda purchased its third mill—Carnauba—in the Mato region near its existing Cotunguba engenho. Six years later the college sent 46 boxes (*caixas*) of sugar to Lisbon and reported that it had another 60 awaiting transportation. Since the size of a sugar chest was then just over 500 kilograms, that report suggests that the two producing estates were capable of exporting nearly 54,000 kilograms of sugar a year. Curiously, in 1716 Monjope resumed production while the other two mills were shut down. Why, we do not know. In the 1730s the Olinda college spent a large sum (about 8 contos) on improvements at Monjope, which, by the late 1740s, was yielding a modest annual income of 200,000 rs., nearly 35.6 percent of the college's income. Thereafter, however, for undisclosed reasons, Monjope's productivity diminished; in 1757 the provincial reported that despite the mill's 130 slaves, it was able to produce only about 25 chests of "inferior" sugar annually.[84]

The college of Recife was more fortunate. In 1739 its sugar-producing property, Nossa Senhora da Luz, shipped to the kingdom 55 caixas. That may have been the plantation's apogee, for its eighteenth-century average was closer to 30 chests per year. Still, its earnings—some 400,000 rs. yearly in the late 1740s—were larger than those of Monjope and accounted for 31 percent of the college's income. With only two-thirds as many slaves as Monjope, Nossa Senhora da Luz shipped 18,636 kilograms of sugar to Lisbon during 1756–57.[85]

During the eighteenth century, sugar also furnished about a third of the income of the college of Bahia. Its mainstay remained the old engenho Pitanga, which annually sent 100 to 150 chests of sugar to the kingdom.[86] In the 1740s and 1750s, the college gained two additional engenhos, one by purchase, the other by bequest. The engenho Pitinga belonged to a heavily indebted couple who, in 1741, sold their plantation to the college for 18,400,000 rs., most of which went to their creditors. That acquisition was of dubious merit, since the property lacked its own firewood source, and fuel represented a fifth of the operating costs of an engenho.[87] Furthermore, although the property had 77 slaves, it lacked skilled workers to process the cane, which could represent another 20 percent of expenditures. The property also shared a tangle of water rights with the adjacent Sergipe do Conde property. To avoid a renewal of unseemly litigation between the two colleges, that of Bahia agreed to sell the estate to that of Santo Antão in 1744 for its original purchase price.

83. *HCJB*, 3: 303–5; "Lista do q. tinhao o coll.º do Pará na faz.ᵈᵃ de Hybrajuba a 8 de junho de 1760," in ARSI, *Bras.*, 28, fol. 12; Manoel Bernardo de Melo e Castro (governor) to Mendonça Furtado, 18 Nov. 1764 (and annexes), AHU/PA/PA, *cx.* 21.

84. The foregoing is based upon the "catalogos trienalis" of 1707, 1739, and 1757, in ARSI, *Bras.*, 6, passim; as well as the "Relação de todos os conventos e hospicios que ha dentro do districto d'este governo de Pernambuco" (ca. 1748), in *ABNRJ* 28 (1908): 416; and the report of the Recife customs house of 13 May 1757, in ANTT/CJ/83, no. 148. See also *HCJB*, 5: 477–79.

85. In addition to the sources cited in note 83, these remarks are based upon a series of affidavits by Fr. Tomás da Costa, the college procurator, extending from 12 May 1756 to 12 May 1757: ANTT/CJ/83, nos. 132–35, 139, 141, 143, and 146.

86. "Catalogos trienalis" of 1722, 1736, 1739, and 1757, in ARSI, *Bras.*, 6, passim; *HCJB*, 5: 258.

87. Schwartz, *Sugar Plantations*, 221–22, tables 8.4 and 8.5.

Santo Antão's resident manager succeeded in boosting the estate's production from about 5,800 kilograms in 1746 to nearly 19,600 kilograms a decade later.[88] In 1755 a benefactor who died a Jesuit brother left the college another mill, Cotegipe. Its lands were located about 40 kilometers northwest of Salvador, close to the town of Abrantes. By the end of the Jesuit regime, Cotegipe was producing over 31,000 kilograms of sugar a year.[89]

The old plantations belonging to Santo Antão fared less well. The output of Sergipe do Conde, which had exceeded 87,000 kilograms a year on several occasions during the seventeenth century, declined by a half or two-thirds during the following century. A survey of the Bahian sugar industry undertaken in 1754–55 revealed that the captaincy had 172 engenhos whose average yield was 30,116.5 kilograms. By then Sergipe's output (37,975.5 kilograms) placed it only 42d on the list, or in the 75th percentile. Thirty lords, led by Simão de Affonseca Pita, owner of three vast properties that produced 228,766.5 kilograms a year, exceeded the output of the onetime king of engenhos. Sergipe do Conde's managers, one of whom was convinced that his assignment represented punishment for his sins, saw their hopes for favorable crops dashed by bad weather, particularly a series of droughts, by a rash of epidemics, and by the flight of their slaves. If Sergipe do Conde produced a modest profit in 1730–31, it contributed nothing but red ink during its final years of Jesuit administration.[90]

Santana suffered a similar decline. When Fr. Pedro Felix reluctantly assumed its management in 1730, he inherited an estate that had been allowed to deteriorate for much of the 27-year regime of his predecessor. Although he sent 21 chests—thirteen of white sugar and eight of brown—to the Lisbon customs house during his first year, he warned his superiors not to expect him to be able to continue to maintain that level of production, because the cane fields were worn out and the 178 slaves were devilish, undisciplined, and unchristian. Many, he affirmed, were useless because of ill health or chronic laziness. Despite his warning, Fr. Felix managed to expand output slightly during his first quinquennium and to increase receipts by 52 percent. Thereafter, however, shipments of the plantation's sugar and timber products declined. By 1739 the amount of sugar produced had fallen by 60 percent, and revenues were only a third of what they had been in 1730. For a few years during the 1740s, income improved, but then it fell once again while the estate's indebtedness rose. During the 1750s, Santana ceased to produce sugar altogether, and its only commercial products became beans, rice, and jacaranda wood.[91]

88. There is substantial documentation on Pitinga, including the terms of its original purchase, in ANTT/CJ, especially *m.* 12, nos. 44 and 154; *m.* 25; and *m.* 54, nos. 27, 36, 37, 39, 58, and 59. Although Pitinga and Sergipe do Conde were separately administered, their managers were expected to work closely together. There is an undated draft of the instructions issued to the Pitinga administrator in ANTT/CJ/14, no. 54.

89. "Catalogo trienal" of 1757, in ARSI, *Bras.*, 6:II, 436–43.

90. The foregoing is based upon ANTT/CJ/54, nos. 30, 31, 35, 46, 49, 54, and 57, as well as /61, no. 513; /58, no. 57; /68, nos. 115 and 346; and /15, no. 25. For the capacities of Bahian mills at mid-century, see José António Caldas, *Notícia geral de toda esta capitania da Bahia desde o seu descobrimento atê o presente ano de 1759* (fasc. ed., Salvador, 1951), fols. 429–38. See also Alden, "Sugar Planters," 153, table II.

91. This paragraph rests upon a mass of documentation in ANTT/CJ, esp. /5, no. 23; /68, nos. 343, 347, and 348; /58, no. 58; /54, nos. 22, 43, 47, 48, 51, and 55. When the estate was confiscated, it was valued, surprisingly, at 24 contos. Joachim Jozé de Andrade, "Engenho chamado de Santa Anna," 27 Aug. 1759, in AHU/PA/BA, 1st. ser., no. 4947.

But while the output of Santo Antão's old properties declined ominously, that of several Jesuit estates along the central littoral grew spectacularly. One was the giant fazenda called Araçatiba in Espírito Santo. In 1721 its wealthy planter donated it to the local college shortly before his demise. By 1722 the college's income had already doubled, in large part because of sales of that plantation's sugar. During the next decade, the college invested heavily in the estate, partly in the construction of hydraulic works but especially in the purchase of slaves. By 1736 the plantation possessed an exceptionally large slave force, some 350 hands. In fourteen years, output had risen by 57 percent. Twenty years later the college's income was three times larger than it had been in the early 1720s, and Araçatiba had lived up to its Indian-derived name (an abundance of fruit), for its 400 slaves were producing 80 caixas of sugar compared with only 22 during the first year of Jesuit management.[92]

The college of Rio de Janeiro was another that impressively expanded its commitment to sugar. By the turn of the eighteenth century it was phasing out its first mill, São Francisco Xavier, and leasing its lands while developing a new engenho beyond the northern confines of the city.[93] That mill would naturally be called *engenho novo*, a name that still survives. By 1706 the two plantations produced as much as 160 chests of sugar a year, a level that they maintained throughout the 1730s. Although their output dropped to only 100 caixas by the early 1740s, that decline was partly offset by the expansion of cane-growing in the famous fazenda do colégio, the Goitacazes property discussed above. Long a major cattle ranch, in the last decades of the Jesuits' administration that estate became their major sugar producer. During the 1740s and 1750s its output grew from a modest 6,000 kilograms to over 107,000 kilograms, more than the combined output of the college's other sugar producers.[94]

It is evident, therefore, that financial exigencies drove one college after another to invest in cane sugar as a means of rescuing itself from alarming indebtedness and to provide income deemed necessary to sustain missions and colleges and to embellish churches. Many of our questions about the operations of the Jesuits' engenhos (or for that matter, about the activities of their ecclesiastical and secular peers) can no longer be answered. Except

92. The economic growth of the Espirituense college of Santiago can be traced in the series of "catalogos trienalis" from 1694 to 1757, in ARSI, *Bras.*, 5:II, 6:I, and 6:II, passim. See also *LAM3*: 172–74, and Alberto Lamego, "As tres grandes fazendas dos Jesuitas: colegio, Muribeca e Santa Ana, em Macaé," *Brasil açucareiro* 24 (1944): 272–75. For the origins of the name Araçatiba, see F. Eugenio de Assis, *Dicionario geografico e historico do estado do Espirito Santo* (Victoria, 1941), 50.

93. Fr. Leite believed that the Jesuits de-emphasized cane planting at the older property because of the city's encroachment; in fact, the estate was still about 5 km west of the metropolis in Joanine times (1808–21). *HCJB*, 6: 67–69; cf. José de Souza Azevedo Pizarro e Araujo, *Memorias historicas do Rio de Janeiro*, 10 vols. (Rio de Janeiro, 1946), 5: 104. I suspect that the real reason why the fathers preferred leasing to cropping the plantation was its diminishing fertility.

94. The "catalogos trienalis" cited in note 84 are essential for tracing the growth of the Rio de Janeiro estates. See also Lamego, "As tres grandes fazendas," 42–44, 72–76; and idem, "Os fazendeiros de Campos, no seculo passado," *Brasil açucareiro* 24 (1944): 86–87. By the late 1750s, the Jesuits appear to have been growing sugar at the fazenda of Macaé, situated between their Goitacazes and Campo Novo properties. According to Lamego, the property consisted of 33 square km of land and two mills. *LAM3*: 166. When crown agents sold it, it was appraised at 30,760,023 rs. "Auto de sequestro e inventario da fazenda de Macaé," 12 Dec. 1759, Museu Historico Nacional, Rio de Janeiro, *armario* 33 (orig.); copy in Arquivo Municipal do Rio de Janeiro, 40-2-21A. Neither refers to an engenho; nor does the 1757 third catalogue. As noted in an earlier section, the Jesuits were also growing cane on the vast Santa Cruz property, and at the time of their ouster they were planning to erect an engenho there.

for the broken series of records concerning Sergipe do Conde and Santana, the ledgers, periodic fiscal reports, operating instructions, and shipping manifests once preserved by estate managers or college procurators no longer survive. Even the periodic provincials' reports that exist provide no more than fragmentary information concerning the changing fortunes of Jesuit facilities that became dependent upon cane sugar, and they fail to illuminate crucial decisions that college officials made with respect to land acquisition and use, production, and the purchase of expensive equipment or of increasingly costly contingents of fresh slaves.

The evidence that remains demonstrates that by the early eighteenth century, the Brazilian colleges were heavily committed to the sugar industry. They continued to be until the end. As Table 16.4 demonstrates, during that century sugar accounted for approximately one-third to three-quarters of the income of five of the colleges in the province of Brazil. In the vice- province of Maranhão, sugar brought in more than two-fifths of the revenues of the college of Pará in 1740, and perhaps even more two decades later.[95] Table 16.5 displays the approximate annual production of the Jesuits' leading sugar estates in the two provinces of Brazil. Altogether they produced more than 300 metric tons, of which 85.3 percent (more than 273 metric tons) came from the engenhos of Brazil's three central sugar captaincies—Pernambuco, Bahia, and Rio de Janeiro. Elsewhere I have suggested that the same captaincies annually dispatched about 10,700 metric tons of sugar to Europe during the 1750s.[96] If that estimate is reasonably correct, the Jesuits' estates contributed just under 3 percent of Brazil's cane exports. Even if one adds a small percentage to cover domestic sales (for the fathers often vended as much as 10 percent of their crop at the plantation), the Jesuits' share of the Luso-Brazilian sugar market was infinitely smaller than that of their colleagues in Peru, where the Society's installations controlled between 20 and 35 percent of the market.[97] It needs to be remembered, however, that Peruvian sugars were inferior to Brazilian sugars, and that the major coastal valleys of Peru produced less than a twentieth of Brazil's tonnage as late as 1804. Furthermore, though the Jesuits were often accused of monopolizing various colonial commodities, no one ever asserted that they were a dominant supplier of sugar. Clearly, they were not.

The Jesuits reluctantly entered the sugar industry at the outset of the seventeenth century because they hoped that their participation would enable them to retire debt and increase income. Assuredly the revenues of each college that turned to cane grew, but so did expenses and debts. In 1701 the income of the college of Rio de Janeiro, for example, stood at 11,400,000 rs.; by 1739 it reached the impressive sum of 19,800,000 rs. And by 1757 earnings exceeded 23,600,000 rs., yet indebtedness then surpassed current revenues by 8,000,000 rs.[98]

95. The only economic report of the vice-province that makes possible a determination of shares of income is the "Catalogus reru' V. Prov^a Maragn^sis," Sept. 1740, in ARSI, *Bras.*, 27, fols. 108–9, which discloses that Ibirajuba and the brandy distillery of Jaguaribe together accounted for 43.5% of Belém's income. Curiously, São Bonifácio supplied only 10% of the earnings of the college of Maranhão at this time.

96. Alden, "Sugar Planters," 159.

97. Cushner, *Lords*, 124; cf. Pablo Macera, "Los Jesuitas e la agricultura de la cana," in *Trabajos de historia*, 4 vols. (Lima, 1977?), 3: esp. 68ff.

98. The statements here are derived from the previously cited third catalogues.

TABLE 16.4

Percentage of Collegial Income Derived from Sugar, 1683–1757

Year	Bahia	Rio de Janeiro	Espírito Santo	Olinda	Recife	Average
1683	—	44.6	—	—	—	—
1694	27.7	37.7	60.0	28.3	—	—
1701	29.9	35.1	66.6	64.1	48.1	48.8
1722	49.2	44.8	76.2	—	43.2	—
1736	—	13.8	—	—	—	—
1739	—	18.2	—	—	—	—
1743	—	6.2	—	35.8	—	—
1757	34.5	33.9	83.6	29.3	32.3	42.7
Average	35.3	29.3	71.6	39.4	41.2	—

SOURCES: ARSI, *Bras.*, 5:I, 5:II, 6:I, 6:II, passim; and 11, fol. 70.

TABLE 16.5

Sugar Output of Leading Jesuit Estates, 1745–60

Estate	Owner college	Production (kg)	Year
Ibirajuba	Pará	5,075	1760
São Bonifáçio	Maranhão	1,617	1760
Nossa Senhora da Luz	Recife	9,505	1756–57[a]
Monjope	Olinda	12,687	1757
Pitanga	Bahia	50,750	1757
Cotegipe	Bahia	30,450	1757
Sergipe do Conde	Santo Antão	42,166	1745–55[a]
Pitanga	Santo Antão	16,385	1746, 1748–51[a]
Santana de Ilhéus	Santo Antão	4,466	1751–52[a]
Araçatiba	Espírito Santo	40,600	1757
Engenho Velho	Rio de Janeiro	20,300	1757
Engenho Novo	Rio de Janeiro	30,450	1757
Fazenda do colégio (Goitacazes)	Rio de Janeiro	56,332	1757
Total		320,783	—

SOURCES: Ibirajuba: ARSI, *Bras.*, 28, fol. 18. São Bonifáçio: AHU/PA/MA, cx. 40. Nossa Senhora da Luz: ANTT/CJ/83, nos. 132, 134–35. Sergipe do Conde: ANTT/CJ/54, nos. 30, 31, 34, 36, 46, 47, 54, 59; Caldas, *Notícia geral*, fol. 429. Pitanga: ANTT/CJ/54, nos. 36 and 39; Caldas, *Notícia geral*, fol. 429. Santana: ANTT/CJ/54, no. 43. Remainder: ARSI, *Bras.*, 6:II, 436–43.

[a] Average production for indicated years.

It may be that the Jesuits stayed with cane too long, for though it was by far Brazil's most attractive export in 1600, that was not true in the 1750s. Brazil no longer dominated the market, and the returns from sugar were not as glittering as they had been.[99] Had the Society endured for the remainder of the century, its colleges might have become leaders in Brazil's agricultural revival, for that revival featured some of the alternative commodities that Jesuit estates were already producing and of which the fathers had been pioneer cultivators.[100] One

99. D. Alden, "Price Movements."
100. D. Alden, "Late Colonial Brazil, 1750–1808," in Leslie Bethell, ed., *The Cambridge History of Latin America*, 11 vols. (New York, 1984–94), 2: 627–53.

thinks, for example, of cacao, coffee, rice, and cotton. But history is full of might-have-beens that never were. At mid-century, the Jesuits' time in Brazil was already running out.

Both directly and indirectly, the Jesuits became successful landlords: directly through their development of large estates in the kingdom, in Brazil, in Africa, and in India, and indirectly through the productivity of their tenants. They received estates that were in decline and restored and expanded them. They cleared and planted virgin lands and reaped abundant harvests. But were they traditionalists or innovators in their agricultural practices and in the crops that they grew? Students of the Spanish and Portuguese assistancies are not in agreement on the answers to those questions. Some, like Chevalier and Disney, admire the fathers for their efficiency and ground-breaking roles as estate managers. Disney, a leading Australian scholar of Portuguese activities in India, writes that "the Jesuits were . . . more efficient farmers and managers than most other landowners, operated on a bigger scale, were more sympathetic to experimentation and improvement, and tended to achieve higher yields. They also . . . advanced seed to farmers who lacked it."[101] Such enthusiasm is matched by the appraisals of the Chilean scholar Francisco Encina and the North American Arnold J. Bauer.[102]

Though such evaluations may be valid, they do pose certain difficulties. What is meant by the term "efficiency"? And how can we compare Jesuit agrarian management or experimental impulses when we lack studies of the agricultural practices of their peers, whether lay or ecclesiastical, in the Americas or in India?

In recent decades several scholars who have studied Jesuit activity in Spanish America, including Ewald, Riley, Konrad, and Cushner, have been impressed by the essential conservativeness of Jesuit estate management.[103] As Cushner summarizes their findings, the fathers

> were conservative, not innovative agriculturalists. They introduced into Mexico no new plants or cattle varieties; their methods of cultivation were those practiced by most of their counterparts; they were hardly leaders in crop rotation or in the use of fertilizer and their cattle ranches and farms were characterized by a high degree of mismanagement and ineptitude . . . their *haciendas* were probably no different than those run by lay persons. . . . Corn, wheat and barley were raised the way the administrators' families had done it back on the family farm. Cattle was raised the way it was done on the ranches of Popayán or Santa Fé . . . apparently not too many new ideas on agricultural techniques were exploited.[104]

Herman Konrad, author of the finest case study of any Jesuit estate, likewise emphasizes the cautious economic behavior of Jesuit owner colleges. They did not "get involved in untried activities, preferring to follow the commercial trends of their regions. They invested

---

101. Anthony Disney, "Goa in the Seventeenth Century," in Malyn Newitt, ed., *The First Portuguese Colonial Empire* (Exeter, 1986), 96; cf. Chevalier, *Land and Society*, 246.

102. The views of Encina and Bauer are outlined in the useful summary of scholarly opinion in Riley, *Hacendados*, 55–56.

103. In addition to the cited works, see Ursula Ewald, *Estudios sobre la hacienda colonial en Mexico: Las propriedades rurales del colegio Espírito Santo en Puebla* (Wiesbaden, 1976).

104. Cushner, *Lords*, 79; and idem, *Farm and Factory: The Jesuits and the Development of Agrarian Capitalism in Colonial Quito, 1600–1767* (Albany, 1982), 87.

in *pulque* and minerals only after these products had become established, proven commodities in reliable markets. This strategy of 'playing safe' avoided the risk of entrepreneurial daring, relying upon superior management to produce steady income levels."[105]

It is easy to find examples to support Konrad's contention, but one may suffice. Some scholars believe that New World corn (*zea mays*) reached Seville during the second decade of the sixteenth century, and that between 1515 and 1525 it entered Portugal via the Mandego River and was first planted near Coimbra, from which it was later disseminated throughout the northern parts of the kingdom. Though other scholars contend that the grain introduced was actually "Guinea corn" or sorghum (*milho zaburro* or *milho da guiné*), there seems no question that New World corn was grown extensively in the kingdom during our period.[106] The Jesuits never grew corn in the kingdom, though they did so in Brazil. But in the Peninsula they were content to rely upon traditional grains—wheat, barley, millet, and rye—for which there was a proven market.

Fr. Serafim Leite, the towering figure whose ten volumes continue to dominate studies of his Order in Brazil, takes a very different view. With obvious pride he points to Jesuit estates in Brazil where cabbages, radishes, lettuce, grapes, eggplant, oranges, and other vegetables and fruits introduced from Portugal were cultivated along with manioc, beans, bananas, pineapples, and exotic fruits from Brazil, as well as jackfruit (*jaca*) from India, oranges from China, cinnamon from Ceylon, and pepper from the Malabar. He credits the Jesuits with having introduced and disseminated each of those commodities in Brazil; he points to the pioneering role of the Jesuits in dispatching feral Amazonian cacao to the kingdom beginning in the late seventeenth century, to their development of a superior rice-husking device in the colony, and to the famous *quinta do tanque*. Situated close to the present state archives of Bahia, the quinta became the favored domicile of António Vieira for nearly seventeen years. It was one of many recreational properties that the Society maintained, but it was also an experimental farm where plants from the four corners of the world were cultivated and from which plantings of cinnamon, pepper, and other commodities were dispatched to the Society's gardens throughout Brazil.[107]

There is something to be said for each of these divergent appraisals. As the preceding chapters have emphasized, the Society of Jesus *was* conservatively administered. During the formative period especially, its leaders were concerned about keeping a low profile, particularly in economic activities, lest the Society be misjudged with respect to its goals. Though the Society gratefully recruited men, especially lay brothers, who possessed farming or stock-raising experience, many of those who were assigned to manage estates began with little practical experience in crop or animal production. Their guides were partly the instructions their superiors handed down to them, sometimes the advice they received from already-tested estate administrators, but often primarily the on-the-job experience they gained through trial and error. It would be a mistake to expect members of the Society to have displayed the "entrepreneurial daring" that Konrad suggests they lacked. Except for their own persons and for certain notoriously large and bad debts, the Society was not

105. Konrad, *Jesuit Hacienda*, 316; see also 317, 325–26.
106. For a summary of the debate, see Maria Olimpia da Rocha Gil, *Arroteias no vale do Mondego durante o seculo XVI: Ensaio de historia agraria* (Lisbon, 1965), 11–12; see also Brandão, *Dialogues*, 198 and 225.
107. *HCJB*, 4: 155–59; 5: 161–63.

geared for risk-taking, and its colleges lacked both the surplus cash and the inclination to attempt to market new commodities on a significant scale.

Slicher van Bath has written with respect to the agricultural practices of medieval Orders that "the novel feature of the great monastic farms was their business-like management; the tillage itself was practised in the same way as on any other mediaeval farm. Cereals were the main crop, and there were no experiments with new implements or crops. There were no model farms for the neighbouring farmers, nor was there any sign of innovation in farming technique."[108] His remarks are equally applicable to Jesuit agriculture in the period studied here. It would be wrong to think of Jesuits in our period as conforming to the image of the modern economic man. Furthermore, considering the Society's leaders' concerns about charges of "mercantile" activities, it is most unlikely that the Jesuits would have attempted to create demand in the kingdom (or elsewhere in Europe) for novel colonial products. It is true that they sent cacao, sugar, and other commodities to the kingdom, but only cacao and sugar were shipped in quantity; most of their other commodity shipments were dispatched in modest amounts and were usually intended as gifts to superiors and to Jesuit facilities in Portugal and elsewhere in Europe. It is true, as Fr. Leite says, that to the extent possible, Jesuits grew overseas foodstuffs they remembered from and had enjoyed in Europe, but they did so primarily to satisfy their own palates, not to improve the quality of life of those outsiders who were dependent upon them.

In modern times, launches belonging to a well-known Protestant church sailed for decades along the backwaters of the Amazon disseminating grapefruit seeds to isolated Indian communities in the hope that the villagers would plant them and that the resulting trees would produce fruit that would alleviate vitamin C deficiencies. The Jesuits in our period never did that; nor did any other religious Order, nor any other organization. But, after all, the Jesuits were educators and soul curers, not public-health officers. It should be remembered that for the Jesuits, the two primary reasons for engaging in agriculture and stock-raising were, first, to provide subsistence for members of the Society and their dependents, and second, to raise revenues to support the Society's vast enterprises, which could not be fully funded in other ways. Just as the fathers were successful in acquiring large landed portfolios, so too were they successful in fulfilling those objectives. But, as the following chapter will demonstrate, the Jesuits' flourishing rural estates made the Society an inviting target for critics who both envied and despised it on other grounds as well.

108. Slicher van Bath, *Agrarian History*, 154.

CHAPTER 17

An Enterprise Under Attack: Attempts to Monitor, Curtail, and Eliminate the Jesuits' Patrimony

> Let our members be cautious of purchasing lands; but if they happen to buy
> such as are well situated, let this be done in the name of some faithful and trusty
> friend: And that our poverty may have the more colorable gloss of reality, let the
> purchases, adjacent to the places wherein our colleges are founded, be assigned
> ... to colleges at a distance; by which means, it will be impossible that princes
> and magistrates can ever attain to a certain knowledge what the revenues of the
> society amount to.
>
> —*Monita Secreta*

THE JESUITS' SUCCESSFUL acquisition and development of lands, a source of pride and sat-isfaction to the members of the Society, became the subject of constant complaints from governors, treasury officers, magistrates, and rival estate owners, who tirelessly warned the crown that the Jesuits and other religious Orders were engrossing a large proportion of its lands in violation of existing laws and at the expense of the king and his subjects. It would be easy to dismiss such critics by accusing them of cupidity, malice, and other base motives, as, indeed, their adversaries did. But that would be a mistake, for their concerns, though frequently exaggerated and resting upon misunderstandings, were often sincerely felt. One of those concerns was the erroneous conviction that the Jesuits' possession of real estate represented a violation of their vow of poverty; but that vow was simply a personal pledge and was never intended to be binding upon the Order itself. Another represented sentiments, repeatedly expressed in Portugal and elsewhere in Europe during the High Middle Ages, that the Church had already become vastly wealthy and that the Jesuits and their ecclesiastical rivals were simply following a baneful pattern by relentlessly amassing a disproportionate share of the available domain at the expense of the king and his faithful subjects.

The first attempts to restrict ecclesiastical landholdings in Portugal occurred in 1211, when the cortes of Coimbra passed legislation that prohibited churches and monasteries from acquiring real property by purchase except during royal anniversaries. However, they were still permitted to obtain lands offered as free gifts and as pious legacies, as well as those contributed by persons taking clerical orders. The first of a long series of royal inquiries into the extent of the holdings of religious bodies was made in 1220.[1] About 1237, Sancho II (1223–45) prohibited churches and monasteries from accepting living trusts or bequests that involved land transfers; however, in an early example of the sort of ambivalence that always characterized the crown's attitude toward ecclesiastical patrimony, the very next year that monarch put aside his own decree when he made large territorial concessions to the archbishopric of Braga. Half a century later, in 1286, the famed Denis the Farmer (1279–1325) undertook what appeared to be further drastic steps against the Church when he forbade religious bodies to purchase any lands and directed that they sell or forfeit within one year all they had bought since the beginning of his reign. Five years later he issued another decree that prohibited religious bodies from inheriting the estates of their recruits. But, like so many such edicts intended to restrain the material appetites of the Church, these measures were not systematically enforced.[2]

Of all this body of legislation, the items that were the most enduring and most frequently cited by opponents of the Jesuits were two articles that first appeared in the initial codification of Portuguese laws, the Afonsinas (1446), and were repeated in its two successors, the Manuelinas (1521) and the Philippinas (1603). One was a provision (book II, tit. 16 of the Philippine Ordinances) that prohibited any religious entity from obtaining crown lands (*realengos, reguengos*) through purchase or other means. This article warned that violators who conspired to evade that injunction would forfeit their interest in those lands. The second article (book II, tit. 18 of the same code) prohibited ecclesiastical bodies from purchasing real property without the king's license and threatened those who sold such lands to religious bodies without the king's consent with the loss of their purchase price.[3]

Precisely what constituted crown lands and whether the Jesuits possessed proper warrants for their lands would become persistent issues between the fathers and their adversaries from the sixteenth to the eighteenth centuries. As will be evident in the next volume of this study, the two laws described above would prove most useful during the fateful 1750s, when the minions of the future marquis of Pombal would employ them as centerpieces of their rationale to justify the confiscation of all the Society's properties. This chapter will demonstrate that the efforts by the crown and its agents and the methods that they employed before 1750 to restrain the ability of the Jesuits and other landholding Orders to acquire lands varied from one regime to another, as did the intensity and severity of complaints agaicomplaints against such ownership. Ironically, despite government threats to sequester the Jesuits' assets, one of the most serious and permanent losses of income-producing property that they sustained prior to 1750 came as a result of a conflict between the fathers and the agents of the English East India Company.

---

1. Maria José Lagos Trindade, "A propriedade das ordens militares nas inquirições gerais de 1220," in Instituto de alta cultura, Centro de estudos historicos, *Do tempo e da historia*, vol. 4 (Lisbon, 1971), 125–38; Henrique da Gama Barros, *História da administração publica em Portugal nos seculos xii a xv*, 2d ed., ed. Torquato de Sousa Soares, 11 vols. (Lisbon, 1945–54), 6: 161–78.

2. The foregoing is based upon *HIP*, 1: 109–13, 309–11; and 2: 81–85.

3. *Codigo philippino ou ordenações e leis do reino de Portugal*, 14th ed., ed. Cándido Mendes de Almeida (Rio de Janeiro, 1870); cf. *Ordenações do Senhor Rey D. Afonso V*, 5 vols. (1792; rpr., Lisbon, 1984), bk. 2, tits. 13–14; and *Ordenações do Senhor Rey D. Manoel*, 3 vols. (Coimbra, 1797), bk. 2, tits. 7–8.

The Benevolent Years, 1541–80

The early Portuguese monarchs were fully supportive of efforts by the Society's leaders to attain financial security. They recognized that the royal exchequer could not fully provide for the Order's financial needs and, as disclosed in Chapter 15, they provided seed grants to enable certain colleges in the kingdom to purchase income-yielding property. They also generously provided land grants (sesmarias) and endowments for several of the early colleges in Brazil. In India, the crown assigned to some Jesuit colleges the income from sequestered temple land. Despite the restrictive articles in the royal ordinances, which were conceived at times when the only lands to which they applied were in the kingdom itself, John III and his immediate successors encouraged Jesuit colleges to accept any properties they were offered. Thus, for example, in 1551 the king authorized the Society in India "to accept and retain any donation of lands that may be made ... in favor of their apostolate." His grandson, Sebastian, signed a similar carte blanche for the Brazil colleges.[4]

It was always assumed, of course, that the fathers would obtain royal license permitting them to hold such properties. Such licenses customarily contained a clause indicating that royal approval represented a specific waiver from the restrictive provisions in the codes mentioned above.[5] But the Jesuits found that procuring those warrants could take years and that the process, especially for overseas properties, could be tedious and troublesome. The lengthy process that led to royal confirmation of the transfer of the temple lands in India to Old St. Paul's provides a good illustration of what proved to be a common experience for Jesuit leaders:

In 1540 the king's forces knocked down all Hindu temples on Tissuary and the other islands near Goa.

In 1545 the governor, Martim Afonso de Sousa, Xavier's voyage companion, awarded the temples' supporting properties to Old St. Paul's, pending ratification by the king.

The college rector applied for such ratification in a petition sent to Lisbon by the next available carrack.

Because the license had not arrived, Governor Jorge Cabral issued a provisional confirmation for two years beginning in July 1550.

In February 1551 John III was prepared to sign the license but elected to wait until a report had been received from the viceroy concerning the status of the temple lands and the Jesuits' need for them.

In 1552 Cabral's successor extended the provisional authorization for another three years.

In March 1553 the license was signed, but because of the proximate departure of the carracks, it was not registered in the royal chancellery before their departure. As a result, when the license reached India, the viceroy refused to accept it and directed the Jesuits to renew their appeal to John III.

---

4. Carlos Merces de Melo, S.J., *The Recruitment and Formation of the Native Clergy in India (16th to 19th Centuries)* (Lisbon, 1955), 89–91; *MB*, 3: 530–31.

5. "Sem embargo da ordenação do Livro II titulo 18 em contrario" was the usual formulation. E.g., ANTT/CJ/83, no. 101.

On 12 March 1556, the king signed the license, and it was subsequently registered and forwarded to Goa.[6]

Thus, between the destruction of the temples and the arrival of an authenticated royal license assigning their supporting lands to the Society, a dozen years elapsed. But even the king's signature did not assure the Jesuits of immunity from future assaults on those properties. On the contrary, in the 1640s another viceroy, hard-pressed (as Portuguese India's governors always were) to find means to defray urgent, defense-related expenditures, insisted that the Jesuits' title to the temple lands was defective and sequestered them for the crown. Upon appeal, John IV set aside his action.[7]

Jesuits in the Portuguese as well as in the Spanish Assistancy confronted another problem during the formative period that would continue to plague them for two more centuries, namely, disputes over land ownership.[8] The sources of those disputes were many and included complaints by disappointed heirs, conflicting titles, disagreements over boundaries, and trespassing. One instance of the last demonstrates how solicitous the crown was of Jesuit territorial claims in this period. In 1574 the provincial of Brazil petitioned the crown that certain persons had allowed their cattle to graze on lands belonging to the college of Rio de Janeiro. He averred that conflicts over those lands were detracting from the fervor and service due God. Sebastian responded by directing his governors and magistrates to prohibit such trespassing.[9]

Despite strong royal support, the Order did not escape criticism during these years. In 1562, for example, one anonymous dissenter seriously questioned the need for Jesuit classes at the University of Coimbra and suggested that the subventions that the crown provided the arts college could be better applied to the Moroccan war and that students who wished to learn ought to go abroad for their studies to the universities of Salamanca or Paris. The same year, complaints registered at the cortes in Évora charged that the Jesuits were already becoming rich and that if they were not prevented from engrossing lands, none would be left for the king's subjects.[10] Before 1580 the sovereigns of Portugal did not take such carping seriously. But when the throne became vacant that year, the Society's honeymoon was over, for the Philippine kings proved to be far less solicitous of the Jesuits, and they and their lieutenants became much more attentive to the complaints of the Society's adversaries concerning its expanding landholdings.

6. Anthony D'Costa, S.J., "The Demolition of the Temples in the Islands of Goa in 1540 and the Disposal of the Temple Lands," *Neue Zeitschrift für Missionswissenschrift* 18 (1962): 161–76.

7. [Fernão de Queiroz, S.J.], "Conquista da India per humas e outras armas reaes e evangelicas," *DUP*, 1: 544.

8. For the Spanish Assistancy, cf. Nicholas P. Cushner, *Lords of the Land: Sugar, Wine and Jesuit Estates of Coastal Peru, 1600–1767* (Albany, 1980), 50–56; idem, *Farm and Factory: The Jesuits and the Development of Agrarian Capitalism in Colonial Quito, 1600–1767* (Albany, 1982), 53–56; and idem, *Jesuit Ranches and the Agrarian Development of Colonial Argentina, 1650–1767* (Albany, 1983), 14, 24–26. Such disputes appear to have been even more common in Spanish America than they were in the Portuguese empire. In Mexico, for example, Herman Konrad found that the Santa Lucia property became the subject of 85 legal actions between 1576 and 1767. *A Jesuit Hacienda in Colonial Mexico: Santa Lucia, 1576–1767* (Stanford, 1980), chap. 7.

9. Provisão, 30 Jan. 1574, in *LTC/RJ*, 15–16.

10. *HCJAP*, I:2, 467; José Maria de Queiroz Velloso, *A universidade de Évora: Elementos para a sua história* (Lisbon, 1949), 57 n. 3.

Philippine Efforts to Check the Growth of Jesuit Latifundia

The coolness of Portugal's Philippine masters toward the Society has already been observed (see Chapter 4). In part, the crown's attitude stemmed from Philip II's skepticism about the activities of an international Order that successfully evaded his efforts to lure its headquarters to the Iberian Peninsula and that enjoyed the protection of a papacy with which the king was often at odds. But the crown's view of the Jesuits was also influenced by its own precarious financial condition by the 1580s, owing to Spain's disastrous wars, especially those with England and Holland, and by reports concerning the unreasonable affluence of the Society.[11]

Both in India and in Brazil, Jesuit leaders soon recognized that different winds were blowing from the court. In 1584 Valignano complained to Aquaviva that there was a definite slowdown in the crown's approval of requests for confirmations of villages acquired for the Japan enterprise.[12] The previous year he had acknowledged that some in India believed that the Society was very rich, and he had insisted that the contrary was true, that of all the Orders in the subcontinent it was the poorest.[13] In 1586 Valignano advised Aquaviva that he had learned that the king had secretly ordered a report of all the Society's sources of income in India. To offset potentially damaging information that might come from the viceregal headquarters, Valignano and his consultores assembled the first comprehensive account of the financial status of each of the Society's units in the East.[14] It was during the 1580s that Jesuit leaders in India and Brazil first complained about the tardiness of the crown's subventions.[15] The vast sums consumed by preparations for the dispatch of the famous armada of 1588 may partly explain those delays, but they also seem to have stemmed from the king's doubts that the Society really needed his financial support.[16] Much to the distress of Francisco Cabral, the provincial, the king ordered an end to the practice of assigning gifts received by the crown from Indian princes to St. Paul's and refused to confirm the donation by D. Pedro de Castro of the villages of Assalona, Velim, and Ambelim to the Society on the ground that they were crown lands (see Chapter 14). In the end, the provincial found it necessary to dispatch a priest to Portugal to gain the king's approval, which was reluctantly conceded in 1594, seven years after the donation had been offered.[17]

The upshot of the increasingly unfriendly attitude of Philip II toward the Society during the first decade of Spanish hegemony was a royal decree signed in 1591. In it, the king stated that he had been informed—presumably in the now-missing secret report concerning Jesuit

---

11. E.g., Jorge de Lemos ("secretary of a fortress") to Philip II, Goa, 5 Dec. 1589, in *DI*, 15: 438–39, advising the king that the Jesuits' revenues in India were "muitas e muito grossas."

12. Valignano to Aquaviva, Cochin, 12 Dec. 1584, in *DI*, 13: 597–98.

13. Valignano, "Regimento e instrução do que ha-de fazer o Padre Nuno Rodriguez que agora vay por procurador a Roma," Goa, 12 Dec. 1583, in *DI*, 13: 420.

14. Valignano to Aquaviva, [Cochin], 22 Dec. 1586, in *DI*, 14: 453; Valignano, "Sumario de todos os colegios e casas . . . rendas e gastos que tem a provincia da companhia na India feito no anno de 1586," in ibid., 463–513.

15. *HCJB*, 2: 156.

16. Philip II to D. Duarte de Menezes (viceroy, India), Lisbon, 21 Jan. 1588, in *APO*:1, 3:1, 110–20; rpr. *DI*, 14: 810–12.

17. Philip II to Duarte de Menezes, Lisbon, 6 Feb. 1589, in *DI*, 15: 256–58; *DI*, 16: 10*–11*.

resources in India—"that the Religious of India" had purchased and were continuing to buy many estates in the subcontinent, resulting in "grave damages and inconveniences," the chief being their refusal to pay tithes upon such estates (see Chapter 18). Accordingly, the king directed that henceforth no religious Order "without exception" could purchase any landed property, and he nullified any authorizations to the contrary.[18] In reporting that edict to Aquaviva, the provincial of Goa observed that the law violated "the liberty of the Church and [was] therefore unjust," but he added that it was reflective of the antipathy that the court was then displaying toward the Society, in marked contrast to the supportive role of Portugal's earlier rulers.[19]

Although the 1591 decree was repeated five years later, there is no evidence that it was ever enforced.[20] On the contrary, the crown soon received additional complaints concerning the Jesuits' continued territorial acquisitiveness. One came from a memorial composed by a famous figure in early Brazilian history, Gabriel Soares de Sousa. A Bahian sugar planter and soon to be a mining prospector, Soares de Sousa was the author of the foremost chronicle of sixteenth-century Brazil. He was also a severe critic of the Jesuits, primarily because of their efforts to protect the Brazilian Indians (see Chapter 19). In 1592 Soares de Sousa composed a lengthy memorial to the crown concerning alleged misdeeds of the fathers, whom he condemned as usurpers of their neighbors' properties and as intimidators who threatened to excommunicate those who opposed their land claims.[21]

Nine years later, the municipal council of Goa warned the new king, Philip III of Spain (1598–1621), that

> if this State . . . is lost, it will be the fault of the Fathers of the Company . . . [who have become] absolute masters of a great part of this island [Goa], and they buy up everything, so that within ten years there will be no house or palm grove left which will not be theirs. . . . The citizens are being dispossessed of them all, which is the reason why this State is so poor.[22]

That alarm found an echo in distant Lima. There, in 1609, a Spanish viceroy assured the king that one-third of the viceroyalty of Peru, the most lucrative among Spain's overseas possessions, was already in the hands of the Jesuits and other ecclesiastics.[23]

Such reports provided part of the motivation for the crown's first serious attempts to compel the Jesuits and other religious Orders to liquidate their landholdings in the kingdom and its empire. But there were surely other factors at work as well. One was the serious financial plight of the government of the dual Iberian empires, which contributed to Madrid's reluctant decision to negotiate a truce with the Dutch rebels in 1609. It is also significant that two other church-related issues in which the Jesuits were deeply involved

18. Provisão of 24 Jan. 1591, in *APO*:1, 5:3, 1280–81.
19. Francisco Cabral to Aquaviva, Cochin, 5 Dec. 1593, in *DI*, 16: 531.
20. Francisco de Gouveia (provincial, Portugal) to Aquaviva, 16 Mar. 1596, in *DI*, 18: 502–3.
21. See Chapter 19, note 28.
22. Quoted in C. R. Boxer, *Portuguese Society in the Tropics* (Madison, Wis., 1965), 17; for a slightly different translation, see Teotónio R. de Souza, S.J., *Medieval Goa: A Socio-Economic Study* (New Delhi, 1979), 72.
23. Conde de Montesclaros to Philip III [of Spain], 5 Apr. 1609, as cited in Paulino Castaneda and Juan Marchena, "Las ordenes religiosas en America: Propriedades, diezmos, exenciones y privilegios," *Anuario de estudos americanos* 25 (1978): 125–58, at 144.

surfaced at this time, namely, the resistance of the Orders to the payment of tithes and their opposition to episcopal visitation.[24]

A royal order in December 1609 to the viceroy of India signaled a toughening of the crown's stance toward the Orders. In effect, it was a more elaborate formulation of the 1591 decree: the king directed that henceforth viceroys were not empowered to award crown lands to ecclesiastics under any circumstances. It also stipulated that no individual might sell, give, or bequeath to the religious such lands upon pain of losing them to the royal exchequer. Fiscal and judicial officers in India were admonished to post the decree prominently and to enforce it rigorously.[25] Three years later those admonitions were repeated in another royal directive, which specifically demanded that the Jesuits disclose the titles they possessed to lands in Goan Salsete.[26]

Before drafting that order, the crown took further steps that appeared to menace the economic future of Jesuit colleges, especially those in the kingdom. In the middle of 1611 it issued two edicts stating that the king had been informed that contrary to the laws of the realm, the religious Orders had purchased many properties without royal license, and insisting that they sell such possessions within a year and a day or suffer their loss to the crown. Those edicts threatened the Jesuits as well as other religious bodies with economic destruction. Consequently, the Orders immediately appealed for reconsideration; in 1612 the crown responded by granting two extensions, each for six months.[27]

Those directives prompted a flurry of activity by the Jesuits. In January 1612 the provincial of Portugal drafted a memorial to the king in which he reminded the sovereign of the many services that the Jesuits had performed for the crown at home and abroad. He stated that if the Society were compelled to dispose of its holdings, the market would inevitably be depressed, and his Order would receive far less than the properties were worth and would be compelled to abandon its colleges.[28] Nevertheless, the provincial ordered each college to submit detailed reports on its properties, including how and when they were acquired, their purchase prices, and their annual yields. The provincial procurator put together the results and in 1612 submitted the first of a series of lengthy accounts to the crown concerning the economic foundations of the province, including the Atlantic islands and Angola. In the most comprehensive version of that report, the leaders of the province were careful to distinguish the properties that each unit possessed before the several royal seed grants were made specifically to enable colleges to purchase income-yielding property, and to demonstrate how those grants had been employed. A close reading of that report discloses that the recipients of those grants actually acquired far more property than they

24. I intend to discuss Jesuit opposition to episcopal visitation throughout the period covered by this study in a future monographic article.

25. Alvará of 24 Dec. 1609, in José Ignácio de Abranches Garcia, comp., *Archivo da relação de Goa*, 2 vols. (Goa, 1872–74), 1:85–86; summarized in *CCLP*, 1: 283.

26. King to D. Jerónimo de Azevedo (viceroy, India), 29 Feb. 1612, in *DRI/LM*, 2: 190–92.

27. Alvarás of 30 July and 23 Aug. 1611, 13 Aug. and 23 Nov. 1612, in ANTT/CJ/57, nos. 2, 3, and 4; *CCLP*, 1: 307, 380, and 388–89. The second of this series is referred to in later documents and appears to have been a reiteration of the first order, for which the text is lacking.

28. Draft of petition of [Jerónimo Dias, provincial] to Desembargo do Paço [the highest tribunal in the realm], ca. Jan. 1612, in ANTT/CJ/57, no. 14. In the same series, another draft (no. 18) places even greater emphasis upon the overseas commitments of the Society.

were authorized to purchase.[29] The degree of the Jesuits' vulnerability to the charge that they held many properties without royal warrant is revealed in the 1619 report of the college of São Lourenço, Porto, which disclosed that of its nearly 170 properties, 162 lacked royal license![30]

Remarkably, the crown does not seem to have been agitated by that disclosure. Yet four years earlier, the king had admonished the viceroy of India that the crown had information that the Jesuits possessed lands and villages in Ceylon for which they did not possess warrants. He had directed that if the charge was true, they were to be sequestered on his behalf.[31]

It is unlikely that the crown really expected the Jesuits and the other ecclesiastical entities to dispose of their landholdings. It is more probable that it intended to compel the religious to restrain their propensities for acquiring territory, to seek with regularity its approval for further land additions, and to accept its determination that their lands were subject to payment of tithes.[32]

Although the crown's directives seem to have been aimed particularly at the Jesuits, its attitude toward the Society soon began to soften. In 1617 the king, upon recommendation from the Desembargo do Paço and despite the opposition of the local episcopal chapter, approved the founding of a new Jesuit college in Santarém, though he stipulated that its endowment be restricted to that already provided by its Jesuit benefactor, Fr. Duarte da Costa.[33] Three years later the crown again called upon the viceroy of India to submit one of the periodic reports concerning the number of religious in each house in the State of India and the sources available to sustain its members. Two years later the new monarch, Philip IV of Spain, conceded that the government had not been able to prevent the faithful in the East from leaving their estates to the Church but insisted that their properties must be judicially inventoried before such bequests could be approved.[34] In 1624 the king authorized the Jesuits' establishment of the Cape Verde mission but declared that they could not receive properties to support it. Interestingly enough, in the same year the crown modified that stipulation: the province could acquire "some farm or orchard" to support the mission provided that it first apply to the crown to license the acquisition.[35] That modification came one year after the papal representative protested to the king that the legislation his ministers had enacted was contrary to well-established papal bulls.[36]

How impressed Philip IV was by the agent's complaint is unknown. What *is* clear is that in 1629, the leaders of the Church received a new royal order giving them a month to disclose the number of houses they possessed, the number of their inmates, and their

29. Although ANTT/CJ/57 contains a number of rather sketchy financial reports for the province prepared at this time, the most thorough is no. 26: "Informaçam dos bens de raiz que os collegios da Companhia de JESV tem neste reyno," n.d. [ca. 1612].

30. "Enformação da fazenda q. tem o coll.º do P.ᵗº em 12 de jan.rº de 1619," in ANTT/CJ/57, no. 31.

31. Alvará, 23 Feb. 1615, in *DRI/LM*, 3: 280.

32. There is an anonymous memo of 1618 (post-24 Oct.) to the provincial, presumably drafted by one of his consultores, that specifically recommends that the Society agree to the first two of these points, though not to the payment of tithes. ANTT/CJ/57, no. 29.

33. *CR*, 11 Sept. 1617, in *CCLP*, 2: 253. On the benefactor, see Chapter 14.

34. *CR*, 5 Mar. 1620, and acknowledgment dated 26 Feb. 1621, in *DHMPPO*, 6: 427–29, and 7: 249; *CR*, 19 Feb. 1622, and *lei* of 24 Feb. 1624, in Abranches Garcia, comp., *Archivo*, 1: 291–92 and 328–29.

35. *CR*s of 3 July and 14 Sept. 1624, in *CCLP*, 3: 123 and 126.

36. *HCJAP*, 3:1, 268–69, which is also the source for the following paragraph.

funding. Upon recommendation of the papal collector, the heads of the Orders delayed in complying with that directive until 1635, when their representatives conferred with the vicereine, Margaret of Savoy, who was finally persuaded that the campaign against the properties of the religious was unwarranted. She therefore ordered that it cease and that the question be subject to perpetual silence.

That directive came too late to prevent further charges of excessive wealth from being leveled against the Jesuits in India. D. Miguel de Noronha, fourth count of Linhares (d. 1647), arrived there in October 1629 to assume his duties as viceroy. The grandson of a former viceroy and son of a governor of Tangier, a post he himself occupied between 1624 and 1628, Linhares served in the State at a critical time amid one disaster after another. During his regime (1629–36), revolts broke out from Ceylon to Mombasa, the Dutch-Sumatran siege of Malacca tightened, state revenues continued to shrink, and the crown's new pepper company proved a failure.[37] About the time of Linhares's departure for the East, Fr. António Collaço, the procurator-general for India, applied to the crown for permission for the northern colleges of Diu, Damão, Taná, and Chaul, as well as that of Mozambique, to purchase or receive donations of income-producing estates, since the royal subventions upon which they had depended no longer reached them. In customary fashion, the crown asked Linhares for his recommendation. After consulting with a desembargador who was probably a member of Goa's High Court, and with others who claimed four decades of experience in the State, Linhares stated emphatically that the petition ought not to be granted because the Jesuits and the other Orders in India were swollen both in number and in revenues. Using the terms favored by Jesuit adversaries, he accused the fathers of being "sovereign and absolute" in Ceylon and "so authoritative in India that they claim that even the viceroys are their lackeys," but, of course, he supplied absolutely no proof of the validity of those charges. He also asserted, on the basis of the opinions of his informants, that the religious Orders in India were enormously wealthy, and he raised the complaint, already discussed in an earlier chapter, that they were luring the king's newly arrived soldiers to join their houses.[38] In view of Linhares's charges, the crown's response was predictable: send a full report of the finances of each religious Order, and do not allow any Order to buy or accept estates. The state of the crown's records was such that it claimed that it had not received such an account in twenty years, although the rector of New St. Paul's said that his predecessor had submitted one as recently as 1628.[39] Linhares detailed his magistrates to survey the holdings of each Order and the results were the highly inflated reports that he forwarded to Madrid in 1635.[40]

By the time those reports reached the court, Linhares himself was approaching the same destination, having so greatly enriched himself during his sojourn in the East that

37. A. R. Disney, *Twilight of the Pepper Empire* (Cambridge, Mass., 1978). Disney is completing what will be the first full biography of this controversial figure.

38. King to viceroy, 16 [month lost] 1630 and undated response, probably composed the same year. HAG/*LM*, 13A, fol. 109[r] (fragments); viceroy to king, 8 Nov. and 2 Dec. 1630, in *BFUP*, 2: 480, 514–16, and 541; viceroy to king, 21 Dec. 1631, quoted in Alberto Carlos Germano da Silva Correa, *Historia da colonização portuguesa na India*, 5 vols. (Lisbon, 1948–62), 4: 98–99.

39. King to Linhares, 22 Feb. 1633 and 7 and 9 Mar. 1634, in *BFUP*, 3: 268, and 4: 304–5 and 331; Francisco de Vergara to king (?), Goa, 24 Jan. 1630, in HAG/*LM*, 13A, fol. 45[r].

40. Many of them are preserved in ANTT/*LM*, 35 and 36. The former also contains a very general report by the provincial to the viceroy dated 3 Jan. 1636, fols. 183[r]–184[r].

he was able to offer the king and queen gifts amounting to four times the Jesuits' annual income from their Indian properties.[41] Within a year or two of Linhares's arrival at court, the crown received three conflicting reports from luminaries in Goa. One came from Jorge Seco de Macedo, apparently an officer of the Holy Office, who, while praising the Jesuits for the extent of their missionary commitment in the East, also insisted that in Goan Salsete and in the northern province they possessed most of the lands and were "almost absolute lords." The second was a carefully phrased refutation of the charges made by Linhares and his informants that had been composed by Fr. Miguel Rangel, a Dominican who was bishop of Cochin and interim governor of the archbishopric of Goa. Fr. Miguel denied that the religious Orders in general and the Jesuits in particular enjoyed excessive revenues and insisted that, on the contrary, each house was burdened with troubling debts, a subject that the crown's reports ignored. The last of this series was an account by one of the magistrates of Goa stating that the Jesuits of that province possessed 26 parcels of unlicensed land.[42] In view of these mixed reports, Margaret of Savoy, soon to be overthrown in the December revolution of 1640, instructed the viceroy of India not to confirm the transfer of a village that a pious woman had left to the college of Damão and insisted that in the future such properties ought to be sold—but only to Portuguese, never to natives of the land![43]

Criticism of Jesuit Landholding During the Restoration and the Petrine Years

As observed in Chapter 5, the Society of Jesus became an indispensable source of support for the restored Portuguese crown beginning with the December 1640 revolution. Consequently the crown was inclined to adopt a policy of tolerance toward further Jesuit land acquisitions, but that did not prevent the Society's properties from becoming a focus of contention in the empire during and after the Restoration. Community organizations—Brazilian cámaras and village assemblies near Goa—became one source of such criticism. In 1641, for example, the municipal council of Rio de Janeiro complained that despite the fact that the Jesuits possessed many properties in the captaincy and were "very rich," the fathers refused to contribute to the cost of strengthening Rio's defenses.[44] In Goan Salsete, the general assembly of villages complained in 1642 and again in 1643 that despite the fact that the Jesuits were among the territory's most important landlords, they refused to contribute to community expenses. The assembly further protested that the king's subjects were unable to obtain justice because of the powerful enemies set against them, especially "the Fathers of the Society of Jesus [who] are the toughest of all [and who] have usurped many lands."[45]

At the end of the 1650s, the cámara of Salvador joined the anti-Jesuit chorus. It complained that "the Religious Orders, which in this captaincy possess much property and many sugar mills, estates, farms, houses, cattle and slaves, refuse to contribute anything . . .

41. *PDH*, 4: 213; third catalogues of the Goan province of 1627 and 1641, in ARSI, *Goa*, 25, fols. 43^v–45^v and 80^r–81^r.

42. Seco de Macedo to king, ca. 20 Jan. 1636, in ANTT/*LM*, 36, fols. 166^r–167^v; "parecer do bispo de Cochim," 22 Jan. 1636, in ibid., 35, fols. 173^r–174^r; and report of Sebastiam Soares Pa[checo?], 24 Jan. 1637, in ibid., 38, fols. 527^r–528^v.

43. To count of Aveiras, 20 Mar. 1640, in *BFUP*, 7: 134.

44. Cámara to John IV, 16 Nov. 1641, in CeA, 7: 16–17.

45. Souza, *Medieval Goa*, 243–46.

to the expenses of the war, so that the rest of the people are heavily burdened."[46]   What especially miffed the local worthies was the arrival of a new Jesuit Visitor, who reviewed the conduct of Jesuit students (many of whom came from some of the best families) and either exiled them from Bahia or dismissed them from the Society altogether. The cámara protested to Afonso VI that the Visitor's action had caused leading families such distress that it could only be alleviated if he ordered the Jesuit inspector and his consultores to retire from Bahia and directed the college of Santo Antão to sell its major sugar estate, Sergipe do Conde, and its other properties in the captaincy.[47] Since the king himself was about to be deposed, it is not surprising that the petition fell upon deaf ears.

Persons of no particular socioeconomic distinction who contested Jesuit property claims constituted another source of conflict. In part, their claims rested upon imprecise boundary descriptions, of which the following is a not-untypical example. On 6 December 1649, a public notary in Salvador met with the rector of the Jesuit college and recorded that institution's purchase of a parcel of land along the São Francisco River. It was sold by Pedro de Abreu de Lima, who swore that "from this day forward" he was prepared to surrender his interest in the property whose boundaries were defined as beginning

> at a cashew tree growing atop a height called Codfish hill and from the said tree toward the bar of the Tabocas river which discharges into a lagoon called Boacucuipe [and] extending along that stream to its source and from there running East-West as far as a brook known as the Cross, and along the said brook which is opposite the lands of Dona Guimar de Melo, returning to the cashew tree and from there running Northeast to the hillock from which the waters descend to the said cashew tree, and from the hillock Southeast until the lands of Dona Guimar de Melo [and he affirms that the parcel so described measures about 4 by 1.5 leagues (about 25.2 by 9.45 kilometers)].[48]

In colonial times, cadastral surveys were rarely undertaken and even more rarely completed. At the end of 1642, the cámara of Rio de Janeiro resolved to end a longtime dispute with the Jesuit college over certain lands by ordering such a survey. But the aldermen and the fathers engaged in a series of legal maneuvers that delayed initiation of the survey until 1667. Subsequently the magistrate in charge became involved in a conflict with the governor, who imprisoned him in a local fortress. That was the last land survey attempted in the captaincy for nearly a century.[49]

Though the Jesuits, like all landowners at the time, experienced their share of litigation over lands, they sought to avoid such unpleasant confrontations wherever possible. For example, in 1663, after the Carmelites in São Paulo protested a testamentary award by a childless couple to the college of São Paulo on the ground that the couple had already offered the Carmelites the inheritance, the college leaders negotiated an agreement with the Carmelites, who, in return for 70 cattle, a Guinea slave cowboy, and 100,000 rs. in cash, "agreed to desist from further complaints and disputes over the said donation."[50] A similar

46. Quoted in Boxer, *Portuguese Society*, 89.

47. Cámara to king, Bahia, 13 Aug. 1666, in AHU/PA/BA, 1st ser. uncat., *cx.* 9, no. 2147.

48. *DH*, 63: 346–47.

49. Roberto Jorge Haddock Lobo, *Tombo das terras municipães . . . da . . . cámara . . . do Rio de Janeiro*, vol. 1 [only] (Rio de Janeiro, 1863): 13–16.

50. *DISP*, 44: 369.

situation arose in the captaincy of Rio de Janeiro. There, around 1605, the college purchased a parcel of land but had no use for it and for some reason did not rent it out. Eventually the fathers noticed that a neighbor was planting cane on their land. They brought suit and won, but the trespasser appealed. Then, belatedly, they offered him a permanent lease. By 1655 the rector was persuaded that it was best to sell the land and to buy another parcel. Accordingly, he requested Goswin Nickel's approval to do so.[51]

Sometimes the Jesuits felt less charitable toward those who violated their lands. Toward 1690 the rector of the college of Bahia complained to Pedro II that two lower-class ruffians, a blacksmith and a plantation overseer, had been found cutting the forest belonging to the Pitanga sugar plantation, timbers needed for fuel and for the construction of sugar crates. Armed with sticks, the trespassers had behaved in an unchristian manner toward the resident Jesuit manager. The rector asked the king to order the trespassers to be arrested and exiled to Angola and to issue a warning to other planters to respect Jesuit property rights.[52]

As the military posture and the financial resources of the kingdom and the empire worsened, desperate governors and viceroys sought scapegoats to explain the collapse of the empire and often conveniently focused their frustration upon the Jesuits and the other religious. In June 1661, for example, the governor-general of Brazil complained that the Orders, especially the religious, were unpatriotic because of their refusal to pay tithes upon their lucrative, abundant properties.[53] In Goa the vitriolic António de Melo de Castro, the viceroy who opposed cession of Bombay to the British (Chapter 8), was equally indignant. In language reminiscent of that of his predecessor, the count of Linhares, he wrote the prince regent that "among the great miseries that this State of India has experienced for many years not the least has been the multitude of priests who are rich and make themselves masters of everything while the poor folk must depend upon alms." He accused the Jesuits of defying the royal magistrates by excluding them from the lands they controlled, of trafficking with Muslim ports, thereby evading His Majesty's customs, and of violating royal ordinances by inducing the terminally ill to make the Society beneficiary of their estates.[54] His immediate successor, João Nunes da Cunha, spoke ardently in the Jesuits' favor, but Manoel Corte Real de Sampaio, a Goan-born member of the triumvirate that ruled Portuguese enclaves in India at the beginning of the 1670s, warned Lisbon that "the major complaint" in the State concerned the landed possessions of the fathers.[55]

The Jesuits were surely not unmindful of the fact that their economic achievements in India were a source of persistent criticism. An anonymous memorial sent to Father General Carlos de Noyelle at the beginning of the 1680s accused his lieutenants in India of deliberately buying lands during the winter months when values were lowest and of charging excessive prices for the commodities they produced. The provincial emphatically denied these allegations and declared that far from owning a majority, the Society did not

51. Francisco Gonzales to Nickel, Rio de Janeiro, 20 Aug. 1655, in ARSI, *Bras.*, 3:I, 286.
52. Overseas Council to king, 20 Oct. 1690, in AHU/PA/BA, 1st ser. uncat., *cx.* 16, no. 3610.
53. Boxer, *Portuguese Society*, 89.
54. Melo de Castro to [prince regent], n.d. [1665–66], in HAG/*LM*, 35, fol. 149; Melo de Castro to prince regent, 18 Jan. 1666, cited in Overseas Council to prince regent, 1 Mar. 1669, in AHU/PA/IN, *cx.* 28, no. 36.
55. To [prince regent], 14 Jan. 1670, in HAG/*LM*, 34, fol. 55^r.

possess "a thousandth" of the estates in Goa, Bardês, or Goan Salsete. But he conceded that its estates were more productive than those of its competitors because they were far more carefully managed.[56] Though he was stung by the criticism and recognized that any additional territorial acquisitions would become sources of further hostility, Fr. Alexandre Cicero, the father Visitor, insisted that it was still legitimate for Jesuit houses to accept estates left as spiritual properties. Ecclesiastics had made that distinction during the Middle Ages, but it was hardly one that impressed envious laymen who coveted prosperous-looking Jesuit estates.[57]

In the face of this conflicting testimony, the crown's response was ambivalent. When Fr. Luís Figueira, the future martyr, was preparing to lead a permanent Jesuit mission to the Amazon in 1642, John IV sanctioned his enterprise but refused to permit the fathers to obtain landed possessions to support it, a restriction that they subsequently quietly ignored.[58] In Goa during the same decade, when a viceroy seized certain Jesuit rental properties belonging to New St. Paul's and confiscated Assalona, Velim, and Ambelim, main supports of the province of Malabar, the crown praised his zeal but, "moved by their services since the discovery of the State," ordered the properties restored to the Jesuits, despite the fact that their ownership was probably in violation of the aforementioned provisions in the royal ordinances.[59]

Beyond that, the crown merely attempted to monitor the status of the religious in India by requiring the submission of comprehensive reports concerning their number and financial status. Between 1662 and 1690 it made such demands on more than half a dozen occasions but, characteristically, completely ignored the laboriously prepared accounts.[60] Seemingly, as long as the Jesuits and the other Orders complied with these periodic demands for such disclosures, the crown would not approve the seizure of their properties. Resistance to its will, however, could imperil their estates, as the crisis that began in the late 1680s demonstrated.

56. Simão Martins to Noyelle, 28 July 1683, in ARSI, *Goa*, 35, fols. 252–57 (Portuguese text) and 258–64 (text in Latin). That the Jesuits took pride in the improved yield of the properties they administered in India is evident throughout their oft-cited 1666 report concerning their finances: "Lista das rendas e despezas da provincia de Goa . . . pera o Snor' Conde V. Rey Joam Nunes da Cunha," Goa, 13 Dec. 1666, in Cámara Municipal, Elvas, ms. 6891.

57. "Ordens que deixou o P. Visitador Alexandre Cicero visitando esta casa professa no anno [1]684," in ARSI, *Goa*, 35, fols. 297–98. For the distinction between temporal and spiritual sources of income, see Robert E. Rodes, Jr., *Ecclesiastical Administration in Medieval England: The Anglo-Saxons to the Reformation* (Notre Dame, 1977), 51; and Donald Matthew, *The Norman Monasteries and Their English Possessions* (Oxford, 1962), 29.

58. Mathias C. Kiemen, O.F.M., *The Indian Policy of Portugal in the Amazon Region, 1614–1693* (Washington, D.C., 1954), 52 and 55.

59. Provisões of 14 Apr. 1649 and 6 Mar. 1651, in *CCLP*, 9: 189 and 198.

60. Such calls and responses are found in HAG/*LM*, 34, fols. 54, 97, 151, 103, and 107; 37, fols. 60 and 85; 51B, fols. 23ʳ–24ʳ, 28ʳ–43ʳ; 53, fol. 185ʳ; 55, fols. 489–90 and 511–12; and in *BFUP*, 9: 504, 511, 518; and 12: 21, 175, and 196. There is no evidence here or in other archival files for the period that the king's ministers paid the slightest attention to the reports. During the seventeenth century, the court seems to have been less interested in obtaining such reports from Brazil, but for one example of an order for an accounting of the properties of the religious in Brazil, see *CR*, 19 Feb. 1687, in *DH*, 68: 118.

*The Second Threat by the State
to Confiscate Jesuit Properties*

In part, the second crisis was reflective of the precarious financial condition of Portugal in the decades immediately before Brazilian gold began to flow to the kingdom (see Chapter 5). Seeking relief for the royal exchequer wherever it might be found, the crown in 1688 renewed its efforts to compel the Jesuits and the other Orders to pay tithes on their properties (see Chapter 18) and, with the apparent concurrence of the papacy, levied a heavy assessment upon ecclesiastical entities and called upon them to disclose the extent of their properties.[61] When Pedro II encountered resistance to his orders, he intensified the pressure. In January 1691 he directed the governor-general of Brazil to notify each ecclesiastical head that he was to submit documentation for each property that his organization possessed within three months for estates in the vicinity of Salvador and no more than six months for those elsewhere in the colony.[62]

Under attack, the Church, which had witnessed so many internal quarrels for more than a millennium, joined forces and presented a lengthy memorial that must have shocked the king's ministers and certainly annoyed the mercurial Pedro II. Prostrating themselves before His Majesty, the Church leaders stated that while they were always willing to sacrifice their blood and their estates in his behalf, they could not comply with royal edicts that were in violation of ecclesiastical immunities and privileges. In a fourteen-point statement, they insisted that the oft-cited provisions of the royal ordinances concerning the possession of properties by the Church had been repeatedly condemned by the holy pontiffs since the thirteenth century and were contrary to the decrees of the Council of Trent. They insisted that the properties conveyed to the Church by the king's predecessors and their pious subjects were irrevocable gifts, that they were not excessive in extent, and that their yield had actually diminished during the past 70 years. In short, while the Church remained firm in its loyalty to the crown, its diverse components could only yield to the crown if ordered to do so by the pope.[63]

Since the extant copies of this memorial, which obviously attempted to pit the papacy against the crown, are regrettably unsigned, it is impossible to be certain that the leaders of the Society in the kingdom also signed the defiant document. There is no evidence that they did not do so. In May 1692, a year or more after the memorial was delivered to the royal palace, the rector of the college of Bahia, Fr. Bernabé Soares, tried a more tactful approach. Without alluding to the current crisis, he addressed a long letter to the newly arrived governor-general of Brazil, D. João de Lencastre. He reminded Lencastre that his Order had performed many services for the crown in times of war and peace in Brazil and that in compensation for such assistance, the rulers of Portugal had granted the Society subventions and lands, which he asked the governor-general to reconfirm.[64]

61. *CR*, 2 June 1688, in BNL/CP/474, fol. 337^r.

62. *CR*, 28 Jan. 1691, in APB/OR/2, no. 13 (orig.); published in *MHB*, 2: 285.

63. "Memorial que as religioens deste reino derao a El Rey Dom Pedro 2.º sobre o decreto em que se mandou exhibir a todas os titulos das fazendas que possuhiao," n.d. [1690 or 1691], in BNL/CP/474, fols. 123^r–145^v. BNL/CP/475, fols. 352–355^v, contains an incomplete draft.

64. Soares to Lencastre, 20 May 1692, in Virginia Rau and Maria Fernanda Gomes da Silva, comps., *Os manuscritos do arquivo da casa de Cadaval respeitantes ao Brasil*, 2 vols. (Coimbra, 1956–58), 1: 292–94. The

For a time the crown played what would now be called hardball. Throughout 1691, 1692, and early 1693, the king continued to insist that his subordinates require Church leaders to submit titles and licenses for each property that their organization possessed and threatened that if they failed to comply, his tribunals would seize the properties and their incomes in his behalf.[65] As late as January 1693, the crown seemed intent on fulfilling its threat, but suddenly in March of that year the king ordered the sequestration suspended.[66]

One may speculate why Pedro II withdrew his threat. The serious illness of Fr. Manuel Fernandes, his longtime Jesuit confessor (d. 10 June 1693), may have been a factor. The intervention of the papal nuncio allegedly cooled the king's temper, but what may have been decisive was the apparent capitulation of the Church, for in his directive suspending the seizure of Church estates, Pedro II observed that his reason for doing so was that its leaders had agreed to provide the crown with the documentation that it demanded concerning their assets. Thus an apparent clash between church and state was averted, and the right of the crown to require an accounting of properties owned by all the entities of the Church was clearly affirmed. In October 1694, the nuncio reported that the crisis was over and that the king had imposed silence upon the entire matter.[67]

As was the case during the aftermath of the first conflict between the crown and the Jesuits over the Society's properties, the crown for a time adopted a stern yet cautiously supportive policy toward Jesuit appeals for income-producing properties to sustain particular enterprises. Thus in 1693, after more than two decades of negotiations, it approved the establishment of the college of Beja, but under exceptionally stringent conditions: the queen's dowry for the institution could never be increased; the Jesuits were not to acquire any income-yielding lands and within one year were to dispose of any they might already possess for its support; and the fathers' request to acquire a recreational estate was simply ignored.[68] That year, however, the Overseas Council approved the petition of the procurator of Japan to acquire the village of Morosi in northern Salsete for the Tonkin mission. The council stated that the royal exchequer would thereby be relieved of supporting the mission.[69] Similarly, in 1700 the crown authorized the procurator of Malabar to buy another village in the same district to support that province's distant and fragile outposts at São Tomé de Meliapor and in Bengal. But the king warned that if the missions were ever withdrawn, the

petition is evidently misdated, since Lencastre only became governor-general in 1694. Bahian-born Soares (ca. 1626–ca. 1705) was a veteran Jesuit administrator. *HCJB*, 9: 128–29.

65. *CR*, 17 Oct. 1691, in APB/OR/2, no. 33; *DH*, 33: 384–85; 34: 53–54 and 65–66.

66. *CR*, 30 Jan. 1693, in APB/OR/2, no. 118 (orig.); copy in BGUC, cod. 706, fols. 10ᵛ–12ᵛ; Overseas Council to António Luís Gonzales da Cámara Coutinho (governor-general, Brazil), 24 Mar. 1693, in ibid., fol. 12 (repeated, fol. 122); acknowledged by Cámara Coutinho on 10 July 1693, in APB/OR/2, no. 118A, published in *DH*, 34: 106–7. An identical order was sent to the captain-general of Pernambuco on 9 Apr. 1693, in IAGHPB/OR 1693–1701, fol. 45ʳ.

67. *HCJAP*, 3:1, 269–70. Rodrigues's account is surprisingly incomplete. The usually dependable Francisco de Almeida ignores the crisis altogether (*HIP*, 2: 81–127), as does Veríssimo Serrão (*HP*, 5).

68. "Difficuldades e inconvenientes q. occurrem acerca das condições com q. se dis que S. Mag.ᵈᵉ ... se ha de servir de dar licencia para a fundação do collegio ... na cidade de Beja," ca. 1693, in ARSI, *Lus.*, 79, fols. 290–290ᵃ. On the 23-year campaign to establish the college, see *HCJAP*, 3:1, 37–47.

69. Overseas Council to Pedro II, 13 Mar. 1693, in AHU/PA/IN, *cx*. 37, no. 14.

villages would have to be sold to seculars.[70] Yet throughout the 1690s, Pedro II repeatedly expressed concern about reports that the religious in India, particularly the Jesuits, were continuing to purchase estates without his consent and directed that all possible measures be taken to prevent the practice.[71] Contemporaneously, the crown approved a number of Jesuit petitions to acquire lands in Maranhão.[72] Finally, four years before his death, Pedro II authorized the professed house in Goa to accept a large bequest (16 contos) from a deceased man in Mozambique. The Jesuits proposed to invest it in a village in India to compensate for the catastrophic loss of properties a dozen years earlier to the East India Company.

The East India Company Versus the Jesuits

Despite all of the posturing by the king's officers, they never deprived the Jesuits of any of their estates in the period covered by this study. Curiously, it was precisely during the 1680s and 1690s, when the Portuguese crown was acting as if it intended to seize Jesuit and other Church properties, that agents of the English East India Company (EIC) actually undertook such a step, the second time within a generation.

It may be recalled that Portuguese authorities, led by Viceroy António de Melo de Castro, were most reluctant to transfer Bombay Island to the English in accordance with the treaty of 1661 (see Chapter 8). In 1665, when the transfer occurred, the viceroy obliged English authorities to agree to a series of articles interpreting the intent of the treaty in a manner highly favorable to the Portuguese. Among other pledges, the English agreed to respect entirely the Catholic faith and churches on the island; they promised that Portuguese property owners would be free to retain ownership or to sell their estates "for just value," and that the island's inhabitants would "not be bound to pay more then [*sic*] the Tribute that they paid to his Majestie," their former sovereign.[73]

Although Portuguese authorities believed that they had made the best bargain possible, their English counterparts had no intention of honoring that accord, and their master, Charles II, later repudiated it. Two years after the transfer was completed, the new English governor, Gervase Lucas, seized the properties of several prominent landowners, including the Jesuits, on the island and the adjacent Mahim Peninsula immediately to the north. But when his successor, Henry Gary, laid claim to the town of Bandorá northwest of Bombay and sent customs officers there to collect duties, they were met by armed inhabitants led by the Jesuit superior of the incipient college. This incident marked the beginning of anti-Jesuit paranoia on the part of the new rulers of Bombay. Gary indignantly wrote the earl of Clarendon that "the great wrongers of His Majesty's rights here have been the Jesuits, who have spared no sweat ... to embroil His Majesty's affairs, endeavouring to divide the inhabitants of the island ... with strange suggestions that ... [it] shall be re-delivered up to the King of Portugal, thereby weakening the hands of ... His Majesty's subjects, and

---

70. Alvará of 10 (or 20) Mar. 1700, in BNL/CP/475, fols. 439^r–439^v; published in *CCLP*, 10: 458. The two sources differ on the authorization's date.

71. King to viceroys of India, 19 Jan. 1695 and 12 Oct. 1697; replies of 12 Dec. 1695 and 1 Jan. 1698; in HAG/*LM*, 59, fols. 92^r–93^r; 61, fols. 7^r–8^r; *CR*, 12 Oct. 1696, in BNL/CP/439, fol. 7.

72. ANTT/CJ/83, nos. 3, 4, and 5, and other licenses in this file.

73. "Auto da entrega da ilha de Bombaim feito em 18 de fevereiro de 1665," arts. 6, 10, 11–13; *CTEIP*, 3: 32–49. Both English and Portuguese texts are included.

endeavouring to shake and falsify their loyalty." He contended that "the Jesuites . . . [were] the greatest bout[e]feu's of the world."[74]

As Table 17.1 indicates, several Jesuit entities had an important economic stake in the Bombay area properties. Consequently, Jesuit leaders worked diligently to recover their own possessions and those of their fellow landowners. To that end, in 1669 they petitioned Sir George Oxenden, the East India Company's president at Surat, for the properties' return. In forwarding that petition, Oxenden, less hot-headed than Gary and less sure of the legalities of the seizure, observed that it was framed in behalf of "the Padres, the better sort of inhabitants, the widows, orphans and poore. . . . Wee hope and pray your answere may come in favour of them, for to us it appeares a mere force, without anything legall proceeding."[75] Later Oxenden complained that he was being deluged by petitions drafted by the fathers and the other concerned landowners.[76]

The land dispute dragged on for several additional years. Gerald Aungier, president of Surat and governor of Bombay, warned his superiors that the Jesuits were extremely obstinate:

> As they are very wise, subtle and powerfull, so in truth they are very troublesome, not to say insolent, and . . . they have used all politick ways to bring their ends about, that these lands might be surrendered without examination. Your President thinks it not fitt to tell you how he hath bin tempted by them to abuse his trust; but . . . when they cannot gaine their desires that way, they use another more dangerous to your government, which is by threatening those your servants [who are Catholic] . . . with severe spirituall censures, with excommunication, pronouncing them damned for serving hereticks, and suchlike illegall pernicious arts they use to weaken the hearts of your people . . . from their duty and obedience to your service.[77]

The Portuguese crown, which was indifferent to the fate of India in this period, made little effort to protest these confiscations.[78] In the end, in February 1672, it was an otherwise unknown Jesuit, Reginaldo Burges, who led the principal landowners in hammering out a settlement with the governor's representatives. Burges, described as a procurator, perhaps the provincial procurator, earned the admiration of even Gerald Aungier, who described him as "a wise and public-spirited man."[79]

Perhaps, but the settlement was a clear victory for the Company's agents. The landowners agreed to pay the Company quitrents amounting to 6 contos a year, more than a quarter of the annual coconut and rice yield.[80] Ironically, the Jesuits promised to

74. Henry Gary, secretary at Surat, to Clarendon, 12 Dec. 1667, quoted in J. H. Gense, S.J., *The Church at the Gateway of India, 1720–1960* (Bombay, 1960), 234–35; Gary to Lord Arlington, 1667, in *EFI* (1665–67), 304.

75. Oxenden to the Company, 15 Jan. 1669, in *EFI* (1668–69), 95–97.

76. Oxenden to the Company, 21 June 1669, in ibid., 230.

77. Aungier to the Company, Surat, 30 Sept. 1671, in *The English Factories in India*, new ser., *1670–84*, ed. Sir Charles Fawcett, 4 vols. (Oxford, 1936–55), 1: 25–26.

78. The only reference that I have found is a casual mention of the unresolved estates question in Pedro Sanches Farinha, "The State of the Account of the 2d Million of the Queen's Portion," Lisbon, 12 Mar. 1669, in PRO/SP/89/10, fols. 37, 39–40, the latter being an English translation of the Portuguese original.

79. Aungier to the Company, post–12 Nov. 1672, in Fawcett, *English Factories*, 1:47.

80. For the text of the agreement of 12 Nov. 1672, see *CTEIP*, 3: 122–28. Among the sixteen signatories is the name of Padre Reginaldo Burges, who is described as the group's secretary. The accord was ratified two years later.

TABLE 17.1

"Manifesto of the Absolutism and Robberies of the English Committed
Contrary to the Transfer Articles of Bombay," 1722

(000 rs.)

Location/owner	Value (1667)	Annual yield (1722)	
		Amount	Percentage of 1667 appraisal
Bombay Island			
Dona Ignez de Miranda, widow of D. Rodrigo de Monsanto	18,000	2,700.0	15.0
Japan province; vice-province of China	15,000	1,680.0	11.2
Chaul college	240	—	—
Bandorá Church (S.J.)	510	66.0	—
Bandorá residents	4,077	609.3	14.9
Francisco Mursello and his father-in-law	—	594.0	—
Bernardino de Távora	1,785	268.5	15.0
Total	39,612	5,917.8	14.9
Mahim Peninsula			
New St. Paul's	27,000	3,900.0	14.4
Agra mission	11,100	1,575.0	14.2
Bernardino de Távora	26,400	3,919.8	14.8
Francisco Mursello Coutinho	1,860	879.0	47.2 [a]
D. Isabel de Miranda	1,380	207.0	15.0
Bandorá residents	—	3,616.8	—
Salsete and Caranja Island residents	—	926.1	—
Total	67,740	15,023.7	22.1
Grand total	107,352 [b]	20,941.5 [c]	19.5

SOURCE: *CTEIP*, 3: 330–36.

[a] Evident scribal error.

[b] Jesuit properties represent 50.2 percent of total.

[c] Jesuit income represents 47.4 percent of total.

contribute to English heretics a far larger proportion of their earnings from their Bombay district lands than they were ever willing to pay the Portuguese crown in the form of tithes (see Chapter 18). But even the accord of 1672 did not assure the fathers of protection against further assaults against their Bombay properties, as the sequel demonstrated.

Throughout the remainder of the century, relations between the English at Bombay and Surat, the Portuguese in Goa and in the northern province, the Marathas, the Mughals, and the Sidis of Rajapore were repeatedly tangled and strained. Each tried to take advantage of the others' weaknesses, and each expressed contempt for its rivals. Although the Jesuits, particularly those at the Bandorá college, tried to abstain from such hostilities, they eventually became their principal victims.

In the mid-1680s, EIC directors, encouraged by their soon-to-be-deposed sovereign, James II, a major Company investor, urged their agents to move aggressively against all of their enemies in the East, including the king of Siam, the Mughals, and the Portuguese. In Bengal they were to capture Chittagong and attack Dacca, and in the Bombay salient they were to expel the Portuguese from that outpost's supposed dependencies. As Sir William Wilson Hunter sarcastically observed, "Of this vast programme, conceived in ludicrous ignorance of the geographical distances and with astounding disregard of the opposing forces, not a single item was carried out."[81]

In fact, the Company's sudden militancy proved disastrous. That was especially true in the West, where EIC officials deliberately quarreled with Mughal officials in Surat. Their conflict began in 1680 when Aurangzeb, the emperor, reimposed a special tax on all infidels. When Company officials refused to pay it, Aurangzeb directed Surat port authorities to double customs duties on English goods entering the EIC factory. Sir John Child, the factory president and governor-general of the Company's eastern outposts from 1686 until his death in 1690, then recklessly seized Mughal ships trading with Red Sea ports and prevented a Sidi merchant fleet from departing Surat.

The Sidis were descendants of Abyssinian traders who had come to India before the arrival of the Portuguese and established themselves, initially as traders and later as sea raiders, at the island fortress of Danda-Rajpuri, 42 kilometers south of Bombay, and at nearby Janjira. Their services were available to the highest bidder, including the rulers of Bijapur and Surat. Their targets included English, Portuguese, and especially Maratha shipping. Indeed, from 1660 onward they were the focus of repeated (but unsuccessful) Maratha attacks, and from time to time they benefited from English assistance. Around 1660 the Sidis became the naval arm of the Mughals, and from about 1672 they regularly brought their fleets for protection and repairs to Bombay during the winter monsoons (generally May to October, but sometimes later).[82]

Child's detention of the Sidi shipping brought devastatingly swift retaliation. At midnight on 14 February 1689, a massive force that the English estimated at 20–25,000 landed on the littoral of Bombay Island, where the island's defenders, outnumbered 10 to 1, were quickly routed, allowing the Sidis to gain control of the entire island save for its castle. For sixteen months they pillaged the island and reduced the castle defenders to a handful. Finally the EIC agents signed a humiliating peace agreement with Aurangzeb. On 22 June 1690, the Sidi leader, Yakut Kahn of Janjira, withdrew his 40,000 men from the island, "leaving," as EIC officials ruefully reported, "therin the marks of ruine and destruct soe deeply engraven as wee believe may require a good competency of tyme to wear out."[83]

Portuguese authorities watched the EIC's debacle closely but resisted the temptation to take sides. The Overseas Council warned the governor at Goa not to offend either the

81. Hunter, *A History of British India*, 2 vols. (New York, 1900), 1: 247. Hunter focused upon the unsuccessful Bengal campaign and ignored the events described here.

82. The value of D. R. Banaji's *Bombay and the Sidis* (Bombay, 1932) is enhanced by its documentary appendix, which, however, is not indexed. It is superior to T. C. Palakshappa, *The Siddhis of North Kanara* (New Delhi, 1976). See also Surendra Nath Sen, *The Military System of the Marathas* (Bombay, 1958), 165–69; and Jivanji Jamshedji Modi, "Rustam Manock (1635–1721), the Broker of the East India Company," *JBBRAS*, n.s. 6 (1930): 1–220, esp. 142–53; and Ashin Das Gupta, *Indian Merchants and the Decline of Surat, c. 1700–1750* (Wiesbaden, 1979), 26.

83. Council of Bombay to EIC directors, 15 Jan. 1691, as quoted in Banaji, *Bombay*, 199. Three EIC employees left accounts of the Sidi occupation: J[ohn] Ovington, *A Voyage to Surat in the Year 1689*, ed. H. G. Rawlinson (London, 1929), 91–96; Alexander Hamilton, *A New Account of the East Indies* [1727], ed. Sir William Foster, 2 vols. (London, 1930), 1: 109–27; and John Burnell, *Bombay in the Days of Queen Anne*, ed. Samuel T. Sheppard, *HS*:2, no. 72 (1933): 18–20, 56–59; see also the map facing p. 90. The most helpful secondary source is John Bruce, *Annals of the Honorable East-India Company, ... 1600 to ... 1707–8*, 3 vols. (London, 1810), 3: 9–11, 95, 631–43.

Mughals or the English.[84] Whether that warning reached the Jesuits and precisely what Fr. José de Pandare, the superior of the residence at Bandorá, did during the invasion is undivinable. What *is* clear is that EIC officials later accused Fr. Pandare of providing the Sidis with rice, coconuts, powder, and gold, of inhibiting the efforts of a Company recruiter, and of failing to answer the call to arms required of all English landowners. As if these allegations were insufficient, the Protestant chaplain, John Ovington, infected with Popish Plot paranoia, insisted that the Bandorá Jesuits "invited the Siddy to exterminate all the Protestants" in Bombay.[85]

Reflecting on these charges, D. R. Banaji observed that "the question naturally arises whether the Senior Padre supplied the Sidis' food supplies of his own free will, or whether he was acting under the constraint of fear," and cautiously concluded, "It is not easy to determine what part the Senior Padre played in the Sidis' invasion."[86] True enough, but it should be obvious that if a garrison of nearly 2,000 English troops could not deter the Sidis, a mere eight Jesuits were quite powerless to resist them. What should be equally evident is that EIC agents deliberately framed these allegations because they coveted Jesuit estates, as did their superiors, who approved of the confiscation.[87]

Every attempt thereafter by Portuguese authorities and the Jesuits themselves to recover those estates failed. In December 1693, the viceroy reported that EIC officials refused to return the properties, claiming that they were not covered by the terms of their convention with Aurangzeb, a preposterous contention since the Jesuits were hardly his subjects. When local Portuguese officials attempted to cut off the shipment of provisions from Salsete Island to Bombay, EIC agents threatened to burn Goa. Led by its president, Francisco de Távora, the count of Alvor, whose tribulations in Goa have been noted in an earlier chapter, the Overseas Council urged that the blockade be continued and that representations be made to London.[88] But the Company maintained its resolve to hold on to the estates and, until the onset of the War of the Spanish Succession (1702–13), ordered its agents to carry on an informal war against Portuguese shipping in the East.[89] The war softened the

84. D. Rodrigo da Costa to king, 24 Jan. 1688; Overseas Council to governor, 14 Oct. 1688, in AHU/PA/IN, *cx.* 34, nos. 84 and 133.

85. Burnell, *Bombay*, 58, n. 1, and Ovington, *Voyage to Surat*, 95–96. Among other studies, see Malcolm V. Hay, *The Jesuits and the Popish Plot* (London, 1934).

86. Banaji, *Bombay*, 46–47.

87. Directors of the EIC to president and council of Bombay and Surat, 29 Feb. 1691–92, in IOL, E/3/92, fol. 103^r. On 18 Mar. 1691, the Court of Directors wrote the council, "Your . . . preserving to the Company for ever the forfeited lands, is very well approved of by us." Gense, *Church at the Gateway*, 241. That dispatch, which Fr. Gense attributes to the Bombay Record Office, is missing from IOL files. For a defense of the EIC's seizure of Jesuit properties by a Company servant, see Bruce, *Annals*, 3: 105.

88. Overseas Council to king, 24 Dec. 1694, in AHU/PA/IN, *cx.* 37, no. 94; Távora to count of Vila Verde (viceroy, India), 5 Mar. 1695, and Vila Verde to Pedro II, 10 Dec. 1695, in *CTEIP*, 3: 170–73; *CR*, 12 Nov. 1696, in BNL/CP/439, fol. 44.

89. EIC directors, "Instructions to Captain John Kempthorne, commander of the *Kempthorne*," 7 Sept. 1699 (OS), in IOL, E/3/91, fols. 292^v–293^r; governor and council, Bombay, to directors, 6 Jan. and 21 Aug. 1699, IOL, G/3/17, no folios. The same year, the Portuguese secretary of state complained to John Methuen about the seizure of a Portuguese China carrack by an EIC corsair, which took it to Bombay and sold it. Methuen insisted that the capture was made by Red Sea pirates. PRO/SP89/17–2, fols. 339 and 341. As late as 1700, EIC directors instructed their Bombay agents to "repel force by force" in dealing with the Portuguese. IOL, E/3/93, fol. 170^v.

Company's belligerence,[90] but the resurgence of Anglo-Portuguese friendship did not enable the Portuguese envoy to London, the celebrated D. Luís da Cunha, to fulfill his promise to the father general to effect the estates' return.[91]

Nor were the fathers themselves any more successful. In 1706, António de Azevedo, superior of the Bandorá house, submitted a plaintive petition to the governor of Bombay in which he denied that his predecessor had ever had any voluntary dealings with the Sidis and in the name of piety urged EIC officials to restore the estates, whose lost income was such a hardship for the Society's colleges.[92] But the governor was unmoved by the father's plea. Nor did another tactic work. In 1713 the father general was advised that a Fr. Benedict Freysleben was about to leave (from where is unclear) for England and urged that he contact a Jesuit friend there, an unnamed EIC official, "a very influential person who formerly held a very high position in Bombay," to support the Society's efforts to recover its estates.[93] Whether such contact was made is unknown; if so, it was ineffective, for the Society's Bombay estates were never restored.

For a time the loss of those properties represented a serious financial setback for several of the Society's facilities. The Mughal mission in Agra was especially hard hit since it was deprived of the village of Parel, whose lands extended north of Bombay for some 6.4 kilometers. But New St. Paul's, the college of Chaul, and both the Japan province and the vice-province of China also experienced losses.[94] A wealthy benefactor soon came to the aid of the Agra station (see Chapter 14), and the administrators of New St. Paul's and the eastern provinces became involved in a protracted squabble concerning their shared losses. In time each unit would recover from what chaplain Ovington approvingly called its "desseizing."[95] Nevertheless, the Society's properties, especially those in India and Brazil, would continue to be targets of opportunity during the eighteenth century.

The Jesuits as Scapegoats: The Case of India

In the late 1720s, the provincial of Goa, on behalf of the four eastern provinces, petitioned the king for relief. He stated that the provinces faced an unprecedented plethora of legal challenges regarding their properties in India. The crown attorney in Goa, he reported,

90. In 1703 the Court of Managers expressed the hope that the Portuguese in India would become more neighborly since they had joined the Grand Alliance. To the general and Bombay council, 4 June 1703, in IOL, E/3/95, fol. 69.

91. D. Luis da Cunha to the general, London, 13 Nov. 1705, in ARSI, *Lus.*, 76, fol. 48. The letter reached Rome after the death of Tirso Gonzalez de Santalla (d. 27 Oct. 1705) and before his successor, Michelangelo Tamburini, assumed office (31 Jan. 1706). Da Cunha later assured the latter of his high personal regard and of his great desire to serve the Society. Luis da Cunha to Tamburini, 9 Aug. 1715, in ibid., fol. 149.

92. Petition to General Nicolus Viotli, n.d. [1706], in ANTT/CJ/90, no. 118.

93. Gense, *Church at the Gateway*, 242–44.

94. See Table 17.1. The late John Humbert, S.J., a usually reliable scholar, was quite mistaken when he stated that "the loss of the Bombay property affected only Agra." H/SAG1: 334. Altogether the Jesuits lost four villages, several smaller territorial units (pacarias and cassabes), salt works, and a coconut wine distillery. João de Saldanha da Gama (viceroy) to king, 18 Jan. 1727 and appendix, in *APO*:1, 6:1, 287–90; rpr. in *CTEIP*, 3: 343–48. Characteristically, the annual letter for the Goa province for 1687–92 ignores the Bombay lands problem. ARSI, *Goa*, 35, fols. 316–40 and 364–85.

95. Ovington, *Voyage to Surat*, 96.

insisted that they submit to the High Court titles for each of their properties within two sessions of the tribunal or face their sequestration for the royal exchequer.[96] In his reply to the Overseas Council's inquiry, the viceroy admitted that the fathers had become very unpopular because they had recently financed the disastrous expedition intended to recover Mombasa.[97]

João de Saldanha da Gama's protective response was only partly true. During the 1720s, 1730s, and 1740s, the fathers became the favorite objects of criticism for disgruntled elements in the crumbling State of India. Spokesmen for those elements warned the crown that the State was in grave peril because its defenses were weak and its leaders did not command respect. They knew that expenditures exceeded revenues with monotonous regularity and that deficits were offset by substantial subsidies (*socorros*) that Lisbon sent to Goa. They also knew that although John V was prepared to commit a large part of the minuscule Portuguese navy to the eastern Mediterranean,[98] the king rarely sent more than one or two East Indiamen a year to Goa; sometimes none arrived. They recognized that all talk about the eventual recovery of Bombay and of Portugal's past glories was a mere pipe dream. But instead of criticizing those responsible for the collapse of the eastern empire, they found it convenient to ascribe its perilous state to the religious Orders, especially the Jesuits, whom they accused of being unacceptably rich and, as in Linhares's time, of luring the king's newly arrived recruits to join their ranks.

The Jesuits' critics included municipal aldermen, High Court magistrates, and some viceroys. In 1732, for example, the cámara of Goa complained that the defenses of the northern province were being neglected because of deficiencies of Jesuit administrators and insisted that an especially critical problem was the continued acquisition of estates by the religious, in defiance of the king's wishes. A few years later, the Eurasian leaders of the village of Chapora in Bardês accused the Jesuits of usurping their river and diverting so much of its water to their own palm groves that it was no longer navigable.[99]

The coterie of thirteen desembargadores residing in the vicinity of Goa were directly responsible for many of the Jesuits' legal problems. They included former and current members of the High Court and those whom the viceroys assigned to other administrative duties. All were Peninsulars, and each had accepted an assignment to Goa in the hope of qualifying for more rapid advancement in the judicial hierarchy of the kingdom than would have been possible at home. As the years passed and the prospect of a summons home faded, most became resigned to spending the rest of their lives in the East and consoled themselves by marrying well (often without the required royal assent) and by enriching themselves, as did their counterparts, the soldier-administrators who staffed the State's outposts. By the 1730s, two justices had become prominent lenders to the royal exchequer, and one had retired to an island near Goa that had become his personal possession.[100]

96. Overseas Council to João de Saldanha da Gama (viceroy, India), 6 Apr. 1729, in AHU/PA/IN, *m*. 46.

97. Saldanha to king, 23 Jan. 1731, in ibid.

98. Eduardo Brazão, *D. João V e a santa sé . . . 1706 a 1750* (Coimbra, 1937), 136ff.

99. Cámara of Goa to king, 25 Jan. 1732, cited in Overseas Council to count of Sandomil (viceroy, India), 6 Mar. 1733, in AHU/PA/IN, *m*. 37; Anon., "Mostrador da parte do rio q. entra pela boca chamada Chapora," ca. 1736, in AHU/PA/IN, *cx*. 46, no. 70.

100. Count of Sandomil to king, 23 Jan. 1735, in AHU/PA/IN, *cx*. 45, no. 32, is a remarkably comprehensive and candid assessment of 53 soldier-administrators and 13 past and present members of

The magistrates' attack on the Jesuits began with a salvo fired in the mid-1720s by a member of the High Court, who accused the Jesuit administrators of the old seminary of Santa Fé of misappropriating the vast income derived from its estates. But, as the rector of New St. Paul's explained, the seminary had absolutely no landed property.[101] A few years later, one of the retired magistrates, José Pedro Emaus, added fuel to the fire. His substantial wealth came from the properties contributed by his two wives and from astute investments, especially in Mozambique. In the course of achieving riches, he made many enemies, especially the Jesuits. He accused the fathers of attempting to usurp an inheritance of his second spouse in the northern province, but in 1730 he announced that because of his "generosity," he had reached an agreement with the fathers, who promised to pay him the staggering sum of 33 contos, more than four times the annual income of New St. Paul's.[102]

During the 1720s and 1730s, the Japan province became embroiled in a serious dispute with the widow of a former High Court judge over the ownership of a lucrative village in the northern province. As reported in Chapter 15, the Jesuits had purchased Malara in 1693 in order to provide the Macao college, especially its pharmacy, with an assured income. For a time the community furnished that college with over 80 percent of its revenues, but in 1727 the widow claimed the village was hers and received support from two crown attorneys whom the fathers accused of being cronies of the late magistrate. We cannot follow the tedious course of the Jesuits' suit through the court, but it is certain that victory eluded them, for they never regained control of the village.[103]

Further attacks on ecclesiastical properties followed. In the mid-1730s, the chancellor of the High Court once again questioned whether church estates were held contrary to the key titles in book II of the Ordinances and insisted that the economic decadence of the State was due to the Church's dominance of available lands in India.[104] About the same time, the fiscal of the exchequer raised questions about the granting of lands (prazos) in Mozambique to the Jesuits and the other religious, claiming that the treasury lost great sums because such properties did not pay taxes.[105]

the High Court. The former had already served an average of 22 years in the East, some as long as 40 years. Many were younger sons of noble families. Two were offspring of Miguel Lopes de Lavre, the longtime secretary of the Overseas Council whose brother, Manoel Caetano Lopes de Lavre, was his successor. The length of service of the magistrates is unfortunately not given. The text is summarized unimaginatively by J. M. do Carmo Nazareth, "No governo do vice-rei conde de Sandomil," *O oriente português*, 2d ser., 6 (May–June 1909): 140–47, who states that it was published in extenso by Pedro Celestino Soares in *Bosquejo das possessões portugueses no oriente*, vol. 3 (Lisbon? 1853).

101. João de Olivares to king, Goa, 22 Dec. 1724, in AHU/PA/IN, *m.* 14, bk. 2; *APO*:1, 6:1, 119–21.
102. Emaus to "Eminentiss.° S.ʳ Cardeal [da Mota]," 1 Jan. 1730, in AHU/PA/IN, *m.* 53.
103. Joseph Anselmo, "Informe das rendas q. tem na India as provincias de Jappam e China," 6 Jan. 1719, in BA/JA/49-V-27, no. 197; Dominicus de Brito Praty Japonica, "Informação do estado temporal da provincia de J[a]p[a]m," 14 June 1727, in BA/JA/49-V-28, no. 107; Overseas Council to viceroy, 11 Apr. 1732, in ACL, ms. Azul 503, fols. 117ʳ–118ʳ; Overseas Council to viceroy, 24 Mar. 1733, in AHU/PA/IN, *m.* 37; Luís Aff.° Dantas (secretary of state, India) to king, 28 Jan. 1735, in ibid., *m.* 34, which indicates that the litigation was continuing.
104. António Freyre de Andrade Henriques to king, cited in Overseas Council to viceroy, 19 Apr. 1736, in ACL, ms. Azul 507, fol. 140ʳ. The viceroy previously had praised the chancellor as zealous in the royal service and as diligent in the performance of his duties. But he had also reported that according to gossip, the judge made money through trade, contrary to Portuguese law. Count of Sandomil to king, 23 Jan. 1735, in AHU/PA/IN, *m.* 32.
105. Verissimo António da Silva to king, 26 Jan. 1736, in AHU/PA/IN, *m.* 36.

But the aldermen, judges, and treasury solicitors were not the only ones who found fault with the Jesuits' economic endeavors; so, too, did some of the viceroys. If João de Saldanha da Gama praised the fathers for their zeal, patriotism, and indispensable financial assistance, his successor, the count of Sandomil, was far less supportive.[106] His concerns about the activities of the religious were virtual echoes of those expressed by Viceroy Linhares precisely a century earlier. Sandomil accepted the contentions of the fathers' critics that they possessed enormous wealth and, ignoring the very comprehensive report that the Jesuits had produced in 1730 in response to a royal order concerning the extent of their holdings, ordered the preparation of a new survey. He first criticized the fathers for their lack of full disclosure, and then submitted an estimate of their income from properties in Goa and Bassein that was four times as great as that in the 1730–31 report.[107] He raised anew the question of whether the fathers legitimately held Assalona and its two sister villages in southern Goa, even though that issue had apparently been settled decades before, and he countenanced the seizure of those villages and other properties belonging to the college of Damão for the crown. In addition, he expressed shock that there were Jesuits living (as estate managers) on plantations and insisted that such conduct was somehow reprehensible and that the fathers should be compelled to live in their colleges.[108]

Sandomil's successor, D. Pedro de Almeida Portugal, third count of Assumar and successively marquis of Castelo Novo and Alorna (1744–50), though more enlightened than his predecessor, was also skeptical of the economic endeavors of the Jesuits and was generally unsympathetic to their requests to have their land titles confirmed. Although he did not single out Jesuits, he criticized the propensity of the religious to reside in the vicinity of Goa rather than in their Orders' distant missions.[109]

The crown took little interest in these complaints. The Overseas Council continued to call for the customary reports concerning the status of ecclesiastical properties,[110] but there was clearly no intention of acting on those reports. Indeed, the king directed that the estates and villages that Goan authorities had taken away from the college of Damão and the Malabar province during the crisis of the 1730s be restored to them.[111] Despite all of the efforts by authorities in Lisbon and India to curtail the growth of the holdings of the Jesuits and other religious, the newly designated marquis of Alorna conceded toward the end of his

106. Saldanha da Gama to king, 23 Jan. 1731, in AHU/PA/IN, *m.* 46.

107. Enc. in Sandomil to king, 22 Jan. 1735, in ACL, ms. Azul 505, fols. 220–23 (draft); AHU/PA/IN, *m.* 31 (orig.). It is obvious that Sandomil never bothered to read the 1730–31 report that his predecessor sent to Lisbon on 23 Jan. 1731.

108. Sandomil to king, 24 Jan. 1735 and 20 Jan. 1736, in AHU/PA/IN, *ms.* 33 and 51. It was well known that estate managers resided for part of the year on the properties they managed and had never been a source of criticism from the king's officers before, but the befuddled Overseas Council, which clearly failed to understand the managerial functions of the procurators, expressed alarm and ordered the Jesuits to cease residing on their plantations. Overseas Council to John V, 30 Jan. 1737 and king's endorsement, in AHU/PA/IN, *m.* 35; Council to viceroy, 21 April 1738, cited in marquis de Castelo Novo (future Alorna, viceroy) to Valentim de Gouvea, S.J. (provincial), 30 Aug. 1747, in NBL/GE 349:3, fol. 91^r.

109. Viceroy to Cardinal da Mota, n.d. [1745], in *Arquivo das colónias,* 4: 239 and 240; viceroy to archbishop of Goa, n.d. [ca. 17 Aug. 1748], in NBL/GE 349:4, fol. 21^r.

110. By the mid-1740s such reports were required annually, but that requirement was never enforced. Castelo Novo to heads of the principal religious Orders, 14 Jan. 1745, in NBL/GE 349:1, fol. 69^v.

111. King to viceroy, 19 Apr. 1743, in AHU/PA/IN, *cx.* 372; Overseas Council to king, 20 Mar. 1744, in ibid., *cx.* 68.

term that churchmen were continuing to gain possession of "the best and most productive estates" in India and that since they did not pay taxes, the king's impoverished subjects were shouldering an insupportable burden.[112] Similar laments reached Lisbon from Brazil.

Increasing Complaints from Brazil

Since the crown deemed Brazil, the source of Portugal's mineral wealth and much of its earnings from re-exported agricultural commodities, far more vital than India, it is not surprising that the crown was more attentive to complaints from Brazil regarding the growth of ecclesiastical properties than to those emanating from the East. In 1706 the Overseas Council considered the offer of Domingo Afonso Sertão to finance a new novitiate for Bahia out of his vast personal estate (see Chapter 14). The crown attorney recommended against the offer because "Brazil already has enough Religious" and he doubted that such a training center was warranted. In the end, the Council strongly endorsed the plan because of the Jesuits' "great zeal and fervor," but one councilor insisted that any properties the novitiate received ought to be sold within a year and a day, according to existing law, since the Jesuits did not pay tithes or other taxes. The terminally ill Pedro II concurred, but somehow that restriction was omitted from the king's order licensing the novitiate's founding.[113]

The Council, however, continued to monitor reports regarding the Church's persistent acquisition of estates. In 1715 it admonished the governors to inform the heads of each Order within their jurisdiction that the king had information that they possessed many lands without title, and that if they failed to obtain confirmation from the king within two years, they would forfeit their holdings.[114] When the Overseas Council then received a petition from the rector of Santo Alexandre in Pará to confirm a land grant disputed by a settler, it called for a full report concerning the extent of the Jesuit college's holdings.[115] A short time later, it directed the viceroy of Brazil and the governors of Rio de Janeiro, São Paulo, and the State of Maranhão to submit comparable statements after receiving a complaint from the cámara of the city of Rio de Janeiro concerning the "inconveniences" to the crown stemming from the growth of ecclesiastical properties, "especially those of the Company [of Jesus] which is today Lord of a greater part of the lands," to the disadvantage of the king and his subjects.[116]

In Maranhão, the religious Orders were given two years to present to local authorities warrants for the properties that they held and were threatened with forfeiture for noncompliance. The State's governor zealously enforced the directive and began reassigning

---

112. Viceroy to archbishop of Goa, ca. 17 Aug. 1748, in NBL/GE 349:4, fol. 21ʳ.

113. Consulta of 15 June 1706 with king's endorsement dated 12 July, in AHU/LR/52, fol. 183, per IHGB/MS, lata 29; *CR*, 9 Sept. 1706, in *MHB*, 2: 313.

114. *CR*, 29 June 1715, in AHU/PA/PA, *cx.* 4. Though directed to the governor of the State of Maranhão, the order was clearly also intended for his counterparts elsewhere in the colony.

115. Overseas Council to Cristóvão da Costa Freire (governor, State of Maranhão), 15 July 1716, in AHU/LR/269, fol. 59ʳ.

116. Overseas Council to António Brito de Menezes, 22 Sept. 1718, in *RADF*, 3: 186–88 (also published in *RIHGB* 47, 1 [1884]: 175–77); conde de Assumar to king, 8 Mar. 1719, in OLL, Alorna ms. no. 1, no fols.; *CR*, 26 May 1722, in APB/OR/116/30; Vasco Fernandes da Cunha e Menezes (viceroy, Brazil) to king, 27 June 1725, in ibid., /19/147. Assumar's dispatch and that of Cunha e Menezes were covers for the required reports, but I have not found them.

the properties of the college of Santo Alexandre until the Jesuits were able to convince the crown of the legitimacy of their holdings and the Overseas Council ordered their assets restored.[117]

During the 1720s and 1730s, boundary disputes between the Jesuits and their neighbors in the northern state became increasingly common. To resolve such differences effectively, the rector of the college in Pará proposed in 1726 that a magistrate be empowered to supervise the survey and enrollment of all lands within the captaincy of Pará. That was a canny suggestion, since the rector doubtless well knew that many settlers there were simply squatters and had never demarcated their holdings or obtained clear title to them.[118] The king approved the scheme in 1728, and the appropriate directive was sent to the local *ouvidor geral* the next year. That magistrate had no sooner begun the cadastral survey than the cámara of Belém protested to Lisbon that he had become an agent of the Society, was dispossessing His Majesty's vassals of their estates to award them to the Indians, and was guilty of "other frivolous" acts. They, therefore, asked for a "disinterested and zealous" minister to replace the offender, who quickly found another job elsewhere. Belém's aldermen received support from their brothers in São Luís do Maranhão, who wrote the king that the missionaries, especially the Jesuits, already possessed "three parts of the lands of this State," and that a majority of the king's subjects were oppressed because they had no land at all. For their part, the Jesuits continued to defend the legitimacy of their possessions and to urge completion of the survey, but the next ouvidor geral declined to continue the work on the pretext that the papers compiled by his predecessor had disappeared. Responding to the settlers' protests, the Overseas Council proceeded to undermine the new magistrate's authority by depriving him of the right to reallocate properties occupied by squatters. Needless to say, the cadastral survey in northern Brazil was never completed, and complaints over lands held by ecclesiastics were unceasing during the remaining years considered in this study.[119]

Throughout the 1740s, the Overseas Council continued its traditional policy of temporizing with respect to Jesuit lands. In 1740 it received still another complaint from the cámara of Belém concerning the economic activities of the religious Orders. It rejected the cámara's plea for new legislation prohibiting them from acquiring further landed property on the ground that the provisions of the 1603 Philippine code were sufficiently comprehensive. But it did call upon colonial governors to file new reports concerning the amplitude of religious real estate and invited those with evidence demonstrating that such lands were held in violation of the ordinances to come forward and denounce them within five years.[120]

117. Overseas Council to Bernardo Pereira de Berredo (governor, Maranhão), 17 May 1718, in AHU/LR/269, fol. 96ᵛ; Berredo to Council, 23 Feb. 1719, in AHU/PA/PA, *cx.* 4; and Council to Berredo, 7 Feb. 1720, in AHU/LR/269, fol. 127ʳ.

118. A point made clearly by an unnamed royal treasurer of Maranhão who advised the king that "a majority of the landholders of this captaincy have not marked their boundaries since they occupy far more land than their grants (*sesmarias*) entitle them to have." Overseas Council to governor of Maranhão, 4 May 1743, in AHU/PA/MA, *cx.* 28.

119. The foregoing is based upon a considerable mass of complaints and protests by the cámaras and the Jesuits and responses by the Overseas Council between 1726 and 1734, mostly in AHU/PA/PA, *cx*s. 5, 7, and 9, as well as AHU/PA/MA, *cx.* 20, and AHU/LR/270, fol. 213ʳ.

120. The Overseas Council directed the preparation of comprehensive reports on ecclesiastical properties in a series of directives in 1740 and 1741. They and the resulting surveys are included in João de

However, when one complainant in the northern part of the captaincy of Rio de Janeiro denounced the Jesuits for improperly holding 12 leagues of land associated with their Macaé estate, the Council rejected his petition to acquire that land on the ground that the Jesuits had been in legal possession of it for many years and that the time for such denunciations had already passed.[121] Yet in 1750, the Council directed the chief treasury official of the State of Maranhão to determine which properties the religious of that state possessed contrary to the standing ordinances and to the "great prejudice" of the royal exchequer, and to proceed with their confiscation.[122] Although the fathers might reasonably have believed that this was simply one further example of the crown's ambivalence toward church lands, it proved to be the beginning of a permanent tilt by the crown in favor of their settler rivals, as the sequel to this study will demonstrate.

When Is Enough Enough?

Almost from the date of their entry into the Portuguese realms, the Jesuits became a leading target of those at home and overseas who expressed misgivings about the growth of ecclesiastical real estate. Yet the Society, as well as those of some (though not all) other religious Orders active in the Portuguese empire, ceaselessly added to their holdings. As suggested in earlier chapters, such additions came about primarily through bequests and purchases. What is striking about the efforts of royal officials and settlers who aimed to check such growth and who called for the literal enforcement of existing legislation restricting the amount of land that the Church could possess is their utter failure. The crown, especially through its Overseas Council, repeatedly expressed alarm when it received accounts, often exaggerated, regarding the extent of ecclesiastical holdings, and it sternly ordered its lieutenants to compel the heads of the Orders to disclose the full extent of their holdings. Countless reports concerning those properties were sent to Lisbon, but there is not a single instance in which any royal representative in the kingdom seems to have analyzed the reports or to have urged remedial action based upon their apparent revelations. They were simply logged in, sometimes (but not always) acknowledged, and buried in the files. Furthermore, at no time did any critic of the holding of lands by ecclesiastics suggest that pious persons be deprived of their right to save their own souls through donations of their estates to the Jesuits or their counterparts. And though royal land grants such as sesmarias always specified that such properties were not to be transferred

---

Abreu de Castelbranco (governor, State of Maranhão) to Overseas Council [late 1740], in AHU/PA/PA, cx. 10; "Reg.ᵗo de huma certidao tirada de huns autos de libello posto por ordem de Sua Mag.ᵈᵉ pelo d.ᵒʳ procurador da coroa contra o rev.ᵈᵒ P.ᵉ procurador do colegio de Jezus," Rio de Janeiro, 26 Aug. 1741, in *RADF*, 2: 366–72; Overseas Council to treasury solicitor, Maranhão, 4 July 1748, in AHU/PA/MA, cx. 32 (again calling for implementation of the 1740 instruction); *CR*, 17 Mar. and 26 July 1743, in IAGHPB/OR, 1742–44, fols. 135ʳ–136ʳ, and 220ʳ–221ᵛ; *CR*, ca. Dec. 1744, in APB/OR/42, index (the text is missing); Overseas Council to governor, Rio de Janeiro, 5 May 1744, in AHU/LR/229, fol. 72ᵛ. See also *DH*, 1: 398–99, and 440–41.

121. Overseas Council, consulta of 28 Apr. 1746, in AHU/LR/229, fol. 126ᵛ; Overseas Council to provedor da fazenda, Rio de Janeiro, 11 Mar. 1747, in ANRJ, col. 60/26, fol. 96ʳ; cf. *LAM3*: 166–70 n. 144.

122. Joseph Machado de Miranda (treasury solicitor, Maranhão) to king, São Luís do Maranhão, 30 July 1750, and Faustino de Affonseca F.ʳᵉ e Melo (State treasurer) to king, São Luís do Maranhão, 5 Aug. 1750, in AHU/PA/MA, cx. 32.

to any agency of the Church, those provisions were never rigorously enforced.[123] Nor did the Jesuits' adversaries offer any reasoned alternative to their reliance upon the fruits of their estates for a substantial share of their expenses. Although in 1750 one treasury official in Maranhão proposed that in lieu of their estates, the Jesuits be paid out of customs revenues from Lisbon, Bahia, and Rio de Janeiro, given the crown's track record in paying promised subventions, the fathers could hardly be expected to rely upon such sources of support.

But did the Jesuits really need all of the lands they possessed? Their adversaries repeatedly said that they did not, but the critics always exaggerated Jesuit income and, of course, lacked access to Jesuit records to verify their surmises. Yet some Jesuits themselves argued that the Society lived too lavishly and possessed more property than was proper for an organization of its character. One of the first to express such misgivings was Fr. Henrique Henriques, that tireless missionary and lexicographer who labored for decades on the Fishery Coast (see Chapter 3). Noting the existence of an estate that served as a recreational facility for members of Old St. Paul's and the construction of the massive professed house (Bom Jesús), he quoted Matthew 8:20: "And Jesus saith unto him, The Foxes have holes, and the birds of the air have nests; but the Son of man hath not where to lay his head."[124] But Henrique Henriques was a New Christian and not a team player. It is not surprising that he was never permitted to take the fourth vow.

The acquisition of a recreational farm by another professed house, Lisbon's São Roque, did become a source of internal controversy. In 1585 the house utilized a silent collaborator, the father of a Jesuit father, to acquire the quinta of Campolide as a place of rest and relaxation, an acquisition noted earlier. Some house members considered it too sumptuous for their needs and, observing that it was obtained about the time that the college of Santo Antão was accumulating Val do Rosal, Enxobregas, and Caniços, feared that its addition would furnish Jesuit critics with more evidence to support their conviction that the Society was only interested in riches. After nearly four decades of debate, the quinta was handed over to the Lisbon novitiate.[125]

Interestingly enough, the 1640s saw Jesuits in Goa, Rio de Janeiro, and Bahia express well-conceived qualms about their Order's ceaseless accumulation of real estate. Though one might suspect that such concerns were tied to a surge of patriotism associated with the proclamation of the new government of John IV, that sentiment appears to have been wholly absent from the minds of Jesuit critics. One such critic was Francisco Ferreira Senior, the Visitor of Goa province, who wrote Vitelleschi in 1642 that an opportunity had arisen for Bom Jesús to purchase a coconut plantation on Chorão Island and that senior fathers (consultores) favored the purchase. He did not. Among his objections were that the plantation would be exposed to adverse winds and therefore would be unhealthy; that its acquisition would require significant and continuing expenses for outfitting, provisioning,

---

123. The standard clause in sesmaria grants stipulated "e sem expressa licença minha se não podem alienar da Coroa, como ficão sendo possuidas pelas religiões, e sem pagarem dízimos, parece fica de nenhum vigor a tal doação, e deixa do testador," but those stipulations were never effectively enforced before 1750. *DI*, 18: 267–68. See also [José da] Costa Porto, *Estudo sobre o sistema sesmarial* (Recife, 1965), 112–16.

124. Henriques to Aquaviva, Tuticorin, 14 Dec. 1589, in *DI*, 15: 452.

125. *HCJAP*, 2:1, 200–203.

and staffing; that it would be within a musket shot of the Santa Ana farm owned by New St. Paul's college, and consequently that its purchase would be unedifying to outsiders, especially because of growing criticism about the large holdings that the Society already possessed in Salsete, Chorão, Divar Island, and Goa itself; and that "the true motive" of some of the fathers urging the estate's purchase was a yearning not for a spiritual retreat but for a place where they could fish and hunt. In the strongest possible terms, Fr. Ferreira Senior urged the father general to prohibit the purchase of that or any similar property.[126]

Less than two months later, Sicilian-born Fr. António Forti, a veteran missionary and administrator in Brazil, wrote the same father general a pair of surprising letters from the college of Rio de Janeiro. He observed that although the local inhabitants revered that facility because of the quality of its spiritual endeavors, they were offended by its material activities, which tarnished its image. And with good reason, he said, for the college owned most of the land, nearly 100 leagues (close to 480 kilometers) along the littoral from the vast Santa Cruz multipurpose estate in the west to the Goitacazes in the northeast. He argued that the institution had no need of so many properties, which were sources of endless expenses and debts, became the sepulchers of too many unconfessed black slaves, and absorbed the energies of too many fathers who could be better used as preachers. His remarkable solution: sell off all the properties save Santa Cruz; concentrate upon its development, so that in time it would become more profitable than all the others; and invest surplus income in an annuity in the kingdom.[127]

Later the same year, a disapproving father living in the college of Bahia reported to Vitelleschi concerning an ongoing debate over a proposal that it dispose of some of its lands. Among the reasons advanced for such action were concerns over the prevalence of criticism of the Jesuits as landlords; the numerous lawsuits properties spawned; and the conviction that it would be less troublesome to buy annuities in the kingdom. However, the reporter, Fr. Belchior Pires, who had spent more than four decades in the province, strongly opposed the sale of the properties, for he was convinced that Brazilian lands were beginning to exhibit signs of wearing out and that even for subsistence purposes, the college needed to retain its estates.[128]

António Vieira was an even more prominent seventeenth-century figure who joined the ranks of that small minority of fathers who seriously questioned the need for the Society to possess large estates. While serving as mission superior of the new enterprise in the State

126. Ferreira Senior to Vitelleschi, 25 Oct. 1642, in ARSI, FG, 1443/9/20.
127. Forti to Vitelleschi, 2 Jan. and 6 Feb. 1643, in ARSI, *Bras.*, 3:I, fols. 216–217ᵛ, and 6:II, fols. 218–19. Forti was a fascinating fellow. Born ca. 1595, he arrived in Brazil in 1622, learned Tupi, spent some years as a missionary, became successively rector of the colleges of Rio de Janeiro and Bahia, and was twice Visitor of the former institution. For reasons unknown, he left the Brazil province and died somewhere in the Río de la Plata after 1671. He also wrote another critique of colleagues who were overly preoccupied with the buying and selling of estates and strongly urged that limitations be placed upon such activities. *HCJB* 8: 258–60.
128. Pires to Vitelleschi, Bahia, 12 Nov. 1643, in ARSI, *Bras.*, 3:I, fols. 231–33 (first orig.) and 234–235ᵛ (second orig.). Pires, born in the Alentejo in 1582, entered the Society at fifteen and sailed for Brazil in 1602. He became a mission superior for fourteen years and helped to rally the Pernambucan resistance to the Dutch invaders. He later served as provincial. *HCJB*, 9: 60–62.

of Maranhão, Vieira dismissed the problem of sustaining such operations as insignificant. He insisted that it did not

> necessitate great revenues because the Indians themselves of their own free will build the churches and the houses. Our clothing is simply cotton, dyed black from a local source and the land also provides material for shoes. The Indians supply us with food for they fish and hunt for us and share with us abundantly everything that their fields produce. Only a few things need come from the kingdom. . . . [If the Maranhão Jesuits engaged in commercial agriculture it would be] the total ruin of this mission. . . . Neither God nor our Holy Patriarch wishes us to have estates except for sheer necessity and in this State we need no more land than we already have . . . and if it does not suffice, then the King will see to our needs.[129]

But most Jesuits in the Assistancy were not content to live as primitively as Vieira was, and, after all, most members resided in urban centers where the thatched huts that the Amazonian Indians built would have been inappropriate and where the cost of living was much higher. Furthermore, as already seen in earlier chapters, Vieira's confidence that the Jesuits could always rely upon the crown's support was often not well founded.

In practice, most Jesuits saw no reason why limits ought to be placed upon the Society's ability to acquire additional real estate that could always be used for some worthwhile purpose.[130]   As Jesuit patrimony continued to grow during the eighteenth century, even fathers general became alarmed. In 1714 Michelangelo Tamburini indignantly wrote the provincial of Paraguay that "the only purpose of superiors [there] seems to be economic gain, a deplorable inversion of means and ends." Twenty years later, his successor, Francisco Retz, worried about the increasingly tarnished image of the Society because of the "costly and useless purchase of haciendas and possessions which the colleges acquired solely out of the vainest ostentation of wealth or to prevent someone else buying them."[131]   Though those observations were directed to a province in the Spanish Assistancy, they were equally applicable to units of the Portuguese Assistancy.

The growth of ecclesiastical, especially Jesuit-owned, latifundia became a continual preoccupation of royal authorities in the Portuguese realm. It was one of the problems that D. Luís da Cunha (b. 1662–d. 1749), Portugal's most illustrious and well-traveled diplomat during the reign of John V, addressed in his famous *Political Testament*, composed toward the end of his life for the use of John's successor, José I (1750–77). Cunha estimated that the Church then controlled "at least" a third of the kingdom. And the only means of preventing

129. The quotations, somewhat freely translated, are from Vieira to Goswin Nickel, Maranhão, 10 Sept. 1658, in *NCJ*, 268; and Vieira to Francisco Gonçalves (provincial, Brazil), 1656, in C. R. Boxer, "Quatro cartas inéditas do Padre António Vieira," *Brotéria* 45, 5 (Nov. 1947): 455–76, at 459–60.

130. The archives of the University of Coimbra contain a curious document that purports to be a patriotic gesture by the province of Portugal to donate to the state the Society's principal estates at home and overseas. The offer was supposedly made in 1704 at the beginning of the War of the Spanish Succession. It is unsigned and quite evidently spurious. Among other obvious flaws in the document are assertions that the Society then possessed "engenhos e fazendas em todo o Mundo," including Malacca, Cape Verde, and Arabia! Province of Portugal to Pedro II, 1704, in BGUC, cod. 617, fols. 40^r–41^r.

131. The sources of these statements are Cushner, *Lords*, 177; and idem, *Jesuit Ranches*, 151–52.

further growth, he declared, was by rigorous application of the provisions of book II of the Philippine Ordinances.[132] As the next volume will demonstrate, it was precisely those provisions that José's regime would employ when it moved against the Jesuits' landholdings. It did so for many reasons, including the conviction of many Jesuit adversaries that the Society for too long had escaped its responsibility to pay tithes upon its possessions. The persistence of that conviction will be considered next.

132. Luis da Cunha, *Testamento politico, ou carta escrita pelo grande D. Luiz da Cunha ao Senhor Rei d. José I* (Lisbon, 1820), 41. See also Luís Ferrand de Almeida, "A autenticidade do 'Testamento politico' de d. Luís da Cunha," Academia portuguesa de historia, *Anais* 17 (1968): 81–105. On D. Luis's eventful career, see Almeida's essay in *DHP*, 1: 770–72.

CHAPTER 18

God's Share or the King's?
Jesuit Resistance to Payment of Tithes

> And all the tithe of the land, whether of the seed of the land, or of the fruit of the tree, is the Lord's: it is holy unto the Lord.
>
> —Leviticus 27:30

> Tithes are to be paid in full; those who withhold them are to be excommunicated.
>
> —Council of Trent, 25th Session

> Every day the Religious [here] inherit or buy estates that are exempted from paying tithes. This is doubly harmful since it deprives the Royal Treasury of funds to which it is entitled but also encourages comparable negligence on the part of the settlers.
>
> —João de Abreu de Castelbranco (governor, Maranhão) to Cardinal da Mota, 14 Oct. 1738

THE REMARKABLE PROLIFERATION of Jesuit properties in the Portuguese Assistancy inescapably aroused the interest of the Jesuits' neighbors and fellow religious as well as royal councilors, governors, treasurers, magistrates, and tax farmers.[1] Whereas the neighbors coveted those properties and other religious sought to emulate Jesuit patrimonialism, the contractors and the crown officers attempted to tax them. In fact, the crown's abiding concern about the growth of Jesuit estates—the subject of Chapter 17—was based not merely upon the belief that the Church, especially the Society, was engrossing too much land, but also upon the Jesuits' insistence that their properties were exempt from tithe assessments because of a series of papal concessions. In the eyes of crown officers, such as Governor Castelbranco of Maranhão, the Jesuits set a poor example for His Majesty's subjects, including members of other religious Orders, for the authorities insisted that everyone ought to be tithed. Moreover, the fact that the Jesuits relied upon an external authority—the papacy—to substantiate their resistance to the payment of tithes made them appear to the increasingly xenophobic officers of the crown to be unpatriotic and perhaps even disloyal to the monarchy.

1. This chapter is a revision of a paper originally presented at a conference on the history of colonial Brazil at the University of Toronto in October 1986. In different form it was published in *Colonial Latin American Review* 1 (1992): 185–200.

Background

Giles Constable, a leading authority on monastic tithes, has observed that "no tax in the history of Europe can compare [with tithes] in the length of duration, extent of application, and weight of economic burden."[2] In fact, God's share, that is, the producer's obligatory payment in recognition of his submission to the deity and to its terrestrial agents—has been collected in Judeo-Christian lands for nearly two millennia. Commonly called tenths, tithe assessments have varied in the burden they have represented according to time and place. Some have amounted to as much as 14 percent, others as little as 2.5 percent of the land's yield.[3]

In theory, tithables included all the fruits of the land and of man's industry. Historically, the most important sources have been cereals, oils, wines, and sweeteners—the bases of predial or major tithes; livestock and fowl, which provided "blood tithes"; and gardens and orchards, which contributed "green tithes." Whereas episcopal chapters, monastic houses, noble families, and states traditionally sought to maximize revenues from each of these sources, parish priests were directly interested in personal tithes, which their parishioners were expected to pay at Eastertide.[4] The great reform council of the sixteenth century, the Council of Trent, issued a strong reminder to the faithful concerning the tithe obligations.

As Constable has said, "Who paid and who received . . . tithes is an important question for historians."[5] But it is one that has received scant attention in Portuguese historiography.[6] That literature also ignores a related subject: who was liable for and who could escape payment of tithes? During the High Middle Ages, for example, when both laymen and monks assiduously appropriated tithe revenues for their own purposes, the religious Orders, led by the remarkably aggressive and successful Cistercians, invoked papal exemptions originally granted for what they themselves produced with their own hands to build up vast estates whose growth, their opponents charged, was achieved at the expense of the parish clergy.[7]

The Jesuits' efforts to evade tithe obligations simply represented another chapter in an old and familiar story. As has been observed in earlier chapters, the fathers acquired impressive landholdings throughout the Assistancy over a period of more than two centuries. Were such lands as liable to tithe assessments as were those of secular producers? Or were they spared such obligations because they were maintained for religious purposes and because of a series of exemptions issued by popes Paul III, Pius IV, and Gregory XIII between 1549 and 1578? Those questions became recurrent sources of conflict between the Society's spokesmen and their adversaries in the kingdom, and especially in Brazil.

2. Constable, *Monastic Tithes from the Origins to the Twelfth Century* (Cambridge, 1964), 2.

3. Emannuel Le Roy Ladurie and Joseph Goy, *Tithe and Agrarian History from the Fourteenth to Nineteenth Centuries*, trans. Susan Burke (New York, 1982), 14–16.

4. On the several classes of tithes, see Christopher Hill, *Economic Problems of the Church from Archbishop Whitgift to the Long Parliament* (Oxford, 1956), chap. 5, and J[ohn] Gilchrist, *The Church and Economic Activity in the Middle Ages* (New York, 1969), 33, 268 n. 117.

5. Constable, *Monastic Tithes*, 2.

6. In addition to the sources cited in the article upon tithes (dízimos) in *DHP*, 1: 842–43, see Aurélio de Araujo Oliveira, *A abadia de Tibães, 1630/80–1813*, 2 vols. (Porto, 1979), 2: chap. 5.

7. Gilchrist, *Church and Economic Activity*, 42–43 and 101.

Tithe Debates in the Kingdom

Typically, disagreements between the Society's leaders and their opponents concerning tithe (dízimo) liability occurred in the kingdom before spreading overseas. The earliest legal challenge to the Society's asserted exemption from tithes occurred in the mid-1560s. Noting that the newly founded college of Santo Antão had acquired properties in the archdiocese of Évora, the attorney for the archdiocese of Lisbon insisted that it should contribute tithes to the capital's archiepiscopal see. The college appealed to its principal patron, Cardinal Henry, who, as regent for his nephew, Sebastian, issued a royal rescript exempting the institution from such assessments.[8] In Spain, the first suits against the Jesuits for payment of tithes were introduced in the 1570s, and the results were likewise favorable to the Society. However, indignant Spanish prelates and their chapters relentlessly campaigned against the Order's exemption, and they were rewarded in 1605 when Pope Leon XI declared that in the future all Jesuit institutions in the Spanish domains would pay one-twentieth of the fruits of their vineyards, olive groves, and orchards, and one-tenth of the proceeds of all other properties that had formerly borne tithes.[9]

Episcopal measures against the Society soon spread to the other kingdom of the dual empire. In 1587, the diocesan chapters of Spain took the unusual step of contacting their counterparts in Braga, Coimbra, Lisbon, and Évora urging them to initiate a comparable campaign against the Society in Portugal. Five years later, the remarkably well-endowed archiepiscopal chapter of Évora wrote to the other twelve archiepiscopal and episcopal chapters of the realm and urged that they maintain a united front against Jesuit assertions of tax immunity. The Évora canons argued that the Society was becoming richer by the day and that its unwillingness to pay tithes defrauded "the good chapters and military orders" of the kingdom of their just revenues.[10] The "good chapters," in turn, organized a writing campaign to their new king, Philip II, and to the pope, Sixtus VI, urging them to force the Society's compliance. Surprisingly, the Spanish monarch, generally hostile to the Society because it successfully resisted full submission to his rule, rose to its defense: the king described the Jesuits as "people who merit respect" and directed his emissary in Rome to protect them.[11]

Despite the king's support of the Society, the Portuguese chapters persisted in their campaign against it. Between 1608 and 1611 they maintained a working committee in Lisbon in order to lobby the regency government installed in the royal palace to endorse their claims against the Society. In 1611 that junta sent a representative to Spain and Italy to present its case to Philip III and Paul V. Although the king did not act in this dispute, the pope did: in 1613 he ruled that the Leonine solution would also extend to Jesuit properties in Portugal.

8. "Provisão do cardeal . . . que nao devem pagar dízimos," 20 Oct. 1567, in *DHJP*, 187–92.

9. *HCJAE*, 5: 233–58.

10. *HCJAP*, 3:1, 247–55. Except as noted, the following paragraphs are based upon Fr. Rodrigues's very useful analysis.

11. Philip II to duke of Sessa (Spanish ambassador to Rome), 18 Nov. 1598, in BNL/CP, 475, fol. 262.

The chapters thus gained a round, but that did not assure them that the bout would end in their favor. Indeed, their zeal to enforce the Pauline brief prompted Jesuits in Portugal to initiate lawsuits defending their immunity claims and led them to appeal to another pope to reverse his predecessor's decision. In 1620 the chapters complained to the king that the intransigent colleges in Portugal still refused to pay their dues.

The next and ultimately decisive round went to the Jesuits. In 1622 Gregory XV issued a new pontifical brief that granted the fathers complete immunity from dízimo levies. Predictably, the chapters promptly launched a vigorous protest. According to the papal collector in Portugal, "At the insistence of some of their leaders the clergy ... are united in a single body against the Fathers of the Company and urge the king to apply to Pope Urban VIII [Gregory's successor] to annul the brief. His Majesty ordered the governors [regents of Portugal] to speak with me about this matter and I responded by defending the Fathers against these unjust persecutions."[12] He went on to advise his superior, the papal cardinal secretary of state, that it was his conviction that the chapters greatly exaggerated the amount of income they had lost because of the Gregorian decision.

Two Jesuit memorials, one drafted about 1622, the other a decade later, advanced the same contention. Though neither is signed, both were probably prepared by the provincial of Portugal or by his deputy, the provincial procurator. The compiler of the first memorial demonstrated that in a worst-case scenario, one in which the Jesuits yielded and paid the sums stipulated by the Pauline award, their ten facilities in the kingdom would owe the chapters only 164,000 rs. per annum, a trifling sum (as the author pointed out) when compared with the chapters' combined yearly income—some 280 contos.[13] The second memorial pointed out that the Society actually did not possess tithable properties in six of the thirteen sees within the kingdom and argued that even if the Pauline brief were revived, the Jesuits would still only be liable for payments amounting to 192,337 rs.[14] Of course, this controversy involved not only money but also principles, especially those concerned with immunities, obligations, control, and submission.[15] But whether persuaded by these memorials or by other considerations, successive pontiffs never reversed the brief of Gregory XV, leaving the frustrated chapters to join with branches of the Holy Office to attack the Society on other grounds thereafter. Curiously, the Portuguese crown never intervened directly in the tithe question at home, but it certainly took an active interest in its ramifications overseas.

12. *HCJAP*, 3:1, 253–54.

13. "Informação dos bens de raiz q' os collegios da Comp.ᵃ de Jesu tem neste reyno de Portugal, por razao dos quaes podiao as igrejas esperar alguns dízimos delles," [ca. 1622], in ANTT/CJ/57, nos. 36 and 37, the latter being the more readable copy.

14. "Informação do estado da causa dos dízimos neste anno de 1632," addressed to Philip IV, in BNL/CP, 475, fols. 263–68ᵛ.

15. That seems clear from an anonymous memorandum completed ca. 1622: "Noticia e informação que deram os PP. da Companhia das pensoes que recebiam, feitas por d. Henrique," in *RIHGB* 43, 1 (1871): 156–63.

Disputes Concerning
Tithes in the State of Brazil

Nowhere in the empire did dízimos play as important a role in royal finances as they did in Brazil. In Portuguese India, for example, they provided only a minor source of revenue. Customs duties, safe-conduct passes (cartazes), and consumptive excises such as the *collecta* were far more lucrative. Until well into the eighteenth century, tithes were levied only on the estates of Christians, and those who were recent converts were for a time exempted.[16] The Jesuits therefore escaped conflicts over tithes in India, and the same was true in Portuguese Africa and in the Atlantic islands. But the situation was far different in Brazil.

Tithe assessments in Brazil date effectively from 1551, when a papal bull conceded to the sovereigns of Portugal in their capacity as Grand Masters of the Order of Christ the responsibility for the collection of dízimos and the allocation of the proceeds. The assumption then was that the crown would simply turn over to the Church the moneys it received; in practice, however, the crown provided the Church with a portion of such funds but utilized the rest to cover its general expenses. Thus, for example, one eighteenth-century official observed that "the proceeds of this contract ... are used to pay the salaries of the governors and troops of dragoons, the salaries and allowances of the ministers of justice, the treasurer and other officials of the exchequer, the vicars, and other expenses to which the exchequer is liable."[17] Such diversions, however, had begun long before.

The government rarely undertook to collect tithes itself. When possible, it farmed out the collection to private persons, who bid for exclusive contracts in public auctions. Successful bidders signed elaborate, usually impressively printed agreements with an agent of the king specifying how much they would put down when they assumed the contract and how much they would pay at the end of each year that it ran. Most contracts spanned a triennium.

In a recently published study, Stuart Schwartz suggests that these leases were signed in Portugal until 1606 but were thereafter consummated in Brazil.[18] In reality, negotiations were less clear cut. During the latter half of the sixteenth century, contracts were sometimes let simultaneously on both sides of the Atlantic, a source of confusion and, inevitably, litigation. In the seventeenth century, contracts were normally finalized in Brazil; thereafter they were subject to approval by the Overseas Council.[19]

During the eighteenth century, a single powerful Lisbon merchant might have enjoyed a monopoly on the supply of salt to Brazil or on whales taken in Brazilian waters, but no central figure ever dominated the collection of tithes there. The vastness of Brazil, the dispersion of its population, the decentralized character of its economic sectors, the primitive state of its communications and transportation, and the tedious mechanics of collection all

---

16. J. M. do Carmo Nazareth, "Dízimos na India," *O oriente português*, 2d ser., 4 (June 1907): 217–26 and (July–Aug. 1907): 267–76, has not been surpassed.

17. Quoted in C. R. Boxer, *The Golden Age of Brazil, 1695–1750* (Berkeley, 1962), 348.

18. Schwartz, *Sugar Plantations in the Formation of Brazilian Society: Bahia, 1550–1835* (Cambridge, 1985), 173.

19. Oscar de Oliveira, *Os dízimos eclesiásticos do Brasil nos períodos da colonia e do imperio* (Juiz de Fora, 1940), has been reprinted in recent years and remains unexcelled.

precluded that. Even in Portugal, it was rare for a single person to be responsible for the gathering of tithes within one parish.[20] Tithe leases in Brazil were customarily let for a single captaincy or captaincy-general but were sometimes awarded for smaller units in the back country.[21]

Brazil was, of course, Portugal's prime agricultural colony. In 1601 tithes provided about two-thirds of the modest income that the crown received from there.[22] During the ensuing century, Brazil's yield appears to have increased more than fourfold, but the rate of growth slackened during the eighteenth century, when prices for Brazil's leading staple, cane sugar, were weak.[23] Although the royal fifths (*quintos*) derived from extracted minerals in the Brazilian interior accounted for far more revenue than did the dízimos during the eighteenth century (as did customs in the case of the port of Rio de Janeiro), tithes continued to furnish between a quarter and a half of the income produced by most Brazilian captaincies and ranked as their second- or third-leading source of revenue.[24] Who did or did not contribute to that income was consequently of great importance to the crown, to its agents overseas, and to the tax collectors there.

The Jesuits were not alone in their claims that the sixteenth-century papal bulls exempted them from tithe liability. The crown deliberately subsidized the Brazilian sugar industry by offering planters ten-year exemptions to undertake production and granting them further grace periods for improvements they claimed to make to their facilities. According to one source, at one stage a quarter of the sugar embarked in Brazilian ports for the kingdom went substantially free of tithe obligations.[25]

The Jesuits, of course, also benefited from tithe receipts. In the kingdom, between 8.1 and 11.2 percent of the yearly revenues of the University of Évora came from dízimos, as did as much as half of the annual receipts of the college of Funchal, Madeira.[26] Those awards, made by the Society's great patron, Cardinal Henry, were confirmed by his successors. As disclosed in Chapter 13, beginning in the mid-1560s and the 1570s, the crown provided three Jesuit colleges—Bahia, Rio de Janeiro, and Olinda—with annual, tithe-derived subventions

20. Araujo Oliveira, *A abadia de Tibães*, 2: 396.

21. Oliveira, *Os dízimos eclesiásticos*, 58–59. In the captaincy-general of Pará, so-called *drogas do sertão*, i.e., extracted forest products such as cacao, cloves, and sarsaparilla, were separately contracted. João de Abreu Castelbranco to treasury superintendent, State of Maranhão, 14 Sept. 1742, in BAPP, cod. 985, no. 384.

22. Luís de Figueiredo Falcão, comp., *Livro em que se contem toda a fazenda . . . dos reynos de Portugal, India, ilhas adjacentes . . . 1607* (Lisbon, 1859), 27.

23. Cf. Schwartz, *Sugar Plantations*, app. B; and D. Alden, "Price Movements in Brazil Before, During, and After the Gold Boom, with Special Reference to the Salvador Market, 1670–1769," in *Essays on the Price History of Eighteenth-Century Latin America*, ed. Lyman L. Johnson and Enrique Tandeter (Albuquerque, 1990), 335–71.

24. In ca. 1774, dízimos provided 27.2% of royal income from Pernambuco; 39.3% of that from Itamaracá; 28.9% of that from Paraíba; 14.9% of that from Ceará; and 100% of that from Rio Grande do Norte. "Resumo do accressimo que houve nos contratos reaes desta capitania de Pernambuco e suas anexas," *ABNRJ* 40 (1918): 94–98; cf. D. Alden, *Royal Government in Colonial Brazil* (Berkeley, 1968), 318, table 2.

25. Schwartz, *Sugar Plantations*, 174.

26. [Anon.], "Historia de la fundacion y progresso del collegio y universidad de Évora," Feb. 1574, in ARSI, *Lus.*, 81:I, fols. 226–27; "Folha da receita e despeza do coll.º de Évora no anno de 1725," in ibid., 81:II, 570–572ᵛ; António Simão Lobo de Matos (ouvidor, Madeira), "Relação da fundação do collegio de Sam João Evangelista da cidade de Funchal," ca. 1761, in AHU/PA/Madeira, *cx.* 1, no. 229; cf. *HCJAP*, 2:1, 49 n. 6, for a different interpretation.

and later underwrote part of the annual expenses of missionaries serving in Maranhão by allotting them another portion of its tithe income.[27]

But, as observed in Chapter 13, the fathers discovered that it was one thing to persuade the king to promise funds to defray the Society's expenses, and it was another to collect them from his agents. From the 1570s on, the Jesuits complained that the stipends derived from tithes were invariably paid tardily. In response, Sebastian directed that Bahia's royal subvention be paid out of customs receipts instead of tithes, but his order provoked sharp protests from the governor-general and his controller, who insisted that these revenues were needed for other purposes. Finally, in 1604, the crown adopted what would become standard practice: each of the three colleges was authorized to collect its stipend in tithable sugar from plantations of its choice. That decision, too, displeased the current governor-general, but his complaint was ignored.[28]

The fathers took great pride in their apparently successful conversion of the Brasis to what they deemed to be the true faith, and the tithe farmers shared their enthusiasm, though for a quite different reason: they viewed the aborigines as potential taxpayers. In 1561, a dozen years after the Jesuits first landed on the Brazilian littoral and began to organize their neophytes into Christian communities, the tax contractors insisted that the converts pay tithes on what they produced. The Society's leaders protested and appealed to the ever-sympathetic Sebastian for relief. After consulting with canonists and theologians, the king ruled in 1576 that for the next six years all tithes collected from the converts would be used to support their newly founded churches and confraternities. Although Visitor Cristóvão de Gouveia applied for an extension of that privilege in 1582, the new Philippine regime did not concede it until 1587, prompting the contractors to demand payment for the intervening years. Eventually the crown granted newly converted Brasis ten-year exemptions, adapting to them therefore the same policy applied to new converts east of the Cape of Good Hope after 1561.[29]

Throughout the sixteenth century, the crown did not contest Jesuit claims that all its properties in Brazil were exempt from payment of tithes,[30] but its views changed during the seventeenth century. The usually very reliable Fr. Serafim Leite maintained that the first serious challenge to Jesuit claims of such immunity arose in the early 1660s as a consequence of the impending settlement of the protracted Sergipe do Conde dispute.[31] But Jesuit claims were challenged at least as early as 1611, when contractors in Brazil's leading sugar

27. The royal subsidies were 1,200,000 rs. for Bahia; 1,000,000 rs. for Rio de Janeiro; and 800,000 rs. for Olinda. Initially the crown contributed 450,000 rs. for the living expenses of Jesuits serving in Maranhão, an amount later raised to 1,000,000 rs. and divided equally between the colleges at São Luís and Belém. *CR*, 29 Nov. 1564, in *DHA*, 1: 175–79; provisões of 11 Feb. 1568 and 19 Nov. 1586, in *DH*, 15: 18–25, and 17: 107–8.

28. Alvará of 20 July 1604, in *DH*, 17: 175–78; king to bishop-viceroy of Portugal, 29 Feb. 1604, in Archivo General de Simancas, Sp. 1489, 22; conselho da fazenda (Lisbon), consultas of 22 June 1613 and 12 Dec. 1620, in ibid., Sp. 1472, 216–17, and 1473, 493–94. (I am indebted to Stuart B. Schwartz for the archival citations.) In 1606 Governor-General Diogo de Menezes wrote with evident disgust that the Jesuits "comerem tudo" in the royal exchequer. [José da] Costa Porto, *Estudo sobre o sistema sesmarial* (Recife, 1965), 107.

29. *HCJB*, 2: 90; Costa Porto, *Estudos*, 98.

30. E.g., provisão of António Salema (governor, Rio de Janeiro and the other southern captaincies of Brazil) to treasurer, Rio de Janeiro, 17 June 1577, in *LTC/RJ*, 21.

31. *HCJB*, 7: 287. Concerning the dispute, see Chapter 10.

captaincies sued the fathers, who, it may be remembered, had begun cane cultivation a decade earlier. In 1614 an anonymous royal official who had served in Brazil for some time and then returned to the kingdom reported that neither the Jesuits, nor the Benedictines, nor the Carmelites were paying dízimos, despite the fact that each possessed extensive, productive lands.[32] The same year, significantly one year *after* the Pauline brief discussed above, the crown itself insisted for the first time that religious Orders in the Atlantic islands and in Brazil should pay tithes upon their estates.[33]

It was about this time that Francisco Lopes Franco, dízimo contractor for the captaincy of Rio de Janeiro, became the first tax farmer to bring suit against the fathers to compel them to pay tithes. In 1621 the ecclesiastical administrator of the captaincy considered the merits of the contractor's case. Although the plaintiff contended that the college and its tenants had an abundance of cane and livestock and should pay tithes on both, the defendants responded that they had been in possession of their lands for 70 years "and longer" and had never been required to pay dízimos since it was well understood that the popes had liberated them from that burden. Moreover, they averred that they lacked the means to do so, since they were still defraying the cost of the construction of their college, which supported 65 to 70 members who lived there or served in the missions or in subordinate houses they assisted in Espírito Santo and Santos. In the end, the administrator found in favor of the fathers and assessed the unsuccessful plaintiff the costs of his suit! Naturally displeased, the plaintiff appealed to the nuncio in Lisbon, but that dignitary reaffirmed the administrator's decision. The Jesuits thereby won another round in a contest that would continue, albeit intermittently, into the eighteenth century.[34]

Beginning in the 1650s, Jesuits in the State of Brazil found themselves again the targets of royal officials, cámaras, and private individuals, who raised serious questions about the fathers' immunity to the payment of tithes and their right to continue to acquire properties in what had become Portugal's most vital remaining colony. In 1656, the crown, faced with the burdensome expense of defending the kingdom against Spain and the empire against Dutch threats, decreed that all regular and secular clergy in Brazil must contribute to the payment of newly imposed taxes intended to finance Brazil's defense. Confronted by the Church's reluctance to comply with the edict, the cámara of Salvador protested the following year to the regency government of Afonso VI that "the Religious Orders, which in this captaincy possess much of the property and many sugar mills, estates, farms, houses, cattle, and slaves, refuse to contribute anything . . . to the expenses of the war, so that the rest of the people are heavily burdened and the poor suffer continual oppression."[35]

32. [Report concerning the estates of the religious Orders in Brazil], 1614, in AHU/LR/284, fols. 162ʳ–63ᵛ.

33. *CR*, 30 July 1614, in *CCLP*, 2: 90; the same order was sent to the archbishop of Lisbon under this date. Archivo General de Simancas, Sp. 1509, fol. 64ᵛ. I am again indebted to Professor Schwartz for the reference.

34. *LTC/RJ*, 345–56. Two years before the nuncio's decision, Fr. Simão de Sottomayor, administrator of the Sergipe do Conde property, insisted that even though estates had paid tithes before they had come into Jesuit hands, those assessments could no longer be collected once they became ecclesiastical patrimony. Declaration of 12 Jan. 1623, in ANTT/CJ/68, no. 392. That became a basic Jesuit position, as evidenced, for example, by a long memorial in defense of the Society's exemption from tithes in Brazil, probably written in the late 1670s. ARSI, *Bras.*, 11:I, fols. 142–144ᵛ.

35. Quoted in C. R. Boxer, *Portuguese Society in the Tropics* (Madison, Wis., 1965), 88–89.

A few years later, the cámara received powerful support from the governor-general, Francisco Barreto, one of the heroes in the war against the Dutch (see Chapter 9). Noting in 1661 that the protracted Sergipe do Conde case was approaching solution, he reminded the crown that "it is the best [sugar estate] in all the State of Brazil," but only one of a large number of plantations that Jesuits, Benedictines, and Carmelites possessed in the colony. He added that the Orders also had extensive cattle ranches and other properties that formerly had paid tithes to the royal exchequer but had ceased to do so as soon as the Orders assumed title to them. As a result, Barreto declared, those organizations which used to be very poor now possessed "great capital," and if not restrained would become "Lords of the greater part of this outpost (*praça*)." He added that if the crown failed to require those Orders to contribute funds to the treasury, it would soon be unable to pay its Brazilian garrisons.[36]

Barreto's long and thoughtful dispatch gave authorities in Lisbon much to contemplate. A crown attorney stated that in view of the apparently flourishing condition of the Jesuits and the other estate-rich Orders and the precarious condition of the exchequer, it would be justifiable for the king to revoke the tithe-funded royal endowments of the three Brazilian colleges and to cancel the subventions of the Maranhão missionaries.[37] The Overseas Council also considered it prudent to terminate the Jesuits' long-standing exemption from customs duties on Society goods shipped between Brazil and the kingdom, a concession first granted by Sebastian in 1573 and renewed by every monarch of Portugal since then (see Chapter 21). The Council observed that according to a report from the treasurer of Bahia, the Jesuits consistently abused that privilege.[38]

But the court did not respond effectively to these concerns. Its failure to do so is probably explained by the political turmoil surrounding the count of Castelo Melhor's successful coup in 1662, his subsequent removal from office in 1667, and the continued wars against Spain and Holland (see Chapters 5, 7, 8, and 9). In any case, attacks on the Jesuits' efforts to preserve their tithe exemptions in Brazil now shifted to the judicial arena.

In the mid-1660s, Domingos Ferreira, a resident of Salvador and Bahia's tithe and whaling contractor from 1661 through 1663, found himself unable to honor the terms of his contract. He insisted that the fault did not lie with him but with the Society of Jesus and the other property-owning Orders. Ferreira asserted that before submitting his bid, he had calculated what the Orders' estates ought to contribute, and he claimed that the Orders' unwillingness to contribute was the reason that he still owed the king the considerable sum of 18 contos. Seeking a way out of his difficulty, Ferreira brought suit against the Jesuit college in 1663, submitting his case first to the local treasury court (*provedoria*) and then to the High Court (the Relação). Insisting that the college could not possibly have owed anything like the amount Ferreira claimed, the Jesuits appealed to the Board of Supplication (casa de suplicação) in Lisbon. The case remained there, undecided, for decades—shades of *Bleak House*![39]

36. Francisco Barreto to king, Bahia, 2 June 1661, in AHU/PA/BA, 1st cat., *cx.* 7; published in *DH*, 4: 409–11.

37. Fiscal to king, 17 Aug. 1662, in AHU/PA/BA, *cx.* 7.

38. Council to king, 3 Oct. 1662, in AHU, *Consultas Mixtas*, 16, fol. 55.

39. Overseas Council to Pedro II, 31 Jan. and 31 Oct. 1681, in *DH*, 87: 192–93 and 213–14.

Ferreira's plight was far from unique among tax contractors in colonial Brazil. In the 1670s three other Bahian tithe farmers also brought suit against the fathers and sought relief from the crown. Sebastião Duarte held the dízimo contract for five years at the beginning of the decade, and Ventura David was his successor during the year 1676–77. They were followed by João Roiz dos Reys, who claimed to have lost 20 contos on his 1677–78 contract. All three told the same story: if only the Jesuits had paid what they legitimately owed, each would have been able to honor his bid. They professed that the fathers' obduracy not only deprived them of anticipated revenue, but also compelled them to undertake legal action against the local college. Each gained a favorable verdict in the colonial tribunals, but, once again, each was stymied when the Jesuits appealed to Peninsular courts and successfully obtained stays preventing the execution of the colonial courts' orders. Each contractor, therefore, declared that it would be unfair for the crown to require him to fulfill the terms of his original agreement and asked forgiveness for the balance still owed. The Overseas Council, more charitable than it was zealous in defense of the crown's rights, sympathized with the contractors' plight and recommended that their pleas be granted.[40]

The Council was exceedingly generous. The contractors' real problems were not the resistance of the three Orders to yield ground they had never been compelled to surrender but slumping sugar prices and the contractors' overly optimistic bids. Even if the Jesuit college had agreed to pay tithes, the sum for which it would have been liable would have amounted to a fraction of what the contractors owed.[41] Still, the contractors found a means of retaliation while the judicial process dragged on: they withheld several years of the crown's subventions to the Jesuits, a practice that the fathers themselves predictably protested and one that the crown itself reproved.[42]

But even if the contractors lost their suits, they had another means to avoid paying a portion of what they owed the crown. Since the early 1660s they had succeeded, with the apparent collusion of treasurers and governors, in inserting an escape clause in their contracts. It provided that if the religious Orders refused to pay whatever sum the contractors deemed that they owed, the contractors might deduct that amount from the sum they paid into the royal exchequer. The crown had never approved that concession and in 1683 denounced it.[43]

Although Bahia was the primary locus of clashes between Jesuits and their adversaries over the payment of tithes, the same issues arose elsewhere in the colony. In Pernambuco, for example, the treasurer appealed to the prince regent for assistance: he reported that in 1679 the Jesuits, Benedictines, and Carmelites had adamantly refused to pay dízimos on

40. Overseas Council to regent, two consultas of 2 Dec. 1678, in AHU/PA/BA, 1st. cat., cx. 13, where there is a notation that the future Pedro II endorsed both on 26 Mar. 1679.

41. The oldest surviving third catalogue for Brazil, that of 1641, reveals that the Bahian college's income from lands that might have been assessed tithes amounted to only 1,100,000 rs., or 12.1% of the college's total income. That of 1679, the next available catalogue in the series, indicates that 1,800,000 rs., or 30% of its properties, could have been tithable. Such sums represented an insignificant part of the vast sums that the contractors owed. ARSI, *Bras.*, 5:I, 163ʳ, and 5:II, 56ʳ.

42. Provisão, 27 May 1675, in *DH*, 25: 460–61; *HCJB*, 7: 288.

43. Overseas Council to prince regent, 17 Dec. 1682, in AHU/PA/BA, 1st cat., cx. 14, no. 3132; prince regent to governor, 30 Jan. 1683, in ANRJ, col. 63/3/36ʳ; Costa Porto, *Estudo*, 110.

formerly tithed properties they had acquired. He observed that these properties included extensive ranch lands as well as three large sugar plantations.[44]

The crown concurred with the treasurer's view and directed each Order to pay tithes on such properties. They refused. Five years later it removed consideration of tithe disputes from colonial courts to the tribunal known as the *juiz dos feitos da coroa e fazenda* in Lisbon, but that move does not seem to have expedited final determinations in such cases. Despite his increasing vexation with the Orders over the tithe issue and also with their unwillingness to disclose the extent of their landed holdings (see Chapter 17), Pedro II instructed his fiscal officers in Brazil to continue to pay the ecclesiastics the sums assured them from the dízimo income.[45]

By the first decades of the eighteenth century, the crown and the Jesuits in the State of Brazil had reached an accommodation of sorts concerning the tithe obligations of religious bodies. John V declared that religious Orders would remain exempt from tithe assessments on properties that they already possessed and directly operated, but insisted that their tenants (lavradores) pay dízimos on what they produced and that the Orders themselves thereafter be liable for payments on all properties they subsequently obtained.[46] In 1711, the year that directive was issued, Giovanni Antonio Andreoni, experienced Jesuit administrator in Brazil, published his famous treatise on the sources of Brazilian wealth.[47] The same year, Fr. Andreoni reported to Rome on the completion of the transfer to the Bahian college of the vast ranching inheritance of Domingo Afonso Sertão (see Chapter 14). He informed the father general that the institution would agree to pay tithes on those 30 ranches because they were being administered as chantries rather than as annexes of the college. "This way," he observed, "we will lessen the outsiders' jealousy, at least in part."[48] Whether Andreoni's strategy worked we cannot say, but the fact remains that from this point until the 1750s, the Jesuits in the State of Brazil seldom found themselves embroiled in the sorts of controversy over dízimos that had repeatedly occurred during the previous century. The new storm center for such disputes became the State of Maranhão.

Persistent Tithe Controversies in the State of Maranhão

Northern Brazil, the State of Maranhão from the 1620s until the 1770s, long remained one of the economic backwaters of the Lusitanian empire. Not only the forest Indians but also most of the Portuguese settlers themselves lived in primitive circumstances, and for reasons discussed in Chapter 19 and elsewhere, the religious Orders, especially the Jesuits, were frequent targets of criticism by the colonists and the king's officers. As noted in the previous chapter, in 1692 Pedro II threatened to seize ecclesiastical landholdings if the Orders persisted in ignoring his demand that they report on the extent of such properties. In

44. Overseas Council to prince regent, 24 Feb. 1680, in IAGHPB, *Consultas do Conselho Ultramarino*, 1, fol. 120ʳ; *CR*, 6 Sept. 1680, in *DH*, 82: 321–22.

45. Alvará of 3 Feb. 1689, in *CCLP*, 10: 186.

46. *CR*, 27 June 1711, in ANRJ, col. 63/1/235ʳ; *ABNRJ* 28 (1908): 340–41. This key directive can be found in many other manuscript collections and published sources.

47. *Cultura e opulencia do Brasil por suas drogas e minas*, of which the edition translated and edited by Andrée Mansuy (Paris, 1965) remains definitive.

48. Andreoni to Tamburini, 26 June 1711, in *HCJB*, 5: 144.

1701 Lisbon instructed the State's treasurer to notify the heads of each Order that henceforth the Orders would pay dízimos on all properties save those recognized as pertaining to their initial seed grants.[49] The treasurer responded that those estates were "the best in the State" and that he would do his best to enforce the directive. He warned, however, that the members of one Order (not specified, but certainly the Society) were threatening the tithe contractor with excommunication when he tried to persuade them to tithe.[50] The court urged the treasurer to defend the contractor and to insist that the Orders pay not only what they currently owed but the arrears as well. Despite that injunction, there is no evidence that the Orders in the State ever contributed to tithe funds.[51]

Nevertheless, the Jesuits in the State found themselves embroiled in a dispute over tithes in the middle of the next decade. That dispute began in 1715, when the Overseas Council instructed the State's governor to compel the Orders to reconfirm all their land titles (see Chapter 17). Three years later, acting on the Council's instruction, the treasurer and the chief judicial magistrate of the State ruled that the college of Pará must pay tithes on some of its properties. But the Jesuits refused and once again appealed to the juiz dos feitos da coroa e fazenda in Lisbon, where, characteristically, the case remained undecided for at least two decades.[52]

Such legal foot-dragging did not prevent complaints against the Jesuits' engrossment of lands in the State and their steadfast refusal to pay tithes throughout the 1720s, 1730s, and 1740s. One of the Society's most influential critics in Maranhão during these years was João de Abreu Castelbranco, the State's unusually conscientious governor (1737–47). Though he sympathized with the fathers' opposition to the enslavement of the Brasis (see Chapter 19), he nevertheless considered the State's "most important" problems to be the religious Orders' continual accretion of lands and their intractability on the tithe issue. Since the Jesuits possessed more property than any other Order, Castelbranco viewed their opposition as most critical. Their unfortunate example, he warned a leading royal minister, was emulated by many seculars who were burdened with bad consciences while the royal exchequer lost much of the revenue to which it was entitled and which it badly needed.[53]

Heretofore Brazil's prelates, who, like their counterparts in the kingdom, reaped handsome amounts from tithe collections, had been strangely silent on the question of the Orders' liability for tithe dues. But in the late 1740s, the bishop of Maranhão joined the governor in criticizing their position. The bishop observed that his clergy received far less income from the crown than did their peers in the State of Brazil, even though their need

49. *CR*, 11 Jan. 1701, in *LGM* 1, 203–4.
50. Provedor (Pará) to king, 28 June 1702, in AHU/PA/PA, *cx*. 3, University of California, Bancroft Library, Microfilm Collection. The document was missing from its archival file when I searched for it.
51. *CR*, 16 Nov. 1702, in *LGM* 1, 225. The statement is based upon an examination of all documents pertaining to the state during the eighteenth century in the AHU, the BAPP, and other archival collections.
52. Rector, college of Santo Alexandre, to king, ca. 1738, in AHU/PA/PA, *cx*. 10. The rector stated that the Jesuits' customs privileges were also first questioned during the 1710s, and that in the 1730s the treasurer advised ship captains not to load Jesuit cargo unless it had been dutied. Two decades later, the Jesuits' most formidable nemesis, Governor Francisco Xavier de Mendonça Furtado, would do the same.
53. Castelbranco to Cardinal da Mota, 14 Oct. 1738, in AHU/PA/PA, *cx*. 10; Castelbranco to king, 12 Oct. 1741, in AHU/PA/MA, *cx*. 28.

was just as great. The obvious solution was to require Jesuits, Carmelites, and Mercedarians, who possessed ample properties in the State, to tithe.[54]

The crown's response to such suggestions was precisely the same as when it received other sorts of complaints regarding the Jesuits and their colleagues. It simply called for further reports on properties said to be liable to dízimos and warned delinquents that failure to pay what they owed would expose them to fines amounting to four times their declared obligations.[55]

For two centuries the Jesuits were remarkably successful in their efforts to resist liability for the payment of tithes, a major source of income in Brazil and of revenues to the secular church in Portugal. But their very success damaged the image the Society's founders had sought to cultivate, that of a poverty-oriented, wholly submissive organization that was firmly supportive of the crown. Regardless of the games that tithe contractors played, there were many persons in Brazil—royal officials, rival religious, and settlers—who believed that a supposedly rich body like the Society ought not to escape the financial burden that many, though not all, planters, farmers, and stockmen bore. Until the 1750s the crown remained largely insensitive to the concerns of such interest groups, but a new leadership would demonstrate how easily and decisively Jesuit resistance could be broken. It would proclaim that the payment of tithes by all of His Majesty's subjects, even those who belonged to religious Orders, was a patriotic as well as a pious obligation. That same regime would act decisively on another issue that had long bedeviled relations between the Society and the settlers of Brazil: the protection of one of the colony's major resources, its indigenous population.

54. Bishop Francisco de Santiago to king, 25 Aug. 1747, in AHU/PA/MA, *cx.* 31.
55. Consulta, 17 May 1742, in AHU/PA/MA, *cx.* 28; provisão of 4 July 1748, in ibid., *cx.* 32.

CHAPTER 19

Jesuit Efforts to Defend the "Freedom" of the Brazilian Indians

> We have against us the people, the religious, the proprietors of the private captaincies and all those who in that Kingdom and in this State are interested in the blood and sweat of the Indians whose inferior status (*minoridade*) we alone defend.
>
> —António Vieira to John IV, Pará, 8 Dec. 1655

> The question of the Indians was always the same throughout Brazil: the Jesuits defended their liberty; the king officially entrusted them with that responsibility; and the colonists acted in defiance against the law [thereby] confronting (*atingindo*) the Jesuits.
>
> —Serafim Leite

BRAZIL ULTIMATELY PROVED to be the most rewarding component of the Lusitanian empire for both Portuguese settlers and the Jesuits, but nowhere within the Portuguese Assistancy did those two elements quarrel as acrimoniously and incessantly as they did in the Portuguese New World.[1] The morally just treatment of the Amerindians and the crown's failure to develop and enforce a defensible Indian policy became the primary sources of those quarrels.

As observed in previous chapters, Jesuits within the Assistancy rarely assumed unpopular positions on issues of concern to the elites they served and upon whom they were dependent. Perennially cautious and acutely sensitive to the views of their lay supporters, the fathers generally adopted mainstream positions on controversial questions. To be sure, there were a few notable exceptions. One was the Society's unsuccessful attempt during the Petrine regime to intervene on behalf of New Christians in the kingdom who were persistently menaced by the Holy Office (see Chapter 5). Another was the Society's long and likewise ultimately inefficacious campaign to persuade the papacy to accept certain Confucian doctrines in imperial China as proximates for Christian values (see Chapter 23). The Jesuits' efforts to protect the Brasis against what they deemed immoral, unjust, and inhumane treatment by the settlers provides a third exception to the Society's usual consensus position

---

1. I have published earlier versions of portions of this chapter in "Black Robes Versus White Settlers: The Struggle for 'Freedom of the Indians' in Colonial Brazil," in Howard Peckham and Charles Gibson, eds., *Attitudes of Colonial Powers Toward the American Indian* (Salt Lake City, 1969), 19–45, and in "Indian Versus Black Slavery in the State of Maranhão During the Seventeenth and Eighteenth Centuries," in Richard L. Garner and William B. Taylor, eds., *Iberian Colonies, New World Societies: Essays in Memory of Charles Gibson* (Pennsylvania State University, 1985), 71–102.

on public issues within the Assistancy. Just as their Chinese Rites campaign ended in failure and damaged their image in the East, so the Jesuits' attempts to safeguard the persons, if not the culture, of the Amerindians seriously undermined their stature in Brazil and served as the rationale for their summary expulsion from various parts of the colony on several occasions, as the following pages will demonstrate.

Perceptions of the Amerindians

Both the settlers and the missionaries viewed the Amerindians through European spectacles. Like other Europeans, the Portuguese were convinced that the Amerindians were their cultural and moral inferiors. Their attitude toward the Brasis was not significantly different from that Englishmen toward Irishmen, Castilians toward the Guanches of the Canaries, or Frenchmen toward the Hurons.[2] Initially both seculars and Jesuit fathers emphasized the childlike innocence of the Brasis, their physical attractiveness, and their malleableness, especially their apparent receptivity to Christianity.[3] Long before John Locke, Fr. Nóbrega considered the Indian's mind to be a tabula rasa ("es todo papel blanco") upon which the missionaries could imprint whatever values they wished.[4] Closer contact, however, corrected such simplistic impressions and led to grim depictions of the indigenes that emphasized their savage qualities, most notably their propensity for gluttony, drunkenness, lasciviousness, cruelty, deceitfulness, and vindictiveness. By the 1570s and 1580s the first descriptions of the Amerindians as something akin to noble savages had been replaced by images that stressed their barbarism, bestiality, and incorrigibility.[5] As

2. Cf. Nicholas Canny, *The Elizabethan Conquest of Ireland: A Pattern Established* (New York, 1976), chap. 6 (and other writings by the same author); Felipe Fernandez-Armesto, *Before Columbus: Exploration and Colonisation from the Mediterranean to the Atlantic, 1229–1492* (London, 1987), chaps. 8–9; J. H. Kennedy, *Jesuit and Savage in New France* (New Haven, 1950), chaps. 7–8; Cornelius J. Jaenen, *Friend and Foe: Aspects of French-Amerindian Cultural Contact in the Sixteenth and Seventeenth Centuries* (New York, 1976); James Axtell, *The Invasion Within: The Contest of Cultures in Colonial North America* (New York, 1985); Bernard W. Sheehan, *Savagism and Civility: Indians and Englishmen in Colonial Virginia* (New York, 1980); Gary B. Nash, "The Image of the Indian in the Southern Colonial Mind," *William and Mary Quarterly*, 3d ser., 29 (1972): 197–230; and Francis Jennings, *The Invasion of America: Indians, Colonialism, and the Cant of Conquest* (New York, 1976), chaps. 4–5.

3. Such qualities are emphasized by Pero Vaz de Caminha in the earliest European report on the Brasis: Vaz de Caminha to Manuel I, Porto Seguro de Vera Cruz, 1 May 1500, in Charles David Ley, ed., *Portuguese Voyages, 1498–1663* (London, 1947), 41–59. For initial Jesuit impressions, see Chapter 3 above.

4. Nóbrega to Dr. Azpilcueta Navarro, Salvador, 10 Aug. 1549, in *MB*, 1: 142. Interestingly enough, the oft-cited Fr. Jerónimo Lobo invoked the same metaphor with respect to the Kaffirs of East Africa: "With little difficulty it was possible to create a flourishing Christianity among these people, because, since their natural disposition is good and they do not have any sect or superstitions to which they are wedded, they are in effect a *tabula rasa* on which the doctrine which is first taught them can be written." *The Itinerário of Jerónimo Lobo*, trans. Donald M. Lockhart, ed. C. F. Buckingham, *HS*:2, no. 162 (1984): 333. See also António da Silva, S.J., *Mentalidade missiológica dos Jesuítas em Moçambique antes de 1759*, 2 vols. (Lisbon, 1967), 1: 301–5, where the author interprets *tabula rasa* to mean the absence of religious convictions. Early Jesuits who served in French Canada began with the same premise: Jaenen, *Friend and Foe*, 41.

5. For important descriptions of the Brasis that reflect settler views, see Pero de Magalhães [de Gandavo], *The History of the Province of Santa Cruz* [1576], in *The Histories of Brazil*, trans. and ed. John B. Stetson, 2 vols. (New York, 1922), vol. 2, esp. chaps. 10 and 11; the references to Soares de Sousa cited in note 28 below; and Ambrósio Fernandes Brandão, *Dialogues of the Great Things of Brazil* [1618], trans. and ed., F. A. H. Hall, W. F. Harrison, and Dorothy W. Welker (Albuquerque, 1987), 307–26. Significant early Jesuit assessments of the Brasis' character include Manuel da Nóbrega, "Informação das terras do Brasil,"

Stuart Schwartz has observed, the colonists clung to such stereotypes for nearly three centuries.[6]

The Mission System and Its Consequences

If Jesuit missionaries refrained from expressing some of the more extreme contentions of the settlers, such as their conviction that the Indians were mindless beasts, they shared with the settlers the view that the Brasis were pagans who lacked the essential institutions of civilized peoples and, like all infidels, must be compelled to embrace Christianity.[7] Experience soon convinced the fathers that the most effective way of indoctrinating the natives was to gather them in mission centers called aldeias.[8]

The fathers organized their first aldeias in Bahia in the early 1550s and established others elsewhere along the length of the Atlantic seaboard during the rest of the century and later. But during the seventeenth and eighteenth centuries, their most visible and controversial missions were situated in the Amazonian interior. Though others viewed these aldeias differently, the Jesuits conceived of them primarily as appropriate communities in which to indoctrinate the Brasis effectively in the precepts of Christianity. Necessarily, that meant persuading the aborigines to abjure some of their traditional practices, such as offensive warfare, anthropophagy, polygamy, reliance upon magic, and excessive consumption of alcohol. It needs to be emphasized that Jesuit superiors always believed that there were never enough missionaries to supervise the large number of natives whom they yearned to save. The formation of the aldeias, whose populations ranged from a few hundred to a few thousand, was intended to place as many Indians as possible under the spiritual supervision of one or more missionaries. Initially the aldeias were situated as close as possible to Portuguese settlements, partly because the fathers themselves were urban-based, but also because it was hoped that the inhabitants of the Portuguese towns would demonstrate Catholic, civilized customs that the Indians would willingly emulate. In practice, that expectation was unfulfilled. Accordingly, by the early seventeenth century, the Jesuits had deliberately erected new aldeias along the middle São Francisco River and in comparable remote locations to protect the Indians from undesirable contact with the settlers.[9]

From the outset until the final removal of the Society, the Jesuits insisted that the aldeias belonged to the Amerindians, not to the Order itself. Although the sponsoring

---

ca. 1549, in *MB*, 1: 145–54; Nóbrega to Simão Rodrigues and to John III, Pernambuco, 11 Aug. 1551, in ibid., 269 and 291–92; Fernão Cardim, "Do principio e origem dos indios do Brasil" [1584], in *Tratados da terra e gente do Brasil*, ed. Rudolfo Garcia (rpr., São Paulo, 1980), 87–106; José de Anchieta, *Informação do Brasil e de suas capitanias (1584)*, intro. Leonardo Arroyo (São Paulo, 1964), esp. 45–52; and Simão de Vasconcelos, *Crónica da companhia de Jesus* [1663], ed. Serafim Leite, 3d ed., 2 vols. (Petropolis, 1977), 97–116.

6. Schwartz, "The Formation of a Colonial Identity in Brazil," in Nicholas Canny and Anthony Pagden, eds., *Colonial Identity in the Atlantic World, 1500–1800* (Princeton, 1987), 26. See also Schwartz, "Indian Labor and New World Plantations: European Demands and Indian Responses in Northeastern Brazil," *AHR* 83, 1 (Feb. 1978): 43–79.

7. Cf. James Muldoon, *The Church and the Non-Christian World, 1250–1550: Popes, Lawyers, and Infidels* (Philadelphia, 1979), 16ff.

8. Except as noted, the statements that follow concerning the functions of the aldeias rely upon *HCJB*, 2: 25–83, and the contemporary Jesuit sources that Fr. Leite utilized.

9. C. R. Boxer, *Salvador de Sá and the Struggle for Brazil and Angola, 1602–1686* (London, 1952), 124–25.

college financially assisted the aldeias in its care as long as necessary, the communities were expected ultimately to become self-supporting. Their inmates raised cereals, vegetables, and meat for their own consumption and sold surpluses to outsiders. The proceeds were used to defray the cost of implements, devotional objects, and other commodities that the fathers believed the aldeias required. The most lucrative among the articles that the missions produced were undoubtedly the so-called spices (*drogas*), cloves, sarsaparilla, cinnamon, and cacao that mission Indians throughout the Amazon collected in the forests beginning in the last quarter of the seventeenth century for sale in the kingdom.

Since aldeias were fundamentally educational and indoctrinational centers, effective communication between the neophytes and the missionaries was a sine qua non. As reported in Chapter 3, to facilitate such communication the Jesuits taught their charges a hybrid language with Tupi-Guarani roots known as the língua geral. One recent scholar has asserted that the Jesuits resorted to that artificial tongue as a means of cultural deprivation and manipulation.[10] Even if we concede that that may have been the result, there is no evidence that the fathers intended to be cultural rapists. It needs to be remembered that in the mid-sixteenth century there were better than 250 linguistic groups in the colony.[11] It was patently impossible for a handful of Jesuits to master all of the dialects spoken by so many aboriginal congeries. The construction of the língua geral was simply an attempt to facilitate effective communication between a few Jesuits and as many aborigines as possible via a commonly understood tongue. The late Adriaan C. Van Oss disclosed that in colonial Guatemala, "Indian languages were considered . . . an obstacle to proper comprehension of the faith,"[12] but neither missionaries nor the crown took that position in early Brazil. Not until 1681 did the crown direct missionaries throughout the Lusitanian empire to instruct native peoples in Portuguese "in order to make our Language universally known and to save the missionaries the burden of learning another tongue."[13] Yet a few years later Lisbon directed the Jesuits in the Amazon to instruct their Portuguese students in the língua geral so that they could later communicate with their Indian workers. Subsequently, in response to an impatient complaint by the aldermen of Belém, who asserted that the fathers had not complied with this directive, the king reprimanded the Jesuit missions' superior.[14] Seemingly the crown took no further interest in the language question for another half century. In the early 1720s, John V directed the heads of various Orders serving in the Amazon to emulate the Jesuits there by undertaking the conversion of the aborigines in their native tongue and only afterward to instruct them in Portuguese.[15] Yet five years later he admonished the governor of the State of Maranhão to maintain vigilance to see that all of the Orders there

10. Stuart B. Schwartz, *Sugar Plantations in the Formation of Brazilian Society: Bahia, 1550–1835* (Cambridge, 1985), 40; cf. David Graham Sweet, "A Rich Realm of Nature Destroyed: The Middle Amazon Valley, 1640–1750," Ph.D. diss., 2 vols., University of Wisconsin, 1974, 2: 75ff.

11. John Hemming, *Red Gold: The Conquest of the Brazilian Indians, 1500–1760* (Cambridge, Mass., 1978), appendix.

12. Van Oss, *Catholic Colonialism: A Parish History of Guatemala, 1524–1821* (New York, 1986), 127.

13. Order of Prince Regent Pedro, 7 Mar. 1681, in ANRJ, col. 63/1, fol. 16, with a notation that the circular was intended for missions in both Brazil and India.

14. Mathias C. Kiemen, O.F.M., *The Indian Policy of Portugal in the Amazon Region, 1614–1693* (Washington, D.C., 1954), 170.

15. Circular of 2 Dec. 1722, in AHU/LR, 269, fol. 222ᵛ.

were teaching their charges Portuguese.[16] But those instructions did not satisfy settlers in Brazil's northern state: for decades to come they would blame the missionaries for their inability to speak with their Indians in Portuguese.[17]

The aldeias also served other functions. Hard-pressed governors sometimes turned to the missions to provide emergency fighting men to repel foreign invaders or to assist in putting down domestic insurrections. In 1605, for example, one governor stated that during the previous eleven years he had frequently called out the Jesuits' neophytes to help meet both kinds of situations and expressed complete satisfaction with their help in protecting the colony's plantations.[18]

But what most attracted the settlers to the missionaries' villages was the pool of labor, which the settlers wished to use on their estates or in their canoes. While it is untrue, as one historian has maintained, that the Jesuits deliberately created the aldeias in order to provide "an indigenous peasantry" that would satisfy the settlers' needs, the fathers certainly recognized that everyone, including the Jesuits themselves, was dependent upon such labor. They simply wanted to mediate between the mission Indians and their secular employers to see that the former were not abused or exploited and were justly compensated for their work. For two centuries the settlers resented such mediation and relentlessly attacked the Jesuits for interfering with their access to indigenous labor.

Another constant settler grievance concerned the temporal administration of the missions. The settlers, who controlled villages on their own plantations and dominated those nearby, contended that only laypersons ought to administer the aldeias. That issue initially arose during Brazil's first documented smallpox epidemic in the early 1560s, when panic-stricken Brasis fled the plantations to the missions and abandoned them for the back country. When colonists later charged the missionaries with providing unwarranted asylum, the fathers urged Governor-General Mem de Sá to designate so-called lay captains to take over the temporal administration of the aldeias, so that the missionaries would retain only their spiritual supervision. Yet because of subsequent complaints concerning the captains' exploitation of the Brasis, the governor-general restored the Jesuits to full administrative authority. In 1583 a committee consisting of leading royal officials and Jesuits met in Salvador and decided that the fathers would continue to control the aldeias but that they would not accept refugees from the plantations, nor would the latter take in neophytes who had left the missions. Nevertheless, Claudio Aquaviva, like Francisco Borgia before him, was uncomfortable with that solution and in 1597 urged the fathers to confine their activities to spiritual matters and leave the administration of the aldeias to the king's functionaries. As the indigenous population by the seacoast continued to diminish alarmingly, the conflict

16. Provisão of 12 Sept. 1727, in ibid., 270, fol. 28ᵛ.

17. As is well known, in early eighteenth-century São Paulo, many Portuguese or *mestiço* settlers could speak the lingua geral more fluently than Portuguese. Why that was not also true in northern Brazil is a puzzle.

18. *HCJB*, 2: 130. A settler in Paraíba observed in 1633 that the only Indians who came to the colonists' assistance in conquering savages and in repelling pirates were those who belonged to the Jesuits. "Informacion q. hize por mandado de VM sobre uns capitulos q. Duarte Gomez de Silveira vizino de Parayba embio a la Mesa de Consciencia," [1633], Archivo General de Simancas, Sp. 1583, fols. 382–89, for which I am indebted to Stuart Schwartz. For the governors' reliance upon Indian militia over a century later, see *DH*, 42: 334–35, and 72: 338–39.

over temporal jurisdiction within the aldeias abated along the littoral, but it would resurface repeatedly throughout the next century and a half elsewhere in Brazil.[19]

Beginnings of the Conflict Between the Jesuits and the Settlers Concerning Indian Slavery

Another source of conflict between the Jesuits and the settlers concerned the enslavement of the indigenes. Soon after Nóbrega, the mission superior, reached Brazil, he reported,

> In this country the majority of the inhabitants have their consciences heavily weighted down because of the slaves whom they hold unjustly besides the many ... who were purchased from their fathers and whom the inhabitants will not free.... Thus Satan has all these souls in his power ... because the men who came out here find no other livelihood than by the work of their slaves.... They are not disturbed at being excommunicated, provided they keep their slaves.[20]

This was the first of many Jesuit warnings condemning the enslavement of the Brasis, which the fathers viewed as morally wrong and as grievously harmful to their efforts to encourage the Indians to lead Christian lives.

As Alexander Marchant showed long ago, by the time the first Jesuits reached Brazil, the Portuguese system of recruiting free Indian laborers through barter had degenerated into blatant slavery.[21] A quarter century after Nóbrega sounded the alarm, a humanist visitor to Brazil observed that "the first thing" newly arrived settlers did was

> to try to obtain ... slaves to work the farms; and any one who succeeds in obtaining two pairs or a half dozen of them (although he may not have another earthly possession) has the means to sustain his family in a respectable way; for one fishes for him, another hunts for him, and the rest cultivate and till his fields, and consequently there is no expense for the maintenance of his slaves or of his household. From this, one may infer how very extensive are the estates of those who own two hundred or three hundred slaves, for there are many ... who have that number or more.[22]

By the time those lines were written, the crown had already begun to formulate an Indian policy, and predictably the Jesuits were involved in its enforcement. In 1566 Sebastian wrote Mem de Sá that he had learned that unjust captures of Indians were occurring in Brazil, and he urged the governor-general to work closely with the bishop and with leading Jesuits to prevent that practice.[23] Four years later, in the first of a long series of statutes that the Portuguese crown enacted concerning Indian-white relations in Brazil, the young monarch prohibited the enslavement of Brasis except for those taken in a just war.[24]

19. *HCJB*, 2: 64–65, 67, 70–71, 73, and 200. See also the "Resoluções da junta da Ba[h]ia sobre as aldeias dos padres e os indios," Bahia, 30 July 1566, in *MB* 4: 354–56.

20. Nóbrega to Rodrigues, 6 Jan. 1550, in *MB*, 1: 166; there is an English translation in Stetson, *The Histories of Brazil*, 2: 214–15 n. 44.

21. Marchant, *From Barter to Slavery: The Economic Relations of Portuguese and Indians in the Settlement of Brazil, 1500–1580* (1942; rpr., Gloucester, Mass., 1966), passim.

22. Magalhães [de Gandavo], *History*, 41.

23. King to Sá, ca. Aug. 1566, in *MB*, 4: 354–56; also quoted in part in *HCJB* 2: 200–201.

24. Kiemen, *Indian Policy*, 4–5.

Sebastian's law came two decades after a famous debate occurred in Valladolid between an Aristotelian scholar and the renowned champion of Indian rights in the Spanish empire, the Dominican Bartolomé de las Casas. That debate centered upon the appropriateness of applying the old principle of just war to Indian-white confrontations in that empire.[25] The concept of just war already had a long history. It found sanctions in the Bible, especially in the Old Testament; in Roman law; and in the writings of the early Church fathers. Aristotle first put forth the concept, but a host of later commentators, including Saint Augustine, Saint Thomas Aquinas, Peter Lombard, and their followers, contributed to its evolution.[26]

Though it is plausible that in sanctioning the 1570 statute the young king was responding to the counsel of his Jesuit advisors, there is no certainty about that. It is, however, evident that the early welcome extended by royal officials and colonists toward representatives of the Society was seriously eroded by the 1580s, when the Jesuits found themselves under attack by an aged governor-general for having allegedly incited an Indian uprising in Bahia.[27] During the same decade, they also became targets of a lengthy, scathing memorial composed by a representative of the sugar planters of Bahia. Its author was the remarkable Gabriel Soares de Sousa.

Soares de Sousa came to Bahia about 1570 and became a cane grower. He is well known as the author of the encyclopedic *Descriptive Treatise on Brazil*, a work that he completed in the 1580s when he returned to the kingdom to secure a royal concession to search in the Bahian backlands for mineral resources. On the few occasions that he mentioned the Jesuits in his *Treatise*, the chronicler spoke of their activities in favorable terms, but he reserved his real sentiments toward them for a memorial that he presented to Philip II's go-between in the kingdom, the quisling Cristóvão de Moura (see Chapter 4). In that memorial, Soares de Sousa charged that the fathers had become deeply involved in political intrigues in the colony; that they had forsaken their spiritual mission for material gain; and that they had behaved unscrupulously in their relations with the Brasis. He was scornful of their claims of a large number of converts, contending that most of their neophytes fled into the forests at the first opportunity. He insisted that the purpose of the fathers' visits to the settlers' plantations was chiefly to incite legitimate Indian slaves to flee to the missions, where their masters were forbidden to pursue them. Lastly, Soares de Sousa alleged that the fathers were not interested in the Indians' welfare but wanted to exploit the natives for their own purposes. Like the early Spanish-American critics of Spain's famous New Laws for the Preservation of the Indians (1542), Soares de Sousa warned the king that unless the planters were assured an ample supply of Indian slaves, Brazil's economy could not survive.[28]

25. Lewis U. Hanke, *The Spanish Struggle for Justice in the Conquest of America* (Boston, 1949), 119ff.; idem, *Aristotle and the American Indians* (London, 1959), chap. 5.

26. Frederick H. Russell, *The Just War in the Middle Ages* (New York, 1975).

27. Alden, "Black Robes," 26, and sources cited there.

28. "Capitulos que Gabriel Soares de Sousa deu em Madrid ao Sr. D. Cristovam de Moura contra os padres da companhia de Jesus ... no Brasil, com umas breves respostas dos mesmos padres." First published, from a copy that remains in ARSI, by Fr. Leite in *Ethnos, Revista do Instituto Portugues de Arquelogia, Historia e Etnografia* (Lisbon, 1941), 2: 5–[36]; rpr. in *ABNRJ* 62 (1940): 341–81. I remain indebted to Stuart Schwartz for providing me with a photocopy of the *Ethnos* edition.

Fr. Serafim Leite rightly called Soares de Sousa's "Charges" the "most anti-jesuitical document of sixteenth-century Brazil."[29] It remains a remarkable document not only because of the severity of the author's allegations but also because many of them were destined to be reiterated in later centuries by the Society's opponents.

The Jesuits never believed in turning the other cheek, and they did not do so in this instance. As soon as word of the memorial reached Salvador, a committee of leading members of the Society assembled in Brazil's capital to prepare a defense. They included the provincial; two former provincials; the procurator; Fernão Cardim, the secretary of a former Visitor and himself the author of a notable treatise on Brazil; and the venerable missionary, linguist, and historian José de Anchieta. In its point-by-point refutation of Soares de Sousa's allegations, the committee candidly admitted that the Society's efforts to protect the Indians against enslavement, sale, and branding made its members unpopular in the colony.

The committee's defense was sent to Madrid in 1592. By then the Society's representatives in Brazil appear to have weathered this particular storm. Both the hostile governor-general and the would-be mining prospector had passed to their rewards. Three years later, in 1595, the new Philippine regime promulgated another law that further narrowed legal grounds for just wars against the Brasis.

At the beginning of the next century, the Spanish crown issued three additional statutes concerning the capture of Brasis. The first two reflected Jesuit convictions, but the third represented a capitulation to the settlers. In a decree framed in 1605, the crown boldly declared that "in no case may the natives of Brazil be taken captive, even though [in the past] there may have been some legal justifications for such seizures, those to the contrary [are] of so much greater consideration . . . that these . . . must be placed before all the rest."[30] Four years later the crown went even further in a statute that seems to have been part of a concerted effort by Madrid to improve the treatment of Indians in its dual empire.[31] That statute declared that all Brasis were free persons, that none might be held in captivity, and that all must be compensated for labor they performed. Only the Jesuits would be permitted to venture into the backlands to bring back natives to the littoral to be housed in aldeias under their control. Colonists who had need for such workers could obtain them through the fathers, but the newly created High Court (Relação) in Bahia would adjudicate all disputes.[32]

Just as the Spanish crown's efforts to enforce the famous New Laws had stirred unexpectedly violent protests in Spanish America, so the statute of 1609 sparked the first of four anti-Jesuit tumults in seventeenth-century Brazil. In each case the fathers, whom the colonists assumed were instigators of legislation they deemed prejudicial to their interests, either were expelled or were threatened with such action. In late June 1610, when Salvador's cámara met to decide how to respond to the offending law, an angry mob gathered outside of the council's chambers. Someone then urged that the Salvadorans

29. "Capitulos," in *Ethnos*, 2: 8.

30. Provisão of 5 June 1605, in *CCLP*, 1: 129. I have followed the translation in Kiemen, *Indian Policy*, 5.

31. Stuart B. Schwartz, *Sovereignty and Society in Colonial Brazil: The High Court of Bahia and Its Judges, 1609–1751* (Berkeley, 1973), 134.

32. Law of 30 July 1609, in *CCLP*, 1: 271–73.

emulate the Venetians, who, four years earlier, had banned the Jesuits from their republic.[33] That cry inspired a march to the Jesuit college, where, however, the provincial and his lieutenants denied that the Society had had any role in the preparation of the law, a plausible contention since, as seen in Chapter 4, the Order did not enjoy a close relationship with the Philippine monarchs.

If the fathers' efforts gave them respite that day, the next proved equally troubling, for several aldermen appeared before the college portal and demanded that senior Jesuits sign a statement that had been framed in the council chambers. Intended for the king himself, it declared that implementation of the offending law would be a disservice "to God and His Majesty" and would be prejudicial to the colony. Although the provincial declined to endorse that memorial, he did agree to sign a declaration that clearly had no legal standing. It assured settlers that the law would not be interpreted to take from them captives sanctioned under previous legislation, that free Indians being "administered" by colonists would not be removed from their domiciles, and that the Jesuits would not attempt to transfer natives from the settlers' care to their own missions.[34]

Evidently that declaration pacified the aldermen and their constituents. Possibly it was transmitted to the court, and conceivably it helped persuade Spain's Philip III to beat a hasty retreat, though it is more probable that in doing so the king was moved by an earlier warning from the governor-general that enforcement of the legislation would pose "a thousand inconveniences" and that continuous levies of Indian laborers obtained from the back country by civilians, not missionaries, were essential to the proper functioning of the colonial economy.[35]

The law of 1611, the last to be enacted by Portugal's Philippine masters, signaled the crown's surrender to the settlers. It again sanctioned the principle of just war under certain conditions; it introduced the notion that colonists who "liberated" natives allegedly intended for cannibalistic feasts were entitled to ten years' labor from those whose lives they had supposedly spared; and it mandated the appointment of lay captains in place of missionaries as the overseers of the temporal affairs of Indian settlements.[36]

It is unlikely that the new regulations had much impact upon the Brasis of the coastal zones of the older captaincies of Brazil, from which most of the indigenous population

33. The pretext for the Jesuits' ouster from Venice was the imposition of an interdict by Paul V in response to the republic's refusal to withdraw several recent laws that were primarily directed against the Jesuits, whose successes there were viewed with alarm by the University of Padua and by other vested interests. Republican authorities demanded that the clergy ignore the interdict (May 1606–April 1607). Some complied, but others, including the Jesuits, did not. Their expulsion was followed by that of the Capuchins and the Theatines. In the end the pope was obliged to back down, but he was compelled, with the concurrence of Aquaviva, to sacrifice the Jesuits, who were banned from the republic for decades. See William J. Bouwsma, *Venice and the Defense of Republican Liberty: Renaissance Values in the Age of the Counter Reformation* (Berkeley, 1968), esp. chap. 7, which is sympathetic to the republic, whereas Ludwig von Pastor, *HP*, 25: chap. 4, is strongly pro-papist. According to Logan Pearsall Smith, the Jesuits were not readmitted to Venice until 1657. *The Life and Letters of Sir Henry Wotton*, 2 vols. (Oxford, 1907), 2: 212 n. 6.

34. The foregoing is based primarily on Henrique Gomes (provincial) to Aquaviva, 5 July 1610, in ARSI, *Bras.*, 8, fols. 114^r–15, transcribed in *HCJB*, 5: 5–8. Precisely what was meant by the settlers' "administration" of the Indians at this time is unclear. As the text will demonstrate, the term would be employed again late in the century to justify what amounted to a sanitized form of Indian slavery, especially in São Paulo.

35. Diogo de Menezes to king, 8 May 1610, in *ABNRJ* 57 (1939): 68–69.

36. Law of 10 Sept. 1611, in *CCLP*, 1: 309–12.

had already disappeared by the early seventeenth century.[37] Many had been killed as a result of punitive campaigns undertaken by the Portuguese or by their Indian allies; others had succumbed to imported diseases of European or African origin;[38] many had expired because of the rigors of forced labor that the Portuguese imposed on plantations and elsewhere; the more fortunate had fled to the interior and mingled with the still "untamed" tribes. Yet elsewhere, particularly throughout the remote southern and northern parts of Brazil, competition between the Jesuits (and other missionaries) and the settlers for control of the Amerindians continued and intensified.

The Great "Tempest"

Beginning in the 1590s, hordes of Tupi-speaking explorer-slavers, many of them mixed bloods (mamelucos) from the captaincy of São Vicente (the future São Paulo), pressed westward and southward from their base in the town of São Paulo in quest of mineral wealth and Indian slaves.[39] During the decade beginning in 1628, these marauders (*bandeirantes*) ravaged two undefended mission fields recently founded west and south of São Paulo by Jesuits from Spanish Paraguay and carried off thousands of neophytes, who were sold to settlers in their captaincy.[40] In 1638 two Spanish Jesuits, Francisco Diaz Taño and Ruiz de Montoya, traveled from Paraguay to Madrid and Rome seeking legal remedies to protect their remaining missions. One result was papal authorization to arm and train the Guaraní in defensive measures. Their surprising success at Mbororé (March 1641) compelled the raiders to seek less hostile environments elsewhere in the Brazilian backlands for future plunder.[41]

The defense of the remaining Paraguayan reductions or missions was, however, offset by ill-timed Jesuit efforts to bring about the liberation of Indian captives held in the captaincies of Rio de Janeiro and São Vicente. Despite the successes of the raiders, Fr. Diaz Taño, the missions' procurator, proved to be an excellent recruiter and sailed from Lisbon with 30 or more fresh missionaries in the late winter of 1640. When adverse winds compelled their ship to put in to Rio de Janeiro (15 April 1641), the Spaniards were warmly welcomed by

37. The presence of Indians is rarely discussed in the most comprehensive report on Brazil's eight northern captaincies completed just after the 1611 law. See Engel Sluiter, ed., "Report on the State of Brazil, 1612," in *HAHR* 29 (1949): 518–62.

38. D. Alden and Joseph C. Miller, "Unwanted Cargoes: The Origins and Dissemination of Smallpox Via the Slave Trade from Africa to Brazil, c. 1560–1830," in Kenneth F. Kiple, ed., *The African Exchange: Toward a Biological History of Black People* (Durham, N.C., 1987), 35–109, and sources cited there.

39. For a summary of the activities of the pathfinders (*bandeirantes*), see Affonso de E. Taunay, *Historia das bandeiras paulistas*, 2d ed., 3 vols. (São Paulo, 1961); or Richard M. Morse, comp., *The Bandeirantes: The Historical Role of the Brazilian Pathfinders* (New York, 1965).

40. By 1632 the Spaniards were compelled to evacuate three recently established towns in Guairá, the larger of the two fields. The indignant viceroy of Peru urged the king either to purchase São Vicente from its owners or to destroy existing Portuguese settlements there. See D. Alden, *Royal Government in Colonial Brazil* (Berkeley, 1968), 63–64 n. 11. Philip Caraman, S.J., *The Lost Paradise* (New York, 1976), chaps. 3 and 4, fails to add anything new to the subject. The number of Indian slaves held by Paulistas may have been far lower than generally assumed. See John Manuel Monteiro, "Os escravos índios de São Paulo nos século xvii: Alguns aspectos demográficos," *Revista da s[ociedade] b[rasileira] de p[esquisa] h[istórica]*, no. 5 (São Paulo, 1989–90): 11ff.

41. Boxer, *Salvador de Sá*, 139, and sources cited there.

local authorities, who called out an honor guard to escort their guests to the Jesuit college on Castle Hill. Little did they know that the procurator brought with him an incendiary brief issued by Urban VIII one year earlier. That brief reiterated the strong language embodied in the bull *Sublimis Deus* by the reforming pope Paul III (29 May 1537). In it Paul declared emphatically that the Amerindians were rational humans and insisted that there could be no ethical basis for their enslavement.[42] Urban's brief, clearly inspired by the bandeirantes' savagery, was directed especially at the settlers in Brazil, Paraguay, and the rest of the Platine area. It threatened those who engaged in Indian enslavement with papal excommunication and enjoined ecclesiastics to oppose the practice vigorously.[43]

That brief, addressed to the acting papal nuncio in Lisbon, triggered a series of events that reflected the breakdown of law in Brazil at the end of the Philippine regime and also the zeal and intransigence, but lack of perspicacity, among Jesuit leaders, as well as the willingness of rival Orders to capitalize upon Jesuit distress. Diaz Taño had left Lisbon with the brief before legal formalities concerning its acceptance by Portuguese authorities had been completed. Not only had the royal chancery not registered the document, as was certainly required in accordance with legal understandings between Rome and Lisbon concerning church matters in the empire (the padroado real), but the customary implementing directives had not been written by superior royal officials to the crown's representatives in Brazil. Nevertheless, when a meeting occurred at the Jesuit college (22 April 1641), neither the ailing governor, the famous Salvador de Sá, nor the acting local ecclesiastical administrator voiced opposition to the publication of the brief. Yet, for obscure reasons, it was actually promulgated in Santos and São Paulo before it was announced in Rio de Janeiro. As soon as rumors of the offending text reached the Carioca community, however, a general meeting was held (4 May) in the Carmelite monastery by invitation only. In what was obviously a studied insult, the governor and the Jesuits were excluded from attendance, but representatives of the other three religious Orders and the ecclesiastical administrator were present. After the administrator had been browbeaten into revealing the text, the assembly agreed to appeal to the king against it and in the interim urged that it not be implemented. Nevertheless, two and a half weeks later, only a week after it had caused a serious riot in Santos, Jesuit leaders decided to go ahead and divulge the text, which was read in the college church during a Sunday service (20 May). They did so, supposedly, because of their conviction that it was urgently necessary to protect the Amerindians, but one wonders if some of those priests were not deliberately seeking martyrdom. In any event, they did not miss such a sanguinary end by much.

The reading of the brief immediately spurred the formation of a mob that climbed Castle Hill, battered down the closed doors of the college, and confronted the fathers with shouts calling for their expulsion or death. Only the timely arrival of the Jesuits' principal protector, the ailing governor, who was borne to the besieged college on a litter, prevented those threats from being translated into action, or so Jesuit accounts would lead us to believe.

Although the mob withdrew, the proslavery forces continued to exert pressure. While they intimidated the pusillanimous ecclesiastical administrator, who was quite content to

---

42. Hanke, *Aristotle*, 19, and more extensively in his "Pope Paul III and the American Indians," *Harvard Theological Review* 30 (1937): 65–102.

43. *HCJB*, 6: 569–71, provides a Portuguese translation of the brief *Commissum nobis*.

allow the fathers to take the heat, and bullyragged the heads of the other Orders as well, each side prepared heated denunciations of the other. The settlers' spokesmen charged the Jesuits with hypocrisy, claiming that they themselves not only had Indian slaves but even peddled them, that they possessed vast revenues in the captaincy, and that there and elsewhere they refused to make their converts available for the defense of the fatherland. The Jesuits not only forcefully denied those charges but suggested that their critics were hardly Christians and were more akin to Jews.[44]

If such language failed to bring credit to the fathers, the notarized statement that their leaders signed with the settlers' spokesmen a month later diminished their prestige even more. By its terms they agreed that they would not attempt to enforce the brief or to remove any Indians performing personal service for the colonists, and that they would restore to their owners any escaped Indian slaves who sought asylum in one of their aldeias. They also promised to pardon the rioters and to refrain from undertaking any legal action against them. The only concession that the settlers' agents made was to refrain from expelling the fathers.[45] Though the agreement's terms represented a repudiation of the position that the fathers had taken a month earlier, their decision to capitulate followed a recommendation by their friend Salvador de Sá. It may also have been influenced by distressing events in the neighboring captaincy of São Vicente.[46]

The trouble started in that captaincy's port of Santos, where the local vicar read Urban's brief in the pulpit of the church belonging to the Jesuit instructional house on 13 May. There, too, a riot ensued, and a mob crying for the heads of the Jesuits threatened to break into their house. It desisted only after the Jesuits' superior surrendered his copy of the brief. Again the rioters proceeded to the Carmelite house and vowed to appeal to Urban himself to remove the offending legislation. Some suggested that even rule by the Dutch heretics would be better than that by the Jesuit fathers, for at least the slavers would be spared threats of excommunication. Angry and armed rioters then returned to the instructional house, where only the intervention of the local governor prevented them from firing upon the fathers.

Urban's bombshell message was first broadcast in the town of São Paulo about 20 June. Four days later, on the feast of St. John the Baptist, delegates from the Paulista cámara met in São Vicente with representatives from its council in its chambers, where they were joined for the next three days by representatives of eight other towns to decide upon a course of common action. Although the brief called upon all ecclesiastics to enforce it, only the Jesuits were willing to do so. Accordingly, the rebels agreed that the fathers, as instigators of the offending legislation, should pay the price—expulsion from the captaincy. It was

44. The settlers' memorial seems to be known only through the Jesuits' indignant refutation: *HCJB*, 6: 572–88.

45. The famous Brazilian historian Francisco Adolfo Varnhagen published the conciliatory agreement of 22 June 1640 in *RIHGB* 3 (1841): 113–17. Signatories included members of the cámara, military officers, and several prominent Jesuits, including the Visitor General, the procurator of the college, and, most curious of all, Francisco Diaz Taño, the bearer of the brief, who had absolutely no authority whatsoever in Brazil or in the Brazil province!

46. Except as noted, the foregoing is based primarily upon the coeval Jesuit sources quoted verbatim in *HCJB*, 6: 32–41, and in Boxer, *Salvador de Sá*, 130–35, though I reach somewhat different conclusions than did Professor Boxer. See also the eyewitness account of Fr. Simon Mendez to Fr. Sebastian Gonzalez, Rio de Janeiro, 15 June 1640, in *MHE*, 19: 231–43, esp. 238–42.

hoped that the Cariocas would follow suit, that the pope would rescind the brief, and that the king, grateful for the revenues deriving from sequestered Jesuit properties, would be understanding.

The first to go were the Jesuits in the Paulista college, who rejected an ultimatum from the town council to disown the brief. At 2 A.M. on 13 July, the cámara expressed the will of "the people," that is, those dependent upon Indian slavery and those who simply detested Jesuits. Escorted by 40 men, the fathers left the town the next day for the port of Cubatão, about 7 kilometers from Santos. If the Paulistas expected that the Jesuits would soon be sent packing, they were disappointed, for the fathers, too, had friends near the port towns. Only the appearance of an armed band of Paulistas accompanied by their Indian servants brought about the desired result: the Jesuits fled Santos for Rio de Janeiro on 3 August.[47]

Less than four months later, the December revolution brought Philippine rule in Portugal and its dominions to an end; but the regime of John IV faced far more serious problems than the Jesuits' ouster from São Paulo (see Chapters 4–5) and did nothing concrete to bring about their return, although Rome declared the captaincy under interdict. In 1642 an angry Salvador de Sá sent the Jesuits back to Santos under an armed escort, but he failed to compel the Paulistas to readmit them or to abide by the terms of the papal brief.[48] Even the four Jesuits stationed in the port found their tenure insecure, for they were forced to leave again in 1646.[49] Not until the early 1650s did Paulista tempers cool sufficiently to permit the negotiations that led to the Jesuits' return to the captaincy in 1653. Toward the middle of that year, a dozen fathers, led by their provincial, triumphantly entered Santos and soon thereafter were warmly welcomed back to São Paulo. Once again the two sides signed a legal agreement (14 May) by which the Jesuits promised their opponents full absolution and gave assurances that they would not press damage claims stemming from the 1640 riots. They also promised not to menace the Indians already in the possession of the settlers. In effect, the fathers recognized that, absent royal support, there was no way to enforce Urban VIII's well-meant brief.[50]

These revealing episodes occurred at a time when the Spanish government and the successor Portuguese regime were preoccupied with far more serious setbacks in Europe and in their empires, so that neither crown could impose its will upon its defiant subjects. Although Fr. Serafim Leite, who mined the sources concerning these anti-Jesuit movements more thoroughly than any other scholar, viewed the 1653 settlement in São Vicente through a roseate lens and concluded that it produced no victors, no vanquished, it is possible to reach a quite different verdict. That settlement, and the events of the thirteen years that led to it, placed the Society very much on the defensive and permanently damaged its credibility in southern Brazil. Though the Jesuits returned to São Vicente, they did so because of popular sufferance, not because the crown resolutely insisted that they ought to be there. And although it is true that because of the benefactions of Salvador de Sá,

47. The previous paragraphs are based upon *HCJB*, 6: 416–23 and 252–53, which consist primarily of coeval Jesuit accounts. See also Boxer, *Salvador de Sá*, 135–37.

48. Boxer, *Salvador de Sá*, 151–53. Strangely, Boxer ignores the fact that the Jesuits were expelled from Santos a second time.

49. *HCJB*, 6: 421–23.

50. The return of the Jesuits to the captaincy of São Vicente is reported in great detail in ibid., 268–79, 282–88.

the house of São Miguel was upgraded to a college in 1653, neither it nor the companion college on the plateau ever grew in students, manpower, or resources to a size comparable to that of Jesuit colleges elsewhere in Brazil.[51]

As their opposition charged, despite their efforts to protect the Amerindians against unwarranted slavery and inhumane treatment, Jesuits in Brazil and elsewhere during the sixteenth to early eighteenth centuries sometimes *did* own Indian chattels.[52] In 1585, for example, José de Anchieta reported that the new college of Olinda possessed "thirty persons of service, Guiné slaves and those of [this] land," and that the college in Bahia possessed 150 service personnel, including Indian slaves. Nearly 40 years later a Paulista couple left the college of Santo Ignácio, São Paulo, a living trust that included "many Indians of the land descended from the backlands and acquired in other ways," and in 1710 a well-known citizen of southern Brazil gave the same college "11 slaves and heathen of the land." Earlier, in 1659, the procurator of the Lisbon college of Santo Antão purchased "40 pieces" consisting of heathens and Guinea slaves for the Santana sugar estate. The price was 2 contos, and the seller was none other than Salvador de Sá![53] Whether the treatment that the Jesuits accorded such slaves was better than that provided by the settlers is debatable but unprovable. Yet it is incontestable that the cassocks of the fathers were not as clean as they or their modern Jesuit interpreter would want us to believe.

António Vieira and the Struggle for Indian Liberty

Though the Jesuits in the south felt compelled to adopt a defensive posture because of the settlers' intransigence concerning their alleged right to utilize the Brasis, their colleagues in the north, led by the redoubtable António Vieira and supported, albeit inconsistently, by the crown, took the offensive, with predictable results. From 1653 until 1662, Vieira, former court preacher and frustrated diplomat (Chapter 5), led a team of nearly 50 missionaries in the State of Maranhão. Convinced of the iniquity of the settlers' exploitation of the natives, he delivered stinging sermons reminiscent of the sixteenth-century Spanish Dominican, Bartolomé de las Casas, condemning Indian slavery and the hypocrisy of the so-called "ransoming" expeditions by which settlers removed Indians from the interior forests to toil for them with minimal compensation for the balance of their shortened lives. When the Jesuits, absent from Maranhão since 1649, returned to the State (see Chapter 9), John IV gave them carte blanche to establish aldeias wherever there were opportunities and authorized

51. Cf. ibid., 286.

52. In his letter of 15 June 1640 (see note 46), Fr. Simon Mendez stated that the settlers' spokesmen contended in their diatribes that the college of Rio de Janeiro possessed more than 600 slaves, but he retorted that "almost all are blacks" (p. 241). Boxer, *Salvador de Sá*, 134, misread that passage and assumed that the critics meant that there were "over six hundred . . . in their Rio college," whereas the passage referred to the total number of slaves, most of whom were on its estates.

53. José de Anchieta, "Informação da província do Brasil para nosso padre" [1585] in A. de Alcântara Machado, ed., *Cartas, informações, fragmentos historicos e sermões de Joseph de Anchieta* (Rio de Janeiro, 1933), 411 and 414; for the Paulista bequests, see *DISP*, 44: 347 and 368; affidavit of Fr. Philippe Franco, procurator of Santo Antão, 1659, in ANTT/CJ/68, no. 122. Cf. François Chevalier, *Land and Society in Colonial Mexico: The Great Hacienda*, trans. Alvin Eustis, ed. Lesley Byrd Simpson (Berkeley, 1966), 249, disclosing that in 1582 the college of St. Peter and St. Paul in Mexico City purchased a band of Chichimecas condemned to twenty years of forced labor.

them to rely upon the personal services of two Amerindian villages, whose workers were to be compensated for their labor. Besides producing food for the fathers' sustenance, such workers helped construct two new colleges, one at the existing house in São Luís and the other a new facility in Belém, where the skeptical citizenry reluctantly admitted the fathers.

The crown's enthusiastic support, the unprecedented number of Jesuits present, and Vieira's remarkable displays of energy—his disturbing sermons, his ceaseless travel (he later claimed to have traversed close to 9,600 kilometers in the State), and his spectacular conversions of hostile tribes—thoroughly alarmed the colonists, who memorialized the crown that Indians were "the most barbaric and the worst people in the world," but that their labor was nevertheless essential to the State's very survival. Vieira himself conceded the settlers' dependency upon indigenous workers.[54] In one of his many famous sermons in behalf of the Brasis, he remarked on the first Sunday of Lent 1653 that he was fully aware that his listeners would maintain that "our people, our country, our government can not be sustained without Indians. Who will fetch a pail of water for us or carry a load of wood? Who will grind our manioc? Will our wives have to do it? Will our sons? I answer yes and repeat yes again yes. You, your wives, your sons, all of us are able to sustain ourselves with our own labor. *It is better to live from your own sweat than from the blood of others.*"[55] Nevertheless, he knew that the settlers would not willingly follow his injunction, and he urged the king to prohibit further ransoming expeditions (*tropas de resgates*) to the interior to bring out so-called captive Indians and to order an inquiry into the proper legal status of all those then held by the settlers.[56] The ailing monarch responded by temporizing: in 1653 he authorized the resumption of ransoming expeditions (suspended in 1651), provided that they be sanctioned by the religious and local officials and that they include missionaries.

Vieira remained deeply troubled by the "greed" of the settlers and their continued "persecution" of the Brasis,[57] and he therefore returned to the kingdom (June 1654) to lobby for a law that would restrict Indian enslavement as much as possible. He was successful. The law of April 1655 gave the Jesuits a decisive voice in the recruitment of Indian labor throughout the State and sanctioned only defensive campaigns against tribes that evinced hostility toward the regime or the spread of the Gospel.

During the next six years, the Jesuits successfully expanded the spiritual conquest from the Serra Ibiapaba in Ceará to the large island of Marajó in the throat of the Amazon, and up that greater river to some of its major affluents. Throughout those years the fathers claimed to have recruited 200,000 neophytes and to have established 54 missions. If those accomplishments pleased the crown, they were disquieting to the settlers, whom Vieira accused of being "solely interested in the sweat and blood of the Indians."[58] He candidly admitted to his friend John IV that "we have against us [here] the people, the [other] religious [Orders], the proprietors of the captaincies, and all those in the Kingdom and in this State who are interested in the blood and sweat of the Indians whose inferior condition we alone

54. Vieira to provincial of Brazil, São Luís, 22 May 1653, in João Lúcio de Azevedo, ed., *Cartas do Padre António Vieira*, 3 vols. (Coimbra, 1925–28), 1: 332. See also note 57.

55. Quoted in Hemming, *Red Gold*, 319.

56. Vieira to provincial of Brazil, 22 May 1653, and to John IV, São Luís, 10 May 1653, in Azevedo, *Cartas*, 1: 322 and 306–12.

57. Vieira to provincial of Brazil, 1654, in ibid., 408.

58. Vieira to an unknown Jesuit, Pará, 16 Apr. 1655, in ibid., 446.

defend."[59] In Lascasian terms, he insisted that "the injustices and tyrannies that have been practiced on the Indians of these lands exceed by far those that have been perpetrated in Africa. In the space of forty years ... more than two million Indians and in excess of 500 Indian settlements ... have been ravaged without any punishments [having been meted out] for such misdeeds."[60] For its part, the cámara of Belém, a leading spokesman for the slaveholding interests, warned the regency governing in the name of Afonso VI that permitting the Jesuits to enjoy temporal jurisdiction within the missions was highly prejudicial to their interests and to those of the crown. A spokesman for the São Luís council raised the charge, destined to be echoed many times in the State during the next century, that the fathers had become "absolute masters" and were bringing about the State's economic ruin.[61] Although such complaints prompted the court to order a further review of the crown's Indian policy in Maranhão, the theologians assigned to investigate the matter concluded that it would be unwise to alter the statute of 1655.[62] Nevertheless, the days of the Jesuits in the State were numbered.

In 1660 fever and smallpox, always harbingers of incipient conflicts between colonists and missionaries in Maranhão because of the ensuing scarcity of Indian workers, ravaged the State. Refusing to recognize that the shortage of laborers was a consequence of disease and the flight of panic-stricken tribesmen, the cámara of Belém remonstrated with the missions superior that the paucity of Indians was a direct consequence of deliberate efforts by the Jesuits to restrict legitimate expeditions in quest of fresh supplies of workers. Vieira responded by denying the culpability of his Order and insisted that the real solution to the labor problem was the one already found in the State of Brazil: the procurement of adequate numbers of Angolan slaves, who were more capable of arduous labor and more resistant to disease than the Amerindians.[63] But the settlers were unconvinced. On 15 May 1661, during the Feast of the Holy Ghost, the colonists of São Luís, goaded by the other religious Orders, who were jealous of the privileged position that the Society enjoyed in the State, rioted and arrested the Jesuits in the town and the nearby missions. A month and two days later the citizens of Belém, led by their cámara, did the same.[64] Although a few missionaries successfully sought safety in the Amazonian rain forest for a time, by 1662 all had been rounded up and packed off to the kingdom.[65]

59. Dispatch of 8 Dec. 1655, in ibid., 452–53.

60. Vieira to Afonso VI, 20 Apr. 1657, in ibid., 468.

61. Jorge de Sampayo e Carvalho to Afonso VI, 1661, in Barão de Studart, ed., *Documentos para a historia do Brasil e especialmente a do Ceará*, 4 vols. (Fortaleza, 1904–21), 4: 109–16. I wish to thank Thomas Cohen for calling this memorial to my attention.

62. Provisão of 10 Apr. 1658, in *LGM* 1: 29.

63. Cámara to Vieira, 15 Jan. 1661, and Vieira to cámara, 12 Feb. 1661, in Bernardo Pereira de Berredo, *Annaes históricos do estado do Maranhão*, 2 vols., 3d. ed. (Florence, 1905), 2: 110–16. Vieira's reply is also in Azevedo, *Cartas*, 1: 579–83.

64. The settlers' view of the expulsions is reflected in [Anon.], "Noticia dos successos e expulsao dos PP. da Comp.ª do estado do Maranhão," São Luís, 8 Aug. 1662, in BNL, cod. 674, fols. 288–312ᵛ. The viewpoint of a noteworthy Jesuit participant is Johan Philipe Betendorf, "Chronica da missão dos padres da Companhia de Jesus no estado do Maranhão," ca. 1699, in *RIHGB* 72 (1909 [1910]): 1 (entire volume), liv. 4.

65. Vieira's years in Maranhão are most fully covered from a Jesuit perspective in Azevedo, *Cartas*, vol. 1; and in Betendorf, "Chronica," liv. 4. For a pro-settler account, see Berredo, *Annaes históricos*, 1: 83–153. See, too, J[oão] Lúcio de Azevedo, *História de António Vieira*, 2d ed., 2 vols. (Lisbon, 1931), 1, esp. 389–99, and idem, *Os Jesuítas no Grão-Pará: Suas missões e a colonização* [1901], 2d ed. (Coimbra, 1930), chap. 3. All of the

In Maranhão, the seventeen years after the removal of the Jesuits were a period that Fr. Mathias C. Kiemen aptly termed one of "retrogression." Although the court welcomed Vieira's return and applauded his "Sermon of the Missions" (6 January 1662), which moved the queen regent, Luísa de Gusmão, to proclaim herself protectress of the Maranhense missions, that display of emotion availed the fathers and the Brasis nothing, for six months later the faction behind Afonso VI executed the palace coup that banished the queen regent to a convent and Vieira to northern Portugal (see Chapter 5). The new regime, headed by the count of Castelo Melhor, immediately became preoccupied with consolidating its own authority and repelling the threatening Spanish armies. It had little knowledge of conditions in Maranhão and little concern for their remedy. It was easier to accommodate the settlers, and that was done. In September 1663, the new regime restored the Jesuits to Brazil's northern State, but deprived them of both temporal authority over the missions and their former spiritual preeminence in the State. The crown doubly rebuffed the Society, first by barring Vieira's return to northern Brazil, and then by pardoning the settlers for their effrontery in ousting the Jesuits. As a further sop to the seemingly vindicated colonists, it also restored the lay captaincy system and assigned the two leading cámaras responsibility for determining the appropriateness of dispatching ransoming expeditions to the interior. Those who presided over the court were evidently more concerned with placating the settlers than with protecting the Amerindians, who inevitably suffered as a consequence.[66]

The Efforts of Pedro II to Protect the Brasis

In the 1680s the pendulum swung against the settlers and toward the missionaries and the Brasis. As noted in other chapters, Portugal's regent, Pedro, who would become Pedro II in 1683, was keenly interested in supporting missions in China, India, and Brazil. In 1679 the prince regent received several reports from Maranhão from experienced royal officials who were highly critical of the settlers' unrestrained enslavement of the aborigines. They urged that the Indians' villages again be placed under the supervision of missionaries, especially Jesuits, and that substantial numbers of African slaves be brought in to replace the Brasis as laborers.[67]

The regency government responded by enacting two critical pieces of legislation. One was the law of 1 April 1680, which again proscribed Indian slavery and authorized the Jesuits, who were declared supervisors of native aldeias, to "descend" heathen Indians from the interior and to supervise the allocation of indigenous workers.[68] To placate the settlers, the crown also sanctioned the establishment of a monopoly company that was expected to furnish the State with 500 to 600 black slaves a year.[69]

---

other standard secondary sources—including Kiemen, *Indian Policy*, chap. 4; *HCJB*, 4: liv. 1, chap. 2; and Hemming, *Red Gold*, chap. 15—devote much space to these years.

66. Kiemen, *Indian Policy*, chap. 5, remains perhaps the best treatment in English of the period; but see also Azevedo, *Os Jesuítas no Grão-Pará*, chap. 5.

67. Kiemen, *Indian Policy*, 137–38, which is superior to Hemming, *Red Gold*, 343, in explaining the background to the resulting statute of 1 April 1680.

68. *LGM* 1: 57–59.

69. Except as noted, the remainder of this section is primarily based upon Alden, "Indian Versus Black Slavery," 77ff., and the sources cited there.

Despite the crown's best intentions, neither the Maranhão Company nor the Company of Jesus survived long in Maranhão. The settlers soon complained that the slave company failed to fulfill its quota of chattels and unfairly charged them for the European goods that it furnished and for the colonial products that its ships took back to the kingdom. They naturally also resented the new authority granted to the Jesuits. In February 1684, the citizens of São Luís again revolted under the direction of a leading planter and another inveterate Jesuit adversary. The rioters declared an end to the slave company's monopoly, deposed their deputy governor, and expelled the 27 Jesuits residing in the captaincy of Maranhão. However, the Maranhenses' efforts to persuade the Parenses to join in their defiance failed.

The settlers' timing had been to their advantage during previous anti-Jesuit uprisings, but on this occasion it worked against them. Their uprising occurred barely five months after Pedro II had assumed the throne and therefore represented an early challenge to the new monarch's authority. The king met that challenge decisively: he dispatched a new governor to the State with orders to deal firmly with the rebels. Two were hanged, and several others received significant sentences.[70]

The crown had further unwelcome surprises for its unruly Maranhense subjects. One was the Overseas Council's enactment of the famous missions ordinances of 1686, which, with modifications, remained in effect for the balance of our period. They designated the missionaries as exclusively responsible for the management of their aldeias but stipulated that they must situate them in places convenient to Portuguese settlements to provide the latter with compensated labor. The workers' distribution became the responsibility of the governor or his deputy, representatives of the dominant cámaras, the Jesuit missions superior, and the resident father. The two Jesuit colleges in the State were each again assigned an aldeia for their support, and other Jesuit residences were awarded 25 Indian families to perform necessary tasks. The Jesuits were also directed to select for each captaincy a reliable person to serve as the Indians' advocate (*procurador dos índios*) in legal matters.[71]

Initially the ordinances proscribed all tropas de resgates, but the crown yielded to the inevitable protests by settlers, and in 1688 it directed that such expeditions might proceed when organized under Jesuit supervision and with the governor's approval. A year later it went even further when it sanctioned private efforts to resettle "uncivilized" Indians at the colonists' own expense. Nevertheless, Pedro II rejected the settlers' demands to restore the lay captaincy system in Maranhão.

To have decided otherwise would have been inconsistent with the policy that the king decided to embark upon in the State of Brazil. There, senior prelates, including the archbishop and the bishop of Olinda, testified that secular control of the villages was

70. *HCJB*, 4: 72–83; Murray Graeme MacNicoll, "Seventeenth-Century Maranhão: Beckman's Revolt," *Estudos Ibero-Americanos* 4 (1978): 129–40. An early indication of Pedro's willingness to support Jesuits against powerful settler interests occurred in northern Bahia, where in 1675 João Peixoto Viegas, a well-known member of a powerful local clan and one of the aldermen of the cámara of Salvador, had attempted to relocate a village of Christian Indians to a site where it could protect his ranches against hostile tribesmen. Though he had the support of the governor-general, the Jesuits objected. In 1680 the prince regent insisted that 230 Indians that Viegas had arbitrarily taken out of a Jesuit aldeia be returned. Prince regent to Roque da Costa Barreto, 26 Aug. 1680, in *RADF*, 4: [253]. See also *HCJB*, 9: 205–8, 279–80.

71. Convenient summaries of the ordinances are *HCJB*, 4: 369–75, and Kiemen, *Indian Policy*, 158–62.

blatantly prejudicial to the Indians' spiritual welfare and urged that missionaries, especially Jesuits, again become responsible for them.[72] As a result, in 1691 Pedro II directed that lay captaincies cease and that the aldeias be turned over to the religious.[73]

Generally that order seems to have been obeyed without provoking violent protests. As was often the case, the captaincy of São Vicente was the exception. There, following reports of the promulgation of the decree of 1 April 1680 abrogating the enslavement of the Brasis, the settlers again made menacing gestures toward the Jesuits, the presumed sponsors of the law.[74] As they did in Maranhão a few years later, the Jesuits seriously considered withdrawing from the region altogether and sought the general's permission to undertake that drastic step. Impressed by the seriousness of the fathers' resolve, the Paulistas backed down: in 1684, both their governor and the cámara of São Paulo beseeched the provincial to reconsider. After some soul-searching, the Jesuits agreed to remain.[75]

The promulgation of the order of 1691 provoked new agitation in the southern captaincy, where many colonists still relied primarily upon Indian slaves, who remained far less expensive than those imported from Africa.[76] To calm the Paulistas, the governor-general sent one of the most respected Jesuits of that day, Alexandre de Gusmão, to serve as the king's spokesman. According to Provincial Gusmão's subsequent report, he found the settlers in the captaincy convinced that "it was lawful to hunt Indians in the backlands, bringing them back in chains, putting them to work, giving them as presents, selling them, or using them to pay debts; . . . and that . . . [the settlers] said that they bring them to the bosom of the Church and give them sufficient food and clothing and that this is more than enough compensation for their labor."[77]

After protracted negotiations, the provincial and the local worthies signed a curious pact. The Paulistas conceded that all Indians must be considered free persons. They pledged that they would not send any more slaving parties to the back country. But the two sides agreed that it was manifestly wrong to return already Christianized Indians to their original homes where, in the absence of pastors, they would certainly revert to their customary bestiality. Consequently, it was decided that the neophytes would stay in the captaincy and labor for the planters, who would remain their "administrators, tutors, and guardians."[78]

---

72. D. Frei Manuel da Resureição (archbishop, Bahia) to king, 23 June 1689, and Overseas Council to king, 10 Oct. 1689, in AHU/PA/BA, 1st ser. uncat., cx. 16. Overseas Council to king, 7 Jan. 1691, in IAGHPB, *Consultas do Conselho Ultramarino*, 1, no. 86.

73. Overseas Council's directive of 18 Jan. 1691, in APB/OR, 1, no. 50; governor-general to king, 19 June 1691, in *DH*, 33: 404, reporting compliance.

74. Some years earlier, in 1677, rumors circulated in the town of São Paulo that the governor of Rio de Janeiro intended to free all Indian captives in São Vicente. Convinced that the Jesuits were responsible for that plan, the Paulistas again threatened to oust the fathers from the college of São Paulo but backed down once persuaded by their governor and the fathers themselves that there was no substance to their fears. Taunay, *Historia*, 1: 123–24; cf. *HCJB*, 6: 306–7.

75. *HCJB*, 6: 310–19.

76. The continued utilization of Indian slaves, identified as "peças do gentio da terra," is evident from testamentary declarations of the last quarter of the seventeenth century. See Archivo do estado de São Paulo, *Inventários e testamentos*, no. 19 (São Paulo, 1921): 20–21, 493–94; no. 22 (1921): [25–27], [74–75], 178–79, 191–92, 217–18, 266, 297–98, 344, 380–81; and no. 24 (1921): 7, 34–38, and 257.

77. Gusmão to Tirso Gonzalez de Santalla (father general), 30 May 1694, in *HCJB*, 6: 323.

78. The pact seems to have been signed toward the middle of 1692. The only copy that I have seen is contained in the annual letter of Gusmão to his general: *HCJB*, 6: 322–28.

Surprisingly, most of the leading Jesuits in the Brazil province concurred with Fr. Alexandre that the pact should be accepted.[79] Its most forceful critic was none other than António Vieira, who had returned to Bahia in 1681. Despite the infirmities resulting from an extraordinarily active, purposeful, contentious life, the 87-year-old father composed a celebrated opinion (*voto*) that demonstrates that he had lost none of his talent for lucid, forceful, incisive expression and that he remained as uncompromising in his defense of Indian freedom as he had been for nearly half a century. He observed that there was no legitimate way that the Indians held by the Paulistas could be deprived of their freedom; that the benefits of the accord would accrue entirely to the settlers and the burdens to the Indians; and that there was no real difference between these Paulista "administrations," as they were termed, and the discredited lay captaincy system. He concluded by assuring the king that if the settlers accorded the Brasis proper treatment, they would have no difficulty recruiting them to work for them for reasonable wages.[80]

Three years and six days after drafting that indictment of the sham concession to the Paulistas, António Vieira died. Very likely he left his comrades recognizing that his final efforts to protect Brazil's first inhabitants against the "avarice" of the settlers would be unavailing, as, indeed, they were, for Pedro II approved the Paulista arrangement in 1696.[81] Within the Brazil province, Vieira became the last of the great Jesuit defenders of Amerindian rights, a tradition that had begun with Nóbrega and Anchieta and had been continued by Figueira. Within that province, Jesuit militancy gave way to accommodation. Accordingly, from the 1680s onward there would be fewer clashes there between the settlers and the Jesuits over the treatment of the aborigines.[82] But a different situation obtained in the vice-province of Maranhão, where the storm clouds were ever present.

The Conflict over "Indian Freedom" in Maranhão

If the crown expected that the legislation of the late 1680s would reduce the conflict between the settlers and the missionaries, that hope was seldom realized. In 1712, for example,

79. António Vieira, the most conspicuous opponent of the agreement, caustically observed that none of its leading supporters had as much missionary field experience as he did. To Fr. Manuel Luís, 21 July 1695, in Azevedo, *Cartas*, 3: 665–70.

80. "Voto do Padre António Vieira sobre as duvidas dos moradores de S. Paulo acerca da administração dos indios," 12 July 1695, in *HCJB*, 6: 330–41.

81. *CR* of 19 Feb. 1696, in *RIHGB* 7 (1845): 282–86.

82. That is not to suggest that conflicts between the two opposing sides were wholly absent; e.g., beginning in 1683, there were persistent disputes between the settlers of Cabo Frio, in the northern part of the captaincy of Rio de Janeiro, and the Jesuits over the level of wages that must be paid to the Amerindians and whether they could be compelled to sell their lands to the secular sugar lords. Overseas Council, consulta of ca. Dec. 1683, in *DH*, 92: 262–63; see also *LAM* 3: 232–39. At the end of the century, the citizens of the town of Porto Seguro complained to the crown that the Jesuits who controlled two nearby aldeias utilized the Indians for their own purposes to the prejudice of the king's subjects. Overseas Council to king, 26 Oct. 1699, in *MHB*, 2: 286. In 1711 the cámara of São Paulo registered the same complaint with respect to the Franciscans, the Benedictines, and the Carmelites in their captaincy but surprisingly did not criticize the Jesuits for "interference" in Indian-white relations. *CR*, 8 Apr. 1713, in AHU/LR/225, fol. 28[r]. The next year, however, the Jesuits in Bahia complained about settlers who persisted in selling brandy to their neophytes and persuaded the governor-general to condemn the practice. *Portaria* of 1 Mar. 1714, in *DH*, 53: 262.

the chief magistrate of Pará bemoaned "the miserable state in which the settlers of this captaincy find themselves because of the lack of Indians," attributable, he thought, to the greedy missionaries—Franciscans, Carmelites, and Mercedarians as well as Jesuits—who sent their charges into the rain forest to collect feral spices. His complaint echoed those made by the cámaras and by governors like Cristóvão da Costa Freire (1707–18), Bernardo Pereira de Berredo (1718–22), and especially Alexandre de Sousa Freire (1728–32), each of whom was far more sympathetic to the settlers' position on the recruitment of Indian labor than to that of the missionaries. What especially vexed the Jesuits' critics was their foot-dragging with respect to authorizations for outfitting the official ransoming expeditions.[83]

The Jesuits naturally had complaints too. They condemned unscrupulous royal officials who requisitioned excessive numbers of mission Indians to serve as paddlers, foragers, and fighting men in the official tropas. They charged that the procurador dos índios, far from being the Indians' advocate, was actually a prime culprit in their exploitation.

The king, John V, was seemingly indifferent to all such allegations. In 1715 the Overseas Council again prohibited Indian slavery, but the same year a magistrate in Maranhão insisted that the Indians must be forcibly removed from their habitats "because they persist in living as brutes and offend the laws of nature and [therefore] must be compelled to abandon their ferocity to learn to live as rational human beings."[84] During the next several years the Council responded by approving offensive operations against Indians who "go naked, recognize neither king nor government and do not live in the form or manner of a republic, trample the laws of nature, make no distinction between mothers and daughters in the satisfaction of their lust, eat one another . . . or are excited by shooting arrows at innocent children." It condemned the Jesuits for preventing departure of official tropas over the course of the previous fourteen years and insisted that the tropas be resumed.[85]

Though the fathers reluctantly complied with the crown's directives, the settlers continued to defy them. In 1722 the Overseas Council dispatched a special investigator to Maranhão to examine the conflicting claims of the missionaries and their adversaries and to make suitable recommendations. The desembargador, Francisco da Gama Pinto, conducted an unusually thorough inquiry, interrogating 121 witnesses, "nobles, artisans, soldiers, boatmasters, and [even] some tamed Indians," throughout the State. Each testified that everyone, including parish priests and missionaries, "with the exception of the Jesuits and the Franciscans," ignored the king's laws concerning the treatment of the Indians and that their unauthorized exploitation was widespread. But the witnesses insisted that such conditions were inevitable, given the poverty of the land, the scarcity of workers, and the character of the "barbarous, ferocious, and inhuman" aborigines.

In view of such testimony, the magistrate's recommendations were shockingly mild, but they accurately reflected the fact that the settlers, rather than the crown or the missionaries, really controlled the State. First, the judge stated that violations of Indian rights were so

83. E.g., Overseas Council, consulta of 15 Oct. 1712; fragment of another dated 26 May 1717; and cámara (Belém) to king, 20 July 1720, in AHU/PA/PA, *cx.* 4.

84. Overseas Council to king, 18 Feb. 1715, in AHU/PA/MA, *cx.* 13.

85. CRs of 9 Mar. 1718, 11 Jan. and 13 May 1721, 25 Mar. 1722, and 10 Mar. 1725, in *LGM* 2: 152–54, 177, 181, and 211. The crown also insisted that missionaries continue to accompany such expeditions. King to superior of Jesuit missions, Maranhão, 9 Feb. 1722, in BPE, CXV-2-12, fol. 183[r].

widespread that the crown's only option was to issue a general pardon. Second, since there was no effective way to monitor the ransom system, he urged that it be abrogated. Third, he renewed the call to end the Indians' enslavement and to release those held in captivity. Last, he declared that if sufficient blacks were introduced into the State, the settlers would cease abusing the indigenous peoples.[86]

But there was part of the rub: despite various schemes proposed to supply the State of Maranhão with thousands of African slaves, none bore fruit in this period.[87] Moreover, by the time the crown considered Gama Pinto's report, the State was afflicted by a serious smallpox epidemic that curtailed the available labor supply just as Maranhão was becoming a significant cacao producer (see Chapter 21).

Precisely because of the increased demand for labor beginning in the mid-1720s, the colonists intensified their efforts to circumvent the Jesuits, who were trying to minimize the recruitment of ransomed captives. The colonists gained a sympathetic ally in Governor Alexandre Sousa Freire, a bitter adversary of the Jesuits.[88] In 1732 Jesuit leaders in the State ardently solicited the governor's removal, stating that they had found it impossible to serve God and king in a land where even the governor encouraged defiance of the law.[89]

Although the governor was replaced, two influential figures at court, both Maranhão veterans, loudly applauded his support of the colonists. Both shared his antipathy toward the Jesuits and his disdain for the aborigines. One was former governor Bernardo Pereira de Berredo, author of a major chronicle of Maranhão's early history, the already-cited *Annaes históricos do Maranhão*; the other was his protégé, Paulo da Silva Nunes, who became the Jesuits' most unrelenting foe during the 1720s and 1730s. Peninsular-born, familiar with Latin and Spanish, and unusually well-read in theological and juridical sources, as well as in the major chronicles of the Spanish empire, Silva Nunes saw military service during the first years of the War of the Spanish Succession (1702–13). Posted to Maranhão in 1708, he became the personal secretary of Governor Costa Freire (1707–18). Under his successor, Pereira de Berredo, he became captain-major of two Amazonian towns, superintendent of fortifications, and commander of an elite militia company. He also entered the pretentious local aristocracy through his marriage to a descendant of the highly esteemed Captain Pedro Teixeira, who during his travels between Belém and Quito in the 1630s had claimed Amazonia for Portugal. Paulo da Silva Nunes thus became intimate with the land- and slaveholding elites of the State and claimed to have traveled to Maranhão's most remote reaches.[90]

Silva Nunes's unceasing campaign against the Jesuits in the State began in 1722. During Judge Gama Pinto's inquiry, he became a prime mover in anti-Jesuit disturbances in Belém, where placards appeared calling for the Society's expulsion. He participated in a heated meeting of the *câmara*, where he presented a forceful statement in behalf of settler control of the Brasis. When the Jesuits complained to Governor João da Maia da Gama that Silva

---

86. Francisco da Gama Pinto to king, 9 Aug. 1723, in AHU/PA/MA, *cx.* 14 and enc.
87. Alden, "Indian Versus Black Slavery," 84–85.
88. Ibid., 85–86.
89. Jesuit leadership to king, ca. 1732, in BNL, 4517, fols. 194[r]–198[v].
90. Silva Nunes provides biographical details in his various petitions to the crown, esp. BPE, CXV-2-13, fols. 193[v]–265[v].

Nunes was fomenting a riot, the governor ordered him placed in irons and confined to a fortress. But Silva Nunes escaped, abandoned his wife and children, and fled to Lisbon.

In the kingdom, the fugitive became the salaried lobbyist for the cámaras of São Luís and Belém, gained entry to the highest royal tribunals, and even managed to kiss the king's feet. In 1725 he submitted to the Overseas Council the first of a plethora of interminably long memorials; in each he enhanced his virulent anti-Jesuit rhetoric with extensive extracts from official documents and quotations from legal authorities ranging from Justinian to Solorzano Pereira, the great jurist of the Spanish empire. His intent was always to discredit the efforts of the missionaries and to reaffirm the settlers' rights to unrestricted Indian labor. His contempt for the Brasis surfaced in his initial memorandum, in which he characterized them as "squalid barbarians, bestial and abject, like wild animals ... brutes incapable of participating in the Catholic faith." Astutely he asked a question that none of his contemporaries was prepared to answer: "If the Ethiopians [Africans] can be enslaved, why not the Indians of Maranhão?"[91]

It was absurd, Silva Nunes argued, for Maranhão to be on the verge of economic ruin when it could become prodigiously wealthy. He argued that its handicaps were bad government and the overwhelming power of the Jesuits, who he insisted were just as interested in the bodies of the Indians as the settlers were. The lobbyist contended that the fathers had forsaken their spiritual mission for their relentless pursuit of Mammon, which drove them to amass enormous profits at the expense of the crown, its loyal subjects, and the poor Indians.[92]

Like the "Charges" of Soares de Sousa 160 years earlier, the fusillades of Paulo da Silva Nunes were too serious to be ignored, and Jesuit spokesmen alertly repelled each attack as soon as it was launched. One of their most articulate and experienced defenders was Jacinto de Carvalho (b. 1677–d. 1744), who served as a missionary in Maranhão for thirteen years until his health broke, leading to his transfer to the College of Arts in Coimbra. Because of his knowledge of local conditions, he was later assigned to Lisbon as procurator for the Maranhão missions, a position he held until João da Maia da Gama prevailed upon him to return to Maranhão. There he served as that governor's confessor and as inspector-general of Jesuit installations in the State. After Maia da Gama retired from his post, Fr. Jacinto agreed to stay on as Sousa Freire's confessor until differences between the two concerning Indian policy resulted in his resignation and return to Lisbon, where he resumed his former post.[93]

91. "Cappitulos sobre os maos procedim[en]tos do gov[ernad]or João da Maya da Gama" [1725], 1st draft, in ibid., fol. 174ʳ.

92. "Cappitulos sobre os maos procedim[en]tos do gov[ernad]or João da Maya da Gama" [1725], 2d draft, in ibid., fols. 258ʳ–69ʳ, which includes the names of 92 supporting witnesses, half of whom identified themselves as citizens of the State. Many were militia officers; others held clerkships and other public positions. The same codex includes many of Silva Nunes's subsequent memorials, composed between 1725 and 1735, and appears to have been his copybook. Still other writings by Silva Nunes on the same themes are published in the complicated notes of Alexandre João Mello Morais, ed., *Corographia do imperio do Brazil*, 4 vols. (Rio de Janeiro, 1860), 2: 474–78 and 4: 286–92, which include his correspondence with the cámara of Belém and criticisms of his views by ex-governor Maia da Gama. See also Alden, "Indian Versus Black Slavery," 88 n. 88.

93. *HCJB*, 8: 149–53, which includes a listing of Fr. Jacinto's writings and demonstrates that he was as prolific as his famous adversary, Silva Nunes.

Jacinto de Carvalho was in all likelihood the author of an unsigned defense of the Jesuits that forcefully denied charges that they had neglected their responsibilities toward the Indians, the settlers, or their sovereign. Its author observed that if the settlers were unable to extract as much cacao from the rain forest as they wanted, it was because they misused their licenses and hunted Indian slaves rather than spices. It warned that if the missionaries were required to surrender their temporal control of native communities, the occupants of those villages would become wholly vulnerable to the "vexations and tyrannies" of the white settlers.[94]

Fr. José Vidigal (b. 1674–d. 1748), vice-provincial of Maranhão, became another conspicuous defender of the Society. In 1733 he, too, wrote a defense of the Society's activities in the State. After recounting his colleagues' efforts to protect Indian lands from assaults by greedy settlers, he declared in language reminiscent of António Vieira that "in a word, the only wrong the Company of Jesus has committed [here] is to defend the liberty of the miserable Indians."[95]

The memorials of the missionaries and Silva Nunes, each reinforced by the testimonials of their supporters, prompted the Overseas Council to dispatch another investigator, Desembargador Francisco Duarte dos Santos, to the State of Maranhão in 1734 to advise it concerning the reshaping of Indian policy. After conferring with public officials and reviewing a vast quantity of records, memorials, petitions, and other self-serving documents, that magistrate concluded that there was far more merit in the statements of the missionaries than in those of their adversaries. He agreed with the Jesuits that they and their fellow missionaries were exceedingly unpopular in the State, where "everyone" opposed them. He found no evidence to support the settlers' claims of abject poverty or of the scarcity of workers. He observed that "there are many households in this state which possess fifty, a hundred, two hundred and even more" Indians, but he conceded that their constitutions made them less durable than African slaves. The judge found that many, including the late archdeacon of Belém, held Indians as slaves illicitly but saw nothing wrong in their actions since they were convinced that the Brasis "do not possess rational souls and were born to be slaves of whites." In response to a specific question that the Council had put to him, Santos averred that the missionaries ought not to be deprived of temporal jurisdiction over the Indian communities, contending that if they were replaced by white captains, those communities "would soon become only a memory."[96]

While the Overseas Council was digesting the judge's report and others that it received, Diogo de Mendonça Corte Real (b. 1658–d. 1736), the secretary of state, mulled over the evidence himself in an effort to determine what Portugal ought to do about the Indian problem in Brazil. He raised again the perplexing question posed earlier by Paulo da Silva Nunes: "Either Hugo Grotius is correct that all forms of slavery are unjust or existing

94. Anonymous critique, ca. 1732, in BPE, CXV-2-12, fols. 293^r–99^r.

95. "Resposta a senistra informação que a S. Mag.^{de} fazem contra os PP da Comp.^{a} do Est[ad]^o do Maranhão," 19 Sept. 1733, in BNL, 4517, fols. 203^r–5^v.

96. Francisco Duarte dos Santos to [Cardinal da Mota], 10 Sept. 1734, in AHU/PA/PA, *m.* 1; Duarte dos Santos to king, 15 July 1735, in Morais, *Corographia*, 4: 123–50n. For more complete documentation on the Santos investigation, see Alden, "Indian Versus Black Slavery," 88–90.

practice is, that is, that all are equally valid, for I do not perceive any difference in the taking of slaves in Angola and the Mina Coast and in this State because some are sold by their fathers, others are stolen or are sold by their rulers." Rather than boldly conceding that no form of slavery could be morally justified, the minister professed himself content to "leave this Question to the theologians."[97]

But the Overseas Council itself proved no more courageous. It concluded that the statutes of the 1680s should remain in effect and ought to be rigorously enforced. How, it did not say.

For the next decade, the production of Amazonian cacao boomed, and the settlers' procurement of Amerindians continued on an unprecedented scale. The conscientious but weak João de Abreu Castelbranco, the state's governor (1737–47), reported in 1739 that despite the Santos investigation and the Overseas Council's directives, the enslavement of aborigines was continuing "in defiance of the missions' ordinances and the laws of Your Majesty." Everyone, including Carmelites and Mercedarians, was guilty, the governor said, but he lamented that he was powerless to prevent such lawlessness.[98]

But what man could not accomplish, lethal epidemics did. In the mid- to late 1740s a succession of them—smallpox followed by catarrhs, pleurisy, bloody flux, and measles— attacked the city of Belém and then spread southward to adjacent Maranhão and westward via the Amazon and its principal affluents.

Those epidemics naturally had devastating consequences. Tens of thousands of persons, a few whites, some mixed bloods, but mostly recently relocated Indians, perished; many others fled their homes in desperate efforts to save their lives. In 1748, for the first time in decades, no ships called at Belém, and the number of canoes outfitted in that port town to gather spices in the interior fell from 150 to a mere 30 a year because there was no manpower to send more. Plantations under cultivation for half a century were abandoned by owners who found no one to work their land. While stocks of cacao in Belém warehouses shrank by 50 percent, the price of manioc, the regional staple, trebled.[99]

Deeply disturbed by reports of the disaster, the government of John V asked João de Abreu Castelbranco what steps he believed it should take to alleviate the widespread regional distress. The former governor's principal recommendations were, first, that the crown reassert the law of 1680 prohibiting Indian slavery altogether, and second, observing as had António Vieira before him that the State of Brazil had not begun to prosper until it had an adequate number of black slaves, that the traditional indigenous workers be replaced by an adequate number of imported African chattels.[100]

Castelbranco's thoughtful analysis prompted the Overseas Council to engage in an unusually candid review of Portugal's Indian policies during the previous two centuries. Not surprisingly, most of the councilors concluded that such policies had failed abjectly and that it was time for a fresh start.[101]

97. Corte Real to José da Serra (governor, Maranhão), 19 Apr. 1736, in AHU/PA/ PA, *cx.* 14.
98. Castelbranco to king, 17 Oct. 1739, in AHU/PA/PA, *cx.* 10.
99. For contemporary sources concerning the scourges and their consequences, see Alden, "Indian Versus Black Slavery," 92–95.
100. [Castelbranco] to king, anterior to 19 Feb. 1750, in AHU/PA/MA, *cx.* 32.
101. Alden, "Indian Versus Black Slavery," 94–95.

But the ailing John V was in no mood to order any such innovations. They would come in the next decade, during the reign of his son. They would include both the definitive legal end of Indian slavery and a new scheme to provide the State of Maranhão with African slaves. And they would include, ironically, the removal of the Amerindians' principal defenders during the past two centuries, the members of the Society of Jesus, and their replacement by the oft-discredited lay captaincy system.

From the outset, Jesuit efforts to convert and protect the Brasis during the centuries considered in this study have drawn extravagant praise from their ardent admirers as well as a mixture of cynicism, scorn, and skepticism from their critics. With the possible exception of the Chinese Rites controversy (Chapter 23), no issue within the Assistancy provoked such heated and persistent debate among contemporaries as the treatment of the Amerindians.

It is evident that the struggle between the Society's representatives and the settlers over the aborigines was rooted in their divergent objectives in the colony. The primary goal of the Jesuits, like that of their fellow missionaries, was the conversion of the heathen to the true faith; the overriding aim of Portuguese colonists, like that of their counterparts in other empires, was the advancement of their own economic welfare. If the Jesuits' basic preoccupation with the Brasis was their spiritual conversion, that of the settlers was their physical exploitation. Those two goals necessarily conflicted, prompting both sides to appeal to the recognized umpires—the crown and its deputies—for support.

As in any human endeavor, the umpires were susceptible to the appeals of the contestants and their supporters—lobbyists, sympathetic royal officials, and rival missionaries—each of whom argued for or against a given proposition. The result was a flood of inconsistent legislation concerning the Indians' material and spiritual welfare. It soon became evident to both sides that the crown was incapable of adopting and enforcing a consistent policy toward its Indian subjects. Each side was therefore left to employ its own weapons in the struggle to control the Amerindians. The Jesuits' weapons consisted of spiritual devices such as excommunication, moral suasion, and vigorously argued remonstrances. Those of the settlers included anti-Jesuit diatribes filled with lurid but unproven charges, and blatant physical intimidation. In several instances, the latter led to the Jesuits' expulsion from Brazil because of suspicions that they were the real authors of royal statutes concerning the treatment of Amerindians that the colonists considered inimical to their own interests. Except on the last occasion, those expulsions were accomplished without penalty to the settlers, a sure indication of the extent of the crown's inability to enforce compliance with its fiat. By accepting the crown's repeated challenges to convert, civilize, and protect the indigenous population, the Jesuits deliberately adopted an unpopular cause, one that made them the focus of incessant and widespread ill will, especially in the impoverished northern and southern peripheries of Brazil, which always relied most heavily upon Indian labor.

It needs to be conceded that both the missionaries, Jesuits and others, and their secular adversaries, like Europeans elsewhere in the New World, held a low opinion of the intellectual capacities of the Amerindians and often referred to them as barbarians and savages who, like

children, needed guardians to look after them.[102] Paternalism was the theoretical justification
for the lay captaincy system, which the colonists always favored and the missionaries and
their supporters consistently opposed.[103] It was likewise the raison d'être for the mission
system. The conflict between the Jesuits and the settlers, therefore, concerned Indian *custody*
more than it did freedom as that concept is understood today.[104] The Jesuits perceived
Indian freedom as connoting liberty of persons and property, but they shared with the
settlers the conviction that the aborigines did not possess the right either to resist by force
peaceful white entry into their lands, or to reject the virtues of Christianity in favor of
pagan traditions. Like the colonists, the Jesuits were also convinced that it was necessary to
subjugate the heathens before their way of life could be fundamentally changed. That it
could and should be changed were their operative premises. The Jesuits contended, and
many of their sympathizers agreed, that the sort of protection they offered the Amerindians
would safeguard them from the physical abuse and moral depravity likely to be their fate
at the hands of the settlers.

Were the Amerindians really better off under the tutelage of missionaries than under
rule by secular overlords? That question has evoked spirited controversy since the sixteenth
century. Some respected scholars have argued that the indigenes were as abused by the
Jesuits as they were by the slavers. Indeed, ever since the appearance of the Gilberto
Freyre's seminal work *The Masters and the Slaves* (1933), it has been fashionable to accuse the
Jesuits who ministered to the Brasis of being guilty of "detribalization," "ethnocide," and
even of heinous crimes approaching "genocide."[105]

One marvels at the restraint of such authors, who must have been terribly tempted
to compare the Jesuits to the Nazis. It is well that they did not, for such criticism is
patently unfair. One could as well condemn medieval chroniclers for plagiarism as the
missionaries of the sixteenth to eighteenth or even nineteenth centuries for what only
modern anthropologists, psychologists, sociologists, and their admirers have decided were
criminal actions.[106] Such critics ignore the fact that no contemporaries in Portuguese
realms or in those of any other European countries regarded the cultures of primitive
peoples as worth preserving. They also pass over in silence the blatant fact that the
settlers were far more guilty of uprooting indigenous folk than were the missionaries. And,

102. A revealing file that demonstrates the persistence of such attitudes for nearly two centuries will be
found attached to Overseas Council to king, 10 Sept. 1742, in AHU/PA/PB, *cx.* 30.

103. Although the religious Orders held divergent views with respect to Indian rights, including
the legitimacy of their title to lands, they and many governors were highly critical of the lay captaincy
system. Especially revealing are the responses of the heads of various Orders in Bahia composed in 1704
in answer to a royal questionnaire: APB/OR/13/83b; published in *Anais do arquivo público da Bahia* 29 (1960):
98–139.

104. No less an authority than Fr. Serafim Leite himself conceded that "*protective* liberty was the
presupposition of all the legislation concerning Indian freedom." *HCJB*, 6: 346.

105. Freyre, *The Masters and the Slaves*, trans. Samuel Putnam, 2d Eng. ed., rev. (New York, 1956),
esp. 107–11; cf. Hemming, *Red Gold*, 111–15, and Schwartz, *Sugar Plantations*, chap. 2, esp. 40. Schwartz
criticizes the Jesuits for not being cultural relativists in Brazil as they were in China and in India, but ignores
the fact that neither the Jesuits nor the Portuguese crown was ever dominant in the eastern lands, and
that even if the missionaries had attempted to preserve indigenous culture in Brazil, there is absolutely no
assurance that the colonists would have respected their efforts.

106. Cf. Mary Noel Menezes, *British Policy Towards the Amerindians in British Guiana, 1803–1873* (Oxford,
1977), 252–53.

conveniently perhaps, they fail to define which aspects of indigenous culture they wanted preserved: tribal warfare? anthropophagy? polygamy? Finally, the Jesuits' modern critics surprisingly ignore the ground where the Society of Jesus *was* most vulnerable to criticism in this Assistancy: its remarkable inconsistency in defending Indian freedom while acquiescing in the denial of liberty to persons of African origin. But, as the following chapter will demonstrate, the Jesuits themselves had a very important stake in the maintenance of black slavery.

CHAPTER 20

Those Who Also Served: Bondsmen and Lay Servants

The state can not survive and increase except with blacks from Angola, as experience throughout Brazil demonstrates.

—António Vieira to Fr. Pedro Luís Gonsalves, 1 Feb. 1679

No one considered that the enslavement of blacks was as unjust as the seizure of native Indians. No Jesuit, not even Vieira, spoke up against this African traffic.

—John Hemming, *Red Gold*

I am convinced that the travail that afflicts Portugal [today] derives from our unjust participation in the slave trade in our conquests and in the places where we trade.

—João Alvares (assistant) to Fr. Baltasar Barreira, 24 July 1604

THE BIBLICAL INJUNCTION, "In the sweat of thy face shalt thou eat bread" (Genesis 3:19), struck a vital chord with many early Christians. During the centuries of the primitive Church, the desert fathers of Egypt adopted the view that "manual labor and poverty ... went hand in hand" and worked to provide their own sustenance. In the early sixth century, when St. Benedict laid down the rule for his Order, he directed that monks not occupied in divine worship, in supping, or in resting ought to engage in useful activities including manual labor, studying, transcribing manuscripts, or teaching.[1] According to Abbot Gasquet, every monastic house in medieval England reserved five hours a day (12 to 5 P.M. in winter and 1 to 6 P.M. in summer) for manual labor, that is, working in the gardens, the fields, or the workshops. Such houses considered physical labor useful to maintain the monks' health and to prevent unseemly idleness.[2] To be sure, with the passage of time many houses, including those who followed the Rule of St. Benedict, relinquished some or all of their physical tasks to their tenants. Consequently, in the twelfth century, the reformist Cistercians, moved by Genesis 3:19 and by the sacrificial example of Christ, reemphasized the importance of manual work as a suitable activity for

1. M. Olphe-Gaillard, S.J., "Evangelical Poverty in Primitive Monasticism," in *Religious Life*, vol. 4, *Poverty*, trans. Lancelot C. Sheppard (1954; rpr. London, 1956), 17; *The Rule of St. Benedict*, trans. and ed. Anthony C. Meisel and M. L. del Mastro (New York, 1975), chaps. 35 and 48.
2. Gasquet, *English Monastic Life* (London, 1904), 147–48.

their monks and insisted that each of their houses ought to try to live by the fruits of its occupants' labors.[3]

Some Orders, like the Carthusians, the Carmelites, and the second Order of Dominicans, continued to emphasize the blessings of manual labor in later centuries, but St. Ignatius rejected such activity as unfitting for the priestly members of his Order. The Society of Jesus was not intended to be a contemplative Order, but rather an activist one, whose qualified members were expected to devote themselves to their own spiritual preparation, to the spiritual instruction of others, to education, and to such administrative tasks as the secular leaders of the lands where they served required of them. In Loyola's view, physical labor could be appropriately reserved for the Society's intellectually less qualified lay brothers and for hired personnel. Though both groups always constituted part of each Jesuit establishment's work force, the Society also made use of a large number of slaves to perform a variety of services. The Order's labor requirements, how it met them, the extent of its reliance upon slave labor, and how its members reconciled themselves to its exploitation constitute the primary themes of this chapter.

The Labor Needs of the Society

Each of the Society's manifold activities necessitated labor support. Its houses always required cooks, stewards, buyers, porters, launderers, gardeners, woodcutters, alms-gatherers, infirmarians, and barbers, and sometimes bookkeepers, clerks, notaries, procurators, solicitors, and surgeons as well. Its estates needed managers, foremen, shepherds, cowhands, and specialists in the production of staples such as coconuts, sugar, and cereal grains. Missionaries in Africa and Southeast Asia found it impossible to travel without bearers, just as their urban colleagues in India required errand boys and umbrella holders. The construction and maintenance of Jesuit churches, dormitories, and other facilities depended upon the services of a host of artisans, including clock repairmen, carpenters, masons, plasterers, and potters.

Seemingly, Loyola and his cofounders expected those recruited as lay brothers (coadjutores temporales) to fulfill many of the Order's labor requirements. Such recruits were to be closely examined to determine their willingness "to exercise themselves in all the low and humble services which are enjoined upon them." They were assured that "they may be employed in more important matters in accordance with the talent God gave them," but they were to be tested to determine "whether ... they will be content and at peace to serve their Creator and Lord in low and humble offices and ministries, of whatever kind they may be, for the benefit of the house and the Society."[4]

Initially the Society was successful in recruiting loyal temporal coadjutors who assisted their priestly superiors in many ways. Some, like Br. Gonçalo Fernandes and Br. Bernabé

---

3. Christopher J. Holdsworth, "The Blessings of Work: The Cistercian View," in Derek Baker, ed., *Sanctity and Security: The Church and the World*, Studies in Church History 10 (Oxford, 1973): 59–76; Hermann Aubin, "Medieval Agrarian Society in Its Prime: The Lands East of the Elbe and German Colonization Eastwards," in *The Cambridge Economic History of Europe*, ed. M. M. Postan (Cambridge, 1966), 1: 474–75.

4. *CSJ(GE)*, chap. 6, pars. 114 and 118. For additional references to the duties of temporal coadjutors, see *CSJ(C)*, pars. 149, 302, 306, and 433.

de Sousa, respectively porter and cook, occupied humble stations in the professed house
of São Roque for decades. Others, like Br. André Gomes, who died at 94 or 95 after more
than 50 years in the Society, mostly as the same house's almoner, held more demanding
positions.[5] Though often passed over by Jesuit historians who prefer to glory in the exploits
of their Order's priestly members, the temporal coadjutors rendered important services
to their houses. Unlike the more peripatetic priests, they tended to be less mobile and to
accumulate valued experience in their dedicated performance of essential tasks.

Nevertheless, the components of the Portuguese Assistancy never succeeded in recruiting as many lay brothers as they needed. In the province of Portugal, for example, there
were only 6 lay brothers for every 10 priests in 1593 and in 1693, and by 1749 that ratio
had fallen to 5.5:10.[6] The ratio of priests to brothers in the Brazil province was close to
1:1 in 1654, but in the vice-province of Maranhão during the eighteenth century, priests
outnumbered coadjutors by a 2 or 3 to 1 margin.[7] In the province of Goa, there were again
only 6 coadjutors for every 10 fathers.[8] Not only was there an insufficient number of lay
brothers to perform all of the nonpriestly tasks of the Society, there was also a scarcity of
specialists, such as lawyers and surgeons, within the Order. Perforce, the Society sought
alternatives.

One was the employment of laymen through annual contracts. Some occupied responsible positions, such as interpreters, solicitors, surgeons, and sugar masters. Whether
such offices became hereditary in Jesuit facilities, as was true in monastic houses in medieval England, is unclear.[9] Certainly many persons served the Jesuits for years in mundane
capacities as personal or house servants in Portugal, Brazil, India, Japan, and other parts
of the Assistancy. Toward the end of the sixteenth century, for example, the rector of the
College of Arts in Coimbra reported that there were 190 inmates attended by more than
40 servants, or a ratio of about 5 to 1. A century and a quarter later, the Jesuit household
of the University of Évora, which boasted some 141 members in 1726, enjoyed the services
of 32 servants and 3 woodcutters.[10] In India the Jesuits, along with Portuguese civilians, were
accustomed to use an umbrella boy (moço de sombreiro) when they ventured into the streets.
The umbrella boy's function was to elevate a parasol to protect them from the direct rays of
the sun or to keep them from being drenched during the saturating monsoon rains.[11] Jesuits

5. For references to these men and to other lay brothers who rendered long service to São Roque,
see *OSR*, nos. 43, 57, 74, 80, 81, 87, 89, 102, 185, and 194.

6. The calculations are derived from the first catalogues of the province during the indicated years
in ARSI, *Lus.*, 44:I, fols. 65–84; 46: fols. 245–298^v; and 49: fols. 8–59^v.

7. ARSI, *Bras.*, 5:I, 183^r–190^v; 27: fols. 95–104, 162–63, and 188–189^v.

8. ARSI, *Goa*, 25, fols. 84^r–92^r; ibid., FG, 627.

9. Cf. Gasquet, *English Monastic Life*, 201.

10. "Informacion de la renta, cargos y numero de personas de la PP de Coimbra," ca. 1600, in ARSI,
Lus., 84:I, fols. 53–54; "Folha da receita e despeza do coll.° de Evora no anno de 1725," in ibid., 81:II,
fols. 570–572^v.

11. Foreign travelers commonly commented on the functions of the umbrella boys: e.g., *The Voyage of
John Huyghen van Linschoten to the East Indies*, ed. Arthur Coke Burnell and P. A. Tiele, *HS*:1, no. 71 (1884): 193;
The Voyage of François Pyrard of Laval to the East Indies, trans. and ed. Albert Gray and H. C. P. Bell, *HS*:1,
no. 77 (1888): 75; *The Travels of the Abbé Carré in India and the Near East, 1672 to 1674*, trans. Lady Fawcett,
ed. Sir Charles Fawcett and Sir Richard Burn, 3 vols., *HS*:2, 96: 342. The directives left by Visitor Francisco
Barreto authorized procurators to possess a scribe and a *moço para o sombreiro* to facilitate their work. "Ordens
que deixou o P. Francisco Barreto . . . pera se goardarem em toda a provincia de Goa . . . 1660," in ARSI,

continued to make use of such servants even when their generals expressed displeasure at the practice.[12] In Southeast Asia, each missionary who served in Siam, Cambodia, and Vietnam was permitted to take with him one servant to cook and do his laundry,[13] while in Japan house servants outnumbered the Jesuits whom they served by a ratio of better than 2 to 1.[14]

In Africa and Brazil, too, the Jesuits considered personal servants indispensable. Early in the seventeenth century, Fr. Baltasar Barreira reported from Luanda that a typical mission to the interior required the services of 22 blacks:

4 litter bearers
2 canoe bearers
4 bearers of the instruments and wine for mass
1 bearer of water
1 bearer of biscuits
2 bearers to carry food for the bearers
1 bearer to carry gifts to the chiefs
1 bearer of dry fish
1 bearer of the chair in which the father preaches
1 bearer of religious images and prizes
1 bearer of pans
1 bearer of two flasks of wine and vinegar
2 tent bearers.[15]

At first, Jesuits in Brazil engaged salaried workers in their houses, but, according to Fr. Leite, by the end of the sixteenth century such personnel were replaced (except in São Paulo, where Amerindians continued to be utilized) by an alternative form of labor—African slaves.[16] Modern writers may perceive a blatant contradiction between the Jesuits' opposition to Amerindian slavery and their countenance of other forms of slavery,[17] but contemporaries, both Jesuits and non-Jesuits, did not discern such an ethical inconsistency.

FG, 1443/9/27, par. 11. Umbrella boys also shaded masters from the sun in tropical Africa. See Michael Angelo of Gattina, "A Voyage to Congo, in the Years 1666 and 1667," in A[wnsham] Churchill, *A Collection of Voyages and Travels*, 6 vols. (1704; London, 1732), I: 561. In Portugal, the statutes of the College of Purification, University of Évora, stipulated that students could have no more than one manservant apiece. ARSI, FG, 1408/19/4.

12. Especially Giovanni Paolo Oliva (1664–81) and Tirso Gonzalez de Santalla (1687–1705). "Alguas ordens' que deixou o P^e Prov.^al Simão M.iz ... 24 de julho de 1682," in ARSI, *Goa*, 35, fol. 23^r, par. 6; and H/SAG2: 99.

13. "Rol do q' se ha de dar p.ª os padres q' fore' as missoens de Siao, Cambodia, Cochinchina e Tunkim," n.d. [seventeenth century], BA/JA/49-V-66, no. 29.

14. João Coelho, "Narração breve do número das casas, da gente, ... da companhia de Jappão," 12 Nov. 1609, in *MHJ*, 537. Cf. *CCJ*, 217.

15. To Assistant General João Alvares, 4–9 Mar. 1607, in ARSI, *Lus.*, 74, fols. 64^r–64^v.

16. *HCJB*, 6: 347–48.

17. Cf. David Brion Davis, *The Problem of Slavery in Western Culture* (1966; rpr., New York, 1988), 193.

Jesuit Attitudes Toward Slavery

If we are to comprehend the stance that Jesuits adopted with respect to other forms of slavery,[18] we must recognize that the Church itself, notwithstanding the efforts of some modern apologists to gloss over its record, long accepted the institution of slavery and was primarily concerned with promoting humane treatment for those who bore its stigma rather than with encouraging its elimination.[19] As is well known, both the Greeks and the Romans accepted the notion of "natural slavery," though, significantly, the former applied that concept primarily to the *barbaroi*, non-Greeks generally thought of as barbarians. The institution enjoyed the sanction of contributors to both the Old and New Testaments and of leading theologians of the Middle Ages, including St. Ambrose (b. ca. 339–d. 397) and St. Augustine (b. 354–d. 430), who, though they recognized that the institution was heinous, nevertheless were convinced that it was divinely inspired and potentially beneficial to the slave. If Ste. Croix is correct, no early Christian authority insisted upon the abandonment of slavery or the liberation of those kept in bondage. By the mid-thirteenth century, according to Fr. Maxwell, "the moral legitimacy of the institution . . . was accepted mainly uncritically not only by civil lawyers but also by Church canonists."[20]

During the centuries-long conflicts between Christians and Muslims of the High Middle Ages and the Early Modern period that followed, both sides reduced war captives to slavery, an inevitable result that the Church accepted. In 1452 Pope Nicholas V gave Afonso V of Portugal "free and full permission to invade, search out, capture, and subjugate the Saracens and pagans and any other unbelievers and enemies of Christ wherever they may be," a license that his successors confirmed and extended during the next six decades.[21] One of those successors, Innocent VIII (1484–92), received 100 Muslim captives as a gift from Ferdinand and Isabella during the Granadan War and assigned them to his cardinals and dependent nobles.[22] Half a century later, when the Council of Trent met to tighten Church machinery and to stiffen Catholic doctrine (1545–63), its members significantly found no need to issue any major directives concerning the institution of slavery,

18. Two previous studies have examined aspects of Jesuit views of black slavery. Magnus Mörner, "Los jesuitas y la esclavitud de los negros," *Revista chilena de historia y geografía*, no. 135 (1967): 92–109, sketches opportunities for research, particularly in the *catalogi rerum temporalium triennales* series in ARSI, but he fails to warn about their limitations. David G. Sweet's "Black Robes and 'Black Destiny': Jesuit Views of African Slavery in 17th-Century Latin America," *Revista de historia de America* no. 86 (July–Dec. 1978): 87–133, is a creditable analysis of Jesuit writings on the question. His summary of António Vieira's advocacy of expanding the slave trade between northern Brazil and Africa is especially helpful.

19. Defenders of the Church's position toward slavery ignore the extent of its own participation in the institution. They include C. Williams, "Slavery (and the Church)," *New Catholic Encyclopaedia*, vol. 13 (New York, 1967): 281–82; Luigi Conti, "The Catholic Church and the Slave Trade," in UNESCO, *The African Slave Trade from the Fifteenth to the Nineteenth Century* (Paris, 1979), 265–68; and most recently, Canon José Geraldo Vidigal de Carvalho, *A igreja e a escravidão: Uma analise documental* (Rio de Janeiro, 1985). Essential antidotes are John Francis Maxwell, *Slavery and the Catholic Church* (London, 1975); and G. E. M. de Ste. Croix, "Early Christian Attitudes to Property and Slavery," in Derek Baker, ed., *Church Society and Politics*, Studies in Church History 12 (Oxford, 1975): 1–38, both of which are followed here.

20. Maxwell, *Slavery*, 19.

21. Ibid., 53–54.

22. Jacob Burkhart, *The Civilisation of the Renaissance in Italy*, trans. S. G. C. Middlemore (London, 1904), 296 n. 2.

even though it had already become one of the inevitable concomitants of the expansion of Europe.[23]

In sixteenth-century Portugal, therefore, kings, nobles, members of the Church, artisans, and even some ordinary working folk owned slaves without experiencing any condemnation for so doing. According to Saunders, by the middle of that century, when the Society was first establishing its roots there, slaves, mostly domestic servants and casual laborers, represented about 10 percent of the population of Lisbon, Évora, and the Algarve, but only 1 to 2 percent of the northern parts of the kingdom.[24] It should cause no astonishment, consequently, that in 1547 Simão Rodrigues reported with satisfaction to Francis Xavier that construction of the Coimbra college was proceeding rapidly, thanks in part to ten black slaves that the king had given him.[25] Five years later Xavier himself urged that *mainatos*, members of the washer caste in India, be purchased along with "some Negroes" for the service of Old St. Paul's.[26] In distant Bahia the same year, Fr. Manuel da Nóbrega took note of the fact that the first regular shipments of Guinea slaves had just begun to arrive and wrote his superior, Simão Rodrigues, to seek permission to purchase a few of them to work in fields that he and his companions had recently laid out to feed their Indian proselytes. He estimated that three or four such chattels would enable his companions to sustain 100 such converts.[27]

Though the founders had contemplated acquiring a few slaves to augment household staffs and to grow subsistence crops,[28] the increasing number of slaves held by Jesuits within the Assistancy soon became a cause of concern to some members and a source of dissension for others. In 1558, after the first contingent of blacks received by the college of Bahia had expired, Manuel da Nóbrega enthusiastically wrote that "the best thing that could happen to this college would be [the procurement of] two dozen males and females from Guinea to till the crops and to fish for the college."[29] But his colleague and later successor Luís de Grã expressed serious misgivings about the propriety of the Society's retaining slaves.[30] Both appealed to Diego Laínez for a ruling. Nóbrega insisted that "we cannot live without some slaves to hew wood and draw water and bake our daily bread and to perform other duties that cannot be carried out by lay brothers since they are so scarce."[31] The second general

---

23. *Canons and Decrees of the Council of Trent*, trans. H. J. Schroeder, O.P. (London, 1941). On the relationship of empire-building to the expansion of the institution of slavery, see Philip D. Curtin, "Slavery and Empire," in Vera Rubin and Arthur Tuden, eds., "Comparative Perspectives on Slavery in New World Societies," *Annals of the New York Academy of Sciences* 292 (1977): 3–11.

24. A. C. de C. M. Saunders, *A Social History of Black Slaves and Freedmen in Portugal, 1441–1555* (Cambridge, 1982), 2, 59–61, and 176.

25. S/*FX*, 3: 526.

26. Ibid., 4: 535.

27. Nóbrega to Rodrigues, 10 July 1552, in *NCJ*, 24; Nóbrega to Rodrigues, Aug. [?] 1552, in *MB*, 1:403.

28. E.g., the *Constitutions* of Old St. Paul's, Goa, specified that the house should make use of "only those servants who are necessary for essential duties," since an excessive number would not be efficacious and would be costly. They authorized the acquisition of half a dozen persons to work in the garden, to bury deceased indigents, to sweep, to cut wood, and to work in the kitchen. "Constitutiones Collegii S. Pauli," Goa, 27 June 1546, in *DI*, 1: 111–29, par. 123; cf. S/*FX*, 3: 461.

29. To Miguel de Torres, Bahia, 8 May 1558, in *MB*, 2: 455.

30. *HCJB*, 2: 348.

31. Nóbrega to Laínez, São Vicente, 12 June 1561, in *MB*, 3: 365.

responded by approving the use of slaves for the purposes Nóbrega had stated but expressed the hope that such bondsmen might be rented rather than owned.[32]

Despite Laínez's sanction for the acquisition of a limited number of slaves by the Brazil province, his three immediate successors—Borgia, Mercurian, and Aquaviva—all expressed serious reservations about the Society's retention of slaves. In 1567 Francisco Borgia asked Inácio de Azevedo, the ill-fated procurator of Brazil, to determine whether the Jesuits in that colony really needed to rely upon slaves and particularly urged him to listen to the views of the experienced Luis de Grã. Two years later Borgia informed the Visitor to India that "my goal and intent is, so far as is possible, to give up slaves and to have the Company rely upon lay brothers . . . or salaried freedmen."[33] The same year he wrote the provincial of Portugal that no house in the kingdom ought to keep slaves, and that every house should liberate those that it then possessed. That order was confirmed by Mercurian in 1576 and by Aquaviva in 1584.[34]

The generals' directives were never fully honored in the kingdom, and they were ignored altogether overseas, where leaders insisted, as have their modern defenders, that there was no alternative to reliance upon slavery. In Brazil, the first provincial congregation resolved in 1568 that houses there might possess slaves so long as there was no other means of support. Three years later, Fr. Gregório Serrão, an experienced administrator in the colony, assured the Roman headquarters that there really was no available substitute for bondsmen.[35]

Jesuits in India shared the same conviction. When Alessandro Valignano reached Goa four years later, he was shocked to discover that the college of St. Paul's alone possessed 48 slaves, but he was assured that the other Orders retained such chattels as well. A year later the Visitor presided over the famous Chorão meeting, which concluded that because of an insufficiency of lay brothers, both servants and slaves were indispensable in the expanding province. The delegates specified, however, that all slaves were to be well treated, instructed in the faith, allowed recreation on feast days, and after some (unspecified) years of service set free and equipped with a means of earning their livelihood.[36] Aquaviva reluctantly concurred, but he insisted that members refrain from buying or selling any slaves where doubt existed as to the legitimacy of their captivity.[37]

As far as two courageous fathers were concerned, there could be no legitimation of slavery or of their colleagues' reliance upon it. Fr. Miguel Garcia served as professor of theology in Bahia from 1576 to 1583. During those years he watched the college acquire

---

32. Lainez to Nóbrega, Trent, 16 Dec. 1562; and Juan Polanco (secretary, on behalf of Laínez) to Fr. Gonçalo Vaz de Melo (provincial, Portugal), 25 Mar. 1563; in *MB*, 3: 514 and 543.

33. Borgia to Azevedo, 22 Sept. 1567, in *MB*, 4: 417; Borgia to Gundislavus Alvares, 2 Nov. 1569, in *DI*, 8: 27–28.

34. *HCJAP*, 2:2, 558.

35. *HCJB*, 2: 350.

36. *VMP*, 1: 153–54. The participants in the meeting again pointed out that the institution of slavery had long been widespread in the subcontinent and that the other Orders utilized both servants and slaves. "Deliberationes . . . in insula Chorão inter 6 et 18 Dec. 1575," in *DI*, 10: 265–66.

37. "Memorial of Fr. Francisco de Monclaro, Procurator, with the Answers of Fr. Claudio Acquaviva" [Aug. 1590], in *DI*, 15: 56. Visitors endeavored to enforce that directive in India: "Orders of Fr. Pimenta . . . Visitor . . . for the Professed House," Goa, June 1597, in *DI*, 18: 808–11, par. 8; "As cousas perpetuas q' ordenou o P.ᶜ Viz.ᵒʳ no coll.º das 11 mil virgens de Damão . . . em fev.ʳº de [1]600," in ARSI, FG, 1407A/44/8.

an increasing number of African slaves until by the latter date it possessed 70 Guineans. Their presence deeply troubled Fr. Garcia, for he became convinced that there was no ethical warrant to hold slaves, whether Brazilian- or African-born. His colleague, Fr. Gonçalo Leite, who had served in Brazil since 1572 and became the first professor of philosophy at the Bahian college, reached the same conclusion and stated publicly that he would no longer confess anyone, even a Jesuit, who made use of slaves. Since their superiors regarded both men as troublemakers, they were silenced and sent back to the Iberian Peninsula.[38]

Those who concurred in the removal of Frs. Garcia and Leite were obviously sending a message to others within the Assistancy. After the two fathers had been muzzled, few Jesuits dared to come forward to denounce the peculiar institution or the Society's growing stake in it. Significantly, when Jesuits did so, they were concerned about slave trades in the Orient, not in Africa, India, or the New World.

Though the Portuguese cannot fairly be burdened with having introduced the institution or the nefarious traffic in bondsmen in East Asia, they willingly joined with unscrupulous indigenous authorities and businessmen in both China and Japan in profiting from such commerce. During the sixteenth century, young Chinese, especially girls, were kidnapped and shipped via Macao to the Goa market, where they became household servants, cooks, and prostitutes for wealthy Portuguese and Indians alike. Nagasaki, the silk port, also became an embarkation point for both Japanese and Korean slaves bound for western buyers. Other chattels came from Ceylon. As Scammell has written, "Slaves built fortresses; served as interpreters; and translators . . . ; carried . . . their masters' weapons in war; transported the spoils of victory, and manned Portuguese ships."[39]

Like other Europeans, the Jesuits simply accepted the existence of slavery throughout the Orient. They did not condemn the Japanese slave trade until prodded to do so by Hideyoshi in 1587 (see Chapter 6). When challenged by the shogun to explain why the Portuguese purchased Japanese chattels and exported them, Fr. Gaspar Coelho, the vice-provincial, shifted the onus to the shogun himself and reminded him that as ruler he could easily end the trade by forthrightly forbidding it. Nevertheless, the Jesuits came to realize that the persistence of the slave trade with Japan and China was inimical to their efforts to convert both empires. Accordingly, they overtly denounced such traffic, which seems to have come to an end in Japan about 1600 and in China some two decades later.[40]

38. *HCJB*, 2: 227–30. Garcia was apparently a Spaniard and is not mentioned again in Portuguese sources. Fr. Leite, who hailed from Bragança and entered the Society in 1563, spent the remainder of his life attached to São Roque in Lisbon, where he ministered to victims of plague until his death in 1603. Significantly, he was never allowed to take the fourth vow. *ASCJ*, 210–11.

39. G. V. Scammell, "Indigenous Assistance in the Establishment of Portuguese Power in Asia in the Sixteenth Century," *Modern Asian Studies* 14, 1 (1980): 10–11.

40. The most recent assessment of the importance of slavery in Southeast Asia is Anthony Reid, *Southeast Asia in the Age of Commerce, 1450–1680*, vol. 1, *The Lands Below the Winds* (New Haven, 1988), 131ff. Although inevitably sketchy, the fullest treatments in English of both the Chinese and the Japanese trades and of Jesuit attitudes toward them remain C. R. Boxer, "The Affair of the *Madre de Deus*: A Chapter in the History of the Portuguese in Japan," Japan Society, *Transactions and Proceedings* 26 (1928–29): 45–46; *CCJ*, 146–47, 226–27. See also Boxer's *Fidalgos in the Far East, 1550–1770: Fact and Fancy in the History of Macao* (1948; rpr., New York, 1968), chap. 13. On the prevalence of slavery in the Chinese empire, see also idem, ed., *South China in the Sixteenth Century*, HS:2, no. 106 (1953): 150–51, 297.

But Jesuits who served in Brazil, Hispanic America, or Africa never campaigned against either the slave trade or the institution of black slavery. On the contrary, some stoutly defended that trade and urged its expansion. One who confidently supported the trade was Pero Rodrigues, Visitor to Angola in the early 1590s. He informed Aquaviva that the Jesuits in Luanda became the beneficiaries of slaves given to them by African chieftains as alms and by others who left them as testamentary awards; that such chattels were simply commodities intended for exchange like any other; and that their sale offered the best means of creating sufficient income to build the planned college at Luanda.[41]

Another who expressed support for the trade was Fr. Luís Brandão, rector of the Luanda college. In 1610 he responded to a query from a fellow Jesuit, Alonso de Sandoval, who labored for many years among newly arrived black slaves in and around the port of Cartagena in the Spanish Indies and was preparing his well-known evaluation of the advantages and abuses of the slave trade, published in Madrid in 1627 and in 1647. When pressed by Sandoval to report whether the slaves sent from Angola had been legally captured, Brandão assured him that he need "have no scruples on this point," because the subject had been reviewed by learned men who served on the Lisbon Board of Conscience and as bishops in several parts of Africa. "We have been here ourselves for forty years," he observed, "and there have been many learned men here and in the province of Brazil who never have considered the trade illicit." He went on to point out that the venerable Tomás Sanchez, a leading Spanish-born Jesuit theologian (b. 1550–d. 1610), had examined the matter in his recently published *Disputations on the Holy Sacrament of Marriage* (1602) and concluded that as long as an owner purchased an article, including a slave, in good faith, he could dispose of it without qualms.[42] He conceded that some blacks were probably obtained unlawfully but insisted that their numbers were few and that their own testimony concerning the circumstances of their confinement could never be trusted. Besides, those who traveled from Luanda to the New World were at least assured of their salvation.[43]

Two decades later, however, a twice-shipwrecked Portuguese Jesuit who sailed from Luanda in a Cartagena-bound ship carrying close to 800 slaves was far less sanguine about the cargo's good fortune. Fr. Jerónimo Lobo was deeply moved by the lot of those with whom he traveled. He lamented "the miserable life and unfortunate fate of those poor creatures, put in the bottom ... as if they were vicious criminals, with no more guilt to justify such treatment, captivity and misery than their colour and our greed." He

41. Pero Rodrigues to Aquaviva, "Apontament°ˢ sobre a fundação de hum collegio no reino de Angola," Luanda, 15 June 1593, in ARSI, *Lus.*, 79, fols. 61–63ᵛ. More will be said in the next chapter about Fr. Rodrigues's justification for Jesuit participation in the slave trade.

42. Fr. Brandão might also have cited another Spanish Jesuit theologian, Fr. Luís de Molina, who wrote favorably concerning the institution of slavery, though he was skeptical of how bondsmen were being obtained in Africa. Molina was born and died in Cuenca but taught at Coimbra (1563–67), at Évora (1568–83), and for some time in Lisbon. For his views on slavery, see Frank Bartholomew Costello, S.J., *The Political Philosophy of Luis de Molina, S.J. (1535–1600)* (Rome, 1974). See also Davis, *Problem of Slavery*, 108.

43. Brandão to Sandoval, 12 Mar. 1610, in José Antonio Saco, *Historia de la esclavitud de la raza africana en el nuevo mundo*, vol. 2 (Havana, 1938): 111–12. For a not wholly reliable English translation, see Elizabeth Donnan, *Documents Illustrative of the History of the Slave Trade to America*, 4 vols. (Washington, D.C., 1930), 1: 123–24. Brandão, born in Porto (1575), joined the Society in 1590 and served as superior of the Angolan mission for nine years. He expired in the late 1640s. *HCJAP*, 3:1, 254 n. 2.

concluded that "God seems to be punishing us for it since we condemn to perpetual captivity free people."[44]

But such candor was as rare among Jesuits as it was among others, ecclesiastics and seculars alike, who witnessed the brutality of the slave system.[45] Somewhat surprisingly, in view of his staunch advocacy of Amerindian "freedom" and his own partly mulatto antecedents, Fr. António Vieira not only failed to oppose Brazil's importation of African slaves but urged that even larger numbers be sent to the State of Maranhão to alleviate the settlers' rapacious demand for aboriginal laborers. Although he consistently urged masters to treat their chattels humanely, he counseled black slaves to be content with their lot. In Augustinian terms, he insisted that they were fortunate to be brought to the New World as converts to the Christian faith and rhapsodized that their sufferings on the sugar plantations rendered them spiritually akin to the crucified Jesus "because you suffer as he suffered. . . . The irons, the shackles, the lash, the open wounds, the insults, of all these your imitation is composed. And if you have patience, you too will have the merit of martyrdom."[46]

But Vieira's onetime companion, Jorge Benci (b. 1650–d. 1708), urged masters not to be excessive in their punishment of misbehaving black slaves. Benci was born in the Adriatic seaport of Rimini not far from Ravenna. He joined the Society at age 15 and volunteered for service in Brazil, where he arrived in 1681 and remained until 1700, eventually returning to Lisbon, where he died. His small treatise, *Economia cristã dos senhores no governo dos escravos*, an expansion of a sermon that he had previously prepared, was published in Rome in 1705, three years before his death. Like nearly all of his contemporaries, ecclesiastics as well as laymen, Benci regarded blacks as unfortunate brutes with limited intelligence, devoid of ambition, and prone to acts of disobedience for which they were deserving of correction. But he insisted that masters bore an obligation to treat bondsmen humanely and to provide them with adequate clothing, sustenance, medical care, and spiritual instruction.[47]

44. *The Itinerário of Jerónimo Lobo*, trans. Donald M. Lockhart, ed. C. F. Beckingham, *HS*:2, no. 162 (1984): 387. Fr. Lobo's compassion for the slaves with whom he sailed was shared by the Capuchin Denisio de Carli of Piacenza, who traveled from Luanda to Salvador da Bahia with 680 slaves in 1667, but neither priest was moved to condemn the trade or the institution of slavery. Michael Angelo, "A Voyage to Congo, in the Years 1666 and 1667," in Churchill, *Collection*, 1: 577–78.

45. One such critic was the author of a memorial to the crown composed at the beginning of the seventeenth century. The memorial severely criticized the slave trades as practiced in Angola and east of the Cape of Good Hope and suggested (1) that their persistence was harmful to evangelical efforts, and (2) that it was inconsistent to enact laws against Amerindian bondage but to permit the enslavement of Africans. Excerpts from the memorial are published by Edmundo Correia Lopes, *A escravatura* (*Subsídios para a sua historia*) (Lisbon, 1944), 171–75. C. R. Boxer has suggested that the author was a Jesuit, but there is no reason to conclude that he was: *Salvador de Sá and the Struggle for Brazil and Angola, 1602–1686* (London, 1952), 237 and n. 32. It is clear that the author was familiar with some of the published portions of Luis de Molina's *De justitia et jure*, of which three (of six) volumes were published in Cuenca between 1592 and 1600. Boxer believed that the author's references to the Asian missions meant that he was probably a member of the Society, but he forgot that Fernão Guerreiro's *RACJ* series, which included detailed reports on the Far Eastern provinces, had been published since 1603.

46. Sermão XIV, as quoted in Sweet, "Black Robes," 107. For an extensive exegesis of Vieira's views on African slavery, see ibid., 101–23.

47. The foregoing is based upon the second edition of Benci's tract, edited by Serafim Leite and published in Porto in 1954. Another Italian priest who formed a low opinion of black slaves in Brazil was the Capuchin Michael Angelo of Gattina, who wrote that while in Bahia in 1666, "to divert us we went one day to see sugar-works. . . . It is wonderful to see the *Blacks*, who are naturally lazy, labour so hard, and clap the cannes so dexterously under that mass of iron [i.e., the grinding apparatus] without leaving their

Benci's book is of interest because it reflects the views of an experienced Jesuit administrator who obviously did not question either the legal or the moral justification for black
slavery. He was simply disturbed about the excesses to which Brazilian masters (and some
mistresses) were prone in dealing with their slaves. To what extent other contemporaries,
including Jesuits, shared his concern is impossible to say. It is likewise difficult to measure
the impact of Benci's book, since only one copy of the first edition is known to survive.
The same limitation applies to the last Jesuit writer in the Assistancy who published advice
concerning the treatment of black slaves, Giovanni Antonio Andreoni.

Andreoni (b. 1649–d. 1716) was born in the Tuscan community of Lucca, studied law
at the University of Perugia, and entered the Society in 1667. He later became one of
at least three Italians who sailed from Lisbon to Bahia with Vieira in 1681.[48] Like Benci,
Andreoni remained close to Vieira. Doubtless with Vieira's support, Andreoni rose to
exercise major administrative duties in the Brazil province, serving twice as rector of the
Bahian college and once as provincial (1705–9).[49] It was during his provincialate that he
labored to complete his magisterial analysis of the roots of Brazil's economic prosperity,
the well-known *Cultura e opulencia do Brasil por suas drogas e minas*, published in Lisbon in 1711
under the pseudonym André João Antonil. That literary device did not prevent the crown
from almost immediately suppressing the book because of fears that it revealed too many
details of the colony's wealth-producing capacities, especially during the War of the Spanish
Succession (1702–13). Fewer than ten copies of the 1711 edition are known to have escaped
the government's destructive efforts.

It is curious that although Andreoni conceded that black slave labor was vital to the
functioning of the colony's economy, he found space to devote only one chapter (out of 72) to
counseling masters on the proper treatment of their slaves. Although he seems to have had a
somewhat higher regard for the intelligence of persons of African origin than did Benci,
Andreoni agreed with his Italian-born colleague that masters ought to see that their slaves
received adequate food, clothing, and medical care. He also shared Benci's abhorrence of
unrestrained cruelty by masters toward their slaves, but, like Benci and so many others,
he refrained from expressing criticism of that system or from suggesting ways by which it
could be ameliorated or even terminated.[50] That is hardly surprising, considering the extent
to which his own Order had become dependent upon black slave labor, especially in Brazil.

---

hands or arms behind them." "A Voyage to Congo, in the Years 1666 and 1667," in Churchill, *Collection*,
1: 559.

48. *HCJB*, 6: 598. Benci supposedly traveled to Brazil the same year, but neither Leite nor any other
source indicates whether he, too, voyaged with Vieira or traveled separately.

49. Ibid., 8: 45–54.

50. The authoritative scholarly edition of Andreoni-Antonil remains that edited and translated by
Andrée Mansuy (Paris, 1965). See bk. 1, chap. 9, 120–32. For an English translation, see Robert Edgar
Conrad, *Children of God's Fire: A Documentary History of Black Slavery in Brazil* (Princeton, 1983), 55–60. It is
possible that Nuno Marques Pereyra was familiar with Benci and/or Andreoni, for he offered slaveholders
quite similar advice concerning the treatment of their bondsmen: *Compendio narrativo do peregrino da America*
(Lisbon, 1731), chap. 13.

Jesuit Reliance upon African Slavery in Portugal, Asia, and Africa

Fragmentary evidence suggests that Jesuits in Portugal and Spain made use of slaves from Guinea and Angola, particularly during the sixteenth century. Upon occasion they also remitted to the Iberian Peninsula a few slaves from the African stations. In 1553 Inácio de Azevedo, rector of Santo Antão, complained to Loyola that four years earlier a returning priest from Kongo had sent seven slaves to labor in the new Lisbon college but that the governor of the island of São Tomé had intercepted the shipment and seized three of the slaves on the pretext that they had escaped payment of customary imposts.[51] In the 1580s, a Jesuit father in Angola also dispatched an unspecified number of slaves to the Portuguese province.[52] It is impossible to say how often that practice occurred during the early years of the enterprise.

Both Iberian crowns joined private benefactors in supplying the Society with chattels to facilitate the completion of its new schools.[53] In the province of Toledo, one Jesuit justified the presence of African bondsmen in Jesuit facilities on the ground that "they serve everywhere within the Company, especially in Évora, Coimbra, and in other parts of Portugal."[54] Though most of the Jesuits' slaves in the Iberian Peninsula were engaged in construction work or household duties, there is a record dating from about 1580 of nine field slaves who belonged to one of the estates owned by the arts college of Coimbra.[55] How widespread that practice was within the Portuguese province is unknown. Although that province continued to receive slaves as gifts down to the late 1580s, the provincial, responding to the edicts cited earlier by Borgia and his successors, directed that no more would be accepted.[56] Even so, there are occasional references to African slaves that units of the province owned as late as the 1750s.[57]

East of the Cape of Good Hope, the Jesuits, like other subjects of the kings of Portugal, obtained slaves from lands as far apart as Mozambique and the Indonesian archipelago. C. R. Boxer remarks that Jesuit house staffs in Japan included slaves who were "Negroes, Indians, Malays, and other Asiatic and Asian races."[58] Blacks were favored not only for their loyalty and durability but also because their imposing presence could be intimidating

51. Azevedo to Loyola, 7 Dec. 1553, in *MB*, 5: 15.

52. Sebastião Morães (provincial) to Aquaviva, Évora, 30 Jan. 1587, in ARSI, *Lus.*, 70, 36^r–36^v. I am indebted to Dr. Nigel Griffin, University of Manchester, for this reference and for the manuscript sources cited in the next two notes.

53. E.g., in Cadiz a Fr. Bernal wrote that "the people are much in favor of the schools we are building and assist us with 400 ducats and many slaves who work on them." Bernal to Francisco Borgia, Cadiz, 25 Apr. 1568, in ARSI, *Hispania*, 108, fol. 169.

54. [Bartolomé de] Bustamante to provincial, Toledo, 14 Sept. 1567, of which an extract was sent to Rome. Ibid., 107, fol. 26^v. Like his grandfather, Sebastian also gave Guinea slaves to the arts college of Coimbra: provisão of 15 July 1561, in *DHJP*, 263.

55. Anon. memo to Jorge Serrão, in ANTT/CJ/32, no. 12.

56. See note 52.

57. E.g., the book of obituaries of São Roque records the death of Luis Correa on 31 May 1618 after a decade of service as an errand boy and baker's helper. He had been given to the house by the widow of a senior royal magistrate. *OSR*, no. 329. In 1754 the procurator-general of the province petitioned the crown to approve the sale of a slave who had served in his office: ANTT/CJ/68, nos. 204–5.

58. *CCJ*, 226.

to hostile Asian crowds. Matteo Ricci testified that soon after his arrival in China, a stone-throwing mob threatened the mission house in Chao-ch'ing but retreated in a hurry after being confronted by "an Ethiopian guard, a black African … Cafir … big and robust and utterly fearless … [who] chased away the whole mob, single handed." He added that "nearly all of our domestics were from India and almost as dark as the Ethiopian."[59] In 1617 the procurator of Macao noted that he had sent a gold chain to the island of Solor to purchase two slaves for his college. Four years earlier the superior of Ternate reported that the mission's recently purchased contingent of nine servants had entirely fled.[60]

The Jesuits' facilities in India utilized a considerable number of low-caste natives of the subcontinent, but they also purchased non-Muslims (Kaffirs) from Mozambique. In Linschoten's day (the 1580s), many of them were sent to the Goan auction market, where they were sold cheaply to Portuguese buyers, who reputedly kept dozens of them in their homes and on their estates.[61] Regrettably, historians have not made much progress in reconstructing the nature and importance of that trade.[62] Most of the bondsmen that Jesuits in India acquired worked in their colleges. Seventeenth-century inspectors of such facilities complained about the "multitude of insolent kaffirs in our houses," the unjustifiable severity of their punishment, and the financial burden that they represented, but they were unspecific about the number present.[63] Whether because of such concerns or for other reasons, the

59. Louis J. Gallagher, S.J., trans., *China in the Sixteenth Century: The Journals of Matthew Ricci, 1583–1610* (1942; rpr., New York, 1953), 191–92.

60. "Contas do padre Manoel Borges … desta procurat.ʳᵃ de Macao … [1]616 … 1617," BA/JA/49-V-712; Pero Gomes to Claudio Aquaviva, Ternate, 15 June 1614, in *DM*, 3: 266.

61. Linschoten, *Voyage*, 71, 185, 193, 275, 277. Cf. S/*FX*, 3: 22; and "Lista das cousas que este anno de 1571 concedeo el-rey de Portugal em favor dos Padres da Companhia de Jesus," in *DI*, 8: 409. The trade continued to flourish in the seventeenth century except when interdicted by the Dutch. See Pyrard de Laval, *Voyage*, 65–67, 75; Nicolao Manucci, *Storia do Mogor or Mogul India*, trans. and ed. William Irvine, 4 vols. (London, 1906–8), 3: 164; *Travels of the Abbé Carré*, HS:2, no. 95 (1947): 168, 172, 242; and Giovanni Francesco Gemelli Careri, *A Voyage Round the World* (1695), in Surendra Nath Sen, ed., *Indian Travels of Thevenot and Careri* (New Delhi, 1949), 188, 272.

62. For one contemporary's observations on the impressive volume of the slave trade between Mozambique and India, see *An Account of Tibet: The Travels of Ippolito Desideri of Pistoia, S.J., 1712–1727*, ed. Filippo de Filippi, intro. C. Wessels, S.J. (rev. ed., London, 1937), 56–57. The secondary literature is uniformly disappointing. See D. R. Banaji, *Slavery in British India* (rev. ed., Bombay, ca. 1933), a legalistic account from 1772 to 1843 that largely ignores Portuguese enclaves; Amal Kumar Chattopadhytay, *Slavery in India* (Calcutta, 1959), is a disappointing, bigoted book (originally an M.A. thesis) that ignores the trans–Indian Ocean slave trade; Joseph E. Harris, *The African Presence in India: Consequences of the East African Slave Trade* (Evanston, Ill., 1971), mistakenly believes (p. 5) that "the slave trade in East Africa seems to have been small in … volume until the nineteenth century." Ann M. Pescatello, "The African Presence in Portuguese India," *Journal of Asian History* 11, 1 (1977): 26–48, is superficial and relies mostly on travel accounts and very little on Goan archives; Hubert Gerbeau, "The Slave Trade in the Indian Ocean," in UNESCO, *The African Slave Trade*, 191–95, is content with telling scholars what research they ought to do. Jeanette Pinto, "Slavery in Portuguese India, 1510–1842," Ph.D. diss., University of Bombay, 1985, of which there is a copy in the library of the Jesuit Historical Institute in Rome, relies largely upon printed sources and adds nothing new; whereas Utsa Patnaik and Manjari Dingwaney, eds., *Chains of Servitude: Bondage and Slavery in India* (Madras, 1985), fails to consider the African slave trade to India. The most recent published study that I have seen is P. P. Shirodkar, "Slavery in Coastal India (With Special Reference to Goa, Daman and Diu)," *Purabhilekh-Puratatva* 3, 1 (1985): 27–43, but, like all previous accounts, it fails to estimate the magnitude of slave imports.

63. "Ordens que deixou o P. Francisco Barreto, visitador … em toda a provincia de Goa … anno de 1660," in ARSI, FG, 1443/9/27; "Ordens quais q. deixou p.ᵃ toda a provincia o P.ᵉ Alexandre Cicero visitador das provincias da India Goa e Malabar," 15 Jan. 1685, in ibid., *Goa*, 35, fols. 291–96, pars. 39 and 53.

TABLE 20.1

*Indian and Kaffir Household Servants in Colleges Belonging to
the Province of Goa, ca. 1730*

Facility	Jesuits (N)	Kaffirs (N)	Indians (N)	Facility	Jesuits (N)	Kaffirs (N)	Indians (N)
New St. Paul's	82	n.a.	n.a.	Taná	6	6	4
Rachol	25	0	10	Diu	4	8	5
Chorão novitiate	25	10	0	Damão	6	9	8
Bassein	20	10	8				

SOURCE: Enc., viceroy to king, 23 Jan. 1731, in AHU/PA/IN, *cx.* 35.

number of Kaffirs and other servants in several of the colleges of the province of Goa was surprisingly modest a half century later (see Table 20.1).

Scattered entries in several codices in the Historical Archives of Goa demonstrate that the colleges continued to purchase slaves from Mozambique until the mid-1750s.[64] One register, for example, shows that an unnamed college, probably Rachol or New St. Paul's, purchased one to three kaffirs a year during the early 1720s, for whom it paid in cash. A day journal of the provincial procurator shows entries for the January monsoon of 1754 in which Goa bartered clothing and comestibles, including butter, cheeses, ham, and peppers, in exchange for Mozambique slaves supplied by Jesuit stations there. Two years later the same procurator entered in his accounts the sum of 240,000 rs. that he had sent to Mozambique for five "large kaffirs."[65] However, that was but a trickle of the estimated 1,000 slaves that the colony annually exported in the mid-eighteenth century.[66]

Since the Jesuits had several installations in two of Portugal's larger slave colonies, it followed that the fathers there became slaveholders too. In Mozambique they possessed 22 large and small estates (prazos) as well as several residences. Those facilities were clustered at the seaport of Quilimane and the Zambesi River stations of Tete and Sena. According

64. One activity that involved Jesuits in India has attracted little attention: their role in placing Indian slaves in the homes of trusted families, who were obliged to teach them "good customs" and to aid them to become Christians, after which they were to be set conditionally free. This was a function of the so-called *pai dos cristãos*. A Jesuit at Bassein and another in Old St. Paul's in Goa held that title. See Josef Wicki, S.J., ed., *O livro do "Pai dos Cristãos"* (Lisbon, 1969). A codex that ought to interest social historians of India is the "L.º de diferentes notas, e outr actos, acorda, treslados e cartas de alforria dadas a alguns escravos, 1682–1759," HAG 860. Most of the slaves appear to have been hill folk from the Western Ghats, described as *casta gatual* or *casta Curumby*. Many were young women between 10 and 30 years of age. In one instance, a married man gave permission for a 20-year-old girl entrusted to him to marry one of his Kaffirs.

65. HAG 2564, fol. 205; 2481, fol. 190^r; and 2094, fol. 60^r. Two other codices that were part of the records of the college of Rachol show occasional entries for the purchase of slaves from Mozambique in 1726 and 1756: HAG 2078, fol. 37^v and 2049 (no fol.). In the first instance, two *cafarinhos* (young boys) were purchased for 63,000 rs., the same price that an adult cost in the latter year. Another entry in codex 2049 records a transfer from Rachol to New St. Paul's of 76,500 rs. to cover the infirmary costs of caring for one of its fathers for 221 days and for "his kaffir" for 213 days, suggesting that even as late as August 1754, Jesuits possessed personal servants, the injunctions of the generals to the contrary notwithstanding.

66. [Anon.], "Memorias da costa d'Africa oriental e algumas reflexões uteis para estabelecer melhor e fazer mais florente o seu commercio," in António Alberto de Andrade, *Relações de Moçambique setesentista* (Lisbon, 1955), 216. Cf. Ralph A. Austen, "The Trans-Saharan Slave Trade: A Tentative Census," in Henry A. Gemery and Jan S. Hogendorn, eds., *The Uncommon Market: Essays in the Economic History of the Atlantic Slave Trade* (New York, 1979), 68, table 2.9.

to one near-contemporary source, by the 1750s the Jesuits possessed about 5,000 slaves distributed among those three centers.[67] But a modern Jesuit scholar insists that those figures are inflated. According to Fr. Rea, the Society possessed about 1,400 slaves in Mozambique during the 1750s. Whatever their actual number, many bondsmen served as domestic servants, others as field hands, and some as gold miners. Still others were skilled workers such as bakers, barbers, fishermen, ironmongers, stonemasons, and tailors.[68]

In the course of the seventeenth century, Angola succeeded Guinea as the primary source of slaves for Brazil and other parts of the New World. As was true in India, freemen, both white and nonwhite, retained a vast number of chattels as their personal servants. Michael Angelo of Gattina reported in the 1660s that it was not uncommon for owners to possess 50, 100, 200, or even as many as 3,000 bondsmen.[69] There, too, the Jesuits received donations of slaves from both African chieftains and Portuguese sojourners.[70] But we have only very sketchy accounts of how many bondsmen the fathers held at any point in time. Indeed, that was the kind of data that the Luanda college rarely transmitted to its Roman headquarters. The earliest inventory (1594) of the new college does report that it possessed 152 slaves: 62 were married, 34 were single, and the remainder were children and aged adults.[71] Four decades later the Jesuits reported that they had "more than 650" persons tilling their lands, of whom nearly two-thirds were freemen.[72]

Considering the turmoil that swept the colony during the Dutch occupation and the subsequent Portuguese recovery in the 1640s (see Chapter 9), it stretches credulity to accept two estimates of Jesuit slaveholdings in Angola made in the late 1650s and the late 1660s. The first came from one of the fathers' militant critics, Governor João Fernandes Vieira, who alleged that they owned "more than 10,000 slaves" and had the capacity to acquire tens of thousands more.[73] The second was written by another rival, Fr. Michael Angelo, an Italian-born Capuchin, who reported in 1666 and 1667 that the Jesuits had been given "12,000 slaves of sundry trades, as smiths, joiners, turners, and stone cutters," who brought them a handsome income.[74] As this report correctly indicates, the Luanda Jesuits derived part of their income from slave artisans whom they owned. According to the crown's inventory of 1760, such craftsmen had provided 7.1 percent of the college's annual income.

67. António Pinto de Miranda, "Memória sobre a costa de Africa," ca. 1766, in Andrade, *Relações*, 255, 259, and 264. The author was a settler on the Zambesi in the 1760s and a conspicuous critic of the notoriously corrupt and inefficient Portuguese regime. Newitt appears to consider him to be more reliable than does Fr. Rea (see note 68).

68. William Francis Rea, S.J., *The Economics of the Zambezi Missions, 1580–1759* (Rome, 1976), 114–30. See also M[alyn] D. D. Newitt, *Portuguese Settlement on the Zambesi: Exploration, Land Tenure and Colonial Rule in East Africa* (New York, 1973), 88–89, 101, 200–201.

69. Michael Angelo, "A Voyage to Congo, in the Years 1666 and 1667," in Churchill, *Collection*, 1: 561.

70. In 1667, when the Capuchin Denisio de Carli of Piacenza was about to leave Kongo to return to Europe, a chieftain sent him several blacks as a gift "which I . . . sent back to him. I afterwards told him I came not into his country to make slaves, but rather to deliver those from the slavery of the devil whom he kept in miserable thraldom." Ibid., 1: 557. I am not aware of any Jesuit who ever spurned such a gift, which, of course, he would have conveyed to the house to which he was attached.

71. ARSI, FG, 1369/6.

72. *HCJAP*, 3:2, 255.

73. Vieira to king, 5 Nov. 1658, as quoted in José António Gonsalves de Mello, *João Fernandes Vieira*, 2 vols. (1956; rpr., Recife, 1967), 2: 189–90.

74. Michael Angelo, "A Voyage to Congo, in the Years 1666 and 1667," in Churchill, *Collection*, 1: 561.

But the same inventory discloses that instead of thousands of slaves, the college possessed 330 slaves who lived in the capital and another 750 who worked on its approximately twenty rural estates (arimos).[75]

Jesuit Dependence upon Black Slaves in Brazil

Brazil became Portugal's largest slave consumer, and because the Society became committed to the commercial production of cane sugar there at the start of the seventeenth century (see Chapter 16), the Brazilian installations came to rely more heavily upon black slavery than did others in the Assistancy. When Fr. Simón Mendez stopped at Rio de Janeiro in 1640 en route to his Paraguayan station, he was impressed by the fact that the Carioca college possessed 600 blacks, of whom 500 toiled on its plantations, while the remainder worked within the college.[76]

Though the household staffs of Jesuit houses in Rio de Janeiro, Goa, and other parts of the Assistancy were much smaller than those of great noble establishments or regal palaces in Europe, the Jesuits' domestic staffs, too, testified to the apparent affluence and might of their owners and aroused the envy of those who were less prosperous in towns where the fathers resided.[77] In the countryside the same was true of the field gangs of slaves that the Jesuits assembled.

Unfortunately Fr. Mendez did not indicate how those in Rio de Janeiro were distributed. Presumably they were assigned to several estates, for it would have been uneconomical to concentrate them on a single fazenda. A Jesuit official had stated three decades earlier that the average sugar estate in Bahia then contained 50 to 60 black slaves, but that the largest plantations sometimes possessed 100 or more.[78] One of the latter was Santo Antão's Sergipe do Conde in Bahia, which averaged about 85 slaves between 1626 and 1638.[79] That was about twice as many as were in the slave gang that António Vieira and his colleagues assembled on a provision farm in Maranhão. In 1661 Vieira reported that that gang contained more than 40 slaves and that the fathers were "bountifully provided with manioc (*pao*), vegetables,

75. António Ferr[eir]a Cardoso, "Relação dos rendimentos certos e incertos que no collegio desta cidade de Loanda do reyno de Angolla tinhao os padres da Companhia de Iezus," 29 July 1760, in Alfredo de Albuquerque Felner, comp., *Angola: Apontamentos sobre a ocupação e inicio do estabelecimento dos portugueses no Congo, Angola e Benguela* (Coimbra, 1933), 462–69. José Carlos Venancio, "A economia de Luanda e hinterland no seculo xviii: Um estudo de etnologia historica," diss., Universidade de Johannes Gutenberg em Monguncia, 1983, 98, accepts the same estimate. I am indebted to Joseph C. Miller for the reference.

76. Mendez to Sebastian Gonzales, 15 June 1640, in *MHE*, 19: 238, 248. C. R. Boxer misread these passages and assumed that the entire contingent of 600 was serving in the college. *Salvador de Sá*, 134. In 1640 there were 79 Jesuits attached to the college, including nine novices. ARSI, *Bras.*, 5:1.

77. On the size of domestic staffs in great European households, see Lawrence Stone, *The Crisis of the Aristocracy, 1558–1641* (Oxford, 1965), 211–13, 556; and Sharon Kettering, *Patrons, Brokers, and Clients in Seventeenth-Century France* (Oxford, 1986), 35, 215–20. Both writers emphasize that the number of servants in noble houses appears to have diminished over time, and the same seems to have been the case in Jesuit houses. See also John Frederick Schwaller, *The Church and Clergy in Sixteenth-Century Mexico* (Albuquerque, N.M., 1988), 103, concerning the number of servants who accompanied the future count-duke of Olivares when he was a student at the University of Salamanca.

78. [Jacomé Monteiro], "Relação da província do Brasil, 1610," in *HCJB*, 8: 404. In 1739, nine sugar plantations in Bahia averaged 67.3 slaves apiece. Stuart B. Schwartz, *Sugar Plantations in the Formation of Brazilian Society: Bahia, 1550–1835* (Cambridge, 1985), 348.

79. Schwartz, *Sugar Plantations*, 347.

and fruits."[80] Several years later, in 1674, when a new manager assumed responsibility for another of Santo Antão's sugar estates in Brazil, specifically Santana de Ilhéus, south of Salvador, he acknowledged receipt of 119 slaves.[81] In the eighteenth century, some Jesuit estates would possess slave gangs that were nearly four times as large.

Slaves who toiled for the fathers were no better off than those who served other owners. Whether in the field or in the sugar factory (engenho), they put in long, arduous, hazardous, and largely thankless days or nights for most of the year.[82] They received about the same amenities as those who served other masters in Brazil. They lived in crude huts and slept upon coarse mats (esteiras). While their ecclesiastical masters, occasional guests, and probably the domestic staff enjoyed partly European diets that included imported wines, cheeses, butter, dried fruit, and nuts, as well as locally produced meats, fruit, and vegetables, the field servants' meals consisted largely of manioc that had been boiled or processed as flour, chickpeas and other legumes, bananas, salt, inferior kinds of fresh and dried fish, whale oil, sometimes whale flesh, and whatever they were able to grow on assigned plots.[83] Infirm slaves could expect the same treatment as their convalescing masters—a diet of eggs and chicken, a variety of medications, and invariably plenty of bleeding. Those who performed their tasks exceptionally well might receive as rewards rations of tobacco and wine, but, during the eighteenth century at least, curiously not sugar brandy (cachaça).[84]

Though Fr. Serafim Leite wished to visualize the Jesuits as generally benevolent masters,[85] there is no persuasive evidence that Jesuit administrators were any more gentle toward their workers than their secular rivals were. If Jesuit managers refrained from delivering the savage punishments that other masters visited upon their chattels, they were equally prone to employ the lash to motivate those deemed slackers, miscreants, and the like.[86] Just as runaways became a constant problem for other owners, so those Jesuits who operated estates like Sergipe do Conde came to expect that each year from one to four slaves of either sex would become fugitives. The usual fate of the runaways was to be returned by professional slave catchers, the infamous capitães do mato, or by nearby Indians who turned in the unfortunates for a small monetary reward.[87]

Despite the recovery of shirkers and the fathers' efforts to preserve the health of their chattels, Jesuit administrators frequently found it necessary to purchase fresh contingents of slaves to replace those who had perished or disappeared. Fr. Estevão Pereira, the controversial manager of Sergipe do Conde from 1629 to 1633, reported that in ordinary

80. Vieira to Goswin Nickel, 21 Mar. 1661, in *NCJ*, 296.

81. "Relação do inventario do eng.º de Santa Anna," 29 July 1674, in ANTT/CJ/54, no.7.

82. Schwartz, *Sugar Plantations*, chaps. 5–6.

83. On differences between masters' and slaves' diets, cf. Michael Craton and James Walvin, *A Jamaican Plantation: The History of Worthy Park, 1670–1970* (Toronto, 1970), 135–37.

84. The accounts in *DHA*, vol. 2, passim, clearly distinguish provisions intended for slaves and for their ecclesiastical managers.

85. *HCJB*, 2: 350–60.

86. Cf. Schwartz, *Sugar Plantations*, 142.

87. Ibid., 144, 157, 174, 210, 250, 265, 322, 482, 486, 527. Fr. Agostinho Quadros discussed the persisting problem of runaways in a report to the rector of the owner college, Santo Antão: Quadros to João de Távora, Sergipe do Conde, 17 Mar. 1660, in ANTT/CJ/68, no. 132.

TABLE 20.2

Slaves Purchased in the Bahian Market for Engenho Sergipe do Conde, 1623–37, 1643–52

Year of harvest	Description	Approximate unit price (000 rs.)	Total cost (000 rs.)
1623–24	6 "slaves"	25.5	153
1625–26	7 "blacks"	20.0	140
1628–29	1 black female	28.0	28
	2 black males and 1 black female	—	90[a]
	1 boatman	40.0	40
1632–33	2 blacks and 1 *moleque*[b]	—	90[a]
1633–34	2 black adults	42.0	84
	1 *moleque*[b]	25.0	25
1634–35	2 males and 1 female	—	126
1635–36	14 Guinea slaves	39.4	552
1636–37	1 slave	50.0	50
1643–44	12 Guinea slaves and *crioulos ladinos*[c]	41.2	494
	10 Cape Verde slaves	44.2	442
	1 *moleque*[b]	28.0	28
	1 mulatto	26.0	26
	2 blacks	35.0	70
	1 black locksmith	60.0	60
	1 purger	60.0	60
	1 black female	40.0	40
	2 *moleques*[b]	28.0	56
1646	12 slaves	42.2	506[a]
1646–47	3 slaves	51.6	155
1650–51	4 Angolans	48.0	192
	10 Guinea slaves	48.5	485
	1 black	55.0	55
1651–52	2 Cape Verdians	70.0	140
	1 *molequão*[b]	30.0	30
	2 *crioulos grandes*[d]	52.5	105

SOURCES: *DHA*, 2: 55, 91, 139, 144, 145, 199, 212, 213, 231, 299, 394, 407, 470, 471, 481, and 521.

[a] Scribal rounding of total cost.

[b] A *moleque* or *molequão* describes a boy or large boy under 12.

[c] A *crioulo ladino* refers to a Brazilian-born slave.

[d] A *crioulo grande* means a large Brazilian-born slave.

years it was necessary to purchase five slaves (about 6.25 percent of the total work force) to replenish those who had died.[88] As Table 20.2 suggests, during the second quarter of the seventeenth century, such recruits were obtained from four different sources: the Guinea Coast, the Cape Verde coast, Angola, and Brazil itself.

The table reveals undulating but generally rising prices for slaves during three decades when Dutch maritime and land forces were disrupting Portugal's Atlantic empire (see Chapter 9). Note, for example, that the price of an unskilled slave doubled between 1623–24 (the eve of the Hollanders' capture of Bahia) and 1637 (when the Dutch seized São Jorge da Mina). Although the creoles appear to have fetched higher prices than African

88. "Da se rezão da fazenda que o colegio de Santo Antão tem no Brasil e de seus rendimentos," Coimbra, 25 Aug. 1635, in Antonil, *Cultura e opulencia*, ed. Mansuy, 524.

imports during the first decades, slaves from the African stations yielded higher prices at the end of the period, that is, immediately after the recovery of Angola (1648), but precisely at a time when Dutch warships were taking a terrible toll of Portuguese shipping in the South Atlantic.[89]

Stuart B. Schwartz contends that the Jesuits were driven to obtain fresh recruits frequently because of their mindless opposition to slave marriages and to the rearing of children on their plantations. He argues that high infant mortality rates and the risks of pregnancy "did not make the fostering of stable unions ... an economic as well as a moral imperative" in the minds of Jesuit administrators, who were less enlightened than Benedictine sugar planters who strove to promote "more balanced sex ratios" on their fazendas. Only in the 1750s, according to Schwartz, is there evidence of "conscious efforts by [Jesuit] administrators to have slaves form 'stable' family units based upon marriage."[90] But it is possible to arrive at different, albeit less dramatic, conclusions by using the same documentation that Schwartz consulted and by placing it within a broader context.

Schwartz relies, in part, upon two inventories from the Jesuits' Santana estate, one dated 1731, the other 1752. Both are part of a longer series of similar documents that reveal significant ethnic and structural changes on that plantation over time. The first of that series was compiled in 1572, upon the death the estate's original owner, Governor-General Mem de Sá. That inventory reveals that only 8.1 percent of the slave force consisted of Guinea slaves; Indians constituted the remainder. Among the Guinea slaves, men exceeded women by a ratio of 19 to 1. Only twelve of the nineteen were married, but the ethnicity of their wives is not indicated. None of those slaves possessed any children. Just over 10 percent of the 222 Indians were children. Men composed 51.4 percent of this group, and 61.1 percent of both sexes was described as married.[91] By 1618 the slave force on that estate consisted entirely of persons of African origin, but by then the gang had shrunk to only 34 slaves, of whom ten were identified as Guinea slaves, one as an Angolan, and the remainder as crioulos. There were seven couples, only three of whom had children. One widow and one single male also each possessed a child.[92]

Four later inventories of the plantation tell a very different story. That of 1674 implies that all of the plantation's slaves had been born in Brazil and that 34 of 44 (77.3 percent) of the adults were married. Nine of the seventeen married couples possessed living offspring. The average couple then had 2.2 children, girls outnumbering boys 11 to 9.[93] The next inventory, completed two years later, reveals that of the 23 two-headed (male and female) households, eleven contained children, an average of 2.3 children per household. Just over 42 percent of the adults were identified as sharing a common household.[94] The third inventory (1730–31) demonstrates that nearly two out of three adults (62.3 percent) lived in a two-headed household. Of 48 couples, 34 (70.8 percent) possessed an average

89. See, for example, Charles R. Boxer, "Padre António Vieira, S.J., and the Institution of the Brazil Company in 1649," *HAHR* 29, 4 (Nov. 1949): 474–97.

90. Schwartz, *Sugar Plantations*, 354–56, 395, 397–400. The quotations appear on pp. 354 and 395.

91. *DHA*, 3: 40–49, 54–55. The coeval inventory for the engenho Sergipe do Conde shows similar values. Ibid., 89–96.

92. "Auto de envent.º da fazenda e engenho de Santa Ana," 13 Aug. 1618, in ANTT/CJ/15, no. 12.

93. "Treslado do inventario do eng.º de Sancta Anna," post–29 July 1674, in ANTT/CJ/54, no. 7.

94. "Treslado do inventario do engenho de Sancta Anna," 13 Aug. 1676, in ibid.

of 2.47 children per household, but if one also includes thirteen single-headed households (widowers, widows, and unmarried males or females), that average declines to 2.3 children per household, precisely the same size indicated by the 1676 listing. All but two of the 178 slaves were born in Brazil.[95] The last of this series, that of 1752, indicates that the percentage of those who married continued to rise—74.1 percent of the adults were members of two-headed households—but the percentage of those with children, in fact, declined to 60.5, and the average number of progeny fell to 2.0, a figure that is increased by only 0.1 percent if one includes offspring with only one parent. Seemingly, all of these chattels were born in the colony.[96]

Ideally, one would like to have a comparable series of inventories from all other Jesuit estates and, indeed, from those of their rivals as well. Regrettably, such documentation has not survived; nor have the registers that estate managers kept concerning marriages, births, and deaths among their slave forces.[97] In their absence, another series of Jesuit estate inventories, compiled within a few years, or at most two decades, after the Society's removal from Brazil, sheds additional light upon the diverse composition and characteristics of the work forces that labored on such properties.

Two of those reports concern the field staffs of Jesuit plantations in the far north, where slaves of African origin remained scarce and dear.[98] According to an inventory of about 1760, the former Jesuit estate of Ibirajuba, Pará, contained a work force of 84. Of 35 conjugal units, 21 (60 percent) possessed an average of just over 2.0 offspring. But what is especially interesting about those couples is that fifteen slave women of African origin were married to freemen, and six slave men also possessed free partners.[99] The near-coeval inventory of the ex-Jesuit estate of Jaguarary in adjacent Maranhão is unique, for it lists the family relationships of resident Indians as well as those of black slaves. The latter numbered 101 in 1760, of whom 50 were adults, all but four of them married. Eight slave women and five slave men had free Indian partners. Sixteen of the 23 couples (69.5 percent) possessed an average of 2.2 children.[100] Among the 63 Indian residents on the property, 24 of the 29 adults were married, and eight couples had an average of three children, nearly one child per household greater than among the slaves. If the children of a single parent are added, that average rises to 3.3. Though most Indians were married to other aborigines, two men were united with *cafuzas* (Indian-Blacks), and one was married to a mulatto.[101]

95. Pedro Teixeira, "Estado em que achey ... eng.° Sta. Anna dos Ilheos," 30 June 1730–30 June 1731, in ANTT/CJ/15, nos. 23 and 24.

96. "Inventario feito pelo P. Joao Cortes ... na entrega q. fis do Eng.° de S. Ana dos Ilheus," 13 Nov. 1752, in ANTT/CJ/544, no. 52.

97. For a study based upon a fragment of one such register for a Jesuit property in the province of Paraguay, see Morner, "Los jesuitas," 95 n. 9.

98. D. Alden, "Indian Versus Black Slavery in the State of Maranhão During the Seventeenth and Eighteenth Centuries," in Richard L. Garner and William B. Taylor, eds., *Iberian Colonies, New World Societies: Essays in Memory of Charles Gibson* (Pennsylvania State University, 1985), 71–102.

99. ARSI, *Bras.*, 28, fols. 21–22.

100. "Relação e avaliação dos escravos pertencentes a fazenda de Jaguarary," 19 Oct. 1761, enc. in [Manuel Bernardo de Melo e Castro (governor-general, Maranhão)] to Francisco Xavier de Mendonça Furtado (colonial secretary), 23 Nov. 1761, in AHU/PA/PA, *cx.* 21.

101. "Relação dos Indios pertencentes a fazenda de Jaguarary," in ibid.

TABLE 20.3

Average Number of Children per Household, Fazenda de Santa Cruz, 1768

	Couples		Widows		Widowers	
Period of birth	(N)	Average number of children	(N)	Average number of children	(N)	Average number of children
Before 1759	33	2.87	23	1.96	18	1.94
After 1759	29	2.82	5	1.40	6	2.83
Before and after 1759	69	4.78	2	3.00	3	4.30

SOURCE: *RADF*, 1 (1894): 189–90, 217, 333–39, and 418–19.

The remaining inventories pertain to former Jesuit properties located in three East Coast captaincies—Espirito Santo, Rio de Janeiro, and São Paulo.[102] One concerns the giant sugar estate of Araçatiba, Espirito Santo. The only available inventory of its slave force dates from 1779, but many of the households indicated there were formed prior to the expulsion. In 1779, 847 slaves resided on the plantation. Sixty-four percent of the adults were married and possessed an average of 3.7 children per household. The number of offspring belonging to single-headed households varied from 2.0 (single females) to 3.8 (widowers).[103]

The most revealing of the inventories of ex-Jesuit plantations in Rio de Janeiro is that of Santa Cruz, compiled in 1768.[104] It is the only known listing of former Jesuit-owned slaves that distinguishes between offspring born before and after the Order's 1759 expulsion. That compilation, summarized in Table 20.3, indicates that the average number of progeny in two-headed households was about 2.8 for those born before or after 1759; among couples who produced offspring both before and after that date, the average nearly doubled.

It appears that widows had fewer children than married couples. Although the number of widowers is small, they appear to have possessed as many children born before 1759 as did married couples, and more children born after that year than did widows. Neither this inventory nor a later series compiled for this property casts light upon the racial composition of the slaves, but the 1768 register does disclose that 40 percent of widowers remarried, twice the percentage of widows who did.[105]

102. Lamentably, none of the inventories of the Society's former estates in Bahia includes a list of its slaves.

103. "Inventario feita na fazenda da Areçetiba por Manoel Carlos da Silva e Susmão, ouvidor da capitania do Espirito Santo," Rio de Janeiro, 20 July 1779, in IHGB, *lata* 339, doc. 1.

104. The 1775 inventory for the Engenho Novo property in the same captaincy provides data on ethnic origins, ages, and appraised values but is not organized by household. The first part of this inventory is published in *RADF*, 3: 517–24, and 4: 14–18, 121–26, 162–67, but a nineteenth-century copy of the entire document exists in AMRJ, 40-2-20.

105. The 1768 inventory appears to be complete, but in fact it omits both females and males who were unmarried. Subsequent inventories of Santa Cruz's slaves were compiled in 1791, 1799, 1816, and 1817. Summaries (for which I am indebted to Mary Karasch) will be found in ANRJ, cod. 808, vol. 4, fols. 184, 191, 194, and 199, and *cx*. 774, pac. 3. The first of that series constitutes the primary source of Richard Graham's "Slave Families on a Rural Estate in Colonial Brazil," *Journal of Social History* 9, 3 (Spring 1976): 382–401. Graham failed to recognize that many of the slaves concentrated on Santa Cruz in 1791 were transferred from other Jesuit properties in the captaincy of Rio de Janeiro that had already been sold. See also Corcino Medeiros dos Santos, "O trabalho escravo numa grande propriedade rural: A fazenda de Santa Cruz," *Estudos históricos* (Marília, São Paulo) 16 (1972): 51–69.

The final inventory is a 1772 register of slaves belonging to five former Jesuit estates in São Paulo. Of the 38 married couples listed there, 73.6 percent possessed children, but the average per household (2.2) was substantially lower than that prevailing in the Santa Cruz estate. Moreover, only 51.2 percent of the adults were members of conjugal unions. Excepting three natives of Angola, all of the 196 slaves registered had been born in Brazil.[106]

As this survey of former Jesuit properties demonstrates, there were substantial differences in the domestic situations and ethnic composition of the chattels and other laborers who toiled on Jesuit plantations. The percentage of adults who formed coresidential unions seems to have increased significantly during the century beginning in the 1670s. The average number of children per family obviously varied from place to place and from time to time, but though the ratios are clearly lower than those found in the British Caribbean, one must remember that the studies of slave families in that region are based upon data deriving from the late eighteenth and the early nineteenth centuries and are therefore not precisely comparable to the evidence presented here.[107] It may be, for example, that the size of completed families of slave couples on both Jesuit and non-Jesuit estates was increasing in Brazil as well by the later eighteenth century. That at least is suggested by Araçatiba and by the Santa Cruz surveys discussed above. The subject warrants further investigation.

It would appear from these inventories that from about the 1670s onward, Jesuit managers preferred to purchase seasoned slaves born in Brazil, creoles or mixed bloods (cafuzos or *cabras*, light-skinned crosses of mulattoes and blacks), rather than freshly arrived bondsmen, whose life expectancy was probably substantially lower than that among those native to Brazil.[108] Certainly Jesuit administrators were undeterred by soaring slave prices during the early eighteenth century,[109] for they fully shared the mania in Brazil to acquire as many slaves as possible.[110] When, for example, one Paulista benefactor left the college of São Paulo lands in the town of Itú in 1710, the fathers promptly sold them "and with

106. "Auto de inventario que mandou fazer o juiz ordinario . . . dos bens dos padres JESUITAS . . . por ordem de Dom Luís António de Souza Botelho Mourão [captain-general, São Paulo]," 3 June 1772, in ANRJ, 481, vol. 1, fols. 102^r–118^r. The inventory represents slaves who resided on the fazendas of Arasiguama, Santa Ana, Cubatão dos Santos, Pitanguy, and Borda do Campo. Most of them continued to live there for the next several decades. "Mappa dos escravos de todas as fazendas que foram dos ex-Jesuitas dos collegios . . . de S. Paulo," ca. 1798, in AHU/PA/SP, 1st ser. cat., *cx.* 35, no. 3507; published in *DISP*, 31: 181.

107. E.g., Craton and Walvin, *Jamaican Plantation*; B[arry] W. Higman, "The Slave Family and Household in the British West Indies, 1800–1834," *Journal of Interdisciplinary History* 6, 2 (Autumn 1975): 261–87, esp. 266, table 1; idem, *Slave Population and Economy in Jamaica, 1807–1834* (New York, 1976), 159ff.; and idem, *Slave Populations of the British Caribbean, 1807–1834* (Baltimore, 1984), esp. 367, table 9.12.

108. In several of his works, C. R. Boxer has quoted the observation of a mid-nineteenth-century British trader that "the average life of a slave on the [Brazilian] plantations or in the mines" was "from seven to ten years." E.g., Boxer, *Race Relations in the Portuguese Colonial Empire, 1415–1825* (Oxford, 1963), 101. There is, however, no assurance that such an estimate was ever accurate or that it held true for the seventeenth and eighteenth centuries. In the British Caribbean, Edward Long estimated that a third of the slaves expired within three years of their arrival. At Worthy Park, Craton and Walvin found that a quarter of the slaves died in the mid-1790s within those bounds. *Jamaican Plantation*, 131, which includes Long's estimate.

109. Bahian slave prices, which varied from 49,000 to 60,000 rs. for a prime slave between 1659 and 1692, rose to 200,000 rs. in the 1720s and 1730s. D. Alden, "Price Movements in Brazil Before, During, and After the Gold Boom, with Special Reference to the Salvador Market, 1670–1769," in *Essays on the Price History of Eighteenth-Century Latin America*, ed. Lyman L. Johnson and Enrique Tandeter (Albuquerque, 1990), 343.

110. Le Gentil [de Barbinais], *Nouveau voyage autour du monde*, 2 vols. (Amsterdam, 1728), 1: 15.

TABLE 20.4

The Slave Population of the Brazil Province, 1694–1757

Owner unit	1694	1701	1707	1736	1739	1743	1757
Paraíba	—	—	—	—	32	40	40
Recife	50	70	n.a.	100+	108	142	262
Olinda	208	200	200	inc.[a]	234	n.a.	253
Bahia	738	738	450+	inc.[a]	889	1,341	1,279
Professed house[b]	—	—	—	—	—	25	3
Ilhéus	—	—	—	18	16	n.a.	6
Porto Seguro	—	—	—	30	—	40	50
Espírito Santo	10	200+	200+	535	583+	633	826
Rio de Janeiro	950	950	900+	1,500	2,340	2,337	2,651
Santos	—	10	10	43	n.a.	n.a.	n.a.
São Paulo	50+	50	50+	153	180	140	210
Paraná	—	—	—	9	61	60	106
Total	2,006+	2,218+	1,810+	2,388+	4,443	4,758	5,686

SOURCES: 1694: ARSI, *Bras.*, 5:II, 136–45. 1701: *HCJB*, 5: app. E. 1707: ARSI, *Bras.*, 6:I, 61ff. 1736: ibid., 230–32. 1739: ibid., 6:II, 276–81. 1743: ibid., 335–40. 1757: ibid., 436–43.

[a] Data too incomplete to be included.

[b] In Bahia.

TABLE 20.5

Jesuit Slaveholding in South America, ca. 1760

Province/vice-province	Number of slaves	Province/vice-province	Number of slaves
Brazil	5,686	Peru	5,224
Maranhão	736	Quito	1,364
Paraguay	3,164	New Granada	358
Chile	1,121	Total	17,653

SOURCES: Brazil: ARSI, *Bras.*, 6:II, fols. 436–43. Maranhão: ibid., 28, fols. 9–22, 39–60. Paraguay: Nicholas P. Cushner, *Jesuit Ranches and the Agrarian Development of Colonial Argentina, 1650–1767* (Albany, 1983), 102. Chile: Gustavo Valdes Bunster, *El poder economico de los Jesuitas en Chile, 1593–1767* (Santiago, 1980), 111. Peru: Pablo Macera, ed., *Instrucciones para el manejo de las haciendas Jesuitas del Peru (ss. xvii–xviii)* (Lima, 1966) 38. Quito: Nicholas P. Cushner, *Farm and Factory: The Jesuits and the Development of Agrarian Capitalism in Colonial Quito, 1600–1767* (Albany, 1982), 136. New Granada: Germán Colmenares, *Las haciendas de los jesuitas en el nuevo reino de granada* (Bogotá, 1969), 95.

their product bought slaves" for the fazenda of Arasiguama, which the same benefactor had also bequeathed to them.[111] Between 1722 and 1725, when slave prices in Bahia were peaking, the local college increased its slaveholdings by purchase from 700 to 1,000.[112]

Until 1694, none of the surviving third catalogues, those indispensable economic summaries that provincials regularly sent the Roman headquarters, supplied global statistics concerning the number of black slaves that each college in Brazil possessed. But from that date until 1757, enough data exist to demonstrate conclusively the increasing commitment of the Jesuits to black bondsmen (see Table 20.4).

Clearly the more the Society expanded its facilities in the Brazil province, the more slaves it required to service them. As should be expected, the three colleges that produced

111. *DISP*, 44: 353.

112. ARSI, *Bras.*, 6:I, fol. 155.

the most sugar—Bahia, Espírito Santo, and Rio de Janeiro—were also the ones that most impressively continued to expand their holdings of slaves during the eighteenth century. By that century's midpoint, the Society possessed far more slaves than any other institution in Brazil or, indeed, in any other part of the Americas.

Brazil was, of course, not the only Jesuit administrative unit where the Society's dependence upon slaveholding intensified during the eighteenth century. In the province of Paraguay, for example, the number of slaves rose from 1,323 in 1710 to 3,164 in 1767, an annual rate of increase of 1.39 percent.[113] Nevertheless, as Table 20.5 indicates, by about 1760, the Brazil province and the vice-province of Maranhão contained more than one-third of all of the slaves that the Society owned in South America.[114]

The Society of Jesus did not set out to become a vast slaveowning Order. Initially its leaders expected that lay brothers and hired personnel would satisfy its labor requirements. To a large extent that remained true in Portugal and in the East, but in Africa, and especially in Brazil, the Jesuits accepted black slavery without much protest and became deeply dependent upon that institution themselves. Of course, theirs was not the only religious Order in the Portuguese empire to do so. Excepting the Franciscans, most of the others who served in Portugal and in its empire also became slaveholders, but none on a scale to match the Jesuits.

In Brazil, in India, and later in Africa, Jesuits at first petitioned the crown only for a small contingent of Africans to perform domestic tasks and to help feed them and their neophytes; but once the early local administrators had persuaded their superiors that slaves were indispensable to their operations, their successors found it possible to justify the Society's increasing commitment to slavery on other grounds. As the number of personnel in the colleges and the missions expanded, so did the need for domestic servants. And in Brazil, once those institutions committed themselves to the production of sugar, not merely to defray the cost of their own needs (for tithe receipts took care of that), but also to sell at a profit in the Peninsular market, there was no turning back. That decision, made by the Bahian college at the beginning of the seventeenth century and emulated by its brother institutions with properties in Brazil throughout that century, inevitably meant the acquisition of an ever-increasing number of slaves, since there, as elsewhere in the New World, the production of sugar always depended upon the toil of slaves.

Because of the Jesuits' opposition to Indian slavery, they followed the prevailing practice among Brazilian planters and acquired as many slaves of African origin as they could afford. At first the fathers appear to have purchased slaves newly arrived from the African stations, but by the late seventeenth century they evidently preferred those born in Brazil and inured to its living conditions.

In time, the Jesuits' commitment to sugar and to slaves became irreversible. The greater their effort to expand production of sugar, the greater their need for slaves. That remained true even after the sugar industry entered a century-long slump, beginning in the 1670s,

113. Morner, "Los jesuitas," 96; Nicholas P. Cushner, *Jesuit Ranches and the Agrarian Development of Colonial Argentina, 1650–1767* (Albany, 1983), 102.

114. I have been unable to find reliable data on Jesuit slaveholding in Spanish North America.

one that witnessed soaring prices for chattels and plummeting prices for cane.[115] But since the Jesuits, along with other religious Orders, were excluded from the newly opened, more lucrative gold washings of the interior, they perceived no easy alternative to earnings derived from sugar. Nor did they come to recognize that free labor might have been less expensive than reliance upon slaves.[116]

The Jesuits thus became the preeminent slaveholders in colonial Brazil. No other corporate body there or elsewhere within the empire came to possess as many chattels as they did. No secular rival could equal the size of the field gangs they accumulated on giant plantations like Araçatiba, Engenho Novo, or Santa Cruz, or the domestic staffs they maintained in their principal colleges.

The prevalence of black slaves in Jesuit facilities became a source of obvious anguish for the Society's leading historian of its activities in colonial Brazil, the frequently cited Fr. Serafim Leite. In several publications Fr. Leite endeavored to rationalize his Order's support of black slavery. His major arguments were both simplistic and ethnocentric: (1) when the Europeans first came to the Americas, the Amerindians were free, and therefore the Jesuits struggled to protect their liberty, but they felt no such obligation with respect to Africans since slavery had existed on the black continent long before the arrival of Europeans; (2) slavery had long been sanctioned by both church law and the laws of leading European nations, so if the Jesuits had opposed the institution, they would have been in opposition to established law; (3) that opposition might have imperiled their educational and evangelical activities, and even their ability to survive in the Lusitanian world; and (4) blacks who voyaged to the New World or who toiled under Jesuit care in Africa benefited from contact with a more advanced culture and with the Christian faith.[117]

Whatever one may think of the merits of those contentions, the fact remains that Fr. Leite consistently ignored the extent of his Order's direct involvement in black slavery. Given the magnitude of its dependency, it patently became impossible for the Society's spokesmen to condemn the institution, since to do so would have been blatantly hypocritical. Admittedly, one might expect an Order known, respected, and detested for its vigorously asserted ethical positions to have assumed as militant a position on the issue of black slavery as the one it maintained with respect to Amerindian slavery. But, as the previous chapter sought to demonstrate, that campaign was hardly crowned with success, and there is no reason to believe that as long as both the church and the leading governments of Europe sanctioned black slavery, Jesuit opposition to it would have been fruitful either.

A noted historian, John Hemming, has written, "No one considered that the enslavement of blacks was as unjust as the seizure of native Indians. No Jesuit, not even Vieira, spoke

115. Alden, "Price Movements," esp. fig. 2.

116. That became the view of some observers in Brazil in the late eighteenth century. See [Luiz António Oliveira Mendes], "Discurso preliminar . . . da comarca e cidade de Salvador" [ca. 1789], *ABNRJ* 27 (1905 [1906]): 293; and Luiz dos Santos Vilhena, *Recopilação de noticias soteropolitanas e brasilicas*, 3 vols. (Bahia, 1921–35), 1: 136–37. According to one historian, by the 1760s Peruvian vintners were replacing slaves with temporary hired workers. Kendall W. Brown, "Jesuit Wealth and Economic Activity Within the Peruvian Economy: The Case of Colonial Southern Peru," *The Americas* 44 (July 1987): 39–40.

117. Leite's argument may be found in many of his writings, especially *HCJB*, 2: 350 and 6: 350–53. His introduction to Benci, *Economia cristã*, 7–10, was a vigorous response to C. R. Boxer's criticism of the Society's uncritical acceptance of black slavery in *Salvador de Sá*, 236–37. His last remarks on the subject were "A Companhia de Jesus e os pretos do Brasil," *Brotéria* 68, 5 (May 1959): 534–38.

up against this African traffic."[118] Hemming is mistaken. There were Jesuits—generals as well as field workers—who expressed misgivings and even opposition to the Society's participation in the African slave trade. Still, such concerns largely ceased to be expressed after the late sixteenth century, for by then most members came to regard their Order's reliance upon black slaves as a necessity. Those who continued to disapprove of Jesuit reliance upon African slaves simply held their tongues.[119] As in so many other respects, most Jesuits preferred to swim with the stream rather than against it. But that may have been to their advantage, for the Society's numerous critics, ever ready to find fault with its actual or alleged practices, never condemned it for the slaves it possessed. More likely, they envied it. The same became true of the real and fancied profits that Jesuits gained through their participation in imperial trade.

118. Hemming, *Red Gold: The Conquest of the Brazilian Indians, 1500–1760* (Cambridge, Mass., 1978), 415.
119. Cf. Cushner, *Jesuit Ranches*, 112–13.

CHAPTER 21

For Piety or Profit?
The Commercial Activities of
the Jesuits in the Portuguese Empire

Non erat mercatura sed opus charitatis.

—Gregory XIII, 1582

Our trade is only that of Souls, nor have we any means of assuring our relationship with God and with the world except to remain completely disinterested
in material considerations.

—António Vieira, 1688

The Society of Jesus sought to erect not only a theocratic territorial empire . . .
but also a gigantic association which should control the world's principal trades,
from the silk of China to the maté tea of Paraguay. This is why it came into
conflict with both State and society, bringing upon its head many riots . . . [the]
first signs of the movement which was to culminate in [its] exclusion.

—Vitorino Magalhães Godinho, 1970

IN THE LATE 1750s, the Pombaline regime professed to be shocked and dismayed by evidence
that the Society had engaged in commercial activities that it claimed were forbidden by the
laws of the Church and State. Its indictment of the Society (later emulated by Bourbon
France) was contrived to justify its predetermined plan to end the Jesuits' presence within its
domains. The charge was a compelling one, for the Society's commercial ventures had been
controversial since its formative years. Although many of those ventures were countenanced
and sometimes approved by the crown, they were always sources of criticism not only for the
Society's adversaries but for some of its most respected members as well.

Francis Xavier, that model of Jesuit rectitude, was among the first to advocate the
Society's participation in a limited form of commerce. Late in 1548, as he was preparing for
his epochal voyage to Japan, he suggested that the best means of providing income for the
remote Moluccas mission was to approach the king for a substantial sum that the rector of the
new college at Goa (later Old St. Paul's) could invest in textiles in Bassein. Xavier predicted
that the cloth could be sent to the islands and sold at a fivefold profit.[1] Such a proposal might
seem in conflict with canon law and with the incipient Society's own rules, but Xavier and
many other Jesuits after him would argue that the aim of the scheme was not *animo lucrandi*

---

1. S/*FX*, 3: 557; cf. António Gomes (Rector) to Simão Rodrigues, 20 Dec. 1548, in *DI*, 1: 418.

(profits for the sake of profits), but rather *charitatis* or *pius* (earnings intended for charitable or pious purposes and therefore licit for a religious Order).[2] But for centuries to come, that distinction would often become blurred in the minds of Jesuit defenders and critics.

As this chapter will indicate, in most places where Jesuits evangelized, they engaged in some form of trading activity. Their endeavors included participation in the fabled silk trade of the Orient, in the sandalwood commerce of Macao, in the cloth, pepper, and gem trades of India, and in the sugar and forest-products trades of Brazil. After their engagement in such commercial ventures has been surveyed, we may appropriately consider whether these activities were conducted on such a vast scale as to threaten the freedom of world commerce, as one prominent Portuguese economic historian has contended.

Royal Ambivalence Toward Jesuit Commercial Activities

Though sixteenth-century Portuguese governments encouraged nominal Jesuit participation in imperial trade, their successors were distinctly less favorably disposed. In the late 1560s, for example, the crown authorized the Jesuits to send 50 quintals of indigo from India to the kingdom annually to defray part of the cost of construction of the churches of São Roque and Santo Antão. Apparently the fathers continued to make use of that privilege until 1583, when Aquaviva, fearing that the practice would scandalize seculars, banned it.[3]

Such scruples seem curious in view of the crown's concession in 1574 to the college of Santo Antão of a share of its income from pepper and other spices brought from the East to the Casa da India in Lisbon. That concession, amounting to 50 rs. per quintal of pepper and 100 rs. per quintal of other so-called "drugs," was repeatedly reconfirmed by Sebastian's successors, but the kings' contractors often refused payment, compelling the Jesuits to sue for their moneys. During the first four decades of the seventeenth century, the college derived as much as 15.7 percent of its annual income from its share of the eastern spices deposited at India House, and spices continued to be a significant source of that institution's income well into the eighteenth century.[4]

Three years earlier, Sebastian conceded the Jesuit mission on Ternate the right to ship 4 *bares* (16 quintals) of cloves per year duty-free to eastern markets. But that was an exceedingly moderate concession when compared with the privilege that the ruler granted four of his

2. Canon law stipulated that ecclesiastics could not purchase objects produced by others with the intent to sell them for a profit, although they could sell articles that they themselves had made or perfected. See Nicholas P. Cushner, *Lords of the Land: Sugar, Wine and Jesuit Estates of Coastal Peru, 1600–1767* (Albany, 1980), 207; and Heribert Jone, *Moral Theology*, trans. and ed. Urban Adelman (London? 1958), 278–79.

3. Francisco Henriques to the general, 25 Apr. 1569, in *DI*, 8: 23* n. 21; H/SAGI: 325.

4. The text of the alvará of 1 Jan. 1574 is in ARSI, *Bras.*, 11:I, fols. 128–130ᵛ. There is much documentation on Santo Antão's income from the pepper trade in ANTT/CJ/4, esp. nos. 2, 3, 4, 5, 12, 14, 16, 35, and 37. For income realized or anticipated from pepper, see the following third catalogues of the province of Portugal: 1599 (*HCJAP*, II:1, 532); 1603, 1611, and 1614 (ARSI, *Lus.*, 44:I); and 1639 (ibid., 44:II). For estimates of yearly exports of spices from India to Portugal, see Vitorino Magalhães Godinho, *Os descobrimentos e a economia mundial*, 2 vols. (Lisbon, 1963–65), 1: 528; and A. R. Disney, *Twilight of the Pepper Empire* (Cambridge, Mass., 1978), 162–68. Another Lisbon house that for a time benefited indirectly from Indian commerce was the Lisbon novitiate, which drew nearly a third of its income from annuities payable in the customs house and in the India House, though the latter were no longer collectable as a result of royal order. "Rol da renda q. tem a casa de N. Sra. da Asunção ... em dezembro de 1607," in ARSI, *Lus.*, 82, fols. 128–29.

officers on the island: they were authorized to export annually 91 bares of cloves plus an additional 86 of nutmeg and mace. Although Aquaviva again worried that Jesuits were being supported by commercial profits, the rulers of Portugal renewed the Society's cloves authorization until the mid-1630s.[5]

But the Philippine rulers of Portugal and the Bragançan kings who followed were conspicuously less willing to grant the Jesuits commercial privileges. Thus, when the missions' procurator approached the crown to propose that Christian supporters of the Jesuit house at São Tomé de Meliapor be permitted to send pepper to the kingdom free of customs duties, Philip II vetoed the plan and suggested that some alternative inducement be found. Moreover, although Cardinal Henry had granted Old St. Paul's, Goa, the right to import 100 quintals of copper from China to India for a period of three years, his Spanish successor sternly rejected Jesuit efforts to extend that privilege for an additional ten years.[6] Toward the end of his life, the ever-suspicious Philip II directed his senior Portuguese minister to write the viceroy of India a dispatch praising the Jesuits for their evangelical efforts but reprimanding them for their involvement in commercial affairs.[7]

A half century later, the Restoration regime of John IV took a dim view of Jesuit efforts to recover from the Dutch intrusions in Brazil (see Chapter 9) by obtaining or confirming commercial concessions in that colony. In 1642, the procurator-general for the Brazil province, citing heavy financial setbacks that the colleges of Olinda and Salvador had sustained in the mid-1620s, asked that the standing prohibition against ginger cultivation in Brazil be set aside and that the Salvador college be authorized to ship 20,000 quintals to the kingdom within fifteen years. But the treasury solicitor opposed that petition, partly on the ground that it was contrary to existing law (which reserved ginger shipments to merchants in the East), but also because of fears that Brazilian farmers would abandon the production of the colony's most vital staple, manioc, in favor of ginger.[8]

5. "Lista das cousas que este anno de 1571 concedeo el-rey de Portugal em favor dos padres da Companhia de Jesus," *DI*, 8: 407. During the Chorão meeting of 1575, senior Jesuits were strongly divided on whether they should sell the king's license or retain it because of adverse publicity. *DI*, 10: 294–95. For the privileges conceded to the king's officers on the island, see Artur Basilio de Sá, comp. and ed., *Documentação para a historia das missões do padroado portugues do oriente: Insulindia*, 5 vols. (Lisbon, 1954–58), 5: 252–53, 260. Aquaviva's reservations are indicated in *DI* 14: 34*–35* and 155, and Valignano's defense follows on 445–46. For renewals of the privilege to the mission, see *DM*, 3: 359–60, 389–90, 460–61, 469, 498.

6. Ruy Vicente to Aquaviva, Goa, 30 Nov. 1581, in *DI*, 12: 340; "D. Henrici, Cardinalis, Regis Lusitaniae, Favores Missionibus Orientis Concessi" [9 Mar. 1579], in *DI*, 11: 541; Philip II to D. Duarte de Menseses (viceroy, India), 22 Feb. 1589, in *DI*, 15: 269, par. VIII. Such copper was used in India both for coinage (bazarucos) and for the casting of cannon. Magalhães Godinho, *Descobrimentos*, vol. 1, chap. 7. According to C. R. Boxer, the price of copper "more than tripled" in Goa between 1545 and 1611. "Macao as a Religious and Commercial Entrepôt in the 16th and 17th Centuries," *Acta Asiatica* 26 (1974): 80. Because of the consequences of internal wars and currency exports, China itself soon became an importer of copper from Japan. George Bryan Souza, *The Survival of Empire* (Cambridge, 1986), 6, 48, 54, 65, 115–16, 145.

7. Francisco Cabral (provincial) to João Alvares (assistant), Goa, 10 Dec. 1596, in *DI*, 18: 620–25. The provincial indicated that, per his instructions, the viceroy summoned both the provincial and the Visitor and read them the relevant paragraphs from the directive of the escrivão da puridade. Cabral consistently opposed the Society's involvement in trade and contended that the scandal attached to its participation outweighed the benefits of such activity.

8. Consultas of 1 Feb. and 8 May 1642, in AHU/LR/44, fols. 137ᵛ and 169ᵛ, per IHGB/MS, *lata* 29. By the latter consulta, the council recommended that the college be given the right to ship 8,000 quintals for eight years, but I have seen no evidence that the Jesuits ever took advantage of that opportunity.

Nor were the Jesuits much more successful in their efforts to secure a share of the exports of brazilwood, always a coveted royal monopoly. In the 1590s, the provincial of Brazil received a gift of 50,000 rs. derived from sales of that dyestuff to spend on installations in the colony.[9] Subsequently, under circumstances far from clear, the Jesuit college in Gante (Flanders) gained the right to ship 3,500 quintals of the dyewood to Europe. That privilege seems never to have been exercised.[10] But that concession encouraged Fr. Francisco Ferreira, the rector of Olinda, whom the Dutch had carried off to Antwerp, to report the loss of his college, valued at 8 contos, and to urge that Vitelleschi apply to the crown for compensation: the right to ship 12,000 quintals of brazilwood to the kingdom.[11] There is no evidence that the general pursued that suggestion, but Fr. Ferreira was not the only Jesuit to make such a request. Six years later, the well-known Simão de Vasconcelos, then a Jesuit representative in the delegation sent from Bahia to congratulate John IV upon his ascendancy, applied for a royal license to ship 8,000 quintals of brazilwood to the kingdom over the next eight years to alleviate his province's debts. His request was granted in 1642, but after the college of Salvador had shipped 1,026 quintals, the treasurer of the State of Brazil questioned the validity of the license and suspended the college's right to export the dyewood. It is most probable that Jesuit authorities in Brazil and in the kingdom protested that suspension, but no trace of their responses survives. However, in the 1670s, when their successors asked the prince regent either to resume dyewood exports or to ship an equivalent value of sugar without payment of convoy taxes, the regent's advisors strongly recommended the second option.[12]

The Vehicles of Jesuit Commerce

Whether in Brazil or in the eastern seas, Jesuits shipped their commodities primarily on commercial carriers, although they themselves owned outright or possessed shares in many different types of vessels. The college of Macao, for instance, possessed two junks in the 1630s and held shares in several other craft. In the 1740s, the *não S. Pedro e S. João* made several trips between Lisbon and the Far East. Its owners were the province of Japan, the vice-province of China, and a former governor of India's northern province.[13]

The dispersed character of Jesuit economic ventures in Brazil and the absence of effective overland communications made water transport essential. Jesuit sugar plantations, like those of secular owners, required various types of small vessels to transport chests of

9. Marcal Belliarte, "O q' gastei parte com os collegios, parte com pessoas de fora necessitados," in ARSI, *Bras.*, 3:II, 358^r–358^v.

10. Order of Mutio Vitelleschi, 6 May 1617, certified as authentic by Francisco de Rop, notary, Gante, 25 Apr. 1657, in ARSI, *Bras.*, 11:II, 321.

11. Francisco Ferreira to Vitelleschi, Antwerp, 26 Sept. 1636, in ARSI, *Lus.*, 74, 270–71.

12. Alvará of 2 June 1642, in ANTT, Chancelaria de D. João IV, 11, 310^r–310^v; consulta of 1 July 1675, in AHU/LR/47, fol. 412^v, per IHGB/MS, *lata* 29.

13. Souza, *Survival of Empire*, 113–14. The "Breve rezumo do estado ... ao prezente se acha esta procuratura da prov.ª de Jappão ... pello discurso do trenio ... [1677–80]," Macao, 20 Dec. 1680, in ARSI, *Goa*, 35, fols. 163^r–166^v, reports that the province possessed "uma barca grande de bom uzo" valued at 4,000 patacas but supplies no further details. In the late sixteenth century, the arts college of Coimbra possessed some kind of ship, but is uses and fate are unknown. The voyages of the *S. Pedro e S. João* are mentioned in ANTT/CJ/68, no. 40, and BA/JA/49-V-29, no. 43.

sugar to warehouses in the major ports.[14] During the seventeenth and eighteenth centuries, when Brazil's northern coastal ports were ill served by ships from the kingdom, the needs of Jesuit facilities there for provisions, livestock, slaves, implements, and the movement of personnel were satisfied by a smack whose purchase in the late 1670s provoked the ire of António Vieira, who contended that the craft was unreasonably expensive.[15]

Initially the crown underwrote the travel expenses of the provincial and his secretary during their triennial visitations of Jesuit installations along the littoral. By the 1590s, however, the Society's leaders had concluded that it would be more practical for the province to possess its own vessel that could sail whenever necessary. Accordingly, around 1592, it purchased two ships. One fell into the hands of English pirates the same year and was lost. Later in the decade, the sister ship, a sailing vessel, was replaced by an oared galley. Why and under what circumstances is uncertain; nor is it known what became of the galley.[16]

Sometime during the seventeenth century, the vessel widely called the *fragata do colégio* made its appearance. It was assigned to the college of Bahia but actually belonged to the province of Brazil. Although it initially accepted paying passengers, Aquaviva ruled that such service violated restrictions against commercial activity and ordered it to cease. Women were never permitted on board, but royal officials—governors and magistrates—frequently took passage on the frigate to their assignments. They also regularly utilized it to send dispatches to their colleagues.[17]

Despite the rendering of such services, royal officials often became suspicious of the activities of the frigate, which was immune to regular cargo searches and could sail whenever Jesuit administrators ordered it to do so rather than after clearing with port authorities. In fact, however, Jesuit leaders were always careful to notify senior royal officials of its sailing plans in case they wished to place cargo or passengers aboard the vessel. On at least one occasion a royal treasurer attempted to tax the frigate's cargo, prompting the provincial procurator to protest strongly against such a violation of the Society's long-established immunity to such levies. John V sustained the Jesuits' claim.[18] Nevertheless, some port officials in Brazil remained convinced that the frigate regularly carried illicit goods, a charge

14. Estêvão Pereira, "Dase rezão da fazenda que o collegio de Santo Antão tem no Brasil" (1635), in ANTT/CJ/13, no. 20, published in André João Antonil [Giovanni Antonio Andreoni], *Cultura e opulencia do Brasil por suas drogas e minas*, trans. and ed. Andrée Mansuy (Paris, 1965), 522–23; Pedro Teixeira to Simão Estivens, 19 Aug. 1731, in ANTT/CJ/68, no. 347. At one point, the college of Bahia possessed three small vessels to service its plantations and the timber facility at Camamú. *HCJB*, 5: 203.

15. Vieira to Fr. Pedro Luíz Gonsalvi, 1 Feb. 1679, in C. R. Boxer, "Quatro cartas inéditas do Padre António Vieira," *Brotéria* 45, 5 (Nov. 1947): 471. The procurator later defended his purchase: Pedro de Pedroso to Estevão Gandolfo (vice-rector), college of N. S. da Luz, 30 Dec. 1681, in ARSI, *Bras.*, 26, fol. 94.

16. At least one Jesuit college in India also owned an oared galley, called a *ballão*. HAG 2049, entry of 1 Oct. 1750.

17. On the origins of the frigate, see *HCJB*, 1: 169–71; and J. Manuel Espinosa, S.J., "Gouveia: Jesuit Lawgiver in Brazil," *Mid-America* 24 (Jan. 1942): 39. For references to its use by crown officers, see *DH*, 38: 397; 39: 82–83; 74: 242–45; 85: 41, 186, 197, 237, 249; and 86: 25, 87, 130. There are further mentions of the use of the frigates as dispatch boats in conde das Galveas (viceroy) to Henrique Luís Pereira Freyre, 20 Aug. 1740, 21 Jan. 1741, 28 Nov. 1743, 10 Aug. 1745, and 17 July 1747, in APB/CGVA/152, fols. 112^v, 127^v, 136^v, 149^v, 179^v, as well as Gomes Freire de Andrada (governor, Rio de Janeiro) to governor of Santos, 19 Feb. 1750, in ANRJ, col. 84/12/74^r–74^v. By the eighteenth century, the frigate was substantial in size and carried a crew of eighteen blacks. *DH*, 54: 197.

18. António de Brito de Menezes to king, Rio de Janeiro, 5 Mar. 1718, in ANRJ, col. 80/1/13^v; provisão of 16 Sept. 1718, in *DH*, 64: 50–52.

also maintained by a well-known ex-Jesuit student, José Basílio da Gama, author of the famous poem *O Uruguai* (1769), but that assertion was never effectively proven.[19]

The canoes, smacks, barks, frigates, galleys, and other vessels that the Society owned in various parts of the Assistancy were visible signs of its apparent commercial affluence. The Society was not, of course, the first religious Order to own commercial vessels. During the late twelfth century, for example, the Cistercian monastery of Les Dunes, situated 40 kilometers west of Bruges, possessed an entire fleet of ships, prompting the general chapter of that Order to condemn the house for engaging in commerce for profit.[20] Within the Spanish Assistancy the Paraguayan missions, like their counterparts in the Amazon, owned river craft to transport their surplus produce to market. But the only unit of that assistancy known to have a large seagoing craft was the province of Mexico, which, in the 1760s, owned a 54-ton vessel.[21] Certainly no unit of the Spanish Assistancy was as active in maritime trade as was the Japan province.

The Jesuits' Role in the Japan Trades

Persistent attacks by so-called Japanese pirates along the Chinese littoral prompted the Mings to sever commercial relations with the Japanese archipelago in 1557. That enabled Portuguese merchants, based in the fledgling town of Macao, to become intermediaries between Chinese suppliers of silk at the biennial Canton fair and Japanese consumers. The Lusitanians furnished raw stuff, white dross, piece goods, and striped cloths in exchange for Japanese silver, copper, and handicraft products.[22] The trade between Macao and Nagasaki from 1571 on proved exceedingly profitable to Portuguese merchants and to the interests they represented.

Scholars are not in agreement as to precisely when the Jesuits gained a share of the silk trade: Boxer and Cooper suggest the mid-1550s, whereas Kōichirō thinks it was "around 1570."[23] Certainly the Jesuits were engaged in some sort of trafficking with the islands

19. Overseas Council, consultas of 1 May and 25 June 1748, in AHU/LR/119, fols. 144^v and 164^v; king to Gomes Freire de Andrada, 25 June 1748, in ANRJ, cod. 60/16/195^v–196^v. Basílio da Gama, *O Uruguai*, Edição comemorativa do segundo centenário, ed. Afrânio Peixoto, Rodolfo Garcia, and Osvaldo Braga (Rio de Janeiro, 1952), 72–73. See, however, Luís Lisanti, ed., *Negocios coloniais*, 5 vols. (Rio de Janeiro, 1973), 4: 21, showing that the Jesuit frigate brought a shipment of salt to Santos for a contractor's agent. How common that practice was remains unknown.

20. R. W. Southern, *Western Society and the Church in the Middle Ages* (New York, 1970), 267.

21. Joseph P. Sánchez, *Spanish Bluecoats: The Catalonian Volunteers in Northwestern New Spain, 1767–1810* (Albuquerque, 1990), 14. Presumably other Spanish Jesuit provinces in South America also owned a number of deepwater craft, but Nicholas P. Cushner never mentions them in his oft-cited studies.

22. Much has been written about the silk trade between Japan and China during the sixteenth and seventeenth centuries. Particularly illuminating are C. R. Boxer, *The Great Ship from Amacon, 1555–1640* (Lisbon, 1963), now also in a Portuguese translation (Macao, 1989); Iwao Seiichi, "Japanese Foreign Trade in the 16th and 17th Centuries," *Acta Asiatica* 30 (1976): 1–18; Kato Eiichi, "The Japanese-Dutch Trade . . . Particularly . . . the Raw Silk Trade, 1620–1640," *Acta Asiatica* 30 (1976): 34–84; and the sources cited below.

23. Takase Kōichirō, "Unauthorized Commercial Activities by Jesuit Missionaries in Japan," *Acta Asiatica* 30 (1976): 19–33, at 20. There is a substantial literature on Jesuit involvement in the silk trade. Of particular note are *CCJ*, index, s.v. "silk and silk trade"; idem, "Missionaries and Merchants of Macao, 1557–1687," in *III Colóquio internacional de estudos luso-brasileiro* (Lisbon, 1960), 2: 210–24; J. L. Álvarez-Taladriz, "El uso y el abuso del contrato de pancada en Macao y Nagasaki (1583)," *Tenri daigaku gakuho* [Bulletin of Tenri University], no. 105 (Sept. 1976): 1–20. Both Michael Cooper, S.J., "The Mechanics of the Macao-Nagasaki

by the late 1560s, when General Francisco Borgia expressed concern about the means subordinates were employing to finance their activities there. The more promising those endeavors became, the more urgent appeared their need for financial security. Prior to 1574, the only assured source of funds was a mere 200,000 rs. that the king promised out of the Malacca customs, but even its collection proved to be illusive. Though the Japan mission had just acquired its first properties in India (see Chapter 15), their yield was still extremely modest. Faced with an alarming deficit in the running expenses of the mission, Alessandro Valignano, that astute and tireless supporter of the Japan enterprise, saw no recourse but to turn to Mammon. Accordingly, in 1578 he negotiated an agreement, subsequently ratified by royal authorities in Macao and Goa, with Macaonese merchants assuring the Society of as much as 100 *piculs* (60 kilograms each) of the fixed annual shipment of 1,600 piculs of silk sent to Japan.

After signing this agreement, Valignano discovered that shortly before his death, Mercurian had issued an order forbidding Jesuits to participate in the silk trade. Nevertheless, the Visitor defended his action on the ground of urgent necessity, but he reported that the mission was willing to forgo profits from the trade as soon as more edifying alternatives could be found. Aquaviva, Mercurian's successor, consulted with the ardently pro-Society Gregory XIII, who agreed to sanction the Jesuits' participation in the silk trade, despite the customary ban upon ecclesiastical trading, since he was persuaded that the Society's interest in the trade was purely charitable in intent. Although his successor, Sixtus V, mandated that the trade must cease, and both he and Philip II of Spain assured the Jesuits that they would find other means to defray the escalating expenses of the Japan enterprise,[24] neither the royal nor the pontifical subventions for that enterprise proved to be dependable sources of income (see Chapters 13 and 14). Accordingly, Valignano, while expressing distaste for the trade and willingness to comply with Rome's instructions, insisted that the only alternatives to adequate funding would be the curtailment or the abandonment of the Japan enterprise, something that neither Rome nor Madrid wanted.[25] By the end of 1587, the pope had removed his ban: the Jesuits' role in the silk trade was again declared to be an inconvenient necessity. And so it remained until about 1620.

Trade," *Monumenta Nipponica* 27, 4 (Winter 1972): 423–33, and J. L. Álvarez-Taladriz, "Un documento de 1610 sobre el contrato de armação de la não de trato entre Macao y Nagasaki," *Tenri Daigaku Gakuho* [Bulletin of Tenri University], no. 29 (July 1959): 1–20, publish the text of an important contemporary source, the 1610 report by Fr. Manoel Dias (Senior), who twice served as rector of the Jesuit college at Macao and later became superior of Jesuit residences in China and Visitor of the vice-province. See also Michael Cooper, S.J., *Rodrigues the Interpreter: An Early Jesuit in Japan and China* (New York, 1974), chap. 12; and Alessandro Valignano, S.J., *Sumario de las cosas de Japon (1583) [y] Adiciones del sumario de Japon (1592)*, ed. José Luis Álvarez-Taladriz, Monumenta Nipponica Monographs, no. 9 (Tokyo, 1954), esp. 40*–50*, 177*–178*, and 309–11. The most important unpublished Jesuit analysis of the Society's involvement in the trade is Luís da Gama to the general, 15 Dec. 1664, a report entitled "Papel sobre a mercancia que exercita a provincia de Japão," which summarizes all available documentation. I have not found the original. There is one complete copy in BA/JA/49-IV-56, no. 21, and three copies, which lack the final numbered paragraph, in ARSI, FG, 721/II/7.

   24. Aquaviva to Valignano, 24 Dec. 1585, in *DI*, 14: 151–52.
   25. Valignano to Aquaviva, Cochin, 20 Dec. 1586, and Valignano to Aquaviva, Goa, 20 Nov.–6 Dec. 1587, in *DI*, 14: 428–32 and 715–17.

Though much has been written about the Jesuits' resort to Mammon in this instance, several points concerning their role in Sino-Japanese commerce need to be clarified. First, the original agreement, which assured the province of the sale of up to 100 piculs of silk, was subsequently revised, reducing the Jesuits' share by 50 percent. Second, the great ships did not sail from Macao to Nagasaki as frequently as might be imagined. Between 1582 and 1620, fourteen ships (36.8 percent of those sailing) failed to reach their Japanese entrepôt or to discharge cargoes at their destinations because of maritime conflict or adverse weather.[26] Third, in addition to the deliberate destruction of the *Madre de Deus* in 1610 (see Chapter 6), which crippled both the Jesuits and their merchant collaborators, the Japan enterprise suffered a number of other costly losses at sea.[27] Fourth, the Society's earnings from the trade were far less than their rivals, notably Franciscan and Dominican friars, contended: instead of the 40 to 80 contos that the critics thought the Jesuits gained from the traffic, their actual profits were, according to Fr. Cooper, normally between 1.2 and 2 contos, "rarely more than that."[28] Fifth, the province's role in the silk trade did not eradicate its chronic debt problem.[29] Sixth, the Jesuits' participation in the trade was not only a continual source of embarrassment to the Society, but also a subject of repeated complaint to the crown by Macaonese merchants and others. In response, between 1607 and 1610, Madrid repeatedly ordered the Jesuits to stop their trading activities, only to have to revoke its prohibition in 1611 when it conceded that it could not, in fact, cover the Jesuits' expenses through increased subventions.[30] Seventh, what the Spanish crown could not do, the bafuku accomplished: as reported in Chapter 6, it expelled the Society of Jesus from the Japanese archipelago. Still, for the next half-dozen years at least, the Jesuits continued to trade with that market through cooperating merchants who secretly handled their goods.[31]

In addition to the official Jesuit silk trade described above, some Jesuits and some Jesuit houses in Japan also engaged in unauthorized, private trade with Macao. The scale of such activity is uncertain, though Japanese scholar Takase Kōichirō, relying upon statements by Jesuit critics and upon certain dubious inferences derived from their complaints, believes that its scale was substantial.[32] In 1583, for example, Francisco Cabral, subsequently Valignano's

26. Boxer, *Great Ship*, 43–100; Eiichi, "Japanese-Dutch Trade," table IV; and Souza, *Survival of Empire*, 55, table 4.2.

27. Notably in 1582, when a junk bound for Japan foundered near Macao with the loss of 3.2 contos; in 1585, when the não *S. Tiago* went down with a loss of 1.6 contos; and in 1586, when the outbound não *S. Felipe* wintered at Mozambique and set course for Europe rather than proceeding on to Goa but was captured by Drake with considerable losses to the Japan mission. Alessandro Valignano, "Sumario de todos os colegios e casas, residencias, e pesoas, rendas e gastos que tem a providencia da Companhia na India . . . 1586," in *MHJ*, 189–90; rpr. in *DI*, 14: 463–513, at 498.

28. Cf. Cooper, *Rodrigues*, 245–46; and "3º Catálogo da província de Japam . . . setembro de 1620," in *MHJ*, 869.

29. Cooper, *Rodrigues*, 241. See also Chapter 24 below.

30. Kōichirō, "Unauthorized Commercial Activities," 25–26. For the text of the royal order of 20 Feb. 1610 and its recision on 1 July 1611, see C. R. Boxer, "The Affair of the *Madre de Deus*: A Chapter in the History of the Portuguese in Japan," Japan Society, *Transactions and Proceedings* 26 (1928–29): 80–82.

31. "Titolo dos bens de raiz de Jappao," post-1616, in BA/JA/49-IV-66, no. 50; there are references to shipments to Japan in "Memorial das couzas da procuratora desta prov.ᵃ e o Padre M.ᵉl Barreto entregou, hindose pᵃ Japao' em agosto de 1616," in BA/JA/49-V-5, no. 79. For details showing precisely what the Jesuits shipped from Macao in 1618, see Boxer, *Great Ship*, 185–91. Significantly, income from the trade was no longer carried in the estimates of the procurate of the province in the last decades of the Japan enterprise.

32. The quotations that follow are from Kōichirō's "Unauthorized Commercial Activities."

opponent in Japan, wrote Aquaviva that he regarded such private trade, which he believed had begun about fifteen years earlier, as "reprehensible." Though it is true that in 1581 the Italian-born Visitor had prohibited such activity, it does not necessarily follow, as Kōichirō avers, that it was, in fact, continuing; nor does Aquaviva's directive of 1585, obviously drafted in response to Cabral's complaint of two years earlier, demonstrate the continuance of illegal trade. In fact, the Visitor himself repeatedly assured the general that the practice did *not* persist. Nevertheless, in 1605 another Jesuit, Diogo de Mesquita, wrote Aquaviva from Nagasaki asserting that "this type of trade is widely practiced . . . [and] is not only a breach of the vow of poverty but also injurious to our faith and to the good nature of the native brothers." But the fact that another Visitor, Francesco Pasio, condemned private trade in his instructions (*Obediencias*) of 1612 again does not necessarily demonstrate, as Kōichirō believes, its persistence, since it was common for inspectors to renew admonitions on subjects of special importance to the fathers general.

Though there is no convincing evidence that the scale of such private trade—seemingly unique to the Japan province—was substantial, another form of trade—the shipment of bullion from the archipelago to Macao—*did* become a matter of serious concern to Jesuit leaders. As Valignano explained in 1592,

> Daimyos want to have their silver sent to Macao through the padres . . . and to get it exchanged for raw silk or gold. In ordinary cases, they want only gold. The practice . . . was carried out at first on a small scale by [certain Christian daimyos]. . . . Later, as . . . [their] number increased, . . . [others] wanted to profit from this practice. When I visited Macao last year [1591], I was given permission by the municipality . . . to send up to 6,000 ducats of silver to Macao to exchange . . . for gold. But this . . . is not sufficient to meet even half the demand for gold by the daimyos . . . and I am afraid that it will increase day by day.[33]

Evidently it did so. Jesuits found themselves in the uncomfortable position of posing as bullion brokers in order to retain the loyalty of Christian daimyos and to protect their converts from the hostility of avaricious non-Christian lords.[34] Even so, some fathers, like procurator Carlo Spinola, a future Nagasaki martyr, were scandalized. As Spinola wrote the general in 1613, "It is indeed true that we have been investing silver in behalf of laymen, and that they in turn have been investing our silver. The padres are engaged in this type of trade so that they can arbitrarily spend the money . . . disregarding the procurator as if it were game they killed with their own spear . . . extravagance. The padres came to be immersed in moneymaking."[35]

Spinola's concern was shared by Fr. Nicolão da Costa, who wrote the assistant that "a considerable sum of money owned by laymen has been remitted to Macao through the Society. Since such acts ruin the commercial interest of Macao, there is a strict embargo laid on them, and those who violate it are subject to excommunication. A certain Japanese brother told me that [the] Provincial gave him permission to remit [800,000 rs.] belonging to some Japanese laymen."

33. As quoted by Seiichi, "Japanese Foreign Trade," 6.
34. Boxer, "Missionaries and Merchants," 212–13.
35. Quoted in Kōichirō, "Unauthorized Commercial Activities," 26 and 32, which is also the source for the remaining quotations in this section.

What the general thought about that practice is unknown, but one may readily infer that he was shocked by such a report. In another instance of bullion-dealing, he reproved Valignano for secretly sending some gold from Macao to India for investment.[36]

Portuguese civilians and the missionaries gained entry into the Japan trade at a time when the islands' demand for raw and processed silk was rapidly expanding. According to Iwao Seiichi, it doubled or trebled between the later sixteenth and early seventeenth centuries, but the Portuguese share remained fixed at 1,600 piculs per annum. In fact, even before the Jesuits were expelled in 1614, the Portuguese were no longer the dominant suppliers, for Japanese licensed (red-seal) ships were going to south Asian and Philippine ports for silk and other commodities; Chinese and Dutch ships were arriving in Japanese ports in increasing numbers; and even the Spaniards based in Manila were attempting to compete for the lucrative Japanese market. As a result, in 1612, the Portuguese sent only 1,300 quintals of raw silk to Japan, while their competitors supplied another 5,000. Unquestionably that competition, encouraged by the bafuku, intensified during subsequent decades. In 1635 the shogunate prohibited Japanese nationals from traveling overseas; four years later it permanently excluded the Portuguese from the archipelago. But the role of Portuguese seculars and of the Jesuits in the economy of Japan had been doomed to extinction long before.[37]

The Macaonese Hub

The expulsion of the Jesuits from Japan and their exclusion from the silk and bullion markets of that archipelago transformed Macao, hitherto but a way station, into the economic hub of the Society's enterprises within the expanding vice-province of China and the restructured province of Japan. Because of the persistence of maritime warfare in Eastern seas throughout the seventeenth century, receipt of both imperial and papal stipends remained problematic, and the same was often true of revenues from the Indian temporalities. As the English adventurer Peter Mundy observed, Jesuit leadership in Macao relied upon "trade in shipping, goodes and building [that is, urban real estate], alleadging the Necessity off itt, As the great Charge they are att in sending their brethren to sundry parts where they have residences, with their Maynetenaunce, etts. there, As upp to Panquinj [Peking] . . . [and] likewise to sundry other places."[38]

The sea was vital to the survival of Jesuit enterprises in the Far East. As Visitor Luís da Gama wrote in 1664, "The wealth of Macao depends upon the sea and the entire City lives off it. There are no more reliable sources of wealth than what the winds and tides bring. If they fail, all else fails. There is no other way for this Province to sustain its missions."[39]

---

36. *CCJ*, 119–20. It is not clear why Boxer insists that the shipment was "not only a crime but a blunder," for, as will be seen below, procurators in Macao followed the custom of sending bullion and gems to Europe on other occasions without suffering reprimand.

37. The foregoing is based partly on C. R. Boxer, "The Rise and Fall of Nicholas Iquan," *T'ien Hsia Monthly* 11, 5 (Apr.–May 1941): 429–34, but primarily upon Seiichi, "Japanese Foreign Trade."

38. *The Travels of Peter Mundy, in Europe and Asia, 1608–1667*, ed. Sir Richard Carnac Temple and L. Anstey, *HS*:2, no. 45 (1919), 292–93. Mundy's observations were recorded in December 1637.

39. Gama to the general, 15 Dec. 1664, par. 30, cited in note 23.

Either independently or, more commonly, in partnership with cooperating Macaonese merchants, the Jesuits traded with the Lesser Sunda Islands, the two Vietnams, and Siam. In the first named, including the islands of Timor, Solor, and the Larantuca Peninsula of the island of Flores, the Portuguese obtained three species of sandalwood, an aromatic wood that one chronicler likened in smell to a combination of cloves and cinnamon. The white and yellow species were widely used in India as ointments to perfume the body, whereas the red served as a medicinal to cure fevers and to desalinate water. India was the primary market for white and yellow sandalwood, but China took most of the red. In fact, China annually purchased up to 4,000 piculs, a third of the shipments from the islands. Profits are said to have ranged between 100 and 200 percent.[40] Fragmentary reports indicate that the Japan province gained 410,400 rs. in 1668–69, proceeds from the sale of over 40 piculs of sandalwood in 1665, and another 900,000 rs. in 1680.[41]

Sandalwood was only one of many commodities that Macao-based Jesuits traded throughout Southeast Asia and parts of the Indonesian archipelago. Others included ivory, rice, pepper, salt, tin, lead, quicksilver, sulphur, seed pearls, strands of coral, and amber, as well as birds' nests and "fish wings." In addition, the warehouse of the Jesuit college in Macao and those of merchants who provided the fathers with storage facilities contained quantities of silk, cotton, and woolen cloth; assortments of mirrors and brass bells; lace towels and fine handkerchiefs, soaps, silver platters, wine cups, and candle holders.[42]

The role of Macao as an investor in sea loans will be considered in Chapter 22. Though the income from trading and such investments defrayed part of the maintenance and evangelical expenses of the Society in the Far East, the procurators used other means to cover the expenses of Jesuit procurators sent to Europe to attend meetings in Rome, to raise funds for the missions, and to recruit additional members for the Far Eastern enterprises. In 1636, for example, when Fr. Alvaro Semedo went on such a mission, the procurator in Macao provided him with 1,796,100 rs. in the form of seed pearls, diamonds, and a small quantity of musk, as well as 285,000 rs. in cash, all of which Semedo handed to the missions' procurator in Lisbon to serve as a credit against which he could draw for his expenses.[43]

40. Humberto Leitão, *Os portugueses em Solor e Timor de 1515 a 1702* (Lisbon, 1948), chap. 17; Artur Teodoro de Matos, *Timor portugués, 1515–1769* (Lisbon, 1974), 163, 183, 202, 341, 347; C. R. Boxer, *Fidalgos in the Far East, 1550–1770* (1948; rpr., New York, 1968), chap. 11; Souza, *Survival of Empire*, 109. John Villiers, "As derradeiras do mundo: The Dominican Missions and the Sandalwood Trade in the Lesser Sunda Islands in the Sixteenth and Seventeenth Centuries," *II Seminário internacional de história indo-portuguesa*, ed. Luís de Albuquerque and Inácio Guerreiro (Lisbon, 1985), 573–600, provides the fullest summary of the inescapably sketchy history of the trade, but see also Roderich Ptak, "The Transportation of Sandalwood from Timor to China and Macao, c. 1350–1600," in *Portuguese Asia: Aspects in History and Economic History (Sixteenth and Seventeenth Centuries)*, ed. Roderich Ptak (Stuttgart, 1987), 87–110.

41. "Receita [e despeza] do cabedal da prov.ª de Japão," late May 1668–late May 1669, in ARSI, *JapSin*, 23, fol. 152; "Breve rezumo do estado . . . se acha esta procuratura da prov.ª de Jappão," Macao, 20 Dec. 1680, in ARSI, *Goa*, 35, fols. 163ʳ–166ᵛ.

42. In addition to the sources cited in note 41, this description is based upon "Memorial das couzas da procuratura desta prov.ª e o padre M.ᵉˡ Barreto entregou, hindose p.a Japao'," Aug. 1616, in BA/JA/49-V-5, no. 79; and "1667: Carregação que Deos salve feita p. my' João do Parado pera Tonkin nesta monção . . . pera a entregar a ordem do P.e Philippe Maximo da Comp.ª de JESUS," in ARSI, *JapSin*, 23.

43. "Informe do irmão Manuel de Figueiredo . . . sobre as contas que tem entre si a provincia de Japam e vice provincia da China desde viagem que fez a Roma o P.ᵉ Alvaro Semedo," post-1642, in BA/JA/49-V-11, nos. 79 and 80.

Since the vice-province of China lacked income-earning property in Europe comparable to the Japan province's invaluable Carcavelos estate (Chapter 15), its administrators were always seeking ingenious ways to defray its European expenses. In 1642, for example, the Visitor of Japan and China directed that a box consisting of 202 pieces of colored taffeta and 39 pieces of damask and satin be sent to Lisbon via Holland to cover the vice-province's expenses. Twenty years later, when Fr. Diogo Fabro was named the vice-province's procurator to Rome, the house procurator in Macao gave him an assortment of cloth and silver amounting to 459,520 rs. to take to Lisbon to defray his expenses.[44] But when the Sicilian Prospero Intorcetta was selected as the next procurator to Rome, Luís Lobo, the Visitor, faced a difficult problem: because of the persecution in China (see Chapter 6), Intorcetta was one of those confined under house arrest in Canton. By a ruse, Lobo smuggled in another father to replace him, and the Sicilian was spirited out of the imperial city and brought to Macao, from which he obtained passage to Goa. When he left there for Lisbon, he took with him a manifest that covered the mixed cargo that accompanied him. It included silver coin, sandalwood, cloth, lead, pepper, tin, incense, rhinoceros horns, and scarlet dye.[45]

As was true of the Jesuits' commercial activities in Japan, their participation in the various branches of Macao's trade exposed them to vigorous criticism. Early in the seventeenth century, for example, a Dominican friar from the Philippines condemned the existence of a Jesuit warehouse adjacent to the Macao college and contended that the fathers "live in great style, one priest having been known to go about in his litter accompanied by sixty horsemen." There is, however, no independent evidence to sustain such an allegation. Later in the century another Dominican, the formidable Domingo Navarrete, a onetime companion of Intorcetta in Canton, labeled the Jesuit college in Macao as "a house of trade and warehouse of merchandise."[46]

One must take such Dominican allegations with more than a few grains of salt. After all, one of their own friars based in Larantuca boasted in the 1650s that he had earned more than 14 contos during his sojourn there. Nearly twenty years later, the Abbé Carré encountered another Dominican on Kharg Island in the Persian Gulf who informed him that he had lived 22 years in China and that he was en route back to Europe with 60,000 *écus* in precious stones. Most remarkable of all was Fr. Pedro da Trindade, a Dominican,

44. "Entrega q. ao P.ᵉ Gon.ˢᵒ da Fon.ᶜᵃ, procurador da vice prov.ⁱᵃ da China ao P.ᵉ Diogo Fabro, procurador eleito a Roma," Macao, 18 Dec. 1661, in ARSI, FG, 722/16. See also note 43 above.

45. Luís Lobo, "Catalogo dos P.ᵉˢ e Irmãos da V. prov.ᵃ da China," Macao, 10 Dec. 1688, in ARSI, *JapSin*, 134, fol. 353ʳ; "Entrega que faz o Irmão Manoel dos Reys, procurador da v. prov.ᵃ da China, ao P.ᵉ Prospero Intorcetta, proc. eleito a Roma," Macao, 10 Dec. 1668, in ARSI, FG, 722/16.

The procurators of China were not the only ones who had difficulty covering their European bills. So, too, did those who served Paraguay. On one occasion during the eighteenth century, the Paraguayan procurator sent silver from Buenos Aires via the Portuguese outpost of Colônia do Sacramento to Rio de Janeiro, where agents of the Portuguese Macao Company exchanged it for 30,000 *pesos fuertes*. The rector of the Carioca college dispatched that money to Fr. Manuel Campos, a mathematician and confessor of one of the sons of John V, whom the Paraguayans called "nuestro amigo de Lisboa." Their "friend" arranged to have the funds sent across the Spanish border in a box dispatched to the prince of Asturias! Magnus Morner, "Un procurador Jesuita del Paraguay ante la corte de Felipe V," *Historiografia y bibliografia americanista* 15, 3 (1971): 367–443.

46. Boxer, *Fidalgos*, 170.

a vicar, and captain-major of Zumbo, Mozambique (1726–51), who amassed a personal estate amounting to some 30 contos, or roughly three times the annual income of the vice-province of China at that time.[47] Nevertheless, the Jesuits were vulnerable to those who found it convenient to attribute their own difficulties to the fathers. Thus in 1669 the cámara of Macao, faced with economic reverses because of the recent disturbances within the Chinese empire and the continued aggressive trade warfare of the Dutch in southeast Asia, lamented that "as long as the Company [of Jesus] was inspired by the zeal of Saint Ignatius, it was the true Company, but now that this has expired and it is solely occupied with merchandising, commerce and trade, it is no longer the [same] Company."[48] Interestingly enough, the Portuguese viceroy of India was reaching the same conclusion at precisely this time.

The Alleged Jesuit Commercial Hegemony in India

The Jesuits had long possessed the reputation of being sharp dealers in the subcontinent. In the 1590s, the former secretary of the archbishop of Goa, Dutch-born Jan Huyghen van Linschoten, asserted that "the Jesuits are so cunning in trade, they traffic in bills of exchange and such-like, that they surpass all the secular merchants, so that in all India there is no place where there is something to be gained but they have a hand in it, so that the other orders and religious bodies and also the ordinary people are starting to murmur greatly about it, and to loathe their avarice and closeness."[49]

Such murmuring continued until the very end of the Jesuits' presence in India. In the 1660s, for example, the combative viceroy, António de Melo de Castro, contended that though Jesuits serving in Spain and Portugal were true members of their religion, those working in India were "the Fathers of the Dutch East India Company," meaning, one supposes, that, like the Dutch, they were preoccupied with Mammon.[50] Twenty years later, an anonymous group of Jesuit critics conveyed the same message to Giovanni Paolo Oliva. They charged that the fathers were neglecting their vows by their relentless acquisition of properties, their monopolistic pharmaceutical enterprises, and their involvement in "infernal trade so prejudicial to the service of God and to the increase of the Faith." When the troubled general forwarded the message to the provincial for his response, the

47. C. R. Boxer, *Portuguese India in the Mid-Seventeenth Century* (Delhi, 1980), 46; see also *The Travels of the Abbé Carré in India and the Near East, 1672 to 1674*, trans. Lady Fawcett, ed. Sir Charles Fawcett and Sir Richard Burn, 3 vols., *HS*:2, no. 95 (1947): 93. In truth it does not follow, as J. S. Cummins assumes (*The Travels and Controversies of Friar Domingo Navarrete, 1618–1686*, *HS*:2, no. 119 [1962]: 254 n. 1), that the friar on Kharg Island was necessarily a jewel smuggler. He may simply have been a courier. For the intriguing case of Fr. Trindade, see S. I. Gorerazvo Mudenge, "The Dominicans at Zumbo: An Aspect of Missionary History in the Zambezi Valley, c. 1726–1836," *Mohlomi, Journal of Southern African Historical Studies* 1 (1976): 32–63, esp. 35–37. (I am indebted to the author for a reprint.)

48. Quoted in Boxer, *Fidalgos*, 170.

49. As quoted in M. A. P. Meilink-Roelofsz, *Asian Trade and European Influence in the Indonesian Archipelago Between 1500 and About 1630* (The Hague, 1962), 130–31.

50. Pedro de Azevedo, "A Inquisição de Goa contra o vicerei Mello de Castro," *Revista de história* 1, 2 (Lisbon, 1912): 175–79.

provincial dismissed the complaints as being entirely without foundation; but that did not silence the Society's foes.[51]

As time passed and the political and economic postures of the Portuguese in India continued to spiral downward, it became all too easy to blame the falloff in trade on the actions of the Jesuits. The English representative to Lisbon who reported in 1753 that "the Jesuits who are the ablest men here and have great power have almost monopolized the country trade in India and from Goa to this city" was doing no more than repeating what some well-placed person in the government of José I had told him. Twenty years later, the preface of the new customs regulations issued to Goan authorities lamented the decadence of that port's trade, explicable, the author contended, by Jesuit "greed" and success in usurping both the internal and the external trade of Portuguese enclaves in the subcontinent.[52]

There is no convincing evidence to support such allegations. However, it is true that the Jesuits had long been vulnerable to criticism because of their participation in certain lines of commerce. The sending of small commodity gifts to friends in Europe persisted, despite Aquaviva's firm opposition to the practice.[53] Upon occasion, the province of Goa also dispatched quantities of Indian products to Europe to settle its obligations. Thus, in 1638, the provincial reported that in order to reduce the province's debt (3.9 contos), he had directed his procurator to dispatch a quantity of unspecified "drugs" to Lisbon. In the 1680s another provincial admitted that occasionally Carcavelos estate wines, the property of the Japan province, were sold in India, and he acknowledged the persistence of complaints about certain "gifts" being sent by sympathetic fathers in India to their always precariously financed colleagues in Mozambique.[54]

Jesuits in India were widely believed to be intimately involved in trade in precious jewels, and it cannot be denied that they became intimately familiar with the gem trades. In 1586 Alessandro Valignano reported to Aquaviva with some embarrassment that he had discharged a commission from Cardinal Tolomeo Galli, papal secretary of state, who asked him to purchase 40 "perfect" pearls from Ormuz, each weighing 3.5 carats, as well as six diamonds (2 carats each), and a half-dozen rubies. He suggested that in the future it would be cheaper (less troublesome?) to buy such items in Lisbon.[55]

The Jesuits' evangelical activities along the Fishery Coast, one of the three major centers of the production of pearls in the East, inevitably brought them into conflict with the local Portuguese captain, a crony of the viceroys, and with the naique of the ancient religious city of Madura.[56] Both were accustomed to exacting as personal tribute a share of the pearls that

51. Simão Martins to Oliva, Goa, 28 July 1683, in reply to Anon., "Cousas que se notaram nos religiosos da Companhia que vivem na India & principalmente na provincia de Goa" (1682), in ARSI, *Goa*, 35, fols. 252–57, 247^r–248^v.

52. Geo[rge] Crowe to C. Amyand, Lisbon, 12 Jan. 1753, in PRO/SP89/49, fols. 87–87^v; "Regimento da alfandega de Goa," Lisbon, 1774, in BNL, cod. 10758.

53. "Memorial of Fr. Francisco de Monclaro . . . procurator, with the answers of Fr. Claudio Aquaviva" [Rome, Aug. 1590], in *DI*, 15: 56.

54. Emanuel de Almeida to Vitelleschi, Goa, 12 Sept. 1638, in ARSI, *Goa*, 22, fols. 136–37; "Ordens perpetuas que deixou o P.^{e} provincial Simão Martins em cada hu' dos collegios do norte e residencia de Bandorá . . . 1683," par. 22, in ibid., 35, fol. 243^v.

55. Valignano to Aquaviva, Cochin, 23 Dec. 1586 and 20 Nov. 1587, in *DI*, 14: 521–27 and 713–14.

56. The best quality pearls were said to come from the Persian Gulf, but those found in the Palk Strait were considered superior to pearls obtained from China and other parts of the East. *The Voyage of John*

local fishermen harvested. The fathers, too, received as alms a portion of what Alexander of Rhodes called "these beautiful heavenly tears," though there is no indication that their income from that source was particularly significant.[57]

It might have become so had a mysterious partnership between Jesuits on the coast and certain Goan merchants persisted. Around 1590 the merchants, whose identities are unknown, apparently gave substantial funds to a missionary departing the capital for the coast. He was to purchase 3.6 contos' worth of seed pearls, and the merchants and the Chorão novitiate were to divide the profits. Though the scheme won the approval of the provincial, his successor, Francisco Cabral, was strongly opposed to it because of the possible scandal of missionaries serving as factors for gem buyers.[58]

The extent to which Jesuits continued to acquire pearls along that littoral is unclear. During the early 1630s, the count of Linhares, well known for his battles with the Jesuits during his viceregency (1629–35) and, like many in his position, himself a diligent collector of precious gems, accused the fathers of dominating the pearl trade there, but he did no more than repeat gossip.[59]

But such gossip persisted. One of its most egregious diseminators was Nicolao Manucci, an Italian mercenary and sometime fraudulent medical practitioner at the Mughal court. According to Manucci, in the mid-1650s a favorite of the Muslim king of Bijapur and keeper of the royal jewels came to Goa for medical treatment. To defray his expenses, he supposedly borrowed the enormous sum of 20,000 *xerafins* (6 contos) from Fr. Gonsalo Martins, whom Manucci describes as "known widely as a great money-dealer." When the treasurer recovered and sought to redeem the gem he had used as collateral for the loan, the Jesuit allegedly denied knowledge of its existence. Subsequently the king of Bijapur sent secret agents, posing as jewel merchants, to Goa, and they reported that Fr. Martins had willingly showed them the stone and demanded a high price for it. When the king's efforts to persuade the Jesuits to surrender the gem failed, he lured several of them, including the culprit, to his interior kingdom, where they were kidnapped and Fr. Martins was severely flogged. According to Manucci, the now-exposed malefactors beseeched their superiors— the presumed custodians of the stone—to the return it, but their efforts, and those of the Portuguese viceroy, were unavailing. At that point, says Manucci, the king dispatched an army into Goa, laying waste to Salsete and Bardês. In response, the viceroy besieged an unspecified Jesuit college and threatened to bombard it with artillery unless the fathers

Huyghen van Linschoten to the East Indies, ed. Arthur Coke Burnell and P. A. Tiele, *HS*:1, no. 71 (1884): 143 and 239; *The Travels of Pedro Teixeira*, trans. and ed. William F. Sinclair and Donald Ferguson, *HS*:2, no. 9 (1902): 175–79.

57. Solange Hertz, trans., *Rhodes of Viet Nam: The Travels and Missions of Father Alexander de Rhodes in China and Other Kingdoms of the Orient* (Westminster, Md., 1966), 19.

58. Cabral to Aquaviva, 15 Dec. 1593, in *DI*, 16: 534. The provincial's views were influenced by two adverse field reports: Francisco Durão to Aquaviva, Fishery Coast, 6 Dec. 1592; and Nuno Rodrigues (superior, Fishery Coast) to Aquaviva, 20 Dec. 1592; in *DI*, 16: 21–22 and 33.

59. Linhares to king, 24 Sept. and 17 Dec. 1631, in Simão José Luz Soriano, *História do reinado de el-rei d. José e da administração do marqués de Pombal*, 2 vols. (Lisbon, 1867), 2: 350–57. Council of Portugal to king, 16 Mar. and 26 Dec. 1636, in BGUC, cod. 459, fols. 184^r–184^v and 201^r–202^v; the former is published under the date of 16 Mar. 1636 in *BFUP*, 5: 89–90. For Linhares's subsequent lavish gifts of diamonds to members of the Spanish court, see Sebastian Gonzalez to Fr. Rafael Pereyra, Madrid, 16 Feb. 1637, in *MHE*, 14: 41–45.

surrendered the stone.[60] It is a good story, but unfortunately there is no evidence in the archives of Goa, Lisbon, or Rome that corroborates Manucci's tale, one of many in his account that makes fascinating reading but must be taken with so many grains of salt.

The same seems to be true of another unverifiable yarn, this one told by a French gem dealer, Jean Baptiste Tavernier, who claims that the Jesuits in India "did a large trade in rough diamonds which they sent to Europe," usually via the caravan route, in which Jesuit messengers traveled in disguise. According to Tavernier, on one occasion Jesuits returning with diamonds from Golconda were seized by agents of the Dutch governor of the Vengurla factory in Goa and were forced to surrender their ill-gotten wealth.[61]

Once again, there is no confirmation of the Frenchman's account, although there *is* evidence that the Jesuits, like other prominent Portuguese in India, did participate in the diamond trade, both on their own account and in behalf of others. In 1681, for example, Fernão de Queiróz, well known as an author and an administrator in India, advised the assistant general that he had remitted 240,000 rs. in diamonds to Lisbon in order to defray the cost of the publication of one of his books and that the stones had been sold for a profit of 100 percent. Viceroys themselves were keen for diamonds. Tavernier reports that "there never was a Viceroy of Goa half so rich as Dom Philippe Mascarenhas [1645–51]. He possessed a quantity of diamonds—all stones of great weight, from 10 to 40 carats. . . . One . . . was a thick stone weighing 57 and the other 67.5 carats, both being fairly clear, of good water, and Indian cut." More than a century later, a waste book belonging to the provincial procurator of Goa records the receipt of three sacks of money from the viceroy, the marquis of Alorna (1744–50), for whom the Jesuits purchased diamonds worth over 4 contos, a transaction that was illegal; a royal edict of 1721 expressly prohibited all higher officials in India from engaging in the gem trades, directly or otherwise.[62]

The Jesuits of Goa also became famous (or infamous) for their production of another kind of stone, variously called Goa stones, snake stones, Bezoar stones, and *pedras cordais*, sometimes corrupted as *Pedro Cordeiro*! Bezoar stones, derived from a concretion formed within the stomach of wild goats found in Iran, Afghanistan, and elsewhere in the East, are said to have varied from the size of a pea to that of a fist, and to be greenish (or greyish) in color, odorless, and tasteless. The true Goa stone, developed by Gaspar António, a seventeenth-century Florentine Jesuit brother who served for many decades in the pharmacy in Goa, consisted of a blending of white and red coral with Bezoar stones. Scrapings were mixed in water with sugar and were considered remedies for the plague and various kinds of fever but, in fact, possessed no therapeutic value. There is no support for the well-known statement of John Fryer that the sale of such a concoction yielded the pharmacy an annual income of 50,000 xerafins.[63] Nor is there any merit to the contention of frustrated Portuguese laymen

60. Manucci, *Storia do Mogor or Mogul India*, trans. and ed. William Irvine, 4 vols. (London, 1906–8), 3: 166–68.

61. Jean Baptiste Tavernier, *Travels in India*, trans. and ed. V. Ball, 2 vols. (London, 1889), 2: 304.

62. Queiróz to Francisco de Almeida, Goa, 15 Dec. 1681, in ARSI, *Goa*, fols. 223–24ᵛ; Tavernier, *Travels*, 1: 182; HAG 2481, fol. 293ʳ; the terms of the alvará of 27 Mar. 1721 were reported by Henry Worsley to Viscount Townshend, 12 Apr. 1721, in PRO/SP89/29, fol. 53ᵛ, and the text was offered for sale by Richard C. Ramer, *Special List*, no. 121 (Nov. 1986), item 31.

63. *HJ*, 90–91; I. H. Burkhill, *A Dictionary of the Economic Products of the Malay Peninsula*, 2 vols. (London, 1935), 1: 321–23; John Fryer, *A New Account of East India and Persia, Being Nine Years' Travels, 1672–1681*, HS:2,

that the Jesuits succeeded in dominating the trade of the Portuguese enclaves in India. As the foregoing demonstrates, they were interested in marketing various commodities, but on an exceedingly modest scale. The story of their hegemony of the subcontinent's commerce is simply a fable, but it is not the only one related to their trading endeavors.

Jesuit Involvement in the African Slave Trade

On Christmas Eve 1978, C. R. Boxer gave an interview in Bombay in which he assured a reporter from the *Times of India* that "the Jesuits were involved in commerce of every form ... including the slave trade.... [They] made a lot of money out of the slave trade." Boxer's contention finds support in the writings of two well-known Africanists, James Duffy and Gerald Bender. Both assure their readers that the Jesuits were "active" in the trade and even possessed ships that specialized in taking the chattels to Brazil.[64] Regrettably, none of these scholars cites contemporary sources to support his position.

There *is*, of course, evidence in the Jesuit archives that affirms Jesuit interest in participating in the slave trade. Francisco Rodrigues, whose multivolume history of the Jesuits in the Portuguese Assistancy is frequently cited in these pages, candidly summarizes some of that documentation. As he observes, by the last quarter of the sixteenth century, the slave trade in Angola was already becoming a large-scale business. Even before the Jesuits possessed a college there, they received hundreds of slaves as gifts from village chieftains (*sobas*).[65] Could they legitimately ship such chattels to Brazil, where the cane-sugar industry was flourishing, to defray their expenses in the African colony? In the early 1590s Pero Rodrigues, a Visitor to both Brazil and Angola, consulted leading Jesuits in both colonies concerning precisely that question. He reported to Aquaviva that since slaves in Angola were considered as much media of exchange as were gold and silver in Europe or sugar in Brazil, it would not be a scandal for the Jesuits to engage in the trade. He observed that they received far more slaves than they required for their services in Luanda and that although they could sell the excess there, it would be far more profitable to send them to Brazil, where they would yield two to two-and-a-half times as much as in Angola. So much for the contention that the Jesuits were never interested in pure profits![66] Undisturbed by the

no. 20 (1912): 11–12; J. Gerson da Cunha, *Origin of Bombay*, *JBBRAS*, extra ser. (1904): 286–87. See also Fr. André Fernandes to Fr. Pedro da Fonseca, Cochin, 16 Jan. 1563, in António da Silva Rego and E. E. Burke, eds., *Documentos de Moçambique* (Lisbon, 1975), 8: 131; Victor von Klarwill, ed., *The Fugger Newsletters* (New York, 1925), 46; Girolamo Franchi di Conestaggio, *The History of the Uniting of the Kingdom of Portugall to ... Castille* [1585], Eng. trans. (London, 1600), 109; and *The Itinerário of Jerónimo Lobo*, trans. Donald M. Lockhart, ed. C. F. Beckingham, *HS*:2, no. 162 (1984): 4–5.

64. James Duffy, *Portugal in Africa* (Baltimore, 1963), 43, 54, and 61; Gerald Bender, *Angola Under the Portuguese: The Myth and the Reality* (Berkeley, 1978), 62 n. 9. On an earlier occasion, Boxer wrote that "the ecclesiastical establishments in São Tomé, Congo, and Angola were maintained almost entirely from the profits of the slave-trade" (*Race Relations in the Portuguese Colonial Empire, 1415–1825* [Oxford, 1963], 9), but he supplied no proof to support his conviction.

65. In 1594 the Luanda Jesuits reported that they possessed 152 slaves: 62 married, 34 bachelors, and the remainder children or persons of advanced years. "Rol do movel das casas da residencia de Angola no año [1594]," in ARSI, FG, 1361/6.

66. Cf. *HCJAP*, 3:2, 319 n. 1, where Fr. Rodrigues attempts to convince his readers that Jesuit sales of slaves to Brazil were not intended for commercial purposes but were simply for housekeeping purposes and were, therefore, "perfectly legal."

implications of his statement, the Visitor argued that such sales would enable the fathers to finance a much-desired college in Luanda. However, Jerónimo Cardoso, procurator for the Indies in Lisbon, strongly opposed the Visitor's views, and about 1604 Aquaviva himself prohibited Jesuit involvement in the trade, much to the annoyance of the fathers in Angola. According to Rodrigues, that ended Jesuit efforts to gain a small share in the slave trade.[67]

There are, however, some indications that Jesuits did dispatch some slaves from Portugal's African enclaves to other parts of the empire (and beyond). In 1621, for example, an agent of the province of Japan reported that a Fr. Wenceslau Pantaleon came to Goa from Mozambique with "some *peças*" (prime slaves) to sell to the Mughals in order to purchase supplies required by the Zambesi missions. In 1707 the rector of the college of New St. Paul's, Goa, advised his successor that the institution had on deposit in Mozambique just over 119 xerafins (35,700 rs.), an amount that appears to have been sufficient to purchase five slaves, presumably for service in the college.[68] Though there is no documentary foundation for the claims of Bender and Duffy that the Jesuits ran a fleet of slave ships between Angola and points west, there are suggestions that the Jesuits sometimes exported (or were asked to ship) a few slaves from Luanda. One intriguing document, a memorandum of understanding between the assistants general for Portugal and Spain prepared in 1646 during the strained Restoration period, authorizes money transfers between those two officials to settle accounts between Luanda and the colleges of Cartagena (present-day Colombia) and Veracruz (Mexico). It is difficult to conceive of shipments other than slaves from the Portuguese colony to those Spanish colleges. Thirteen years later, the rector of Santo Antão advised the general that because slave prices in Angola were excessively high, he was sending olive oil, wheat, and wine to Angola with instructions to the procurator of Luanda to dispatch two slaves on each Bahia-bound *tumbeiro* (slave ship) to meet the labor demands of the college's Bahian estates. Toward the end of the seventeenth century, the governor of Angola reported that it was the custom of the Jesuits in the colony to send incorrigible slaves from their arimos to Brazil, thereby emulating the crown's practice of dispatching undesirables from the kingdom to various parts of the empire.[69] Despite such occasional shipments, it appears that in Brazil, where, as reported in Chapter 20, the Jesuits became the colony's largest institutional

67. The key document is Pero Rodrigues to Aquaviva, "Apontamentos sobre a fundação de hum collegio no reino de Angola," Luanda, 15 June 1593, in ARSI, *Lus.*, 79, fols. 61–63ᵛ. See also *HCJAP*, 2:2, 557–64. Jerónimo Cardoso (procurator) to Aquaviva, Lisbon, 6 Sept. 1586, in *DI*, 14: 335–36. In 1609 the Luanda Jesuits again appealed either for authorization to participate in the slave trade or, alternatively, for their withdrawal from Angola. M.ᵉˡ Pereyra (governor) to king, Luanda, 14 May 1609, in ARSI, *Lus.*, 74, fol. 113 (copy). Neither sanction was forthcoming.

68. Manoel Coelho to Vitelleschi, 12 Dec. 1621, in ARSI, *Goa*, 18, fols. 54ʳ–55ᵛ; "Entrega q. faz o P.ᵉ Reytor Manoel Sarayva a seu successor, o P.ᵉ António de Payva, deste coll.º de S. São Paulo . . . ao derrad.ʳᵒ de novembro de 1707," in ARSI, *Goa*, 9:2, fols. 400–404ᵛ. For the approximate value of Mozambique slaves at this time, see William Francis Rea, S.J., *The Economics of the Zambezi Missions, 1580–1759* (Rome, 1976), 85 n. 166.

69. Anon., memorandum, Rome, 13 June 1646, in ARSI, *Lus.*, 79, fol. 91; Fr. Felippe Franco to Fr. Antão G.lz, Lisbon, 22 Jan. 1659, in ANTT/CJ/68, no. 45; Gonçalo de Alcaçova Carneiro da Costa de Menezes (governor, Angola) to king, ca. 1691, in BNL, cod. 1587, fol. 137ʳ. In the 1750s, the provincial ordered a mulatto slave on the Paulista estate of Arasiguama sent to Colônia do Sacramento for sale because he had been the leader of an uprising. "Relações dos bens apprehendidos e confiscados aos Jesuitas da capitania de S. Paulo," 14 Dec. 1762, in *DISP*, 44: 358. Brazilian planters likewise got rid of rebellious slaves by the same strategy.

slaveholders, the fathers acquired most of their chattels the same way their colleagues in Peru did, namely, in the open market.[70]

The Jesuits and the Brazil Trades

Certainly no critic in Brazil ever accused the Jesuits of dominating the slave trade; nor did anyone ever assert that the fathers controlled the colony's sugar trade. Despite the vital importance of that trade to their activities, and despite the notoriety attached to their large, much-envied plantations, the fathers' total share of the sugar trade appears to have been small. In 1648 Simão de Vasconcelos reported that the value of the province's exports to the kingdom that year reached the staggering sum of 32 contos, but those shipments represented the yield from the previous two and a half years' crops and amounted to about 2.4 percent of Brazil's sugar exports at that time.[71] During the next century, cane production in Brazil continued to expand, northward to Maranhão and Pará and southward to São Paulo. As indicated in Chapter 16, the Jesuits increased cane cultivation in the same captaincies; however, by the 1750s their share of Brazil's cane exports was no more than 2.5 percent, about the same as it had been a century earlier.[72]

Although the Jesuits' participation in Brazil's sugar trade did not arouse settler antipathy, the same cannot be said for their role in the so-called spice trade of the Amazon. That trade included two forms of cloves, sarsaparilla, and vanilla, but the most important export was cacao. Its cultivation dates from the 1670s. Serafim Leite credited the Jesuits with having been the pioneer growers. His claim is unverifiable, but two facts seem irrefutable: first, because of the absence of a European market, cacao did not became a significant Brazilian export until the mid-1720s, and second, most Amazonian cacao was harvested "wild" in the forests rather than on plantations, unlike cacao grown in Venezuela, Ecuador, and elsewhere in the New World. By the 1730s cacao had become the Amazon's dominant export staple, a position it would maintain for more than a century.

The Jesuits, along with the other missionary Orders active in the Amazon, produced some cacao on their own plantations, but they depended primarily upon their Amerindian charges in the interior missions to collect it. Such reliance brought the fathers into direct conflict with vested settler interests. As early as 1704, the cámara of Belém complained about such competition and echoed the common anti-Jesuit lament throughout the empire when it charged that the missionaries were forsaking their spiritual obligations and, by depriving the settlers of the workers they needed to gather spices, were responsible for their continued impoverishment. In 1734 the crown sent desembargador Francisco Duarte dos Santos from

---

70. Cf. Cushner, *Lords,* 90.

71. Vasconcelos to Carafa, Bahia, 30 Aug. 1648, in ARSI, *Bras.,* 3:I, fols. 266ʳ–266ᵛ. The estimate is based upon calculations derived from Stuart B. Schwartz, *Sugar Plantations in the Formation of Brazilian Society: Bahia, 1550–1835* (Cambridge, 1985), 176–77, 499. It assumes that Jesuit plantations were producing about 336,096 kg of cane annually, compared with 13,789,440 kg for all of Brazil. The latter estimate was made prior to the second Dutch invasion of the northeast (1630ff.). Overall production may well have been lower when Vasconcelos wrote.

72. D. Alden, "Sugar Planters by Necessity, Not Choice: The Role of the Jesuits in the Cane Sugar Industry of Colonial Brazil, 1601–1759," in Jeffrey A. Cole, ed., *The Church and Society in Latin America* (New Orleans: Tulane University, Center for Latin American Studies, 1984), 157–59.

TABLE 21.1

Exports by Religious Orders from Belém to Lisbon, 1743–45

(kilograms)

Order	Cacao	Cloves	Coffee	Sarsaparilla	Sugar
Jesuits	154,816	24,905	824	5,068	4,595
Carmelites	38,015	45	170	145	2,120
Mercedarians	3,803	377	—	58	—
Franciscans	25	13	9	—	—
Total	196,659	25,340	1,003	5,271	6,715

SOURCE: Pedro Cavalleyro e Cavalleyro (*escrivão proprietario*, Pará customs), 18 Sept. 1747, enc. in Lour[en]ço d'Anv.ᶜᵉ Pacheco to king, 20 Oct. 1747, in AHU/PA/PA, *cx.* 14.

Lisbon to the Amazon to investigate such charges. The desembargador concluded that the settlers' complaints were unfounded. That did not prevent their reiteration, however. In the mid-1740s, the royal treasurer in Pará, pursuant to an order from the Overseas Council, examined the customs files that recorded all spice shipments by the religious Orders between 1743 and 1745. His report, summarized in Table 21.1, tells part of the story. The rest of it is that the share of the spice trade for the Jesuits and the other three principal missionary Orders then amounted to only 6.6 percent, hardly the monopoly that their adversaries asserted they possessed.[73] Still, the assertion that the Jesuits, the dominant Order in the Amazon, controlled the great river's spice trade continued to be widely believed both in Brazil and in the kingdom.

Another source of settler envy in Brazil concerned the Jesuits' exemption from all customs duties on goods they shipped to or from the colony. First granted by Sebastian in 1573 and renewed by subsequent monarchs until at least 1710, that exemption was among the Society's most prized privileges in the Portuguese Assistancy. At one point it was even construed as applying to Jesuit wine purchases from the Canary Islands, which, of course, belonged to Spain.[74] Other religious Orders in Brazil envied the Jesuits' customs exemption, but their efforts to gain equal treatment were unavailing.[75] Six years after the concession was first issued, Cardinal Henry also spared the Society from payment of all excise duties on foodstuffs that it shipped, purchased, or exchanged within the kingdom or its empire.[76]

73. The foregoing is based upon my "The Significance of Cacao Production in the Amazon Region During the Late Colonial Period: An Essay in Comparative Economic History," American Philosophical Society, *Proceedings* 120, 2 (Apr. 1976): 103–35, esp. 115–23. One acerbic critic also accused the Society of controlling the production of Malmsey, one of the varietals of Madeira dessert wine. J[ohn] Ovington, *A Voyage to Surat in the Year 1689*, ed. H. G. Rawlinson (London, 1929), 13. Ovington insisted that on Madeira, "among the Merchants, the *Jesuits* are none of the meanest ... and have ... secured the Monopoly of *Malmsey*, of which there is but one good Vineyard in the Whole Island which is entirely in their possession." I know of no evidence to sustain his charge.

74. For the text, see *CCLP*, 10: 22–23, where the date 1643 is an obvious printer's error. In addition to the renewals of 1632 and 1684 recorded here, that of 14 Feb. 1686 is recorded in ANRJ, col. 61/6/167ʳ–179ʳ. The alvará of 21 Nov. 1710, in AHU/PA/PA, *cx.* 14, further renews the long-standing privilege.

75. For the unsuccessful efforts of the Benedictines to gain the same privilege, see AHU/PA/BA, 1st ser. uncat., *cx.* 8 (no. 1896) and *cx.* 9 (no. 2131). In the Amazon, the crown granted exemptions to other Orders to export small amounts of spices. E.g., in 1698 Pedro II enlarged the right of the Franciscans to ship from 1,451 to 2,902 kg of cacao and cloves per year without payment of customs. AHU/PA/PA, *cx.* 14.

76. Alvará of 22 May 1579, *HCJB*, 1: 141 n. 2.

An order of 1688 required all ship captains sailing between the Amazon and Portugal's Atlantic islands to accept whatever cargo the Jesuits wished to dispatch.[77] Such privileges were naturally galling to the Jesuits' rivals and were sometimes challenged by the crown's legal officers, but they were never rescinded in this period.[78]

Myths and Realities Concerning the Jesuits' Trading Network

The Portuguese Assistancy was one of several trading networks within the Society.[79] As in other assistancies, units within this one exchanged locally available goods with one another. In the Far East, the college of Macao, for example, supplied Jesuit institutions in India, Brazil, and Portugal with chinaware, silks, teas, and lacquered boxes. Jesuit installations in India furnished fine cloth and precious stones to their counterparts in the kingdom and exchanged cloth and foodstuffs with other institutions within the subcontinent and in distant Mozambique. They also sent to Brazil altar cloths, worked silver, and Chinese porcelains. Colleges in the Atlantic islands sent wheat and wines to their overseas partners, and Peninsular installations also contributed wines to the same destinations. The Brazil colleges furnished sugars, tobacco, and cacao to colleges in Angola and in the kingdom. But the quantity of goods involved in these exchanges was moderate, and the goods were primarily intended for use by the Jesuits themselves. The volume of this trade never approached the magnitude that Jesuit adversaries—contemporary or modern—suspected.[80] Procurators of each house regularly adjusted balances of amounts earned and owed to brother institutions and, absent goods to exchange, sent letters of credit drawn upon houses where they possessed favorable balances to settle accounts.[81] But there does not exist a single Jesuit ledger that separates profits derived from commercial transactions from those made on other kinds of transactions.

Of course, the Jesuits' opponents often complained that the Society utilized its trading connections and its network to benefit its friends. The author of the *Monita Secreta*, for example, insisted that "the Society may also advantageously traffick under the borrow'd name of some rich merchants, our friends; but never without a prospect of certain and abundant gain; and this may be done even to the Indies which hitherto . . . have furnished us not only

77. *CR*, 23 Mar. 1688, in *LGM* 1: 94.

78. E.g., in 1731 one of Santo Antão's agents in Bahia reported that customs officials had attempted to prevent him from importing wine for use on the college's plantations without payment of duties, but that he had finally compelled the official to accept the king's exemption. Ant.º Jorge Miz. to Simão Estivens, Bahia, 30 July 1731, in ANTT/CJ/68, no. 345.

79. Cf. Cushner, *Lords*, chap. 7; idem, *Jesuit Ranches and the Agrarian Development of Colonial Argentina, 1650–1767* (Albany, 1983), 146ff.

80. These observations are based primarily upon ANTT/CJ/58 and /68; HAG 2094 and 2557; and the many college accounts cited throughout this study. ANTT/CJ/58 contains fragments of many early-seventeenth-century accounts that Portuguese colleges in the kingdom maintained with each other, whereas CJ/68 includes several hundred accounts that they kept concerning their exchanges with overseas Jesuit institutions. There are similar accounts in ANTT/CJ/54, esp. nos. 16 and 17, and CJ/90, nos. 122 and 124. In addition, several surviving bills of lading provide further detail on the commodities sent by one facility to another (e.g., BA/JA/49-V-29, no. 43), whereas the mistitled HAG 833 contains the commercial correspondence of the procurator of New St. Paul's, Goa, with his counterparts in Bahia and Lisbon between 1744 and 1759.

81. In addition to Cushner, *Lords*, and idem, *Jesuit Ranches*, see Gustavo Valdes Bunster, *El poder economico de los Jesuitas en Chile, 1593–1767* (Santiago, 1980), chap. 4.

with souls, but also plenteously supplied our coffers with wealth."[82] It is easy to dismiss such assertions as simply the prattle of a malicious, cashiered ex-Jesuit. Nevertheless, there are documentary fragments that suggest the existence of undeclared partnerships between units of the Society and secular merchants. One arrangement already noted involved the Fishery Coast pearl beds. Another is revealed in an eighteenth-century memorandum detailing shipments by a Lisbon merchant to the Luanda Jesuits. It includes a simple numerical code by which baize, woolen stuffs such as *serafines*,[83] and other fabrics, as well as olive oil, wheat, brandy, and other items, could be ordered directly and secretly from the Lisbon supplier. Since the Angolan Jesuits shared the services of a procurator in Lisbon, it is difficult to understand why they required an external commercial connection unless they were trading on the side.[84] Another example concerns a commercial agreement of the late 1750s involving the substantial sum of 3 contos. The signatories were the procurator of Malabar and a Saraswat Brahman merchant in Goa, and their negotiation concerned a shipment of cloth and crockery. Curiously, the procurator voided that agreement in 1759, on the eve of the expulsion.[85]

Though it is impossible to know how frequently Jesuits served as conduits, enabling their friends to obtain wanted commodities, it is not hard to find examples demonstrating that they provided such service. Two have already been instanced in this chapter: the purchase of diamonds for the marquis of Alorna and the dispatch of silver by Jesuit intermediaries from Japan to Macao to obtain raw silk or gold for Christian daimyos. In the 1580s, one Jesuit informant in Malacca advised the father general, "Our Fathers who travel from Goa to Japan customarily carry with them some money belonging to our friends to be invested in China," and asseverated that "the superiors who reside in Goa authorize this practice." About the same time, a Ming viceroy in Canton publicly informed the Jesuits that he could not accept gifts from them and ostentatiously gave them silver for certain items they presented to him. Later he secretly informed them that the bullion was, in fact, intended to pay for another consignment of European "novelties." During the same decade, when the royal court of Wan-li wanted to procure certain purple draperies from Portuguese merchants in Macao, it asked Matteo Ricci to facilitate the purchase.[86] The vital role of the Jesuits in facilitating the silk trade between Macaonese merchants and the Japanese is, of course, another example of such service.

Nor are further examples hard to discern. In the 1630s, when an Augustinian friar visited Jesuit missions in Cochin China, he came to the conclusion that the fathers were permitted to function there only because they paid bribes to the "chief mandarins" and arranged for their purchase of goods from Macao.[87] A short time after, agents of the English East India

82. Jerome Zahorowski, *Monita Secreta Societatis Jesu: The Secret Instructions of the Jesuits* (London, 1722), 77.

83. Serafines consisted of woolen cloths used for curtains and for the lining of coats. They were evidently very fashionable during the eighteenth century

84. "Ordens q. dou a Theodozio Alz' Lima, morador em L.xa, para fazer o seguinte" [1738], in BNL/FG, 7211, no. 20.

85. HAG 2130 contains various affidavits concerning the procurator's negotiations with Suba Camotim (Kamath) in 1758.

86. Domingos Alvarez to Aquaviva, Malacca, 28 Dec. 1583, in *DI*, 13: 474; Louis J. Gallagher, S.J., trans., *China in the Sixteenth Century: The Journals of Matthew Ricci, 1583–1610* (1942; rpr., New York, 1953), 137 and 208.

87. *The Travels of Fray Sebastien Manrique, 1629–1643*, trans. C. Eckford Luard, assisted by H[enry] Hosten, S.J., *HS*:2, no. 61 (1927): 60–65.

Company reported the safe arrival in Goa of some carpets that the Jesuit resident in Agra had obtained for the viceroy, the count of Aveiras. When the agents turned them over to the viceroy, he first denied that they were his property, but then sent the president of the Surat factory expensive presents to indicate his appreciation for the transport of his purchases.[88]

These examples provide further illustrations of a point emphasized in an earlier chapter: Jesuits often found themselves in situations where they could not avoid doing favors for powerful friends, whether merchants or administrators or court dignitaries. It was their conviction that failure to provide such services could adversely affect their evangelical enterprises, and it was those activities rather than the commercial endeavors that claimed the highest priority in Jesuit thinking.

It is worth noting that the services described above were not profit-making ventures for the Jesuits, who asked for no more than compensation for their expenses. Still, some Jesuit leaders were strongly opposed to the practice of providing commercial assistance to seculars, no matter who they were. Thus, when Francisco Cabral, provincial of Goa, discovered that the viceroy had asked the superior of the Fishery Coast to purchase rice and arrange for its shipment to Ceylon, he vigorously opposed that command on the ground that compliance was contrary to the Society's Institute.[89] Later, when Francisco Barreto was Visitor of the Goa province, he directed that no member should proceed from the capital to Surat on behalf of merchants, suggesting thereby that the practice did, in fact, exist.[90]

Whether such prohibitions were actually observed is, of course, impossible to determine. Nicholas Cushner assures his readers that in the Spanish Assistancy, "[the Jesuits] were forbidden under pain of mortal sin to sell or exchange silver belonging to private persons, or to transport to Europe anything not belonging to Jesuits." Despite the severity of the penalty, such activity was not unknown, for Cushner tells us about the misadventure of Fr. Nicolás de Mirabel, who, in 1697, attempted to send 347,000 pesos in silver from Peru to Spain for friendly merchants. In order to evade customs duties, he had their chest placed in the personal luggage of a returning viceroy! When his scheme was exposed, his superiors suffered considerable embarrassment.[91] It is rare to discover comparable instances of misdeeds by Jesuits in the Portuguese Assistancy,[92] but just as it is clear that they continued to perform commercial services for important friends until the end of their enterprise, so, too, Jesuits sometimes entrusted cargoes to friendly laymen and asked them to dispose of the goods.[93]

88. *EFI* (1642–45): 60, 63, 66. See also *EFI* (1646–50): 127, for details of another shipment of carpets to Aveiras's successor. It is not clear whether Jesuits again served as intermediaries.

89. Cabral to Aquaviva, 15 Dec. 1593, in *DI*, 16: 534.

90. "Ordens que deixou o P. Francisco Barreto ... pera se goardarem em toda a provincia de Goa ... 1660," in ARSI, FG, 1443/9/27, par. 12.

91. Cushner, *Lords*, 178.

92. One interesting example: in 1674 the provincial of Goa dispatched an inspector to Mozambique and informed him that the previous year he had received a report that "a bag sent by one of Ours with the name of the Provincial on it contained gold biscuits, none of which belonged to the Society, but ... were sent to his many native friends in Salsete," and forbade the practice. Letter of Fr. Teotonio de Souzsa to the Open Forum of the *Sunda Times* [India], 16 Feb. 1979. I am indebted to Fr. John Correia-Afonso for a photocopy.

93. In 1758 the conde de Redondo sent the Goan Jesuits 2,324,000 rs. to be forwarded to Macao for an undisclosed purchase on his behalf. He was still trying to recover his money as late as 1781. D. Frederico Guilherme de Sousa (governor, India) to Martinho de Melo e Castro (colonial secretary), 2 Jan. 1781 and enc. in AHU/PA/IN, *m*. 133. In the late 1720s, some Jesuit official in Goa entrusted a box containing 40 napkins,

The trading ventures discussed in this chapter were sources of concern to both the Jesuits and their critics. There were always some Jesuits, like Francisco Cabral and António Vieira, who were adamantly opposed to the Society's involvement in any form of commercial activity, since it seemed to violate both canon law and the Institute. Moreover, the Society's mercantile ventures exposed it to endless gossip and seemingly provided substance for the assertion that its members had forsaken their initial spiritual mission and had become preoccupied with Mammon. That became the conviction not only of carping religious rivals, competing merchants and planters, and disgruntled royal officials, but even of the highest members of the Society itself. In 1714 the general, Michelangelo Tamburini, excoriated the fathers in Paraguay, whose "only purpose ... seems to be economic gain, a deplorable inversion of means and ends." The provincial himself admitted "the overconcern of many priests in things temporal."[94] Three-quarters of a century earlier, a Jesuit stationed on the Malabar coast uttered the same complaint against the rector of Cranganore: "The Rector carries on commerce, he sells coconuts, milk, wine. Yet he has no money for the Missions. He has even reduced the fare of the Community. Prayer is neglected. He builds much. It is there that he spends money."[95] That criticism was in some respects on the mark, for although there are no data that suggest that individual Jesuits became high livers, the assertions of the acerbic Domingo Navarrete and other ecclesiastics notwithstanding, some Jesuit managers did become very much concerned about the perfection of infrastructure—well-appointed churches, chapels, libraries, and other image-making facilities. But it was precisely such installations, together with Jesuit-owned ships and warehouses, that contributed to the popular perception of the Society's apparent affluence.

The Society's commercial operations and trading facilities were obviously limited when compared with those of the great merchants of the day. Certainly there is no evidence to confirm the hysterical allegation of Magalhães Godinho that "the Society of Jesus sought to erect not only a theocratic territorial empire ... but also a gigantic association which should control the world's principal trades," though his statement would obviously gain the nodding approval of the Jesuits' archfoe, the marquis of Pombal.[96] Neither Magalhães Godinho nor any other scholar has ever been able to demonstrate that Jesuits dominated a single branch of imperial trade, or ever had any aspiration to do so. Still, it must be admitted that through its commercial endeavors, the Society projected an image of financial well-being that its accounts do not confirm. As is often the case, the myth of Jesuit wealth was more pervasive than the reality of Jesuit poverty. In retrospect, the Society might have aroused far less suspicion, animosity, and enmity had it been able to rely more heavily upon its invisible investment portfolios, the subject of the next chapter.

---

20 hand towels, and a tablecloth to a ship's passenger with instructions that the contents be sold in Bahia and that the proceeds be delivered to the procurator of India or his agent in Lisbon. Statement by António Teixeira, Goa, 2 Jan. 1730, in ANTT/CJ/54, no. 16.

94. Cushner, *Lords*, 177.

95. F/*JM*, 1: 389–90.

96. The statement appears in Magalhães Godinho, "Portugal and Her Empire, 1680–1720," *The New Cambridge Modern History*, vol. 6, ed. J. S. Bromley (Cambridge, 1970), 537.

CHAPTER 22

Alternative Forms of Risk-Taking: The Jesuits as Lenders and Borrowers

> Thou shalt not lend upon usury to thy brother . . . usury of any thing that is lent upon. . . . Unto a stranger thou mayest lend upon usury; but unto thy brother thou shalt not lend upon usury.
>
> —Deuteronomy 23:19–20

WITHIN THE PORTUGUESE ASSISTANCY, the Society possessed both visible and invisible assets. The former included its novitiates, colleges, seminaries, and retreats, its churches and other devotional buildings, rented shops and houses, and productive estates. The latter consisted of interest-bearing loans made to a variety of borrowers, property liens (*census realis*), and both government and personal annuities. Most of the funds belonging to the Jesuits of the Portuguese Assistancy were invested in lands under Portuguese control, but some were deposited in Italy, Austria, and the Germanies. Together with sea loans and the acquisition, by purchase or bequest, of quitrents derived from individual estates or from entire communities, discussed in preceding chapters, such investments constituted an alternative form of risk-taking by units of the Society.

Along with other contemporary lenders—episcopal chapters; other religious Orders, female as well as male; and especially the Holy Houses of Mercy (Santa Casa da Misericórdia)—Jesuit managers learned through experience that some kinds of borrowers were more dependable than others. The least risky naturally received loans at the lowest rates of interest, in Portugal generally 2 to 4 percent, but those for whom repayment was less certain were charged up to 6.25 percent in the Atlantic world, and even more in the East.[1]

---

1. In exceptional circumstances, such as long delays in the arrival of the convoys from the kingdom, interest rates in Brazil could soar to as much as 18% per annum. João Francisco Muzzi and Luiz Alv[a]res Pretto to Francisco Pinheiro, 14 Oct. 1721, in Luís Lisanti, ed., *Negocios coloniais*, 5 vols. (Rio de Janeiro, 1973), 2: 187. In 1757 the crown arbitrarily rolled back the prevailing interest rate throughout its domains to 5%. Alvarás of 17 Jan. and 6 Aug. 1757, *CCLP*, 4: 8–11 and 79–80. Some writers have assumed that lenders, particularly those in Brazil, immediately complied with the crown's fiat, but that was far from the case. The edict was not even published in Salvador until 1761, and the old legal rate still prevailed four years later.

The list of preferred borrowers was headed by other Jesuit entities and other religious congregations, notably monasteries, convents, and third orders. In the next rank were prominent landowners, leading merchants, and eminent government officials, particularly judicial officers. Less dependable, particularly in the Indian subcontinent, were farmers, moneylenders, and shopkeepers, each of whom borrowed from the fathers at higher rates. The most risky borrowers were the government itself and members of the high nobility (see Chapter 13 and below).

The society itself was also a borrower, especially during its formative period and whenever its facilities required renovation or replacement because of damage or destruction. Its need for funds was naturally great when its colleges and churches were initially constructed. Following the recovery of Bahia, Recife, and Luanda from the Dutch, the Society's facilities in those towns had to be rebuilt (see Chapter 9). Fires were especially devastating in India, where New St. Paul's sustained five conflagrations during the seventeenth century.

The Society borrowed from several sources. It was common for the overseas procurators based in Lisbon to borrow from each other and from the college of Santo Antão, where they resided. Regular lenders also included other religious houses, heads of families, widows, and secular priests. In times of crisis, sympathetic high government officials sometimes extended personal loans to Jesuit facilities.

The Society's investment practices within the Assistancy varied with the times. Initially, units of the Assistancy had little surplus capital available for loans because of the construction of infrastructure and the financing of far-flung educational and evangelical programs. Then, too, during the formative period, Jesuits and other theologians still had serious misgivings about the legitimacy of lending, scruples that were conveniently overcome by the beginning of the seventeenth century, when the Society became less preoccupied with the cultivation of its public image.[2] Also, the extent to which units of the Society borrowed or lent money in the communities they served varied considerably within the Assistancy and depended in part upon an array of alternatives.

The College of Santo Antão as Borrower and Lender

Most of what we know about investment practices among Jesuit colleges in seventeenth-century Portugal comes from the surviving records of the Lisbon college of Santo Antão, which are preserved in Portugal's National Archives. That college became the domicile of the overseas procurators, who regularly lent money to and borrowed it from each other. A report from the mid-1620s, for example, shows that the procurators for Japan, Goa, and Malabar owed the college 2,066,583 rs., while that institution held deposits for half a dozen persons, mostly nuns it would appear, totaling 3,114,000 rs.[3]

Francisco Xavier de Mendonça Furtado (colonial secretary) to interim governors of Brazil, 20 Apr. 1761, in APB/OR/64, fol. 267[r]; António Roiz Lopes (*juiz ordinario*, Rio das Contas, Bahia) to king, 25 June 1765, in APB/CGVA/24, fol. 175[r].

2. For introductions to the vast contemporary and secondary literature, see Benjamin Nelson, *The Idea of Usury*, 2d. ed. (Chicago, 1969); and John T. Noonan, Jr., *The Scholastic Analysis of Usury* (Cambridge, Mass., 1957), esp. 217–41.

3. Jorge de Gouvea, "Orsamento de contas do anno de [1]625 de todas as provincias," Santo Antão, 23 Mar. 1627, authenticated copy signed by Pedro da Cunha, 6 Aug. 1629, in ARSI, *Lus.*, 77, fols. 92–93. The

The intent behind those deposits is not evident from this report. However, other records demonstrate that Santo Antão, along with other Jesuit facilities and certain other religious corporations at the time, performed a little-noticed social-security service. It accepted what are termed conditional deposits, distinguished from general or demand obligations. According to A. P. Usher, "Conditional deposits were a characteristic feature of the primitive bank of deposit ... they consisted of actual deposits of specie to be paid to a designated party at a fixed date.... The payor placed the funds in the hands of the banker with an explicit understanding that they would be transferred to the payee when the conditions of their agreement had been fulfilled."[4] The deposits that the Jesuits received represented a variation of this form of capital transfer. Those who assumed the burden of financial care of members of their families assigned the colleges that responsibility and the capital necessary to discharge it. Usually the providers were brothers, fathers, husbands, or uncles, and sometimes aunts. The recipients were commonly women living in convents.[5] At the beginning of the seventeenth century, for example, Duarte da Costa, grandson of Brazil's second governor-general and a wealthy landowner before he became a Jesuit, not only endowed the incipient college of Santarém but also left funds with the managers of Santo Antão to provide periodic cash payments and a jar of olive oil for each of his four sisters, who were living in a convent.[6] In return for the use of the givers' capital, the college promised to pay the maintenance costs of the recipients for as long as they lived. The account managers (usually the procurators acting upon the directive of the rectors) made quarterly or semestrial payments, in the latter instance traditionally on St. John's Day (24 June) and at Christmas. After the recipients' demise, the college was sometimes free to utilize the remainder of the fund in whatever ways the rector and his consultores deemed appropriate, although contributors often specified that residuals were to be used to support a chantry they had already established.[7] Though it may be presumed that most contributors resided in the kingdom, some, like a royal treasurer in Rio de Janeiro, lived abroad and utilized the services of the college to send regular contributions to their relatives in Portugal.[8] In

---

procurators' accounts cited elsewhere in this study reveal many instances of such transactions. Others in the files of the college of Santo Antão are in ANTT/CJ/59, nos. 337, 357, and 395.

4. Abbott Payson Usher, "The Origins of Banking: The Primitive Bank of Deposit, 1200–1600," *Economic History Review* 4 (1932–34): 399–428, at 413–14.

5. James Denson Riley reports that in Mexico City, the college of San Pedro y San Pablo received moneys from sons with instructions to pay installments derived from earned interest to their parents. *Hacendados jesuitas en Mexico: El colegio maximo de San Pedro y San Pablo, 1685–1767* (Mexico City, 1976), 27. I have not found that practice observed in the Portuguese Assistancy, but it is not unlikely.

6. "Visita da provincia de Portugal pelo P. João Alvares," in ANTT/AJ, *cx.* 1, *m.* 5, tit. 10, cap. 4, par. 23.

7. There are several hundred specimens of the rectors' acknowledgments of the obligations of such annuities extending from 1618 to the early 1730s in ANTT/CJ/59 and 60. Other Jesuit colleges clearly performed the same services. E.g., the third catalogue of the Portuguese province in 1633 reports that Coimbra paid out 20,000 rs. a year from a fund of 620,000 rs. to a nun for the balance of her life. ARSI, *Lus.*, 44:II, fols. 512–518ᵛ. In the eighteenth century, the college of Bahia was obligated to pay 240 rs. per day to Theresa de Jesus from a fund left by her brother and 200,000 rs. "for her lifetime only" to a widow. ATC/CJ no. 266, fols. 10ʳ–10ᵛ. The monastic practice of receiving annuities and corodies was common in medieval England. G. W. O. Woodward, *The Dissolution of the Monasteries* (New York, 1966), 24–27. Evidently Jesuit houses in France also dealt in life annuities. *EJF*, 3: col. 283.

8. Francisco Cordovil de Siqueira Melo to Raphal Mendes, S.J., Rio de Janeiro, 28 Apr. 1739, in ANTT/CJ/68, no. 277. The writer was a prominent landowner in Rio de Janeiro and the captaincy's treasurer during the 1730s and 1740s. CeA, 7: index, s.v. Francisco de Cordovil de Sequeira e Mello.

all probability the Jesuits performed such services, as they did others, for selected dignitaries rather than for the king's ordinary subjects.

Interest from annuities provided an important share of Santo Antão's income. In the early 1620s it amounted to as much as 26.5 percent.[9] But the college was also a frequent borrower. Its lenders, who received returns that ranged from 2.5 to 5 percent, included convents, widows, landowners, merchants, and sympathetic royal officials. The college, which was always hard-pressed to meet its expenses despite the acquisition of landed estates both in the kingdom and in Brazil, regularly borrowed to undertake repairs, to maintain its facilities, and especially to pay off other short-term obligations. Sometimes it discharged the principal that it owed; in other cases it renegotiated the debt and merely continued to pay regular interest.[10]

The Aveiro Loan Debacle

Santo Antão was rarely in the position of becoming a significant lender. In one instance its managers unwisely extended its credit for a prominent noble, and both the college and the entire province suffered the consequences.

It is curious that each of the Latin assistancies was rocked by major financial scandals at different times. The best known is the so-called Lavalette affair. Fr. Antoine Lavalette was assigned by the French provincial to the Caribbean in 1741. By 1753 he became superior of the French insular missions there. With great enthusiasm but ill luck, he undertook a rapid expansion of the missions' sugar plantations and actively traded with leading ports in France and Holland. But a series of disasters befell him, including hurricanes, the loss of ships laden with sugar cargoes captured by the English enemy during the Seven Years War, and lethal disease that severely reduced his slave forces. Each disaster caused him to borrow more funds from Marseilles lenders, one of whom was compelled to declare bankruptcy in 1756 because of Lavalette's inability to meet his obligations. By the time Lavalette returned to Europe in 1762 (when he resigned from the Society), his mission owed vast sums to 126 creditors. The collapse of his enterprises led to major judicial inquiries into the economic activities of the Society in the French Assistancy and hastened its expulsion from French domains a few years later.[11]

A century and a quarter earlier, the Spanish Assistancy had experienced a similar financial disaster. Although its consequences were not fatal, they were nevertheless grievous and embarrassing to the Society. At the beginning of the 1630s, the college of San Hermenegildo in Seville was one of the brightest ornaments of the Spanish Assistancy. Its staff numbered between 80 and 90, about twice the size of Santo Antão and comparable

9. "Primeira receita que se offereceo nos livros em que se davao' as contas aos padres provinciaes," summarizing Santo Antão's income for the years 1619–25, in ARSI, *Lus.*, 77, fols. 304ʳ–304ᵛ.

10. There are hundreds of examples of such borrowings in ANTT/CJ/59–61 extending from the 1620s as far as the late 1730s.

11. Two recent but hardly sympathetic descriptions of the Lavalette affair are by Canadian historian Dorothy G. Thompson: "The Fate of the French Jesuits' Creditors Under the Ancien Regime," *English Historical Review* 91 (1976): 255–77; and "French Jesuit Wealth on the Eve of the Eighteenth-Century Suppression," in W. J. Sheils and Diana Wood, eds., *The Church and Wealth*, Studies in Church History 24 (Oxford, 1987), 307–19. Despite its age, *HP*, 36: 383ff. remains a more detailed, better-balanced treatment.

to Goa's New St. Paul's. The college, the largest in the Spanish kingdom, served upwards of 900 students. Its large refectory was one of the most impressive dining facilities in Seville, the economic nerve center of Spain and its empire. In 1632 the college gained a new procurator, a Basque lay brother from the Biscay province. Andres Villar Goitia had served for five years as the procurator of the novitiate. He had given a good account of himself there and was considered knowledgeable about business affairs. According to Jesuit apologists, the college administrators trusted his judgment so much that they gave him full control over the institution's finances. The ledgers that Br. Villar periodically displayed to his superiors showed that the college was becoming increasingly prosperous under his stewardship: herds of cattle and other livestock multiplied marvelously; wheat and barley production sextupled; the production of olive oil grew rapidly; and the college enjoyed the benefits of extensive trade not only with the Biscayan ports but with those in the Indies as well. It also acquired new facilities, including a tennis court that the procurator purchased from the venerable duke of Medina Sidonia, a descendant of the commander of the ill-fated armada of 1588.

All went well until 1644 or 1645, when a newly appointed rector became suspicious about evident falsifications in the procurator's books and demanded a full accounting. Because of the complexity of Villar's financial juggling, the college's leaders confessed their inability to determine how bad the damage was. Accordingly, they secured the services of the treasurer of the Seville cathedral, who soon concluded that Villar had swindled the college out of hundreds of thousands of ducats in order to benefit members of his family. The procurator was promptly incarcerated and for a time was not permitted to see or speak with anyone. At some point, however, he established contact with the papal nuncio, to whom he complained about his mistreatment. He was then transferred to the local English college and assigned a Basque-speaking companion to keep watch over him. Meantime, shocked college authorities learned from the interventor and the clamoring creditors that the institution's debts had reached a staggering sum, somewhere between 350,000 and 450,000 ducats, the equivalent of 160 contos. In order to discharge those massive burdens, the college was obliged to dispose of most of its patrimony and to reduce its once-impressive staff to a mere fourteen members. But Br. Villar was not among them, for after years of confinement he was dismissed from the Society under cloudy circumstances.[12]

The same conditions characterize the Aveiro affair, which, although it involved a large loan rather than dubious commercial transactions, bore certain similarities to the two fiscal misadventures just described. In 1615 the third duke of Aveiro, D. Alvaro de Lencastre, headed one of the leading families of the kingdom. His family was related to the English ducal family of Lancasters through D. Felipa, wife of King John I, who founded the Aviz dynasty in 1385. D. Alvaro's uncle, the second duke, and his elder brother both perished at Alcázarquibir in 1578, when Sebastian went to his reward. The third duke possessed

---

12. The standard account of the Villar affair is *HCJAE*, 5: 40–47. The well-known polemic by J[ames] Brodrick, S.J., *The Economic Morals of the Jesuits: An Answer to Dr. H. M. Robertson* (London, 1934), 94–99, relies entirely upon Astráin but goes even farther than the Spaniard in attempting to level exclusive blame for the college's plight upon Br. Villar. At least Astráin recognizes "the lamentable neglect" of the procurator's superiors (p. 47). Important documents concerning the college's bankruptcy are published in *MHE*, 18: 46–52 and 105–17, including the damning testimony of a mysterious courtier, Juan Onofre de Salazar, who rightly criticized the procurator's superiors for failing to maintain proper supervision over Villar; but neither Astráin nor Brodrick paid serious attention to Onofre.

palaces in Lisbon and Setúbal as well as a country house in Azeitão, and was the patron of the monastery of Arrabida. He and his wife, a near cousin, produced sixteen children, three of whom died in infancy; four became nuns and one a Dominican priest. Strangely, none joined the Society, although the family engaged the services of a Jesuit confessor.[13]

In 1615 three matters preoccupied the duke. The first was that he had successfully negotiated the approaching marriage of D. Jorge de Lencastre (b. 1594), the son expected to succeed him, with D. Ana Doria Colonia, the daughter of a supposedly wealthy Spanish noble, and he yearned to put on a sumptuous wedding that would bring credit to his house. The second was an impending visit to Portugal by Philip III of Spain, whom the duke wished to entertain in impressive style. The third was his lack of the means to put on either entertainment. To raise the money to achieve both objectives, the duke turned to a New Christian moneylender, from whom he had borrowed funds in the past and for whom he had obtained a habit in the Order of Christ. This time, however, the lender declined to come to his aid, contending that all his capital was tied up in government contracts. Accordingly, the duke approached several prominent Jesuits, including Cristóvão de Gouveia, at different times provincial of both Brazil and Portugal, and Francisco Pereira, a distinguished jurist and longtime advisor of high ecclesiastical and secular officials, who served as provincial of Portugal between 1615 and 1618. The duke asked them to agree to a loan of about 40 contos, promising that he would repay his indebtedness speedily because he expected that his daughter-in-law would bring a large dowry. The senior Jesuits then consulted Diogo Luís, a man who had entrée to the moneylenders of Lisbon.

Br. Luís was an experienced procurator. Born in Évora in 1574, he entered the Society about 1598 and served for a time as procurator in the Azores before assuming the duties of that office in Santo Antão.[14] According to his later (but uncorroborated) testimony, Br. Luís visited the duke at Azeitão with his superiors but was most reluctant to agree to the loan, despite the fact that the duke insisted that he had arranged previous borrowings through another Jesuit procurator, João Soeiro (d. 1604), who had served for many years as procurator of India and Brazil,[15] that he had always paid his bills, and that the college had previously guaranteed loans for several other nobles. Br. Luís tells us that he continued to have misgivings despite several later visits with the duke, who on one occasion fell to his knees and with tears in his eyes pleaded for the loan. Since Luís's superiors insisted that the duke's word must be honored—so he informs us—the procurator was eventually persuaded to support the loan request. According to his account, he did not actually arrange for the large loans to the duke. Instead, he enlisted the aid of another procurator, Fr. Mateus Tavares, to obtain them.

Mateus Tavares remains a shadowy figure. The 1600 personnel catalogue of the Brazil province lists him as assistant to the procurator of the college of Bahia. In 1604 he served as

13. In 1601 the duke's wife protested to the provincial about the impending assignment to Brazil of her confessor and asked that his departure be delayed until she could persuade Aquaviva how much she needed him. Duchess to provincial, 31 Aug. 1601, in ANTT/CJ/68, no. 4. The basic study of the dukes of Aveiro is Francisco Ferreira Neves, "A casa e ducado de Aveiro: Sua origem, evolução e extinção," *Revista do arquivo do distrito de Aveiro* 38 (1972).

14. "Primeiro catalogo da provincia de Portugal," 1614, 1619, 1622, and 1625, in ARSI, *Lus.*, 44:II, 307[v], 355–57, 387, and 413.

15. For Fr. Soeiro, see *ASCJ*, 184.

companion of a Jesuit inspector sent from Brazil to Angola. The 1617 catalogue for the Brazil province informs us that he was then living at Santo Antão as the procurator for the province.[16] Why Br. Luís involved him in the deal is unclear. He says that he did so because he was no longer serving as Santo Antão's procurator in 1616 but was living at the professed house (São Roque), but the personnel catalogues for the period do not bear him out. Equally puzzling is why Fr. Mateus would have agreed to become the front man for such a transaction without the express approval of his superiors.[17]

What *is* known is that during 1615 and 1616 the duke borrowed through the Jesuits about 42 contos, large sums by Portuguese standards—thirteen times the annual income of Santo Antão in this period—but barely a quarter of the funds Villar was said to have misappropriated in Seville. Whether the Jesuits were uneasy about their involvement in the Aveiro loans is unrecorded, but they should have been. The marriage of D. Jorge to D. Ana Doria Colonia occurred in 1619 but ended disastrously, without issue, a year later when D. Ana Doria died. Her chagrined father-in-law gave assurances to the fathers that he would discharge his obligations, and by the time of his own death (1626) he reputedly paid about 60 percent of them, though the balance that actually remained is uncertain.

By then, senior Jesuits were clearly worried about the heavy debt cloud that hung over Santo Antão. Some person or persons decided to place all the blame for the unwise loan guarantee upon the two procurators, and from this time to the end of the century Jesuit commentators on the affair insisted that those two alone were responsible for the debacle and condemned them for having failed to consult their superiors before committing the college so disastrously. But Br. Luís steadfastly maintained, both orally and in a written deposition composed in 1629, after he had been removed from Santo Antão and transferred to St. Patrick's seminary in the capital, that he had acted only after being pressured to do so by his superiors. Unfortunately for him, the two most important among them, Francisco Pereira and Cristóvão de Gouveia, were unable to corroborate his version, since the former had expired in 1619 and the latter in 1622. Equally regrettable from his perspective, another senior administrator whom Br. Luís claimed had full knowledge of the affair chose (or was ordered) to remain silent. Within a few years Br. Luís's name disappears from the personnel catalogues. Whether he died or was dismissed from the Order remains uncertain.[18] Fr. Tavares was also removed from office in the mid-1620s, but he was sent to Évora, where he

---

16. There are scattered references to Mateus Tavares in *HCJB*, 1: 578; 2: 354; and 7: 270.

17. A retrospective account of the debacle refers to the Brazil procurator as Matheus Sandres, but no such person held that office at this or any other time. Gabriel Diaz, "Fundamentos de q. hu. procurador do collegio de S.ᵗᵒ Antão tire noticia ... sobre ... a divida ... pella casa de Aveiro," Lisbon, 13 June 1684, in ARSI, *Lus.*, 78, fol. 25. The 1617 personnel catalogue for the Brazil province lists Fr. Mateus Tavares as residing in Lisbon and serving as procurator. In the only surviving reference to his role in the Aveiro loan, Simão de Vasconcelos explained that the reasons for the delay of the completion of the college church in Bahia were the Dutch capture of Salvador (1624), "e dividas que no reino se achou dever este colegio, feitas pelo padre procurador Mateus Tavares." *HCJB*, 5: 107. Curiously, the normally exhaustive Serafim Leite made no mention of the role of the Brazil province in the Aveiro loan.

18. The first catalogue of the province lists Br. Luís at St. Patrick's in 1628 but makes no mention of him in 1633 or later. ARSI, *Lus.*, 44:II, fols. 450 and 481ff. In his account of his conduct, Br. Luís indicates that he had disclosed everything that he knew repeatedly during the previous decade. Diogo Luís to António de Abreu (provincial), 27 July 1629, in ANTT/CJ/68, no. 265.

died while confined to a cell in one of the Jesuit colleges of the university in 1635. Strangely, he apparently did not leave any written explanation of his role in the Aveiro transactions.[19]

Meanwhile the Jesuits attempted to persuade the Lencastre family to honor the duke's pledges of repayment. Initially both the duke's widow and D. Jorge, who had acquired another Spanish wife, a lady-in-waiting of the queen of Spain, refused to pay the huge debt. The fathers then enlisted the aid of the papal collector in Portugal, King Philip IV of Spain, and the courts to persuade the two to change their stance. Finally, in 1631, they signed agreements to share the unpaid balance, declared to be 31.5 contos, between them and promised to pay off most of the remainder within three years and the balance as soon thereafter as possible. But the next year D. Jorge expired, and four years later his mother followed him to the grave, leaving most of the residual still unsettled. When the Jesuits applied to D. Jorge's widow, D. Ana Manrique de Cardenas, her lawyers insisted that she had no obligation to pay her father-in-law's debts because they did not directly concern her and because the estate left in her custody consisted of properties exempt from the collection of familial debts, specifically her personal dowry and the dukedom's entailed estates. The family maintained that position throughout the remainder of the century.

The family's intransigence left Santo Antão holding the bag. In 1636 the provincial congregation held a heated debate over whether the college ought to bear the full burden of the debt or whether each of the other colleges should assume a share. The father general, Mutio Vitelleschi, clearly favored the latter solution and ordered a pro rata division of the debt among all units of the province. But many of Santo Antão's fellow colleges were debt-ridden and reluctant to take on additional burdens not of their own making. Somehow, by the 1690s, most of the debt had mysteriously melted away, leaving one to speculate that the New Christian moneylenders who provided the loans either had surrendered their claims or had forgiven them twenty years earlier, when the Society fought unsuccessfully to exempt their estates from confiscation by the Inquisition (see Chapter 5).[20]

Investments by the Portuguese Province During the Eighteenth Century

There appears to have been a deliberate cover-up of the Aveiro scandal by Jesuit officials, who recognized that it brought discredit to the Society. Who those officials were cannot be known at this point. Certainly the Order tried to be more careful after that to prevent the mixing of its funds with those of seculars.[21] Indeed, for a time the Roman headquarters proscribed loans to laymen.[22] At some point that ban was patently lifted, for, as will be seen

19. The statement that Fr. Tavares died in a Jesuit cell in Évora is based upon the previously cited "Fundamentos" by Gabriel Diaz (note 17). Tavares was not the only Jesuit confined to a jail cell in one of the Society's facilities. For other examples of such confinement, see ARSI, *Lus.*, 44:II, fol. 357, and 37:I, fol. 196. Cf. the contradictory statements concerning the existence of Jesuit jails in A. Lynn Martin, *The Jesuit Mind: The Mentality of an Elite in Early Modern France* (Ithaca, N.Y. 1988), 117–18.

20. The foregoing is based upon the documents in ARSI, *Lus.*, 77, 78, and 82, as well as ANTT/CJ/68, esp. nos. 4, 44, 265, and 436. It is clear from a 1684 inventory of the papers concerning the case (ARSI, *Lus.*, 78, fols. 22^r–22^v) that many illuminating records were at some point destroyed. The account in *HCJAP*, 3:1, 279–83, is cautious and terse but generally fair.

21. H/SAG2: 72–73.

22. E.g., "Ordens que deixou o P. Francisco Barreto, visitador, pera se goardarem em toda a provincia de Goa ... anno de 1660," in ARSI, FG, 1443/9/27. Par. 26 states that "experience has shown that

below, units of the Society continued to lend funds to outsiders, including their aristocratic friends; but the sums involved were much smaller than those committed in the Aveiro scandal.[23]

In the eighteenth century, the Portuguese province invested in two sorts of annuities. One consisted of property liens termed census. Rooted in the Middle Ages, such encumbrances represented annual returns derived from fruitful properties.[24] The province's colleges had possessed a number of such liens since early in the seventeenth century. In its comprehensive report of 1619, for example, the college of São Lourenço disclosed that it owned about 35 census on both urban and rural properties.[25] By the beginning of the eighteenth century, the province itself had purchased such annuities from a number of religious houses in Italy. Among them was a Dominican monastery in Ferrara; two colleges, one there and one in Milan, both possibly Jesuit facilities; and several other Italian congregations. The sums involved were modest (6.5 contos) and so were the interest rates (between 2.6 and 3 percent).[26]

The second type of annuity was a charge or rent (juro) on a source of crown income. A retrospective report of 1791 discloses that four Lisbon houses, the colleges of Santo Antão and St. Francis Xavier, and the novitiates of Cotovia and Arroios possessed government annuities with a book value of slightly in excess of 65 contos. Their yield—4 and 5 percent per annum—amounted to 3.3 contos. All those annuities were acquired between 1696 and 1731, some by purchase, others by gift. The sources included excises on fruit, fish, and meat collected in Lisbon, the Setúbal salt revenues, the house of the heir apparent (infante), and tax revenues derived from assessments on brazilwood and bullion from Brazil, as well as receipts from customs houses in the northern reaches of the kingdom. Most of the funds

---

grave damage results from monetary loans to seculars" and directs "in virtue of Holy Obedience that no procurator loan money to any person of any quality whatsoever" save those who are members of the Society. Interestingly enough, 80 years later a Visitor to Jesuit missions in northwestern Mexico admonished that "the missionaries should not contract debts with laymen even if they need something for their own maintenance. Let the superior be of assistance by getting a loan from some nearby missionary." "Remarks of an Unknown Father Visitor, about 1740," in Charles W. Polzer, S.J., trans. and ed., *Rules and Precepts of the Jesuit Missions of Northwestern New Spain* (Tucson, 1976), 120.

23. E.g., a report of 1758–59 reveals that for the previous dozen years, the marquis of Alegrete had failed to pay the 5% interest that he owed the province of Malabar on a loan of 400,000 rs. ATC/CJ, no. 266, fol. 3^v.

24. Noonan, *Scholastic Analysis*, chaps. 7 and 11. There is an increasing volume of literature concerning the importance of census obligations in Colonial Spanish America, notably Asunción Lavrin, "The Role of the Nunneries in the Economy of New Spain in the Eighteenth Century," *HAHR* 46 (Nov. 1966): 371–93; Brian R. Hamnett, "Church Wealth in Peru: Estates and Loans in the Archdiocese of Lima in the Seventeenth Century," *Jahrbuch für Geschichte von Staat, Wirtschaft und Gesellschaft Lateinamerikas* 10 (1973): 113–32; Arnold J. Bauer, "The Church in the Economy of Spanish America: *Censos* and *Depositos* in the Eighteenth and Nineteenth Centuries," *HAHR* 63 (1983): 707–33; Nicholas P. Cushner, *Lords of the Land: Sugar, Wine and Jesuit Estates of Coastal Peru, 1600–1767* (Albany, 1980), 49–50 and 138–39; Ermilia Troconis de Veracoechea, ed., *Los censos en la iglesia colonial Venezolana*, vol. 1 (Caracas, 1982); and Gisela von Wobeser, "Los censos como mecanismo de endeudamiento de las haciendas en la epoca colonial," in *De la historia: Homenaje a Jorge Gurria Lacroix* (Mexico City, 1985). (For the last two items I am indebted to Professor Lavrin.) The only comparable work that I have seen on the Lusitanian world is *DHP*, 4: 393–96.

25. "Enformação da fazenda o q. tem o coll.º do P.^{to} ... 1619," in ANTT/CJ/57, no. 31.

26. "Censuum activorum provincia lusitaniae [July] 1702," in ARSI, *Informationum*, procurator general, lib. 142, fols. 677^r–677^v; Francisco da Fonseca, S.J., "Livro da fazenda ou noticia das rendas e obrigações das provincias da assistencia de Portugal ... anno 1730," in ARSI, FG, 627/B, fol. 3.

were invested in behalf of chantries, such as that of St. Francis Xavier in the college of Santo Antão, or for the training of missionaries bound for Meliapor or China.[27]

Another source, a book of accounts spanning the years 1756–61, provides further clues to the question of Jesuit investments in the kingdom. It reveals that nearly all the houses in the Peninsular province and most of the overseas provinces possessed annuities issued by nineteen different government agencies. Among them were the two largest maritime customs houses, Lisbon and Porto; the leading salt-exporting center, Setúbal; the network of interior customs, called *portos secos*; the royal mint; the treasury council; the Overseas Council; and the excise tax board. Those annuities provided Peninsular houses with 14.3 percent of their annual income during the 1750s.[28] Such income was especially important to the overseas provinces that did not share the Japan province's advantage of having a steady income supplier, the Carcavelos property, in the kingdom (see Chapter 15). Conspicuously missing among Jesuit shareholders of those government annuities, however, were the Brazil provinces.

The Anomaly of the Brazil Provinces

A few years ago, Dr. Rae Jean Flory completed an impressive dissertation in which she analyzed lending patterns in Salvador, Brazil's first administrative center, and its environs between 1680 and 1725. Not surprisingly, her study reveals that the capital's religious institutions provided nearly half (45.3 percent) of the capital that was lent, followed by merchants (24.8 percent), lawyers and other professionals (12.5 percent), mill owners (7.3 percent), and minor lenders.[29] Among the institutional creditors, by far the largest was the local charitable agency, the Santa Casa da Misericórdia, which supplied 26.4 percent of all loans. One of many such agencies that Portuguese philanthropists established in communities at home and throughout the empire, the Bahian house was certainly the best endowed in Brazil and was easily the source of the largest loans.[30] Between 1699 and 1726, that is, during the first decades of the Brazilian gold rush (about 1690–1760), the level of its loans increased dramatically to an average of 1,427,150 rs. per year, compared with an average of only 627,642 rs. annually during the years 1677–98. Remarkably, the house was able to lend as much as 25 contos a year during the first quarter of the eighteenth century, a sum that was about twice the average income of the Jesuit college in Salvador at that time.[31]

27. "Relação dos juros reaes que existem' nesta contadoria geral que ficarão dos que se sequestrarão aos regulares da Companhia . . . de Jezus," Lisbon, 9 Aug. 1791, in ATC/CJ, no. 268.

28. Calculations based upon "Livro da receita de juros, tenças, e ordinarias confiscados em virtude da sentença de 12 janeiro de 1759," in ATC/CJ, no. 281, an account book of 221 folios. The last available economic report from the province is the "Catalogus 3us rerum provincia Lusitana an. 1754," in ARSI, *Lus.*, 49, fols. 200–204^v.

29. Flory, "Bahian Society in the Mid-Colonial Period: The Sugar Planters, Tobacco Growers, Merchants, and Artisans of Salvador and the Recôncavo, 1680–1725," Ph.D. diss., University of Texas, 1978, 72.

30. The standard study is A. J. R. Russell-Wood, *Fidalgos and Philanthropists: The Santa Casa da Misericórdia of Bahia, 1550–1755* (Berkeley, 1968).

31. "Memoria do cabedal pertencente a Santa Caxa da Miz.^{a} desta cid.^{e} . . . dado a rezao de juro a seis e quarto por cento feito por ordem de Sua Mag.^{de} no anno de 1727," BPE, CXVI/2–13, fols. 100^r–119^r.

What has escaped Dr. Flory and those who have followed her is the conspicuous omission of the Salvadoran college from the list of major lenders in the Brazilian capital. The fact is that Jesuit colleges in the Brazil province or in the vice-province of Maranhão did *not* become prominent lenders in the colony,[32] although their brother colleges often performed that service in the Spanish empire.[33] Why, then, did Brazilian colleges, unlike those in the Spanish empire and, indeed, unlike those in other parts of the Portuguese Assistancy, abstain from lending in their own local markets?

Since no directive from Rome required Jesuit managers in Brazil to refrain from investing in that colony, we are left with several possible explanations. First, during most of the inclusive years of this study, the expanding infrastructure of colleges, especially those that became heavily committed to slave-produced cane sugar, absorbed a large proportion of the earned income, leaving at best modest surpluses. Second, it is possible that the demand for investment funds in the colony was adequately filled by the branches of the Santa Casa and the other types of lender discussed by Dr. Flory. Third, it is also conceivable that Jesuit leaders regarded the practice of lending in Brazil to be exceptionally risky. The experience of the Bahian Holy House of Mercy demonstrates that such activity could indeed become perilous. According to the Holy House's records, by 1772 it was owed 227,331,693 rs. for funds lent during the course of the preceding century to 203 borrowers, many of them prominent members of the local aristocracy. Of that amount, the directors of the House wrote off 85 contos as uncollectable; they optimistically regarded the balance, 25 percent of which had been owed prior to 1740, as still recoverable.[34] It is unlikely that the problems of the Holy House, echoes of those that beset other branches in places as far removed as Goa and Macao, were unknown to Jesuit leaders, and they may have dampened whatever interest the Society may have had in lending funds in Brazil.[35]

But there is another consideration, and this introduces a fourth point: far more than any of the other overseas provinces, those of Brazil were so actively engaged in trade with the kingdom through sales of their sugars, hides, cacao, and other forest products that they

---

Flory, who consulted a copy of this manuscript in the IHGB, provides an excellent analysis of the categories of the Santa Casa's borrowers during these years. "Bahian Society," 76.

32. The emphasis is upon *prominent*, for it is clear that the colleges and their managers did extend at least short-term credit to their debtors. In an undated memo of about 1575, Cristóvão de Gouveia observed that "ciertas personas en Perna'buco [deven] ao dicho collegio 600U," that "diversas personas desta cidade [Salvador deven] ao dicho collegio 800U," and that "Deve el collegio de la Baya a diversas personas en la mesma cidade 900U." ARSI, *Bras.*, 11. However, the surviving economic reports from the Brazilian colleges show no significant source of income deriving from funds or goods lent.

33. Cf. Kendall W. Brown, "Jesuit Wealth and Economic Activity Within the Peruvian Economy: The Case of Colonial Southern Peru," *The Americas* 44 (July 1987): 23–43, at 35 and 39; and Nicholas P. Cushner, *Jesuit Ranches and the Agrarian Development of Colonial Argentina, 1650–1767* (Albany, 1983), 18–19. Cf. idem, *Farm and Factory: The Jesuits and the Development of Agrarian Capitalism in Colonial Quito, 1600–1767* (Albany, 1982), 167–69, concerning limited opportunities for investment in Quito.

34. "Livro de contas de diversos devedores antigos, 1671–1772," in Archives of the Santa Casa da Misericórdia, Bahia, cod. 1360 (cod. 1336, which begins in 1773, is the continuation). Another codex in the Overseas Council's archives casts further light upon the burden of debts that the Santa Casa bore between 1676 and 1744 and indicates that there was scant likelihood of recovering many of them. AHU/LR/1265.

35. As one viceroy observed, "The collection of debts everywhere is difficult but especially so in America," because of the propensity of both principals and their bondsmen (*fiadores*) to abscond, leaving behind assets insufficient to defray their obligations. Count of Galveas to Duarte Sodre P[erei]ra (captain-general, Pernambuco), 11 Oct. 1735, in APB/CGVA/152, fol. 22.

inevitably accumulated relatively large cash balances in Lisbon. Rather than send such surplus funds back across the Atlantic, it made more sense for the procurators to invest them in Europe and to utilize the accrual to defray expenses they incurred in behalf of the provinces they served. That, in fact, did happen, as we know from two statements concerning the Brazil province accounts. One, already mentioned in the previous section, indicates that the province held annuities worth 3.5 contos belonging to a Dominican house in Ferrara and to another religious congregation in Italy.[36] The second is a summary of the accounts of the Lisbon procurate of the Brazil province compiled for an internal inspection in the mid-1690s. It lists the amount of principal and the interest rate for fifteen loans outstanding within the kingdom. Altogether they were valued at 20.95 contos. The borrowers, who paid interest installments of 4 to 6.25 percent yearly, included the Cotovia novitiate in Lisbon, the procurator of the province of Goa, several convents, individual priests, and others who may have been merchants or landowners.[37] Whether the Brazil province subsequently increased such investments and whether the vice-province of Maranhão did so as well remains to be determined. What seems clear, at any rate, is that the eastern provinces followed a very different pattern in their investments.

Investment Patterns Among the Eastern Provinces

Proceeds from investments were an especially important source of income for the two Far Eastern provinces. In Macao, one distinctive source of such income was sea loans (*respondência*, *respondêntia*) made upon the cargoes of third parties. Issuance of such loans traces back to Greek and Roman antiquity. They were high-risk ventures, since lenders were not assured of the payment of either their principal or a premium if the voyage failed. For that reason, one procurator recommended against investing in them. Nevertheless, the Macao college received certain legacies whose donors specified that the moneys they left were to be invested in respondência until the funds they established became large enough to fulfill a prescribed pious purpose.[38] Between December 1661 and June 1667, sea loans provided just over 51 percent of the reported income of the vice-province of China.[39] As Portugal's political and economic position in the East deteriorated, the making of this type of loan appears to have declined as well sometime before the end of that century.

36. Those annuities, reported in 1702, were still owned in 1730 but were omitted from the crown's analysis of the overseas procurates' accounts at the end of the 1750s.

37. Enc. in "Exemplum de Ratiocensus etatis a P. Balthassar . . . proveratoris Brasiliae P. Dominico Ramos," 24 Aug. 1695, in ARSI, *Bras.*, 3:II, 347–348[v].

38. On the origins of sea loans, see Robert S. Lopez and Irving W. Raymond, *Medieval Trade in the Mediterranean World* (New York, [1967]), 169–73. For juridical aspects, consult John E. Hall, trans. and ed., *An Essay on Maritime Loans from the French of M. Bathazard Marie Emerignon* (Baltimore, 1811), 17, 22, and 28; Alexandre Annesley, *A Compendium of the Law of Maritime Insurance, Bottomry, Insurance on Lives, and Insurance Against Fire* (Middleton, Conn., 1808), 173–96; and Samuel Marshall, *A Treatise on the Law of Insurance* (Boston, 1805), 633. C. R. Boxer confuses bottomry with respondência ("Macao as a Religious and Commercial Entrepôt in the 16th and 17th Centuries," *Acta Asiatica* 26 [1974]: 80), while the editors of the *DI* series confuse respondência with *correspondencia*. See *DI*, 16: 32 n. 13, which is the only reference I have seen to the letting of sea loans by Jesuits in India.

39. "Receita do cabedal da v. prov.ᵃ da China . . . 18 de dezembro de 1661 ate o fim de junho de 1667," in ARSI, FG, 721/II/6.

At the beginning of the 1660s, the vice-province of China became the beneficiary of a respectable legacy of 2,160,000 rs., which it invested, apparently in Macao, at 10 percent.[40] One suspects that the fund managers must have been tempted by the extraordinary interest rates prevailing in mainland China—rates that at various times in the seventeenth century mushroomed to between 30 and 50 percent per annum—to invest the legacy in loans to the emperor's subjects.[41] There is no evidence that they or their successors ever did so. Their restraint may have stemmed from concerns regarding the unstable political conditions within the empire and the long-precarious position of the Society's representatives there (see Chapter 6), from misgivings about possible charges of usury, or simply from a lack of interest among potential Chinese customers. In any case, the vice-province did earn income from investments in two distant places, Europe and India.

As observed in Chapter 14, a number of wealthy Europeans promised and sometimes actually provided funds for the support of the vice-province. One was a duke of Bavaria who in 1616 left 500 florins a year to the enterprise for the balance of his life. His heirs continued to honor that pledge until 1689, by which time the fund had grown to 20,200 florins invested at 4 to 6 percent interest. But that year, the Turks overran the estates that had been the source of the income, and the fund subsequently disappeared. As already noted, however, some German nobles came forward to assist the vice-province with funds that its agents were able to invest in the Germanies, Austria, or Italy. In the early eighteenth century, several Portuguese aristocrats also promised legacies to be invested in the East, but the money was never forthcoming; however, the vice-province did share the fabulous estate of the famous admiral of Castile (see Chapter 14).[42] Parts of its share were invested in banks in Vienna and Milan and in a chantry in Naples. The deposit in the *giro* bank in Vienna amounted to 400,000 florins and, at 4 percent, netted as much as 16,000 florins a year in interest.[43]

The same source provided much, if not all, of the money that the Lisbon procurate of the vice-province employed when it purchased annuities in four government treasuries in the kingdom during the 1710s or 1720s. In 1731, income from government annuities in the kingdom and from several other legacies was a modest 388,750 rs. Yet by the late 1750s, the yield from the same annuities had grown to about 2.6 contos a year. Such earnings became vital to the operations of the vice-province and at one point during the eighteenth century provided 44.3 percent of its annual income.[44]

40. "Treslado da escritura q. o proc.^or da prov.^a de Japan passou ... [do] legado ... deixou a vice prov.^a da China" (1662), in ARSI, *JapSin*, 23, fol. 13^v.

41. For testimony concerning the prevalence of such rates, at least in Canton and its vicinity, see Manuel Ramos (ouvidor, Macao) to Viceroy Linhares, 11 Dec. 1635, in C. R. Boxer, "The Swan Song of the Portuguese in Japan, 1635–39," Japan Society, *Transactions and Proceedings* 27 (1929–30): 4–11, at 8–9, and Fr. Buenaventura Ibañez to missions procurator, province of Canton, 25 Feb. 1682 and 7 Jan. 1683, in Anastasius Van den Wyngaert, O.F.M., and Fabian Bollen, O.F.M., eds., *Sinica Franciscana*, vol. 3, *Relationes et epistolas fratrum minorum saeculi xvii* (Quarachi, 1936), 242, 251, and 255.

42. Fonseca, "Livro da fazenda ... da assistencia de Portugal," fols. 11^v, 12, 15^r, and 89ff.

43. "Copia de padrão dos juros do banco do giro da cid.^e de Vienna ... 1730," in ARSI, *Lus.*, 80:II, fol. 514, is a summary of the yield of that account from 1718, the year after it was opened, until 1732. On the functions of giro banks, see Frederick C. Lane, "Venetian Bankers, 1496–1533," reprinted in Lane, *Venice and History* (Baltimore, 1966), 69 and 72.

44. "Estado de todas as rendas da v. provincia da China em 1731," in ARSI, FG, 627; "Livro da receita de juros, tenças, e ordinarias" (see note 28 above), passim.

Much of the rest came from India. Earlier chapters have pointed to the revenue-producing estates that the vice-province maintained in the Indian subcontinent. Its resident procurator utilized part of the income derived from those properties to lend money to Indian borrowers. A report of 1717 lists 27 persons who between 1694 and 1716 borrowed 29.8 contos from the procurate at rates that varied from a low of 1.5 to a high of 15.3 percent.[45] The principals of many of those loans were probably lost during the war with the Marathas in the late 1730s when the vice-province experienced severe financial losses in India (see Chapter 23).

The Japan province also lost revenue as a result of the Maratha capture of revenue-producing lands in the northern province, but it was in a better position to withstand such a blow because it possessed greater resources. As observed in earlier chapters, its most lucrative source of income during the late sixteenth and early seventeenth centuries was the silk trade, followed by royal and papal subventions. After Japanese authorities terminated trade between their archipelago and Macao, and Anglo-Dutch intrusions in the eastern seas made the dispatch of the subventions increasingly sporadic and undependable, the provincial managers pursued other forms of commerce, especially with South Asia and with the Indonesian archipelago (see Chapter 21), and invested in respondência.[46]

By the eighteenth century, however, the Japan province also became an active lender in conventional paper. Unlike the vice-province of China, it lent some funds (2.4 contos) to half a dozen religious congregations in Italy. Their proceeds probably covered its expenses in Rome.[47] The province also acquired a few investments to support its general expenses, the college of Macao, and the Vietnam missions, but in 1719 their yield was only about 4.4 percent of its total income.[48] Of greater consequence, especially after the province lost some of its Indian holdings, was income from government and other annuities that it acquired in the kingdom during that century. In the 1750s their yield reached as much as 6 contos, a sum that exceeded the province's entire reported income for 1730.[49] Yet that sum was insignificant when compared with Jesuit investments in eighteenth-century India.

In 1660, when Francisco Barreto served as Visitor, he left an instruction to be observed by each procurator in the Goan province. He admonished them to abstain from lending to secular persons because of the difficulties of collection.[50] A few years later, the college of Bassein revealed that it was the only Jesuit institution in the province that gained a significant portion of its income (16.7 percent) from loans to Indian villages.[51] The Visitor's directive, of

45. "Lista ou balança geral que o mandou a Goa o Irmao M.ᵉˡ Simões quando entro a ser pro[curador] no norte . . . 1717," HAG 1497, fols. 317ʳ–324ᵛ.

46. Two sources that indicate the making of sea loans on behalf of the Japan province during the 1660s and 1680s are "Receita [e despeza] do cabedal da prov.ᵃ de Japão," May 1668 to May 1669, in ARSI, *JapSin*, 23, fols. 152–155ᵛ; and "Breve rezumo do estado . . . ao prezente se acha esta procuratura da prov.ᵃ de Jappao," Macao, 20 Dec. 1680, in ARSI, *Goa*, 35, fols. 163ʳ–166ᵛ.

47. "Censuum activorum provincia lusitaniae [July] 1702" (note 26 above).

48. Joseph Anselmo, S.J., "Informe das rendas q. tem na India as provincias de Jappam e China," 6 Jan. 1717, BA/JA/49-V-27, no. 197.

49. "Livro da receita de juros, tenças, e ordinarias" (see note 28 above); report of provincial secretary to viceroy, enc. in João de Saldanha da Gama to king, 23 Jan. 1731, in AHU/PA/IN, *m*. 35.

50. See note 22.

51. "Lista das rendas e despezas da provincia de Goa," Goa, 13 Dec. 1666, in Câmara Municipal, Elvas, ms. 6891.

course, did not preclude loans to the royal exchequer in Goa and, as noted in Chapter 13, the exchequer borrowed rather frequently from the Jesuits from this time onward. Such borrowings naturally restricted the funds the Jesuits were able to make available to others from their own assets. However, the fathers also controlled another source of loan money that was specifically entrusted to them for the making of loans so that the proceeds could be used to defray the cost of masses as well as the purchase of wax, wafers, wine, and candles. In 1710 the provincial reported that 22 persons had left 20.5 contos in chantries in the church of the professed house, Bom Jesús, to defray such expenses.[52] That was ten times as much as was in a similar loan fund that the church of New St. Paul's college maintained to purchase materials required for its masses.[53] Furthermore, the interest the fathers charged, a mere 5.3 percent, was extremely modest by Indian standards, especially during the seventeenth century.[54]

Early in the eighteenth century, Manoel Pereira, provincial of the fragile Malabar province (1711–14), responded to a number of queries from General Tamburini. He was asked why the province did not invest in land and responded that because of the frequency of wars in the south it did not make sense to do so. He was asked why his province did not earn money through loans extended in Goa and answered that it lacked opportunities to do so.[55] Such opportunities subsequently materialized for the administrators of Malabar, but in the northern province rather than in Goa. According to a report of 1734, the province had lent the astounding sum of 133 contos at an average rate of 7.9 percent to unnamed borrowers in the north.[56] But units of the Goan province advanced even more funds in the northern province and supposedly earned returns of as much as 10 percent. According to a viceregal report of 1735, they lent 805 contos in the Bassein district and another 360.6 contos to borrowers in the vicinity of Goa.[57]

Such investments far outweighed the annuities that the two provinces acquired in Europe. Like several other provinces of the Assistancy, both Malabar and Goa lent money to Italian congregations, three in the case of Malabar and six in that of Goa.[58] In addition, Goa (but not Malabar) acquired government securities amounting to 16.6 contos and loaned, at 3 percent, another 4.2 contos to the overseas procurate of Brazil.[59] Earnings from those

52. Manoel Carvalho (provincial), [report on chantries], professed house, Goa, 5 Sept. 1710, in ARSI, *Goa*, 9:II, fols. 467–73ᵛ.

53. "Livro da receita e despeza dos ganhos do colegio de S. Paulo 1705–1714," HAG 2107. This is one of a series of eight codices showing income and expenditures relating to a fund of 2.7 contos lent at 5.3% interest.

54. During that century, rates along the Coromandel coast reached as much as 4% and 5% per month. At Surat they varied from 0.5% to 3% per month, about the same as in North India. Tapan Raychaudhuri, *Jan Company in Coromandel, 1605–1690* (The Hague, 1962), 12; Irfan Habib, "Usury in Medieval India," *Comparative Studies in Society and History* 6, 4 (1964): 393–423, esp. 401–4. In the 1750s an archbishop of Goa undertook a visitation of his domain and was shocked to learn that non-Christian Indians lent Catholics money at 25% to 50% per year and concealed the extent of their extortion by manipulating their books. António, archbishop of Goa, to king, 19 Jan. 1754, in AHU/PA/IN, *m.* 56.

55. F/JM, 2: 269.

56. Ibid., 347.

57. Pedro Mascarenhas, count of Sandomil (viceroy), to king, 22 Jan. 1735, in ACL, ms. Azul, 505, fols. 220–23 (draft); AHU/PA/IN, *m.* 31 (orig.).

58. The "Censuum activorum" cited in note 26 above indicates that Goa's holdings amounted to 2,665,000 rs., while Malabar's amounted to 1,033,000 rs.

59. "Conta que derão os pp. procuradores das prov.ᵃˢ da companhia de Jesus em o ultramar" (Dec. 1758–Feb. 1759), ATC/CJ/266, fol. 1.

sources remained secure until the expulsion, but most, if not all, of those contracted in the northern province were lost a few years later as a result of the Maratha invasion. Apparently Jesuit managers simply wrote off most of them, for when royal authorities seized their records in 1761 they found evidence of only 134.4 contos owed by 136 persons to units of the Goan province. But those debts included delinquent rent and service obligations as well as loans, some of which dated from the 1720s. Surprisingly, crown investigators discovered only sixteen borrowers who, in 1761, owed an additional 3.7 contos to the enfeebled Malabar province.[60]

From the evidence that survives, it appears that Jesuit facilities in the Portuguese Assistancy began expanding their investment portfolios in the seventeenth century and continued to do so, either through purchase or gift of annuities, census, or obligations, well into the 1750s. Such investments appeared to be attractive alternatives to more traditional sources of income, such as the yield of estates or earnings from leased urban holdings. Since they were invisible to the Society's critics, their growth did not invite the sort of virulent criticism that the Society's expanding rural and urban properties provoked. For the same reason, they were immune to the jealousy that, for example, canoe-laden cargoes of cacao and other forest products attracted in northern Brazil or that Jesuit-owned frigates inspired when they cleared colonial ports. With the exception of the conditional deposits held by Santo Antão and probably certain other colleges, the administrative burdens of managing annuities held in European banks and loans made to dependable ecclesiastical borrowers were minimal. Absent the onset of war, or acts of arbitrary confiscation by states, or the insolvency of borrowers, such investments may not have involved substantially greater risks than insuring the cargo of a merchant vessel sailing in perilous eastern seas or attempting to forecast the price of sugar on the Lisbon market a year and a half after planting canes. Though income from investments for most Jesuit entities still provided only a small share of total receipts by the mid-eighteenth century, it is entirely possible that Jesuit leaders would have expanded that source in years to come. But, of course, that is mere speculation, since the Society was destined to lose all of its assets within Portuguese domains during the late 1750s and early 1760s. As we shall see next, the Society's situation in the Assistancy became increasingly perilous during the first half of the eighteenth century.

60. "Relação do que esta por cobrar dos rendimentos e dividas preteritas e prezentes pertencentes a admin. do confisco . . . de [*sic*] Est.° da India, ate o fim de dezembro de 1775," in AHU/LR/348.

PART V

An Enterprise Questioned

CHAPTER 23

Vicissitudes of a Beleaguered Enterprise: The Society on the Defensive, 1700–1750

Maintaining their East Indies has for many years cost this crown more than it has gotten, nor is there any likelihood it should be otherwise hereafter.

—Charles Fanshaw to earl of Sunderland, Lisbon, 20 Nov. 1684

Tournon's embassy led not only to the destruction of the mission, it was also fraught with the worst consequences for the Jesuits in China.

—Ludwig von Pastor

It is doubtful if a worse or more fruitless struggle has ever shaken Catholic Christendom.

—J. S. Cummins, ed., *The Travels and Controversies of Friar Domingo Navarrete, 1618–1686*

EACH CENTURY PRODUCED new challenges for the Society in its Portuguese Assistancy. The sixteenth witnessed the Order's foundation, its spectacular growth, its initial entry into Portugal, its expansion to the furthest reaches of the globe, and the foundations of its educational, evangelical, and economic infrastructures. But during the ensuing century, it, along with the Portuguese crown, suffered serious setbacks, from which, to some extent, both eventually recovered. It is true that the Jesuits were definitively expelled from Japan, Malacca, Ceylon, and Ethiopia and, together with other agents of the Lusitanian regime, were largely eliminated by the Dutch from South India; but they returned to both northeastern Brazil and Angola after the Dutch intruders had been driven out and attained a dominant position in the spiritual life of Amazonia, the theater where their missions in Brazil became most numerous. In the kingdom, the Society remained the crown's most favored Order and continued to dominate its higher-education facilities and to offer spiritual advice to the royal family and to the families of leading nobles. Although Portugal experienced a long succession of military and naval reverses in the Estado da India, Jesuits remained the most conspicuous missionaries there. Though Southeast Asia proved to be a less rewarding mission field than Japan had once been, the Society's leaders could point to the growing number of Christians and to its representatives' entry into the high levels of the Manchu court of imperial China as providing compensation for the lost enterprise in the Japanese isles.

However, during the first half of the eighteenth century (the Joanine period, as these years are often called after the reigning monarch, John V [1706–50]), Jesuits in the Portuguese Assistancy found themselves beset by a new series of reverses. They included the loss of a substantial part of the economic basis of support for Jesuit endeavors in Indian provinces and in the Far East; the serious impairment of missionary activities in China, for which the Society became the accepted scapegoat; the intensification of criticism of its wide-ranging activities throughout Brazil; its diminished presence in the Portuguese court; and the loss of its dominant position in higher education in the Portuguese kingdom. Though many of these reverses failed to catch the attention of Europeans outside the Lusitanian world, that could hardly be said of the celebrated Chinese Rites affair.

Of Rites and Wrongs: The Erosion of the Enterprise in Southeast Asia and China

As reported in Chapter 6, the Jesuits reached a milestone in the celestial empire in the 1690s when the emperor K'ang-hsi sanctioned their right to preach publicly and the number of Christians in his domain reputedly approached 300,000. In 1700 there were nearly a hundred Jesuits serving in the two Far Eastern Portuguese provinces, and perhaps another twenty attached to the French mission to China.[1] Although the Japan province, primarily Southeast Asia, remained much smaller than it had been at the beginning of the seventeenth century, it continued to attract more than half the number of Jesuits serving in the two Portuguese provinces. Some members of that province, in fact, assisted in China. According to a report of 1730, eight missionaries attached to that province worked in the Chinese provinces of Kwantung and Kwansi, compared with 32 serving in the two Vietnams, Siam, and Cambodia; 36 were members of the Macao college, whereas four were stationed in India.[2] An even higher portion of the vice-province's membership was then ministering within the empire: an estimated 39 out of 50.[3] As Table 23.1 suggests, the membership of the two provinces fluctuated considerably throughout the first half of the eighteenth century, when the long-standing Chinese Rites controversy reached the boiling point, with serious consequences for both provinces.[4]

1. The only estimate that I have seen for the French mission is that of 1717 in *RJC*, 338.

2. Jesuit authorities in Macao reported that members of the Society continued to suffer martyrdoms in Southeast Asia during the eighteenth century. In the mid-1730s a contingent of four young fathers entered North Vietnam via Tonkin Gulf and were promptly expelled. When they persisted in returning, they were apprehended, tried, and executed by having their throats slit. *Relação da prizão e morte dos quatro veneraveis padres da companhia, Bartholomeo Alvarez, Manoel de Abreu, Vicente da Cunha (Portuguezes) e João Gaspar Cratz (Alemão), mortos ... na corte de Tumkin aos 12 de janeiro de 1737* (Lisbon, 1739). James Ford Bell Library, University of Minnesota.

3. Enc. in João de Saldanha da Gama (viceroy, India) to king, 23 Jan. 1731, in AHU/PA/IN, *cx.* 35, no. 46.

4. The literature concerning the Rites controversies is voluminous. See *HP*, 33: 394 n. 1; *BHCJ*, 2: 351–53; and John W. Witek, S.J., "From India to Japan: European Missionary Expansion, 1500–1650," in John W. O'Malley, S.J., ed., *Catholicism in Early Modern History: A Guide to Research* (St. Louis, 1988), 208–9. Despite its age, Arnold H. Rowbotham, *Missionary and Mandarin: The Jesuits at the Court of China* (Berkeley, 1942), chaps. 9–12, is still worth reading, though it makes no use of Jesuit archival sources and is hostile toward the Society. Antonio Sisto Rosso, O.F.M., *Apostolic Legations to China of the Eighteenth Century* (South Pasadena, 1948), offers a Franciscan perspective and supplies a valuable documentary appendix. J. S. Cummins, ed., *The Travels and Controversies of Friar Domingo Navarrete, 1618–1686*, 2 vols., *HS*:2, nos. 118–19 (1962), 118: xxxviii–

TABLE 23.1

Growth and Decline of the Japan Province and the Vice-Province of China,
1700–1755

Year	Japan	China	Year	Japan	China
1700	63	36	1734	87	—
1702	—	46	1741	—	45
1703	57	—	1742	61	—
1706	—	38	1751	—	47
1714	54	—	1753	59	—
1723	—	26	1755	—	46
1730	80	50			

SOURCES: For 1730: viceroy to king, 23 Jan. 1731, in AHU/PA/IN, *cx.* 35, no. 46. For the remainder: ARSI, *JapSin,* 25, 26/D, and 134, fols. 301–447.

That fundamental dispute, whose substance was political as well as theological, traces back to the beginning of the seventeenth century, when Matteo Ricci, the founding architect of Jesuit endeavors in the empire, tried to build a firm cultural bridge between Chinese and Western culture to facilitate China's conversion. His studies of Chinese classics led him to conclude that certain Chinese practices, notably those involving the veneration of ancestors and periodic ceremonies honoring Confucius, could be construed as proximates of Christian customs and that certain terms, notably *T'ien* and *Shang-ti,* could be employed to denote Heaven and the Lord on high or God. Although his superior, Alessandro Valignano, concurred with Ricci's relativism, the founder's successor, Niccolò Longobardo, strongly dissented and wrote a series of treatises denying Ricci's contentions. Despite his efforts and those of his many supporters, Longobardo was eventually ruled out of order by his superiors. As a result, the Riccian interpretation would remain the official Jesuit position and would be endorsed by a prominent Chinese emperor.[5]

The arrival of the Mendicants inevitably brought new challenges to Jesuit syncretism, for China became a new arena of dissension between Jesuits and friars, who, as seen earlier, had already squabbled in Japan. Although initially excluded from China, too, the Mendicants obtained papal support to enter the empire in the early 1630s. The Spanish-born Dominicans and the Franciscans who first arrived in the empire during that decade discovered Jesuit tolerance of Chinese religious practices that they deemed as corrupting and

lxxii, provides an astute analysis of the conflict between the Jesuits and the friars. See also idem, "Two Missionary Methods in China: Mendicants and Jesuits," reprinted in *Jesuit and Friar in the Spanish Expansion to the East* (London, 1986). Pastor (*HP,* 33: 31–35, passim) places the controversies in a European perspective. George Minamiki, S.J., *The Chinese Rites Controversy from Its Beginning to Modern Times* (Chicago, 1985), adds nothing new to our understanding of that conflict during the seventeenth and eighteenth centuries. See also David E. Mungello, *Curious Land: Jesuit Accommodation and the Origins of Sinology* (Stuttgart, 1985); and Jacques Gernet, *China and the Christian Impact: A Conflict of Cultures,* trans. Janet Lloyd (New York, 1985). The contributions of other writers are indicated below. The late Philip Robinson assembled a major collection of rare published sources on the Rites question and other aspects of Jesuit activities in China, but unhappily it was dispersed at an auction: *The Library of Philip Robinson,* pt. 2, *The Chinese Collection* (London, 1988).

5. On divisions within the Society concerning these matters, see especially George H. Dunne, S.J., *Generation of Giants: The Story of the Jesuits in China in the Last Decades of the Ming Dynasty* (Notre Dame, 1962), chap. 17.

threatening the very fabric of Catholicism. They therefore challenged Jesuit superiors to an unwanted debate. As James Cummins has wisely observed, the clash between the Jesuits and their rivals "was first and foremost a struggle between two types of Western mind— the one traditional and conservative, the other progressive and adventurous. . . . [It was a] clash . . . exacerbated by nationalism and institutional rivalries" and fueled by "misguided patriotism," since the Jesuits who then operated in China did so under Portuguese patronage, whereas the friars served under that of Spain. It was, as Cummins says, inevitable that the two sides would engage in bitter conflict, since one attacked the issues from a Probalist viewpoint, and the other came from a Rigorist perspective.[6]

Having failed to reach a meeting of minds with Jesuits in the field, the leader of the opposition, the Dominican Juan Bautista de Morales, went to Rome to present his case to Urban VIII, who referred Morales's complaint to the Congregation of the Propaganda of the Faith. The first of many papal findings was issued in 1645: having accepted Morales's arguments, Innocent X condemned the Rites as depicted by the Dominicans. A decade later, the Jesuits dispatched one of their leading scholars, Fr. Martino Martini, the compiler of the first atlas of China, to represent their views before another supreme pontiff, Alexander VII, who concurred with Martini that the contested ceremonies were civic and social but not religious in intent. Accordingly, in 1656 the pope issued another decree supportive of the Jesuits' position. Dominicans naturally protested that these two decrees were contradictory, so Rome further muddled the situation by issuing still another decree in 1669, one that was, as Fr. Minamiki has written, "in reality no decision at all," since it left the determination of the legitimacy of the Rites "to the consciences of the missionaries" themselves.[7]

If Rome was content to leave such thorny questions up to missionaries in the field and to their immediate superiors, the Jesuits' critics clearly were not. One of the Society's most formidable adversaries was the Spaniard Domingo Navarrete (b. 1618–d. 1686), a Dominican who spent nine years in the Philippines before coming with Morales to China, where after some years in the field he became head of his Order. Dissatisfied with the 1669 decree, he traveled to Rome and submitted to the Propaganda a lengthy statement in which he denounced Jesuit interpretations of Chinese moral and religious values. Subsequently he expanded his views in a highly influential anti-Jesuit scholarly treatise, part of which was published in Madrid in 1676. His sources included not only Confucian and neo-Confucian commentaries but also some of Longobardo's critique.[8]

But although Navarrete offered a serious scholarly critique of the Rites question that influenced later Jesuit opponents, his efforts did not bring about papal action. Those of Charles Maigrot did. Maigrot, a secular priest with close connections to the anti-Jesuit Society of Foreign Missions of Paris,[9] in his capacity as vicar apostolic of Fukien province, issued a pastoral letter condemning accommodation and proscribing the use of the terms T'ien and Shang-ti. Ironically, his letter was issued exactly one year after the Jesuits'

---

6. Cummins, ed., *Travels*, 1: l–li.
7. Minamiki, *Chinese Rites Controversy*, 36.
8. Cummins, ed., *Travels*, 1: lxxxiv–cxiv.
9. Founded in 1658–63 by two vicars apostolic of North and South Vietnam, the Society of Foreign Missions was a congregation of secular priests whose center was a Parisian seminary. *The Catholic Encyclopedia*, special ed. (New York, 1912), 14: 79.

great triumph, the imperial decree upholding the right of the religious to proselytize freely. Undaunted, in 1697 Maigrot, whose deficient knowledge of the Chinese language Emperor K'ang-hsi later ridiculed, labeled Jesuit neophytes as "Jesuit converts" rather than Christians and confidently appealed to Rome for support.

This time the Vatican responded decisively, with devastating results. In 1701 Clement XI named Carlo Tommasco Maillard de Tournon, patriarch of Antioch, as his special envoy to the Chinese court. Tournon (b. 1668–d. 1710), as he is usually called, was the first papal legate sent to the Far East since the thirteenth century, but he proved to be a most unfortunate choice. A member of the Savoyard nobility, he was youthful, supercilious, imperious, moody, and ignorant, for he had no knowledge of the language or culture of China nor any capacity for compromise. He was prone to find fault on all possible occasions, and during his ill-fated years in the Far East the Jesuits were his most frequent targets.[10] His mission began inauspiciously: in an obvious power play, Clement XI directed him to avoid Lisbon and ignored Pedro II's insistence that, in accordance with the padroado real, his government must review the legate's credentials. Instead, Tournon made a leisurely three-year trip (1702–5) to Canton via Pondichery and Manila. If Jesuits in China initially rejoiced at the dispatch of the papal envoy, they soon braced themselves for the worst after learning that he had ruled against the Society in the Malabar Rites case brought against the Jesuits by a French Capuchin during the legate's stay in Pondichery. In effect, Tournon overturned the accommodationist approach of Roberto de Nobili and his successors in South India, one that Rome had approved for nearly a century.[11] During his subsequent sojourn in Manila, the legate severely reproved a Jesuit procurator whom he accused of being guilty of usurious practices.[12]

In China, Tournon had three objectives, none of which he was able to realize. First, as he stated to the emperor K'ang-hsi during the first of their three audiences (December 1705–June 1706), he wanted to establish a permanent papal representative at the imperial court; but he summarily rejected the emperor's proposal that an experienced Jesuit be selected for that position. Second, he hoped to realize Rome's long-standing ambition to make the emperor a Chinese Constantine. Since, however, the emperor's attitude toward religion approximated that of Akbar the Great, that is, one of curiosity but not of profound commitment, Tournon stood no chance of success on that score.[13] Third, he intended to promulgate the pope's decree of 20 November 1704 proscribing Riccian accommodation altogether.

10. Francis A. Rouleau, S.J., "Maillard de Tournon, Papal Legate at the Court of Peking: The First Imperial Audience (31 December 1705)," *AHSI* 31 (1962): 264–323, is a foretaste of a projected two-volume study that the author never lived to complete. It is not only erudite but exceptionally fair to a subject who was far less generous to the Jesuits he encountered in the East. Rowbotham, *Missionary and Mandarin*, chap. 11, is markedly pro-Tournon; Rosso, *Apostolic Legations*, chap. 7, is less so, whereas Pastor is highly critical, esp. *HP*, 33: 412–28, and 35: 461ff. For recent Jesuit assessments of the legate's mission, see John W. Witek, S.J., *Controversial Ideas in China and in Europe: A Biography of Jean-François Foucquet, S.J. (1665–1741)* (Rome, 1982), 130–38; and Minamiki, *Chinese Rites Controversy*, 53–56.

11. *HP*, 33: 485–90; and 34: 204.

12. So, according to Rowbotham, *Missionary and Mandarin*, 149. Strangely, the normally reliable Fr. Horacio de la Costa makes no mention of the incident in his account of the legate's stop in the Philippine capital: *The Jesuits in the Philippines, 1581–1768* (Cambridge, Mass., 1967), 573.

13. Huang Song-Kang, "Kangxi's Attitude in the Rites Controversy," *Heythrop Journal* 28, 1 (Jan. 1987): 57–67.

But the legate concealed his third objective from the emperor until it became evident that his mission to Peking was a failure, one that he attributed (without any shred of evidence) to the machinations of the so-called court Jesuits, especially the highly regarded Tomás Pereira. Accepting the word of a defaulting Chinese debtor, he reproached the fathers for being scandalous lenders, though he suggested no alternatives for defraying their local expenses.

The first of a series of gestures that soured relations between the proud, astute emperor and the Church's representatives came in 1706, when K'ang-hsi summoned Bishop Maigrot to his presence and expelled him and two other vicars from the empire. For good measure, he also consigned Luigi Appiani, a Lazarist priest who had served as the legate's interpreter and prime advisor during his court sojourn, to what proved to be a twenty-year prison term. Since the legate's conduct had made him increasingly suspicious of the intentions of European churchmen, K'ang-hsi effectively revoked his protective decree of 1692. In its stead, he directed that all missionaries take a pledge to adhere to Riccian accommodation and stipulated that only those willing to do so would be issued a certificate (*p'iao*) permitting them to remain in the empire; but even then they would no longer be permitted to spread their faith. To explain why such measures were necessary, the emperor dispatched the first of what proved to be a series of unfruitful Jesuit embassies to Rome.[14]

In retaliation, the retiring legate, Tournon, issued an order, known as the Nanking decree, that effectively proscribed the emperor's order to the missionaries and admonished them to refrain from any compromise with Confucian practices. That mandate led to his arrest by Chinese officials and to his detention in Macao, where the dying prelate spent the balance of his life feuding with local authorities and with the Jesuits. In his frustration, he placed the latter's Macaonese facilities under interdict and excommunicated several Loyolans.[15]

The Tournon mission had several consequences, none of which were beneficial to the China enterprise. First, it represented a serious setback to the Jesuits and to other missionaries, whose position in the empire reverted to that set forth by the imperial edict of 1669, which permitted them to observe their own faith in China privately but not to disseminate it.[16] Second, it divided the missionaries: some took the forbidden oath and

14. Rouleau, "Maillard de Tournon," 265 n. 3 and 281 n. 34; *HP*, 33: 448 and 470; 34: 70–72 and 85; Rosso, *Apostolic Legations*, 333–34; and Song-Kang, "Kangxi's Attitude," 61.

It is significant that whereas the emperor relied upon Jesuits for such missions, the eighteenth-century popes always excluded them from the embassies they sent to the Orient. It seems evident that there was a deliberate policy by the pontiffs and their advisors to strengthen the Vatican's role in China at the expense of the Jesuits.

15. *HP*, 33: 454. "Relação sincera e verdadeira do que fez . . . na missão da China e em Macao o patriarch . . . de Tournon," in Joaquim Heliodoro da Cunha Rivara, ed., *O Chronista de Tissuary* 1 (Nova Goa, 1866): 21–28, 44–49, 85–88, 110–15, 131–36, 159–64, 187–92, 220–23, 249–52, 273–77, 303–9, 321–34; and 2 (1867): 20–25 and 46–50. See also "Primeiro relatorio do capitão geral da cidade de Macao, Diogo de Pinho Teixeira, ao vice rei sobre as cousas do patriarcha de Antiochia," 1 Dec. 1707, in ibid., 2–4, passim; as well as C. R. Boxer, "The Portuguese Padroado in East Asia and the Problem of the Chinese Rites, 1576–1773," *Boletim do Instituto Portuguese de Hong Kong* 1 (July 1948): 199–226, which includes an important appendix. Both the Jesuits and Macaonese civil authorities were targets of severe criticism by partisans of Tournon, who failed to recognize that they were simply obeying instructions from Lisbon. See *APO*:2, 1:3:2, 6–8, 27–34, and 57.

16. Cf. Song-Kang, "Kangxi's Attitude," 60–61.

remained in the empire, others avoided it by going underground, and the remainder—43 until December 1708—suffered banishment from China.[17]

The failure of the Tournon embassy became a cause of deep concern in Lisbon and Goa and led to a bizarre, unofficial Jesuit diplomatic mission to China. The government of John V was very much annoyed that Rome had dispatched Tournon to the East without first notifying the Portuguese court, as had always been customary, and had authorized him to bypass Lisbon. In an effort to offset the damage to the China missions, for which the court held the papal legate responsible, the king directed the viceroy of Goa to identify a worthy person within his territory to dispatch as an "envoy extraordinary" to the emperor with gifts and his personal reassurances that the king had no role in the Tournon affair.[18]

As soon as that instruction reached Goa, the viceroy consulted with the Jesuit Visitor. They both knew bitterly that one of the reasons that the French Jesuits had gained entrée to the celestial court was their knowledge of trigonometry, a form of mathematics with which few Portuguese were familiar.[19] They reasoned that the easiest way to convey the king's message to the emperor was to send a Portuguese father posing as a mathematician. The Visitor soon discovered his man. In November 1709 he addressed a worried letter to the provincial of Goa. He observed that the legate's debacle placed at risk not only the missions in China but also those in Southeast Asia (the Japan province) as well as the Society's essential support base, Macao, which imperial forces might easily overrun. It was imperative to prevent such a catastrophe and to reassure K'ang-hsi, who would surely be upset once he knew that the Jesuit emissaries he had dispatched to Europe had perished at sea. What he would not know, continued the Visitor, was that as soon as the king had learned of their deaths, he had dispatched another religious to reassure the emperor, but his ship had been diverted to Bahia because of leaky seams. It was therefore necessary to detail someone already in the East to the emperor to reassure him as quickly as possible.[20]

Fortunately there was a partially qualified person available, a so-called "master of mathematics" who had taken (but not completed) a course in geometry at Évora, João Francisco Cardozo, assigned to the Malabar province. Initially neither its provincial nor the bishop of Meliapor was willing to part with his services, but the Visitor urged the provincial to consult with the viceroy about sending Fr. Cardozo to China for the good of the Society.[21] The provincial and the prelate bowed to the crown's wishes, and Fr. Cardozo, bearing diplomatic instructions signed by the viceroy and messages to Portuguese Jesuits

17. "Catalogo dos missionarios lançados da China nos annos 1706, [1]707, e [1]708, e dos q. ficaram nella athe Dez.^bro de 1708," in ARSI, FG, 722/5; another copy is in BA/JA/49-V-25, fols. 204^v–207^v; cf. Rouleau, "Maillard de Tournon," 268 n. 7.

18. King to D. Rodrigo da Costa (viceroy), 3 Apr. 1709, in *APO*:2, 1:3:2, 6–8; "Recurso do P.^e Miguel de Amaral ao R.^do P. Manoel Sarayva, provincial da provincia de Goa," 23 Nov. 1709, in ARSI, *Goa*, 9:II, 446–448^v, which is followed by copies of exchanges between the provincial and the viceroy concerning efforts to implement the king's directive.

19. In 1715 the crown ordered the Portuguese province to establish chairs in higher mathematics and music at both the arts college of Coimbra and at the University of Évora but offered no funds to aid their creation. Diogo de Mendonça Corte Real to provincial, Lisbon, 28 Feb. 1715, in ARSI, *Lus.*, 76, fol. 147. A course in geometry was being taught at Évora before that date.

20. "Recurso do P.^e Miguel de Amaral ao R.^do P. Manoel Sarayva," cited in note 18 above.

21. D. Rodrigo da Costa (viceroy) to Manoel Saraiva (Visitor), 27 Nov. 1709; Saraiva to Costa, 28 Nov. 1709; Costa to Saraiva, 28 Nov. 1709; and Saraiva to Costa, 29 Nov. 1709, in ARSI, *Goa*, 9:II, fols. 450–450^v.

at the imperial court, arrived in Macao on 6 December.[22] Less than two months later, on 5 February 1711, he gained an audience with K'ang-hsi and presented gifts and reassurances from John V. What K'ang-hsi thought about either is unfortunately unrecorded.[23]

The curious mission of Fr. Cardozo was Portugal's only active response to the Rites crisis. If his mission was of no vast consequence, the same cannot be said of that of the next papal envoy, Mgr. Carlo Ambrogio Mezzabarba. The new legate departed from Lisbon on a Portuguese warship on 25 March 1720 and reached the Chinese mainland exactly nine months later.[24] His primary mission was to consult with K'ang-hsi about the enforcement of the apostolic constitution *Ex illa die* (1715), in which Clement XI reiterated the Vatican's refusal to permit Christians to employ Confucian terms for heaven or the deity, to participate in ceremonies honoring Confucius, to retain ancestral tablets in their homes, or to practice other so-called superstitious observances. Though the new legate proved more tactful than his predecessor, he was no more successful, and after a series of audiences (January–March 1721), it became obvious that no meeting of minds between Rome and Peking was possible on the matter of Rites.

There could be no question of who was responsible for that impasse. As K'ang-hsi astutely observed,

> Maigrot and other ignorant small people, by sending false letters have confounded right and wrong and accused the late Ricci, Schall, Verbiest, Buglio, Magalhães, Ciceri, Pereira and other Westerners of having practiced things contrary to your religion. Such libels . . . ought not to be perpetuated. . . . The Prohibitions of your King of religion are greatly opposed to the Chinese principles. Your Catholic religion is impractical in China and must be forbidden. . . . Westerners allowed to remain [here] may live in accordance with the Prohibitions . . . but they are . . . not to propagate their religion among the people.[25]

Although the Mezzabarba mission was, as Pastor rightfully said, "a complete failure," it, too, had important consequences.[26] One was an intensified campaign of vilification by churchmen against the court Jesuits, who, in the minds of the disappointed legate and of several ecclesiastical rivals in the East, were primarily responsible for the stalemate between the two courts. The campaign had begun with the apologetic dispatches of Tournon, which asserted that the Jesuits had thwarted his efforts to reach an accommodation with the emperor, and with the reports of the banished Bishop Maigrot, who asserted that in the Orient the Jesuits were more powerful than the Holy See. His contentions were reinforced

22. Viceroy to king, 4 Dec. 1710 and 6 Dec. 1711, in *APO*:2, 1:3:1, 42–43, 62–63.

23. Rosso, *Apostolic Legations*, 188. Cardozo's instructions, properly dated 6 May 1710, are printed with a transposed date in *APO*:2, 1:3:2, 113–16. Dehergne, *RJC*, 44–45, mistakenly believed that he came to China directly from the kingdom. Fr. Cardozo spent the balance of his life as a missionary in Shantung, dying there in 1723.

24. Chinese officials were apprehensive when they learned about the dispatch of the new legate. The viceroy of Canton, normally very restrained, heatedly told a Jesuit informant that if the envoy dared to approach his city he would sink all ships entering the port of Macao and burn the city to the ground. João Laureate, S.J., to Fr. Miguel de Amaral, Canton, 5 Oct. 1720, in *Arquivos de Macao*, 3d ser., 6:1 (July 1966): 3.

25. The source is the so-called Mandarins' Diary printed in Rosso, *Apostolic Legations*, 342–74, but I have followed the translations in Song-Kang, "Kangxi's Attitude," 63–64. Apart from Song-Kang (62–64), assessments of the Mezzabarba debacle include Rowbotham, *Missionary and Mandarin*, 168–70; Rosso, *Apostolic Legations*, chap. 9; Minamiki, *Chinese Rites Controversy*, 62–65; and *HP*, 33: 468–84, and 35: 433–42.

26. *HP*, 33: 480.

by those of a disgruntled Dominican missionary in China, who uttered the same complaint, as did the Lazarist Theodore Pedrini, who seems to have attributed his imprisonment during the latter part of K'ang-hsi's reign to Jesuit machinations. In time, Mezzabarba jumped aboard the same bandwagon.[27]

An early manifestation of papal involvement in this anti-Jesuit movement, one that would grow in momentum with the passing of time, especially amid Jansenist circles in France, as well as in Rome and throughout the Portuguese Assistancy, was the devastating papal brief of 13 September 1723, prepared by the papal secretary of Propaganda in the name of Innocent XIII (1721–24) and addressed to Michelangelo Tamburini, the Jesuit general. In it, the pope averred that the behavior of Jesuit missionaries in China could no longer be ignored. They were accused of conniving to obstruct the expressed will of a succession of pontiffs. Even their general was accused of failing to assure the Society's compliance with papal edicts. Accordingly, Tamburini was admonished that he must compel his subjects in China and in Vietnam to comply with Rome's position on the Rites question and to furnish proof within three years that they were doing so; failure would compel the pope to withhold permission for the Society to admit any more novices, but during the interim Tamburini was forbidden to send fresh missionaries to the eastern empire. Not surprisingly, the Society's Jansenist adversaries gleefully published that remarkable edict.[28]

This astounding papal reprimand reveals more about Rome's frustrations in attempting to delineate the parameters of Catholicism in China and its susceptibility to the fulminations of the Society's adversaries than it does about the actual misdeeds of that Order's members. Since it was not based upon any objective factual inquiry, it also demonstrates cogently a point made by K'ang-hsi in his talks with Mezzabarba, namely, that the pope was not an umpire but a partisan.[29] Because the directive was issued in the name of Innocent XIII, it is hard to agree with Pastor that the pope could not "be held responsible for [its] harsh language." Obviously stunned, Tamburini defended his subjects and asked for a display of the specific evidence against them. None was forthcoming. Instead, the papal secretary of state sent the general a letter containing further allegations concerning presumed missionary improprieties in the Orient, prompting the father general to draft still another defense of the Society. Finally, Benedict XIII (1724–30) wearied of the assault on the Society, and in February 1725 he quashed the substance of the original accusatory brief.[30] Meanwhile, the Jesuits in China had lost one of their greatest defenders: K'ang-hsi expired on 20 December 1722.

Conditions for the Jesuits worsened under the next emperor, Yung Cheng, a usurper who was possibly guilty of patricide and more certainly of fratricide. He quickly made it clear that he had little use for the emissaries of Christ. Upon his direction, in September 1723 the viceroy of Fukien, the province situated opposite Taiwan, issued an edict requiring Christians to give up their faith and surrender their churches. Except for those deemed

27. Pedrini, a musical-instrument maker, was sent by Rome to be its permanent representative in Peking and arrived in China after a harrowing trip from Mexico and the Philippines. For his activities in the empire, see *HP*, 33: 459–61, 463–65, 470–73, 474, 479–81. On the anti-Jesuit campaign, *HP*, 34: 74–83, and 35: 436–45 are fundamental.

28. *HP*, 34: 83–85.

29. Cf. Song-Kang, "Kangxi's Attitude," 63.

30. *HP*, 34: 86–93, and 195–97.

useful to the court, all missionaries were ordered rounded up and sent to Macao. Just as the seventeenth-century Hollanders turned Jesuit churches into schools, so the agents of Yung Cheng converted them into storehouses, schools, and pagodas. In explaining his actions, the emperor claimed to honor all religions, but he insisted (not unreasonably) that if he had not acted to prevent Christianity from sweeping China, the empire would soon have become a mere satellite of Europe.[31] In 1726, João Mourão, a former Jesuit mission superior and a well-respected court participant, was strangled in a temple in Tartary as a result of an imperial order. Although he was charged with conspiracy and treason, Fr. Mourão's real crime was that of being the confidant of the late emperor's reputedly ablest son, who was the new emperor's perceived rival. Fr. Mourão thus became the first Jesuit in China to die as a result of an imperial command (in marked contrast with the experience of Jesuits in seventeenth-century Japan), but he would not be the last of his Order to become a victim of guilt by association.[32]

Yung Cheng expired in 1735, but the position of the Jesuits in China did not improve under his successor, the durable Ch'ien Lung (1736–95).[33] On the contrary, in 1742 Benedict XIV (1740–58) issued what became the final papal statement on the Rites question for more than two centuries: the constitution *Ex quo singulari*, which effectively reinforced the 1715 constitution and authorized no exceptions to compliance with it. Indeed, the pope insisted that all missionaries must take an oath to observe the new Roman edict and to refrain from further discussion of the question.[34]

Though Benedict XIV reassured the missionaries that the Lord would bless their efforts, that did not prove to be the case. Instead, a new wave of persecution occurred, not only in the empire but in Vietnam as well: Jesuits as well as Dominicans and secular priests perished (1745–48) at the hands of government officials who condemned them as subversives.[35] By 1750 the Jesuits' position in China and Vietnam was more precarious than it had been at any time since the entry of Matteo Ricci in 1583.

The Rites controversy was an unmitigated disaster for all concerned.[36] The physical privations experienced by members of the vice-province as a result of the so-called persecutions, first by Chinese authorities and later by those of Portugal, undoubtedly help

31. *HP*, 34: 72–74.

32. Cf. Chapter 6. There would be other victims of guilt by association in Portugal during the 1750s as a result of an alleged regicide conspiracy, as volume 2 of this study will disclose. On the fate of Fr. Mourão, see Rosso, *Apostolic Legations*, 214, 219–21. See also *RJC*, 183.

33. The viceroy of India wrongly forecast that the ascendancy of a new emperor would bring about a relaxation of restrictions upon the missionaries. Conde de Sandomil to Fray João Mascarenhas, 2 Jan. 1737, in ACL, ms. Azul, 511, fol. 69ʳ. For visual impressions of the Ch'ien Lung regime, see Cecile and Michel Beurdeley, *Giuseppe Castiglione: A Jesuit Painter at the Court of the Chinese Emperors*, trans. Michael Bullock (Tokyo, 1971). Castiglione, an Italian portraitist, landscapist, and genre painter, served in the empire from 1715 until his death in Peking in 1766.

34. Joseph Krahl, S.J., *China Missions in Crisis: Bishop Laimbeckhoven and His Times, 1738–1787* (Rome, 1964), 34–48; Minamiki, *Chinese Rites Controversy*, 69–76; *HP*, 35: 448–58. Rosso, *Apostolic Legations*, 229, curiously defends the constitution of 1742.

35. Krahl, *China Missions*, chap. 3; *HP*, 35: 459–61. Barbara Widenor Maggs, "'The Jesuits in China' Views of an Eighteenth Century Russian Observer," *Eighteenth-Century Studies* 8, 2 (Winter 1974–75): 137–52, is an uncritical, disappointing summary of the observations of a Russian Orthodox priest who lived in Peking from 1745 to 1755.

36. For an excellent assessment, see Cummins, ed., *Travels*, 1: 1.

TABLE 23.2

Average Age at Death of Missionaries Serving in the
Vice-Province of China and the Province of Japan, 1500–1749

Quarter of birth	China[a]		Japan[b]	
	(N)	Average age	(N)	Average age
1500–1524	7	61.0	—	—
1525–1549	25	55.3	15	57.1
1550–1574	39	62.8	3	36.6
1575–1599	48	56.9	1	43.0
1600–1624	80	55.0	2	33.5
1625–1649	54	58.7	2	34.0
1650–1674	126	60.5	3	37.0
1675–1699	58	64.6	4	40.5
1700–1724	66	57.4	5	40.2
1725–1749	28	50.6	2	37.5

SOURCE: *RJC*, passim.
[a] Excluded from the China list are 38 missionaries (6.7 percent) who died en route, mostly at sea, to their stations.
[b] For 1600 on, the data are for the "New Province" of Japan, which was basically Southeast Asia.

explain why the average age at death of missionaries serving in eighteenth-century China significantly diminished (see Table 23.2).

Table 23.2 suggests that the missionaries who served in Southeast Asia bore greater hardships and appear to have therefore experienced shorter lives than those who labored within the Chinese empire. But it also demonstrates that the life spans of those who resided within the empire shrank during the eighteenth century, initially as a result of the persecution that ensued after papal pronouncements on Rites matters, and later as a consequence of Portugal's suppression of the Society within spiritual jurisdictions under its control. The Rites dispute was surely partially responsible for the vice-province's precarious condition at mid-century, but its economic foundations, as well as those of the Japan province, had already been seriously eroded by the achievements of the Marathas in distant India.

The Beleaguered Provinces of Goa and Malabar

In India, too, the Jesuit provinces experienced serious personnel problems. By 1700 membership in the two provinces had declined about 41 percent from its peak in 1627. Goa's had shrunk by a quarter, but Malabar's had fallen by 72.1 percent. Of the two provinces, Malabar had lost the most stations. In 1627 that province had consisted of a half-dozen centers, including Cochin, Quilon, Madura, the Fishery Coast, Meliapor, and Bengal. By 1734 there were only three Jesuits residing along the entire east coast, from Coromandel to Bengal; by 1742 the college at Bengal was closed after its last member expired.

Until the devastating Maratha invasions of the late 1730s, the Goan province suffered less than its partner. There remained a cluster of five houses in or near the capital (Old and New St. Paul's, the professed house, the probationary house on Chorão, and the college of Salsete or Rachol). To the north along the littoral were the colleges of Chaul, Bassein, Taná, Bandorá, Damão, and Diu, whereas inland the province maintained half a dozen missions, of which the one at the Mughal court of Agra was the best known.[37] Across the Indian Ocean lay three Jesuit clusters in Mozambique: the insular college and the upriver stations at Sena and Tete.[38] Both provinces continued to rely heavily upon external sources of recruits. Though many of them came from the kingdom, others were natives of Italy, the Germanies, Austria, and even Brazil.[39] Even so, there were never enough. The statistics summarized in Table 23.3 are incomplete, but the two provinces appear to have commanded over half the recruits sent East: Goa received about four per annum and Malabar about half that many. In 1722 the provincial of Goa declined the king's suggestion that the Society send a contingent to Timor, pointing out that the number of new arrivals did not compensate for those the province lost by death. The provincial noted that during the previous three years fewer than 20 recruits had been received while 36 had died, and that among the thirteen new arrivals who were welcomed that year, one had already expired and six were mere novices.[40]

The dispatch of such raw recruits proved increasingly common during the eighteenth century. In 1712, for example, eight of the thirteen who sailed to India were novices, and the average age of the entire contingent was only 21.3.[41] Gone were the days when India could depend upon a steady flow from Europe of mature, experienced, well-trained men. Even Rome recognized as much. In 1725, a clearly concerned father general, Michelangelo Tamburini, wrote the provincial of Portugal and appealed for neophytes willing to serve in the Malabar province; only a handful responded to that call.[42]

One problem that did not confront the Goan province until the 1740s was a scarcity of revenue. As Table 23.4 indicates, the units of that province enjoyed incomes that rose spectacularly from the 1690s until the end of the 1730s. Whether such gains were the products of increasing land values, of strong demand for Jesuit-produced commodities, especially coconuts and rice, or of successful investments is entirely unclear from Jesuit accounts, which are silent on the sources of the colleges' remarkable growth in income during those decades.[43] Although there is a paucity of such data for the Malabar province,

37. Some sketchy details concerning the modest progress that the Jesuits achieved in those interior missions are contained in the annual reports of 1711, 1724, 1731, 1733 and 1734: ARSI, *Goa*, 36:I, fols. 218–21; 36:II, 312–327ᵛ, 391–400ᵛ, 403–426ᵛ, and 435–458ᵛ.

38. The two preceding paragraphs are based upon analyses of the provincials' reports in ARSI, *Goa*, 26 and 27, and on F/*JM*, 2: app. 1.

39. On average, recruits reached India about every other year between 1700 and 1750. *LJI*, 313–30. For those who came from Brazil (some of them being natives of Portugal), see Serafim Leite, S.J., "Movimento missionário do Brasil para a India (1637–1748)," *Boletim do Instituto Vasco da Gama*, no. 69 (1952): 107–18.

40. João de Olivares (provincial) to crown, 25 Oct. 1722, in Artur Teodoro de Matos, *Timor portugués, 1515–1769* (Lisbon, 1974), 356–57. The Overseas Council advised the king that the provincial's arguments appeared persuasive but made no suggestion as to how recruitment might be improved. Council to king, 23 Feb. 1724, in ibid., 366–67.

41. "Missionarios q.' forao' p.ᵃ a India em 1712," in ARSI, *Goa*, 9:II, fol. 522.

42. Tamburini to Joseph de Almeida, 1 Dec. 1725, in ANTT/CJ/68, no. 137. Among many other sources, this dispatch belies the allegation of some writers that Jesuit generals arbitrarily and capriciously detailed their subordinates to whatever posts they deemed necessary.

43. There were serious, recurrent famines in the Deccan in 1705–8, in the vicinity of Surat in 1717–18, and in Bombay in 1722 and 1728. Rice and other commodities advanced substantially in price during such

TABLE 23.3

Jesuits Sent from Europe to the Eastern Provinces, 1700–1759

Period	Total	Goa	Malabar	Japan	China	Unspecified
1700–1709	133	44	56	20	13	—
1710–1719	98	13	5	16	4	60
1720–1729	100	39	10	3	9	39
1730–1739	151	68[a]	40	25	11	7
1740–1749	98	25	10	32	3	28
1750–1759	142	47	13	23	21	38
Total	722[b]	236	134	119	61	172

SOURCE: *LJI*, 313–44.

[a] Includes 10 "to India," some of whom may have been assigned to Malabar.

[b] 21 died en route to their assignments.

TABLE 23.4

Estimated Income of the Provinces of Goa and Malabar, 1699–1746

(000 rs.)

Year	Goa	Malabar	Year	Goa	Malabar
1699	22,200	24,205	1728	66,209	—
1706	27,900	—	1730	40,491	—
1713	41,572	—	1731	68,706	—
1716	48,665	—	1734	104,003	—
1719	39,304	—	1741	21,000	6,656
1727	56,746	—	1746	—	6,370

SOURCES: Goa: for 1730, viceroy to king, 23 Jan. 1731, in AHU/PA/IN, *cx.* 35, no. 46; for remainder, ARSI, *Goa*, 26. Malabar: F/*JM*, 2: 346 and 349.

it is evident from Table 23.4 that its resources were much more modest than those of its brother province.

Undoubtedly the viceroys and other officials observed increasing Jesuit affluence with keen interest. Until the troubled 1730s, the Jesuits generally enjoyed cordial relations with the viceroys. In 1707, for example, Caetano de Melo e Castro (1702–7) strongly defended the missionaries against charges made by a member of the Goan High Court, Desembargador Domingos Dourado de Oliveira. The judge wrote an alarmist memorial to

periods of distress, but scholars have provided meager specific evidence of the levels attained. E.g., Irfan Habib, "The Monetary System and Prices," in Irfan Habib and Tapan Raychaudhuri, eds., *The Cambridge Economic History of India*, 2 vols. (New York, 1982), 1: 376. Employing a weighted (but unspecified) moving average, K. N. Chaudhuri concluded that the price of ordinary rice generally moved upward from 1660 to 1760: *The Trading World of Asia and the English East India Company, 1660–1760* (New York, 1978), 102. However, an unweighted moving average for the same commodity and market in Brij Narain, *Indian Economic Life, Past and Present* (1929; rpr., Delhi, 1984), 96, suggests a steep upward movement from 1700 to 1710, and then a gradual decline for the next decade, followed by a leveling-off until 1735 and a further slide thereafter. See also Radhakamal Mukerjee, *The Economic History of India, 1600–1800* (Allahabad, 1967), 19–20; Mohammad Azhar Ansari, "A Short Survey of Cereal Prices in Northern India During the 18th Century," Indian History Congress, *Proceedings* 31 (1969): 255–59; and Muzaffar Alam, *The Crisis of Empire in Mughal North India: Awadh and the Punjab, 1707–1748* (Delhi, 1986), 26–27, 31–32, and 47–48. The upward movement of rice and wheat prices in the city of Goa during the seventeenth century is apparent in Teotonio R. de Souza, S.J., *Medieval Goa: A Socio-Economic History* (New Delhi, 1979), 172, but there are no comparable published data for the eighteenth century.

Pedro II in which he attributed the military setbacks that the crown repeatedly sustained in the State of India to the negligence of the religious, especially their passive role in seacoast spiritual citadels and their failure to evangelize in the State's interior. Melo e Castro, a distinguished veteran of many years of both land and maritime service in Brazil, Mozambique, and India, concluded that the judge's fault-finding was without foundation.[44] The count of Ericeira (1717–20) strongly praised the "singular zeal and disinterest" of the Jesuits, who performed services in behalf of the crown and took an avid interest in the China missions.[45] A third ardent viceregal supporter was João de Saldanha da Gama (1725–32), who wrote Tamburini praising the zeal of those members of the Society who particularly attracted his attention.[46]

But such cordiality was not universal and certainly did not characterize relations between the Society and D. Inácio de Santa Teresa, the long-serving, talented, tempestuous archbishop of Goa (1721–39). Born in Porto, the archbishop studied in the local Jesuit college, where his teachers, impressed by his erudition, hoped to recruit him. Instead, he followed an uncle and became an Augustinian. In 1711 he became a doctor of theology at Coimbra and distinguished himself so well that a chair in philosophy was created to exploit his talents. He remained in that position for nearly a decade, until the king nominated him to become archbishop of Goa. He sailed in the company of Viceroy Francisco José de Sampaio e Castro, who concluded that he was a religious fanatic and pleaded for his recall. Instead, the archbishop became one of the triumvirate who succeeded Sampaio e Castro upon his death. Throughout his stormy years in Goa, D. Inácio quarreled with several viceroys and various churchmen, especially the Jesuits.[47]

Such quarrels began soon after the archbishop's arrival in Goa, when he accompanied the newly consecrated Jesuit patriarch of Ethiopia and the bishop of Malacca to Old St. Paul's, where they witnessed a solemn baptism of 409 persons. Far from being pleased by the proceedings, the prelate condemned them as being too lavish and accused the Society of having abandoned its original humble demeanor, a charge that was destined to be repeated frequently during the next two centuries, but one that was never uttered with any degree of precision.[48]

The archbishop also revived a perennial source of conflict between the college of Rachol and the archiepiscopal see when he charged that the missionaries were improperly occupying the Salsete parishes (see Chapter 13). As was customary, the fathers responded by first denying the prelates' authority, and then by offering to surrender the parishes. The viceroy and his council of state sought to mediate the dispute, but without success. After the

44. Dourado de Oliveira to king, Goa, 19 Jan. 1703, in *APO*:1, 6:1, 161–73; viceroy to king, 10 Jan. 1707, in HAG/*LM*, 69–70, fols. 158ʳ–163ʳ.

45. Ericeira to Fr. João Mourão, 18 Feb. 1719, in British Library, Add. mss. 20906, fol. 27ʳ; Ericeira to Mourão, 20–21 Apr. 1720, in *Boletim eclesiástico de Macau* 36 (1938?): 453–57.

46. Saldanha da Gama to Tamburini, 28 May 1729, in ARSI, *Bras.*, 4, fol. 382. As noted elsewhere, the viceroy had formerly enjoyed a close relationship with the Society in Maranhão, and in India he was grateful to its leaders for backing his ill-fated Mombasa recovery venture. See below, this section.

47. The best sketch of D. Inácio's career remains the article in *PDH*, 6: 600–601, probably written by Ferreira Martins. It was cribbed by A. Gonçalves Pereira, *Tratado de todos os vice-reis e governadores da India* (Lisbon, 1962), 177–79, who includes two portraits of the contentious archbishop.

48. Francisco de Sousa, S.J., *Oriente conquistado a Jesus Cristo pelos padres da Companhia de Jesus da província de Goa* [1710], ed. M. Lopes de Almeida (Porto, 1978), 162.

parishes had passed into the archbishop's control, the provincial insisted that the property of their churches be properly inventoried, but D. Inácio ignored their request. The provincial then appealed to the viceroy, who dispatched two magistrates to accompany the rector of the college of Rachol and began to compile the inventory. Incensed, the archbishop insisted that the inquiry be stopped, claiming that it represented a usurpation of his authority. One of the judges responded that the archbishop was ill informed, that they were merely proceeding in accordance with the laws of the realm, which, he added tartly, "Your Grace must also respect."

Such an unwanted reminder merely prompted the archbishop to increase the pressure. He directed the posting of public notices excommunicating the Rachol college rector, Fr. António de Betancurt, for cooperating with the judges and for being guilty of other previously undisclosed crimes. When the Jesuits, whose defense was then led by one of their oldest, most respected members, Manuel de Sá, superior of Bom Jesús, appealed to the heads of the other religious Orders to support their view that the excommunication was illegal, the religious leaders unanimously sided with the Jesuits. The ball was thus tossed back into the archbishop's court. Advantage archbishop, for he enjoyed John V's favor more than did the Jesuits. The king summoned Frs. Betancurt and Sá to the kingdom. There neither Jesuit was given a hearing. On the contrary, a royal decree barred Fr. Betancurt from visiting either Évora or Coimbra and banished him to the furthest reaches of the kingdom. Although such treatment would become common for Jesuits during the next regime, it was exceedingly rare until this time. Fr. Sá, who had spent 45 years in the East and had become blind, avoided such humiliation by expiring almost immediately.[49]

If, from the Jesuits' perspective, D. Inácio was an ill wind that blew in from the West, he was only one of many that beset the remnants of the heartland of the State of India during the period. In 1702, a "dismal calamity" struck Bombay and uprooted an estimated 20,000 to 30,000 coconut trees as well as mangoes and jack trees. Houses "lay in ruinous heaps," and small and large ships alike were destroyed.[50] Very likely the "dismal tempest" also afflicted the intensely cultivated Portuguese island of Salsete do Norte immediately north of Bombay, where the Jesuits possessed extensive holdings, but available sources are silent on possible damage there. They do indicate that the costly raids by the Omani against Portuguese enclaves along the north coast (see Chapter 8) diminished at the beginning of the eighteenth century, when the Arabs appear to have shifted their attention to attacks on shipping in the Red Sea.[51]

49. The foregoing is based primarily upon two lengthy files, one prepared by the Jesuits, the other by the staff of the archbishop. The first is BNL, cod. 519, and the latter, entitled "Memorias do Estado da India, 1725–1732," is part of the Portuguese history manuscript collection of the Lilly Library, Indiana University, where it constitutes part of the Boxer collection. I am indebted to John V. Lombardi, now president of the University of Florida and formerly a member of the History Department at Indiana University, for a microfilm of that codex. For a brief summary based only on Jesuit sources, see *HCJAP*, 4:1, 208–11.

50. Bombay Council to Surat factors, 14 Nov. 1702, in IOL, G/3/17, no fol.; EIC directors to general and Bombay Council, 18 Jan. 1703, in IOL, E/3/93, fol. 335. That blow was the second severe one in six years. *The Gazetteer of Bombay City and Island* (1909; fasc. ed., Pune, India, 1977), 97–100.

51. The Omani caused considerable damage to Salsete do Norte in 1699, but their attack on Damão in 1704 was beaten off. Concerning Omani attacks on Red Sea shipping, see Ashin Das Gupta, *Indian Merchants and the Decline of Surat, c. 1700–1750* (Wiesbaden, 1979), 159–60.

The withdrawal of the Omani in the Indian Ocean was offset by the appearance of three sorts of pirate.[52] One consisted of English freelances such as George Taylor, who gravely embarrassed the Portuguese government in January 1721, when he successfully attacked a storm-damaged Portuguese 70-gun ship in a harbor of the French island of Reunion and captured and later marooned its most distinguished passenger, the count of Ericeira, the retiring viceroy of India.[53] The second maritime foe consisted of the Sidis of the island of Janjira, whose devastating occupation of Bombay in the 1690s has been considered elsewhere (see Chapter 17). By the early eighteenth century, the Sidis became nominal protectors of the trade of Surat. Sometimes they were in the pay of the English of Bombay, but at other times they were at odds with the English and joined the most feared maritime adversary of the period, Kanhoji Angria, who led the third piratical force.[54]

The origins of this storied Maratha admiral remain unclear.[55] Some writers believe his roots were Arabian, others Abyssinian. His family came from the village of Angarvadi (hence the name Angria) near Poona, but its primary base was the island of Kolaba, about 30 kilometers south of Bombay.[56] As a sea marauder, Angria took on all customers as long as his guns were more powerful than theirs. By 1712 he was fighting simultaneously with the Portuguese and the Sidis, and he was close to war with the English as well. On one occasion he seized a Portuguese pal-of-war, a large three-masted craft with a square stern, and captured and caused the death of the retiring governor of Chaul. Several times he menaced communications between Goa and its northern outposts, and he repeatedly ravaged Chaul's trade. The Bombay Council rejected a Portuguese proposal for an alliance against Angria in 1712, after he had seized its governor's armed yacht, but they agreed to a joint offensive in 1721 that miscarried.[57] Consequently, in 1722, the Portuguese signed a separate peace with Angria, much to the annoyance of the agents of the East India Company.[58]

The following year, a long-simmering dispute between the English and the Portuguese over the right of free passage along the Bandorá River separating the islands of Bombay and Salsete do Norte came to a boil. Since an award made by Sebastian to Old St. Paul's in 1570, the Jesuits had collected tolls upon shipping in that river. The English persistently termed

52. For a succinct survey of international piracy in the Indian Ocean at this time, see Auguste Toussaint, *History of the Indian Ocean*, trans. June Guicharnaud (Chicago, 1966), 140–46.

53. The account given by Holden Furber, *Bombay Presidency in the Mid-Eighteenth Century* (New York, 1965), 17, differs from that in Gonçalves Pereira, *Tratado de todos*, 174–75.

54. Das Gupta, *Indian Merchants*, 260.

55. Much has been written about Angria. He occupies a central place in John Biddulph, *The Pirates of Malabar and an Englishwoman in India Two Hundred Years Ago* (London, 1907), an undocumented work based upon East India Company files but marred by its blatant biases. Manohar Malgonkar, *Kanhoji Angrey Maratha Admiral* (New York, 1959), purports to be "a true story" but is undocumented. Much the best account, solidly based upon contemporary, especially Portuguese, archival sources, is Surendra Nath Sen, *The Military System of the Marathas* (Bombay, 1958), chap. 11, the source primarily followed here.

56. B[halchandra] K[rishna] Apte, *A History of the Maratha Navy and Merchant Ships* (Bombay, 1973), 18–20, includes a description of the fortress at Kolaba and its environs together with a map. It also contains excellent sketches of various types of ships operating in Indian waters during this period.

57. For a terse English summary attributing the expedition's failure to "the cowardice and treachery of the Portugeez," see Clement Downing, *A History of the Indian Wars*, ed. William Foster (1924; rpr., Lahore, 1978), xx–xxi.

58. *APO*:2, 1:3:3, 60–96, 98–100.

Jesuit claims "frivolous" and in 1701 erected the fortress of Mahim at the north end of Bombay Island, opposite Bandorá, to defend their asserted right of free navigation throughout the waters bathing Salsete do Norte. In early June 1722 they suddenly discharged an estimated 400 salvos upon the port of Bandorá, the nearby village of Corlem, and especially the Jesuit college, which was largely destroyed as a result. Each side naturally blamed the other for the ensuing skirmishes, but although both referred the dispute to their European principals, the Portuguese viceroy yielded to English demands by replacing Fr. Manoel Diniz, the superior of the Bandorá college, who supposedly asserted the Society's rights too heatedly. The provincial detailed one of his staff to Lisbon to defend the Society's position, but, as will soon be seen, the Anglo-Portuguese dispute quickly became moot.[59]

The foregoing pages amply testify to the enfeeblement of Portuguese defenses throughout the Indian Ocean. That was a well-recognized fact among Portuguese authorities in both Lisbon and Goa, as well as among their adversaries throughout this period. In 1703 the Overseas Council warned Pedro II that every bastion within the State of India was ill provided with men, powder, balls, arms, and other munitions, and that there was no easy remedy for that situation.[60] Each newly arrived viceroy warned his superiors that his regime lacked sufficient manpower or revenues to defend the State. In 1713, for example, Vasco Fernándes César de Meneses stated that he had only 750 European troops at his disposal.[61] Both then and later, the backbone of Portuguese land defenses consisted of Indian mercenaries (sepoys) and topazes, Eurasians who claimed descent from Portuguese ancestors, neither of whom proved reliable in combat, especially when outnumbered by their enemies. But the reinforcements that the crown sent out periodically were no better. They consisted primarily of a few "volunteers," who were probably impressed, convicts (*degredados*), and officers, many of whom were failed and pampered sons of nobles who owed their appointments and opportunities for self-aggrandizement to their personal connections at home or in India.[62] Not a few died in transit, and others arrived so ill that they soon expired in the Jesuit-administered hospital in Goa.[63]

59. The fullest coeval Portuguese summary is Francisco José de Sampaio e Castro (viceroy) to king, 14 Sept. 1722, in *APO*:2, 1:3:3, 126–36; but see also ibid., 96–98, 111–21, and 142–47, as well as *CTEIP*, 3: 297–320. For an English perspective, see Biddulph, *Pirates of Malabar*, 192–94.

60. Council to king, 13 Mar. 1703, in AHU/PA/IN, *cx.* 44, no. 27.

61. Viceroy to king, n.d. [ca. Jan. 1713], in *APO*:2, 1:3:2, 79; count of Ericeira to D. Cristóvão de Melo, 11 Mar. 1720, in British Library, Add. mss. 20906, fol. 50[r]; Francisco José de Sampaio e Castro to king, 22 Jan. 1721 and 12 Dec. 1722, in *APO*:2, 1:3:3, 46 and 141. In his regular January reports, the count of Sandomil repeatedly warned about his state's fragile military and fiscal condition: viceroy to king, 11 Jan. 1733, 19 Jan. 1734, and 25 Jan. 1736, in ACL, ms. Azul, cod. 503, fols. 176[r]–177[v]; cod. 504, fol. 148[r]; and cod. 505, fol. 238[r]. In 1732, the câmara of Goa warned the king that the State had almost reached the point of exhaustion, "not the least reason being the damage experienced here by permitting the Religious to buy landed estates contrary to the king's orders." Câmara to king, 6 Mar. 1733, in AHU/PA/IN, *m.* 37. There can be no question that the Overseas Council recognized the State's desperate straits. E.g., consulta of 26 Nov. 1738, in AHU/PA/IN, *m.* 29.

62. See Chapter 17, note 100.

63. In 1685, of 2,500 men who sailed from Lisbon to Goa, 720 expired en route, and another 600 perished soon after reaching the viceregal center. Lotika Varadarajan, trans. and ed., *India in the 17th Century: Memoirs of François Martin at Surat (1670–1694)*, 2 vols. in 4 (New Delhi, 1981), 2: 977. Of the 900 men who left Lisbon in 1699, 300 perished before reaching India; 360 were admitted to the military hospital, where another 100 succumbed. Justus Strandes, *The Portuguese Period in East Africa* [1899], trans. Jean F. Wallwork, ed. J. S. Kirkman (Nairobi, 1961), 273. According to C. R. Boxer, "A death-rate of over fifty

It is not surprising, therefore, that Archbishop Santa Teresa wrote in the mid-1720s that the State contained only half as many troops as it had had at the beginning of the century.[64] Nor is it astonishing that the marquis of Abrantes, Portuguese envoy extraordinary to Rome, casually suggested that Portugal ought to sell its interests in India and withdraw entirely from the subcontinent. When Jesuits learned of that suggestion, Manuel de Sá, soon to be banished from India, addressed a curious memorial to John V written in the name of Saint Francis Xavier. In it, he protested that the principal value of India was the opportunity to win converts, and he pleaded for continued support of the missions so that the king might establish the fifth empire, a reference to a controversial vision of António Vieira.[65]

There is no evidence that the crown was then seriously considering giving up its remaining enclaves in India. On the contrary, there were still officials who believed in the possibility of restoring the State of India to its former glory. An upheaval on the east coast of Africa seemed to assure a step in that direction: the reoccupation of the old fortress of Mombasa, Fort Jesús, key to control of the Swahili coast. Following its loss in 1698 (see Chapter 8), the Portuguese undertook a series of abortive efforts to recover that fortress. Nevertheless, the crown continued to insist that any reasonable opportunity be exploited to regain that lucrative littoral.[66]

Such an occasion arose in 1727, after a civil war between Mombasa and the Zanzibar Omani. When the latter were defeated, they fled to Pate, where the sultan initially welcomed but later extirpated them. Having thereby incurred the wrath of two Arab factions, the sultan sent an emissary to Goa seeking Portuguese help against the Omani. Viceroy Saldanha dispatched a large squadron, whose expenses were substantially defrayed by a loan from the Jesuits (see Chapter 13), to the island of Pate. There the expedition learned that rebellious African slaves had gained control of Fort Jesús and had placed themselves under the sultan's protection. With the sultan's blessing, the Portuguese reentered the base, and for a brief time the entire coast recognized Portuguese authority. But the tactless, caretaker Portuguese governor soon stirred up a series of anti-Lusitanian eruptions that led to the siege of the Portuguese garrison by April 1729. Despite the fact that the besiegers lacked artillery and possessed few firearms, the fort commander surrendered on 26 November with the loss of 34 bronze and 110 iron cannon. A relief expedition arrived two months later, two months too

---

percent of the personnel on board was nothing unusual" for outbound voyages to India. "The Carreira da India," in Centro de estudos históricos ultramarinos, *As comemorações henriquinas* (Lisbon, 1961), 33–81, at 58.

64. "Estado do prezente estado da India," Lilly Library, Indiana University, Portuguese Manuscripts, Miscellaneous, untitled codex concerning India, fol. 88ᵛ.

65. "Discurso contra o voto do Marquez de Abrantes que quieria se vendesse a India," BPE, cod. CXII/2–21, fol. 19; "Carta feita pelos padres da companhia de Jesus em nome de S. Francisco Xavier ao ... João o 5 para conservar a India" (1722), BPE, cod. CV/1–9, fol. 29; copy in BNL, cod. 6620, no fol. Curiously, Eduardo Brazão makes no reference to the envoy's proposal. *D. João V e a santa sé ... 1706 a 1750* (Coimbra, 1937), chap. 3. A few years later, the crown rather wistfully asked the viceroy to determine what it might cost to repurchase Bombay Island. He reported that its annual income from trade amounted to 533 contos! Had the king been prepared to shelve plans for construction of the palace-monastery of Mafra (see below), it is conceivable that the crown could have raised the funds necessary to reacquire Bombay, but there is no indication that the East India Company had any inclination to sell its lucrative holding. João de Saldanha da Gama to king, 18 Jan. 1727, in *CTEIP*, 3: 343–50.

66. Such instructions were issued in 1712, 1720, 1721, and 1724. *APO*:2, 4:2:2, 342–43.

late. When that force attempted to return to Goa, it suffered heavy losses, including the flagship, which went down with 557 men.[67]

The men, the arms, and the ships so tragically lost during this fiasco (*fracaço*, as the Portuguese would call it) were badly missed a few years later when the Portuguese and the Jesuits faced their most serious challenge in eighteenth-century India—the resurgent Marathas, the ascendant power in the Deccan. As Sir Jadunath Sarkar has written, the Mughals were no longer the dominant force in India: "At the end of the seventeenth century the great empire founded by Akbar and raised to world-famed prosperity and splendor by Shah Jahan, was in a state of hopeless decay; administration, culture, economic life, military strength and social organization—all seemed to be hastening to utter ruin and dissolution."[68] When Aurangzeb, the last of the dominant Mughal rulers, expired in February 1707, two of his sons divided the decadent empire, but the most important figure became the Nizam-ul-Mulk, viceroy of the Deccan and for two decades the archfoe of the Marathas.

As disclosed in Chapter 8, Aurangzeb succeeded in capturing and executing the last powerful Maratha leader of the seventeenth century, Sambhaji, in 1689. Thereafter he kept Sambhaji's son a state prisoner until his own death. The new leader of the Marathas was not their nominal chieftain, but their principal minister (*Peshwa*). It was the second Peshwa, Bajirao (variously spelled), who became a serious menace to both the Mughals and the Portuguese.[69]

Even though Bajirao's forces were concentrated primarily against those of the Nizam until the mid-1730s, the Marathas began probing Portuguese weaknesses in the vicinity of Bassein as early as 1717, when 500 mounted troops ravaged Goan Salsete, sacking various towns and withdrawing with 120 contos in loot, mostly in silver.[70] But Bassein, a city of nearly

---

67. The foregoing is based upon Strandes, *Portuguese Period*, chap. 18; C. R. Boxer and Carlos de Azevedo, *Fort Jesus and the Portuguese in Mombasa* (London, 1960), 75–82; as well as João de Saldanha da Gama to king, 20 Jan. 1728, in AHU/PA/IN, *m.* 14; Saldanha da Gama to R.[no] D. M.[el] Caetano de Sousa, 6 Jan. 1731, in BNL, cod. 177, fol. 146; and [Anon.], "Mapa das embarcacoens' armas e petrechos q. se perderão desde Mayo de [1]728 ate setembro de [1]730," 25 Jan. 1731, in AHU/PA/IN, *m.* 29; and *APO*:2, 4:2:2, 343–60.

68. Sarkar, *History of Aurangzib* [1919], 2d ed., 5 vols. (Bombay, 1972–74), 5: 181.

69. The rise of the Peshwas and the final days of Portugal's northern province are covered by a number of sources. Pro-Maratha interpretations include H. N. Sinha, *Rise of the Peshwas* [1931], 2d ed. (Allahabad, 1954); Rajaram Vyankatesh Nadkarni, *The Rise and Fall of the Maratha Empire* (Bombay, 1966), esp. 172–95; and V. G. Dighe, *Peshwa Bajirao I and Maratha Expansion* (Bombay, 1944). Though brief, Apte's *History of the Maratha Navy* is very useful. Apart from the manuscript materials cited below, there is a published coeval Portuguese summary: Diogo da Costa, *Relaçam das guerras da India desde . . . 1736 até 1740* (Porto, 1741), Boxer Collection, Lilly Library, Indiana University, no. 171. Pro-Portuguese analyses begin with the pioneering work of J. A. Ismael Gracias's series, "Os últimos cinco generaes do norte (Dezembro de 1730 a Abril de 1739)," and "Os últimos dias de Baçaim," in *O oriente português*, 2d ser., 3 (1906) and 4 (1907) passim, which is based upon HAG materials, as are Alexandre Lobato, *Relações Luso-Maratas, 1658–1737* (Lisbon, 1965), an eccentric, highly partisan, anti-Jesuit account, and the badly translated but fundamental Pandurang S. S. Pissurlencar [Pissurlenkar], *The Portuguese and the Marathas*, trans. P. R. Kakodkar (Bombay, 1975), esp. chaps. 6–14. See also Pissurlencar, "The Luso-Maratha Campaign of Bassein," Indian History Congress, *Transactions*, 5th sess. (Hyderabad, 1941), 416–27. A. G. Pawar, "English Records on the Conquest of Salsette by the Marathas in 1737," *Journal of the University of Bombay* 11, 1 (July 1962): 29–79, is invaluable for assessing the perspectives and interests of Bombay in the Luso-Maratha conflict. I am indebted to Dr. M. D. David (Wilson College, Bombay) and to my colleague Frank F. Conlon for a photocopy.

70. F. C. Danvers, ed., *Report of Portuguese Records Relating to the East Indies*, 2 vols. in 1 (London, 1892), 1: 78, citing a report by the archbishop of Goa.

60,000 in 1720, became a special Maratha target. It had been a Portuguese possession since 1534 and rivaled Goa and at one time Cochin in its commerce, opulence, and luxury-loving, indolent, largely Indian inhabitants, for there were fewer than 800 Europeans there in 1720. Although it had long since been superseded economically by Bombay, Bassein continued to be the capital of Portugal's northern province.[71] That province extended from Damão in the north to Chaul in the south and comprised an irregular rectangle measuring about 145 by 30 kilometers. Its heartland was the verdant island of Salsete do Norte, long coveted by the English, situated between Bassein and Bombay and measuring 40 by 16 kilometers. Its principal communities were Taná in the northeast, Bandorá in the south, and the deepwater harbor of Versova in the west.[72]

Previous chapters have emphasized the Jesuits' vital interests in the northern province, the home of five of their colleges (Damão, Bassein, Taná, Bandorá, and Chaul). In addition, rents from rice and coconut estates on Salsete do Norte contributed vital income to the Society's four eastern provinces. The fathers must, therefore, have shared the anxiety widespread among the northern province's inhabitants because of its notoriously inadequate garrisons. In a survey that he took in 1728, for example, the constable of Bassein fortress reported that the province's regular forces scarcely numbered 1,500, many of them non-Europeans.[73]

In 1730 the Marathas threatened to occupy Salsete Island via lightly defended Taná, and the alarmed Portuguese commanding general of the north appealed to his British counterpart for urgently needed reinforcements. Bombay answered by sending 700 men to hold the town at a cost of some £5,000.[74] It was presumably because he recognized Taná's vulnerability that Pedro Mascarenhas, count of Sandomil, Saldanha's successor as viceroy (1732–41), ordered the erection of the Dos Reis fortress to protect Taná and the rest of the island. Construction began in 1734, and during the following two years Portuguese authorities received repeated warnings from several of the Marathas' rivals, including English authorities, that the Marathas were preparing to launch a major invasion of the northern province.[75]

Such warnings fell upon deaf ears. The first of a series of calamities to befall Portuguese defenders of the province occurred on 6/7 April 1737, when an advance party of Maratha warriors landed near Taná, quickly overran an outpost, and ambushed a scouting force that the fortress's governor, D. Luís Botelho, the viceroy's nephew, sent against it. Rather than defend their position, that unworthy officer and a large

71. For descriptions of Bassein, see *The Travels of the Abbé Carré in India and the Near East, 1672 to 1674*, trans. Lady Fawcett, ed. Sir Charles Fawcett and Sir Richard Burn, 3 vols., *HS*:2, 95 (1947): 178; Giovanni Francesco Gemelli Careri, *A Voyage Round the World* [1695], in Surendra Nath Sen, ed., *Indian Travels of Thevenot and Careri* (New Delhi, 1949), 167–69; and Alexander Hamilton, *A New Account of the East Indies* [1727], ed. Sir William Foster, 2 vols. (London, 1930), 1: 104–5.

72. The Bombay Council, which repeatedly advocated the acquisition of Salsete do Norte, described as "our Granary" as well as that of the Portuguese, estimated that it was capable of producing over 900 metric tons of rice worth £47,250, as well as other marketable fruits. Pawar, "English Records," 48 and 55.

73. André Ribeiro Coutinho, "Extracto individual do estado em que se acha a infantaria, cavallaria, presidios, praças, fortes e barras da província do norte no anno de 1728," in J. H. Cunha Rivara, ed., *O Chronista de Tissuary* 1 (Nova Goa, 1866): 29–35 and 50–59.

74. Pissurlencar, "Luso-Maratha Campaign," 421; Furber, *Bombay Presidency*, 421.

75. Pissurlencar, "Luso-Maratha Campaign," 422.

part of the garrison and citizenry pusillanimously abandoned the fortress and fled to Karanja Island, 15 kilometers east of Bombay.[76] Predictably, the caretaker force that was left behind gave up the still-unfinished fort the next day and did not even bother to spike its guns.[77]

The Marathas quickly pressed their attack on two fronts. One force, consisting of several thousand men, spread rapidly over the island and confidently attacked Versova and Bandorá, but both proved tough nuts to crack, the latter especially, because the Jesuits appealed for British aid to hold the fortification they themselves had constructed. The British responded by dispatching 350 men to Bandorá, not because they had developed a sudden fondness for the fathers, but because they preferred weak Portuguese neighbors to "the more troublesome" Marathas.[78] Contemporaneously, another Maratha contingent assaulted the powerful citadel of Bassein, an imposing fortress protected by black stone walls nearly 1.5 meters thick and as much as 13.7 meters high. The strong points along those ramparts, which measured 2.4 to 3.2 kilometers in circumference, were eleven quadrangular bastions containing a total of 114 guns. The western approaches to the citadel were bathed by the Arabian Sea; the east was bounded by marshes, and the south by Bassein Creek. The easiest approach seemed to be via the north, but there unwanted intruders were exposed in sandy, open country to the fort's heavy guns.[79] As a result, the first Maratha attempts to storm the fortress failed at the cost of heavy casualties. The same was true on two later occasions, when the Marathas attempted to scale the walls by *escalade* and again suffered heavy losses.

In December 1737, Fr. António Gablesperger began his review of the year's events affecting the Goan province by proclaiming dramatically, like a medieval chronicler of bygone centuries, that "India is aflame with war" (*ardente India bellorum incendus*).[80] Yet, despite the reverses of that year, Portuguese defenders in the northern province, strengthened by several contingents of reinforcements and resupplied with funds—the products of forced loans—grimly held on to Bassein and most of its dependencies. However, the odds soon turned against them. On 7 January 1738, the Peshwa achieved a major victory over the Nizam at Bhopal (northeast of Surat), thereby enabling him to send his brother thousands of reinforcements, both mounted and foot soldiers, on a scale that neither the Portuguese nor

76. Previously the viceroy had assured the king that his nephew was "capable of discharging all assignments within this State because he possesses sound judgment, great capacity, much valor and probity." Sandomil to king, 23 Jan. 1735, in AHU/PA/IN, *cx.* 45, no. 32. His confidence was patently misplaced.

77. Sandomil to king, 25 Jan. 1738, in AHU/PA/IN, *m.* 77. In his detailed report concerning the debacle, the viceroy was very protective of his own conduct and that of his nephew and reserved his criticism for a mortally wounded captain who fell with his minuscule garrison following the initial Maratha incursion into Taná. Cf. Pissurlencar, *Portuguese and Marathas*, 185–88; and Dighe, *Peshwa Bajirao*, 168–69, who employs Old Style dates throughout his narrative. It should be noted that important documents concerning the victorious Maratha campaign in the northern province were removed from the AHU/PA/IN, *ms.* 79 and 80, in 1959 and loaned to the Centro de Estudos Históricos, which neither published nor returned them.

78. Minutes of Bombay Council, 28 Mar. 1737, in Pawar, "English Records," 34. Cf. James Douglas, *Bombay and Western India*, 2 vols. (London, 1893), 1: 133.

79. [Anon.], "Descripçao' da cid.ᶜ de Bacay. e sua jurisdiçao' ocupada actualm.ᵗᵉ do inymigo Marata" [ca. Jan. 1738], in AHU/PA/IN, *cx.* 77. For a sketch of the fortress, see Apte, *History of the Maratha Navy*, 16, fig. 3. Braz A. Fernandes, *A Guide to the Ruins of Bassein*, 2d ed. (Bombay, 1948), is very helpful.

80. "Lettera annuae prov.ᵃ Goanam anni 1737," 20 Dec. 1737, in ARSI, *Goa*, 36:II, fol. 480ʳ.

the British could match.[81] Still, the following November, a daring Portuguese general led a force of 1,000 men in an effort to recover Taná, hoping thereby to regain mastery over Salsete do Norte. That effort failed miserably after the general was felled by a lucky shot from a Maratha gun and his lieutenants proved unable to rally their men.

The Marathas then began to apply pressure simultaneously along several fronts. They ransacked the agricultural lands around Damão and Chaul. They captured one after another of the smaller Portuguese outposts along the littoral: Versova's two-year resistance finally collapsed, as did that of Bandorá.[82] At the same time, the Peshwa's troops commenced the first of five incursions into the territory of Goa, repeatedly occupying most of Salsete and Bardês and making it impossible for the befuddled viceroy to send further assistance northward.[83] They also brought up heavy artillery that hurled 45,000 shells into beleaguered Bassein, the Louisbourg of the East, within the span of three months. In desperation, Portuguese commanders appealed to Bombay for an alliance or at least stepped-up assistance; Bombay responded that it would accept cash-and-carry only and demanded the cession of all of Salsete Island to the East India Company.[84]

The siege of Bassein, a rare example of Portuguese valor during the eighteenth century, reached its inevitable climax in May 1739. In the preceding month, the Marathas had defied heavy fire from the fort by laying a dozen mines under its ramparts. Beginning on 13 May,

81. In 1737 the East India Company possessed only 2,623 soldiers and sailors to defend Bombay and its approaches. Two-thirds were sepoys and topazes. In October 1737, the president of Bombay reported that his sources indicated that the Marathas already possessed 10,000–12,000 men in Bassein and Salsete and were expecting additional reinforcements of "upwards of twenty thousand," far greater than what he and the Portuguese could raise. John Horne to Onslow Burrish, 3 Oct. 1737 (OS), in Pawar, "English Records," 40 and 59.

82. Despite Jesuit protests, the college and its strong fortifications were blown up with British encouragement to prevent the Marathas from gaining a stronghold that might "incommode" the British in Bombay. George W. Forrest, ed., *Selections from the Letters, Despatches, and Other State Papers Preserved in the Bombay Secretariat, Maratha Series*, 3 vols. (Bombay, 1885), I:1, iii.

83. In Salsete, Maratha forces captured Assalona and Margão and reached the outskirts of Rachol. The state of mind of the viceroy, who was primarily preoccupied during these years with his own debts, with efforts to augment his income by illegal trading between Lisbon, Bahia, and Goa, and with concern over the future of his bastard daughter, is fully revealed in his personal correspondence. His copybooks are in ACL, ms. Azul, cods. 504–11; his official dispatches are in AHU/PA/IN, esp. *cxs.* 45–49.

84. The appeal from the general of the north was personally conveyed by Fr. Manuel Rodrigo de Estrada, S.J. (See Pawar, "English Records," 42ff.) The directors of the EIC responded to a complaint from the Portuguese government concerning their lack of support with a defense of the conduct of its agents there and observed that the Company had not been repaid for the £5,000 expended in support of Taná in 1730 or the £4,000 advanced to defend Bandorá. They noted that although the rector of the latter college "amused our Governour with a Bill of Exchange drawn for part thereof on their Provincial at Goa, the said bill was returned unpaid." EIC directors to duke of Newcastle, 5 June 1735 and 18 Jan. 1737, and "Answer of the East India Company to a Paper Given in by Mr. Azevedo (Portuguese minister to London)," 4 Nov. 1738, in PRO/SP89/36, 122–23ᵛ. Cf. Pawar, "English Records," 72–75, who prints the Company's reply from a different text. The EIC was still attempting to collect loans that it had made to the viceregal exchequer and its dependencies half a century later. By 1781 it claimed that the loans had reached the equivalent of 139.7 contos. "Accounts Between the Crown of Portugal and the Hon.rable English East India Company," 31 July 1781, in AHU/PA/IN, *m.* 132; D. Federico Guilherme de Sousa (governor, India) to colonial secretary, ca. Apr. 1782, in ibid., *m.* 10; and marquis de Alorna (viceroy) to Marco António de Azevedo Coutinho, 5 Jan. 1750 and encs., in ANTT/Ministério do Reino, *m.* 602 (orig.). The statement by Fr. John Correia-Afonso that "the English were indeed of little help to the Portuguese in this campaign" is ill informed. "The Jesuits and the Fall of Bassein," *Indica* 15, 2 (1978): 107–20, at 119.

several were exploded, enabling hordes of troops to pour through the resulting breaches. Although they were repelled after bitter hand-to-hand fighting, the fortress commander, Caetano de Sousa Pereira, knew that the game was up. Many of his men were ill or wounded, all were exhausted and discouraged, supplies of munitions and provisions were nearly expended, and there was no hope of relief.[85] Accordingly, the commander capitulated on honorable terms. On 23 May, he and his troops boarded a flotilla of small boats that the governor of Bombay had provided, and the jubilant Marathas entered the rubble that was once the proud fortress of Bassein.[86]

It was not until September 1740 that the Marathas and the Portuguese agreed to a new peace. The results for the Portuguese generally and for the Society in particular were devastating. The state had been deprived of the entire northern province, including its onetime jewels, Bassein and Salsete do Norte. In addition to Bassein, it lost 8 cities, 377 villages, 20 fortresses, and revenues in excess of 32 contos.[87] The Marathas agreed to evacuate the Goan territories, but at the additional cost of extracting heavy tribute from the inhabitants of those territories; and in exchange for evacuating Assalona and its fellow villages, they acquired Chaul, which Goan authorities first tried to sell to the British.[88]

The failed defense of the north also cost the Society dearly. The province of Goa lost four colleges (Bassein, Taná, Bandorá, and Chaul), which in 1731 had been staffed by 17.1 percent of its members. Each of the eastern provinces lost substantial income derived from landed revenues from Salsete do Norte as well as loans made in the lost province.[89] In addition, the surviving Jesuit facilities in Goa found themselves cut off from the cloth

85. The Maratha commander reported that the defense of Bassein had cost the Portuguese in excess of 500 Europeans besides 350 topazes and unnumbered sepoys. At the time of the capitulation, there were 130 wounded out of a force of ca. 800 men. Pissurlencar, *Portuguese and Marathas*, 328 and 340 n. 15. How many were seriously ill is not revealed. Unfortunately, the admission and discharge records of Bassein's hospital, which begin in January 1733, stop in July 1737. The "Livro de matricula dos doentes do hospital de S. João de Deus," HAG 865, is a unique and grim register. It gives the soldiers' names, units, places of origin, lengths of hospital stay, and dates of discharge but not their infirmities. Admissions varied from 180 to 1,167 and the number "cured" from a mere 24 to 113.

86. There is a competent summary of the last days of Bassein by an anonymous Jesuit who wrote his report from Bombay a few days after the survivors' arrival there: ARSI, *Goa*, 36:II, 496ᵛ–497ᵛ. See also Dighe, *Peshwa Bajirao*, 187–91; Pissurlencar, *Portuguese and Marathas*, 325–40. Forrest, *Selections*, 1:1, 39–41 and 47–49, includes key documents on the capitulation and on subsequent British financial aid to the defeated Portuguese forces. For the unhappy end of Caetano de Sousa Pereira, see C. R. Boxer, "O plano da reconquista da província do norte elaborato pelo capitão Caetano de Sousa Pereira," *Boletim do Instituto Vasco da Gama*, no. 29 (1936): 1–12.

87. Encs. in viceroy to king, 25 Jan. 1738, in AHU/PA/IN, *m.* 77. Cf. Frederick Charles Danvers, *The Portuguese in India* [1894], 2 vols. (rpr., London, 1966), 2: 412.

88. Anthony D'Costa, "The Rendition of Chaul," *Indica* 5 (1968): 53–63.

89. In 1735 the viceroy stated that estimates of Jesuit investments on the island amounted to 80.5 contos. Enc. in Sandomil to king, 22 Jan. 1735, in ACL, ms. Azul, 505, fols. 220–223ʳ (draft) but missing from the original: AHU/PA/IN, *m.* 31. The Jesuits reported much lower figures: the procurator of New St. Paul's declared that the college had lost 11.7 contos in income in the entire northern province. Procurator to Fr. M.ᵉˡ de M[agalhã]ᵉˢ, 8 Jan. 1746, in HAG 833, fol. 5ʳ. The income of the province of Japan, the Vietnam missions, and the college of Macao from the northern estates averaged 5.5 contos between 1729 and 1736. HAG 1497. Malabar's losses from investments were much heavier, amounting to 133.5 contos. F/*JM*, 2: 347. Obviously the earnings of the college of Bassein also disappeared. Those of its seminary, mostly in rice, are reported for 1709 in ARSI, *Goa*, 9:II, 441ʳ. The crown also had an exaggerated notion of the extent of Jesuit holdings on the island. One minister stated that the Order administered 67 out of 79 villages there. António Guedes Pereira to Sandomil, 17 Oct. 1738, in ACL, ms. Azul, 509, fols. 21ʳ–23ʳ.

and foodstuffs they had formerly obtained from Bassein and Salsete do Norte.[90] But, of course, other entities of the Church also suffered heavy losses in the war, as did the Holy Brotherhood of Mercy of Goa, which claimed to have made estate loans amounting to 39.7 contos in the lost province.[91]

Following the conclusion of the conflict, there occurred the customary scramble among Portuguese officials to distance themselves from any charge of wrongdoing and to suggest that the debacle was the fault of others. The viceroy naturally absolved himself and his principal officers of any responsibility. Nor did any contemporary have the courage to blame the crown for its belated and inadequate response, though such criticism was surely warranted.[92] Not surprisingly, the Jesuits soon emerged as leading culprits, and the viceroy himself became their leading critic. It is true that in January 1734 he had expressed full satisfaction in their diplomatic and evangelical skills,[93] but already Sandomil had raised questions about their willingness to aid his imperiled regime financially. In 1733, when the provincial had invoked the old ploy of ecclesiastical immunity to avoid assessments that the treasury attempted to levy on the Society's villages in Salsete do Norte in order to secure funds for the financing of the Taná fortress, Sandomil had convoked a board of jurists and church leaders who unanimously concurred with the viceroy that the Jesuits ought to pay up. Later Sandomil condemned the fathers in Salsete for setting a poor example by failing to comply with the local commandant's orders to supply lime from their villages for the fortress's construction, a charge that led a modern historian to the bizarre (and wholly unfounded) conclusion that the Jesuits were primarily responsible for the loss of Taná and Salsete do Norte.[94]

By 1735, Sandomil had become increasingly disenchanted with the Jesuits. Revealing a not-uncommon paranoia, he wrote a royal minister that he suspected that the fathers were sending the court adverse reports concerning his administration. He professed to believe that they were enormously rich and enjoyed a fantastic income amounting to 2,400 contos, more than nine times that of the royal exchequer in Goa, Bardês, and Salsete. There is

90. Those imports can be traced, for example, in HAG 2048, the accounts of the college of Rachol from 1725 to 1730.

91. Overseas Council to count of Ega (viceroy, India), 17 Mar. 1758, in AHU/PA/IN, *m.* 99. For Franciscan losses in the province and in Chaul, see Fr. Achilles Meersman, O.F.M., ed., *Annual Reports of the Portuguese Franciscans in India, 1713–1833* (Lisbon, 1972), 11–12.

92. No ships from Portugal reached Goa during 1736 and possibly not the following year, presumably because of Portugal's near war with Spain over control of southern Brazil. D. Alden, *Royal Government in Colonial Brazil* (Berkeley, 1968), 77–78 n. 66; Sandomil to Fr. João Mascarenhas (his Augustinian brother), 2 Jan. 1737, in ACL, ms. Azul, cod. 511, fol. 69ʳ. On 17 Mar. 1738, the king "resolved" to send a couple of frigates to India, but they were still awaiting a favorable wind that October. Marginal note, consulta of 13 Mar. 1738, in AHU/PA/IN, *m.* 53, no. 30; António Guedes Pereira (secretary of state) to Sandomil, 22 Oct. 1738, in ACL, ms. Azul, 509, fols. 24ʳ–25ʳ. In 1740, Sandomil learned through Jesuit sources that a squadron of four large ships, 3,500 men, and 240 contos was sailing to Goa. Sandomil to Francisco Xavier de Miranda Henriques, 15 Dec. 1740, in ibid., 511, fol. 98ʳ. In fact, it took 372 days for that squadron to reach its destination, and many of its passengers had been grievously ill with scurvy. Boxer, "Carreira da India," 75–78.

93. Sandomil to king, 14 Jan. 1734, in ACL, ms. Azul, 504, fol. 97ʳ.

94. Resolutions of the *junta de theologos e juristas*, Goa, 5 Dec. 1733, in *ACE*, 5: 394–96. Lobato, *Relações Luso-Maratas*, 149; but cf. 163–65, where the author concedes that the fortress was largely completed before the Marathas intimidated its commander into fleeing his post, misconduct for which the Jesuits can hardly be held responsible.

absolutely no reliable evidence that the Society possessed revenues on such a scale, but viceroys of India had always believed that the Order was exceedingly opulent.[95]

As the military situation in the north became increasingly bleak, the viceroy's impatience with leaders of the Society intensified. As early as December 1734, the Goan council of state had supported his decision to remove the Jesuit administrator of military stores in Bassein because of a dispute with its commander, who claimed that the administrator refused to release urgently needed powder.[96] In August 1737, four months after the fall of Taná, the viceroy advised the provincial of Goa that the committee of the three estates had agreed that each entity of the Church must contribute silver to defray the extraordinary defense expenditures occasioned by the current war.

The provincial delayed compliance as long as possible, but Sandomil was persistent. In hopes of preventing his churches from being stripped of their silver, the provincial ultimately agreed to loan the royal treasury 9 contos. That was not what Sandomil had had in mind, and he insisted that the provincial submit to him a complete inventory of the silver holdings of his churches within three days. Noting that the Bandorá college had already contributed heavily to the cost of fortifying that community, a service for which it had not been compensated, the provincial again declined, but he increased his loan offer to 12 contos, a sum equal to 28.6 percent of the Church's contribution to the forced loan.[97] Yet the viceroy was persuaded that that did not begin to dent the Society's annual income. Accordingly, he insisted that the provincial comply with his original demand, and his council of state sent the same administrator a sharp reprimand that came close to charging him with lèse-majesté.[98]

The viceroy's accusations that the Jesuits lacked a proper sense of patriotism need to be taken with so many grains of salt. As recently as 1728, the Society had lent the crown the not-inconsiderable sum of 41.7 contos to defray expenses of the Mombasa misadventure at a time when, as the Overseas Council later acknowledged, no one else was willing to advance the exchequer a real (see Chapter 13).[99] Three years later the provincial again came to the aid of the viceregal treasury with a further noninterest-bearing loan of 12 contos as well as a "gift" of 3.9 contos.[100] The forced loan that the provincial attempted to resist in 1737 was, therefore, far from the first that the Society had been called to furnish within the decade. Less than three weeks before the fall of Bassein, the last rector of that city's college

95. Sandomil to Diogo de Mendonça Corte Real, 26 Jan. 1735, in ACL, ms. Azul, 511, fol. 34[v]. In January 1733, the exchequer's receipts were reported to be 162,480,000 rs., but expenses amounted to 207,123,000 rs. "Extracto das rendas reaes e dispezas de Goa, Salcete e Bardes como da praça de Angediva," 27 Jan. 1733, in AHU/PA/IN, *cx*. 40, no. 37.

96. Deliberations of the council of state, 7 Dec. 1734 and 5 Jan. 1735, in *ACE*, 5: 396–400.

97. During 1737, the viceregal exchequer collected 95.6 contos from private individuals as well as entities of the Church for the defense of the northern province. Treasurer, Goa, to king, 20 Jan. 1738, in AHU/PA/IN, *m*. 77. One of the documents missing from these archives is a twelve-page list of contributors. A possible copy of that list is in the Lilly Library, Indiana University, in the C. R. Boxer manuscript collection, in a codex entitled "Governo na India e Africa Oriental," doc. 18, fols. 61[r]–64[r].

98. *ACE*, 5: 435–46, and 452–53. Cf. Correia-Afonso, "Jesuits," 115–16.

99. Overseas Council to viceroy, 18 Mar. 1729, in *APO*:2, 4:2:2, 351. The magnitude of the Jesuit loan is understated in the consulta, where it is given as 31.5 contos.

100. João de Saldanha da Gama to king, 14 Jan. 1732, in AHU/PA/IN, *m*. 43. Sandomil seemingly deliberately minimized Jesuit financial assistance by reporting that the Dominicans had furnished 2.7 contos, the four eastern provinces of the Jesuits 2.4 contos, and the Augustinians 0.45 contos. Sandomil to king, 26 Jan. 1734, in AHU/PA/IN, *m*. 38.

TABLE 23.5

Membership of the Provinces of Goa and Malabar, 1697–1756

Year	Goa	Malabar	Year	Goa	Malabar
1697	—	46	1728	165	—
1699	231	—	1731	163	51
1706	205	—	1734	—	54
1708	—	51	1737	—	59
1709	170	—	1740	—	62
1718	—	54	1741	138	—
1719	181	—	1756	161	45

SOURCES: Goa: ARSI, *Goa*, 26 and 27. Malabar: F/*JM*, 2: app. 1.

agreed to raise 12 contos in Bombay on the college's credit to buy urgently needed supplies for the fortress's garrison. The fact that the city fell shortly thereafter did not prevent its former military governor from demanding that British officials in Bombay compel Jesuit refugees in the city to honor that pledge, a demand that those officials rejected as beyond their authority.[101]

Soon after, someone framed a diatribe whose thesis was that the Religious served no useful purpose in India and that the Jesuits in particular were guilty of serious shortcomings. As Soares de Sousa had done in the sixteenth century, the anonymous writer accused the fathers of meddling in politics, attempting to poison the viceroy, and facilitating the entry of the Marathas into Salsete do Norte. Just as the Jesuits in sixteenth-century Salvador moved with alacrity to refute Soares de Sousa's allegations, so the provincial of Goa directed Fr. Rodrigo de Estrada, formerly of the college of Bassein and subsequently procurator-general of Goa in Lisbon, to assemble a large array of witnesses in India to testify in behalf of the Society. They included military and civil officers and the heads of the other religious Orders: all absolved the Society of any wrongdoing.[102]

As far as is known, the crown did not take official notice of the defamatory memorial. Though symptomatic of the times and the seemingly insurmountable problems that confronted Portugal in the East, it caused the Society far less damage than the Marathas did. By 1741, when the last personnel listing of the period was assembled, there remained in the province of Goa only 130 members of the Society, and in the neighboring province of Malabar about another 50 (see Table 23.5). That was a smaller representation for the Society in India and Mozambique than at any time in 180 years. The *catalogus rerum* of the same year, the last of the series that began in the sixteenth century, is the most incomplete of all. Its numerous lacunae offer mute testimony to the chaos that confronted the Society in India; nor would the Jesuits' position there improve during their remaining years in the subcontinent.[103] But if reports from the eastern segments of the Assistancy made grim reading for the Roman headquarters, those from Brazil were far more encouraging.

101. Forrest, *Selections*, 45–47; cf. Correia-Afonso, "Jesuits," 117.

102. The testimonials are scattered in several maços in ANTT/CJ, especially /83. Correia-Afonso, "Jesuits," 117–20, provides a fair summary of their substance.

103. "Catalogus rerum provinciae Goanae," Dec. 1741, in ARSI, *Goa*, 26, fol. 249ʳ–249ᵛ.

Brazil:
An Expanding Enterprise

Though the Portuguese were barely able to retain the remnants of their once-vaunted eastern empire during the first half of the eighteenth century, Brazil became the brightest star of the Lusitanian thalassocracy, thanks to the discovery of alluvial gold and later of diamonds. The first major gold finds were made in the mid-1690s in the interior province of Minas Gerais; later strikes of varying magnitude occurred in the interiors of half a dozen captaincies. Such discoveries had far-reaching results for both the colony and the kingdom. Immigrants, both voluntary and involuntary (African slaves), swarmed to the littoral, and many of them quickly advanced to the backlands. For about 60 years, some in Brazil and in Portugal enjoyed far greater prosperity than they had ever known before.[104]

Although this period can hardly be called a golden age for the Society, it, too, prospered and expanded in personnel, facilities, and missions during those decades, in marked contrast to its severe contraction in the East. During the Joanine period, Jesuits could be found from one end of Brazil to the other, from the Platine outpost of Colônia do Sacramento to the furthest reaches of the Amazon. The only administrative unit where the Order did not flourish was Minas Gerais, from which all religious Orders were theoretically banned.[105] As Table 23.6 demonstrates, between 1690 and the late 1740s, membership of the Brazil province increased by nearly 52 percent, while that of the vice-province of Maranhão soared by 174 percent during roughly comparable years.

The growth of the Brazil province owed less to its attraction of new members from abroad than to its successful recruiting within the colony itself. Between 1702 and 1709 it gained only 2.3 members per annum from abroad, an average that fell to 1.2 during the following decade. It is true that the average rose somewhat during the 1720s (1.7 per year) and the 1730s (2.5 per year), but no recruits joined the province from outside in the 1740s. During these decades, the Brazil province, in fact, received fewer external recruits than did the eastern provinces. The figures for the younger vice-province more closely resembled Goa's pattern: the number of external recruits reaching Maranhão increased from 3.3 per year (1702–9) to 6.8 (1720–29), then declined to 4.9 per annum during the 1730s and 1740s.[106]

The personnel catalogues, especially the last ones of the province and the vice-province, shed further light on the geographic origins of their memberships. Portugal continued to furnish Maranhão with most of its recruits. Some 73.3 percent of them came from the kingdom's central bishoprics, compared with 20 percent representing those in the north; but only 6.6 percent came from those in the south. Though Brazil supplied only 5 percent of those who served in the vice-province, it actually contributed a greater percentage of those who labored in the Brazil province than did the kingdom itself. As would be

---

104. A. J. R. Russell-Wood, "Colonial Brazil: The Gold Cycle, *c.* 1690–1750," in Leslie Bethell, ed., *The Cambridge History of Latin America*, 11 vols. (New York, 1984–94), 2: 547–600.

105. Because some religious allegedly engaged in contraband in Minas Gerais, the crown attempted to restrict the number of clergy permitted to reside there. *CRs* of 18 May and 19 Oct. 1709, in APB/OR/7, nos. 576 and 607. Two Jesuits served there briefly in 1719 and 1720, but none apparently did so thereafter. *HCJB*, 6: 192–94. Cf. C. R. Boxer, *The Golden Age of Brazil, 1695–1750* (Berkeley, 1962), 170, 180.

106. BGJ, 258–68, conveniently assembles lists of external recruits for the province and the vice-province from appendixes in *HCJB*.

TABLE 23.6

Growth of the Brazil Province and the Vice-Province of
Maranhão, 1690–1751

Year	Brazil	Maranhão	Year	Brazil	Maranhão
1690	—	54	1735	417	117
1694	310	—	1740	—	128
1716	324	64	1742	—	138
1720	—	64	1745	447	—
1722	367	—	1748	471	—
1730	—	102	1751	—	148
1732	362	118			

SOURCES: ARSI, *Bras.*, 6 and 27, passim.

expected, Bahia furnished the largest share of the Brazilian-born (34.6 percent), followed by Pernambuco (22.4 percent) and Rio de Janeiro (13.6 percent). Rather surprisingly, Minas Gerais, the primary focus of the eighteenth-century gold boom, provided 10.2 percent of the recruits, with the remainder coming from São Paulo and the more southerly parts of the colony. Interestingly enough, among the Peninsulars who reached the province, more than half (56.7 percent) came from the northern bishoprics, compared with 41.3 percent who came from the central sees and a mere 1.9 percent who were natives of the southern bishoprics. Despite the paranoia that afflicted government leaders during the 1750s, less than 10 percent of those who served in either province were foreign-born, though their number was conspicuously greater in the north than in the rest of Brazil.[107]

Table 23.7 indicates that although the number of personnel attached to the two colleges of the vice-province was about the same in the first half of the eighteenth century, that was not true within the Brazil province. In those decades the college of Bahia and its dependencies, including the novitiate and the Belém seminary, became one of the largest facilities in the Assistancy. There were about a third more Jesuits attached to Bahia than to the entire province of Goa in the mid-eighteenth century, when it equaled Coimbra, until then the largest entity within the Assistancy, in size. Rio de Janeiro and its dependencies, which included a two- or three-man contingent at the Platine outpost of Colônia do Sacramento, opposite Buenos Aires, and incipient houses in Parnaguá and Desterro (Santa Catarina), clearly constituted the second most rapidly growing unit of the Brazil province, a not-unexpected development, since the southern city was becoming a more vital metropolis than Salvador during the gold boom.

Although many Jesuits remained attached to urban educational and training facilities, the Society was still the primary missionary Order in Portugal's principal colony. In each captaincy it continued to maintain more missions (aldeias) and more inmates than did any of its rivals.[108] Some were situated in remote backlands; others were located in the littoral

107. This analysis is based upon the last available personnel catalogues for the Brazil province (1757) and for the vice-province of Maranhão (1760). See *HCJB*, 4: 363–67, and 7: 421–34.

108. E.g., [Anon.], "Relação das aldeas, que há no districto deste governo de Pernambuco e a capitania da Paraiba" [ca. 1748], *ABNRJ* 28 (1908): 419–22; "Mapa geral de todas as misoens ou aldeias de gentio manso que estaó nesta capitania da Bahia e nas mais q. comprehende o seo governo," 20 Dec. 1758, in

TABLE 23.7

Distribution of Members of the Brazil Province and the Vice-Province of Maranhão, 1701–57

Year	Bahia	Rio de Janeiro	Olinda	Recife	Espírito Santo	São Paulo	Santos	Maranhão	Pará
1701	171	63	40	16	12	13	6	—	—
1722	191	82	33	22	13	18	6	—	—
1723	—	—	—	—	—	—	—	40	29
1726	—	—	—	—	—	—	—	50	45
1732	195	83	17	24	19	23	6	—	—
1736	200	111	23	24	19	20	6	—	—
1739	190	110	25	27	19	19	7	57	68
1744	199	99	30	21	16	23	7	84	58
1751	—	—	—	—	—	—	—	56	66
1753	—	—	—	—	—	—	—	82	64
1757	220	145	33	22	21	32	8	—	—

SOURCES: ARSI, *Bras.*, 5:I, 5:II, 6:I, 6:II, and 27.

within a few kilometers of Portuguese settlements. Those administered by the Pernambucan colleges extended from Ceará and Rio Grande do Norte to Alagoas; those belonging to the college of Bahia ranged from Sergipe d'Elrey in the north to Porto Seguro in the south.[109] In contrast with the Maranhense missions, which relied especially upon the harvesting of the forest for their income, those in the Brazil province depended primarily upon small-scale ranching, as indicated by Table 23.8. A considerable number of Brasis remained under Jesuit care, though far fewer than in the sixteenth century.

Surprisingly enough, in 1730 there were about as many mission Indians within the Brazil province as there were in Maranhão. The provincial's report of that year records the existence of 21,031 aborigines living on 29 aldeias and nine of the Society's estates.[110] Yet the vice-province was patently the Society's primary mission frontier in Brazil: by the 1750s, despite occasional setbacks and various consolidations, the number of missions there reached 52.[111]

Largely because of the northern State's poverty, the existence of the Maranhense missions had long been a source of bitter controversy for the fathers and the settlers. As stated in Chapter 19, that conflict intensified during the first half of the eighteenth century. But there was also persistent criticism of the mission system within the State of Brazil. One such critic was a Pernambucan, Diogo de Conceição, who had come to Salvador after his wife's death and joined that city's famous third order of Saint Francis.[112] From there he made his way to the court, where he spent nine years (doing what, we do

José António Caldas, *Notícia geral de toda esta capitania da Bahia desde o seu descobrimento atê o presente ano de 1759* (fasc. ed., Salvador, 1951), facing fol. 60.

109. In addition to the sources cited in the preceding note, the fullest coeval description of the aldeia system within the Brazil province is João Pereira (provincial) to general, 5 July 1702, in *HCJB*, 5: 569–73. Fr. Leite discussed the development of the aldeias in several of his volumes in *HCJB*, especially vols. 3, 5 and 6.

110. "Numerus personaru' in Indoru' pagis qui Nostris regu'tuo de gentiu' in Maragnonis 1730," in ARSI, *Bras.*, 10:II, fol. 338r.

111. *LAM*3: 363–64.

112. See A. J. R. Russell-Wood, "Prestige, Power, and Piety in Colonial Brazil: The Third Orders of Salvador," *HAHR* 69, 1 (Feb. 1989): 61–89.

TABLE 23.8

Jesuit Missions in the Province of Brazil, 1702–57

	Missions (N)	Indians	Africans	Cattle and oxen	Horses	Goats and sheep
1702						
Bahia	10	4,850	—	—	—	—
Rio de Janeiro	4	1,800	—	—	—	—
Olinda	6	6,700	—	—	—	—
São Paulo	3	1,000	—	—	—	—
Espírito Santo	2	1,100	—	—	—	—
Total	25	15,450	—	—	—	—
1739						
Bahia	10	4,159	40	582	122	719
Rio de Janeiro	4	1,713	—	345	11	199
Olinda	3	4,100	14	1,971	170	—
São Paulo	4	1,040	—	117	62	30
Espírito Santo	2	3,117	—	79	—	—
Total	23	14,129	54	3,094	365	948
1743						
Bahia	10	3,719	29	630	118	522
Rio de Janeiro	4	1,889	—	240	18	262
Olinda	7	10,526	10	2,110	120	—
São Paulo	4	1,176	—	150	22	—
Espírito Santo	2	2,450	—	60+	—	—
Total	27	19,760	39	3,190+	278	784
1757						
Bahia	10	4,145	26	—	411	354
Rio de Janeiro	5	1,810	—	364	—	149
Olinda	7	12,723	7	180	—	—
São Paulo	7	1,395	—	89	14	—
Espírito Santo	2	2,580	—	67	—	20
Total	31	22,653	33	700	425	523

SOURCES: 1702: ARSI, *Bras.*, 10:I, fols. 25–25ᵛ. Remainder: ibid., 6:II, fols. 276–81, 335–40, and 436–43.

not know) before submitting to the king his curious proposal in 1738. In that petition he claimed that years of experience in Brazil's backlands had convinced him, as it had Soares de Sousa long before, that the mission system was a failure. He insisted that the aldeias were prisons rather than training centers, and that despite the efforts of the fathers, their inmates retained their heathenish ways and continued to be lazy, brutish, and unreasonably fearful of white settlers. His solution was similar to that advocated by the formidable Paulo da Silva Nunes: the secularization of all missions within 120 kilometers of white settlements and their assignment to parisent to parish priests.[113]

In 1738 and again in 1746, the crown referred that proposal to the governors-general of Bahia and directed them to solicit the opinions of the religious leaders there. The response was precisely what one would expect: the Jesuits, supported by the superiors of the other

113. Br. Diogo de Conceição to king, Lisbon, Day of Monte do Carmo, [1738], in APB/OR/34, fol. 108. Unlike Silva Nunes, the author expressed no animus toward the Jesuits and insisted that he had no ax to grind but was simply doing his Christian duty.

Orders, insisted that secularization had always brought baneful results for the Brasis and that the aldeia system had functioned beneficially for nearly two centuries. Understandably, the president of the archdiocese chapter, who was also procurador dos índios, took a very different view, that of the settlers generally: he maintained that Indians were "brutes without any remedial qualities" and that they harbored deeply rooted propensities toward idleness, theft, drink, and murder. He agreed that the missionaries had failed to reshape their character, but he argued that if long-sought episcopal seminaries were established, their graduates might persuade the natives to change their ways.[114]

The extension of the debate over the persistence of the missions to the Brazil province was only one of several controversies that Jesuits endured there during these years. As was the case in both India and the State of Maranhão, the primary vehicle for the expression of the settlers' grievances against the religious Orders remained the municipal council (cámara). In 1718, for example, the cámara of Rio de Janeiro wrote John V urging strict enforcement of existing legislation intended to prevent the religious from engrossing lands. The aldermen stated that the religious, "principally those of the Company [of Jesus] are today the masters of the greater part of our lands with pernicious inconvenience" to the king and his subjects. They continued that most of those lands lay fallow and paid no tithes, and that the ecclesiastics wrongly utilized Indians, who were intended to serve the settlers. Typically, the crown referred that complaint to the local governor, renewing its earlier directive to undertake a survey of the properties that the religious held and to respond to the aldermen's complaints. Like many such executives, the governor contended that the allegations were mostly unfounded. He noted that during the French invasion of 1711, the Jesuits had furnished Indians to defend the city of Rio de Janeiro and had provided beef and other provisions for its relief, and that during a recent smallpox epidemic, the rector of the Jesuit college had gone about the city with a cart distributing chickens and bread to the victims. Probably naively, the governor reported that after consulting the heads of the three land-owning Orders, he had learned that the legislation restricting their ability to acquire lands had never been enforced in the colony.[115] Whether the Overseas Council was impressed by the governor's findings cannot be determined, but it is clear that settlers' criticisms of land acquisition by Jesuits and by other Orders continued throughout the Joanine years.[116]

Another complaint by the same council demonstrates how Jesuits were perceived to be arrogant, unfair competitors of local merchants. In 1729 the courts of Lisbon and Madrid arranged one of their customary marriage alliances, for which the Portuguese were obliged to contribute a large dowry. Part of the burden was passed on to the Brazilians, who were required to raise money through excise taxes on food, in Rio de Janeiro's case

114. Governor-general to king, Bahia, 1 Oct. 1738 and encs., in APB/OR/34, fols. 103–11; revised petition, 18 Mar. 1745; *CR*, 21 May 1746, and governor-general's reply, 10 Mar. 1747, in APB/OR/44, nos. 3, 3A, and 3B.

115. Cámara to king, 14 Mar. 1718, in *RADF*, 2: 372; Overseas Council to Ayres de Saldanha de Albuquerque Coutinho Matos e Noronha, 22 Sept. 1718, and the latter's reply of 10 July 1719, in ANRJ, cod. 80, vol. 1, fols. 54^r–56^r. Concerning the French invasions of Rio in 1710 and 1711, see Boxer, *Golden Age*, chap. 4.

116. E.g., from the late 1720s until the mid-1750s, the cámara of Cabo Frio, Rio de Janeiro, tirelessly but unsuccessfully complained to the crown about the Jesuits' landholdings, control over the indigenes, and contempt for local justices. *LAM*3: 250–53, 267–68, and 166–67 n. 144.

including beef. The next year the cámara, perhaps emboldened by the new governor, the irascible Luís Vaía Monteiro (1725–32), who bore no love for the Society, remonstrated with the rector of the local college for opening a butcher shop near that institution. The council's concern was twofold: first, the college was in competition with other merchants; and second, it claimed exemption from the local meat tax. The council therefore demanded that the rector either furnish royal authorization for the shop or shut its doors. The rector responded unconvincingly that the authorization had been lost during the French invasions but that the college had sold meat at retail in the past and that previous councils had not complained.[117] That may have been true, but the incident made the college appear in a bad light and demonstrated a kind of insensitivity that would have shocked the Society's sixteenth-century image makers.[118]

The outcome of that dispute is unknown, but another that occurred in Salvador a few years later produced a surprising result. For many years there had been a cove along the city's waterfront where small craft bringing manioc and other provisions from across All Saints Bay to sustain the city customarily anchored. In January 1736 the Jesuits closed the cove to outsiders and began to build a large wharf there to house their sugar and other commodities awaiting overseas shipment. That project was, in fact, a realization of twenty-year-old plans that had long enjoyed the crown's sanction, since the fathers promised to provide equipment on their wharf to offload artillery for the defense of the city. Though that wharf was designed by a military engineer and was destined to become the city's largest, the cámara protested that the fathers were exceeding the dimensions prescribed in their license and appealed successively to the local royal magistrate (*juiz de fóra*), to the High Court, and to the crown for remedy.

The king's reaction was hardly what the aldermen had expected. He denied that they had any jurisdiction in the matter or any legal authority to block a project that he had long ago sanctioned. Describing the councilmen's behavior as "absurd" and "frivolous," he ordered their arrest and the election of a new council, whose members the viceroy was to impress with the need to display proper respect for the royal will.[119]

The Jesuits' apparent "victory" in this instance seems to reflect the Society's continued ability to cultivate the high and mighty. During this period it still relied upon traditional techniques to achieve its objectives. Thus, sympathetic administrators like Cristóvão da Costa Freire, governor of Maranhão (1707–17), received letters of greeting from Father General Michelangelo Tamburini, who conferred upon him a charter of brotherhood in the Society and declared him to be its "great Defender" in the state.[120] And when two

117. *RADF*, 3: [225]–29.
118. E.g., one warning from the Roman headquarters during the formative period contained the following admonition: "Sepan los nuestros que les está prohibido todo lo que tenga apariencia de nego-ciaciones seglares en cultivar los campos y vender sus frutos o productos similares en la plaza." Quoted by Félix Zubillaga, "La provincia jesuítica en Nueva España: Su fundamento económico: Siglo XVI," *AHSI* 38 (Jan.–June 1969): 57.
119. Cámara to governor-general, 22 Feb. 1736, in AMB, *Ofícios ao govêrno, 1712–1737*, fols. 378^r–390^v; cámara to king, 5 Sept. 1736, in AMB, *Cartas do senado a sua magestade*, 28:9, fols. 167^r–172^r; Overseas Council, consulta, ca. 1737, AHU/LR/254, no fol.; king to viceroy, 6 Jan. 1737, in BNRJ, II, 33, 48; governor-general to king, 15 July 1738 and related documents, in APB/OR/34, nos. 66, 87, and 108. There is, curiously, no mention of this contretemps in *HCJB*.
120. Tamburini to Costa Freire, 13 July 1715, in ARSI, *Bras.*, 25, fol. 6^v.

India-bound carracks made an unplanned stop at Rio de Janeiro in 1738, José da Silva Pais, the acting governor, insisted that one of the passengers, an aristocrat named D. Luís de Mascarenhas, stay at the governor's palace but found himself outmaneuvered by the Jesuits, who had already offered the noble their own hospitality. As Silva Pais, founder of the new captaincy of Rio Grande de São Pedro (later do Sul), unhappily remarked, "I was unable to separate him from the cassock."[121] Such a candid confession, so alien to officially expressed sentiments during the formative period of the Society, is one of many indications that the organization was no longer as highly respected as it had once been. Its tribulations in the kingdom during these decades provide further illustrations of its diminished position within the Lusitanian world.

Tribulations of the Society in Joanine Portugal

The membership of the Society in the kingdom continued to expand moderately during the eighteenth century, but at a rate that was hardly commensurate with Portugal's newfound affluence. At the beginning of the century, membership stood at 716; by 1749 it would peak at 855, representing a gain of 19.4 percent. The central bishoprics continued to be the Order's most fertile recruiting grounds: nearly two-thirds (62.7 percent) of its personnel came from there, compared with 23.4 percent from the northern bishoprics and only 13.8 percent from those south of the Tagus.[122] By the end of the period, the Society ranked third, behind the Franciscans and the Dominicans, in the number of facilities that it possessed in the kingdom and in the Atlantic islands.[123]

During this period concerned critics like D. Luís da Cunha (b. 1662–d. 1749), dean of the Portuguese diplomatic corps, contended that the kingdom possessed too many religious houses and that young people would better serve their sovereign in secular capacities.[124] If contemporary reckonings are to be believed, the number of such houses, male and female, grew by some 61.6 percent between about 1600 and 1763. Whether the number of inmates increased proportionately is entirely uncertain.[125]

The Jesuits added surprisingly few facilities in the kingdom at this time.[126] Provincial leaders, anxious to execute the terms of the bountiful will of the admiral of Castile (see Chapter 14) by erecting a special probationary house in Lisbon for recruits pledged to serve

121. Silva Pais to Gomes Freire de Andrada (governor, Rio de Janeiro and southern Brazil), 27 Dec. 1738, in ANRJ, col. 84/9/190ʳ.

122. The province's first and third catalogues, in ARSI, *Lus.*, 47, 48, and 49, make it possible to chart the fluctuations in the Society's membership during these five decades. For the "Catalogus primus" of 1749, see 49, fols. 8–59ᵛ, for which fols. 2–7ᵛ provide a helpful index.

123. *HIP*, 3: 138–39.

124. Pedro de Azevedo, ed., *Instruções inéditas de d. Luís da Cunha a Marco António de Azevedo Coutinho* (Coimbra, 1930), 49ff.

125. *HIP*, 2: 20; 3: 138–39. Cf. José-Augusto França, *Lisboa pombalina e o iluminismo* (Lisbon, 1965), 33, who contends, unconvincingly, that the number of convents in Lisbon grew by 300% between the early seventeenth and mid-eighteenth centuries while the capital's population, estimated at 250,000 around 1755 and thought to have represented about a tenth of the kingdom's inhabitants, increased by only 150%. Whatever the number of such houses in the eighteenth century, the real concern of Church critics was how many occupants they contained, and we have no data on that.

126. The Society achieved most of its institutional growth before the onset of the eighteenth century. In France, for example, only 5.3% of its facilities were initiated between 1700 and 1760. *EJF*, passim.

in the empire, found themselves frustrated by obstructive litigation and were unable to open that house before the end of our period.[127] Even though two benefactors left bequests in 1697 for a novitiate to house recruits bound for the Orient, sufficient funds did not become available to open the novitiate of Arroios in the outskirts of the capital until 1735.[128] Four years later, despite bitter opposition from parish authorities, Franciscans, and a convent of Santa Clara nuns, the college of Gouveia in the diocese of Guarda was finally able to open its doors, thereby fulfilling the terms of a bequest by a childless couple who had left their estate to the Society for that purpose a dozen years earlier. Even so, the college remained unfinished in 1759.[129]

At first sight, it seems shocking that far more benefactors in this supposedly gilded age did not come forth with offers of estates to the Society. It appears, however, that Jesuits were no longer as successful as they had been during the formative period in establishing close bonds with members of Portugal's high aristocracy. If many sons of that aristocracy were attracted to the Order during its formative period, they were wholly absent from its rosters during the Joanine era. If many nobles left estates to the Society in the sixteenth and early seventeenth centuries, virtually none did so after that time. And if many members of great families yearned to be buried in Jesuit churches during the formative period, hardly any did so later. Indeed, a survey of over twenty prominent persons who died between 1721 and 1750 reveals that only two elected to be interred in a Jesuit facility. One, Giovanni Bautista Carbone, of whom more will be said later, was himself a Jesuit; the other, a bishop of Leiria, had been Jesuit-trained. The rest, including ministers of state, prelates, viceroys, palace equerries, councilors of the realm, and senior magistrates, opted for burial in the churches of other religious Orders such as the Benedictines, Capuchins, Carmelites, Dominicans, and Franciscans, or in parish churches long supported by their families.[130] Since the aristocracy continued, as it had for centuries, to take its cue from the king, it is reasonable to conclude that when John V (1706–50) elected to distance himself from the Society, the nobles simply followed suit.

John V, who was only 17 when he ascended the throne to become one of his nation's longest-serving monarchs, was generally accorded high marks by foreign diplomats who served in his court, and their commendatory portraits have generally (though not universally) been echoed by later Portuguese historians.[131] Although liberals, led by J. P. Oliveira Martins, describe the king as a bloated, sybaritic, bigoted, ultra-pious, spendthrift simpleton,[132] most

127. *HCJAP*, 4:1, 169–86.
128. Ibid., 160–66.
129. Ibid., 258–65.
130. Fr. Claudio da Conceição, *Gabinete historico*, 7 (Lisbon, 1820): 120 and 206–7; 9 (1823): 5, 56–62, 64–66, 68, 102–5, 119–20, 142, 248–49, and 252; 10 (2d ed., 1871): 97–99, 133, 134, 146–47, 160, 284–86, 292, 294, and 297–300.
131. E.g., Angelo Ribeiro, "D. João V," in Damião Peres, ed., *História de Portugal*, 10 vols. (Barcelos, [1937]), 6: 179–93; João Ameal and Rodrigues Cavalheiro, *De d. João V a d. Miguel* (Porto, 1939), 5–45; Jaime Cortesão, *Alexandre de Gusmão e o tratado de Madrid (1750)*, pt. III:1 (Rio de Janeiro, 1951), 11; *DHP*, 2: 623–26, which includes a useful but dated bibliography; and VS/*HP*, 5: 270–72. For a useful introduction to the period, see M. Lopes de Almeida, "Portugal na época de d. João V," *Proceedings of the International Colloquium on Luso-Brazilian Studies* (1953): 253–59. The author's call for a sophisticated study of the era still awaits an effective response.
132. Joaquim Pedro Oliveira Martins, *Historia de Portugal*, 2 vols. (Lisbon, 1879), 2: 121–38. The author (b. 1845–d. 1895) was a multitalented historian, engineer, businessman, and politician. His depiction of the

Portuguese historians have been conservatives who have insisted that John was exceedingly conscientious about his responsibilities, forceful in the exercise of his duties, sagacious, judicious, pious, enlightened, abstemious, and, as contemporaries dubbed him, magnanimous.

It is easy enough to agree with some of these descriptive labels. As the king's marginalia on the thousands of royal dispatches that he scrutinized and his private correspondence with his most valued minister, Cardinal da Mota, attest, he was deeply concerned about the management of his kingdom and empire.[133] Like his father, John was moderate in his consumption of alcohol, but he shared his father's proclivity for sexual adventures, three products of which became the famous *meninos de Palhavã*, so named after a Lisbon suburb (today a metropolitan subway stop) where they once lived.[134] Although unpaid soldiers and sailors who had to beg for their food and travelers who risked their lives sailing along the pirate-infested coast or traversing the kingdom's wretched highways would have been unlikely to term their monarch magnanimous, he was uncommonly generous toward those who caught his fancy. Such recipients included a Sicilian-born architect, a ship captain who captured an Algerian pirate after an eight-hour combat, and a plethora of ambassadors, both Portuguese and foreign, who enjoyed the king's bounty amounting to hundreds of contos in Brazilian gold and diamonds at a time when John's lieutenants in India were frantically searching for every xerafin to save his crumbling eastern empire.[135] Prideful, pompous, and prickly, the monarch allowed himself to be closely guided by his advisors during his first years in office but soon began to assert himself in unexpected ways and permitted no one to doubt who was governing his realm.[136] Among those who learned that lesson forcefully were the Jesuits.

Like his father and his grandfather before him, John had been educated and spiritually supported by Jesuits. He continued to rely upon three Jesuit tutors during his first years in office, but between 1707 and 1712 two of his Jesuit confessors died, and in the latter year the king made the decision not to engage any more members of that Order as his spiritual counselors, preferring the advice of other priests, especially the Oratorians, a congregation of secular priests active in the kingdom since the reign of his father. John never explained why he no longer wanted Jesuit confessors and never barred other members of his family (including his brothers and his wife, Queen Mariana of Austria, sister of Charles VI, the

---

king still seems closer to the mark than those of the sovereign's ardent defenders, such as those cited in the preceding note.

133. For a sampling of his correspondence with the cardinal, see Eduardo Brasão, *D. João V: Subsídios para a história do seu reinado* (Porto, 1945), 51–177; and Cortesão, *Alexandre de Gusmão*, III:1, 344–45, 349–50, and 355–57.

134. António Ferrão, *O Marquês de Pombal e os "Meninos de Palhavã"* (Coimbra, 1923). One of the three, D. José, became grand inquisitor, while another, D. Gaspar, served as archbishop of Braga. The latter's mother was an attractive nun with whom the king carried on a decade-long affair. The third, D. António, was the product of a liaison with an unknown French girl. When the king first became seriously ill with epilepsy in 1742, he recognized the trio. Their fates during the next regime will be discussed in volume 2 of this study.

135. For examples of the king's prodigality, see Manoel de Barros Sousa (visconde de Santarém) and L. A. Rebello da Silva, eds., *Quadro elementar das relações políticas e diplomáticas de Portugal com as diversas potências do mundo*, 18 vols. (Lisbon and Paris, 1842–60), 5: cclvii–cclxii.

136. Like his father, who last convoked a legislative body (cortes) in 1698 to assure his son's succession, John had no use for shared government. No cortes assembled during his reign. In a revealing passage, Ameal and Cavalheiro assure their readers that the king "happily was not a democrat but a lover of his people (*demófilo*)." *De d. João V a d. Miguel*, 19.

onetime pretender to the Spanish throne) from continuing to engage them. Although he sometimes accompanied the queen to São Roque to participate in vigils for Saint Francis Xavier, John evidently did not share his family's passion for Saint Dominic. On the other hand, he lavishly supported the half-dozen divisions of Franciscans in the kingdom as well as the Carthusians, the Oratorians, and, of course, the secular church. The creation of the patriarchate of Lisbon with its large and costly ceremonial staff (1716) represented the fulfillment of the king's personal ambition.[137]

Although one must always guard against enticing *post hoc ergo propter hoc* analyses, it seems likely that the monarch's decision to distance himself from the Jesuits was related to his obvious annoyance over what became known as the *quindénio* affair. The quindénio (or *quindennia*) originated as a service charge levied by popes upon vacant benefices before their transfer to new holders. During the fifteenth century, popes permanently assigned many such properties to hospitals and ecclesiastical congregations, which assumed an obligation to render periodic payments to the papacy. In 1469 Pius II issued a decree stipulating that such payments must be made every fifteen years or the property would revert to the papacy.[138]

Between 1548 and 1575, Paul III, Pius V, and Gregory XIII authorized the permanent assignment of the income from thirteen benefices to five Jesuit institutions (Coimbra, Évora, Braga, Bragança, and Porto) subject to the quindénio.[139] Whether it was remitted periodically before 1640 is not clear. Certainly such remissions ceased during the long, mid-century hiatus when Rome refused to recognize Portugal's resumed independence; nor were they begun again until at least 1679, when a concerned provincial wrote the father general and proposed their resumption. Evidently they were forwarded without incident until the end of the Petrine regime, when the duke of Cadaval notified Pope Clement XI that the king had doubts whether the remittances were legal.[140] The source of such concern was legislation dating from the Middle Ages, when Portugal often experienced shortages of specie and those who exported bullion without license were threatened with dire penalties. That hardly seemed to have been a problem during the gilded age. The king himself sent large remittances to Rome and elsewhere to support favored causes,[141] and Portugal's persisting adverse balance of payments with its principal trading partner, Great Britain, was

137. On the royal family's participation in the *novena* honoring Xavier, see *Gazeta de Lisboa*, 9 Mar. 1719; Manuel Bernardes Branco, *Portugal na epocha de d. João V* (Lisbon, 1885), 55; king to Cardinal da Mota, 2 Dec. [1738?], in Brasão, ed., *D. João V*, 85; during the royal progress to Vila Viçosa in 1717, the king was accompanied by high nobles and an Oratorian father but not by a Jesuit. Conceição, *Gabinete historico*, 6: 399–400; the queen and four of her children as well as the inquisitor general and the patriarch all received habits in the Dominican Order. For the crown's beneficence to Franciscans and Carthusians, see Branco, *Portugal na epocha de d. João V*, 47, 49, 154–55, 160, 271. The king's role in the negotiations leading to the establishment of the patriarchate is evident in Eduardo Brazão, *Subsídios para a história do patriarcado de Lisboa (1716–1740)* (Porto, [1943?]).

138. William E. Lunt, *Papal Revenues in the Middle Ages*, 2 vols. (New York, 1934), 1: 102–3; 2: 386–88.

139. Francisco da Fonseca, S.J., "Livro da fazenda, ou noticia das rendas e obrigações das provincias da assistencia de Portugal ... anno 1700," in ARSI, FG, 727/D. There exist several lists of the churches and incomes involved in ARSI, especially *Lus.*, 78, fols. 34 and 42 and 84:1, fol. 108.

140. Adrian Pedroso to Oliva, Lisbon, 20 [month missing] 1679, in ARSI, *Lus.*, 75, fol. 21ᵛ; Cadaval to Clement XI, 24 Dec. 1705, in ibid., 76, fol. 50ʳ.

141. Oliveira Martins seems to be the source for the common assertion that the Joanine regime sent more than 80,000 contos to Rome (*História de Portugal*, 2: 124), but the author cites no documentation to support that fantastic statement.

always settled by specie transfers; yet the eighteenth-century governments of the kingdom remained suspicious of unauthorized monetary transfers.

In 1707 Diogo de Mendonça Corte Real, the secretary of state, informed the provincial, Fr. Manoel Dias, that his master had learned that the procurator had sent Rome quindénios amounting to 2.8 contos, a small sum compared with the magnitude of the king's gifts, but without royal consent. In the king's name, the minister indignantly ordered the provincial denaturalized and expelled from the realm. The sovereign directed that no Jesuit facility send funds to Rome without his express authorization, and that no Jesuit communicate with Tamburini as long as he lived! Precisely why the crown became quite so furious is unclear, but the order expelling the provincial remained active (though unfulfilled) until mid-summer 1711. The controversy persisted until 1716, when it was finally resolved by a new concordat with the pope, who agreed to designate Lisbon as a patriarchate.[142]

Whether this dispute really reflected the sentiments of the king or those of his well-traveled senior advisor cannot be easily determined.[143] It may have been intended as an early warning to a powerful entity of the Church that the professedly absolutist regime of the new monarch was not to be trifled with. There are numerous examples throughout the reign of the crown's acute sensitivity where its prerogatives were concerned and its insistence that members of the Church recognize their status as its subordinate instruments. From time to time nuns and priests, religious as well as secular, Jesuits as well as members of other Orders, were summarily removed by royal fiat from their positions, usually on grounds of disobedience or lack of respect for royal authority.[144] As already remarked, such treatment of Jesuits was hitherto uncommon, but it would occur far more readily during the next reign.

142. The analysis given here is based upon the documents in ARSI, *Lus.*, 76, fols. 93, 96, 97, 106, 112, and 124. The accounts in *HCJAP*, 3:2, 120–21 and 4:1, 432 are not wholly accurate. For some reason the leading historian of Portugal's diplomatic relations with Rome during this period, Eduardo Brazão, totally ignores the quindénio problem in his published studies. One consequence of its establishment was the division of the capital into two cities, East and West Lisbon, a distinction abolished in 1740. Ribeiro, "D. João V," 184–85.

143. Born in Tavira in the Algarve, Diogo de Mendonça Corte Real (b. 1658–d. 1736), related on both sides of his family to members of the highest aristocracy in both Spain and Portugal, earned a doctorate in canon law at Coimbra before being sent as envoy extraordinary to Holland in 1691. While serving in the same capacity in Madrid, he fathered an illegitimate son by the same name who also served as secretary of state. In 1703, Mendonça the elder became Pedro II's private secretary and was named secretary of state early in 1707, a position he held until his death. *PDH*, 4: 1034–36; John Norris and Lord Tyrawly to duke of Newcastle, 10 May 1736, in PRO/SP89/39/40.

144. E.g., José Soares da Silva, *Gazeta em forma de carta (anos de 1701–1716)*, vol. 1 (only) (Lisbon, 1933), 118 (concerning the removal of the rector of Setúbal college); opinion of duke of Cadaval, 11 Mar. 1720, in Virginia Rau and Maria Fernanda Gomes da Silva, comps., *Os manuscritos do arquivo da casa de Cadaval respeitantes ao Brasil*, 2 vols. (Coimbra, 1956–58), 2: 266 (approving removal from the captaincy of São Paulo of certain Capuchins and Carmelites because of "scandalous excesses"); viceroy to king, Bahia, 22 Mar. 1728, in APB/OR/23, no. 22 (acknowledging a directive to withdraw an offending priest from Rio das Contas because of settler complaints); Overseas Council, consulta of 14 June 1736, in *DH*, 100: 174–76, and *CR* to governor of Pernambuco, 15 Apr. 1737, IAGHPB, OR, *1733–1736*, fols. 256ᵛ–257ᵛ (concerning a dispute between a local bishop and the rector and four colleagues of the college of Recife over the right of asylum); "Relig.ᵃˢ degregadas do most.ʳᵒ de S.ᵗᵃ Clara de Santarém por ordem de Sua Mag.ᵈᵉ ano de 1749," in BNL/FG, no. 5258 (inside fly leaf) (ordering relocation of six misbehaving nuns). The Joanine regime also revived the old medieval offense termed *desacato* (disrespect for authority) and applied its penalties to priests, a practice that became far more common during the subsequent Pombaline regime. Branco, *Portugal na epocha de d. João V*, 148–49. See also Oliveira Martins, *Historia de Portugal*, 2: 130–31.

Like his predecessors, John strongly supported the activities of the Inquisition, and with other members of his family he witnessed the public ceremonies, that is, the acts of faith (autos-de-fé) that took place in the capital several times a year and often included deviant churchmen among the penitents.[145]

Indubitably, the Joanine regime intervened in the internal affairs of the Society to a far greater extent than any Iberian regime since that of Spain's Philip II. That is apparent from the notorious partridge affair. Both John and Mariana customarily went to São Roque to participate in the mass for Saint Francis Xavier (2 December). But on that feast in 1724, the queen went by herself with a newborn son and his nurse. During the service the nurse became faint and asked for something to eat. Two Jesuit residents, one of them the king's former longtime tutor, went to the kitchen and prevailed upon their cook to supply the stricken aide with a roasted partridge. When the house rector, Fr. João Tavares, learned of the cook's action, he sternly rebuked him for having acted without his express consent. The two fathers came to the cook's defense and, since they considered their superior's censure as applying to themselves as well, appealed to the Visitor and vice-provincial, Carlos António Casnedi, formerly the confessor of the famous admiral of Castile (see Chapter 14), to transfer them to another house. Casnedi directed them to remain silent and to obey their superior. Still piqued, the two fathers utilized their palace connections and appealed over Casnedi's head.

When the king learned about this absurd fracas he acted, or rather overreacted. He directed that the two be permitted to remove to any residence of their choice but barred Frs. Tavares and Casnedi from the royal palace. For good measure, he instructed his ambassador to Rome not to receive either the father general or his Portuguese assistant. Both the rector and the Visitor subsequently confessed their errors and attempted to regain the king's favor, but John remained obdurate, and Tamburini was obliged to express profuse apologies to the irate monarch and to order the two offenders to relinquish their posts. Casnedi soon left the country but died, supposedly of humiliation, two weeks after crossing into Spain. João Tavares followed him to the grave seven months later.[146]

The treatment of these two former senior administrators was a shocking but quite deliberate manifestation of royal power, more reminiscent of its exercise in the France of Louis XIV and his successors than of the conduct of previous Portuguese rulers. It is difficult to measure the impact of the partridge affair upon the Society, although Fr. Rodrigues argued that it marked the low point in relations between the Society and the king. Perhaps, yet there are indications that the Society was no longer prepared to play as vigorous a role in the kingdom as it long had done. Certainly it was not the dominant cultural force there that it had once been. Though Jesuits attended the half-dozen meetings of the *academia de historia ecclesiástica*, which met in Lisbon in 1715–16, they were not leaders in its deliberations.[147] Jesuits participated in its successor, the royal academy of history, which

145. Thomas Burnett to James Craggs, Lisbon, 23 June 1720, in PRO/SP/28/93. Thirty autos-de-fé occurred in the capital between 1707 and 1729. Castelo Branco Chaves, trans. and ed., *O Portugal de D. João visto por três forasteiros* (Lisbon, 1983), III n. 64.

146. *HCJAP*, 4:1, 436–41.

147. Conceição, *Gabinete historico*, 6: 274–82. A single Jesuit, Fr. Manoel de Oliveira, spoke at the second session.

first gathered in 1720, but they did not play a major role in its activities either.[148] "Three grave [Jesuit] fathers" assisted, one suspects uneasily, in the consecration in 1730 of the basilica at Mafra, that vast, incredibly costly "palace-convent" that the king commenced in 1717 to house hundreds of members of a rival Order, the Capuchins.[149]

Nor were any of the most conspicuous learned works of the age the products of Jesuit energies. They included a pioneering and still useful bibliography, Diogo Barbosa Machado's *Biblioteca Lusitana* (1741–59); João Baptista de Castro's geographical handbook, the *Mapa de Portugal* (1745–58); António Caetano de Sousa's *Historia genealógica familiae regiae Portugaliae* (1735–50), a remarkably industrious verification of aristocratic pedigrees; and that prolix philosophical and pedagogical critique of prevailing Jesuit educational practices, Luís António Vernei's *Verdadeiro methódo de estudar* (1746). Significantly, each writer was a priest, but none belonged to the Society.[150]

Vernei's critique has inspired many Portuguese scholars to argue that the content and approach of courses that the Jesuits offered in their colleges and universities in the kingdom had become badly outdated by the eighteenth century.[151] But although it is common for modern critics to censor the fathers for failing to introduce their students to Bacon, Descartes, Leibnitz, Locke, Gassendi, and others, it is equally customary for them to ignore the passive role that the crown still maintained in the pedagogical realm. The only significant positive measures that it undertook in higher education were the financing of the sumptuous but hardly practical library of the University of Coimbra (built 1716–28), the establishment of the large Mafra library, whose use was restricted to its inmates, and the creation (1745) of a school of humanities with a 30,000-volume library and a large stipend. That school, entrusted to the Oratorians, represented the first breach of the long-standing Jesuit dominance of higher education in Portugal.[152] Yet what critics seem to ignore is that in an age in which the crown itself placed such heavy emphasis upon orthodoxy and the

148. Ibid., 7: 100–106. Joaquim Veríssimo Serrão, *A historiografia portuguesa*, 3 vols. (Lisbon, 1972–74), 3: 56–59, 62–79. The academy of history, whose members initially included 23 religious, of whom six were Jesuits, and 27 nobles, magistrates, and secular priests, met semi-monthly from 1720 to 1737 and irregularly thereafter until 1760, when it was suppressed.

149. Conceição, *Gabinete historico*, 8: 272. The king took greater personal interest in the construction of that 4,000-square-meter edifice, in which as many as 45,000 craftsmen and 7,000 soldiers labored, than he did in his crumbling Eastern empire. Mafra epitomizes not only the religiosity and antediluvian spirit of the regime, but also its lamentable dependence upon external sources of materials and design. See José Hermano Saraiva, *História concisa de Portugal*, 4th ed. (n.p., 1979), 234ff.

150. Conceição, *Gabinete historico*, 9: 68–69 and 72–73; Veríssimo Serrão, *A historiografia portuguesa*, 3: 53–184; António Alberto de Andrade, *Vernei e a cultura do seu tempo* (Coimbra, 1966).

151. E.g., Teofilo Braga, *História da universidade de Coimbra*, 4 vols. (Lisbon, 1892–1902), 3: chaps. 2–3; see also essays by Joaquim de Carvalho in Damião Pires, ed., *Historia de Portugal*, 8 vols. (Barcelos, 1928–37) 5: 564ff., and by Newton de Macedo, in ibid., 6: 432–34. See also José Calvet de Magalhães, *História do pensamento económico em Portugal da idade-média ao mercantilismo* (Coimbra, 1967), 169–74. In part, criticism of Jesuit pedagogy in Joanine Portugal relies upon [Anon.], "Breve noticia dos estudos que os Jesuitas exerciam na universidade de Évora ao tempo que forão expulsos" [ca. 1775], *Revista de historia* 10 (Lisbon, 1921): 299–305. The author claims to have been a student at the University of Évora for ten years and to have returned to help sort out its books in 1775, i.e., sixteen years after the university had been closed. There is, however, no assurance that the library had not been pillaged before that date. Certainly generalizations based upon its extant materials can hardly be deemed reliable.

152. Hernani Cidade, *Lições sôbre a cultura e a literatura portuguesa*, 2 vols. (Coimbra, 1933), vol. 2 (2d ed. 1940), 123–40.

subordination of the clergy, it could have required the Jesuits to update their philosophical and scientific programs by royal fiat, just as it did with respect to higher mathematics.[153] Neither the king nor his ministers ever did so.[154]

No Jesuit ever occupied a ministerial position during the Joanine regime. As stated above, Diogo de Mendonça Corte Real, a doctor in canon and civil law and an experienced diplomat, served as sole minister from the beginning of the reign until his sudden death in 1736. Subsequently, Marco António de Azevedo Coutinho (b. 1688–d. 1750), a former diplomat and uncle of the future marquis of Pombal, became foreign secretary, while the obscure António Guedes Pereira (b. 1679–d. 1747) served as secretary for the empire. The position of chief minister (though without the title) was occupied first by the king's former librarian, Cardinal D. João da Mota e Silva (b. 1685–d. 1747), brother of D. Pedro, a well-known diplomat, and after his death by another ecclesiastic, Fr. Gaspar da Encarnação (b. 1685–d. 1754).[155]

One name that needs to be added to this small group of royal advisors is that of Giovanni Bautista Carbone (b. 1694–d. 1750), the most influential and widely respected Jesuit in the kingdom. Carbone came to Lisbon in 1722 with another Neapolitan member of the Society, Domingos Capassi, who shared his interests in mathematics and astronomy. Both volunteered to serve in the Maranhão missions, but the king was so impressed by their abilities that he detained them at court. Capassi passed to Brazil in 1729, where he contracted a fever and died six years later. Carbone continued to serve his royal master for the balance of their respective lives. Initially he tutored the royal princess, D. Maria Barbara, later wife of Spain's lackluster Ferdinand VI (1746–59), but John V soon named him as a high-level bureaucratic troubleshooter. Carbone resided in a special apartment in Santo Antão and, doubtless in accord with the ruler's wishes, enjoyed special privileges there.[156]

Although he was primarily concerned with facilitating negotiations with the papacy, Fr. Carbone also conducted a wide-ranging correspondence with high officials throughout the empire and with certain Portuguese diplomats, including the Society's future nemesis, Sebastião José de Carvalho e Melo.[157] So far as his surviving correspondence permits

153. See above, note 18.

154. In fact, in 1713 the king specified that no alterations were to be introduced to the philosophy offerings in the arts college at Coimbra. Braga, *História da universidade de Coimbra*, 3: 298–99. It does not necessarily follow, as the Jesuitophobic author maintained, that John's order was dictated by the Jesuits themselves. Nor is it reasonable to suppose that the edict of the rector of the arts college in 1746 forbidding the teaching of "new philosophy," including Descartes, Gassendi, and Newton, could have been issued without the approval of the crown or its agents. Ibid., 3: 47.

155. Concerning Marco António de Azevedo Coutinho and António Guedes Pereira, see Conceição, *Gabinete historico*, 10 (2d ed., Lisbon, 1871): 133 and 299–300; for Mota e Silva, see *Grande encyclopédia portuguesa e brasileira*, 40 vols. (Lisbon, 1936–60), 28: 799–800. The lineage of Fr. Gaspar, born D. Gaspar Moscoso da Silva, is discussed by Ferrão, *O Marquês de Pombal*, 17–18.

156. "Licenças que pede ao R. P. provincial o Pe João Baut.ª Carbone," 26 Aug. 1725, BNL/CP/474, fol. 263. Such privileges included the right to use large sums of (the king's) money; to consume chocolate and tobacco; to drink outside of the customary hours; to arise and sleep according to his wants; and to leave the premises whenever he chose. Because of his standing with the king, he was exempt from having someone else read his mail. Carbone to Manoel Pereira de Sampaio, 1 Feb. 1735, in BA/49-X-31, fol. 15ᵛ. At the end of his life, Carbone served briefly as rector of Santo Antão, his only administrative position within the Society.

157. Carbone's correspondence with the sometime Portuguese minister to Rome, Manuel Pereira de Sampaio, extends from 1736 to 1750 and may be consulted in BA, especially 49-IX-1, 49-X-1, 49-X-31, and

judgment, he seems to have discharged his sometimes delicate responsibilities efficiently and with one exception, without any effort to secure favor for his Order. That exception was his forceful opposition to efforts by the Spanish government to advance the cause in Rome of one of the Society's most detested adversaries, the famous Bishop Palafox of Mexico.[158]

Fr. Carbone's talents earned him high praise from an unlikely quarter, members of the British diplomatic corps. In 1732 the often petulant Lord Tyrawly wrote the duke of Newcastle that he enjoyed the confidence of "a Jesuit friend, one of the most considerable men here of that order[,] extremely in the King's favour and confidence, and personally better with him than any man in Portugal ... a very sensible, agreeable man, and for my great good fortune ... a particular and warm Friend.... This person gets twenty little jobbs done for me every day that Mons.ʳ Mendo[n]ça does not care to meddle with.... I find his advise good ... tho confidential since he [is] not caring that our acquaintance or commerce should be publickly known."[159]

Newcastle was obviously pleased and urged the envoy to "cultivate and improve" that relationship.[160] Later, when Benjamin Keene, former envoy to Lisbon, learned of Carbone's terminal illness, he remarked "God grant Padre Carboni may recover. He is worth the whole Order, and its chief into the bargain."[161] After Carbone expired, Keene's friend and successor in Lisbon, Abraham Castres, lamented his passing: "He was not only a man of parts and great application, but likewise of the strictest honour and integrity, and as such had been employed by the King, particularly since the late Cardinal Mota's death [1747], in his most secret affairs, tho' without the character of a Minister which he is said to have constantly refused. No man has died here in my time so much regretted as he is, not only by the King ... but by all ranks of people as well natives as foreigners."[162]

Carbone's demise (5 April 1750) was one of a series of deaths of prominent governmental figures whose expiration brought the regime—and an era—to a close. On 29 May 1749, the venerable duke of Cadaval, whose family had been cherished advisors of the Braganças since the Restoration, died, as did the marquis of Valença, master of the queen's household, the following September. On 13 February 1750, Carbone's longtime confidant in Rome, Manuel Pereira de Sampaio, passed away. Five weeks after Carbone succumbed to a particularly lethal form of cancer, Marco António, the foreign minister, expired (19 May). Then came the king's final illness.

John V had never been favored with a robust constitution. His health began to deteriorate seriously in May 1742, when he suffered the first of a long series of strokes

51-X-31. Brazão, *D. João V,* 20–36, utilized this material, but the codices have been renumbered since he consulted it. Carbone frequently mentioned his dispatches to other prominent persons abroad in his letters to Pereira de Sampaio.

158. Carbone to Pereira de Sampaio, 12 Sept. 1741, in BA, 51-X-32, fols. 31ʳ–31ᵛ.

159. Tyrawly to Newcastle, Lisbon, 6 June 1732, in PRO, SP89/37, 181ᵛ.

160. Newcastle to Tyrawley [*sic*], Kensington, 22 Aug. 1732, in ibid., /36, fol. 56ʳ.

161. Keene to Abraham Castres, Madrid, 10 Apr. 1750, in Sir Richard Lodge, ed., *The Private Correspondence of Sir Benjamin Keene, K.B.* (Cambridge, 1933), 222.

162. Castres to the duke of Bedford, Lisbon, 11 Apr. 1750, in PRO/SP89/49, fols. 93ᵛ–94ʳ. I am indebted to C. R. Boxer for having provided me with a transcription of the text, which may also be found in the British Library, Add. mss. 9244, fols. 6ʳ–6ᵛ. For a similar appraisal of Carbone by a Lisbon advocate, see F. X. Teixeira de Mendonça to a Spanish noble, Lisbon, 26 Feb. 1756, in Cortesão, *Alexandre de Gusmão,* 2:2, 264. Carbone is an obvious candidate for a biography.

that left him partially paralyzed. While the king's illness proved to be a bonanza for the religious, for the royal physicians, and for those who attended his repeated progresses to Caldas da Rainha, situated north of Obidos, neither restorative waters, nor repeated bleedings, nor constant prayers enabled the monarch to regain his health. Finally, having been attended by several prominent ecclesiastics, including Gabrial Malagrida, the veteran Jesuit missionary who had recently returned from Brazil and had earlier administered the last rites to Fr. Carbone, John V breathed his last at 7 P.M. on 31 July 1750.[163] From the Jesuits' perspective, that seemed to be an especially propitious day, since it was the feast of Saint Ignatius.[164] Yet, the sequel to this volume will demonstrate, it proved to be precisely the opposite.

If the Portuguese assistant had been directed by his superior[165] to assess the Jesuits' gains and losses within the Assistancy during the previous half century, he would have understandably produced a grim report. It would have emphasized the ruin of the two oft-celebrated Far Eastern enterprises, both once so promising, both theaters where some of the most noted members of the Society had fearlessly acted out their lives. It would have conceded that the two Indian provinces were also failed enterprises, particularly since the dismal 1730s. It would have conceded that the African outposts, Mozambique and Angola, were really mere holding operations, and that neither had ever displayed any great promise as missionary centers. Even in the kingdom of Portugal itself, the Society no longer commanded the prestige or attracted the spectacular bequests or the illustrious recruits that it formerly enjoyed. Only in Brazil were the Society's colleges, missions, and supporting real-estate holdings continuing to expand, but even there Jesuits were barred from functioning within the most lucrative of the mining complexes.

The assistant might have attributed these setbacks to the will of God, but he would have recognized that unwise judgments had also contributed to many of them. Such judgments were made not by the Jesuits themselves but by those who were their recognized superiors. It was, after all, the papacy that yielded to the Jesuits' critics and sent out two legates who destroyed the basis for the cultural bonding in China and India that the Jesuits had so diligently striven to construct over the centuries. It was a Portuguese government incapable of recruiting an adequate number of able soldier-administrators to hold its positions in India and of supporting them with a sufficient number of well-paid troops that was ultimately responsible for the Marathas' victories, so costly to both the crown and to the Society.

Neither the assistant nor any objective interpreter would concede that the Jesuits were responsible for these losses. They were bit players in dramas where others assumed the major roles. Nevertheless, the Assistant would have been compelled to recognize that throughout the Assistancy, from China to Brazil, the Society had become virtually every

163. Fr. Carbone's correspondence, cited in note 157 above, often alludes to the state of the king's health, which also became the subject of many dispatches by British representatives to Lisbon between 1742 and the monarch's death. See PRO/SP89/42, 44, and 47, passim. Ironically, eleven years later, John's successor, his son José I, would sanction the public burning of Malagrida (b. 1689–d. 1761).

164. Gomes Freire de Andrada (governor, Rio de Janeiro) to Luís Garcia de Bivar (governor, Colônia do Sacramento), 20 Nov. 1750, in ANRJ, 84/12/123ᵛ.

165. Francisco Retz, the father general since 1730, also expired in 1750 and was succeeded by his vicar general, Ignácio Visconti.

articulate person's favorite scapegoat for the ills of the empire and that the allegations concerning the Order's shortcomings were increasing in number and intensity with each passing decade.

No such report is known to have been prepared by any assistant. But even if one had been, not even the most prescient person, Jesuit or non-Jesuit, friend or foe, could have anticipated that the demise of one of the church's most highly esteemed organizations would occur within the next quarter century or that the process would begin in the very kingdom that had been the first to welcome the sons of Loyola and to send them into its expanding empire. Why and how Portugal became the leader in the suppression of the Society of Jesus and the consequences of its actions will be considered in the second volume of this study. The following chapter will evaluate the oft-stated charge that for nearly two centuries the Society had abandoned its spiritual mission and had become preoccupied with Mammon.

CHAPTER 24

Striking a Balance:
For God or Mammon?

No servant can be a slave to two masters: you cannot serve God and money.
—Matthew 6:24

The frugality with which the Company sustains its subjects is well known.
—Anonymous defense of Jesuit economic activities, ca. 1630

The Jesuits indulged themselves much more than would be expected in a religious
order whose founder placed special emphasis on the virtue of poverty.
—A. Lynn Martin, *The Jesuit Mind*

CONTEMPORARY OPPONENTS as well as certain modern critics have incessantly charged that members of the Society of Jesus abandoned their original commitment to serve God at some unspecified point in time in order to pursue Mammon. Such detractors could point to the commodious, richly adorned churches that the Society maintained as well as to its equally impressive colleges, professed houses, and novitiates, almost always conspicuously situated and complemented by attractive, ample, restful gardens. They could also identify some of the Society's vast real-estate holdings, especially its coveted rural properties, which supported its enterprises at home and abroad. However, since Jesuit accounts, like those of the crown itself, were always closely guarded secrets to which only key members of the Society were privy on a need-to-know basis, the Society's denigrators have never successfully documented their contention that its members became untrue to their callings. The aims of this chapter are to examine patterns of income growth among units of the Portuguese Assistancy, to identify their major sources of expenditure, and to compare levels of individual Jesuit support with those enjoyed by their secular peers. At the outset, however, it is necessary to consider further the nature of the Society's initial commitment to poverty and to ascertain whether its agents really endeavored to enforce that pledge and, if so, with what degree of success.

Poverty, "The Strong Wall"

The *vita apostolica* is a tradition that runs deep in the history of the Catholic Church. It began with Christ himself, when he acclaimed the state of poverty as blessed (Luke 6:20). St. Paul taught that Christ deliberately made himself poor in order to make his followers rich (2 Cor. 8:9). During the era of the primitive church, the desert fathers deliberately cultivated poverty, and it became an essential feature of the Benedictine Order, whose founder stipulated that no member could possess a thing, "neither a book, nor tablets, nor a pen—nothing at all," and directed abbots to conduct frequent bed searches for private property. Offenders were threatened with "the most severe discipline."[1] "The veneration of poverty," as Leff reminds us, "was common to most medieval movements of religious reform: it had inspired heretical groups, like the Arnoldists and Waldenses, as well as those recognized by the church. In the thirteenth century its foremost exponents were the mendicant orders."[2] The Dominicans and the Franciscans extended the concept of Christlike adherence to poverty from the status of individual preference to a primary tenet of their apostolate. The founders of both Orders urged their followers to embrace poverty as fervently as passionate lovers clung to each other, and each spoke of poverty as a revered female. While Saint Dominic conceived of "Queen Poverty" as his spouse, Saint Francis spoke of "Lady Poverty" as his constant companion.[3] If the influential polemicist Marsilius of Padua (b. ca. 1275–d. 1342) preferred to depersonalize poverty, he still insisted that "the status of poverty and contempt for the world is that which befits every perfect man, especially the disciple and successor of Christ in the pastoral office."[4]

There were, of course, several aspects to the notion of ecclesiastical poverty. Its acceptance required the subject to divest himself (or herself) of all worldly goods upon entering the religious life. It also involved a renunciation of all inheritances received after the taking of vows. Further, depending upon the severity of the Order's rule, it promised members a more or less austere existence within the religious community. Such conditions were entirely personal; the concept of ecclesiastical poverty did not necessarily imply, as critics presumed, that the religious corporation itself renounced the right to acquire secular wealth in the form of lands and fixed incomes. Some Orders, such as those of the Mendicants and the Theatines, did (or did at some point), but others, including the Society of Jesus, did not.[5]

When Ignatius and his companions assembled at Montmartre in August 1534, they pledged themselves to observe strict personal poverty thereafter. Later, when the founder

1. The quotations are from Dom O. Rousseau, "Poverty of St. Benedict," in *Religious Life*, vol. 4, *Poverty*, trans. Lancelot C. Sheppard (London, 1956), 26–27.

2. Gordon Leff, *Paris and Oxford Universities in the Thirteenth and Fourteenth Centuries: An Institutional and Intellectual History* (New York, 1968), 256. For a recent appraisal of the Waldenses and their dedication to personal poverty, see Gabriel Audisio, "How to Detect a Clandestine Minority: The Example of the Waldenses," *Sixteenth Century Journal*, 21, 2 (Summer 1990): 205–16.

3. Cf. William A. Hinnebusch, *The History of the Dominican Order: Origins and Growth to 1500*, vol. 1 (Staten Island, 1966), chap. 5.

4. *Marsilius of Padua: The Defender of Peace*, trans. and ed. Alan Gewirth (New York, 1956), 183. For other references to the virtue of poverty, see 183–215.

5. The literature on ecclesiastical poverty is vast. See, e.g., Sheppard, *Poverty*; Réginald Grégoire, "La Place de la pauvreté dans la conception et la pratique de la vie monastique médiévale latine," in *Il monarchesimo e la riforma ecclesiastica (1049–1122), Miscellanea del Centro di Studi Medioevali*, vol. 6 (Milan, 1971), 173–92; Michel Mollat, *Études sur l'histoire de la pauvreté*, 2 vols. (Paris, 1974); M. D. Lambert, *Franciscan Poverty: The Doctrine of Absolute Poverty of Christ and the Apostles in the Franciscan Order, 1210–1323* (London, 1961); and Lester K. Little, *Religious Poverty and the Profit Economy in Medieval Europe* (Ithaca, N.Y., 1978). For monastic poverty in medieval Portugal, see José Mattoso, "O ideal de pobreza e as ordens monásticas em Portugal durante os séculos XI–XIII," in Mattoso, *Religião e cultura na idade média portuguesa* (Lisbon, 1982), 281–323. *Poverty and Religion: A Bibliography Selected from the ATLA Religion Database*, rev. ed. (Chicago, 1982), emphasizes modern writings.

submitted the *Formula* of 1550 to Pope Julius III for his approval, he explained that he and his companions were seeking a life far removed from "the contagion of avarice" and as near to "apostolic poverty" as possible. In the *Constitutions*, he stipulated that candidates for admission ought to surrender all actual or future property before entering the Order or, if that proved impossible, at least must do so before reciting final vows. No member could accept money or gifts for himself or his house for services rendered; no Jesuit church would contain an alms box. Colleges and houses of formation could derive income from real property, but professed houses must depend exclusively upon alms rather than fixed revenues. Ignatius reminded his followers that they must love poverty as "the strong wall," the "bulwark" that assures the purity of religious life, and that they should regard temporal things with "total contempt," because to do otherwise would be to follow the dictates of Satan.[6]

Obviously it proved easier to verbalize such ideals than it did to enforce them, but there can be no question that Loyola, his successors, and their subordinates attempted to do precisely that. In 1542, for example, when a student at Padua complained to Ignatius about the restricted fare served at the newly founded college, the Society's first secretary, Juan Polanco, responded for the general by extolling the virtue that Christ perceived in poverty: "Wisdom ... according to St. Bernard, [shows] how precious a jewel is poverty. He chose it for Himself, so that His teaching 'Blessed are they that hunger and thirst, blessed are the poor etc. [Matt. 5:3, 6; Luke 6:20]' should not be out of harmony with His life." Polanco, therefore, urged, "Love holy poverty." A decade later, Ignatius issued a general circular in which he exhorted his brethren to confront poverty cheerfully: "Suppose we compare ourselves with our brothers in India, who in such corporal and spiritual toil are so ill provided with food, in some places not even having bread, to say nothing of wine for their drink. They must get along with a bit of rice and water.... They are ill clothed and have a minimum of bodily comfort. If we compare ourselves with them, I cannot think that our suffering is excessively hard."[7] Though this statement might seem to suggest that Loyola sympathized with his companions in India, there is evidence that he was pleased by reports of the hardships they sustained and urged them to rely as much as possible upon alms.[8] But, as previous chapters have demonstrated, the Jesuits soon found it impossible to rely upon such an uncertain source of income.

During the seventeenth century, both the Roman headquarters and field inspectors (Visitors and provincials) emphasized the need to avoid excesses and to live as modestly as possible. In the late 1630s, for example, Vitelleschi wrote to one Visitor of the colleges in India's northern province to express his strong disapproval of three practices that conflicted with strict adherence to poverty. The first concerned a father who had been given a portable writing desk and kept it with him when he was transferred to another post. (It belonged to the house he had left.) Second, Vitelleschi complained that some Jesuits were retaining

6. *CSJ(C)*, pt. 4, chaps. 4 and 15; pt. 6, chap. 2; pt. 8, chap. 1, par. 671; and pt. 10, par. 816. See also J. Creusen, S.J., "The Poverty of St. Ignatius," in Sheppard, *Poverty*, 69–81.

7. Polanco to the Members of the Society in Padua, 7 Aug. 1547; Ignatius to the members of the Society in Europe, 24 Dec. 1552, in William J. Young, S.J., trans. and ed., *Letters of St. Ignatius of Loyola* (Chicago, 1959), 147, 281–82.

8. Ignatius to Fr. António Gomes, 27 Jan. 1552, in BNL, cod. 662, published in *DI*, 2: 315. Cf. Gomes to Ignatius, Cochin, 16 Jan. 1551, in *DI*, 2: 177.

excessive amounts of cash (as much as 9,000 rs.) in their personal possession. Third, he reiterated his opposition to the use of tobacco by members of the Society (see Chapter 11).[9]

Later field administrators emphasized other concerns that they felt were inconsistent with the Society's devotion to poverty. In the 1680s, for example, the provincial of Goa and a provincial Visitor cautioned that members of the province ought to exercise moderation in the number of courses they consumed at mealtimes, and that no one, not even a house superior, ought to possess a personal servant, or to display white handkerchiefs in public, or to utilize striped towels or tablecloths, or to consume expensive, imported Portuguese wines. The provincial also insisted that his subordinates wear resoled shoes in place of new ones, that when they traveled they make use of small rather than large containers to carry their modest possessions, and that they always reflect upon their adherence to "holy poverty, our Mother."[10] Such injunctions reflect the leaders' efforts not only to enforce the vow of individual poverty but also to strengthen the sanitary public image of the Society that its heads were anxious to project. The repetition of such admonitions, of course, also suggests that practice did not always conform to the Order's ideals.[11] Yet the best available evidence illuminating the quality of life of members of the Assistancy consists of the Society's fiscal records, whose meticulous compilation was a manifestation of the Order's determination to account fully for its stewardship of what God provided.

Scrupulosity: Jesuit Record-Keeping

Each custodian of the enterprise was required to maintain complete records of his stewardship. Whether in China, India, Africa, or Brazil, every missionary kept a record of all moneys, goods, and equipment entrusted to him and of all expenditures that he made in pursuance of his duties.[12] Plantation managers kept accounts of workers, whether slave or free, including dates of baptism, marriage, and death for the former, and wages paid to the latter. They also maintained accounts displaying all goods received from owner colleges and commodities dispatched to them; estate inventories; copies of legal documents pertaining to land titles; directives from the fathers general, Visitors, provincials, and their immediate chiefs, the college rectors; ledgers displaying rents paid by tenants or lessees; and detailed records of the commodities the property produced.[13] Each college functionary preserved accounts of the areas of responsibility assigned to him: cooks maintained records of all

9. H/SAG1: 336–37. Earlier a Visitor to the college of Damão stipulated that no superior could keep more than 10 pardãos (3,000 rs.) in his quarters. ARSI, FG, 1407, no. 8, par. 12.

10. "Ordens perpetuas que deve guardar os subditos deste coll.º de Rachol . . . postas pello P.ᵉ Provincial Simão Martins," 3 July 1682; "Alguas ordens' que deixou [o mesmo] . . . visitando esta casa professa em 24 de julho de 1682" and "Ordens quais q. deixou p.ª toda a provincia o P.ᵉ Alexandre Cicero visitador das provincias da India, Goa e Malabar," 15 Jan. 1685, in ARSI, *Goa*, 35, fols. 234ʳ–235ʳ, 23ʳ, and 291–96.

11. For a recent assessment of the Jesuits' dedication to Ignatian poverty, see T. M. McCoog, S.J., "The Finances of the English Province of the Society of Jesus in the Seventeenth Century: Introduction," *Recusant History* 18, 1 (May 1986): 14–33.

12. H/SAG2: 96; cf. Charles W. Polzer, S.J., trans. and ed., *Rules and Precepts of the Jesuit Missions of Northwestern New Spain* (Tucson, 1976), 67, par. 6, 111, pars. 39–40. For one example of such record-keeping, see Appendix E.

13. ARSI, *Bras.*, 11:I, 132–134ᵛ. Cf. Herman W. Konrad, *A Jesuit Hacienda in Colonial Mexico: Santa Lucia, 1576–1767* (Stanford, 1980), 117–19.

equipment and foodstuffs in their custody, infirmarians accounted for all medical supplies on hand, librarians kept a full inventory of all books and manuscripts entrusted to them. The house minister (ministro da casa) kept a roll of all members and servants residing in the house and of the wages paid out to the latter.

Summaries of such records were reported to the house procurator, who, often with an assistant, maintained a series of ledgers. They included an inventory of every article of furniture and all equipment that belonged to the house as well as current stocks of all implements, clothing, bedding, and other supplies. Procurators also kept up-to-date accounts with supporting estates, with brother colleges at home and abroad, and between their colleges and the province, as well as copies of the standing orders from all superior authorities. They, too, retained files of legal documents that included legacies, bequests, and other donations; land titles; and lease agreements. Last, the procurators guarded both a cash book showing funds received and expended on behalf of the house, and one of three keys necessary to open the strongbox, the others being in the possession of the rector and the eldest consultor.[14]

Other custodians also kept books recording income and expenses for their constituencies. As discussed elsewhere, they included the Japan and China procurators based in Goa, the overseas procurators who resided in Lisbon, the office of the Portuguese assistant in Rome, and the various provincials.

Only tantalizing examples of this once-abundant corpus of records survive. Several Lisbon archives, notably the National Archives (the Torre do Tombo), the National Library, the Ajuda palace archives, and especially those of the Tribunal of Accounts, possess single codices that were once parts of long chronological series of accounts kept by the procurators of various Peninsular colleges. Some fine, generally well-preserved specimens of the accounts of Jesuit facilities in the vicinity of Goa (but not elsewhere in India) remain in the Historical Archives of Goa. Although none of these sources dates from the sixteenth century, a fair number exist for the seventeenth and even more for the eighteenth century. The sixteenth-century accounts of the Peninsular colleges are largely lost, though a few specimens survive in the Society's Roman archives. Few records pertaining to the Jesuits' colleges and estates in Brazil survive. Apart from illuminating fragments found in the Jesuits' Roman archives, the most extensive collection of Jesuit estate accounts for the Brazil province concerns the plantations that belonged to the Lisbon college of Santo Antão, whose records were retained in the Peninsular capital.

All known extant accounts of the Assistancy were consulted for this study. Aside from the substantive data they contain, they reveal some of the strengths, weaknesses, and limitations of Jesuit accounting methods. First, Luís de Bivar Guerra's contention that Jesuit ledgers were constructed according to a uniform model proves to be utterly unfounded. Some bookkeepers were extremely orderly in their monthly and yearly entries, but others were absolutely chaotic. The house procurator of Porto's college of São Lourenço, for example, continually forgot to enter the payment of bills during the month or year that they were settled

---

14. Although not wholly reliable, Luís de Bivar Guerra, "A administração e contabilidade dos colégios da companhia de Jesus, nos séculos xvii e xviii," Instituto Nacional de Estatística, *Revista do centro de estudos económicos* 13 (Lisbon, 1953), remains a useful, albeit enthusiastic, introduction.

and customarily itemized them months or even a year after they had been liquidated.[15] The same was true of other procurators as well. One must again remember, however, that such accountants were self-trained, that most of them had no special preparation for their jobs, and that the intellectually more gifted fathers had little appreciation for or understanding of their work. As a Benedictine father once rather contemptuously observed, "Accountancy, rather than a science or an art, is a craft. One of minor importance, no doubt, but the discipline of every craft benefits those who welcome it. In this case it calls for the virtues of justice and prudence and inspires a fondness for order and clarity; the finest spiritual ideal has nothing to fear from what contributes … to a realistic outlook."[16] That is a view that most Jesuits then (and I suspect today) could easily endorse.

In the sixteenth century, such accounts were generally mere listings (and often were so labeled) rather than analyses by categories of income and expenditure. Thus, though a codex might be labeled "Income and Expenditures," each category was kept in a separate part of the ledger and the results of the two were never displayed side by side for reconciliation, as in double-entry practice. Beginning in the last years of the seventeenth century, entries became increasingly detailed: instead of merely itemizing how much was spent on food or clothing or estates, accountants began to indicate precisely how much was spent on various kinds of food, clothing, labor, estates, and so on.[17] Students of the history of prices will still be frustrated, however, because the accountants failed to reveal the quantities of goods and services purchased or sold. Yet by the 1720s and 1730s, the inclusion of such precise information became standard practice, as is evident from the ledgers of the professed house of Bom Jesús, the college of Rachol, and the college of Bragança.[18]

As was the case with medieval ecclesiastical accounts, the Jesuits did not distinguish between capital and regular income;[19] nor did they include any reserve funds to cover unanticipated emergencies. Further, though other Jesuit records, notably the so-called third catalogues mentioned below, contained estimates of income and expenditures, none of the accounts described here show any evidence of planning or budgeting. It is true that, unlike the keepers of medieval ledgers, the Society's record-keepers were expected to strike balances between income and expenditures and to identify far from uncommon and always distressing deficits. But when Visitors, provincials, and rectors periodically examined the books, as they did about every trivium, their major concerns were simply to verify the accuracy of the figures and to insist that bills be paid and debts be collected rather than to suggest how particular categories of expenses might be lessened or sources of income might be augmented.[20]

15. BNL, cod. 4512. As noted elsewhere, this codex spans the years 1714 to 1721.

16. Dom Pierre Doyere ("monk of Wisques"), "The Need for Accountancy," in Sheppard, *Poverty*, 247.

17. A good example of increasingly sophisticated entries by Jesuit accountants may be seen in the "Livro da receita e despeza geral" of the college of Setúbal (ANTT/CJ/102, no. 6), which runs from December 1696 through August 1711.

18. E.g., Tables 24.3 and 24.4 and sources cited there.

19. Cf. Dom David Knowles, *The Religious Orders in England*, vol. 2 (Cambridge, 1955), 319; and Nicholas P. Cushner, *Farm and Factory: The Jesuits and the Development of Agrarian Capitalism in Colonial Quito, 1600–1767* (Albany, 1982), 146.

20. Bivar Guerra, "A administração e contabilidade," 180–85, prints examples of such verifications. Cushner, *Farm and Factory*, 146, states that in the Spanish empire, Jesuit books were audited "by the provincial superior's office" about every four years. That practice sometimes obtained in the Portuguese Assistancy,

One final observation concerning these institutional accounts: when the compilers and the inspectors reconciled their monthly and yearly levels of income and expenditures, the results, when positive, were expressed as "liquid" or "remains," but rarely as "profits" (*proveito, ganho, lucro*) in Portuguese, or their Latin equivalents, *lucrum, quaestus,* or *fructus*). For one who does not subscribe to the notion that Jesuit enterprise was or became primarily capitalist in its objective, such terms are unsurprising.

There remains another source that partially compensates for the lost accounts and also helps to measure levels of income and expenditure by units of the Assistancy, namely, the set of documents known as the third catalogue (*catálogo terceiro* or *catalogus tertius*). The third catalogue was one of a group of periodic reports that provincials regularly submitted to the Society's Roman headquarters, where many specimens are still available in its central archives. The preparation of such reports began during the last decades of the sixteenth century, but for some parts of the Assistancy there are extensive lacunae, so that, for example, only five remain for the Brazil province between 1631 and 1694. Most of those for the Malabar province are also missing, and large gaps remain in the series compiled for the Japan province and the vice-province of China. Still, one must be grateful for what is available. The remaining triennial accounts were often, though not always, estimates of expected levels of receipts and expenses as well as of active and passive debts incurred by each unit of the province. Some include breakdowns of yearly income and expenditures for one of the years spanned by the report. The third catalogues obviously must be used with caution, as Fr. Thomas M. McCoog admonishes us, but so must all historical documents.[21] Since these reports were never challenged by authorities in Rome, they may be assumed to have depicted their fiscal situations reasonably well. Despite lacunae and inescapably rough computations, these sources are the best available instruments for measuring the shifting fortunes of the components of the Assistancy.

Patterns of Income

Previous chapters have examined the variety of sources of income that units of the Assistancy relied upon for their support. Those sources included royal subsidies, private bequests, and other forms of gifting, as well as income derived from loans, rentals, the yield of farms and estates, and the sale of articles of commerce. Table 24.1 demonstrates the income levels of each major component of the Assistancy from the late sixteenth to the mid-eighteenth century. As would be expected, the income of the province of Portugal appears to have grown markedly during the critical 1570s: in that decade receipts increased by 141 percent, a higher rate than in any other period.[22] By contrast, during the 85 years between the

---

for when superior officials went on their periodic inspection tours, they regularly reviewed the accounts of each entity they visited. As Bivar Guerra correctly observes (p. 186), such inspectors were constantly changed, perhaps to prevent any possible charge of collusion.

21. McCoog, "'Laid Up Treasure': The Finances of the English Jesuits in the Seventeenth Century," in W. J. Sheils and Diana Wood, eds., *The Church and Wealth*, Studies in Church History 24 (Oxford, 1987), 257–66, at 258. Cf. Cushner, *Farm and Factory*, 148.

22. It should be remembered that the province of Portugal also included Jesuit installations in the Azores, the Madeiras, and Angola.

onset of the Philippine regime and the climax of the struggle for independence (1580–1665), the province's rate of income growth fell to 33.8 percent. Curiously, despite the economic doldrums during the next quarter century, the province's revenues grew by 47.5 percent, but that was the last significant spurt: during the Joanine regime, receipts increased by only 8.4 percent.

It would appear that the province of Goa followed the Peninsular model and that its earnings even briefly exceeded those of the home province before shrinking spectacularly. Between 1575 and 1599, the Indian province's revenues went up by just over 100 percent. The increase was less spectacular between 1605 and 1666, but at 43.6 percent exceeded the performance of the Peninsular province. Despite the continued military reverses that the State of India sustained during the second half of the seventeenth century, the Goan province's receipts grew by 90.2 percent, but the best was yet to come: between 1699 and 1734 revenues expanded by an astounding 388 percent. However, the devastating Maratha campaigns of the 1730s (see Chapter 23) deprived the province of 79.8 percent of its income between 1734 and 1741, the last available economic survey.

Table 24.1 also suggests several observations about the income levels of the remaining provinces. The first is that the combined income of the Japan province and the vice-province of China was always substantially lower than that of India or perhaps even Brazil during the seventeenth century. That was certainly true from 1694 onward. Despite the Brazil province's heavily capitalized sugar plantations and other properties, its income level did not consistently exceed that of the Goan province until the late 1730s. By the late 1750s, however, receipts from the Brazil province were on the verge of eclipsing those of the home province.

At first sight, therefore, it appears that Jesuit enterprises prospered from the sixteenth to the mid-eighteenth century, despite the state's long series of disastrous military and economic reverses. But the data presented in Table 24.1 are expressed in so-called "money of account," what Carlo M. Cipolla termed "ghost money." The purpose of the Portuguese real, the xerafim, and the other monetary units employed in the eastern empire, like that of the French *livre tournois*, the Spanish *maravedi*, the Dutch *guilder*, the English pence, and other comparable value systems, was, as Frank C. Spooner has reminded us, "to produce a homogeneous system from a variety of currency in circulation—gold, silver, and copper, both domestic and foreign."[23] Jesuit accounts, like those of the state, were consequently computed in multiples of such units—hundreds, thousands, millions, and fractions thereof. But, as Gustave Dupont-Ferrier suggested long ago, such a procedure failed to take into consideration variations in the *value* of money expressed in terms of gold or silver, and, one must add, it also ignored the fluctuating costs of goods and services that Jesuits, like everyone, were obliged to pay over time.[24]

23. Cipolla, *Money, Prices, and Civilization in the Mediterranean World, Fifth to Seventeenth Century* (New York, 1967), chap. 4; Spooner, *The International Economy and Monetary Movements in France, 1493–1725* (Cambridge, Mass., 1972), 90, 98–99.

24. Dupont-Ferrier, *Du collège de Clermont au lycée Louis-le-Grand (1563–1920)*, 3 vols. (Paris, 1921–25), 1: 93. Dupont-Ferrier observed that even though the college Louis le Grand, the richest in France, enjoyed an income of 44,000 livres, its purchasing power was less than 20,000 livres during the sixteenth century; but he failed to develop the implications of his insightful suggestion, which seems to have been virtually ignored by other writers.

TABLE 24.1

Estimates of Income by Major Units of the Portuguese Assistancy, ca. 1570–1757

(000,000 rs.)

Years	Portugal	Brazil	Maranhão	Goa	Malabar	Japan	China
ca. 1570	9.2	—	—	—	—	—	—
1575	—	—	—	5.8	—	—	—
1579	—	—	—	—	—	5.9	—
ca. 1580	22.2	—	—	—	—	—	—
1585	—	—	—	—	—	3.3	—
1586	—	—	—	6.3	—	—	0.1
1590	23.8	—	—	—	—	—	—
1599	29.6	—	—	11.8	—	—	—
1602–5	—	—	—	—	—	4.7	—
1603	28.2	—	—	—	—	—	—
1605	—	—	—	7.8	4.1	—	—
1609	—	—	—	—	—	2.9	—
1611	24.9	—	—	—	—	—	—
1617–18	—	—	—	—	—	2.9	—
1619	26.6	—	—	—	—	—	—
1620–24	—	—	—	—	—	2.5	—
1624	—	—	—	—	—	—	1.1
1624–25	—	—	—	—	—	3.2	—
1627	—	—	—	10.7	—	—	—
1628	27.4	—	—	—	—	—	—
1631	—	7.6	—	—	—	—	—
1639	26.4	—	—	—	—	—	—
1641	—	—	—	9.6	—	—	—
1646	—	—	—	—	—	4.5	4.9
1649	24.2	—	—	10.6	—	—	—
1653	—	—	—	12.9	—	—	—
1658	29.7	—	—	—	—	—	—
1659	—	—	—	15.3	—	—	—
1661–67	—	—	—	—	—	—	1.2
1662	—	—	—	14.3	—	—	—
1663–67	—	—	—	—	—	4.0	—
1664	—	—	—	16.1	—	—	—
1665	29.7	—	—	—	—	—	—
1666	—	—	—	14.1	—	—	—
1669	—	—	—	—	—	—	5.1
1677	—	—	—	18.6	—	—	—
1678	42.8	—	—	—	—	—	—
1679	—	14.9	—	—	—	—	—
1681	41.6	—	—	—	—	—	—
1689	—	—	—	21.6	—	—	—
1690	43.8	—	—	—	—	—	—
1690–91	—	—	—	—	—	—	0.8
1694	—	26.2	—	18.4	—	—	—
1694–96	—	—	—	—	—	12.0	—
1698–99	—	—	—	—	—	4.2	—

Continued on next page

TABLE 24.1 *(continued)*

Years	Portugal	Brazil	Maranhão	Goa	Malabar	Japan	China
1699	—	—	—	21.3	—	—	—
1700	51.0	—	—	—	—	—	—
1701	—	28.3	—	—	—	—	—
1705	54.3	—	—	—	—	—	—
1706	—	—	—	24.3	—	—	—
1707	—	40.5	—	—	—	—	—
1711	54.6	—	—	—	—	—	—
1713	—	—	—	41.6	—	—	—
1719	—	—	—	39.3	—	8.5	—
1720	48.7	36.9	—	—	—	—	—
1722	—	—	6.0	—	—	—	—
1726	61.2	—	—	—	—	—	—
1730	—	—	—	36.7	—	5.6	1.3
1731	—	—	—	68.6	—	—	7.2
1732	—	39.4	—	—	—	—	—
1734	50.6	—	—	104.0	6.6	—	—
1739	—	42.7	—	—	—	—	—
1740	—	—	6.1	—	—	—	—
1741	—	—	—	21.0	—	—	—
1743	—	36.2	—	—	—	—	—
1746	—	—	—	—	6.4	—	—
1749	61.8	—	—	—	—	—	—
1751	—	—	5.5	—	—	—	—
1754	55.3	—	—	—	—	—	—
1757	—	54.8	—	—	—	—	—

SOURCES: Portugal, 1570 and 1580: ARSI, *Lus.*, 78, fols. 43, 49–50; remainder: ibid., 44:I, 44:II, 45, 46, 47, 48, and 49. Brazil: ARSI, *Bras.*, 5:I, 5:II, 6:I, and 6:II. Maranhão: ARSI, *Bras.*, 27. Goa, 1575 and 1586: *DI*, 10: 51–59 and 14: 463–513; 1599–1664: ARSI, *Goa*, 24:II and 25; 1666: Cámara Municipal de Élvas, ms. 6891; 1667–1741: ARSI, *Goa*, 25 and 26. Malabar: F/*JM*, 2: 346 and 349. Japan, 1579, *DHMPPO*, 12: 543–44; 1585–1646 (except for 1617–24): *MHJ*, 185–200, 343–45, 535–37, 966–69, and 1026–28; 1617–18, 1620–25: ARSI, *JapSin*, 23, fols. 51r–60v; 1663–67: ibid., fols. 138–39; 1694–96, 1698–99: ARSI, *Goa*, 36:I, fol. 65; 1719: BA/JA/49-V-27, no. 197; 1730: AHU/PA/IN, *cx.* 35. China, 1586: *DI*, 14, 463–513; 1624: *MHJ*, 969; 1618–46: BA/JA/49-V-11, no. 76; 1661–67: ARSI, FG, 721/II/6; 1669: ARSI, *JapSin*, 134, fols. 360–61; 1690–91: ibid., fols. 170–171v; 1730: ibid., fol. 425v; and 1731: ARSI, FG, 627/II/6.

Unfortunately, our knowledge of currency fluctuations and prices in the Portuguese Assistancy remains rudimentary. It *is* clear that the Portuguese governments, like those of France and Spain, repeatedly devalued the coins they issued throughout the period considered in this study and that the intrinsic value of such coins diminished relative to the more stable English or Dutch coinage. Between 1580 and 1640, the Lisbon mint issued coins at a fixed ratio of 2,800 rs. per mark of silver, but the financially hard-pressed regimes of John IV (1640–56) and Afonso VI (1656–68) repeatedly devalued the silver content of its issues, whose value per mark of silver diminished 22.4 percent by 1663 and fell an additional 35.4 percent as a result of the Petrine devaluation of 1688 and another 36 percent in the devaluation of 1734.[25] The ratio of the Portuguese *milréis* (1,000 rs.) to pence sterling between 1619 and 1750 roughly followed the downward movement of the intrinsic value of Portuguese coinage: between 1619 and 1642 the milréis lost 13.2 percent of its sterling exchange value; by 1676 it was worth only 47.4 percent as much as it was in 1619; and between 1700 and 1750 its value declined another 6 to 10 percent.[26]

No history of commodity prices for Portugal during this period yet exists,[27] but the general advances in the prices of several basic commodities—wheat, olive oil, and rice—and one luxury item—saffron—during the period are unmistakable. Évora was not only a major Jesuit learning center but also a major wheat market. Between 1582 and 1599 wheat prices there rose as much as 55 percent; during the 1620s and 1630s they weakened significantly, but they ended the seventeenth century 73.7 percent higher than they were at its beginning. The Lisbon price of olive oil per *cántaro* (13 liters) more than doubled between the late 1560s and the late 1590s. By the 1640s, it stood 40.5 percent higher than it had 80 years before. Yet during the ensuing six decades, it again doubled before entering a long period of weakened prices that prevailed from the end of the century until the 1720s. Throughout our period, Portugal depended upon foreign (Italian or British North American) sources for rice, whose price on the Lisbon market rose by 45.8 percent between the late 1660s and the late 1690s. By the late 1740s, rice prices had risen another 10.7 percent. Jesuit cooks lavishly used saffron, a yellowish, perennially expensive aromatic food coloring imported from Spain and France. Between the late 1560s and the late 1590s, the average Lisbon price of saffron rose 83.3 percent, and by the 1640s it had advanced another 69.4 percent.[28]

Much remains to be learned about the behavior of prices in the kingdom during this period, but even less is known about commodity movements in the Portuguese empire and beyond. As far as I am aware, no such studies exist for the Far East during these decades, nor are there any for the Portuguese enclaves in India.[29] The only available proxy for those outposts are studies of price movements in the Mughal empire. They suggest that prices in that empire doubled between about 1590 and the early 1660s, and that they declined somewhat during the 1670s, remained flat until about 1710, and redoubled between about

25. T. Bentley Duncan, *Atlantic Islands: Madeira, the Azores, and the Cape Verdes in Seventeenth-Century Commerce and Navigation* (Chicago, 1972), app. III. Cf. Spooner, *International Economy*, 290–91, for the generally downward movement of the French *écu d'or au soleil* relative to the Dutch guilder between 1620 and 1726.

26. John J. McCusker, *Money and Exchange in Europe and America, 1600–1775* (Chapel Hill, 1978), tables 2.23 and 2.32; also H. E. S. Fisher, *The Portugal Trade: A Study of Anglo-Portuguese Commerce, 1700–1770* (London, 1971), app. VI.

27. The distinguished economic historian Vitorino Magalhães Godinho has promised to publish such a study for the past four decades. See his pioneering essay, "A 'revolução dos preços' no século xvi," reprinted in his *Ensaios*, vol. 2 (Lisbon, 1968), 157–74, which republishes a useful series of wheat prices for the Azorean island of São Miguel between 1500 and 1600. This series demonstrates that cereal prices there increased 37.6% between 1540 and 1544, i.e., the founding years of the Society of Jesus, and between 1580 and 1584, the beginning of the Philippine era, and that a decade later they had advanced an astounding 171.4%.

28. This analysis rests primarily upon the several price series in *DHP*, 4: 501–8. See also Virgínia Coelho, "Preços do azeite em Lisboa: 1626–1733," *Revista de historia economica e social* 4 (July–Dec. 1979): 15–39.

29. The surviving Jesuit accounts in the HAG could be extremely useful for determining price levels in Goa and its vicinity from the early eighteenth century through the 1730s, but unfortunately not before or after.

that date and mid-century. Assuming the accuracy of such estimates, the annual rate of increase between 1600 and 1750 was about 1.93 percent.[30]

One cannot even be certain of that for early colonial Brazil. It is reasonable to conjecture that prices there advanced sharply, as they did in Portugal and elsewhere in the Atlantic world during the famous sixteenth-century price revolution. Doubtless they also rose substantially during the years of the Dutch intrusion (1624–54) and probably throughout most of the Restoration (1640–68), but no studies confirm such surmises. There are enough data, however, to demonstrate that prices, especially for cane sugar, the dominant export of Brazil and the Jesuits, turned sharply downward between the 1670s and the 1690s, and that prices of both local and imported products generally soared during the early decades of the Golden Age (between the 1690s and the 1730s) but slackened thereafter.[31]

The foregoing suggests, albeit imprecisely, that Jesuit income growth in various parts of the Assistancy was substantially consumed over time by added costs of goods and services. And the burdens upon that income would have increased in proportion to the increases in personnel and students, as well as the growth of Jesuit enterprises and the aging of the Society's facilities.

Patterns of Expenditure

Though other studies of Jesuit financial activities emphasize sources of the Society's income, few explain how such funds were expended. Considering the belief among contemporaries and even some writers today that the Society was blessed with vast, unneeded riches, it is important to examine the other side of the ledger.

Loyola did not promise his recruits sumptuous meals. On the contrary, he warned that "if [the candidate] is pleased to remain in the Society, his food, drink, clothing, shoes, and lodging will be what is characteristic of the poor; and he should be persuaded himself that it will be what is worst in the house, for his greater abnegation and spiritual progress."[32] Nevertheless, despite the fact that many Jesuit colleges possessed supporting estates, food costs always loomed large in their accounts (see Tables 24.2 and 24.3, as well as Table 24.4 below). To be sure, those situated in the kingdom procured most of their meat, grains, fruits, and vegetables from their own estates. However, fish, wine, olive oil, domestic and imported cheeses, and spices were purchased in the open market and came from many parts of the kingdom and abroad. At the beginning of the seventeenth century, for example, the University of Évora obtained tunny fish and almonds from the Algarve, cod from Lisbon

30. Tapan Raychaudhuri and Ifran Habib, eds., *The Cambridge Economic History of India*, 2 vols. (Cambridge, 1982), 1: 375–76; cf. Joseph J. Brennig, "Silver in Seventeenth-Century Surat: Monetary Circulation and the Price Revolution in Mughal India," in J. F. Richards, ed., *Precious Metals in the Later Medieval and Early Modern Worlds* (Durham, N.C., 1985), 477–96. Brennig does not proceed beyond 1700 but argues that seventeenth-century prices remained more stable than Raychaudhuri and Habib contend. See also Chapter 23, note 43.

31. D. Alden, "Price Movements in Brazil Before, During, and After the Gold Boom, with Special Reference to the Salvador Market, 1670–1769," in *Essays on the Price History of Eighteenth-Century Latin America*, ed. Lyman L. Johnson and Enrique Tandeter (Albuquerque, 1990), 335–71.

32. *CSJ(GE)*, 81. A. Lynn Martin, *The Jesuit Mind: The Mentality of an Elite in Early Modern France* (Ithaca, N.Y., 1988), 144, incorrectly attributes this passage to the *Constitutions*. The passage also appears in Loyola, *Regras da companhia de Iesu* (Évora, 1603), 15, par. 25.

TABLE 24.2
Patterns of Expenditure in Six Jesuit Colleges

Category	Santo Antão (1567)	Setúbal (1704–5, 1710–11)	São Lourenço (1714)	Macao (1719)	Bahia (1722)	Évora (1725)
Total rs. (00)	1,002.6	348.4	3,775.7	1,208.4	18,507.0	19,199.5
Foodstuffs	43.1%	25.4%	32.5%	78.6%	30.8%	49.4%
Clothing	10.7	9.3	7.7	12.5	19.3	4.2
Fabric	22.0	6.9	20.0	—	17.8	1.9
Supplies	5.2	—	6.5	2.9	6.7	3.1
Salaries and wages	—	0.6	7.4	—	2.4[a]	5.3
Estates	—	20.7[b]	—	—	—	22.1
Health care	5.9	—	2.0	—	7.8[c]	1.3
Church	3.9	5.4	9.3	5.8	—	1.9
Alms	—	—	2.0	—	—	1.7
Provincial assessment	—	—	—	—	—	3.8
Miscellaneous	8.6	30.7	12.4	—	14.8	5.3
Total	99.4	99.0	99.8	99.8	99.6	100.0

SOURCES: Santo Antão: ARSI, FG, 1453/5, no. 4. Setúbal: ANTT/CJ, 102, no. 104. São Lourenço: BNL, cod. 4512. Macao: ARSI, *JapSin*, 23, fols. 376–379ᵛ. Bahia: ARSI, *Bras.*, 6:I, fols. 127ᵛ–128ʳ. Évora: ARSI, *Lus.*, 81:II, fols. 570–572ᵛ.

[a] Cost of slaves purchased during the year.

[b] Includes an estate and a salt pan (*marinha*).

[c] Health care for members (5.5 percent) and slaves (2.3 percent).

TABLE 24.3
Expenditures of the College of Bragança, 1565–1756

Category	1565–68	1699–1700	1710	1721–22, 1724–25	1736–37	1754–56
Total rs. (00)	389.3	2,046.4	1,644.8	2,093.9	1,179.7	2,330.3
Foodstuffs	39.5%	24.7%	36.9%	20.9%	24.1%	47.3%
Clothing	28.2	12.5	16.1	5.7	4.7	3.4
Fabric	7.5	7.8	10.6	8.4	1.1	0.5
Supplies	—	3.3	3.9	2.5	1.0	12.3
Salaries and wages	0.8	5.1	6.7	4.9	7.7	5.7
Health care	1.9	1.1	0.1	0.7	11.2	—
Estates	8.9	8.3	7.9	12.9	6.9	8.8
Travel and carriage	—	7.0	0.9	1.3	2.2	5.6
Church	3.5	7.0	5.5	1.8	9.7	0.2
Alms	—	0.5	1.2	0.2	0.6	0.9
Province	—	7.8	3.2	16.6	—	9.1
Miscellaneous	9.5	14.7	6.8	21.6	30.7	6.1
Total	99.8	99.8	99.8	100.1	99.9	99.9

SOURCES: 1565–68: ARSI, FG, 1379/2. Remainder: ATC/JI, cods. 33, 34, and 35.

and Porto, mixed nuts from Estremoz, dried fish from Lisbon, sardines from Setúbal, lentils from Évora, and saffron from Spain.³³ The proportion and variety of foodstuffs each community consumed naturally varied with the institution and with time. During the formative period, for example, cereals represented nearly half (49.4 percent) of Bragança's food purchases, followed by meat (18.7 percent), wine (14.7 percent), fish (8.8 percent), olive oil (7.8 percent), and fruit (0.5 percent).³⁴

Students attending the College of Purification (Évora) prepared themselves for long days of study and contemplation as well as restricted diets. They were expected to rise for morning prayers at 5 A.M. and afterward to partake of a light (unspecified) repast. Dinner was set for 11 A.M. in winter and 10 A.M. in summer; supper followed at 7 P.M. in winter or an hour earlier in summer. Candles were to be out by 10 P.M. in winter and an hour earlier during summer. At dinner members received bread (amount unspecified), water, 680 grams of meat (beef or pork or both), mustard, and a variety of vegetables including amaranth, onions, and squashes. Dessert consisted of fresh or dried fruit, nuts, and cheese. On meatless days the fare included fresh fish (sardines or tunny) with vinegar and olive oil and three eggs, along with a porringer of vegetables. During Lent, inmates received an orange, some sardines, a dish of rice, and other fruit in season.³⁵

But members of other houses ate far less spartan meals. In remote northeastern Portugal the seventeen or eighteen members of the college of Bragança enjoyed a remarkably varied diet during the eighteenth century. Besides wheat, their grains included barley, rye, and rice; their meats included beef, beef tongue, ham, lamb, and occasionally goat and rabbit. Chickens constituted the major fowl served at their table, but they sometimes also had partridge and turkey. Although cod and sardines were probably their predominant fish, they also had lamprey, eel, trout, whiting, octopus, and assorted shellfish. Their vegetables included two kinds of beans, cabbages, cucumbers, peas, and turnips. They enjoyed an even wider array of fruits, notably apples, cherries, fresh and dried figs, peaches, pears, plums, quinces, grapes, raisins, oranges, and both musk and watermelon. Water and wine appear to have been their principal beverages, but they also drank an occasional cup of chocolate. Desserts included almonds, chestnuts, and walnuts, and both domestic and imported (English and Dutch) cheese.³⁶

Meat or fish always figured prominently in Jesuit diets. Early in the seventeenth century, a provincial of Brazil stipulated that the standard allotment of meat or fish should be 450 grams at dinner in winter and 300 in summer. By the early eighteenth century, dinner at Santo Antão was also restricted to 450 grams of beef or lamb per person in addition to 45 grams of bacon. Still, meat remained the heaviest expenditure for victuals: in 1711 it

33. "Varias lembranças pera hum procurador . . . feito no anno de [1]606," in BNL/FG, 4254, fols. 28ʳ–29ʳ.

34. "Renta, gasto y deudas del collegio de Bragança de los años 1565, 1566, '67, 1568," in ARSI, FG, 1379/2. The account shows no funds expended for vegetables, which, as shown below, the Jesuits certainly ate.

35. "Varias lembranças . . . [1]606," fol. 73 (note 33); "Statutos do collegio da Purificação que mandou fazer el rei d. Henrique" (1579), in ARSI, FG, 1408/19, no. 4. Cf. English Benedictine practice: Abbot Gasquet, *English Monastic Life* (London, 1904), 120, 136, and 150. The mealtimes given here represent modifications of those initially prescribed by Fr. Jerónimo Nadal in 1553–54: *RSI*, 451, par. 3.

36. ATC/JI, cod. 35.

represented 22 percent of the daily allotment, compared with 17.6 percent for vegetables, and 17.5 percent each for bread and wine.[37]

Procurators were instructed to take great care in assembling rations for members of the Society bound for overseas assignments. The check-off list for a member proceeding from Lisbon to Madeira, normally a nine- to eleven-day voyage, included 32.3 kilograms of ships' biscuit, six loaves of fresh bread, an unspecified quantity of dried and fresh fish, a half dozen chickens, 7.25 kilograms of sugar, an equal quantity of marmalade, 8.5 liters of wine, 7.25 kilograms of sugar plums, and other fruits and vegetables (unspecified as to quantity) in season.[38]

Those procurators responsible for organizing contingents of missionaries bound for the East were admonished to assemble their charges fifteen days before sailing because, wrote the provincials of Goa and Malabar, "experience" and "the doctors" had demonstrated that it was better for them to sail well rested than exhausted. They enjoined procurators to see that all perishables, including hams, pork, fish, and sweets, were carefully stowed below deck and to give the voyage superior, normally the eldest member, a complete inventory of all stores and where they were located. The provincials directed that during the long voyages each Jesuit ought to have a small glass of wine and a bit of biscuit before breakfast, stipulated to occur at 8:30 A.M. and to include something cooked. At night the voyagers were to partake of meat, fruit, raisins, figs, olives, almonds, and a slice of something sweet, probably marmalade. The live chickens the contingent brought were reserved for light meals on Sundays and particularly for those brothers and fathers who were under the weather. At the end of the voyage all surplus stocks, especially wine, vinegar, and empty casks, were to be turned over to the procurator of the port where the contingent arrived, in the early days either Cochin or Goa, but later always the eastern capital.[39]

Not a few of the sailings from Lisbon were aborted because of damage sustained in combat, leaks, and excessive time lost in the West African doldrums. Despite their fervor for the overseas missions, Jesuits, like their shipmates, rejoiced upon returning to Lisbon, for entry into the Tagus meant swarms of small boats ready to sell the carrack's passengers fresh water, fresh bread, and especially fresh fruit, all of which soon disappeared.[40]

In 1604 Alessandro Valignano drew up a list of stores to sustain China-bound members of the Society sailing between Goa and Macao, ordinarily a voyage of four to five months. That list included quantities of wheat, vermicelli, fresh beef and pork, 100 sucklings, twenty chickens, sausages, dried fish, olives, olive oil, fruits and vegetables in season, vinegar, butter, salt, seasonings, raisins, and marmalade.[41]

Other early-seventeenth-century directives specify rations to be provided missionaries entering China and parts of Southeast Asia. Those venturing into the empire were to take

37. The size of meat rations was first stipulated by Provincial Henrique Gomes around 1611, in ARSI, FG, 721:I:1. The 1711 rations for Santo Antão are in ARSI, *Lus.*, 77, fols. 68–69.

38. "Visita da província de Portugal pelo P. João Alvares (1610/1613)," in ANTT/AJ, *cx.* 1, *m.* 5, fol. 152ʳ.

39. "Regimento pera os P.ᵉˢ e Irs' da comp.a que se embarcao' de Portugal pera a India feito em janeiro de [1]616," in ARSI, FG, 721:II/3/2.

40. *The Itinerário of Jerónimo Lobo*, trans. Donald M. Lockhart, ed. C. F. Beckingham, *HS*:2, no. 162 (1984): 162.

41. "Rol de matalotagem de Goa pᵃ a China feito por ordem de P. Visitador de Japão [Alessandro Valignano]," Jan. 1604, in BA/JA/49-IV-66, no. 6.

along quantities of mass wine, chickens, fried and salted fish, rice, butter, and an assortment of herbs and sweets. Their comrades sent from Macao to Vietnam, Cambodia, and Siam carried with them similar stocks of food as well as sausages, strips of pork, eggs packed in sugar, rice, biscuit, table wine, cabbages, onions, radishes, and available fruit.[42]

Other chapters have emphasized that most of those who served in the Portuguese Assistancy were European by birth. Whether they labored in Europe or abroad, they were expected to adapt themselves to the lands where they ministered. Such adaptation included the consumption of local foods, seasonings, and drinks. Nevertheless, as the specifications summarized above suggest, Jesuits preferred European provisions when they were available. Other sources sustain that conclusion. A 1603 want list for the Japan province called for annual shipments from Goa of 1,192 liters of "very good and pure" mass wine, olive oil, Flemish cheeses preserved in butter (so that they would keep better), and olives. The college of Macao ordered nearly identical supplies.[43] In 1747, when the rector of the college of Luanda, Angola, submitted his annual requests to Lisbon, he asked for olive oil (950 liters), butter (29 kilograms), two dozen Alentejo cheeses, a dozen Flemish cheeses, hams and sausages ("in good condition, not rotten as they sometimes reach us"), a barrel of olives, 45 kilograms of codfish, 900 grams of saffron, 450 grams of cinnamon, 225 grams of cloves, and an unspecified quantity of wheat. Considering the fact that there were then only fourteen Jesuits stationed in Angola, such requests suggest that Jesuits there ate rather well.[44]

Still, most of these items were delicacies, reserved for holidays and religious feasts. In large measure Jesuits, like others, adapted to local foods and supplemented them with the produce of their own gardens. When Fernão Cardim visited the college of Bahia in 1583, he was impressed by its ample garden, which contained a large fish tank, grapevines, eggplant, lettuce, cabbages, radishes, bananas, squashes, calabashes, pineapples, and coconuts.[45] Six decades later, a Jesuit guest in the Goan seminary observed that "the refectory was well stocked with fruit, which grows in that land all year long, seafood of various kinds, which is excellent and in great abundance ... and shellfish of all kinds." Obviously such seafood came from local catches, yet during the Friday meal that he took there, "the choicest morsel on the table and the one most esteemed by everyone was a saucer given to each religious with two salted sardines with oil just as they may have arrived from the ... voyage." He added that "everyone ate these including the bones ... because of what it represented of our Portugal."[46]

During the heat of conflict between the Jesuits and their rivals, it was not uncommon for opponents of the Society to charge that the fathers lived far better than did members of the Mendicant Orders. Jesuit spokesmen were sensitive to such criticism. Recalling the discrimination that had existed in the halls of some of the early monastic Orders, one defender observed that among Jesuits, "Their Rectours eat and drink no better than their Porters and Cooks do; all out of the same pot, and all at the same table. . . . All Jesuits fare

42. The lists are in BA/JA/49-V-66, nos. 32 and 29.
43. BA/JA/49-IV-66, nos. 4 and 5.
44. Rector to procurator general, Lisbon, 26 Sept. 1747, in ANTT/CJ/68, no. 234 (postscript).
45. Cardim, "Narrativa epistolar de uma viagem e missão Jesuítica," in *Tratados da terra e gente do Brasil* (rpr., São Paulo, 1980), 144–45.
46. Lobo, *Itinerário*, 296.

ande lodge alike, all clad alike. There is no difference, save only the respect due to age and superiority."[47] Nevertheless, modern writers, led by C. R. Boxer, have concluded that Jesuits generally ate quite well.[48] In certain places, especially in urban situations, they did, but one must not forget that such comforts had not always existed and that many Jesuits who served in the field never partook of the varied cuisine enjoyed by their citified brethren. In his third year in India, Xavier wrote Ignatius, "There are few provisions for the body, and these are without exception rice, fish, and chickens. There is no bread or wine, nor other things that your lands have in great abundance."[49] Nearly 120 years later, Fr. Cinnami, a missionary working in Mysore, testified,

> Our ordinary food consists of rice, vegetables, milk, butter, and water. The men who live here the life of a penitent loath flesh, meat, eggs, and wine. These are our sumptuous banquets; and what is taken in Europe on fast days is eaten here on the greatest solemnities. There is no difference between Friday and Sunday, between Lent and Easter tide. Fasting is not different, for our life is a perpetual fast.[50]

Fr. Cinnami's statement would have been understood in parts of Brazil, where in the 1570s a Jesuit critic observed that the new college of Olinda was so impoverished that its members did not ordinarily eat wheaten bread or drink a glass of undiluted wine.[51] More than a century later, a Luxembourg priest in the Amazon reported that his only luxuries were a bottle of olive oil and three small containers of brandy, which one presumes he sipped on lonely evenings after long days of frustrating toil.[52] Both the brandy and the sardines were symbolic gustatory ties with a distant Europe to which only a few Jesuits would ever return.

What is indisputable is that Jesuit fare, whether the spartan diets of isolated missionaries or the more bountiful repasts of the best-equipped colleges, was exceedingly modest when compared with that enjoyed by Europe's great noble houses. In the 1720s, for example, a French medical naturalist visited Portugal and was entertained by the royal minister Diogo de Mendonça Corte Real on his country estate outside of Lisbon. There the Frenchman and his host shared 40 plates "very well cooked."[53] Although we do not know what those dishes contained, there can be little doubt that the tables of high nobles and prelates were far more lavish than were those of the Society of Jesus.[54]

47. M[artin] G[rene], *An Account of the Jesuites Life and Doctrine* (London, 1661), 85.

48. Cf. *CCJ*, 216–17, and 479 n. 13; Martin, *Jesuit Mind*, 144; and John Patrick Donnelly, S.J., "Religious Order of Men, Especially The Society of Jesus," in John W. O'Malley, S.J., ed., *Catholicism in Early Modern History: A Guide to Research* (St. Louis, 1988), 153.

49. Xavier to Ignatius, Jan. 1545, in S/*FX*, 2: 537.

50. Quoted in D. Ferroli, S.J., *The Jesuits in Mysore* (Kozhikode, India, 1955), 58. See also Filippo de Filippi, ed., *An Account of Tibet: The Travels of Ippolito Desideri of Pistoia, S.J., 1712–1727*, intro. by C. Wessels, S.J., rev. ed. (London, 1937), 334–35.

51. Belchior Cordeiro, "Enformação dalgumas cousas do Brasil" (1577), ed. Serafim Leite, Academia portuguesa de historia, *Anais*, 2d ser., 15 (1965): 186.

52. Johan Philipe Betendorf, "Chronica da missão dos padres da Companhia de Jesus no estado do Maranhão," *RIHGB* 72, 1 (1909 [1910]): 159.

53. Charles Fréderic de Merveilleux, "Memoirs instructifs pour un voyageur dans les divers états de l'Europe" (Amsterdam, 1738), trans. and ed. in Castelo Branco Chaves, *O Portugal de D. João V visto por três forasteiros* (Lisbon, 1983), 152.

54. I intend to examine Jesuit diets in this assistancy more closely in a subsequent study that bears the working title "Food and Drink for Holy Men."

TABLE 24.4

Patterns of Expenditure of the Colleges of the Province of Goa, 1730

Category	New St. Paul's	Old St. Paul's	Chorão novitiate	Rachol	Bassein	Taná	Diu	Damão	Chaul
Total rs. (000)	12,360	1,155	4,819	5,591	3,360	2,093	1,401	2,337	831
Foodstuffs and clothing	59.5%	47.3%	46.7%	28.5%	49.1%	17.2%	29.9%	41.0%	54.1%
Fabric	4.8	—	—	—	6.2	—	8.6	8.9	7.2
Salaries and wages	8.0	10.4[a]	9.3[a]	4.3	7.1[a]	15.7[b]	15.7	0.9	10.8
Estates	—	—	—	—	23.0	—	—	—	—
Health care	16.9	—	—	4.8	1.8	—	4.3	1.3	3.6
Church	—	41.3	29.7[c]	40.6[d]	12.1	25.8[e]	22.6[f]	33.8[g]	18.0
Alms	1.5	—	8.7	5.4	1.8	2.8	4.3	7.7	3.6
Provincial assessment	—	—	5.5	—	8.2	8.8	6.8	5.9	—
Miscellaneous	9.2[h]	—	—	16.3	13.4	6.4	7.5	—	2.5
Total	99.9	99.0	99.9	99.9	99.7	99.7	99.7	99.5	99.8

SOURCE: AHU/PA/IN, *m.* 35.

[a] Subsistence and clothing for servants and/or slaves.

[b] Includes 10 percent of total for subsistence and clothing for servants and slaves.

[c] Includes 15.1 percent for the Lisbon novitiate and 3.6 percent to assist the missions of Mysore and Qatar.

[d] Includes a 7.3 percent subsidy for the Mysore mission and a contribution of 0.5 percent sent to the Lisbon novitiate to train future missionaries for India.

[e] Includes 14.3 percent for the Mysore mission and 0.7 percent for the Lisbon novitiate.

[f] Includes 6.4 percent for the Mysore mission and 1.1 percent for the Lisbon novitiate.

[g] Includes 12.8 percent for the Mysore mission and 0.9 percent for the Lisbon novitiate.

[h] For the Holy Faith Seminary, which consisted of three fathers and 30 natives.

Clothing was also a substantial expense for each college. The outfit issued to recruits in the Lisbon novitiate included a linen cassock, linen and woolen hats, a quilt, a coverlet, and bed boards.[55] The jottings of the Évora procurator frequently cited in this chapter indicate that the clothing room of the College of Purification in that city kept 64 different articles in stock.[56] Jesuits did not universally wear the same garb but adjusted their dress to what they considered most acceptable in the lands where they served. The 1616 instructions to the Lisbon procurator for the eastern provinces directed him to be sure that those who sailed on the Indian carracks had ample supplies of white clothing to lessen the effects of excessive heat.[57] Because of that heat, missionaries who served in the tropics needed substantial wardrobes to permit frequent changes. Those who served at the Cape Verde residence, for example, found it necessary to change shirts two to three times a day and to have three changes of sheets apiece.[58]

As Tables 24.4, 24.5 and 24.6 indicate, Jesuit bookkeepers sometimes lumped together charges for food and clothing since both, together with lodging, became an index of how

55. "Papel do q. pode o noviciado de Lx.ª p.ª ... todos os novicios," n.d. [1660s], in ARSI, *Lus.*, 82, fol. 243.

56. "Varias lembranças," fols. 5ʳ–6ᵛ (see note 33 above).

57. "Regimento pera os P.ᵉˢ e Irs' ... que se embarcao' de Portugal pera a India," pt. 5, par. 2 (see note 39 above).

58. "Dos que pode sostentar a residencia do Cabo Verde" [1632], in ARSI, *Lus.*, 83, fols. 343–344ᵛ.

TABLE 24.5

Patterns of Expenditure in the Provinces of Malabar, China, and Japan, 1730

Category	Malabar	China	Japan
Total rs. (000)	14,883.0	1,414.7	9,629.9
Foodstuffs and clothing	58.0%	64.5%[a]	85.6%[b]
Estates and remittances	—	—	14.4
Church	24.5	3.3	—
Miscellaneous	17.3	31.8	—
Total	99.8	99.6	100.0

SOURCE: See Table 24.4.

[a] Members accounted for 27 percent, catechists and servants for 37.5 percent.

[b] Missionaries within China accounted for 15.6 percent, missionaries serving in Southeast Asia for 37.4 percent, and members based in Macao for the remainder.

many members a particular institution could support. The data assembled in Table 24.6 are incomplete but nevertheless revealing. Costs in Portugal appear to have remained stable until the 1590s, but in 1596 Pope Clement VIII authorized a doubling of the personal allowance because of recent advances in prices.[59] That allowance remained the average in the kingdom for the balance of the century; however, as in other assistancies, there were substantial variations in the per-person costs of individual houses.[60] For example, in 1606 the *porção* or personal allowance in five Peninsular colleges ranged from 25,300 to 40,000 rs., whereas the personal ration in the probationary house was only 12,000 rs.[61]

It is clear from Table 24.6 and from other evidence that the weakening acceptance of Portuguese coinage and mounting prices drove up the cost of personal allowances in Portugal, especially during the eighteenth century. The same was true elsewhere, notably in the Far East, where expenditures in behalf of missionaries in Southeast Asia and China became the highest in the Assistancy and obviously restricted the ability of the eastern provinces to supply missionaries to fields where opportunities seemed especially promising. In France, too, the cost of personal allowances advanced at levels comparable to those noted here, probably for the same reasons.[62]

As the tables in this section suggest, maintenance of the fabric was a continuing financial burden whose magnitude varied from house to house. The fabric of a college, as D. G. Thompson reminds us, "consisted of . . . gardens, courtyards, entrance ways, and

59. ARSI, *Lus.*, 80, fols. 219–25.

60. In the Jesuit provinces in eighteenth-century South America, for example, Nicholas P. Cushner found that the allowances varied from 120 pesos for Jesuits attached to the college of Asunción to 290 pesos for those in the Paraguayan missions and 350 pesos for members of the Peruvian colleges. *Lords of the Land: Sugar, Wine and Jesuit Estates of Coastal Peru, 1600–1767* (Albany, 1980), 6; but cf. idem, *Jesuit Ranches and the Agrarian Development of Colonial Argentina, 1650–1767* (Albany, 1983), 130 and 130 n. 22, where Cushner offers different estimates.

61. "Varias lembranças," fol. 125 (see note 33 above).

62. E.g., the per-person allowances in the college of Ardeche (southeastern France) rose 52% between 1621 and 1717 and another 16.2% between 1717 and 1743; those of the royal college of Orléans (Loiret) gained 78.1% between 1617 and 1675 and another 63.6% between the latter date and 1757. In the department of Nord, the allowances of the college of Valenciennes soared 91.7% between 1619 and 1651; at the college of Roanne (Loire), they increased 69.6% during the period 1635–1726. *EJF*, 1: col. 371; 3: col. 1010; and 4: cols. 446, 448, and 1612.

TABLE 24.6

Estimated Cost of Maintaining a Single Jesuit for One Year, 1550–1750

(000 rs.)

Year(s)	Portugal	Brazil	Goa	Japan	China	Other	
1550	20.0	—	—	—	—		—
1577	—	20.0	—	—	—		—
1579	20.0	—	—	—	—		—
1593	—	—	18.7	—	—	Angola:	42.5
1596	20.0[a]	—	—	—	—		—
1598	—	—	—	8.0	—		—
1603	40.0	—	21.6	7.2[b]	—		—
1606	30.6[c]	—	—	—	—		—
1607	43.0	—	—	—	—		—
1608	—	—	43.2	—	—		—
1616	—	—	—	—	—	Angola:	80.0;
						Macao:	18.0[d]
1618	—	—	—	12.3	—		—
1621	40.0	—	—	—	—		—
1624–39	—	—	—	—	—	Macao:	22.0
1626	—	—	—	—	—	Mozambique:	25.0
1628	40.0	—	—	—	—		—
1632	—	—	—	—	—	Cape Verde:	40.0
1639	45.0	—	—	—	—	Madeira:	50.0
1643	—	20.0	—	—	—		—
1645	—	—	—	—	30.0		—
1648	—	—	—	—	—	Malabar:	45.0
1652	—	—	—	—	—	Maranhão:	35.0
1678	36.5	—	—	—	—		—
1711	54.7–82.8[e]	—	—	—	—		—
1722	67.0	47.0	—	—	—		—
1730	—	—	82.8	187.5[f]	62.6	Vietnam &	
						Cambodia:	112.5;
						Siam & Macao:	87.2
1735	80.3	—	—	—	—		—
1746	80.3	—	—	—	—		—
1750	73.0–80.0	—	—	—	—		—

SOURCES: Portugal, 1550: ARSI, *Lus.*, 80, fols. 219–25; 1579: ibid., 84:I, fols. 69–71; 1596: ARSI, FG, 1408–19; 1603: "Varias lembranças," fol. 125 (see note 33); 1606: ARSI, *Lus.*, 44:I, fols. 157ᵛ–158ʳ; 1607: *HCJAP*, 2:1, 575; 1621: ARSI, *Lus.*, 80, fols. 219–25; 1628: ibid., *Lus.*, 44:II, fol. 478; 1639: ARSI, *Lus.*, 44:II, fol. 594ᵛ; 1678: ibid., 78, no fol.; 1711: ibid., 77, fol. 62; 1722: ANTT/CJ/80, no. 49; 1735, 1746, and 1750: ibid., nos. 50, 64, 81, and 83. Cape Verde, 1632: ARSI, *Lus.*, 83, fols. 343–344ᵛ. Brazil, 1577: Belchior Cordeiro, "Enformação dalgumas cousas do Brasil," ed. Serafim Leite, Academia portuguesa de historia, *Anais*, 2d ser. 15 (1965): 187; 1643: ARSI, *Bras.*, 3:I, fol. 229; 1722: ibid., 6:I, fols. 126–30. Goa, 1593: *DI*, 16: 9* and 14–15; 1603: *APO*:1, 6:2, 759; 1608: *APO*:1, 4:2:3; 1730: AHU/PA/IN, m. 35. Japan, 1598: ARSI, *JapSin*, 43, fol. 85ᵛ; 1602–5: *MHJ*, 345; 1618: ibid., 797; 1730: BA/JA/49-V-28, no. 130. China, 1645: BA/JA/49-V- 11, no. 81; 1730: AHU/PA/IN, m. 35. Angola, 1593: ARSI, *Lus.*, 79, fol. 61; 1617: William Francis Rea, S.J., *The Economics of the Zambezi Missions, 1580–1759* (Rome, 1976), 56–57. Mozambique, 1626: ibid. Macao, 1616–39: BA/JA/49-IV-66, no. 44; 1730: AHU/PA/IN, m. 35. Madeira, 1639: ARSI, *Lus.*, 44:II, fol. 594ᵛ. Malabar, 1648: *CCLP*, 9: 184–85, 200–201. Maranhão, 1652: *DH*, 64: 101–3. Vietnam, Cambodia, Siam, 1730: AHU/PA/IN, m. 35.

[a] Because of rising prices, Clement VIII authorized a doubling of the personal allowance at this time.

[b] Average for 1602–5.

[c] Average for Coimbra and Évora.

[d] Average for the period 1616–23.

[e] Range recorded for several colleges within the province.

[f] Unit cost for one of the eight missionaries and their assistants from the Japan province who served in the imperial provinces of Kwantung and Kwansi.

outbuildings, as well as the actual college building or buildings."[63] In the early 1580s, Valignano estimated that in Japan the building of a seminary cost between 200,000 and 300,000 rs., a mission station 130,000 rs., and a college 1,000,000 rs.[64] Normally the principal benefactor or benefactors paid for the construction of a college and its church. Though we often know the extent of their commitment (see Chapter 14), we lack information concerning the full costs they promised to defray. It is evident from the third catalogues, especially those for Goa, that reported debts were often related to building expenditures. As was commonly true in this period and sometimes even today, the completion of churches took a long time: for example, the first stone of the church of New St. Paul's in Goa was laid in 1601, but the last one was not in place until 1710.[65]

The adornment of Jesuit churches, like those of their rivals, was a continual process and became a source of pride, the very existence of which would have been deeply troubling to Ignatius, Xavier, and the other founding members. In 1717, an anonymous father wrote that although the church of the college of Recife was not the grandest in the State of Brazil, it was one of its best embellished. A few years later, an early Jesuit chronicler of the Maranhão missions insisted that the church of the college of S. Alexandre (Belém) exceeded in "sumptuousness, magnificence ... and majesty" all of the other churches in the colony and compared favorably with the best in Europe.[66]

The cost of maintenance of the church was supposed to be defrayed by alms contributions but often became a burden on the college itself.[67] As the tables in this chapter suggest, however, the sums that the colleges expended in behalf of the faith were generally less than what they spent upon clothing. The college of Rachol constitutes an exception (see Table 24.4), but it was responsible for a score or so of parishes in the Salsete district. It may at first sight seem surprising that the level of alms contributions by Jesuit colleges was generally modest, but ecclesiastical entities were never known for being lavish with such expenditures. Snape, for example, estimated that in medieval England, the ratio of alms-giving to total income was about 5 percent. There were well-known French monasteries, such as Mont-Saint-Michel, whose records of alms contributions were even more modest than that. In medieval Portugal, the famous Alcobaça monastery expended only 2.3 percent of its income on alms. But it was not until the eighteenth century that the niggardliness of monastic charity became a significant source of ridicule by critics of the Church.[68]

63. Thompson, "French Jesuit Wealth on the Eve of the Eighteenth-Century Suppression," in Shiels and Wood, eds., *Church and Wealth*, 308.

64. Hubert Cieslik, S.J., "The Training of a Japanese Clergy in the Seventeenth Century," in J. Roggendorf, S.J., ed., *Studies in Japanese Culture* (Tokyo, 1963), 66. The estimates are given in terms of gold ducats, here assumed to be each about 1,000 rs.

65. *APO*:2, 4:2:2, 627.

66. Anonymous report on college of Recife, 1717, in ANTT, *Brasil*, 41, fol. 39, as noted in IHGB/MS, *lata* 6; Fr. Domingos de Araujo, "Chronica da companhia de Jesus da missão do Maranhão" (1720), in BNRJ, 11, 2, 7 (a nineteenth-century copy).

67. Visitor Fr. Luís da Gama informed Oliva that such a problem existed in Macao and that the annual maintenance cost of both facilities was 1.2 contos and was one of many reasons for the college's heavy indebtedness. Gama to Oliva, 20 Dec. 1664, in Hubert Jacobs, S.J., trans. and ed., *The Jesuit Makasar Documents* (Rome, 1988), 192.

68. R. H. Snape, *English Monastic Finances in the Later Middle Ages* (Cambridge, 1926), 116; Iria Gonçalves, *O património do mosteiro de Alcobaça nos séculos xiv e xv* (Lisbon, 1989), 323.

TABLE 24.7

Wages of Hired Workers, Évora, ca. 1606

(rs. per year)

Occupation	Yearly salary	Occupation	Yearly salary
Household servants	4,000–10,000	Cook's helper	4,000–5,000
Carter	9,000–10,000	Laundryman	6,000–7,000
Carter's assistant	6,000–7,000	Woodsplitter	7,000–8,000
Kiln minder	5,000–6,000	Miller	7,500–8,000
Chief gardener	8,000–9,000	Mule driver	7,000–7,500
Gardener's assistant	5,000–6,000	Estate guard	4,000
Carpenter	7,500–8,000	Steward	7,500–8,000
Pharmacist's assistant	5,500–6,000	Shepherd	2,500

SOURCE: "Varias lembranças" (see note 33), fols. 27^r and 34^r.

The upkeep of churches and colleges, especially in the tropics, was a continual problem because of rot, infestation, and damage by water and fire, as well as expanding needs for accommodations, library facilities, and the like. In the month of February 1725, for example, the professed house of Bom Jesús spent 323,380 rs. on materials and labor necessary for the construction of a new well. In 1749 the rector of Lisbon's Santo Antão acknowledged that he had expended 3.27 contos on upkeep, mostly to panel the college library with woods from Brazil, a practice very much in vogue in Joanine Portugal but one that was hardly in keeping with the spartan image projected by the early Society.[69]

The craftsmen and their assistants who toiled on such construction projects constituted part of the extensive work force that Jesuit houses regularly employed. The variety of employees and their wages at the Évora colleges in 1606 are indicated in Table 24.7. Even small colleges like that of Bragança hired an impressive number and variety of workers. Among them were three stewards, three cowboys, two shepherds, two cooks, a baker, a physician, a farrier, a wax chandler, a barber-surgeon, a washerman, a tailor, a shoemaker, a farm guard, a muleteer, a fisherman who doubled as baker's assistant, a butcher, a swineherd, a turkey keeper, a farm tenant, and an errand boy.[70] In Goa during the 1720s and 1730s, the professed house paid monthly wages to a laundryman, a surgeon-bleeder, an herbalist (*pandito*), a barber, a clocksetter, and unspecified house servants.[71] Although the college of Rachol possessed only eleven members in the 1720s, its auxiliary staff numbered between 29 and 32. It included three scribes, a chapelmaster, a pedagogue, a clothes master, a porter, a surgeon, an infirmarian, a tailor, four cooks, and a solicitor.[72] In the past, Jesuits themselves had discharged some of those duties.[73] Both the paneling of Santo Antão's library and Rachol's abundance of servants suggest ways in which the Society's standards relaxed and adjusted to changing times.

69. João Fernandes, S.J., "Not.^{a} do estado em q. achei e deixo o coll.^{o} de S^{to} Antão," 6 Feb. 1749, in BNL, *cx.* 26, 5, 8, no. 5.

70. Bivar Guerra, "A administração e contabilidade," 176 n. 1.

71. HAG 2098, covering the years 1724–36.

72. HAG 2048, fols. 76–77.

73. For further details concerning those who worked for the Jesuits, see Serafim Leite, S.J., *Artes e ofícios dos Jesuítas no Brasil (1549–1760)* (Rio de Janeiro, 1953), passim.

Most of the remaining categories in these tables warrant only brief comments. The sums expended for health care, for example, were usually well below the 10 percent level. Apparently, Bragança's health costs ballooned in the mid-1730s because that college then offered some sort of clinic to the public.

The amount spent on supplies was usually close to what was expended on health care. Like comparable secular establishments, Jesuit houses kept a wide variety of supplies on hand. They included continual supplies of firewood for cooking and sometimes heating, bedding, towels, articles of clothing, leather for shoemaking, candles, kettles and pots, china, tableware, tablecloths, cooking utensils and other sorts of equipment, lamps, portable bathtubs, and impressive stocks of paper and quills.[74]

Various writers have called attention to the fact that Jesuits traveled a lot in this period and that it was very costly to do so.[75] With certain qualifications, it is quite possible to agree with such observations. During the Middle Ages, land travel was markedly expensive.[76] Yet in early-seventeenth-century Portugal it was possible to travel by carriage from Coimbra to Évora for 200 to 300 rs. and from Faro to the Alentejo walled town for between 180 and 250 rs.[77] The accounts suggest that in the kingdom and in India, Jesuits often traveled over land by mule rather than by horse. In the subcontinent and elsewhere in the East, their use of litters and sedan chairs, condemned by the generals (Chapter 11), was no longer prevalent by the eighteenth century. When going on short trips, as between the college of Rachol and Goa, they usually proceeded by distinctive dugouts called baloons (balloons or *balões*).[78] Some Jesuits, especially priests concerned with administration, moved about a good deal, but brothers, like cooks and porters, rarely had that opportunity.

Since the distances covered were small, transport costs within the kingdom and from port to port within the province of Goa were not onerous. In 1730, for example, the travel expenses of a half dozen of the Goan colleges ranged between 1 percent and 5.7 percent per annum.[79] Long sea voyages represented considerable burdens for distant overseas provinces. Beginning with Xavier's departure from the Tagus, the crown provided partial subsidies for Jesuits sailing between Lisbon and Goa, but the Society's leaders frequently complained that the allowances were never sufficient. In 1576 the subsidy was 40,000 rs. per man, an amount raised to 44,000 rs. a decade later but reduced again to 40,000 rs. by the mid-1630s, despite advancing prices.[80] The expenses of such travel included not only the cost of the food, clothing, and miscellaneous articles mentioned above, but also the cost of persons to serve Jesuit voyagers. Initially the fathers, like most shipboard passengers, were obliged to cook for themselves unless the captain took pity upon them and provided a cook. By the 1750s

---

74. An excellent but very rare example of an inventory of supplies on hand is the certified transfer of the rectorate of New St. Paul's from Fr. Manoel Saraiva to Fr. António de Paiva on 31 Nov. 1707, in ARSI, *Goa*, 9:II, fols. 400–404ᵛ. The accounts cited in this chapter, of course, contain many entries concerning the acquisition of supplies of all sorts. See Appendix E.

75. E.g., H/SAG1: 85; Thompson, "French Jesuit Wealth," 309.

76. Cipolla, *Money, Prices, and Civilization*, chap. 5.

77. "Varias lembranças," fol. 58ᵛ (note 33 above).

78. *HJ*, 53.

79. AHU/PA/IN, *m.* 35.

80. *DI*, 9: 378; 14: 112; ARSI, *Goa*, 25, fols. 62–63.

TABLE 24.8

Comparative Expenditures by Four Contemporary Colleges, 1675–1700

Category	San Pablo 1675	Collège de l'Arc 1677–78	St. Germain des Prés 1679	Bragança 1699–1700
Food and clothing	66.4%	70.8%	22.5%	37.2%
Fabric	10.3	4.4	9.5	7.8
Supplies	—	—	4.5	3.3
Salaries and wages	—	—	—	5.1
Debt retirement	15.8	16.9	33.8[a]	—
Estates	—	—	22.2	8.3
Travel	1.3	3.7	1.7[b]	7.0
Litigation	—	1.5	—	—
Church	—	—	2.5	7.0
Alms	6.3	—	0.4	0.5
Health	—	—	2.2	1.1
Miscellaneous	—	2.7	0.5	22.5
Total	100.1	100.0	99.8	99.8

SOURCES: College of San Pablo (Lima): Cushner, *Lords*, 144. Collège de l'Arc (Department of Jura): *EJF*, 2: col. 148. St. Germain des Prés, Paris: Maarten Ultee, *The Abbey des Prés in the Seventeenth Century* (New Haven, 1981), 97. College of Bragança: ATC/CJ, cod. 33.

[a] Includes wages, rents, and other charges.

[b] Travel and legal expenses.

it had become customary for groups of Jesuits sailing to the East to employ a cook, a barber, and a bleeder.[81]

Surviving accounts suggest that the royal allowance covered less than half the actual expense of the long voyage to India.[82] The king also contributed to the expenses of Jesuits sailing from Goa to Japan via Malacca and Macao, but Valignano stated that the sums represented no more than the cost of clothing needed for the trip.[83] Even so, such contributions were unmatched for the Maranhão missions, where travel costs initially fell upon the older Brazil province.[84]

As observed in earlier chapters, Jesuits dispatched overseas sometimes returned to Europe either as procurators on the Society's business or because they had incurred the displeasure of the crown. Such trips were even more burdensome than outbound voyages, but, as noted earlier, the crown contributed nothing to defray their expense.[85]

81. HAG 2099.

82. E.g., the provisions alone for six fathers sent out from Lisbon in 1615–16 amounted to 580,987 rs., or 96,831 rs. per man, i.e., 41.3% of the allowance. The food costs of the next contingent, eight who sailed in 1616–17, were even higher, 113,307 rs. per man or 35.35% of the subsidy. "Livro da receita e despeza da provincia de Goa . . . de [1613 até 1624]," in ARSI, FG, 1443/9/16. HAG 1890 provides further examples of the cost of Lisbon-to-Goa voyages by Jesuits during the Philippine period.

83. The crown provided 6,000 rs. for voyages between Goa and Malacca and an equal amount for continuations from Malacca to Macao. *DI*, 14: 499.

84. "Comueniensiaz q. a missão teve em se comprar o barco," Maranhão, ca. 1693, in ARSI, *Bras.*, 9, fol. 389.

85. Provincial to viceroy, Goa, ca. 1636, in ARSI, *Goa*, 25, fols. 62–63. See "Rol da matolotagem que se dá a cada hum dos padres que vão pera o reino . . . janeiro de 1576," in *DI*, 10: 429–31. Procurators' trips within Europe could also incur heavy costs: travel and clothing expenses for one who went from Lisbon to Rome in 1616 amounted to 960,796 rs. "Livro da receita e despeza da provincia de Goa" (see note 82).

Also, haulage costs, generally overlooked, were at least as heavy for every college as was staff transportation. The accounts are replete with sums paid to those who brought the colleges foodstuffs, building materials, firewood, and other articles that they regularly required.

A question that easily arises at this point is whether the expenditures of colleges within this assistancy were unique to it or were, in fact, typical of Jesuit colleges elsewhere as well. Much more work needs to be done on the surviving accounts of other Jesuit colleges before one can offer firm judgments on such a question. However, Table 24.8 offers some comparisons for four ecclesiastical institutions at roughly the same time. Three were Jesuit colleges—Lima's San Pablo, Portugal's Bragança, and the college de l'Arc in the Department of Jura in southeast central France—and the fourth was a large Benedictine monastery in Paris. Though there are obvious differences in the percentage of expenditures for personal allowances and in some categories distinctive to a particular institution, there is also a substantial measure of comparability among many of the categories of expenditure.[86] But what the budgets for the non-Portuguese institutions do not include are items that represented considerable encumbrances for colleges in the Portuguese Assistancy, namely, shared financial expenses.

Parameters of Shared Costs

The Society of Jesus was intended to be an evolving enterprise consisting of interdependent, cooperative units. Sometimes it was and sometimes it was not. In theory each facility was responsible for its own income and expenditures, but in practice certain entities were heavily dependent upon others. Since each manager was obliged to be the ever-watchful guardian of the resources of his own house and was always convinced that his facility needed greater income than it possessed, managers often resented financial demands made upon them by other entities.

Those charged with maintaining Jesuit accounts operated on the principle of "no free lunch." That is, some house or province was charged for every expenditure made in behalf of a member affiliated with that institution. If, for example, a Jesuit and a companion traveled from their own college (college *A*) to another college (college *B*) and remained there for some days for reasons of health, spiritual needs, or business, college *B* debited college *A* for each day's lodgings and food provided for them.[87] If the Jesuit and/or his companion became ill during their sojourn in college *B*, the billing was reduced by one-half to reflect the days when the guests were unable to eat. In the event that a particular Jesuit stayed at college *B* while awaiting transportation to a new post, the latter would be billed for expenses incurred during his stay.[88]

86. There are other surviving budgets for several French colleges that demonstrate similar comparability; e.g., the college of Saint-Louis, Angoulême, in southwest France (1714), that of Fontenay-Le-Comte in Vendée in the southwest (1762), and that of Godrans, Dijon (Côte d'Or), in the central southeast (1763). *EJF*, 1: col. 269; 2: cols. 55–56 and 489.

87. If, however, the Jesuit was summoned from his station by the provincial, his expenses during his sojourn were paid out of the provincial procurate. Brolhas António Brandolini (provincial) to province of Goa, 21 Dec. 1740, in HAG 2092, fols. 23^r–24^r.

88. Order of Oliva, 24 June 1665, in H/SAG2: 84.

Certain colleges, notably those situated at maritime crossroads, provided dormitory facilities for a large number of Jesuits in transit from one place to another. That was especially true of Lisbon's Santo Antão, Brazil's Bahia and (especially during the eighteenth century) Rio de Janeiro, Mozambique, Goa's Bom Jesús, Malacca, and Macao. For centuries the residents of Santo Antão were accustomed to having a varying number of "guests" awaiting shipping to the overseas provinces or expecting transfers to other colleges within the kingdom.[89] In 1722, for example, 37 guests stayed there, most of them voluntarily, though Fr. Manuel Gomes was sent there from Setúbal "for his confinement." Their length of stay varied from a single day to as many as 134 days.[90] The college in Bahia served partly as a dormitory for members in transit to Maranhão or elsewhere within the State of Brazil, and both it and the college of Rio de Janeiro played host, sometimes for several months, to members journeying between the Orient or Angola and Europe.[91] Mozambique, Bom Jesús, Malacca, and Macao provided comparable services to those awaiting ships to carry them to their next destinations. Between 1616 and 1639, the badly overcrowded college of Macao put up a total of 1,358 members of the Society, most of them bound for assignments in Southeast Asia or China.[92]

The college of Santo Antão and the professed house in Goa were also the headquarters of the several procurators who, with their assistants and amanuensis, represented the overseas provinces. Except for bedding and laundry services, the procurator's expenses were charged to the province he served. What those charges ought to be frequently became sources of conflict between the provincial procurators and the house procurators.[93] Until the 1680s, procurators and their companions who were absent from their residences on inspection tours received a credit of 25 percent since they did not eat in their residences, but because of "difficult times and rising prices" the Visitor ordered that discount eliminated.[94]

The tours of inspection that Visitors and provincials undertook represented substantial expenses to the provinces they served. In 1587 Fr. Marçal Belliarte (b. ca. 1543–d. 1596) devoted a year to an examination of the Brazil province. His expenses, mostly supplies that he distributed to the various installations that he examined, amounted to 478,100 rs. Seven years later, Provincial Pero Rodrigues (b. 1542–d. 1628) and two companions conducted an

89. Initially Jesuits bound for the Spanish Indies were lodged in the college of San Hermenegildo in Seville. Later the Spanish Province established a 100-bed residence in Santa María, near Cadiz, as a domicile for Jesuits in transit to the New World, but the Province of Portugal never erected a comparable facility. Pedro Borges Moran, *El envio de misioneros a America durante la epoca español* (Salamanca, 1977), 385–87; and David Block, *Mission Culture on the Upper Amazon: Native Tradition, Jesuit Enterprise, and Secular Policy in Moxos, 1660–1880* (Lincoln, Neb., 1994), 111.

90. "Anno de 1722: Contas do prov.ᵒʳ com o coll.º de S.ᵗᵒ Antão," in ANTT/CJ/58, no. 49. The same bundle contains a series of such accounts from this date until 1750.

91. *HCJB*, 5: 100–101.

92. BA/JA/49-IV-66, no. 44.

93. E.g., anonymous memorandum entitled "Nam basta p.ª satisfazer ao gasto da porção quotidiana . . . q. se costuma pagar no collegio de S.ᵗᵒ Antam" (1678), in ARSI, *Lus.*, 78, fols. 80ʳ–90ᵛ; and Joseph de Paiva [proposal by procurator of Santo Antão to increase charges for guests, 16 Sept. 1711], in ARSI, *Lus.*, 77, fols. 62ʳ–69ʳ.

94. "Ordens que deixou o P. Visitador Alexandre Cicero visitando esta casa professa no anno [1]684," in ARSI, *Goa*, 35, fols. 297–98, par. 20.

inspection of the Society's colleges between Olinda and São Paulo and spent—mostly on alms and supplies—302,400 rs.[95]

There is one further example of expenditures by a Jesuit examiner in Brazil. At the end of 1681, Fr. Pedro de Pedrosa submitted a detailed report of what he had spent during a tour of the future vice-province of Maranhão. He included the cost of his passage, that of a companion, and that of several craftsmen who accompanied him, as well as the cost of horses, slaves, and other commodities that he took with him, altogether the impressive sum of 5,002,000 rs.[96]

Only two specimens of the accounts of a Visitor and a provincial who served in India seem to have survived. The first concerns the expenditures of Fr. Miguel de Amaral, Visitor of the province of Goa during a thirteen-month period beginning in March 1704. The principal items he listed for himself and his companion were transportation, alms and gifts, wages for those who served them, clothing, pay for a secretary, official documents, paper, and books. Fr. Amaral was clearly a heavy smoker, for he consumed a pound of tobacco a month, the total cost of which amounted to four months' worth of alms that he distributed. During those thirteen months Fr. Amaral expended nearly 357,000 rs. That, however, was about half of what his successor, Provincial Manoel Carvalho, spent during the first year of his administration (1705–6).[97]

Among the facilities that provincials and Visitors examined were the Society's missions. Their support initially became a charge upon the sponsoring college. Such was the case in the province of Brazil and the vice-province of Maranhão. As soon as possible, however, such missions were expected to become self-sustaining. In the eighteenth century, for example, those in the Amazon gathered spices and sent them downriver in order to purchase the spiritual and material goods they required (see Chapter 21). Elsewhere in Brazil, the aldeias produced livestock and barnyard animals and sold surpluses to defray their expenditures.

None of the missions in India, of which there were a half dozen in the eighteenth century, was ever able to meet its expenses by the sale of goods that it produced. All relied upon income supplied by villages whose tax revenues the Jesuits purchased for that purpose. When shortfalls existed, as in 1730, a half dozen of the colleges of the littoral made up the difference through assessments proportionate to their incomes.[98] Thanks to the legacy of D. Juliana Dias da Costa (see Chapter 14), the Agra mission was by far the most securely funded, but that security disappeared as a result of the Maratha conquests of the northern province. Their successes also imperiled the funding of Jesuit missions in the Sund, Mysore, and elsewhere.

Such contributions to the missions and the finta assessments mentioned in Chapter 12 are but two examples of the practice of sharing financial burdens within the Society. As noted earlier, when the overseas provinces sent procurators to Lisbon and Rome, each college assisted in defraying its representative's expenses. The colleges also jointly bore the

95. Marçal Belliarte, "O q' gastei parte como os collegios, parte com pessoas de fora necessitados" (1587), and visitation expenses of Fr. Rodrigues, 9 Dec. 1594, in ARSI, *Bras.*, 3:II, 358ʳ–358ᵛ.

96. "Carta corrente do Pᵉ Pedro de Pedrosa com a missam," 30 Dec. 1681, in ARSI, *Bras.*, 26, fol. 93ʳ–93ᵛ.

97. ARSI, *Goa*, 9:II, fols. 378–81ᵛ.

98. Viceroy to king, 23 Jan. 1731, in AHU/PA/IN, *m.* 35.

expenses of the missions' procurators who resided in Lisbon (see Chapter 12). During the Philippine period, the Assistancy maintained a special procurator at the Spanish court to represent its interests. The province of Portugal paid half his expenses, the Indian provinces contributed two-sixths, and Brazil provided one-sixth, but the Far Eastern provinces paid nothing.[99]

Initially, external units of the Society were not required to contribute to the maintenance of the father general or his secretariat.[100] By 1564, however, it was evident that the Society's business in Rome warranted the creation of the office of procurator-general, and Father General Laínez directed that each province contribute to its expenses.[101] Each component also contributed to the expenses of the office of the assistant to the father general.[102]

One of the common bonds of the Society was the joy its members felt when the papacy recognized the exceptional spiritual contributions of certain of their illustrious companions. The promotion of such causes in the bureaucratic labyrinth of the Roman curia was extremely time-consuming and expensive. During the seventeenth century, for example, the missions' procurator of the eastern provinces in Lisbon spent as much as 23.4 percent of his resources to promote the canonization of Francis Xavier.[103] Not only the province of Brazil but also the Far East provinces supplied moneys in support of the cause of Brazil's Forty Martyrs (1570) and the beatification of José de Anchieta.[104]

Though Jesuit leaders did not oppose sending money to Rome to meet these obligations, they were also acutely aware that the Iberian crowns viewed such activities with dark suspicion and that there were circumstances in which it was unwise, even dangerous, to attempt to remit funds to the Eternal City. Thus, at the beginning of the seventeenth century, when Aquaviva appealed to the province of Portugal for alms to support the professed house (known as the Gesù) in Rome, the provincial delicately declined to comply. As he explained to the assistant general, there were several reasons why such contributions could not be made. First, the Spanish crown was always suspicious when ecclesiastical funds were sent out of the realm and insisted that approval be granted before any such transaction occurred. Second, if the king discovered that the province had sufficient revenues to afford such a contribution, he was likely to reduce the crown's subsidies to the Society. Because many of the newer colleges were far from self-supporting, the provincial insisted that such subsidies were still vital. Third, compliance would establish an uncertain precedent: who could anticipate what financial demands future generals might make for the support of the Gesù or for other purposes? He added that his views were shared by his consultores and by other experienced members of his province.[105] Aquaviva's response, if any, remains

99. "Varias lembranças," fol. 102ᵛ (see note 33 above).

100. *DI*, 14: 510 n. 208.

101. *MB*, 4: 116–20, 346–47, 347 n. 1; *DI*, 7: 11 n. 1. The accounts of the missions' procurator in Lisbon for the eastern provinces between 1613 and 1626 show regular payments to the office of the procurator-general for the processing of legal papers. ARSI, FG, 1443/9/16.

102. The oft-cited "Livro da fazenda ou noticia das rendas e obrigações das provincias da assistencia de Portugal ... anno 1730," in ARSI, FG, 627/B, is fundamental for an understanding of the precarious funding for this position.

103. See note 101.

104. "O dinheiro que deve vice provincia da China a prov.ᵃ de Japam" (1659), in BA/JA/49-V-11, no. 76, fol. 508; ARSI, *Bras.*, 11:II, 465–70ᵛ (entries for 1707 and 1713).

105. João Correa to João Alvares (assistant general), Porto, 16 July 1602, in ARSI, *Lus.*, 74, fols. 15–16.

unknown. There is no record in the files of this assistancy of further solicitations by the generals for the support of the Gesù. The Portuguese crown's reaction to the quindénio remittances a century later demonstrates that the provincial's concerns were not ill founded (see Chapter 23).

Despite the provincial's negative response to Aquaviva's solicitation, he may well have wanted to aid the financially strapped Gesù. Within all the assistancies, the spiritual and intellectual welfare of members was always a vital concern and one of the shared fiscal burdens of each college. Each was expected to contribute to the incomes of novitiates, probationary houses, and the institutions that were best equipped to provide advanced training. In 1589, for example, Aquaviva ruled that if a bequest for the establishment of the probationary house in Goa proved insufficient, each college and residence would render financial aid according to its means. Similarly, when it was discovered that the income left by Domingo Afonso Sertão was inadequate to cover the costs of the novitiate of Jiquitaia, situated outside of Salvador and opened in 1728, each college in the province of Brazil, save that of Rio de Janeiro, provided it with financial aid.[106] And, as mentioned in the previous chapter, when a novitiate was created in Lisbon to prepare candidates to serve in India, the colleges of Goa province shared its expenses.

Upon occasion there were complaints that constituent units were delinquent in rendering such payments, or that they had declined to honor their obligations altogether. That was true during the turbulent 1630s, for example, when the superior of the Lisbon novitiate reported that it had substantial debts, partly because of the failure of the Atlantic island colleges to send their contributions. And during the same decade, the rector of Santo Antão made a similar complaint about sums that the far better financed arts college of Coimbra owed it.[107]

Normally such issues were quickly resolved without the need for the Roman headquarters' intervention. However, that was not the case with a dispute between the rector of New St. Paul's college in Goa and the Far Eastern provinces at the end of the seventeenth century. At the time, the Goan institution had recently experienced two severe financial jolts, both discussed elsewhere. The first was the seizure of its Bombay properties by agents of the East India Company; the second was a devastating typhoon that destroyed its Bandorá estate. Since those properties contributed about a quarter of the college's income, its superior appealed to other institutions within the province, especially the college of Rachol, to provide relief. In 1694 the rector informed the local procurator of the Far Eastern provinces that although New St. Paul's college had always trained novices for the eastern provinces gratis, because of its financial plight it could no longer afford to do so. He therefore asked each province to furnish subventions. The rector also advised the general of his request and justified it by stating that he and his consultores deemed it inappropriate for the college to continue to expend its patrimony in support of the "subjects of other provinces" and that the other colleges within Goa province shared their conviction.

As might be expected, the provincials of the always precariously financed eastern provinces protested vigorously. The provincial of Japan submitted a surprisingly emotional

106. *DI*, 15: 248; *HCJB*, 5: 141–48.
107. ARSI, *Lus.*, 44:II, fols. 512–18^v; 74, fols. 261^r–261^v.

memorandum to a Jesuit adjudicator in Rome in which he observed that Xavier had founded the original St. Paul's "especially for the Japan missions," that New St. Paul's was intended to be the "common seminar" of all the eastern missions, that the eastern provinces had never been billed for the training of their students, and that to demand payment now would be to deprive the college's own "sons" of their bread and to compel them to die of hunger. In a supporting statement, the Far Eastern provinces' procurator in Rome effectively demonstrated that their income was vastly inferior to that of the colleges in Goa province. In the end, the general, Tirso Gonzalez de Santalla, sided with the Far Eastern provinces' position.[108]

Since it was the responsibility of each administrator to defend what he and his advisors considered to be the legitimate concerns of his constituency, the existence of such disputes is not surprising. But their occurrence ought not obscure the evidence of financial cooperation that took place in times of emergency both within and even without the Portuguese Assistancy. One instance discussed elsewhere is the response of the brother colleges in Portugal to Santo Antão's distress over the defaulted Aveiro loan (see Chapter 22).[109] Another was the decision of Simão de Vasconcelos, rector of the college of Rio de Janeiro, and presumably his consultores, to use surplus funds of his college to pay the debts of less-affluent colleges in the province during the critical mid-1640s.[110] Later during the same century, when the college of Recife was founded (1678), the nearby college of Olinda annually contributed nearly 3,000 kilograms of sugar for its support, and when the casa of Maranhão was upgraded and became a college, the college of Pará supplied 600,000 rs. toward its increased expenses.[111] And in seventeenth-century India, when the Dutch devastated the Malabar province, the brother province of Goa provided asylum and financial aid for its refugees (Chapter 8).

In 1587 Fr. Amador Rebêlo, procurator for the overseas provinces, suggested to Aquaviva that he and his successors ought to have the freedom to use the funds of one province to fill urgent needs of another.[112] Though such authority was never conceded, the proximity of brother provinces (Japan and China, Goa and Malabar, Brazil and Maranhão), especially during critical times, made fiscal cooperation inevitable. Still, in the case of Japan and China, that did not prevent vitriolic disagreements over who should pay what.[113]

108. Provincial, Japan, to Cardinal Barbonier, prefect, [1701], in BA/JA/49-V-24, no. 14[A]; Jacobus Vidal to Gonzalez de Santalla, professed house, Rome, 11 Feb. 1702, in ARSI, *JapSin*, 23, fol. 251; ARSI, *Goa*, 36:I, fols. 27r–27v, 36r, 56r–57v, and 84r–88v.

109. A student of the French Assistancy contends that "the provincial ... could not apply the revenues of one college to the debts of another [but] he might instruct [his] procurator ... to make payments to colleges if the general funds of the province ... would permit." Thompson, "French Jesuit Wealth," 309. The reprimand issued by Vitelleschi to the provincial of Goa for ordering his colleges to contribute moneys to the professed house of that city would seem to bear out Professor Thompson. See H/SAG1: 330. Nevertheless, provincials evidently could persuade better-off colleges to assist distressed brothers, as the Aveiro case indicates.

110. Vasconcelos to Vicente Carafa, Rio de Janeiro, 6 July 1646, in ARSI, *Bras.*, 3:I, fol. 248.

111. *HCJB*, 5: 462; 4: 178.

112. Rebêlo to Aquaviva, 18 July 1587, in *DI*, 14: 623ff.

113. E.g., António Francisco Cardim, the mordacious procurator of the Japan province, once accused the members of the vice-province of China of being lazy, dishonest, and bent upon stealing his province's college of Macao. "Informação sobre a pretenção dos p.es da China em destruir a prov.a de Jappam," Lisbon, 3 Oct. 1648, in ARSI, FG, 721/II/6.

In rare instances, provinces of one assistancy provided urgently needed financial help to elements of another assistancy. The vice-province of China provides examples of such aid. In the late 1690s, the procurator of that vice-province wrote Pedro II stating that his colleagues faced severe financial problems and appealed for assistance. The king, in turn, asked the viceroy of India what the Goan exchequer could contribute. His lieutenant replied that the cupboard was bare. The vice-province also tried elsewhere and received alms from as far away as Manila and even New Spain.[114] The famous Lavalette debacle, which contributed to the decision to expel the Jesuits from French realms, offers a further example, for the English province provided a substantial portion of the money the unfortunate French procurator borrowed.[115] What happened to the French might easily have befallen other branches of the Society, including many units within the Portuguese Assistancy, for the burden of debt was an all-too-common experience.

The Persistent Preoccupation with Debts

Pierre Delattre, editor of a major compilation of studies concerning Jesuit colleges in France, entitled one subsection "Richesse apparente; misère endémique." That designation was appropriate, suggesting that a college that appeared to outsiders to be extremely wealthy was, in fact, burdened by its continual indebtedness.[116] Depending upon the place and period, the same was often true within the Portuguese Assistancy; but such a condition was hardly limited to Jesuit establishments.

Among religious houses, indebtedness had long been an unwanted, sinister companion. According to C. H. Lawrence, "Monastic indebtedness is a recurrent theme of the chronicles and visitation records of the thirteenth century."[117] In the Portuguese Assistancy, as elsewhere, there were many causes of such indebtedness, some of them evident to contemporaries, others not. They included the costs of initial construction, later additions, and repairs to infrastructure; these costs were only partly covered by subventions from either the crown or private donors. Crop failures, dismal markets, and unsuccessful investments also contributed their share of fiscal adversities. Throughout much of the period, the Society's entities sustained substantial property losses on land and sea as consequences of military or naval operations or of natural calamities, notably storms and fires. Shortfalls in expected income from the crown, the papacy, or private benefactors as well as "bad debts" (defaults by private borrowers in loan payments or by purchasers of commodities sold by Jesuit facilities) were among the other causes. Ironically, so were the Jesuits' very successes, for colleges, especially during the late sixteenth century, often grew in personnel

---

114. King to viceroy, 22 Mar. 1697, and response dated 2 Feb. 1698, in HAG/*LM* 61, fol. 91ʳ; "Contas da v. prov.ᵃ começada ao 1° de julho de 1690 athe fim de julho de 1691," in ARSI, *JapSin*, 23, fols. 170–71; "Ratio eorum ... v. provinciae sinensis [1730]," in ibid., 134, fols. 426ʳ–426ᵛ; and "Estado de todas as rendas da v. provincia da China em 1731," in ARSI, FG, 627. Manila's contributions varied from 42,000 to 1,000,000 rs., whereas New Spain's amounted to 400,000 rs.

115. Geoffrey Holt, S.J., "The Fatal Mortgage: The English Province and Père La Valette," *AHSI* 38 (July–Dec. 1969): 464–78. See also Chapter 22.

116. *EJF*, 2: col. 1399.

117. C. H. Lawrence, *Medieval Monasticism: Forms of Religious Life in Western Europe in the Middle Ages* (New York, 1984), 113.

and in students more rapidly than did their sources of income. Although surviving accounts disclose little evidence of mismanagement, it may have been a contributory factor; Jesuit superiors, however, more commonly charged their colleagues with being incautious spendthrifts.[118] That charge may well have been unfounded, and, at least in the case of the expenses of procurators in Lisbon and Rome, more likely reflected the consequences of inflationary spirals of which Jesuit functionaries posted in distant overseas headquarters were simply unaware.[119]

It needs to be remembered that the Society's accountants, like those of the crown, distinguished between debts owed by their house to private contractors or to other Jesuit establishments and moneys due their house from others.[120] Within the Assistancy, the former generally outweighed the latter by a large margin. In their periodic summaries, Jesuit record-keepers also defined as debt a negative balance between income and outlays. Their superiors were as troubled by what may have been temporary shortfalls as they were by less tractable burdens.

The debt burden of the Peninsular province can be traced from 1599, when it stood at 5.7 contos. Four years later it had grown to 15.3 contos; by 1614 it rose to 20.1 contos. It peaked for the Philippine period in 1628 at 26.8 contos but diminished to 22.5 contos five years later. That load became much heavier during the Restoration, reaching 71.6 contos (1649) before gradually falling to 39.5 contos (1678), when seven units reported substantial encumbrances. Thereafter, however, most of the colleges declared themselves debt-free.[121] By 1690 only Santo Antão, Évora, and Faro reported debts; they totaled 28.9 contos, an amount reduced to 23.2 contos by 1700. The downward trend of the Peninsular colleges' indebtedness continued during most of the Joanine years, reaching a low point of 11 contos in 1737 before more than doubling to 36.3 contos in 1749.[122]

There is evidence that the debt problems of the province of Brazil began during the Philippine period. In 1575 the college of Bahia was debt-free; eight years later it owed creditors 1.1 contos. By 1593 its debts had risen to 2 contos, and by 1604 they stood at 8 contos, a 300 percent increase in scarcely more than a decade. Similarly, the new college of Rio de Janeiro had no obligations in the 1570s, but its burdens had reached 2 contos by the beginning of the seventeenth century. Significantly, by 1604 the crown's arrears to those colleges amounted to 6.8 contos.[123]

118. For examples of such mismanagement, see Konrad, *Jesuit Hacienda*, 77–78, and 97n. I know of no comparable cases in the Portuguese Assistancy.

119. That would seem to be the basis for the criticisms of such procurators expressed in the Chorão meeting's complaints of 1575, as well as those of Fr. Jerónimo Xavier (provost) to Aquaviva, Goa, 12 Nov. 1593, and Fr. Francisco Fernández to Aquaviva, Goa, 7 Nov. 1594, in *DI*, 10: 246 and 16: 248, 759–60; and Emanuel de Almeida (rector) to Vitelleschi, Goa, 12 Sept. 1638, in ARSI, *Goa*, 22, fols. 136ʳ–137ʳ. Fr. Almeida confessed that neither he nor his colleagues could imagine how their Lisbon procurator could spend so much money and incur so many debts.

120. Cf. Thompson, "French Jesuit Wealth," 310, for a different sort of distinction.

121. One conspicuous example: the college of Angra, which reported in 1669 that it owed no debts and announced with evident pride in 1693 that it was so committed to the avoidance of encumbrances that it did not owe a single real. ARSI, *Lus.*, 75, fols. 121 and 271.

122. The foregoing is based upon analyses of the third catalogues in ARSI, *Lus.*, 44:I and II, 45, 46, 47, and 48.

123. *HCJB*, 1: 127 n. 1.

We possess only fragmentary evidence concerning the Brazilian province's debt load during the seventeenth century. In 1631, at the beginning of the Dutch invasions, the debts of the three colleges in the province reached 16.4 contos.[124] Soon after, when the Dutch took over the college of Olinda and its properties, losses must have been substantial, but no record of them has surfaced. As observed above, in the mid-1640s the rector of Rio de Janeiro reported that his college had paid the debts of the other Jesuit installations within the province, but he did not indicate the sums involved.

As far as the colleges of the Brazil province were concerned, the Golden Age was far from lustrous. Indeed, every fiscal summary sent to Rome indicates that their debt load increased steadily between 1694 (13.5 contos) and 1739 (94.7 contos)—significantly, years when they were expanding the production of cane sugar and when slave prices were ascending at an alarming rate. Thereafter, however, the colleges' administrators succeeded in erasing much of that massive burden, which diminished to 32.2 contos in 1757. Although eight established colleges and the incipient college of Paraná reported themselves to be indebted in 1739, only four institutions disclosed significant obligations eighteen years later.[125]

The colleges in the East never experienced debt loads as great as those in the western provinces, but most of them never enjoyed comparable resources either. The fragmentary evidence that remains suggests that both the Japan province and the fiscally much weaker vice-province of China were almost hopelessly in debt throughout the seventeenth and eighteenth centuries.[126] For much of the seventeenth century, the Japan province's principal debtor was its brother, the vice-province of China. Between 1618 and 1656, the cumulative debts of the vice-province to the Japan province reached more than 10 contos, or more than twice the Japan province's annual income.[127] In 1730, the last year for which data are available, the expenses of the vice-province exceeded its income by a ratio of nearly 6 to 1.[128]

The colleges of the province of Goa, which possessed far more abundant and certain sources of income than did the eastern provinces, were rarely in as precarious shape as those of the Far East. Xavier himself was very much concerned about indebtedness. On more than one occasion, he urged his lieutenants to be thrifty, to remember that whatever they spent in Goa meant less for missionaries in the field, and to avoid undertaking any new construction until existing structures had been paid for.[129] Before long, however, the number of recruits and students to be accommodated made it necessary to violate Xavier's injunction.

By the mid-1570s, the Goan college's obligations had reached an alarming 8.5 contos, and the Chorão assembly desperately sought ways of lightening that burden, including

124. "Catalogus tertius rerum provincia Brasilia," Aug. 1631, in ARSI, *Bras.*, 5:I, fols. 144ʳ–145ʳ.

125. Third catalogues, 1694, 1701, 1707, 1722, 1736, 1739, 1743, and 1757, in ARSI, *Bras.*, 5:II and 6:I and II.

126. As indicated elsewhere, some of these accounts are published in *MHJ*, such as those for 1609 (537–39), 1624 (969), and 1654 (1026–28); others are scattered in ARSI, *JapSin*, 23; *Goa*, 35, 36:1; FG, 721/II/6 and 722/16; BA/JA/49-V-27, no. 197, and 49-V-28, nos. 107 and [130]; and AHU/PA/IN, *m.* 46.

127. BA/JA/49-V-11, nos. 76 and 77. Most of the bills were for shared transportation and freight expenses between Goa and Macao, temporary housing (notably, 667,800 rs. to cover the cost of nine missionaries who wintered in Mozambique), the rescue of prisoners (e.g., 176,880 rs. expended to ransom four fathers and two brothers captured by the Dutch), cloth, books, and incidentals.

128. AHU/PA/IN, *m.* 46.

129. S/*FX*, 4: 481–82 and 534–35.

restricting the number of novices that the college might admit, imposing strict economies in the operation of the college, and directing that the Lisbon missions' procurator make no extraordinary commitments on behalf of the province without specific license.[130] But the debt problem continued throughout the 1580s and early 1590s, not only for São Paulo but also for the colleges of Cochin and Bassein, each of which reported "heavy" obligations ranging between 1.2 and 1.8 contos. Administrators wrote their superiors in despair, stating that their institutions were "very poor" and that no easy remedy was in sight.[131]

Despite such despair, remedies were somehow gradually discovered. By the end of the century, only two of the province's institutions disclosed debts, amounting to only 600,000 rs. Except for 1614, when the province mysteriously disclosed an unexplained obligation of 22.2 contos, which later was somehow miraculously liquidated, and despite the intensification of maritime warfare, most of the colleges in the province appear to have managed to live within their means throughout the seventeenth century. Only three colleges reported debts, totaling 5.3 contos, in 1627; five admitted 5.7 contos in 1653. During most of the second half of the century, the province's economic reports are silent on the existence of debts. With two exceptions, the catalogues for 1713 and 1741, the same is true of the eighteenth-century series. But the latter provides evidence of the catastrophic losses in the northern province. Some colleges failed to show any income at all, and five other institutions identified burdens amounting to 8.2 contos, higher than at any time since the 1590s. The 1741 catalogue would be the last of the long series sent from Goa to Rome, but there is no indication that the finances of the province ever improved thereafter.[132]

As is evident from this analysis, the custodians of Jesuit houses experienced the same types of financial demand that beset administrators of other religious bodies as well as rulers and subjects in the lands where the Society functioned. Most of the funds the Jesuits earned went for the customary essentials—food, clothing, and shelter—although the very nature of the Society necessitated expenditures in behalf of its causes in Rome, its missions, its churches, its schools, and its other facilities, as well as the shifting of its personnel. Though incomes generally increased over time, such gains were offset by currency devaluations and by rising expenditures. Some types of expenditure sanctioned during the eighteenth century would have prompted severe scolding by the generals and other senior officials at earlier times. Such disbursements included the relentless acquisition of African slaves for the Brazilian plantations (see Chapter 20), the lavish use of house servants in colleges like Rachol, the sumptuous ornamentation of churches and libraries in the kingdom and overseas, and the efforts of some overseas houses to import European delicacies for their tables.

Whether or not one agrees with Fr. Leite that none of these sorts of expenditure was intended to benefit individual Jesuits, the question that inevitably recurs is whether such outlays constituted serious violations of the Society's commitment to personal poverty. Contemporaries were divided on that question, and modern scholars are as well. Thirty years ago François Chevalier, a distinguished French scholar, insisted that the large sums

130. *DI*, 10: 246 and 419.
131. Ibid., 12: 200, 222, 232, 491; 15: 54, 431, 588, 632, 724, 727–28; 16: 208, 248, and 872.
132. The foregoing is based largely upon the series of third catalogues in ARSI, *Goa*, 24:II, 25, and 26.

that the Society acquired in colonial Mexico "were spent, not on individuals, but on the betterment of the order."[133]   Like Chevalier, Serafim Leite, doyen of Jesuit scholars concerned with colonial Brazil, always maintained that a distinction must be made between the persistent adherence to poverty by individual Jesuits and the apparent affluence of certain of their houses.[134] Leite's colleague, Fr. Ernest J. Burrus, among the most respected scholars studying the Jesuits in colonial Mexico, went even further and insisted that in both Spanish America and the Philippines, the Jesuits survived with "a standard of living that not one of their critics would have dared attempt to share."[135]

But such defenses of the Society do not always persuade its modern critics, who seem convinced that, as some contemporaries of an earlier age never tired of saying, the Jesuits somehow enjoyed far more wealth and a better quality of life than they ought to have in conformity with their *Constitutions*. To cite but two examples of such critics, A. Lynn Martin, author of a recent study that purports to reveal "the Jesuit mind" in sixteenth-century France, repeatedly contends that Jesuits "indulged themselves" in the kinds of construction they erected as well as in the quality of the food they consumed and even the cloth they wore.[136] At no point does Martin define precisely what he means by the verb "indulge" (Lat. *indulgere*: to be kind to, to yield, to give way to, to gratify one's tastes or desires) or by what objective standard his Jesuits are to be measured. Nicholas P. Cushner, himself a former Jesuit, maintains that in Spanish America, the Society owned and developed far more property than was needed for the maintenance of its members. One presumes that he also means the maintenance of their students and/or neophytes. Still, Cushner is never very precise about how many material possessions the Jesuits ought to have retained for their needs, since he does not systematically examine how they spent the income they gained.

To be fair to Cushner, he does cite several leading Jesuits of the seventeenth and eighteenth centuries, who complained that some Jesuits in Paraguay were engaging in forbidden economic behavior and were guilty of vain ostentation.[137] No doubt such concerns were sincerely expressed, and they may have been valid with respect to the Paraguayan enterprise. Even so, that would not substantiate assertions by contemporaries and later writers that most Jesuits in most parts of the world, including the Portuguese Assistancy, violated their absolute vow of poverty once, often, or always. There is, in fact, no evidence, in the Portuguese Assistancy at least, that they ever did so.

As Fr. Burrus contended, the standard of living of members of the Order was both absolutely and relatively modest. True, Jesuits did not endure as spartan an existence as, for example, the Carthusians did, but neither their *Constitutions* nor the succession of popes whom they served ever required them to do so. Beyond question, individual Jesuits survived on far less income than did most of their equally visible contemporaries. During the early 1590s, Robert Tofte, a London-born, Oxford-educated sometime poet, sojourned in Rome, where in the space of under four years he witnessed the coming and going of no less than

133. François Chevalier, *Land and Society in Colonial Mexico: The Great Hacienda*, trans. Alvin Eustis, ed. Lesley Byrd Simpson (Berkeley, 1966), 242.

134. E.g., *HCJB*, 1: 107–10.

135. Burrus, "A Diary of Exiled Philippine Jesuits," *AHSI* 20 (1951): 275.

136. Martin, *Jesuit Mind*, 39, 146, 148, and 157.

137. Cushner, *Lords*, 6; and idem, *Jesuit Ranches*, 151–52.

TABLE 24.9
Selected Salaries of Ecclesiastical and Imperial Officials, 1549–1750s

(000 rs.)

Office	Date	Amount	Office	Date	Amount
Portugal			Treasurer/Maranhão	1751	350
Archbishop/Braga	1606	22,000	Chief Judge/Maranhão	1751	400
Archbishop/Évora	1606	20,800	Viceroy	1750s	4,800
Archbishop/Lisbon	1606	20,000	Desembargador/High Court	1750s	600
Bishop/Coimbra	1606	16,400	District Magistrate (*ouvidor*)	1750s	400
Archbishop/Porto	1606	6,000	Crown Judge (*juiz de fóra*)	1750s	200
Dean/Évora	1606	2,600	Treasury Superintendent	1750s	400
Canons/Évora	1606	350–700	Chief of Customs/Bahia	1750s	400
Councilor, Overseas Council	1664	50	Archbishop/Bahia	1750s	2,400
Brazil			Dean of Cathedral/Bahia	1750s	400
Governor	1549	400	Canon of Cathedral/Bahia	1750s	250
Treasurer	1549	200	India		
Chief Judge	1549	200	Viceroy	1584	7,340
Bishop	1551	200	Archbishop	1584	1,600
Dean of Cathedral/Salvador	1608	120	Chief Inquisitor	1584	400
Canon	1608	40	Captain of the City/Goa	1584	600
Vicar/Rio de Janeiro	1608	50	Chancellor	1584	300
Governor/Rio de Janeiro	1616	2,000	Captain/Malacca	1584	200
Bishop/Rio de Janeiro	1616	1,200	Archbishop	1605	3,600
Vicar/Rio de Janeiro	1616	74	Viceroy	1605	7,200
Coadjutor/Maranhão	1616	25	Desembargador/High Court	1605	400
Bishop/Rio de Janeiro	1681	800	Viceroy	1630s	7,339
Dean of Cathedral/Rio de Janeiro	1681	100	Desembargador	1630s	414
Canon of Cathedral/Rio de Janeiro	1681	60	Captain of the City/Goa	1630s	600
Bishop/Rio de Janeiro	1702	1,000	Treasury Superintendent	1630s	200
Archbishop/Bahia	1717	1,910	Keeper of the Archives	1630s	90
Treasurer/Rio Grande do Norte	1717	120	Viceroy	1690	7,340
Bishop/Pará	1724	800	Archbishop	1690	3,600
Bishop/Maranhão	1724	800	Treasury Solicitor	1690	400
Archbishop/Bahia	1725	1,600	Treasury Inspector	1690	320
Governor/Pernambuco	1727	2,800	Viceroy	1737	7,819
Treasurer/Pernambuco	1727	350	Archbishop	1737	3,600
Chief Judge/Pernambuco	1727	300	Treasury Superintendent	1737	800
Bishop/Pará	1751	1,400	Desembargadors/High Court	1737	475–528
Governor/Pará	1751	1,600	Captain/Goa	1737	711
Bishop/Maranhão	1751	500	Magistrate/Goa	1737	100
Governor/Maranhão	1751	400			

SOURCES: Portugal, 1606: "Varias lembranças" (see note 33); 1664: Ignácio Accioli de Cerqueira e Silva, *Memórias históricas e políticas da Bahia*, 6 vols. (Bahia, 1925), 2: 113. Brazil, 1549, 1551: *DH*, 35: 4, 9, 24, 25; 1608: ibid., 78: 338–43; 1616: *ABNRJ* 27 (1906): 351–76; 1681: ANRJ, col. 63/1/16ᵛ; 1702 (Bishop/Rio de Janeiro): APB/OR/11/29; 1717, 1724, 1725: AHU/LR, 1276; 1727: *ABNRJ* 28 (1908): 314–27; 1751: AHU/LR, 485, fols. 241ʳ, 296ʳ–304ʳ; 1750s: José António Caldas, *Notícia geral de toda esta capitania da Bahia desde o seu descobrimento atê o presente ano de 1759* (fasc. ed., Salvador, 1951), 205 and 25. India, 1584: Duarte de Meneses, "The Receipt of Revenues of the State of India," in Samuel Purchas, *Hakluytus Postumus, or Purchas, His Pilgrimes*, vol. 9 (Glasgow, 1905), 160–90; 1605: Luiz de Figueiredo Falcão, comp., *Livro em que se contem toda a fazenda . . . dos reynos de Portugal, India, ilhas adjacentes . . . 1607* (Lisbon, 1859); 1630s: *APO*:2, 4:2:224ff.; 1690: HAG/*LM* 54, fols. 24ʳ–49ᵛ; 1737: AHU/PA/IN, *cx.* 40, no. 37.

five popes and observed the behavior of 60 cardinals who resided in the city. According to his report to the bishop of London, ten cardinals enjoyed incomes that in Portuguese equivalencies ranged between 5 and 10 contos a year; another ten possessed annual incomes between 10 and 20 contos; fourteen made do on 20 to 30 contos; seven received between 40 and 50 contos; and eight enjoyed between 50 and more than 100 contos per year.[138]

It is interesting to compare such staggering incomes with the yearly allowances of individual Jesuits in the Portuguese Assistancy, summarized in Table 24.6. And it is likewise revealing to compare those allowances with the authorized salaries of various ecclesiastical and secular officials who served in the Portuguese world during the period of this study (see Table 24.9). But Table 24.9 only identifies the sanctioned incomes of such officials, many of whom were accustomed to exact rake-offs that far exceeded their legitimate sources of income. There can scarcely be any doubt that every one of these officials, like the Church's leadership in Rome, enjoyed a vastly higher income than did a single Jesuit or, indeed, a house full of Jesuits. In sum, the notion that Jesuits in this assistancy fled from the embraces of the virtuous Lady Poverty to the seductive arms of that vile, base slut called Materialism is unsupported by any available evidence. To the best of their abilities, the Jesuits served only one master. It was not the devil.

138. Robert C. Melzi, ed., *Robert Tofte's "Discourse" to the Bishop of London* (Geneva, 1989), [xiii], xxxv–xxxvi.

CHAPTER 25

An Enterprise with a Rich Past but an Uncertain Future

The Company originated in extravagance and madness: in its progress it was supported and aggrandized by fraud and falsehood; and its history is stained by actions of the darkest die.

—Robert Southey, *A History of Brazil*

Whatever the human failings of the sons of Loyola . . . the impartial historian is bound to admit with Protestant Peter Mundy: "And to speak truly, they neither spared cost nor labour, diligence nor danger to attain their purpose": *Ad majorem Dei gloriam.*

—C. R. Boxer, *The Church Militant and Iberian Expansion, 1440–1770*

THE CENTURY THAT began with Portuguese probes approaching the Indian Ocean in the 1480s and concluded with the establishment of the dual Iberian empires and with Spain's abortive effort to recatholicize England was an extraordinary time in European and indeed global history. It witnessed the culmination of more than half a century of efforts to link by sea most of the world's continents, including the previously unknown Americas. Effective linkages led inevitably to conquest and to the beginning of Europeans' efforts to dominate the globe with their technology, institutions, and faith, and to exploit the non-European world's human, mineral, and plant wealth.[1] That century witnessed the flourishing of the High Renaissance, but it also saw the emergence of powerful Protestant alternatives to traditional Catholicism. The papacy's responses to those threats included the deliberations and seminal reforms enacted by one of the great Church conclaves, the Council of Trent, and the sanctioning of new religious Orders. The Society of Jesus became the most aggressive, prominent, popular, and polemical among them. From its inception to the present, no agency of the Church has aroused such contrary sentiments as that Order.

Starting without a fixed agenda, the Society's organizers eagerly and pragmatically accepted the spiritual, confessional, and educational challenges offered them with an abundance of confidence and conviction that their subjects' spiritual preparation, their zeal, and their devotion to their leader, to Jesus Christ, and to His terrestrial vicars, the supreme pontiffs, would assure them of victory over their opponents. Their adversaries came to include Protestant heretics, Brazilian shamans, Buddhist and Shinto priests, Muslim

---

1. Fernand Braudel, *Civilization and Capitalism, 15th–18th Century*, trans. Sian Reynolds, 3 vols. (New York, 1981–84); Vitorino Magalhães Godinho, *Os descobrimentos e a economia mundial*, 2 vols. (Lisbon, 1963–65).

mullahs, other Catholic priests, dissenting Catholic officials, and laymen. In Europe, the new Order was particularly associated with the Counter-Reformation, with the training of elites, and with the spiritual counsel that its members provided the continent's leading families. Overseas, it became one of the Church's most conspicuous evangelical forces.

No assistancy offered the new Order challenges as many and as varied as did the Portuguese. When the first Jesuits, so warmly solicited by John III, entered Portugal in June 1540, they became the harbingers of thousands, mostly Portuguese but also Italians, Germans, Spaniards, and a few Poles, Bohemians, Austrians, Irishmen, Englishmen, and others, who would serve as priests and lay brothers in a variety of capacities throughout the kingdom, its empire, and beyond for nearly 220 years. Within the kingdom, Jesuits became conspicuous educators, preachers, and diplomats, as well as advisors to the rulers and their families and confessors of other leading houses. As the operators of more than a score of colleges, including those strategically situated in Portugal's two national universities, Coimbra and Évora, the Jesuits trained recruits, initially drawn especially from the upper ranks of society but later from more plebeian strata, particularly from the kingdom's northern and central dioceses, where the Order was most effectively established. Many were then dispatched to the overseas branches of the Society's global enterprise.

The Portuguese Assistancy was geographically the most extensive and ethnically the most diverse among the Order's half dozen such administrative entities. In the West it extended from Portugal to Brazil, including Portugal's Atlantic islands, as well as Kongo and Angola; in the East it reached from riverain Mozambique and the Ethiopian highlands to the vast and populous Indian subcontinent, Ceylon, Malacca, the Indonesian archipelago, that of Japan, the empire of China, and the kingdoms of Southeast Asia. In all of these domains, the Society established distinctive churches, missions, colleges, and other facilities. Some thrived; others (such as the Cape Verde mission and that of Ormuz) failed quickly; still others were ultimately overrun by hostile Protestant or indigenous forces.

During the formative period, the eastern branches of the enterprise appeared the most promising. The Society's agents successfully established strings of missions or colleges from the Zambesi to the Pearl rivers; from the littoral of western India to the remote outposts of Malacca, the Moluccas, and Macao; from the Japanese archipelago to the heavily forested kingdoms of Southeast Asia and the western desert provinces of imperial China. Although preceded in India and Ceylon by their Franciscan rivals, the Jesuits were the first missionaries to reach the Japanese isles and the first in centuries to gain entry to the vast Chinese empire. Respected fathers, suitably attired, fluent in the languages of their hosts and knowledgeable about their cultures, became familiar figures in the palaces of the shoguns, of the emperors of China, of Mughal India, and of the Ethiopian highlands, just as their brethren did in the more familiar courts of Europe. While they were winning tens (possibly hundreds) of thousands of converts throughout the East and were optimistically predicting their ability to win over entire nationalities, their companions elsewhere in Africa and in Brazil struggled amid smaller, less culturally advanced populations and achieved more modest successes. Meantime, the original province in Portugal prospered and expanded to embrace the Azores and the Madeiras, both of which later helped to staff the more distant overseas branches of the Assistancy.

The successful establishment of such a far-flung enterprise presented the Society with a set of complex, enduring problems whose solutions contributed, despite the wishes of its leaders, to its image as a pampered, controversial, unconventional religious Order. But the intent of those solutions was often misunderstood by the Society's critics, and their implications have eluded many of its later interpreters. First, there was the problem of governance. Although the Society was structured as a highly centralized, hierarchical organization in which all power was concentrated in the hands of the fathers general, the generals were rarely able to exercise their authority, especially in distant lands, as decisively as their critics or their defenders have assumed. If, for example, the generals' authority had been absolute, how can one explain the recurrent quarrels between provinces (Japan versus China, Malabar versus Goa and Goa versus the eastern provinces) or the bitter divisions among provinces in seventeenth-century Europe that led to the splintering of the Portuguese province and several others? If the generals' directives had commanded the universal compliance that is sometimes assumed, how can the persistence of divisions based upon nationality within the Society be understood? If the generals' authority had been truly imperious and they really had possessed the capacity to shunt from place to place levies of priests and brothers who responded like automatons, why did each overseas province regularly send recruiters to Europe to appeal for volunteers to serve in their stations? Or, indeed, why did directors of such provinces continually emphasize the spiritual gains to be made if only they possessed sufficient hands to seize the opportunity?

Although the fathers general were nominally commanders-in-chief, the vast distances separating their headquarters from the Order's units obliged them to delegate much of their authority to trusted lieutenants—provincials, Visitors, rectors, and other superiors. And just as the general congregations and the units they represented placed their absolute trust in the fathers general, so the latter were compelled to rely upon their subordinates for personnel recommendations and for the initiation and execution of policies whose local implications those subordinates understood far better than did Jesuit authorities in the Eternal City. Of course, the subordinates remained answerable for their actions to the assistants, and through them to the fathers general. Their accountability was manifested by means of frequent, detailed communications. Their conduct was also monitored by their immediate superiors and by their advisors (consultores), who wrote directly to headquarters. All administrators also reported regularly upon the spiritual and intellectual promise of their subordinates, who rendered obeisance, but hardly "blind obedience," to their superiors.

The Society certainly emphasized discipline, but not in the heavy-handed manner that some writers imagine. It established a record of personal morality that few other Church entities could match. Its members took their vows of personal poverty with utmost seriousness, and especially during the formative period (1540–1615), its leaders were quick to censor those who seemingly violated those vows and therefore besmirched the Order's public image. In keeping with the times and the values of the secular world in which it functioned, the leadership was also prone to discipline those at the bottom of the hierarchical ladder more severely than it did those further up: there were far more novices, coadjutor priests, and lay brothers dismissed, especially during the formative period, than senior priests, in whom the Society had both a greater investment and greater confidence. From beginning to end, the Society of Jesus was run by elites and was especially solicitous of the support of elites, whether Europeans or others.

The founders had expected that most Jesuits would reside in professed houses, but Loyola and his successors discovered that there was little interest among laymen in sponsoring such facilities. Such benefactors preferred to finance colleges that would provide a rigorous classical education for favored members of their community. Accordingly, the Jesuits agreed to assume the responsibility for such educational facilities, many of which in Portugal, as in France, were created not through their own initiative but by heads of government, bishops, wealthy laymen, and others.

With few exceptions, the colleges in the Portuguese Assistancy were situated in urban rather than rural areas, for the Jesuits, like the Mendicants, had a strong urban bent despite the profusion of their rural missions. The most important of those colleges, like the colleges of their religious rivals, were established in key imperial cities—Lisbon, Porto, Évora, Braga, Bahia, Rio de Janeiro, Goa, Cochin, Bassein, Malacca, and Macao—each a recognized center of political, religious, and sometimes economic power. Such facilities, usually the largest structures in their communities, served multiple purposes. They were not only preparatory schools but also dormitories for resident staff and sojourners, as well as the administrative centers of dependent houses, missions, and estates. Their rectors and procurators were invariably highly visible in their communities, in part because of their efforts to defend the college's interests against censorious secular and ecclesiastical officials and hostile laymen.

Once recruits had survived their novitiates and probationary periods, they became collegial residents, then were assigned duties elsewhere. Despite the fact that during the formative years the Society's directors were nearly overwhelmed by the number of young people who were anxious (or whose parents were anxious for them) to join, the Order, as already remarked, never possessed as many members as its leaders wanted to meet its manifold needs. In the Portuguese Assistancy, both the leadership and the government that it served bore responsibility for continual manpower shortages. The leadership, largely European by birth and Eurocentric in outlook, yielded to the prevailing prejudices of the European governments and societies upon which it was heavily dependent and turned its back on prospective New Christian recruits, despite the fact that some of its early leaders were of Jewish origin. It also viewed with deep suspicion supposedly intellectually and morally inferior colonial-born whites and, together with other religious Orders, effectively barred the entry of persons of mixed blood as well as those of African origin. It reluctantly admitted a token number of Asiatics to its priestly ranks but remained bitterly divided on the wisdom of such action.

The state, too, handicapped the Society's ability to meet its staffing needs, at least overseas. It did so inadvertently when it lost control of the seas, beginning in the 1570s, which delayed departures and led to the loss of men as a result of piracy, naval warfare, and inexpert seamanship. It did so quite deliberately when the Portuguese regime's increasing xenophobia, like that of the government of Spain, led the crown to order the exclusion of non-Portuguese, especially from leadership positions, measures that more readily commanded compliance within the empire than beyond the imperial reach, especially in Southeast Asia and the Chinese empire. Such prohibitions were sometimes applied to foreigners generally, sometimes to particular nationalities suspected of disloyalty (like Spaniards after the Restoration). Nevertheless, some of the most distinguished Jesuits to serve in the Assistancy were not, in fact, Portuguese (Francis Xavier, Rudolfo Aquaviva, Matteo Ricci, Alessandro Valignano, Adam Schall, Ferdinand Verbiest, José de Anchieta, Johan Philipe Betendorf, and Giovanni Antonio Andreoni, for example). Despite all the obstacles, slightly more than half of the Jesuits who served in this assistancy between 1600 and 1754 resided outside of the Portuguese kingdom (see Appendix D).

The ethnic composition of the Society discussed here is, of course, very different from the mix that characterizes its modern successor, which contains a large number of persons of African or Asian origin. Indeed, it can be argued that the modern Society far more closely resembles the international organization that Loyola envisaged than did the original Society. The founder intended his subjects to be exclusively apolitical in their behavior and to be vertically bound together by means of their common submission to the fathers general and the supreme pontiffs, the vicars of Christ, and, of course, ultimately to their deity. But there remained other compelling bonds of loyalty that prevented the harmonious cohesion that the founder expected. Efforts by the leadership to sever ties between recruits and their parents and other members of their families were never uniformly successful: though some recruits did turn their backs on their families, others continued to correspond with them and retained an interest in their parents' and siblings' welfare. Since the Society was established at a time of incipient nationalism, it is not surprising to discover the existence of both pride in native origins and contempt for other nationalities within the Society (such as the rivalry between Portuguese members and the Spaniards, the French, the Germans, and the Italians, notably throughout Asian branches of the enterprise).[2]

As this study has demonstrated, there were other ties of loyalty as well. They included the attachment of lay brothers to the estates they managed or of all members to the province or the house with which they were identified. Such bonds resulted in the unseemly rivalry, for example, between the stronger Goan and the weaker Malabar provinces and between the stronger Japanese province and the weaker vice-province of China. They also produced that embittering internecine factionalism between the Lisbonian and the Évora-based fathers from the 1640s to the 1660s that seriously diminished the stature of the oldest province within the Assistancy.

The Society was formed at a time when rulers, especially those in Latin Europe, were intent upon extending their own authority at the expense of noble, ecclesiastical, and popular interests. Consequently, those who governed Spain, France, and Portugal always insisted that all religious who served within their domains owed allegiance to them as well as to their ecclesiastical heads and were, therefore, subject to secular discipline. Jesuits suspected of engaging in actions contrary to national laws, as interpreted by the kings' ministers, were not infrequently threatened with severe punishment, including expulsion, especially during the Joanine period (1706–50).[3]

2. Some present and former Jesuits would argue that ethnic pride and antipathies still exist within the Order.

3. As will be seen in the next volume, the regime of Joseph (José) I (1750–77) frequently disciplined Jesuits and other religious accused of crimes against the state (*desacato*) by arresting, imprisoning, banishing, and expelling them. Though more frequently employed then than earlier, such practices were far from new.

The insistence by state authorities that Jesuits, like other religious, owed their primary allegiance to the heads of state is but one example of the degree to which the Society remained dependent upon the whims of secular authorities. From the outset Jesuit administrators were compelled to rely upon the support and protection of the governments of the nations in which their Order served and to yield to the constraints they imposed. Whether European, Ethiopian, or Asiatic, those rulers determined how and where representatives of the Society could function and under what conditions. (For example, in imperial China during certain times in the seventeenth and eighteenth centuries, Jesuits were permitted to worship only within their own compounds and were forbidden to engage in public-conversion exercises.) The notion that the Society was an independent, powerful firm, able to act at will on its own impulses irrespective of the admonitions of secular authorities, an idea espoused especially in the eighteenth century, is entirely chimerical.

The heads of state supported, tolerated, and/or encouraged the activities of the Society because they perceived that it was in their own interests to do so. Potentates in Ethiopia, Japan, China, and India and tribal leaders in central Africa and Brazil valued the Jesuits because of their knowledge of the Western world, their ability to serve as interpreters, and their talent as commercial facilitators. John III of Portugal, his two immediate successors, and two of the first three Braganças applauded Jesuit efforts to spread the faith at home and abroad, partly because of their own religious convictions but also because converts were expected to become tractable, tax-paying subjects and auxiliary defenders of the empire. Such rulers admired the Jesuits because of their intellectual preparation, personal rectitude, moral fervor, courage, resourcefulness, and linguistic and diplomatic skills. Accordingly, they were lavish in their support of the Society, endowing it with lands, rents, subventions, customs exemptions, and other aids.

The Society responded to such assistance by rendering many important services for the crown. The Jesuits' roles as leading educators, confessors of the high and mighty, restorers of purified pietism, and trusted advisors on public policies have been examined in earlier chapters. Both at home and abroad they, like other religious, emphasized in their relations with the faithful the necessity for obedience and submissiveness to legitimate Portuguese authority. If Jesuit missionaries encouraged revolutionary conduct by neophytes abroad, who were persuaded to reject non-Christian spiritual and political leaders and to give up traditional pagan practices inconsistent with the tenets of their new faith (polygamy, infanticide, concubinage, intertribal warfare, and suttee), they were staunch advocates of political and religious orthodoxy among Old Christians.[4] Although two prominent Spanish Jesuit writers advocated regicide under extreme circumstances, no Jesuit within the Portuguese Assistancy is known to have done so.[5] Thus although Portuguese Jesuits strongly

4. Two writers who emphasize the excessive zeal of the Jesuits as cultural destroyers within the Assistancy ignore the fact that their actions not only were approved by the crown and its agents but were consonant with those undertaken by other religious and by laymen as well. Teotonio R. de Souza, S.J., *Medieval Goa: A Socio-Economic History* (New Delhi, 1979), 92–93; and Stuart B. Schwartz, *Sugar Plantations in the Formation of Brazilian Society: Bahia, 1550–1835* (Cambridge, 1985), 40–41.

5. The best-known Jesuit advocates of regicide under extreme conditions (usurpation, tyrannicide, and doctrinal deviancy) were Francisco Suarez (d. 1617) and Juan de Mariana (d. ca. 1623), but in 1610 Aquaviva strongly repudiated such views. Franklin L. Ford, *Political Murder: From Tyrannicide to Terrorism* (Cambridge, Mass., 1985), 156–57 and 182–83. See also John Laures, S.J., *The Political Economy of Juan de Mariana* (New

favored a Portuguese candidate during the crisis of 1578–80, they did not participate in the popular opposition to the Spanish intruders. Nor did they become prime movers in the coup that overthrew the Spanish regime 60 years later, an action that Spanish Jesuits strongly denounced. Nor were Portuguese Jesuits directly involved in the subsequent coup that toppled the incompetent Afonso VI in 1667, though they clearly approved both operations and facilitated the divorce of the demented ruler's wife so that she could marry his successor. No religious organization did as much to promote loyalty to the Bragança regime, both at home and abroad, as the Society. Nor did any other Order yield so completely to the demands of the Portuguese crown to perform administrative and diplomatic tasks that lay far beyond the bounds of the Society's spiritual mission.

As the most conspicuous and the most favored religious Order in the Portuguese world, the Society was always a source of sharply divided opinions among both European and non-European peoples. Its defenders included sovereigns and members of their families, many heads of noble houses, some prelates, some pro-Jesuit families, couples, and bachelors, some governors-general and viceroys of India, some magistrates, and even some members of rival religious bodies. But its adversaries included members of many of the same groups, as well as fellow landowners, municipal authorities, tax farmers, treasurers, lawyers, crown law officers, some high civil and religious administrators, and some members of other Church agencies.[6]

Despite (or perhaps because of) the fact that the Society became the most favored religious Order in the Portuguese world, it also became the focus of persistent criticism that began within a few decades of its entry into Portugal and grew in intensity with almost every passing decade throughout the period. Such criticism took various forms, some of which proved more compelling in one part of the Assistancy than in others.

One contention was that Jesuits were somehow responsible for Portugal's military reverses. In the 1560s, one anonymous critic suggested that royal expenditures in behalf of the arts college of Coimbra could be better spent on a Moroccan campaign. Yet when the youthful Sebastian recklessly led his nation to disaster at Alcázarquibir (1578), it was not the fallen king but his Jesuit advisors who were blamed for imperiling the nation's future. In India during the 1630s, when a hard-pressed viceroy found himself with insufficient soldiery and an inability to turn back relentless Dutch aggressors, he condemned the religious, notably the Jesuits, for providing asylum for recruits rather than blaming his masters, who were unable to raise a sufficient number of mature, adequately trained, dedicated soldiers to serve in his State. Half a century later, when the Marathas first successfully invaded Goan Salsete, the failure of the troops to man their guns went ignored while critics condemned Jesuit priests for failing to rally their parishioners against the numerically vastly superior intruders. And when the Marathas returned in the 1730s and overran Goan Salsete once more, destroying its northern province, the viceroy censored the Jesuits for niggardly financial contributions to the defense effort rather than admit his own incompetence and that of his kinsman

---

York, 1928), 3–5, 61–69, and 237. Fr. Laures observed that Saint Thomas Aquinas also advocated tyrannicide in the case of usurpers but contended that Mariana "went too far" and "erred" in his advocacy of such action by private citizens.

6. One could, of course, add to this list many indigenous leaders as well as many Englishmen, seemingly all Hollanders, and many other Europeans.

charged with the protection of the northern bastions. But memorialists and viceroys were not alone in assigning the Society responsibility for disastrous reverses: when it became clear that efforts to promote Christianity in eighteenth-century China were doomed to failure, Church critics placed the blame for China's "loss" upon interfering court Jesuits rather than ill-informed, uncompromising papal emissaries.

Another set of charges concerned presumed Jesuit political influence both in the royal palace and in the seats of governance overseas. The fact that the fathers were the confessors of members of the royal family and of some (but not all) of the viceroys and governors who served abroad made such a complaint plausible and difficult to refute. Thus in 1579 one memorial warned the citizens of Lisbon that only Jesuit wire-pullers in the palace could expedite their petitions. In the 1590s, the Portuguese-born chronicler Gabriel Soares de Sousa charged that in Brazil, the fathers were deeply involved in political intrigue. And in the 1630s, a disdainful count of Linhares, viceroy of India, asserted that Jesuits were so contemptuous of the holders of his office that they considered them to be their toadies.

But the most persistent and vigorously debated complaints against the Jesuits pertained to economic issues. The occupants of the State of Brazil and the State of Maranhão were acutely concerned about Jesuit positions on two of them—their defense of the Brasis and their claims of tithe exemption. Although the production of cane sugar, meat, and minerals in Brazil depended upon the sweat of black slaves, most of them imported, the settlers in both the far south and the far north continued to rely upon Indian labor, which they naturally preferred to exploit without ecclesiastical interference. Though the Jesuits seldom adopted an unpopular position, they continually sought to protect the Amerindians against settler abuses and, along with other religious, were assigned by the crown responsibilities for mediating between employers and Indian laborers. The colonists, with the support of some royal officials and churchmen, consistently opposed ecclesiastical restraints upon their use of Amerindians, complained that the missionaries' interest in them was primarily to exploit them for their own enrichment, and, despite the toll taken by catastrophic epidemics in the Amazon, denounced the Jesuits for withholding the Brasis from those who claimed that they could not survive without them.

One of the standard arguments of the planters was that by restricting or denying them necessary Indian workers, the Jesuits were responsible not only for the planters' impoverishment but that of the royal exchequer as well. Tithe farmers in Brazil repeatedly invoked the same claim to explain their failure to meet their bids. Both there and in the kingdom, agents of the crown, strongly supported by the prelates, attempted to compel the Jesuits to pay tithes upon their estates because the government and the prelates shared the proceeds.

Although Jesuit leaders long avoided compliance—in Brazil more successfully than in the kingdom—their resistance exposed the Society to a further series of allegations. One was that the Society was simply an instrument of an alien regime with which the Portuguese government was often at odds—the papacy. Another was that their unpatriotic position served as a baneful example to the king's subjects, who felt that they had an equal right to avoid payments. Finally, Jesuit opposition to tithe payments seemed especially callous to those who were persuaded that the Society was enormously rich.

Other economically rooted allegations against the Jesuits were vented throughout the empire. Many believed that the Society engaged in trade on a grand scale, thereby providing unfair competition for secular traders; others were convinced that the Society was a dangerous patrimonial power inimical to the interests of the state and its subjects. The first rulers of Portugal adopted a more tolerant view of Jesuit trading than did their successors. Since neither the crown nor the papacy could ensure that promised subventions for the favored Japan missions would arrive in timely fashion, the crown countenanced Jesuit participation in the silk trade between Nagasaki and Canton via Macao. However, the Jesuits profited far less from their involvement in such trade than their critics imagined. Because of their commercial connections, Jesuits were often compromised by doing favors for important personages, including Christian daimyos, Church cardinals, and viceroys. Thus they brokered bullion shipments to China for the daimyos and the purchase of gems and carpets in India for high churchmen and viceroys, even though the law prohibited the latter from making such purchases. At various times, spokesmen in Macao, Goa, and Belém do Pará complained that the Jesuits were dominating the trade of their area to the grave disadvantage of the kings' subjects, but there is little evidence to sustain such assertions. Though units of the Assistancy sent commodity gifts to important personages within and without the Society and engaged in small-scale intraenterprise trade, there is no support for the belief that the Society was a pioneer multinational trading company (see Appendix B) or that its commercial activities adversely affected the profits of merchants, many of whom, in the East, were non-Portuguese.

Without question, the Society became a highly visible patrimonial power in the Assistancy. That was surely not by intent. The founders expected that the enterprise's financial needs would be met by grateful monarchs and private benefactors, and in part they were. During the sixteenth century, both the crown and admiring prelates in the kingdom assigned Jesuit colleges underutilized monastic lands and properties sequestered from New Christians at home and indigenous peoples abroad. Private benefactors, both Old Christians and recent converts, also contributed income-producing estates, particularly during the sixteenth and seventeenth centuries. Such properties were intended to provide subsistence for the Jesuits and those in their care (staff, students, and recent converts) and to generate sufficient income to defray essential expenses. But the Jesuits became victims of their own success: the more their educational and evangelical activities prospered, the greater their financial requirements. Beginning early in the Philippine era (1580–1640), however, the crown's ability to deliver its promised material support diminished because of deficiencies in fiscal management and the onset of costly maritime and land wars. Accordingly, those Jesuits charged with funding the enterprise felt compelled to develop and to continue to expand their landholdings and to sell unneeded surpluses to outsiders. The Society leased some of its holdings and directly operated others.

The growth of such estates met some of the Society's financial requirements, but it also created new problems. First, although those who labored on Jesuit estates in the kingdom and in India were free workers, the accepted labor regime for the production of cane sugar required costly black slaves. But although the Society became the largest institutional holder of slaves in Brazil, it continued to oppose the enslavement of Amerindians on grounds that mystified not only impoverished colonists who believed their survival depended upon such workers but even royal ministers. Second, the existence of carefully, albeit conservatively, managed grain farms and vineyards in Portugal and the Atlantic islands, livestock ranches and especially large-scale, slave-operated sugar plantations in Brazil, extensive subsistence estates (arimos and prazos) in Angola and Mozambique, and rice-paddy lands and large coconut orchards in India appeared to confirm the widespread belief that the Society had become extremely wealthy and that its leadership had forsaken its spiritual mission and had become preoccupied with material gain. The Évora cortes of 1562 became the first representative body in the Lusitanian world to warn about the Jesuits' putative engrossment of lands, and its concerns would be echoed by cámaras, high royal officials, and ordinary subjects throughout the empire for nearly two centuries. All would adopt the same refrain: the fathers were becoming land-rich at the expense of His Majesty's loyal subjects, who were becoming increasingly marginalized by the aggressive churchmen. Such a charge might have made sense in medieval Portugal, when legal restrictions against ecclesiastical landlordism were first enacted, though indifferently enforced; but it hardly did so in the vast reaches of Brazil, Angola, Mozambique, or even the western littoral of India. Third, the growth of Jesuit latifundia, together with other forms of infrastructure, notably novitiates, probationary houses, professed houses, retreats, and even ships, convinced many opponents that the Order had abandoned its commitment to ecclesiastical poverty and had become preoccupied with Mammon.

One of the many myths that beset the Society, both in this assistancy and elsewhere, concerned its supposed riches. Those who subscribed to the notion of the Order's affluence never questioned the right of members of the royal family, of those belonging to the great noble houses in the kingdom, of prominent prelates, or of merchant princes to enjoy vast wealth. Somehow they assumed that the vows of personal poverty that Jesuits and some other ecclesiastics took represented commitments to beggary by their organizations. Nor did they realize that for much of the period covered by this study, many of the components of the enterprise were burdened with heavy debts. As Jesuit records convincingly demonstrate, most of the Society's income was expended in ways necessary for the religious to support their distinctive lifestyles. The greatest outlay was for foodstuffs, followed by shelter, fabric, clothing, church maintenance, supplies, and health care. Depending upon the location and the extent of the unit's infrastructure, estates, transport, and wages also constituted substantial burdens. Though Jesuits enjoyed greater creature comforts than did their slaves or salaried employees, they never lived as lavishly as their opponents imagined. Certainly the per-person expenditures necessary to sustain Jesuits throughout the Assistancy were infinitely more modest than those enjoyed by prelates, magistrates, governors, viceroys, merchants, or adventurers.

Yet the more impoverished the kingdom and the empire became during the seventeenth and eighteenth centuries (notwithstanding the so-called "golden age," whose benefits few shared), the more difficult it became for anti-Jesuit elements to comprehend why the government should support or continue to sanction the presence of an agency whose members claimed primary allegiance to alien superiors. But despite the multitude of recriminations, most rulers of Portugal protected the Society against its critics down to the mid-eighteenth century. As already indicated, they had good reason to do so. But where the crown's vital interests seemed to be involved, as in the case of tithe payments and charges that the Society's vast landholdings were obtained in defiance of existing law and royal fiat, it responded by demanding reports on the extent of ecclesiastical holdings and incomes, and, especially during the Petrine years, it threatened to confiscate the assets of all noncompliant religious bodies. But that was mere bluster, for, in fact, no properties were ever expropriated.

From the perspective of 1750, leaders of the Assistancy could take satisfaction in the undeniable exploratory, proselytizing, scientific, theological, artistic, and other achievements of those who had created and nourished their vast global enterprise during the previous two centuries. Nevertheless, they must have been sobered by several reflections. The first was the obvious fact that areas that had once been sources of special rejoicing—the flourishing provinces of Goa, Malabar, and Japan, and the vice-province of China—were in irretrievable decline; that despite repeated promises, the African outposts had never truly prospered; and that the only branch of the enterprise that was still expanding was Brazil, where, however, settler hostility, abetted by unfriendly royal officials and rival churchmen, was continuing to mount. Second, despite the fact that there were then more members of their Order in the kingdom than at any time in the past, the Society was no longer the preeminent cultural force in Portugal. Third, despite vigorous, learned, and inspired defenses mustered by Jesuit spokesmen in behalf of the enterprise, the complaints—against its continued engrossment of lands; its avoidance of taxes, customs duties, and other levies; its varied commercial activities; its intimate relations with senior government officials—many of them issues that also arose in the French and Spanish assistancies, never seemed to cease. On the contrary, the more the empire slumbered, the more frustrated and resentful its officials and the king's subjects became, and the more frequently they targeted the Society as the obvious scapegoat for their perceived disappointments and failures. The tempo of such complaints noticeably intensified throughout the ultramar during the 1720s, 1730s, and 1740s. Fourth, although leaders of the Society had long enjoyed a closer relationship with the crown than any other Church entity save the Inquisition, the Order lost some of its luster during the long regime of John V, who (with the exception of his reliance upon Fr. Carbone) seems to have deliberately distanced himself from the Jesuits. Whether his successor, Joseph I, would restore the close relationship that had long existed between the Society and the crown was unclear. But if he and his ministers proved unfriendly, and if they heeded the simmering complaints against the Society leveled by royal officials, prelates, planters, farmers, merchants, and others throughout the empire, the future of the enterprise could well be perilous. As the sequel to this volume will show, the fateful 1750s would demonstrate that it was.

Appendixes

APPENDIX A

Concerning Coinage, Money of Account, and Conversions

Persisting debasement rather than intrinsic stability characterized Portuguese coinage issues throughout much of the period considered in this study. The history of the famed *cruzado* easily illustrates the point. When it was introduced during the long reign of Afonso V (1438–81), it was a gold coin weighing 71.25 grams. Later it became a silver issue, with a nominal value of 400 *réis* in 1517. By the reign of the first Philip, its weight was reduced to 64.41 grams, a level maintained until the financially troubled reign of Pedro II (1683–1706), when the *cruzado novo* was issued with a nominal value of 480 rs., though it weighed only 21.6 grams, or 31.5 percent of its initial value. That level was maintained throughout the balance of our period. Still, as observed in Chapter 24, declining ratios of the cruzado and other Portuguese issues relative to pence sterling continued throughout the seventeenth and the first half of the eighteenth centuries.[1]

In the Atlantic world, Jesuit account keepers avoided the problem of computing alterations in the intrinsic values of such coins and rates of exchange by keeping their records in moneys of account. During the formative period they sometimes calculated incomes and expenditures in terms of cruzados (400 rs.), but for much of our period they recorded them in multiples of fictive réis, most commonly units of 1,000 (*milréis*) or 1,000,000 (*contos*). About 1700, however, they began reporting the fiscal status of the colleges in the Atlantic provinces in terms of Roman *scudi*, which, though rated at 2 cruzados apiece in Xavier's time, were then reckoned at 1,000 rs.[2]

East of the Cape of Good Hope, the Portuguese and their European rivals encountered various currency systems, many of which were derived from those developed in Babylonia and Iran between about 600 and 330 B.C. As Henry T. Grogan once observed, the Portuguese missed an opportunity to dominate exchange rates in Asian and East African markets.[3] After all, they were the first Europeans in these areas, with what appeared to be overwhelming seapower. Had they been able to maintain the integrity of their coinage issues, they

1. The standard work on Portuguese coinage remains A. C. Teixeira de Argão, *Descripção geral e historia das moedas cunhadas . . . de Portugal*, 3 vols. (Lisbon, 1874–80). See esp. 3: 237–42.

2. *HCJB*, 5: 589 n. 1.

3. Henry T. Grogan, "The Silver Issues of Goa:—The Saint Type," in Spink and Sons, *Numismatic Circular* (Sept. 1912): cols. 13865–72, at col. 13866.

TABLE A.1

The Debasement of Xerafins and Tangas, 1569–1858

| | Weight in grams | | Percentage of original value | |
Year	Xerafins	Tangas	Xerafins	Tangas
1569	19	4.4	100	100
1594	19	3.6	100	81.8
1614	19	3.0	100	68.2
1640–50	11	2.2	57.9	50.0
1650–1727[a]	10.4	2.0	54.7	45.5
1727–1858[a]	5.8	1.2	30.5	27.3

SOURCES: See note 4.

[a] For xerafins, the periods are 1650–1726 and 1726–1858.

might have been able to establish their own issues as standard media of exchange. By the early 1550s, the Goan mint was producing silver pieces called São Thomés, bearing a likeness of the saint presumed to have ended his life at Meliapor. Initially the São Thomés or *patacões* bore a nominal value of 360 rs. and weighed 27.2 grams each, but their weight was soon reduced to 24.3 grams and was repeatedly lowered thereafter, though the coins always retained the same nominal value. Debasement also characterized other Portuguese coins, such as the *xerafins* and *tangas*. The former, whose etymology is Persian and Arabic (*asrafi* or *sharifi*) but also Konkan (*asurpi*), were initially gold coins but were later minted in silver. Gold xerafins bore a nominal value of 360 rs., whereas the more common silver ones were declared to be worth 300 rs., the equivalent of 5 tangas (60 rs. each) or 5 *larins*. The subsequent debasement of the xerafins and tangas is indicated in Table A.1.

The same erosion occurred in issues of the *pardão* (var. *pardau*, also *pardão de tangas*), nominally worth 1 xerafim.[4] During the late seventeenth century, the xerafim was accepted as the equivalent of 3 rupees, but a half century later, following Maratha successes in the northern province (Chapter 23), the rupee was valued at 2 xerafins.[5] Because of the instability of Portuguese issues, Jesuits followed the practice of both merchants and government officials in the subcontinent—they kept their records in moneys of account: xerafins (300 rs.), tangas (60 rs.), and réis.

According to Cunha Rivara, it was presumed that "the réis of Goa were equal to the réis of Portugal."[6] It was further assumed that the xerafim was the equivalent of 0.75 cruzados or 0.75 ducats or 0.75 Spanish "pieces of eight," or *pesos del ocho*. Silver pesos, distributed throughout the East beginning in the late sixteenth century via the China trade with Manila, became the predominant barter coins in maritime Asia until the end of the nineteenth century because they remained intrinsically stable.

In Southeast Asia, Jesuit fiscal reports were displayed in Chinese monetary units, beginning with the *tael*, a silver coin but also money of account, and various fractional

4. The foregoing is based upon Grogan, "Silver Issues"; H. W. Codrington, "The Pedigree of the Pardaõ [*sic*]," *Ceylon Antiquary* 1 (Colombo, 1915–16): 24–28; and C. R. Boxer, *The Great Ship from Amacon, 1555–1640* (1959; rpr., Lisbon, 1963), appendix.

5. Lotika Varadarajan, trans. and ed., *India in the 17th Century: Memoirs of François Martin at Surat (1670–1694)*, 2 vols. in 4 (New Delhi, 1981), 2:2, 1660; P. S. S. Pissurlencar [Pissurlenkar], *The Portuguese and the Marathas*, trans. P. R. Kakodkar (Bombay, 1975), 339 and 384.

6. *APO*:1, 5:2, 878n.

units thereof. Like cruzados, ducats, and pesos, taels were reckoned to be the equivalent of 400 rs. or 1.33 xerafins.[7]

To facilitate comparisons between Jesuit units in the western and eastern portions of the Assistancy, all accounts in this book have been converted to réis and contos.

7. Lotika Varadarajan, "Seventeenth Century Coins and Mensuration in Some Parts of Asia," *Journal of the Andhra Pradesh Archives* 5, 1 (1977): 23–49, at 36.

APPENDIX B

The Society of Jesus as the
Alleged First Multinational Firm

In 1978, when C. R. Boxer gave the Heras Memorial Lectures at St. Xavier's College, Bombay, he resorted to his penchant for striking analogies by observing that the Jesuits' "economic activities were . . . far greater in scope than those of either the Dutch or the English East India Companies, which are sometimes termed the first multinationals. Moreover, whereas the directors of both Jan Compagnie and John Company were nationals of their respective nations, the Jesuit Generals at Rome, and the Provincials, superiors, and heads of missions abroad were truly international."[1] In a subsequent interview Boxer was quoted as remarking that "the world's first multinational corporation was the Company of Jesus."[2]

While I hold Professor Boxer in the highest regard, I must question the aptness of these assertions. First, as suggested by Chapter 21, there is absolutely no evidence that the scale of intra-Society trading operations ever approximated that of either the Dutch or the English firms. On the contrary, the Jesuits' commercial exchanges were invariably modest in scale. Second, most scholars restrict the use of the term "multinational" to organizations formed after our own Civil War, when firms national in scope began to reach out to gain access, sometimes ultimately to attain dominant positions, in foreign markets. What did those firms and their modern successors have to offer? Capital; goods; demand for raw materials such as ores, timber, and unrefined hydrocarbons; and expertise. Precisely where and what share of the firm's capital and human resources were or are invested was and is determined by the parent firm, that is, by the corporate headquarters, which was and is the destination of a substantial portion of the returns or profits.[3]

During the period spanned by this study, was the Society of Jesus an appropriate model for such firms? Hardly. The Roman headquarters rarely involved itself in basic decisions affecting the economic life of its "subsidiaries" (provinces, colleges, missions), such as the opening or closing of stations, movement into new territory, or withdrawal from existing outposts. Its restraint was certainly not constitutionally mandated but was

1. C. R. Boxer, *Portuguese India in the Mid-Seventeenth Century* (Delhi, 1980), 50.

2. *Times of India*, 24 Dec. 1978. I am indebted to Fr. John Correia-Afonso, S.J., former director of the Historical Institute, Xavier College, Bombay, for sending me a copy of this interview.

3. Mira Wilkins, *The Emergence of Multinational Enterprise: American Business Abroad from the Colonial Era to 1914* (Cambridge, Mass., 1970), chaps. 1–3.

necessitated by the fact that events changed too rapidly overseas for such decisions to be feasible (for example, the 1614 expulsion of the Society from Japan and the later expulsion from Ethiopia). Communications, whose rapidity is essential for the conduct of modern multinational corporate operations, were far too slow to permit swift decision-making.[4] Nor were "policies ... framed with the intention of ensuring the profitable operation of the company," unless profits can be interpreted in sixteenth-century missionary terms as the harvesting of souls.[5] The only "goods and services" the Society could provide its host lands were Christian indoctrination and education, plus, in some areas (Brazil, Paraguay, and India, for example), agricultural and handicraft training. But, contrary to the impressions of some of the Society's critics, there were no significant capital "transfers" from the overseas "subsidiaries" to the central headquarters, nor any shifting of personnel, assets, or priorities from one overseas branch to another to achieve economic advantages (see especially Chapter 22). Nor did the Society possess "a hierarchy of middle- and top-salaried managers who supervise[d] the work of the units under its control." Indeed, such a supervisory class did not exist until after the mid-nineteenth century.[6] The Roman headquarters was *not* the equivalent of the modern economic concept of "owners" who "often for extended periods ... have a say in critical policy decisions about products, services, volume of output, rate of return, and the allocation of resources."[7]

Although Boxer's generalization is clearly tied to "economic activities," a case can be made for the Society as an early (but not the first) multinational firm providing a *service*, a definition that fits one offered by Brooke and Remmers, who state, "Our definition of a *multinational company* is any firm which performs its main operations, either manufacture or the provision of service, in at least two countries."[8] But they go on to point out that the *parent company* (head office, headquarters) "owns and controls direct foreign investment" and describe the foreign subsidiary as "sometimes ... [an] *affiliate* or *local company*," thereby defining a relationship entirely alien to the one that prevailed between the Roman headquarters and its overseas provinces. Whatever "benefits" accrued from the activities of Jesuit "subsidiaries" did not redound to "the parent company" (the headquarters), but rather to the residents of the host land. And "power" (such as superiors' orders framed "by holy obedience") was never "wielded by economic means for economic aims."[9] Nor was the Society ever integrated horizontally, vertically, or in any other manner comparable to the familiar structures of modern multinational firms. In conclusion, therefore, Boxer's suggested analogy appears forced, anachronistic, and inappropriate. When closely examined, the operations, organizational structure, and decision-making character of the Society of Jesus in our period bear no discernible resemblance to those of the modern multinational corporation.

4. Cf. Alfred D. Chandler, Jr., "The United States: Seedbed of Managerial Capitalism," in Chandler and Herman Daems, eds., *Managerial Hierarchies: Comparative Perspectives on the Rise of the Modern Industrial Enterprise* (Cambridge, Mass., 1980), 15–16.

5. Cf. Michael Z. Brooke and H. Lee Remmers, *The Strategy of Multinational Enterprise: Organization and Finance* (New York, 1970), 10.

6. Chandler, "United States," 11.

7. Ibid., 13.

8. Brooke and Remmers, *Strategy of Multinational Enterprise*, 5.

9. Ibid., 10.

APPENDIX C

Relations Between the Society and
the Portuguese Inquisition

Many years ago, Fr. Henry Heras, Director of the Indian Historical Research Institute, St. Xavier's College, Bombay, assured his readers that "the Jesuits had nothing to do with the Inquisition not only in Goa, but even in Portugal and in Spain."[1] Two leading Jesuit historians of the Portuguese Assistancy, Francisco Rodrigues and Serafim Leite, knew better, but even they understated the extent of relations between members of the Society and the Holy Office, both in the kingdom and in the empire. Whereas Rodrigues emphasized the celebrated seventeenth-century battles between the Society and the Inquisition within the kingdom, Leite insisted that although Jesuits and inquisitors respected each other, theirs was never a cordial relationship.[2] In fact, Jesuits were often more active partners of the Holy Office than these scholars were prepared to recognize. That much has been conceded recently by the American Jesuit historian John W. O'Malley, who has observed that from the outset Loyola and his confidants were generally supportive of the establishment of inquisitorial tribunals in Portugal and in Rome.[3]

Loyola, in fact, supported the application of John III to the papacy to confirm the formation of the Portuguese Inquisition. It was provisionally created in 1536 and definitively established by 1547. Although six tribunals were initially formed, by 1548 only two—Lisbon and Évora—remained. They were joined in 1560 by the Goan court, the only overseas tribunal in the Lusitanian empire, and by the restored Coimbra branch in 1565. As Charles Amiel has observed, the Portuguese inquisitorial apparatus was modeled on that of Spain. A general council, headed by the inquisitor general and his deputies, set policy and supervised the work of the local tribunals. These tribunals consisted of two or three inquisitors and their staffs and were assisted by external experts (*calificadores*), who evaluated suspicious writings submitted to them, and by other priests, who confessed prisoners, accompanied them in the public processions (*autos-de-fé*), and delivered didactic sermons that preceded the execution of the victims' sentences. Where no tribunals existed, the general council enjoyed the services of designated ecclesiastics, who bore the title of commissioners (*comissários*). The commissioners were

1. Henry Heras, S.J., *The Conversion Policy of the Jesuits in India* (Bombay, 1933), 62.
2. *HCJB*, 4: 9–10. For citations to Rodrigues's view ʒ, see Chapter 5 above.
3. John W. O'Malley, S.J., *The First Jesuits* (Cambridge, Mass., 1993), 310–20.

charged with gathering testimony concerning suspects, and were assisted by unpaid lay informers (*familiares*).[4]

At one time or another, almost every one of these offices was occupied by a Jesuit. Indeed, the Order nearly administered two of the tribunals. In 1555 John III notified Provincial Diego Mirón that he was considering assigning the Lisbon office to the Society and asked whether such action would contravene the Society's Institute. The monarch's proposal provoked a good deal of soul-searching within the Order, both in Lisbon and in Rome. In the Eternal City, the founder convoked a special advisory commission consisting of his most trusted colleagues. Although that group recommended acceptance and Loyola concurred, the king had changed his mind: he decided instead to name a Dominican to supervise the Lisbon branch. Fr. Rodrigues suggests that it was the Jesuits' great benefactor, Cardinal Henry, who persuaded John III to spare the Society direct involvement with the Inquisition in order to guard it from attacks by that tribunal's opponents. That contention is hard to square with the monarch's subsequent request that the Society administer the Coimbra branch. Since the king insisted that its administrator be answerable to him and not to the father general, Loyola declined the offer.[5]

Nevertheless, Jesuits were closely associated with the operations of the tribunals in the kingdom for many years. António Quadros, provincial of Goa (d. 1572), was the brother of D. Manuel de Quadros, one of the first inquisitors of the realm and a member of the general council. Bishop D. Fernão Mascarenhas (d. 1628), a sometime inquisitor general, was the brother of four prominent Jesuits and an important Jesuit benefactor.[6] It was Bishop Mascarenhas who ordained the oft-cited Jerónimo Lobo as a subdeacon to facilitate his rapid advancement to the priesthood, which qualified him for missionary service in Ethiopia.[7]

During these decades, several Jesuits figured prominently in the activities of the Holy Office in the kingdom. Simão Rodrigues, the Society's founder in Portugal, bore the dubious distinction of having twice denounced to the Holy Office the humanist Damião de Góis.[8] Two of his successors, provincials Leão Henriques (b. ca. 1524–d. 1589) and Jorge Serrão (b. ca. 1528–d. 1590), became deputies of the Évora office. The latter for a time even served as its president. Upon Serrão's death, his colleagues in the Lisbon tribunal conducted a solemn mass in the church of São Roque and extolled the virtues of their "well-merited" late collaborator. One of Serrão's successors, the respected Dr. Francisco Pereira (b. 1551–d. 1619), an advisor to several prelates and a confidant of Sebastian's mentor, Martim Gonçalves da Cámara, became a member of the general council.[9] Another was the mysterious Manuel Alvares Tavares, head inquisitor of the Lisbon branch, who allegedly "never missed" an auto-de-fé between 1594 and 1611 and was reputedly its "most cruel and heartless" and visible member.[10]

4. For a useful introduction to the literature and to surviving archival sources, see Charles Amiel, "The Archives of the Portuguese Inquisition: A Brief Survey," in Gustav Henningsen, John Tedeschi, and Amiel, eds., *The Inquisition in Early Modern Europe: Studies on Sources and Methods* (DeKalb, Ill., 1986), 79–99.

5. *HCJAP*, 1: 693–97.

6. António Franco, *Imagem da virtude em o noviciado da companhia de Jesus no real collegio de Jesus de Coimbra em Portugal*, 2 vols. (Évora and Coimbra, 1719), 1: 747; *OSR*, no. 142.

7. *The Itinerary of Jerónimo Lobo*, trans. Donald M. Lockhart, ed. C. F. Beckingham, *HS*:2, no. 162 (1984): 1.

8. Damião de Góis, *Descrição da cidade de Lisboa*, trans. and ed. José da Felicidade Alves (Lisbon, 1988), 7–8.

9. *ASCJ*, 437–38, 629–32, and 685–86.

10. H. P. Salomon, *Portrait of a New Christian: Fernão Alvares Melo (1569–1632)* (Paris, 1982), 73, 111–12. Curiously, there is no reference to Tavares in any published Jesuit source.

Jesuits were also closely associated with the Goan tribunal of the Holy Office. As early as 1545 Francis Xavier urged its founding in order to defend the faith. To be sure, not all Jesuits agreed with him,[11] and though no Jesuit ever headed that tribunal, between 1560 and 1718 Jesuits constituted 20 percent of its deputies.[12] During the sixteenth century and perhaps beyond, the traditional incendiary sermon delivered during the auto-de-fé was customarily given by a Jesuit. The aforementioned provincial, António Quadros, performed that service, as did Fr. Nicolas Pimenta, the latter while he was in the kingdom and later when he became Visitor of the Indian provinces.[13]

The Holy Office never established a permanent branch in Brazil, although on at least four occasions it sent truth squads from the kingdom to investigate the state of the colony's morals. So far as is known, Jesuits were not directly involved in those inquiries. However, in late 1645 the general committee of the Holy Office received an alarming report from Bahia alleging that there was a large number of relapsed Jews of questionable loyalty living there. As a result, the ministers of the Inquisition directed the Jesuit provincial, Francisco Carneiro, to conduct an investigation that became known as "the great inquest." That inquiry was held in the college of Bahia during three months in 1646. Among the 120 deponents were the governor, António Teles da Silva, a strong supporter of the hearings and himself an informer (familiar), and four Jesuits. A total of 118 persons, most of them residents of Bahia, were implicated by witnesses, but there is no indication of any punishments being meted out.[14]

As the Jesuit chronicler Sebastiam Gonçalves wrote, members of the Society, like other ecclesiastics, also served as commissioners of the Holy Office throughout the Portuguese Assistancy.[15] At the beginning of the seventeenth century, Fr. António Marta, a missionary serving in the Moluccas, held that office, as did Manuel da Lima, who sailed to Pará with António Vieira in the early 1650s.[16] In the province of Brazil, the well-known chronicler and administrator Simão de Vasconcelos was named to that position, as was an early Jesuit chronicler and administrator in the Amazon, Johan Philipe Betendorf.[17] Despite the cooling relationship between the Society and the crown during the eighteenth century, Jesuits continued to assist the Holy Office as commissioners in places as far removed as Macao and Rio de Janeiro.[18]

Of course, it does not follow that Jesuits eagerly sought inquisitorial responsibilities, which appear to have been thrust upon them, as were so many other tasks (see Chapter 14). On the contrary, there is evidence that at least some Jesuits bore their inquisitorial responsibilities reluctantly. Valignano argued that although it was appropriate for members of the

11. S/FX, 3: 44; cf. Anthony D'Costa, S.J., *The Christianisation of the Goa Islands* (Bombay, 1965), 196.

12. António Baião, *A inquisição de Goa*, 2 vols. (Lisbon, 1930–49), 1: chap. 3; D'Costa, *Christianisation*, 197.

13. Franco, *Coimbra*, 1: 491–98; *DI*, 18: 768–70. For the names of other prominent Jesuits in Goa who also delivered the traditional sermon, see D'Costa, *Christianisation*, 196–97.

14. Anita Waingort Novinsky, *Cristãos novos na Bahia* (São Paulo, 1972), 130–40, and app. 3.

15. Gonçalves, *Primeira parte da historia dos religiosos da companhia de Jesus … nos reynos e provincias da India oriental*, 2 vols. (Coimbra, 1960), 2: 322.

16. Hubert Jacobs, S.J., "The Portuguese Town of Ambon, 1576–1605," *II seminário internacional de história indo-portuguesa* (Lisbon, 1985): 603–14; António Vieira to Francisco Gonçalves (provincial, Brazil), 14 Nov. 1562, in João Lúcio de Azevedo, ed., *Cartas do Padre António Vieira*, 3 vols. (Coimbra, 1925–28), 1: 286.

17. Novinsky, *Cristãos novos*, 117; *HCJB*, 4: 9.

18. In Macao the college rector was charged with that responsibility: Miguel(?) de Amaral to câmara (Macao), 12 Feb. 1721, in *Arquivos de Macao*, 3d ser., vol. 6, no. 1 (July 1966): 28; "Modo de proceder na controversia do Padre Gaspar de Amaral, rector do collegio … comissario do Santo Officio," in BNL, cod. 722, fols. 490ᵛ–508ᵛ. According to José Gonçalves Salvador, *Cristãos-novos jesuítas e inquisição* (São Paulo, 1969), 150, the same was true of Estévão Gandolfi, the rector of the college of Rio de Janeiro in 1713. There is no mention of such a responsibility in *HCJB*, 8: 266.

Society to utilize their expertise to evaluate suspicious written materials, it was unfitting for his subjects to occupy positions within the inquisitorial hierarchy. More than half a century later, António Vieira urged Goswin Nickel, the father general, to arrange for Manuel de Lima to be relieved of his duties as commissioner because the position was burdensome and he could be more productively utilized as a missionary.[19]

As often happened with requests that they considered beyond the scope of their service mission, Jesuits found it difficult to refuse assignments to assist the Holy Office. The cases of two Jesuits virtually drafted to serve as deputies of the Goan tribunal illustrate the point. In 1711, Fr. Manuel de Sá had just arrived in the State's capital from Lisbon and found himself named a deputy to the tribunal. He protested that such service was not only contrary to the Society's Institute but also to several papal edicts; but the chief inquisitor brushed aside his objections, and Fr. Sá was still serving as a deputy a decade later.[20] A year later a second Jesuit, Fr. Joseph Pereira, was also directed by the tribunal to become one of its deputies. He raised the same objections that Fr. Sá had and was supported by his provincial. As in the case of Fr. Sá, the chief inquisitor argued that the tribunal possessed papal authority that superseded that of the Society and even the stipulated papal exemptions, but in this instance he agreed to submit the question to the inquisitor general in Lisbon for resolution.[21] How the appeal was resolved remains unknown.

There can be little question, then, that despite some famous feuds between the Society and the Holy Office, Jesuits in the Portuguese Assistancy did aid and abet the Inquisition's activities. But that was also true of members of other religious Orders. Whether Jesuits were more reluctant or zealous collaborators in the defense of orthodoxy than were other religious cannot, of course, be ascertained. What is incontestable is that members of the Society played a more conspicuous role in the operations of the Holy Office than some Jesuit scholars have been willing to admit.

19. Valignano, "Summary of the Rules for the Province of India," Apr. 1588, in *DI*, 14: 849–50; Vieira to Nickel, 14 May 1654, in Azevedo, *Cartas*, 3: 710–11.

20. ARSI, *Goa*, 9:II, fols. 529^r–532; 36:II, fol. 310.

21. Ibid., 9:II, fols. 546^r–550^v.

APPENDIX D

Number of Jesuits Serving in
the Portuguese Assistancy, 1549–1760

Year	Portugal	Goa[a]	Malabar	Japan[b]	China	Brazil	Maranhão	Approximate Total
1549	—	42	0	3	0	6	0	—
1558	—	—	0	—	0	25	0	—
1559	—	112	0	8	0	—	0	—
1560	350	—	0	—	0	—	0	500
1568	—	—	0	—	0	61	0	—
1571	—	194	0	13	4	—	0	—
1574	552	—	0	—	—	—	0	—
1579	484	—	0	—	—	—	0	—
1582	—	302	0	—	—	—	0	—
1584	—	—	0	82	—	140	0	—
1587	—	311	0	—	12	—	0	—
1588	—	—	0	113	—	—	0	—
1590	533	—	0	—	—	—	0	—
1593	570	—	0	138	—	—	0	—
1599	591	321	0	—	—	—	0	—
1600	—	—	0	109	30	169	0	1,230
1603	620	—	—	—	—	—	0	—
1605	—	258	—	—	—	—	0	—
1606	644	—	—	—	—	176	0	—
1607–1608	—	—	—	140	17	—	0	—
1609	—	—	—	233	—	—	0	—
1610	—	—	—	—	—	165	0	—
1612	680	—	—	—	—	—	0	—
1614	659	266	135	—	—	—	0	—
1615	665	—	141	—	—	—	0	—

Continued on next page

Year	Portugal	Goa	Malabar	Japan	China	Brazil	Maranhão	Approximate Total
1619	643	—	—	—	—	—	0	—
1620	—	245	149	115	—	—	0	1,350
1624	—	—	—	106	28	—	0	—
1626	—	—	—	165	—	—	0	—
1627	—	304	—	—	—	—	0	—
1628	634	—	—	—	—	—	0	—
1631	—	—	—	—	—	176	0	—
1632	—	—	180	—	—	—	0	—
1633	662	261	140	—	—	—	0	—
1634	—	—	—	—	28	—	0	—
1639	639	—	—	—	30	—	0	—
1640	—	—	160	—	—	—	0	—
1641	—	268	—	—	—	159	0	—
1646	—	—	—	75	24	—	0	—
1648	—	—	142	—	29	—	0	—
1649	649	229	—	—	—	—	0	1,260
1654	—	—	—	—	—	162	26[c]	—
1664	—	265	—	—	—	—	11[c]	—
1665	630	—	—	45	—	—	—	—
1666	—	—	—	—	27	—	—	—
1667	—	—	36	—	—	—	—	—
1671	—	—	—	—	—	—	20	—
1672	655	—	—	—	—	—	—	—
1673	—	245	—	—	—	—	—	—
1674	—	—	54	47	—	—	—	—
1675	657	—	—	43	—	—	—	—
1677	—	—	64	—	—	—	—	—
1678	700	210	—	—	—	—	—	—
1679	—	—	—	44	—	188	34	—
1681	700	—	—	—	21	—	—	—
1683	—	—	—	—	—	252	—	1,340
1688	—	—	49	—	—	—	—	—
1689	—	226	—	—	—	—	—	—
1690	701	—	—	—	—	—	54	—
1691	—	—	—	45	35	—	—	—
1694	—	—	—	—	—	310	—	—
1696	665	—	—	—	—	—	—	—
1697	—	—	42	—	—	—	—	—
1699	—	231	—	—	—	—	—	—
1700	716	—	—	—	36	—	—	1,440
1705	732	—	—	—	—	—	—	—
1706	—	205	—	—	38	—	—	—
1711	736	—	—	—	—	—	—	—

Continued on next page

Year	Portugal	Goa	Malabar	Japan	China	Brazil	Maranhão	Approximate Total
1713	—	205	—	—	—	—	—	—
1714	—	—	—	54	—	—	—	—
1716	—	—	—	—	—	324	—	—
1720	706	—	—	—	—	—	64	—
1721	—	—	—	49	—	—	—	—
1722	—	175	—	—	—	367	69[c]	1,460
1726	717	—	—	—	26	—	—	—
1728	—	165	—	—	—	—	—	—
1730	—	—	—	—	—	—	102	—
1732	—	—	—	—	—	362	118	—
1734	796	—	56	61	—	—	—	—
1735	—	—	—	—	—	417	117	1,625
1737	755	—	—	—	—	—	—	—
1738	—	—	—	—	—	423	—	—
1740	789	62	—	—	—	—	—	—
1741	—	134	—	—	45	431	—	—
1743	799	—	—	—	—	447	—	—
1748	—	—	—	—	—	471	—	—
1749	855	—	—	—	—	—	—	—
1751	—	—	—	—	47	—	148	—
1753	—	—	—	59	—	—	136	—
1754	818	161	—	—	—	—	—	1,760
1756	—	—	45	—	—	—	—	—
1757	—	—	—	—	—	476	—	—
1760	—	—	—	—	—	—	155	—

SOURCES: Portugal, 1560–79: *HCJAP*, 2:1, 3–4, 531–36; remaining years: first and third catalogues, in ARSI, *Lus.*, 44:I to 49. Goa, 1549–87: *DI*, 1: 516–23; 4: 301–6, 466–76; 8: 414–18, 602–26; 14: 788–800; remaining years: third catalogues, in ARSI, *Goa*, 25–26. Malabar: F/JM, 2, app. 1. Japan, 1549– 87: see Goa; 1600–1608, *RACJ*, 1: 179; 3: 115; 1604–46: *MHJ*, 579–1054, passim; remaining years: ARSI, *JapSin*, 134, fols. 301–447. Brazil, 1558 and 1568: *MB*, 2: 459–66; 4: 475–82; remaining years: first and third catalogues, in ARSI, *Bras.*, 5 and 6. Maranhão, 1652–55 and 1663: *HCJB*, 4: 338–40; remaining years: ARSI, *Bras.*, 27.

[a] The original province of Goa, or India, embraced all installations east of the Cape of Good Hope. Consequently, sixteenth-century personnel reports included personnel outside the subcontinent in places like Malacca, Ormuz, and the Moluccas.

[b] As noted in Chapter 6, the Japan province was really Southeast Asia after the expulsion of 1614.

[c] The estimates for Maranhão are for the years 1655, 1663, and 1723.

Inventory of Supplies,
New St. Paul's College, Goa, 1707

Articles	Quantity	Articles	Quantity
		Clothing	
Shirts	368	Pants	540
Handkerchiefs, white	2,600	Socks (pairs)	3,400
		Bedding for guests	
Bed made of yellow gauze	1	Canopy (satin)	1
Quilt from Diu	1	Damask coverlet	1
Pillowcases, large	13	Sheets	21
Pillowcases, small	20	Tablecloth from Portugal	1
Tablecloths	16	Napkins	50
Hand towels	13		
		Foodstuffs	
Pepper (kg)	170	Cloves (kg)	4.5
Cardamom (kg)	0.9	Marmalade (boxes)	150
Pear preserves (boxes)	4	Cherry preserves (box)	1
		Candles, hides, incense, sealing-wax, and writing materials	
Large wax candles	6	Yellow candles for Holy Week	20
Pilgrimage candle	1	Candle wax (kg)	793.8
Hides, cordovan for shoes	40	Hides, unspecified, for shoes	80
Hides from Diu	20	Sheepskins for books	45
Genoa paper (reams)	31	Venice paper (reams)	5
Imperial paper (sheets)	70	Pens (bundles)	9
Sealing-wax (kg)	1.8	Incense (bundles)	2

Continued on next page

Articles	Quantity	Articles	Quantity
Pots, copper			
Kettles, large	9	Kettles, medium	5
Kettles, small	4	Kettles, extra small	11
Pots (*tachos*), large	11	Pots, medium	15
Pots, small	6	Pans (*panelas*)	19
Frying pans, large	8	Frying pans, small	6
Indian earthen vessels (*calões*), large	4	Great pitcher (*tambio*)	2
Indian earthen vessels, small	13	Oven	1
Nails (*belmazes*)	800		
Brass articles			
Tumblers, large	14	Tumblers, small	6
Candlesticks, large	8	Lamps	3
Spoons	200	Forks	250
Lavatory faucets	16	Wire (kg)	4.5
Pestle	1	Bathtub	1
Half bathtub	1		
Iron articles			
Scissors	30	Shoemaker's scissors	4
Shoemaker's knife	6	Wedding hooks	8
Knives for festivals	230	Knives, ordinary	130
Hoes	4	Hatchets	8
Handpike	1	Lamps from Portugal	26
Tin teapots	16	Balances, small	1
Balances, large	2		
China			
Plates	900	Plates, small	380
Tamarind juice cups	960	Ordinary cups	220
Tea cups	380	Other cups	30
Infirmary saucers	30	Other saucers	230
Salt cellars	40	Wine decanters	60
Cruets	40	Vinegar cruets	40
Pitchers (*guindes*) and plates	8	Wash basins	10
Capuchos (?)	3	Preserve pots	13
Mustard dishes	300		

Continued on next page

Articles	Quantity	Articles	Quantity
Pantry supplies			
Wine for masses (liters)	954	Arrack wine (liters)	2,285
Wine from Portugal (liters)	954	Raisin wine (liters)	7,631
Sugar (kg)	163	Marinated raisins (kg)	163
Butter (kg)	22	White raisins (kg)	34
Coconut oil (liters)	982	Portuguese vinegar (liters)	367
Portuguese olive oil (liters)	257	Tamarind, tub	1
Olives (liters)	27	Rice for Jesuits (kg)	3,563
Cheese, Dutch (kg)	33	Rice for servants (kg)	7,620
Cheese, Alentejo (kg)	7	Wheat (kg)	16,482
Miscellaneous			
Linen pieces for cassocks	40	Linen for caps (meters)	33
Damão handkerchiefs	323	Spools of white ribbon for pants	52
Spools of rope for Kaffirs' beds	46	Cotton for lamps (kg)	4
White thread (kg)	3	Black thread (kg)	3
Coverlets, grey	60	Coverlets, red	27
Gingham for doublets (piece)	1	Linen, amber-colored (pieces)	140
Druggett (pieces)	20	Thin muslin (pieces)	9
Ordinary muslin (pieces)	110	Coarse muslin (pieces)	100
Hand towels	120	Towels for church	20
Bright cloth for Kaffirs	60	Other cloth for Kaffirs	10
Napkins	1,600	Black sheets	420
Pillowcases, large	100	Pillowcases, small	500
Quilts, grey	65	Cotton cloth for servants' trousers (pieces)	60
Cotton cloth for Kaffirs	52	Writing desks	3
Bandorá planks	90	Brazilian tobacco (kg)	23

SOURCE: "Entrega q. faz o P.ᶜ Rector Manuel Sarayua a seu successor o Pᶜ António de Payva deste coll.º de S. Paulo. Provimentos q. ficao' na procurat.ᵃ," 31 Nov. 1707, in ARSI, *Goa*, 9:II, 400–404ᵛ. There were 77 residents in the college and 2 in Old St. Paul's at this time. "Catalogus rerum provinciae Goane," Aug. 1706, in ARSI, FG, 627.

APPENDIX F

The Fate of the Jesuits Serving in the College of Olinda and Its Dependencies at the Time of the Second Dutch Invasion, 1630

As mentioned in Chapter 9, the Dutch invasion of Pernambuco disrupted the lives of the 33 Jesuits serving there in 1630. The identities and subsequent careers of most of them are summarized below.[1]

Name	Age in 1630	Birthplace	Careers
Leonardo Mercúrio	44	Italy	Vice-rector of college; captured at the defense outpost of Arraial de Bom Jesús (close to Olinda and Recife) in 1635; died at sea.
José da Costa	66	Portugal	Minister of college; captured (where unclear) and sent to Holland; repatriated to Portugal, but died at sea en route back to Brazil in 1636 or 1637.
Belchior Pires	49	Portugal	Longtime missionary in Pernambuco, who died in 1668.
Manuel Teneiro	58	Portugal	Captured by the Dutch in 1624 and again in 1635; perished in Dutch hands in 1636.
Gaspar de Semperes	79	Spain	Engineer and architect; designer of Fort Reis Magos in Natal; captured at Arraial de Bom Jesús; deported to Cartagena, where he died (when unknown).
Pero de Castilho	59	Brazil	No information.
Manuel do Couto	70	Portugal	Retired to Bahia, where he died in 1639.
Domingos Ferreira	78	Madeira	Died during or soon after invasion.

1. The following is based on *HCJB*, 5: 383–88 and 365–68; see also Serafim Leite, "A Companhia de Jesús no Brasil e a restauração de Portugal," Academia portuguesa da história, *Anais*, ser. 1, no. 7 (1942): 119–61.

Name	Age in 1630	Birthplace	Careers
Francisco de Vilhena	48	Portugal	Fought in the resistance under Matias de Albuquerque but was captured at Fort Nazaré; exiled to Spanish empire (where unspecified); for later career, see Chapter 9.
Manuel de Araujo	41	Portugal	No information.
Francisco da Costa	41	Portugal	No information.
António de Oliveira	22	Portugal	Student and companion of Manuel de Morais in Paraíba; captured and sent to Antwerp; released and returned to Bahia, where he died at age 33.
Francisco Ribeiro	21	Brazil	Student; captured at Fort Nazaré and sent to Holland; see Chapter 9; died in 1666.
Sebastião da Cruz	68	Portugal	Lay brother; fate unknown.
João Gonçalves	54	Portugal	Lay brother; collected tithes in Pernambuco for college in Rio de Janeiro; captured and sent to Holland. Following release returned to Bahia, where he died in 1644.
Rodrigo Alvares	69	Portugal	Lay brother; captured and sent to Amsterdam, where he died in 1636.
Afonso Luiz	66	Portugal	Lay brother; captured and sent to Amsterdam, where he died in 1636.
Francisco Martins	65	Spain	Lay brother; captured and brutally tortured; died at sea in 1636.
Pedro Alvares	75	Portugal	Lay brother; captured; tortured; became blind and died in Zeeland in 1636.
Manuel Pereira	28	Portugal	Captured at Arraial de Bom Jesús in 1635; died at sea in 1637.
Gaspar da Costa	31	Portugal	No information.
Manuel de Morais	35	Brazil	Missionary who became a resistance leader; captured in 1635; for his later career, see Chapter 9; died ca. 1651.
António Bellaiva	38	Italy	Died in combat while attending the wounded in 1633.
Manuel de Oliveira	38	Portugal	Missionary; participated in the resistance but retired to Bahia in 1635; died there in 1657.
Domingos Pires	68	Portugal	Lay brother; fate unknown.
António Antunes	57	Brazil	Missionary; captured and exiled to Holland, but returned to Brazil and died in Rio de Janeiro in 1638.
António Caminha	36	Portugal	Missionary; returned to Bahia in 1635 and died there in 1676.

Name	Age in 1630	Birthplace	Careers
Gonçalo Fernandes	29	Portugal	Student; withdrew to Bahia in 1635, where he completed his studies and died in 1666.
Manuel Ferreira	18	Portugal	Student; captured by Dutch but escaped and fought with distinction at battle of Porto Calvo.
António Ferraz	42	Portugal	Missionary; captured and transported to Holland; returned to Rio de Janeiro in 1641; died in 1646.
Manuel Gomes	58	Portugal	Missionary in the northeast and later in Maranhão; died in Rio de Janeiro ca. 1648.
Francisco da Fonseca	54	Brazil	Missionary; retired to Alagoas in 1635; died in Rio de Janeiro in 1645.
Matias da Costa	42	Brazil	Missionary; role in resistance unknown; died in Rio de Janeiro in 1675.

The 33 men averaged 49.9 years in age in 1630, or 53.7 years if the four students are excluded. The age at death of 23 of the men is known. Despite their travail during and after the Dutch intrusion, they lived an average of 65.9 years, a figure remarkably close to the sample for the Brazil province during the years 1661–65 (see Table 11.7). Evidently these men clung to life as tenaciously as they did to their faith.

Bibliographical Note

This study and its sequel rest upon a wide array of sources, printed and manuscript. Within North America, the major libraries that I have consulted for books and manuscripts are the Ames Library and the James Ford Bell Library of the University of Minnesota; the John Carter Brown Library at Brown University; the libraries at the University of California, Berkeley, the University of Chicago, and Columbia University; the Library of Congress; the Lilly Library and the general library of the University of Indiana; the general library of the University of Michigan; the Newberry Library, Chicago; the New York Public Library; the Oliveira Lima Library, Catholic University of America; the Pius XII Memorial Library, St. Louis University; the general library of the University of British Columbia, Vancouver; the Nettie Lee Benson Library, University of Texas; the Seattle University Library; and the libraries of the University of Washington. The notes that accompany the text adequately disclose the printed sources utilized, obviating the need for a conventional listing.

As the Preface indicates, I have been privileged to work in archives situated on several continents. I began manuscript research for this project in Portugal in 1968 and returned to work there for extended periods on three other occasions. Despite the devastating 1755 earthquake, a cluster of archives in Lisbon still possesses an abundance of documentation relevant to all aspects of this study.[1] The richest and most diverse of these depositories are the ex-imperial archives known as the Overseas Archives (the Arquivo

---

1. Although inevitably dated, Virgínia Rau, "Arquivos de Portugal: Lisboa," *Proceedings of the International Colloquium on Luso-Brazilian Studies* (Nashville, 1953), 189–213, remains a useful introduction. It was reprinted in Lisbon in 1961 for the use of Fulbright students by the Luso-American Educational Commission. The best-informed recent description of the holdings of Portuguese and Goan archives and libraries is Timothy J. Coates, "Sources in Portuguese and Goan (Indian) Archives and Libraries (1500–1755): A Guide and Commentary," in *Discovery in the Archives of Spain and Portugal: Quincentenary Essays, 1492–1992*, ed. Lawrence J. McCrank (Binghamton, N.Y., 1993), 291–318. I wish to acknowledge the kindness of Fr. Mathias C. Kiemen, O.F.M., of the now-defunct American Academy of Franciscan History, Potomac, Maryland, who invited me in 1968 to consult his extensive collection of 25 oversize, bound volumes of photocopies of the documents that he filmed in Portuguese and Spanish archives for a planned expansion of his seminal study of missionaries and Indians in the Amazon. Together with the rest of the Academy's impressive library, that collection is currently housed at the Franciscan School of Theology in Berkeley, California, and ought to be consulted by students interested in the themes that it illuminates before they venture to Peninsular archives.

Histórico Ultramarino, or AHU), housed in the former residence of an eighteenth-century viceroy of India, the Palácio da Ega, in west Lisbon. It is the counterpart, though on a smaller scale, of the Spanish General Archives of the Indies in Seville. Its resources include a vast array of administrative correspondence, reports, and recommendations (*consultas*) of the Overseas Council (Conselho Ultramarino), the reports of administrative, ecclesiastical, judicial, and military officials within the empire, as well as petitions of colonists and ecclesiastics residing there.[2] Some of these materials, which begin early in the seventeenth century and extend well beyond the period covered by this study, are bound in codices (*livros de registro*), but vastly more are preserved in metal boxes (*caixas*) and bundles (*maços*).[3] Whereas the codices emphasize imperial directives that applied to particular jurisdictions or sometimes to the entire empire, the caixas and maço series are more or less chronologically and geographically ordered correspondence focused on particular segments of the former empire. To the extent possible, I examined boxes and bundles in each series from its beginning until the end of the eighteenth century. Of the 400 or more boxes and bundles devoted to Portuguese enclaves in India, I examined 124, mostly those pertaining to the late seventeenth and eighteenth centuries. With respect to Brazil, I concentrated upon the documentary series pertaining to the captaincies of Pará, Maranhão, Bahia, and Rio de Janeiro, reviewing about 50 boxes or bundles for each. In addition, I read selectively boxes concerning the remaining maritime captaincies and some of the interior captaincies (such as Piauí).[4] I also consulted the small collection of boxed documents on Madeira and the Azores and many of those concerning Angola and Mozambique.

The single greatest documentary mine in Lisbon is the venerable Arquivo Nacional da Torre do Tombo (ANTT), the central state archives whose origins trace back to the fourteenth century. From 1757 until 1990 they were inadequately housed in the Palácio de São Bento, a former Benedictine monastery in central west Lisbon, but since 1990 they have been situated in more spacious quarters in the Cidade Universitária district of northern Lisbon. Despite the existence of several published guides, consultation of the richness of these archives is still handicapped by inadequate finding aids.[5] For this study I consulted some of the 72-volume series known as the *Documentos remettidos da India* or *Livros das monções do reino*, files of correspondence between Lisbon and Goa during the seventeenth century,

2. For a description of the origins of the Overseas Archives, see Alberto Iria, "Introdução," *Boletim de Arquivo Histórico Colonial*, 1 (only volume) (Lisbon, 1950): 5–15.

3. Though not free from error, M. A. Hedwig Fitzler, "Relação dos códices do 'extinto conselho ultramarino,' " in Fitzler and Ernesto Ennes, eds., *A Secção ultramarina da Biblioteca Nacional* (Lisbon, 1928), 69–184, remains a helpful guide. It was completed shortly before the papers of the Overseas Council were shifted from the National Library to the present Overseas Archives.

4. Unfortunately there are no published calendars of the documents on India. There are two published guides to some of the materials on Brazil: that compiled by Eduardo de Castro e Almeida (CeA), which focuses upon one of the series of caixas concerning Bahia and Rio de Janeiro, and "Catálogo de documentos sôbre a história de S. Paulo, existentes no arquivo histórico ultramarino, de Lisboa," *RIHGB*, Tomo[s] Especia[is], 7 vols. (Rio de Janeiro, 1956–57). In addition, there are also several typescript inventories, such as one on the "first catalogue" series on Bahia and another concerning documents on Pernambuco.

5. See, however, Pedro A. de Azevedo and António Baião, *O Arquivo da Torre do Tombo: Sua história, corpos que o compõem e organização* (1905; facs. ed., Lisbon, 1989); A. Mesquita de Figueiredo, *Arquivo Nacional da Torre do Tombo: Roteiro prático* (Lisbon, 1922); João Martins da Silva Marques, *Arquivo Nacional da Torre do Tombo*, vol. 1 (only), *Index indicum* (Lisbon, 1935); and Joel Serrão, Maria José da Silva Leal, and Miriam Halpern Pereira, *Roteiro de fontes da história portuguesa contemporanea: Arquivo Nacional da Torre do Tombo*, 2 vols. (Lisbon, 1984). There are several hundred handwritten "catalogues" of individual collections, but they tend to be sketchy and are not always reliable.

especially its first half.[6] Ten codices (nos. 597–606) from the extensive series of the former Ministério do Reino records produced unexpectedly revealing materials concerning Brazil, Angola, and Mozambique during the eighteenth century. But the most extensive and most vital collection in the ANTT for this study is the vast and miscellaneous "Cartório Jesuítico." That cartulary consists of some of the original files of the missions procurators who resided at Santo Antão (see Chapter 13). Each of the cartório's 106 bundles contains hundreds of pages of documents, some bound but many loose. They provide vital economic data concerning how the Society functioned in India, in Brazil, and elsewhere within the Assistancy. Included, for example, are estate inventories, records of sugar production, registers of plantation slaves, bills of lading, deeds of donation, royal licenses, and correspondence by both Jesuits and royal officials posted throughout the empire.[7]

The manuscript (*reservados*) section of the Biblioteca Nacional (BNL) contains an old but still serviceable file drawer catalogue of its extensive holdings.[8] This collection includes remnants of the files of a number of Jesuit houses and offices in Portugal. Among them are a half dozen codices (nos. 1587, 4517, 4518, 4529, 4532, and 4534) that contain eighteenth-century correspondence of Jesuit leaders in Maranhão and Pará. Fr. Francisco Rodrigues once suggested that such files may have belonged to the University of Coimbra, but I think it more likely that they were also part of the records of the missions procurator for Maranhão and Pará. One priceless codex that belonged to the University of Évora is no. 4254, the notes of its market buyers between 1606 and 1631, including their food purchases at local fairs and the daily rations prescribed for college residents; another (no. 4214) is a Portuguese translation of a handbook of rules of conduct prepared by Loyola for the Society's students, one that was issued to those attending the same institution. There are also a few account books that once belonged to Jesuit colleges, the most important being the previously unidentified codex 4512, early-eighteenth-century accounts of the college of São Lourenço, Porto. Though most of the 758 codices of the library's well-known Coleção Pombalina contain documents consulted for the sequel to this volume, several concern Jesuit disputes in the period covered here.[9] Three codices, for example (nos. 176, 177, and 519), concern disagreements between the archbishop of Goa and the Society, whereas no. 475 provides documentation of the Jesuits' land disputes in Brazil.

Overlooking the western outskirts of Lisbon is the Palácio da Ajuda. The former royal library (BA) housed there includes judicial papers, correspondence between the crown

6. About one-seventh of this series is published in Raymundo António de Bulhão Pato, ed., *Documentos remettidos da India, ou Livros das monções*, 5 vols. (Lisbon, 1880–1935). António da Silva Rego resumed publication of that series and issued vols. 6–8 (Lisbon, 1974–77). Most of the "Livros das monções" are preserved in the HAG archives. See below.

7. Catalogue 305 in the ANTT provides a superficial summary of the Cartório and of the smaller collection called the "Armário Jesuítico," the latter being some of the surviving files belonging to the college of Santo Antão. The best, though partial, introduction to the Cartório Jesuítico is Fr. John Correia-Afonso's "Indian History in the 'Cartório dos Jesuitas' " (n.d., mimeographed).

8. A useful index of some of its documents concerning the history of colonial Brazil is the "Inventário dos documentos relativos ao Brasil, existentes na Biblioteca Nacional de Lisboa," *ABNRJ* 75 (1955 [1957]), covering the years 1534–1692, and ibid., 93 (1973 [1974]), spanning the years 1693–1702 and 1723–1825. The first of these two calendars contains the better of the two analytical indexes. It is evident from Coates, "Sources" (see note 1), that the Biblioteca Nacional in Lisbon has been extensively modernized since I was last privileged to work there.

9. The National Library acquired the collection in July 1886. Three years later it issued a highly detailed inventory that remains indispensable: Biblioteca Nacional de Lisboa, *Inventario . . . Collecçao Pombalina* (Lisbon, 1889).

and its agents overseas, and extensive ecclesiastical records, including the illuminating correspondence between Fr. Carbone and the Portuguese representative to Rome (1734–50; see Chapter 23) and the famed "Jesuítas na Asia" collection of transcripts.[10] That extensive collection provides exceptional detail concerning the economic and evangelical activities of Jesuits serving in the Japan province and the vice-province of China down to the mid-eighteenth century. Consultation of its 61 codices is facilitated by a handwritten index in the library.[11] The transcripts were laboriously but lucidly copied in the college of São Paulo, Macao, between the early 1740s and the late 1750s and were sent for safekeeping to the Far Eastern missions procurate in Lisbon on the eve of the Society's expulsion. Their originals were long considered lost, but in the early 1960s Fr. Josef Schütte discovered that some of them survive in three Madrid depositories.[12] The Jesuítas na Asia collection discloses much about the Jesuits' commercial and investment practices in the East and their tribulations there as missionaries.

Two other especially useful Lisbon manuscript repositories may be briefly mentioned. The manuscripts of the library of the Academia das Ciências de Lisboa (ACL) consists of two collections: the first, the "green" (verde) series, came from the convent N. S. de Jesus and includes copies and some originals dating from the sixteenth to eighteenth centuries. The 980 codices of this collection emphasize ecclesiastical, genealogical, and literary themes. By contrast, the "blue" (azul) series represents a variety of manuscripts contributed to the Academy since its founding (1779) by its many patrons. That series includes, for example, the papers of some of the governors and viceroys who served in Brazil and India.[13] Especially important for this study are the nine codices (mss. 503–11) of the count of Sandomil, viceroy of India from 1733 to 1741, which reveal as much about the state of the viceroy's mind as they do about the reasons for the catastrophic loss of Bassein (see Chapter 23).

Finally, among the Lisbon repositories, there is the Arquivo do Tribunal das Contas (ATC), the accounting bureau archives that possess priceless collections of fiscal records from the mid-eighteenth century until the present. Two of its collections proved to be especially important. The first is the "Cartório da junta da inconfidência"—the cartulary of the treason board's archives, which includes registers of income and expenditures of several of the Jesuits' colleges in the kingdom, most notably a unique series for the Bragança college (nos. 31–35) that extends from 1649 to 1759, and less extensive runs of the accounts of colleges of Setúbal, Santarém, and Elvas (nos. 133, 135, and 196). The second collection consists of the records of the centralized royal treasury (Real Erário or Erário Régio) from 1761 until 1834. Among its holdings is an indispensable series of large folio volumes (nos. 368–75) that concerns income and expenditures of former Jesuit facilities in the kingdom, Brazil, Angola, Mozambique, and India between 1759 and the end of the eighteenth century. Although that

10. For a brief but informative description of the Ajuda library, see *PDH*, 1: 107–8. See also Carlos Alberto Ferreira, *Inventário dos manuscritos da Biblioteca da Ajuda referentes a América do Sul* (Coimbra, 1956). In the 1970s the indefatigable Fr. António da Silva Rego supervised the preparation of a two-volume calendar of the library's holdings, but a subsequent reorganization of the collections diminished the calendar's utility.

11. Between 1955 and 1960, Jacques Braga published excerpts from this collection in *Boletim eclesiastico da diocese de Macao*, vols. 53–56. Braga's own collection, mostly copies rather than original documents, is in the national library of Australia in Canberra but proved to be disappointing when I examined it.

12. Schütte's discovery was first reported in *Brotéria* 72 (Jan. 1961): 88–90. For a nice piece of detection, see Josef Franz Schütte, S.J., *El "Archivo del Japon," Vicisitudes del Archivo Jesuítico del extremo oriente y descripción del fondo existente en la real academia de la historia de Madrid* (Madrid, 1964). Schütte found other parts of the college's archives in the Archivo Nacional and in the Biblioteca Nacional.

13. The "blue" series is calendared in *BFUP*, 6: 177–261, and the "green" series in ibid., 263–325. But see alternatively ACL, *Catálogo de manuscritos: Série vermelha*, 2 vols. (Lisbon, 1986).

group of codices is primarily useful for the sequel to this study, it also includes documents that illuminate Jesuit fiscal practices before the expulsion.[14]

Outside of Lisbon, three Portuguese archives contributed important data to this study. First is the Biblioteca Pública de Évora (BPE), for which Cunha Rivara's old guide remains the best introduction to its manuscript resources.[15] The manuscripts there emphasize diplomatic and ecclesiastical themes for the empire, especially Brazil and India, during the seventeenth and eighteenth centuries. Five codices (CXV/2-12 to CXV/2-16), for example, contain fundamental evidence pertaining to the activities and controversies of the Jesuits in northern Brazil, especially the Amazon, between the 1660s and the 1730s. Second is the Biblioteca Geral da Universidade de Coimbra (BGUC), which possesses an extensive collection of letter books for this period.[16] A few of them provide additional evidence of Jesuit disputes over the possession of landed property, the payment of tithes, and asserted exemption from the jurisdiction of bishops in Brazil, as well as the only document that I have found in which the province of Portugal purportedly offered to surrender all of its landed holdings for the defense of the realm (1704). Third, the municipal archives of the city of Elvas proved to have a unique and vital document, ms. 6891.[17] This invaluable account is a very detailed report, dated 31 December 1666, by the provincial of Goa to the viceroy concerning his Order's assets and expenses in the province. I know of no other copy.

The numerous municipal, state, and federal archives and historical institutes of Brazil also contributed to this study but proved most useful for the companion volume to follow. For the colonial period, those archives are strongest for the eighteenth and early nineteenth centuries and are relatively weakest before then. That is true, for example, of the colonial section of the state archives of Pará, which is kept in a large room in the public library of Belém. The original edition of the initial volume of the *Annaes da Bibliotheca e Archivo Publico* (10 vols., Belém, 1902–26) contained a very helpful inventory of the several hundred codices that constitute that collection. Unfortunately, it was omitted from the facsimile edition (1968). When I consulted the collection in 1976, some of the codices listed were missing, and others had become unreadable. Still, I discovered important dispatches and enclosures, both originals and copies, in more than 50 codices in four series that I explored from their beginnings until the end of the eighteenth century: (1) correspondence of the governor's office with local authorities (1740–1844); (2) replies by local authorities (1733–1854); (3) correspondence of Lisbon with subordinates in Pará (1752–1841); and (4) their dispatches to Lisbon (1717–1836).

My efforts to work in one group of archives in 1976–77 proved disappointing. The state archives of Maranhão were then warehoused in total disarray while their quarters were supposedly being renovated, a situation that had already endured for some years, during which serious historical research in São Luís was impossible. The badly lit and poorly

14. See Luis Bivar Guerra and Manuel Maria Ferreira, *Catálogo do Arquivo do Tribunal de Contas* (Lisbon, 1950); and Alzira Teixeira Leite Moreira, *Inventário do fundo geral do Erário Régio* (Lisbon, 1977).

15. Joaquim Heliodoro da Cunha Rivara, comp., *Catálogo dos manuscritos da Biblioteca Eborense*, 4 vols. (Lisbon, 1850–71). Cunha Rivara (b. 1809–d. 1879) was one of the giants of nineteenth-century Portuguese historiography.

16. The library maintains a unique, very helpful ongoing series of *Catálogos de manuscritos da Biblioteca da Universidade de Coimbra* (Coimbra, 1931–). For its holdings on Brazil especially, see Francisco Morais, *Catálogo dos manuscritos da Biblioteca da Universidade de Coimbra relativos ao Brasil* (Coimbra, 1931).

17. Domingos Lavadinho, *Manuscritos e otros documentos da biblioteca municipal de Elvas* (Elvas, 1945). (I am indebted to Fritz Berkmeier of the Livraria Histórica Ultramarina, Lisbon, for making available to me a copy of this rare work.) The 1666 manuscript is mentioned on p. 48, where it bears a different call number than that employed today.

ventilated state archives of Pernambuco in Recife proved to have little of interest, and the same may be said for that city's once-famed historical institute.[18]

In Salvador (Bahia), the most fruitful archives for this study were the state archives (Arquivo Publico do Estado da Bahia) (APB) and the municipal archives (AMB), both well organized, both equipped with reliable published guides.[19] The historical section of the APB possesses several series that proved vital for this study: (1) "Ordens régias," consisting of directives from the crown to authorities in Bahia (I read the first 76 codices, 1648–1786); (2) dispatches from the government in Bahia to Lisbon (in this fragmented series I examined five codices, 1664–1799); (3) dispatches from the government in Bahia to various functionaries (I consulted a half dozen codices, 1730–77); and (4) responses from various functionaries to the government in Bahia (I examined nine codices, 1726–81). In the municipal archives I found useful information in 34 codices in eight series, of which the following were especially helpful: (1) "Atas da cámara" (1702–75); (2) "Cartas do senado [da cámara]" (1678–1741); (3) "Cartas do senado a sua magestade" (1640–1822); and (4) "Oficios ao govêrno" (1712–1807).

In Rio de Janeiro I examined materials in the Arquivo Nacional (ANRJ), the Biblioteca Nacional (BNRJ), the Arquivo Municipal (AMRJ), the historical institute (IHGB), and several other repositories. The footnotes reveal my occasional indebtedness to these sources. However, most of my research in these depositories focused upon themes analyzed in the second volume, where my use of these facilities can more appropriately be indicated.

The Historical Archives of Goa (HAG), situated 400 kilometers south of Bombay, have long been recognized as a rich mine of information concerning the operations of royal government there, and especially the economic activities of the Jesuits in India in support of their endeavors in the subcontinent and those in the Far East.[20] One of the archives' fundamental collections is the famous "Livros das monções do reino," the official correspondence between Lisbon and the viceroys and governors of India, a series of 467 folio volumes that extends from 1574 to 1914. I consulted about 30 codices numbered between 13 and 65 in the Livros das monções with emphasis upon the second half of the seventeenth century. But even more important were a score of codices concerning the Jesuits' estate management, commerce, receipts, and expenditures incurred by Jesuit facilities in India and related correspondence.[21]

In England, documents in the Public Record Office (PRO) proved to be more illuminating than were the Portuguese manuscripts that I saw in the British Library. The PRO's important "State Papers, Portugal" (SP 89), which begins in 1661, includes consular and diplomatic reports from Lisbon to London on a variety of topics. They include economic conditions within the kingdom, prospects for diplomatic or economic

18. But at least it was open when its well-known director chose to be there. In Belém the historical institute was shut up and its president was away from the city with what was seemingly the only set of keys.

19. Arquivo do Estado da Bahia, *Guia do Arquivo do Estado da Bahia* (Salvador, n.d.); Prefeitura Municipal do Salvador, *Catálogo dos manuscritos: Documentos do século xvii ao século xx* (Salvador, 1972).

20. Though none is as complete or as accurate as one might wish, the following are essential guides to the resources of this depository: C. R. Boxer, "A Glimpse of the Goa Archives," *Bulletin of the School of Oriental and African Studies* 14 (June 1952): 299–324; P. S. S. Pissurlencar, *Roteiro dos arquivos da India Portuguesa* (Bastorá, 1955); M. N. Pearson, "The Goa Archives and Indian History," *Quarterly Review of Historical Studies* 13 (1973–74): 205–11; V. T. Gune, *A Guide to the Collections of Records from the Goa Archives* (Panaji, 1973); Teotónio R. de Souza, S.J., *Medieval Goa: A Socio-Economic History* (New Delhi, 1979), 199–205; and P. P. Shirodkar, "Records on Jesuits in Goa Archives," in Teotónio R. de Souza and Charles J. Borges, eds., *Jesuits in India: In Historical Perspective* (Goa, 1992), 21–33.

21. It would serve no useful purpose to list each of the codices consulted concerning Jesuit economic activities in the East: the footnotes provide sufficient testimony of their importance to this study.

gain there by England, ship movements, and assessments of key personnel, including Jesuits, whom the English feared were influential at court. For this volume I consulted SP89/16 to /47.[22]

The last archives where I was privileged to work proved to be the most illuminating of all for this study. Although once closed to laymen, the Roman archives of the Society of Jesus, the Archivum Romanum Societatis Iesu (ARSI), are today accessible to qualified scholars interested in the history of the Society from its founding until the early twentieth century.[23] Two of the ARSI's many collections especially engaged my attention.[24] The smaller of the two, the Fondo Gesuitico, is a series of loose bundles that once belonged to the office of the solicitor general of the Society, an intriguing medley of legal papers concerning problems that regularly confronted administrators of Jesuit colleges. The other, far more ample collection consists of the surviving files of the secretariat of the generalate pertaining to the Portuguese Assistancy. They are preserved in several series of bound volumes that average about 400 pages. They are geographically and to some extent chronologically organized. Particularly important were the periodic personnel and economic reports (catalogues) that illuminated patterns of recruitment, training, assignment, leadership, and death of members (especially prominent ones) of the Society and fiscal gains and losses experienced by colleges throughout the Assistancy from the Society's beginning until 1750. Both series provide detailed information on the Jesuits' participation in imperial commerce, their investment strategies, levels of income and expenditure, the Assistancy's major and lesser beneficiaries, the administrative and economic roles of major administrators, and Jesuit conflicts with representatives of other Orders and with royal officials. Altogether I examined seventeen bundles pertaining to the Fondo Gesuitico (nos. 627, 720–22, 757, 1269, 1361/6, 1373, 1369, 1376, 1443/4, 1443/9, 1469, 1477, 1536/4, 1569, and 1587), and 73 codices: *Lus.* (Portugal, the Atlantic islands, and Angola): nos. 13, 14:I, 14:II, 37:I, 40, 44:I, 44:II, 45, 46, 47, 48, 49, 74, 75, 76, 77, 78, 79, 80, 81:I, 82, 83, 84:I, 84:II, 87, and 88. *Bras.*, (Brazil): nos. 1, 2, 3:I, 3:II, 5:I, 5:II, 6:I, 6:II, 7, 8:I, 8:II, 9, 10:I, 10:II, 11:I, 11:II, 12, 13, 14, 15:I, 15:II, 16, 25, 26, and 28. *Goa* (includes Malabar): nos. 9:II, 18, 19, 20, 22:I, 22:II, 23, 24:I, 24:II, 25, 26, 27, 35, 36:I, 36:II, and 60. *JapSin* (the Japan province and the vice-province of China): nos. 23, 26, 35, 48, 134, and 166.

22. The splendid calendar, *Descriptive List of the State Papers, Portugal, 1661–1780, in the Public Record Office, London*, prepared by C. R. Boxer (3 vols. [Lisbon, 1979–83]), greatly facilitated my labors in the PRO. I wish to thank Professor Boxer for allowing me to consult the first two of these volumes in typescript.

23. Cf. Azevedo and Baião, *Torre do Tombo*, 55. After describing briefly the Cartório Jesuítico, the two authors observed sarcastically that the collection was "much consulted by the fathers of the Company of Jesus," which kept its own archives in Rome sealed. The statement was ill informed. In 1893 the leaders of the Society, convinced that the Italian state was about to seize their records, had their archives secretly transported by sea to Holland, where they remained until their return in 1939. The Italian government *did* seize the Fondo Gesuitico collection, but handed it back to the Society "on loan" in 1924. This information was supplied primarily by Fr. Charles O'Neill, S.J.

24. The best brief introduction to the archives is that of their late longtime archivist, Edmond Lamalle, S.J., "L'archivio di un grande ordine religioso: L'Archivio Generale della Compagnia di Gesu," *Archiva ecclesiae* (1981–82): 89–120; and idem, "La Documentation d'histoire missionaire dans le *Fondo Gesuitico* aux archives romaines de la Compagnie de Jésus," *Euntes Docete* 21 (1968): 131–76. A basic inventory of the *Bras.* section will be found in *HCJB*, 1: xxi. For *JapSin*, see Juan Ruiz de Medina, S.J., "La sección Japsin del Archivo Romano de la Compañía de Jésus," *El Extremo Oriente Ibérico* (Madrid, 1989): 117–24. To my knowledge there are no published catalogues of ARSI's holdings for the remainder of the old Assistancy. An opportunity to work in the Vatican Film Library, Saint Louis University, before going to Rome gave me some important preliminary knowledge of what I would find in the ARSI as far as its holdings on Brazil are concerned.

INDEX

In this index an "f" after a number indicates a separate reference on the next page, and an "ff" indicates separate references on the next two pages. A continuous discussion over two or more pages is indicated by a span of page numbers, e.g., "57–59." *Passim* is used for a cluster of references in close but not consecutive sequence. Inclusive dates placed immediately after a name indicate lifespans; when situated after the title of an office holder, they refer to years in office. Portuguese names are usually indexed under the last surname.

Acquisition of lands, licensing procedure, 432. *See also* Lands, Jesuit

Acuña, Cristobal de, Jesuit explorer and author, 222

Administration of Indians, Paulista-Jesuit agreement concerning, 492f

Admiral of Castile, *see* Cabrera, D. Juan Tomás Enrique de

Afonso V, king of Portugal (1438–81), 84

Afonso VI, king of Portugal (1656–83), 109, 331; character, 110; restricts foreign-born Jesuits in *ultramar*, 268, 271

Agra mission, 359, 360n60, 382, 394, 450, 582, 640

Aguiar, D. Isabel de, Jesuit benefactor, 366, 378

Ahmadnagar, sultanate of, 197

Akbar, Jalal-ud-din Muhammad, Mughal ruler (1556–1605), 51

Alcázarquibir, battle of (1578), 657; cost, 329f; Jesuits as scapegoats for, 88; Portuguese defeat, 85; redemption of captives after, 86

Aldeias, *see* Missions, Jesuit, in Brazil

Alexander VI, Pope (1492–1503), 233

Alexander VII, Pope (1655–67), 574

Almeida, Luís de (1525–83), Jesuit benefactor, 349

Alms, 634, 641

Alorna, Marquis of, viceroy of India (1744–50), 453, 543

Alvares, Gaspar, Jesuit benefactor, 351, 378

Alvares, Gonçalo, Visitor, 262

Alvares, João, 285

Ambalakad, 204f

Amerindians, *see* Brasis

Anchieta, José de (1534–97), missionary and linguist, 73, 92, 481

Andreoni, Giovanni Antonio (1649–1716), Jesuit administrator and writer, 409f; accepts African slave trade, 512; and António Vieira, 269; calculates numbers dismissed from Brazil province, 292f; strategy concerning tithe payments, 471

Anglo-Portuguese relations, *see* Luso-English relations

Angola: captured by Dutch, 214; Jesuit beginnings in, 75; liberation of, 214f; limited Jesuit achievements in, 612

Angra, Jesuit college at, 412; debt-free in seventeenth century, 645n121; endowment of, 323; origins, 73f

Anti-Jesuit riots: in Maranhão and Pará (1662), 224; in Maranhão (1684), 123, 225

António, prior of Crato (1531–95), 87–91

Appiani, Luigi, 576

Aquaviva, Claudio, general (1581–1615), 233, 307, 642; against long-term leases, 404; appeals to province of Portugal for alms, 641; approves Jesuits' production of sugar, 416; bans Jesuits' role in indigo trade, 529; career, need for study of, 15n49; cautions confessors, 15, 80; concerns regarding Jesuit deportment, 284; deplores nationalist sentiments by Jesuits, 92; directs Jesuits to abstain from politics, 92; opponents in Fifth Congregation, 258; opposes admission of colonial-born, 259; and *Ratio Studiorum*, 18; rules against Jesuits fighting other Catholics, 91n56; rules against paying passengers on *fragata do colégio*, 532; supports Cape Verde mission, 212f; and temporal administration of *aldeias*, 478; and use of black slaves, 508

Aquaviva, Rudolfo, 46, 51, 67, 393

Araçatiba, sugar estate, 424, 522

Araujo family of Rio de Janeiro, Jesuit benefactors, 358

Arima seminary and college, Japan, 63, 131

Arimos, estates, 217

Arneiro, *quinta de*, 385, 412

Assalona, Velim, Ambelim, villages of, 361; acquisition, 392f; captured by Marathas, 592; confirmation of title to, 434; confiscation and restoration, 442; second confiscation, 453

Assistants (general), 234f

Astráin, António, 288f

Augustinians, 8; arrival in India, 43; arrival at Ormuz, 53; failure to enter China, 67

Aungier, Gerald, 446

Aurangzeb, Mughal Emperor (1659–1707), 448

Aveiras, count of, D. João da Silva Teles e Menezes, viceroy of India (1640–45), 182

Aveiro, D. Alvaro de Lencastre, third duke of Bragança, Jesuit debtor, 556f

Azeitão, country house of, 557

Azevedo, Inácio de, procurator of Brazil (ca 1527–70): canonization sought, 124; complains about interception of African slaves, 513; costs of canonization, 641; ill-fated expedition of, 74f; Jesuit benefactor, 348

Azevedo, Jerónimo de, captain-general of Ceylon (1594–1612) and viceroy of India (1612–17), 393; Jesuit benefactor, 153, 164

Azuchi seminary, Japan, 63

Bahia, college of: founding, 73; garden of, 629; "great inquest" at, 672; growth of during eighteenth century, 598; land acquisition of, 380; loss and recovery of, 207f; ranches of, 407; and tithes, 466f; urban properties of, 398f

Bahia de Todos os Santos: Dutch attack and Portuguese recovery of, 168, 206ff; Jesuit beginnings at, 69f; sugar estates in, 416–20. *See also* Salvador, city of

Bandeirantes (slave raiders), 483

Bandorá, college at, 48, 445, 447, 587, 590; alleged role of superior of during Sidi invasion, 449f; Jesuit-led defense of, 197; loss of, 593

Bardês, parishes of, 45

Barnabites, 3, 7

Barreto, Francisco, governor of India (1555–58), 54f

Barreto, Francisco, Jesuit Visitor, 565

Barreto, João Nunes, patriarch of Ethiopia, 53f

Barreto (de Menezes), Francisco, governor-general of Brazil (1657–63) and Jesuit critic, 469

Barzaeus, Gaspar, 53, 326, 366

Bassein, college of, 43, 47, 381, 415; debts of, 647; as lender, 565

Bassein, town of: captured by Portuguese, 43, 47; coveted by England, 114n55, 190, 326; siege and fall, 592f; Xavier visits, 43

Batticaloa (Ceylon), 169, 179

Bavaria, duke of, Jesuit benefactor, 564

Bazarucos, as petty market coins, 343

Beja, college of: founding, 123; terms of authorization, 444

Belém da Cachoeira, Bahia, seminary of, 332, 369f, 373; endowment of, 349

Belém do Grão Pará, Santa Maria de, city of: founding, 222; anti-Jesuit disturbances in, 495

Belém do Pará, cámara of, 489

Belém do Pará, college (Santo Alexandre) of: contribution to expenses of college of Maranhão, 643; disturbances at (1722), 495; expulsion of Jesuits from (1661–63), 489f; expulsion of Jesuits avoided (1684), 491; ordered to pay tithes, 472; origins, 224; properties of, 381 (*see also* Ibirajuba); ranches of, 408; sugar production of, 421

Benci, Jorge, 511

Benedict XIV, Pope (1740–58), 580

Benedictine, Order of, 8. *See also* St. Benedict, Rule of

Benefactors, Jesuit, 346. *See also*, Azevedo, Inácio de; Azevedo, Jerónimo de; Brandão, Diogo; Cabral, Francisco, Jesuit benefactor; Castro, D. Pedro de; Costa, Sebastião da; Sá, Mem; Sá, Salvador de

Bengal, bay of, 150, 356

Berredo (e Castro), Bernardo Pereira de, governor of Maranhão (1718–22) and Jesuit critic, 495

Betendorf (Bettendorff), Johan Philipe (1625–98), inquisition commissioner, 225f, 672

Betim (Bety), estate of, 390f

Bezoar stones, Jesuit sales of, 543f

Bijapur, 42, 45, 542; sultan invades Bardês, 188; sultanate of, 197

Bishops and tithes, 463

Bom Jesús, professed house of, Goa, 566; complaints concerning resident procurators, 314n67; endowment of, 350, 362; loss of endowment, 373; origins, 45; proposed assignment to Poor Clares, 79; Xavier interred in, 202

Bombay, town of: "dismal calamity" afflicts, 585; establishment of, 190–96; Jesuit opposition to transfer of, 114; Portuguese proposal to repurchase, 588n65; Portuguese resistance to transfer of, 191–96; Sidi invasion of, 491

Bombay lands, Jesuit, 196, 449f

Borba, Diogo de, founder of seminary in India, 44

Borgia, Francisco, general (1565–72), 20, 34, 83, 258; and admission of natives of India, 262; and establishment of colleges in Portugal, 33; favors ending Jesuit reliance upon black slaves, 508; founder of college of Gandia, 16; opposes Jesuits' role as stockmen or sugar planters, 407, 416

Borja [y Aragón], Francisco [de], general (1565–72), *see* Borgia, Francisco

Botelho, Simão, critic of ecclesiastical wastage, 326

Boxer, C. R., 9f, 668f

Braga, college of (São Paulo): origins, 33, dispersion of properties, 385; extent of landholding, 381

Bragança, Catherine (1540–1614), claimant of Portuguese throne, 87

Bragança, D. Theodósio, heir of John IV (d. 1643), 105–9 *passim*

Bragança, college of, 411, 627; endowment of, 352, 366; extent of holdings, 381; niggardliness of, 354

Bragança family, and Society of Jesus, 35, 87, 97, 109, 271, 354n36

Brandão, Diogo, Jesuit benefactor, 349, 390

Brasis, 72; character assessments of, 475, 492, 494, 499f, 601; conversion of to 1600, 73; Jesuit enslavement of, 487; Jesuit opposition to enslavement of, 479–90 *passim*; laws concerning enslavement, 479, 481f, 490f, 494; estimated number ca. 1500, 72

Brazil province, *see* Province of Brazil

Brazilwood, Jesuit trade in, 531

Brisacier, Jean, 249

Brito, João de, Jesuit martyr, 205

Bullion trade, Jesuit role in, 536

Burrus, Ernest J., defender of Jesuit poverty, 648

Buzoni, Francesco (1576–1635), mission superior in Vietnam, 138

Cabo Frio, cámara of, 601n116

Cabral, Francisco (1528–1609), Jesuit administrator, 61f; criticizes admission of Japanese clergy, 62–65, 264; opposes admission of colonial-born, 259; opposes Jesuit involvement in gem trade, 542; opposes Jesuit participation in imperial trade, 530n7, 550; urges replacement of missions procurator, 300

Cabral, Francisco, Jesuit benefactor, 348

Cabrera, D. Juan Tomás Enrique de, Admiral of Castile, Jesuit benefactor, 355f

Cacao, Amazonian boom, 498

Cafilas (convoys), 175

Camamú, engenho of, 417

Cámara, Luís Gonçalves da, confessor of King Sebastian, 81–84

Cámara, Martim, confidential secretary of King Sebastian, 81–84, 671

Campolide, novitiate in Lisbon, 30; disputed quinta of, 379, 412, 457

Campos de Goitacazes, *see* Goitacazes, Campos de

Campos Novos (de São João), Jesuit estate of, 380, 409f

Canal, quinta of, 381

Caniços, quinta of, 349, 381, 385, 412

Cannanore, 43

Cano, Melchior, Dominican critic of Jesuits, 22, 92

Cape Verde mission, 212, 382, 437, 631, 652

Capuame, Bahia, livestock fair, 409

Capuchins, 21; enter Cape Verdes, 213; enter Kongo and Angola, 214n17, 215f

Carafa, Vicente, general (1646–49), 233, 237

Carbone, Giovanni Bautista, 610f

Carcavelos, estate of Japan province, 349f, 383, 390

Cardim, António Francisco (1596–1659), procurator of Japan province, 643n113

Cardim, Fernão (ca. 1549–1625), Jesuit administrator and chronicler, 73, 251f, 352, 417, 481, 629

Cardinal Henry (D. Henrique, 1512–80), king of Portugal (1578–80), 26; authorizes transfer of monastic lands to Jesuits, 377; exempts college of Santo Antão from tithes, 463; exempts Society from payment of excises, 547; generosity toward Society, 321f; opposition to admission of New Christians by the Society, 258; as regent of Sebastian, 81; and succession problem, 85–90 passim

Cardozo, António, 302

Cardozo, João Francisco, mathematician, 577f

Cardozo, Miguel, 302

Careri, Giovanni Francisco, globetrotter and Jesuit critic, 339

Carmelites, Order of, 43, 503

Carmona, village of, 350

Carneiro, Melchior Miguel, 33, 53

Cárquere, N. S. de, monastic source of Jesuit income, 28ff, 322

Carthusians, Order of, 503

Carvalho, Jacinto de (1677–1744), missionary and missions procurator of Maranhão, 303, 496f

Casa da India, see India House

Casas (incipient colleges), see Espírito Santo; Porto, college of; College of São Paulo de Piratininga; São Vicente, settlement of

Casnedi, Carlos António, confessor and Visitor (1721–24), 250, 356, 608

Castelbranco, João de Abreu, governor of Maranhão (1737–47) and Jesuit critic, 472, 498

Castelo Melhor, count of, Luís de Vasconcelos e Sousa, 271; coup of, 111; fall of, 116f; and Jesuits, 122n90, 469; and transfer of Bombay, 194

Castracani, Alexandre de, papal collector, 98

Castro, António de Melo de, viceroy of India (1662–66): critic of Jesuits, 192n48, 331, 342, 371, 441, 540; opposition to transfer of Bombay, 192–96; and Portuguese lands in Bombay, 445

Castro, Caetano de Melo e, viceroy of India (1702–7), Jesuit defender, 583

Castro, João Baptista de, 609

Castro, Matias de, bishop of Chrysopolis, 263f

Castro, D. Pedro de, Jesuit benefactor, 361, 393

Catherine of Bragança, (1638–1706): dowry of, 191n45, 331; Jesuit benefactor, 114, 354

Censos (liens), 385, 560

Centurione, Luís, general (1755–57), 233

Cereal production, 411–16

Cerqueira, Luís de, bishop of Japan, 133

Ceuta, 24, 83f

Ceylon (Sri Lanka), 43, 178; Jesuit enterprise in, 152ff; Portuguese efforts to conquer, 152f, 168f; Lusitanian military reverses in and exclusion from, 169, 178f, 188

Chao-ch'ing, 68

Chaul, college at, 48, 450, 593

Cheira, quinta of, 381

Chichorro, Luis Martins de Sousa, governor of Angola and Jesuit critic, 216

Ch'ien Lung, Emperor of China (1736–95), 580

Child, Sir John, president of East India Company stations, 448

China, French Jesuit mission to, 148f

China, vice-province of, see Vice-province of China

Chorão, novitiate of, 350, 361, 393

Chorão conference (1575), 57, 398, 508, 530n5, 646f

Church, as landowner, 377f

Churches, Jesuit, embellishment of, 634

Cistercian, Order of, 12

Clement VIII, Pope (1592–1605), 232, 351

Clement IX, Pope (1667–69), 118

Clement XI, Pope (1700–1721), 578, 606

Cloth trade, Jesuit role in, 539

Cluny, Congregation of, 8

Coadjutors, spiritual, 12

Coadjutors, temporal, 12, 503f

Cochin, college of (Madre de Deus), 48, 58, 68, 361, 392; "academy" at, 251; debts of, 647

Cochin, port of, 167, 189f, 350

Cochin, raja of, 42

Coconut estates, 315f, 382, 415

Coelho, Gaspar (1531–90), first vice-provincial of Japan, 63, 509

Coen, Jan Pieterzoon, Dutch governor-general, 166

Coimbra, College of Arts and Humanities: administration assigned to Jesuits, 31f; beginnings, 31; curriculum, 610n154; endowment, 322; estates, 381; sale of property by, 383f; slaves owned by, 513

Coimbra, University of, 17, 30. *See also* Coimbra, College of Arts and Humanities

College Espírito Santo (Évora), 33, 387. *See also* Évora, University of

College of Espírito Santo (Brazil), *see* Santiago, college of

College of Olinda, *see* Olinda, college of

College of Rio de Janeiro, *see* Rio de Janeiro, college of

College of Salvador (Bahia), *see* Bahia, college of

College of São Alexandre (Pará), *see* Belém do Pará, college of

College of São Paulo (*o novo*), Goa, *see* New St. Paul's, college of

College of São Paulo (*o velho*), Goa, *see* Old St. Paul's, college of

College of São Paulo de Piratininga, 74. *See also* São Paulo, cámara of

Colleges as dormitory facilities, 639

Collegial rivalries, 235f

Colombo, Jesuit college at, 154, 188

Colônia do Sacramento, 597f

Comorin, Cape, 49

Company of Jesus, *see* Jesuits; Society of Jesus

Conceição, Diogo de, Jesuit critic, 599f

Confessors, Jesuit, *see* Aquaviva, Claudio; Cámara, Luís Gonçalves da; Casnedi, Carlos António; Fernandes, André; Fernandes, Manuel; Henriques, Leão; Magalhães, Sebastião; Serpe, Maurício; Vitelleschi, Mutio. *See also* Jesuits as confessors

Congregations, general: 18f, 231ff, 258

Congregations, provincial, 232n8

Conspiracy of 1641, 102f

Constitutions of the Society, 8–23 *passim*, 365, 371; and novices' property, 347; silence of, 232, 305n27, 402. *See also* Loyola, St. Ignátius

Consultores, 242

Cooke, Humphrey, second English governor of Bombay, 195

Coromandel coast, 50f, 188

Corruption, endemic to State of India, 185f, 344

Corte Real, Diogo de Mendonça (1658–1736), secretary of state, 497f, 607, 610

Costa, Duarte da, Jesuit benefactor, 349, 388, 554

Costa, José, defender of Society, 260

Costa, José, provincial of Brazil, and "Jacintada," 251

Costa, D. Juliana Dias da, Jesuit benefactor, 366f, 640

Costa, Sebastião da, secretive Jesuit benefactor, 362

Cotegipe, Jesuit sugar estate, 349, 409, 423

Cotovia, novitiate in Lisbon, 30

Cotunguba, engenho of, 420

Council of Portugal, 92, 164–71 *passim*

Council of the Indies (Spanish), 165

Coutinho, Miguel Vaz, 44

Couto, Sebastião (1570–1639), Jesuit leader during Évora rebellion, 97f

Cranganore, 43, 49, 189

Criminale, António, Jesuit martyr, 50

Critics of the Society, *see* Society of Jesus, critics

Cunha, D. Luís, Portuguese diplomat (1709–49), 450, 459f, 603

Cunha, Nuno da, Jesuit administrator and diplomat, 98, 106, 238

Cunha, Pero (Pedro), 301

Currency, Portuguese, fluctuations of, 623f

Customs duties, Brazil, Jesuits exempted from, 547

Dalva, D. Juliam, Jesuit benefactor, 352

Damão, college of (11,000 Virgins), 171, 371, 381, 415, 453; founding, 48; sources of income, 394

Deathbed bequests, 347n5, 370f

December (1640) revolution, 100, 107f, 182

Desacato, crime of, 607n144

Destêrro, Santa Catarina, incipient college at, 598

Dionisio, Francisco, dismissed mulatto ex-Jesuit, 291

Diplomats, Jesuits as: in Bengal, 151; in China, 148f; and East India Company, 163f, 171–74; and the Marathas, 198; during the Restoration, 104ff; during the succession crisis (1579–80), 89f; in western India, 164, 171–74, 198

Diu, college of, 47f, 196, 361

Diu, port, 187, 328ff; Omani attacks on, 196; siege of (1534), 47

Divar, island of, 392

Dojuku (acolytes), 62f

Dominican Order, 8; arrival in China, 573, 580; arrival in India, 43; arrival in Japan, 65, 132; arrival in Mozambique, 154; growth, 23; inability to enter China, 57; Irish seminary established by, 34n40; and manual labor, 503; opposition to admission of Chinese candidates, 266; and poverty, 615; and Queen Mariana of Austria, 606n137; and trade, 539

Downs, battle of the (1639), 99

Duarte, Baltasar, missions procurator, 302

Dutch: assaults on Portugal's eastern empire, 159–63, 166ff, 175–80, 182f, 188ff; invasions of Brazil, 206–9 passim; invasion of Angola, 214f. See also Bahia de Todos os Santos; Goa, port and city of; Macao, city of; Mozambique; Pernambuco

East India Company (English) (EIC), 160, 163, 171; and acquisition of Bombay, 190–95; and Jesuits, 163f, 171–74, 445–50; as a multinational firm, 668; quarrel with Mughals, 448ff; and racism, 294f; troops of (1737), 592n81

Ecclesiastical lands, acquisition of, 430–45

EIC, see East India Company

Elvas, college of, 107

Elvas, town of, 25, 106f, 110

Embassy, first Japanese to Europe, 64

Engenho Novo, sugar estate of (Rio de Janeiro), 424

Engenho Velho, sugar estate of (Rio de Janeiro), 404; origins, 420; lands leased, 424

Enxobregas, quinta of, 381, 412

Episcopal discipline, Jesuit denial of, 584

Erédia, António, Jesuit critic, 290

Erédia, Manuel Godinho de, cosmographer, 290f

Espírito Santo, college of (Brazil), see Santiago, college of

Espírito Santo, college of (Évora), 390

Estado da India: corruption in, 185f, 342; extent, 42; loss conceded by John IV, 187; loss of shipping sent to (1580–1640), 184; mortality among troops sent to, 587n63; problems of manpower, 184; proposal to sell portions of, 588

Estate managers, Jesuit, 311–17

Ethiopia, 158; beginnings of Jesuit enterprise in, 53f; funds promised uncollectible, 328; growth and destruction, 154–57

Évora, city of, 25, 90n55, 96ff

Évora, University of, 411; debts, 645; dissidents at, 241; and the Inquisition, 112; origins, 32f; reception of Philip II, 92; recipient of tithes, 466; servant staff, 504; sources of income, 385; and tenancy, 403; urban holdings of, 396

Expulsion of Jesuits, see Society of Jesus, expulsion of

Fabric, expenses of, 632f

Faro, college of, 34, 381, 645

Fayãa, quinta of (Madeira), 412

Fazenda do Colégio, see Goitacazes, Campos de

Fernandes, André (d. 1660), confessor of John IV, 104, 110

Fernandes, Manuel (1614–93), Jesuit administrator and confessor, 121ff, 128, 444

Ferreira, Cristóvão (1580–1650), Jesuit apostate, 136

Figueira, Luís, 221ff, 442

Fintas (assessments), 306

Fishery Coast (India), 43, 49f, 393, 541f

Forti, António, 458

Fortresses in India, 341f

Fragata do colégio, 532f

Franciscan Order, 8n15; arrival in China, 67, 573; arrival in Ceylon, 153; arrival in India, 43, 47f; arrival in Japan, 65, 132; concept of poverty, 615; crucifixions in Japan, 65; disputes within, 21; failure to gain entry to China, 67; growth, 23; preceded Jesuits, 652; responsibility for Bardês parishes, 46

Franco, António, Jesuit biographer, 35

French mission to China, 46

Funai, college at, 61

Funai (Oita), Japan, hospital at, 59, 340f, 349

Funchal, Madeira, college of (São João Evangelista), 412; hosts governor-general of Brazil, 352f; membership during seventeenth century, 211f; origins, 34, 378; and payment of tithes, 466

Gama, João da Maia da, Jesuit defender, 495f

Gandía, Jesuit college at, 16, 20

Gantacomprem, village of, 394

Gary, Henry, English governor of Bombay, 445f

Gaya, Maria, benefactress of college of Macao, 368

General, Fathers: age range of, 233f, 280f; authority, 8f; practical limits of authority, 229, 653. See also by individual names

General congregations, *see* Congregations, general

General Examen, *See* Loyola, St. Ignátius

Gerbillon, Jean François, 148

Goa, cámara of, 435, 587n61

Goa, port and city of: conquest, 42; coveted by England, 114n55; Dutch blockade of, 94, 182, 188; Dutch naval victory at, 176; East India Company threatens to burn, 449; as Jesuit hub, 44–54 *passim*, 150; planned removal of, 332f; as redeployment center, 150; royal exchequer drained, 330

Goa, province of, *see* Province of Goa

Godinho, Manuel, Jesuit messenger and overland traveler, 193

Godolphin, William, 374

Goitacazes, Campos de (*Fazenda do Colégio*), 379f, 409f, 424

Golconda, sultanate of, 196

Gomes, António, first director of seminary of Santa Fé, 45, 289, 361

Gonzalez de Santalla, Tirso, general (1687–1705), 383, 643

Gottifredi, Aloysius, general (1651–52), 239f

Gouveia, André de, pedagogue and founder of Jesuit college at Coimbra, 31

Gouveia, Cristóvão (1542–1622), provincial of Brazil, 251ff, 352, 357, 467, 557; favors admission of colonials, 259; seeks renewal of tithe exemption, 467

Gouveia, Dr. Diogo de, 5, 25, 31

Gouveia, Francisco de, first mission superior in Angola, 76

Gouveia, Jesuit college of, 372, 604

Grã, Luís de (ca. 1523–1609), provincial of Brazil, 244, 507

Granaries (in India), 343

Gregory XIII, Pope (1572–85), 62; authorizes subvention for Japan province, 351; confirms Jesuit exclusivity in Japan, 65; opposes Spaniard as Society's general, 231; receives Japanese embassy, 64; sanctions Jesuit role in silk trade, 534

Gregory XV, Pope (1621–23), 464

Gregory, John, Jesuit interpreter, 192

Guerreiro, Francisco, 238

Guidiccioni, Cardinal Bartolomeo, early Jesuit supporter, 7

Gusmão, Alexandre de, 492

Gusmão, Luísa, Queen of Portugal (1640–56) and regent (1656–62), 109, 240, 490

Hawkins, William, 163f

Health care, 636

Henriques, Francisco, lay brother and procurator, 309

Henriques, Henrique (1520–1600), 50, 56, 455

Henriques, Leão, Jesuit administrator and confessor of Cardinal Henry, 82, 671

Heredia, Pedro de, rejected Jesuit benefactor, 373

Hideyoshi, *see* Toyotomi Hideyoshi

High Court of Goa, *see* Relação of Goa

Holy Faith, seminary of (India), 44f, 262, 452

Holy Office, *see* Inquisition, Goa; Inquisition, Portugal

Horta, college at (Azores), 359

Hospitals, 185, 338–41. *See also* Funai

House ministers, Jesuit, 308f, 618

Hsü Kuang-ch'i, 142f

Hugli, college at, 151

Ibirajuba (São Francisco de Borja), Jesuit estate in Pará, 421, 521

Ilha Verde (Macao), 391

India House, 327

Innocent VIII, Pope (1484–92), 506

Innocent X, Pope (1644–55), 232f

Innocent XIII, Pope (1721–24), 579

Inquisition, Goa, 673

Inquisition, Portugal: awards estate to College of Arts (Coimbra), 387; intervention in College of Arts (Coimbra), 31; opposes formation of Brazil Company, 113; relations with the Society, 124–27, 670–73. *See also* Vieira, António

Interest rates: in Brazil, 552n1; in India, 566n54

Jaffna, *see* Ceylon

Jaguary, estate of (Pará), 521

Jahangir, Mughal Emperor (1605–27), 52, 163f

Japan province, *see* Province of Japan

Japan trade, *see* Silk trade

Japanese mission to Rome, 62f

Jask, EIC factory at, 166

Jesuit deportment prescribed, 282–87

Jesuit diets, 625, 627–30

Jesuit estates, prominent, 459n130. *See also* Araçatiba; Arneiro; Betim; Campolide; Canal; Caniços; Carcavelos; Cheira; Cotegipe; *Engenho Novo*; *Engenho Velho*; Enxobregas; Fayãa; Goitacazes, Campos de; Ibirajuba; Labruja; Loredo;

Luz, Nossa Senhora da; Macaé; Monjope; Monte Olivete; Pico do Cardo; Pitanga; Pitinga; Santa Cruz; Santana de Ilhéus; São Bonifáçio; Sergipe do Conde; Taleigão; Val do Rosal; Vila Franca

Jesuits: comparative longevities of, 278–82; German, 267, 269; Italian, 267–71, 274; novices, 347f; Spanish, 267. *See also* Jesuits and; Jesuits as; Society of Jesus

Jesuits and: accountability, 653; agriculture (cereal and wine production), 411–16; alleged illicit recruitment in India, 171n46, 185; Amerindian slavery, 479–101; black slavery, 506–37 *passim*; bonds of loyalty, 655; bullion trade, 306f, 536; the Catalán rebellion, 107ff; coinage, 342 (*see also* Portugal); defective land titles, 437; discipline, 285, 296, 653; eurocentrism, 255, 264ff; health care, 636; indigenous clergy (Japan), 131; the inquisition (*see* Inquisition, Goa; Inquisition, Portugal); the jewel trade, 538, 541f; land disputes, 433, 435, 440–50, 455, 601; military service, 106, 166; nationalism, 108f; New Christians (*see* New Christians; Society of Jesus and New Christians); personal servants, 285, 504f, 635, 647; poverty, 284, 615ff, 648–53 *passim*; profits, 620; racism, 56, 262n32; record-keeping, 617–20; regicide, 656n5; revolution, 129; sugar, 425f; tenancy, 403, 406; tithe payments, 463–73; tobacco consumption, 286f; trade on behalf of friends, 536, 541, 548f; travel, 284, 286, 325, 636ff; women benefactresses, 364–67. *See also* Loyola, St. Ignátius; Valignano, Alessandro; Xavier, St. Francis

Jesuits as: confessors, 658; conservative agriculturalists, 427ff; diplomats (*see* Diplomats); fortress administrators, 341f, 451; grain storage administrators, 343; hospital administrators, 338–41; lenders, 552–67 *passim*; novices, 12; parish priests, 317n77, 335f, 584f; pharmacists, 307, 337f; ranchers, 406–8; scapegoats, 450–54, 594ff, 657f; sugar planters, 416–26; trustees, 336f

Jiquitaia, novitiate, 302, 370

John III, king of Portugal (1521–57), 7, 81, 652; appeals for Jesuits to come to Portugal, 26; authorizes land grants to Jesuits, 378, 432; endows Jesuit facilities, 322f, 378f; establishes royal government in Brazil, 321ff; proposes Jesuit administration of Inquisition in Lisbon, 701

John IV, king of Portugal (1640–56), 108; accepts loss of *Estado da India*, 187; assessments of, 101f; demands financial contributions, 330; and division of province of Portugal, 237–41 *passim*; and the Inquisition, 112; Jesuit application for lands, 442; opposes Jesuit efforts to obtain commercial concessions, 530; orders Jesuits to Maranhão, 223f; reliance upon Jesuits, 101–6; restricts sending of foreign-born Jesuits to ultramar, 268, 271; and truce with Dutch, 182

John V, king of Portugal (1706–50), 610; character, 604f; defends Jesuits, 602; and diminishing Jesuit influence, 605–7; indifference to Jesuit complaints, 494; opposes Tournon mission, 577; restricts foreign-born Jesuits, 268, 271; supports archbishop of Goa against Jesuits, 585; terminal illness of, 611f; visits to São Roque, 606

Juana of Portugal, queen and queen mother (d. 1573), 20, 81, 83

Juros, 560–66 *passim*

Just war, and enslavement of the Brasis, 479f

Kaffirs, 475n4, 514f

K'ang-hsi, emperor of China (1654–1722), 145, 575–79

Kanhoji Angira, Maratha admiral, 586

Kibi, Pedro Casui, Japanese Jesuit martyr, 264f

Kirwitzer, Wenzel Pantaleon, agent of vice-province of China, 385

Kongo (Zaire), 75, 351; Capuchins, 214f

Kung (Kongo), 187, 332n54

Labruja, quinta of, 383, 388f, 412; account of (1610–12), 413

Laerzio, Alberto, vice-provincial and provincial of Malabar (1602–11), 236f, 252, 327f

Laínez, Diogo, general (1558–65), 5, 233, 416; as a New Christian, 257; sanctions procurement of black slaves, 507f; at Trent, 234

Lands, Jesuit: dispersed patterns of, 385f; exchanges, 378, 389; extent of, 381f; extent criticized by Jesuits, 457ff; licenses, 377f; sales, 383; state confiscation threatened, 436f, 443f. *See also* East India Company and Jesuits; Jesuits and land disputes

Lands, monastic, *see* Cárquere; Longosvalles; Paço de Sousa; São Fins; São Jorge

Lay captaincies, 478, 489, 491f, 500

Legacies, 345–75 *passim*

Leite, Serafim, 278, 389, 467, 486, 546; defense of Jesuits' reliance upon black slaves, 505, 518, 526; and Jesuit poverty, 647f

Leo XI, Pope (1605), 463

Lesser Sunda Islands, 534

Língua geral, 223, 477

Linhares, conde de, D. Miguel de Noronha, viceroy of India (1629–35), 173f; as Jesuit critic, 170f, 270, 438, 542

Linschoten, Jan Huyghen van, 540

Lisboa, Fr. Gaspar de, Franciscan critic of Jesuits in India, 79

Lisbon, city of, 25, 107f, 607

Lobo, Jerónimo, 286; and African slave trade, 510f; opposes admission of colonial-born, 259; rapid assignment of, 257–58

Longobardo, Niccolò (1565–1655), 140, 142f; favors admission of Chinese, 265; opposes Riccian accommodation, 573

Longosvalles, S. João, monastery of, 322, 336, 388

Loredo, quinta of, 387

Loyola, St. Ignátius (1491–1556): drafts *Constitutions*, 8–10, 17–20; early years, 4f; and the Five Chapters, 7, 13; and the *Formula Instituti*, 7; and General Examen, 11, 13n; and manual labor, 503; and obedience, 283, 312f; and personal poverty, 615f, 625; and the Portuguese Inquisition, 67of; and Spiritual Exercises, 5 (*see also* Spiritual Exercises); and women, 19–21

Luanda, Jesuit college at, 510; captured by Dutch and recovered, 214f; dispute with *cámara*, 217; endowment of, 351; extent of landholding, 381

Luís, Diogo, provincial procurator, 557f

Luís, Pero, ordained Indian, 263

Luso-English relations: deterioration in India (1690s–1702), 449f; during Maratha campaign, 590ff; and treaty of 1662, 113; unauthorized accord, 172–75

Luz, Nossa Senhora da, sugar estate, 420, 422

Macaé, Jesuit estate of, 380, 424n94

Macao, cámara of, 333, 540

Macao, *casa* of São José, 236

Macao, city, 66, 133; as commercial hub, 537; execution of embassy from, 137; failure of Dutch attacks upon, 166; Jesuits' arrival, 66; Jesuits' trade with, 535–40; shipping harassed by Dutch, 160

Macao, college of Madre de Deus at, 68, 133, 137, 236, 333, 368; farm owned by, 391; income, 382n31; income lost, 593n89; and Indian village of Malara, 452; junks owned by, 531; recipient of legacies, 563; residents of, 572

Macedo, Jorge Seco de, 439

Machado, Diogo Barbosa, 609

Madre de Deus, ship, 134

Madura mission and college, 157, 205, 350, 391. *See also* Nobili, Roberto de

Mafra, consecration of, 609

Magalhães, Sebastião (1635–1709), Jesuit academician and confessor, 122f

Magistris, Jacinto de and "Jacintada," 250f, 419

Mahim Peninsula, 445, 447, 587

Maigrot, Charles, Jesuit critic in China, 574f

Maintenance costs of Jesuit churches and colleges, 632–35

Malabar, province of, *see* Province of Malabar

Malabar Coast, 43, 48

Malacca (Melaka), bastion of, 57, 385; administration of hospital abandoned by Jesuits, 341; customs duties, 324f; Dutch siege, 161, 166, 176; fall of, 177f, 180; Jesuit college at, 57f; Jesuit losses at, 178; number of Jesuits stationed at, 55f; Portuguese defense of (1629), 172; shipping attacked, 160; Xavier's visits, 43

Malagrida, Gabriel, 612

Malara, village of, 394, 452

Mamô, engenho of, 417

Manar island, 49f, 188

Manila, 162, 166

Manpower problem of Jesuits, 47; in Brazil and Maranhão, 597; in China, 70, 266, 293f; loss of missionaries en route to China, 141n49; responsibility for, 63, 258–66, 654

Manrique, Sebastien, Augustinian critic of Jesuits, 139

Manucci, Nicolao, Jesuit critic and fabricator, 542f

Manuel "the Fortunate," king of Portugal (1495–1521), 27, 84

Marajó, island of, 408, 488

Maranhão, college of (Nossa Senhora da Luz), 384, 408, 421. *See also* São Bonifáçio

Maranhão, State of: conflict over Indian freedom, 493–99; founding, 222; expulsion of Jesuits, 123, 489ff; tithe controversies, 471ff

Maranhão Company, 491

Marathas, 197–202, 589ff

Margão, college of, 46f, 335

Margaret of Savoy, regent of Portugal, 95–102 *passim*, 438f

Mariana de Austria (1683–1754), queen of Portugal and Jesuit benefactress, 354, 605f

Marie François Isabelle of Savoy (d. 1684), queen of Portugal and wife of Afonso VI and Pedro II, 116–23 *passim*

Martini, Martino, 271, 574

Martins, Gonçalo, Jesuit diplomat, 198

Mártires, Bartolomeu, archbishop, 33, 35

Martyrs and martyrdom, Franciscan, 64

Martyrs and martyrdom, Jesuits: in Ethiopia, 157; in Japan, 135f; in Vietnam, 572n2. *See also* Aquaviva, Rudolfo; Azevedo, Inácio de; Brito, João de; Criminale, António; Mourão, João; Moureira, Maurício; Serpe, Maurício; Silveira, Gonçalo de

Mascarenhas, António, assistant (1607–15), 234, 238

Mascarenhas, D. Fernão, 671

Mascarenhas, D. Jerónimo, 373

Mascarenhas, Nuno, assistant (1615–37), 234

Masuliptam, 161

Mateo Sánchez, *see* Juana of Portugal

Maurits, Johan, governor of Dutch Brazil, 209–14 *passim*

Mendes, D. Afonso, 156f, 263

Mendes, António, 312

Meninos de Palhavã, 605

Mercurian, Everard, general (1573–80): bars admission of Asians and Eurasians, 263; opposes admission of colonial-born, 259; orders end to Jesuit reliance upon black slaves, 508; urges dismissal of confessor of Cardinal Henry, 88; why selected, 231

Methwold, William, 172ff, 190

Mezzarbarba, Carlo Ambrogio, papal envoy to China, 578f

Mina, São Jorge da, 214

Minas Gerais, 598

Ministers, *see* House ministers

Mirón, Diego, 249, 288

Mission ordinances (1686) and Jesuits, 491

Mission procurators, *see* Procurators, missions

Missions, expenses of, 640

Missions, Jesuit: Angola, 507; Brazil, 73, 476ff, 598ff; Cape Verdes, 212f; India, 382, 582, 630; Maranhão, 488 (*see also* Figueira, Luís; Vieira, António; Vice-province of Maranhão); Moluccas, 43, 58, 161, 162n14,

174, 353n36, 373; Mozambique, 330, 386; Southeast Asia (*see* Vietnam missions)

Moluccas, *see* Missions, Jesuit

Mombasa: attempted recovery of, 451, 588f, 595; Jesuit contributions to relief expedition, 334; Omani attacks, 196f; uprising, 169

Monastic lands, *see* Cárquere; Longosvalles; Paço de Sousa; São Fins; São Jorge

Money of account defined, 621

Monita Secreta, 358, 548f

Monjope, sugar plantation, 420

Monserrate, António de, 51, 154

Monte Agraço, Sobral de, 322, 385, 391

Monte Olivete, quinta of, 359

Monteiro, Luís Vaía, governor of Rio de Janeiro (1725–32) and Jesuit critic, 602

Montmartre oath, 6, 13, 615

Morais, Manuel de, Jesuit resistance leader and renegade, 209f

Morais, Sebastião de (1535–88), confessor of duke of Parma, provincial of Portugal, and bishop-elect of Japan, 243

Morales, Juan Bautista, Dominican critic of Jesuits in China, 574

Mormugão harbor, 176, 332

Morosi, village of, 394, 444

Mota, Cardinal da, 605

Moura, D. Cristóvão (1538–1613), agent of Philip II of Spain, 87

Mourão, João, Jesuit martyr in China, 580

Moureira, Maurício, Jesuit martyr at Goa, 176

Mozambique, 361; beginnings of Jesuit enterprise in, 54f; Dutch naval victory at, 166f; Jesuits criticized, 452; modest Jesuit achievements in, 612; Omani attack on, 196f; return of Jesuits, 154

Mughal court, 46, 51f, 582

Muribeca ranch, 408f

Muscat, 187, 196, 332n54

Mwene Mutapa, kingdom of, 54, 154

Mysore mission, 382, 630

Nadal, Jerónimo (1507–80), key Jesuit administrator, 13, 29, 37, 267

Nagasaki, college of, 61f, 131

Nagasaki, port of: conversions near, 131f; crucifixions at, 65; embarkation point for Asian slaves, 509; governor as Jesuit benefactor, 357; "Great Martyrdom" (1622), 135f; provincial congregation at, 236

Nanchiang, 70

Nanking (Nanjing), 70; decree of, 576

Nargol, village of, 394

Nationalism and Society of Jesus, 655

Navarrete, Domingo (1618–86), Dominican critic of Jesuits in China, 574

Negapatam, Dutch capture of, 182, 188

Negombo, 179, 182

Nerchinsk, Treaty of (1689), 149

New Christians: and conspiracy of 1641, 103; financiers of the Brazil Company, 112; lenders, 559; and the Portuguese Inquisition, 126f. *See also* Society of Jesus and New Christians

New St. Paul's college, Goa: beginnings, 45, 566; coconut production, 415; extent of lands, 381f; fires afflicting, 553; founding, 56; impact of confiscation of Bombay estates, 450; inventory of, 677–79; quarrel with Japan province, 642f

Nicholas V, Pope (1447–55), 506

Nickel, Goswin, general (1652–64), 233, 237, 240, 261

"No free lunch," principle of, 638f

Nobili, Roberto de (1577–1657), 49, 151f, 157, 350, 575; letters to the powerful, 353

Nobility of Portugal, 355

Nóbrega, Manuel da (1517–70), superior and provincial of Brazil, 71; appeals for black slaves, 507; assessment of Brasis, 70f; concerns about late crown payments, 326; favors Jesuit role in sugar production, 416

Noronha, D. Miguel de, *see* Linhares, conde de

Northern Province, *see* Salsete do Norte

Novais, Paulo Dias de, Portuguese captain and Jesuit benefactor, 75f

Novices, *see* Jesuits as novices

Nunes, Paulo da Silva, persistent Jesuit critic, 495ff

Oda Nobunaga (1534–82), shogun, 61, 63

Old St. Paul's, college of (Goa): origins, 44f; sources of revenue, 393

Olinda, college of, 72, 466; captured by Dutch, 209, 680–82; contributes to expenses of college of Recife, 643; Jesuit losses at, 210; origins, 72, 74, 368f; ranches, 408; royal subvention in behalf of, 466f; sales of property, 384; sugar plantations, 420, 422; urban income, 398n122

Oliva, Giovanni Paolo, general (1664–81), 122; and division of province of Portugal, 240; favors limited admission of Chinese, 266;

rebukes leaders of Brazil province over "Jacintada," 251

Oliveira, Manuel de, estate manager, 313

Omani Arabs, raids of, 196f, 585

Oratorians, 609f

Ormuz (Hormuz), 42, 48, 52f, 373, 652; fall of, 94, 165ff; Jesuit residence at, 51f; recovery planned, 174; trading center, 42

Overseas Council, Portugal, 453n108, 454ff, 470ff, 494–98 *passim*; favors return of Jesuits to Cape Verdes, 213; orders blockade of Bombay, 449; warns about precarious state of Portuguese positions in India, 587

Oviedo, André, 53f

Ovington, John, East India Company chaplain and Jesuit critic, 449f

Oxenden, Sir George, East India Company president, 446

Paço de Sousa, São Salvador de, monastery of, 322, 385

Pagodas, 44

Pais, José da Silva, acting governor of Rio de Janeiro and Jesuit critic, 603

Pais, Pero (Pedro Paes) (1563–1622), Jesuit missionary in Ethiopia, 154ff

Paraíba, Jesuit college at, 359n59

Paraná, incipient college of, 408, 598

Parel (Parela), village of, 359, 360n60, 393, 450

Partridge affair, 608

Parvas (pearl fishers), 49

Paul III, Pope (1534–49), 6f, 484

Paul V, Pope (1605–21), 132, 463

Pedania mission, 382

Pedro II, regent and king of Portugal (1668–1706), 118, 644, 665; character, 120f; demands religious Orders in Brazil disclose properties, 443f; and Maranhão missions, 226; opposes Sertão land grant, 454; restricts dispatch of foreign-born Jesuits, 228, 271; interest in China enterprise, 148n80; urges physicians be sent to India, 390

Peking (Beijing), 70

Pereira, Estevão, Jesuit estate manager, 313, 419, 518f

Pereira, Tomás, 148f, 576

Pernambuco, Dutch invasion of, 208–9

Pessoa, André, governor of Macao, 133f

Philip II, king of Spain (1556–98) and Portugal (1581–98), 52, 76, 83, 665; attempts to gain control of Society, 232; defends Jesuits concerning tithe liability, 463; disapproves of ecclesiastical acquisitions of lands, 445; hostility toward Society, 434; prohibits Jesuit participation in pepper trade, 530; and Portuguese succession, 89–94 *passim*; urges Jesuits to assume administration of hospital at Goa, 338, 340

Philip III, king of Spain and Portugal (1598–1621): advocates Jesuit mission to Cape Verdes, 212; tries to compel Jesuit general to visit Spain, 232; visits Portugal, 557

Philip IV, king of Spain (1621–65) and Portugal (1621–40), 97; mandates invasion of Portugal, 110; orders inventory of lands bequeathed to Church, 437

Philippine Ordinances, 431, 452

Piauí, Jesuit cattle ranches in, 408f. *See also* Sertão, Domingo Afonso

Piccolomini, Francisco, general (1649–51), 233, 237, 239

Pico do Cardo, farm, 378

Pimenta, João, mission procurator, 301f

Pimenta, Nicolas, Jesuit administrator in India, 150f, 248, 251f; laments Jesuit administration of Goa hospital, 340; preaches for the inquisition, 671

Pinto, Fernão Mendes, merchant and ex-Jesuit brother, 290

Pinto, Francisco da Gama, 494

Pirates, Algerian, 332

Pitanga, Jesuit sugar plantation, 409, 417, 422, 441

Pitinga, sugar estate, 422

Polanco, Juan (1517–76), secretary to generals Loyola, Laínez, and Borja, 14, 258, 616

Ponta Delgada, college of (Azores), 34, 403

Portalegre, college, 34, 349, 382

Portalegre, town, 25

Porto, city of, 25

Porto, college of, *see* São Lourenço, college of

Portugal, D. Pedro de Almeida, *see* Alorna, Marquis of

Portugal, kingdom of: debasement of coinage by, 665ff; districts supplying Jesuit recruits, 272; origins, 24f; population in sixteenth century, 25; shipping losses sustained by (1622–25), 165; teaching of language prescribed, 477

Portuguese Inquisition, *see* Inquisition, Portugal

Possevino, António, 268

Poverty, 346, 614. *See also* Jesuits and poverty

Prices, advancement in Portugal, 624

Procurador da corte, 304n24

Procurators, college, 308–9

Procurators, missions, 298–303 *passim*, 553

Procurators, provincial, 231, 305–6

Professed houses: 20, 654. *See also* Bom Jesús, São Roque, Vila Viçosa

Propaganda Fide, 13

Province of Brazil: beginnings, 71–75, 235, 597; colleges inactive as lenders, 562; exclusion of mulatto students, 262n32; geographic origins of members, 272f, 597f; growth, 74, 219f, 597ff, 674–76; income (1631–1757), 621ff; increase in native-born members, 261; increasing debts, 645f; Jesuits dismissed from (1566–1707), 292f; Jesuits sent to, 71–74 *passim*, 219

Province of Goa: beginnings, 41–70 *passim*; contraction of income of by Maratha campaigns, 621; debts, 646; geographic origins of members, 273f; growth, 44–71 *passim*, 203, 596, 674–76; income (1575–1741), 583, 621ff; Jesuits sent to, 47, 219, 582f; peak and decline of membership, 203, 581f, 596

Province of Japan, 324, 381f, 386, 415; beginnings, 59–66; clashes with province of Goa, 642f; converts within, 131; Jesuits expelled from (1614) but remain underground, 135; geographic origins of members, 274f; growth, 46, 137, 572f; income, 324, 621ff; income lost, 593n89; indebtedness, 646; as lender, 565; and loss of Bombay estates, 450; papal subventions for, 306; properties in India and Portugal, 382, 394; restructuring of, 137; urban income, 397. *See also* Silk trade

Province of Malabar: beginnings, 150, 235; impoverishment, 350; income, 393, 622f; income lost, 593n89; loans by, 566; membership peak and decline, 204, 581, 596; opposes reunification with Goa, 237; precarious finances, 390f. *See also* Bengal; Ceylon; Cochin, port of; Coromandel coast; Malacca; Moluccas; São Tomé de Meliapor

Province of Paraguay, 347f

Province of Portugal: beginnings, 25–36, 235; debts, 645; geographic origins of members (1593–1750), 276f; growth, 36, 94, 256, 674–76; income, 620–23; movement to divide, 237–41; purge of members (1552), 288f

Provincial rivalries, 235ff

Provincials and vice-provincials: ages, 244f; broad authority of, 242–45; duration in office, 244

Pulicat, 49, 161f, 174

Pyrard [de Laval], François, testimony of, 339

Qatar, mission of, 382

Quadros, António, vice-provincial and provincial of Goa, 244, 671f

Queiróz, Fernão de, chronicler and consultor, 336, 543

Quilon (Coulão), 49, 189, 357

Quindénio affair, 606f

Quirol (Kirol), 392

Rachol, college of, 46, 382, 415

Ranching, as a source of Jesuit income, 407–8

Rebêlo, Amador, missions procurator (1539–1622), 81, 300, 643

Recife, college of: establishment, 362f; ranches, 408; sugar estate, 420, 422; urban properties, 398

Rectors, 246f

Reimão, Paulo, Jesuit diplomat, 172ff

Relação of Goa, 451f

Rentals and leases, extent and duration of, 403f

Retz, Francisco, general (1730–50), 459

Rho, Giacomo (1592–1638), 141, 143

Rhodes, Alexander of (1593–1660), 138f, 256ff, 286

Ricci, Lourenço, general (1758–73), 234

Ricci, Matteo (1552–1610), pioneer Jesuit missionary in China, 67–70 *passim*, 140, 573

Rice as a source of Jesuit income, 415

Rio de Janeiro, cámara of, 601

Rio de Janeiro, college of: beginnings, 72; estate sold by, 384; land acquisitions, 380; land sales, 383; ranches, 407f; royal subventions in behalf of, 466f; tenancy terms, 404f; and tithes, 466; tumult against, 483f; urban properties, 398f

Rites, Chinese, 572–81 *passim*

Rites, Malabar, 575

Rodrigues, Francisco, Jesuit historian, 97, 288f

Rodrigues, João, Jesuit interpreter and cultural historian in Japan and China (1561–1634), 133f, 143, 264

Rodrigues, Simão, superior and provincial of Portugal (1510–79), 25–28, 74; denunciations of to Inquisition, 671; opens college in future University of Évora, 33; opposes admission of New Christians, 257; seeks to lead Jesuits to Brazil, 71f; and stringent recruitment, 36

Roe, Sir Thomas, 164

Roser, D. Isabel, 19

Rougement, François (1624–76), 266, 296

Ruggieri, Michele, 67

Sá, D. Felipa de, countess of Linhares and Jesuit benefactor, 364f

Sá, Mem, governor-general of Brazil (1557–72), 358; acquisition of Santana de Ilhéus and Sergipe do Conde, 418f; collaborates with Jesuits in Brasis' pacification, 72; Jesuit benefactor, 72; names first lay captains, 478

Sá, Salvador de (1602–86), administrator, Jesuit benefactor, and warrior 218, 358; confronts anti-Jesuit tumults in Rio de Janeiro and São Paulo, 484, 486; facilitates Jesuit acquisition of Goitacazes' lands, 379; founds college of São Miguel (Santos), 221; liberates Angola, 214f; loyalty questioned, 104; purchases Indian slaves, 487

Sabino, Sebastiano, 299

St. Benedict, Rule of, 12, 502

Saint Francis, 14

St. Patrick, Lisbon, seminary of, 34, 359n59

Salsete, Goa, 45, 356; Maratha invasions of, 202, 589; parishes and Jesuit administration, 335f, 584f; villages as Jesuit critics, 439

Salsete, Goa, Jesuit college at, 46f, 634. *See also* Margão, college of; Rachol, college of

Salsete do Norte, 45, 48, 356, 366; coveted by English, 194, 590n72; Jesuit loans to inhabitants, 566f; Maratha invasions of, 201, 590–93; source of Jesuit income, 382n31, 392; tolls dispute with English East India Company, 586f; villages assigned to Japan province, 324, 444

Salvador (da Bahia), cámara of: calls for sale of Sergipe do Conde, 440; complains Jesuits discriminate against native sons, 260; complains religious Orders not contributing to war expenditures, 440f; criticizes Jesuit-built wharf, 602; opposes Indian protective laws, 481f; protests religious Orders' refusal to tithe, 468

Salvador (da Bahia), city of, 94, 206ff

Sambhaji, Maratha successor of Sivaji, 199

San Hemengildo, college of, 555f

Sancian island, 67

Sandalwood trade, Jesuit role in, 538

Sandomil, count of, Pedro Mascarenhas, viceroy of India (1732–41), 453, 594f

Santa Casa da Misericórdia, Bahia, 375n126, 398, 418, 561f

Santa Casa da Misericórdia, branches, 334

Santa Casa da Misericórdia, Goa, 45, 334n63

Santa Cruz, estate of, 72, 315, 389, 458, 522

Santa Fé, seminary of, see Holy Faith, seminary of

Santa Teresa, D. Inácio, archbishop of Goa and Jesuit critic (1721–39), 584

Santana, São Paulo, Jesuit estate, 409

Santana de Ilhéus, estate of, 313, 379, 385, 417; decline of, 423; Indian purchased for, 487; slaves on, 518, 520f

Santarém, college at, 34, 93f, 349, 382f, 389

Santarém, town, 25

Santiago, college of, Espírito Santo, Brazil, 74, 221, 408, 424. See also Araçatiba

Santo Alexandre, college of, see Belém do Pará, college of

Santo Antão, canons of, 322n3

Santo Antão, college of, 323, 411; as asylum for refugees, 91; benefactors, 348; as borrower and lender, 553ff; debts, 645; dispersed lands, 385; dispute over ownership of Sergipe do Conde, 417ff; endowment, 323, 365; exemption from tithe payments, 463; as holder of government annuities, 560; income from annuities, 555, 560; land acquisitions, 381; meeting at concerning division of province of Portugal, 239; origins, 28f; purchase of slaves, 487; as residence of missions procurators, 296n4, 639; and spice trade, 529; and tenancy, 403; urban properties, 396. See also Pitinga; Santana de Ilhéus; Sergipe do Conde

Santos, Francisco Duarte dos, 497, 546f

Santos, college of, see São Miguel (Santos), college of

Santos, port of, 485

São Bonifáçio, estate (Maranhão), 315, 381, 421

São Fins, monastery of, 346, 388

São Jorge, monastery of, 322

São Lourenço, college of (Porto), 33, 380f, 385, 396

São Luís do Maranhão, cámara of, 489ff

São Miguel (Azores), college of, 412

São Miguel (Santos), college of, 220f, 381f, 487. See also Sá, Salvador de

São Paulo, cámara of, 485, 492

São Roque, professed house in Lisbon: beginnings, 29f; chapel built by Queen Marie Anna de Neuberg, 123; and division of

province of Portugal, 241; internal disputes concerning lands, 457; and negotiations to depose Afonso VI, 116; as recreational facility, 379

São Tomé de Meliapor, 47, 51, 188, 394, 444; college at, 49; occupied by French and Golcondans, 196; pepper trade proposed by Jesuits at, 530

São Vicente, count of, João Nunes da Cunha, viceroy of India (1666–68), 198

São Vicente, settlement of (1653), 486

Sarmento, Francisco, procurator of Goa, 353

Schall, Johann Adam (von Bell) (1592–1666), 141, 143ff, 166

Schomberg, Count Frederic Armand, 115, 119

Schreck, Johann Terrenz, see Terrentius

Schwartz, Stuart B., modern critic of Jesuits, 520

Sea loans, 538, 563ff

Sebastian, king of Portugal (1557–78), 34, 657; approves of Jesuits' acquisition of lands, 432; character, 83; endowments by, 378; exempts college of São Antão from tithes, 463; exempts province of Brazil from customs duties, 469, 547; fixation on conquest of North Africa and death, 84–85; generosity toward the Society, 321–24; Jesuit advisors of, 81–84; opposition to Society's admission of New Christians, 258; sanctions transfer of monastic lands to Jesuits, 377; urges prevention of illicit Amerindian enslavement, 479

Sebastianism, 92

Seminary of Santa Fe, Goa, see Holy Faith, seminary of

Sergipe do Conde (Sergipe da Condessa), 313, 365; beginnings, 418–19; decline, 423; engenho of, 385; land sales, 384; slave gangs on, 517, 519; tenants of, 405

Serpe, Maurício, confessor of King Sebastian, 85

Serra Ibiapaba, Ceará, 488

Serrão, Gregório, 508

Serrão, Jorge, provincial of Portugal (1570–74), 268, 671

Sertão, Domingo Afonso ("Mafrense"), Jesuit benefactor, rancher, and pathfinder, 363f, 408f, 454, 471, 642

Setúbal, college of Saint Francis Xavier at, 359

Setúbal, town of, 25

Shah Jahan, Mughal Emperor (1628–58), 170

Shimabara rebellion (1637–38), 137

Shipman, Sir Abraham, first English governor of Bombay, 191f

Shipping losses by Portugal, 184

Siam, 137, 140n42, 538, 572

Sidis, 448, 586

Silk trade, Jesuits' share in, 306f, 533ff

Silveira, Gonçalo de, Jesuit martyr in Mozambique, 54

Siqueira, Emmanuel de, first Chinese-born Jesuit, 265

Sivaji (ca. 1630–80), Maratha leader, 198f

Sixtus V, Pope (1585–90), 64, 232, 351, 534

Slave trade, 510, 544ff

Slavery, black, and the Jesuits: in Africa, 510, 513–17, 544ff; in Brazil, 507, 511, 517–26; in East Asia, 385, 509; in India, 508, 514f; in Portugal, 507f, 513

Slavery and the Brasis, 479–501 *passim*

Slavery and the Church, 506

Smallpox, outbreaks of, 489, 495, 498

Soares, Bernabé, Jesuit defender, 443

Société des Missions Étrangères, 139

Society of Jesus: conception of, 655; founding, 6f; growth, 16f, 674–76; and New Christians, 125–28, 257f; periods of development, 230; and royal subventions, 325–29, 372, 467n27; as an urban Order, 34, 654

—critics, 441, 451. *See also* Aungier, Gerald; Barreto, Francisco (governor); Berredo, Bernardo Pereira de; Cano, Melchior; Castelbranco, João de Abreu; Castro, Matias de; Chichorro, Luis Martins de Sousa; Conceição, Diogo de; Erédia, António; Gary, Henry; Innocent XIII; Linschoten, Jan Huyghen van; Lisboa, Fr. Gaspar de; Macedo, Jorge Seco de; Maigrot, Charles; Manucci, Nicolao; Manrique, Sebastien; Monteiro, Luís Vaía; Morales, Juan Bautista; Navarrete, Domingo; Nunes, Paulo da Silva; Ovington, John; Pais, José da Silva; Santa Teresa, D. Inácio; Sousa, Ayres de Saldanha de Menezes e; Sousa, Gabriel Soares de; Tavernier, Jean Baptiste; Vieira, João Fernandes. *See also* Belém do Pará, cámara of; Cabo Frio, cámara of; Goa, cámara of; Macao, cámara of; *Monita Secreta*; Rio de Janeiro, cámara of; Salsete, Goa; Salvador, cámara of

—expulsion of, *see* Belém do Pará, college of; Ethiopia; Maranhão, State of; Province of Japan; Rio de Janeiro, college of; Santos,

port of; São Paulo, cámara of; Venice

—myths concerning: affluence, 551, 660; efficiency of, 229f; internal discipline, 285, 296f, 653; as a machine, 229; as a pioneer multinational firm, 668–69; as a state within a state, 656; as a trading network, 548–51

—policies of, concerning: abandonment of unprofitable enterprises (*see* Cape Verde mission; Ormuz; Maranhão, state of); admission of non-white clergy, 262–67; dismissal of unfit members, 287–93; Eurocentrism, 255, 264–66; exclusion of New Christians from membership, 257f; host states, 655f; nationalism, 230; non-Portuguese European members, 267–72; Portuguese independence (1580–1640), 80; public image, 257, 265, 282–87, 559; racism, 55, 158, 295; separation of members from families and friends, 241; social security, 554; tobacco smoking, 286f

Sousa, António Caetano de, 609

Sousa, Ayres de Saldanha de Menezes e, 217–18

Sousa, Gabriel Soares de, Jesuit critic, 79, 435, 480f

Spice trade: Amazon, 170, 546; Asia, 529f

Spínola, Francesco, 67

Spiritual Exercises, 27, 211. *See also* Loyola, St. Ignátius

Stephens, Thomas, 46, 335

Stipends, royal, 325–29, 434, 466f

Sunda mission, 382

Surat (India), 170, 448

Susinyos, soldier of fortune in Ethiopia, 155

Swally Hole, 171, 190

Tabula rasa, 475

Taleigão estate, 315, 350; coconut orchard on, 415; importance of income for Japan province, 390; purchase of, 384; rice tenants on, 406

Tamburini, Michelangelo, general (1706–30): apologizes to John V, 608; condemns Jesuits for preoccupation with economic gain, 551; criticized by pope and defends subjects, 579; criticizes Society's acquisition of lands, 459; and recruitment for province of Malabar, 582; writes to colonial governors, 602f

Taná, 48, 194, 381, 415

Taná, college of, 593

Tangier, 114f

Tavares, Mateus, missions procurator, 557f

Tavernier, Jean Baptiste, 543

Távora, Francisco, first count of Alvor, governor of Angola (1669–76) and viceroy of India (1681–86), 199–202, 218, 332, 353, 449

Taylor, George, piracy of, 586

Teive, Diogo de, 31

Teixeira, Pedro, estate manager, 312f

Temple lands, India, 432f

Temples, Hindu, destruction of, 44n9, 323, 432f

Ten Years Truce, Luso-Dutch, 182

Tenancy, 403, 406

Terrentius (Johann Terrenz Schreck) (1576–1630), 141, 143

Theatine Order, 3, 6f

Thirty Years War (1618–48), 165

Thomas Christians, 48f

Tibet, Jesuit mission in, 137, 359

Tidore, island of, 160

Tithes, 462–69 passim

Tobacco, 286f

Tokugawa Ieyasu (1542–1616), shogun, 132

Toledo, Francisco de, 249

Torres, Cosme de, Xavier's successor in Japan, 59n67, 61

Torres, Dr. Miguel de, 82, 249, 288

Tournon, Carlo Tommasco Maillard de (1688–1710), 575–77

Toyotomi Hideyoshi (1536–98), shogun of Japan, 63ff, 70, 130

Travancore, raja of, 357

Travancore Coast, 43, 48f, 188

Travel expenses, Jesuits', 325, 636ff

Treaty of Pyrenees (1659), 110

Trent, Council of (1545–63), 3, 16, 27, 443, 462; and slavery, 506f

Trigault, Nicholas (1577–1628), procurator for China missions, 140, 270

Trincomalee, Dutch capture of, 179

Trinitarian friars, 86n34

Tropas de resgates (ransoming expeditions), 488

Tupinambá, 72

Tuticorin, 188

Tuticorin, college at, 49

Twelve Years Truce, 162

United Netherlands East India Company (VOC), 160, 163, 182, 184

University of Coimbra, 30, 93

Urban VIII, Pope (1623–44), 98, 484

Urban income of Jesuits, 382, 395–401

Vaipicota (Vaipikotta), 41, 49

Val do Rosal, estate of, 381, 385, 390, 412

Valbom, quinta de, 387, 390

Valignano, Alessandro (1539–1606), Jesuit administrator in India and Japan, 45, 247, 371, 401, 434, 573, 634; author of "Indian Summary," 56; author of "Japan Summary," 65; and China, 65; cultivates the powerful, 321; early life, 55; on exclusion of ex-members, 288, 290; favors Jesuit cooperation with inquisition, 672f; and Japan enterprise, 60ff; on Jesuit participation in pearling trade, 541; obtains license to purchase villages, 392; opposes admission of New Christians, 257; opposes purchase of lands in Japan, 405f; orchestrates Society's role in silk trade, 534; organizes Japan embassy, 64; pessimism concerning admission of Asians and Eurasians, 55, 263; and racism, 56; a realist, 157; recommends caution concerning admission of colonial-born, 259; recruitment of a murderer, 295; and slavery, 508

Vallareggio, Alessandro (1529–80), first missions procurator, 267, 299

Van Diemen, Antonie, Dutch governor-general, 175f

Van Goens, Rijcklof, 188f

Vargas, Diogo Ximenes, slave merchant and Jesuit benefactor, 369

Vasconcelos, Miguel de, Portuguese quisling, 95, 97f

Vasconcelos, Simão de (1596–1671), Jesuit administrator and chronicler, 104, 260, 531, 546, 672

Veloso, Luís, estate manager, 313, 315

Venice, 482n33

Verbiest, Ferdinand, missionary and administrator in China (1628–88), 145ff, 236

Vernei, Luís António, Jesuit critic, 609

Versova, port of, 590, 592

Vice-province of China: beginnings, 66–71; deaths of missionaries assigned to, 141; debate over effectiveness of Jesuits' intellectual transmission to, 143n58; enthusiasm of German students to serve in, 147; ethnic origins of members, 275; funds, 144; growth, 46, 144, 149, 573; income, 385, 621; indebtedness, 646; land route to Europe, 271; and legacies, 564; loss of Bombay estates, 450; possession of lands in India, 382; and papacy, 576n14; paucity of converts in, 69; persecution in

(1665–71), 146; purchases income from villages, 394f; state of after Ricci's death, 140; urban income, 397f; zenith of conversions within, 572. *See also* Ricci, Matteo; Rites, Chinese

Vice-province of Maranhão: establishment (1727), 225; ethnic origins of members, 219f; growth of Jesuit presence, 225f, 597ff; expulsion of Jesuits from, 123, 489ff; paucity of Brazilian-born members, 261. *See also* Figueira, Luís; Vieira, António

Vidigal, José, 497

Viegas, Gaspar, 350

Vieira, António (1608–97), Jesuit missionary, preacher, diplomat, 104f, 247; condemns Society's smack, 532; critic of Jesuit compromise with Paulistas, 493; critic of Jesuit land acquisitions, 458f; and defense of Indian liberty, 487–90; favors African slave imports, 511; last years, 128; leads mission to Amazon, 113, 224; letters to the powerful, 353; and New Christians, 125–28; and Portuguese Inquisition, 113, 673; proposes Brazil Company, 111ff; role in division of province of Portugal, 141n32; writes *Life* of Francis Xavier, 123

Vieira, Damião, 198

Vieira, Francisco, Visitor to Japan province, 264

Vieira, João Fernandes, 216f, 516

Vieira, Miguel (1681–1760), estate manager in India, 313

Vietnam missions, 137f, 382n31, 397n112, 444, 538, 572, 580; income lost, 593n89; number of Jesuits serving in, 572

Vijayanagar, sultanate of, 41, 197, 356

Vila Franca, estate, 378n6, 381, 387f, 390

Vila Viçosa, Jesuit professed house at, 34, 56, 93

Vilhena, Francisco, Jesuit missionary, academician, and diplomat, 104f

Villages and towns as sources of Jesuit income, 324, 391–95, 444, 565. *See also* Assalona, Velim, and Ambelim; Ceylon; Malara; Monte Agraço, Sobral de; Morosi; Nargol; Parel; Quirol

Villes, François de, Jesuit confessor, 116

Visconti, Inácio, general (1751–55), 233

Visitors, 247–53, 639f

Vitelleschi, Mutio, general (1615–45), 80, 107f, 213, 238, 393

VOC, *see* United Netherlands East India Company

Xavier, Jerónimo, 52, 164

Xavier, St. Francis (1506–51), 5, 25, 326; achievements, 42f, 47f; activities and impressions in Japan, 59f; advocates Society engage in trade, 528; canonization, 641; crypt of, 45; and defense of Goa, 202; exclusion of unfit members, 289f; favors establishment of Goan inquisition, 672; questions admission of creoles, 258f; reports on restricted diet customary in India, 630; and sources of political power, 79–80, 321; troubled by indebtedness, 646; warns against admission of Indians (from India), 262; and women, 283f

Xenophobia, Iberian crowns and, 654

Yakut Kahn, Sidi leader at Janjira, 448

Yate, John Vincent, English-born Jesuit in Brazil, 292

Yung Cheng, Emperor of China (1723–35), 579f

Yusuf bin Hasan, apostate Christian, 169

Zambesi River, 54

Zu'lqarnai, Mirza, Jesuit benefactor, 359f, 393

Library of Congress Cataloging-in-Publication Data

Alden, Dauril.
    The making of an enterprise : the Society of Jesus in Portugal,
its empire, and beyond : 1540–1750 / Dauril Alden.
        p.   cm.
    Includes index.
    ISBN 0-8047-2271-4
    1. Jesuits—Portugal—History.   2. Jesuits—Portugal—Colonies—
History.   3. Portugal—Church history.   4. Portugal—Colonies—
Religion.   I. Title.
BX3742.A1A53   1995
271′.530469—dc20   94-4820   CIP   Rev.

    ⊗This book is printed on acid-free, recycled paper.
        It was typeset in 10/13 Baskerville by
        Humanist Typesetting & Graphics.

            Original printing 1996

    Last figure below indicates year of this printing:

    05   04   03   02   01   00   99   98   97   96